Today's most **popular authors** have collaborated on this exciting new series, which combines **great literature** with remarkably **effective instruction,** bringing real writers and real tools together for real results.

Give your students

Real writers

unprecedented access to award-winning authors (see page NC T2)

Real tools

remarkably effective tools for differentiated instruction (see page NC T4)

Real results

built-in benchmarking to guarantee Standard Course of Study mastery and North Carolina Writing Assessment success (see page NC T6)

"This project is what I wish I'd had when I was in school . . . a resource where I could not only read really good writing, but also get a sense about how the authors actually felt!"

—Cornelius Eady
featured unit author

NORTH CAROLINA

North Carolina

Professional Development Handbook

TEACHER'S EDITION

GRADE TEN
VOLUME ONE

Upper Saddle River, New Jersey
Boston, Massachusetts

ISBN 0-13-190805-7
3 4 5 6 7 8 9 10 09 08 07 06

Real writers

Fifty-three of today's most popular writers have collaborated on this extraordinary new program.

Now your students can learn about reading, writing, and literature from the authors themselves, as they share their personal experiences, insights, and expertise while presenting key instructional concepts.

It's a little bit like having you, the students, come backstage with Tim O'Brien, a writer.

—Tim O'Brien
Grade 11, Unit 5 author

From the Scholar's Desk

JUDITH ORTIZ COFER INTRODUCES
"Ithaka" by Constantine Cavafy

An Interview with Judith Ortiz Cofer
Conducted by Prentice Hall

What aspect of the ancient Greek epic the *Odyssey* would most help someone reading Cavafy's "Ithaka"? The *Odyssey* contains worlds. It's a love story. It's a story of a man trying to get back home to his wife after fighting and suffering in a long war. It's a story of a king and a story of loyalty. But to Cavafy, I think it was especially a story of the journey in between here and there. He shows you how the journey becomes a symbolic journey, standing for your life and goals

...poem is so often recited at graduations ...nies? Yes, the theme is that, when you go

Judith Ortiz Cofer

Judith Ortiz Cofer has won numerous awards for her work as a poet, an essayist, and a novelist. In 1994, she won the O. Henry Prize for short story. Or...

Each **unit** in *Prentice Hall Literature* is hosted by one of the featured **authors**. Each author serves as a **guide** for your students, taking them on an unforgettable journey through the writer's world and introducing them to a universe of great literature.

Give your students unprecedented access to award-winning authors!

JAMAICA KINCAID INTRODUCES

from Annie John: A Walk to the Jetty

Making Memories and Stories

I come from a small island in the Caribbean that was part of the British Empire until the early 1970s when it gained political independence. Everyone I knew was literate and everyone I knew told stories.

My mother, in particular, not only knew how to read, she did so for sheer pleasure. At the time, she was the only person I ever saw do this, sit and read just for the sake of reading.

She also told me stories but these stories were not folk tales or stories about revered ancestors; they were stories about what she was like as a child, what her mother and father did, what had happened to her before I was born, what the world into which I was born was like before I was born, what the day was like when I took my first steps, the first words I said, the things I liked to eat. I was too young then to make proper memories for myself and so the memory I have of that time are the memories she created for me.

It was at that time, the time before I could make my own memories, that she taught me to read. I believe now that this set of circumstances, my mother telling me stories and teaching me to read, led to my own obsession with literature and writing and especially writing about her.

The Influence of Autobiography

Walk to the Jetty

novel traces th

Jamaica Kincaid won the Morton Dauwen Zabek Award for *At the Bottom of the River* (1983) and she was a finalist for the PEN Faulkner Award for *The Autobiography of My Mother* (1995). Kincaid's stories often focus on the development of relationships between women, especially between mothers and daughters.

Each author

- hosts a unit in *Prentice Hall Literature*
- introduces a literary genre or historical period
- provides insight into the "story behind the story"
- answers questions about writing and literature from real students
- shares his or her expertise as scholars or translators of great works of literature

***From the Author's Desk* DVD**

A corresponding video program brings your students into the writer's world, as the authors explain how their personal experiences shaped their writing and how they use the world around them to create the stories that inform, engage, and entertain readers around the world.

Real tools

Presenting: QuickTake™
instant progress monitoring
as easy as 1, 2, 3!

1. Pose questions to the entire class
2. Students answer via response pads
3. Results are recorded and displayed instantly

Deliver differentiated instruction easily and seamlessly.

For every selection:

- **Leveled Reading Warm-ups**
  Brief reading passages comprising high-interest text and low-level Lexile™ vocabulary preteach essential reading skills.
- **Leveled Vocabulary Warm-ups**
  Lexiled™ word lists and activities prepare students for reading selections.
- **Leveled Assessment**
  Two levels of selection tests allow you to provide assessment targeted for different ability levels.
- **Reader's Notebook series**
  Three levels of interactive readers support every selection.

Technology to help you Plan, Teach, and Assess:

- **TeacherEXPRESS™**
  Powerful lesson-planning, resource-management, and standards-aligned assessment tools, all in one place, make class preparation quick and easy!
- **StudentEXPRESS™**
  An interactive textbook, electronic worksheets, and links to online activities make this the perfect student tool for studying or test review.
- **Exam*View*™ Test Generator**
  Create standards-aligned tests in seconds or customize tests to suit individual student's needs.

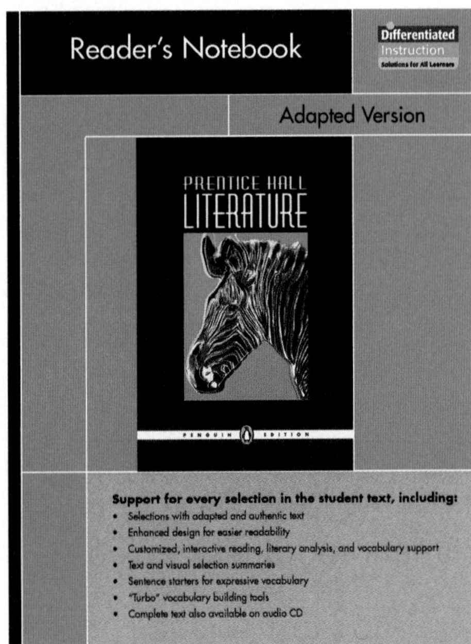

Three levels of Reader's Notebooks ensure that all students get the help they need.

The Reader's Notebook is an interactive companion to the student text that provides additional support for the skills presented. The Adapted version provides additional scaffolding through the use of modified text summaries and partially filled-in graphic organizers, while the English Learner's version provides additional language and vocabulary support.

Accessibility at a Glance charts help you find the best fit for your students.

These charts, at the beginning of each selection grouping, provide a quick way to determine which selections will be more accessible—and more challenging—for your students.

Differentiated Instruction Solutions for All Learners

Accessibility at a Glance

	Creation Hymn	Night
Context	Hindu speculations about the world's origin	Hindu belief in nature's protective forces
Language	Abstract nouns and several series of short questions	Concrete nouns and different personal pronouns referring to a goddess
Concept Level	Accessible (The origin of the world is mysterious.)	Accessible (Think of night as a protective goddess.)
Literary Merit	Vedic hymn from the *Rig Veda*	Vedic hymn from the *Rig Veda*
Lexile	590	590
Overall Rating	Average	Average

Differentiated Instruction Solutions for All Learners

Strategy for Less Proficient Readers
Have students identify three of the four short story elements—main characters, setting, and main events of the plot. Have them use these three elements to try to establish the story's theme or themes.

Strategy for English Learners
Have students diagram the story's plot. Remind them that plot consists of exposition, rising action, climax, falling action, and resolution. Can students find all five stages in this story, or do they think it is missing one or more stages? Which ones?

Strategy for Advanced Readers
Have students discuss which narrative element—plot, character, setting, or theme—is most important to this story. Have them explain their answers in brief essays.

Differentiated instruction for every selection.

These notes provide specific strategies you can use to tailor instruction for all students, including English language learners, gifted students, and less proficient readers.

Real results

Catch small learning problems before they become big ones!

Diagnose Readiness

Brief assessments at the beginning of each part determine student readiness to learn new skills.

Monitor Progress

Assessment Practice features after each selection group check skills proficiency and make sure students are on track.

Benchmark Mastery

Frequent benchmark tests gauge standards mastery and determine whether intervention is needed.

Online Reading Intervention

Introducing: Prentice Hall Success Tracker™

Help your students make real progress!

This fully automated, interactive online diagnostic and remediation system provides:

- Diagnosis and benchmarking of skills
- Customized skills practice
- At-a-glance standards reporting

See page T82 for more information.

Built-in benchmarking ensures success.

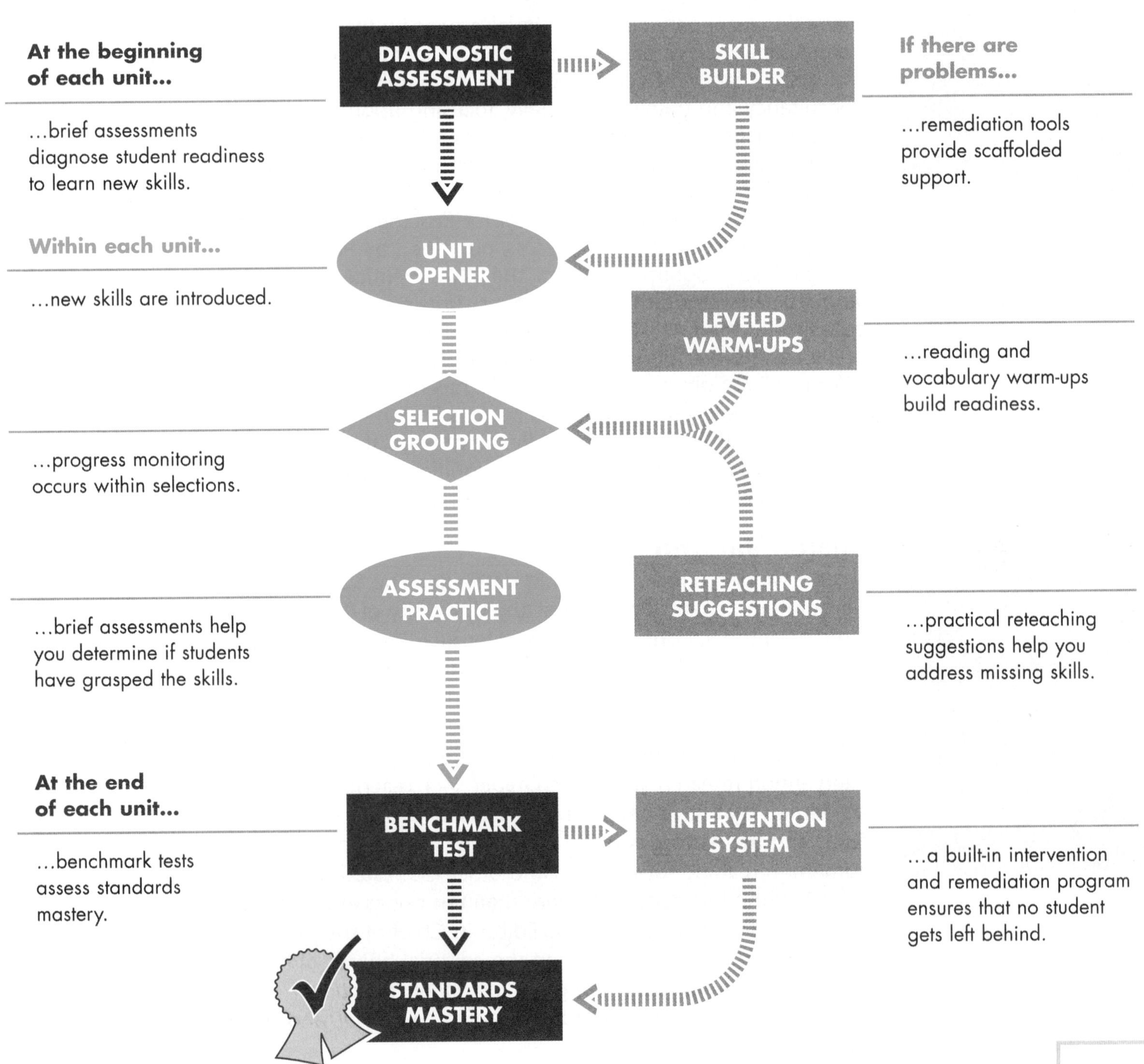

At the beginning of each unit...
...brief assessments diagnose student readiness to learn new skills.
DIAGNOSTIC ASSESSMENT
SKILL BUILDER
If there are problems...
...remediation tools provide scaffolded support.
Within each unit...
...new skills are introduced.
UNIT OPENER
LEVELED WARM-UPS
...reading and vocabulary warm-ups build readiness.
SELECTION GROUPING
...progress monitoring occurs within selections.
ASSESSMENT PRACTICE
RETEACHING SUGGESTIONS
...brief assessments help you determine if students have grasped the skills.
...practical reteaching suggestions help you address missing skills.
At the end of each unit...
BENCHMARK TEST
INTERVENTION SYSTEM
...benchmark tests assess standards mastery.
...a built-in intervention and remediation program ensures that no student gets left behind.
STANDARDS MASTERY

CONTRIBUTING AUTHORS

The contributing authors guided the direction and philosophy of *Prentice Hall Literature: Penguin Edition.* Working with the development team, they helped to build the pedagogical integrity of the program and to ensure its relevance for today's teachers and students.

Kate **Kinsella**

Kate Kinsella, Ed.D., is a teacher educator in the Department of Secondary Education at San Francisco State University. She teaches coursework addressing academic language and literacy development in linguistically and culturally diverse classrooms. Dr. Kinsella maintains secondary classroom involvement by teaching an academic literacy class for adolescent English learners through the University's Step to College Program. She publishes and provides consultancy and training nationally, focusing upon responsible instructional practices that provide second language learners and less proficient readers in grades 4–12 with the language and literacy skills vital to educational mobility.

Dr. Kinsella is the program author for *Reading in the Content Areas: Strategies for Reading Success,* published by Pearson Learning, and the lead program author for the 2002 Prentice Hall secondary language arts program *Timeless Voices: Timeless Themes.* She is the co-editor of the *CATESOL Journal* (California Association of Teachers of ESL) and serves on the editorial board for the *California Reader.* A former Fulbright scholar, Dr. Kinsella has received numerous awards, including the prestigious Marcus Foster Memorial Reading Award, offered by the California Reading Association in 2002 to a California educator who has made a significant statewide impact on both policy and pedagogy in the area of literacy.

Sharon **Vaughn**

Sharon Vaughn, Ph.D., is the H.E. Hartfelder/The Southland Corporation Regents Professor at the University of Texas and also director of the Vaughn Gross Center for Reading and Language Arts at the University of Texas (VGCRLA). As director of the VGCRLA, she leads more than five major initiatives, including The Central Regional Reading First Technical Assistance Center; the Three-Tier Reading Research Project; a bilingual-biliteracy (English/Spanish) intervention research study; the Grades 1–4 Teacher Reading Academies that have been used for teacher education throughout Texas and the nation; and the creation of online professional development in reading for teachers and other interested professionals.

Dr. Vaughn has published more than ten books and over one hundred research articles. She is Editor in Chief of the *Journal of Learning Disabilities* and serves on the editorial boards of more than ten research journals, including the *Journal of Educational Psychology,* the *American Educational Research Journal,* and the *Journal of Special Education.*

Kevin **Feldman**

Kevin Feldman, Ed.D., is the Director of Reading and Intervention for the Sonoma County Office of Education and an independent educational consultant. He publishes and provides consultancy and training nationally, focusing upon improving school-wide literacy skills as well as targeted interventions for struggling readers, special needs students, and second language learners. Dr. Feldman is the co-author of the California Special Education Reading Task Force report and the lead program author for the 2002 Prentice Hall secondary language arts program *Timeless Voices: Timeless Themes.* He serves as technical consultant to the California Reading and Literature Project and the CalSTAT State Special Education Improvement Project. Dr. Feldman has taught for nineteen years at the university level in Special Education and Masters' level programs for University of California, Riverside, and Sonoma State University.

Dr. Feldman earned his undergraduate degree in Psychology from Washington State University and has a Master's Degree from UC Riverside in Special Education, Learning Disabilities, and Instructional Design. He has an Ed.D. from the University of San Francisco in Curriculum and Instruction.

Differentiated Instruction Advisor

Don **Deshler**

Don Deshler, Ph.D, is the Director of the Center for Research on Learning (CRL) at the University of Kansas. Dr. Deshler's expertise centers on adolescent literacy, learning strategic instruction, and instructional strategies for teaching content-area classes to academically diverse classes. He is the author of *Teaching Content to All: Evidence-Based Inclusive Practices in Middle and Secondary Schools,* a text which presents the instructional practices that have been tested and validated through his research at CRL.

UNIT AUTHORS

An award-winning contemporary author hosts each unit in each level of *Prentice Hall Literature: Penguin Edition.* In the upper-level courses, some of these authors are renowned scholars or translators, while others are famous for their own contributions to literature. All serve as guides, helping to introduce a unit, discussing the work of a traditional author or their own work in a translation, and revealing their own writing processes. Following are the featured unit authors who guide students for *World Masterpieces.*

Coleman **Barks**

Coleman Barks, who serves as a guide for this unit, is a critically acclaimed and popular translator of one of the unit's major authors, the Persian poet Rumi. Professor Barks explains the cultural and religious context of Rumi's work.

Wendy **Doniger**

An authority on Hindu literature and a translator of the *Rig Veda,* Professor Wendy Doniger is the perfect choice for this unit's guide. Her books include *The Origins of Evil in Hindu Mythology,* and she is a distinguished professor at the University of Chicago.

Royall **Tyler**

Royall Tyler is highly qualified to be this unit's guide. He has taught Japanese literature, language, and culture at many universities. His acclaimed translations include *The Tale of Genji,* which is widely recognized as the world's first novel.

David **Mamet**

A major playwright and a brilliant student of the theater, David Mamet is well suited to introduce Greek drama. His works include the Pulitzer Prize-winning play *Glengarry Glen Ross* and *Three Uses of the Knife: On the Nature and Purpose of Drama.*

Marilyn **Stokstad**

Marilyn Stokstad, the guide for this unit, is the author of the widely used textbook *Art History* and a specialist in medieval art. She brings an art historian's perspective to medieval literature, helping students picture the grail castle in *Perceval.*

NORTH CAROLINA

State of North Carolina

Program Advisors

Shanita Anderson
Grays Creek Middle School
Hope Hills, NC

Michael D. Blas
Lowe's Grove Middle School
Durham, NC

Karen C. Lilly-Bowyer
Winston-Salem/Forsyth County Schools
Winston-Salem, North Carolina

Amanda Grose
Lufkin Road Middle School
Apex, NC

Stephanie S. Kestner
Providence High School
Charlotte, NC

Mark Kozlowski
Winston-Salem/Forsyth County Schools
Winston-Salem, NC

Erin McDermott
Brogden Middle School
Durham, NC

Suzanne V. Micallef
John T. Hoggard High School
Wilmington, NC

Donna H. Morris
South Mecklenburg High School
Charlotte, North Carolina

Melaine Rickard
Alamance-Burlington Schools
Burlington, NC

Andrea Rumley
Alamance-Burlington Schools
Graham, NC

Tara Alexandra Thomas
South Mecklenburg High School
Charlotte, North Carolina

Betty S. Tunks
North Rowan High School
Spencer, North Carolina

Stephanie J. Wallace
East Forsyth High School
Kernersville, NC

Harriett Wilson
Vance High School,
Charlotte-Mecklenberg Schools
Charlotte, NC

Susanna Quick Winton
Lufkin Road Middle School
Apex, NC

João **Magueijo**

João Magueijo is a theoretical physicist and author whose ideas challenge some cherished beliefs of science. As a contemporary rebel, he is ideally suited to help students understand that scientific rebel of the Renaissance, Galileo.

W. S. **Merwin**

One of the best poets now writing in English, W. S. Merwin has received the Pulitzer Prize and many other honors. He has been deeply influenced by the Romantic tradition, and as this unit's guide, comments on French Romantic poetry and two of his own poems.

Judith Ortiz **Cofer**

Poet, essayist, and novelist Judith Ortiz Cofer has won many awards for her work, including a nomination for the Pulitzer Prize. As this unit's guide, she describes her experiences with modern world literature and introduces "Ithaka" by Constantine Cavafy.

Jamaica **Kincaid**

A leading figure in world literature, Jamaica Kincaid is a natural choice to serve as a guide for this unit. She describes her sudden discovery of contemporary literature, at age nineteen, and she introduces an excerpt from her own book *Annie John*.

Chinua **Achebe**

Chinua Achebe, nominated for the Nobel Prize in Literature in 2000, introduces his story "Marriage Is a Private Affair." Mr. Achebe's novel *Things Fall Apart* is widely acknowledged as both an inaugurator and a classic of postcolonial African literature.

North Carolina

Academic Achievement Handbook

Unit 1

Origins and Traditions

Ancient Worlds (c. 3000 B.C.–A.D. 1400)

All selections and workshops in this unit support your North Carolina standards.

Unit 2

Sacred Texts and Epic Tales

Indian Literature (c. 1400 B.C.–A.D. 500)

NC

All selections and workshops in this unit support your North Carolina standards.

Skills Workshops

SAT PREP ACT

Unit 3

Wisdom and Insight

Chinese and Japanese Literature (1000 B.C.–A.D. 1890)

Japanese Literature

Comparing Literary Works

Comparing Literary Works

Reading Informational Materials: Reference Materials

Skills Workshops

SAT PREP ACT

NC ***All selections and workshops in this unit support your North Carolina standards.***

Unit 4

Classical Civilizations

Ancient Greece and Rome (c. 800 B.C.–A.D. 500)

Roman Literature

Skills Workshops

All selections and workshops in this unit support your North Carolina standards.

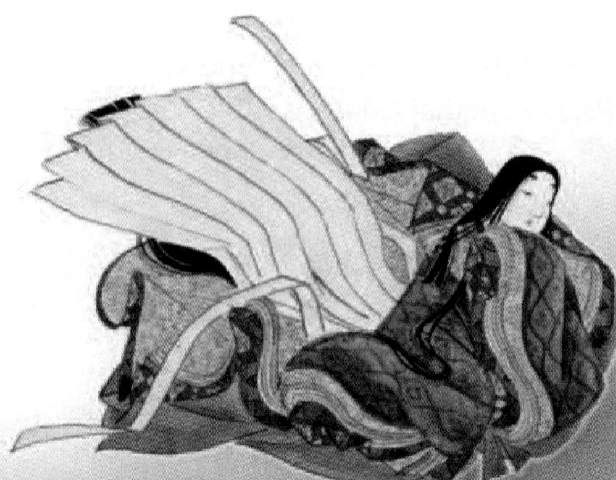

Unit 5

From Decay to Rebirth

The Middle Ages (A.D. 450–1300)

Unit 6

Rebirth and Exploration

The Renaissance and Rationalism (1300–1800)

All selections and workshops in this unit support your North Carolina standards.

Skills Workshops

SAT PREP ACT

Unit 7

Revolution and Reaction

Romanticism and Realism (1800–1890)

NC ***All selections and workshops in this unit support your North Carolina standards.***

Skills Workshops

SAT PREP ACT

Unit 8

From Conflict to Renewal

The Modern World (1890–1945)

All selections and workshops in this unit support your North Carolina standards.

Skills Workshops

SAT PREP ACT

Unit 9

Voices of Change

The Contemporary World (1945–Present)

All selections and workshops in this unit support your North Carolina standards.

INFORMATIONAL TEXT AND OTHER NONFICTION

Reading Informational Materials—Instructional Workshops

Additional Nonfiction—Selections by Type

Historical and Literary Background

Themes in World Masterpieces—Reading in the Humanities

INFORMATIONAL TEXT AND OTHER NONFICTION (cont.)

Literature in Context—Reading in the Content Areas

A Closer Look

Focus on Literary Forms

SKILLS WORKSHOPS

Writing Workshops

SAT PREP ACT

SKILLS WORKSHOPS

Vocabulary Workshops

SAT PREP ACT

Assessment Workshops

SAT PREP ACT

Communications Workshops

Connections to Literature

Literature of the Americas

American Literature

British Literature

Your Guide to North Carolina Standards and Testing

NORTH CAROLINA

What's a GLC?

Grade Level Competencies (GLCs) are part of the North Carolina Standard Course of Study. Your teachers are responsible for helping you master all of the GLCs for language arts. Here is a sample English II GLC as well as a sample writing prompt that tests your understanding of it.

Standards Groupings

To help you better understand the GLCs, we've assigned them names and abbreviations that relate to what they cover. For example, Competency Goal 1 covers the area of Written Language, so we've assigned it the name **Written Language** or **WL** to make it a bit more clear.

SAMPLE QUESTION

"Imagination is more important than knowledge..."
Albert Einstein (1879–1955)

"Memory feeds imagination."
Amy Tan (1952–)

"Everything you can imagine is real."
Pablo Picasso (1881–1973)

Write an essay for your principal describing the meaning of imagination and its importance in education. You may use the ideas presented above, your own experiences, observations, and/or readings.

SAMPLE GLC

WL-1.03.8 Demonstrate the ability to read, listen to and view a variety of increasingly complex print and non-print expressive texts appropriate to grade level and course literary focus, by:

making connections between works, self and related topics.

As a grade 10 student in North Carolina, you are required to take the **Writing Assessment**, which requires you to write an informational composition. You may also take the PSAT or SAT as you prepare for college.

View of North Carolina Mountains from Round Bald, Roan Mountain, NC

Standard Course of Study

English II

The following pages list the North Carolina English II Standard Course of Study, which specifies what you are expected to learn this year in language arts class.

WL Written Language

<u>Competency Goal 1</u>: The learner will react to and reflect upon print and non-print text and personal experiences by examining situations from both subjective and objective perspectives.

WL-1.01 Produce reminiscences (about a person, event, object, place, animal) that engage the audience by:

WL-1.01.1 using specific and sensory details with purpose.

WL-1.01.2 explaining the significance of the reminiscence from an objective perspective.

WL-1.01.3 moving effectively between past and present.

WL-1.01.4 recreating the mood felt by the author during the reminiscence.

WL-1.02 Respond reflectively (through small group discussion, class discussion, journal entry, essay, letter, dialogue) to written and visual texts by:

WL-1.02.1 relating personal knowledge to textual information or class discussion.

WL-1.02.2 showing an awareness of one's own culture as well as the cultures of others.

WL-1.02.3 exhibiting an awareness of culture in which text is set or in which text was written.

WL-1.02.4 explaining how culture affects personal responses.

WL-1.02.5 demonstrating an understanding of media's impact on personal responses and cultural analyses.

WL-1.03 Demonstrate the ability to read, listen to and view a variety of increasingly complex print and non-print expressive texts appropriate to grade level and course literary focus, by:

WL-1.03.1 selecting, monitoring, and modifying as necessary reading strategies appropriate to readers' purpose.

WL-1.03.2 identifying and analyzing text components and evaluating their impact on the text.

WL-1.03.3 providing textual evidence to support understanding of and reader's response to text.

WL-1.03.4 demonstrating comprehension of main idea and supporting details.

WL-1.03.5 summarizing key events and/or points from text.

WL-1.03.6 making inferences, predicting, and drawing conclusions based on text.

WL-1.03.7 identifying and analyzing personal, social, historical or cultural influences, contexts, or biases.

WL-1.03.8 making connections between works, self and related topics.

WL-1.03.9 analyzing and evaluating the effects of author's craft and style.

WL-1.03.10 analyzing and evaluating the connections or relationships between and among ideas, concepts, characters and/or experiences.

Key to Standard Codes

LA Language
IR Informational Reading
FA Foundations of Argument
CT Critical Thinking
LT Literature
GU Grammar and Usage

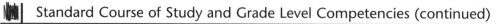

WL-1.03.11 identifying and analyzing elements of expressive environment found in text in light of purpose, audience, and context.

Competency Goal 2: The learner will evaluate problems, examine cause/effect relationships, and answer research questions to inform an audience.

IR
Informational Reading

IR-2.01 Demonstrate the ability to read, listen to and view a variety of increasingly complex print and non-print informational texts appropriate to grade level and course literary focus, by:

- **IR-2.01.1** selecting, monitoring, and modifying as necessary reading strategies appropriate to readers' purpose.
- **IR-2.01.2** identifying and analyzing text components and evaluating their impact on the text.
- **IR-2.01.3** providing textual evidence to support understanding of and reader's response to text.
- **IR-2.01.4** demonstrating comprehension of main idea and supporting details.
- **IR-2.01.5** summarizing key events and/or points from text.
- **IR-2.01.6** making inferences, predicting, and drawing conclusions based on text.
- **IR-2.01.7** identifying and analyzing personal, social, historical or cultural influences, contexts, or biases.
- **IR-2.01.8** making connections between works, self and related topics.
- **IR-2.01.9** analyzing and evaluating the effects of author's craft and style.
- **IR-2.01.10** analyzing and evaluating the connections or relationships between and among ideas, concepts, characters and/or experiences.
- **IR-2.01.11** identifying and analyzing elements of informational environment found in text in light of purpose, audience, and context.

IR-2.02 Create responses that examine a cause/effect relationship among events by:

- **IR-2.02.1** effectively summarizing situations.
- **IR-2.02.2** showing a clear, logical connection among events.
- **IR-2.02.3** logically organizing connections by transitioning between points.
- **IR-2.02.4** developing appropriate strategies such as graphics, essays, and multi-media presentations to illustrate points.

IR-2.03 Pose questions prompted by texts (such as the impact of imperialism on *Things Fall Apart*) and research answers by:

- **IR-2.03.1** accessing cultural information or explanations from print and non-print media sources.
- **IR-2.03.2** prioritizing and organizing information to construct a complete and reasonable explanation.

Competency Goal 3: The learner will defend argumentative positions on literary or nonliterary issues.

FA
Foundations of Argument

FA-3.01 Examine controversial issues by:

- **FA-3.01.1** sharing and evaluating initial personal response.
- **FA-3.01.2** researching and summarizing printed data.
- **FA-3.01.3** developing a framework in which to discuss the issue (creating a context).
- **FA-3.01.4** compiling personal responses and researched data to organize the argument.
- **FA-3.01.5** presenting data in such forms as a graphic, an essay, a speech, or a video.

NORTH CAROLINA

FA-3.02 Produce editorials or responses to editorials for a neutral audience by providing:

- **FA-3.02.1** a clearly stated position or proposed solution.
- **FA-3.02.2** relevant, reliable support.

FA-3.03 Respond to issues in literature in such a way that:

- **FA-3.03.1** requires gathering of information to prove a particular point.
- **FA-3.03.2** effectively uses reason and evidence to prove a given point.
- **FA-3.03.3** emphasizes culturally significant events.

FA-3.04 Demonstrate the ability to read, listen to and view a variety of increasingly complex print and non-print argumentative texts appropriate to grade level and course literary focus, by:

- **FA-3.04.1** selecting, monitoring, and modifying as necessary reading strategies appropriate to readers' purpose.
- **FA-3.04.2** identifying and analyzing text components (such as organizational structures, story elements, organizational features) and evaluating their impact on the text.
- **FA-3.04.3** providing textual evidence to support understanding of and reader's response to text.
- **FA-3.04.4** demonstrating comprehension of main idea and supporting details.
- **FA-3.04.5** summarizing key events and/or points from text.
- **FA-3.04.6** making inferences, predicting, and drawing conclusions based on text.
- **FA-3.04.7** identifying and analyzing personal, social, historical or cultural influences, contexts, or biases.
- **FA-3.04.8** making connections between works, self and related topics.
- **FA-3.04.9** analyzing and evaluating the effects of author's craft and style.
- **FA-3.04.10** analyzing and evaluating the connections or relationships between and among ideas, concepts, characters and/or experiences.
- **FA-3.04.11** identifying and analyzing elements of argumentative environment found in text in light of purpose, audience, and context.

Key to Standard Codes

- **LA** Language
- **IR** Informational Reading
- **FA** Foundations of Argument
- **CT** Critical Thinking
- **LT** Literature
- **GU** Grammar and Usage

Competency Goal 4: The learner will critically interpret and evaluate experiences, literature, language, and ideas.

CT Critical Thinking

CT-4.01 Interpret a real-world event in a way that:

- **CT-4.01.1** makes generalizations about the event supported by specific references.
- **CT-4.01.2** reflects on observation and shows how the event affected the current viewpoint.
- **CT-4.01.3** distinguishes fact from fiction and recognizes personal bias.

CT-4.02 Analyze thematic connections among literary works by:

- **CT-4.02.1** showing an understanding of cultural context.
- **CT-4.02.2** using specific references from texts to show how a theme is universal.
- **CT-4.02.3** examining how elements such as irony and symbolism impact theme.

CT-4.03 Analyze the ideas of others by identifying the ways in which writers:

- **CT-4.03.1** introduce and develop a main idea.
- **CT-4.03.2** choose and incorporate significant, supporting, relevant details.
- **CT-4.03.3** relate the structure/organization to the ideas.
- **CT-4.03.4** use effective word choice as a basis for coherence.
- **CT-4.03.5** achieve a sense of completeness and closure.

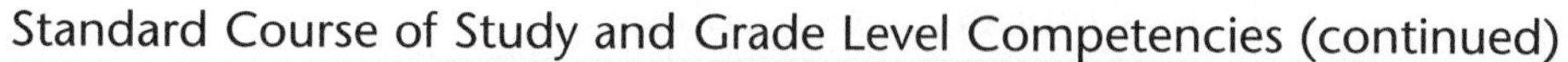

Standard Course of Study and Grade Level Competencies (continued)

NORTH CAROLINA

CT-4.04 Evaluate the information, explanations, or ideas of others by:

CT-4.04.1 identifying clear, reasonable criteria for evaluation.

CT-4.04.2 applying those criteria using reasoning and substantiation.

CT-4.05 Demonstrate the ability to read, listen to and view a variety of increasingly complex print and non-print critical texts appropriate to grade level and course literary focus, by:

CT-4.05.1 selecting, monitoring, and modifying as necessary reading strategies appropriate to readers' purpose.

CT-4.05.2 identifying and analyzing text components (such as organizational structures, story elements, organizational features) and evaluating their impact on the text.

CT-4.05.3 providing textual evidence to support understanding of and reader's response to text.

CT-4.05.4 demonstrating comprehension of main idea and supporting details.

CT-4.05.5 summarizing key events and/or points from text.

CT-4.05.6 making inferences, predicting, and drawing conclusions based on text.

CT-4.05.7 identifying and analyzing personal, social, historical or cultural influences, contexts, or biases.

CT-4.05.8 making connections between works, self and related topics.

CT-4.05.9 analyzing and evaluating the effects of author's craft and style.

CT-4.05.10 analyzing and evaluating the connections or relationships between and among ideas, concepts, characters and/or experiences.

CT-4.05.11 identifying and analyzing elements of critical environment found in text in light of purpose, audience, and context.

Competency Goal 5: The learner will demonstrate understanding of selected world literature through interpretation and analysis.

LT
Literature

LT-5.01 Read and analyze selected works of world literature by:

LT-5.01.1 using effective strategies for preparation, engagement, and reflection.

LT-5.01.2 building on prior knowledge of the characteristics of literary genres, including fiction, non-fiction, drama, and poetry, and exploring how those characteristics apply to literature of world cultures.

LT-5.01.3 analyzing literary devices such as allusion, symbolism, figurative language, flashback, dramatic irony, situational irony, and imagery and explaining their effect on the work of world literature.

LT-5.01.4 analyzing the importance of tone and mood.

LT-5.01.5 analyzing archetypal characters, themes, and settings in world literature.

LT-5.01.6 making comparisons and connections between historical and contemporary issues.

LT-5.01.7 understanding the importance of cultural and historical impact on literary texts.

LT-5.02 Demonstrate increasing comprehension and ability to respond personally to texts by:

LT-5.02.1 selecting and exploring a wide range of works which relate to an issue, author, or theme of world literature.

LT-5.02.2 documenting the reading of student-chosen works.

LT-5.03 Demonstrate the ability to read, listen to and view a variety of increasingly complex print and non-print literary texts appropriate to grade level and course literary focus, by:

LT-5.03.1 selecting, monitoring, and modifying as necessary reading strategies appropriate to readers' purpose.

LT-5.03.2 identifying and analyzing text components and evaluating their impact on the text.

LT-5.03.3 providing textual evidence to support understanding of and reader's response to text.

LT-5.03.4 demonstrating comprehension of main idea and supporting details.

LT-5.03.5 summarizing key events and/or points from text.

LT-5.03.6 making inferences, predicting, and drawing conclusions based on text.

LT-5.03.7 identifying and analyzing personal, social, historical or cultural influences, contexts, or biases.

LT-5.03.8 making connections between works, self and related topics.

LT-5.03.9 analyzing and evaluating the effects of author's craft and style.

LT-5.03.10 analyzing and evaluating the connections or relationships between and among ideas, concepts, characters and/or experiences.

LT-5.03.11 identifying and analyzing elements of literary environment found in text in light of purpose, audience, and context.

Competency Goal 6: The learner will apply conventions of grammar and language usage.

GU
Grammar and Usage

GU-6.01 Demonstrate an understanding of conventional written and spoken expression by:

GU-6.01.1 employing varying sentence structures (e.g., inversion, introductory phrases) and sentence types (e.g., simple, compound, complex, compound-complex).

GU-6.01.2 analyzing authors' choice of words, sentence structure, and use of language.

GU-6.01.3 using word recognition strategies to understand vocabulary and exact word choice (Greek, Latin roots and affixes, analogies, idioms, denotation, connotation).

GU-6.01.4 using vocabulary strategies such as context clues, resources, and structural analysis (roots, prefixes, etc.) to determine meaning of words and phrases.

GU-6.01.5 examining textual and classroom language for elements such as idioms, denotation, and connotation to apply effectively in own writing/speaking.

GU-6.01.6 using correct form/format for essays, business letters, research papers, bibliographies.

GU-6.01.7 using language effectively to create mood and tone.

GU-6.02 Edit for:

GU-6.02.1 subject-verb agreement, tense choice, pronoun usage, clear antecedents, correct case, and complete sentences.

GU-6.02.2 appropriate and correct mechanics (commas, italics, underlining, semicolon, colon, apostrophe, quotation marks).

GU-6.02.3 parallel structure.

GU-6.02.4 cliches, trite expressions.

GU-6.02.5 spelling.

Key to Standard Codes

LA Language
IR Informational Reading
FA Foundations of Argument
CT Critical Thinking
LT Literature
GU Grammar and Usage

Writing Assessment
Scoring Model

The following rubrics are similar to those used to score your response on the North Carolina Writing Assessment, which you are required to take this year. The Conventions Rubric is used to assign a score for form—how well your writing conforms to the conventions of English grammar. The Composing Rubric is used to assign a score for the content of what you write—how well you express and organize your ideas.

Find Formative Rubrics with individual Writing Workshops

NORTH CAROLINA

Conventions Rubric

Points	*Description*
2	**Exhibits reasonable control of grammatical conventions appropriate to the writing task** • Exhibits reasonable control of sentence formation • Exhibits reasonable control of standard usage including agreement, tense, and case • Exhibits reasonable control of mechanics including use of capitalization, punctuation, and spelling
1	**Exhibits minimal control of grammatical conventions appropriate to the writing task** • Exhibits minimal control of sentence formation • Exhibits minimal control of standard usage including agreement, tense, and case • Exhibits minimal control of mechanics including use of capitalization, punctuation, and spelling
0	**Lacks control of grammatical conventions appropriate to the writing task** • Lacks control of sentence formation • Lacks control of standard usage including agreement, tense, and case • Lacks control of mechanics including use of capitalization, punctuation, and spelling

Composing Rubric

Points	Description
4	• Topic/subject is clear, though it may or may not be explicitly stated • Maintains focus on topic/subject throughout the response • Organizational structure establishes relationships between and among ideas and/or events • Consists of a logical progression of ideas and/or events and is unified and complete • Support and elaboration are related to and supportive of the topic/subject • Consists of specific, developed details • Exhibits skillful use of vocabulary that is precise and purposeful • Demonstrates skillful use of sentence fluency
3	• Topic/subject is generally clear, though it may or may not be explicitly stated • May exhibit minor lapses in focus on topic/subject • Organizational structure establishes relationships between and among ideas and/or events, although minor lapses may be present • Consists of a logical progression of ideas and/or events and is reasonably complete, although minor lapses may be present • Support and elaboration may have minor weaknesses in relation to and support of the topic/subject • Consists of some specific details • Exhibits reasonable use of vocabulary that is precise and purposeful • Demonstrates reasonable use of sentence fluency
2	• Topic/subject may be vague • May lose or may exhibit major lapses in focus on topic/subject • Organizational structure may establish little relationship between and among ideas and/or events • May have major lapses in the logical progression of ideas and/or events and is minimally complete • Elaboration may have major weaknesses in relation to and support of the topic/subject • Consists of general and/or undeveloped details, which may be presented in a list-like fashion • Exhibits minimal use of vocabulary that is precise and purposeful • Demonstrates minimal use of sentence fluency
1	• Topic/subject is unclear or confusing • May fail to establish focus on topic/subject • Organizational structure may not establish connection between and among ideas and/or events • May consist of ideas and/or events that are presented in a random fashion and is incomplete or confusing • Elaboration attempts to support the topic/subject but may be unrelated or confusing • Consists of sparse details • Lacks use of vocabulary that is precise and purposeful • May not demonstrate sentence fluency
NS	This code may be used for compositions that are entirely illegible or otherwise unscorable: blank responses, responses written in a foreign language, restatements of the prompt, and responses that are off-topic or incoherent.

Writing Assessment Practice

NORTH CAROLINA

This year, you are required to take the North Carolina Writing Assessment. This test requires you to write an informational composition in response to a prompt. Below is one sample prompt. Use the prompt to practice writing in the test format. Then use the North Carolina Scoring Model to evaluate how well you did.

North Carolina Writing Assessment Sample Prompt

Read the following quotations about power, which is possession of control, authority, or influence over others.

"Nearly all men can stand adversity, but if you want to test a man's character, give him power."
Abraham Lincoln (1809–1865)

"You see what power is—holding someone else's fear in your hand and showing it to them!"
Amy Tan (1952–)

"Ultimately, the only power to which man should aspire is that which he exercises over himself."
Elie Wiesel (1928–)

"Knowledge is power."
Sir Francis Bacon (1561–1626)

"We have, I fear, confused power with greatness."
Stewart L. Udall (1920–)

Write an essay explaining how power can be used in both positive and negative ways. You may use the ideas presented above, your own experiences, observations, and/or readings.

As you write, remember to:

- Focus on the meaning of power.
- Consider the audience, purpose and context of your writing.
- Organize the ideas and details effectively.
- Include specific examples that clearly develop your writing.
- Edit your writing for standard grammar, spelling and punctuation.

Standardized Test Practice

Standardized Test and North Carolina Writing Assessment Practice

This year, your mastery of the Standard Course of Study for English language arts is measured by the North Carolina Writing Assessment. You may also take the PSAT as you begin to prepare for college. To do well on these exams, you'll need to practice.

The following pages provide four short tests with questions just like those you'll encounter on standardized tests. Your teacher will set the pace for the practice. As you work through the material, note the Skill Focus for each test and the types of questions that pose a struggle for you.

The Countdown

Test	Use After Unit	Skill Focus	Text Pages
1	3	Making Inferences Drawing Conclusions Poetic Forms Cultural Context	1–345
2	5	Analyzing Purpose Analyzing Imagery Summarize Archetypes and Symbols	346–711
3	7	Drawing Conclusions Reading Sonnets Allegory, Parody and Satire Historical Context Fables	712–1047
4	9	Character Symbolism Author's Voice Reading Contemporary Literature	1048–1365

A Note to Parents

The North Carolina Standard Course of Study outlines the knowledge that your child needs to pass the North Carolina Writing Assessment. Using the chart to the left, you can help your child review the skills covered in the textbook and monitor your child's progress toward mastering these concepts.

Standardized Test Practice

NORTH CAROLINA

Read the following poems and answer the questions that follow.

Hokku Poems in Four Seasons

by Yosa Buson

It penetrates into me;
stepping on the comb of my gone wife,
in the bedroom.

More than last year,
I now feel solitude;
this autumn twilight.

This being alone may even be a kind of happy
—in the autumn dusk.

Moon in the sky's top,
clearly passes through this
poor town street.
This feeling of sadness—
a fishing string being blown by the autumn wind.

1. How is the speaker of the poems different from the way he was last year?
   A. He misses his wife less.
   B. He is happier now.
   *C. He feels more alone.
   D. He enjoys the autumn dusk less.

2. Which characteristic of the selection is similar to that of a haiku?
   *A. It links nature to human nature.
   B. It contains only seventeen syllables.
   C. It tells a story.
   D. It has no distinct form.

3. What does the speaker mean when he says, "This feeling of sadness—a fishing string being blown by the autumn wind"?
   A. The start of autumn always brings a feeling of sadness.
   *B. Sadness can leave one feeling directionless and lost.
   C. People should let go of their sadness quickly.
   D. Sadness is an easy condition to overcome.

4. Which of the following statements is an example of a paradox?
   A. A fishing string being blown by the autumn wind.
   B. More than last year, I now feel solitude.
   C. It penetrates into me; stepping on the comb of my gone wife.
   *D. This being alone may even be a kind of happy.

5. Which of the following statements is ***best*** supported by the selection?
   *A. The speaker has grown accustomed to being alone.
   B. The speaker is happier now than he has been in the past.
   C. The speaker equates autumn with his late wife.
   D. The speaker has removed all reminders of his late wife from his life.

6. What is the significance of the author's references to autumn in the poem?
   *A. The moon and winds of autumn illuminate the speaker's sadness.
   B. The positive images of autumn serve as a contrast to the speaker's loneliness.
   C. Autumn represents a renewal of spirit and rebirth for the speaker.
   D. The autumn season was a favorite of the speaker's late wife.

Writing Prompt

Read the following quotations about education, which is the knowledge or skill obtained or developed by a learning process.

"Everyone has a right to a university degree in America, even if it's in Hamburger Technology."
–**Clive James**

"The foundation of every state is the education of its youth."
–**Diogenes Laertius,** 1732

"Only the educated are free."
–**Epictetus** (55 A.D.–135 A.D.), *Discourses*

"America believes in education: the average professor earns more money in a year than a professional athlete earns in a whole week."
–**Evan Esar** (1899–1995)

"Education is like a double-edged sword. It may be turned to dangerous uses if it is not properly handled."
–**Wu Ting-Fang**

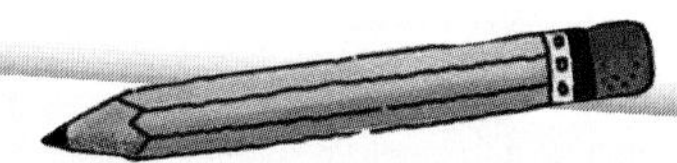

As you write, remember to:

- **Focus on the meaning of education.**
- **Consider the audience, purpose and context of your writing.**
- **Organize the ideas and details effectively.**
- **Include specific examples that clearly develop your writing.**
- **Edit your writing for standard grammar, spelling and punctuation.**

Write a speech for your class on the successes and failures of education in America.

You may use the ideas presented above, your own experience, observations, and/or readings.

Standardized Test Practice

An excerpt from a poem is included below. Read the selection and answer the questions that follow.

NORTH CAROLINA

The Wasteland

by T.S. Eliot

Unreal City,
Under the brown fog of a winter dawn,
A crowd flowed over London Bridge, so many,
I had not thought death had undone so many.
Sighs, short and infrequent, were exhaled,
And each man fixed his eyes before his feet.
Flowed up the hill and down King William Street,
To where Saint Mary Woolnoth kept the hours
With a dead sound on the final stroke of nine.
There I saw one I knew, and stopped him, crying "Stetson!"
"You who were with me in the ships at Mylae!"
"That corpse you planted last year in your garden,"
"Has it begun to sprout? Will it bloom this year?"
"Or has the sudden frost disturbed its bed?"

1. In this selection, which ***best*** describes the tone created by the author?
   A. despondent
   B. festive
   *C. tranquil
   D. hazardous

2. What does the frost symbolize?
   *A. the rebirth that occurs after death
   B. the cold winter climate
   C. the stagnancy of life
   D. the wilted garden

3. What effect does the author achieve with the image of the "brown fog"?
   A. It shows that the city described in the poem is fictional.
   B. It sheds light on how dark and dreary life is for the speaker.
   C. It describes how the winter season has changed the atmosphere.
   *D. It symbolizes the finality of death.

4. When describing the march of the crowd, the author writes, "each man fixed his eyes before his feet." What does this statement suggest?
   A. The people were walking with a decided purpose.
   *B. The people were ashamed to be a part of the march.
   C. The people were unable to see their way through the fog.
   D. The people were blindly following one another.

5. What characteristic of surrealism does the poem contain?
   *A. It is made up of the speaker's subconscious thoughts.
   B. It provides a philosophy about life.
   C. It describes ordinary people in everyday situations.
   D. It contains references to actual places and events.

6. What ***most likely*** causes the speaker to cry out to Stetson in the poem?
   A. The speaker wants to know what has become of Stetson's garden.
   B. The speaker wants to know the purpose of the crowd's march through London.
   *C. The speaker is desperate for a connection with someone he knows.
   D. The speaker is interested in learning about Stetson's life.

Standardized Test Practice

The following is a passage from *Candide* by Voltaire. Read this passage from a novel and answer the questions that follow.

Candide

by Voltaire

[Candide] asked charity of several grave-looking people, who one and all answered him, that if he continued to follow this trade they would have him sent to the house of correction, where he should be taught to get his bread.

He next addressed himself to a person who had just come from haranguing a numerous assembly for a whole hour on the subject of charity. The orator, squinting at him under his broadbrimmed hat, asked him sternly, what brought him thither and whether he was for the good old cause?

"Sir," said Candide, in a submissive manner, "I conceive there can be no effect without a cause; everything is necessarily concatenated (*connected*) and arranged for the best. It was necessary that I should be banished from the presence of Miss Cunegund; that I should afterwards run the gauntlet; and it is necessary I should beg my bread, till I am able to get it. All this could not have been otherwise."

1. Which of the following is an example of satire?
   A. The orator questions Candide's dedication to a cause.
   B. Candide implies that he is in want of food.
   *C. Candide seems to mock his own misfortune.
   D. The orator requires an hour to make his point.

2. Which **best** describes how suffering is portrayed in this selection?
   *A. with scorn
   B. with tolerance
   C. with empathy
   D. with justification

3. Based on the selection, which statement **most** closely explains the philosophy of Voltaire's day?
   A. One's fate is based on the will to change.
   *B. One's fate—whether good or bad—must be accepted.
   C. One may learn simply by observing others.
   D. One should seek advice from those who speak knowledgeably.

4. Based on the selection, which **best** defines the word haranguing?
   A. ignoring
   B. mocking
   C. alarming
   *D. criticizing

5. Which statement **best** describes Candide's interactions with people?
   A. People seem sympathetic toward Candide.
   *B. People seem to be lecturing Candide.
   C. People appear to listen intently to Candide.
   D. People appear to be ignoring Candide.

6. Based on the selection, what is the **most** supportable inference to make about Candide?
   A. He seems depressed about his lack of fortune.
   B. He appears unsympathetic to the needs of others.
   *C. He seems naive about what is wrong with the world.
   D. He appears interested in righting the wrongs of the world.

Standardized Test Practice

This selection is an excerpt from *The Iliad* by Homer. Read this passage and answer the questions that follow.

NORTH CAROLINA

from The Iliad

translated by Ian Johnston

The meeting came to order. Swift-footed Achilles rose to speak: "Son of Atreus, I fear we're being beaten back, forced home, if we aren't all going to be destroyed right here with war and plague killing off Achaeans. Come now, let's ask some prophet, priest, interpreter of dreams—for dreams, too, come from Zeus—a man who might say why Apollo is so angry, whether he faults our prayers and offerings, whether somehow he'll welcome sacrificial smoke from perfect lambs and goats, then rouse himself, to release us from this plague."

Achilles spoke and took his seat. Then Calchas, Thestor's son, stood up before them all, the most astute interpreter of birds, who understood present, future, past. His skill in prophecy, Apollo's gift, had led Achaean ships to Troy. He addressed the troops, thinking of their common good:

"Achilles, friend of Zeus, you ask me to explain Apollo's anger, the god who shoots from far. And I will speak. But first you listen to me. Swear an oath that you will freely help me in word and deed. For I think I may provoke someone who wields great power over Argives, a man who is obeyed by everyone. An angry king overpowers lesser men. Even if that day his anger is suppressed, resentment lingers in his chest, until one day he acts on it. So speak. Will you protect me?"

1. Based on the selection, what is the meaning of *astute?*
   *A. insensitive
   B. unusual
   C. perceptive
   D. eager

2. Based on his actions and words, which ***best*** describes Achilles?
   A. determined
   B. apprehensive
   *C. reserved
   D. angry

3. Which of the following ***best*** describes the purpose of the selection?
   A. to instruct the reader about a period in history
   *B. to relate a story from the author's childhood to the reader
   C. to inform the reader about ancient prophecies
   D. to entertain the reader with a tale about ancient warriors

4. What characteristic of epic poetry does this selection exhibit?
   A. It uses exaggeration to describe ordinary events.
   B. It involves a character interacting with the gods.
   C. It is based on real individuals from history.
   *D. It describes an intense battle.

5. Which of the following best summarizes the selection?
   *A. Achilles seeks the answer to what has angered Apollo.
   B. Calchas asks Achilles for his protection.
   C. Achilles describes the plight of the Achaeans.
   D. Calchas fears the wrath of an angry king.

6. What is the importance of the image of the angry king?
   A. It illustrates why Achilles and his men are unable to defeat Apollo.
   B. It shows why Apollo is killing off the Achaeans.
   *C. It explains why Calchas is reluctant to share his prophecy with Achilles.
   D. It describes why Zeus has not stepped in to help the Achaeans.

Writing Prompt

Read the following quotations about risk, which is the possibility of loss, injury or peril.

"The policy of being too cautious is the greatest risk of all."
–**Jawaharlal Nehru**

"Everything is sweetened by risk."
–**Alexander Smith**

"Nothing is worth doing unless the consequences may be serious."
–**George Bernard Shaw**

"Progress always involves risk; you can't steal second base and keep your foot on first base."
–**Fredrick Wilcox**

"You may be disappointed if you fail, but you are doomed if you don't try."
–**Beverly Sills**

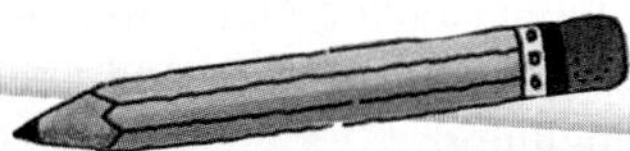

As you write your essay, remember to:

- Focus on the meaning of risk.
- Consider the audience, purpose and context of your writing.
- Organize the ideas and details effectively.
- Include specific examples that clearly develop your writing.
- Edit your writing for standard grammar, spelling and punctuation.

Write an essay about the importance and dangers of taking risks as a young adult. You may use the ideas presented above, your own experiences, observations, and/or readings.

PRENTICE HALL LITERATURE: A RICH TRADITION OF LEARNING SUCCESS

The Research Process

Since 1988, *Prentice Hall Literature* has been at the forefront of language arts instruction, providing teachers and their students with quality instruction and assessment tools to ensure success. Each successive edition builds on the strong heritage of *Prentice Hall Literature.*

To develop the current edition of *Prentice Hall Literature,* we conducted a variety of research studies, yielding three key elements of an effective language arts program: clean, clear, non-distracting design with considerate text; systematic, consistent skills instruction; and built-in benchmarking to ensure learning success. Our research comprised these three design stages:

1 EXPLORATORY NEEDS ASSESSMENT

In conjunction with Prentice Hall authors, we conducted research to explore proven educational reading methodologies. The results of this research were incorporated into our instructional strategy and pedagogy to create a more effective literature program. This stage included:

- Reading research
- Review of state standards
- Teacher interviews

2 FORMATIVE RESEARCH, DEVELOPMENT, AND FIELD-TESTING

During this phase of the research, we developed and field-tested prototype material with students and teachers. Results informed revisions to the final design and pedagogy. Formative research included:

- Field testing of prototypes in classroom pilots
- Classroom observations
- Teacher reviews
- Supervisor reviews
- Educator advisory panels

3 SUMMATIVE RESEARCH, VALIDATION RESEARCH

Finally, we have conducted and will continue to conduct longer-term research under actual classroom conditions. Research at this phase includes:

- Pilot-testing
- Prepublication learner verification research
- Postpublication validation studies, including validation of test questions
- Evaluation of results on standardized tests

RESEARCH BIBLIOGRAPHY

Reading

Alexander, Patricia A., and Tamara Jetton. "Learning from Text: A Multidimensional and Developmental Perspective." *Handbook of Reading Research*, vol. 3, ed. M. L. Kamil, P. B. Mosenthal, P. D. Pearson, and R. Barr. Mahwah, NJ: Lawrence Erlbaum Associates, 2000. 285–310.

Finders, Margaret J., and Susan Hynds. *Literacy Lessons: Teaching and Learning with Middle School Students.* Upper Saddle River, NJ: Merrill, 2003.

Guthrie, John T., and Allan Wigfield. "Engagement and Motivation in Reading." *Handbook of Reading Research,* vol. 3, ed. M. L. Kamil, P. B. Mosenthal, P. D. Pearson, and R. Barr. Mahwah, NJ: Lawrence Erlbaum Associates, 2000. 403–422.

Harvey, Stephanie, and Anne Goudvis. "Determining Importance in Text: The Nonfiction Connection." *Strategies That Work: Teaching Comprehension to Enhance Understanding.* Portland, ME: Stenhouse Publishers, 2000.

Langer, Judith. "Beating the Odds: Teaching Middle and High School Students to Read and Write Well," 1999. Center on English Learning and Achievement. May 2003. <http://cela.albany.edu/eie2/main.html>

National Reading Panel. *Teaching Children to Read: An Evidence-Based Assessment of the Scientific Research on Reading and Its Implications for Reading Instruction.* NIH Publication 00-4769. Bethesda, MD: U.S. Department of Health and Human Services, 2000.

Pressley, Michael. "What Should Comprehension Instruction Be the Instruction Of?" *Handbook of Reading Research*, vol. 3, ed. M. L. Kamil, P. B. Mosenthal, P. D. Pearson, and R. Barr. Mahwah, NJ: Lawrence Erlbaum Associates, 2000. 545–562.

Vocabulary

Baumann, J.F., and E.J. Kame'enui. *Vocabulary Instruction: From Research to Practice.* New York: Guilford Press, 2004.

Blachowicz, Camille, and Peter Fisher. *Teaching Vocabulary in All Classrooms*, 2nd ed. Upper Saddle River, NJ: Merrill, 2002.

Coxhead, Averil. "A New Academic Word List." *TESOL Quarterly*, 2000.

Kinsella, Kate. "Strategies to Teach Academic Vocabulary." Strategies to Promote Academic Literacy for Second Language Learners Within the English Language Arts Classroom, 2005.

Kinsella, Kate, and Kevin Feldman. *Narrowing the Language Gap: The Case for Explicit Vocabulary Instruction.* New York: Scholastic, Inc., 2005.

Marzano, Robert J. "The Developing Vision of Vocabulary Instruction." *Vocabulary Instruction: From Research to Practice.* New York: Guilford Press, 2004

Differentiated Instruction

Allington, Richard L. *What Really Matters for Struggling Readers: Designing Research-Based Programs.* New York: Longman, 2001.

Armbruster, Bonnie, and Thomas H. Anderson. "On Selecting 'Considerate' Content Area Textbooks." *Remedial and Special Education*, vol. 9 (1): 47–52.

Carnine, Douglas, Jerry Silbert, and Edward J. Kame'enui. *Direct Instruction Reading. 3rd ed.* Upper Saddle River, NJ: Prentice Hall, 1997.

Deshler, Donald D., Keith B. Lenz, and Brenda R. Kissam. *Teaching Content to All: Evidence-Based Inclusive Practices in Middle and Secondary Schools.* Boston: Allyn and Bacon, 2004.

Moore, David. W., and Kathleen A. Hinchman. *Starting Out: A Guide to Teaching Adolescents Who Struggle with Reading.* Boston: Allyn and Bacon, 2003.

Vaughn, Sharon, Candace S. Bos, and Jeanne Shay Schumm. *Teaching Exceptional, Diverse, and At-Risk Students in the General Education Classroom.* Boston: Allyn and Bacon, 2002.

FIELD-TESTING OF *PRENTICE HALL LITERATURE, PENGUIN EDITION*

Background In May 2004, six Language Arts teachers and 133 students field-tested Grade 7 and Grade 9 prototypes. Each teacher taught the prototype with one or more classes for three weeks. The students involved in the study represented a wide range of backgrounds and ability levels.

Prentice Hall researchers and editors used a variety of tools to gather information, including classroom observation and weekly debriefings with teachers who kept weekly lesson logs to note their experiences and observations about the prototype. In addition, we reviewed the results of pre-tests and post-tests to assess students' knowledge of the skills addressed in the prototypes.

Key Findings Reaction to the prototype from both teachers and students was highly favorable. The most highly-praised features of the program included the following:

Paired Selections: Teachers liked choosing which selection to teach. They agreed that this organization was useful for differentiated instruction.

Skills Instruction: Teachers praised the systematic skills instruction in the prototype. Classroom observation, teacher lesson logs, and student post-test results confirmed student mastery of the skills taught in the prototype.

Literature Selections: Students praised the selections as "interesting" and "fun-to-read," while teachers also noted that the content of the prototype was appropriate for their students' grade and ability levels.

Unit Authors: Teachers felt the featured unit authors added value by providing the writers' insights into their works.

Program Design and Organization: Both students and teachers enjoyed the bright, vibrant pictures. Teachers also commended the ratio of text to visuals, the consistent organization, and the ease of navigation.

How Field Testing Informed Development

Field Testing Finding	Result
Pacing The prototype included more material than could be taught in a three-week cycle.	The final product includes fewer part-level features and provides suggestions for revised pacing.
Reading Informational Materials Students and teachers commented that the prototype selection was not age-appropriate.	Editors identified selections for the feature that would be more relevant to students' everyday lives, such as articles, recipes, applications, and schedules.
Practice and Assess Questions Students and teachers told us that some questions were too complicated.	Questions in the final product are direct, clear, and concise.
Vocabulary Instruction Teachers told us that they wanted to see more vocabulary development.	We expanded the part vocabulary preview and review. For each selection, we developed Vocabulary Warm ups to increase the number of words taught per selection.

PRENTICE HALL LITERATURE: PROVEN TO GET RESULTS

National Effect-Size Study: Student Performance of *Prentice Hall Literature,* Users vs. Non-Users

This quasi-experimental study examined longitudinal test results of 976 closely matched user and non-user districts as a point of comparison across the same time periods and achievement tests.

Prentice Hall users performed as well or better than their counterparts, achieving approximately a 56% gain in the percentage of students meeting or exceeding state reading/ELA standards and a 62% gain in national percentile ranking after one or more years of program implementation. A sustained gain was noted in districts that have implemented the program for two or more years.

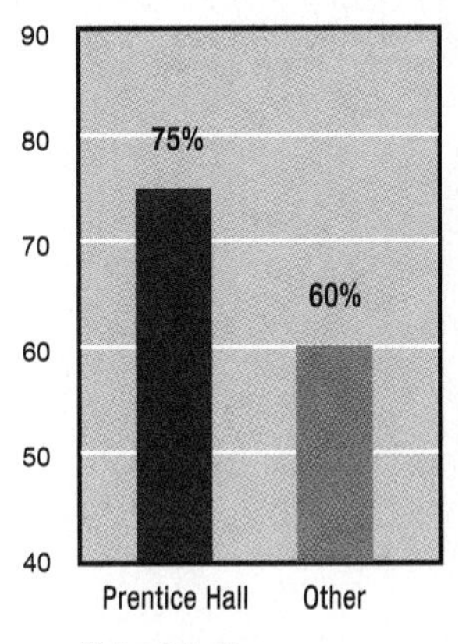

State: Colorado
Number of Districts: 10
Assessment: CSAP

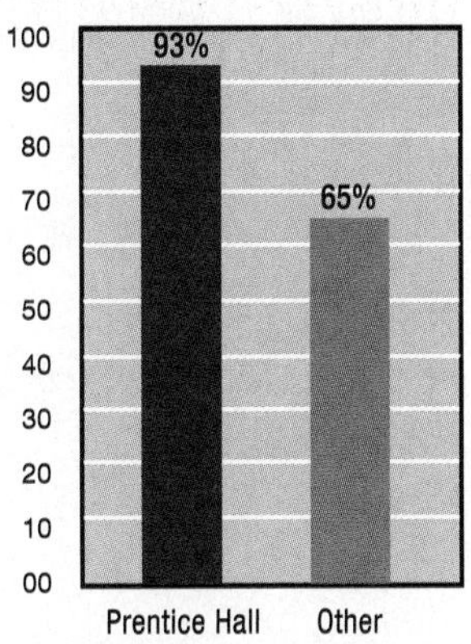

State: Arizona
Number of Districts: 34
Assessment: Stanford

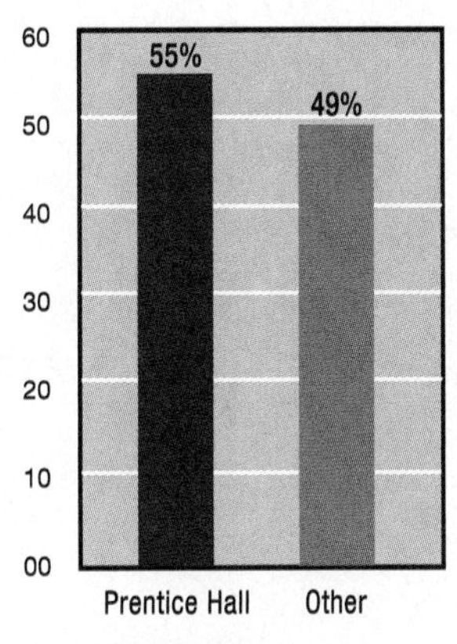

State: Tennessee
Number of Districts: 117
Assessment: Terra Nova

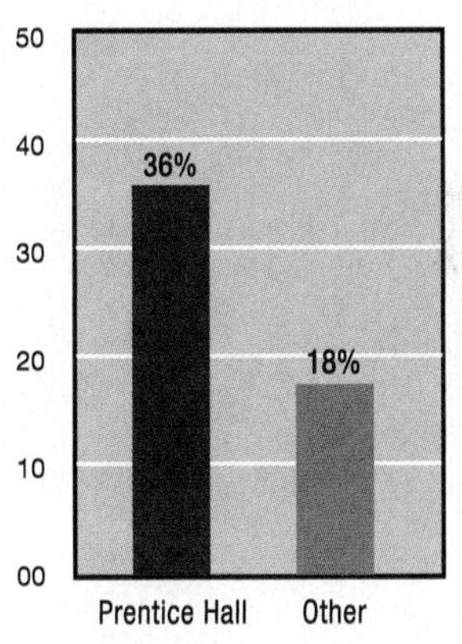

State: Ohio
Number of Districts: 43
Assessment: OPT

Learner Verification Research

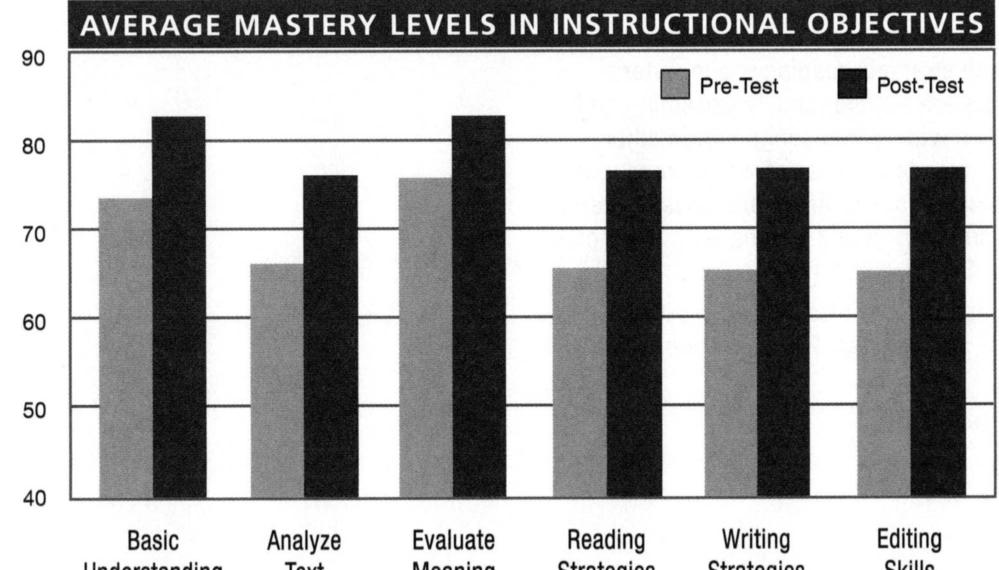

In a yearlong learner verification study, students using *Prentice Hall Literature* increased their mastery levels in several diagnostic skill areas for reading/language arts.

All students were tested at the start of the year with a nationally normed standardized test, the TerraNova™ Complete Battery Plus exam. At the end of the study period, students were retested with the same standardized test. Only students who completed both the pre- and post-tests were included in this analysis. All tests were scored by CTB/McGraw Hill, publisher of the TerraNova™.

PROFESSIONAL DEVELOPMENT GUIDEBOOK

The Prentice Hall contributing authors and advisors guided the pedagogical design and content of Prentice Hall Literature Penguin Edition. *Their expertise informed the development of instruction and support. In these pages, we share the authors' expertise on some of the key issues in language arts education.*

BECOMING A STRATEGIC READING TEACHER

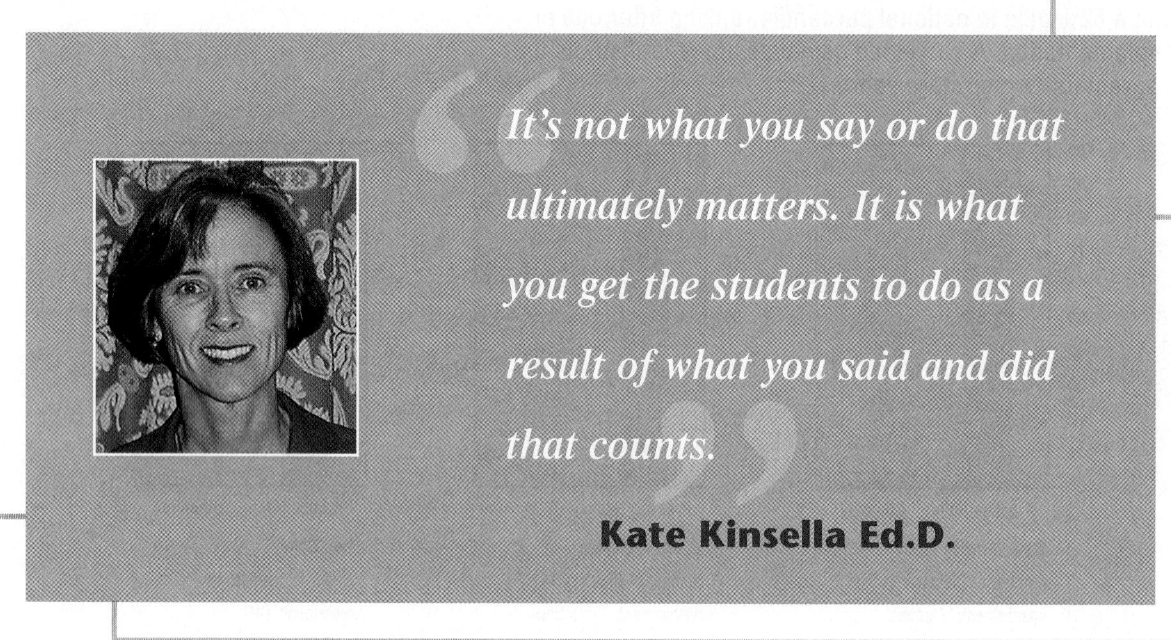
It's not what you say or do that ultimately matters. It is what you get the students to do as a result of what you said and did that counts.
Kate Kinsella Ed.D.

Strategic Reading

Recent research suggests that skillful and strategic reading is a long-term developmental process in which "readers are simultaneously extracting and constructing meaning" through interaction with written language. In other words, successful readers know how to decode all types of words, read with fluency and expression, have well-developed vocabularies, and possess various comprehension strategies such as note-taking and summarizing to employ as the reading task demands (Snow and Sweet, 2003).

Research illustrates that virtually all students benefit from direct, systematic, and explicit instruction in reading (Baker and Gersten, 2000). There are three stages to the instructional process:

- **Instructional Frontloading** (before reading)
- **Guided Instruction** (during reading)
- **Reflection and Study** (after reading)

Instructional Frontloading

If teachers emphasize preteaching, or frontloading instruction, they will help structure learning to ensure student success. Frontloading instruction is especially critical in mixed-ability classrooms with English language learners, students with special needs, and other students performing below grade level in terms of literacy. Before reading, prepare students with the following prereading activities and instruction:

- Introduce the big concepts.
- Provide direct teaching of vocabulary necessary to comprehend key ideas.
- Build academic vocabulary.
- Build, activate, and elaborate on background knowledge.
- Pique curiosity and guide students to generate questions.
- Use launch activities that incorporate key vocabulary.

Guided Instruction

In guided instruction, the teacher models approaches for how to actively engage with the text to gain meaning. The teacher guides the students through the text using reading strategies and then guides discussion about the content using participation strategies.

Structured Accountable Responses

During the instructional frontloading and the guided instruction, it is important to ensure participation by all students in a nonthreatening environment. The following strategies are ways to structure your instruction so that all students are accountable and prepared to participate.

Use partners. Partner response increases active language use, attention, and higher order thinking during instruction.

- Choose partners, alternating ranking based on literacy/social skills.
- Assign roles—such as *A* and *B*. *"A's tell B's two things we have learned about. . . ."*
- Give a specific topic. *"What do you predict. . . ?" "What are two things we have learned about. . . . ?"*
- Allow a brief time of exchange: *"A's tell B's two things we have learned about. . . ."*
- Call on students to share with the class after they have practiced with a partner.

Write first. Writing first increases thinking, accountability, and focus. It provides you as the teacher with concrete formative feedback. Having students write before responding connects written language to oral language, and it provides an opportunity for students to target academic language.

Nominate volunteers. Choosing volunteers based on your observations during partner work or written work allows you to ensure that all students participate and succeed. Circulate and observe as students discuss or write about the topic. Ask students to share their responses with you. Then, "nominate" the students you will ask to share with the class—that is, alert the student that he or she will be sharing with the class, so that the student can practice with a partner or with you before sharing with the larger group.

PRENTICE HALL LITERATURE

Putting Research Into Practice

You can introduce the big concepts for each selection using the **Connecting to the Selection** feature in the **Student Edition.**

You will find teaching plans for instructional frontloading in the ***General Resources*** including plans and student pages for the following activities:

- Anticipation Guide
- KWL Chart
- Idea Wave

PRENTICE HALL LITERATURE

Putting Research Into Practice

You can use questions and prompts provided in the **Student Edition** and the **Teacher's Edition** as prompts for structured accountable responses.

Language for Active Classroom Participation

Explicitly teach students ways to express themselves in class discussions. Model the use of these phrases, and encourage students to use them in responding.

Expressing an Opinion
I think that ____________.
I believe that ____________.
In my opinion, ____________.

Asking for Clarification
What do you mean?
Will you explain that again?
I have a question about that.

Soliciting a Response
What do you think?
Do you agree?

Individual Reporting
I discovered from ______ that ______.
I found out that ____________.
______ pointed out that ______.

Disagreeing
I don't agree with you because ______.
I got a different answer from yours.
I see it a different way.

Affirming
That's an interesting idea.
I hadn't thought of that.
I see what you mean.

Predicting
I predict that ____________.
I imagine that ____________.
Based on ______, I predict that ______.

Paraphrasing and Clarifying
So you are saying that ______.
In other words, you think that ______.
What I hear you saying is ______.

Acknowledging Ideas
My idea is related to ______'s idea.
My idea is similar to ______'s idea.
My idea builds on ______'s idea.

Partner and Group Reporting
We agreed that ____________.
We decided that ____________.
We had a different approach.
We had a similar idea.

Offering a Suggestion
Maybe we could ____________.
What if we ____________.
Here's something we might try.

Holding the Floor
As I was saying, ____________.
What I was trying to say was ______.

PRENTICE HALL LITERATURE

Putting Research into Practice

- Questions and notes in the **Student Edition** provide frequent, regular opportunities for applying the strategies.
- In the Reading and Vocabulary Preview, in the **Student Edition**, students learn the academic vocabulary needed to write and speak about the concepts taught in the parts of the unit.
- The **Teachers' Edition** provides strategies for ensuring student participation.
- You will find teaching plans and student pages in the ***General Resources*** for participation strategies, including
  - Oral Cloze
  - Choral Reading
  - ReQuest

Works Cited

Gersten, Russell and Scott K. Baker. "What We Know About Effective Instructional Practices for English-Language Learners." *Exceptional Children,* Vol. 66(4), 2000. 454-470.

Snow, Catherine E. and Anne Polselli Sweet. "Reading for Comprehension." *Rethinking Reading Comprehension.* New York: Guilford Press, 2003.

ENERGIZING VOCABULARY INSTRUCTION

> *Educators need to make robust intentional vocabulary instruction a high priority.*
>
> **Kevin Feldman Ed.D.**

Vocabulary Instruction

There is a clear consensus among literacy researchers that accelerating vocabulary growth is a vital and often neglected component of comprehensive language arts instruction (Baumann and Kame'enui, 2004). Numerous studies have documented the strong and reciprocal relationship between vocabulary knowledge and reading comprehension. Research focused on school-age second language learners similarly concludes that vocabulary knowledge is the single best predictor of their academic achievement across subject matter domains. Therefore, educators need to make robust intentional vocabulary instruction a high priority. Intensive instruction should focus on words related to central lesson concepts and high-use academic words. Academic word lists developed by researchers can help educators determine appropriate high-use academic words (Coxhead, 2000; Xue and Nation, 1984).

Big Ideas in Vocabulary Teaching

Connect
Assess students' current knowledge of the target lesson vocabulary. Give explanations before definitions. Use student-friendly explanations. Use language students already know. Use examples from students' experiential realm. Use synonyms.
Process
Have students give examples and images. Have students use "show you know" sentences. Have students generate synonyms and antonyms.
Practice
Have students use graphic organizers and webs. Have students use the words in new contexts.

Rationale for Direct Vocabulary Instruction

Over the past two decades, mounting research has challenged traditional views regarding the role of direct teaching in vocabulary development. Numerous studies have documented the positive impact of direct, explicit vocabulary instruction on both immediate word learning and longer-term reading comprehension (Baker, Simmons, and Kame'enui, 1995; Beck, McKeown, and Kucan, 2002; Biemiller, 2004; Marzano, 2004).

PRENTICE HALL LITERATURE

Putting Research Into Practice

- You can preteach academic vocabulary in the **Reading and Vocabulary Preview** at the beginning of each part of the **Student Edition**.
- All vocabulary activities in the **Student Edition** are structured to be generative, "show you know" types of activities.
- You can develop students' expressive vocabulary for talking about the big concepts and themes of the literature with the **Connecting to the Literature** feature that precedes every selection in the **Student Edition**.
- The **Teacher's Edition** provides consistent support for introducing vocabulary at the beginning of every selection.
- The ***Unit Resources*** provide generative activities for all vocabulary instruction and activities.

A Powerful Teaching Routine

The following steps can be elaborated and adapted, depending on the relative importance of the words in question and the students' background knowledge.

1) **Pronounce** The first step in teaching a new term is guiding students in correctly pronouncing the word. This will support learners in decoding the word confidently, while also supporting both auditory and muscle memory (Shaywitz, 2003).
2) **Explain** Understanding a new term requires a clear explanation of the meaning, using language familiar to the students (Beck et al., 2002; Stahl, 1999). Provide a synonym to solidify the connection between the new vocabulary term and students' prior knowledge.
3) **Provide examples** Students will usually need at least two or three examples of a new term to firmly grasp the meaning of it. Moreover, these examples should be drawn from a variety of contexts, not only the one used in the reading or lesson.
4) **Elaborate** Research in cognitive psychology consistently indicates that learners understand and remember information better when they elaborate on it themselves (Marzano et al., 2001). Thus, students' understanding of new vocabulary terms is strengthened when they are given opportunities to elaborate word meanings by generating their own examples.
5) **Assess** Research, such as Baker et al., (1995) and Marzano (2004) have documented the importance of incorporating regular informal assessment into the instructional process, especially with academically diverse learners. Assessment of vocabulary involves both formative evaluation (quick checks for understanding) and summative evaluation (formal quizzes or tests).

PRENTICE HALL LITERATURE

Putting Research Into Practice

- Use the Vocabulary notes in the **Teacher's Edition** for consistent, predictable vocabulary instruction structure.
- Use the **Vocabulary Knowledge Rating Sheet** in **General Resources** to assess students' current knowledge.
- Use the **Academic Vocabulary** lessons in the **Vocabulary Preview and Review** to introduce high-frequency words.
- Use the sample sentences in the **Vocabulary Builder** feature with each selection in the **Student Edition** to preteach words.

Works Cited

Baker, Scott, Deborah C. Simmons, and Edward J. Kame'enui. *Vocabulary Acquisition: Synthesis of the Research.* (Tech. Report No. 13). Eugene: University of Oregon, National Center to Improve the Tools of Educators, 1995.

Baumann, James F., and Edward J. Kame'enui. Eds. *Vocabulary Instruction: From Research to Practice.* New York: Guilford Press, 2004.

Beck, Isabel L., Margaret G. McKeown, and Linda Kucan. *Bringing Words to Life: Robust Vocabulary Instruction Solving Problems in the Teaching of Literacy.* New York: Guilford Publications, 2002.

Biemiller, Andrew. "Teaching Vocabulary in the Primary Grades: Vocabulary Instruction Needed." Eds. J.F. Baumann and Edward J. Kame'enui. *Vocabulary Instruction: From Research to Practice.* New York: Guilford Press, 2004.

Coxhead, Averil. "A New Academic Word List." *TESOL Quarterly,* 2000.

Marzano, Robert J., Debra J. Pickering, and Jane E. Pollock. *Classroom Instruction That Works: Research-Based Strategies for Increasing Student Achievement.* Alexandria, Virginia: Association for Supervision and Curriculum Development, 2001.

Marzano, Robert J. "The Developing Vision of Vocabulary Instruction." Eds. J.F. Baumann and E.J. Kame'enui. *Vocabulary Instruction: From Research to Practice.* New York: Guilford Press, 2004.

Shaywitz, Sally E. *Overcoming Dyslexia: A New and Complete Science-Based Program for Reading Problems at Any Level.* New York: Knopf, 2003.

Stahl, Steven A. *Vocabulary Development.* Cambridge: Brookline, 1999.

Xue, Guoyi, and I. S. P. Nation. "A University Word List." *Language Learning and Communication.* Vol. 3(2), 1984, 215-229.

GIVING HOPE TO STRUGGLING READERS

"Students with reading difficulties are very aware that they struggle. What is amazing is that despite these challenges, students are motivated to improve when given stimulating text, good instruction, and opportunities."

Sharon Vaughn, Ph.D.

Middle and high school students are expected to read at proficient levels and possess vocabularies and comprehension skills for understanding complex reading material. However, despite reading intervention programs during the primary grades, many students continue to experience learning problems well into their adolescent years. Many of these students experience difficulty in word recognition skills, decoding, reading fluency, and vocabulary development (Biancarosa and Snow, 2004). Moreover, besides their scant word recognition skills and poor reading fluency, students with low reading skills may demonstrate significant deficits in reading comprehension. Unfortunately, findings from previous research indicate that adolescents with reading-related learning disabilities become further behind in reading each year in school and risk losing the skills they acquired during elementary school.

Older students with reading disabilities need explicit and systematic instruction in reading. In addition, their instruction in reading is enhanced by experiences that are designed explicitly to foster vocabulary development, background knowledge, the ability to detect and comprehend relationships among verbal concepts, and the ability to actively use strategies to ensure understanding and retention of material.

PRENTICE HALL LITERATURE

Putting Research Into Practice

- **The Vocabulary and Reading Warm-ups** in the ***Unit Resources*** are explicitly designed to foster vocabulary development and build background knowledge.
- Use the ***Reader's Notebook*** series to enhance students' ability to actively use reading strategies taught in the **Student Edition.**

Attitudes Toward Reading

In general, students with low reading skills perceive reading as a difficult, unsuccessful, and unappealing activity (McKenna, Kear, and Ellsworth, 1995). Increasingly, researchers have used qualitative studies to describe middle and high school students' reading opportunities and reader characteristics. Kos (1991), for example, explores the reasons why middle school students reading problems persist. Using a case study approach, Kos identified three reasons why middle school students make limited progress in reading.

- First, although students are cognizant of their deficiencies in reading and in the instruction they have received and are motivated to improve their reading, they feel hopeless to do so in their current school situations.
- Second, reading problems may manifest themselves in stress-related behaviors and distraction from instruction.
- Third, even when students attempt to use reading strategies, they often fail to use them efficiently.

Bintz (1993) examined reasons for declining interest in reading during the middle and high school years. According to Bintz, although students, interest in school reading declines, they do not necessarily lose interest in pleasure reading and informational reading outside of school. Second, students are not nonstrategic in their approach to reading, nor do they use dysfunctional strategies. Rather, Bintz maintains, middle and high school students use different strategies for in-school and out-of-school reading. For instance, in school, students were observed using shortcut strategies to assist them in completing assignments. Outside of school, however, these students were more inclined to use higher-level strategies because the material was personally interesting. Third, students do not fit into developmental categories such as avid, passive, or reluctant readers, but instead demonstrate different literate behaviors depending on the tasks they perform, the texts they read, and the interpretive stances they adopt.

Likewise, Worthy and McKool (1996), through analysis of student interviews of sixth-grade students who were good readers but who also had negative attitudes toward reading, suggested that students' negative attitudes toward reading may be related to their limited opportunities in reading instruction. Students who indicated negative attitudes toward reading also indicated that they had limited opportunities to read independently, select reading materials, or read personally interesting materials in school. Moreover, their feelings about reading instruction and materials used in school might have distorted their opinion about reading in general and thus their willingness to read.

PRENTICE HALL LITERATURE

Putting Research Into Practice

- Use the **On Your Own** feature and the **For Further Reading** pages in the **Student Edition** to encourage independent reading.

Works Cited

Biancarosa, Gina, and Catherine E. Snow. "Reading Next—A Vision for Action and Research in Middle and High School Literacy: A Report to Carnegie Corporation of New York." Washington, DC: Alliance for Excellent Education, 2004.

Bintz, William P. "Resistant Readers in Secondary Education: Some Insights and Implications." *Journal of Reading.* Vol. 36(8), May 1993. 604-615.

Kos, Raylene. "Persistence of Reading Disabilities: The Voices of Four Middle School Students." *American Educational Research Journal.* Vol. 28(4), Winter 1991, 875-895.

McKenna, Michael C., Dennis J. Kear, and R. A. Ellsworth. "Children's Attitudes Toward Reading: A National Survey." *Reading Research Quarterly,* Vol. 30(4), 1995, 934-956.

Worthy, Jo, and S. McKool. "Students Who Say They Hate to Read: The Importance of Opportunity, Choice, and Access." Eds. Donald J. Leu, Charles K. Kinzer, and Kathleen Hinchman, *Literacies for the 21st Century: Research and Practice.* Chicago: National Reading Conference, 1996, 245-256.

MAKING THE DIFFERENCE MATTER

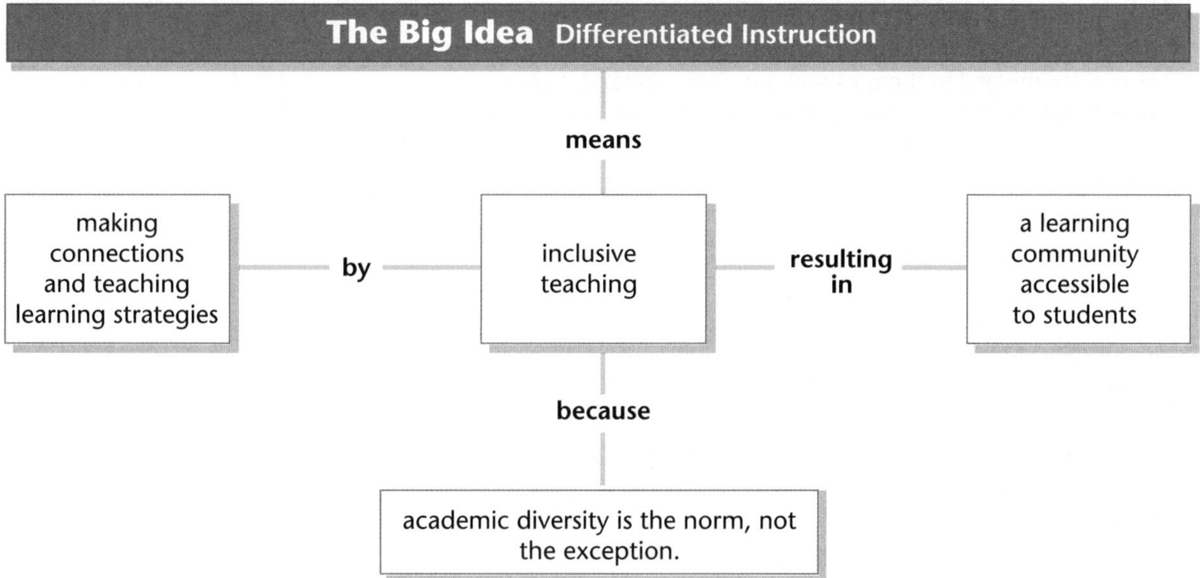
The Big Idea Differentiated Instruction
means
making connections and teaching learning strategies
by
inclusive teaching
resulting in
a learning community accessible to students
because
academic diversity is the norm, not the exception.

Why do we need differentiated instruction?

The wide range of academic diversity in schools today presents both a challenge and an opportunity to all teachers. Because the challenge is so great and the need to accommodate all students so urgent, we need to think about the problem of planning and teaching to include all learners in a new way.

Diversity is the norm. Thinking about diversity among students as the norm rather than as something out of the ordinary is the first step in building inclusive teaching practices. Diane Ferguson (1995) has noted that "Meaningful change will require nothing less than a joint effort to reinvent schools to be more accommodating to all dimensions of human diversity" (282). She argues that we must change our view of the school's role from one of providing educational services to one of providing educational support for learning:

> Valuing diversity and difference, rather than trying to change or diminish it so that everyone fits some ideal of similarity, leads to the realization that we can support students in their efforts to become active members of their communities....Perhaps the most important feature of support as a concept for schooling is that it is grounded in the perspective of the person receiving it, not the person providing it.

This is not to say, however, that differences should be ignored. It is important to respect differences and to incorporate them into the classroom and the curriculum, so that learning is grounded in what is familiar to students.

Don Deshler, Ph.D.

Works Cited

Ferguson, Diane L. "The Real Challenge of Inclusion: Confessions of a 'Rabid Inclusionist.'" *Phi Delta Kappan.* Vol. 77(4), 1995, 281-87.

How do we provide inclusive instruction?

Make connections. What does it mean to make connections? It means that as a teacher you need to be as concerned about understanding your students and what is important and meaningful to them as you are about understanding your content and how to teach it. Making connections means that students need to believe that what you want to teach is important and relevant to them and that you can and will help them learn. Making connections also means that you as the teacher need to believe it is worthwhile to build a learning community in your classroom, to know and understand your students well enough to make choices about content and instruction so that all students have an opportunity to learn. Every good teacher aspires to these goals, and many teachers successfully realize them. But as academic diversity among students grows in secondary schools, teachers need more support and more tools to be effective with all learners. Support can be gained, we believe, by thinking about a classroom as a learning community where teacher and students work together to ensure that everyone is learning. More tools become available with the implementation of teaching routines and learning strategies that make learning more accessible to more learners.

Understand what students already know. What students already know, or their "prior knowledge," comes not only from what students have previously learned in school, but also from their lived experiences. Lived experience includes all the differences that students bring with them into the schools, such as culture, language, ethnic background, as well as previous learning successes or failures. Valuing and using the prior knowledge of students allows teachers to link new knowledge to what students already know, thereby making learning more meaningful for students. It also allows students to construct new knowledge for themselves.

Teach learning strategies. Finally, students are more likely to make connections in learning the content in your class if they know how to learn. All good listeners use strategies to learn new things. Some students are better than others at developing strategies to learn. Inclusive teaching means that you have to take into account whether all your students are good strategic learners, and the only way to do this is to teach them—explicitly—how to use and develop learning strategies.

What is the result of differentiated instruction?

A learning community. Making connections and building a learning community in your classroom will establish an environment where learning, cooperation, and respect for differences are all valued. The "work" of this community is learning. Everyday practices and routines are based on cooperation in accomplishing this work, and the interests and learning needs of everyone in the community are taken seriously.

PROGRAM CONSULTANTS

The Prentice Hall national language arts consultants advised on many aspects of this program, particularly the professional development strand. The professional development notes in this textbook represent successful strategies acquired and applied during their many years of experience in classrooms.

Yvonne R. Cadiz
Language Arts, ESOL, and Spanish teacher
Curriculum Specialist for ESOL
Hillsborough County, Tampa, FL
Director of the MERIT Program (Multilingual Educational Resource Information and Training Program), University of South Florida

Anita Clay
District Coordinator, Gateway Institute of Technology
St. Louis, MO

Nancy McDonald
K-12 Reading Specialist
Waterloo School District, Waterloo, WI
Belleville School District, Belleville, WI
Title I Language Arts Teacher, 6-8
Beloit Turner Middle School, Beloit, WI
Grade 8 Language Arts Teacher
Olson Junior High School, Woodstock, IL

Jean Ripple
Language Arts Teacher, 1-10
Model Classroom for Inclusion
Pennsylvania

John R. Scannell
Teacher, 9-12 English, Writing, Acting and Drama, Debate and Public Address
Newport HS, Bellevue, WA
Lykens Jr. HS, Lykens, PA
Nazareth HS, Nazareth, PA

Kathryne Lewis Stewart
Director of Humanities Instruction
Tomball Independent School District
Tomball, TX
Teacher/GT Specialist
Burleson High School
Burleson Independent School District
Burleson, TX

Joseph A. Wieczorek, Ph.D.
Instructor, Georgetown University
College of Notre Dame
University of Maryland, Baltimore County
Howard County Public Schools, MD
Language Specialist, FBI

LITERATURE REVIEW PANEL

These teachers helped develop the Penguin Edition of *Prentice Hall Literature* by testing new selections by contemporary authors and gathering student questions for these authors to answer. The work of these teachers helped ensure that the program would be truly interactive, with a built-in dialogue between authors and students.

Sherry Abner
Two Rivers Middle School
Covington, KY

Heather Barnes
Central Crossing High School
Grove City, OH

Bonnie Bellows
Humboldt Senior High School
St. Paul, MN

Shawn L. Brumfield
Los Angeles Unified School District
Los Angeles, CA

Donna Burch
Southern Middle School
Somerset, KY

Susanne Buttrey
Sycamore Middle School
Pleasant View, TN

Denise Campbell
Cherry Creek School District
Centennial, CO

Holly Carr
Central Crossing High School
Grove City, OH

Vanessa Carroll
LBJ High School
Austin, TX

Joanne Chambers
Swiftwater Intermediate School
Swiftwater, PA

Susan Cisna
East Prairie Junior High School
Tuscola, IL

Nancy DiGasso
Pine Bush High School
Pine Bush, NY

Karen Gibson
Appleton North High School
Appleton, WI

Margaret Jan Graham
Cobb Middle School
Tallahassee, FL

Doris Sue Hawkins
C. W. Otto Middle School
Lansing, MI

Deanna Hilliard
Soddy Daisy Middle School
Soddy Daisy, TN

Helen Hudson
Crawfordsville High School
Crawfordsville, IN

Gisele Le Duc
East Lyme Middle School
Niantic, CT

Greg MacAvoy
Pine Bush High School
Pine Bush, NY

Deb Madej
Norris Middle School
Omaha, NE

Nancy Mast
Hobart Middle School
Hobart, IN

Nancy Monroe
Bolton High School
Alexandria, LA

Suzanne Moore
Sunrise Middle School
Clackamas, OR

Paul Putnoki
Torrington Middle School
Torrington, CT

Herb Ranlose
Zion Benton High School
Zion, IL

Robert Rarrick
Union Endicott Senior High
Endicott, NY

Margaret St. Sauver
St. Paul Public Schools
St. Paul, MN

Denise Greer Wallace
Western Valley Middle School
Phoenix, AZ

Debbie Watts
Jacobs Fork Middle School
Newton, NC

Melissa Williams
Delsea Regional High School
Franklinville, NJ

Charles Youngs
Bethel Park High School
Bethel Park, PA

1 WHERE DO I START?

Right here! These pages will guide you through the program's organization and describe the resources you have available to enrich your teaching. *Prentice Hall Literature, Penguin Edition,* is carefully designed to make pacing, lesson planning, teaching, and assessment easier.

2 HOW DO I INTRODUCE THE UNIT?

Each unit in this book presents the literature of a specific time period. The unit is hosted by a featured contemporary author, scholar, or translator who introduces a literary trend or theme in the **Setting the Scene** essay.

The *From the Author's Desk* orange banner appears throughout the unit when the featured author appears.

Use the unit **Introduction** to develop students' understanding and appreciation for literature in its broader context.

The timeline shows the literature in the context of key world events and other literary milestones.

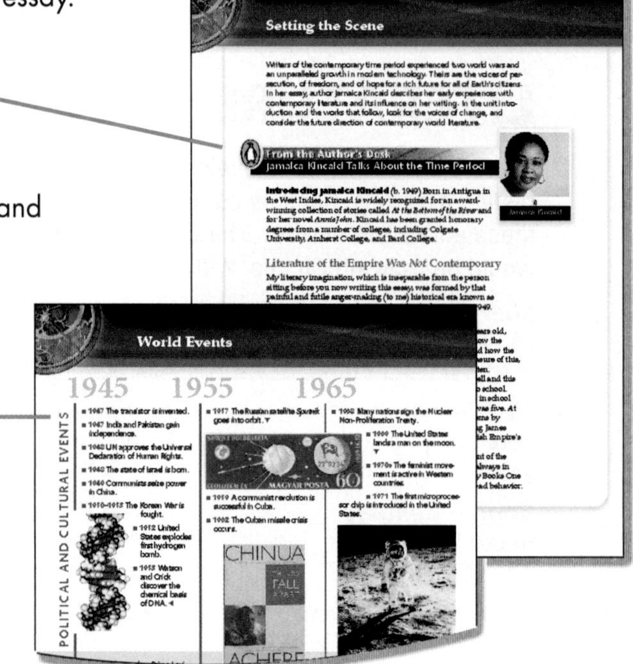

Technology

From the Author's Desk

Stimulate students' interest with this engaging DVD featuring in-depth interviews with unit authors discussing unit concepts, literature, history, reading, and writing.

Use the **History of the Period** and the **Literature of the Period** essays to introduce the major events, influential people, critical themes, and important trends of the time period. This background information will build a strong foundation for the literary exploration to follow in the unit selections.

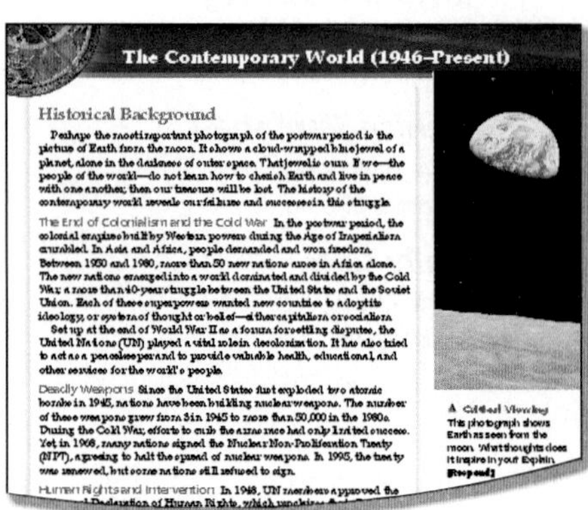

3 WHAT SHOULD I USE TO PLAN AND PREPARE?

Start your planning with the **Time and Resource Manager** before every selection or selection grouping. This guide provides these tools:

- a detailed lesson plan
- suggestions for incorporating program resources into your instruction
- recommendations for pacing each element of your lesson
- information about lesson objectives

Meeting Your Standards
Standards coverage information

Step-by-Step Teaching Guide
A systematic approach to teaching the literature

Pacing Guide
Suggested pacing information

Resources
Suggested resources for differentiated instruction

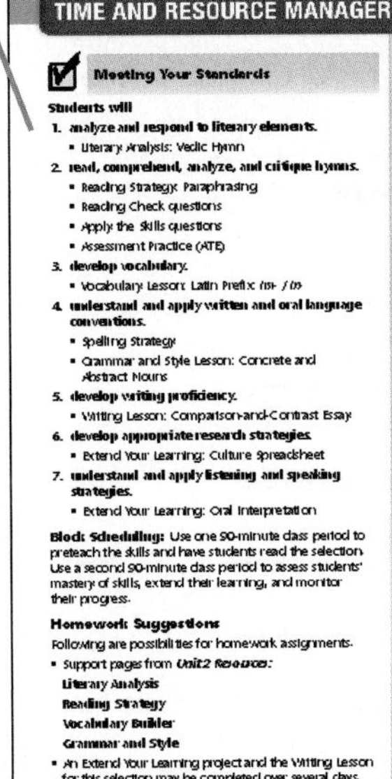

TIME AND RESOURCE MANAGER

Meeting Your Standards

Students will

1. **analyze and respond to literary elements.**
   - Literary Analysis: Vedic Hymn
2. **read, comprehend, analyze, and critique hymns.**
   - Reading Strategy: Paraphrasing
   - Reading Check questions
   - Apply the Skills questions
   - Assessment Practice (ATE)
3. **develop vocabulary.**
   - Vocabulary Lesson: Latin Prefix *im-* / *in-*
4. **understand and apply written and oral language conventions.**
   - Spelling Strategy
   - Grammar and Style Lesson: Concrete and Abstract Nouns
5. **develop writing proficiency.**
   - Writing Lesson: Comparison-and-Contrast Essay
6. **develop appropriate research strategies.**
   - Extend Your Learning: Culture Spreadsheet
7. **understand and apply listening and speaking strategies.**
   - Extend Your Learning: Oral Interpretation

Block Scheduling: Use one 90-minute class period to preteach the skills and have students read the selection. Use a second 90-minute class period to assess students' mastery of skills, extend their learning, and monitor their progress.

Homework Suggestions

Following are possibilities for homework assignments.

- Support pages from *Unit 2 Resources:*
  Literary Analysis
  Reading Strategy
  Vocabulary Builder
  Grammar and Style
- An Extend Your Learning project and the Writing Lesson for this selection may be completed over several days.

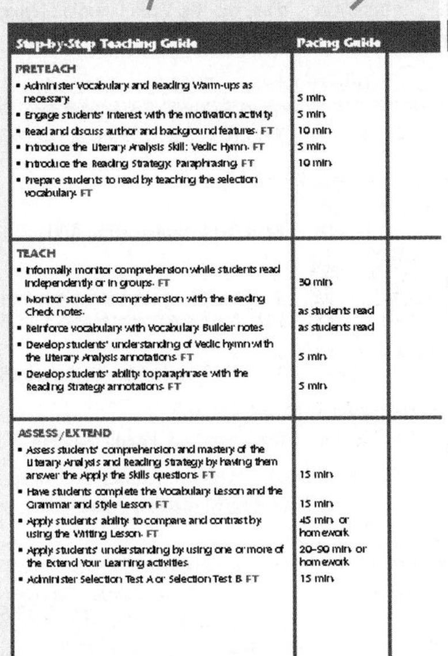

from the Rig Veda

Step-by-Step Teaching Guide	Pacing Guide
PRETEACH	
• Administer Vocabulary and Reading Warm-ups as necessary.	5 min.
• Engage students' interest with the motivation activity.	5 min.
• Read and discuss author and background features. FT	10 min.
• Introduce the Literary Analysis Skill: Vedic Hymn. FT	5 min.
• Introduce the Reading Strategy: Paraphrasing. FT	10 min.
• Prepare students to read by teaching the selection vocabulary. FT	
TEACH	
• Informally monitor comprehension while students read independently or in groups. FT	30 min.
• Monitor students' comprehension with the Reading Check notes.	as students read
• Reinforce vocabulary with Vocabulary Builder notes.	as students read
• Develop students' understanding of Vedic hymn with the Literary Analysis annotations. FT	5 min.
• Develop students' ability to paraphrase with the Reading Strategy annotations. FT	5 min.
ASSESS/EXTEND	
• Assess students' comprehension and mastery of the Literary Analysis and Reading Strategy by having them answer the Apply the Skills questions. FT	15 min.
• Have students complete the Vocabulary Lesson and the Grammar and Style Lesson. FT	15 min.
• Apply students' ability to compare and contrast by using the Writing Lesson. FT	45 min. or homework
• Apply students' understanding by using one or more of the Extend Your Learning activities.	20–90 min. or homework
• Administer Selection Test A or Selection Test B. FT	15 min.

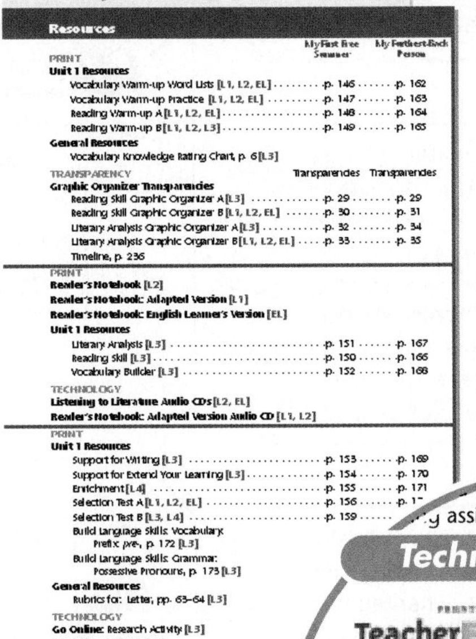

Resources	My First Free Summer	My Farthest-Back Person
PRINT		
Unit 1 Resources		
Vocabulary Warm-up Word Lists [L1, L2, EL]	p. 146	p. 162
Vocabulary Warm-up Practice [L1, L2, EL]	p. 147	p. 163
Reading Warm-up A [L1, L2, EL]	p. 148	p. 164
Reading Warm-up B [L1, L2, L3]	p. 149	p. 165
General Resources		
Vocabulary Knowledge Rating Chart, p. 6 [L3]		
TRANSPARENCY	Transparencies	Transparencies
Graphic Organizer Transparencies		
Reading Skill Graphic Organizer A [L3]	p. 29	p. 29
Reading Skill Graphic Organizer B [L1, L2, EL]	p. 30	p. 31
Literary Analysis Graphic Organizer A [L3]	p. 32	p. 34
Literary Analysis Graphic Organizer B [L1, L2, EL]	p. 33	p. 35
Timeline, p. 236		
PRINT		
Reader's Notebook [L2]		
Reader's Notebook: Adapted Version [L1]		
Reader's Notebook: English Learner's Version [EL]		
Unit 1 Resources		
Literary Analysis [L3]	p. 151	p. 167
Reading Skill [L3]	p. 150	p. 166
Vocabulary Builder [L3]	p. 152	p. 168
TECHNOLOGY		
Listening to Literature Audio CDs [L2, EL]		
Reader's Notebook: Adapted Version Audio CD [L1, L2]		
PRINT		
Unit 1 Resources		
Support for Writing [L3]	p. 153	p. 169
Support for Extend Your Learning [L3]	p. 154	p. 170
Enrichment [L4]	p. 155	p. 171
Selection Test A [L1, L2, EL]	p. 156	p. 1–
Selection Test B [L3, L4]	p. 159	
Build Language Skills: Vocabulary: Prefix *pre-*, p. 172 [L3]		
Build Language Skills: Grammar: Possessive Pronouns, p. 173 [L3]		
General Resources		
Rubrics for: Letter, pp. 63–64 [L3]		
TECHNOLOGY		
Go Online: Research Activity [L3]		
Go Online: Self-test [L3]		
ExamView®, **Test Bank** [L3]		

Technology

PRENTICE HALL **Teacher EXPRESS™** Plan · Teach · Assess — Use this complete suite of powerful teaching tools to make lesson planning and testing quicker and easier.

PRENTICE HALL **Student EXPRESS™** Learn · Study · Succeed — Use the Interactive Textbook (online and on CD-ROM) to make selections and activities come alive with audio and video support and interactive questions.

4 HOW DOES THE PROGRAM HELP ME WITH PACING?

The **Diagnostic and Benchmark Tests** divide the program into three-week instructional blocks, with each segment focusing on core skills and standards. This consistent organization ensures thorough skills coverage presented in manageable chunks. A benchmark test is provided for each part, allowing you to administer assessment at 3-, 6-, or 9-week intervals. This systematic, logical organization with built-in progress monitoring allows you to make sound instructional choices for your class without missing any skills or standards.

5 HOW DO I TEACH EACH UNIT?

A Start each unit with the **Introduction,** featuring the unit author and providing key literary and historical background.

B Teach literary analysis with representative literature of the period. (See p. T53 for more information.)

C Develop student mastery of literary elements with the instruction in **Focus on Literary Forms** and the selections that follow.

D Use **A Closer Look** features for an in-depth exploration of trends in literature.

E Teach **Comparing Literary Works** groupings to help students analyze literary elements in two or more selections. (See p. T53 for more information.)

F Present **Connections** features to show the thematic relationship among works from different literary heritages.

G Show students how to apply reading skills to real-life reading situations with the **Reading Informational Materials** features.

H Use the Skills Workshops to provide opportunities for skills practice and high-stakes test preparation.

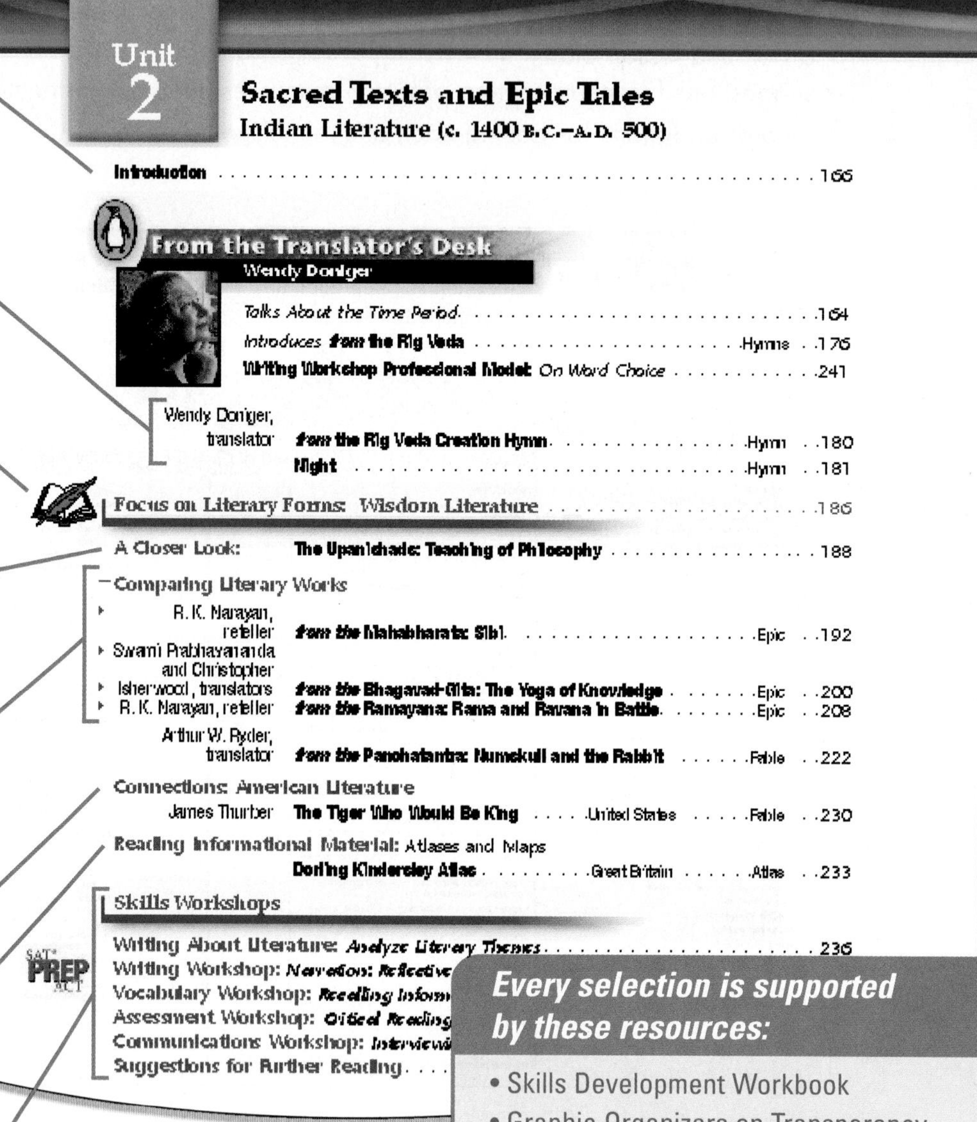

Unit 2

Sacred Texts and Epic Tales
Indian Literature (c. 1400 B.C.–A.D. 500)

SAT PREP ACT

Every selection is supported by these resources:

- Skills Development Workbook
- Graphic Organizers on Transparency
- Selection Tests
- Reader's Notebook series
- Listening to Literature audio program
- Student Express
- Teacher Express

6 HOW DO I TEACH A SELECTION?

Each selection or selection grouping follows a consistent pattern. This allows you and your students to appreciate significant works of literature by developing essential literary analysis and critical reading skills.

Check the **Accessibility at a Glance** chart in the Teacher's Edition for an analysis of the factors influencing accessibility, and choose the most appropriate literature for your students.

Use the **Build Skills** pages to present a full author biography and instruction on literary analysis, reading strategy, and vocabulary. Build context with the **Background** notes that appear at the beginning of each selection.

After completing the selection, use the **Critical Reading** and **Apply the Skills** pages to assess students' understanding. For grammar, vocabulary skills, and writing practice, use the **Build Language Skills** pages.

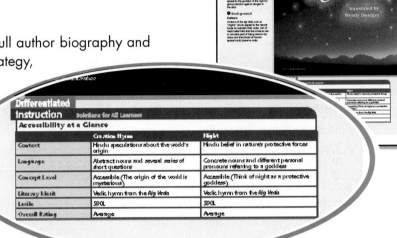

Differentiated Instruction Solutions for All Learners

Accessibility at a Glance

	Creation Hymn	Night
Context	Hindu speculations about the world's origin	Hindu belief in nature's protective forces
Language	Abstract nouns and several series of short questions	Concrete nouns and different personal pronouns referring to a goddess
Concept Level	Accessible (The origin of the world is mysterious)	Accessible (Think of night as a protective goddess)
Literary Merit	Vedic hymn from the *Rig Veda*	Vedic hymn from the *Rig Veda*
Lexile	590L	590L
Overall Rating	Average	Average

7 HOW DO I DIFFERENTIATE INSTRUCTION?

Prentice Hall Literature provides unprecedented opportunities for differentiated instruction:

- **Teacher's Edition:** Use the strategies and techniques geared toward different reading levels and learning styles.
- **Reader's Notebooks:** Customize instruction for every selection with reading support for struggling readers and English learners.
- **Leveled Vocabulary and Reading Warm-ups:** For each selection, build background, fluency, and vocabulary.
- **Leveled Selection Tests:** Choose from two tests for each selection, according to your students' ability levels.
- **Graphic Organizers:** Give struggling readers additional support with completed versions of all organizers in the Student Edition.

Differentiated Instruction Solutions for All Learners

Support for Special Needs Students
Students may have difficulty understanding that the dialogue between Jean and Priscilla is imaginary. Make certain that they understand the purpose of the note at the bottom of the previous page. Then remind students that the Pilgrims were the first people from Europe to move to America and that some of them arrived on the *Mayflower*. Explain that when Jean opens the book, she imagines the Pilgrims are with her and on their way to America just as she will be one day soon.

Enrichment for Gifted/Talented Students
Ask students to consider why Jean probably relates to Priscilla. Have them think of story characters with whom they identify or admire. Have them create an imaginary discussion with the character of their choice. Their discussion should consider an issue or solve a problem. Encourage students to choose their individual tone (e.g., serious, formal, humorous) and perform the dialogue for the class.

8 WHEN DO I TEACH WRITING?

This program incorporates opportunities in every unit for both process writing and writing for assessment.

Process Writing In each unit, a **Writing Workshop** with step-by-step instruction guides students to develop their ideas into full-length compositions, addressing these key stages in the writing process:

- Prewriting
- Drafting
- Revising
- Editing and Proofreading
- Publishing and Presenting

In addition, a **Writing About Literature** workshop in each unit provides practice in analytical writing, guiding students through the key areas of writing a thesis statement, gathering evidence, and drafting a response to a specific literature-based prompt.

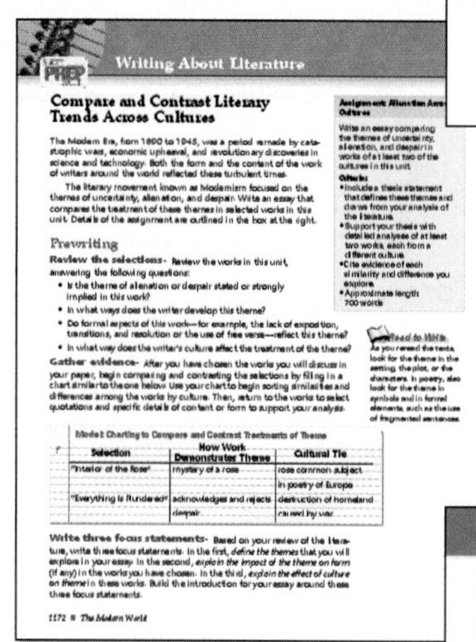
Writing About Literature

Compare and Contrast Literary Trends Across Cultures

Timed Writing To address the growing call for on-demand writing and to prepare students for college entrance exams, the program provides many opportunities in each unit to help students practice writing for assessment. Timed Writing prompts ask students to produce brief expository or persuasive writing relating to the literature they have read.

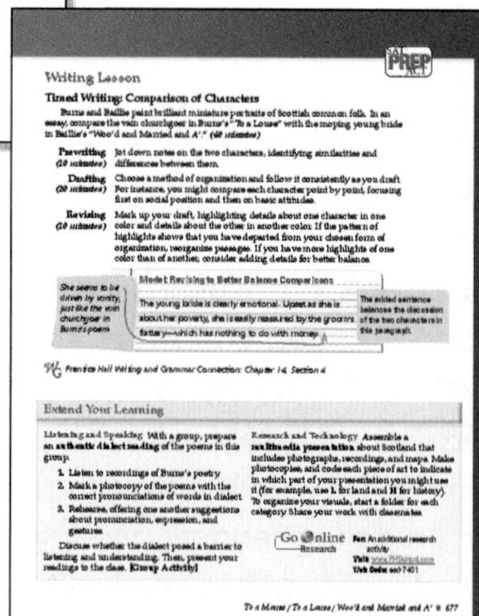
Writing Lesson

Timed Writing: Comparison of Characters

Extend Your Learning

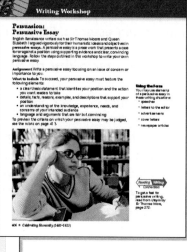

Technology

Score student essays in seconds.

Finally, to facilitate your teaching of writing, the Prentice Hall **Online Essay Scorer** provides instant scoring and feedback, plus tips for revision. You save time and your students become better writers!

9 HOW DO I MONITOR STUDENT PROGRESS?

Prentice Hall makes progress monitoring easy with frequent opportunities to evaluate student progress and to reteach material.

- Use the **Diagnostic Tests** as indicated to determine readiness. You will find frequent reading checks and suggestions in the Teacher's Edition for monitoring student progress during reading.
- After reading the selections, use the **Selection Tests** to assess comprehension and mastery of the reading and literary analysis skills.
- As you teach the unit, use the **Monitor Your Progress** pages in standardized-test format. These appear after the Reading Informational Materials section and in unit workshops to give students practice in applying specific skills under test-taking conditions.
- Use the **Benchmark Tests** to monitor progress at regular, frequent intervals. For your convenience, tests are provided at 3-week intervals.

Technology

Monitor student progress instantly in an interactive format.

Access companion Web sites for self-tests.

Use the electronic test generator to customize assessment.

10 HOW DOES PRENTICE HALL LITERATURE HELP ME DEVELOP AS A TEACHER?

The Teacher's Edition provides built-in professional development. Look for these special features:

- **Step-by-Step Teaching:** Margin notes provide strategies, tips, and examples for teaching skills.
- **Differentiated Instruction:** Notes provide support, strategies, and enrichment for learners of varied abilities.
- **Professional Development:** Pedagogical explanations of specific techniques enhance your effectiveness as a teacher.

Using *Prentice Hall Literature* to Prepare Students for the North Carolina

Writing Assessment

NORTH CAROLINA

The North Carolina testing system includes a Writing Assessment, which is administered in English II.

In English II, students in North Carolina are required to take the North Carolina Writing Assessment. In addition to this assessment, students may also take standardized tests, such as the PSAT or SAT, as they begin to prepare for college.

The North Carolina Writing Assessment was developed with the understanding that an emphasis on writing instruction was necessary and that measurement of writing would enhance instruction. Students in English II are assessed on the informational mode, and the prompt will be either definition, cause/effect, or problem/solution. Sample prompts are provided in the North Carolina Student Edition, as well as in the *North Carolina Test Preparation Workbook*.

Students' written responses are then evaluated against the North Carolina Writing Assessment Scoring Model, which includes the 4-point Content Rubric and the 2-point Conventions Rubric.

The North Carolina Writing Assessment and standardized tests such as the PSAT and SAT challenge students to apply their critical thinking and writing skills. This feature explains how you can use the *Prentice Hall Literature* textbook to facilitate your students' mastery of standards and prepare them for the North Carolina Writing Assessment and other standardized tests.

1 *Use the Writing Workshop features to provide ongoing practice with the skills that students will use on the North Carolina Writing Assessment.*

The North Carolina Writing Assessment, administered in English II, requires students to demonstrate proficiency in the informational mode of writing. Typically, the prompt consists of a series of quotes that focus on a theme on which students are asked to reflect personally.

Each of the nine **Writing Workshops** offer short prompts and brainstorming opportunities. These then culminate in the drafting of a complete response, followed by the proofing and publishing phases. Repeatedly following each of these steps will help students hone their composition and conventions skills, both of which are the focus of the North Carolina Scoring Model.

Writing Workshop

Narration: Autobiographical Narrative

Some of the best stories you may read are not made up—they tell of real events in the writer's life. Such stories are called autobiographical narratives (see the definition at right). Follow the steps outlined in this workshop to write your own autobiographical narrative.

Assignment Write an autobiographical narrative about an event in your life that helped you grow or changed your outlook.
- a short story
- a poem

NC Standard Course of Study
- Elaborate upon a past experience from current perspective. (L.1.01.1)
- Edit for correct spelling and punctuation. (GU.6.02.6)

2 Use North Carolina Writing Assessment Sample Prompts in the Student Edition and North Carolina Test Preparation Workbook to provide ongoing practice leading up to the assessment.

Prentice Hall Literature's North Carolina World Masterpieces Student Edition includes three sample prompts, which can be found on pages NC 36, 39, and 43. These three prompts are a direct model of the type to which North Carolina students will be required to respond. In addition, the *North Carolina Test Preparation Workbook* also provides additional prompts as well as samples of different levels of student responses.

North Carolina Writing Assessment Sample Prompt

Read the following quotations about imagination, which is the act or power of forming a mental image of something not present to the senses or never before wholly perceived in reality; creative ability.

"The secret to creativity is knowing how to hide your sources."
Albert Einstein (1879 – 1955)

"Creativity is a drug I cannot live without."
Cecil B. DeMille (1881 – 1959)

"To live a creative life, we must lose our fear of being wrong."
Joseph Chilton Pearce (1856 – 1950)

"Every child is an artist. The problem is how to remain an artist once he grows up."
Pablo Picasso (1881 – 1973)

Use the blank sheet of paper given to you by your teacher to plan your writing. Anything you write on the blank sheet will not be scored. You must write the final copy of your speech on a blank sheet.

As you write, remember to:

- Focus on the meaning of imagination.
- Consider the audience, purpose and context of your writing.
- Organize the ideas and details effectively.
- Include specific examples that clearly develop your writing.
- Edit your writing for standard grammar, spelling and punctuation.

3 Familiarize students with the rubric scoring system as well as the criteria used in the North Carolina Scoring Model.

In addition to familiarizing students with the types of prompts to which they will be required to respond, it is also important that students are exposed to the criteria against which their written responses will be assessed. Students' responses will be judged against the 4-point **Content Rubric** and the 2-point **Conventions Rubric.**

Once students are familiar with these rubrics, you should also offer models of what constitutes the various points on the rubric scale. You may also ask students to use the rubrics to assess their peers' writing.

The complete **North Carolina Scoring Model** is included on pages NC 34-35 of the North Carolina Student Edition, and the formative rubric is included on the last page of each **Writing Workshop** in the interior of the textbook. Make it an ongoing practice to review student work against these criteria. This practice will provide students with continued exposure to the rubric.

NC Writing Assessment Scoring Model	Rating Scale: not very				very
How clearly is the sequence of events presented?	1	2	3	4	5
How well linked are details to the central conflict and change?	1	2	3	4	5
How vividly described are details?	1	2	3	4	5
How effectively is dialogue used to introduce characters?	1	2	3	4	5
How precise are the nouns chosen?	1	2	3	4	5

Each rubric is aligned to an individual writing assignment.

Provide high quality writing experiences on a daily basis.

Each selection in the *Prentice Hall Literature* student edition provides several questions that require students to articulate their thoughts on related topics. The questions may simply assess recall or comprehension, but many require students to reflect on the major elements in writing.

This daily writing practice is key to developing students' communication skills. When students are consistently held accountable for expressing their ideas clearly in writing, even in the area of reading and literature, this knowledge and skill set will transfer to their performance on both the North Carolina Writing Assessment as well as the PSAT and SAT. The following exercises featured in every unit provide writing practice that students need.

- **Writing Questions**
- **Literary Analysis Questions**
- **Reading Skill Questions**

These features can be found on Apply the Skills pages that follow each reading selection.

Writing

Write a **two-paragraph essay** in which you compare and contrast Harry's behavior before and after he entered junior high school. Gather details from the story in a two-column chart.
Write a **two-paragraph essay** in which you compare and contrast Harry's behavior before and after he entered junior high school. Gather details from the story in a two-column chart.
Harry's behavior before and after he entered junior high school.

- In the first column, list details that show what Harry was like before junior high school.
- In the second column, list details that show his behaviors and thoughts while he is in junior high school.

Use details from your chart in your essay.

Literary Analysis

7. Using a chart like the one shown, review the course of events in the life of Madame Loisel. Based on those events, what would you say is the theme of "The Necklace"? Explain.

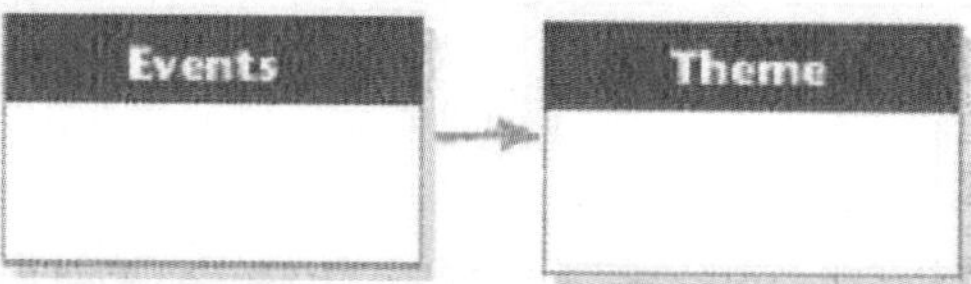

Reading Skill

6. **(a)** Make a timeline like the one shown to show the **sequence of events** in the story. **(b)** Based on your timeline, what might happen between Harry and his father in the future?

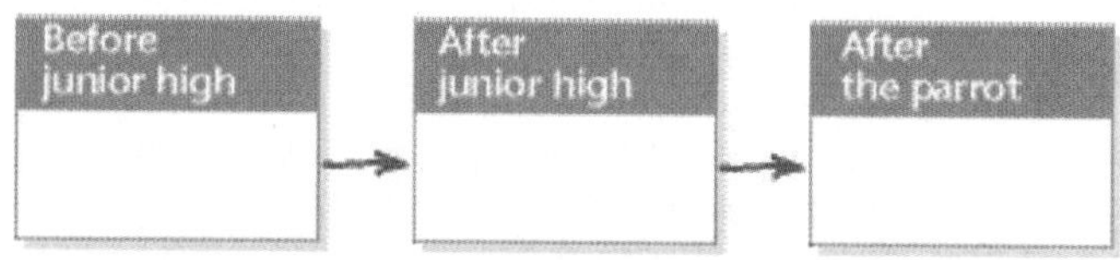

7. How might the story have turned out if Mr. Tillian had bought the parrot before Harry stopped coming to the store? Explain.

5 Prepare for the PSAT and SAT by reinforcing the strategies students will use to tackle multiple-choice questions each and every day.

- **Tip 1** Encourage students to **read the passage carefully** and refer to it if the question requires them to do so.
- **Tip 2** Look for **key words** or **facts** before looking for the correct answer. For example, a question may ask students to define a word as it is used in a passage or provide a synonym or antonym for the word.
- **Tip 3** Remind students that **underlined words** in a question indicate that the words are important in determining the correct answer.
- **Tip 4** Always remind students to be sure that the question number on the answer sheet is the same as the question they are answering. One way to reinforce this skill is to **provide bubble-sheets** for daily assessments.

6 Monitor your students' skill levels on an ongoing basis.

- Use the **Build Skills** section at the beginning of every selection grouping to familiarize students with comprehension, literary analysis, vocabulary, writing, and spelling skills that they will be using in conjunction with a particular selection.

Use the questions within the Monitor Your Progress, Vocabulary Workshop and Assessment Workshop features to assess student mastery of related skills.

Multiple opportunities to monitor progress can be found in each unit.

Monitor Your Progress — Test Practice

Reading: Chronological Order

Directions: *Read the passage. Then answer the questions that follow on a separate piece of paper.*

On Saturday morning Leon woke up early. He wanted to finish his chores so he could go to a football game. He took the dog for a quick walk, then made himself some breakfast. After he finished eating, Leon helped his father fix a broken fence post. Then he raked the leaves in the back yard, bagged the leaves, and dragged the bags to the curb. He was finished in time to see the kickoff.

1. According to the passage, what was the first thing Leon did after he woke up?
- **A** He made breakfast.
- **B** He walked the dog.
- **C** He got dressed.
- **D** He raked leaves.

2. Select the correct sequence of events
- **A** Eat breakfast, walk dog, rake leaves
- **B** Walk dog, fix fence, eat breakfast
- **C** walk dog, go to game, fix fence
- **D** fix fence, rake leaves, go to game

3.Which set of events could not have occurred in any other order?
- **A** Walk dog, make breakfast, bag leaves
- **B** rake leaves, bag leaves, drag leaves to curb
- **C** make breakfast, finish eating, fix fence
- **D** fix fence, rake leaves, see kickoff

4. Which word helps you identify a sequence of events?
- **A** After
- **B** Finished
- **C** Early
- **D** so

Curriculum Progression

Use this feature to acquaint yourself with how and what students were taught in previous years, what they should learn this year, and how their studies will progress moving forward.

English II

Competency Goal 1: The learner will react to and reflect upon print and non-print text and personal experiences by examining situations from both subjective and objective perspectives.

WL-1.01 Produce reminiscences (about a person, event, object, place, animal) that engage the audience by:

1. using specific and sensory details with purpose.
2. explaining the significance of the reminiscence from an objective perspective.
3. moving effectively between past and present.
4. recreating the mood felt by the author during the reminiscence.

WL-1.02 Respond reflectively (through small group discussion, class discussion, journal entry, essay, letter, dialogue) to written and visual texts by:

1. relating personal knowledge to textual information or class discussion.
2. showing an awareness of one's own culture as well as the cultures of others.
3. exhibiting an awareness of culture in which text is set or in which text was written.
4. explaining how culture affects personal responses.
5. demonstrating an understanding of media's impact on personal responses and cultural analyses.

Key to Standard Codes

WL	Written Language
IR	Informational Reading
FA	Foundations of Argument
CT	Critical Thinking
LT	Literature
GU	Grammar and Usage

Progression of Learning

PRIOR YEARS

Students developed a personal style and voice in their narrative writing. Students responded to expressive texts in a manner that demonstrated knowledge of how personal experiences and cultural and societal issues influenced those responses.

THIS YEAR

In English II, students will continue to develop their personal voice and style. Students will move skillfully between past and present in their writing and remain objective when relaying events to the reader. Students will begin to develop an increased awareness of their own culture as well as the cultures of others, and will be able to explain how one's culture affects one's response to texts. They will analyze how the media may influence personal responses to texts.

GOING FORWARD

Students will create memoirs that demonstrate how the past can affect the present. They will write reflective essays that develop voice and address a specific purpose and audience. As students continue to analyze expressive writing, they will uncover multiple perspectives in a given work. They will understand how a reader's past experiences can influence the present reading of a text.

WL-1.03 Demonstrate the ability to read, listen to and view a variety of increasingly complex print and non-print expressive texts appropriate to grade level and course literary focus, by:

1. selecting, monitoring, and modifying as necessary reading strategies appropriate to readers' purpose.
2. identifying and analyzing text components (such as organizational structures, story elements, organizational features) and evaluating their impact on the text.
3. providing textual evidence to support understanding of and reader's response to text.
4. demonstrating comprehension of main idea and supporting details.
5. summarizing key events and/or points from text.
6. making inferences, predicting, and drawing conclusions based on text.
7. identifying and analyzing personal, social, historical, or cultural influences, contexts, or biases.
8. making connections between works, self, and related topics.
9. analyzing and evaluating the effects of author's craft and style.
10. analyzing and evaluating the connections or relationships between and among ideas, concepts, characters, and/or experiences.
11. identifying and analyzing elements of expressive environment found in text in light of purpose, audience, and context.

Progression of Learning

PRIOR YEARS

Students learned to select reading strategies appropriate to their purpose. They identified and analyzed organizational features and structures of text. They worked on supporting their claims about text with evidence directly from the text. Students distinguised between main ideas and supporting details and summarized both. They learned to make inferences and predictions and to draw conclusions about text, based partly on the historical, cultural, and personal context of what they read. Students began to develop a critical eye for text and made connections between and among ideas and characters.

THIS YEAR

In English II, students both select and monitor their reading strategies based on the specific text and their purpose for reading. They develop a deeper understanding of how the organizational structure of a text affects the reader. Students are expected to support increasingly subtle interpretations with solid textual evidence. They hone in on main ideas as distinguised from supporting details. Students become more sophisticated in placing a text in historical, cultural, and personal context, and they critique texts against various criteria.

GOING FORWARD

Students will continue to build on their comprehension, interpretation, and critical skills with increasingly more complex materials. They will make more informed and subtle connections among texts, authors, ideas, characters, and cultural/historical contexts. Students will become informed critics of print and non-print texts.

NORTH CAROLINA

Competency Goal 2: The learner will evaluate problems, examine cause/effect relationships, and answer research questions to inform an audience.

IR-2.01 Demonstrate the ability to read, listen to and view a variety of increasingly complex print and non-print informational texts appropriate to grade level and course literary focus, by:

1. selecting, monitoring, and modifying as necessary reading strategies appropriate to readers' purpose.
2. identifying and analyzing text components (such as organizational structures, story elements, organizational features) and evaluating their impact on the text.
3. providing textual evidence to support understanding of and reader's response to text.
4. demonstrating comprehension of main idea and supporting details.
5. summarizing key events and/or points from text.
6. making inferences, predicting, and drawing conclusions based on text.
7. identifying and analyzing personal, social, historical, or cultural influences, contexts, or biases.
8. making connections between works, self, and related topics.
9. analyzing and evaluating the effects of author's craft and style.
10. analyzing and evaluating the connections or relationships between and among ideas, concepts, characters, and/or experiences.
11. identifying and analyzing elements of informational environment found in text in light of purpose, audience, and context.

IR-2.02 Create responses that examine a cause/effect relationship among events by:

1. effectively summarizing situations.
2. showing a clear, logical connection among events.
3. logically organizing connections by transitioning between points.
4. developing appropriate strategies such as graphics, essays, and multimedia presentations to illustrate points.

IR-2.03 Pose questions prompted by texts and research answers by:

1. accessing cultural information or explanations from print and non-print media sources.
2. prioritizing and organizing information to construct a complete and reasonable explanation.

Progression of Learning

PRIOR YEARS

Students applied the information acquired from informational texts to a variety of situations. They integrated their own knowledge with ideas in texts. They learned to discriminate between essential and nonessential information. Students wrote informational essays to instruct an audience. Students also used informational materials to answer research questions and appropriately cited those sources in their writing.

THIS YEAR

In English II, students will continue to read informational texts with a discriminating eye. They will recognize how the author employs style and evaluate the effects of that style. Students will produce research papers that show organization of thought and ideas. Students will write informational essays that analyze cause-and-effect relationships. They will use appropriate media to illustrate their ideas.

GOING FORWARD

Students will use research to present ideas and events related to U.S. culture. They will continue to distinguish between relevant and extraneous information and will provide accurate documentation for research. Students will produce research projects that explain how culture influences language in the United States.

Competency Goal 3: The learner will defend argumentative positions on literary or nonliterary issues.

FA-3.01 Examine controversial issues by:

1. sharing and evaluating initial personal response.
2. researching and summarizing printed data.
3. developing a framework in which to discuss the issue (creating a context).
4. compiling personal responses and researched data to organize the argument.
5. presenting data in such forms as a graphic, an essay, a speech, or a video.

FA-3.02 Produce editorials or responses to editorials for a neutral audience by providing:

1. a clearly stated position or proposed solution.
2. relevant, reliable support.

FA-3.03 Respond to issues in literature in such a way that:

1. requires gathering of information to prove a particular point.
2. effectively uses reason and evidence to prove a given point.
3. emphasizes culturally significant events.

FA-3.04 Demonstrate the ability to read, listen to and view a variety of increasingly complex print and non-print argumentative text appropriate to grade level and course literary focus, by:

1. selecting, monitoring, and modifying as necessary reading strategies appropriate to readers' purpose.
2. identifying and analyzing text components and evaluating their impact on the text.
3. providing textual evidence to support understanding of and reader's response to text.
4. demonstrating comprehension of main idea and supporting details.
5. summarizing key events and/or points from text.
6. making inferences, predicting, and drawing conclusions based on text.
7. identifying and analyzing personal, social, historical, or cultural influences, contexts, or biases.
8. making connections between works, self, and related topics.
9. analyzing and evaluating the effects of author's craft and style.
10. analyzing and evaluating the connections or relationships between and among ideas, concepts, characters, and/or experiences.
11. identifying and analyzing elements of argumentative environment found in text in light of purpose, audience, and context.

Progression of Learning

PRIOR YEARS

Students analyzed the strategies writers employ to develop an argument. Students began writing their own arguments. They expressed informed opinions and supported their opinions with evidence. Students used language to engage and excite their readers.

THIS YEAR

In English II, students will continue to explore argumentation. They will use research to examine controversial ideas and will create a context for discussion and response. Students will produce editorials. They will create reasoned argumentative responses to literature.

GOING FORWARD

Students will continue to use research to help them develop organized and well-supported arguments. They will use persuasive language to establish and defend a point of view, and will respond to various viewpoints and biases respectfully. They will continue to read and analyze argumentative texts.

NORTH CAROLINA

Competency Goal 4: The learner will critically interpret and evaluate experiences, literature, language, and ideas.

CT-4.01 Interpret a real-world event in a way that:

1. makes generalizations about the event supported by specific references.
2. reflects on observation and shows how the event affected the current viewpoint.
3. distinguishes fact from fiction and recognizes personal bias.

CT-4.02 Analyze thematic connections among literary works by:

1. showing an understanding of cultural context.
2. using specific references from texts to show how a theme is universal.
3. examining how elements such as irony and symbolism impact theme.

CT-4.03 Analyze the ideas of others by identifying the ways in which writers:

1. introduce and develop a main idea.
2. choose and incorporate significant, supporting, relevant details.
3. relate the structure/organization to the ideas.
4. use effective word choice as a basis for coherence.
5. achieve a sense of completeness and closure.

CT-4.04 Evaluate the information, explanations, or ideas of others by:

1. identifying clear, reasonable criteria for evaluation.
2. applying those criteria using reasoning and substantiation.

CT-4.05 Demonstrate the ability to read, listen to and view a variety of increasingly complex print and non-print critical texts appropriate to grade level and course literary focus.

1. selecting, monitoring, and modifying as necessary reading strategies appropriate to readers' purpose.
2. identifying and analyzing text components and evaluating their impact on the text.
3. providing textual evidence to support understanding of and reader's response to text.
4. demonstrating comprehension of main idea and supporting details.
5. summarizing key events and/or points from text.
6. making inferences, predicting, and drawing conclusions based on text.
7. identifying and analyzing personal, social, historical, or cultural influences, contexts, or biases.
8. making connections between works, self, and related topics.
9. analyzing and evaluating the effects of author's craft and style.
10. analyzing and evaluating the connections or relationships between and among ideas, concepts, characters, and/or experiences.
11. identifying and analyzing elements of critical environment found in text in light of purpose, audience, and context.

Progression of Learning

PRIOR YEARS

Students began to determine the effectiveness of communication by applying their own analytic standards to a literary work. Students judged the impact of stylistic and literary devices on a text.

THIS YEAR

In English II, students will apply their critical skills to experiences, literature, and ideas. They will interpret an event by making generalizations and observations. Students will understand universal themes. They will identify introductions, conclusions, and text structures.

GOING FORWARD

Students will critically analyze texts by examining narrative strategies. They will study how different figures of speech and sound devices affect texts. Students will show how culture helps to shape texts. Students will evaluate and critique how an author develops an argument.

Competency Goal 5: The learner will demonstrate understanding of selected world literature through interpretation and analysis.

LT-5.01 Read and analyze selected works of world literature by:

1. using effective strategies for preparation, engagement, and reflection.
2. building on prior knowledge of the characteristics of literary genres, including fiction, non-fiction, drama, and poetry, and exploring how those characteristics apply to literature of world cultures.
3. analyzing literary devices such as allusion, symbolism, figurative language, flashback, dramatic irony, situational irony, and imagery and explaining their effect on the work of world literature.
4. analyzing the importance of tone and mood.
5. analyzing archetypal characters, themes, and settings in world literature.
6. making comparisons and connections between historical and contemporary issues.
7. understanding the importance of cultural and historical impact on literary texts.

Progression of Learning

PRIOR YEARS

Students improved their analysis of literary texts by delving deeper into literary elements. Students studied the way history and culture impact literary texts. They produced creative responses to literary texts. Students analyzed characteristics of literary genres. Students produced responses to literature that modeled the conventions of a particular genre.

THIS YEAR

In English II, students will apply literary analysis skills to world literature. They will examine how the characteristics of genre relate to the literature of various world cultures. Students will analyze the use of literary elements in texts and explore the importance of culture and history in world literature. They will examine literary devices and explain their effect on texts.

GOING FORWARD

Students will continue to study how the use of a particular literary genre helps shape the meaning of a text. They will study literature from various time periods and literary movements of the United States. Students will be able to identify works from a specific movement of United States literature and compare ideas, styles, and themes within each movement.

NORTH CAROLINA

LT-5.02 Demonstrating increasing comprehension and ability to respond personally to texts by:

1. selecting and exploring a wide range of works which relate to an issue, author, or theme of world literature.
2. documenting the reading of student-chosen works.

LT-5.03 Demonstrate the ability to read, listen to and view a variety of increasingly complex print and non-print literary texts appropriate to grade level and course literary focus, by:

1. selecting, monitoring, and modifying as necessary reading strategies appropriate to readers' purpose.
2. identifying and analyzing text components (such as organizational structures, story elements, organizational features) and evaluating their impact on the text.
3. providing textual evidence to support understanding of and reader's response to text.
4. demonstrating comprehension of main idea and supporting details.
5. summarizing key events and/or points from text.
6. making inferences, predicting, and drawing conclusions based on text.
7. identifying and analyzing personal, social, historical, or cultural influences, contexts, or biases.
8. making connections between works, self, and related topics.
9. analyzing and evaluating the effects of author's craft and style.
10. analyzing and evaluating the connections or relationships between and among ideas, concepts, characters, and/or experiences.
11. identifying and analyzing elements of literary environment found in text in light of purpose, audience, and context.

Progression of Learning

PRIOR YEARS

Students increased their comprehension of literature. Students demonstrated the skills to analyze plot, and made inferences and conclusions based on information from texts. They made connections between their experiences and texts, and provided evidence to support their responses to texts.

THIS YEAR

In English II, students will demonstrate an increased ability to comprehend literary texts. Students' personal responses to texts will show a sophistication of thought. Students will develop an understanding of the themes used in world literature. They will learn to make connections between world literature and their own experiences.

GOING FORWARD

Students will study and analyze the relationships between the lives of United States authors and their texts. Students will make comparisons between texts to show similarities and differences among themes, characters, or ideas.

Competency Goal 6: The learner will apply conventions of grammar and language usage.

GU-6.01 Demonstrate an understanding of conventional written and spoken expression by:

1. employing varying sentence structures and sentence types.
2. analyzing author's choice of words, sentence structure, and use of language.
3. using word recognition strategies to understand vocabulary and exact word choice.
4. using vocabulary strategies such as context clues, resources, and structural analysis to determine meaning of words and phrases.
5. examining textual and classroom language for elements such as idioms, denotation, and connotation to apply effectively in own writing/speaking.
6. using correct form/format for essays, business letters, research papers, bibliographies.
7. using language effectively to create mood and tone.

GU-6.02 Edit for:

1. subject-verb agreement, tense choice, pronoun usage, clear antecedents, correct case, and complete sentences.
2. appropriate and correct mechanics.
3. parallel structure.
4. clichés and/or trite expressions.
5. spelling.

Progression of Learning

PRIOR YEARS

Students used a variety of sentence types in their writing. They used strategies to determine the meanings of unknown words. Students edited their writing for spelling and grammatical errors.

THIS YEAR

In English II, students will introduce new sentence structures into their writing. They will develop word recognition skills to help them understand vocabulary and word choice. They will be able to use the correct format for different types of writing. Students will continue to edit their writing for clarity and mechanics.

GOING FORWARD

Students will continue to use vocabulary strategies to determine meanings. They will begin to recognize relationships of meaning between pairs of words. Students will make revisions to their writing that enhance the voice and style as well as sentence variety.

Fast Track to Standards Mastery

Your Essential Course of Study

The North Carolina edition of *Prentice Hall Literature, The Penguin Edition* was built to give you strong standards coverage and lots of options to create the course that best meets the needs of your students.

Use this chart to target selections and workshops that will most efficiently facilitate your students' mastery of the North Carolina Standard Course of Study and preparation for the North Carolina Writing Assessment.

Pacing	Unit	Selection Pairing	Standards Covered
20 Days * 10 Blocks	*1. Ancient Worlds*	*Teach* ***THE FOLLOWING*** *selections:* • **from *The Epic of Gilgamesh*** • **Genesis 1-3 (The Creation and the Fall), Genesis 6-9 (The Story of the Flood)** • **from the *Qur'an*** • **African Proverbs**	**NC** CT.4.01.1, LT.5.01.2, LT.5.01.3, LT.5.01.5, LT.5.01.6, LT.5.01.7, LT.5.02.1, LT.5.03.1, LT.5.03.2, LT.5.03.4, LT.5.03.5, LT.5.03.9, GU.6.01.2
14 Days * 7 Blocks	*2. Indian Literature*	*Teach* ***THE FOLLOWING*** *selections:* • **from the *Mahabharat*** • **from the *Bhagavad Gita*** • **from the *Ramayana***	**NC** WL.1.02.3, WL.1.02.4, LT.5.01.5, LT.5.01.7, LT.5.02.1, LT.5.03.6
16 Days * 8 Blocks	*3. Chinese and Japanese Literature*	*Teach* ***THE FOLLOWING*** *selections:* • **from the *Tao Te Ching*** • **from *The Analects*** • **Tanka, Haiku** • **from *The Pillow Book***	**NC** WL.1.02.1, WL.1.03.6, WL.1.03.9, WL.1.03.10, IR.2.02.1, CT.4.04.1, CT.4.04.2, LT.5.01.3, LT.5.03.6, GU.6.01.2
22 Days * 11 Blocks	*4. Ancient Greece and Rome*	*Teach* ***THE FOLLOWING*** *selections:* • **from *the Iliad*: from Book 1; from Book 6** • **from *the Apology*** • **from the *Aeneid*: from Book 1: How They Took the City**	**NC** WL.1.02.2, FA.3.01.3, FA.3.02.1, FA.3.03.1, CT.4.02.2, LT.5.03.7, LT.5.03.9, GU.6.01.2, GU.6.01.4

Unit	Reading Informational Materials	Connections	Writing About Literature	Writing Workshop	Assessment Workshop	Communication Workshop	
1. Ancient Worlds (cont.)	Brochure: The Quest for Immortality **NC** IR.2.01.5, CT.4.05.1	from *Popol Vuh: The Wooden People* **NC** CT.4.01.1, CT.4.02.2, LT.5.03.8	Analyze Literary Periods **NC** WL.1.02.2, WL.1.03.1, LT.5.01.5				**20 Days * 10 Blocks**
2. Indian Literature (cont.)	Atlases and Maps: Dorling Kindersley Atlas **NC** IR.2.01.1, IR.2.01.8				Sequential Order **NC** IR.2.02.1, IR.2.02.3		**14 Days * 7 Blocks**
3. Chinese and Japanese Literature (cont.)	Reference Materials: Origami **NC** IR.2.01.1	Poor Richard's Almanack **NC** CT.4.02.1		Persuasion: Persuasive Essay **NC** FA.3.01.5, FA.3.02.2, FA.3.04.11	Cause-and Effect Relationships **NC** IR.2.01.2		**16 Days * 8 Blocks**
4. Ancient Greece and Rome (cont.)	Web Research Sources: Perseus Web site **NC** IR.2.01.11, IR.2.03.1, FA.3.03.1	The Gettysburg Address **NC** FA.3.04.7, LT.5.01.6	Analyze Cultural Ideas **NC** CT.4.02.1, CT.4.02.2, LT.5.03.9	Exposition: Problem and Solution Essay **NC** IR.2.02.3, IR.2.03.2, FA.3.02.1			**22 Days * 11 Blocks**

Fast Track, continued

Pacing	Unit	Selection Pairing	Standards Covered
14 Days * 7 Blocks	*5. The Middle Ages*	*Teach* ***THE FOLLOWING*** *selections:* • **from *Perceval*** • ***The Lay of the Werewolf*** • **from the *Divine Comedy: Inferno***	**NC** CT.4.02.3, CT.4.04.2, LT.5.01.3, LT.5.01.5, LT.5.01.10, LT.5.03.10, GU.6.01.7
18 Days * 9 Blocks	*6. The Renaissance and Rationalism*	*Teach* ***THE FOLLOWING*** *selections:* • **from the *Decameron*** • **from *The Starry Messenger* (from Astronomical Message), from the Assayer** • **from *Candide***	**NC** WL.1.03.11, IR.2.01.10, FA.3.04.9, FA.3.04.11, CT.4.03.1, CT.4.05.4, LT.5.01.6, LT.5.03.8
22 Days * 11 Blocks	*7. Romanticism and Realism*	*Teach* ***THE FOLLOWING*** *selections:* • **from Faust** • **"Two Friends," "How Much Land Does a Man Need?" "A Problem"**	**NC** CT.4.03.1, CT.4.03.2, CT.4.03.3, LT.5.01.2, LT.5.03.6, LT.5.03.10, LT.5.03.11, GU.6.01.2
14 Days * 7 Blocks	*8. The Modern World*	*Teach* ***THE FOLLOWING*** *selection:* • **"The Metamorphosis"**	**NC** WL.1.03.9, FA.3.03.3, CT.4.04.2, LT.5.01.7, LT.5.02.1
20 Days * 10 Blocks	*9. The Contemporary World*	*Teach* ***THE FOLLOWING*** *selections:* • **from *Survival in Auschwitz*, from *Night*, "When in early summer"** • **"Half a Day"** • **"Comrades," "Marriage is a Private Affair"**	**NC** WL.1.02.3, WL.1.03.5, WL.1.03.11, FA.3.01.4, CT.4.01.2, LT.5.01.3, LT.5.01.4, LT.5.01.6, LT.5.03.7, LT.5.03.8, LT.5.03.11

Unit	Reading Informational Materials	Connections	Writing About Literature	Writing Workshop	Assessment Workshop	Communication Workshop	
5. The Middle Ages (cont.)	Interviews: Comic Fan **NC** IR.2.03.1, CT.4.05.1		Evaluate Literary Themes **NC** LT.5.01.5	Research: Research Paper **NC** IR.2.01.4, IR.2.03.1, IR.2.03.2	Comparing and Contrasting **NC** CT.4.03.3	Analyzing the Impact of Media **NC** WL.1.02.5	**14 Days * 7 Blocks**
6. The Renaissance and Rationalism (cont.)	Feature Articles: Leonardo da Vinci **NC** IR.2.01.10, CT.4.03.2, CT.4.04.1		Analyze Literary Periods **NC** WL.1.02.2, LT.5.02.1		Critical Reasoning **NC** WL.1.03.6, CT.4.02.1, LT.5.03.4		**18 Days * 9 Blocks**
7. Romanticism and Realism (cont.)	Critical Reviews: A Doll's House **NC** CT.4.05.3, CT.4.05.5, CT.4.05.9	from *The Tragical History of Doctor Faustus* **NC** LT.5.01.5	Compare and Contrast Literary Periods **NC** CT.4.02.2, LT.5.01.7, GU.6.02.3	Exposition: Response to Literature **NC** FA.3.03.1, CT.4.02.2			**22 Days * 11 Blocks**
8. The Modern World (cont.)	Scientific Text: What is an Insect? **NC** IR.2.01.5, IR.2.01.9	The Corn Planting **NC** LT.5.03.8		Exposition: Multimedia Report **NC** IR.2.02.4, IR.2.03.1		Analyzing a Media Presentation **NC** WL.1.02.5, IR.2.03.1, CT.4.01.3	**14 Days * 7 Blocks**
9. The Contemporary World (cont.)	Magazine Article: Holocaust Haggadah **NC** IR.2.01.1, IR.2.01.3, CT.4.03.2	from *Hiroshima* **NC** IR.2.01.9, CT.4.04.1, LT.5.01.2	Compare and Contrast Literary Themes Across Cultures **NC** LT.5.01.5, LT.5.01.7, LT.5.03.7		Analyzing an Author's Meaning **NC** FA.3.04.4, FA.3.04.6, CT.4.04.2, CT.4.05.5	Delivering a Multimedia Presentation **NC** WL.1.02.5, CT.4.03.3	**20 Days * 10 Blocks**

Units 1–9

World Masterpieces

	Unit	From the Author's Desk	Focus on Literary Forms	A Closer Look	Connections	Reading Informational Materials
1	**Origins and Traditions** (c.3000 B.C.–A.D. 1400)	Coleman Barks pp. 114–115	Epic pp. 14–15	Bible pp. 74–75	*from* **Popol Vuh: The Wooden People** pp. 54–57	Brochures: Adjusting Your Reading Rate pp. 144–147
2	**Sacred Texts and Epic Tales** (c.1400 B.C.–A.D. 500)	Wendy Doniger pp. 176–177	Wisdom Literature pp. 186–187	The Upanishads pp. 188–189	James Thurber, **The Tiger Who Would be King** pp. 230–231	Atlases and Maps: Locating Information Using Atlases and Maps pp. 232–235
3	**Wisdom and Insight** (1000 B.C.–A.D. 1890)	Royall Tyler pp. 294–295	Poetry pp. 276–277	Women Writers in Japan pp. 316–317	Benjamin Franklin, **Poor Richard's Almanac** pp. 274–275	Reference Materials: Following Directions pp. 326–331
4	**Classical Civilizations** (c.800 B.C.–A.D. 500)	David Mamet pp. 463–465	Drama pp. 460–461	Oedipus: The Myth p. 462	Abraham Lincoln, **The Gettysburg Address** pp. 436–437	Web Research Sources: Analyzing the Usefulness and Credibility of Web Sources, pp. 528–531
5	**From Decay to Rebirth** (A.D. 450–1300)	Marilyn Stokstad pp. 626–627	Medieval Romance Saga pp. 596–597	The Art of Translation pp. 694–695	Alfred Lord Tennyson, **Sir Galahad** pp. 652–655	Interviews: Analyzing Purpose pp. 622–625
6	**Rebirth and Exploration** (1300–1800)	João Magueijo pp. 754–755	Sonnet pp. 726–727	Great Minds Do Not Think Alike pp. 798–799	William Shakespeare, **Sonnets 29 and 116** pp. 740–741	Feature Articles: Evaluating Support pp. 810–815
7	**Revolution and Reaction** (1800–1890)	W.S. Merwin pp. 898–900	Lyric Poetry pp. 872–873	The Slamming of the Door pp. 1026–1027	Christopher Marlowe, *from* **the Tragical History of Dr. Faustus** pp. 866–871	Critical Reviews: Comparing and Contrasting Critical Reviews pp. 1028–1033
8	**From Conflict to Renewal** (1890–1945)	Judith Ortiz Cofer pp. 1142–1143	Short Story pp. 1062–1063	The Nobel Prize: A Dynamite Idea pp. 1158–1159	Sherwood Anderson, **The Corn Planting** pp. 1136–1141	Scientific Texts: Analyzing Text Features pp. 1112–1115
9	**Voices of Change** (1946–Present)	Jamaica Kincaid pp. 1216–1217 Chinua Achebe pp. 1338–1339	Nonfiction pp. 1250–1251	I, Witness pp. 1214–1215	John Hersey, *from* **Hiroshima** pp. 1318–1321	Magazine Articles: Establishing a Purpose for Reading pp. 1274–1277

Technology

Go Online PHSchool.com	From the Author's Desk DVD				ExamView® QuickTake
• Author Biographies • Self-tests • Research Activities	Bring real writers into your classroom.				Monitor student progress instantly.

Prentice Hall StudentEXPRESS™ Learn · Study · Succeed — Prentice Hall TeacherEXPRESS™ Plan · Teach · Assess — Instant access to all program resources with the click of a mouse

Skills Navigator Overview

Writing About Literature	Writing Workshop	Vocabulary Workshop	Assessment Workshop	Communications Workshop
Analyze Literary Periods pp. 148–149	Narration: Autobiographical Narrative pp. 150–157	Define, Identify p. 158	Conventions of Grammar and Language Usage p. 159	Delivering a Speech p. 160
Analyze Literary Themes pp. 236–237	Narration: Reflective Essay pp. 238–245	Recall, Summarize p. 246	Sequential Order p. 247	Interviewing Techniques p. 248
Analyze Literary Trends pp. 332–333	Persuasion: Persuasive Essay pp. 334–341	Predict, Apply p. 342	Cause and Effect Relationships p. 343	Delivering a Persuasive Argument p. 344
Analyze Literary Themes pp. 568–569	Exposition: Problem-and-Solution Essay pp. 570–577	Describe, Infer p. 578	Inferences and Generalizations p. 579	Listening to Speeches p. 580
Evaluate Literary Themes pp. 696–697	Research: Research Paper pp. 698–707	Categorize, Differentiate p. 708	Comparing and Contrasting p. 709	Analyzing the Impact of Media p. 710
Analyze Literary Periods pp. 816–817	Exposition: Comparison-and-Contrast Essay pp. 818–825	Illustrate, Interpret p. 826	Critical Reasoning p. 827	Presenting a Literary Interpretation p. 828
Compare and Contrast Literary Periods pp. 1034–1035	Response to Literature pp. 1036–1043	Demonstrate, Analyze p. 1044	Strategy, Organization, and Style p. 1045	Delivering an Oral Response to Literature p. 1046
Compare and Contrast Literary Trends Across Cultures pp. 1172–1173	Exposition: Multimedia Report pp. 1174–1181	Conclude, Deduce p. 1182	Writer's Point of View p. 1183	Analyzing a Media Presentation p. 1184
Compare and Contrast Literary Themes Across Cultures pp. 1352–1353	Workplace Writing: Job Portfolio and Résumé pp. 1354–1361	Evaluate, Judge p. 1362	Analyzing an Author's Meaning p. 1363	Delivering a Multimedia Presentation p. 1364
	 PH Online Essay Scorer: electronic essay grader		 Monitor student progress instantly	

Instant access to all program resources with the click of a mouse

UNIT 1

Origins and Traditions (3000 B.C.–A.D. 1400)

Selection	Reading Strategy	Literary Analysis	Vocabulary
Focus on Epic			
from *The Epic of Gilgamesh*: Prologue/Battle with Humbaba (MC), SE, p. 18; **from *The Epic of Gilgamesh*: The Death of Enkidu** (MC), SE, p. 23; **from *The Epic of Gilgamesh*: The Story of the Flood** (MC), SE, p. 25; **from *The Epic of Gilgamesh*: The Return** (MC), SE, p. 30	**Understanding the Cultural Context,** SE, p. 17; *UR1,* p. 12; **Reading Warm-ups A and B,** *UR1,* pp. 9–10; **Reading Strategy Graphic Organizers A and B,** *GOT,* pp. 1-2	**Archetype: The Hero's Quest,** SE, p. 17; *UR1,* p. 11; **Literary Analysis Graphic Organizers A and B,** *GOT,* pp. 3-4	**Vocabulary Builder,** SE, p. 17: *immolation, succor, somber, incantation, ecstasy, teemed, babel, subsided* **Latin prefix** *sub-,* SE, p. 34; *UR1,* p. 13
from the *Bible: Genesis 1–3, The Creation and the Fall* (A), SE, p. 38; **from the *Bible: Genesis 6–9, The Story of the Flood*** (A), SE, p. 44	**Identifying Chronological Order,** SE, p. 37; *UR1,* p. 29; **Reading Warm-ups A and B,** *UR1,* pp. 26-27; **Reading Strategy Graphic Organizers A and B,** *GOT,* pp. 5-6	**Archetypal Setting,** SE, p. 37; *UR1,* p. 28; **Literary Analysis Graphic Organizers A and B,** *GOT,* pp. 7-8	**Vocabulary Builder,** SE, p. 37: *void, expanse, shrewdest, duped, enmity, corrupt, covenant, comprised* **Latin prefix** *com-,* SE, p. 52; *UR1,* p. 30
from the *Bible: The Book of Ruth* (A), SE, p. 60; **from the *Bible: Psalm 8*** (A), SE, p. 67; **from the *Bible: Psalm 19*** (A), SE, p. 68; **from the *Bible: Psalm 23*** (A), SE, p. 68; **from the *Bible: Psalm 137*** (A), SE, p. 70;	**Using Context Clues,** SE, p. 59; *UR1,* p. 46; **Reading Warm-ups A and B,** *UR1,* pp. 43-44; **Reading Strategy Graphic Organizers A and B,** *GOT,* pp. 9-10	**Parallelism,** SE, p. 59; *UR1,* p. 45; **Literary Analysis Graphic Organizers A and B,** *GOT,* pp. 11-12	**Vocabulary Builder,** SE, p. 59: *glean, reapers, redeem, avenger, precepts, lucid, steadfast* **Anglo-Saxon Root:** *-stead-,* SE, p. 72; *UR1,* p. 47
from the *Qur'an: The Exordium/Night/Daylight/ Comfort* (A), SE, p. 78	**Setting a Purpose for Reading,** SE, p. 77; *UR1,* p. 63; **Reading Warm-ups A and B,** *UR1,* pp. 60-61; **Reading Strategy Graphic Organizers A and B,** *GOT,* pp. 15-16	**Imagery,** SE, p. 77; *UR1,* p. 62; **Literary Analysis Graphic Organizers A and B,** *GOT,* pp. 13-14	**Vocabulary Builder,** SE, p. 77: *compassionate, incurred, affliction, recompense, abhor, chide, renown, fervor* **Latin Prefix:** *ab-,* SE, p. 82; *UR1,* p. 64
from *The Thousand and One Nights: The Fisherman and the Jinnee* (MC), SE, p. 86	**Summarizing,** SE, p. 85; *UR1,* p. 80; **Reading Warm-ups A and B,** *UR1,* pp. 77-78	**Folk Tales,** SE, p. 85; *UR1,* p. 79; **Literary Analysis Graphic Organizers A and B,** *GOT,* pp. 17-18, 19-20	**Vocabulary Builder,** SE, p. 85: *inverted, blasphemous, adjured, indignantly, resolutely, enraptured, munificence, ominous* **Latin Root:** *-vert-,* SE, p. 98; *UR1,* p. 81
from *The Rubáiyát* (MC), Omar Khayyám, SE, p. 102; **from *The Gulistan*: from *The Manners of Kings*** (A), Sa'di, SE, p. 106	**Breaking Down Long Sentences,** SE, p. 101; *UR1,* p. 106; **Reading Warm-ups A and B,** *UR1,* pp. 103-104; **Reading Strategy Graphic Organizers A and B,** *GOT,* pp. 21-22	**Didactic Literature,** SE, p. 101; *UR1,* p. 105; **Literary Analysis Graphic Organizers A and B,** *GOT,* pp. 23-24	**Vocabulary Builder,** SE, p. 101: *repentance, pomp, myriads, piety, beneficent, extortions* **Latin Root:** *-tort-,* SE, p. 112; *UR1,* p. 107

Key to Program References:
SE: Student Edition **UR:** Unit Resources **GOT:** Graphic Organizer Transparencies **GR:** General Resources **WG:** Writing and Grammar
MA: More accessible **A:** Average **MC:** More Challenging. See Accessibility at a Glance chart on selection pages.

Skills Navigator

Grammar	Writing	Extend Your Learning	Assessment
Commonly Confused Words: *in* and *into*, SE, p. 34; *UR1*, p. 14; *WG*, Ch. 26, Section 2	**Writing Lesson:** Comparison-and-Contrast Essay, SE, p. 35; *UR1*, p. 15; *WG*, Ch. 9	**Listening and Speaking:** Press Conference, SE, p. 35 **Research and Technology:** Research Report, p. 35, *UR1*, p. 16	**Diagnostic Test 1,** *UR1*, pp. 2-4; **Selection Tests A and B,** *UR1*, pp. 18-23; **Rubrics for Research: Research Report,** *GR*, pp. 51-52; **Rubrics for Exposition: Comparison-and-Contrast Essay,** *GR*, pp. 53-54
Punctuation in Dialogue, SE, p. 52; *UR1*, p. 31; *WG*, Ch. 28, Section 4	**Writing Lesson:** Extended Definition, SE, p. 53; *UR1*, p. 32; *WG*, Ch. 10, Section 3	**Listening and Speaking:** Choral Reading, SE, p. 53 **Research and Technology:** Written Report, p. 53, *UR1*, p. 33	**Selection Tests A and B,** *UR1*, pp. 35-40; **Rubrics for Exposition: Cause-and-Effect Essay,** *GR*, pp. 61-62; **Rubric for Speaking: Narrative Account,** *GR*, p. 88
Compound Predicates, SE, p. 72; *UR1*, p. 48; *WG*, Ch. 19, Section 1	**Writing Lesson:** Response to a Biblical Narrative, SE, p. 73; *UR1*, p. 49; *WG*, Ch. 13	**Listening and Speaking:** Improvised Dialogue, SE, p. 73 **Research and Technology:** Multimedia Report, p. 73, *UR1*, p. 50	**Selection Tests A and B,** *UR1*, pp. 52-57; **Rubrics for Response to Literature,** *GR*, pp. 55-56; **Rubrics for Research: Research Report,** *GR*, pp. 51-52
Parallelism, SE, p. 82; *UR1*, p. 65; *WG*, Ch. 27, Section 4	**Writing Lesson:** Guidelines for Personal Behavior, SE, p. 83; *UR1*, p. 66; *WG*, Ch. 11	**Listening and Speaking:** Speech, SE, p. 83 **Research and Technology:** Magazine Article, p. 83, *UR1*, p. 67	**Selection Tests A and B,** *UR1*, pp. 69-74; **Rubrics for Exposition: Problem-Solution Essay,** *GR*, pp. 49-50
Action and Linking Verbs, SE, p. 98; *UR1*, p. 82; *WG*, Ch. 16, Section 1	**Writing Lesson:** Critique of a Work, SE, p. 99; *UR1*, p. 83; *WG*, Ch. 9, Section 4	**Listening and Speaking:** Panel Discussion, SE, p. 99 **Research and Technology:** Written Report, p. 99, *UR1*, p. 84	**Selection Tests A and B,** *UR1*, pp. 86-91; **Rubrics for Exposition: Cause-and-Effect Essay,** *GR*, pp. 61-62; **Rubrics for Research: Research Report,** *GR*, pp. 51-52; **Benchmark Test 1,** *UR1*, pp. 92-97
Interjections, SE, p. 112; *UR1*, p. 108; *WG*, Ch. 18, Section 2	**Writing Lesson:** Fable, SE, p. 113; *UR1*, p. 109; *WG*, Ch. 5	**Listening and Speaking:** Panel Discussion, SE, p. 113 **Research and Technology:** Annotated Anthology, p. 113, *UR1*, p. 110	**Diagnostic Test 2,** *UR1*, pp. 98-100; **Selection Tests A and B,** *UR1*, pp. 112-117; **Rubrics for Narration: Short Story,** *GR*, pp. 63-64

All Selections are supported in the Reader's Notebooks.

UNIT 1

Origins and Traditions (3000 B.C.–A.D. 1400) *(continued)*

Selection	Reading Strategy	Literary Analysis	Vocabulary
Elephant in the Dark, (MA), Rumi, SE, p. 118; ***Two Kinds of Intelligence,*** (A), Rumi, SE, p. 120; ***The Guest House,*** (A), Rumi, SE, p. 122; ***Which Is Worth More?,*** (MA), Rumi, SE, p. 124	**Making Generalizations,** SE, p. 117; *UR1,* p. 125; **Reading Warm-ups A and B,** *UR1,* pp. 122-123; **Reading Strategy Graphic Organizers A and B,** *GOT,* pp. 25-26	**Analogy,** SE, p. 117; *UR1,* p. 124; **Literary Analysis Graphic Organizers A and B,** *GOT,* pp. 27-28	**Vocabulary Builder,** SE, p. 117: *competence, conduits, malice, solitude* **Latin Prefix:** *com- or con-,* SE, p. 126; *UR1,* p. 126
African Proverbs: *Uganda: The Baganda,* (A), SE, p. 130; ***Liberia: The Jabo,*** (A), SE, p. 130; ***South Africa: The Zulu,*** (A), SE, p. 130; ***Ghana: The Ashanti,*** (A), SE, p. 131; ***Nigeria: The Yoruba,*** (A), SE, p. 131; ***Tanzania and Kenya: The Masai,*** (A), SE, p. 131; **from *Sundiata: An Epic of Old Mali,*** (MA), D.T. Niane, SE, p. 132	**Rereading for Clarification,** SE, p. 129; *UR1,* p. 142; **Reading Warm-ups A and B,** *UR1,* pp. 139-140; **Reading Strategy Graphic Organizers A and B,** *GOT,* pp. 29-30	**Epic Conflict,** SE, p. 129; *UR1,* p. 141; **Literary Analysis Graphic Organizers A and B,** *GOT,* pp. 31-32	**Vocabulary Builder,** SE, p. 129: *fathom, taciturn, malicious, infirmity, innuendo, diabolical, estranged* **Latin Root:** *-firm-,* SE, p. 142; *UR1,* p. 143

UNIT 2

Sacred Texts and Epic Tales (c. 1400 B.C.–A.D. 500)

Selection	Reading Strategy	Literary Analysis	Vocabulary
from the *Rig Veda: Creation Hymn* (A), SE, p. 180; **from the *Rig Veda: Night*** (A), SE, p. 182	**Paraphrasing,** SE, p. 179; *UR2,* p. 11; **Reading Warm-ups A and B,** *UR2,* pp. 8-9; **Reading Strategy Graphic Organizers A and B,** *GOT,* pp. 34-35	**Vedic Hymn,** SE, p. 179; *UR2,* p. 10; **Literary Analysis Graphic Organizers A and B,** *GOT,* pp. 36-37	**Vocabulary Builder,** SE, p. 179: *immortality, distinguishing, stems, palpable* **Latin Prefix** *im-/in-,* SE, p. 184; *UR2,* p. 12
Focus on Wisdom Literature			
from *The Mahabharata: Sibi* (A), SE, p. 192; **from *The Bhagavad-Gita: The Yoga of Knowledge*** (A), SE, p. 200; **from *The Ramayana: Rama and Ravana in Battle*** (A), SE, p. 208	**Inferring Beliefs of the Period,** SE, p. 191; *UR2,* p. 28; **Reading Warm-ups A and B,** *UR2,* pp. 25-26; **Reading Strategy Graphic Organizers A and B,** *GOT,* pp. 41-40	**The Indian Epic,** SE, p. 191; *UR2,* p. 27; **Literary Analysis Graphic Organizers A and B,** *GOT,* pp. 38-39	**Vocabulary Builder,** SE, p. 191: *mitigated, caricature, scruples, pervades, manifested, dispel, invoked, pristine* **Latin Root** *-voc-/ -vok-,* SE, p. 218; *UR2,* p. 29
from *The Panchatantra: Numskull and the Rabbit* (A), SE, p. 222	**Reread for Clarification,** SE, p. 221; *UR2,* p. 45; **Reading Warm-ups A and B,** *UR2,* pp. 42-43; **Reading Strategy Graphic Organizers A and B,** *GOT,* pp. 44-45	**Indian fable,** SE, p. 221; *UR2,* p. 44; **Literary Analysis Graphic Organizers A and B,** *GOT,* pp. 42-43	**Vocabulary Builder,** SE, p. 221: *obsequiously, rank, elixir, accrue, tardily, reprobate, extirpate, skulks* **Latin Prefix** *ex-,* SE, p. 228; *UR2,* p. 46

Key to Program References:
SE: Student Edition **UR:** Unit Resources **GOT:** Graphic Organizer Transparencies **GR:** General Resources **WG:** Writing and Grammar
MA: More accessible **A:** Average **MC:** More Challenging. See Accessibility at a Glance chart on selection pages.

Skills Navigator

Grammar	Writing	Extend Your Learning	Assessment
Agreement and the Indefinite Pronouns *each* and *no one*, SE, p. 126; *UR1,* p. 127; *WG,* Ch. 24, Section 1 and 2	**Writing Lesson:** Poem with an Insight, SE, p. 127; *UR1,* p. 128; *WG,* Ch. 10, Section 4	**Listening and Speaking:** Group Discussion, SE, p. 127 **Research and Technology:** Research Report, p. 127, *UR1,* p. 129	**Selection Tests A and B,** *UR1,* pp. 131-136; **Rubrics for Poem (Rhyming),** *GR,* pp. 73-74
Sentence variety, SE, p. 142; *UR1,* p. 144; *WG,* Ch. 21, Section 3	**Writing Lesson:** Storytelling Notes, SE, p. 143; *UR1,* p. 145; *WG,* Ch. 5	**Listening and Speaking:** Oral Retelling, SE, p. 143 **Research and Technology:** Booklet of Proverbs, p. 143, *UR1,* p. 146	**Selection Tests A and B,** *UR1,* pp. 148-153; **Rubrics for Narration: Short Story,** *GR,* pp. 63-64; **Rubric for Speaking: Narrative Account,** *GR,* p. 88

Grammar	Writing	Extend Your Learning	Assessment
Concrete and Abstract Nouns, SE, p. 184; *UR2,* p. 13; *WG,* Ch. 16, Section 1	**Writing Lesson:** Comparison-and-Contrast Essay, SE, p. 185; *UR2,* p. 14; *WG,* Ch. 9	**Listening and Speaking:** Oral Interpretation, SE, p. 185 **Research and Technology:** Culture Spreadsheet, p. 185, *UR2,* p. 15	**Selection Tests A and B,** *UR2,* pp. 17-22; **Rubrics for Exposition: Comparison-and-Contrast Essay,** *GR,* pp. 53-54; **Rubric for Peer Assessment: Oral Interpretation,** *GR,* p. 129
Participles as Adjectives, SE, p. 218; *UR2,* p. 30; *WG,* Ch. 20, Section 1	**Writing Lesson:** Editorial, SE, p. 219; *UR2,* p. 31; *WG,* Ch. 7	**Listening and Speaking:** TV News Report, SE, p. 219 **Research and Technology:** Oral Presentation, p. 219, *UR2,* p. 32	**Selection Tests A and B,** *UR2,* pp. 34-39; **Rubrics for Persuasion: Persuasive Essay,** *GR,* pp. 47-48; **Rubric for Speaking: Presenting an Oral Response to Literature,** *GR,* p. 91
Adjective Clauses, SE, p. 228; *UR2,* p. 47; *WG,* Ch. 20, Section 2	**Writing Lesson:** Animal Fable, SE, p. 229; *UR2,* p. 48; *WG,* Ch. 5	**Listening and Speaking:** Retelling, SE, p. 229 **Research and Technology:** Multimedia Report, p. 229, *UR2,* p. 49	**Selection Tests A and B,** *UR2,* pp. 51-56; **Rubrics for Narration: Short Story,** *GR,* pp. 63-64; **Rubrics for Multimedia Report,** *GR,* pp. 57-58; **Benchmark Test 2,** *UR2,* pp. 64-69

All selections are supported in the Reader's Notebooks.

UNIT 3

Wisdom and Insight (1000 B.C.–A.D. 1890)

Selection	Reading Strategy	Literary Analysis	Vocabulary
from ***The Tao Te Ching: I and III*** (MC), Lao Tzu, SE, p. 266; **from *The Analects*** (A), Confucius, SE, p. 268	**Questioning Causes and Effects,** SE, p. 265; *UR3,* p. 12; **Reading Warm-ups A and B,** *UR3,* pp. 9-10; **Reading Strategy Graphic Organizers A and B,** *GOT,* pp. 47-48	**Aphorisms,** SE, p. 265; *UR3,* p. 11; **Literary Analysis Graphic Organizers A and B,** *GOT,* pp. 49-50	**Vocabulary Builder,** SE, p. 265: *manifestations, contention, calamity, submissive, homage, chastisements, ritual, bias* **Latin Suffix** *-ment,* SE, p. 272; *UR3,* p. 13
Focus on Poetry			
from ***The Book of Songs: I Beg of You, Chung Tzu*** (A), SE, p. 280; from ***The Book of Songs: Thick Grow the Rush Leaves*** (A), SE, p. 281; ***Form, Shadow, Spirit,*** (A), T'ao Ch'ien, SE, p. 282; ***I Built My House Near Where Others Dwell,*** (MA), T'ao Ch'ien, SE, p. 285; ***The River-Merchant's Wife: A Letter,*** (A), Li Po, SE, p. 286; ***Addressed Humorously to Tu Fu*** (MA), Li Po, SE, p. 288; ***Jade Flower Palace*** (A), Tu Fu, SE, p. 289; ***Sent to Li Po as a Gift*** (A), Tu Fu, SE, p. 290	**Responding,** SE, p. 279; *UR3,* p. 29; **Reading Warm-ups A and B,** *UR3,* pp. 26-27; **Reading Strategy Graphic Organizers A and B,** *GOT,* pp. 53-54	**Chinese Poetic Forms,** SE, p. 279; *UR3,* p. 28; **Literary Analysis Graphic Organizers A and B,** *GOT,* pp. 51-52	**Vocabulary Builder,** SE, p. 279: *bashful, eddies, scurry, pathos, imperceptibly* **Greek Root** *-path-,* SE, p. 292; *UR3,* p. 30
When I Went to Visit (MA), Ki Tsurayuki, SE, p. 298; ***Went to Sleep,*** (MA), Ono Komachi, SE, p. 299; ***Loneliness*** (MA), Priest Jakuren, SE, p. 299; ***Sun's Way/ Clouds Come/Cuckoo/Seven Sights/Summer Grasses,*** (MA), Matsuo Bashō, SE, p. 300; ***Four Views of Spring Rain*** (MA), Yosa Buson, SE, p. 301; ***Beautiful/ Far-Off Mountain Peaks/World of Dew/Bland Serenity*** (MA), Kobayashi Issa, SE, p. 302	**Picturing Imagery,** SE, p. 297; *UR3,* p. 48; **Reading Warm-ups A and B,** *UR3,* pp. 45-46; **Reading Strategy Graphic Organizers A and B,** *GOT,* pp. 55-56	**Japanese Poetic Forms,** SE, p. 297; *UR3,* p. 47; **Literary Analysis Graphic Organizers A and B,** *GOT,* pp. 57-58	**Vocabulary Builder,** SE, p. 297: *veiled, bland, serenity* **Connotations and Denotations,** SE, p. 304; *UR3,* p. 49
from ***The Pillow Book: In Spring/The Cat/Things That Arouse/I Remember*** (A), Sei Shonagon, SE, p. 308	**Relating to Your Own Experiences,** SE, p. 307; *UR3,* p. 65; **Reading Warm-ups A and B,** *UR3,* pp. 62-63; **Reading Strategy Graphic Organizers A and B,** *GOT,* pp. 61-62	**Journal,** SE, p. 307; *UR3,* p. 64; **Literary Analysis Graphic Organizers A and B,** *GOT,* pp. 59-60	**Vocabulary Builder,** SE, p. 307: *earnest, chastised, loathsome, indefinitely* **Latin Prefix** *in-,* SE, p. 314; *UR3,* p. 66
Zen Parables: *A Parable* (A), SE, p. 320; **Zen Parables: *Publishing the Sutras*** (A), SE, p. 321; **Zen Parables: *The Taste of Banzo's Sword*** (A), SE, p. 321	**Interpreting Paradox,** SE, p. 319; *UR3,* p. 82; **Reading Warm-ups A and B,** *UR3,* pp. 79-80; **Reading Strategy Graphic Organizers A and B,** *GOT,* pp. 63-64	**Zen Parables,** SE, p. 319; *UR3,* p. 81; **Literary Analysis Graphic Organizers A and B,** *GOT,* pp. 65-66	**Vocabulary Builder,** SE, p. 319: *sustained, epidemic, mediocre, anticipate, rebuked* **Latin Prefix** *ante-/anti-,* SE, p. 324; *UR3,* p. 83

Key to Program References:
SE: Student Edition **UR:** Unit Resources **GOT:** Graphic Organizer Transparencies **GR:** General Resources **WG:** Writing and Grammar
MA: More accessible **A:** Average **MC:** More Challenging. See Accessibility at a Glance chart on selection pages.

Skills Navigator

Grammar	Writing	Extend Your Learning	Assessments
Infinitives and Infinitive Phrases, SE, p. 272; *UR3,* p. 14; *WG,* Ch. 20, Section 1	**Writing Lesson:** Critical Comparison, SE, p. 273; *UR3,* p. 15; *WG,* Ch. 9	**Listening and Speaking:** Philosophical Debate, SE, p. 273 **Research and Technology:** Research Presentation, p. 273, *UR3*, p. 16	**Diagnostic Test 3,** *UR3,* pp. 2-4; **Selection Tests A and B,** *UR3,* pp. 18-23; **Rubrics for Exposition: Comparison-and-Contrast Essay,** *GR,* pp. 53-54
Prepositional Phrases, SE, p. 292; *UR3,* p. 31; *WG,* Ch. 18, Section 1	**Writing Lesson:** Response to Criticism, SE, p. 293; *UR3,* p. 32; *WG,* Ch. 13	**Listening and Speaking:** Oral Report, SE, p. 293 **Research and Technology:** Poster, p. 293, *UR3*, p. 33	**Selection Tests A and B,** *UR3,* pp. 35-40; **Rubrics for Response to Literature,** *GR,* pp. 55-56; **Rubrics for Research: Research Report,** *GR,* pp. 51-52
Participial Phrases, SE, p. 304; *UR3,* p. 50; *WG,* Ch. 20, Section 1	**Writing Lesson:** Short Story, SE, p. 305; *UR3,* p. 51; *WG,* Ch. 6	**Listening and Speaking:** Poetry Reading, SE, p. 305 **Research and Technology:** Climate Report, p. 305, *UR3*, p. 52	**Selection Tests A and B,** *UR3,* pp. 54-59; **Rubrics for Narration: Short Story,** *GR,* pp. 63-64; **Rubrics for Multimedia Report,** *GR,* pp. 57-58
Noun Clauses, SE, p. 314; *UR3,* p. 67; *WG,* Ch. 20, Section 2	**Writing Lesson:** Journal Entry, SE, p. 315; *UR3,* p. 68; *WG,* Ch. 5	**Listening and Speaking:** Oral Report, SE, p. 315 **Research and Technology:** Graphic Presentation of Poll Results, p. 315, *UR3*, p. 69	**Selection Tests A and B,** *UR3,* pp. 71-76; **Rubrics for Narration: Autobiographical Narrative,** *GR,* pp. 43-44
Adverb Clauses, SE, p. 324; *UR3,* p. 84; *WG,* Ch. 20, Section 2	**Writing Lesson:** Annotated Bibliography, SE, p. 325; *UR3,* p. 85; *WG,* Ch. 12, Section 5	**Listening and Speaking:** Panel Discussion, SE, p. 325 **Research and Technology:** Multimedia Report, p. 325, *UR3*, p. 86	**Selection Tests A and B,** *UR3,* pp. 88-93; **Rubrics for Research: Research Report,** *GR,* pp. 51-52; **Benchmark Test 3,** *UR3,* pp. 101-106

All Selections are supported in the Reader's Notebooks.

UNIT 4 Classical Civilizations (c. 800 B.C.–A.D. 500)

Selection	Reading Strategy	Literary Analysis	Vocabulary
from *The Iliad:* from *Book 1: The Rage of Achilles* (MC), Homer, SE, p. 363; **from *The Iliad:* from *Book 6: Hector Returns to Troy*** (MC), Homer, SE, p. 374	**Analyze Confusing Sentences,** SE, p. 362; *UR4*, p. 12; **Reading Warm-ups A and B,** *UR4*, pp. 9-10; **Reading Strategy Graphic Organizers A and B,** *GOT*, pp. 68-69	**Theme,** SE, p. 362; *UR4*, p. 11; **Literary Analysis Graphic Organizers A and B,** *GOT*, pp. 70-71	**Vocabulary Builder,** SE, p. 362: *incensed, plunder, sacrosanct, brazen, harrowed, bereft* **Latin Root:** *-sacr-*, SE, p. 381; *UR4*, p. 13
from *The Iliad:* from *Book 22: The Death of Hector* (MC), Homer, SE, p. 383; **from *The Iliad:* from *Book 24: Achilles and Priam*** (MC), Homer, SE, p. 397	**Picture the Action,** SE, p. 382; *UR4*, p. 28; **Reading Warm-ups A and B,** *UR4*, pp. 25-26	**Imagery,** SE, p. 382; *UR4*, p. 27; **Literary Analysis Graphic Organizers A and B,** *GOT*, pp. 72-73, 74-75	**Vocabulary Builder,** SE, p. 382: *implore, marshals, whetted, brandished, stinted, lustrous, gaunt, illustrious* **Latin Root:** *-lustr-*, SE, p. 410; *UR4*, p. 29
"You Know the Place: Then" (MA), Sappho, SE, p. 414; **"He Is More Than a Hero"** (A), Sappho, SE, p. 416; **"Olympia 11"** (A), Pindar, SE, p. 418	**Responding to Imagery,** SE, p. 413; *UR4*, p. 45; **Reading Warm-ups A and B,** *UR4*, pp. 42-43; **Reading Strategy Graphic Organizers A and B,** *GOT*, pp. 78-79	**Lyric Poetry,** SE, p. 413; *UR4*, p. 44; **Literary Analysis Graphic Organizers A and B,** *GOT*, pp. 76-77	**Vocabulary Builder,** SE, p. 413: *sleek, murmur, tenuous, suffuses, endeavor, accordance* **Echoic Words,** SE, p. 420; *UR4*, p. 46
Pericles' Funeral Oration* from *History of the Peloponnesian War (MC), SE, p. 424	**Recognizing Cultural Attitudes,** SE, p. 423; *UR4*, p. 62; **Reading Warm-ups A and B,** *UR4*, pp. 59-60; **Reading Strategy Graphic Organizers A and B,** *GOT*, pp. 80-81	**Speech,** SE, p. 423; *UR4*, p. 61; **Literary Analysis Graphic Organizers A and B,** *GOT*, pp. 82-83	**Vocabulary Builder,** SE, p. 423: *incredulous, manifold, tangible, consummation, culmination, commiserate* **Latin Root:** *-cred-*, SE, p. 434; *UR4*, p. 63
from *The Apology* (MC), Plato, SE, p. 440	**Challenging the Text,** SE, p. 439; *UR4*, p. 88; **Reading Warm-ups A and B,** *UR4*, pp. 85-86; **Reading Strategy Graphic Organizers A and B,** *GOT*, pp. 84-85	**Monologue,** SE, p. 439; *UR4*, p. 87; **Literary Analysis Graphic Organizers A and B,** *GOT*, pp. 86-87	**Vocabulary Builder,** SE, p. 439: *eloquence, affidavit, lamented, avenged, exhorting, impudence, indictment, piety* **Legal Terminology,** SE, p. 458; *UR4*, p. 89
Focus on Drama			
Oedipus the King, Part I (MC), Sophocles, SE, p. 468	**Reading Drama,** SE, p. 467; *UR4*, p. 107; **Reading Warm-ups A and B,** *UR4*, pp. 104-105	**Tragedy,** SE, p. 467; *UR4*, p. 106; **Literary Analysis Graphic Organizers A and B,** *GOT*, pp. 88-89, 90-91	**Vocabulary Builder,** SE, p. 467: *blight, pestilence, induced, dispatch, invoke, prophecy, countenance, malignant* **Greek Prefix:** *pro-*, SE, p. 501; *UR4*, p. 108
Oedipus the King, Part II (MC), Sophocles, SE, p. 503	**Questioning the Characters' Motives,** SE, p. 502; *UR4*, p. 123; **Reading Warm-ups A and B,** *UR4*, pp. 120-121; **Reading Strategy Graphic Organizers A and B,** *GOT*, pp. 92-93	**Irony,** SE, p. 502; *UR4*, p. 122; **Literary Analysis Graphic Organizers A and B,** *GOT*, pp. 94-95	**Vocabulary Builder,** SE, p. 502: *fettered, beneficent, consonant, gratify, infamous, reverence* **Latin Prefix:** *con-*, SE, p. 526; *UR4*, p. 124

Key to Program References:
SE: Student Edition **UR:** Unit Resources **GOT:** Graphic Organizer Transparencies **GR:** General Resources **WG:** Writing and Grammar
MA: More accessible **A:** Average **MC:** More Challenging. See Accessibility at a Glance chart on selection pages.

Skills Navigator

Grammar	Writing	Extend Your Learning	Assessment
Compound Adjectives, SE, p. 381; *UR4,* p. 14; *WG,* Ch. 17, Section 1	**Writing:** Everyday Epic, SE, p. 381; *UR4*, p. 15	**Research and Technology:** Multimedia Map, SE, p. 381	**Diagnostic Test 4,** *UR4*, pp. 2-4; **Selection Tests A and B,** *UR4*, pp. 17-22
Commas With Quotations, SE, p. 410; *UR4,* p. 30; *WG,* Ch. 28, Section 2	**Writing Lesson:** Editorial, SE, p. 411; *UR4*, p. 31; *WG*, Ch. 8, Section 4	**Listening and Speaking:** Movie Preview, SE, p. 411 **Research and Technology:** Archeological Oral Report on Troy, SE, p. 411; *UR4*, p. 32	**Selection Tests A and B,** *UR4*, pp. 34-39; **Rubrics for Persuasion: Persuasive Essay,** *GR*, pp. 47-48
Direct Address, SE, p. 420; *UR4,* p. 47; *WG*, Ch. 28, Section 2	**Writing Lesson:** Comparative Analysis of Translations, SE, p. 421; *UR4*, p. 48; *WG*, Ch. 9, Section 3	**Listening and Speaking:** Recitation, SE, p. 421; *UR4*, p. 49 **Research and Technology:** Illustrated Report, SE, p. 421	**Selection Tests A and B,** *UR4*, pp. 51-56; **Rubrics for Exposition: Comparison-and-Contrast Essay,** *GR*, pp. 53-54
Colons, SE, p. 434; *UR4,* p. 64; *WG*, Ch. 28, Section 3	**Writing Lesson:** Essay About Leadership, SE, p. 435; *UR4*, p. 65; *WG*, Ch. 13, Section 3	**Listening and Speaking:** Oral Interpretation, SE, p. 435 **Research and Technology:** Chart Evaluating Pericles' Claims, SE, p. 435; *UR4*, p. 66	**Selection Tests A and B,** *UR4*, pp. 68-73; **Rubrics for Response to Literature,** *GR*, pp. 55-56; **Benchmark Test 4,** *UR4*, pp. 74-79
Transitions and Transitional Phrases, SE, p. 458; *UR4,* p. 90; *WG,* Ch. 10, Section 4	**Writing Lesson:** Account of a Remarkable Person, SE, p. 459; *UR4*, p. 91; *WG*, Ch. 6, Section 2	**Listening and Speaking:** Interview, SE, p. 459 **Research and Technology:** Research Report, SE, p. 459; *UR4*, p. 92	**Diagnostic Test 5,** *UR4*, pp. 80-82; **Selection Tests A and B,** *UR4*, pp. 94-99; **Rubrics for Descriptive Essay,** *GR*, pp. 67-68; **Rubrics for Research: Research Report,** *GR*, pp. 51-52
Participial Phrases, SE, p. 501; *UR4,* p. 109; *WG,* Ch. 20, Section 1		**Listening and Speaking:** Dramatic Reading, SE, p. 501 **Writing:** News Article, SE, p. 501; *UR4*, p. 110	**Selection Tests A and B,** *UR4*, pp. 112-117; **Rubrics for Response to Literature,** *GR*, pp. 55-56
Gerunds and Gerund Phrases, SE, p. 526; *UR4,* p. 125; *WG*, Ch. 20, Section 1	**Writing Lesson:** Character Study, SE, p. 527; *UR4*, p. 126; *WG*, Ch. 14, Section 2	**Listening and Speaking:** Debate, SE, p. 527 **Research and Technology:** Illustrated Report on Greek Theaters, SE, p. 527; *UR4*, p. 127	**Selection Tests A and B,** *UR4*, pp. 129-134; **Rubrics for Response to Literature,** *GR*, pp. 55-56

All selections are supported in the Reader's Notebooks.

UNIT 4

Classical Civilizations (c. 800 B.C.–A.D. 500) *(continued)*

Selection	Reading Strategy	Literary Analysis	Vocabulary
from the *Aeneid:* from *Book II: How They Took the City* (MC), Virgil, SE, p. 534	**Applying Background Information,** SE, p. 533; *UR4*, p. 140; **Reading Warm-ups A and B,** *UR4*, pp. 137-138; **Reading Strategy Graphic Organizers A and B,** *GOT*, pp. 96-97	**National Epic,** SE, p. 533; *UR4*, p. 139; **Literary Analysis Graphic Organizers A and B,** *GOT*, pp. 98-99	**Vocabulary Builder,** SE, p. 533: *notions, perjured, guile, tumult, unfettered, blasphem-ing, desecrating, portents* **Latin Root:** *-jur-*, SE, p. 546; *UR4*, p. 141
from *Metamorphoses: The Story of Daedalus and Icarus* (A), Ovid, SE, p. 550	**Anticipating Events,** SE, p. 549; *UR4*, p. 157; **Reading Warm-ups A and B,** *UR4*, pp. 154-155; **Reading Strategy Graphic Organizers A and B,** *GOT*, pp. 100-101	**Narrative Poetry,** SE, p. 549; *UR4*, p. 156; **Literary Analysis Graphic Organizers A and B,** *GOT*, pp. 102-103	**Vocabulary Builder,** SE, p. 549: *dominion, sequence, poised* **Latin Root:** *-domin-*, SE, p. 554; *UR4*, p. 158
from *The Annals:* from *The Burning of Rome* (MC), Tacitus, SE, p. 558	**Recognize Author's Bias,** SE, p. 557; *UR4*, p. 174; **Reading Warm-ups A and B,** *UR4*, pp. 171-172; **Reading Strategy Graphic Organizers A and B,** *GOT*, pp. 104-105	**Annals,** SE, p. 557; *UR4*, p. 173; **Literary Analysis Graphic Organizers A and B,** *GOT*, pp. 106-107	**Vocabulary Builder,** SE, p. 557: *conflagration, unham-pered, destitute, antiquity, pre-cipitous, demarcation, munifi-cence* **Latin Suffix:** *-tion*, SE, p. 566; *UR4*, p. 175

UNIT 5

From Death to Rebirth (A.D. 450–1300)

Selection	Reading Strategy	Literary Analysis	Vocabulary
Focus on Medieval Romance Saga			
from *The Song of Roland* (MC), SE, p. 600; **from *The Nibelungenlied: How Siegfried Was Slain*** (MC), SE, p. 610	**Recognizing Feudal Values,** SE, p. 599; *UR5*, p. 12; **Reading Warm-ups A and B,** *UR5*, pp. 9-10; **Reading Strategy Graphic Organizers A and B,** *GOT*, pp. 109-110	**Medieval Epic,** SE, p. 599; *UR5*, p. 11; **Literary Analysis Graphic Organizers A and B,** *GOT*, pp. 111-112	**Vocabulary Builder,** SE, p. 599: *vassal, prowess, exult-ing, unrestrained, malice, sinis-ter, intrepid, thwarted* **Latin Prefix** *mal-*, SE, p. 620; *UR5*, p. 13
from *Perceval: The Grail* (A), Chrétien de Troyes, SE, p. 630; ***The Lay of the Werewolf*** (MC), Marie de France, SE, p. 642	**Interpreting Symbols,** SE, p. 629; *UR5*, p. 31; **Reading Warm-ups A and B,** *UR5*, pp. 28-29; **Reading Strategy Graphic Organizers A and B,** *GOT*, pp. 113-114	**Archetypes,** SE, p. 629; *UR5*, p. 30; **Literary Analysis Graphic Organizers A and B,** *GOT*, pp. 115-116	**Vocabulary Builder,** SE, p. 629: *sovereign, navigated, elated, serene, nimble, esteemed, importunity, abases* **Latin Root** *-naviga-*, SE, p. 650; *UR5*, p. 32
from *The Inferno: Canto I: The Dark Wood of Error* (MC), Dante Alighieri, SE, p. 658; **from *The Inferno: Canto III: The Vestibule of Hell/The Opportunists*** (MC), Dante Alighieri, SE, p. 665	**Interpreting Imagery,** SE, p. 657; *UR5*, p. 48; **Reading Warm-ups A and B,** *UR5*, pp. 45-46; **Reading Strategy Graphic Organizers A and B,** *GOT*, pp. 117-118	**Allegory,** SE, p. 657; *UR5*, p. 47; **Literary Analysis Graphic Organizers A and B,** *GOT*, pp. 119-120	**Vocabulary Builder,** SE, p. 657: *flounders, tremulous, zeal, putrid, despicable, lamen-tation, scorn, reprimand* **Latin Root** *-trem-*, SE, p. 673; *UR5*, p. 49

Key to Program References:
SE: Student Edition **UR:** Unit Resources **GOT:** Graphic Organizer Transparencies **GR:** General Resources **WG:** Writing and Grammar
MA: More accessible **A:** Average **MC:** More Challenging. See Accessibility at a Glance chart on selection pages.

Skills Navigator

Grammar	Writing	Extend Your Learning	Assessment
Sentence Beginnings: Adverb Phrases, SE, p. 546; *UR4,* p. 142; *WG,* Ch. 21, Section 3	**Writing Lesson:** Analysis of Storytelling Technique, SE, p. 547; *UR4*, p. 143; *WG*, Ch. 9, Section 4	**Listening and Speaking:** Persuasive Speech, SE, p. 547 **Research and Technology:** Travelogue, SE, p. 547; *UR4*, p. 144	**Selection Tests A and B,** *UR4*, pp. 146-151; **Rubrics for Response to Literature,** *GR*, pp. 55-56; **Rubrics for Research: Research Report,** *GR*, pp. 51-52
Appositives and Appositive Phrases, SE, p. 554; *UR4*, p. 159; *WG*, Ch. 20, Section 1	**Writing Lesson:** Multimedia Script, SE, p. 555; *UR4*, p. 160; *WG*, Ch. 28, Section 3	**Listening and Speaking:** Videotaped News Report, SE, p. 555 **Research and Technology:** Map of the Roman Empire, SE, p. 555; *UR4*, p. 161	**Selection Tests A and B,** *UR4*, pp. 163-168; **Rubrics for Multimedia Report,** *GR*, pp. 57-58
Commonly Confused Words: *less* and *fewer*, SE, p. 566; *UR4*, p. 176; *WG*, Ch. 26, Section 2	**Writing Lesson:** Eyewitness Narrative Essay, SE, p. 567; *UR4*, p. 177; *WG*, Ch. 9, Section 4	**Listening and Speaking:** Skit, SE, p. 567; *UR4*, p. 178 **Research and Technology:** Illustrated Timeline of Roman History, SE, p. 567	**Selection Tests A and B,** *UR4*, pp. 180-185; **Rubrics for Narration: Autobiographical Narrative,** *GR*, pp. 43-44; **Benchmark Test 5,** *UR4*, pp. 193-198

Grammar	Writing	Extend Your Learning	Assessment
Interrupting Phrases and Clauses, SE, p. 620; *UR5*, p. 14; *WG*, Ch. 27, Section 5	**Writing Lesson:** Persuasive Essay on Values, SE, p. 621; *UR5*, p. 15; *WG*, Ch. 7, Section 2	**Listening and Speaking:** Press Conference, SE, p. 621 **Research and Technology:** Informative Poster, p. 621, *UR5*, p. 16	**Diagnostic Test 6,** *UR5*, pp. 2-4; **Selection Tests A and B,** *UR5*, pp. 18-23; **Rubrics for Persuasion: Persuasive Essay,** *GR*, pp. 47-48
Compound-Complex Sentences, SE, p. 650; *UR5*, p. 33; *WG*, Ch. 13, Section 4	**Writing Lesson:** Modern Symbolic Tale, SE, p. 651; *UR5*, p. 34; *WG*, Ch. 5, Section 4	**Listening and Speaking:** Panel Discussion, SE, p. 651 **Research and Technology:** Research Presentation, p. 651, *UR5*, p. 35	**Selection Tests A and B,** *UR5*, pp. 37-42; **Rubrics for Narration: Short Story,** *GR*, pp. 63-64
Present Perfect Verb Tense, SE, p. 673; *UR5*, p. 50; *WG*, Ch. 21, Section 2		**Listening and Speaking:** Presentation, SE, p. 673 **Writing:** New Version, p. 673, *UR5*, p. 51	**Selection Tests A and B,** *UR5*, pp. 53-58; **Benchmark Test 6,** *UR5*, pp. 59-64

All selections are supported in the Reader's Notebooks.

UNIT 5 From Death to Rebirth (A.D. 450–1300) *(continued)*

Selection	Reading Strategy	Literary Analysis	Vocabulary
from *The Inferno: Canto V: Circle Two: The Carnal* (MC), Dante Alighieri, SE, p. 675; **from *The Inferno: Canto XXXIV: Cocytus*** (MC), Dante Alighieri, SE, p. 683	**Distinguishing Between the Speaker and the Poet,** SE, p. 674; *UR5,* p. 73; **Reading Warm-ups A and B,** *UR5,* pp. 70-71; **Reading Strategy Graphic Organizers A and B,** *GOT,* pp. 121-122	**Characterization,** SE, p. 674; *UR5,* p. 72; **Literary Analysis Graphic Organizers A and B,** *GOT,* pp. 123-124	**Vocabulary Builder,** SE, p. 674: *grotesque, degree, anguish, tempest, perilous, awe, writhes, nimble* **Related Words: *Awe,*** SE, p. 692; *UR5,* p. 74

UNIT 6 Rebirth and Exploration (1300–1800)

Selection	Reading Strategy	Literary Analysis	Vocabulary
Focus on Sonnet **from *Canzoniere:* "Laura"** (A), Petrarch, SE, p. 730; **from *Canzoniere:* "The White Doe"** (MC), Petrarch, SE, p. 732; **from *Canzoniere:* "Spring"** (MC), Petrarch, SE, p. 733; **"To Hélène"** (MC), Pierre de Ronsard, SE, p. 734; **"Roses"** (MC), Pierre de Ronsard, SE, p. 736	**Reading in Sentences,** SE, p. 729; *UR6,* p. 9; **Reading Warm-ups A and B,** *UR6,* pp. 6-7; **Reading Strategy Graphic Organizers A and B,** *GOT,* pp. 128-129	**The Sonnet,** SE, p. 729; *UR6,* p. 8; **Literary Analysis Graphic Organizers A and B,** *GOT,* pp. 126-127	**Vocabulary Builder,** SE, p. 729: *sated, exults, sojourn, crone, languishing, reposes* **Related Words:** *languish,* SE, p. 738; *UR6,* p. 10
from the *Decameron:* "Federigo's Falcon" (MC), Giovanni Boccaccio, SE, p. 744	**Identifying with Characters,** SE, p. 743; *UR6,* p. 26; **Reading Warm-ups A and B,** *UR6,* pp. 23-24; **Reading Strategy Graphic Organizers A and B,** *GOT,* pp. 132-133	**Novella,** SE, p. 743; *UR6,* p. 25; **Literary Analysis Graphic Organizers A and B,** *GOT,* pp. 130-131	**Vocabulary Builder,** SE, p. 743: *courtly, sumptuous, frugally, deference, affably, impertinence, despondent* **Latin Suffix** *-ence,* SE, p. 752; *UR6,* p. 27
from *Starry Messenger:* from "Astronomical Message" (A), Galileo Galilei, SE, p. 758; **from *The Assayer*** (A), Galileo Galilei, SE, p. 762	**Breaking Down Long Sentences,** SE, p. 757; *UR6,* p. 45; **Reading Warm-ups A and B,** *UR6,* pp. 42-43; **Reading Strategy Graphic Organizers A and B,** *GOT,* pp. 134-135	**Narrative Accounts,** SE, p. 757; *UR6,* p. 44; **Literary Analysis Graphic Organizers A and B,** *GOT,* pp. 136-137	**Vocabulary Builder,** SE, p. 757: *manifest, conspicuous, multitude, impelled, derive, diffidence* **Latin Root** *-pel-,* SE, p. 766; *UR6,* p. 46
from *Don Quixote* (A), Miguel de Cervantes, SE, p. 770	**Comparing and Contrasting,** SE, p. 769; *UR6,* p. 62; **Reading Warm-ups A and B,** *UR6,* pp. 59-60; **Reading Strategy Graphic Organizers A and B,** *GOT,* pp. 138-139	**Parody,** SE, p. 769; *UR6,* p. 61; **Literary Analysis Graphic Organizers A and B,** *GOT,* pp. 140-141	**Vocabulary Builder,** SE, p. 769: *constitution, conjectures, infatuation, ingenuity, incongruous, appropriate, illustrious* **Latin Root** *-ject-,* SE, p. 786; *UR6,* p. 63
"The Fox and the Crow" (A), Jean de La Fontaine, SE, p. 790; **"The Oak and the Reed"** (A), Jean de La Fontaine, SE, p. 792	**Drawing Conclusions,** SE, p. 789; *UR6,* p. 88; **Reading Warm-ups A and B,** *UR6,* pp. 85-86; **Reading Strategy Graphic Organizers A and B,** *GOT,* pp. 142-143	**Fables,** SE, p. 789; *UR6,* p. 87; **Literary Analysis Graphic Organizers A and B,** *GOT,* pp. 144-145	**Vocabulary Builder,** SE, p. 789: *buffeted, hazards, impervious, prone* **Latin Prefix** *im-,* SE, p. 796; *UR6,* p. 89

Key to Program References:
SE: Student Edition **UR:** Unit Resources **GOT:** Graphic Organizer Transparencies **GR:** General Resources **WG:** Writing and Grammar
MA: More accessible **A:** Average **MC:** More Challenging. See Accessibility at a Glance chart on selection pages.

Skills Navigator

Grammar	Writing	Extend Your Learning	Assessment
Past Perfect Verb Tense, SE, p. 692; *UR5,* p. 75; *WG,* Ch. 21, Section 2	**Writing Lesson:** Response to Criticism, SE, p. 693; *UR5,* p. 76; *WG,* Ch. 14, Section 3	**Listening and Speaking:** Movie Proposal, SE, p. 693 **Research and Technology:** Biographical Analysis Chart, p. 693, *UR5,* p. 77	**Diagnostic Test 7,** *UR5,* pp. 65-67; **Selection Tests A and B,** *UR5,* pp. 79-84; **Rubrics for Response to Literature,** *GR,* pp. 55-56

Grammar	Writing	Extend Your Learning	Assessment
Predicate Adjective, SE, p. 738; *UR6,* p. 11; *WG,* Ch. 18, Section 3	**Writing Lesson:** Journal Passage, SE, p. 739; *UR6,* p. 12; *WG,* Ch. 4, Section 3	**Listening and Speaking:** Dramatic Reading, SE, p. 739 **Research and Technology:** Informative Essay, SE, p. 739; *UR6,* p. 13	**Selection Tests A and B,** *UR6,* pp. 15-20; **Rubrics for Reflective Essay,** *GR,* pp. 45-46; **Rubrics for Research: Research Report,** *GR,* pp. 51-52
Varying Sentence Beginnings, SE, p. 752; *UR6,* p. 28; *WG,* Ch. 20, Section 3	**Writing Lesson:** Literary Analysis, SE, p. 753; *UR6,* p. 29; *WG,* Ch. 14, Section 3	**Listening and Speaking:** Storytelling Circle, SE, p. 753 **Research and Technology:** Classroom Display, SE, p. 753; *UR6,* p. 30	**Selection Tests A and B,** *UR6,* pp. 32-37; **Rubrics for Response to Literature,** *GR,* pp. 55-56; **Rubrics for Research: Research Report,** *GR,* pp. 51-52
Comparative and Superlative Adjectives and Adverbs, SE, p. 766; *UR6,* p. 47; *WG,* Ch. 25, Section 1	**Writing Lesson:** Response to Literature, SE, p. 767; *UR6,* p. 48; *WG,* Ch. 6, Section 4	**Listening and Speaking:** Dramatic Reading, SE, p. 767 **Research and Technology:** Scrapbook, SE, p. 767; *UR6,* p. 49	**Selection Tests A and B,** *UR6,* pp. 51-56; **Rubrics for Response to Literature,** *GR,* pp. 55-56; **Rubrics for Descriptive Essay,** *GR,* pp. 67-68
Gerunds, SE, p. 786; *UR6,* p. 64; *WG,* Ch. 19, Section 2	**Writing Lesson:** Profile of a Comic Hero, SE, p. 787; *UR6,* p. 65; *WG,* Ch. 6, Section 4	**Listening and Speaking:** Role-play, SE, p. 787 **Research and Technology:** Visual Essay, SE, p. 787; *UR6,* p. 66	**Selection Tests A and B,** *UR6,* pp. 68-73; **Rubrics for Descriptive Essay,** *GR,* pp. 67-68; **Rubrics for Multimedia Report,** *GR,* pp. 57-58; **Benchmark Test 7,** *UR6,* pp. 74-79
Adjective Clauses Using *who, whom,* and *whose,* SE, p. 796; *UR6,* p. 90; *WG,* Ch. 19, Section 3	**Writing Lesson:** A Children's Story, SE, p. 797; *UR6,* p. 91; *WG,* Ch. 27, Section 4	**Listening and Speaking:** Dramatic Reading, SE, p. 797 **Research and Technology:** Research Report, SE, p. 797; *UR6,* p. 92	**Diagnostic Test 8,** *UR6,* pp. 80-82; **Selection Tests A and B,** *UR6,* pp. 94-99; **Rubrics for Narration: Short Story,** *GR,* pp. 63-64; **Rubrics for Research: Research Report,** *GR,* pp. 51-52

All selections are supported in the Reader's Notebooks.

UNIT 6 Rebirth and Exploration (1300–1800) *(continued)*

Selection	Reading Strategy	Literary Analysis	Vocabulary
from *Candide* (A), Voltaire, SE, p. 802	**Connecting to Historical Context,** SE, p. 801; *UR6,* p. 105; **Reading Warm-ups A and B,** *UR6,* pp. 102-103; **Reading Strategy Graphic Organizers A and B,** *GOT,* pp. 146-147	**Satire,** SE, p. 801; *UR6,* p. 104; **Literary Analysis Graphic Organizers A and B,** *GOT,* pp. 148-149	**Vocabulary Builder,** SE, p. 801: *endowed, candor, vivacity, prodigy, clemency* **Latin suffix** *-ity,* SE, p. 808; *UR6,* p. 106

UNIT 7 Revolution and Reaction (1800–1890)

Selection	Reading Strategy	Literary Analysis	Vocabulary
from *Faust:* "Prologue in Heaven" (MC), Johann Wolfgang von Goethe, SE, p. 846; **from *Faust:* from "The First Part of the Tragedy"** (MC), Johann Wolfgang von Goethe, SE, p. 851	**Drawing Inferences,** SE, p. 845; *UR7,* p. 9; **Reading Warm-ups A and B,** *UR7,* pp. 6-7; **Reading Strategy Graphic Organizers A and B,** *GOT,* pp. 151-152	**Romanticism,** SE, p. 845; *UR7,* p. 8; **Literary Analysis Graphic Organizers A and B,** *GOT,* pp. 153-154	**Vocabulary Builder,** SE, p. 845: *envoys, fervent, primal, obstinate, fetters, tenacity, insatiableness* **Related Words:** *prime,* SE, p. 864; *UR7,* p. 10
"I Have Visited Again" (A), Alexander Pushkin, SE, p. 876; **"The Lorelei"** (A), Heinrich Heine, SE, p. 879; **"The Lotus Flower"** (A), Heinrich Heine, SE, p. 880	**Reading Between the Lines,** SE, p. 875; *UR7,* p. 26; **Reading Warm-ups A and B,** *UR7,* pp. 23-24; **Reading Strategy Graphic Organizers A and B,** *GOT,* pp. 155-156	**Lyric Poetry,** SE, p. 875; *UR7,* p. 25; **Literary Analysis Graphic Organizers A and B,** *GOT,* pp. 155-156	**Vocabulary Builder,** SE, p. 875: *painstakingly, fathomless, ancestral, morose, resplendent, mutely* **Anglo-Saxon suffix** *-less,* SE, p. 882; *UR7,* p. 27
Focus on Lyric Poetry **"Invitation to the Voyage"** (MC), Charles Baudelaire, SE, p. 886; **"The Albatross"** (MC), Charles Baudelaire, SE, p. 888; **"The Sleeper in the Valley"** (MC), Arthur Rimbaud, SE, p. 889; **"Ophelia"** (MC), Arthur Rimbaud, SE, p. 890; **"Autumn Song"** (MC), Paul Verlaine, SE, p. 894	**Judging a Poet's Message,** SE, p. 885; *UR7,* p. 43; **Reading Warm-ups A and B,** *UR7,* pp. 40-41; **Reading Strategy Graphic Organizers A and B,** *GOT,* pp. 159-160	**Romantic Poetry,** SE, p. 885; *UR7,* p. 42; **Literary Analysis Graphic Organizers A and B,** *GOT,* pp. 161-162	**Vocabulary Builder,** SE, p. 885: *proffering, nonchalantly, sovereign, adroit, flourish, strains, monotone* **Greek prefix** *mono-,* SE, p. 896; *UR7,* p. 44
"Two Friends" (A), Guy de Maupassant, SE, p. 906; **"How Much Land Does a Man Need?"** (A), Leo Tolstoy, SE, p. 913; **"A Problem"** (A), Anton Chekhov, SE, p. 928	**Evaluating Characters' Decisions,** SE, p. 905; *UR7,* p. 62; **Reading Warm-ups A and B,** *UR7,* pp. 59-60; **Reading Strategy Graphic Organizers A and B,** *GOT,* pp. 165-166	**Dynamic and Static Characters,** SE, p. 905; *UR7,* p. 61; **Literary Analysis Graphic Organizers A and B,** *GOT,* pp. 163-164	**Vocabulary Builder,** SE, p. 905: *pillaging, superimposed, placidly, discord, prostrate, taciturn, benevolent* **Latin prefix** *dis-,* SE, p. 938; *UR7,* p. 63
***A Doll House,* Act One** (A), Henrik Ibsen, SE, p. 942	**Reading Drama,** SE, p. 941; *UR7,* p. 88; **Reading Warm-ups A and B,** *UR7,* pp. 85-86; **Reading Strategy Graphic Organizers A and B,** *GOT,* pp. 167-168	**Modern Realistic Drama,** SE, p. 941; *UR7,* p. 87; **Literary Analysis Graphic Organizers A and B,** *GOT,* pp. 169-170	**Vocabulary Builder,** SE, p. 941: *spendthrift, squandering, prodigal, indiscreet, frivolous, contraband, subordinate* **Word Analysis:** Coined Words, SE, p. 973; *UR7,* p. 89

Key to Program References:
SE: Student Edition **UR:** Unit Resources **GOT:** Graphic Organizer Transparencies **GR:** General Resources **WG:** Writing and Grammar
MA: More accessible **A:** Average **MC:** More Challenging. See Accessibility at a Glance chart on selection pages.

Skills Navigator

Grammar	Writing	Extend Your Learning	Assessment
Parallel Structure, SE, p. 808; *UR6,* p. 107; *WG,* Ch. 20, Section 6	**Writing Lesson:** Short Satirical Story, SE, p. 809; *UR6,* p. 108; *WG,* Ch. 5, Section 2	**Listening and Speaking:** Group Discussion, SE, p. 809 **Research and Technology:** Visual Report, SE, p. 809; *UR6,* p. 109	**Selection Tests A and B,** *UR6,* pp. 111-116; **Rubrics for Narration: Short Story,** *GR,* pp. 63-64; **Rubrics for Research: Research Report,** *GR,* pp. 51-52

Grammar	Writing	Extend Your Learning	Assessment
Usage: *who* and *whom*, SE, p. 864; *UR7,* p. 11; *WG,* Ch. 23, Section 2	**Writing Lesson:** Writing a Film Script, SE, p. 865; *UR7,* p. 12; *WG,* Ch. 2, Section 2	**Listening and Speaking:** Brief Dialogue, SE, p. 865 **Research and Technology:** Film, SE, p. 865; *UR7,* p. 13	**Selection Tests A and B,** *UR7,* pp. 15-20; **Rubric for Speaking: Narrative Account,** *GR,* p. 88
Pronouns and Antecedents, SE, p. 882; *UR7,* p. 28; *WG,* Ch. 24, Section 2	**Writing Lesson:** Analytical Essay, SE, p. 883; *UR7,* p. 29; *WG,* Ch. 10, Section 4	**Listening and Speaking:** Oral Interpretive Reading, SE, p. 883 **Research and Technology:** Museum Exhibit, SE, p. 883; *UR7,* p. 30	**Selection Tests A and B,** *UR7,* pp. 32-37; **Rubrics for Response to Literature,** *GR,* pp. 55-56
Adjectival Modifiers, SE, p. 896; *UR7,* p. 45; *WG,* Ch. 20, Sections 1 and 2	**Writing Lesson:** Comparison-and-Contrast Essay, SE, p. 897; *UR7,* p. 46; *WG,* Ch. 9, Section 3	**Listening and Speaking:** Discussion, SE, p. 897 **Research and Technology:** Multimedia Travelogue, SE, p. 897; *UR7,* p. 47	**Selection Tests A and B,** *UR7,* pp. 51-56; **Rubrics for Exposition: Comparison-and-Contrast Essay,** *GR,* pp. 53-54
Restrictive and Nonrestrictive Adjective Clauses, SE, p. 938; *UR7,* p. 64; *WG,* Ch. 20, Section 2	**Writing Lesson:** Analyzing a Character's Decision, SE, p. 939; *UR7,* p. 65; *WG,* Ch. 3, Section 2	**Listening and Speaking:** Monologue, SE, p. 939 **Research and Technology:** Coat of Arms, SE, p. 939; *UR7,* p. 66	**Selection Tests A and B,** *UR7,* pp. 68-73; **Rubrics for Narration: Short Story,** *GR,* pp. 63-64; **Rubric for Speaking: Narrative Account,** *GR,* p. 88; **Benchmark Test 8,** *UR7,* pp. 74-79
Compound Predicates, SE, p. 973; *UR7,* p. 90; *WG,* Ch. 19, Section 1	**Writing:** Monologue, SE, p. 973	**Research and Technology:** Rendering of the Set, SE, p. 973; *UR7,* p. 91	**Diagnostic Test 9,** *UR7,* pp. 80-82; **Selection Tests A and B,** *UR7,* pp. 93-98; **Rubrics for Response to Literature,** *GR,* p. 55-56

All selections are supported in the Reader's Notebooks.

UNIT 7 Revolution and Reaction (1800–1890) *(continued)*

Selection	Reading Strategy	Literary Analysis	Vocabulary
***A Doll House,* Act Two** (A), Henrik Ibsen, SE, p. 975	**Inferring Beliefs of the Period,** SE, p. 974; *UR7,* p. 104; **Reading Warm-ups A and B,** *UR7,* pp. 101-102; **Reading Strategy Graphic Organizers A and B,** *GOT,* pp. 171-172	**Characterization in Drama,** SE, p. 974; *UR7,* p. 103; **Literary Analysis Graphic Organizers A and B,** *GOT,* pp. 173-174	**Vocabulary Builder,** SE, p. 974: *proclaiming, intolerable, impulsive, tactless, excruciating, retribution, disreputable* **Latin prefix** *re-,* SE, p. 999; *UR7,* p. 105
***A Doll House,* Act Three** (A), Henrik Ibsen, SE, p. 1001	**Recognizing Dramatic Tension,** SE, p. 1000; *UR7,* p. 120; **Reading Warm-ups A and B,** *UR7,* pp. 117-118; **Reading Strategy Graphic Organizers A and B,** *GOT,* pp. 175-176	**Theme,** SE, p. 1000; *UR7,* p. 119; **Literary Analysis Graphic Organizers A and B,** *GOT,* pp. 177-178	**Vocabulary Builder,** SE, p. 1000: *calculating, evasions, naturalistic, proprieties, hypocrite, grafter, bewildered* **Greek prefix** *hypo-,* SE, p. 1024, *UR7,* p. 121

UNIT 8 From Conflict and Renewal (1890-1945)

Selection	Reading Strategy	Literary Analysis	Vocabulary
Focus on Short Story			
"The Metamorphosis" (MC), Franz Kafka, SE, p. 1066	**Applying the Author's Biography,** SE, p. 1065; *UR8,* p. 12; **Reading Warm-ups A and B,** *UR8,* pp. 9-10; **Reading Strategy Graphic Organizers A and B,** *GOT,* pp. 180-181	**Modernism,** SE, p. 1065; *UR8,* p. 11; **Literary Analysis Graphic Organizers A and B,** *GOT,* pp. 182-183	**Vocabulary Builder,** SE, p. 1065: *impracticable, obstinacy, exuded, rectify, imminent, gyration, pallid, debacle* **Latin prefix** *im-,* SE, p. 1110; *UR8,* p. 13
"The Bracelet" (A), Colette, SE, p. 1118	**Drawing Conclusions,** SE, p. 1117; *UR8,* p. 29; **Reading Warm-ups A and B,** *UR8,* pp. 26-27; **Reading Strategy Graphic Organizers A and B,** *GOT,* pp. 186-187	**Epiphany,** SE, p. 1117; *UR8,* p. 28; **Literary Analysis Graphic Organizers A and B,** *GOT,* pp. 184-185	**Vocabulary Builder,** SE, p. 1117: *supple, connoisseur, convalescent, enraptured, iridescent, serpentine, congealed* **Latin prefix** *en-,* SE, p. 1124; *UR8,* p. 30
"War" (A), Luigi Pirandello, SE, p. 1128	**Comparing and Contrasting Characters,** SE, p. 1127; *UR8,* p. 46; **Reading Warm-ups A and B,** *UR8,* pp. 43-44; **Reading Strategy Graphic Organizers A and B,** *GOT,* pp. 188-189	**Setting,** SE, p. 1127; *UR8,* p. 45; **Literary Analysis Graphic Organizers A and B,** *GOT,* pp. 190-191	**Vocabulary Builder,** SE, p. 1127: *plight, paternal, discrimination, vitality, retorted, stoically, incongruous, harrowing* **Latin root** *-patr-,* SE, p. 1134; *UR8,* p. 47
"The Guitar" (MC), Federico García Lorca, SE, p. 1146; **"Ithaka"** (A), Constantine Cavafy, SE, p. 1148; **"Fear"** (MA), Gabriela Mistral, SE, p. 1150; **"The Prayer"** (A), Gabriela Mistral, SE, p. 1151; **"Green"** (A), Juan Ramón Jiménez, SE, p. 1154	**Reading Stanzas as Units of Meaning,** SE, p. 1145; *UR8,* p. 65; **Reading Warm-ups A and B,** *UR8,* pp. 62-63; **Reading Strategy Graphic Organizers A and B,** *GOT,* pp. 192-193	**Lyric Poetry and Epiphany,** SE, p. 1145; *UR8,* p. 64; **Literary Analysis Graphic Organizers A and B,** *GOT,* pp. 194-195	**Vocabulary Builder,** SE, p. 1145: *monotonously, exalted, sensual, invokes, anoint, sheaves* **Greek prefix** *mono-,* SE, p. 1156; *UR8,* p. 66

Key to Program References:
SE: Student Edition **UR:** Unit Resources **GOT:** Graphic Organizer Transparencies **GR:** General Resources **WG:** Writing and Grammar
MA: More accessible **A:** Average **MC:** More Challenging. See Accessibility at a Glance chart on selection pages.

Skills Navigator

Grammar	Writing	Extend Your Learning	Assessment
Commas After Introductory Words, SE, p. 999; *UR7*, p. 106; *WG*, Ch. 28, Section 2	**Writing:** Letter, SE, p. 999	**Listening and Speaking:** Radio Play, SE, p. 999; *UR7*, p. 107	**Selection Tests A and B,** *UR7*, pp. 109-114; **Rubric for Speaking: Narrative Account,** *GR*, p. 88
Infinitives and Infinitive Phrases, SE, p. 1024; *UR7*, p. 122; *WG*, Ch. 20, Section 1	**Writing Lesson:** Writing a Persuasive Essay, SE, p. 1025; *UR7*, p. 123; *WG*, Ch. 7, Section 4	**Listening and Speaking:** Round-table Discussion, SE, p. 1025 **Research and Technology:** Costume Design Display, SE, p. 1025; *UR7*, p. 124	**Selection Tests A and B,** *UR7*, pp. 126-131; **Rubrics for Persuasion: Persuasive Essay,** *GR*, pp. 47-48; **Rubric for Listening: Evaluating a Persuasive Presentation,** *GR*, p. 83; **Benchmark Test 9,** *UR7*, pp. 80-82

Grammar	Writing	Extend Your Learning	Assessment
Adverb Clauses, SE, p. 1110; *UR8*, p. 14; *WG*, Ch. 20, Section 2	**Writing Lesson:** Essay Responding to a Critical Perspective, SE, p. 1111; *UR8*, p. 15; *WG*, Ch. 13, Section 3	**Listening and Speaking:** Eulogy, SE, p. 1111 **Research and Technology:** Multimedia Classroom Presentation, SE, p. 1111; *UR8*, p. 16	**Diagnostic Test 10,** *UR8*, pp. 2-4; **Selection Tests A and B,** *UR8*, pp. 18-23; **Rubrics for Response to Literature,** *GR*, pp. 55-56
Commonly Confused Words: *sit* and *set*, SE, p. 1124; *UR8*, p. 31; *WG*, Ch. 22, Section 1	**Writing Lesson:** Analytical Essay, SE, p. 1125; *UR8*, p. 32; *WG*, Ch. 13, Section 2	**Listening and Speaking:** Monologue, SE, p. 1125 **Research and Technology:** Set and Costume Design, SE, p. 1125; *UR8*, p. 33	**Selection Tests A and B,** *UR8*, pp. 35-40; **Rubrics for Response to Literature,** *GR*, pp. 55-56
Adjective Clauses, SE, p. 1134; *UR8*, p. 48; *WG*, Ch. 20, Section 2	**Writing Lesson:** Newspaper Article, SE, p. 1135; *UR8*, p. 49; *WG*, Ch. 2, Section 2	**Listening and Speaking:** Dramatic Reading, SE, p. 1135 **Research and Technology:** Multimedia Report, SE, p. 1135; *UR8*, p. 50	**Selection Tests A and B,** *UR8*, pp. 52-57;
The Understood *You* in Imperative Sentences, SE, p. 1156; *UR8*, p. 67; *WG*, Ch. 19, Section 2	**Writing Lesson:** Interpretive Essay, SE, p. 1157; *UR8*, p. 68; *WG*, Ch. 13, Section 4	**Listening and Speaking:** Oral Interpretation, SE, p. 1157 **Research and Technology:** Color Chart, SE, p. 1157; *UR8*, p. 69	**Selection Tests A and B,** *UR8*, pp. 71-76; **Rubrics for Response to Literature,** *GR*, pp. 55-56

All selections are supported in the Reader's Notebooks.

UNIT 8 From Conflict and Renewal (1890-1945) *(continued)*

Selection	Reading Strategy	Literary Analysis	Vocabulary
Focus on Short Story **"The Artist"** (A), Rabindranath Tagore, SE, p. 1162	**Identifying Cause and Effect,** SE, p. 1161; *UR8,* p. 82; **Reading Warm-ups A and B,** *UR8,* pp. 79-80; **Reading Strategy Graphic Organizers A and B,** *GOT,* pp. 198-199	**Conflict,** SE, p. 1161; *UR8,* p. 81; **Literary Analysis Graphic Organizers A and B,** *GOT,* pp. 196-197	**Vocabulary Builder,** SE, p. 1161: *meager, terminology, frugality, connotations, equable, squandered, disdain, myriad, enumerating* **Greek word part** *-logy,* SE, p. 1170; *UR8,* p. 83

UNIT 9 Voices of Change (1946–Present)

Selection	Reading Strategy	Literary Analysis	Vocabulary
"The Handsomest Drowned Man in the World" (A), Gabriel García Márquez, SE, p. 1202	**Hypothesizing,** SE, p. 1201; *UR9,* p. 12; **Reading Warm-ups A and B,** *UR9,* pp. 9-10; **Reading Strategy Graphic Organizers A and B,** *GOT,* pp. 201-202	**Magical Realism,** SE, p. 1201; *UR9,* p. 11; **Literary Analysis Graphic Organizers A and B,** *GOT,* pp. 203-204	**Vocabulary Builder,** SE, p. 1201: *bountiful, labyrinths, haggard, resistant, destitute* **Latin prefix** *re-,* SE, p. 1212; *UR9,* p. 13
"A Walk to the Jetty" from *Annie John* (MA), Jamaica Kincaid, SE, p. 1220	**Understanding Spatial Relationships,** SE, p. 1219; *UR9,* p. 31; **Reading Warm-ups A and B,** *UR9,* pp. 28-29; **Reading Strategy Graphic Organizers A and B,** *GOT,* pp. 205-206	**Point of View,** SE, p. 1219; *UR9,* p. 30; **Literary Analysis Graphic Organizers A and B,** *GOT,* pp. 207-208	**Vocabulary Builder,** SE, p. 1219: *jetty, loomed, wharf, scorn, stupor, cue* **Latin root** *-stup-,* SE, p. 1228; *UR9,* p. 32
"The Guest" (MC), Albert Camus, SE, p. 1232	**Inferring Cultural Attitudes,** SE, p. 1231; *UR9,* p. 48; **Reading Warm-ups A and B,** *UR9,* pp. 45-46; **Reading Strategy Graphic Organizers A and B,** *GOT,* pp. 209-210	**Existentialism,** SE, p. 1231; *UR9,* p. 47; **Literary Analysis Graphic Organizers A and B,** *GOT,* pp. 211-212	**Vocabulary Builder,** SE, p. 1231: *plateau, siege, fore-taste, mobilized, denounce, fraternized, furtive* **Anglo-Saxon prefix** *fore-,* SE, p. 1248; *UR9,* p. 49
Focus on Nonfiction **from *Survival in Auschwitz*** (A), Primo Levi, SE, p. 1254; **from *Night*** (A), Elie Wiesel, SE, p. 1261; **"When in Early Summer"** (MC), Nelly Sachs, SE, p. 1270	**Connecting to Historical Context,** SE, p. 1253; *UR9,* p. 65; **Reading Warm-ups A and B,** *UR9,* pp. 62-63	**Autobiography,** SE, p. 1253; *UR9,* p. 64; **Literary Analysis Graphic Organizers A and B,** *GOT,* pp. 213-214, 215-216	**Vocabulary Builder,** SE, p. 1253: *sordid, prophetic, intuition, affinity, plaintive, beseeching, liquidated, deportees* **Latin root** *-port-,* SE, p. 1272; *UR9,* p. 66
"A Song on the End of the World" (A), Czesław Miłosz, SE, p. 1280; **"The End and the Beginning"** (A), Wisława Szymborska, SE, p. 1282	**Evaluating the Writer's Statement of Philosophy,** SE, p. 1279; *UR9,* p. 91; **Reading Warm-ups A and B,** *UR9,* pp. 88-89; **Reading Strategy Graphic Organizers A and B,** *GOT,* pp. 217-218	**Irony,** SE, p. 1279; *UR9,* p. 90; **Literary Analysis Graphic Organizers A and B,** *GOT,* pp. 219-220	**Vocabulary Builder,** SE, p. 1279: *glimmering, prophet, shards, glaze, gawking* **Related words:** *glaze and glimmering,* SE, p. 1286; *UR9,* p. 92

Key to Program References:
SE: Student Edition **UR:** Unit Resources **GOT:** Graphic Organizer Transparencies **GR:** General Resources **WG:** Writing and Grammar
MA: More accessible **A:** Average **MC:** More Challenging. See Accessibility at a Glance chart on selection pages.

Skills Navigator

Grammar	Writing	Extend Your Learning	Assessment
Appositives and Appositive Phrases, SE, p. 1170; *UR8*, p. 84; *WG*, Ch. 20, Section 1	**Writing Lesson:** Newspaper Editorial, SE, p. 1171; *UR8*, p. 85; *WG*, Ch. 7	**Listening and Speaking:** Themed Reading, SE, p. 1171 **Research and Technology:** Group Report, SE, p. 1171; *UR8*, p. 86	**Selection Tests A and B,** *UR8*, pp. 88-93; **Rubrics for Persuasion: Persuasive Essay,** *GR*, pp. 47-48; **Benchmark Test 10,** *UR8*, pp. 101-106

Grammar	Writing	Extend Your Learning	Assessment
Punctuating Dialogue, SE, p. 1212; *UR9*, p. 14; *WG*, Ch. 28, Section 4	**Writing Lesson:** Essay Tracing the Development of a Character, SE, p. 1213; *UR9*, p. 15; *WG*, Ch. 10, Section 4	**Listening and Speaking:** Interactive Story, SE, p. 1213 **Research and Technology:** Collage, SE, p. 1213; *UR9*, p. 16	**Diagnostic Test 11,** *UR9*, pp. 2-4; **Selection Tests A and B,** *UR9*, pp. 18-23; **Rubrics for Response to Literature,** *GR*, pp. 55-56; **Rubric for Speaking: Narrative Account,** *GR*, p. 88
Adjective Clauses, SE, p. 1228; *UR9*, p. 33; *WG*, Ch. 20, Section 2	**Writing Lesson:** A Reminiscence, SE, p. 1229; *UR9*, p. 34; *WG*, Ch. 4, Section 2	**Listening and Speaking:** Discussion, SE, p. 1229 **Research and Technology:** Map, SE, p. 1229; *UR9*, p. 35	**Selection Tests A and B,** *UR9*, pp. 37-42; **Rubrics for Narration: Autobiographical Narrative,** *GR*, pp. 43-44
Prepositional Phrases as Adjectives and Adverbs, SE, p. 1248; *UR9*, p. 50; *WG*, Ch. 20, Section 1	**Writing Lesson:** Essay Evaluating Fiction as an Expression of Philosophy, SE, p. 1249; *UR9*, p. 51; *WG*, Ch. 9, Section 2	**Listening and Speaking:** Play, SE, p. 1249 **Research and Technology:** Timeline, SE, p. 1249; *UR9*, p. 52	**Selection Tests A and B,** *UR9*, pp. 54-59; **Rubrics for Exposition: Comparison-and-Contrast Essay,** *GR*, pp. 53-54; **Rubric for Speaking: Narrative Account,** *GR*, p. 88
Absolute Phrases, SE, p. 1272; *UR9*, p. 67; *WG*, Ch. 20, Section 1	**Writing Lesson:** Persuasive Essay, SE, p. 1273; *UR9*, p. 68; *WG*, Ch. 7, Section 4	**Listening and Speaking:** Group Discussion, SE, p. 1273 **Research and Technology:** Multimedia Presentation, SE, p. 1273; *UR9*, p. 69	**Selection Tests A and B,** *UR9*, pp. 71-76; **Rubrics for Persuasion: Persuasive Essay,** *GR*, pp. 47-48; **Benchmark Test 11,** *UR9*, pp. 77-82
Indefinite and Demonstrative Pronouns, SE, p. 1286; *UR9*, p. 93; *WG*, Ch. 16, Section 2	**Writing Lesson:** Narrative About a Quiet Hero, SE, p. 1287; *UR9*, p. 94; *WG*, Ch. 6, Section 2	**Listening and Speaking:** Multimedia Reading, SE, p. 1287 **Research and Technology:** Map or Set of Maps, SE, p. 1287; *UR9*, p. 95	**Diagnostic Test 12,** *UR9*, pp. 83-85; **Selection Tests A and B,** *UR9*, pp. 97-102; **Rubrics for Narration: Short Story,** *GR*, pp. 63-64

All selections are supported in the Reader's Notebooks.

Voices of Change (1946–Present) *(continued)*

Selection	Reading Strategy	Literary Analysis	Vocabulary
"Freedom to Breathe" (A), Alexander Solzhenitsyn, SE, p. 1290; **from *Nobel Lecture*** (A), Alexander Solzhenitsyn, SE, p. 1291; **"Visit"** (MC), Yevgeny Yevtushenko, SE, p. 1295	**Inferring the Speaker's Attitude,** SE, p. 1289; *UR9,* p. 98; **Reading Warm-ups A and B,** *UR9,* pp. 105-106; **Reading Strategy Graphic Organizers A and B,** *GOT,* pp. 221-222	**Speaker,** SE, p. 1289; *UR9,* p. 107; **Literary Analysis Graphic Organizers A and B,** *GOT,* pp. 223-224	**Vocabulary Builder,** SE, p. 1289: *glistens, reciprocity, assimilate, inexorably, oratory, fungus, clenched* **Forms of *reciprocity,*** SE, p. 1298; *UR9,* p. 109
"Half a Day" (A), Naguib Mahfouz, SE, p. 1302	**Determining the Author's Purpose,** SE, p. 1301; *UR9,* p. 125; **Reading Warm-ups A and B,** *UR9,* pp. 122-123; **Reading Strategy Graphic Organizers A and B,** *GOT,* pp. 227-228	**Surrealism,** SE, p. 1301; *UR9,* p. 124; **Literary Analysis Graphic Organizers A and B,** *GOT,* pp. 225-226	**Vocabulary Builder,** SE, p. 1301: *unmarred, intimacy, intricate, presumed, throngs, hordes, hastened* **Connotations:** words for crowds, SE, p. 1308; *UR9,* p. 126
"Pride" (A), Dahlia Ravikovitch, SE, p. 1312; **"The Diameter of the Bomb"** (MC), Yehuda Amichai, SE, p. 1313; **"From the Book of Esther I Filtered the Sediment"** (A), Yehuda Amichai, SE, p. 1314	**Evaluating a Writer's Message,** SE, p. 1311; *UR9,* p. 142; **Reading Warm-ups A and B,** *UR9,* pp. 139-140; **Reading Strategy Graphic Organizers A and B,** *GOT,* pp. 229-230	**Imagery,** SE, p. 1311; *UR9,* p. 141; **Literary Analysis Graphic Organizers A and B,** *GOT,* pp. 231-232	**Vocabulary Builder,** SE, p. 1311: *flourishes, considerably, solitary, sediment, vulgar* **Latin word origins:** *vulgar,* SE, p. 1316; *UR9,* p. 143
"Comrades" (A), Nadine Gordimer, SE, p. 1324; **"Marriage Is a Private Affair"** (A), Chinua Achebe, SE, p. 1329	**Identifying With a Character,** SE, p. 1323; *UR9,* p. 159; **Reading Warm-ups A and B,** *UR9,* pp. 156-157; **Reading Strategy Graphic Organizers A and B,** *GOT,* pp. 233-234	**Atmosphere,** SE, p. 1323; *UR9,* p. 158; **Literary Analysis Graphic Organizers A and B,** *GOT,* pp. 235-236	**Vocabulary Builder,** SE, p. 1323: *assent, euphemisms, furtively, revelation, disposed, vehemently, deference, perfunctorily* **Greek prefix** *eu-,* SE, p. 1336; *UR9,* p. 160
"Thoughts of Hanoi" (A), Nguyen Thi Vinh, SE, p. 1342; **"All"** (MC), Bei Dao, SE, p. 1346; **"Also All"** (MA), Shu Ting, SE, p. 1347; **"Assembly Line"** (A), Shu Ting, SE, p. 1348	**Connecting to Historical Context,** SE, p. 1341; *UR9,* p. 176; **Reading Warm-ups A and B,** *UR9,* pp. 173-174; **Reading Strategy Graphic Organizers A and B,** *GOT,* pp. 237-238	**Political Poetry,** SE, p. 1341; *UR9,* p. 175; **Literary Analysis Graphic Organizers A and B,** *GOT,* pp. 239-240	**Vocabulary Builder,** SE, p. 1341: *jubilant, obsolete, lamentation, heralds, reverberates, chasm, monotony, tempo* **Latin root** *-temp-,* SE, p. 1350; *UR9,* p. 177

Key to Program References:
SE: Student Edition **UR:** Unit Resources **GOT:** Graphic Organizer Transparencies **GR:** General Resources **WG:** Writing and Grammar
MA: More accessible **A:** Average **MC:** More Challenging. See Accessibility at a Glance chart on selection pages.

Skills Navigator

Grammar	Writing	Extend Your Learning	Assessment
Using Dashes, SE, p. 1298; *UR9,* p. 110; *WG*, Ch. 28, Section 5	**Writing Lesson:** Persuasive Speech, SE, p. 1299; *UR9*, p. 111; *WG*, Ch. 7, Section 3	**Listening and Speaking:** Oral Description, SE, p. 1299 **Research and Technology:** Annotated List, SE, p. 1299; *UR9*, p. 103	**Selection Tests A and B,** *UR9,* pp. 114-119; **Rubrics for Persuasion: Persuasive Essay,** *GR*, pp. 47-48
Agreement in Inverted Sentences, SE, p. 1308; *UR9*, p. 127; *WG*, Ch. 24, Section 1	**Writing Lesson:** Surrealistic Descriptive Essay, SE, p. 1309; *UR9*, p. 128; *WG*, Ch. 6, Section 4	**Listening and Speaking:** Discussion Panel, SE, p. 1309 **Research and Technology:** Multimedia Presentation, SE, p. 1309; *UR9*, p. 120	**Selection Tests A and B,** *UR9,* pp. 131-136; **Rubrics for Descriptive Essay,** *GR*, pp. 67-68
Elliptical Clauses, SE, p. 1316; *UR9,* p. 144; *WG*, Ch. 22, Section 2	**Writing Lesson:** Poem With a Strong Central Image, SE, p. 1317; *UR9*, p. 145; *WG*, Ch. 6, Section 4	**Listening and Speaking:** Oral Interpretation, SE, p. 1317 **Research and Technology:** Multimedia Presentation, SE, p. 1317; *UR9*, p. 146	**Selection Tests A and B,** *UR9,* pp. 148-153
Noun Clauses, SE, p. 1336; *UR9*, p. 152; *WG*, Ch. 20, Section 2	**Writing Lesson:** Manual on How to Change a Story's Atmosphere, SE, p. 1337; *UR9*, p. 162; *WG*, Ch. 6, Section 4	**Listening and Speaking:** Dramatization, SE, p. 1337 **Research and Technology:** Presentation, SE, p. 1337; *UR9*, p. 163	**Selection Tests A and B,** *UR9,* pp. 165-170
Parallelism, SE, p. 1350; *UR9,* p. 178; *WG*, Ch. 21, Section 4	**Writing Lesson:** Literary Analysis, SE, p. 1351; *UR9*, p. 179; *WG*, Ch. 21, Section 3	**Listening and Speaking:** Dialogue, SE, p. 1351 **Research and Technology:** Multimedia Report, SE, p. 1351; *UR9*, p. 180	**Selection Tests A and B,** *UR9,* pp. 182-187; **Rubrics for Response to Literature,** *GR*, pp. 55-56; **Benchmark Test 12,** *UR9*, pp. 195-200

All selections are supported in the Reader's Notebooks.

Standards-at-a-Glance

This chart provides an overview of where you'll find the North Carolina Standard course of Study addressed in ***Prentice Hall Literature, Penguin Edition.*** For more detailed information regarding skills coverage, see the **Skills Navigator**, found on page NC T86, which provides an overview of Student Edition content and related skills. The **Time and Resource Manager** will show the standards breakdown for each selection grouping.

North Carolina Standard Course of Study

UNIT	1	2	3	4	5	6	7	8	9
Competency Goal 1: The learner will react to and reflect upon print and non-print text and personal experiences by examining situations from both subjective and objective perspectives.									
WL.1.01.1 Produce reminiscences that use specific and sensory details with purpose.	•	•							•
WL.1.01.2 Explain the significance of a reminiscence.	•				•				
WL.1.01.3 Move effectively between past and present in a reminiscence.	•	•							
WL.1.01.4 Produce reminiscences that recreate the mood felt during the experience.	•						•	•	
WL.1.02.1 Relate personal knowledge to textual information in a written reflection.	•		•	•		•			
WL.1.02.2 Show awareness of culture in personal reflections.		•		•		•	•	•	•
WL.1.02.3 Exhibit an awareness of cultural context.	•				•		•	•	•
WL.1.02.4 Explain how culture affects personal responses.		•		•	•				•
WL.1.02.5 Demonstrate an understanding of media's impact on analyses and personal reflection.		•			•	•		•	•
WL.1.03.1 Select, monitor, and modify reading strategies appropriate to personal reflection.	•							•	
WL.1.03.2 Identify and analyze text components and evaluate impact on personal reflection.	•	•				•	•		
WL.1.03.3 Provide textual evidence to support understanding and response to personal reflection.	•						•		
WL.1.03.4 Demonstrate comprehension of main idea and supporting details in personal reflection.				•	•	•			
WL.1.03.5 Summarize key events and points from personal reflection.		•				•			•
WL.1.03.6 Make inferences and draw conclusions based on personal reflection.			•	•		•	•		
WL.1.03.7 Analyze influences, contexts, or biases in expressive texts.	•		•	•			•	•	•

• *Supports standard mastery*

North Carolina Standard Course of Study

UNIT	1	2	3	4	5	6	7	8	9
WL.1.03.8 Make connections between works, self and related topics in response and reflection.				●	●		●	●	
WL.1.03.9 Analyze effects of author's craft and style in reflection.			●		●			●	●
WL.1.03.10 Analyze connections between ideas, concepts, characters and experiences in reflection.			●	●	●				
WL.1.03.11 Identify and analyze elements of expressive environment in personal reflections.						●	●		
Competency Goal 2: The learner will evaluate problems, examine cause/effect relationships, and answer research questions to inform an audience.									
IR.2.01.1 Select, monitor, and modify reading strategies appropriate to research.			●						●
IR.2.01.2 Analyze text components and evaluate their impact on research questions.							●		
IR.2.01.3 Provide evidence to support understanding of and response to research text.				●					
IR.2.01.4 Demonstrate comprehension of main idea and supporting details in answering research questions.	●			●	●				●
IR.2.01.5 Summarize key events and/or points from research text.	●				●			●	
IR.2.01.6 Make inferences, predict and draw conclusions based on research questions.			●	●				●	
IR.2.01.7 Analyze influences, contexts, or biases in research texts.		●							
IR.2.01.8 Make connections between works, self and related topics in research texts.		●		●		●			
IR.2.01.9 Analyze and evaluate author's craft and style in research texts.			●						
IR.2.01.10 Analyze the connections between ideas, concepts, characters and experiences in research.			●			●			
IR.2.01.11 Identify and analyze information in light of purpose, audience, and context.	●			●				●	●
IR.2.02.1 Summarize situations to examine cause/effect relationships.		●	●			●	●	●	
IR.2.02.2 Show clear, logical connection among cause/effect events.		●	●	●				●	
IR.2.02.3 Use transitions to make logical connections.	●	●		●			●	●	
IR.2.02.4 Develop appropriate strategies to illustrate points about cause/effect relationships.		●				●		●	●

North Carolina Standard Course of Study

UNIT	1	2	3	4	5	6	7	8	9
IR.2.03.1 Access cultural information from media sources.		●	●	●	●			●	●
IR.2.03.2 Prioritize and organize information to construct an explanation to answer a question.		●	●				●		
Competency Goal 3: The learner will defend argumentative positions on literary or nonliterary issues.									
FA.3.01.1 Share and evaluate initial personal response to a controversial issue.			●				●		●
FA.3.01.2 Research and summarize printed data about a controversial issue.	●				●	●			●
FA.3.01.3 Develop a framework in which to discuss controversial issues.	●			●					
FA.3.01.4 Compile response and research data to organize argument about controversial issues.	●		●	●	●		●		
FA.3.01.5 Present data about controversial issues in multiple forms.	●		●					●	●
FA.3.02.1 State position or proposed solution in an editorial or response.	●		●	●					
FA.3.02.2 Provide relevant, reliable support in editorials.			●	●		●			
FA.3.03.1 Gather information to prove a point about issues in literature.		●		●		●			●
FA.3.03.2 Use reason and evidence to prove a given point.						●	●		●
FA.3.03.3 Produce responses to literature that emphasize culturally significant events.				●		●			●
FA.3.04.1 Select, monitor, and modify reading strategies appropriate to argument.						●			
FA.3.04.2 Analyze text components and evaluate their impact on argumentative texts.	●						●		
FA.3.04.3 Provide textual evidence to support understanding of and response to argumentative text.			●						●
FA.3.04.4 Demonstrate comprehension of main idea and supporting details in argument.					●			●	●
FA.3.04.5 Summarize key events and/or points from argumentative text.						●			●
FA.3.04.6 Make inferences and draw conclusions based on argumentative text.					●		●		●
FA.3.04.7 Identify and analyze influences, contexts, or biases in argument.	●		●	●		●			
FA.3.04.8 Make connections between works, self and related topics in argument.	●		●	●				●	

North Carolina Standard Course of Study

UNIT	1	2	3	4	5	6	7	8	9
FA.3.04.9 Analyze and evaluate the effects of author's craft and style in argument.						●			●
FA.3.04.10 Analyze connections between ideas, concepts, characters and experiences in argumentative work.						●			●
FA.3.04.11 Analyze elements of argumentative environment.			●				●		
Competency Goal 4: The learner will critically interpret and evaluate experiences, literature, language, and ideas.									
CT.4.01.1 Interpret and make generalizations about events supported by specific references.	●			●					
CT.4.01.2 Reflect on and show how a real-world event affects viewpoint.									●
CT.4.01.3 Distinguish fact from fiction and recognize personal bias in interpretation.						●		●	
CT.4.02.1 Show an understanding of cultural context in analyzing thematic connections.	●			●		●			●
CT.4.02.2 Use specific references from texts to show theme.				●		●	●		
CT.4.02.3 Examine how elements such as irony and symbolism impact theme.	●		●	●	●				●
CT.4.03.1 Analyze how writers introduce and develop a main idea.						●	●		
CT.4.03.2 Analyze how writers choose and incorporate significant, supporting details.		●			●			●	
CT.4.03.3 Analyze how writers relate the organization to the ideas.					●			●	●
CT.4.03.4 Analyze how writers use effective word choice as a basis for coherence.				●					
CT.4.03.5 Analyze how writers achieve a sense of completeness and closure.		●		●		●			
CT.4.04.1 Identify clear criteria for evaluation of work of others.	●					●	●		●
CT.4.04.2 Apply criteria to evaluate others using reasoning and substantiation.		●			●				
CT.4.05.1 Select, monitor, and modify reading strategies appropriate to critical interpretation.	●				●				●
CT.4.05.2 Analyze text components and evaluate impact on critical interpretation.						●		●	●
CT.4.05.3 Provide evidence to support understanding of and response to critical interpretation.	●					●	●		●
CT.4.05.4 Comprehend main idea and supporting details in critical text.		●		●		●			

North Carolina Standard Course of Study

UNIT	1	2	3	4	5	6	7	8	9
CT.4.05.5 Summarize key events and points from critical text.	•			•					
CT.4.05.6 Make inferences and draw conclusions based on critical text.			•				•	•	
CT.4.05.7 Identify and analyze influences, contexts, or biases in critical text.	•				•			•	•
CT.4.05.8 Make connections between works, self and related topics in critical texts.						•	•		
CT.4.05.9 Analyze and evaluate the effects of craft and style in critical text.		•							•
CT.4.05.10 Analyze connections between ideas, concepts, characters and experiences in critical text.			•		•			•	
CT.4.05.11 Identify and analyze elements of critical environment.		•		•					•
Competency Goal 5: The learner will demonstrate understanding of selected world literature through interpretation and analysis.									
LT.5.01.1 Use strategies for preparation, engagement, and reflection on world literature.	•	•			•	•		•	
LT.5.01.2 Build knowledge of literary genres, and explore how characteristics apply to literature of world cultures.	•	•	•	•	•		•	•	
LT.5.01.3 Analyze literary devices and explain their effect on the work.	•	•	•	•	•	•	•		•
LT.5.01.4 Analyze the importance of tone and mood in world literature.			•				•		•
LT.5.01.5 Analyze archetypal characters, themes, and settings in world literature.	•	•	•		•			•	•
LT.5.01.6 Make connections between historical and contemporary issues in world literature.	•				•	•	•	•	
LT.5.01.7 Understand the cultural and historical impact on world literature texts.	•	•			•		•	•	•
LT.5.02.1 Explore a range of works which relate to an issue, author, or theme.	•	•	•	•		•	•	•	
LT.5.02.2 Document the reading of student-chosen works.	•						•		
LT.5.03.1 Select, monitor, and modify reading strategies appropriate to reader's purpose.	•	•	•			•	•		•
LT.5.03.2 Analyze text structure and components and evaluate impact.	•			•			•		•
LT.5.03.3 Provide textual evidence to support understanding of and response to world literature.			•				•		
LT.5.03.4 Demonstrate comprehension of main idea and supporting details.	•	•	•	•	•	•	•	•	•
LT.5.03.5 Summarize key events and points from the text.	•	•	•	•			•		

NORTH CAROLINA

North Carolina Standard Course of Study

UNIT	1	2	3	4	5	6	7	8	9
LT.5.03.6 Make inferences, predict, and draw conclusions based on world literature.		•	•	•		•	•	•	•
LT.5.03.7 Analyze influences, contexts, or biases in world literature.				•			•		•
LT.5.03.8 Make connections between works, self and related topics in world literature.	•				•	•			•
LT.5.03.9 Analyze and evaluate the effects of author's craft and style in world literature.	•			•				•	•
LT.5.03.10 Analyze connections between ideas, concepts, characters and experiences in world literature.			•	•	•		•		
LT.5.03.11 Analyze elements of literary environment in world literature.				•			•	•	•
Competency Goal 6: The learner will apply conventions of grammar and language usage.									
GU.6.01.1 Employ varying sentence structures and sentence types.	•					•			
GU.6.01.2 Analyze author's use of language to demonstrate understanding.	•		•	•			•	•	
GU.6.01.3 Use recognition strategies to understand vocabulary and exact word choice.				•				•	•
GU.6.01.4 Use vocabulary strategies to determine meaning.			•	•					•
GU.6.01.5 Examine language for elements to apply effectively in own writing/speaking.				•	•		•		•
GU.6.01.6 Use correct format for writing.				•		•			•
GU.6.01.7 Use language effectively to create mood and tone.	•	•			•				
GU.6.02.1 Edit for agreement, tense choice, pronouns, antecedents, case, and complete sentences.	•								
GU.6.02.2 Edit for appropriate and correct mechanics.	•				•				
GU.6.02.3 Edit for parallel structure.	•	•		•		•		•	
GU.6.02.4 Edit for clichés/trite expressions.	•		•				•	•	•
GU.6.02.5 Edit for spelling.		•		•	•			•	•

Instant intervention, tailored for each student!

Catch small problems *before* they become big ones.

How it works:
Success Tracker diagnoses student readiness to learn new skills and benchmarks their progress towards standards mastery.

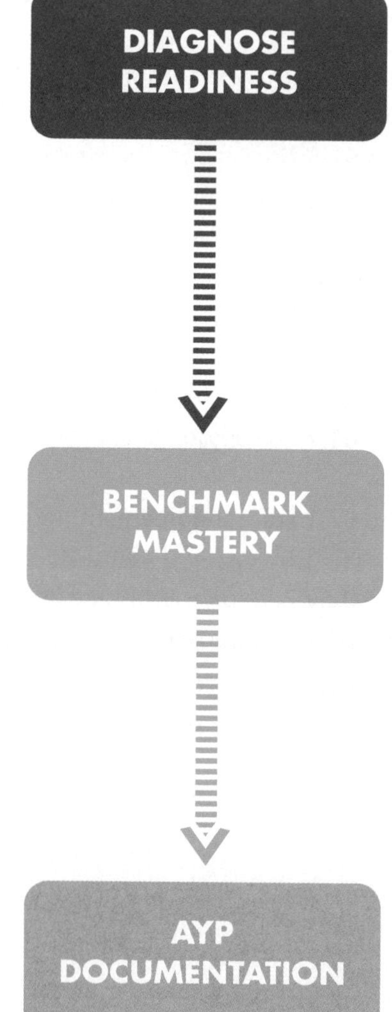

1 AT THE BEGINNING OF EACH UNIT OR PART:

- Students take Diagnostic Tests online.
- Tests measure skills necessary to successfully complete the unit.
- Tests are scored instantly and results trigger one of three levels:

High Score	=	No remediation required
Medium Score	=	Level B remediation
Low Score	=	Level A remediation

- Success Tracker provides a list of recommended remediation assignments to students automatically.

2 AT THE END OF EACH UNIT OR PART:

- Students take Benchmark Tests online.
- Tests measure mastery of skills covered in the unit.
- Tests are scored instantly, and a list of "mastered" and "unmastered" skills are reported to the teacher.
- Remediation activities are automatically assigned, based on "unmastered" skills.
- Benchmark retests can be assigned online to students by the teacher, if needed.

3 AS YOU DOCUMENT ADEQUATE YEARLY PROGRESS (AYP):

Success Tracker's easy-to-use reporting system lets you see at a glance where students may be having trouble mastering standards. These reports give you the kind of data you need to make decisions that will positively affect student performance on high-stakes tests.

Welcome to your new classroom!

PRENTICE HALL LITERATURE

WORLD MASTERPIECES

Batik Sarong, Javanese c. 1920, on glazed cotton: This image is a detail from a sarong, a traditional type of clothing consisting of a long strip of cloth worn like a skirt. This particular sarong hails from Java, an island in the Indonesian archipelago. The fabric features a design called *batik*, meaning "to dot" in Javanese. The herons featured in the design of this sarong have many symbolic meanings throughout Asia.

PENGUIN  EDITION

Upper Saddle River, New Jersey

Boston, Massachusetts

ISBN 0-13-131737-7

2 3 4 5 6 7 8 9 10 09 08 07 06

Cover: A detail of the design on a batik sarong which incorporates herons and other birds, flowers and water plants. c. 1920. Javanese. Glazed cotton, Werner Forman/Art Resource, NY

ACKNOWLEDGMENTS

Grateful acknowledgement is made to the following for copyrighted material:

The Asia Society and Dr. Nguyen Ngoc Bich "Thoughts of Hanoi," by Nguyen Thi Vinh from *A Thousand Years of Vietnamese Poetry*, edited by Nguyen Ngoc Bich. Copyright © 1962, 1967, 1968, 1969, 1970, 1971, 1974 by The Asia Society, Inc. and Nguyen Ngoc Bich. Reprinted by permission.

Georges Borchardt, Inc. "The Metamorphosis," by Franz Kafka, editor and translated by Stanley Corngold. Copyright © 1972 by Stanley Corngold.

Geoffrey Bownas and Anthony Thwaite "Tanka: "Was it that I went to sleep…," 5 lines by Ono Komachi, "Tanka: "When I went to visit…,"" 5 lines by Ki Tsurayuki, "Tanka: "One cannot ask loneliness…,"" 4 lines by Priest Jakuren, "Haiku: "The cuckoo…, "Seven sights were veiled…," and "Summer grasses…,"" 9 lines by Matsuo Basho, "Haiku: "A World of Dew…" "Far-off mountain peaks…," "With Bland Serenity…,"" and "Beautiful, seen through holes…,"" 12 lines by Yosa Buson, "Haiku: "Spring Rain: Telling a tale as they go…," "Soaking on the roof…," "A man lives here…," and "In our sedan…,"" 12 lines by Yosa Buson, from *The Penguin Book of Japanese Verse* translated by Geoffrey Bownas and Anthony Thwaite (Penguin Books 1964, Revised edition 1998). Translation copyright © Geoffrey Bownas and Anthony Thwaite, 1964, 1998. Reprinted by permission.

Toby Cole, Actors & Authors Agency "War" from *The Medals and Other Stories* by Luigi Pirandello. © E.P. Dutton, NY, 1932, 1967. Reprinted by permission of Toby Cole, Agent for the Pirandello Estate. All rights reserved. For performance rights in all media apply to Toby Cole, Agent for the Pirandello Estate, 295 Derby Street, #225, Berkeley, CA 94705.

Copper Canyon Press c/o The Permissions Company T'ao Ch'ien, "Form, Shadow, Spirit," translated by David Hinton, from *Selected Poems of T'ao Ch'ien*. Copyright © 1993 by David Hinton. Reprinted with permission of Copper Canyon Press, P.O. Box 271, Port Townsend, WA 98368-0271, c/o The Permissions Company, High Bridge, New Jersey.

Joan Daves Agency/Writer's House, Inc. c/o The Permissions Company Gabriela Mistral, "Fear" translated by Doris Dana, from *Selected Poems of Gabriela Mistral: A Bilingual Translation* (Baltimore: The Johns Hopkins University Press, 1971). Copyright © 1961, 1964, 1970, 1971 by Doris Dana. Reprinted with the permission of Joan Daves Agency/Writer's House, Inc., New York, on behalf of the proprietors; c/o The Permissions Company, High Bridge, New Jersey.

Doubleday, a division of Random House, Inc. "Marriage is a Private Affair," from *Girls at War and Other Stories* by Chinua Achebe, copyright © 1972, 1973 by Chinua Achebe. "Half a Day," from *The Time and the Place and Other Stories* by Naguib Mahfouz, translated by Denys Johnson-Davies. Copyright © 1991 by the

(Continued on page R55, which is hereby considered an extension of this copyright page.)

PRENTICE HALL LITERATURE

PENGUIN  EDITION

WORLD MASTERPIECES

VOLUME I

Standard Course of Study

WL.1.03.1	Select, monitor, and modify reading strategies appropriate to personal reflection.
CT.4.01.1	Interpret and make generalizations supported by specific references.
CT.4.02.1	Show an understanding of cultural context in analyzing thematic connections.
LT.5.01.5	Analyze archetypal characters, themes, and settings in world literature.
LT.5.03.4	Demonstrate comprehension of main idea and supporting details in world literature.
GU.6.01.2	Analyze author's use of language to demonstrate understanding of expression.

Unit Instructional Resources

In *Unit 1 Resources,* you will find materials to support students in developing and mastering the unit skills and to help you assess their progress.

Vocabulary and Reading

Additional vocabulary and reading support, based on Lexile scores of vocabulary words, is provided for each selection or grouping.

- **Word Lists A and B** and **Practices A and B** provide vocabulary-building activities for students reading two grades or one grade below level, respectively.
- **Reading Warm-ups A and B,** for students reading two grades or one grade below level, respectively, consist of short readings and activities that provide a context and practice for newly learned vocabulary.

Selection Support

- Reading Strategy
- Literary Analysis
- Vocabulary Builder
- Grammar and Style
- Support for Writing
- Support for Extend Your Learning
- Enrichment

PRENTICE HALL TeacherEXPRESS™ Plan · Teach · Assess You may also access these resources at TeacherExpress.

Unit 1 Origins and Traditions

c. 3000 B.C.–A.D. 1400

Assessment Resources

Listed below are the resources available to assess and measure students' progress in meeting the unit objectives and your state standards.

Skills Assessment

Unit 1 Resources
Selection Tests A and B

TeacherExpress™
ExamView® Test Bank Software

Adequate Yearly Progress Assessment

Unit 1 Resources
Diagnostic Test 1
Benchmark Test 1

Standardized Assessment

Standardized Test Preparation Workbook

Walking Lion in Relief **(detail)**, 605–562 B.C., Babylonian mosaic, Mesopotamia

Ancient Worlds

Standard Course of Study
In This Unit You Will

- Produce reminiscences that recreate the mood felt during the experience. (WL.1.01.4)
- Identify and analyze information in light of purpose, audience, and context. (IR.2.01.11)
- Interpret and make generalizations supported by specific references. (CT.4.01.1)
- Analyze literary devices and explain their effect on the work. (LT.5.01.3)
- Analyze archetypal characters, themes, and settings in world literature. (LT.5.01.5)
- Understand the cultural and historical impact on text. (LT.5.01.7)
- Analyze text structure and components and evaluate impact. (LT.5.03.2)
- Edit for parallel structure. (GU.6.02.3)

◀ In ancient Babylon, the lion—shown in this mosaic—symbolized the goddess Ishtar, who was associated with love, fertility, and war.

Introduce Unit 1

- Direct students' attention to the title and time period of this unit. Have a student read the quotation. **Ask** them: What does the quotation suggest about the values of Hammurabi?
  Possible response: The quotation suggests that he valued righteousness, and during his rule, he would have protected vulnerable people by destroying those who would have tried to take advantage of or harm them.
- Have students look at the art. Read the Humanities note to them, and ask the discussion questions.
- Then **ask:** What kinds of literature or themes in literature do you think might come out of this period in literary history?
  Possible response: The quotation mentions God and violence, and the art is of a fierce-looking lion that represented a Babylonian god, so the literature might be about ancient people's religious beliefs or practices, war, and the uses of power.

Humanities

Walking Lion in Relief **(detail)**

The Babylonians carried images of gods along the main street of Babylon during their New Year Festival. This processional road was decorated with more than 100 lions in relief. The lion symbolized the goddess Ishtar, who was associated with love, fertility, and war.

Use these questions for discussion:

- How do you think the Babylonians felt as they marched in processions?
  Possible response: They might have felt pride in their culture.
- What are some animals that have symbolic value for Americans? What do they represent?
  Possible response: The eagle represents power and war. The turtle represents determination.

Unit Features

Coleman Barks
Each unit features commentary by a contemporary writer or scholar under the heading "From the Author's Desk." Translator Coleman Barks introduces Unit 1 in Setting the Scene, in which he discusses Persian mystical poetry and the contributions of the mystical poet, Rumi. Later in the unit, he introduces selections of Rumi's poetry. He also contributes his insights on word choice in the Writing Workshop.

Connections
Every unit contains a feature that connects literature to a related topic, such as art, science, or history. In this unit, students will read ***from*** **Popol Vuh: The Wooden People** on p. 55.

Use the information and questions on the Connections pages to help students enrich their understanding of the selections presented within the unit.

Reading Informational Materials
These selections will help students learn to analyze and evaluate informational texts, such as workplace documents, technical directions, and consumer materials. They will expose students to the organization and features unique to nonnarrative texts.

In this unit, the focus is on Brochures. The brochure for the exhibition **The Quest for Immortality: Treasures of Ancient Egypt** is on p. 145.

 **From the Translator's Desk**

Introduce Coleman Barks

- Coleman Barks, a poet and translator, introduces the unit and provides insight into the poetry of the Persian-speaking Islamic culture of the Middle East. His introduction to the poetry of Rumi appears later in this unit on pages 114–115.
- Have students read the introductory paragraph about Coleman Barks. Tell them that he is most famous for his translations of the poetry of Rumi, a Persian poet. Barks said that each afternoon he would translate poems over a pot of hot tea.
- Use the ***From the Author's Desk DVD*** to introduce Coleman Barks. Show Segment 1 to provide insight into his writing career. After students have watched the segment, **ask:** What does Barks believe that young students can learn from poetry?
  Answer: Poetry makes us "see" from the perspective of our soul and helps us to live in a "deeper place."

Mystical Poetry in the Persian Tradition

- After students have read Barks's commentary on mystical poetry in the Persian tradition, **ask:** Explain in your own words Barks's explanation of the meaning of the term *mystic.*
  Possible response: Barks says that although *mystic* is not a precise term, it refers to experiencing a sense of joyful union with all things.
- **Ask:** Why might poetry be an effective means to express mystical experience?
  Possible response: The metaphors, rhyme, and figurative language of poetry help to express the powerful experiences and insights of the mystic which otherwise are difficult—or even impossible—to express adequately.
- Tell students that they will also read Coleman Barks's introduction to a selection of Rumi's poetry later in this unit. Barks will explain how he translated the poetry of Rumi as well as how he became a translator.

Critical Viewing

Possible response: The dancing dervishes are one part of the overall action of the community. Rumi believed that everything a community did—from dancing to cooking meals—was meant to "open the heart."

Setting the Scene

Unit 1 features writing from many different ancient cultures in the Middle East and Africa. The following essay by Coleman Barks introduces you to an important poet and the literary tradition from one of those civilizations: the Persian-speaking Islamic culture of the Middle East. As your read his essay, the unit introduction that follows, and the literature in Unit 1, immerse yourself in the diversity of writing and ideas that these ancient cultures produced.

From the Translator's Desk

Coleman Barks Talks About the Time Period

Coleman Barks

Introducing Coleman Barks (b. 1937) Born in Chattanooga, Tennessee, Barks is a poet and translator who has earned great praise and a vast readership for his translations of the thirteenth-century Persian poet Rumi. Barks taught poetry and creative writing at the University of Georgia for thirty years.

Mystical Poetry in the Persian Tradition

From the twelfth to the fourteenth century, the Persian-speaking culture in the Middle East produced several world-class poets: Attar, Sanai, Hafiz, and Rumi. They were all mystics as well as poets. *Mystic* is an imprecise term, meaning different things to different people. I use it to mean someone who has a way of seeing, a way of being, within which he or she *experiences* the interconnectedness of all beings—and a joy and a longing inherent in that experience.

Persian mystics explored many metaphors for their core experience: a moth dying in the flame, a drop of rain falling into the sea, the sense of individual boundaries dissolving into something larger. Mystical experience is real, even if difficult to define. But the depth of our love for a person is also difficult—some would say impossible—to express, and surely that is the most real thing in our lives.

Molecules and Galaxies The poet Rumi, one of the writers in this unit, spoke his poems spontaneously as part of his work within a spiritual community known as the "Whirling Dervishes." A *dervish* is a "holy one," and the whirling dervishes practiced a type of twirling, hypnotic dance as a path to enlightenment. Rumi was the original whirling dervish. One day he heard music coming from a shop where craftsmen were pounding gold bars into gold leaf. He heard inside the hammering such beauty

▼ **Critical Viewing** This Persian miniature shows whirling dervishes dancing during the preparation of a meal. How does this painting reflect Rumi's belief that work within a community is an essential part of the spiritual process? **[Connect]**

Teaching Resources

The following resources can be used to enrich or extend the instruction for Unit 1 Introduction.

From the Author's Desk DVD
Coleman Barks, Segment 1

Unit 1 Resources
Names and Terms to Know, p. 5
Focus Questions, p. 6
Listening and Viewing, p. 119

that he began turning. He would say later that he was turning with the molecules and the galaxies.

In contemporary America, Grateful Dead concerts used to begin with spontaneous turners in the audience. We've seen children, and we've *been* them, turning to make the whole horizon turn until they fall. The dervish dance, like the children's spin, is abandon and discipline at once.

Rumi's Community Rumi's "work" within the dervish community was the attempt to open the heart. Members of this community studied texts. They tended gardens and orchards. They sat in silence, and they sat in a conversational practice sort of like the Quaker circles, where everyone is encouraged to speak openly. They played music and told stories. They listened to poetry and watched animals, whose behavior was a kind of scripture that they read for signs. Rumi's community was not a monastery. Its members had families, and each knew a craft, whose performance in the community was an essential part of the spiritual process.

Opening the Heart Rumi and his dervish community were Sufis, members of a mystical sect of Islam known as Sufism. Yet I prefer not to use the term *Sufism* at all, because it leads us into *-isms,* those systems of beliefs that are the source of religious bickering and wars. Instead, let's call the Sufis *people of the heart*.

Rumi, like other mystical writers, knew that the most important thing happens *inwardly,* and that it does not matter what we call it: opening the heart, being born again, finding the kingdom within. That inner opening is the same, and it can only be *lived,* not explained. But it can also be *approached* with words, and that is why I love the mystical poets.

Go Online — Author Link

For: An online video
Visit: www.PHSchool.com
Web Code: ete-8101

For: More about Coleman Barks
Visit: www.PHSchool.com
Web Code: ete-9101

Reading the Unit Introduction

Reading for Information and Insight Use the following terms and questions to guide your reading of the unit introduction on pages 6–13.

Names and Terms to Know
Mesopotamia
Sumerians
Hammurabi
Nile
Pyramid
Hebrews
Islam
Griot

Focus Questions As you read this introduction, use what you learn to answer these questions:

- Why do you think that the legal code of Hammurabi played such an important role in the development of civilization?
- List two or more reasons for the importance of the Nile in the development of Egyptian civilization.
- What was the role of the griot in the literature of Africa?

Reading the Unit Introduction

Tell students that the terms and questions listed here are the key points in this introductory material. This information provides a context for the selections in this unit. Students should use the terms and questions as a guide to focus their reading of the unit introduction. When students have completed the unit introduction, they should be able to identify or explain each of these terms and answer or discuss the Focus Questions.

Concept Connector

After students have read the unit introduction, return to the Focus Questions to review the main points. For key points, see p. 13.

Go Online — Author Link Typing in the Web Code when prompted will bring students to a video clip and more information on Coleman Barks.

Using the Timeline

The Timeline can serve a number of instructional purposes, as follows:

Getting an Overview

Use the Timeline to help students get a quick overview of themes and events of the period. This approach will benefit all students but may be especially helpful for Visual/Spatial Learners, English Learners, and Less Proficient Readers. (For strategies in using the Timeline as an overview, see the bottom of this page.)

Thinking Critically

Questions are provided on the facing page. Use these questions to have students review the events, discuss their significance, and examine the "so what" behind the "what happened".

Connecting to Selections

Have students refer to the Timeline when they begin to read individual selections. By consulting the Timeline regularly, students will gain a better sense of the period's chronology. In addition, they will appreciate world events that gave rise to these works of literature.

Projects

Students can use the Timeline as a launching pad for projects like these:

- **Finding Significance** Ask students to choose one of the events on the Timeline and list two or three reasons why it is important enough to be included in the timeline. Have students do additional research to find reasons to support or alter their conclusions.
- **News Presentation** Have students select one of the events on the Timeline and do additional research to learn more about it. Then, have them prepare and present to the class a brief television news presentation about the event.

Ancient World Events

3000 B.C. | 2000 B.C. | 1000 B.C.

CULTURAL AND HISTORICAL EVENTS

- c. 3000 **(Sumeria)** Sumerian civilization begins.
- c. 2900 **(Egypt)** The ruler Menes joins Upper Egypt and Lower Egypt.
- c. 2925–c. 2575 **(Egypt)** This is the Early Dynastic Period.
- c. 2575–c. 2130 **(Egypt)** This is the era called the Old Kingdom.

- c. 2500 **(Egypt)** The pharaoh Khufu has the Great Pyramid built at Giza.
- c. 2334–2279 **(ancient Middle East)** King Sargon reigns in Mesopotamia. ▲
- c. 2000 **(Mesopotamia)** Amorites found the city of Babylon.
- c. 2000 **(Mesopotamia)** The Hebrew patriarch Abraham leaves the Sumerian city of Ur.
- 1938–c. 1600 **(Egypt)** This is the era called the Middle Kingdom.
- c. 1800 **(Canaan)** Famine forces some Hebrews to migrate to Egypt, where they are enslaved.
- c. 1792–1750 **(Mesopotamia)** King Hammurabi reigns over Babylonian empire.
- c. 1540–1075 **(Egypt)** This is the era called the New Kingdom. ▶

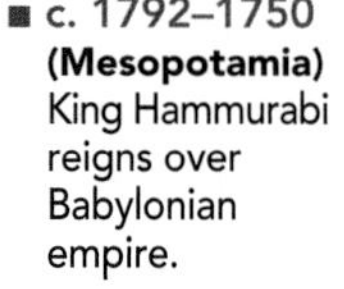

- 1000 **(Mesopotamia)** A tribal group called the Parsa settles in what is now southern Iran; they become the Persians.
- c. 628–c. 551 **(Persia)** Zoroaster, founder of Zoroastrianism, lives.
- 500s **(Persian Empire)** King Cyrus the Great of Persia establishes an empire.
- c. 330 **(Persian Empire)** Alexander the Great conquers the Persian Empire. ▲

LITERARY EVENTS

- c. 2200–2100 **(Mesopotamia)** Earliest written texts about King Gilgamesh appear. ▼

- c. 1792–1750 **(Mesopotamia)** The Code of Hammurabi, one of the world's first legal codes, is compiled.
- c. 2000–1600 **(Mesopotamia)** *The Epic of Gilgamesh* is written.
- c. 1540–1075 **(Egypt)** Love poetry of the New Kingdom is written.
- c. 1200 **(ancient Middle East)** This is the earliest date for the composition of biblical writings.
- 100 **(ancient Middle East)** This is the latest date for the composition of biblical writings. ▼

Getting an Overview of the Period

Introduction To give students an overview of the period, have them indicate the span of dates in the title of the Timeline. Next, point out that the Timeline is divided into Cultural and Historical Events (on the top) and Literary Events (on the bottom). Have students scan the Timeline, looking at both the Cultural and Historical Events and the Literary Events. Finally, point out that the events in the Timeline often represent beginnings, turning points, and endings (for example, the establishment of the Persian Empire by King Cyrus in the 500s B.C.).

Key Events Have students **select** events from the Timeline that demonstrate intellectual advances.

Possible response: The Code of Hammurabi (c. 1792–1750 B.C.) and the establishment of an official version of the Qur'an (c. A.D. 650) are intellectual advances.

What four major kingdoms emerged in West Africa during the period covered on the Timeline?

Answer: The four major kingdoms are the Ghana, the Benin, the Mali, and the Songhai.

0 A.D. 1000 A.D. 2000

- c. 570 **(Arabia)** Muhammad, the founder of Islam, is born in Mecca.
- c. 600s **(West Africa)** Kingdom of Ghana begins to thrive.
- c. 610 **(Arabia)** Muhammad experiences his first revelation.
- 632 **(Arabia)** Muhammad dies; Arabia is united as an Islamic nation.
- 636–637 **(Iran)** Muslim Arabs begin to conquer Iran. ▶

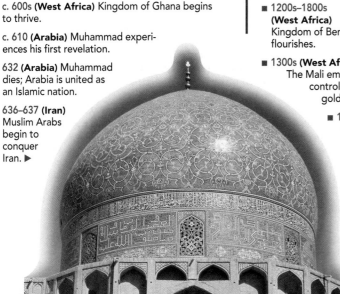

- 1076 **(West Africa)** Kingdom of Ghana ends.
- 1200s–1800s **(West Africa)** Kingdom of Benin flourishes.

- 1300s **(West Africa)** The Mali empire controls the gold trade.
- 1324 **(West Africa)** The Muslim emperor of Mali, Mansa Musa, makes a religious pilgrimage to Mecca.
- 1400s **(West Africa)** The Songhai kingdom emerges. ▲

- c. 650 **(Arabia)** A Muslim leader directs learned men to establish an official version of the Qur'an.
- c. 850 **(Persia)** A Persian storybook called *The Thousand Tales* is translated into Arabic and becomes known as *The Thousand and One Nights.*
- c. 935–c. 1020 **(Persia)** The Persian poet Firdawsi, author of the *Shah-nama* ("Epic of Kings"), lives.

- c. 1207–1273 **(Turkey)** Rumi, celebrated mystic and poet in the Persian language, lives.
- 1255 **(West Africa)** This is the death date of Sundiata, founder of the Kingdom of Mali and protagonist of the epic that bears his name. ▼

Analyzing the Timeline

1. (a) What are two events that show stages in Egypt's development? (b) How did the first of these events help make possible the building of the Great Pyramid? **[Draw Conclusions]**
   Answer: (a) Upper Egypt and Lower Egypt united under Menes. The pharaoh Kufu had the Great Pyramid built at Giza. (b) The unification of Egypt brought together the entire civilization's political, economic, and cultural strength, which were necessary for building a great monument.
2. (a) What does the c. that appears before dates mean? (b) Do the inexact dates for the events affect the Timeline's reliability? Explain. **[Make a Judgment]**
   Answer: (a) The c. that appears before dates is the abbreviation for circa, which means that the date is not exact. (b) No; the events appear in chronological order relative to one another.
3. (a) What types of events occurred in 100 B.C., A.D. 632, and A.D. 1324? (b) What can you infer from these events? **[Infer]**
   Answer: (a) Important religious events occurred during these years. (b) Religious beliefs developed over time in different places.
4. (a) What did King Hammurabi accomplish during his reign between 1792 and 1750 B.C.? (b) How might this accomplishment have affected people's lives? **[Analyze Causes and Effects]**
   Answer: (a) He produced the Code of Hammurabi, a written set of laws. (b) It gave his people a consistent, predictable legal code.
5. (a) How many major kingdoms and empires flourished in Africa from A.D. 100 to 1000, according to the Timeline? (b) What does this information tell you about the vitality of civilization in Africa? **[Deduce]**
   Answer: (a) Four kingdoms flourished. (b) Civilization was thriving in Africa during this period.

Critical Viewing

1. Compare the style of Egyptian art during the New Kingdom (1540–1075 B.C.) with the Middle Eastern art of 100 B.C. **[Compare and Contrast]**
   Possible response: The Egyptian art is more formalized than later Middle Eastern art, which is more realistic with natural poses and settings.
2. What does the dome of the temple tell you about the Arabic civilization at this time (A.D. 636–637)? **[Deduce]**
   Possible response: Arabia had a prosperous civilization with skilled artisans.
3. What mood does the artist establish in the picture of Sundiata (A.D. 1255)? Explain. **[Interpret]**
   Possible response: The artist establishes a mood of joy and happiness. The people are happy and relaxed. The bright colors evoke feelings of energy and joy.

Literature of the Period

- *The Epic of Gilgamesh,* p. 18, is one of the oldest works of literature known today. It is another of the "firsts" contributed by the Sumerian civilization.
- In selections such as "The Fisherman and the Jinnee," p. 86, and *Sundiata,* p. 132, students will learn about some of the values, joys, and passions of the ancient peoples of the world.

Background

Fertile Crescent

The Tigris-Euphrates Valley, home of the ancient Mesopotamian civilization, forms the eastern part of the Fertile Crescent. Shaped like a semicircle, this fertile strip of land stretches from the Persian Gulf around to the Mediterranean Sea. Not only was the Fertile Crescent agriculturally productive at this time, but it was also ideally situated for trade because of its location at the point where three continents—Asia, Africa, and Europe—meet.

Critical Viewing

Possible response: The parallel lines through the middle of the map represent the Euphrates River, and the rectangle across these lines stands for the city of Babylon. The double circular lines represent the ocean.

Historical Background

Ancient Middle East: Origins About 5,000 years ago, several major civilizations developed in the fertile river valleys of southwest Asia. The region between the Tigris and Euphrates rivers, in modern Iraq, was one of these sites. Mesopotamia (mes′ ə pə tā′ mē ə), the Greek name for this region, means "the land between two rivers." (See the map on page 7.)

Even today, scholars disagree about the identity of the people or peoples who spoke and wrote Sumerian and who lived in ancient Sumer (so͞o′ mər). In the succession of civilizations that arose in this region, however, theirs was the first, and it influenced the Babylonian and Assyrian civilizations that followed.

As the founders of Mesopotamian civilization, the Sumerians have many "firsts" to their credit: the region's earliest system of writing—cuneiform (kyo͞o nē′ ə fôrm′), or wedge-shaped, characters; a number system based on sixty that led to our 60-second minute, 60-minute hour, and 360-degree circle; the first wheeled vehicles; and the earliest city-states.

The Babylonians One of the greatest Mesopotamian kings was Sargon (reigned c. 2334–2279 B.C.). His new capital city of Agade, located near the site of Babylon, was north of Sumer—the northward shift of power in Mesopotamia became a trend. Agade contributed its name to the region where Sargon lived, Akkad (ak′ ad′), and to the language he spoke, Akkadian (ə kā′ dē ən). A Semitic language related to modern Hebrew and Arabic, Akkadian in its various forms became the tongue of the new northern centers of power, Babylon and Assur.

Those who spoke Semitic languages, the Semites, were nomadic peoples who had migrated to Mesopotamia from the Arabian peninsula. One such group, the Amorites, founded the village of Babylon on the Euphrates River (c. 2000 B.C.).

Not until the reign of Hammurabi (c. 1792–1750 B.C.), however, did Babylon come into its own as the capital of a great empire. (See the map on page 7.) Hammurabi's famous legal code was an important step in the development of civilization. Engraved on a stone slab, this code contains 282 laws covering all aspects of daily life.

Ancient Egypt: "The gift of the Nile" At the time that Sumerian civilization was developing along the Tigris and Euphrates rivers, Egyptian civilization arose along the banks of the Nile in northeastern Africa. The Greek historian Herodotus called Egypt

▼ Critical Viewing
This clay tablet shows an ancient Babylonian map of the world. After comparing this map with the one on page 7, answer this question: What do you think some of the circles and lines on the ancient map represent? Explain. **[Speculate]**

Enrichment

Sumerian Cities

Perhaps the most famous Sumerian "first" was the creation of cities. Many of these urban centers, which were like mini-nations, were actually within sight of one another. At first, the main institution in each city was a temple. This temple contained the image of the city's chief god—the Sumerians worshiped many gods—and housed the temple staff: priests who ruled the city, scribes who recorded the crops that the temple received from its lands, and artisans. The largest building in the temple complex, and in the city itself, was the ziggurat, a six- or seven-story tower that Sumerians believed the gods could use as a ladder in descending from heaven.

As city-states grew and came into conflict, military leaders replaced priests as rulers. These military leaders eventually became kings, and the king's palace, with its own staff, rivaled the temple in importance.

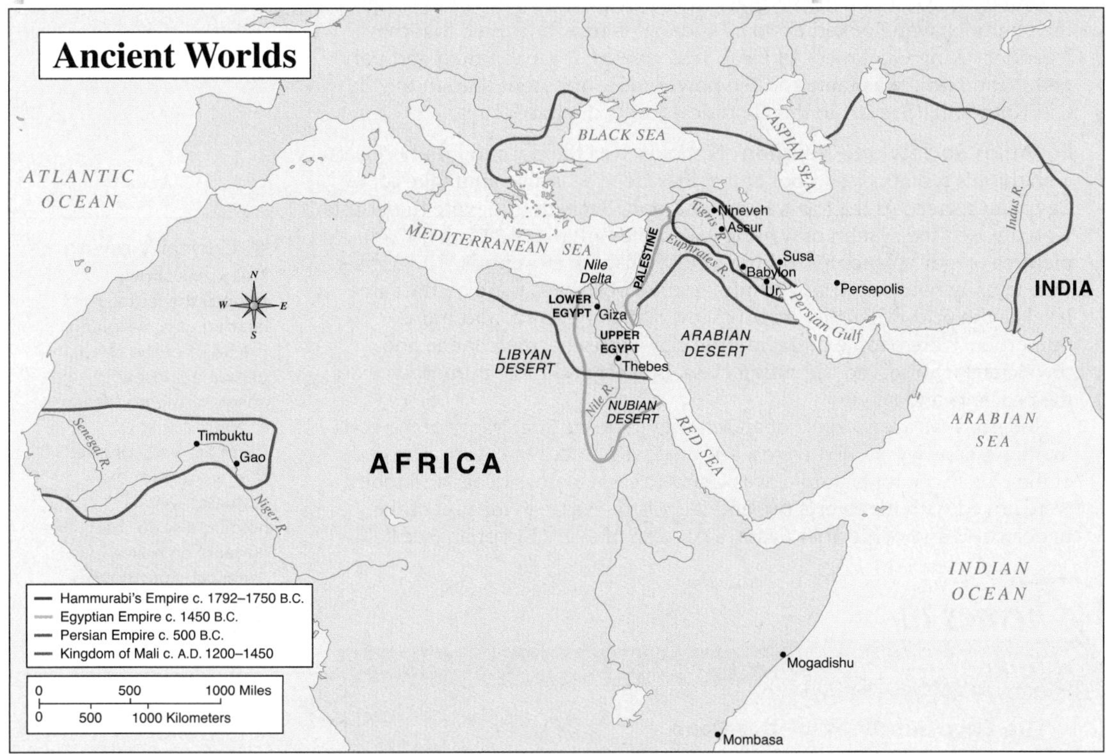

"the gift of the Nile," and he was right. Every July the river would flood, replenishing farmland along its banks with moisture and rich silt. In addition to fertile land, the river provided a watery highway for travel and trade. It was also a source of fish. Without the river's life-giving bounty, Egypt would be as barren as the deserts that surround it.

At first, the villages along the Nile were divided into two countries: Upper Egypt in the south and Lower Egypt in the north. Around 2900 B.C., a ruler joined the two kingdoms to create a single realm. The history of the pharaohs (far′ ōz), or rulers, who then led Egypt for almost two thousand years can be divided into the following periods: Early Dynastic Period (c. 2925–c. 2575 B.C.), the Old Kingdom (c. 2575–c. 2130 B.C.), the Middle Kingdom (1938–c. 1600 B.C.), and the New Kingdom (c. 1540–1075 B.C.). In the periods between these eras, Egypt was prey to invasions and civil wars. By and large, however, the geographical barriers of desert and sea protected Egypt from its neighbors and made for a long-lived, stable, and conservative civilization.

▲ Critical Viewing
What does this map suggest about the relationship between rivers and civilizations? Explain. **[Read a Map]**

Background

Literature in the Middle Kingdom

Explain to students that Egyptian literature and art started to flourish during the Middle Kingdom, when Egyptians began to have more contact with other peoples. A famous story written at this time is the *Tale of Sinuhe,* which tells about the adventures of an Egyptian traveling in foreign lands. This tale later inspired stories about Sindbad the Sailor, one of which found its way into the Persian book of tales entitled *The Thousand and One Nights.* (For an excerpt from this classic—not the story of Sindbad, however—see "The Fisherman and the Jinnee" on p. 86.)

Critical Viewing

Possible response: Early civilizations were built along rivers. Civilizations relied on rivers for transportation, food, water, and irrigation.

Differentiated Instruction Solutions for All Learners

Strategy for Less Proficient Readers
Have students preview the introduction by looking at the art and illustrations and reading the heads and subheads. Ask students what they think the text will be about. Then, have them compile a list of questions they would like to answer by reading the material. Tell them to look for answers to their questions as they read.

Strategy for English Learners
If any of your students have special knowledge of the Middle East or Africa, invite them to share their knowledge. Ask them to talk about the history, geography, and culture of the region.

Strategy for Advanced Readers
After students have read pp. 6–13, ask them to work together to create a Venn diagram showing similarities and differences between two of the civilizations discussed. Have them present their conclusions to the class.

Background

Hieroglyphics

The Egyptian system of writing, called hieroglyphics, appeared in the earliest stages of Egyptian history. From its first appearance, this system makes use of a rebus-principle. In other words, taking an example from English, the pictures of a bee and of a leaf might be put together to sound out the word *belief.* The rebus-principle usually takes some time to develop, so it is surprising to find it in use from the beginning of a people's history. Some scholars theorize that the Egyptians may have borrowed this principle from the Mesopotamians.

Critical Viewing

Possible response: Anubis and Ma'at are gods of the ancient Egyptians, so justice may be a religious function. Also, Anubis is weighing the soul of the dead person. In the United States today, the scale of justice is usually associated with government rather than with religion and symbolizes the weighing of truth in this life.

Themes in World Literature

Close-up on Culture

- Tell students that papyrus was a tall sedge plant that grew in the Nile River Valley in Egypt. The plant was cut and pressed into a material to write on.
- **Ask** students to explain why Egyptians collected such notes for their Book of the Dead.
  Answer: Egyptians believed in eternal life after death. They thought these notes would help them travel through the afterlife.
- **Ask** how the Book of the Dead influenced the way Egyptians buried the dead.
  Answer: The Egyptians mummified the dead because they believed that the preserved bodies would have a better afterlife.

Unlike the Mesopotamian kings, who were powerful but human figures, the pharaohs were looked upon as gods. (It is true, however, that the legendary King Gilgamesh of Uruk was viewed as part human and part god.) At no time was their godlike power more apparent than in the Old Kingdom. (See Art in the Historical Context, page 9.)

Egyptian Society and Religion Not only was the pyramid that housed a pharaoh's remains a symbol of the afterlife, it was also an image of Egyptian society. At the top was the pharaoh. Beneath him were the priests, who devised the system of writing called hieroglyphics (hī′ ər ō glif′ iks), pictures or symbols representing words, syllables, or sounds. The nobles, who usually held important administrative positions, were on the same level as the priests. Farther down on the social pyramid, and more numerous, were people of the middle class: artisans, merchants, and physicians who served the ruling class. Lowest and most numerous were the peasants and slaves.

Religion was a key aspect of ancient Egyptian culture. Many of the gods that Egyptians worshiped were associated with forces of nature. The god of the Nile River, for example, was Osiris (ō sī′ ris), whose death and rebirth were linked with the river's rise and fall. Osiris was also the god of the underworld and of life after death, a concern of every Egyptian (see below).

▼ **Critical Viewing**
This scene shows Anubis, the jackal-headed god, weighing the heart of the dead person against an image of the goddess of truth, Ma'at. Compare and contrast this image with the statue of Justice holding a scale that appears on many American courthouses. **[Compare and Contrast]**

Themes in World Masterpieces

Close-up on Culture

The Egyptian Book of the Dead

Ancient Egyptians believed that, after death, the soul journeyed in the underworld in search of eternal life. To prepare for the afterlife, they collected the numerous spells, confessions, and words of power known as the Egyptian Book of the Dead. This title refers not to a single volume but to many different texts. Written on long papyrus scrolls entombed with the deceased, these texts were like travel guides telling Egyptians what to do and say in the strange country of the hereafter.

The most dramatic moment of the underworld journey was the judgment of the dead by Osiris (ō sī′ ris). This god's story involved suffering, death, and resurrection, and he could grant eternal life to the deceased. First, however, the candidate's heart was weighed against a figure of Ma'at, goddess of law, truth, and justice. (See the picture.) Souls that failed this test of goodness were tortured and destroyed, while those who passed lived eternally.

Although everyone was judged, the afterlife continued the class divisions of Egyptian society. Pharaohs and wealthy bureaucrats were buried with a deluxe Book of the Dead, rendered by an expert scribe. Less-important Egyptians had to settle for a cut-rate edition. Presumably, the expensive text offered upper-class Egyptians a better chance for eternal life.

The famous burial practice of mummification was associated with the Book of the Dead. Egyptians used this method of embalming in the belief that preserving the body would ensure a satisfactory afterlife.

Enrichment

Book of the Dead

John A. Wilson explains how, as the Old Kingdom ended, a new emphasis on good deeds emerged:

> *Ma'at,* "truth, justice, righteousness, right dealing, order," had thus become critically important for the supreme prize of eternal happiness. Meri-ka-Re was advised by his father [the king] "to do *ma'at* whilst thou endurest upon earth." Why? The text goes on to relate royal justice upon earth to the judgment at death: "The council which judges the deficient, though knowest that they are not lenient on that day of judging the miserable, the hour of doing (their) duty. . . . A man remains over after death, and his deeds are placed beside him in heaps. However, existence yonder is for eternity. . . . He who reaches it without wrongdoing shall exist yonder like a god, stepping out freely like the lords of eternity." Whereas those of earlier times had tried to purchase their immortality, the new emphasis on character shifted the focus from goods to good.

Themes in World Masterpieces

Art in the Historical Context

The Great Pyramid at Giza: The One and the Many

During the 4th dynasty (c. 2575–c. 2465 B.C.), the power of the pharaohs was at its height. A symbol of this power is still visible today at Giza, on the west bank of the Nile just south of Cairo. It is the Great Pyramid, built to house the remains of the pharaoh Khufu. Almost 500 feet tall and consisting of more than 2 million stones, this pyramid was meant to be Khufu's home forever—and, so far, forever has lasted about 4,500 years!

Seen from a distance, this structure seems to proclaim the power of one mighty ruler. Viewed more closely, however, it is a well-engineered assembly of many stone blocks (see the face of the pyramid in shadow). Thousands of sweating men dragged those blocks up ramps and then fit them together with stunning accuracy. These workers—either a special crew or farmers taking off during Nile floods—labored twenty years to build their pharaoh an eternal life.

▲ Critical Viewing This picture shows the Great Pyramid. Are there any modern buildings or monuments that are comparable to the Great Pyramid in size or purpose? Explain. **[Connect]**

The Hebrews: People of the Covenant Not too long after the Amorites were founding the village of Babylon (c. 2000 B.C.), another Semitic group migrated westward from Mesopotamia to Palestine, or Canaan (kā′ nən), which corresponds to modern Israel and Lebanon. (In dating events, Jewish people normally use B.C.E., "Before the Common Era," rather than B.C., "Before Christ.") This group, the Hebrews, recorded their history in a sacred text that we now call the Bible. Unlike the Mesopotamians or Egyptians, the Hebrews believed in one God and the covenant, or solemn agreement, between God and the Hebrew people. This covenant provided that God would protect the Hebrews from their enemies as long as the Hebrews obeyed him.

Toward the beginning of the second millennium, famine forced some of the Hebrews to migrate from Canaan to Egypt. There, they were enslaved by the pharaohs. The Bible tells, however, that God inspired a leader called Moses to lead the Hebrews out of their captivity and back to Canaan (c. 1200s B.C.). Through Moses, God gave the Hebrews a set of laws called the Ten Commandments. In return for their obedience to these laws and their worship of him, the Hebrews believed, God granted them the land of Canaan.

The Kingdom of Israel For several hundred years, the Hebrews battled the Philistines and other peoples for control of this promised land. They finally conquered the region in about 1000 B.C. under the leadership of David. He became the ruler of the new Hebrew kingdom of Israel, and Solomon, his son, made Jerusalem into an impressive national capital. He erected a temple there that became the center of worship for the entire nation. After his death in the tenth century B.C., however, quarrels led to the division of the country into the northern kingdom of Israel and the southern kingdom of Judah.

Themes in World Literature

Art in the Historical Context

The Great Pyramid is one of ten pyramids that were built in the town of Giza, an ancient Egyptian necropolis, or city of the dead. The ten were built between about 2600 and 1500 b.c. Scholars estimate that it took twenty years for as many as 100,000 men, working four-month shifts, to build the Great Pyramid. Because the ancient Egyptians had no machinery, they cut the limestone with copper chisels and saws. Groups of men dragged the blocks to the site. The upper layers of blocks were dragged up long ramps. Workers then covered the pyramid with an outer coating of white casing stones. The outer stones were laid so exactly that from a distance the pyramid appeared to have been cut from a single white stone. These outer stones have since disappeared.

- **Ask** students what motivated the builders of the Great Pyramid.
  Answer: The builders wanted to create a home for eternity for the remains of the pharaoh Khufu.

Critical Viewing

Possible response: The Lincoln Memorial and the Washington Monument are similar structures because they memorialize past leaders.

Background

Origin of the Hebrews

The Hebrews trace their origin to Abraham, who migrated from Ur in southern Babylonia to Canaan, the ancient country known today as Israel. Abraham did not travel as an individual but as the head of a family caravan. Although scholars cannot trace his route with certainty, they guess that he followed the Euphrates River past Babylon and Mari, then continued on to Harran, and traveled south through Aleppo, Ebla, Qatna, Damascus, and Hazor, finally entering Canaan. Scholars disagree about when this migration took place. Suggested dates range from 3000 to 1000 B.C.

Background

Administration of the Persian Empire

The Persians were adept at retaining order throughout their huge empire. They divided the empire into twenty provinces, each with its own governor, who collected taxes and administered the Persian code of laws. To connect these provinces, they built a sophisticated system of roads and established relay stations with fresh horses along the main roads. By doing so, the Persians made it possible for royal messengers to cover up to 1,500 miles in only ten days.

Critical Viewing

Possible response: The beautiful equipment worn by Cyrus, his soldiers, and his horse and the look of pride on the face of Cyrus and his followers all suggest that warfare was glorified.

In 721 B.C., Israel fell to the Assyrians. Not long after, in 587–586 B.C., Judah was conquered by the Babylonians, who destroyed the temple in Jerusalem and carried away many Hebrews to Babylon. At the end of the sixth century B.C., however, another turn of events led to the conquest of the Babylonians by the Persians. Cyrus, the Persian king, allowed the Hebrews to return to their homeland and rebuild the temple.

While ancient Israel never again achieved the power and independence it had enjoyed under David, the Hebrew contribution to Western culture has been great. (For more about this contribution, see pages 36 and 74–75.)

The Persian and Islamic Empires: Origins About 1000 B.C., a group of Aryan tribes arrived in the mountainous region that is now known as Iran. A tribal group called the Parsa settled in southern Iran. Gradually, this group became known as the Persians. Calling their language Persian and their region Persia, they emerged as a great power in the ancient Middle East.

The Persian Empire During the sixth century B.C., the Persian king Cyrus the Great established a vast and powerful empire. This Cyrus was the same king who conquered the Babylonian Empire and allowed the Hebrews to return to their homeland. By the time of his death, the Persian Empire stretched from the border of India to Asia Minor and from the edge of Egypt to the coasts of the Black Sea and the Caspian Sea. (See the map on page 7.) About 200 years later, this empire, weakened by its unsuccessful attempts to conquer Greece, fell to the forces of Alexander the Great.

Religion in Ancient Persia Although the Persian Empire was short-lived, its official state religion continued to thrive long after its downfall. Founded by a man whom the Greeks called Zoroaster (zō´ rō as´ tər) (c. 628 B.C.–c. 551), this religion taught that two gods—one good and one evil—battle each other and that the good god will prevail. Zoroastrianism remained dominant in Persia for over one thousand years. Then, it was replaced by Islam in the seventh century A.D.

▲ **Critical Viewing** What does this picture of Cyrus the Great and his followers suggest about the nature of warfare in ancient Persia? Explain. **[Infer]**

Islam Muhammad, the founder of Islam, was born in about A.D. 570 in Mecca, a large town in what is today Saudi Arabia. At the time, Mecca was a city of extremes, where the rich lived in luxury and the poor lived in despair. Profoundly disturbed by these conditions, Muhammad frequently retreated to a mountain cave to meditate. At the age of forty, he had an experience during one of his retreats that dramatically changed his life. He believed that the angel Gabriel came to him and told him that he had been chosen to serve as God's prophet. Muhammad continued to receive such revelations throughout the rest of his life, and he recited them to his followers.

Although Muhammad taught people to recognize Allah (al´ ə) as the only God, he did not discount the principles of Judaism and Christianity.

Enrichment

Unity of Persian Empire

The Persian empire was an amalgam of many different conquered peoples, yet despite rebellions from Egypt, Lydia, and Babylon, the empire was remarkably stable during its short-lived history. One of the most important reasons for this stability was the Persians' general tolerance toward the people under their rule. Not only did they allow conquered peoples to retain some degree of political freedom, but they also allowed them to continue their customs and religions. This tolerance resulted in part from the teachings of Zoroastrianism, the principal religion of the Persians. According to Zoroaster, all the gods worshipped by people were indeed gods, although subservient to either Ahura-Mazda, the good god, or Ahriman, the evil god. Cyrus and the other Persian kings saw it as their duty to support the gods of Ahura-Mazda and to destroy those supporting Ahriman. By demonstrating this type of tolerance, the Persians minimized dissent and reduced the frequency of rebellion within the empire.

Instead, he believed that he was the last in a long line of prophets, including Moses and all of the other prophets mentioned in the Bible.

The Spread of Islam Because Muhammad preached the importance of establishing a just and pious society on Earth, his message had great appeal among the poor in Arabian towns such as Mecca and Medina. These people converted to Islam in large numbers, enabling Muhammad to assemble an army and spread his message throughout the Arabian peninsula.

By the time of Muhammad's death in 632, all of Arabia had been united into an Islamic nation. Then, within a remarkably brief period, Arab armies established a massive Islamic empire that extended from Spain and North Africa to Central Asia.

Although they were deeply committed to the idea of converting people to Islam, Arab leaders did not force people to abandon their cultural traditions. Instead, the Arabs themselves embraced much of the heritage of their conquered peoples, even as these peoples were embracing elements of Arab culture. This blending of heritages resulted in the establishment of a vibrant and diverse Islamic civilization.

▲ **Critical Viewing** Which details on these pages of the Qur'an indicate that it is a sacred book? Explain. **[Infer]**

Africa: Kingdoms and Trading States From early times, people traded across a long route that stretched from the Middle East and North Africa to the savanna lands, or grasslands, of West Africa. Camel caravans crossed the Sahara, carrying valuable cargoes of gold or salt.

In time, trading empires arose in West Africa. Ghana flourished from the 600s to the 1200s A.D. By the 1300s, Mali controlled the gold trade. The Muslim emperor of Mali, Mansa Musa, won widespread fame when he made a religious pilgrimage to the Arabian city of Mecca in 1324. In the 1400s, a new empire, Songhai, arose in the savanna. Its great city of Timbuktu was a center of learning, attracting scholars from all over the Muslim world.

The kingdom of Benin, which flourished from the 1200s to the 1800s, arose in West African forests. Farther inland, the rulers of Great Zimbabwe (zim bä′ bwā), a city built of stone, controlled rich gold mines and established a trading empire. In East Africa, city-states such as Mogadishu (mō′ gä dē′ sho͞o), Kilwa, and Mombasa formed part of a prosperous trade route across the Indian Ocean.

Humanities

Qur'an

The Qur'an represents the highest form of Islamic religious art. It is written in Arabic calligraphy. Continuing patterns of geometric and natural adornment suggest infinite repetition, triggering the deliberation of the nature of God. Islamic religious art avoids any representation of the human form, which might be mistaken for the worship of idols, a practice prohibited by the Qur'an.

Critical Viewing

Possible response: The use of calligraphy, the lack of human form, and the repetition of patterns indicate that the Qur'an is a sacred book.

Historical Background

Comprehension Check

1. For what great achievement is the Sumerian king Hammurabi famous?
   Answer: Hammurabi created a legal code composed of 282 laws.
2. Why was Egypt called the "gift of the Nile"?
   Answer: Every July, the Nile would flood, replenishing its banks with moisture and silt, thus creating fertile land.
3. How was the religion of the Hebrews different from that of the Mesopotamians and Egyptians?
   Answer: Unlike the Mesopotamians and Egyptians, the Hebrews believed in one God and in a covenant between God and the Hebrew people.
4. Why did the teachings of Muhammad appeal so strongly to the poor people of the Arabian Peninsula?
   Answer: Muhammad's teachings appealed to them because he taught the importance of establishing a just and pious society.
5. What was the significance of the city of Timbuktu?
   Answer: The city attracted scholars from all over the Muslim world.

Critical Thinking

1. What can you infer from the pyramids about the political and economic conditions of Egypt's Old Kingdom? **[Infer]**
   Possible response: The Old Kingdom was wealthy, and its pharaohs were powerful.
2. How did the Hebrews' migration to Canaan reinforce their belief in a covenant with God? **[Analyze]**
   Possible response: The Hebrews believed that God had given them a set of laws, called the Ten Commandments, and had inspired Moses to lead them out of slavery to a land granted to them by God.
3. Compare and contrast Zoroastrianism and Islam. **[Compare and Contrast]**
   Possible response: Whereas Zoroastrianism taught that there were two gods, Islam taught that there was one God. Each religion was once dominant in Persia.

Background

The Bible

The Bible is the foundation of both Judaism and Christianity. However, the sacred writings used in the two religious traditions are somewhat different. The Hebrew Bible consists of thirty-nine books that were originally written primarily in Hebrew. (A few sections were composed in Aramaic.) These thirty-nine books are divided into three parts: the Torah, or Law, which is sometimes called the books of Moses; the Nebiim, or Prophets; and the Ketubim, or Writings, which include Psalms and other writings. The Christian Bible includes the Hebrew Bible, which is called the Old Testament, as well as twenty-seven books that make up the New Testament and describe the lives of Jesus and his followers. Even among Christian groups, versions of the different Bibles are used.

Themes in World Literature

A Living Tradition

- **Ask** students to give an example of *Ecclesiastes* as a living musical tradition.
  Answer: Pete Seeger used some words of *Ecclesiastes* in a folk song that later became a popular rock 'n' roll version.
- Have a student read the quote from *Ecclesiastes.*
- **Ask** students how they can make these words a living tradition in their own lives. What key words helped them decide?
  Possible response: "All is vanity" suggests that, although one should strive for high achievement, one must not become self-centered.

Literature

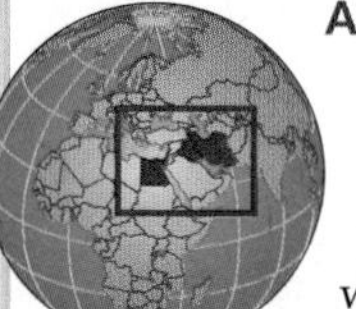

Ancient Middle Eastern Literature: Babylonia Babylonians had a reverent attitude toward Sumerian culture. Yet they were far more than slavish imitators. Reshaping a group of Sumerian tales about a legendary king, Babylonian scribes fashioned a brilliant work that we know today as *The Epic of Gilgamesh.*

Egyptian Literature Egyptian literature varied with the mood of the times. In the Old Kingdom, when the power of the pharaohs was unquestioned, literature was characterized by sacred hymns as cold and formal as the great pyramids themselves. As society became less rigidly structured in the Middle Kingdom, literature began to reflect personal feelings. The love poetry of the New Kingdom continued this trend.

Hebrew Scripture: The Bible Hebrew monotheism, or belief in a single God, served as a basis for two other world religions, Christianity and Islam. In addition, Hebrew law demonstrated a greater respect for human life than

Themes in World Masterpieces — A Living Tradition

Ecclesiastes Becomes a Musical Hit

Ecclesiastes (e klē´ zē as´ tēz´), a book of the Bible dating from the third century B.C., furnished the lyrics for a 1960s rock hit. Earlier, the folk singer Pete Seeger had used words from Ecclesiastes to write the song "Turn! Turn! Turn!" Then, in the mid-1960s, Roger McGuinn of the Byrds did a rock version of the song that climbed to the top of the charts.

Here is what McGuinn said about this version: "It was a standard folk song by that time, but I played it, and it came out rock 'n' roll because that's what I was programmed to do like a computer. . . ."

[from Johnny Rogan's *The Byrds: Timeless Flight Revisited: The Sequel* (Rogan House, 1998)]

The Greek word Ecclesiastes, meaning "member of an assembly," comes from the Hebrew kohelet, "someone who calls together an assembly—a preacher." Ecclesiastes, a book of wise sayings attributed to a "Preacher," stresses the "vanity" of ambition and the need to accept life's different seasons:

> . . . saith the Preacher . . . all is vanity. What profit hath a man of all his labor which he taketh under the sun? . . . To every thing there is a season, and a time to every purpose under the heaven: A time to be born and a time to die, a time to plant and a time to pluck up that which is planted. . . .

Seeger had used the section about different seasons, adding the refrain "Turn! Turn! Turn!" to suggest, perhaps, how Earth's turning brings different times and purposes. The song's final plea—"a time for peace, I swear it's not too late"—appealed to Vietnam War protesters in the United States.

Enrichment

History of Sumerian Literature

The Sumerian culture produced the world's oldest literature of record. Recorded on clay tablets, it dates from between about 2100 and 1650 B.C. Currently, an estimated 400 works of Sumerian literature, running to more than 50,000 lines, have been identified. This vast body of work remains largely unpublished. Sumerian literature was produced in a scribal tradition; many scribes over several centuries made copies of certain works. The versions often vary, and archaeologists must work with thousands of tablet fragments. The work of assembling complete, reliable texts is underway, but progress is slow. In addition, advances in the knowledge of the Sumerian language continue, making older translations unacceptable. To facilitate the translation and editing of Sumerian literature and to make it widely available, Oxford University's Oriental Institute is collecting the works and preparing them for electronic publication.

had previously existed in the ancient Near East. Also new was the Hebrews' deep concern with moral behavior.

All these qualities are evident in the Hebrew Bible, a series of books written during the period 1200 to 100 B.C. These books have deeply influenced Western morality and religious beliefs and, together with Greek thought, form the foundation of Western civilization.

The Simurgh Brings Zal to Sam, Leaf from Shah-nameh by Ferdowsi, 14th century. The Metropolitan Museum of Art

▲ **Critical Viewing** Which details on this page of the *Shah-nama* suggest that it is a book about kings? Why? **[Infer]**

Arabic and Persian Literature: Folk Tales In addition to appreciating poetry and prose of all kinds, Islamic Arabs enjoyed listening to fables and folk tales. Many anonymous collections of such stories exist, but the one entitled *The Thousand and One Nights* is by far the most famous.

Islamic Scripture: The Qur'an Shortly after Muhammad's death, the revelations he had received were arranged into a book called the Qur'an (ko͞o rän′), which became the sacred scripture of all Muslims. The central message of the Qur'an is that Allah is the single, unique God who is the creator and sustainer of all things: Allah means "the God" in Arabic. According to the Qur'an, all Muslims should submit their wills to Allah because he is not only their creator but also the one who will judge them at death. This duty is evident in the fact that *Islam* actually means "submission."

Persian Literature During the ninth and tenth centuries A.D., several poets attempted to write epic poems in Persian describing Persian history. The most famous of these poems, the *Shah-nama,* or "Epic of Kings," by Firdawsi (fir dou′ sē; also spelled Ferdowsi) is still considered a national treasure in Iran. Another Persian poetic form, the rubái—a poem in four-line stanzas—has been immortalized in the Western world through the translation of *The Rubáiyát.* This book is a collection of verse by the Persian scientist and poet Omar Khayyám (kī yäm′).

Many gifted Persian poets were Sufis (so͞o′ fēz), members of an Islamic sect known as Sufism (so͞o′ fiz′ əm). Sufis withdrew from society to live solitary lives of worship and piety in order to achieve a sense of oneness with Allah. Their attachment to Allah was similar to being in love and caused them to experience such feelings as intoxication, bliss, and pain. Sufi poets like Sa'di (sä′ dē) and Rumi (rü′ mē) wrote exquisite verses expressing their spiritual feelings in the language of love.

African Literature: Oral Literature Africa has a rich heritage of oral literature. In traditional societies, the griot (grē′ ō), or storyteller, held a place of honor. The griot spoke the praises of the ruler, retold events from history, challenged listeners with riddles and proverbs, and recited poems and folk tales. *Sundiata* (so͞on dyä′ tä), by D. T. Niane, is named for the founder of the Kingdom of Mali and retells stories about him from the oral tradition.

Humanities

The Simurgh Brings Zal to Sam

Emphasize that griots tried both to entertain their audiences and to preserve the traditions of their society. Display Art Transparency 11: Benin Bronze Plaque in the **Fine Art Transparencies** booklet. Ask students why the Benin warrior-king represents a good subject for a griot's tale.

Critical Viewing

Possible response: The illustration shows a man dressed as a king might be dressed, along with three other figures who appear to be assisting him. Also, a presentation is being made to the man.

Literature of the Period

Comprehension Check

1. What new element did Hebrew law introduce into the Near Eastern culture of the ancient world?
   Answer: Hebrew law introduced a respect for human life and a concern for moral behavior.
2. What book contains the Islamic scriptures?
   Answer: The Qur'an contains Islamic scriptures.
3. What theme characterized the poetry of the Persian Sufi poets?
   Answer: The theme that characterized the poetry of Sufis was their love for Allah.

Critical Thinking

1. What can you conclude about the Babylonians on the basis of their regard for Sumerian culture? **[Draw Conclusions]**
   Possible response: The Babylonians had great regard for learning and literature.
2. How are Islam and the Hebrew religion alike? **[Compare and Contrast]**
   Possible response: Both religions worship one God.
3. Why were griots shown great honor in traditional African societies? **[Infer]**
   Possible response: Griots were shown great honor because they helped preserve the values, traditions, and histories of the people.

Concept Connector

Have students discuss the Focus Questions on p. 3. Students' discussions should include the following points:

The role of the code of Hammurabi:

- The code's 282 laws provided order and structure to developing civilizations.
- The code's laws covered all aspects of life.

The importance of the Nile in the development of Egyptian civilization:

- The Nile annually overflowed its banks and made the surrounding land fertile.
- The river provided a means for travel and trade.
- The river was a source of fish.

Role of the griot in African literature:

- The griot praised the ruler, retold events from history, challenged listeners with riddles and proverbs, and recited poems and folk tales.

PRETEACH/TEACH

Standard Course of Study

LT.5.01.2 Build knowledge of literary genres and explore how characteristics apply to literature of world cultures.

LT.5.01.3 Analyze literary devices and explain their effect on the work of world literature.

❶ Types of Epic

- Tell students that they will learn about epics in Unit 1. Have students read the quotation and the first paragraph, which defines an epic. **Ask** students: How is an epic different from other types of poetry that you have read?
  Possible response: Other forms of poetry usually are shorter than epics, may not deal with a hero or a hero's quest, and may not have begun as oral tradition.
- **Ask:** Why might the poetic form have been useful to storytellers who traveled from place to place telling the story of the epic hero?
  Possible response: The rhyme helped storytellers remember the content.
- Discuss the differences between the folk and literary epic. **Ask:** What do folk and literary epics have in common?
  Possible response: Literary epics usually borrow the characteristics of the folk epic, and some literary epics draw upon stories that originally were orally transmitted, as folk epics were.
- Tell students that the story of the Trojan War and Odysseus' journeys are part of the epics the *Iliad* and the *Odyssey,* attributed to Homer.

❷ Elements of the Epic

- Ask students: What does an epic conflict tell about the culture of a country?
- Point out that the conflict shows the dangers the society faced as well as what the culture considers important enough for a hero's struggle.
- Suggest that students refer to these pages as they read the excerpted portions of the epics in their books.

Unit 1 Focus on Literary Forms: The Epic

Defining the Epic

An **epic** is a long narrative poem about a larger-than-life hero who is engaged in a dangerous journey, or quest, that is important to the history of a nation or people.

THE EPIC IS NOT MERELY A GENRE, BUT A WAY OF LIFE. — *Harry Levin*

❶ Types of Epic

There are two main types of epic—the folk epic, created and developed through the oral tradition, and the literary epic, a story attributed to a single identified author.

- **Folk epics** are stories about heroes that were originally recited or sung as entertainment at feasts. Over the generations, these stories were passed down orally from storyteller to storyteller until eventually they were written down.
- **Literary epics** were written by a specific author, usually borrowing the style and characteristics of the folk epic. Some literary epics draw upon well-known stories, characters, and myths that were passed down through the oral tradition. For example, Homer's *Illiad* and *Odyssey* and Valmiki's *Ramayana* are often classified as folk epics, although ultimately they were attributed to these authors

The chart at the right shows examples of folk epics and literary epics in world literature.

Folk Epics	Literary Epics
The Epic of Gilgamesh (Sumerian), p. 18	The *Odyssey* and the *Illiad* by Homer (ancient Greek), p. 363
Sundiata (West African), p. 132	the *Ramayana* by Valmiki (ancient Indian), p. 208
the *Mahabharata* (Indian), p. 192	the *Aeneid* by Virgil (ancient Rome), p. 534
the *Song of Roland* (French), p. 600	the *Divine Comedy* by Dante Alighieri (Italian), p. 658
the *Nibelungenlied* (German), p. 610	*Paradise Lost* by John Milton (English)
Beowulf (Anglo-Saxon)	*Orlando Furioso* by Ariosto (Italian)

❷ Elements of the Epic

Both epics are characterized by certain key elements.

- **An Epic Hero** An epic focuses on the adventures of a larger-than-life main character called the **epic hero.** This hero is strong, brave, loyal, and virtuous—although he is sometimes flawed. For example, in Homer's *Iliad,* Achilles is a courageous warrior whose weakness is his temper. The epic hero also occupies an elevated position in society. He may even be semidivine. Achilles, for example, is the son of a mortal king and a sea goddess.
- **An Epic Conflict** The plot of an epic centers on the hero's struggle against an obstacle or series of obstacles. The hero proves his strength,

Extend the Lesson

Activity

- Ask students to re-read the quotation by Harry Levin.
- Review the elements of the epic. Then **ask** students the following questions:
  1. In what ways does an epic suggest a way of life?
     Answer: It shows what is important to the culture that created it, and the epic helps shape the identity of a nation or people and how they relate to the world.
  2. What elements demonstrate a way of life?
     Answer: What the hero seeks, how he acts, what he struggles against, and how the supernatural forces intervene show what the culture values.

bravery, wisdom, and virtue through valorous deeds—success in battle or adventure. For example, in the *Ramayana,* Prince Rama defeats an evil giant.

- **A Heroic Quest** Often, the hero's adventure takes the form of a perilous journey, or **quest,** in search of something of value to his people. In *The Epic of Gilgamesh,* the hero embarks on a quest for the secret of immortality.
- **Divine Intervention** The epic hero often receives help from a god or some other supernatural force. However, a different god may also work against the hero. For example, in Homer's *Odyssey,* the goddess Athena helps Odysseus, but the god Poseidon repeatedly tries to destroy him.

▲ Critical Viewing 5
This vase shows Aeneas, hero of Virgil's epic the *Aeneid*, carrying his father, Anchises, from burning Troy. How does this scene reflect the qualities of the epic hero? **[Connect]**

3 Epic Conventions

In addition to these key elements, epics also share certain literary characteristics, called **epic conventions.**

- An epic usually begins with an **opening statement of theme,** followed by an **invocation,** or appeal for supernatural help in telling the story.
- The story begins ***in medias res*** (Latin for "in the middle of things"). Readers are plunged right into the action, and then flashbacks and other narrative devices report on earlier events.
- An epic has a **serious tone** and an **elevated style** that reflect the importance of its characters and theme.
- Epics often include **epic similes,** elaborate extended comparisons using *like* or *as*. For example, in the *Illiad,* a twelve-line simile compares Achilles' pursuit of Hector to a mountain hawk swooping down on a dove.
- Epics typically include **epithets,** or stock descriptive words or phrases. Because these poems were originally composed and recited orally, epithets were a kind of shorthand that allowed the poet to describe a character or an object quickly in terms the audience would recognize. **Homeric epithets** are compound phrases such as "the gray-eyed goddess Athena," "man-killing Hector," and "the wine-dark sea."

4 Strategies for Reading Epics

Use these strategies as you read epic literature.

Focus on the Epic Hero Analyze the hero's virtues, strengths, and weaknesses. Make sure you understand what the hero seeks on his quest, and consider how the object of his quest will help his people.

Identify Cultural Values Consider the values the epic conveys about the culture that produced it. To pinpoint this cultural context, identify the values the hero embodies and the values he learns to respect on his quest.

3 Epic Conventions

- Review the epic conventions. **Ask** students: Why do epics begin *in media res?*
- Explain that epics were often told orally, and the storyteller needed to capture the listener's interest quickly.
- Point out that the epic usually begins with an opening statement of theme. **Ask** students: Why might this statement of theme be helpful to the listeners?
- Discuss how this statement helps the listener because the epic begins in the middle of the action.

4 Strategies for Reading Epics

- Tell students not to read epics as they would read other poetry. Suggest that students read an epic as they would read a story because an epic tells the tale of a hero's quest. As they read, students may want to keep a log of the main events and the characters to understand more easily the hero's quest.
- Point out that students should pay attention to the importance of the cultural values in an epic and how the epic hero should reflect these values.

5 Critical Viewing

Answer: This scene reflects the qualities of the epic hero in Aeneas' actions. Aeneas is carrying his father in an effortless manner, displaying great strength and courage under terrifying circumstances. His armor and weaponry also reveal that he is a great warrior.

Standard Course of Study

Goal 1: WRITTEN LANGUAGE

WL.1.02.2 Show awareness of culture in personal reflections.

Goal 3: FOUNDATIONS OF ARGUMENT

FA.3.01.3 Develop a framework in which to discuss controversial issues.

Goal 5: LITERATURE

LT.5.01.2 Build knowledge of literary genres, and explore how characteristics apply to literature of world cultures.

LT.5.01.5 Analyze archetypal characters, themes, and settings in world literature.

LT.5.01.7 Understand the cultural and historical impact on text.

Goal 6: GRAMMAR AND USAGE

GU.6.01.2 Analyze author's use of language to demonstrate understanding of expression.

GU.6.01.6 Use correct format for writing.

Step-by-Step Teaching Guide	Pacing Guide
PRETEACH	
• Administer Vocabulary and Reading Warm-ups as necessary.	5 min.
• Engage students' interest with the motivation activity.	5 min.
• Read and discuss author and background features. **FT**	10 min.
• Introduce the Literary Analysis Skill: Archetype: The Hero's Quest. **FT**	5 min.
• Introduce the Reading Strategy: Understanding the Cultural Context.	10 min.
• Prepare students to read by teaching the selection vocabulary. **FT**	
TEACH	
• Informally monitor comprehension while students read independently or in groups. **FT**	30 min.
• Monitor students' comprehension with the Reading Check notes.	as students read
• Reinforce vocabulary with Vocabulary Builder notes.	as students read
• Develop students' understanding of archetype: the hero's quest with the Literary Analysis annotations. **FT**	5 min.
• Develop students' ability to understand the cultural context with the Reading Strategy annotations. **FT**	5 min.
ASSESS/EXTEND	
• Assess students' comprehension and mastery of the Literary Analysis and Reading Strategy by having them answer the Apply the Skills questions. **FT**	15 min.
• Have students complete the Vocabulary Lesson and the Grammar and Style Lesson. **FT**	15 min.
• Apply students' ability to focus on organization by using the Writing Lesson. **FT**	45 min. or homework
• Apply students' understanding by using one or more of the Extend Your Learning activities.	20–90 min. or homework
• Administer Selection Test A or Selection Test B. **FT**	15 min.

Resources

Print

Unit 1 Resources

- Vocabulary Warm-up Word Lists **[L1, L2, EL]** .... p. 7
- Vocabulary Warm-up Practice **[L1, L2, EL]** .... p. 8
- Reading Warm-up A **[L1, L2, EL]** .... p. 9
- Reading Warm-up B **[L1, L2, L3]** .... p. 10

Transparency

Graphic Organizer Transparencies

- Timeline .... p. 253
- Literary Analysis Graphic Organizer A **[L3]** .... p. 3
- Literary Analysis Graphic Organizer B **[L1, L2, EL]** .... p. 4
- Reading Strategy Graphic Organizer A **[L3]** .... p. 1
- Reading Strategy Graphic Organizer B **[L1, L2, EL]** .... p. 2

Print

Reader's Notebook [L2]

Reader's Notebook: Adapted Version [L1]

Reader's Notebook: English Learner's Version [EL]

Unit 1 Resources

- Literary Analysis **[L3]** .... p. 11
- Reading Strategy **[L3]** .... p. 12
- Vocabulary Builder **[L3]** .... p. 13

Technology

Listening to Literature Audio CDs [L2, EL]

Reader's Notebook: Adapted Version Audio CD [L1, L2]

Print

Unit 1 Resources

- Grammar and Style **[L3]** .... p. 14
- Support for Writing Lesson **[L3]** .... p. 15
- Support for Extend Your Learning **[L3]** .... p. 16
- Enrichment **[L4]** .... p. 17
- Selection Test A **[L1, L2, EL]** .... pp. 18–20
- Selection Test B **[L3, L4]** .... pp. 21–23

General Resources

- Rubrics for Exposition: Comparison-and-Contrast Essay .... pp. 53–54
- Rubric for Research: Research Report **[L3]** .... pp. 51–52

Technology

- **Go Online:** Research **[L3]**
- **Go Online:** Self-test **[L3]**
- *ExamView®*, **Test Bank [L3]**

Choosing Resources for Differentiated Instruction

[L1] Special Needs Students

[L2] Below-Level Students

[L3] All Students

[L4] Advanced Students

[EL] English Learners

For Vocabulary and Reading Warm-ups and for Selection Tests, **A** signifies "less challenging" and **B** "more challenging." For Graphic Organizer transparencies, **A** signifies "not filled in" and **B** "filled in."

FT Fast Track Instruction: To move the lesson more quickly, use the strategies and activities identified with **FT**.

Scaffolding for Less Proficient and Advanced Students

The leveled Critical Thinking questions after selections progress in the levels of thinking required to answer them. To address the needs of your different students, you may use the (a) level questions for your less proficient students and the (b) level questions with your on-level and advanced students. The occasional (c) level questions are appropriate for your advanced students.

PRENTICE HALL **TeacherEXPRESS™** Plan · Teach · Assess — Use this complete suite of powerful teaching tools to make lesson planning and testing quicker and easier.

PRENTICE HALL **StudentEXPRESS™** Learn · Study · Succeed — Use the interactive textbook (online and on CD-ROM) to make selections and activities come alive with audio and video support and interactive questions.

Monitoring Progress

Before students read the excerpts from *The Epic of Gilgamesh*, administer **Diagnostic Test 1** (***Unit 1 Resources*, pp. 2–4**). This test will determine students' level of readiness for the reading and vocabulary skills.

For: Information about Lexiles
Visit: www.PHSchool.com
Web Code: eue-1111

PRETEACH

Motivation

Ask students to think about heroes of today and of earlier times. What qualities make these people heroes? How are heroes of the past different from those of the present? After students share their ideas, tell them that they are going to read about a hero of very early times, one of the world's first heroes ever to be the subject of a literary work.

❶ Background

More About the Selection

Although this translation of the epic is in prose, the original epic consists mostly of long, unrhymed lines of poetry, divided in half by a caesura, or pause. Each half-line contains two beats, or stresses. The following is an excerpt of a scholarly translation of the poem by E. A. Speiser that gives some idea of its original form. The bracketed material indicates portions of the tablet where the cuneiform cannot be clearly read:

The [hi]dden he saw, [laid bare]
the undisclosed

He brought report of before the
Flood,

Achieved a long journey, weary
and [w]orn.

Although few people in ancient Mesopotamia could read this poem, it is probable that a wider, less-educated audience heard versions of the poem recited.

Geography Note

Draw students' attention to the map at the top of the page. Remind them that ancient Mesopotamia, the region in which *The Epic of Gilgamesh* takes place, is mostly the present-day nation of Iraq. Point out that the dry climate is the reason the sun-baked clay tablets of cuneiform writing survived over the centuries.

Build Skills | Epic

from The Epic of Gilgamesh ❶

The Gilgamesh Epic A long narrative poem named for a Sumerian king who lived between 2700 and 2500 B.C., the Gilgamesh epic describes an era about twenty-three times more distant from us than our own Revolutionary War. Its concerns, however, are timeless and universal: how to become known and respected, how to cope with the loss of a dear friend, and how to accept one's own inevitable death. It is also an action-packed story, featuring battles, gods and goddesses, heroes, tests of strength and wisdom, and arduous journeys.

How the Epic Endured Stories about King Gilgamesh were told and handed down by Sumerians for hundreds of years after his death. By the twenty-first century B.C., however, these tales existed in written form. When the Babylonians conquered the Sumerians soon afterward, they inherited the Sumerian cultural tradition. A Babylonian author, borrowing from some of these tales, created the start of the unified *Gilgamesh* epic that we have today. Other Babylonian writers modified the epic, adding the prologue and the flood story and emphasizing the friendship between Gilgamesh and Enkidu. Most important, these writers gave the narrative its central theme: the search for immortality. By the seventh century B.C., a written version was included in the library of the Assyrian king Ashurbanipal.

After the fall of Babylonia, the written epic was lost. The story survived only in folklore until archaeologists excavated Ashurbanipal's library in the mid-1880s. They discovered the poem on clay tablets in cuneiform, the wedge-shaped writing used by the Babylonians. Archaeologists were especially excited by the portion of the epic describing a great flood, an account remarkably similar to the story of Noah and the ark in the Bible.

The Story of "The Arrogant King" As the story begins, Gilgamesh is king of Uruk, an ancient Sumerian city. He is an arrogant king who is eager for fame. Periodically, the gods and goddesses intervene in his life to provide challenges, obstacles, and challenging tests of Gilgamesh's mettle. The goddess Aruru creates Enkidu to provide such a challenge to Gilgamesh. Enkidu begins his life as a wild man who lives on friendly terms with gazelles and other beasts. He confronts Gilgamesh just as the king is about to claim certain rights that anger the men of Uruk. Gilgamesh and Enkidu become engaged in a heated wrestling match, which Gilgamesh wins after a hard-fought battle with his opponent. In spite of the contentious start to their relationship, the two men become close friends.

A Name for Himself As he searches to make a name for himself, the king battles the giant Humbaba, the Bull of Heaven, as well as lions that he encounters along a great journey. Worried about his mortality, Gilgamesh goes in search of everlasting life. He seeks out Utnapishtim, the sole survivor of a great flood that had destroyed humanity centuries before. On his quest, Gilgamesh has many adventures. He passes through the mysterious Mount Mashu, guarded by Man-Scorpions, and crosses the waters of death with the ferryman, Urshanabi. Gilgamesh seeks immortality, but instead he learns that, for him, there is no permanence. Sometime later, Gilgamesh dies and is lamented by his people. Death, then, completes the cycle of life.

Preview

Connecting to the Literature

You may have tried to imagine what it would mean to live forever. The hero of *Gilgamesh* can think of nothing else. He is desperate to find the one man who has the secret to everlasting life.

❷ Literary Analysis

Archetype: The Hero's Quest

An **archetype** is a basic plot, character, symbol, or idea that recurs in the literature of many cultures. One archetype is the **hero's quest,** a plot in which an extraordinary person goes on a difficult journey or mission. The hero may search for a person, place, or object of value; the answer to a problem or puzzling question; or some other kind of special knowledge.

In *Gilgamesh,* a heroic king searches for the secret of immortality. As you read, think about why Gilgamesh might want that knowledge.

Connecting Literary Elements

Part of telling a quest story is providing details about the extraordinary person at the center of the action. **Characterization** is the means by which characters are created and developed. Authors reveal characters' personalities through direct statements; through characters' actions, speech, and thoughts; or through descriptive details. Look for these methods of characterization in *Gilgamesh.*

❸ Reading Strategy

Understanding the Cultural Context

Gilgamesh was a real Sumerian king, and learning about the culture in which he lived—and in which his story grew and changed—will illuminate this work. Follow these steps to help you **understand the cultural context:**

- Before you read, use the unit introduction on pages 2–11 to get an overview of Sumerian and Babylonian civilization.
- As you read the selection, look for details about the way people lived, worked, and believed. For example, notice the writing materials, the agriculture, and the powers of the gods.
- On a chart like the one shown, record details that provide clues to the culture that created this epic.

Detail

The gods gave Gilgamesh beauty and courage.

↓

What It Suggests About the Culture

Gods provided physical and emotional qualities to humans.

Vocabulary Builder

immolation (im´ ə lā´ shən) *n.* offering or killing made as a sacrifice (p. 20)

succor (suk´ ər) *n.* aid; relief (p. 20)

somber (säm´ bər) *adj.* dark; gloomy (p. 23)

incantation (in´ kan tā´ shən) *n.* chant (p. 24)

ecstasy (ek´ stə sē) *n.* great joy (p. 24)

teemed (tēmd) *v.* was full of; swarmed (p. 25)

babel (bab´ əl) *n.* confusion of voices or sounds (p. 25)

subsided (səb sīd´ ed) *v.* settled; lessened; died down (p. 27)

NC Standard Course of Study

- Analyze archetypal characters, themes, and settings in world literature. (LT.5.01.5)
- Understand the cultural and historical impact on text. (LT.5.01.7)

❷ Literary Analysis

Archetype: The Hero's Quest

- Read aloud the Literary Analysis instruction. Make sure that students understand that a quest is a journey in search of something.
- Explain that the term *archetype* contains the Greek root *-arch-*, which means "first" or "main." Tell students that an *archetype* is a "main type" that reoccurs in literature.
- Have students identify modern heroes engaged in quests. For instance, in the film *Raiders of the Lost Ark,* Indiana Jones searches for the Ark of the Covenant. As students cite examples, have them explain why those making the quests are considered heroes.

❸ Reading Strategy

Understanding the Cultural Context

- After students have read the Reading Strategy instruction, clarify that a work's cultural context is the culture in which the work is produced and/or in which it takes place.
- Have students brainstorm additional examples of the cultural context from this epic (for example, jobs, cities, education, and transportation).
- Then, call their attention to the graphic organizer. Give students this example detail: The center of a Sumerian city was a temple. Tell students that the detail suggests the importance of religion to this culture.
- Give students a copy of **Reading Strategy Graphic Organizer A** in ***Graphic Organizer Transparencies,*** p. 1. Have them use it to chart cultural details as they read.

Vocabulary Builder

- Pronounce each vocabulary word for students, and read the definitions as a class. Have students identify any words with which they are already familiar.

Differentiated Instruction Solutions for All Learners

Support for Special Needs Students

Have students read the adapted version of "The Death of Enkidu" in the ***Reader's Notebook: Adapted Version.*** This version provides basic-level instruction in an interactive format with questions and write-on lines. Completing these pages will prepare students to read the selection in the Student Edition.

Support for Less Proficient Readers

Have students read "The Death of Enkidu" in the ***Reader's Notebook.*** This version provides basic-level instruction in an interactive format with questions and write-on lines. After students finish the selection in the ***Reader's Notebook,*** have them complete the questions and activities in the Student Edition.

Support for English Learners

Have students read "The Death of Enkidu" in the ***Reader's Notebook: English Learner's Version.*** This version provides basic-level instruction in an interactive format with questions and write-on lines. Completing these pages will prepare students to read the selection in the Student Edition.

TEACH

Facilitate Understanding

Discuss with students whether a relationship begun in rivalry could turn into friendship. Tell students to consider, as they read, the origins and strength of the friendship between Gilgamesh and Enkidu.

❶ About the Selection

One of the world's oldest written works of literature, *The Epic of Gilgamesh* tells of a hero's quest for fame, knowledge, and immortality. Gilgamesh is an ancient Sumerian king who, in this excerpt, slays a giant named Humbaba and loses his best friend, Enkidu.

❷ Humanities

Relief Sculpture of King Gilgamesh, c. 725 B.C.

A relief is a sculpture carved into a background, such as the exterior or interior wall of an important building. Created by the Assyrians (a later people in the area), the sculpture on this page is from a relief at the palace of the ruler Sargon II at Khorsabad. It depicts King Gilgamesh as a colossus, or giant figure, holding a lion.

Use the following question to initiate discussion:

What qualities of Gilgamesh can you infer from this depiction of him as a colossus?
Possible responses: The depiction stresses Gilgamesh's power, size, high rank, and importance in history.

❸ Critical Viewing

Possible response: Gilgamesh has the body of a man but his ability to master a lion is godlike.

❶ *from* The Epic of Gilgamesh

translated by
N. K. Sandars

❷ 

Background *Gilgamesh* is a story shaped by centuries of storytellers who lived in ancient Mesopotamia, a region between the Tigris and Euphrates rivers. Life in the desert region was simultaneously subject to poverty and plenty, opportunity and danger. Frequent floods enriched the soil, but they were also violent and unpredictable. The flat terrain left cities open to invaders. Ancient Near-Eastern religion reflected the insecurities of life in the region. For Mesopotamians, the underworld was a dreary, inhospitable place, and the quarreling, all-too-human gods had absolute control over human destiny.

The hero's quest is a theme found in the literature of many peoples. Usually, the hero must suffer a number of ordeals in the course of this search, yet this suffering leads to a special knowledge or understanding that could not otherwise have been gained. Gilgamesh's bravery, both during his journey and in battle, was legendary; such a role model may have been exceedingly necessary in a culture and time of tribal invasions. Nonetheless, accounts of this famous king—two thirds a god and one third a man—and his quest for everlasting life may have served as a lesson in accepting one's mortality for generations of listeners.

❸ Critical Viewing ▶ In this statue of Gilgamesh holding a lion, which details reflect the legend that Gilgamesh was two thirds a god and one third a man? **[Explain]**

Differentiated Instruction Solutions for All Learners

Accessibility at a Glance

	from The Epic of Gilgamesh
Context	Culture of Ancient Sumeria
Language	Formal with complex syntax; challenging vocabulary and pronunciation of characters' unfamiliar names
Concept Level	Accessible (Rivalry, friendship, and a hero's quest for fame, knowledge, and immortality)
Literary Merit	Heroic epic
Lexile	1100L
Overall Rating	More challenging

Prologue

4 I will proclaim to the world the deeds of Gilgamesh. This was the man to whom all things were known; this was the king who knew the countries of the world. He was wise, he saw mysteries and knew secret things, he brought us a tale of the days before the flood. He went on a long journey, was weary, worn-out with labor, returning he rested, he engraved on a stone the whole story.

When the gods created Gilgamesh they gave him a perfect body. Shamash the glorious sun endowed him with beauty, Adad the god of the storm endowed him with courage, the great gods made his beauty perfect, surpassing all others, terrifying like a great wild bull. Two thirds they made him god and one third man.

5 In Uruk he built walls, a great rampart, and the temple of blessed Eanna[1] for the god of the firmament Anu, and for Ishtar the goddess of love. Look at it still today: the outer wall where the cornice runs, it shines with the brilliance of copper; and the inner wall, it has no equal. Touch the threshold, it is ancient. Approach Eanna the dwelling of Ishtar, our lady of love and war, the like of which no latter-day king, no man alive can equal. Climb upon the wall of Uruk; walk along it, I say; regard the foundation terrace and examine the masonry: is it not burnt brick and good? The seven sages[2] laid the foundations.

The Battle With Humbaba

When the people of Uruk complain about Gilgamesh's arrogance, the goddess Aruru creates Enkidu to contend with the king and absorb his energies. At first, Enkidu lives like a wild animal and has no contact with other humans. Later, he enters Uruk, loses a wrestling match to Gilgamesh, and becomes his faithful friend. Then the two set off to destroy Humbaba, the giant who guards the cedar forest. As Gilgamesh prepares for battle, Enkidu expresses his fears.

1. **In Uruk . . . Eanna** Uruk was an important city in southern Babylonia, with temples to the gods Anu and Ishtar. Eanna was the temple site where these gods were worshiped.
2. **seven sages** legendary wise men who civilized Mesopotamia's seven oldest cities.

Literary Analysis
Archetype: The Hero's Quest What hints does the Prologue give about Gilgamesh's quest?

Reading Strategy
Understanding the Cultural Context What can you conclude about life in Gilgamesh's day from the importance placed on the rampart, or defensive wall, and other city walls?

Reading Check 6
Why does the goddess Aruru create Enkidu?

Differentiated Instruction — Solutions for All Learners

Strategy for Less Proficient Readers
To give students a context for the story and to model how to recognize and understand that context, give them a copy of **Reading Skill Graphic Organizer B** in ***Graphic Organizer Transparencies,*** p. 2. The completed graphic organizer will give students insight into the process of understanding cultural context. They can use it as a model for independently identifying cultural details as they read.

Strategy for English Learners
Lead a quick "selection tour" before students read, focusing their attention on the selection title and subtitles, illustrations, questions and vocabulary in the side margins, Reading Check questions, and footnotes. Also point out the italicized summaries beneath each subtitle and explain that these tell readers what has happened before the episode begins.

4 Literary Analysis
Archetype: The Hero's Quest

- Remind students that the hero's quest is a literary plot in which an extraordinary person goes on an extraordinary mission.
- Ask a volunteer to read aloud the bracketed passage. Then, **ask** the Literary Analysis question: What hints does the Prologue give about Gilgamesh's quest?
  Answer: The Prologue hints that Gilgamesh will see mysteries, gain knowledge of the world's secrets, and go on a long, exhausting journey.
- Read aloud the second paragraph of the Prologue. Have students **consider** how Gilgamesh is characterized as an extraordinary person.
  Possible response: Gilgamesh is physically perfect and possesses great courage and strength.

5 Reading Strategy
Understanding the Cultural Context

- Review with students how understanding cultural context will enhance their understanding of a story.
- Tell them to look for details about the way people lived as you read aloud the bracketed passage.
- Encourage students to use the description in the Prologue to visualize the rampart, or protective walls. Explain that the purpose of the rampart is to protect the city from a military attack.
- **Ask** students the Reading Strategy question: What can you conclude about life in Gilgamesh's day from the importance placed on the rampart, or defensive wall, and other city walls?
  Possible responses: Walls were used for military defense; warfare was frequent; defense of the city was important.

6 Reading Check

Answer: Aruru created Enkidu to curb Gilgamesh's arrogance. Enkidu "absorb[ed]" Gilgamesh's "energies" and was someone with whom Gilgamesh could "contend."

7 Literary Analysis

Archetype: The Hero's Quest and Characterization

- Have students independently read the bracketed passage. Explain that Gilgamesh is responding to Enkidu's concerns about the danger of fighting Humbaba.
- **Ask** students: What is Gilgamesh predicting when he says that immolation and sacrifice are not yet for him?
  Answer: Gilgamesh is predicting that he will not die in this battle.
- **Ask** students the first Literary Analysis question: According to Gilgamesh, what character traits are required to battle a fierce enemy like Humbaba?
  Possible response: Traits required to battle Humbaba include strength of purpose, determination, courage, power, and confidence.

Monitor Progress Have students explain what a hero does on a quest and what makes this literary element archetypal. Then, **ask** students why the battle with Humbaba is an archetypal quest.
Answer: The hero goes on an important mission or journey. The quest is archetypal because such quests recur in literature.

8 Literary Analysis

Archetype: The Hero's Quest and Characterization

- Have students read the bracketed passage.
- Explain that Shamash is one of the gods whom Gilgamesh worships. **Ask** students what Gilgamesh wants Shamash to do.
  Answer: Gilgamesh wants Shamash to keep him safe and help him win the battle with Humbaba.
- **Ask** the second Literary Analysis question: What do Gilgamesh's calls to Shamash—and Shamash's tremendous response—reveal about Gilgamesh's own powers and their limitations?
  Possible response: Gilgamesh sometimes needs the help of powerful forces.

Then Enkidu, the faithful companion, pleaded, answering him, "O my lord, you do not know this monster and that is the reason you are not afraid. I who know him, I am terrified. His teeth are dragon's fangs, his countenance is like a lion, his charge is the rushing of the flood, with his look he crushes alike the trees of the forest and reeds in the swamp. O my lord, you may go on if you choose into this land, but I will go back to the city. I will tell the lady your mother all your glorious deeds till she shouts for joy: and then I will tell the death that followed till she weeps for bitterness." But Gilgamesh said, "Immolation and sacrifice are not yet for me, the boat of the dead[3] shall not go down, nor the three-ply cloth be cut for my shrouding. Not yet will my people be desolate, nor the pyre be lit in my house and my dwelling burnt on the
7 fire. Today, give me your aid and you shall have mine: what then can go amiss with us two? All living creatures born of the flesh shall sit at last in the boat of the West, and when it sinks, when the boat of Magilum sinks, they are gone; but we shall go forward and fix our eyes on this monster. If your heart is fearful throw away fear; if there is terror in it throw away terror. Take your ax in your hand and attack. He who leaves the fight unfinished is not at peace."

Humbaba came out from his strong house of cedar. Then Enkidu called out, "O Gilgamesh, remember now your boasts in Uruk. Forward, attack, son of Uruk, there is nothing to fear." When he heard these words his courage rallied; he answered, "Make haste, close in, if the watchman is there do not let him escape to the woods where he will vanish. He has put on the first of his seven splendors but not yet the other six, let us trap him before he is armed." Like a raging wild bull he snuffed the ground; the watchman of the woods turned full of threatenings, he cried out. Humbaba came from his strong house of cedar. He nodded his head and shook it, menacing Gilgamesh; and on him he fastened his eye, the eye of death. Then Gilgamesh called to Shamash and his tears were flowing, "O glorious Shamash, I have followed the road you commanded but now if you send no succor how shall I escape?" Glorious Shamash heard his prayer and he summoned the
8 great wind, the north wind, the whirlwind, the storm and the icy wind, the tempest and the scorching wind; they came like dragons, like a scorching fire, like a serpent that freezes the heart, a destroying flood and the lightning's fork. The eight winds rose up against Humbaba, they beat against his eyes; he was gripped, unable to go forward or back. Gilgamesh shouted, "By the life of Ninsun my mother and divine Lugulbanda my father, in the Country of the Living, in this Land I have discovered your dwelling; my weak arms and my small weapons I have brought to this Land against you, and now I will enter your house."

So he felled the first cedar and they cut the branches and laid them at the foot of the mountain. At the first stroke Humbaba blazed out, but still they advanced. They felled seven cedars and cut and bound the

Vocabulary Builder
immolation (im´ ə lā´ shən) *n.* offering or killing made as a sacrifice

Literary Analysis
Archetype: The Hero's Quest and Characterization According to Gilgamesh, what character traits are required to battle a fierce enemy like Humbaba?

Vocabulary Builder
succor (suk´ ər) *n.* aid; relief

Literary Analysis
Archetype: The Hero's Quest and Characterization What do Gilgamesh's calls to Shamash—and Shamash's tremendous response—reveal about Gilgamesh's own powers and their limitations?

3. **boat of the dead** ceremonial boat on which the dead were placed.

Enrichment

The Cedars of Lebanon

The illustration on these two pages shows a cedar forest like the one where Humbaba lives. Cedars are pinelike evergreen trees known for their fine wood and strong fragrance. The cedar forest in the early Sumerian tales of Gilgamesh was probably located in the mountains northeast of the city of Uruk. However, in the full-length Babylonian epic that students are reading, the cedar forest is associated with the Cedars of Lebanon, which are famous trees in the Mount Lebanon area west of Mesopotamia.

The battle with Humbaba probably reflects Gilgamesh's desire to gain control of valuable woodland. In the dry, open environment of the Middle East, a forest would be an extremely valuable holding, even though most scholars believe that there were more forests in the region during that time period than there are today. In fact, one likely reason for the fall of ancient Sumer was deforestation, or extensive cutting down of forests. This led to an increase in desert conditions and an eventual loss of prosperity.

branches and laid them at the foot of the mountain, and seven times Humbaba loosed his glory on them. As the seventh blaze died out they reached his lair. He slapped his thigh in scorn. He approached like a noble wild bull roped on the mountain, a warrior whose elbows are bound together. The tears started to his eyes and he was pale, "Gilgamesh, let me speak. I have never known a mother, no, nor a father who reared me. I was born of the mountain, he reared me, and Enlil
9 made me the keeper of this forest. Let me go free, Gilgamesh, and I will be your servant, you shall be my lord; all the trees of the forest that I tended on the mountain shall be yours. I will cut them down and build you a palace." He took him by the hand and led him to his house, so that the heart of Gilgamesh was moved with compassion. He swore by the heavenly life, by the earthly life, by the underworld itself: "O Enkidu, should not the snared bird return to its nest and the captive man return to his mother's arms?" Enkidu answered, "The strongest of men will fall to fate if he has no judgment. Namtar, the evil
10 fate that knows no distinction between men, will devour him. If the snared bird returns to its nest, if the captive man returns to his mother's arms, then you my friend will never return to the city where the mother is waiting who gave you birth. He will bar the mountain road against you, and make the pathways impassable."

Humbaba said, "Enkidu, what you have spoken is evil: you, a hireling, dependent for your bread! In envy and for fear of a rival you have spoken

Reading Check 11
Which god helps Gilgamesh in the battle against Humbaba?

9 Critical Thinking

Infer

- Ask a volunteer to read aloud Humbaba's speech in the bracketed passage. Encourage the student to imbue it with the emotions that he or she thinks Humbaba would be feeling.
- **Ask** students to infer the chief emotion that Humbaba feels.
  Answer: The chief emotion Humbaba feels is fear.

10 Critical Thinking

Compare and Contrast

- Have one student read Gilgamesh's question and another student read Enkidu's response in the bracketed passage. Then, **ask** students to contrast the two men's attitudes.
  Answer: Gilgamesh seems willing to grant Humbaba mercy, but Enkidu argues that showing the monster mercy would endanger Gilgamesh's life.
- **Ask** students to compare and contrast Gilgamesh and Enkidu on the basis of the bracketed passage.
  Possible responses: Gilgamesh is more trusting, and Enkidu is more suspicious; Gilgamesh is bolder, and Enkidu is more cautious; Gilgamesh is more compassionate than Enkidu.
- Invite students to compare and contrast Gilgamesh's dilemma with similar leadership choices today. Elicit from students that leaders or public policy makers are, like Gilgamesh, often torn between the desire to be compassionate and the need to administer justice, or between the hope of achieving safety by improving relations with former enemies and the fear that security can be achieved only through harsh measures.

11 Reading Check

Answer: Shamash, the sun god, helps Gilgamesh.

Differentiated Instruction

Solutions for All Learners

Enrichment for Gifted/Talented Students

Remind students that *The Epic of Gilgamesh* was originally written in cuneiform. Have students use the Internet or library resources to research the subject of cuneiform writing. Then, have them create five of their own cuneiform-style symbols, each representing a term present in the text. For example, they might create a cuneiform symbol for the word "cedar." Students can pool their symbols to fashion a single-sentence summary of the selections.

Enrichment for Advanced Readers

Organize students in small groups. Have each group draw a historical map of the Middle East that includes the ancient area of Mesopotamia, the Tigris and Euphrates Rivers, and other places mentioned in the selection. Then, have groups show on a clear overlay the same area with modern-day place names. Have students consult reliable sources to find the locations of ancient places and their modern locales. Groups should present their final work to the class.

12 Literature in Context

Ancient Gods and Goddesses
At one time the Sumerians believed Anu, the god of the heavens, to be the greatest god; however, his supreme position was eventually taken over by Enlil, god of the air. Anu was worshiped primarily at Uruk, Gilgamesh's city.

Connect to the Literature
Encourage students to give at least two examples with an explanation for each.
Possible responses: *Aruru:* The goddess creates Enkidu to help tone down Gilgamesh's arrogance, but then Enkidu becomes a faithful companion and helps Gilgamesh in the battle against Humbaba. *Shamash:* The sun god sends a violent storm of strong winds that weaken Humbaba and help Gilgamesh avoid being killed.

13 Critical Thinking

Evaluate

- Read aloud the bracketed passage.
- **Ask** students: Do you think Gilgamesh was right to heed Enkidu and ignore Humbaba's pleas for mercy? Why or why not?
  Possible responses: Gilgamesh is right because Humbaba is evil and not to be trusted; Gilgamesh is wrong because the powerful god Enlil champions Humbaba and now may seek revenge on Gilgamesh and his people.

14 Humanities

Sculpture of the God Abu,
c. 2700–2600 B.C.

This sculpture depicting the Sumerian god Abu, the lord of vegetation, is from the Sumerian early dynastic period. The gesture of clasped hands offering a cup is a typical sign of religious devotion.

Use the following questions to initiate discussion:

- What can you conclude about men's facial hair and hair styles in ancient Sumer?
  Possible response: Men often wore beards and long hair.
- What do you find unusual about the sculpture?
  Possible response: The huge eyes are unusual.

evil words." Enkidu said, "Do not listen, Gilgamesh: this Humbaba must die. Kill Humbaba first and his servants after." But Gilgamesh said, "If we touch him the blaze and the glory of light will be put out in confusion, the glory and glamour will vanish, its rays will be quenched." Enkidu said to Gilgamesh, "Not so, my friend. First entrap the bird, and where shall the chicks run then? Afterwards we can search out the glory and the glamour, when the chicks run distracted through the grass."

13 Gilgamesh listened to the word of his companion, he took the ax in his hand, he drew the sword from his belt, and he struck Humbaba with a thrust of the sword to the neck, and Enkidu his comrade struck the second blow. At the third blow Humbaba fell. Then there followed confusion for this was the guardian of the forest whom they had felled to the ground. For as far as two leagues the cedars shivered when Enkidu felled the watcher of the forest, he at whose voice Hermon and Lebanon used to tremble. Now the mountains were moved and all the hills, for the guardian of the forest was killed. They attacked the cedars, the seven splendors of Humbaba were extinguished. So they pressed on into the forest bearing the sword of eight talents.[4] They uncovered the sacred dwellings of the Anunnaki[5] and while Gilgamesh felled the first of the trees of the forest Enkidu cleared their roots as far as the banks of Euphrates.[6] They set Humbaba before the gods, before Enlil; they kissed the ground and dropped the shroud and set the head before him. When he saw the head of Humbaba, Enlil raged at them. "Why did you do this thing? From henceforth may the fire be on your faces, may it eat the bread that you eat, may it drink where you drink." Then Enlil took again the blaze and the seven splendors that had been Humbaba's: he gave the first to the river, and he gave to the lion, to the stone of execration[7] to the mountain and to the dreaded daughter of the Queen of Hell.

O Gilgamesh, king and conqueror of the dreadful blaze; wild bull who plunders the mountain, who crosses the sea, glory to him, and from the brave the greater glory is Enki's![8]

14

---

4. **talents** large units of weight and money used in the ancient world.
5. **Anunnaki** gods of the underworld.
6. **Euphrates** (yo͞o frāt′ ēz) river flowing from eastern Turkey generally southeastward through Syria and Iraq.
7. **execration** (ek′ si krā′ shən) *n.* cursing, denunciation.
8. **Enki's** belonging to Enki, god of wisdom and one of the creators of human beings.

Literature in Context

Cultural Connection

12 ***Ancient Gods and Goddesses***
The Babylonians adopted much of the religion of the ancient Sumerians, including their gods and goddesses, though they often used different names for them. Listed below are some of the gods and goddesses mentioned in *Gilgamesh:*

- **Adad** (ā′ dad): god of storms and weather
- **Anunnaki** (ä no͞o nä′ kē): Anu's sons, gods of the underworld
- **Anu** (ā′ no͞o): father of gods; the god of the heavens
- **Aruru** (ä ro͝o′ ro͞o): goddess of creation
- **Ea** (ā′ ä), also called **Enki** (eŋ′ kē): god of waters and wisdom
- **Enlil** (en lil′): god of earth, wind, air, and agriculture
- **Irkalla** (ir kä′ lə), also called **Ereshkigal** (er esh kē′ gäl): queen of the underworld
- **Ishtar** (ish′ tär): goddess of love and war; patron goddess of the city of Uruk
- **Namtar** (näm′ tär): god of evil fate
- **Ninurta** (nə nʉr′ tə): god of war wells, and irrigation
- **Samuqan** (säm′ o͞o kän): god of cattle
- **Shamash** (shä′ mäsh): the sun god; also a lawgiver
- **Siduri** (sə do͞o′rē): goddess of wine

Connect to the Literature

Which of these gods or goddesses have the most impact on the characters in *Gilgamesh?*

Enrichment

Political Leaders

Gilgamesh appears to have been a great leader of his people and embraced by them as a hero. Yet the people's feelings about their leaders mattered little in ancient Sumer, where rulers were not elected. It is only in modern democracies that people are able to choose their leaders. Doing so is a great responsibility, and citizens of a democracy should weigh carefully the qualities they want in a leader.

The Death of Enkidu

15 *Gilgamesh rejects the advances of Ishtar, goddess of love. In revenge, she brings the mighty Bull of Heaven down to threaten Uruk. Gilgamesh and Enkidu kill the bull, but Enkidu dreams that the gods have decreed his death for helping to slaughter the bull and Humbaba. Enkidu is furious at his fate until Shamash, the sun god, allays some of his anger. Then Enkidu describes another dream about death.*

As Enkidu slept alone in his sickness, in bitterness of spirit he poured out his heart to his friend. "It was I who cut down the cedar, I who leveled the forest, I who slew Humbaba and now see what has become of me. Listen, my friend, this is the dream I dreamed last night. The heavens roared, and earth rumbled back an answer; between them stood I before an awful being, the somber-faced man-bird; he had directed on me his purpose. His was a vampire face, his foot was a lion's foot, his hand was an eagle's talon. He fell on me and his claws were in my hair, he held me fast and I smothered; then he transformed me so that my arms became wings covered with feathers. He turned his stare towards me, and he led me away to the palace of Irkalla, the Queen of Darkness, to the house from which none who enters ever returns, down the road from which there is no coming back.

"There is the house whose people sit in darkness; dust is their food and clay their meat. They are clothed like birds with wings for covering, they see no light, they sit in darkness. I entered the house of dust and I saw the kings of the earth, their crowns put away for ever; rulers and princes, all those who once wore kingly crowns and ruled the world in the days of old. They who had stood in the place of the gods like Anu and Enlil, stood now like servants to fetch baked meats in the house of dust, to carry cooked meat and cold water from the water-skin. In the

Vocabulary Builder
somber (säm´ bər) *adj.* dark; gloomy

Reading Check 16
According to Enkidu, what actions resulted in dreams about his own death?

17

18 ◀ **Critical Viewing**
Which details in this crown make it a worthy symbol for a king? **[Speculate]**

15 Critical Thinking

Cause and Effect

- **Ask** a volunteer to read aloud the bracketed passage. Have students state the cause or reason that the Bull of Heaven comes to threaten Uruk.
  Answer: Because Gilgamesh rejects Ishtar's advances, she sends the bull to menace the city.
- **Ask** how the appearance of the Bull of Heaven leads to Enkidu's dreams of his own death.
  Answer: Ishtar and other gods send Enkidu those dreams partly because he helps Gilgamesh kill the bull.
- Have a student **describe** Enkidu's initial reaction to the dreams of his own death and explain why he might react that way.
  Possible response: Enkidu recognizes that the dreams foretell his doom, and he is angry about it. He may feel that way because he finds it unfair that he should be punished for helping save Uruk from the bull.

16 Reading Check

Answer: Enkidu believes that his dreams are the result of his cutting down the cedar forest and killing Humbaba.

17 Humanities

Gold Crown,
c. first century B.C.–first century A.D.

This gold crown was taken from the excavations of the necropolis at Tilya Tepe, Afghanistan. This area is far to the northeast of Mesopotamia.

Use the following question for discussion:

Why do you think crowns were made of gold?
Possible responses: Gold made the crowns sparkle in the sun; gold was valuable, worthy of kings.

18 Critical Viewing

Possible response: The crown's ornate workmanship and its being made of gold make it a worthy symbol for a king.

Differentiated Instruction
Solutions for All Learners

Support for Special Needs Students
Students may struggle with the concept of cultural context. To aid their comprehension, have them read along with the recording on **Listening to Literature Audio CDs.** After they listen, point out that Gilgamesh and Enkidu's behavior when they offer Humbaba's head to Enlil shows how the people of this culture relate to the gods. Then ask students to share any other ideas they may have about the cultural context. Encourage them to add details that depict this culture in their graphic organizer.

Enrichment for Advanced Readers
Explain that the ancient Sumerians viewed the underworld as a bleak place, where little distinction was made between those who did evil on Earth and those who did good. Then, have students find out more about ancient religious beliefs in an afterlife or underworld and compare and contrast their findings with the descriptions in this section. Have students conduct research using online sites or printed sources.

ASSESS

Answers

1. **Possible response:** Gilgamesh's courage, strength, and dedication is admirable, but he may be too trusting and lacking in wisdom.
2. (a) Gilgamesh is two thirds god and one third man. (b) **Possible responses:** The combination might make Gilgamesh arrogant; it might make him yearn for the immortality that only gods have; it might allow him to call on the gods for help.
3. (a) Aruru creates Enkidu to curb Gilgamesh's arrogance. (b) **Possible response:** Gilgamesh and Enkidu become friends because they share qualities such as strength and courage and because they admire each other.
4. (a) Enkidu tells Gilgamesh that Humbaba is a dangerous monster. (b) Gilgamesh does not fear death, although he thinks it will not come as a result of his fight with Humbaba.
5. (a) Humbaba has used cedar to build his house. (b) Cedar trees were a valuable and sought-after resource in the Sumerian culture.
6. (a) With the help of Shamash, the sun god, Gilgamesh and Enkidu cut down trees, enter Humbaba's house, and debate whether to kill him. Gilgamesh considers granting Humbaba mercy, but Enkidu talks him out of it. They then kill Humbaba. (b) **Possible response:** Enkidu is more cautious, more practical, less favored by the gods, and perhaps less civilized than Gilgamesh.
7. (a) **Possible response:** Enkidu will die, causing Gilgamesh to fear for his life. (b) **Possible response:** Enkidu's vision of the afterlife and Gilgamesh's attitude about death support this conclusion.
8. (a) **Possible response:** Gilgamesh's wisdom, courage, and ability to protect his people make him an effective leader. He is less effective when he is absent too long or relies too much on physical strength. (b) **Possible response:** Like other leaders, Gilgamesh listens to the advice of people around him; unlike other leaders, much of Gilgamesh's power comes from his physical strength.

house of dust which I entered were high priests and acolytes[9] priests of the incantation and of ecstasy; there were servers of the temple, and there was Etana, that king of Kish whom the eagle carried to heaven in the days of old. I saw also Samuqan, god of cattle, and there was Ereshkigal the Queen of the Underworld; and Belit-Sheri squatted in front of her, she who is recorder of the gods and keeps the book of death. She held a tablet from which she read. She raised her head, she saw me and spoke: 'Who has brought this one here?' Then I awoke like a man drained of blood who wanders alone in a waste of rushes; like one whom the bailiff[10] has seized and his heart pounds with terror."

Vocabulary Builder

incantation (in′ kan tā′ shən) *n.* chant

ecstasy (ek′ stə sē) *n.* great joy

9. **acolytes** (ak′ ə līts′) *n.* attendants; faithful followers.
10. **bailiff** (bāl′ if) *n.* court officer; law officer.

Critical Reading

1. **Respond:** Is Gilgamesh the kind of hero that you admire? Why or why not?
2. **(a) Recall:** According to the Prologue, what combination of god and man is Gilgamesh? **(b) Analyze Cause and Effect:** How might this combination affect him as a leader?
3. **(a) Recall:** Why does the goddess Aruru create Enkidu? **(b) Infer:** Why do you think Enkidu and Gilgamesh eventually become good friends?
4. **(a) Recall:** Before the battle, what does Enkidu tell Gilgamesh about Humbaba? **(b) Interpret:** In his response, what attitude does Gilgamesh display toward death?
5. **(a) Recall:** What material has Humbaba used to build his house? **(b) Draw Conclusions:** What do the repeated references to cedar trees and Humbaba's offer of them in exchange for his life suggest about their value to this culture?
6. **(a) Summarize:** Summarize the battle with Humbaba, and identify Enkidu's role in it. **(b) Compare and Contrast:** What differences between Gilgamesh and Enkidu does the battle reveal?
7. **(a) Speculate:** What do you think will happen to Enkidu, and how do you think Gilgamesh will react? **(b) Support:** Which details led you to this conclusion?
8. **(a) Evaluate:** How effective is Gilgamesh as a leader? **(b) Apply:** In what way is he both like and unlike other strong leaders you have seen or read about?

Enrichment

The Latin Root *-cant-*

Enkidu dreams of "priests of the incantation." *Incantation* contains the Latin root *-cant-*, which means "song." The root appears not only in English but also in Spanish, Italian, and French. In French the sound and spelling change—the Latin /k/ sound, spelled *c,* becomes a /sh/ sound, spelled *ch,* as in the word *chanteuse,* French (and now also English) for a female singer. In words with this root borrowed earlier from French, the French /sh/ sound often turns into the English /ch/: *chant, enchant.*

The root appears in several English words related to music and literature. For example, a *cantor* is a synagogue official who sings liturgical music or a church choir leader; in English, a *canto,* from the Italian for "song," refers to a poem division; French fables—and their English versions—traditionally name the rooster character *Chanticleer* because roosters sing loudly in the morning. A related spelling appears in the Spanish *canción,* or "song," and the French *chanson de geste,* "song of heroic deeds," which refers to French epics.

19 from *The Epic of Gilgamesh*

Background

In the early sections of *Gilgamesh*, the goddess Aruru creates Enkidu to temper Gilgamesh's arrogance and his dynamic energies. Enkidu quickly becomes the king's valued companion. After many glorious battles, Enkidu dies, and Gilgamesh, greatly saddened by his death, goes on a quest for immortality. He seeks Utnapishtim and his family, the only humans who have defeated death. Will Utnapishtim explain how a human might achieve immortality? Will the king return to his people with the knowledge of everlasting life? Find the answers to these questions in "The Story of the Flood" and "The Return" from *Gilgamesh*.

The Story of the Flood

"You know the city Shurrupak, it stands on the banks of Euphrates?
That city grew old and the gods that were in it were old. There was Anu,
lord of the firmament, their father, and warrior Enlil their counselor,
Ninurta the helper, and Ennugi watcher over canals; and with them
also was Ea. In those days the world <u>teemed</u>, the people multiplied, the
world bellowed like a wild bull, and the great god was aroused by the
clamor. Enlil heard the clamor and he said to the gods in council, 'The
uproar of mankind is intolerable and sleep is no longer possible by reason of the <u>babel</u>.' So the gods agreed to exterminate mankind. Enlil did
this, but Ea because of his oath warned me in a dream. He whispered
their words to my house of reeds, 'Reed-house, reed-house! Wall, O
20 wall, harken reed-house, wall reflect: O man of Shurrupak, son of
Ubara-Tutu; tear down your house and build a boat, abandon possessions and look for life, despise worldly goods and save your soul alive.
Tear down your house, I say, and build a boat. These are the measure-
ments of the barque as you shall build her: let her beam equal her
length, let her deck be roofed like the vault that covers the abyss;[1] then
take up into the boat the seed of all living creatures.'

"When I had understood I said to my lord, 'Behold, what you have commanded I will honor and perform, but how shall I answer the people, the city, the elders?' Then Ea opened his mouth and said to me, his

Vocabulary Builder

teemed (tēmd) *v.* was full of; swarmed

babel (bab′ əl) *n.* confusion of voices or sounds

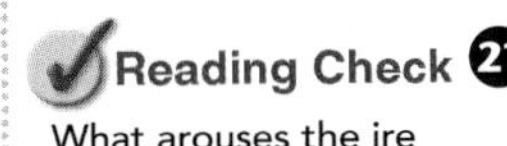

Reading Check 21

What arouses the ire and frustration of Enlil?

1. **like ... abyss** like the firmament, or heaven, that covers the depths.

19 About the Selection

In this excerpt from *The Epic of Gilgamesh,* Gilgamesh journeys to the underworld to find the secret of immortality. On this journey he hears a remarkable tale of a devastating flood ordered by the gods to cleanse the world of evil. It is a tale that resembles the biblical account of Noah and his ark.

20 Reading Strategy

Understanding the Cultural Context

- Remind students that as they read, identifying details of the cultural context will give them deeper insight into a story.
- Ask a volunteer to read aloud the bracketed passage. Explain that Ea is bound by his oath to the other gods not to warn anyone of the impending disaster. Have students **explain** how Ea is able to warn Utnapishtim about the flood without breaking his oath.
  Answer: Ea whispers to the reed walls of Utnapishtim's house and to Utnapishtim in a dream so that he can claim he never directly warned Utnapishtim.
- **Ask** students: What does Ea's cunning suggest about the value that Sumerians and Babylonians placed on this kind of slyness?
  Answer: Sumerians and Babylonians obviously valued cleverness.

21 Reading Check

Answer: Enlil is angry with the noise and confusion of humanity.

Differentiated Instruction Solutions for All Learners

Strategy for Less Proficient Readers

Have students describe floods they have experienced, read about, or seen on television news programs. Discuss why a flood would have been even more devastating in ancient times. Then, give students a brief synopsis of "The Story of the Flood" before they begin reading.

Enrichment for Gifted/Talented Students

Ask students to consider the setting and mood of each excerpt from *The Epic of Gilgamesh.* Have each student select an excerpt and imagine the kind of music that might accompany it in a performance. Have students offer an oral description of this music for classmates. Then, discuss as a class how the setting and mood changes in each excerpt.

㉒ Critical Thinking

Assess

- Have a student read aloud Ea's advice in the bracketed passage.
- **Ask:** Is Ea advising Utnapishtim to tell the whole truth? Explain Ea's actions.
  Possible response: Ea advises Utnapishtim to tell the others a half-truth. He may have done this because he does not want the gods to know that he broke his oath.
- **Ask:** What does Ea's behavior suggest about him?
  Possible responses: Ea cares about humanity so much that he will not let a good man perish; he is willing to play favorites and save one person but not others; he is dishonest.

㉓ Humanities

Front of Lyre from Tomb of Queen Pu-Abi at Ur, c. 2685–2290 B.C.

This lyre, or harplike stringed instrument, is made of wood. It was meant to give the appearance of a bull making noise. The figure of the bull was treated by the Sumerians as a natural deity. Its head, the only part of its body represented on this lyre, is covered with gold leaf and overlaid with lapis lazuli, a semiprecious blue stone.

Use the following questions for discussion:

- What facial feature does this bull share with the sculptures on pp. 18 and 22? What might be the reason for this similiarity?
  Possible response: All the sculptures show a long, curly beard. Mesopotamians may have seen such beards as symbols of power and majesty, characteristics shared by gods and rulers.
- What does the gold and lapis lazuli ornamentation suggest about the lyre?
  Possible response: The lyre was a valued object.

㉔ Critical Viewing

Possible response: Music may have made the story more appealing and memorable.

㉒ servant, 'Tell them this: I have learnt that Enlil is wrathful against me, I dare no longer walk in his land nor live in his city; I will go down to the Gulf[2] to dwell with Ea my lord. But on you he will rain down abundance, rare fish and shy wild-fowl, a rich harvest-tide. In the evening the rider of the storm will bring you wheat in torrents.'

"In the first light of dawn all my household gathered round me, the children brought pitch and the men whatever was necessary. On the fifth day I laid the keel and the ribs, then I made fast the planking. The ground-space was one acre, each side of the deck measured one hundred and twenty cubits[3] making a square. I built six decks below, seven in all, I divided them into nine sections with bulkheads between. I drove in wedges where needed, I saw to the punt-poles[4] and laid in supplies. The carriers brought oil in baskets, I poured pitch into the furnace and asphalt and oil; more oil was consumed in caulking[5] and more again the master of the boat took into his stores. I slaughtered bullocks for the people and every day I killed sheep. I gave the shipwrights wine to drink as though it were river water, raw wine and red wine and oil and white wine. There was feasting then as there is at the time of the New Year's festival; I myself anointed my head. On the seventh day the boat was complete.

"Then was the launching full of difficulty; there was shifting of ballast above and below till two thirds was submerged. I loaded into her all that I had of gold and of living things, my family, my kin, the beasts of the field both wild and tame, and all the craftsmen. I sent them on board, for the time that Shamash had ordained was already fulfilled when he said, 'In the evening, when the rider of the storm sends down the destroying rain, enter the boat and batten her down.' The time was fulfilled, the evening came, the rider of the storm sent down the rain. I looked out at the weather and it was terrible, so I too boarded the boat and

▼ Critical Viewing ㉔ Recitations of epics like *Gilgamesh* may have been accompanied by music from lyres like this one. In what ways would music contribute to such a reading? **[Hypothesize]**

㉓

2. **Gulf** the abyss, the great depths of the waters, where Ea, also called Enki, was supposed to dwell.
3. **cubits** (kyo͞o′ bitz) ancient units of linear measure, about 18–22 inches (originally, the distance from the elbow to the tip of the middle finger).
4. **punt-poles** poles that are pushed against the bottom of a shallow river or lake in order to propel a boat.
5. **caulking** (kôk′ iŋ) *v.* stopping up cracks or seams with a sealant.

Enrichment

Appreciating an Akkadian Pun

Ea, the god of the waters, was also the god of wisdom. When Utnapishtim wonders what he will tell his fellow citizens about the ark he is building, Ea gives him a clever speech to recite. In Akkadian, the language of ancient Babylon, this speech contains the words *kukku* and *kibati,* which can mean either "bran and wheat" or "misfortune and sorrow." When Utnapishtim uses these words, his listeners believe that Enlil "will rain down abundance . . . and a rich harvest-tide." The real message, however, is that the god will shower the people with misfortune.

battened her down. All was now complete, the battening and the caulking; so I handed the tiller to Puzur-Amurri the steersman, with the navigation and the care of the whole boat.

"With the first light of dawn a black cloud came from the horizon; it thundered within where Adad, lord of the storm, was riding. In front over hill and plain Shullat and Hanish, heralds of the storm, led on. Then the gods of the abyss rose up; Nergal pulled out the dams of the nether[6] waters, Ninurta the war-lord threw down the dykes, and the seven judges of hell, the Anunnaki, raised their torches, lighting the land with their livid flame. A stupor of despair went up to heaven when the god of the storm turned daylight to darkness, when he smashed the land like a cup. One whole day the tempest raged, gathering fury as it went, it poured over the people like the tides of battle; a man could not see his brother nor the people be seen from heaven. Even the gods were terrified at the flood, they fled to the highest heaven, the firmament of Anu; they crouched against the walls, cowering like curs. Then Ishtar the sweet-voiced Queen of Heaven cried out like a woman in travail:
25 'Alas the days of old are turned to dust because I commanded evil; why did I command this evil in the council of all the gods? I commanded wars to destroy the people, but are they not my people, for I brought them forth? Now like the spawn of fish they float in the ocean.' The great gods of heaven and of hell wept, they covered their mouths.

"For six days and six nights the winds blew, torrent and tempest and flood overwhelmed the world, tempest and flood raged together like warring hosts. When the seventh day dawned the storm from the south
26 subsided, the sea grew calm, the flood was stilled; I looked at the face of the world and there was silence, all mankind was turned to clay. The surface of the sea stretched as flat as a roof-top; I opened a hatch and the light fell on my face. Then I bowed low, I sat down and I wept, the tears streamed down my face, for on every side was the waste of water. I looked for land in vain, but fourteen leagues[7] distant there appeared a mountain, and there the boat grounded; on the mountain of Nisir the boat held fast, she held fast and did not budge. One day she held, and a second day on the mountain of Nisir she held fast and did not budge. A third day, and a fourth day she held fast on the mountain and did not budge; a fifth day and a sixth day she held fast on the mountain. When the seventh day dawned I loosed a dove and let her go. She flew away, but finding no resting-place she returned. Then I loosed a swallow, and she flew away but finding no resting-place she returned. I loosed a raven, she saw that the waters had retreated, she ate, she flew around, she cawed, and she did not come back. Then I threw everything open to the four winds, I made a sacrifice and poured out a

6. **nether** (neth′ ər) *adj.* below the earth's surface; lower.
7. **leagues** units of linear measure, varying in different times and countries; in English-speaking countries, a league is usually about three miles.

Reading Strategy
Understanding the Cultural Context What does the reaction of the gods to the flood tell you about their powers?

Vocabulary Builder
subsided (səb sīd′ ed) *v.* settled; lessened; died down

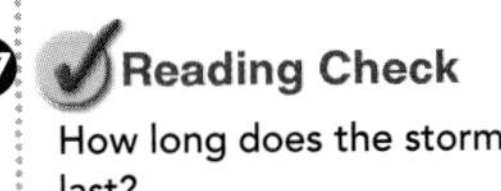

How long does the storm last?

25 Reading Strategy

Understanding the Cultural Context

- Call students' attention to the bracketed passage. After students read it, have them **summarize** the reaction of the gods to the flood.
  Answer: The gods are upset and frightened by the flood.
- **Ask** students to contrast the gods' present reaction with their earlier attitude toward destroying mankind.
  Possible response: Most of the gods seemed not to worry before, when they agreed to destroy humanity in a flood. They care only about the devastation when it gets so out of hand that they fear for their own lives.
- **Ask** students the Reading Strategy question: What does the reaction of the gods to the flood tell you about their powers?
  Possible response: The gods' reaction reveals that they are not all-powerful. All-powerful beings would not be frightened.

26 Vocabulary Builder

Latin Prefix *sub-*

- Direct students' attention to the word *subsided* and its use in the story.
- Explain that *subsided* includes the Latin root *-sid(e)-*, which means "settle," and the prefix *sub-*, which means "under," "lower," or "down." *Subsided* literally means "settled down."
- Have students **offer** other examples of words that contain the prefix *sub-*. Write the words on the board.
  Possible response: Students might mention *subplot, subdivide, subhuman,* and *substandard.*

27 Reading Check

Answer: The storm lasts for six days and six nights.

Differentiated Instruction Solutions for All Learners

Vocabulary for English Learners

Students may have difficulty with the sailing jargon in this section—words such as *battening, tiller, steersman,* and *navigation.* Post meanings for such specialized vocabulary. In addition, model the strategy of using context clues when possible to determine the meanings of unfamiliar words. Point out context clues such as *raged, gathering fury,* and *poured over people like the tides of battles* that will help students see that the meaning of *tempest* is "a violent storm," in this case, causing a flood.

Enrichment for Advanced Readers

Pose these questions to students: What role did clay play in cuneiform writing? What role did a stylus play, and just what *is* a stylus? What did cuneiform look like? Did it have real letters, or was the writing pictographic? How was cuneiform deciphered by modern scholars? Have students address some or all of these questions in a research report that includes photocopies or other illustrations of cuneiform.

28 Reading Strategy
Understanding the Cultural Context

- Read aloud with students the bracketed passage. Help students understand that Utnapishtim offers the gods a sacrifice in this passage.
- **Ask** students the Reading Strategy question: What does Utnapishtim's sacrifice suggest about the relationship between the people of his culture and their gods?
  Possible response: The people believed that by making sacrifices, or offerings, to the gods, they could obtain the gods' favor.

➤ **Monitor Progress** Stress that details often reveal historical information. **Ask** students what this passage suggests about these resources in ancient Mesopotamia.
Answer: Because these resources were offered to the gods, the materials must have had great value.

➤ **Reteach** To guide students in making additional cultural inferences, have them reread the Reading Strategy text on p. 17. Then, ask them to share the cultural details they have collected on their graphic organizer. Encourage them to stay alert for such details as they continue reading.

29 Background
History

Lapis lazuli, the semiprecious blue gemstone, has been widely used in the Middle East throughout history. Ancient people fashioned lapis lazuli into decorative objects. The Egyptians mixed powdered lapis lazuli into a paste for the eyelids—an early form of makeup. People from different cultural groups have also used lapis lazuli as a symbol of knowledge, success, wisdom, and insight.

30 Critical Thinking
Interpret

- Have a volunteer read aloud the bracketed passage.
- **Ask** students to summarize the message in those lines.
  Answer: Ea asks Enlil to be more merciful toward humankind. He does not deny the need to punish sin but stresses that punishment must be tempered with mercy.

---

libation[8] on the mountain top. Seven and again seven cauldrons I set
up on their stands, I heaped up wood and cane and cedar and myrtle.
28 When the gods smelled the sweet savor, they gathered like flies over the
sacrifice. Then, at last, Ishtar also came, she lifted her necklace with
the jewels of heaven that once Anu had made to please her. 'O you gods
29 here present, by the lapis lazuli[9] round my neck I shall remember these
days as I remember the jewels of my throat:
these last days I shall not forget. Let all the gods gather round the sacrifice, except Enlil. He shall not approach this offering, for without reflection he brought the flood; he consigned my people to destruction."

"When Enlil had come, when he saw the boat, he was wrath and swelled with anger at the gods, the host of heaven, 'Has any of these mortals escaped? Not one was to have survived the destruction.' Then the god of the wells and canals Ninurta opened his mouth and said to the warrior Enlil, 'Who is there of the gods that can devise without Ea? It is Ea alone who knows all things.' Then Ea opened his mouth and spoke to warrior Enlil, 'Wisest of gods, hero Enlil, how could you so senselessly bring down the flood?

Lay upon the sinner his sin,
Lay upon the transgressor his transgression,
Punish him a little when he breaks loose,
Do not drive him too hard or he perishes;
Would that a lion had ravaged mankind
30 *Rather than the flood,*
Would that a wolf had ravaged mankind
Rather than the flood,
Would that famine had wasted the world
Rather than the flood,
Would that pestilence had wasted mankind
Rather than the flood.

It was not I that revealed the secret of the gods; the wise man learned it in a dream. Now take your counsel what shall be done with him.'

"Then Enlil went up into the boat, he took me by the hand and my wife and made us enter the boat and kneel down on either side,

Reading Strategy
Understanding the Cultural Context What does Utnapishtim's sacrifice suggest about the relationship between the people of his culture and their gods?

8. **libation** (lī bā′ shən) *n.* liquid poured out as a sacrifice to a god.
9. **lapis lazuli** (lap′ is laz′ yo͞o lī′) *n.* sky-blue semiprecious gemstone.

Enrichment
Floods in the United States

Floods have always been considered devastating natural disasters. Generally caused by too much rain or too much snow melting quickly, floods often involve bodies of water spilling over their banks. From ancient times to the present, populations have always gathered near water, in areas at risk for floods.

Have students choose a famous flood from United States history and prepare a class presentation about it. Ask them to explore the flood's causes and effects, the preparedness of the affected region, and its social, personal, and environmental costs. Some of the floods they might explore include the Johnstown, Pennsylvania, flood of 1889; the Galveston, Texas, flood of 1900; the Midwest flood of 1993; and the Red River flood, along the North Dakota-Minnesota border, of 1997.

Encourage students to include different media in their presentations, such as photos, videos, recordings, and diagrams. Their research might include printed works, interviews of survivors, and/or reliable Web sites.

31 he standing between us. He touched our foreheads to bless us saying. 'In time past Utnapishtim was a mortal man; henceforth he and his wife shall live in the distance at the mouth of the rivers.' Thus it was that the gods took me and placed me here to live in the distance, at the mouth of the rivers."

32 

Reading Check

Why is Enlil enraged when he sees the boat?

33

◀ **Critical Viewing** 34
Which details from this mosaic accurately illustrate the end of the flood in *Gilgamesh*? **[Analyze]**

31 Critical Thinking

Speculate

- Have students read the bracketed passage. Help them recognize that Enlil has granted what Gilgamesh is searching for: immortality.
- **Ask** students why Enlil might have granted immortality to Utnapishtim and his wife.
  Possible responses: Enlil had decreed that no mortal should survive the flood, so by making Utnapishtim and his wife immortal, he ensures that his decree has been obeyed. Enlil now recognizes the senselessness of his effort to destroy humanity, and he wants to reward the couple who bravely withstood that destruction.

32 Reading Check

Answer: Enlil is enraged because he had planned to destroy all human beings.

33 Humanities

Noah Releases a Dove from a Window in His Ark

This mosaic, which appears in the Basilica of San Marco in Venice, Italy, depicts the Bible story of Noah and the Flood, which is similar to the story that Utnapishtim relates. The mosaic is from the Byzantine Empire, the Christian empire that survived the fall of Rome and flourished in Eastern Europe from the fourth to fifteenth centuries. The Byzantine capital, called Byzantium, became known as Constantinople as early as A.D. 330 and is located on the site of the present-day city of Istanbul, Turkey.

Use the following question for discussion:

What features of this mosaic do you find striking?
Possible response: The water with its snakelike shapes is the most striking feature.

34 Critical Viewing

Possible response: The mosaic shows a man, like Utnapishtim, releasing a bird to see whether the flood waters have receded.

Differentiated Instruction

Solutions for All Learners

Strategy for Special Needs Students

To assist students in their understanding of Utnapishtim's account of the flood, remind them that Gilgamesh is still on his quest for immortality, and he thinks that Utnapishtim can give him advice because he had survived the deadly flood. Then give students a copy of the **Timeline Graphic Organizer** in ***Graphic Organizer Transparencies,*** p. 253. Have students work in pairs, discuss characters' actions, and do a timeline of the key events in "The Story of the Flood."

Strategy for Advanced Readers

Encourage students to compare Utnapishtim's account with the story of the flood in the Bible (Genesis 6–9), which appears on pp. 44–50 of their textbook. Have students make charts comparing and contrasting details, including the reasons for the flood, the characterization of Utnapishtim or Noah, the things either man was able to save, the experience of the flood itself, and the aftermath of the event.

35 Literary Analysis

Archetype: The Hero's Quest and Characterization

- Remind students that an extraordinary person undertaking a dangerous journey quest is a theme that appears in literature from around the world.
- Call students' attention to Utnapishtim's remarks in the bracketed passage. **Ask:** What does Utnapishtim mean by the "life for which you are searching"?
  Answer: "Life" refers to immortality. Gilgamesh is searching for the immortality that the god Enlil granted Utnapishtim.
- **Ask** students the Literary Analysis question: What effect has Gilgamesh's quest had on him, in spite of his remarkable strength?
  Answer: The quest has exhausted Gilgamesh.

▶ **Monitor Progress Ask** students to explain why Gilgamesh's adventures are a hero's quest.
Answer: Gilgamesh has extraordinary, godlike powers. His journey is fraught with challenges and dangers.

▶ **Reteach** To guide students in further exploration of Gilgamesh's archetypal quest, have students reread the **Literary Analysis** instruction on p. 17. Then assign the **Literary Analysis** support page in *Unit 1 Resources*, p. 11.

36 Critical Thinking

Explain

- Read aloud the bracketed passage while students follow along in their textbooks.
- **Ask** students: Why does Utnapishtim tell his wife to bake the loaves of bread?
  Answer: The loaves at varying stages of decay will prove the length of Gilgamesh's slumber.
- **Ask** students to speculate about why Utnapishtim wants to prove how long Gilgamesh slept.
  Possible response: Utnapishtim wants to show Gilgamesh the difficulty of the task and the extent to which he failed at it.

37 Critical Viewing

Possible responses: The serpent is under the water; it looks powerful and devious.

The Return

35 Utnapishtim said, "As for you, Gilgamesh, who will assemble the gods for your sake, so that you may find that life for which you are searching? But if you wish, come and put it to the test: only prevail against sleep for six days and seven nights." But while Gilgamesh sat there resting on his haunches, a mist of sleep like soft wool teased from the fleece drifted over him, and Utnapishtim said to his wife, "Look at him now, the strong man who would have everlasting life, even now the mists of sleep are drifting over him." His wife replied, "Touch the man to wake him, so that he may return to his own land in peace, going back through the gate by which he came." Utnapishtim said to his wife, 36 "All men are deceivers, even you he will attempt to deceive; therefore bake loaves of bread, each day one loaf, and put it beside his head; and make a mark on the wall to number the days he has slept."

So she baked loaves of bread, each day one loaf, and put it beside his head, and she marked on the wall the days that he slept; and there came a day when the first loaf was hard, the second loaf was like leather, the third was soggy, the crust of the fourth had mold, the fifth was mildewed, the sixth was fresh, and the seventh was still on the embers. Then Utnapishtim touched him and he woke. Gilgamesh said to Utnapishtim the Faraway, "I hardly slept when you touched and roused me." But Utnapishtim said, "Count these loaves and learn how many days you slept, for your first is hard, your second like leather, your third is soggy, the crust of your fourth has mold, your fifth is mildewed, your sixth is fresh and your seventh was still over the glowing embers when I touched and woke you." Gilgamesh said, "What shall I do, O Utnapishtim, where shall I go? Already the thief in the night has hold of my limbs, death inhabits my room; wherever my foot rests, there I find death."

Then Utnapishtim spoke to Urshanabi the ferryman: "Woe to you Urshanabi, now and for ever more you have become hateful to this harborage; it is not for you, nor for you are the crossings of this sea. Go now, banished from the shore. But this man before whom you walked, bringing him here, whose body is covered with foulness and the grace of whose limbs has been spoiled by wild skins, take him to the washing-place. There he shall wash his long hair clean as snow in the water, he shall throw off his skins and let the sea carry them away, and the beauty of his body shall be shown, the fillet[10] on his forehead shall be renewed, and he shall be given clothes to cover his nakedness. Till he reaches his own city and his journey is accomplished, these clothes will show no sign of age, they will wear like a new garment." So Urshanabi took Gilgamesh and led him to the washing-place, he washed

Literary Analysis Archetype: The Hero's Quest and Characterization What effect has Gilgamesh's quest had on him, in spite of his remarkable strength?

37 ▼ **Critical Viewing** In what ways is this serpent similar to the one Gilgamesh sees? **[Analyze]**

10. **fillet** (filʹ it) *n.* narrow band worn around the head to hold the hair in place.

his long hair as clean as snow in the water, he threw off his skins, which the sea carried away, and showed the beauty of his body. He renewed the fillet on his forehead, and to cover his nakedness gave him clothes which would show no sign of age, but would wear like a new garment till he reached his own city, and his journey was accomplished.

Then Gilgamesh and Urshanabi launched the boat onto the water and boarded it, and they made ready to sail away; but the wife of Utnapishtim the Faraway said to him, "Gilgamesh came here wearied out, he is worn out; what will you give him to carry him back to his own country?" So Utnapishtim spoke, and Gilgamesh took a pole and brought the boat in to the bank. "Gilgamesh, you came here a man wearied out, you have worn yourself out; what shall I give you to carry you back to your own country? Gilgamesh, I shall reveal a secret thing,
38 it is a mystery of the gods that I am telling you. There is a plant that grows under the water, it has a prickle like a thorn, like a rose; it will wound your hands, but if you succeed in taking it, then your hands will hold that which restores his lost youth to a man."

When Gilgamesh heard this he opened the sluices so that a sweet-water current might carry him out to the deepest channel; he tied heavy stones to his feet and they dragged him down to the water-bed. There he saw the plant growing; although it pricked him he took it in
39 his hands; then he cut the heavy stones from his feet, and the sea carried him and threw him onto the shore. Gilgamesh said to Urshanabi the ferryman, "Come here, and see this marvelous plant. By its virtue a man may win back all his former strength. I will take it to Uruk of the strong walls; there I will give it to the old men to eat. Its name shall be 'The Old Men Are Young Again'; and at last I shall eat it myself and have back all my lost youth." So Gilgamesh returned by the gate through which he had come, Gilgamesh and Urshanabi went together. They traveled their twenty leagues and then they broke their fast; after thirty leagues they stopped for the night.

Gilgamesh saw a well of cool water and he went down and bathed; but deep in the pool there was lying a serpent, and the serpent sensed

Literary Analysis
Archetype: The Hero's Quest How does the plant relate to Gilgamesh's quest?

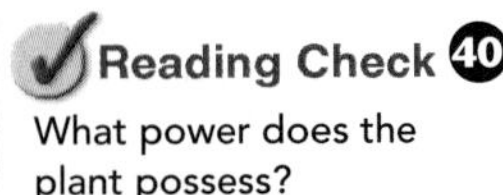

Reading Check 40
What power does the plant possess?

41

Differentiated Instruction Solutions for All Learners

Strategy for English Learners

Have students share with the class summaries of a legend or tale from their own cultures. Tell them to include any lesson or moral that the story aims to instill. Also, ask students to describe the circumstances under which they first heard the tale and to explain whether the tale is used to teach children good behavior, celebrate a great hero, or the like.

Strategy for Gifted/Talented Students

Have students draw Gilgamesh's journey, briefly noting the various adventures that occur along the way. Make sure that students use evidence from the text to create their maps; however, where the text does not specify a direction or distance, give students latitude in imagining Gilgamesh's quests. Display students' completed maps in the classroom.

38 Literary Analysis

Archetype: The Hero's Quest

- Direct students to read the bracketed passage.
- **Ask** students the Literary Analysis question: How does the plant relate to Gilgamesh's quest?
  Answer: In his quest, Gilgamesh sought the secret of immortality, which the plant provides.
- **Ask** students why they think Utnapishtim now makes this offer.
  Possible responses: Utnapishtim admires Gilgamesh; he recognizes how exhausted Gilgamesh is.

39 Literary Analysis

Archetype: The Hero's Quest

- Have a volunteer read aloud the bracketed passage.
- **Ask** what adjectives students would use to describe the actions Gilgamesh takes to obtain the plant.
  Possible responses: Students may suggest *difficult, dangerous, unpleasant,* and *painful.*
- **Ask** students how the difficulty and danger are in keeping with the nature of Gilgamesh's quest.
  Possible responses: An archetypal quest cannot be something easily accomplished; to win a great prize takes great effort; Gilgamesh is a hero and must perform tasks that seem heroic.

40 Reading Check

Answer: The plant restores a person's youth.

41 Humanities

Sea Serpent and Ship from Historiae animalium

Konrad Gesner was a German scholar with an interest in the natural world. From 1551 to 1556, he published the five-volume *Historiae animalium,* an encyclopedia of real and mythological animals. Included in the set were woodcuts such as the one pictured here.

Use the following question for discussion:

What feelings are evoked by this woodcut?
Possible response: The image seems sinister and threatening.

the sweetness of the flower. It rose out of the water and snatched it away, and immediately it sloughed its skin and returned to the well. Then Gilgamesh sat down and wept, the tears ran down his face, and he took the hand of Urshanabi; "O Urshanabi, was it for this that I toiled with my hands, is it for this I have wrung out my heart's blood? For myself I have gained nothing; not I, but the beast of the earth has joy of it now. Already the stream has carried it twenty leagues back to the channels where I found it. I found a sign and now I have lost it. Let us leave the boat on the bank and go."

42 After twenty leagues they broke their fast, after thirty leagues they stopped for the night; in three days they had walked as much as a journey of a month and fifteen days. When the journey was accomplished they arrived at Uruk, the strong-walled city. Gilgamesh spoke to him, to Urshanabi the ferryman, "Urshanabi, climb up onto the wall of Uruk, inspect its foundation terrace, and examine well the brickwork; see if it is not of burnt bricks; and did not the seven wise men lay these foundations? One third of the whole is city, one third is garden, and one third is field, with the precinct of the goddess Ishtar. These parts and the precinct are all Uruk."

This too was the work of Gilgamesh, the king, who knew the countries of the world. He was wise, he saw mysteries and knew secret things, he brought us a tale of the days before the flood. He went a long journey, was weary, worn out with labor, and returning engraved on a stone the whole story.

Reading Strategy
Understanding the Cultural Context These last two paragraphs echo the first paragraphs of *Gilgamesh's* Prologue. How might Sumerian and Babylonian values be revealed in these repeated descriptions of the city and its king?

Critical Reading

1. **Respond:** Did the gods and goddesses in *Gilgamesh* behave in ways you expected? Explain.
2. **(a) Recall:** How does Gilgamesh come to hear the story of the flood? **(b) Make Inferences:** Relative to the other events in *Gilgamesh,* when did the flood happen? **(c) Draw Conclusions:** Why is Utnapishtim able to tell about it?
3. **(a) Recall:** Why do the gods decide to destroy humanity? **(b) Analyze Cause and Effect:** Why do they soon question the wisdom of their decision? **(c) Interpret:** What lessons might Gilgamesh draw from the gods' experiences?
4. **(a) Recall:** After telling the story of the flood, what mysterious gift does Utnapishtim direct Gilgamesh to find? **(b) Recall:** What happens to this gift? **(c) Interpret:** What lesson might Gilgamesh draw from this experience?
5. **Modify:** What changes would you make to *Gilgamesh* if you were adapting it into an adventure or science-fiction film for today's audiences? Explain.

42 Reading Strategy
Understanding the Cultural Context

- Allow students time to reread the Prologue on p. 19. Then, have them read the bracketed passage on this page.
- **Ask** students the Reading Strategy question: These last two paragraphs echo the first paragraphs of *Gilgamesh's* Prologue. How might Sumerian and Babylonian values be revealed in these repeated descriptions of the city and its king?
Possible response: The descriptions reveal the value that both cultures place on security, wisdom, faith, nature, enterprise, strength, and endurance.

ASSESS
Answers

1. **Possible response:** Some students may say that the gods behaved far more selfishly and "ungodly" than they expected; others may say that the gods' behavior was similar to those they have encountered in other mythologies.
2. (a) Utnapishtim, a human who survived the flood, tells Gilgamesh the story of the flood. (b) The flood happened long ago, before Gilgamesh's battle with Humbaba. (c) Utnapishtim is able to tell the story of the flood because he was granted immortality.
3. (a) There are so many people that their noise disturbs the gods' sleep. (b) The gods question their wisdom when they become terrified by the flood. (c) **Possible responses:** It is difficult to predict the future; actions often have unintended consequences.
4. (a) Utnapishtim directs Gilgamesh to a magical plant that grants immortality. (b) A serpent steals the plant from Gilgamesh. (c) **Possible response:** Human beings cannot achieve immortality; Gilgamesh cannot succeed in all his quests.
5. **Possible response:** Students might change Utnapishtim's boat to an airplane.

Apply the Skills

from *The Epic of Gilgamesh*

Literary Analysis

Archetype: The Hero's Quest

1. **(a)** How does *The Epic of Gilgamesh* fit the **archetype** of a **hero's quest**? **(b)** How does Gilgamesh respond to the difficult obstacles he encounters?
2. Would you say Gilgamesh's quest is a selfish or an altruistic one? Cite details to explain your opinion.
3. **(a)** What does the outcome of Gilgamesh's quest suggest about human limitations? **(b)** How might the tale he brings home to Uruk eventually grant Gilgamesh the immortality he seeks?

Connecting Literary Elements

4. List at least three examples of actions, speech, or thoughts that contribute to the **characterization** of Gilgamesh as a hero. Use a chart like the one shown to explain what each example reveals about Gilgamesh's personality, values, or talents.

Example of Indirect Characterization	What It Shows About Gilgamesh

5. **(a)** What part does Gilgamesh's nature—two thirds god, one third man—play in his behavior? **(b)** What part does his nature play in motivating his quest?
6. What drawbacks or limitations on Gilgamesh's powers and talents seem to exist?

Reading Strategy

Understanding the Cultural Context

7. **(a)** Identify three qualities or beliefs in *Gilgamesh* that the Sumerians and Babylonians seemed to value. **(b)** For each one, cite supporting evidence in the selection that suggests this **cultural context.**
8. Identify three details that show that Sumerian or Babylonian society was highly organized. Consider such things as where people lived, what jobs they held, and their common beliefs.

Extend Understanding

9. **Cultural Connection:** What personal goals set by people today might be considered quests for immortality? Explain.

QuickReview

An **archetype** is a basic plot, character, symbol, or idea that recurs in the literature of many cultures. The **hero's quest** is an archetype in which an extraordinary person goes on a difficult journey to find something important.

Characterization is the means by which characters are developed. Authors may reveal characters' personalities directly, through statements and descriptions, or indirectly, through characters' actions, speech, and thoughts.

To **understand the cultural context,** look for details in ancient works about the way people lived and worked and what they believed.

For: Self-test
Visit: www.PHSchool.com
Web Code: eta-6104

Answers

1. (a) An extraordinary leader goes on a difficult journey in search of the secret of immortality. (b) Gilgamesh bravely faces and tries to overcome all the obstacles he encounters.
2. **Possible response:** It is selfish because most of the time Gilgamesh seems to want immortality for himself alone.
3. (a) Even the strongest, noblest, and most accomplished human beings have limitations. (b) Gilgamesh may not be literally immortal, but his story and achievements will be recounted for years to come.
4. **Possible response: Example:** Gilgamesh's speech to Enkidu to "throw away fear" and "attack" Humbaba; **What It Shows:** Gilgamesh is powerful and brave. **Example:** Gilgamesh asks Shamash for help; **What It Shows:** Gilgamesh knows that he is not all-powerful. **Example:** Gilgamesh says that he will share the magical plant with the old men of Uruk; **What It Shows:** Gilgamesh is a generous ruler.
Another sample answer can be found on **Literary Analysis Graphic Organizer B,** p. 4 in ***Graphic Organizer Transparencies.***
5. (a) Gilgamesh's nature influences him to act courageously and at times recklessly; it gives him great confidence. (b) Being only partly a god, Gilgamesh is not fully immortal, and he may want to attain complete immortality.
6. Gilgamesh does not have unlimited strength and power; he has human needs such as sleep.
7. (a) **Possible response:** Sumerians and Babylonians value bravery, cleverness, and generosity. (b) **Possible response:** Valuing bravery is illustrated by Gilgamesh's willingness to fight Humbaba; cleverness, by Ea's way of communicating with Utnapishtim; generosity, by Gilgamesh's desire to share the magical plant with the old men of Uruk.
8. **Possible response:** Evidence of organization includes special sages laying out the foundations of city walls, complicated and formal rituals surrounding death, and the special temples built for specific gods.

Answers continued

9. **Possible response:** A person's efforts to find a cure for a disease might be considered a quest for immortality because his or her discovery will affect others far into the future.

Go Online Assessment Students may use the **Self-test** to prepare for **Selection Test A** or **Selection Test B.**

Answers

❶ Vocabulary Lesson

Word Analysis: Latin Prefix *sub-*

1. *submarine:* undersea ship
2. *submerge:* plunge under water
3. *subterranean:* under the earth; underground
4. *subtraction:* the act of pulling or making lower; taking away from

Spelling Strategy

1. transmission
2. pretension
3. commission

Vocabulary Builder: Context

1. succor
2. immolation
3. incantation
4. somber
5. ecstasy
6. teemed
7. babel
8. subsided

❷ Grammar and Style Lesson

1. in
2. into
3. in
4. in
5. into

Writing Application

Sample sentences:

In a few weeks, Gilgamesh returned to Uruk. He went into his palace. On his return, his subjects came in to greet him. After his experiences, he turned into a better ruler.

WG Writing and Grammar Platinum Level

For support in teaching the Grammar and Style Lesson, use Chapter 26, Section 2.

Build Language Skills

❶ Vocabulary Lesson

Word Analysis: Latin Prefix *sub-*

Subsided contains the prefix *sub-*, which means "under," "lower," or "down." *Subsided,* therefore, means "died down," or "lessened." Use the prefix *sub-* with the roots below to form familiar words, and then define each one.

1. *-mar-* (sea)
2. *-merg-* (plunge)
3. *-terra-* (earth)
4. *-tract-* (pull)

Spelling Strategy

The *shun* sound is often spelled *-tion.* When a root word ends with the *s* or *d* sound, the suffix is spelled *-sion: tense* becomes *tension; extend* becomes *extension.* When the root ends in *-mit,* the suffix is spelled *-ssion: permit* becomes *permission.* Use these rules to add the correct form of the suffix to each word below.

1. transmit
2. pretend
3. commit

Vocabulary Builder: Context

Complete each sentence below with the appropriate word from the list on page 17.

1. When afraid, Gilgamesh pleads to the gods for __?__.
2. The Sumerian high priestess was in charge of __?__ and sacrifice.
3. When Enkidu died, the priestess chanted an __?__.
4. Residents of the Underworld seem __?__ and submissive.
5. Gilgamesh would be in __?__ if he could learn the secret of immortality.
6. Long before, when the world __?__ with people, the gods caused a great flood.
7. They objected to the __?__ of human voices.
8. Finally the violent storm __?__.

❷ Grammar and Style Lesson

Commonly Confused Words: *in* and *into*

In *Gilgamesh,* the English translator correctly uses both *in* and *into*— two prepositions that are commonly confused. As the following examples from the epic *Gilgamesh* indicate, the preposition *in* refers to place or position, while *into* suggests motion.

Place or Position: "O Gilgamesh, remember now your boasts *in* Uruk."

Motion: "O my lord, you may go on if you choose *into* this land, but I will go back to the city."

Practice Choose the correct preposition to complete each sentence.

1. Gilgamesh was king (in, into) Uruk.
2. Humbaba retreated (in, into) his house of cedar.
3. (In, Into) the forest, it became dark.
4. The goddess spoke to Enkidu (in, into) a dream.
5. Gilgamesh went (in, into) the mysterious mountain of Manshu.

Writing Application Write four sentences about what might happen after Gilgamesh returns to Uruk. Use *in* in two of your sentences, and use *into* in the other two.

WG *Prentice Hall Writing and Grammar Connection: Platinum Level, Chapter 26, Section 2*

34 ■ *Ancient Worlds*

Assessment Practice

Using Context Clues to Determine Meaning

(For more practice, see *Test Preparation Workbook,* p. 1.)

Students taking standardized tests will encounter vocabulary questions that require them to use context clues to determine meaning. Use this sample test question from *The Epic of Gilgamesh* to give students practice with context clues.

The world bellowed like a wild bull, and the great god was aroused by their clamor.

In this sentence, the word *clamor* most likely means—

A noise.
B boredom.
C elegance.
D harmonious.

B can be eliminated as illogical, because boredom tends to calm, not arouse; *C* and *D* can be eliminated because the bellow of a bull does not sound elegant or harmonious. This leaves the correct choice, *A*.

❸ Writing Lesson

Timed Writing: Comparison-and-Contrast Essay

Gilgamesh is a hero on a quest for the secret of immortality. Think about one modern-day hero—from books, movies, or TV—who is also on a quest of some kind. In an essay, compare and contrast Gilgamesh to this modern hero. ***(40 minutes)***

Prewriting *(10 minutes)* Brainstorm for similarities and differences between the two heroes. Consider the personality and talents of each hero, the goal of each quest, the obstacles that must be overcome, and his or her ultimate success or failure. Gather details in a chart like the one shown.

Model: Gathering Details

Points of Comparison	Gilgamesh	Modern-Day Hero

Drafting *(20 minutes)* Organize your essay by comparing the two heroes point by point or by detailing all the points about Gilgamesh before moving on to the modern hero. Include specific details to support each general point you make.

Revising *(10 minutes)* Check your draft against your prewriting chart to confirm that you have presented each point of comparison, discussing it in relation to each hero. Make sure that the details about each character are accurate.

WG *Prentice Hall Writing and Grammar Connection: Platinum Level, Chapter 9, Section 3*

❹ Extend Your Learning

Research and Technology Find out more about the rediscovery of *Gilgamesh* in the nineteenth century. Use these questions to guide your research:

- Where and when was the discovery made?
- In what form was *Gilgamesh* preserved?
- What other poems or stories about Gilgamesh have survived?

Find information in reliable Internet sources, or consult the i ntroductory material in a translation of *Gilgamesh.* Present your findings in a brief **research report.**

Listening and Speaking Hold a **press conference** in which the returning Gilgamesh answers questions about his quest. Review the selection to find the details Gilgamesh could report. Then, with several classmates, take on the roles of Gilgamesh, his advisers, and the reporters who ask questions. **[Group Activity]**

For: An additional research activity
Visit: www.PHSchool.com
Web Code: etd-7103

Assessment Resources

The following resources can be used to assess students' knowledge and skills.

Unit 1 Resources
- **Selection Test A,** pp. 18–20
- **Selection Test B,** pp. 21–23

General Resources
- **Rubrics for Exposition: Comparison-and-Contrast Essay,** pp. 53–54
- **Rubrics for Research: Research Report,** pp. 51–52

Go Online Assessment Students may use the **Self-test** to prepare for **Selection Test A** or **Selection Test B.**

❸ Writing Lesson

You may use this Writing Lesson as a timed-writing practice, or you may allow students to develop the Comparison-and-Contrast Essay as a writing assignment over several days.

- To give students guidance in writing this comparison-and-contrast essay, give them **Support for Writing Lesson** in ***Unit 1 Resources,*** p. 15, to organize their essay information.
- Read aloud the Writing Lesson instruction. Tell students that a comparison-and-contrast essay examines similarities and differences between two or more things.
- Remind students that they may organize the essay by making point-by-point comparisons between the two heroes or by first making all the points about one hero and then making all the points about the other hero.
- Use the Exposition: Comparison-and-Contrast Essay rubrics in ***General Resources,*** pp. 53–54, to evaluate students' work.

WG **Writing and Grammar Platinum Level**

To give students further instruction for writing a comparison-and-contrast essay, use Chapter 9, Section 3.

❹ Research and Technology

- Tell students that in the nineteenth century, archaeologists rediscovered cuneiform tablets containing the Babylonian epic version of *Gilgamesh.*
- Remind students to include a Works Cited page with their research reports.
- Use the Research: Research Report rubrics in ***General Resources,*** pp. 51–52, to evaluate students' work.

The **Support for Extend Your Learning** page (***Unit 1 Resources,*** p. 16) provides guided note-taking opportunities to help students complete the Extend Your Learning activities.

Go Online Research Have students type in the Web Code for another research activity.

Standard Course of Study

Goal 1: WRITTEN LANGUAGE

- **WL.1.03.1** Select, monitor, and modify reading strategies appropriate to personal reflection.
- **WL.1.03.5** Summarize key events and points from personal reflection.
- **WL.1.03.11** Identify and analyze elements of expressive environment in personal reflections.

Goal 2: INFORMATIONAL READING

- **IR.2.02.2** Show clear, logical connection among cause/effect events.

Goal 5: LITERATURE

- **LT.5.01.5** Analyze arthetypal characters, themes, and settings in world literature.

Goal 6: GRAMMAR AND USAGE

- **GU.6.02.2** Edit for appropriate and correct mechanics.

Step-by-Step Teaching Guide	Pacing Guide
PRETEACH	
• Administer Vocabulary and Reading Warm-ups as necessary.	5 min.
• Engage students' interest with the motivation activity.	5 min.
• Read and discuss author and background features. **FT**	10 min.
• Introduce the Literary Analysis Skill: Archetypal Setting. **FT**	5 min.
• Introduce the Reading Strategy: Identifying Chronological Order.	10 min.
• Prepare students to read by teaching the selection vocabulary. **FT**	
TEACH	
• Informally monitor comprehension while students read independently or in groups. **FT**	30 min.
• Monitor students' comprehension with the Reading Check notes.	as students read
• Reinforce vocabulary with Vocabulary Builder notes.	as students read
• Develop students' understanding of archetypal setting with the Literary Analysis annotations. **FT**	5 min.
• Develop students' ability to identify chronological order with the Reading Strategy annotations. **FT**	5 min.
ASSESS/EXTEND	
• Assess students' comprehension and mastery of the Literary Analysis and Reading Strategy by having them answer the Apply the Skills questions. **FT**	15 min.
• Have students complete the Vocabulary Lesson and the Grammar and Style Lesson. **FT**	15 min.
• Apply students' ability to revise to add specific examples by using the Writing Lesson. **FT**	45 min. or homework
• Apply students' understanding by using one or more of the Extend Your Learning activities.	20–90 min. or homework
• Administer Selection Test A or Selection Test B. **FT**	15 min.

Resources

Print

Unit 1 Resources

Transparency

Graphic Organizer Transparencies

Print

Reader's Notebook [L2]

Reader's Notebook: Adapted Version [L1]

Reader's Notebook: English Learner's Version [EL]

Unit 1 Resources

Technology

Listening to Literature Audio CDs [L2, EL]

Print

Unit 1 Resources

General Resources

Technology

Go Online: Research **[L3]**
Go Online: Self-test **[L3]**
ExamView®, **Test Bank [L3]**

Choosing Resources for Differentiated Instruction

[L1] Special Needs Students
[L2] Below-Level Students
[L3] All Students
[L4] Advanced Students
[EL] English Learners

For Vocabulary and Reading Warm-ups and for Selection Tests, **A** signifies "less challenging" and **B** "more challenging." For Graphic Organizer transparencies, **A** signifies "not filled in" and **B** "filled in."

FT Fast Track Instruction: To move the lesson more quickly, use the strategies and activities identified with **FT**.

Scaffolding for Less Proficient and Advanced Students

The leveled Critical Thinking questions after selections progress in the levels of thinking required to answer them. To address the needs of your different students, you may use the (a) level questions for your less proficient students and the (b) level questions with your on-level and advanced students. The occasional (c) level questions are appropriate for your advanced students.

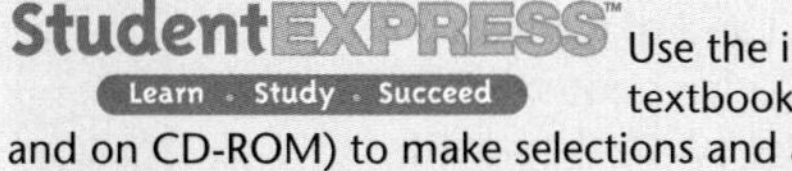

Use this complete suite of powerful teaching tools to make lesson planning and testing quicker and easier.

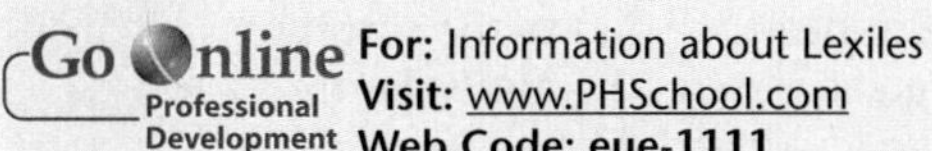

Use the interactive textbook (online and on CD-ROM) to make selections and activities come alive with audio and video support and interactive questions.

Go Online Professional Development
For: Information about Lexiles
Visit: www.PHSchool.com
Web Code: eue-1111

PREHEACH

Motivation

Tell students that people in all cultures have speculated on the origins of the universe and of humans. For instance, contemporary scientists believe that they can trace the origins of our universe to a time a split second after the Big Bang, when all the matter and energy of today's galaxies were concentrated in a tiny point of unimaginable density and heat. Ask students whether they have contemplated these origins or whether they have any images in mind about the origins. Tell students that in the biblical story of Genesis, they can read a different version of the events surrounding the birth of the universe.

❶ Background

More About the Selections

The Bible contains many books—Genesis, Exodus, and so on. Each book is divided into chapters that are further divided into numbered verses. When people refer to the Bible, they refer to book, chapter, and verse. For example, *Genesis 1:3* means the book of Genesis, Chapter 1, verse 3:

God said, "Let there be light"; and there was light.

Geography Note

Draw students' attention to the map at the top of the page. Explain that the Promised Land of Canaan written about in the early chapters of the Bible comprises parts of present-day Syria, Lebanon, Israel, Jordan, and the West Bank and Gaza Strip. The area is bordered to the west by the Mediterranean Sea and to the east by the Arabian desert. The area's diverse landforms and bodies of water give it a wide range of habitats, plants, and animals.

Build Skills *Scripture*

from the Bible: Genesis 1–3 (The Creation and the Fall) ❶ *and* Genesis 6–9 (The Story of the Flood)

The Hebrew Bible The most important example of Hebrew literature is the Hebrew Bible, known by Christians as the Old Testament. Translated into many languages, it has influenced three major religions: Judaism, Christianity, and Islam.

The word *Bible* comes from the Greek word *biblia,* meaning "a collection of writings." It is accurate to call the Bible a collection—even a library—rather than a single book. Like a library, it contains many types of books.

Traditionally, the books of the Hebrew Bible have been divided into three main sections. The Torah—from the Hebrew word *tora,* meaning "law"—consists of the first five books of the Bible (Genesis, Exodus, Leviticus, Numbers, and Deuteronomy). While the Torah is largely concerned with the law, it contains important narratives and an account of the world's creation. Another section, called Nevi'im, or Prophets, contains historical accounts, such as the Book of Samuel, and the writings of the prophets, those who summoned the Jews to the path of justice and faith in God. Still another section, called Ketuvim, or Writings, consists of a variety of works: poetry like the Psalms, short stories like the Book of Ruth, and religious dialogues like the Book of Job.

The Bible's Origins The Bible's authorship is a question that has intrigued people over the centuries. Many believe that the Bible is the word of God. Through the workings of divine inspiration, human beings wrote down God's message. It was once believed that Moses himself wrote the first five books of the Bible and that King David composed the Psalms. In the nineteenth century, however, some scholars began to theorize that differences in style and content suggest multiple sources for the Bible. Today, some experts infer that the oldest source for the Torah, for instance, dates back to the tenth century B.C. and the most recent dates to about the fifth century B.C.

A Book of Great Influence For Jews, the Bible was a "Written Temple," sustaining Jewish culture and beliefs when the actual Temple in Jerusalem was destroyed in 586 B.C. and again in A.D. 70. The Bible has also had major importance for Muslims and Christians, who, like Jews, worship a single God. In the sixteenth century, Martin Luther translated the Bible into German and stressed its importance for the individual believer, thereby inaugurating Protestantism. Still another famous translation of the Bible is the English version written by a committee of scholars for King James in 1611. The poetic phrasing and cadences of the King James version have influenced the prose and poetry of the English language for nearly four hundred years.

Themes of the Bible

Despite the diversity of the Bible, the text is unified by a few constant themes, or insights into life. These themes often address the power, goodness, and mercy of a single God; the covenant, or solemn agreement, into which God enters with the Hebrew people; the tendency of humans to stray from a right, or moral, path; and the forgiveness they can win from God. Such messages can be found in the various chapters of the Bible.

Within the Bible are numerous stories called *parables,* in which writers present themes that can be interpreted as life-lessons. Biblical parables teach lessons of deep personal strength in the face of overwhelming adversity; of the remarkable capacity of even the weak to survive the harshest of circumstances; and of the consequences of vices, such as greed and betrayal. Although such lessons are an integral part of parables in world literature, themes in the Bible are specifically rooted in the spirituality it presents.

Preview

Connecting to the Literature

Nearly everyone has a vision of paradise, or an ideal place. The Garden of Eden is one such paradise, described in the opening chapters of the Bible.

Standard Course of Study

- Analyze archetypal characters, themes, and settings in world literature. (LT.5.01.5)

2 Literary Analysis

Archetypal Setting

An **archetypal setting** is a time, place, or landscape feature that has similar significance for different peoples and therefore connects to powerful, universal human experiences. One example is a paradise like the Bible's Garden of Eden. Common archetypal setting details include

- a universe of opposites
- a landscape that emerges from watery chaos
- a circle that symbolizes completion
- a great tree that connects the realms of heaven and earth

As you read, think about why the archetypal settings you encounter have been significant to so many cultures.

Connecting Literary Elements

To bring its archetypal settings to life, the writings of the Bible include **dialogue,** or conversation between characters. Dialogue can also

- reveal information about characters
- present events
- add variety to narratives
- arouse the reader's interest

As you read, consider how the dialogue reinforces the meanings of the archetypal settings.

3 Reading Strategy

Identifying Chronological Order

Chronological order is the order in which events happen in time. Transitional words and phrases like *first, later, on the next day,* or *after that* often help make the chronological order clear. Use a chart like the one shown to track the sequence of events in Genesis 1–3.

Chronological Order of the Creation

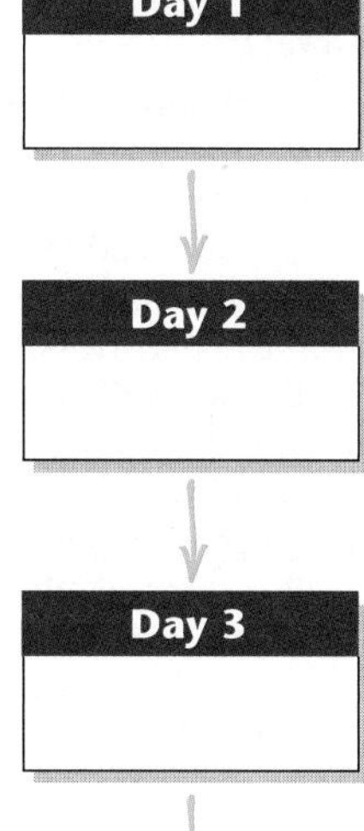

Vocabulary Builder

void (void) *n.* empty space; total emptiness (p. 38)

expanse (ek spans′) *n.* very large open area (p. 38)

shrewdest (shrōōd′ est) *adj.* most cunning or clever (p. 41)

duped (dōōpt) *v.* tricked; fooled (p. 42)

enmity (en′ mə tē) *n.* state of being enemies; antagonism; hostility (p. 42)

corrupt (kə rupt′) *adj.* spoiled by sin or dishonesty; rotten (p. 45)

covenant (kuv′ ə nənt) *n.* serious, binding agreement (p. 45)

comprised (kəm prīzd′) *v.* included; consisted of (p. 46)

2 Literary Analysis

Archetypal Setting

- Remind students that *setting* refers to the time and place in which a work or scene unfolds. Then, have them read the Literary Analysis instruction.
- Explain that in order to occur so often, an archetypal setting must involve experiences or traits common to much of humanity.
- Discuss with students other works they have read that feature the archetypal setting of a paradise, or ideal place. Mention Sir Thomas More's *Utopia,* a famous sixteenth-century British work about an ideal island of peace and plenty. Note that the words *Eden* and *utopia* have come to be used generically to refer to any ideal place.

3 Reading Strategy

Identifying Chronological Order

- Read aloud the Reading Strategy instruction.
- Have students **offer** more examples of transitional words and phrases that signal chronological order. Write their responses on the board. **Possible responses:** Words and phrases such as *second, third, then, now, at the same time, a day later, last,* and *finally* signal chronological order.
- Review the graphic organizer. Give students a copy of **Reading Strategy Graphic Organizer A** in ***Graphic Organizer Transparencies,*** p. 5, to use to track the chronological order of events in the Bible chapters as they read.

Vocabulary Builder

- Pronounce each vocabulary word for students, and read the definitions as a class. Have students identify any words with which they are already familiar.

Differentiated Instruction Solutions for All Learners

Support for Special Needs Students
Have students complete the **Preview** and **Build Skills** pages for the selections from *Genesis* in the ***Reader's Notebook: Adapted Version.*** These pages provide a selection summary, an abbreviated presentation of the reading and literary skills, and the graphic organizer on the **Build Skills** page in the student book.

Support for Less Proficient Readers
Have students complete the **Preview** and **Build Skills** pages for the selections from *Genesis* in the ***Reader's Notebook.*** These pages provide a selection summary, an abbreviated presentation of the reading and literary skills, and the graphic organizer on the **Build Skills** page in the student book.

Support for English Learners
Have students complete the **Preview** and **Build Skills** pages for the selections from *Genesis* in the ***Reader's Notebook: English Learner's Version.*** These pages provide a selection summary, an abbreviated presentation of the reading and literary skills, additional contextual vocabulary, and the graphic organizer on the **Build Skills** page in the student book.

TEACH

Facilitate Understanding

Discuss with students what they already know about Creation, the Garden of Eden, and Adam and Eve, and have them offer summaries of these topics. As students read, have them consider how reading the account is more powerful and compelling than simply summarizing it.

❶ About the Selection

The first three chapters of the Bible offer an account of God's creation of the universe, including the stars, the sun, the moon, the Earth, and the plants and animals on Earth. Also included is the story of the Fall, in which Adam and Eve—the first man and woman—are tempted by an evil serpent into committing the original sin of eating the fruit of the Tree of Knowledge. For breaking God's commandment and eating the forbidden fruit, they are banished from the paradise of the Garden of Eden, and all subsequent generations of humanity are forced to know suffering and hard labor.

❷ Background

Culture

The Hebrews, or Jews, trace their history to Abraham, a descendant of Noah (whom students will encounter when they read the next section, the Flood). According to later chapters in the Book of Genesis, the Lord guided Abraham and his wife Sarah (then called Abram and Sarai) to leave Ur of Chaldees (in present-day Iraq) for the Promised Land of Canaan. After spending some time in Egypt, Abraham and Sarah resettled in Canaan, where they prospered. Eventually Sarah bore Abraham a son named Isaac. Isaac's son Jacob had twelve sons, who became the founders of the twelve tribes of Israel.

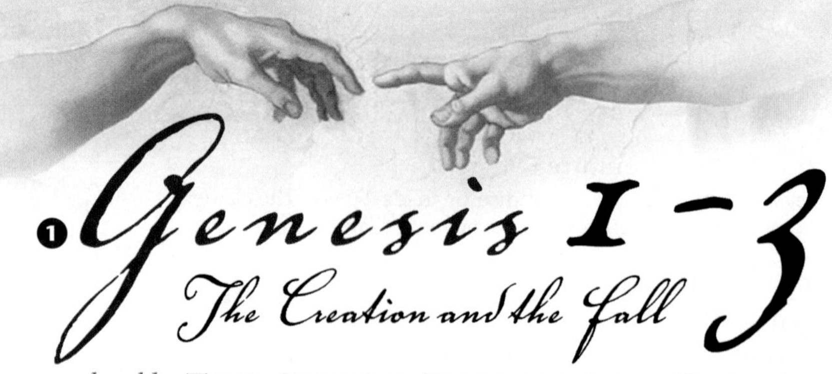

❶ Genesis 1–3
The Creation and the Fall

translated by THE JEWISH PUBLICATION SOCIETY

❷ Background The Jews of antiquity, the Hebrews, originated as a nomadic tribe in Iraq sometime around 2000 B.C. By 1600 B.C., they had arrived in the Promised Land of Canaan (now known as Israel and Lebanon). After migrating to Egypt to escape famine, the Hebrews suffered centuries of enslavement by the Egyptians and were ultimately liberated by Moses around 1200 B.C. By 1000 B.C., a monarchy was established by King David as a permanent institution in the city of Jerusalem. In subsequent ages, the Jews lost their established nation but reestablished one again in 1948, nearly 2000 years later. Resilient amid the upheavals of history, the Hebrews documented their nation's beginnings and other details of their history within the work now called the Bible. All of the English translations of the Bible presented here are from the Tanakh, the Jewish Publication Society edition translated from the original Hebrew.

CHAPTER 1

1 When God began to create heaven and earth—
2 the earth being unformed and void, with darkness over the surface of the deep and a wind from God sweeping over the water—
3 God said, "Let there be light"; and there was light.
4 God saw that the light was good, and God separated the light
from the darkness.
❸ 5 God called the light Day, and the darkness He called Night. And
there was evening and there was morning, a first day.
6 God said, "Let there be an expanse in the midst of the water,
that it may separate water from water."
7 God made the expanse, and it separated the water which was below
the expanse from the water which was above the expanse. And it was so.
8 God called the expanse Sky. And there was evening and there
was morning, a second day.
9 God said, "Let the water below the sky be gathered into one area,
that the dry land may appear." And it was so.

Vocabulary Builder
void (void) *n.* empty space; total emptiness

Vocabulary Builder
expanse (ek spans′) *n.* very large open area

Differentiated Instruction Solutions for All Learners

Accessibility at a Glance

	Genesis 1–3 The Creation and the Fall	Genesis 6–9 The Story of the Flood
Context	God's creation of the universe	Role of Noah and the ark
Language	Transitional words and phrases signifying chronological order	Complex syntax with some quotations embedded within quotations
Concept Level	Accessible (God punishes those who defy him.)	Accessible (God's mercy and the survival of the species)
Literary Merit	Classic: Scripture	Classic: Scripture
Lexile	1010L	1010L
Overall Rating	Average	Average

10 God called the dry land Earth, and the gathering of waters He called Seas. And God saw that this was good.

11 And God said, "Let the earth sprout vegetation: seed-bearing plants, fruit trees of every kind on earth that bear fruit with the seed in it." And it was so.

12 The earth brought forth vegetation: seed-bearing plants of every kind, and trees of every kind bearing fruit with the seed in it. And God saw that this was good.

13 And there was evening and there was morning, a third day.

14 God said, "Let there be lights in the expanse of the sky to separate day from night; they shall serve as signs for the set times—the days and the years;

15 and they shall serve as lights in the expanse of the sky to shine
3 upon the earth." And it was so.

16 God made the two great lights, the greater light to dominate the day and the lesser light to dominate the night, and the stars.

17 And God set them in the expanse of the sky to shine upon the earth,

18 to dominate the day and the night, and to separate light from darkness. And God saw that this was good.

19 And there was evening and there was morning, a fourth day.

20 God said, "Let the waters bring forth swarms of living creatures, and birds that fly above the earth across the expanse of the sky."

21 God created the great sea monsters, and all the living creatures of every kind that creep, which the waters brought forth in swarms, and all the winged birds of every kind. And God saw that this was good.

22 God blessed them, saying, "Be fertile and increase, fill the waters in the seas, and let the birds increase on the earth."

4 23 And there was evening and there was morning, a fifth day.

24 God said, "Let the earth bring forth every kind of living creature: cattle, creeping things, and wild beasts of every kind." And it was so.

25 God made wild beasts of every kind and cattle of every kind, and all kinds of creeping things of the earth. And God saw that this was good.

26 And God said, "Let us make man in our image, after our likeness. They shall rule the fish of the sea, the birds of the sky, the cattle, the whole earth, and all the creeping things that creep on earth."

27 And God created man in His image, in the image of God He created him; male and female He created them.

28 God blessed them and God said to them, "Be fertile and increase, fill the earth and master it; and rule the fish of the sea, the birds of the sky, and all the living things that creep on earth."

29 God said, "See, I give you every seed-bearing plant that is upon all the earth, and every tree that has seed-bearing fruit; they shall be yours for food.

30 And to all the animals on land, to all the birds of the sky, and to everything that creeps on earth, in which there is the breath of life, [I give] all the green plants for food." And it was so.

31 And God saw all that He had made, and found it very good. And there was evening and there was morning, the sixth day.

Literary Analysis
Archetypal Setting What role do opposites play in the settings that God creates in the first four days?

Reading Strategy
Identifying Chronological Order In the description of each day, which sentence signals the end of one day and the start of another?

What does God create on the fourth day?

Differentiated Instruction
Solutions for All Learners

Support for Special Needs Students
To model for students how to identify chronological order, give them a copy of **Reading Strategy Graphic Organizer B** in ***Graphic Organizer Transparencies,*** p. 6. This completed graphic organizer will give students insight into the process of identifying chronological order. They can use it as a model to track events as they read.

Enrichment for Gifted/Talented Students
Ask students to find artistic renderings of the Creation on a museum's Web site or in illustrated books or magazines. Have them then bring to class photocopies or computer printouts of a piece of art that appeals to them, along with some information about it—the name of the artist, when it was painted, and so on. Encourage students to share their examples and information in a class "art show."

3 Literary Analysis
Archetypal Setting

- Review with students the information on p. 37 about archetypal settings. Remind them that a universe created from opposites is an archetypal setting.
- **Ask** students why the idea of a universe created from opposites would be widespread enough to be considered archetypal.
  Possible response: The idea of opposites helps capture concepts about good and evil or right and wrong. It also reflects the human condition and the world of nature (for example, day and night and spring and fall are part of nature).
- Have students read the bracketed passage. Then, **ask** them the Literary Analysis question: What role do opposites play in the settings that God creates in the first four days?
  Possible response: Opposites, such as heaven and earth, day and night, water and land, the sun and the moon, and plants and animals form the foundations of the universe.

4 Reading Strategy
Identifying Chronological Order

- Remind students that chronological order is the order in which events happen in time. Explain that transitional words and phrases often signal this order.
- Ask a volunteer to read aloud the bracketed verse. Have students skim the previous text for verses that discuss the other four days.
- Then, **ask** students the Reading Strategy question: In the description of each day, which sentence signals the end of one day and the start of another?
  Answer: The sentence "And there was evening and there was morning" signals the end of one day and the start of another.
- Elicit that each repetition of the sentence includes a different ordinal number—*first, second, third,* and so on—which signals chronological order by clarifying time relationships.

5 Reading Check
Answer: On the fourth day, God creates the sun, moon, and stars.

❻ Critical Thinking

Compare and Contrast

- Ask a volunteer to read aloud the bracketed verse. Then, ask another volunteer to read aloud verse 1:27 on p. 39.
- Have students contrast the two descriptions of creation. **Ask:** Which creation scene is more vivid? Why? **Possible response:** The verse on this page is more vivid because of the descriptive image of God breathing life into man's nostrils.

❼ Literary Analysis

Archetypal Setting

- Read aloud the bracketed passage. Then, **ask** students to identify the two positive qualities that verse 9 stresses about the trees found in the Garden of Eden.
  Answer: The trees are beautiful in appearance and are good sources of food.
- **Ask** students to identify the positive quality that verse 10 stresses about the Garden of Eden.
  Answer: The garden has a river that provides water for the area's vegetation.
- Point out that in the Middle East, where so much of the climate is desert, the availability of water for irrigation would be especially valued.
- Then, **ask** students the Literary Analysis question: Why do you think the Bible suggests a garden as the ideal setting for human beings?
  Possible response: A garden is beautiful and bountiful—a refreshing and healthful place in which to live. A garden is a place where things grow, which enhances the theme of creation.

❽ Critical Viewing

Answer: The painting depicts God's creation of Adam.

CHAPTER 2

1 The heaven and the earth were finished, and all their array.
2 On the seventh day God finished the work that He had been
doing, and He ceased on the seventh day from all the work that He had
done.
3 And God blessed the seventh day and declared it holy, because
on it God ceased from all the work of creation that He had done.
4 Such is the story of heaven and earth when they were created.
When the LORD God made earth and heaven—
5 when no shrub of the field was yet on earth and no grasses of
the field had yet sprouted, because the LORD God had not sent rain
upon the earth and there was no man to till the soil,
6 but a flow would well up from the ground and water the whole
surface of the earth—
❻ 7 the LORD God formed man from the dust of the earth.[1] He blew
into his nostrils the breath of life, and man became a living being.
8 The LORD God planted a garden in Eden, in the east, and placed
there the man whom He had formed.
9 And from the ground the LORD God caused to grow every tree
❼ that was pleasing to the sight and good for food, with the tree of life in
the middle of the garden, and the tree of knowledge of good and bad.
10 A river issues from Eden to water the garden, and it then
divides and becomes four branches.
11 The name of the first is Pishon, the one that winds through the
whole land of Havilah, where the gold is.
12 (The gold of that land is good; bdellium[2] is there, and lapis lazuli.)[3]
13 The name of the second river is Gihon, the one that winds
through the whole land of Cush.
14 The name of the third river is Tigris, the one that flows east of
Asshur. And the fourth river is the Euphrates.[4]
15 The LORD God took the man and placed him in the garden of
Eden, to till it and tend it.
16 And the LORD God commanded the man, saying, "Of every tree
of the garden you are free to eat;
17 but as for the tree of knowledge of good and bad, you must not
eat of it; for as soon as you eat of it, you shall die."
18 The LORD God said, "It is not good for man to be alone; I will
make a fitting helper for him."
19 And the LORD God formed out of the earth all the wild beasts
and all the birds of the sky, and brought them to the man to see what

Literary Analysis
Archetypal Setting Why do you think the Bible suggests a garden as the ideal setting for human beings?

▼ Critical Viewing ❽ What moment from Genesis is depicted in the painting shown here? **[Analyze]**

1. **the Lord God . . . earth** The name Adam is said to come from the Hebrew word *'adhāmāh,* meaning "earth."
2. **bdellium** (del′ ē əm) deep red gem.
3. **lapis lazuli** (lap′ is laz′ yo͞o lē) sky-blue semiprecious stone.
4. **Asshur . . . Euphrates** (yo͞o frāt′ ēz) Asshur was the capital city of Assyria, an ancient empire in southwestern Asia; the Euphrates River flows from East Central Turkey southward through Syria and Iraq.

Enrichment

Snakes

The serpent in Chapter 3 is a key figure in the fall of mankind. Snakes are limbless reptiles closely related to lizards. They are coldblooded, which means that they absorb the heat around them instead of creating their own heat. The almost three thousand varieties of snakes around the world can range in length from four inches to more than thirty feet. Most snakes are patterned in a way that helps them blend into their surroundings.

Most snakes live on land, but some live in the water or in trees. Having no legs, they usually propel themselves forward by a combination of thrusts and side-to-side movements.

Snakes consume small animals such as insects, mice, and frogs. With no paws to hold their food, they do not chew but swallow their prey whole. Some snakes crush their prey to death or stun or kill their prey with poison called venom.

he would call them; and whatever the man called each living creature, that would be its name.

20 And the man gave names to all the cattle and to the birds of the sky and to all the wild beasts; but for Adam no fitting helper was found.

21 So the LORD God cast a deep sleep upon the man; and, while he slept, He took one of his ribs and closed up the flesh at that spot.

22 And the LORD God fashioned the rib that He had taken from the man into a woman; and He brought her to the man.

23 Then the man said,
"This one at last
Is bone of my bones
And flesh of my flesh.
This one shall be called Woman,
For from man was she taken."

24 Hence a man leaves his father and mother and clings to his wife, so that they become one flesh.

CHAPTER 3

The two of them were naked, the man and his wife, yet they felt no shame.

1 Now the serpent was the shrewdest of all the wild beasts that the LORD God had made. He said to the woman, "Did God really say: You shall not eat of any tree of the garden?"

2 The woman replied to the serpent, "We may eat of the fruit of the
9 other trees of the garden.

3 It is only about fruit of the tree in the middle of the garden that God said: 'You shall not eat of it or touch it, lest you die.'"

4 And the serpent said to the woman, "You are not going to die,

5 but God knows that as soon as you eat of it your eyes will be opened and you will be like divine beings who know good and bad."

6 When the woman saw that the tree was good for eating and a delight to the eyes, and that the tree was desirable as a source of wisdom, she took of its fruit and ate. She also gave some to her husband, and he ate.

7 Then the eyes of both of them were opened and they perceived that they were naked; and they sewed together fig leaves and made themselves loincloths.

8 They heard the sound of the LORD God moving about in the garden at the breezy time of day; and the man and his wife hid from the LORD God among the trees of the garden.

9 The LORD God called out to the man and said to him, "Where are you?" 11

Vocabulary Builder
shrewdest (shrōōd′ est) *adj.* most cunning or clever

Reading Check 10

From what tree does God forbid Adam to eat?

The Creation of Adam, Michelangelo, Scala

9 Critical Thinking

Cause and Effect

- Have students read the bracketed passage independently.
- **Ask** students: What does the serpent say will happen if Eve eats the forbidden fruit?
  Answer: The serpent says that Eve will gain knowledge of good and bad and become like a divine being.
- Discuss with students what, in addition to the snake's promises, might cause Eve to eat the fruit. Elicit from them that people are often curious about things that are labeled "forbidden."

10 Reading Check

Answer: God forbids Adam to eat from the "tree of knowledge of good and bad."

11 Humanities

The Creation of Adam, by Michelangelo

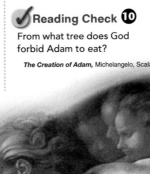

Michelangelo Buonarroti (1475–1564) was truly a Renaissance man. In addition to being a painter, Michelangelo was a sculptor, an architect, an engineer, and a poet. Michelangelo used biblical themes in his most famous painting, the ceiling and wall of the Sistine Chapel in Rome. In addition to *The Creation of Adam,* the Sistine ceiling shows *The Flood* and many other scenes and figures from the Bible.

The Creation of Adam depicts a dynamic creator, cloaked in a billowing cape and surrounded by angels. God is shown reaching out to the creation made in His own image—Adam, the first man. In the full depiction, God is floating in the air, and Adam is rooted on the earth.

Use the following questions to initiate discussion:

- What might be the significance of God's finger touching Adam's?
  Possible responses: God may be giving Adam the spark of life. He may be blessing his creation and leading Adam toward goodness.
- How would you describe the expression on Adam's face?
  Possible responses: Adam seems to be showing reverence toward God. He looks pure and innocent.

Differentiated Instruction

Solutions for All Learners

Support for Less Proficient Readers

Students may have difficulty with some of the more difficult vocabulary in these selections. To aid students' comprehension, suggest that they listen to the recording of the story on the **Listening to Literature Audio CDs** as they follow the text. After they listen to each chapter, invite students to restate the main events of the chapter in their own words.

Strategy for Advanced Readers

Have students consider the implications of the biblical claim that human beings were created in the image of God. Organize students into groups, and ask each group to create a list that shows the ways humans are similar to God, according to Genesis, and the ways they are different. Encourage them to respond to these questions: What positive characteristics does the claim suggest that human beings possess? What responsibilities does the claim imply that human beings have?

⓬ Humanities

Expulsion From Paradise, c. 1500s

This tapestry, which was created in Brussels, now hangs at the Gallerie dell'Accademia in Florence, Italy. The tapestry shows God in midair, casting Adam and Eve out of the Garden of Eden.

Use the following questions to initiate discussion:

- How would you characterize God's facial expression?
  Possible response: God seems firm and strict yet sad to be casting out Adam and Eve.
- Which details of the tapestry suggest the beauty and bounty of Eden?
  Possible response: The lush fields, the tree, the monkey, and the plants suggest Eden's beauty and bounty.

⓭ Critical Viewing

Possible response: Adam and Eve's expressions and bowed heads show their shame and sorrow.

⓮ Critical Thinking

Analyze

- Choose volunteers to read aloud the dialogue in the bracketed passage.
- Before students read the text, **ask** what emotion the student reading Adam's part should try to convey in verse 10.
  Possible response: Emotions for Adam's part include guilt and shame.
- Then, **ask** what tone would be appropriate for God in verses 11 and 13.
  Possible responses: God might be angry or accusatory. He might be saddened yet resolute.
- After students read the passage, note the similarity of Adam and Eve's reactions to God's questions. Discuss with students how Adam and Eve both try to blame their actions on someone else.
- **Ask** students: Are Adam and Eve's reactions believable? Explain.
  Answer: The tendency to feel ashamed to admit the truth and to try to evade responsibility and punishment are common human foibles that most students are likely to find believable.

⓬

⓭ ◀ **Critical Viewing** Which details in this tapestry illustrate the intense emotions at the end of Genesis, Chapter 3? **[Interpret]**

⓮

10 He replied, "I heard the sound of You in the garden,
and I was afraid because I was naked, so I hid."
11 Then He asked, "Who told you that you were naked? Did you
eat of the tree from which I had forbidden you to eat?"
12 The man said, "The woman You put at my side—she gave me of
the tree, and I ate."
13 And the LORD God said to the woman, "What is this you have
done!" The woman replied, "The serpent duped me, and I ate."
14 Then the LORD God said to the serpent,
"Because you did this,
More cursed shall you be
Than all cattle
And all the wild beasts:
On your belly shall you crawl
And dirt shall you eat
All the days of your life.
15 I will put enmity
Between you and the woman,
And between your offspring and hers;
They shall strike at your head,
And you shall strike at their heel."
16 And to the woman He said,
"I will make most severe
Your pangs in childbearing;
In pain shall you bear children.
Yet your urge shall be for your husband,
And he shall rule over you."
17 To Adam He said, "Because you did as your wife said and ate of
the tree about which I commanded you, 'You shall not eat of it,'
Cursed be the ground because of you;

Vocabulary Builder
duped (do͞opt) *v.* tricked; fooled

Vocabulary Builder
enmity (en′ mə tē) *n.* state of being enemies; antagonism; hostility

Enrichment

Community Rules

As students read the account of the Garden of Eden in Genesis, encourage them to think of Eden as a kind of community, albeit one nearly perfect in its comforts. In that community there was a rule, established by God, and Adam and Eve were called on to live according to God's rule. They did not; instead, they broke the rule by eating the forbidden fruit. As a result, the community was broken for all time. Not only were Adam and Eve cast from Eden, but according to Genesis, humans from that point on would live with multiplied sorrows and earn their bread through wearying labor.

Suggest to students that most communities today are similar to the Garden of Eden community in this respect: They rely on rules to direct and harmonize the sometimes chaotic ways that people are inclined to behave. Without the structure offered by such rules, communities can disintegrate with surprising speed.

By toil shall you eat of it
All the days of your life:
18 Thorns and thistles shall it sprout for you.
But your food shall be the grasses of the field;
19 By the sweat of your brow
Shall you get bread to eat,
Until you return to the ground—
For from it you were taken.
For dust you are,
And to dust you shall return."

20 The man named his wife Eve, because she was the mother of all the living.

21 And the LORD God made garments of skins for Adam and his wife, and clothed them.

22 And the LORD God said, "Now that the man has become like one of us, knowing good and bad, what if he should stretch out his hand and take also from the tree of life and eat, and live forever!"

23 So the LORD God banished him from the garden of Eden, to till the soil from which he was taken.

24 He drove the man out, and stationed east of the garden of Eden the cherubim and the fiery ever-turning sword, to guard the way to the tree of life.

Critical Reading

1. **Respond:** In what ways did you find this account of the Creation and the Fall interesting?
2. **(a) Recall:** What is the first thing God creates? **(b) Interpret:** What meanings does the first chapter of Genesis seem to give to light and darkness?
3. **(a) Recall:** What does God command human beings to do on the sixth day? **(b) Draw Conclusions:** Why is it significant that man is created in God's image?
4. **(a) Recall:** Find four places where God names things. **(b) Connect:** How does the act of naming seem related to the act of creation? **(c) Compare and Contrast:** What does Adam's naming of the animals reveal about him?
5. **(a) Interpret:** Explain two ways in which Adam and Eve change after they eat the forbidden fruit. **(b) Evaluate:** By the end of Chapter 3, are Adam and Eve more human than they were when they were first created? Explain.
6. **Apply:** What common problems of human existence does this section of Genesis help explain?

15 Reading Strategy

Identifying Chronological Order

- Elicit from students that chronological order is the order in which events happen in time.
- Read aloud the bracketed passage, and note that Adam and Eve's expulsion is the end result of the events described in Chapter 3.
- **Ask** students to list the events, in chronological order, that lead to this banishment.
  Answer: The serpent encourages Eve to eat from the tree of knowledge; Eve does so and shares the fruit with Adam; God discovers their betrayal; God punishes Adam, Eve, and the serpent.

ASSESS

Answers

1. **Possible response:** Points of interest may include the humanity of Adam and Eve and the tragedy of their sin.
2. (a) The first thing God creates is light. (b) **Possible response:** Darkness is associated with formlessness and confusion; light with form and all that is "good."
3. (a) God commands human beings to populate the earth and rule its creatures. (b) **Possible response:** Man's creation stresses his potential for goodness, the value of human life, and man's difference from other animals.
4. (a) **Possible response:** "God called the light Day" (1:5); "the darkness He called Night" (1:5); "God called the expanse Sky" (1:8); "God called the dry land Earth" (1:10). (b) **Possible response:** Naming something calls it into being. (c) **Possible response:** Adam's ability to name things reveals a godlike capacity.
5. (a) **Possible response:** Adam and Eve hide their nakedness and hide from God. (b) **Possible response:** Adam and Eve are more human because they display shame and guilt.
6. **Possible response:** Common problems include the toil of labor, the pain of childbirth, and the strife of the world.

Differentiated Instruction Solutions for All Learners

Support for Special Needs Students

Tell students who have difficulty following the written selection to work in pairs and review their graphic organizers on chronological order. Have them reread to make sure that they have included all events. Then assign the **Reading Strategy** support page in ***Unit 1 Resources,*** p. 29.

Enrichment for Gifted/Talented Students

Have students interested in music work in small groups to find appropriate pieces to accompany the first or third chapter of Genesis. Each group should select one piece of music, bring to class the chosen recording, play it for classmates, and then explain what it is and why group members find it appropriate. Students might consider classical music, jazz, New Age instrumentals, film soundtracks, or any other type of music.

16 About the Selection

Chapters 6 through 9 of Genesis offer the biblical account of the Flood, the result of forty days of rain that God visits on earth to destroy humanity for its sins. Recognizing Noah as a pious human being, the Lord decides to spare him and his family and gives him instructions for building an ark in which they will survive the Flood. Noah also is told to take into the ark male and female pairs of the earth's animals, ensuring that each species will survive.

17 Reading Strategy

Identifying Chronological Order

- Have a volunteer read aloud the bracketed passage.
- **Ask** students which word in the first three verses helps show a time relationship.
  Answer: The word *when* in verse 1 helps show a time relationship.
- Discuss how the details in the third verse might help students calculate time relationships. Elicit that if the Bible lists generations of descendants, a reader might—on the basis of the Lord's decision in verse 3—assign 120 years to each generation to figure out time in the Bible.
- **Ask** students the Reading Strategy question: Which words in verse 4 help clarify the order of events?
  Answer: The words *then, later,* and *when* help clarify the order of events.

16

Background In Genesis 1–3, God creates the heavens, the earth, and Adam and Eve, who serve as the parents of humanity. Throughout the generations, God maintains a deep concern about humankind and their earthly doings. He establishes a covenant, or solemn agreement, with humans as a way to protect those who remain faithful and loyal to him. When he finds them threatening this sacred covenant, God appoints one man, Noah, to act as a mediator between God and his people. Will God exact a punishment on those who have violated his covenant? What purpose will Noah have in protecting not only the Hebrew people but also the viability of humanity? Find the answers to these questions in Genesis 6–9.

CHAPTER 6

1 When men began to increase on earth and daughters were born
to them,
2 the divine beings saw how beautiful the daughters of men were
and took wives from among those that pleased them.—
17 3 The Lord said, "My breath shall not abide in man forever, since
he too is flesh; let the days allowed him be one hundred and twenty
years."—
4 It was then, and later too, that the Nephilim appeared on earth—
when the divine beings cohabited with the daughters of men, who bore
them offspring. They were the heroes of old, the men of renown.
5 The Lord saw how great was man's wickedness on earth, and
how every plan devised by his mind was nothing but evil all the time.

Reading Strategy
Identifying Chronological Order Which words in verse 4 help clarify the order of events?

Enrichment

Jewish Dietary Laws

The reference in 7:2 to clean and unclean animals relates to Jewish dietary laws about which animals are clean enough to eat and which are not. These laws are spelled out in Leviticus and Deuteronomy, the third and fifth books of the Bible. The body of these laws is called *kashrut,* from the Hebrew for "fitting" or "proper." The related adjective, describing food fitting or proper to eat, is *kosher.*

According to these laws, kosher animals must have cloven hooves and chew their cud. Thus, cattle, sheep, and goats are among those animals that are kosher, but pigs, camels, and rabbits are among those that are not. Water creatures must have fins and scales, as regular fish do; shellfish, such as lobsters, clams, and shrimp, are forbidden. Birds are permitted except for scavengers. Rodents, reptiles, amphibians, and most insects are also not permitted.

6 And the Lord regretted that He had made man on earth, and His heart was saddened.

7 The Lord said, "I will blot out from the earth the men whom I created—men together with beasts, creeping things, and birds of the sky; for I regret that I made them."

8 But Noah found favor with the Lord.

9 This is the line of Noah.—Noah was a righteous man; he was blameless in his age; Noah walked with God.—

10 Noah begot three sons: Shem, Ham, and Japheth.

11 The earth became corrupt before God; the earth was filled with lawlessness.

12 When God saw how corrupt the earth was, for all flesh had corrupted its ways on earth,

13 God said to Noah, "I have decided to put an end to all flesh, for the earth is filled with lawlessness because of them: I am about to destroy them with the earth.

14 Make yourself an ark of gopher wood; make it an ark with compartments, and cover it inside and out with pitch.

18 15 This is how you shall make it: the length of the ark shall be three hundred cubits,[1] its width fifty cubits, and its height thirty cubits.

16 Make an opening for daylight in the ark, and terminate it within a cubit of the top. Put the entrance to the ark in its side; make it with bottom, second, and third decks.

17 "For My part, I am about to bring the Flood—waters upon the earth—to destroy all flesh under the sky in which there is breath of life; everything on earth shall perish.

18 But I will establish My covenant with you, and you shall enter the ark, with your sons, your wife, and your sons' wives.

19 And of all that lives, of all flesh, you shall take two of each into the ark to keep alive with you; they shall be male and female.

20 From birds of every kind, cattle of every kind, every kind of creeping thing on earth, two of each shall come to you to stay alive.

21 For your part, take of everything that is eaten and store it away, to serve as food for you and for them."

22 Noah did so; just as God commanded him, so he did.

CHAPTER 7

1 Then the Lord said to Noah, "Go into the ark, with all your household, for you alone have I found righteous before Me in this generation.

2 Of every clean animal you shall take seven pairs, males and their mates, and of every animal that is not clean, two, a male and its mate;

3 of the birds of the sky also, seven pairs, male and female, to keep seed alive upon all the earth.

1. **cubits** ancient units of linear measure, about 18–22 inches each.

Vocabulary Builder
corrupt (kə rupt′) *adj.* spoiled by sin or dishonesty; rotten

Literary Analysis
Archetypal Setting and Dialogue Which precise details in God's instructions help readers picture the ark?

Vocabulary Builder
covenant (kuv′ ə nənt) *n.* serious, binding agreement

19  **Reading Check**

What reason does God give for putting an end to all living things on earth?

18 Literary Analysis

Archetypal Setting and Dialogue

- Remind students that an archetypal setting is one that occurs again and again in the literature of many cultures. Then, have them independently read the bracketed passage.
- Have a student reread aloud verses 12–13. Explain that a corrupt place destroyed for its sins is an archetypal setting. Support this idea with another biblical example, the cities of Sodom and Gomorrah, which God later destroys because of the cities' sinfulness (Genesis 18–19).
- Discuss how special boats or ships are another type of archetypal setting. Have students **offer** examples from books and films of this archetype.
  Possible responses: Fictional examples include the *Argo* of Greek mythology or the *Pequod* in *Moby-Dick*. Real ships, such as the *Bounty* or the *Titanic,* also have acquired legendary status.
- **Ask** students the Literary Analysis question: Which precise details in God's instructions help readers picture the ark?
  Answer: Details include the gopher wood, the compartments and decks, the pitch on the inside and outside, and the information about the size.

▶ **Monitor Progress** **Ask** students: What additional archetypal setting is referred to in this passage?
Answer: The passage also refers to a great Flood that will cover the land.

▶ **Reteach** Help students recognize the characteristics of archetypal settings by reviewing with them the Literary Analysis instruction on p. 37. Then assign the **Literary Analysis** support page in ***Unit 1 Resources,*** p. 28.

19 Reading Check

Answer: God's reason for putting an end to all living things on earth is that he sees the pervasiveness of humanity's wickedness.

Differentiated Instruction
Solutions for All Learners

Support for English Learners
Have students identify the words that the Lord speaks in verses 6:1–7. Clarify that in most works, each new paragraph of speech begins with open quotation marks. In the Bible, however, verses of the same paragraph sometimes look like new paragraphs; that is why there are no open quotation marks at the start of verses 14, 15, or 16. Despite this peculiarity, dialogue ends only when there are closed quotation marks. Have students find where God's speech starting in verse 13 ends (at the end of verse 21).

Enrichment for Gifted/Talented Students
Students interested in science and nature might work together to create animal charts to show some of the different animals that Noah would have taken on the ark. Have students include on the charts some information about each animal's appearance, characteristics, and habitat, perhaps with a picture or sketch of the animal. Encourage students to focus especially on animals found in the Middle East in ancient times.

20 Reading Strategy

Identifying Chronological Order

- Read aloud the bracketed passage.
- **Ask** students the Reading Strategy question: Which precise details help readers pinpoint when the Flood took place and when Noah entered the ark?
  Answers: Details include "on the seventh day," "the six hundredth year of Noah's life," "the second month," "the seventeenth day of the month," and "that same day."

21 Vocabulary Builder

Latin Prefix *com-*

- Call students' attention to the word *comprised,* its definition, and its use in verse 16.
- Explain that *comprised* includes the prefix *com-,* which means "with" or "together," and the Latin root *-pris-,* which means "caught" or "held." *Comprised* means "included" or "consisted of." In other words, the animals entering the ark in verse 16 included males and females.
- Tell students that the root *-pan-* means "bread." **Ask** them to use their knowledge of the root and the prefix *com-* to explain the meaning of the word *companion.*
  Answer: *Companion* means someone you break bread with, or a friend.
- Explain that the prefix *com-* sometimes changes its spelling to *co-,* especially before vowel or *h* sounds. It changes its spelling to *con-* before *c, d, g, j, n, q, s, t, v,* and sometimes *f.* Have students **give** examples of words using these spellings of the prefix.
  Possible responses: Words with *co-* include *coauthor, copilot,* and *cohabitate.* Words with *con-* include *concept, conduct, congestion, connect, conquer, consent, contract,* and *convene.*
- Have students work together to find definitions for the words discussed in class.

4 For in seven days' time I will make it rain upon the earth, forty days and forty nights, and I will blot out from the earth all existence that I created."

5 And Noah did just as the Lord commanded him.

6 Noah was six hundred years old when the Flood came, waters upon the earth.

7 Noah, with his sons, his wife, and his sons' wives, went into the ark because of the waters of the Flood.

8 Of the clean animals, of the animals that are not clean, of the birds, and of everything that creeps on the ground,

9 two of each, male and female, came to Noah into the ark, as God had commanded Noah.

10 And on the seventh day the waters of the Flood came upon the earth.

11 In the six hundredth year of Noah's life, in the second month, on the seventeenth day of the month, on that day.

20 All the fountains of the great deep burst apart,
And the floodgates of the sky broke open.

12 (The rain fell on the earth forty days and forty nights.)

13 That same day Noah and Noah's sons, Shem, Ham, and Japheth, went into the ark, with Noah's wife and the three wives of his sons—

14 they and all beasts of every kind, all cattle of every kind, all creatures of every kind that creep on the earth, and all birds of every kind, every bird, every winged thing.

15 They came to Noah into the ark, two each of all flesh in which there was breath of life.

21 16 Thus they that entered comprised male and female of all flesh, and God had commanded him. And the Lord shut him in.

17 The Flood continued forty days on the earth, and the waters increased and raised the ark so that it rose above the earth.

18 The waters swelled and increased greatly upon the earth, and the ark drifted upon the waters.

19 When the waters had swelled much more upon the earth, all the highest mountains everywhere under the sky were covered.

20 Fifteen cubits higher did the waters swell, as the mountains were covered.

21 And all flesh that stirred on earth perished—birds, cattle, beasts, and all the things that swarmed upon the earth, and all mankind.

22 All in whose nostrils was the merest breath of life, all that was on dry land, died.

23 All existence on earth was blotted out—man, cattle, creeping things, and birds of the sky; they were blotted out from the earth. Only Noah was left, and those with him in the ark.

Reading Strategy
Identifying Chronological Order Which precise details help readers pinpoint when the Flood took place and when Noah entered the ark?

Vocabulary Builder
comprised (kəm prīzd′) *v.* included; consisted of

Enrichment

Noah's Flood in Literature

The biblical account of Noah is very spare, but it has inspired many folk tales, legends, and other literary works that contain specific, and often entertaining, details. According to one folk tale, the ass was slow in boarding the ark and Noah shouted in exasperation, "Hurry, even though Satan be with thee." Hearing this curse, the devil interpreted it as an invitation to enter the ark with the ass. This detail, of course, explains why there was still evil in the world after the flood subsided.

A more recent expansion of the story of the Flood is the poem "The Unicorn" by American humorist and children's author Shel Silverstein (1932–1999), best known as a recording by the Irish Rovers. According to this piece, when all the animals were entering the ark, the unicorns were hiding outside, playing in the rain. The rain had begun to pour, and Noah had to leave without them. For that reason, the song concludes, no unicorns are seen today.

CHAPTER 8

22

And when the waters had
swelled on the earth one hundred and
fifty days,
1 God remembered Noah and all
the beasts and all the cattle that were
with him in the ark, and God caused
a wind to blow across the earth, and
the waters subsided.
2 The fountains of the deep and
the floodgates of the sky were stopped
up, and the rain from the sky was
held back;
3 the waters then receded
steadily from the earth. At the end of
one hundred and fifty days the waters
diminished,
4 so that in the seventh month,
on the seventeenth day of the month,
the ark came to rest on the mountains of Ararat.
5 The waters went on diminish-
ing until the tenth month; in the
tenth month, on the first of the
month, the tops of the mountains
became visible.
6 At the end of forty days, Noah
opened the window of the ark that he
had made
7 and sent out the raven; it went
to and fro until the waters had dried
up from the earth.
8 Then he sent out the dove to
see whether the waters had decreased from the surface of the ground.
9 But the dove could not find a resting place for its foot, and
returned to him to the ark, for there was water over all the earth. So
putting out his hand, he took it into the ark with him.
10 He waited another seven days, and again sent out the dove
from the ark.
25 11 The dove came back to him toward evening, and there in its bill
was a plucked-off olive leaf! Then Noah knew that the waters had
decreased on the earth.
12 He waited still another seven days and sent the dove forth; and
it did not return to him any more.
13 In the six hundred and first year, in the first month, on the first
of the month, the waters began to dry from the earth; and when Noah
removed the covering of the ark, he saw that the surface of the ground
was drying.

▲ Critical Viewing 23
Compare and contrast the details in this image to the events in Genesis, Chapter 8. **[Compare and Contrast]**

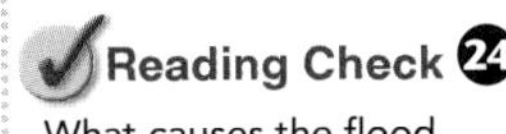

Reading Check 24
What causes the flood waters to subside?

22 Humanities

Decorative art, Derbyshire, England

Decorative art showing Bible scenes was popular in Europe for centuries. Europeans and Americans were familiar with stories from the Bible, so artists could rely on their audience's knowledge of key scenes. This decorative image illustrates the familiar scene of Noah releasing the dove from the ark.

Use the following questions to initiate discussion:

- Which of the three incidents in which Noah releases the dove does this image seem to reflect? Explain.
Answer: The art reflects the second release of the dove, when it returns with an olive leaf in its beak.
- Which details in the image suggest that Noah has brought the ark safely through the danger of the storm?
Possible response: The presence of a dove and Noah's focus on it, the position of his hands, and the rainbow all suggest safety or comfort. The proximity of the jagged mountains to the ark suggests the danger that the ark has already faced.

23 Critical Viewing

Possible response: Similarities include the ark resting on a mountain as the flood waters ebb, Noah at the ark's window, the dove that Noah has released, and the branch in the dove's beak. Differences include the size of the ark, which in comparison to the ark described in Genesis seems far smaller, and the simultaneous appearance of the dove and the rainbow, which the Bible says happens separately.

24 Reading Check

Answer: God sends a wind across the earth.

Differentiated Instruction
Solutions for All Learners

Strategy for Less Proficient Readers
Graphic organizers might help students better understand Noah's experiments with the dove. Have each student complete a simple chart in which the first column lists the four separate releases of the birds. In the second column, students should record the bird's actions or discoveries. In the third column, students should explain what the bird's actions or discoveries show about the state of the flood waters.

Enrichment for Advanced Readers
Have students research a major flood of more recent times, such as the Johnstown, Pennsylvania, flood of 1889, the flooding in Bangladesh in 1987, or the Midwestern summer floods of 1993. Ask students to report their findings in the form of newspaper articles. The article should report where and when the flood took place, factors that led to the flooding, effects of the flood on people and property, and action being taken—if any—to prevent future floods in the same area.

25 Reading Strategy
Identifying Chronological Order

- Have students independently read the bracketed passage on pp. 47–48.
- **Ask** students to respond to the Reading Strategy item: In chronological order, list three significant events that occur at the end of the forty-day flood.
  Possible response: Noah releases the dove to test whether the flood waters have subsided, he and his family are able to leave the ark, and the Lord promises never again to destroy all of Earth because of human corruption.

26 Humanities

Noah's Ark, by Aaron Douglas

Midwestern-born artist Aaron Douglas (1899–1979) studied art in New York City and Paris and later chaired the art department at Fisk University in Tennessee. A leading figure of the Harlem Renaissance of the 1920s and 1930s, Douglas is known for monochromatic (single-color) paintings influenced by Egyptian art and the Art Deco movement. He completed *Noah's Ark* in 1927.

Use the following questions for discussion:

- How do the animals shown in the painting reflect the biblical description?
  Answer: The animals are shown entering the ark in pairs.
- Who do you think the people in the painting are, and what does Douglas suggest about them?
  Possible response: The people are probably Noah and his family. Douglas suggests that they are reacting with efficiency but urgency.

27 Critical Viewing

Possible response: The lightning, the animals hurrying into the ark, the rising waters, and the gesture of the figure (presumably Noah) atop the ark all convey a sense of urgency.

14 And in the second month, on the twenty-seventh day of the
month, the earth was dry.
15 God spoke to Noah, saying,
16 "Come out of the ark, together with your wife, your sons, and
your sons' wives.
17 Bring out with you every living thing of all flesh that is with
you: birds, animals, and everything that creeps on earth; and let them
swarm on the earth and be fertile and increase on earth."
18 So Noah came out, together with his sons, his wife, and his
sons' wives.
19 Every animal, every creeping thing, and every bird, everything
that stirs on earth came out of the ark by families.
25 20 Then Noah built an
altar to the LORD and, taking
of every clean animal and of
every clean bird, he offered
burnt offerings on the altar.
21 The LORD smelled the
pleasing odor, and the LORD
said to Himself: "Never again
will I doom the earth because
of man, since the devisings of
man's mind are evil from his
youth; nor will I ever again
destroy every living being, as I
have done.
22 So long as the earth
endures,
Seedtime and harvest,
Cold and heat,
Summer and winter,
Day and night
Shall not cease."

Reading Strategy
Identifying Chronological Order In chronological order, list three significant events that occur at the end of the forty-day flood.

▼ **Critical Viewing** 27 Which details in the scene depicted here convey a sense of urgency? **[Interpret]**

 26

Noah's Ark, Aaron Douglas, Fisk University Fine Art Galleries, Nashville, Tennessee

Enrichment

Noah's Flood in History

Scientists have long debated the historical accuracy of the Flood. In the 1920s, while excavating the site of the Sumerian city of Ur, archaeologist Leonard Wooley found evidence of a major flood in the area.

Some geologists and oceanographers have speculated about the possibility of a flood of a much larger scale a few thousand years earlier. This theory is that in about 5000 B.C., melting European glaciers caused the Mediterranean Sea to overflow and turn a freshwater lake into the Black Sea. Beginning in 1999, a team of explorers led by Robert Ballard found shell evidence supporting a Black Sea shift from freshwater to saltwater and artifacts suggesting that humans once lived in an area now under the Black Sea.

CHAPTER 9

1 God blessed Noah and his sons, and said to them, "Be fertile and
increase, and fill the earth.
2 The fear and the dread of you shall be upon all the beasts of the
earth and upon all the birds of the sky—everything with which the
earth is astir—and upon all the fish of the sea; they are given into your
hand.
3 Every creature that lives shall be yours to eat; as with the green
28 grasses, I give you all these.
4 You must not, however, eat flesh with its life-blood in it.
5 But for your own life-blood I will require a reckoning: I will
require it of every beast; of man, too, will I require a reckoning for
human life, of every man for that of his fellow man!
6 Whoever sheds the blood of man,
By man shall his blood be shed;
For in His image.
Did God make man.
7 Be fertile, then, and increase; abound on the earth and increase
on it."
8 And God said to Noah and to his sons with him,
9 "I now establish My covenant with you and your offspring to
come,
10 and with every living thing that is with you—birds, cattle, and
every wild beast as well—all that have come out of the ark, every living
thing on earth.
11 I will maintain My covenant with you: never again shall all flesh
be cut off by the waters of a flood, and never again shall there be a flood
to destroy the earth."
12 God further said, "This is the sign that I set for the covenant
between Me and you, and every living creature with you, for all ages to
come.
13 I have set My bow in the clouds, and it shall serve as a sign of
the covenant between Me and the earth.
29 14 When I bring clouds over the earth, and the bow appears in the
clouds,
15 I will remember My covenant between Me and you and every
creature among all flesh, so that the waters shall never again become a
flood to destroy all flesh.
16 When the bow is in the clouds, I will see it and remember the
everlasting covenant between God and all living creatures, all flesh that
is on earth.
17 "That," God said to Noah, "shall be the sign of the covenant
that I have established between Me and all flesh that is on earth."

18 The sons of Noah who came out of the ark were Shem, Ham,
and Japheth—Ham being the father of Canaan.
19 These three were the sons of Noah, and from these the whole
world branched out.

Literary Analysis
Archetypal Setting and Dialogue Where will God place a sign of His covenant?

Reading Check 30
What covenant does God establish with Noah and all living creatures?

Differentiated Instruction Solutions for All Learners

Strategy for English Learners
To assist students with comprehension of the events in Chapter 9, point out that in verses 1–17, the Lord speaks. Ask students what message God delivers. (Do not shed the blood of another man, or your blood may be shed.) Then ask a volunteer to explain God's promise to Noah. (God will never again threaten life on Earth with a deadly flood.) Finally, point out that verses 18–29 resume Noah's story. Encourage students to list the events in that passage.

Enrichment for Gifted/Talented Students
Have students adapt the key elements of the Flood story to write a science-fiction movie in an outer-space setting. Students should include ideas for specific shots, music, and sound effects that will impress an audience. Encourage students to share their story summaries with one another.

28 Critical Thinking
Compare and Contrast
- Invite volunteers to read aloud the bracketed passage.
- Have students compare and contrast the passage with Genesis 1:26–30 on p. 39. **Ask** students to name at least three similarities between the passages.
  Possible response: In both passages, the Bible indicates that human beings are made in God's image, God says that human beings rule all other living things, and God says that plants and animals can serve as food for human beings.
- **Ask:** Why is it appropriate for the ideas of the Creation to be repeated after the Flood?
  Possible response: The survival of Noah and his family is like a new beginning for humanity. They are again the only people and must be fruitful and multiply in order to populate the world.

29 Literary Analysis
Archetypal Setting and Dialogue
- Draw students' attention to the word *covenant* in verse 11. Explain that in the Bible, the word *covenant* refers to a divine-human relationship that is warm and intense. It is almost like a marriage bond.
- Have students read the bracketed passage independently. Then, have them **respond** to the Literary Analysis question: Where will God place a sign of His covenant?
  Answer: God will place a sign of His covenant in a "bow in the clouds," or a rainbow.
- **Ask** students: Why is a rainbow an appropriate sign of God's covenant?
  Possible response: Rainbows often appear after storms and are seen as a positive or hopeful sign after a period of unhappiness or suffering.
- Discuss with students how a rainbow is an archetypal setting in literature, art, films, and religious works.

30 Reading Check
Answer: God promises never again to destroy the whole world with a flood.

ASSESS

Answers

1. **Possible response:** Floods and other natural disasters are dramatic events that human beings always remember.
2. (a) Humanity has become corrupt. (b) In both accounts, God is responding to humanity's disobedience or evil. In the case of Adam and Eve, however, evil results in the loss of the Garden of Eden; in the case of Noah, it almost results in the loss of the earth itself.
3. (a) God pledges that never again will a flood destroy the whole earth or cause all of humanity to perish at once. (b) The fact that all of humanity will now descend from Noah, who is holy and virtuous, prompts God to make the covenant.
4. (a) Noah is a just and righteous man who obeys God. (b) **Possible response:** God wants humanity to begin anew from the virtuous line of Noah and his family.
5. (a) **Possible response:** It is important to obey God's laws. (b) **Possible response:** God rewards Noah for his piety and destroys most of humanity because of its sinfulness and disobedience.
6. **Possible response:** Noah and his family may have felt fearful of the flood and sorrowful for those who were lost. They may have experienced a sense of duty or responsibility to save God's creatures and carry on the human race.

20 Noah, the tiller of the soil, was the first to plant a vineyard.
21 He drank of the wine and became drunk, and he uncovered
himself within his tent.
22 Ham, the father of Canaan, saw his father's nakedness and
told his two brothers outside.
23 But Shem and Japheth took a cloth, placed it against both
their backs and, walking backward, they covered their father's nakedness; their faces were turned the other way, so that they did not see
their father's nakedness.
24 When Noah woke up from his wine and learned what his
youngest son had done to him,
25 he said,
"Cursed be Canaan;
The lowest of slaves
Shall he be to his brothers."
26 And he said,
"Blessed be the LORD,
The God of Shem;
Let Canaan be a slave to them.
27 May God enlarge Japheth,
And let him dwell in the tents of Shem;
And let Canaan be a slave to them."
28 Noah lived after the Flood 350 years.
29 And all the days of Noah came to 950 years; then he died.

Critical Reading

1. **Respond:** Why do you think the story of Noah has such universal and timeless appeal?
2. **(a) Recall:** What reason does God give for destroying humanity? **(b) Compare and Contrast:** How is his reaction here both similar to and different from his earlier reaction to Adam and Eve?
3. **(a) Recall:** What covenant, or pact, does God make after the Flood? **(b) Analyze Cause and Effect:** How does Noah's behavior help prompt this covenant?
4. **(a) Compare and Contrast:** In what ways is Noah different from the rest of humanity in his day? **(b) Speculate:** In addition to Noah's virtues, what reason might God have for sparing Noah and his family?
5. **(a) Draw Conclusions:** What main moral lesson might readers draw from the story of the Flood? **(b) Support:** Cite details to support your conclusion.
6. **Synthesize:** What emotions do you think Noah and his family might have felt during the Flood? Why?

Apply the Skills

from the *Bible: Genesis 1–3 (The Creation and the Fall)* and *Genesis 6–9 (The Story of the Flood)*

Literary Analysis

Archetypal Setting

1. **(a)** Which details in these sections of the Bible reveal the **archetypal setting** of a universe consisting of opposites? **(b)** What other important opposites appear in the first three chapters of Genesis?
2. What evidence is there that the tree from which Eve eats an apple is an archetypal world-tree, or a link between the human and divine realms?
3. **(a)** Which adjectives would you use to describe the archetypal event of the Flood? **(b)** What does the setting of the Flood have in common with the setting of the Creation?

Connecting Literary Elements

4. **(a)** What is the first example of **dialogue** in Genesis 1? **(b)** How does this statement alter the archetypal setting? **(c)** What do you think this much-quoted statement has come to signify?
5. In the exchange between Eve and the serpent, how does the serpent demonstrate that he is a master of psychology?
6. **(a)** In a chart like the one shown, note the opposites that appear in the words God speaks in Genesis 8:22. **(b)** In general, what is God talking about in this section?

List of Opposites	

Reading Strategy

Identifying Chronological Order

7. **(a)** Make a list that **identifies in chronological order** what God does on each of the seven days of the Creation. **(b)** What significance does the seventh day continue to have for many people?
8. **(a)** During the Flood, how long does the rain last? **(b)** How long does the water swell? **(c)** In chronological order, explain how Noah uses birds to check on the flood waters.

Extend Understanding

9. **Science Connection:** What knowledge of the natural world is displayed in these chapters from Genesis?

QuickReview

An **archetypal setting** is a time, place, or landscape feature that has similar meaning for many different cultures.

Dialogue is a conversation between characters.

To **identify chronological order**, notice the order in which events happened in time.

For: Self-test
Visit: www.PHSchool.com
Web Code: eta-6105

Answers

1. (a) **Possible response:** Details include light and dark, day and night, evening and morning, sky and earth, land and water, sun and moon, and plants and animals.
   (b) **Possible response:** Additional opposites include male and female, good and evil, and corrupt humanity contrasted with the righteousness of Noah and his family.
2. **Possible responses:** The tree is described as giving knowledge and evil, which the serpent indicates is divine knowledge.
3. (a) **Possible response:** Appropriate adjectives include *cataclysmic, catastrophic, disastrous, long, gigantic, monumental,* and *awesome.* (b) **Possible responses:** Both settings involve God's direct involvement and are archetypal.
4. (a) God says, "Let there be light." (b) **Possible response:** The statement brings light to the universe. (c) **Possible responses:** This statement may be used to mean *Let there be good; Let there be knowledge;* or *The universe is created.*
5. The serpent downplays Eve's fears and tempts her with the divinity that she desires.
6. (a) Opposites include "seedtime and harvest," "cold and heat," "summer and winter," and "day and night." (b) God is talking about the cycles of time. Another sample answer can be found on **Literary Analysis Graphic Organizer B**, p. 8 in ***Graphic Organizer Transparencies.***
7. (a) The chronology of God's creations is as follows: Day 1: light (day) and dark (night); Day 2: sky and water; Day 3: land (Earth), seas, and vegetation; Day 4: the sun, moon, and stars; Day 5: birds and sea creatures; Day 6: land creatures and man; Day 7: God rests. (b) Many people continue to observe the seventh day as a day of rest.
8. (a) The rain lasts for forty days and forty nights. (b) The water swells for 150 days. (c) Noah sends out a raven that just flies back and forth, waiting for the waters to dry. Then, Noah sends out a dove three times until it does not return, indicating that the dove was able to land.

Answers continued

9. **Possible response:** Details about plants, animals, floods, topography, and the heavenly bodies are mentioned in these chapters.

Go Online Assessment Students may use the **Self-test** to prepare for **Selection Test A** or **Selection Test B.**

EXTEND/ASSESS

Answers

❶ Vocabulary Lesson

Word Analysis: Latin Prefix *com-*

1. to press together
2. to find similarities and differences
3. to put things together
4. to understand

Spelling Strategy

1. toil
2. boyhood
3. oily
4. destroyed
5. avoid
6. oyster
7. decoy
8. moisture

Vocabulary Builder: Sentence Completions

Answers: void; expanse; comprised; shrewdest; duped; enmity; corrupt; covenant.

❷ Grammar and Style Lesson

1. "Be fertile and increase," God told the first human beings. "Fill the earth and master it."
2. God asked Adam, "Where are you?"
3. Was it Adam who said, "I was naked and so I hid from You"?
4. After that God exclaimed, "What is this you have done!"
5. "The serpent duped me, and I ate," Eve explained.

Writing Application

Sample dialogue:

"I can't believe it's still raining!" Noah's wife exclaimed.

"Neither can I," said Noah.

Noah's wife sighed. "Do you think it will ever stop?"

"One of these days," Noah responded.

Build Language Skills

❶ Vocabulary Lesson

Word Analysis: Latin Prefix *com-*

The word *comprised* contains the Latin prefix *com-*, which means "with" or "together," and the root *-pris-*, which means "caught; held." *Comprised* means "included" or "consisted of." Define the following words.

1. compress
2. compare
3. combine
4. comprehend

Spelling Strategy

The *oy* sound is usually spelled *oi* or *oy: void, toy.* Complete each word below with the correct spelling of the *oy* sound.

1. t_?_l
2. b_?_hood
3. _?_ly
4. destr_?_ed
5. av_?_d
6. _?_ster
7. dec_?_
8. m_?_sture

Vocabulary Builder: Sentence Completions

Fill in each blank below with the appropriate words from the vocabulary list on page 37.

Before the Creation, there was nothing but the black __?__ of space. God set the sun, moon, and stars in the vast __?__ of sky. Beneath the sky, Earth __?__ land and water. Here Adam and Eve dwelled in the Garden of Eden until the serpent, who was the __?__ of animals, __?__ Eve into eating the forbidden fruit. Since then, there has been __?__ and fear between serpents and human beings. When humanity became more __?__, God destroyed everyone but Noah and his family in a great flood. With Noah, God made a pact, or __?__, promising not to destroy the whole earth ever again.

❷ Grammar and Style Lesson

Punctuation in Dialogue

In dialogue, a speaker's exact words are placed within opening (") and closing (") **quotation marks.** A period or a comma goes inside the closing quotation mark. A question mark or exclamation point goes inside only if it is the end punctuation of the quotation itself; otherwise, it goes outside.

God said, "Let there be light."

"You are not going to die," the serpent told Eve.

"Did you eat of the forbidden tree?" God asked.

Who said, "Let there be light"?

Practice Copy these sentences, adding the necessary quotation marks.

1. Be fertile and increase, God told the first human beings. Fill the earth and master it.
2. God asked Adam, Where are you?
3. Was it Adam who said, I was naked and so I hid from You?
4. After that God exclaimed, What is this you have done!
5. The serpent duped me, and I ate, Eve explained.

Writing Application Write a brief dialogue to show what Noah and his wife might have said during the Flood. Use correct punctuation.

WG *Prentice Hall Writing and Grammar Connection: Platinum Level: Chapter 28, Section 4*

Assessment Practice

Using Context Clues to Determine Meanings

(For more practice, see *Test Preparation Workbook*, p. 3.)

Students taking standardized tests will encounter vocabulary questions that require them to use context clues to determine meaning. Use this sample test item from Genesis 8:2–3 to give students practice with context clues.. . . the rain from the sky was held back; the waters then <u>receded</u> steadily from the earth.

In this sentence, the word *receded* most likely means—

A asked.
B strengthened.
C spilled.
D withdrew.

A can be eliminated because waters do not ask. *B* and *C* can be eliminated because the waters would not strengthen or spill after the rain stopped. The correct answer is *D* because it makes sense in the context of the sentence.

❸ Writing Lesson

Timed Writing: Extended Definition

Suppose that you had to define the meaning of paradise to someone unfamiliar with this archetypal setting. Using the descriptions of Eden in Genesis 2–3, write an extended definition of paradise. ***(40 minutes)***

Prewriting *(10 minutes)* In a sentence, formulate a general definition of paradise, and then list more specific qualities based on the details in Genesis. For each detail, note the verse where you will gather support: *No death (see 3:19–23)* or *Humans can talk with animals (see 3:1–5).*

Drafting *(20 minutes)* Begin with your general definition. Then, create an extended definition by explaining the qualities you listed and providing details from Genesis that illustrate each quality.

Revising *(10 minutes)* Review your draft, underlining each main quality you cite and placing a check mark beside each supporting detail. If there are not enough details, go back to the text to find additional examples.

Model: Revising to Add Examples

Eden is a paradise where life is easy. ^One important asset is the ready availability of food.^ Adam need not toil to survive, as he must after his exile.

Additional details from the text strengthen the explanation.

WG Prentice Hall Writing and Grammar Connection: Platinum Level, Chapter 10, Section 3

❹ Extend Your Learning

Listening and Speaking With a group, prepare and perform a **choral reading** from Genesis. Choose one of these sections:

- The Creation: Genesis 1 and Genesis 2:1–7
- The Fall: Genesis 2:8–24 and Genesis 3
- The Flood: Genesis 6–7
- After the Flood: Genesis 8–9

Decide whether any passages will be read by individuals. Discuss the appropriate tone and pace for the piece. Rehearse several times before performing for your classmates. **[Group Activity]**

Research and Technology Research and prepare a **written report** on flood stories as they appear in the literature or history of another culture. Use the Internet or your library's electronic sources to search for information. Be sure to identify the sources you use.

For: An additional research activity
Visit: www.PHSchool.com
Web Code: etd-7104

Assessment Resources

The following resources can be used to assess students' knowledge and skills.

Unit 1 Resources
- **Selection Test A,** pp. 35–37
- **Selection Test B,** pp. 38–40

General Resources
- **Rubrics for Exposition: Cause-and-Effect Essay,** pp. 61–62
- **Rubric for Speaking: Narrative Account,** p. 88

Go Online Assessment Students may use the **Self-test** to prepare for **Selection Test A** or **Selection Test B.**

❸ Writing Lesson

You may use this Writing Lesson as a timed-writing practice, or you may allow students to develop the Extended Definition as a writing assignment over several days.

- To give students help with this Writing Lesson, give them the **Support for Writing** page in ***Unit 1 Resources,*** p. 32, to organize their examples.
- Tell students that an extended definition includes explanations and examples. It usually begins with a basic definition and then elaborates on it.
- Use the Writing Lesson to guide students in developing their definitions.
- Use the Exposition: Cause-and-Effect Essay rubrics in ***General Resources,*** pp. 61–62, to evaluate students' work.

WG Writing and Grammar Platinum Level

To give students further instruction for writing this essay, use Chapter 10, Section 3.

❹ Listening and Speaking

- Read aloud the Listening and Speaking instruction.
- Organize the class into four groups and assign each of the four specified sections to a different group.
- Encourage students to assign most of the lines of dialogue to individual members but to consider group readings for the narrative.
- Use the Speaking: Narrative Account rubric in ***General Resources,*** p. 88, to evaluate students' performances.
- The **Support for Extend Your Learning** page (***Unit 1 Resources,*** p. 33) provides guided note-taking opportunities to help students complete the Extend Your Learning activities.

Go Online Research Have students type in the Web Code for another research activity.

Standard Course of Study

CT.4.01.1	Interpret and make generalizations supported by specific references.
CT.4.02.2	Use specific references from texts to show theme.
LT.5.03.8	Make connections between works, self and related topics in world literature.

Connections

Literature of the Americas

Just as the Judeo-Christian tradition draws its creation story from the Hebrew Bible, other traditions have their own accounts of creation. After students have read "The Wooden People," have them return to the account of creation in *Genesis* on pp. 38–50. Ask students what similarities and differences they can find between the Quiché Mayan and Hebrew accounts of creation.

The Beginning of the World

- Point out to students that most societies have a creation story that explains the origins of their people, as well as their relationship with the beings they worship. The Quiché Mayan story shares elements with other stories.
- Have students read the introductory text. Then, **ask** them what the Hebrew and the Quiché Mayan traditions have in common.
  Answer: Both traditions have a flood story.
- As students read the selection, have them look for similarities between the Quiché Mayan and Judeo-Christian views of humankind. **Ask** students what they think the Quiché Maya thought of the nature of human beings and why it was necessary that a flood destroy them.
  Possible response: The Quiché Mayan view was that human beings were ungrateful and did not take care of their world or respect their creator.

Literature of the Americas

Guatemala

The Beginning of the World

Explaining the emergence of the world from the chaos of nothingness has been a challenge for every civilization. Explanations vary from culture to culture, but there are remarkable elements of similarity. The Judeo-Christian tradition finds its explanation of creation in the account of the Hebrew Bible. In the excerpt from Genesis in this unit (page 38), God creates the heavens and the earth and populates the world with creatures, including man and woman. Later, as humans descend into wickedness, God destroys the evil in a great flood. The just Noah and his family, however, warned by God in time, save themselves and two of every species in an ark that they build—and they survive to repopulate the earth.

The Maker, Modeler On the other side of the world, in Central America, the Quiché Maya people call their God the Maker, Modeler, and their account of creation also includes a destruction by flood. "The Wooden People" describes a sort of rough draft of human beings—creatures made of wood who are not competent and do not speak. Overthrown and destroyed, they are left as a sign in a form that may surprise you.

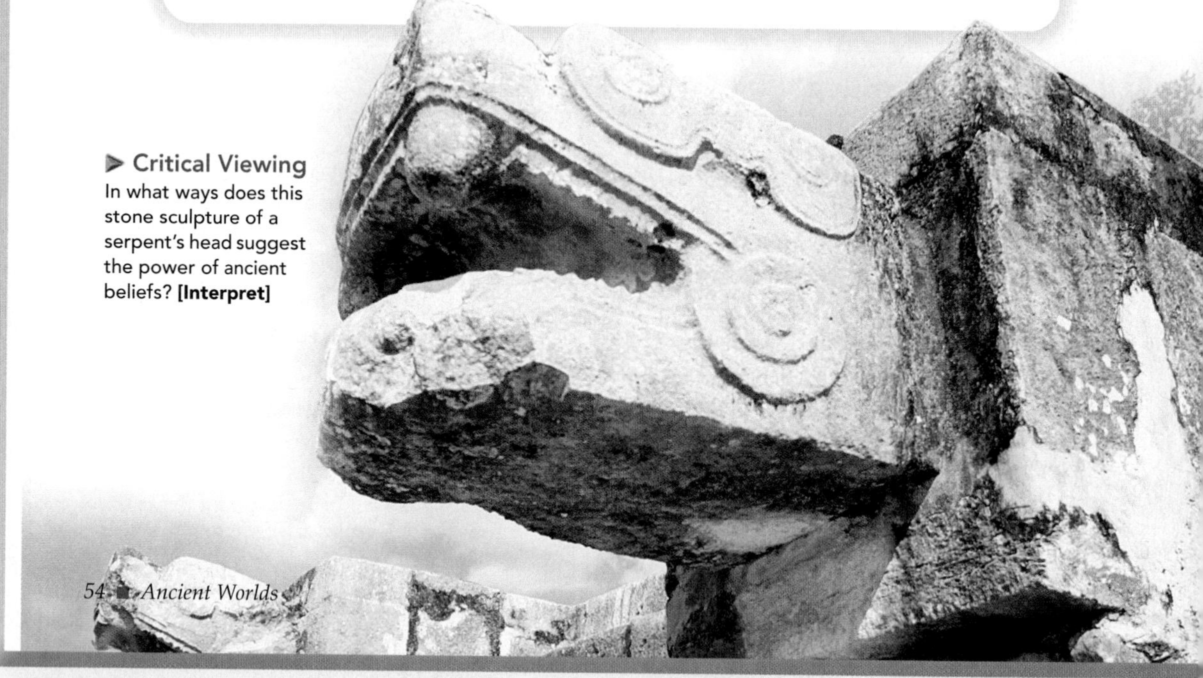

▶ Critical Viewing
In what ways does this stone sculpture of a serpent's head suggest the power of ancient beliefs? **[Interpret]**

- Have students review the *Genesis* account of creation and the flood. Then, **ask** them about the nature of human beings as shown in *Genesis* and the reason for the flood.
  Possible response: Human beings disobeyed God and were ungrateful, so God destroyed all but Noah, his family, and the animals on the Ark.

Humanities

This serpent sculpture is part of the ruined ancient Mayan city of Chichén Itzá. The city was founded about the sixth century A.D. This carving is symbolic of Quetzalcóatl, a main deity of the Mayan people.

Use the following question for discussion:

What does this sculpture reveal about the civilization that created it?
Possible response: To create a sculpture of this size, a culture would have to possess the human resources and knowledge to engineer incredible works of stone.

Critical Viewing

Possible response: Humankind has little power in comparison to the gods and nature.

from *Popol Vuh*

The Wooden People

A Quiché Mayan Myth

This was the peopling of the face of the earth: They came into being, they multiplied, they had daughters, they had sons, these manikins,[1] woodcarvings. But there was nothing in their hearts and nothing in their minds, no memory of their mason and builder. They just went and walked wherever they wanted. Now they did not remember the Heart of Sky.

And so they fell, just an experiment and just a cutout for humankind. They were talking at first but their faces were dry. They were not yet developed in the legs and arms. They had no blood, no lymph. They had no sweat, no fat. Their complexions were dry, their faces were crusty. They flailed their legs and arms, their bodies were deformed.

And so they accomplished nothing before the Maker, Modeler who gave them birth, gave them heart. They became the first numerous people here on the face of the earth.

Again there comes a humiliation, destruction, and demolition. The manikins, woodcarvings were killed when the Heart of Sky devised a flood for them. A great flood was made; it came down on the heads of the manikins, woodcarvings.

The man's body was carved from the wood of the coral tree by the Maker, Modeler. And as for the woman, the Maker,

Reading Check
What was missing from the first people created?

1. **manikin** (man' i kin) *n.* little man; model.

▲ **Critical Viewing** How does this Mayan figure emerging from a water lily relate to the beings described in these paragraphs? **[Connect]**

Background
from *Popol Vuh*

Popol Vuh is a Quiché Mayan account of the history and culture of the people of Guatemala before 1550. This document includes the Quiché Mayan creation account, the activities of the gods, the beginning of the Quiché people, as well as the history of their kings. In the early eighteenth century, a priest in Guatemala found *Popol Vuh* and translated the work into Spanish. The original text has been lost.

Reading Check
Answer: The first people lacked anything in their hearts and minds and did not remember their creator.

Critical Viewing
Answer: The figure is made of wood and is undeveloped.

Enrichment
The Quiché Civilization

The Quiché, who have about 700,000 members living in Guatemala, are the descendants of the advanced Mayan civilization that existed before Columbus landed in the Western Hemisphere. The pre-Columbian Quiché culture had a well-developed political and social structure with a well-defined class structure. Their centers of population are believed to have been large.

The modern Quiché are primarily farmers who work their land by hand, growing beans, squash, strawberries, and peaches. They live mainly in thatched huts, and most identify themselves as Roman Catholics, although many still follow pagan rituals.

Humanities

The Codex Fejervary-Mayer is a Mesoamerican artifact made of deerskin. It consists of twenty-three painted pieces folded together into a book called a codice. Codices were folded for the dual purpose of easy storage and the ability to view all of the pages at one time. These books consisted of pictures instead of writing and depicted ceremonies, calendars, and stories about the gods.

Critical Viewing

Answer: The images of the corn planter and the descriptions of the newly created beings both depict hardship and suffering.

▲ Critical Viewing Compare the images in this depiction of the life of a corn planter with the descriptions of newly created beings in these paragraphs. **[Compare and Contrast]**

Modeler needed the pith[2] of reeds for the woman's body. They were not competent, nor did they speak before the builder and sculptor who made them and brought them forth, and so they were killed, done in by a flood:

There came a rain of resin from the sky.

There came the one named Gouger of Faces: he gouged out their eyeballs.

There came Sudden Bloodletter: he snapped off their heads.

There came Crunching Jaguar: he ate their flesh.

There came Tearing Jaguar: he tore them open.

They were pounded down to the bones and tendons, smashed and pulverized even to the bones. Their faces were smashed because they were incompetent before their mother and their father, the Heart of Sky, named Hurricane. The earth was blackened because of this; the black rainstorm began, rain all day and rain all night. Into their houses came the animals, small and great. Their faces were crushed by things of wood and stone. Everything spoke: their water jars, their tortilla griddles, their plates, their cooking pots, their dogs, their grinding stones, each and every thing crushed their faces. Their dogs and turkeys told them:

"You caused us pain, you ate us, but now it is *you* whom *we* shall eat." And this is the grinding stone:

"We were undone because of you.

> Every day, every day,
> In the dark, in the dawn, forever,
> r-r-rip, r-r-rip,
> r-r-rub, r-r-rub,
> right in our faces, because of you.

This was the service we gave you at first, when you were still people, but today you will learn of our power. We shall pound and we shall grind your flesh," their grinding stones told them.

And this is what their dogs said, when they spoke in their turn:

"Why is it you can't seem to give us our food? We just watch and you just keep us down, and you throw us around. You keep a stick ready when you

---

2. **pith** *n.* soft, spongy tissue in the center of certain plant stems.

Enrichment

Mayan City-States

Between A.D. 300 and 900, Mayan city-states flourished from Mexico's Yucatán Peninsula through much of Central America. Temple-pyramids and artifacts in the jungles of Central America testify to the artistic skills of the Mayans.

The most famous Mayan site is Chichén Itzá, where thousands of tourists visit the remains of the Mayan pyramids, temples, an observatory, and a ball court. Other Mayan sites on the Yucatán Peninsula include Uxmal, Tikal, and on the Caribbean coast, Tulum.

eat, just so you can hit us. We don't talk, so we've received nothing from you. How could you not have known? You *did* know that we were wasting away there, behind you.

"So, this very day you will taste the teeth in our mouths. We shall eat you," their dogs told them, and their faces were crushed.

And then their tortilla griddles and cooking pots spoke to them in turn:

"Pain! That's all you've done for us. Our mouths are sooty, our faces are sooty. By setting us on the fire all the time, you burn us. Since *we* felt no pain, *you* try it. We shall burn you," all their cooking pots said, crushing their faces.

The stones, their hearthstones were shooting out, coming right out of the fire, going for their heads, causing them pain. Now they run for it, helter-skelter.

They want to climb up on the houses, but they fall as the houses collapse.

They want to climb the trees; they're thrown off by the trees.

They want to get inside caves, but the caves slam shut in their faces.

Such was the scattering of the human work, the human design. The people were ground down, overthrown. The mouths and faces of all of them were destroyed and crushed. And it used to be said that the monkeys in the forests today are a sign of this. They were left as a sign because wood alone was used for their flesh by the builder and sculptor.

So this is why monkeys look like people: they are a sign of a previous human work, human design—mere manikins, mere woodcarvings.

The Quiché Maya

The Quiché Maya, an Indian people living in Guatemala, in Central America, come from a civilization that was politically and socially advanced in pre-Columbian times. *Popol Vuh,* which is the record of the history and the mythol-ogy of the Quiché Maya, was originally written in hieroglyphics. After the Quiché Maya were conquered by the Spanish in 1524, the *Popol Vuh* was written down in the Quiché language using the Latin alphabet. Dennis Tedlock, the award-winning translator of this excerpt from *Popol Vuh,* is also a poet and a cultural anthropologist.

Connecting Literature of the Americas

1. **(a)** What is the reason for the flood in "The Wooden People"? **(b)** Why does God destroy by flood in Genesis? **(c)** Identify the elements that make these floods similar and those that make them different.
2. Compare the accounts of the creation of woman in Genesis and in "The Wooden People." **(a)** In what ways are the two accounts similar? **(b)** How are they different?
3. What do these creation stories suggest about the differences between Hebrew and Quiché Maya culture?

ASSESS

Answers

1. (a) The flood destroys the people because they have accomplished nothing. They have nothing in their hearts and minds and do not remember the Heart of Sky. (b) God destroys by flood in *Genesis* because humans had only wickedness in their hearts and had broken their covenant with God. (c) The floods cover the Earth in both accounts, and humans are destroyed for their failure to remember their creator. The accounts are different because in the *Genesis* account, Noah and his family are preserved. In the Quiché Mayan account, the flood destroys all of humankind.
2. (a) In both accounts, man is created first. (b) In *Genesis,* woman is created from Adam's rib and is to be his companion because Adam is lonely. In "The Wooden People," woman is created from the pith of reeds.
3. The *Genesis* creation story shows that God is more involved in humans' lives and is willing to spare Noah and his family. Also, in the *Genesis* account, humans are made in God's image and have a covenant with Him that they are supposed to uphold. The Quiché Mayan account shows a more distant god that makes wooden people without a heart and not in his likeness. These wooden people are a reminder to humans to be aware of their creator.

Differentiated Instruction Solutions for All Learners

Strategy for Less Proficient Readers
This piece, although written in fairly simple vocabulary, may present a challenge for students because of its style and structure. Have students write a brief summary of each major event and create a timeline of the major events. Then, have them compare these events with the *Genesis* account.

Strategy for English Learners
Ask students whether they are familiar with any other creation stories. If so, have students share the stories aloud or in written paragraphs. They should also explain whether there are any similarities between the creation stories they know and the *Genesis* and Quiché Mayan accounts.

Enrichment for Advanced Readers
Have students research another creation account, such as one from an Eastern religion or a Native American tradition. Then, have them write reports on the similarities and differences between their information and the two accounts in the text. Ask students to share their findings with the class.

Standard Course of Study

Goal 1: WRITTEN LANGUAGE

WL.1.02.1	Relate personal knowledge to textual information in a written reflection.

Goal 5: LITERATURE

LT.5.01.6	Make connections between historical and contemporary issues in world literature.
LT.5.01.7	Understand the cultural and historical impact on world literature texts.
LT.5.03.2	Analyze text structure and components and evaluate impact.
LT.5.03.3	Provide textual evidence to support understanding of and response to world literature.

Goal 6: GRAMMAR AND USAGE

GU.6.02.3	Edit for parallel structure.

Step-by-Step Teaching Guide	Pacing Guide
PRETEACH	
• Administer Vocabulary and Reading Warm-ups as necessary.	5 min.
• Engage students' interest with the motivation activity.	5 min.
• Read and discuss author and background features. **FT**	10 min.
• Introduce the Literary Analysis Skill: Parallelism. **FT**	5 min.
• Introduce the Reading Strategy: Using Context Clues.	10 min.
• Prepare students to read by teaching the selection vocabulary. **FT**	
TEACH	
• Informally monitor comprehension while students read independently or in groups. **FT**	30 min.
• Monitor students' comprehension with the Reading Check notes.	as students read
• Reinforce vocabulary with Vocabulary Builder notes.	as students read
• Develop students' understanding of parallelism with the Literary Analysis annotations. **FT**	5 min.
• Develop students' ability to use context clues with the Reading Strategy annotations. **FT**	5 min.
ASSESS/EXTEND	
• Assess students' comprehension and mastery of the Literary Analysis and Reading Strategy by having them answer the Apply the Skills questions. **FT**	15 min
• Have students complete the Vocabulary Lesson and the Grammar and Style Lesson. **FT**	15 min
• Apply students' ability to include quotations from the text by using the Writing Lesson. **FT**	45 min. or homework
• Apply students' understanding by using one or more of the Extend Your Learning activities.	20–90 min. or homework
• Administer Selection Test A or Selection Test B. **FT**	15 min.

Resources

Print

Unit 1 Resources

Transparency

Graphic Organizer Transparencies

Print

Reader's Notebook [L2]

Reader's Notebook: Adapted Version [L1]

Reader's Notebook: English Learner's Version [EL]

Unit 1 Resources

Technology

Listening to Literature Audio CDs [L2, EL]

Reader's Notebook: Adapted Version Audio CD [L1, L2]

Print

Unit 1 Resources

General Resources

Technology

Go Online: Research **[L3]**
Go Online: Self-test **[L3]**
ExamView®, **Test Bank [L3]**

Choosing Resources for Differentiated Instruction

[L1] Special Needs Students
[L2] Below-Level Students
[L3] All Students
[L4] Advanced Students
[EL] English Learners

For Vocabulary and Reading Warm-ups and for Selection Tests, **A** signifies "less challenging" and **B** "more challenging." For Graphic Organizer transparencies, **A** signifies "not filled in" and **B** "filled in."

FT Fast Track Instruction: To move the lesson more quickly, use the strategies and activities identified with **FT**.

Scaffolding for Less Proficient and Advanced Students

The leveled Critical Thinking questions after selections progress in the levels of thinking required to answer them. To address the needs of your different students, you may use the (a) level questions for your less proficient students and the (b) level questions with your on-level and advanced students. The occasional (c) level questions are appropriate for your advanced students.

Use this complete suite of powerful teaching tools to make lesson planning and testing quicker and easier.

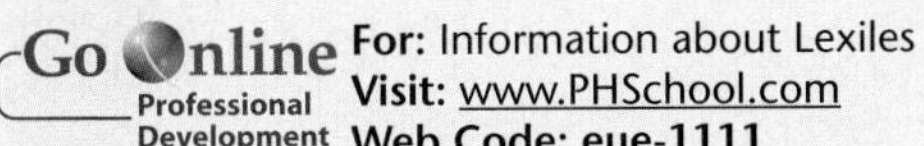

Use the interactive textbook (online and on CD-ROM) to make selections and activities come alive with audio and video support and interactive questions.

Go Online Professional Development **For:** Information about Lexiles
Visit: www.PHSchool.com
Web Code: eue-1111

PRETEACH

Motivation

Ask students to recall stories or films that show what it is like to be a stranger in a new place. Have them describe vivid details from these stories or films. Then, tell them that the Book of Ruth deals with a similar subject.

❶ Background

More About the Selections

Many English biblical terms, such as *psalm,* come from the Greek language. This derivation reflects the influence of the Septuagint, a Greek translation of the Jewish Bible made from the third through second centuries B.C. At this time, a large group of Jews lived in Alexandria, Egypt, then under Greek domination, and knew Greek better than Hebrew. Jewish leaders wanted a Bible translation that would be understood by these Greek-speaking Jews. Later they went back to more authentic Hebrew sources, but early Christians continued to use the Septuagint. Furthermore, the New Testament of the Christian Bible was originally written in Greek.

Geography Note

Draw students' attention to the map at the top of the page. Explain that in biblical times, the Moabites were neighbors of the Jews. Their homeland of Moab was located between the Dead Sea and the Arabian Desert in what is now part of the nation of Jordan.

Build Skills *Scripture*

❶

from the Bible: Book of Ruth • Psalms 8, 19, 23, and 137

Book of Ruth (400s or 300s B.C.)

The Book of Ruth, in the part of the Hebrew Bible called the Writings, appeared in written form after the Jews returned from their exile in Babylon (597–538 B.C.).

Speaking for the Outsider Ruth, the central character, is not a Jew but displays exceptional loyalty toward her Jewish mother-in-law. The book's purpose, therefore, was to show the worth of an outsider at a time when the Jews, recalling their forced exile, were less willing to accept outsiders.

The Hebrew Short Story The Book of Ruth is also an excellent example of the Hebrew short story. Such a form was something new in the literature of the ancient Middle East. For the most part, such stories dispensed with the obvious magical and fairy-tale elements that characterized other Middle Eastern tales. As this story shows, they might also have had a serious purpose.

A Story That Speaks to Us The Book of Ruth still speaks to us today. Contemporary novelist Cynthia Ozick, for example, sees special meaning in it. In this brief story, she says, "death, loss, displacement, destitution" give rise to "mercy and redemption."

Book of Psalms (c. 900s – c. 400s B.C.)

Like the Book of Ruth, the Book of Psalms (sämz) is in the part of the Hebrew Bible called the Writings. The Book of Psalms, however, is not a short story but a collection of 150 religious poems that were set to music.

A Greek Name for Hebrew Poems The English word *psalms* comes from the Greek *psalmos,* meaning "a song accompanied by a plucked instrument." This Greek word, in turn, is the translation of the Hebrew terms for "song" and "praise." That is how Hebrew religious poems came to be called by an English word derived from Greek!

Many Authors, Different Moods The Hebrew psalms praised a single God, but they did not have a single author. The traditional belief was that King David (reigned c. 1000–962 B.C.) wrote them. In truth, however, the psalms were composed by many authors over a long period of time. They were included as part of religious ceremonies and expressed the different moods inspired by the relationship between God and the Hebrew people. These moods could vary from despair to joy.

Enduring Poems The psalms are among the most influential poems in the Western tradition. They have played a central role in both Christian and Jewish religious ceremonies. They have also influenced poets as diverse as John Milton, Walt Whitman, and Dylan Thomas.

Psalms and Bible Stories in the Oral Tradition

Before it was written down, the Book of Ruth was probably told orally. Just who told it—and where—is a matter for speculation. It may have been told in the small towns that dotted the countryside. Townsfolk might have gathered in the evening at the town spring or gate to hear the story of Ruth and her mother-in-law, Naomi.

The storytellers themselves may have been Levites, members of a Hebrew tribe whose role was to assist with religious ceremonies. An even more interesting possibility is that "wise women" told this tale. Such female storytellers are mentioned in a number of biblical narratives.

In contrast to the mysterious origins of the Book of Ruth, the background on the Psalms is clearer. The psalm is a literary form borrowed by the Jews from the peoples of Mesopotamia and Egypt. When the Jews borrowed this form, however, they made one crucial change. Their Middle Eastern neighbors used psalms to worship many gods, whereas the Jews used them to express emotions arising from their belief in a single God. Despite their differences, both groups of people used psalms as part of their respective religious services.

Preview

Connecting to the Literature

Living among people who view you as an outsider can both pose problems and offer opportunities. The heroine of the Book of Ruth finds herself in just such a situation.

❷ Literary Analysis

Parallelism

Both the Book of Ruth and the Psalms use **parallelism**—a style that involves stating an idea in the first half of a verse and then, using a similar grammatical structure, repeating, negating, completing, or otherwise elaborating on it in the second half.

- completion of an idea (Ruth 2:20): *"[T]he man is related to us; he is one of our redeeming kinsmen."*
- repetition with variations (Psalms 8:4): *what is man that You have been mindful of him, / mortal man that You have taken note of him ...*

Parallelism creates balance, variation, and flowing rhythm in prose and poetry alike. Look for examples of this style as you read.

Comparing Literary Works

Parallelism—especially repetition with variation—can communicate a work's **theme,** or central idea. Ruth's repeated phrases suggest a theme of loyalty: "Wherever you go, I will go; wherever you lodge, I will lodge." In Psalm 23, parallelism underscores the central ideas of guidance and trust: "He leads me to water . . . He renews my life; He guides me. . . ." Look for such themes as you read these selections from the Bible.

❸ Reading Strategy

Using Context Clues

Use context clues, or hints in the surrounding passage, to determine the meanings of unfamiliar words as you read. Common context clues are synonyms, antonyms, and examples that clarify a word's meaning. Use a chart like the one shown to find context clues as you read.

Vocabulary Builder

glean (glēn) *v.* collect grain left by reapers (p. 62)

reapers (rē´ pərz) *n.* those who gather a crop by cutting (p. 62)

redeem (ri dēm´) *v.* buy back; fulfill a promise (p. 64)

avenger (ə venj´ ər) *n.* one who takes revenge (p. 67)

precepts (prē´ septs´) *n.* rules of conduct (p. 68)

lucid (lo͞o´ sid) *adj.* clear; apparent (p. 68)

steadfast (sted´ fast´) *adj.* firm; not changing (p. 68)

NC Standard Course of Study

- Analyze text structure and components and evaluate impact. (LT.5.03.2)
- Edit for parallel structure. (GU.6.02.3)

Passage
"Day to day makes utterance, night to night speaks out."

↓

Unfamiliar Word
utterance

↓

Context Clue
night to night speaks out

↓

Relation to Unfamiliar Word
synonym

↓

Conclusion
If *makes utterance* means *speaks out,* then *utterance* probably means "speech."

❷ Literary Analysis

Parallelism

- Read aloud the Literary Analysis instruction.
- Then, point out the two examples of parallelism. Offer students an example of parallelism used to negate an idea:
  I went away full, and the Lord brought me back empty.
- Explain that parallelism was common in ancient Middle Eastern poetry. It occurs sometimes in the Book of Ruth, but it is even more common in the Psalms.
- Note that although parallelism sometimes involves the use of similar grammatical structures, it is not rigid or mechanical. In the hands of ancient Hebrew poets, parallelism was a means of introducing balance and variation into their work.

❸ Reading Strategy

Using Context Clues

- Read aloud the Reading Strategy instruction. Then, review the example in the chart. Clarify that "speaks out" means the same as "makes utterance"; this context clue indicates the meaning of *utterance.*
- Give students a copy of **Reading Strategy Graphic Organizer A** in ***Graphic Organizer Transparencies,*** p. 9, and encourage them to use it when they read.
- Remind students to use dictionaries to check the word meanings that they guess from context clues.

Vocabulary Builder

- Pronounce each vocabulary word for students, and read the definitions as a class. Have students identify any words with which they are already familiar.

Differentiated Instruction Solutions for All Learners

Support for Special Needs Students
Have students read the adapted version of the Book of Ruth in the ***Reader's Notebook: Adapted Version.*** This version provides basic-level instruction in an interactive format with questions and write-on lines. Completing these pages will prepare students to read the selection in the Student Edition.

Support for Less Proficient Readers
Have students read the Book of Ruth in the ***Reader's Notebook.*** This version provides basic-level instruction in an interactive format with questions and write-on lines. After students finish the selection in the ***Reader's Notebook,*** have them complete the questions and activities in the Student Edition.

Support for English Learners
Have students read the Book of Ruth in the ***Reader's Notebook: English Learner's Version.*** This version provides basic-level instruction in an interactive format with questions and write-on lines. Completing these pages will prepare students to read the selection in the Student Edition.

TEACH

Facilitate Understanding

Students may enjoy the Book of Ruth more if you encourage them to predict what is going to happen. At the end of each chapter, pause to allow them to guess what might happen next and to speculate about what they think will happen at the end of the selection.

❶ About the Selection

In just eighty-five verses, the Bible tells one of the world's best-known stories of suffering, love, and redemption. After Naomi loses her husband and her sons, she mournfully decides to leave Moab and return to her homeland of Bethlehem. Her daughter-in-law Ruth, although a Moabite, insists on accompanying her and adopting her Jewish ways. Impressed by Ruth's loyalty and self-sacrifice, Naomi's wealthy kinsman, Boaz, protects the young Moabite from discrimination and gladly allows her to glean in his fields. Eventually he weds her in accordance with Jewish law. Also by this law, their first son becomes the heir of Ruth's first husband, thus providing Naomi with the grandson she desires.

❷ Critical Thinking

Hypothesize

- Invite a volunteer to read aloud the bracketed passage. **Ask** students why there is no longer a famine in Bethlehem.
  Answer: The Lord has provided food to His people who live there.
- Have students **hypothesize** why Naomi might want to move back to Bethlehem.
  Possible response: Naomi is saddened by the deaths of her husband and sons. Because the famine has ended in Bethlehem, Naomi feels that she can return to the place where her family was once together and happy.

❶ Book of Ruth

translated by The Jewish Publication Society

Background The written version of the Book of Ruth dates from after the Babylonian exile (538 B.C.), but the story it tells is set around 1100 B.C. This era, called in the story "the days when the chieftains ruled," predates by about 100 years King David's reign over a united Israel. In fact, as the story establishes, David was Ruth's great-grandson.

Moab, Ruth's country, was a kingdom east of the Dead Sea. The story explains that Naomi's family fled there to escape a famine, and their reasons for doing so are easy to infer: Moab was near Bethlehem, Naomi's home, and the Moabites were closely linked with the Jews.

CHAPTER 1

1 In the days when the chieftains ruled, there was a famine in the
land; and a man of Bethlehem in Judah, with his wife and two sons,
went to reside in the country of Moab.[1]
2 The man's name was Elimelech, his wife's name was Naomi, and
his two sons were named Mahlon and Chilion—Ephrathites of Bethlehem in Judah.[2]
3 Elimelech, Naomi's husband, died; and she was left with her two
sons.
4 They married Moabite women, one named Orpah and the other
Ruth, and they lived there about ten years.
❷ 5 Then those two—Mahlon and Chilion—also died; so the woman
was left without her two sons and without her husband.
6 She started out with her daughters-in-law to return from the
country of Moab; for in the country of Moab she had heard that the
LORD had taken note of His people and given them food.

1. **Moab** (mō ab´) ancient kingdom east and south of the Dead Sea, and east of the Jordan River.
2. **Judah** Jewish kingdom in the southern part of Palestine.

Differentiated Instruction Solutions for All Learners

Accessibility at a Glance

	Book of Ruth Chaps. 1–4	Psalms 8, 19, 23, 137
Context	Jewish biblical history	The Judeo-Christian tradition: God's relationship to man
Language	Syntax: Long sentences featuring parallelism	Syntax: Long sentences with embedded clauses
Concept Level	Accessible (Suffering, love and redemption; God rewards the obedient.)	Accessible (the comfort of the Lord's gifts to man; the torment of exile)
Literary Merit	Classic: Scripture	Classic: Scripture
Lexile	940L	940L
Overall Rating	Average	Average

7 Accompanied by her two daughters-in-law, she left the place
where she had been living; and they set out on the road back to the
land of Judah.
8 But Naomi said to her two daughters-in-law, "Turn back, each of
you to her mother's house. May the LORD deal kindly with you, as you
have dealt with the dead and with me!
9 May the LORD grant that each of you find security in the house of
a husband!" And she kissed them farewell. They broke into weeping
10 and said to her, "No, we will return with you to your people."
11 But Naomi replied, "Turn back, my daughters! Why should you
go with me? Have I any more sons in my body who might be husbands
for you?
12 Turn back, my daughters, for I am too old to be married. Even
3 if I thought there was hope for me, even if I were married tonight and I
also bore sons,
13 should you wait for them to grow up? Should you on their
account debar yourselves from marriage? Oh no, my daughters! My lot
is far more bitter than yours, for the hand of the LORD has struck out
against me."
14 They broke into weeping again, and Orpah kissed her mother-
in-law farewell. But Ruth clung to her.
15 So she said, "See, your sister-in-law has returned to her people
and her gods. Go follow your sister-in-law."
16 But Ruth replied, "Do not urge me to leave you, to turn back
4 and not follow you. For wherever you go, I will go; wherever you lodge,
I will lodge; your people shall be my people, and your God my God.
17 Where you die, I will die, and there I will be buried. Thus and
more may the LORD do to me[3] if anything but death parts me from you."
18 When [Naomi] saw how determined she was to go with her, she
ceased to argue with her;
19 and the two went on until they reached Bethlehem.
When they arrived in Bethlehem, the whole city buzzed with
excitement over them. The women said, "Can this be Naomi?"
20 "Do not call me Naomi," she replied. "Call me Mara,[4] for
Shaddai[5] has made my lot very bitter.
21 I went away full, and the LORD has brought me back empty.
How can you call me Naomi, when the LORD has dealt harshly with me,
when Shaddai[5] has brought misfortune upon me!"
22 Thus Naomi returned from the country of Moab; she returned
with her daughter-in-law Ruth the Moabite. They arrived in Bethlehem
at the beginning of the barley harvest.

Literary Analysis
Parallelism What is an example of parallelism in Ruth 1:16? Explain.

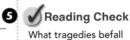

5  **Reading Check**
What tragedies befall Naomi and her family in the country of Moab?

3. **do to me** punish me.
4. **Naomi . . . Mara** In Hebrew, Naomi means "my delight" and Mara means "bitter."
5. **Shaddai** usually, "the Almighty."

Differentiated Instruction Solutions for All Learners

Strategy for Special Needs Students
Direct students' attention to verse 22, the last verse of Chapter 1. Point out that this verse serves as a kind of summary of what has happened in the chapter. It also helps make a transition to events in the next chapter, which will apparently take place in Bethlehem at the beginning of the barley harvest. Tell students to look for other summarizing or transitional paragraphs in the Book of Ruth. Stress that such paragraphs, which often come at or near the ends of the chapters, can help students follow and anticipate the story's events.

Strategy for English Learners
To help students develop an ear for the balance and flowing rhythm of parallelism, have them read along with the recording on **Listening to Literature Audio CDs.** After they listen, explain that elaboration of an idea is one form of parallelism. Point out that in verse 2, parallelism is caused by the second clause *his wife's name was Naomi* adding to the idea in the first clause *The man's name was Elimelech.* The third clause *and his two sons were named Mahlon and Chilion* further elaborates, with variation, that idea. Ask students what repeated words add to the rhythm. *(name was, was named)*

3 Critical Thinking
Compare and Contrast
- Have students read the bracketed passage independently. Point out that the Book of Ruth often conveys character by means of contrast.
- Have students **compare** and **contrast** Orpah and Ruth in terms of their devotion to Naomi.
  Answer: Orpah and Ruth are both devoted to Naomi, but Orpah stays in Moab.
- Then, have students **compare** and **contrast** how Ruth and Naomi react to the deaths of their husbands.
  Possible response: Both women are saddened by the loss of their husbands. Naomi, however, complains bitterly about God for having "struck out" against her, whereas Ruth seems more accepting of the situation.
- **Ask** students what these contrasts reveal about Ruth.
  Possible response: Ruth is loyal, willing to go beyond the call of duty, and accepting of her lot in life.

4 Literary Analysis
Parallelism
- Remind students that in parallelism, a biblical verse states an idea in the first half and then repeats, negates, completes, or otherwise elaborates on it in the second half. Note that parallelism can also occur within smaller units of a verse or between two verses.
- Have a volunteer read aloud Ruth's words in the bracketed passage.
- **Ask** students the Literary Analysis question: What is an example of parallelism in Ruth 1:16? Explain.
  Possible response: The phrase "to turn back and not follow you" restates the first part of that sentence, "Do not urge me to leave you." In the rest of 1:16—for example, "wherever you lodge, I will lodge"—the second clause repeats the idea of the first clause.
- **Ask** students to explain parallelism in verse 17.
  Answer: "Where you die, I will die" continues the pattern in which the second clause repeats the idea of the first clause.

5 Reading Check
Answer: Naomi loses her husband and both sons; her daughters-in-law lose their husbands.

❻ Humanities

Ruth in the Field of Boaz, c. 1860s

This Bible illustration shows Ruth holding sheaves of wheat in Boaz's field. Leviticus 23:22 instructs those who farm crops to leave the corners of their fields for strangers and the poor to make use of: "And when ye reap the harvest of your land, thou shalt not make clean riddance of the corners of thy field when thou reapest, neither shalt thou gather any gleaning of thy harvest: thou shalt leave them unto the poor, and to the stranger: I am the Lord your God." This helps explain why Ruth is permitted to glean in Boaz's field.

Use the following questions to initiate discussion:

- Which details in the image suggest Boaz's wealth and power?
  Possible response: Boaz's opulent gown, thick gold-trimmed robe, golden neck ornament, and outstretched arm all suggest wealth and power. The deference of the people around him also suggests his status in the community.
- What adjectives would you use to describe Ruth in this image?
  Possible response: Ruth appears respectful, humble, thankful, and graceful.

❼ Critical Viewing

Answer: The image illustrates the exchange between Boaz and Ruth in verses 8–13, specifically showing how Ruth prostrates herself before Boaz in verse 10.

❽ Reading Strategy

Using Context Clues

- Remind students that a word's context refers to the surroundings in which the word appears.
- Invite a volunteer to read aloud the bracketed passage. Then, **ask** students the Reading Strategy question: Based on the context clues, what does *partake* mean?
  Answer: *Partake* means "take part."
- Have students **explain** how the context clarifies the meaning of *partake.*
  Possible response: Boaz asks Ruth to "partake of the meal," and Ruth sits down and eats. The cause-and-effect relationship suggests that *partake* means "to take part."

CHAPTER 2

❻

1 Now Naomi had a kinsman on her husband's side, a man of substance, of the family of Elimelech, whose name was Boaz.

2 Ruth the Moabite said to Naomi, "I would like to go to the fields and glean among the ears of grain, behind someone who may show me kindness." "Yes, daughter, go," she replied;

3 and off she went. She came and gleaned in a field, behind the reapers; and, as luck would have it, it was the piece of land belonging to Boaz, who was of Elimelech's family.

4 Presently Boaz arrived from Bethlehem. He greeted the reapers, "The LORD be with you" And they responded, "The LORD bless you!"

5 Boaz said to the servant who was in charge of the reapers, "Whose girl is that?"

6 The servant in charge of the reapers replied, "She is a Moabite girl who came back with Naomi from the country of Moab.

7 She said, 'Please let me glean and gather among the sheaves behind the reapers.' She has been on her feet ever since she came this morning. She has rested but little in the hut."

8 Boaz said to Ruth, "Listen to me, daughter. Don't go to glean in another field. Don't go elsewhere, but stay here close to my girls.

9 Keep your eyes on the field they are reaping, and follow them. I have ordered the men not to molest you. And when you are thirsty, go to the jars and drink some of [the water] that the men have drawn."

10 She prostrated herself with her face to the ground, and said to him, "Why are you so kind as to single me out, when I am a foreigner?"

11 Boaz said in reply, "I have been told of all that you did for your mother-in-law after the death of your husband, how you left your father and mother and the land of your birth and came to a people you had not known before.

12 May the LORD reward your deeds. May you have a full recompense from the LORD, the God of Israel, under whose wings you have sought refuge!"

❽ 13 She answered, "You are most kind, my lord, to comfort me and to speak gently to your maidservant—though I am not so much as one of your maidservants."

14 At mealtime, Boaz said to her, "Come over here and partake of the meal, and dip your morsel in the vinegar." So she sat down beside

▲ **Critical Viewing** ❼ What verses from Chapter 2 might this painting illustrate? Why? **[Speculate]**

Vocabulary Builder

glean (glēn) *v.* collect grain left by reapers

reapers (rē′ pərz) *n.* those who gather a crop by cutting

Reading Strategy
Using Context Clues
Based on the context clues, what does *partake* mean?

Enrichment

Grain and Its Cultivation

The barley and wheat in Boaz's field are types of grain, or grassy plants bearing dried fruits that are used for food. Each seedlike fruit is also called a grain. Grain is the principal food of human beings and animals around the world. In the Middle East and Europe, wheat is the chief grain used as food, although barley was once more widely used than it is today. In eastern Asia, rice is the staple; in the Americas, wheat is the staple, although it was corn before Europeans brought over wheat in the seventeenth century.

Evidence suggests that in the Middle East, wheat and barley have been cultivated since perhaps as early as 8000 B.C. For wheat to be used as food, the grains must be separated from the husks, or "chaff," by a process of threshing (beating) or winnowing (blowing). The dried grains are then usually ground into coarse meal or fine flour, which can be baked into bread.

the reapers. He handed her roasted grain, and she ate her fill and had some left over.

9 15 When she got up again to glean, Boaz gave orders to his workers, "You are not only to let her glean among the sheaves, without interference,

16 but you must also pull some [stalks] out of the heaps and leave them for her to glean, and not scold her."

17 She gleaned in the field until evening. Then she beat out what she had gleaned—it was about an *ephah*[6] of barley—

18 and carried it back with her to the town. When her mother-in-law saw what she had gleaned, and when she also took out and gave her what she had left over after eating her fill,

19 her mother-in-law asked her, "Where did you glean today? Where did you work? Blessed be he who took such generous notice of you!" So she told her mother-in-law whom she had worked with, saying, "The name of the man with whom I worked today is Boaz."

20 Naomi said to her daughter-in-law, "Blessed be he of the LORD, who has not failed in His kindness to the living or to the dead! For," Naomi explained to her daughter-in-law, "the man is related to us; he is one of our redeeming kinsmen."

21 Ruth the Moabite said, "He even told me, 'Stay close by my workers until all my harvest is finished.'"

10 22 And Naomi answered her daughter-in-law Ruth, "It is best, daughter, that you go out with his girls, and not be annoyed in some other field."

23 So she stayed close to the maidservants of Boaz, and gleaned until the barley harvest and the wheat harvest were finished. Then she stayed at home with her mother-in-law.

CHAPTER 3

1 Naomi, her mother-in-law, said to her, "Daughter, I must seek a home for you, where you may be happy.

2 Now there is our kinsman Boaz,[7] whose girls you were close to. He will be winnowing barley on the threshing floor tonight.

3 So bathe, anoint[8] yourself, dress up, and go down to the threshing floor. But do not disclose yourself to the man until he has finished eating and drinking.

4 When he lies down, note the place where he lies down, and go over and uncover his feet and lie down. He will tell you what you are to do."

5 She replied, "I will do everything you tell me."

6 She went down to the threshing floor and did just as her mother-in-law had instructed her.

6. ***ephah*** (ē′ fə) ancient Hebrew unit of dry measure, estimated at from one third of a bushel to a little over one bushel.
7. **our kinsman Boaz** According to Jewish law, the closest unmarried male relative of Ruth's deceased husband was obligated to marry her.
8. **anoint** (ə noint′) *v.* rub oil or ointment on.

Reading Strategy
Using Context Clues
Which context clues in verse 16 help define the word *sheaves* in verse 15?

11 
Reading Check
What reasons does Boaz give for helping Ruth?

9 Reading Strategy
Using Context Clues

- **Ask** a volunteer to read aloud the bracketed passage.
- Then, have two volunteers **remind** the class of the meanings of the vocabulary words *glean* and *reapers.* **Answer:** *Glean* means "to collect grain left by reapers." *Reapers* are "those who gather a crop by cutting."
- Explain that when grain is harvested, it is reaped or cut down and put into heaps. At the time of the Book of Ruth, it was the custom to allow the poor or strangers to follow the reapers and gather the loose grain that had been dropped.
- **Ask** students the Reading Strategy question: What context clues in verse 16 help define the word *sheaves* in verse 15? **Answer:** The context clues are "pull some [stalks]" and "heaps."
- Have students use those clues to **determine** the meaning of *sheaves.* **Answer:** *Sheaves* are stacked piles; in this case they are piles of grain.
- Remind students that when they use context clues, they should check their guesses in a dictionary.

10 Critical Thinking
Analyze Causes and Effects

- Read aloud the bracketed passage. **Ask** what might cause Ruth to be "annoyed" in other fields. **Answer:** Because Ruth is an attractive young woman who is a stranger from an alien land, she might be harassed in other fields.
- **Ask** students why Ruth might fare better working in Boaz's field. **Possible response:** In Boaz's field, she is under his protection and will not be bothered by his workers, whom he has ordered to leave her alone.

11 Reading Check

Answer: Boaz thinks highly of Ruth because of her devotion to Naomi and her courage in coming to a strange land.

Differentiated Instruction Solutions for All Learners

Enrichment for Gifted/Talented Students
Have students research the subject of agriculture and then prepare graphic aids about their findings. For example, one student might prepare a diagram showing the different steps in growing wheat and turning it into food—planting, threshing or winnowing, grinding, and so on. Another might prepare a chart showing the appearance of different types of grain. A small group might work on a timeline showing early advances in agriculture or farming in general. Some students might create a map showing widely grown crops.

Enrichment for Advanced Readers
The Book of Ruth has influenced a great many writers, including John Keats. In his poem "Ode to a Nightingale," Keats uses Ruth as a powerful symbol of unhappy exile. Have students read "Ode to a Nightingale" and write responses to Keats's symbolic use of Ruth. Have them compare and contrast the way Ruth is portrayed in "Ode to a Nightingale" with her portrayal in the Book of Ruth.

⓬ Reading Strategy

Using Context Clues

- Read aloud the bracketed passage.
- **Ask** students to use the context to decide whether *stealthily* means "in an open way" or "in a quiet or sneaky way." Have students explain how they came to their conclusions.
  Answer: *Stealthily* means "in a quiet or sneaky way." The meaning is indicated in verse 8, in which Boaz is surprised to find Ruth at his feet; this reaction implies that she got there in a quiet or sneaky way.
- Point out the word *start* in verse 8. Elicit from students that *start* can mean "to begin," "the beginning," or "to be startled."
- **Ask** students the Reading Strategy question: Which context clues reveal the correct meaning of *start* in Ruth 3:8? Explain.
  Answer: The context clue of Boaz's surprised exclamation at finding Ruth indicates the meaning of "to be startled."

➤ **Reteach** Remind students that they can use context clues to determine the meanings of unfamiliar words. Break down the steps used to find the meanings of *stealthily* and *start* by working through the chart on p. 59 with students.

Ask volunteers to use dictionaries to find the definitions of *stealthily* and *start* and to write the appropriate meanings for each word on the board.

⓬ 7 Boaz ate and drank, and in a cheerful mood went to lie down beside the grainpile. Then she went over stealthily and uncovered his feet and lay down.

8 In the middle of the night, the man gave a start and pulled back—there was a woman lying at his feet!

9 "Who are you?" he asked. And she replied, "I am your handmaid Ruth. Spread your robe over your handmaid, for you are a redeeming kinsman."

10 He exclaimed, "Be blessed of the LORD, daughter! Your latest deed of loyalty is greater than the first, in that you have not turned to younger men, whether poor or rich.

11 And now, daughter, have no fear. I will do in your behalf whatever you ask, for all the elders of my town know what a fine woman you are.

12 But while it is true I am a redeeming kinsman, there is another redeemer closer than I.

13 Stay for the night. Then in the morning, if he will act as a redeemer, good! let him redeem. But if he does not want to act as redeemer for you, I will do so myself, as the LORD lives! Lie down until morning."

14 So she lay at his feet until dawn. She rose before one person could distinguish another, for he thought, "Let it not be known that the woman came to the threshing floor."

15 And he said, "Hold out the shawl you are wearing." She held it while he measured out six measures of barley, and he put it on her back. When she got back to the town,

16 she came to her mother-in-law, who asked, "How is it with you, daughter?" She told her all that the man had done for her;

17 and she added, "He gave me these six measures of barley, saying to me, 'Do not go back to your mother-in-law empty-handed.'"

18 And Naomi said, "Stay here, daughter, till you learn how the matter turns out. For the man will not rest, but will settle the matter today."

Reading Strategy
Using Context Clues
Which context clues reveal the correct meaning of *start* in Ruth 3:8? Explain.

CHAPTER 4

1 Meanwhile, Boaz had gone to the gate and sat down there. And now the redeemer whom Boaz had mentioned passed by. He called, "Come over and sit down here, So-and-so!" And he came over and sat down.

2 Then [Boaz] took ten elders of the town and said, "Be seated here"; and they sat down.

3 He said to the redeemer, "Naomi, now returned from the country of Moab, must sell the piece of land which belonged to our kinsman Elimelech.

4 I thought I should disclose the matter to you and say: Acquire it in the presence of those seated here and in the presence of the elders of my people. If you are willing to redeem it, redeem! But if you will not redeem, tell me, that I may know. For there is no one to redeem but you, and I come after you." "I am willing to redeem it," he replied.

Vocabulary Builder
redeem (ri dēm´) *v.* buy back; fulfill a promise

Enrichment

Moab and Israel

Ruth is a stranger in Judah; she comes from the land of Moab. *The Harper Atlas of the Bible* explains the political relationship between Moab and Israel:

> The Israelites and Moabites were close neighbors who shared a common culture and whose respective histories were intertwined. Periods of peaceful relations (as depicted in the Book of Ruth) were interrupted occasionally by periods of hostilities . . . .

Encourage interested students to research the histories of the Israelites and Moabites. Ask them to focus on what led to problems between the two countries and what eventually became of Moab. Invite volunteers to share their findings with the class.

5 Boaz continued, "When you acquire the property from Naomi and from Ruth the Moabite, you must also acquire the wife of the deceased, so as to perpetuate the name of the deceased upon his estate."

6 The redeemer replied, "Then I cannot redeem it for myself, lest I impair my own estate. You take over my right of redemption, for I am unable to exercise it."

7 Now this was formerly done in Israel in cases of redemption or exchange: to validate any transaction, one man would take off his sandal and hand it to the other. Such was the practice in Israel.

8 So when the redeemer said to Boaz, "Acquire for yourself," he drew off his sandal.

9 And Boaz said to the elders and to the rest of the people, "You are witnesses today that I am acquiring from Naomi all that belonged to Elimelech and all that belonged to Chilion and Mahlon.

10 I am also acquiring Ruth the Moabite, the wife of Mahlon, as my wife, so as to perpetuate the name of the deceased upon his estate, that the name of the deceased may not disappear from among his kinsmen and from the gate of his home town. You are witnesses today."

11 All the people at the gate and the elders answered, "We are. May the LORD make the woman who is coming into your house like Rachel and Leah,[9] both of whom built up the House of Israel! Prosper in Ephrathah and perpetuate your name in Bethlehem!

12 And may your house be like the house of Perez whom Tamar bore to Judah[10] —through the offspring which the LORD will give you by this young woman."

14 | 13 So Boaz married Ruth; she became his wife, and he cohabited with her. The LORD let her conceive, and she bore a son.

14 And the women said to Naomi, "Blessed be the LORD, who has not withheld a redeemer from you today! May his name be perpetuated in Israel!

15 He will renew your life and sustain your old age; for he is born of your daughter-in-law, who loves you and is better to you than seven sons."

16 Naomi took the child and held it to her bosom. She became its foster mother,

9. **Rachel . . . Leah** wives of Jacob, whose sons, along with those of their handmaids Bilhah and Zilpha, became the founders ot the twelve tribes of Israel.

10. **Perez . . . Judah** Ruth, like Tamar, was a childless widow who conceived a son with her husband's kinsman.

13 Literature in Context

Cultural Connection

Jewish Marriage Customs in Biblical Times

According to Jewish customs of Ruth's day, as a widow without a son, she could expect her deceased husband's closest male relative to marry her. Also, the first son of the new marriage would be considered the deceased man's heir. This custom provided the widow with a man who could support her. It also gave the first husband an heir who could inherit family property and take on family obligations, such as saying mourning prayers for the first husband.

A document that spells out Jewish marriage customs in legal form is a ketubba (k' to͞o´ bə), or Jewish marriage contract. The ketubba shown here is recent, but the use of such documents dates back to ancient times. One purpose of the ketubba is to safeguard a woman's right to property if her husband dies.

Connect to the Literature

What are the advantages Ruth will receive from the marriage to Boaz?

Literary Analysis
Parallelism and Theme
In what way does the parallelism in Ruth 4:13 help emphasize Ruth's new position in the Jewish community?

15  **Reading Check**

In what two ways does Boaz fulfill his obligations to his kinsman Elimelech?

13 Literature in Context

Jewish Marriage Customs In addition to protecting a woman's right to property in the event of her husband's death, a ketubba spells out the woman's right to food, pleasure, shelter, and clothing. Many of the contracts are still written in Aramaic, the ancient language Jewish people began to speak after their defeat by the Babylonians in 586 B.C.

Today the groom signs the ketubba at the wedding reception, in the presence of two witnesses. In addition to being binding legal documents, many ketubbot are beautiful works of art decorated with images specific to the couple's family history. A couple often frames and displays their ketubba in their home.

Connect to the Literature
Encourage students to list at least four advantages.
Possible responses: Ruth will enjoy Boaz's kindness and protection, his wealth, a new son from their marriage, and a new home.

14 Literary Analysis

Parallelism and Theme

- **Ask** students to identify which parallelism in verse 13 involves repetition and which parallelism completes information.
  Answer: "So Boaz married Ruth," "she became his wife," and "he cohabited with her" all involve repetition. "And she bore him a son" completes "The Lord let her conceive" by indicating what she conceived; in addition, the entire sentence completes the first part of the verse by indicating what happened as a result of the marriage.
- **Ask** students the Literary Analysis question on this page.
  Answer: The parallelism stresses that Ruth is now Boaz's wife and has produced the much-valued male heir for Elimelech and Naomi as well as for Boaz.

15 Reading Check

Answer: Boaz takes on Elimelech's land and marries his widowed daughter-in-law.

Differentiated Instruction Solutions for All Learners

Enrichment for Gifted/Talented Students

Have a group of students role-play the scene at the gates of Bethlehem in which Boaz gathers the people to decide on what should be done with Naomi's land and with Ruth. Students should expand on the dialogue in the Bible story and should also use appropriate body language and gestures to act out what happens. Encourage students to rehearse the scene and then perform it for classmates.

Enrichment for Advanced Readers

Ask students to write modern stories based on the Book of Ruth. The story might focus on a young American woman who marries someone from another country, loses her husband, and then returns to her husband's native land with her mother-in-law. Or, the story could feature the reverse situation. Encourage students to include in their stories the modern equivalent of such ancient customs and events as the barley harvest and the proceeding by the town gate. Invite volunteers to share their stories with the class.

17 and the women neighbors gave him a name, saying, "A son is
born to Naomi!" They named him Obed; he was the father of Jesse,
father of David.
18 This is the line of Perez: Perez begot Hezron,
19 Hezron begot Ram, Ram begot Amminadab,
20 Amminadab begot Nahshon, Nahshon begot Salmon,
21 Salmon begot Boaz, Boaz begot Obed,
22 Obed begot Jesse, and Jesse begot David.

Critical Reading

1. **Respond:** Do you think Ruth behaved heroically? Why or why not?
2. **(a) Recall:** What happens to Naomi's family during the time they live in Moab? **(b) Infer:** How do these events affect Naomi's attitude toward life?
3. **(a) Recall:** What decisions do Orpah and Ruth make about traveling to Judah with Naomi? **(b) Analyze Cause and Effect:** What motivates Ruth's decision?
4. **(a) Recall:** What reason does Boaz give for welcoming Ruth? **(b) Analyze Cause and Effect:** How might Boaz have learned about Ruth?
5. **(a) Recall:** In what way does Ruth respond to Naomi's instructions in Ruth 3:1–4? **(b) Infer:** What does Ruth's response reveal about her?
6. **(a) Recall:** What does Boaz do when he finds Ruth in his tent? **(b) Assess:** Is Boaz an honorable man? Why or why not?
7. **(a) Recall:** What status does Ruth achieve in Ruth 4:10–15? **(b) Connect:** How has her status changed from what it was in Ruth 1:5? **(c) Infer:** In what way does Naomi's action in Ruth 4:16 suggest that her attitude toward life has changed?
8. **Analyze:** What is significant about Ruth's relationship to David, one of Israel's greatest kings?
9. **Interpret:** In what way is God, who does not appear directly in the story, present throughout the story?
10. **Evaluate:** Does this story teach an effective lesson against prejudice? Why or why not?

ASSESS

Answers

1. **Possible responses:** Students who find Ruth heroic may praise her loyalty and willingness to go among strangers and adopt their ways. Others may think she is too timid and too willing to let others tell her what to do.
2. (a) Naomi's husband dies. Her sons wed Moabite women; then, the sons die. (b) Naomi thinks of herself as unlucky and "harshly dealt" with by God.
3. (a) Ruth decides to travel with Naomi, but Orpah decides to stay behind. (b) **Possible response:** Ruth has a deep sense of loyalty to Naomi and feels obliged to stay with her and make sure that she is all right. She may want to care for Naomi for the sake of her deceased husband.
4. (a) Boaz welcomes Ruth because of her loyalty and devotion to Naomi. (b) **Possible response:** Boaz might have learned about Ruth from others in the community.
5. (a) Ruth follows Naomi's instructions exactly. (b) **Possible response:** Ruth is obedient, trusting, and willing to accept Jewish customs even when she does not completely understand them.
6. (a) Boaz is startled but lets her spend the night. (b) Boaz is honorable because he is kind to Ruth, rewards her loyalty, does not take advantage of her, and is willing to follow Jewish law when considering whether to marry her.
7. (a) Ruth becomes the wife of a wealthy, influential man and bears a son whose descendant will one day be king. (b) In Ruth 1:5, Ruth was a poor, childless widow. (c) Naomi shows love for her grandson, a sign that she has lost her bitter attitude about life.
8. The fact that Ruth turns out to be the great-grandmother of Israel's greatest king shows what a valuable person Ruth has become to the Jewish community.

Answers continued

9. **Possible response:** Throughout the story, the good fortune that comes to the characters is credited to God and seen as his blessing. In addition, obedience to God's laws is rewarded.
10. **Possible response:** The story is an effective lesson against prejudice because it shows the benefits of welcoming strangers like Ruth into a community.

The Psalms (16)

translated by
The Jewish Publication Society

(17)

Background The ancient Hebrew instrument that may have accompanied the Psalms was called a kinnor. It had from three to twelve strings, which a musician could pluck with his or her fingers or with a thin piece of metal or bone.

The "lyre" to which Psalm 137 refers is probably a kinnor. The bitterness in this Psalm, expressed as an unwillingness to play the lyre, arises from the time when the Jews were held captive in Babylon (597–538 B.C.).

PSALM 8

1 O LORD, our Lord, How majestic is Your name throughout the
earth, You who have covered the heavens with Your splendor!
2 From the mouths of infants and sucklings
You have founded strength on account of Your foes, to put an end to
enemy and avenger.
3 When I behold Your heavens, the work of Your fingers, the moon
and stars that You set in place,
4 what is man that You have been mindful of him, mortal man
that You have taken note of him,
5 that You have made him little less than divine, and adorned him
with glory and majesty;
(18) 6 You have made him master over Your handiwork, laying the
world at his feet,
7 sheep and oxen, all of them, and wild beasts, too;
8 the birds of the heavens, the fish of the sea, whatever travels the
paths of the seas.
9 O LORD, our Lord, how majestic is Your name throughout
the earth!

Vocabulary Builder
avenger (ə venj´ ər) *n.* one who takes revenge

Reading Strategy
Using Context Clues
Based on context clues in Psalm 8, what is the meaning of the word *handiwork*? Explain.

Reading Check (19)
According to Psalm 8, what power has God granted to humans?

(16) About the Selections

The four psalms presented here express the relationship between God and human beings that is at the center of Judeo-Christian tradition.

(17) Humanities

The Good Shepherd, fourth century A.D.

The origin of this Roman statuette, of which the upper portion is shown here, is unknown. The image of the shepherd was an important one for the people of the ancient Mediterranean world. Sheep and lambs were largely defenseless against wolves and other predators, depending entirely on the shepherd for protection. This connection is seen in the word *pastor,* which means "leader of a Christian congregation," and is derived from the Latin word for shepherd.

Use the following question to initiate discussion:

Why do you think the shepherd is holding the lamb?
Possible response: The shepherd is helping the lamb. It might be a lost lamb that he is returning to the fold.

(18) Reading Strategy

Using Context Clues

- Remind students that examples in the context can help clarify the meanings of unfamiliar words.
- Have a student read aloud the bracketed passage. Then, **ask** the Reading Strategy question: Based on context clues in Psalm 8, what is the meaning of the word *handiwork*? Explain.
Answer: *Handiwork* means "creation." The context clues of sheep, oxen, wild beasts, birds, fish, and so on are all examples of God's creations.

(19) Reading Check

Answer: God has made humans master over the world's animals.

Differentiated Instruction Solutions for All Learners

Strategy for Special Needs Students
Students may have difficulty with the poetic language in the Psalms. Point out that the Psalms include a great deal of repetition, so students may be able to grasp the general idea without having to understand every detail. To increase students' understanding, have the class work in pairs to summarize the main idea of each verse. When students have the main idea of a verse, they should then reread it to appreciate the power of its imagery and emotions.

Strategy for Less Proficient Readers
Students may have some difficulty with the long sentences in the Psalms. Encourage students to work in pairs, breaking each sentence into parts and then considering one part at a time. Note that punctuation can often be used as a guideline for taking apart sentences. For example, in Psalm 8, students should mentally break verse 3 into at least three parts, indicated by the commas. Then, they should focus on one part at a time.

⑳ Literary Analysis

Parallelism

- Read aloud the bracketed verses.
- Call students' attention to the first sentence of verse 4. Then, have them **explain** the relationship of the first and second parts of the sentence.
  Answer: The second part repeats with variation the idea in the first clause.
- **Ask** students the Literary Analysis question: Is the type of parallelism that occurs in Psalm 19:5 the completion of an idea or a repetition with variation? Explain.
  Answer: The parallelism in 19:5 is repetition with variation. The first half of the verse compares the sun to a groom eagerly leaving his chamber; the second half compares the same image to an athletic hero eager to run his race.

➤ **Monitor Progress** Have students reread verse 6. **Ask** them to explain what the parallelism indicates about the sun.
Answer: The parallelism describes the great power of the sun.

㉑ Reading Strategy

Using Context Clues

- Have a volunteer read aloud the bracketed passage.
- Elicit from students the following meanings for the word *comb:* "an object with teeth used in the hair as an ornament or to untangle it"; "to carefully examine or search through"; "the structure of six-sided wax cylinders in which bees hold their honey or eggs."
- Then, **ask** students the Reading Strategy question: Based on the context clues in Psalm 19:11, which of the several meanings of *comb* did the author intend? Why?
  Answer: The intended meaning of *comb* is "the structure of six-sided wax cylinders in which bees hold their honey or eggs" because the author is talking about honey.

㉒ Reading Check

Possible response: The Lord leads the speaker to water and guides the speaker along a righteous path of life.

PSALM 19

1 The heavens declare the glory of God, the sky proclaims His handiwork.

2 Day to day makes utterance, night to night speaks out.

3 There is no utterance, there are no words, whose sound goes unheard.

⑳ 4 Their voice carries throughout the earth, their words to the end of the world. He placed in them a tent for the sun,

5 who is like a groom coming forth from the chamber, like a hero, eager to run his course.

6 His rising-place is at one end of heaven, and his circuit reaches the other; nothing escapes his heat.

7 The teaching of the LORD is perfect, renewing life; the decrees of the LORD are enduring, making the simple wise;

8 The precepts of the LORD are just, rejoicing the heart; the instruction of the LORD is lucid, making the eyes light up.

㉑ 9 The fear of the LORD is pure, abiding forever;
the judgments of the LORD are true, righteous altogether,

10 more desirable than gold, than much fine gold;

11 sweeter than honey, than drippings of the comb. Your servant pays them heed; in obeying them there is much reward.

12 Who can be aware of errors? Clear me of unperceived guilt,

13 and from willful sins keep Your servant; let them not dominate me; then shall I be blameless and clear of grave offense.

14 May the words of my mouth and the prayer of my heart be acceptable to You, O LORD, my rock and my redeemer.

* * *

PSALM 23

1 The LORD is my shepherd; I lack nothing.

2 He makes me lie down in green pastures; He leads me to water in places of repose;

3 He renews my life; He guides me in right paths as befits His name.

4 Though I walk through a valley of deepest darkness; I fear no harm, for You are with me; Your rod and Your staff—they comfort me.

5 You spread a table for me in full view of my enemies; You anoint my head with oil;
my drink is abundant.

㉓ 6 Only goodness and steadfast love shall pursue me all the days of my life, and I shall dwell in the house of the LORD for many long years.

Literary Analysis
Parallelism Is the type of parallelism that occurs in Psalm 19:5 the completion of an idea or a repetition with variation? Explain.

Vocabulary Builder
precepts (prē′ septs′) *n.* rules of conduct

lucid (lo͞o′ sid) *adj.* clear; apparent

Reading Strategy
Using Context Clues Based on the context clues in Psalm 19:11, which of the several meanings of *comb* did the author intend? Why?

Vocabulary Builder
steadfast (sted′ fast′) *adj.* firm; not changing

㉒ **Reading Check**
In Psalm 23, what are two actions that the Lord performs as a shepherd?

Enrichment

English Translations of the Bible

Students are reading just one of the many translations of the Bible. During the Middle Ages, western Christians used St. Jerome's Latin translation of the Bible, called the Vulgate, although a handful of scholars translated sections of the Bible into Old English. In the 1500s, as the Protestant Reformation swept western Europe, Bible translation without Church approval was banned, and Protestant reformers who made translations were considered heretics.

That did not stop William Tyndale, who completed an English translation of the New Testament and was executed for heresy in 1536. By the time King James I came to the throne in 1603, people wanted an English version of the Bible. James commissioned the task, which produced the King James Version of the Bible in 1611.

David Composing the Psalms, from the Paris Psalter, 10th century, Photo Bibliothèque Nationale, Paris

25 ▲ Critical Viewing This illustration shows David composing psalms. What qualities of the psalms do the details in the image suggest? **[Interpret]**

Differentiated Instruction Solutions for All Learners

Strategy for English Learners

Have students read each psalm silently. As they read, they should write down questions concerning words or passages they find difficult. Encourage students to go back after reading each psalm to answer as many of their questions as they can. They should then reformulate their remaining questions for a class discussion.

Enrichment for Advanced Readers

Have students compare and contrast the translations of the Psalms that appear in their texts with the translations in the King James version of the Bible. Students should then hold a panel discussion on the similarities and differences between the two translations. Do students prefer the sparer, leaner translations in their texts or the more ornate diction of the King James versions? Which do they think better conveys the concept of God and the emotions associated with God? Why?

23 Vocabulary Builder

Anglo-Saxon Root *-stead-*

- Draw students' attention to the use of the word *steadfast* in verse 6, and read its definition aloud.
- Tell students that the root *-stead-* means "place."
- **Ask** students how the meaning of the root *-stead-* contributes to the meaning of the word *steadfast*.
  Possible response: The word *fast* can mean, "firmly fixed." Therefore, *steadfast* essentially means "firmly fixed in place."

24 Humanities

David Composing the Psalms, tenth century A.D.

This picture comes from an illustrated French psalm book. Such books——collections of the psalms used for religious worship—are also called *psalters.* David, the biblical figure who slew Goliath, is sometimes credited with composing or collecting the Psalms.

Use the following questions to stimulate discussion:

- Which figure is David, and how can you tell?
  Answer: David is the central figure in the picture, the one playing the lyre. This is revealed by the title of the picture; a person composing a psalm would probably be using a musical instrument.
- How would you describe the mood of this picture?
  Possible response: The scene suggests serenity and reverence.

25 Critical Viewing

Possible response: The image suggests that psalms were a central part of the culture and tradition during the time of David. The details of the image emphasize humans, animals, nature, and even structures; this emphasis suggests that the psalms are addressed to God, who is the creator of all.

26 Critical Thinking

Interpret

- Read aloud the bracketed passage. Remind students that after Jerusalem fell, the Jews were exiles in Babylon. Then, have a student read aloud the bracketed passage.
- **Ask** why the captors request the Jewish poets to sing.
  Answer: The captors wish to be amused and want to torment the Jewish poets.
- **Invite** students to interpret the meaning of verse 4.
  Possible response: The poets cannot sing of the Lord without being reminded that they have been cast out of their homeland.

ASSESS

Answers

1. **Possible response:** Psalm 23 offers words of reassurance that God will defend a person from all enemies.
2. (a) The verses say that humans have dominion over the created world. (b) Human beings are the most powerful mortal creatures and rule the natural world.
3. (a) The heavens declare God's glory, and the sky "proclaims His handiwork." (b) The verses praise God as the creator of the material universe. (c) The verses praise God's law and judgments.
4. (a) The first line compares God to a shepherd. (b) The believer is compared to sheep, which follow the shepherd and rely on him for safety and comfort. (c) **Possible response:** Humans who follow God's teachings are taken care of and blessed by God.
5. (a) The verses sing of Jerusalem, or Zion. (b) The poets said that they could not sing of Jerusalem because they were too sad about losing it and refused to amuse their captors, but in fact they do sing of it to one another. (c) The verses show that even though the poets are not singing of God, He is always in their thoughts.
6. **Possible response:** Songs or poetry help people endure the hardship of captivity and provide a way to preserve their culture, dignity, and faith.

PSALM 137

1 By the rivers Babylon, there we sat, sat and wept, as we thought
of Zion.
2 There on the poplars we hung up our lyres,
3 for our captors asked us there for songs, our tormentors, for
amusement, "Sing us one of the songs of Zion."
4 How can we sing a song of the LORD on alien soil?
5 If I forget you, O Jerusalem, let my right hand wither;
6 let my tongue stick to my palate if I cease to think of you, if I do
not keep Jerusalem in memory even at my happiest hour.

7 Remember, O LORD, against the Edomites[1] the day of Jerusalem's fall; how they cried, "Strip her, strip her to her very foundations!"
8 Fair Babylon, you predator, a blessing on him who repays you in
kind what you have inflicted on us;
9 a blessing on him who seizes your babies and dashes them
against the rocks!

1. **Edomites** (ē´ dəm ītz) the people of Edom, an ancient kingdom in southwest Asia, south of the Dead Sea and east of the Jordan River.

Critical Reading

1. **Respond:** Which of these psalms might you find most comforting in a time of crisis? Why?
2. **(a) Recall:** What does Psalm 8: 6–7 say about "mortal man"? **(b) Interpret:** According to Psalm 8, what role do human beings play in the universe?
3. **(a) Recall:** According to Psalm 19, what do the heavens declare and the sky proclaim? **(b) Interpret:** What achievement of God do verses 2–6 celebrate? **(c) Generalize:** What aspect of God do verses 7–14 praise?
4. **(a) Recall:** To what does the first line of Psalm 23 compare God? **(b) Infer:** Given this comparison, to what can the believer be compared? Explain. **(c) Analyze:** What do these comparisons convey about the relationship between God and human beings?
5. **(a) Connect:** In what way are verses 5–9 of Psalm 137 an answer to the command in verse 3? **(b) Analyze:** What is ironic or unexpected about this answer? **(c) Interpret:** In what way are verses 5–9 also an answer to the question in verse 4?
6. **Apply:** Why do you think songs or poetry—like Psalm 137—are especially valuable to people in exile or captivity? Explain.

Apply the Skills

from the *Bible: Book of Ruth* • *Psalms 8, 19, 23, and 137*

Literary Analysis

Parallelism

1. In a chart like the one shown, identify an example of each type of **parallelism** from the Book of Ruth or the Book of Psalms. Then, explain your choice.

Type of Parallelism	Example	Explanation
repetition with variation		
completion of an idea		
elaboration of an idea		

2. Is the effect of the parallelism in Psalm 19:1– 4 mainly to repeat ideas with variation, to complete ideas, or to elaborate on them? Explain.
3. Psalms were composed to be sung. How might parallelism make it easier to perform them aloud?

Comparing Literary Works

4. Review the parallelism in Ruth 4:9–12. In what ways does this parallelism emphasize the **theme** of making an outsider part of the community?
5. **(a)** What theme do you think the speaker expresses in Psalm 8? **(b)** Which words or phrases support this theme?

Reading Strategy

Using Context Clues

6. **(a)** Using the **context clues** in Ruth 1:11–13, what does *lot* seem to mean? **(b)** Based on clues in this passage, what do you think *debar* means?
7. What word in these Psalms was unfamiliar to you? Explain how context clues helped you determine its meaning.
8. Which context clues in Psalm 137 might help readers define the meaning of the word *palate*? Explain.

Extend Understanding

9. **Music Link:** Which of these Psalms do you think would work best set to music? Explain.

QuickReview

Using **parallelism,** biblical authors state an idea in the first half of a verse and then, using a similar grammatical structure, repeat, complete, negate, or otherwise elaborate on it in the second half.

A **theme** is a central idea that a literary work reveals or explores.

When you **use context clues,** you check the passage surrounding an unfamiliar word for clues to its meaning.

For: Self-test
Visit: www.PHSchool.com
Web Code: eta-6106

Go Online Assessment Students may use the **Self-test** to prepare for **Selection Test A** or **Selection Test B.**

Answers

1. **Possible response: Repetition with variation:** Example: "The man's name was Elimelech, his wife's name was Naomi, and his two sons were named Mahlon and Chilion." Explanation: The naming of different people is repeated. **Completion of an idea:** Example: "Elimelech, Naomi's husband, died; and she was left with her two sons." Explanation: The second clause completes the idea of Elimelech's death. **Elaboration of an idea:** Example: "They married Moabite women, one named Orpah and the other Ruth." Explanation: The second clause elaborates on the Moabite women.
2. The verses repeat with variation the idea of the world testifying to the greatness of God.
3. **Possible response:** Parallelism would make the words easier to recall and would create a rhythm suited to musical accompaniment.
4. The parallelism emphasizes the steps Boaz takes to marry Ruth and the blessings the community gives them.
5. (a) **Possible response:** The Lord is all powerful, and all human powers derive from Him. (b) **Possible response:** Phrases that support this theme include "How majestic is Your name," and "You have made [man] master over Your handiwork."
6. (a) *Lot* seems to mean "fate" or "the future that has been allowed me." (b) To *debar* seems to mean "to prevent or keep from" or "to hinder."
7. **Possible response:** Some students may mention the word *circuit* in 19:6. The example of the sun traveling its path clarifies the meaning of *circuit.*
8. The use of *palate* in "let my tongue stick to my palate" makes it clear that the palate is something with which the tongue would come in contact and to which it would stick in order to prevent speech.
9. **Possible response:** Students may choose Psalm 23 because of the rhythm and brevity of the lines.

EXTEND/ASSESS

Answers

❶ Vocabulary Lesson

Word Analysis: Anglo-Saxon Root *-stead-*

1. remaining in place
2. in place of
3. framework for supporting a mattress

Spelling Strategy

1. reapers
2. evening
3. cheerful
4. ceased

Vocabulary Builder True/False

1. true
2. true
3. false
4. false
5. true
6. false
7. true

❷ Grammar and Style Lesson

1. Subject: Naomi; verbs: lost, had; conjunction: but
2. Subject: women; verbs: returned, worked; conjunction: and
3. Subject: people; verbs: did like, took; conjunction: or
4. Subject: Ruth; verbs: came, partook, dipped; conjunction: and
5. Subject: she; verbs: married, bore; conjunction: and

Writing Application

Sample sentences:

The community *accepted* Boaz's marriage and *welcomed* Ruth to the fold. They still *viewed* her as something of an outsider but *respected* her devotion to Naomi and her adherence to Jewish law. Everyone also *respected* Boaz's decision or *considered* Naomi's needs for a grandson. The birth of an heir *delighted* the community and *won* them over completely.

Build Language Skills

❶ Vocabulary Lesson

Word Analysis: Anglo-Saxon Root *-stead-*

The word *steadfast,* which appears in Psalm 23, contains the Anglo-Saxon root *-stead-*, meaning "place." *Steadfast* love is love that stays fixed in one place, or love that endures. Using the meaning of this word root, define each of the following words:

1. steady **2.** instead **3.** bedstead

Spelling Strategy

The sound of long *e* is often spelled *ea* or *ee*, as in *glean* or *redeeming*. It is sometimes spelled *e*, as in the first syllable of *precepts.*

Complete each word below with the correct spelling of the long *e* sound.

1. r_?_pers **2.** _?_vening **3.** ch_?_rful **4.** c_?_sed

Vocabulary Builder: True/False

Review the vocabulary list on page 59 and notice the way each word is used in the context of the selections. Then, use your knowledge of the italicized word's meaning to decide whether each statement below is true or false.

1. You can rely on a *steadfast* person.
2. When you *glean* information, you gather it bit by bit from one or more sources.
3. An upright citizen does not follow *precepts.*
4. A *lucid* argument will probably puzzle others.
5. An *avenger* might make sure that a criminal is caught and punished for his or her crimes.
6. *Reapers* work in early spring, turning the soil and planting seeds in the ground.
7. You *redeem* a mortgage when you pay it off.

❷ Grammar and Style Lesson

Compound Predicates

The **predicate** is the part of the sentence that tells what the subject does or is. In a **compound predicate**—also called a **compound verb**—two or more verbs that have the same subject are joined by a conjunction such as *and, but,* or *or.*

> She *came* and *gleaned* in a field, . . .
>
> Naomi's son *had married* Ruth but then *died.*

Poets may use compound predicates to create effects similar to parallelism—repeating, varying, or contrasting actions and events through their choice of verbs joined in the predicate.

Practice Copy each sentence. Put a box around the subject, underline the verbs, and circle the conjunction that joins the compound predicate.

1. Naomi lost her husband but still had Ruth.
2. The two women returned to Bethlehem and worked on Boaz's lands.
3. Many people in the community did not like the outsider or at least took no interest in her.
4. Ruth came to Boaz's table, partook of the meal, and dipped her morsel in the vinegar.
5. Later she married Boaz and bore him a son.

Writing Application Write four sentences describing the community's reaction to Boaz's marriage. Use compound predicates in each sentence.

WG *Prentice Hall Writing and Grammar Connection: Platinum Level, Chapter 19, Section 1*

Assessment Practice

Using Context Clues to Determine Meanings

(For more practice, see *Test Preparation Workbook*, p. 4.)

Students taking standardized tests will encounter vocabulary questions that require them to use context clues to determine meaning. Use this sample question to practice this skill.

> The heavens declare the glory of God,
> the sky proclaims His handiwork.
>
> —Psalm 19

In this sentence, the word *proclaims* most likely means

A owns.
B announces.
C whispers.
D denies.

A is illogical; *D* can be eliminated as an antonym; and *C* is unlikely because declarations are not made in a whisper. Thus, *B* is the correct response.

❸ Writing Lesson

Timed Writing: Response to a Biblical Narrative

As you read the Book of Ruth, you probably reacted to the words and decisions of the characters, the sequence of events, and the ideas that the story suggests. Write a response to this biblical narrative, focusing on any one of these elements. ***(40 minutes)***

Prewriting *(10 minutes)* Identify the element that affected you most strongly, and summarize your reaction to it. Then, find details in the work that you can focus on to help clarify and explain your response.

Drafting *(20 minutes)* Use the summary of your reaction to write a thesis statement. Support your thesis by discussing the ways in which your chosen element affected you at different points in the story. Include quotations from the story as well.

Model: Adding Quotations From the Selection

The language of the characters is simple but eloquent. In Ruth 1:21, Naomi expresses her unhappiness in a single sentence. "I went away full, and the LORD has brought me back empty," she says.

The added quotation shows the simplicity and eloquence of a character's language.

Revising *(10 minutes)* Make sure that you review the quotations and their verse numbers for accuracy. If your support seems weak, consider adding quotations.

WG Prentice Hall Writing and Grammar Connection: Platinum Level, Chapter 13, Section 3

❹ Extend Your Learning

Research and Technology Research musical settings of the Psalms, and prepare a **multimedia report** on your findings. Include live or recorded music, written or oral explanations, and sheet music. Here are some sources to consider:

- library or other music collections
- local churches or choirs
- Web sites about religious music
- nonfiction books about religious music

Present your report to your classmates.

Listening and Speaking Working with other students, develop an **improvised dialogue** to add to the Book of Ruth. Assign roles and decide which situations to enhance with added dialogue. Develop and rehearse your dialogue, then perform it for classmates. **[Group Activity]**

For: An additional research activity
Visit: www.PHSchool.com
Web Code: etd-7105

Assessment Resources

The following resources can be used to assess students' knowledge and skills.

Unit 1 Resources
- **Selection Test A**, pp. 52–54
- **Selection Test B**, pp. 55–57

General Resources
- **Rubrics for Response to Literature,** pp. 55–56
- **Rubrics for Research: Research Report,** pp. 51–52

Go Online Assessment — Students may use the **Self-test** to prepare for **Selection Test A** or **Selection Test B.**

❸ Writing Lesson

You may use this Writing Lesson as a timed-writing practice, or you may allow students to develop the Response to a Biblical Narrative as a writing assignment over several days.

- You might have students use the **Support for Writing** page in ***Unit 1 Resources***, p. 49, to help them develop their responses.
- Read aloud the Writing Lesson instruction.
- Use the Writing Lesson to guide students in developing their responses. Encourage students to respond to the story element that interests them the most. They may choose from character, plot, setting, or theme.
- Remind students that when they quote from the Bible, they should use the standard format of book, chapter, and verse, with a colon between chapter and verse (or verse span). For instance, *Ruth 2:1–2* means the Book of Ruth, Chapter 2, verses 1–2.
- Use the Response to Literature rubrics in ***General Resources***, pp. 55–56, to evaluate students' work.

WG Writing and Grammar Platinum Level

To give students further instruction for writing a response to literature, use Chapter 13, Section 3.

❹ Research and Technology

- Read aloud the Research and Technology instruction.
- Tell students with musical skills that they may choose to perform musical versions of the psalms for the class as part of their multimedia presentations.
- Use the Research: Research Report rubrics in ***General Resources***, pp. 51–52, to evaluate students' presentations.
- The **Support for Extend Your Learning** page (***Unit 1 Resources***, p. 50) provides guided note-taking opportunities to help students complete the Extend Your Learning activities.

Go Online Research — Have students type in the Web Code for another research activity.

Standard Course of Study

IR.2.01.6 Make inferences, predict, and draw conclusions based on research questions.

IR.2.03.1 Access cultural information from media sources.

LT.5.01.7 Understand the cultural and historical impact on world literature texts.

Background

King James I

James I of England was the son of Mary, Queen of Scots. He was born and raised in Scotland and was a Presbyterian. He was later appointed the leader of Scotland's Presbyterian Church.

James had been king of Scotland since the age of one, when his mother abdicated the throne. In 1603, at the age of 36, he became king of England when Elizabeth I died. James I died in 1625.

Background

William Tyndale

Because of the increased demand for Bibles written in English in the 1500s, William Tyndale decided to prepare a new translation of the Bible. Faced with clerical opposition at home, Tyndale fled to what is now Germany and there published his English translation of the New Testament. However, he was still working on his translation of the Old Testament when he was arrested and executed.

A Closer Look

The King James Version of the Bible

Commissioned by King James I of England and completed in 1611, the English translation of the Bible known as the King James Version has influenced countless poems, novels, sermons, and speeches. A sacred book for Christians, it is considered one of the greatest works to come from the English Renaissance.

"In the beginning . . ." So powerful is its influence that Chapter 1 of Genesis is, without rival, the sound of creation in English:

1 In the beginning God created the heaven and the earth.
2 And the earth was without form, and void; and darkness *was* upon the face of the deep. And the Spirit of God moved upon the face of the waters.
3 And God said, Let there be light: and there was light . . . .

Although it speaks so majestically of beginnings, the King James Version itself came rather late in the life of the Bible.

The Hebrew Bible is a collection of books written from 1200 to 100 B.C. (For the Jewish Publication Society translations of portions of the Bible, see pages 38 and 60.) Christians refer to this Bible as the Old Testament, and they refer to the smaller collection of books they added to it as the New Testament. The King James Version is a translation into English of the Hebrew of the Old Testament and the Greek of the New Testament.

> *"The combination of Protestantism and the modern printing press encouraged new translations of the Bible."*

Protestantism and the Printing Press The King James Version was not the first English translation of the Bible. In the 1500s, the Christian movement called Protestantism emerged and began to emphasize the Bible as a source of religious authority. At the same time, Gutenberg's invention of movable type was making possible the widespread distribution of the Bible for the first time. The combination of Protestantism and the modern printing press encouraged new translations of the Bible into English and other languages.

One influential English translation was that of William Tyndale, a Protestant whose act of translating the Bible from the Latin resulted in his execution for heresy. As England became more Protestant, however, Tyndale came to be viewed not as a heretic but as a hero. King James's translators closely followed the magnificent diction and rhythms of Tyndale's groundbreaking translation.

Enrichment

Biblical Translations

The Bible has undergone many translations since it was first written. The Old Testament was originally written in Hebrew but eventually needed to be translated into Aramaic because that was the language spoken by many of the Hebrew people. When Greek became the common language in the third century B.C., the Jewish scriptures were translated into Greek. This translation was called the Septuagint and took over a century to finish.

Early Christians used the Septuagint, and as the New Testament developed, it was written in Greek and Aramaic. The New Testament was not translated into Latin until A.D. 406. This translation by St. Jerome was called the Vulgate and was used for over a thousand years.

A Classic "created by a committee . . ." In 1603, James I ascended to the English throne. The Bible project he approved a year later was ambitious. It involved the work of forty-seven scholars divided into six groups at three different locations. The result of their labors has been called "the only classic ever created by a committee."

A Sample of Riches The sample that follows comes from the New Testament Gospels, which record the words of Jesus. His speeches contain memorable sayings and parables, brief stories that teach moral lessons. In a famous passage from Chapter 6 of the Gospel According to Saint Matthew, Jesus warns about the love of money and possessions (*mammon* is "money" and *raiment* is clothing):

24 No man can serve two masters: for either he will hate the one, and love the other; or else he will hold to the one, and despise the other. He cannot serve God and mammon.
25 Therefore I say unto you, Take no thought for your life, what ye shall eat, or what ye shall drink; nor yet for your body, what ye shall put on. Is not the life more than meat, and the body more than raiment?
26 Behold the fowls of the air: for they sow not, neither do they reap, nor gather into barns; yet your heavenly Father feedeth then. Are ye not much better than they?

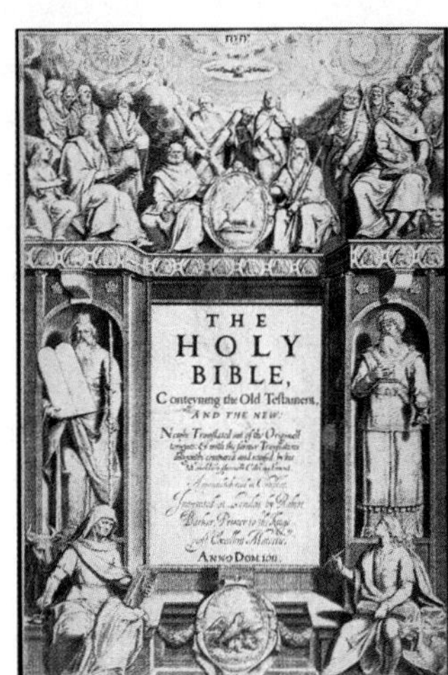

▲ **Critical Viewing** What connection is there between the literary style of the King James Version and the style of art on its title page? Explain. **[Connect]**

From Renaissance England to America The King James Version of the Bible has enriched our language with many phrases, such as "out of the mouths of babes" and "fat of the land." Its words, rhythms, and images have influenced English authors like John Milton and William Blake, as well as Americans like Walt Whitman and Abraham Lincoln. In an important way, therefore, this Bible from the English Renaissance has helped shape our own nation's literature and public life.

Activity

Cultural Influence

In previous centuries, the King James Version of the Bible was one of the most influential books in the English language. With a gorup, discuss whether there is a book, poem, song, movie, or television show that exerts as powerful a cultural influence today. Use these questions to guide your discussion:

- Is there a work of literature, art, music, or popular culture with which most contemporary Americans are familiar? Defend your opinion.
- Are there generational, regional, educational, or other differences in our cultural knowledge? If so, what are the effects of these differences?

Choose a point person to share your group's views with the class.

Background

The Gutenberg Bible

The Gutenberg Bible was printed in Germany in 1455. It was the first book printed on Johannes Gutenberg's press. Printed in Latin, this Bible did not have page numbers or a title page. Of the forty known copies of this work, some can be found in the United States Library of Congress.

Critical Viewing

Possible Response: The language of the King James Version is formal and majestic; the style of the art on its title page is also formal and majestic.

Critical Thinking

1. Why do you think King James appointed so many scholars to translate the King James Version of the Bible? **[Infer]**
   Possible response: Because several translations of the Bible existed, including those in Greek and Hebrew, King James wanted all of them compared and considered in the new translation. This work would require a number of people with knowledge of different languages. Many translators, instead of just one, would reflect different interpretations of the original work.
2. Why was Gutenberg's invention of the printing press so vital to the translation of the Bible? **[Deduce]**
   Possible response: The invention of the printing press allowed for a wider distribution of the Bible. Because many people read only their native language, it was important to have the Bible written in the vernacular. Also, the rise of Protestantism placed new emphasis on the use of the Bible.

Activity

Form students into groups. Encourage each group to first make a list of choices, comparing the universality of each work. Then, have students pool their opinions about one work they would most like to defend in a discussion. Next, ask students to list effects of differences in our cultural knowledge and determine whether these effects enrich our society. Before speaking, a point person should organize the group's opinions of a work and of the effects of differences in our cultural knowledge. Finally, advise students to be courteous throughout the discussion and avoid interrupting the speakers.

Standard Course of Study

Goal 1: WRITTEN LANGUAGE

WL.1.01.1	Produce reminiscences that use specific and sensory details with purpose.
WL.1.02.1	Relate personal knowledge to textual information in a written reflection.
WL.1.03.1	Select, monitor, and modify reading strategies appropriate to personal reflection.

Goal 5: LITERATURE

LT.5.01.3	Analyze literary devices and explain their effect on the work of world literature.
LT.5.03.11	Analyze elements of literary environment in world literature.

Goal 6: GRAMMAR AND USAGE

GU.6.02.3	Edit for parallel structure.

Step-by-Step Teaching Guide	Pacing Guide
PRETEACH	
• Administer Vocabulary and Reading Warm-ups as necessary.	5 min.
• Engage students' interest with the motivation activity.	5 min.
• Read and discuss author and background features. **FT**	10 min.
• Introduce the Literary Analysis Skill: Imagery. **FT**	5 min.
• Introduce the Reading Strategy: Setting a Purpose for Reading.	10 min.
• Prepare students to read by teaching the selection vocabulary. **FT**	
TEACH	
• Informally monitor comprehension while students read independently or in groups. **FT**	30 min.
• Monitor students' comprehension with the Reading Check notes.	as students read
• Reinforce vocabulary with Vocabulary Builder notes.	as students read
• Develop students' understanding of imagery with the Literary Analysis annotations. **FT**	5 min.
• Develop students' ability to set a purpose for reading with the Reading Strategy annotations. **FT**	5 min.
ASSESS/EXTEND	
• Assess students' comprehension and mastery of the Literary Analysis and Reading Strategy by having them answer the Apply the Skills questions. **FT**	15 min.
• Have students complete the Vocabulary Lesson and the Grammar and Style Lesson. **FT**	15 min.
• Apply students' ability to revise for organization by using the Writing Lesson. **FT**	45 min. or homework
• Apply students' understanding by using one or more of the Extend Your Learning activities.	20–90 min. or homework
• Administer Selection Test A or Selection Test B. **FT**	15 min.

Resources

Print

Unit 1 Resources

Vocabulary Warm-up Word Lists **[L1, L2, EL]** .... p. 58
Vocabulary Warm-up Practice **[L1, L2, EL]** .... p. 59
Reading Warm-up A **[L1, L2, EL]** .... p. 60
Reading Warm-up B **[L1, L2, L3]** .... p. 61

Transparency

Graphic Organizer Transparencies

Literary Analysis Graphic Organizer A **[L3]** .... p. 13
Literary Analysis Graphic Organizer B **[L1, L2, EL]** .... p. 14
Reading Strategy Graphic Organizer A **[L3]** .... p. 15
Reading Strategy Graphic Organizer B **[L1, L2, EL]** .... p. 16

Print

Reader's Notebook [L2]

Reader's Notebook: Adapted Version [L1]

Reader's Notebook: English Learner's Version [EL]

Unit 1 Resources

Literary Analysis **[L3]** .... p. 62
Reading Strategy **[L3]** .... p. 63
Vocabulary Builder **[L3]** .... p. 64

Technology

Listening to Literature Audio CDs [L2, EL]

Print

Unit 1 Resources

Grammar and Style **[L3]** .... p. 65
Support for Writing Lesson **[L3]** .... p. 66
Support for Extend Your Learning **[L3]** .... p. 67
Enrichment **[L4]** .... p. 68
Selection Test A **[L1, L2, EL]** .... pp. 69–71
Selection Test B **[L3, L4]** .... pp. 72–74

General Resources

Rubrics for Exposition: Problem-Solution Essay **[L3]** .... pp. 49–50

Technology

Go Online: Research **[L3]**
Go Online: Self-test **[L3]**
***ExamView®*, Test Bank [L3]**

Choosing Resources for Differentiated Instruction

[L1] Special Needs Students
[L2] Below-Level Students
[L3] All Students
[L4] Advanced Students
[EL] English Learners

For Vocabulary and Reading Warm-ups and for Selection Tests, **A** signifies "less challenging" and **B** "more challenging." For Graphic Organizer transparencies, **A** signifies "not filled in" and **B** "filled in."

FT Fast Track Instruction: To move the lesson more quickly, use the strategies and activities identified with **FT**.

Scaffolding for Less Proficient and Advanced Students

The leveled Critical Thinking questions after selections progress in the levels of thinking required to answer them. To address the needs of your different students, you may use the (a) level questions for your less proficient students and the (b) level questions with your on-level and advanced students. The occasional (c) level questions are appropriate for your advanced students.

PRENTICE HALL **TeacherEXPRESS™** Plan · Teach · Assess
Use this complete suite of powerful teaching tools to make lesson planning and testing quicker and easier.

PRENTICE HALL **StudentEXPRESS™** Learn · Study · Succeed
Use the interactive textbook (online and on CD-ROM) to make selections and activities come alive with audio and video support and interactive questions.

For: Information about Lexiles
Visit: www.PHSchool.com
Web Code: eue-1111

PRETEACH

Motivation

Ask students why it is useful to learn about different religions. How can people who are not Muslims benefit from reading the Qur'an? How can Muslims benefit from reading the Bible or the writings of Buddhism, Hinduism, and other faiths? How does learning about other religions help us understand people from different cultures?

❶ Background

More About the Selections

The belief that the words used in the Qur'an are divine has had a tremendous impact on the development of the Arabic language. Because the Qur'an contains God's speech, and God does not make mistakes, Muslims believe that the Qur'an is grammatically and stylistically perfect. For this reason, the Qur'an is regarded as the best model of Arabic and is the basis for all Arabic grammar to this day.

Geography Note

Call students' attention to the map on this page. Explain that the present-day country of Saudi Arabia is the largest nation on the highlighted Arabian peninsula. Mecca and Medina, two holy cities of the Islamic faith, are both located in Saudi Arabia.

Mecca, the city of Muhammad's birth, is the holiest city. All practicing Muslims are expected to make at least one pilgrimage to Mecca in their lifetimes. Medina is holy because Muhammad fled there to escape persecution for his religious teachings. This famous flight, called the Hegira (also spelled *Hejira*), took place in A.D. 622, the year that marks the beginning of the Muslim calendar.

Build Skills Scripture

from the Qur'an ❶

In the eyes of Muslims, the Qur'an (sometimes referred to as the Koran) is viewed as the most important scripture in the world, but not the only one. Muslims believe that Allah sent a series of heavenly books, or scriptures, to the world. These include the Torah (see pages 44–56), the Psalms (see pages 67–70) and the New Testament. The last of these heavenly books is the Qur'an, which Muslims believe to be the final revelation of Allah.

The Prophet Muhammad In the latter third of his life, revelations started coming to the prophet Muhammad as he meditated in a cave outside his hometown of Mecca, now in Saudi Arabia. Suddenly, the angel Gabriel came to him and commanded him to recite something. When Muhammad asked the angel what it was that he wanted him to recite, Gabriel said in Arabic, "Recite in the name of the Lord Who creates." This command was followed by the first of the revelations, and as a result it is the first line of the Qur'an. In fact, the name of the book may be taken from this line, because the word *Qur'an* means "recitation" in Arabic.

It is held that, from the age of forty, Muhammad continued to receive such revelations until his death approximately twenty years later. He repeated them to his followers, who either memorized them or wrote them down on bits of parchment, pieces of leather, or clay tablets. In the years after Muhammad's death, his followers organized the fragments into a book and named it the Qur'an. Copies of the Qur'an were sent to all major cities in the Islamic world, with orders that other unofficial versions should be destroyed, and the Qur'an was made the official scripture of the Islamic religion.

The Organization of the Qur'an The revelations of Muhammad are arranged in chapters called *Surahs.* There are 114 Surahs in the Qur'an, varying in length from three or four verses to well over 200. Each Surah's title is generally an unusual word or phrase appearing early in the Surah.

The earliest copies of the Qur'an were written in an imperfect Arabic script that included no vowels and used the same symbols for many different consonants. When Arabic script was reformed in the eighth century, the Qur'an was recopied in this script, and it has remained virtually unchanged to this day.

Revelations from God Although Muhammad uttered the words of the Qur'an, he is not considered its author; rather, he is viewed as the transmitter of Allah's message to humanity. Muslims believe that the Qur'an, word for word and syllable for syllable, is the exact message of Allah. Because this belief means that the words used in the Qur'an are Allah's words, and any translation loses some of its religious value, most Muslims feel that the Qur'an should be read in Arabic and that translations are only approximations of the real text. The vast majority of today's Muslims do not know Arabic and can only read the translations. However, all scholars of Islam use the original Arabic text for their studies.

Islam and the Five Pillars of Wisdom

The word *Islam* means "submission to the will of God" (who is called *Allah* in Arabic). Members of the Islamic faith are known as Muslims, and the Muslim creed states: "There is no god but Allah; Muhammad is his prophet." Muslims are expected to perform the following five acts of worship, known as the Five Pillars of Wisdom:

1. express one's faith by reciting the creed
2. pray five times each day (facing Mecca, the birthplace of the prophet Muhammad)
3. give alms, or charity, to the poor
4. fast from sunrise to sundown during the holy month of Ramadan, the ninth month of the Islamic calendar
5. make, in one's lifetime, at least one pilgrimage to Mecca; this trip is called a *hajj* or *hadj* in Arabic

Preview

Connecting to the Literature

Perhaps the world would be a kinder place if compassion and mercy filled more hearts. In the Qur'an, every Surah opens by calling on "God, the Compassionate, the Merciful."

❷ Literary Analysis

Imagery

Imagery is language used to create word pictures by appealing to one or more of the five senses—sight, hearing, taste, smell, and touch. An **image** is a single instance of imagery: "hot dry wind," for example, or "cold wet rain." Imagery makes descriptions more vivid and abstract ideas more concrete.

As you read the selections from the Qur'an, track the images on a chart like the one shown.

Image	"straight path"
Selection	Exordium
Sense(s)	sight

Connecting Literary Elements

One form of imagery highlights contrasts and differences. **Antithesis** is the use of strongly contrasting language, images, or ideas. Antithesis can be expressed in various ways:

- two long contrasting pieces meant to be read together and balanced against each other
- shorter contrasts in words, phrases, clauses, or sentences that express their contrasting ideas in similar grammatical structures (parallelism): "By the light of day, and by the dark of night. . . ."

Notice how often the Qur'an employs antithesis to reinforce images and make them more memorable.

❸ Reading Strategy

Setting a Purpose for Reading

When you **set a purpose for reading,** you decide beforehand why you are reading and what to focus on as you read. For example, if you read the Qur'an to learn more about Islamic culture, you may focus on its guidelines for human behavior. Identify your purpose before you begin to read and then read to achieve that goal.

Vocabulary Builder

compassionate (kəm pash′ ən it) *adj.* feeling or showing sympathy or pity (p. 78)

incurred (in kʉrd′) *v.* brought about through one's own actions (p. 78)

affliction (ə flik′ shən) *n.* something that causes pain or distress (p. 79)

recompense (rek′ əm pens′) *n.* payment of what is owed; reward (p. 79)

abhor (ab hôr′) *v.* feel disgust for; hate (p. 80)

chide (chīd) *v.* scold (p. 80)

renown (ri noun′) *n.* fame (p. 80)

fervor (fʉr′ vər) *n.* strong or heated feeling; zeal (p. 80)

NC Standard Course of Study

- Analyze literary devices and explain their effect on the work. (LT.5.01.3)
- Select and modify reading strategies appropriate to reader's purpose. (LT.5.03.1)

❷ Literary Analysis

Imagery

- Have students read independently the Literary Analysis instruction.
- Explain that imagery helps make feelings, moods, and other abstract ideas more concrete and powerful. As an example, have students consider which statement has more impact: "It was raining" or "Rain drizzled from the gray sky." Discuss how the sensory details in the second statement create a concrete image that is more powerful and memorable.
- Lead a discussion about why imagery might be valuable in religious writings. Elicit that images can help make abstract religious concepts and teachings more concrete.
- Give students a copy of **Literary Analysis Graphic Organizer A** in ***Graphic Organizer Transparencies,*** p. 13. Encourage them to record details about the imagery in the selections as they read.

❸ Reading Strategy

Setting a Purpose for Reading

- Read aloud the Reading Strategy instruction.
- Elicit from students some of the possible reasons that people might have for reading excerpts from the Qur'an. For example, someone reading it for religious purposes might focus on the inspiration it provides; someone reading it for literary purposes might focus on its style.

Vocabulary Builder

- Pronounce each vocabulary word for students, and read the definitions as a class. Have students identify any words with which they are already familiar.

Differentiated Instruction Solutions for All Learners

Support for Special Needs Students
Have students complete the **Preview** and **Build Skills** pages for these passages from the Qur'an in the ***Reader's Notebook: Adapted Version.*** These pages provide a selection summary, an abbreviated presentation of the reading and literary skills, and the graphic organizer on the **Build Skills** page in the student book.

Support for Less Proficient Readers
Have students complete the **Preview** and **Build Skills** pages for these passages from the Qur'an in the ***Reader's Notebook.*** These pages provide a selection summary, an abbreviated presentation of the reading and literary skills, and the graphic organizer on the **Build Skills** page in the student book.

Support for English Learners
Have students complete the **Preview** and **Build Skills** pages for these passages from the Qur'an in the ***Reader's Notebook: English Learner's Version.*** These pages provide a selection summary, an abbreviated presentation of the skills, additional contextual vocabulary, and the graphic organizer on the **Build Skills** page in the student book.

Facilitate Understanding

You may want to read these selections aloud to help students appreciate the power and beauty of the Qur'an's language and imagery. Encourage them to ask questions after you have finished reading.

❶ About the Selections

Presented here are four Surahs, or chapters, from the Qur'an.

The first Surah is probably the most frequently recited prayer in the Islamic faith. Translator N.J. Dawood calls it "The Exordium," a term used for the opening of a formal speech or another important work; other translators have called it "The Opening."

❷ Reading Strategy

Setting a Purpose for Reading

- Have the class **suggest** purposes for reading the Qur'an. **Possible response:** Purposes might include reading to learn about world cultures or reading to compare and contrast religious teachings.
- Then, read aloud the Background note to give students a sense of what they are about to read.

❸ Critical Thinking

Compare and Contrast

- Have students read "The Exordium." Then, direct their attention to the bracketed passage.
- Have students **contrast** the two groups described in the passage. **Answer:** The lines discuss those who obey God and gain His favor and those who sin and incur His anger.

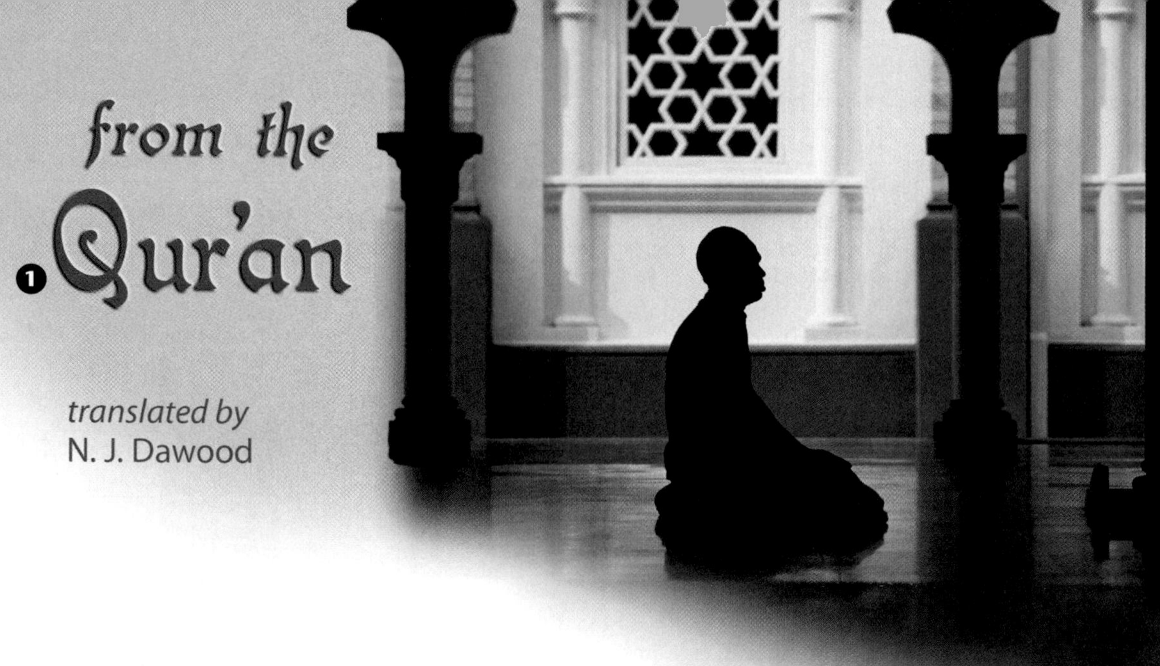

from the ❶ Qur'an

translated by
N. J. Dawood

❷ **Background** The fundamental message of all the Surahs of the Qur'an is that there is but one God who has created the world and everything in it. This God is all-powerful and all-knowing; just, loving, and merciful; the protector and sustainer of all life; and the final judge at death. As a result, the Qur'an says, it is the duty of all people to praise him, glorify him, and submit to him.

The Exordium

IN THE NAME OF GOD
THE COMPASSIONATE
THE MERCIFUL

Praise be to God, Lord of the Universe,
The Compassionate, the Merciful,
Sovereign of the Day of Judgment!
You alone we worship, and to You alone we turn for help.
❸ *Guide us to the straight path,*
The path of those whom You have favored,
Not of those who have incurred Your wrath,
Nor of those who have gone astray.

Vocabulary Builder

compassionate (kəm pash′ ən it) *adj.* feeling or showing sympathy or pity

incurred (in kʉrd′) *v.* brought about through one's own actions

Differentiated Instruction Solutions for All Learners

Accessibility at a Glance

	From the Qur'an
Context	Religious beliefs of Islamic Muslims
Language	Formal, with a variety of shifting capitalized pronouns that refer to God
Concept Level	Accessible: To win God's comfort and love, man must be charitable to others and work hard.
Literary Merit	Classic: Muslim Scripture
Lexile	930L
Other	Features imagery and antithesis
Overall Rating	Average

Night

In the Name of God, the Compassionate, the Merciful

4 By the night, when she lets fall her darkness, and by the radiant day! By Him that created the male and the female, your endeavors have varied ends!

For him that gives in charity and guards himself against evil and believes in goodness, We shall smooth the path of salvation; but for him that neither gives nor takes and disbelieves in goodness, We shall smooth the path of affliction. When he breathes his last, his riches will not avail him.

It is for Us to give guidance. Ours is the life to come, Ours the life of this world. I warn you, then, of the blazing Fire, in which none shall burn save the hardened sinner, who denies the Truth and pays no heed. But the good man who keeps himself pure by almsgiving shall keep away from it: and so shall he that does good works for the sake of the Most High only, seeking no recompense. Such men shall be content.

Literary Analysis
Imagery and Antithesis What image contrasts with night in the first paragraph?

Vocabulary Builder

affliction (ə flik′ shən) *n.* something that causes pain or distress

recompense (rek′ əm pens′) *n.* payment of what is owed; reward

5

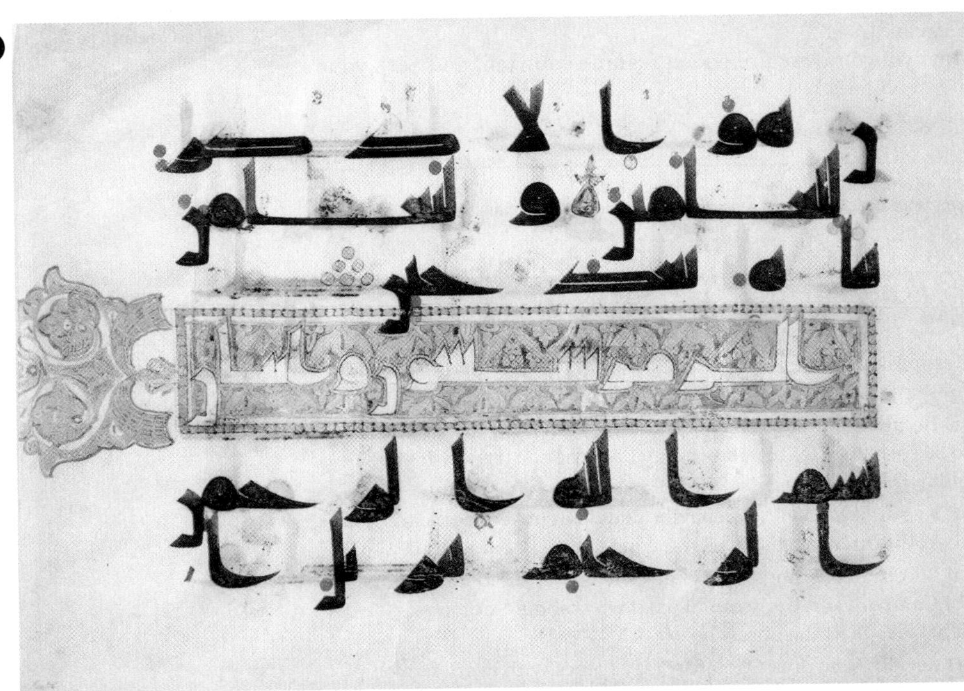

6 ▲ Critical Viewing What effect does the artist achieve by using stylized lettering and graphics in this page from an illuminated Qur'an? **[Make a Judgment]**

4 Literary Analysis

Imagery and Antithesis

- Remind students that imagery creates word pictures by using language that appeals to the senses.
- Ask a volunteer to read aloud the bracketed passage.
- Then, **ask** students the Literary Analysis question: What image contrasts with night in the first paragraph?
  Answer: The image of day contrasts with night.
- Explain to students how the second paragraph contrasts good behavior, which results in salvation, with sinful behavior, which results in affliction.
- Have students **identify** the image in the second paragraph that helps convey the idea of salvation or affliction.
  Answer: The image of a path conveys the idea of salvation or affliction.

5 Humanities

Arabic manuscript page, eighth or ninth century

This folio, or manuscript page, comes from a Qur'an. It shows the end of one Surah and the beginning of another, with a chapter heading in between. The chapter heading, illuminated in gold leaf, has an elegant palm design to the left. The widely spaced rectangular Arabic script, in black with red vowel marks, is a style of writing called *kufic* that is typical of this early era.

Use the following question to initiate discussion:

What might the first words under the chapter heading say?
Possible response: The words say, "In the Name of God, the Compassionate, the Merciful."

6 Critical Viewing

Possible response: The lettering and graphics convey the artist's reverence for the Qur'an. They stress the holy, serious nature of the text.

Differentiated Instruction — Solutions for All Learners

Support for Special Needs Students
Students may have difficulty with the shifting pronouns that refer to God in the different Surahs. Point out that pronouns used for God are often capitalized as a sign of respect. For example, the capital *Y* of "You" in "The Exordium" suggests that the word refers to God; have students consider the content of the lines to check whether this suggestion makes sense. Then, conduct similar exercises with other Surahs, eliciting or explaining that in "Night" and "Daylight," "Him" and "He" refer to God; in "Comfort," "We" refers to God.

Enrichment for Gifted/Talented Students
Have interested students research Lawrence of Arabia or another Westerner who was interested in or adopted the Islamic religion. For example, students might choose a famous athlete, such as Muhammad Ali or Kareem Abdul Jabbar. When conducting their research, students should focus on the role of Islam in the life of the figure they have chosen. After students have finished their research, have them present their findings to the class.

7 Vocabulary Builder

Latin Prefix *ab-*

- Draw students' attention to the word *abhor.* Then, tell students that the prefix *ab-* means "away" or "from."
- **Ask** students to suggest other words that use the prefix *ab-*. **Possible responses:** *Abnormal, abduct,* and *absent* use the prefix *ab-*.

8 Literary Analysis

Imagery

- Ask a volunteer to read aloud the bracketed passage.
- **Ask** students the Literary Analysis question: What image helps make the abstract idea of the afterlife more concrete?
  Answer: The prize image helps make the concept more concrete.

▶ **Monitor Progress** Have students discuss the contrasting images in the opening line.

▶ **Reteach** Review with students the Literary Analysis instruction on p. 77 and the images and sensory details they charted.

ASSESS

Answers

1. **Possible response:** "The Exordium" is the most interesting because it is a powerful way to open the Qur'an.
2. (a) "The Exordium" addresses God. (b) The speaker is a follower of Islam. (c) The speaker needs help staying on the "straight path."
3. (a) "Night" equates charitable actions with goodness. (b) A person's hope of salvation and fear of eternal punishment drive charitable behavior.
4. (a) The Lord has not forsaken his people, nor does he hate them. (b) Humans should be charitable and kind.
5. (a) Ease follows every hardship. (b) **Possible response:** This Surah suggests an eventual reprieve from the toil of life.
6. **Possible response:** People who treat others kindly and give to those in need are considered "good people" today.

Daylight

In the Name of God, the Compassionate, the Merciful

7 By the light of day, and by the dark of night, your Lord has not forsaken you[1] nor does He abhor you.

8 The life to come holds a richer prize for you than this present life. You shall be gratified with what your Lord will give you.

Did He not find you an orphan and give you shelter?

Did He not find you in error and guide you?

Did He not find you poor and enrich you?

Therefore do not wrong the orphan, nor chide away the beggar. But proclaim the goodness of your Lord.

Comfort

In the Name of God, the Compassionate, the Merciful

Have we not lifted up your heart and relieved you[2] of the burden which weighed down your back?

Have We not given you high renown?

With every hardship there is ease. With every hardship there is ease.

When your prayers are ended resume your toil, and seek your Lord with all fervor.

Vocabulary Builder

abhor (ab hôr′) *v.* feel disgust for; hate

chide (chīd) *v.* scold

Literary Analysis

Imagery What image helps make the abstract idea of the afterlife more concrete?

Vocabulary Builder

renown (ri noun′) *n.* fame

fervor (fur′ vər) *n.* strong or heated feeling; zeal

---

1. **you** here, Allah's prophet, Muhammad.
2. **you** here, Mecca, a city in Saudi Arabia and the birthplace of Muhammad.

Critical Reading

1. **Respond:** Which of these selections from the Qur'an did you find most interesting? Why?
2. **(a) Recall:** Whom does the Exordium address? **(b) Infer:** Who seems to be speaking? **(c) Interpret:** Why does the speaker wish to be guided?
3. **(a) Recall:** What kind of behavior does "Night" equate with goodness? **(b) Infer:** What drives someone to be a good person?
4. **(a) Recall:** According to "Daylight," what has the Lord *not* done? **(b) Compare and Contrast:** In what ways should human behavior reflect the Lord's behavior?
5. **(a) Recall:** What does "Comfort" say comes with every hardship? **(b) Evaluate:** In what ways does this Surah offer comfort?
6. **Apply:** "Night" describes the behavior of a good man. In what ways is this description applicable to good people today?

Apply the Skills

from the *Qur'an*

Literary Analysis

Imagery

1. To which senses does the **imagery** in "Night" appeal? Cite examples of images to support your answer.
2. In "Daylight," what does the image of the orphan given shelter help express about God?
3. **(a)** What abstract idea does the imagery in "Comfort" help you perceive? **(b)** Which concrete aspects of the image help you perceive the abstract idea?

Connecting Literary Elements

4. Identify five examples of **antithesis** that help make the ideas and imagery in these selections clearer.
5. **(a)** Which two Surahs have titles that suggest an antithesis between them? **(b)** Does their content actually contrast? Explain by summarizing the main points of each one.

Reading Strategy

Setting a Purpose for Reading

6. Imagine that your **purpose for reading** is to learn about the Islamic view of Allah, or God. Reread the selections, and jot down five main characteristics of Allah. Record your examples in a chart like the one shown.

Selection	Characteristic of Allah

7. **(a)** If your purpose for reading is to learn about Islamic views of the afterlife, which of these Surahs contains information on which you might focus? **(b)** What does that information tell you about the afterlife?
8. Reread the selections with the purpose of learning more about Islamic values. What do you think are the three most important values of Islam?

Extend Understanding

9. **Social Studies Connection:** Based on these Surahs, what social practices would you expect to find in Islamic nations? Explain.

QuickReview

Imagery is the use of language that appeals to one or more of the five senses—sight, hearing, taste, smell, and touch. A single instance of imagery is called an **image.**

Antithesis is the use of strongly contrasting language, images, or ideas.

To **set a purpose for reading,** decide why you are reading and focus on the details that help you achieve that goal as you read.

For: Self-test
Visit: www.PHSchool.com
Web Code: eta-6107

Answers

1. "Night" appeals to the senses of sight and touch. Examples include "radiant day," "smooth the path," and "blazing fire."
2. The image expresses the idea that God offers comfort and love and welcomes people into the spiritual community.
3. (a) The imagery shows the lifting of a burden. (b) The imagery speaks of hardship, toil, and a "burden which weighed down your back."
4. **Possible response:** Examples of antithesis include "Not of those who have incurred Your wrath" and "Nor of those who have gone astray" in "The Exordium"; "We shall smooth the path of salvation" and "We shall smooth the path of affliction" in "Night"; "By the light of day" and "By the dark of night" in "Daylight"; "find you an orphan" and "give you shelter" in "Daylight"; "find you in error" and "guide you" in "Daylight"; and "find you poor" and "enrich you" in "Daylight."
5. (a) "Night" and "Daylight" are antithetical titles. (b) The content of the two Surahs does not necessarily contrast. "Night" stresses charity and faith leading to contentment in the afterlife, and sin and lack of charity leading to blazing fire; "Daylight" suggests that people should treat others with the same compassion and mercy that God has shown them.
6. **Possible response:** In "The Exordium," Allah offers guidance; in "Night," Allah is powerful; in "Daylight," Allah is merciful and caring; in "Comfort," Allah offers succor.
   Another sample answer can be found on **Reading Strategy Graphic Organizer B,** p. 16 in ***Graphic Organizer Transparencies.***
7. (a) "Night" contains the most information on the afterlife.
   (b) The Surah says that there will be a Day of Judgment; those judged to be good will enjoy the life to come (heaven), but those judged to be bad will burn in the afterlife (hell).
8. The three most important values are faith, charity, and hard work.

Answers continued

9. **Possible response:** Because Muslims are expected to follow the Five Pillars of Wisdom, Islamic nations might have a large number of charitable institutions and might allow time for daily prayers.

Go Online Assessment Students may use the **Self-test** to prepare for **Selection Test A** or **Selection Test B.**

EXTEND/ASSESS

Answers

1 Vocabulary Lesson

Word Analysis: Latin Prefix *ab-*

1. b 2. a

Spelling Strategy

1. sinned, sinning
2. begged, begging
3. abhorred, abhorring
4. favored, favoring

Vocabulary Builder: Synonyms

1. c 2. a 3. b 4. c 5. a 6. b 7. c 8. b

2 Grammar and Style Lesson

1. In 622, Muhammad fled from Mecca and arrived in Medina.
2. The Islamic calendar has twelve months per year and about thirty days per month.
3. During Ramadan, Muslims fast from sunrise to sunset.
4. The Qur'an stresses the value of work, prayer, and charity.
5. Just as Jews and Christians consider the Bible sacred, Muslims consider the Qur'an sacred.

Writing Application

Sample sentences: 1. If you are kind to others, they will be kind to you. 2. It is better to give than to receive. 3. To be or not to be: that is the question. 4. Self-confidence will take you down the boulevard to success; fear will take you down a one-way road to failure.

Writing and Grammar Platinum Level

For support in teaching the Grammar and Style Lesson, use Chapter 7, Section 4.

Build Language Skills

1 Vocabulary Lesson

Word Analysis: Latin Prefix *ab-*

The word *abhor* combines the Latin prefix *ab-*, meaning "away" or "from," with the root *-hor-*, meaning "shudder." To *abhor* is to shudder from something or find it disgusting. Match each numbered word below with its meaning.

1. abduct
2. abrupt

a. happening suddenly
b. kidnap

Spelling Strategy

If a verb ends in a single stressed vowel followed by a single consonant, you usually double the consonant before adding *-ed* or *-ing: incur + -ed = incurred; incur + -ing = incurring.* Do not double *w, x,* or *y*. Add *-ed* and *-ing* to the verbs below, making sure that they are spelled correctly.

1. sin 2. beg 3. abhor 4. favor

Vocabulary Builder: Synonyms

Choose the letter of the word that is closest in meaning to the first word.

1. incurred: (a) paid, (b) delivered, (c) caused
2. recompense: (a) repayment, (b) fullness, (c) whining
3. compassionate: (a) angry, (b) sympathetic, (c) emotional
4. fervor: (a) shine, (b) grief, (c) enthusiasm
5. affliction: (a) calamity, (b) vibration, (c) accent
6. renown: (a) wisdom, (b) celebrity, (c) perseverance
7. chide: (a) slice, (b) ignore, (c) reprimand
8. abhor: (a) distribute, (b) detest, (c) spend

2 Grammar and Style Lesson

Parallelism

Parallelism presents equal ideas in similar grammatical structures. Using parallelism often makes writing more rhythmic, powerful, and memorable.

Not Parallel: He *created* the heavens, and the earth *was created* by Him.

Parallel Sentences: He *created* the heavens, and He *created* the earth.

Practice Revise the italicized section in each sentence below so that parallel ideas are expressed in parallel grammatical structures.

1. In 622, Muhammad fled from Mecca and *Medina was the town in which he arrived.*
2. The Islamic calendar has twelve months per year, and *in a month there are about thirty days.*
3. During Ramadan, Muslims fast from sunrise to *when the sun goes down.*
4. The Qur'an stresses the value of work, prayer, and *being charitable.*
5. Just as Jews and Christians consider the Bible sacred, so *is the Qur'an considered sacred by Muslims.*

Writing Application Write four sentences about human behavior, giving advice or making observations. Use parallelism in each sentence.

Prentice Hall Writing and Grammar Connection: Platinum Level, Chapter 7, Section 4

Assessment Practice

Vocabulary (For more practice, see *Test Preparation Workbook*, p. 5.)

Use this sample question from "The Exordium" to give students practice with vocabulary questions.

Praise be to God, Lord of the Universe / The Compassionate, the Merciful, / Sovereign of the Day of Judgment!

In this passage, the word *sovereign* most likely means

A a type of coin.
B defendant.
C fearful.
D ruler.

Students should consider the context by testing possible definitions in place of the word. *Sovereign* can mean a type of coin, but it does not fit in this passage; therefore, *A* is incorrect. *B* and *C* are not supported by the context—the Lord is not the defendant, nor is He fearful. The correct choice is *D*.

❸ Writing Lesson

Guidelines for Personal Behavior

After thinking about the Five Pillars of Wisdom and the passages you read from the Qur'an, create your own guidelines for personal behavior.

Prewriting Jot down five or six human qualities that you think are important and the kinds of behavior you associate with each. Number each quality, using *1* for most important, *2* for next most important, and so on.

Drafting For your guidelines, write a short paragraph identifying each quality and describing behavior that exemplifies or illustrates it. Organize your guidelines in order of importance, moving from least to most important or vice versa.

Revising As you revise, focus on organization. Shift the positions of your guidelines, if necessary. Then, underline the clauses or sentences that introduce each guideline and make sure that they provide clear signals of your organization.

Model: Revising to Clarify Organization

Most important of all,
Kindness is crucial to a worthy life. A worthy person is kind to his or her equals and especially to those who are weaker or less fortunate.

The transitional phrase helps make it the order of importance.

Prentice Hall Writing and Grammar Connection: Platinum Level, Chapter 11, Section 3

❹ Extend Your Learning

Listening and Speaking Prepare and give a brief **speech** on what compassion and mercy mean to you. Follow these guidelines:

- Define *compassion* and *mercy* and provide examples for each one.
- Draft an opening statement addressing the importance of compassion and mercy.
- As you speak, do not read your notes, but use them as a guide.

Practice your speech in front of a mirror or before friends or family. Then, present your speech to classmates.

Research and Technology In a small group, research the role that the Qur'an plays in Islamic life. Present your findings in a **magazine article** that includes copies of photos or paintings illustrating aspects of Islamic life. Assign some students to research the information and others to find the illustrations. Be sure to cite all sources. **[Group Activity]**

For: An additional research activity
Visit: www.PHSchool.com
Web Code: etd-7106

❸ Writing Lesson

You may use this Writing Lesson as timed-writing practice, or you may allow students to develop the guidelines as a writing assignment over several days.

- Use the Writing Lesson to help students develop their guidelines. Have students use the **Support for Writing Lesson** page in ***Unit 1 Resources***, p. 66, to organize their essays.
- Read aloud the Writing Lesson instruction. Point out that students' final guidelines will be in paragraph form, not list form.
- Explain some of the transitional words and phrases students might use in a composition arranged in order of importance. For instance, if they elevate a quality, they might use phrases such as "even more important" and "most valuable of all."
- Use the Exposition: Problem-Solution Essay rubrics in ***General Resources***, pp. 49–50, to evaluate students' work.

Writing and Grammar Platinum Level

To give students further instruction for this writing lesson, use Chapter 11, Section 3.

❹ Listening and Speaking

- Encourage students to draw ideas for speeches from the Qur'an or other selections in Unit 1.
- Have students work in pairs to rehearse their speeches. Each student should give his or her speech to a partner and get feedback on ways to improve it.
- **The Support for Extend Your Learning** page (***Unit 1 Resources***, p. 67) provides guided note-taking opportunities to help students complete the Extend Your Learning activities.

Go Online Research Have students type in the Web Code for another research activity.

Assessment Resources

The following resources can be used to assess students' knowledge and skills.

Unit 1 Resources
- **Selection Test A**, pp. 69–71
- **Selection Test B**, pp. 72–74

General Resources
- **Rubrics for Exposition: Problem-Solution Essay**, pp. 49–50

Go Online Assessment Students may use the **Self-test** to prepare for **Selection Test A** or **Selection Test B**.

Standard Course of Study

Goal 1: WRITTEN LANGUAGE

- **WL.1.02.2** Show awareness of culture in personal reflections.
- **WL.1.03.1** Select, monitor, and modify reading strategies appropriate to personal reflection.
- **WL.1.03.5** Summarize key events and points from personal reflection.

Goal 4: CRITICAL THINKING

- **CT.4.02.1** Show an understanding of cultural context in analyzing thematic connections.

Goal 5: LITERATURE

- **LT.5.01.3** Analyze literary devices and explain their effect on the work of world literature.

Goal 6: GRAMMAR AND USAGE

- **GU.6.02.1** Edit for agreement, tense choice, pronouns, antecedents, case, and complete sentences.

Step-by-Step Teaching Guide	Pacing Guide
PRETEACH	
• Administer Vocabulary and Reading Warm-ups as necessary.	5 min.
• Engage students' interest with the motivation activity.	5 min.
• Read and discuss author and background features. **FT**	10 min.
• Introduce the Literary Analysis Skill: Folk Tales. **FT**	5 min.
• Introduce the Reading Strategy: Summarizing.	10 min.
• Prepare students to read by teaching the selection vocabulary. **FT**	
TEACH	
• Informally monitor comprehension while students read independently or in groups. **FT**	30 min.
• Monitor students' comprehension with the Reading Check notes.	as students read
• Reinforce vocabulary with Vocabulary Builder notes.	as students read
• Develop students' understanding of folk tales with the Literary Analysis annotations. **FT**	5 min.
• Develop students' ability to summarize with the Reading Strategy annotations. **FT**	5 min.
ASSESS/EXTEND	
• Assess students' comprehension and mastery of the Literary Analysis and Reading Strategy by having them answer the Apply the Skills questions. **FT**	15 min.
• Have students complete the Vocabulary Lesson and the Grammar and Style Lesson. **FT**	15 min.
• Apply students' ability to use transitions effectively by using the Writing Lesson. **FT**	45 min. or homework
• Apply students' understanding by using one or more of the Extend Your Learning activities.	20–90 min. or homework
• Administer Selection Test A or Selection Test B. **FT**	15 min.

Resources

Print

Unit 1 Resources

Transparency

Graphic Organizer Transparencies

Print

Reader's Notebook [L2]

Reader's Notebook: Adapted Version [L1]

Reader's Notebook: English Learner's Version [EL]

Unit 1 Resources

Technology

Listening to Literature Audio CDs [L2, EL]

Print

Unit 1 Resources

General Resources

Technology

Go Online: Research [**L3**]
Go Online: Self-test [**L3**]
***ExamView®*, Test Bank [L3]**

Choosing Resources for Differentiated Instruction

[**L1**] Special Needs Students
[**L2**] Below-Level Students
[**L3**] All Students
[**L4**] Advanced Students
[**EL**] English Learners

For Vocabulary and Reading Warm-ups and for Selection Tests, **A** signifies "less challenging" and **B** "more challenging." For Graphic Organizer transparencies, **A** signifies "not filled in" and **B** "filled in."

FT Fast Track Instruction: To move the lesson more quickly, use the strategies and activities identified with **FT**.

Scaffolding for Less Proficient and Advanced Students

The leveled Critical Thinking questions after selections progress in the levels of thinking required to answer them. To address the needs of your different students, you may use the (a) level questions for your less proficient students and the (b) level questions with your on-level and advanced students. The occasional (c) level questions are appropriate for your advanced students.

Use this complete suite of powerful teaching tools to make lesson planning and testing quicker and easier.

Use the interactive textbook (online and on CD-ROM) to make selections and activities come alive with audio and video support and interactive questions.

Benchmark

After students have completed reading *The Fisherman and the Jinnee,* administer **Benchmark Test 1 (*Unit 1 Resources,* pp. 92–97).** If the Benchmark Test reveals that some of the students need further work, use the **Interpretation Guide** to determine the appropriate reteaching page in the **Reading Kit** and on **Success Tracker.**

Go Online Professional Development **For:** Information about Lexiles
Visit: www.PHSchool.com
Web Code: eue-1111

PRETEACH

Motivation

Have students discuss experiences they might have had in finding unusual objects that have washed ashore. Then, ask them to imagine that they find an old bottle on a beach and open it. Out pours a swirling column of smoke that assumes a surprising shape. Invite students to share their reactions and expectations. Explain that they will meet a jinnee (genie) in this tale.

❶ Background

More About the Selection

The first standard printed text of *The Thousand and One Nights* appeared in the fifteenth century. After the French scholar Antoine Galland (1646–1715) introduced the Western world to the stories, many English translations of the work were produced. In fact, many of the tales have become so well known in the West that they have almost become integrated into Western folklore.

Geography Note

Draw students' attention to the map at the top of the page, which highlights the Arabian peninsula. Point out the peninsula's location in Asia, near Africa and Europe. Stress that such a location would make the Arabian Peninsula a crossroads in the trading of stories as well as goods.

Build Skills | Folk Tale

from The Thousand and One Nights: ❶ The Fisherman and the Jinnee

About *The Thousand and One Nights*

The Thousand and One Nights is the most famous work of Arabic prose known to the Western world. Many of the stories, including those of Sindbad the Sailor, Ali Baba, and Aladdin, have become integral parts of Western literary and popular culture.

The Frame Story *The Thousand and One Nights* is actually a collection of unrelated tales pieced together into one long narrative. The connecting framework is the tale of King Shahriyar (depicted above), whose wife's betrayal has filled him with hatred for all women. Every night, motivated by vengeance and fear, he marries a different woman only to put her to death the following morning. Finally, a young woman named Scheherazade (shə her′ ə zäd′) devises a scheme to stop the bloodshed. She weds the king, and on the first night of their marriage, she tells him a spellbinding story. At daybreak, she has not yet finished. As the executioners await their orders, Scheherazade promises Shahriyar that she will finish the story that evening. Captivated by the tale, Shahriyar stays the order of execution. That night, Scheherazade finishes the first story but immediately starts another that is just as exciting as the first. In this way, she enthralls the king and prolongs her life for a thousand and one nights. By the time she has finished telling her final story, almost three years have passed. King Shahriyar, now in love with Scheherazade, decides not to kill her.

Varied Origins Most likely, King Shahriyar and Scheherazade never existed. Nor was there a single author who wrote all of *The Thousand and One Nights*. The book we know today is based on an ancient Persian work entitled the *Hazar Afsaneh (A Thousand Legends)*. When the book was translated into Arabic around the year A.D. 850 and renamed *The Thousand and One Nights*, it quickly became popular throughout the Arab world. People would gather around professional storytellers in marketplaces and shops to hear the fantastic tales retold. Over the years, storytellers embellished the original collection of tales with new stories they had invented or heard from other sources. They also changed the names of people and places as well as other details. Reshaped and enlarged by this battalion of anonymous storytellers, *The Thousand and One Nights* finally took the form with which modern readers are familiar. In 1704, Antoine Galland produced a French version of the book, its first major translation into a European language. An English version followed in 1708.

The Three Cultural Strands *The Thousand and One Nights* evolved over the course of centuries, incorporating three distinct cultural strands. The first strand is the original Persian book, which includes tales that many scholars believe originated in Persian folklore. The frame story of Princess Scheherazade is part of this strand. The second strand of tales is set in the Arabic city of Baghdad, which is now the capital of Iraq. These stories focus on the reign of King Harun ar-Rashid. Among the stories included in this strand are those of Sindbad and Aladdin. The final strand consists of many short, humorous tales that originated in the city of Cairo, which is now the capital of Egypt. All three strands are now woven together like a tapestry, containing stories within stories. Rich in characters, imagery, adventure, moral lessons, and humor, this collection of stories has inspired countless dramatizations, musical compositions, and other literary works.

Preview

Connecting to the Literature

For many people, the idea of finding a magical jinnee—also spelled genie or jinni—in a bottle is the stuff of pleasant daydreams. However, for the luckless fisherman in this story, the discovery soon leads to trouble.

❷ Literary Analysis

Folk Tales

Folk tales are part of the oral tradition, the body of stories, poems, and songs that are passed down by word of mouth from generation to generation. Most folk tales include the following characteristics:

- a lesson about life
- magical or supernatural elements
- characters who possess one or two main traits
- a clear separation between good and evil

In addition, folk tales may share plot patterns and deceptively ordinary characters. As you read, look for these distinctive elements.

Connecting Literary Elements

Narrative structure refers to the way in which a work of fiction is organized. *The Thousand and One Nights* contains framed stories, or stories-within-a-story. That narrative structure occurs as characters in one story tell other stories. As you read, use a chart like the one shown to map the narrative structure of "The Fisherman and the Jinnee" and to identify similarities among the stories.

❸ Reading Strategy

Summarizing

A summary is a brief statement expressing the key details of a literary work. To **summarize**, identify the details that are essential to your understanding of a story. Then, organize those details into a concise statement. As you read, summarize to aid your understanding.

Vocabulary Builder

inverted (in vʉrt´ id) *adj.* upside down (p. 87)

blasphemous (blas´ fə məs) *adj.* showing disrespect toward God or religious teachings (p. 88)

adjured (ə jo͝ord´) *v.* ordered solemnly (p. 88)

indignantly (in dig´ nənt lē) *adv.* in a way showing righteous anger or scorn (p. 89)

resolutely (rez´ ə lo͞ot´ lē) *adv.* in a determined way (p. 89)

enraptured (en rap´ chərd) *adj.* completely delighted; spellbound (p. 91)

munificence (myo͞o nif´ ə səns) *n.* great generosity (p. 92)

ominous (äm´ ə nəs) *adj.* hinting at bad things to come (p. 92)

NC Standard Course of Study

- Build knowledge of literary genres and explore how characteristics apply to world literature. (LT.5.01.2)
- Summarize key events and points from the text. (LT.5.03.5)

First Story
Narrator: Scheherazade
Story: "The Fisherman and the Jinnee"

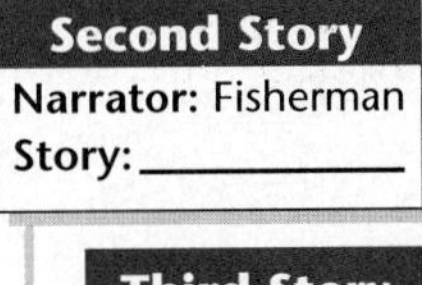

Third Story
Narrator: ________
Story: ________

Similarities Among All Three Stories

❷ Literary Analysis

Folk Tales

- Have students read the Literary Analysis feature while you list on the board the four bulleted items plus *oral composition and transmission, repeated plot patterns,* and *seemingly ordinary characters.*
- Stress that because folk tales were composed and transmitted orally, their authors are seldom known. Add *unknown authors* to the list on the board.
- Point out that through the process of oral retelling, details of folk tales may have changed over time, even as their basic plots and characters remained the same.
- Review the graphic organizer. Tell students that this selection consists of three related stories in which a character in one narrates the next, and so on. Give students a copy of **Literary Analysis Graphic Organizer A** in ***Graphic Organizer Transparencies,*** p. 17. Have them use it to convey this structure by summarizing all three stories.

❸ Reading Strategy

Summarizing

- Read aloud the definitions of *summary* and *summarize* in the Reading Strategy feature.
- Point out that summarizing will help students focus on main ideas and key details of a work.
- Explain that summarizing is also useful when taking notes or writing reviews or critical essays.

Vocabulary Builder

- Pronounce each vocabulary word for students, and read the definitions as a class. Have students identify any words with which they are already familiar.

Differentiated Instruction Solutions for All Learners

Support for Special Needs Students
Have students complete the **Preview** and **Build Skills** pages for "The Fisherman and the Jinnee" in the ***Reader's Notebook: Adapted Version.*** These pages provide a selection summary, an abbreviated presentation of the reading and literary skills, and the graphic organizer on the **Build Skills** page in the student book.

Support for Less Proficient Readers
Have students complete the **Preview** and **Build Skills** pages for "The Fisherman and the Jinnee" in the ***Reader's Notebook.*** These pages provide a selection summary, an abbreviated presentation of the reading and literary skills, and the graphic organizer on the **Build Skills** page in the student book.

Support for English Learners
Have students complete the **Preview** and **Build Skills** pages for "The Fisherman and the Jinnee" in the ***Reader's Notebook: English Learner's Version.*** These pages provide a selection summary, an abbreviated presentation of the skills, additional contextual vocabulary, and the graphic organizer on the Build Skills page in the student book.

TEACH

Facilitate Understanding

Remind students that most folk tales were passed down by word of mouth for centuries before being written down. Have students discuss what usually happens to a story that gets passed around by word of mouth: Does it grow more accurate? More entertaining? Have them consider how oral transmission might affect these folk tales.

❶ About the Selection

Each of the three stories woven together in "The Fisherman and the Jinnee" conveys a lesson about the importance of compassion, forgiveness, and trust. Each tale features a seemingly simple character who shows virtues that others lack. Each tale raises questions about the struggle for justice.

❷ Humanities

The artifact shown here represents the sort of lamp in which the supernatural creatures known as jinnees, jinn, or genies, supposedly were found. Typically, a human character finds the lamp (or bottle or jar) and unwittingly releases the jinnee, who, despite granting wishes, often causes more harm than good.

Use the following questions for discussion:

- How would having the jinnee hide in a lamp, bottle, or jar enhance the effectiveness of his appearance?
Possible response: Lamps and bottles are everyday objects, and the appearance of a jinnee from one would seem surprising.
- How do you think a jinnee would feel about being released?
Possible response: The jinnee may want to be released, or the jinnee may not want to be disturbed.

from The Thousand and One Nights

❶ The FISHERMAN and the JINNEE

translated by N. J. Dawood

Background Most of the tales in *The Thousand and One Nights* are set in the Middle East, especially Egypt, Baghdad (now the capital of Iraq), and Persia (now Iran). In all of these areas, the dominant religion is Islam. "The Fisherman and the Jinnee" is typical of the tales that make up *The Thousand and One Nights*—two of the three interlocking stories presented here are set in Persia and all of them feature Muslim characters.

In Muslim folklore, a jinnee is a supernatural creature that can take human or animal form and exert powerful influences on human affairs. While many Westerners are familiar with the image of the all-powerful jinnee trapped in a bottle, the jinnee who makes his appearance in this story offers several surprises.

❷

Differentiated Instruction Solutions for All Learners

Accessibility at a Glance

	The Fisherman and the Jinnee
Context	Ancient Persian and Muslim folklore
Language	Challenging vocabulary: pronunciation and meanings clarified in sidenotes and footnotes
Concept Level	Accessible (the struggle for justice between the powers of good and evil)
Literary Merit	Classic: Folk tale
Lexile	1030L
Other	Has the story-within-a-story structure, magical details, and supernatural elements
Overall Rating	Challenging

3 Once upon a time there was a poor fisherman who had a wife and three children to support.

He used to cast his net four times a day. It chanced that one day he went down to the sea at noon and, reaching the shore, set down his basket, rolled up his shirt-sleeves, and cast his net far out into the water. After he had waited for it to sink, he pulled on the cords with all his might; but the net was so heavy that he could not draw it in. So he tied the rope ends to a wooden stake on the beach and, putting off his clothes, dived into the water and set to work to bring it up. When he had carried it ashore, however, he found in it a dead donkey.

"By Allah,[1] this is a strange catch!" cried the fisherman, disgusted at the sight. After he had freed the net and wrung it out, he waded into the water and cast it again, invoking Allah's help. But when he tried to draw it in he found it even heavier than before. Thinking that he had caught some enormous fish, he fastened the ropes to the stake and, diving in again, brought up the net. This time he found a large earthen vessel filled with mud and sand.

Angrily the fisherman threw away the vessel, cleaned his net, and cast it for the third time. He waited patiently, and when he felt the net grow heavy he hauled it in, only to find it filled with bones and broken glass. In despair, he lifted his eyes to heaven and cried: "Allah knows that I cast my net only four times a day. I have already cast it for the third time and caught no fish at all. Surely He will not fail me again!"

With this the fisherman hurled his net far out into the sea, and waited for it to sink to the bottom. When at length he brought it to land he found in it a bottle made of yellow copper. The mouth was stopped with lead and bore the seal of our master Solomon son of David.[2] The fisherman rejoiced, and said: "I will sell this in the market of the coppersmiths. It must be worth ten pieces of gold." He shook the bottle and, finding it heavy, thought to himself: "I will first break the seal and find out what is inside."

The fisherman removed the lead with his knife and again shook the bottle; but scarcely had he done so, when there burst from it a great column of smoke which spread along the shore and rose so high that it almost touched the heavens. Taking shape, the smoke resolved itself into a jinnee of such prodigious[3] stature that his head reached the clouds, while his feet were planted on the sand. His head was a huge dome and his mouth as wide as a cavern, with teeth ragged like broken rocks. His legs towered like the masts of a ship, his nostrils were two
5 inverted bowls, and his eyes, blazing like torches, made his aspect fierce and menacing.

The sight of this jinnee struck terror to the fisherman's heart; his limbs quivered, his teeth chattered together, and he stood rooted to the ground with parched tongue and staring eyes. 6

1. **Allah** (al´ ə) Muslim name for God.
2. **Solomon . . . David** In the Old Testament, David and his son Solomon are both kings of Israel and are considered prophets by Muslims.
3. **prodigious** (prō dij´ əs) *n.* wonderful; amazing.

Literary Analysis
Folk Tales Which details in the first two paragraphs show that the fisherman is an ordinary person, perhaps less fortunate than most?

Literary Analysis
Folk Tales What supernatural element is introduced here?

4

Vocabulary Builder
inverted (in vurt´ id) *adj.* upside down

Reading Check
What does the fisherman catch when he casts his net for the fourth time?

3 Literary Analysis
Folk Tales
- Have students read the first two paragraphs of the tale.
- **Ask** students the first Literary Analysis question: Which details in the first two paragraphs show that the fisherman is an ordinary person, perhaps less fortunate than most?
Answer: The fisherman is poor and has a wife and three children to support. His first cast nets a dead donkey.

4 Literary Analysis
Folk Tales
- Remind students that folk tales usually contain magical details.
- Have students focus on the details in the second bracketed passage.
- **Ask** students the second Literary Analysis question: What supernatural element is introduced here?
Answer: A jinnee emerges from the bottle.

5 Vocabulary Builder
Latin Root *-vert-*
- Draw students' attention to the word *inverted*, and read its definition. Tell students that *inverted* includes the Latin root *-vert-*, which means "turn."
- **Ask** students to discuss how the meaning of the root *-vert-* relates to the meaning of *inverted*.
Answer: *Inverted* means turned upside down or on end.
- **Ask** students to suggest other words with the root *-vert-*, and list them on the board. Then, have students use each suggested word in a sentence that demonstrates their understanding.
Possible response: *Vertigo, subvert, extrovert,* and *introvert* all contain the root *-vert-*.

6 Reading Check
Answer: The fisherman catches a bottle that contains a jinnee.

Differentiated Instruction Solutions for All Learners

Support for Special Needs Students
Some students may have difficulty identifying narrators and summarizing stories within stories. Remind students that the main narrator of this folk tale is the woman Scheherazade. To model how to summarize, give them a copy of **Literary Analysis Graphic Organizer B** in ***Graphic Organizer Transparencies,*** p. 18. The completed graphic organizer will give students insight into the process of summarizing. They can use it as a model for writing their own summaries as they read.

Vocabulary for English Learners
Students whose native language is Latin-based may gain better understanding of many unfamiliar English words by focusing on the Latin roots. For example, the vocabulary word *inverted* contains the root *-vert-*, which means "turn." Spanish speakers may recognize this root from words such as *convertir,* "to convert," *revertir,* "to revert," and *vertiginoso,* "dizzy," as well as the Spanish for *inverted* itself, *invertido.* Assign the **Vocabulary Builder** support page in ***Unit 1 Resources,*** p. 81.

7 Background
Culture
Muslims believe that Solomon was a part of a long line of prophets whose purpose was to guide humankind toward salvation. It is also believed that Muhammad, the founder of Islam, was the last of these prophets.

8 Critical Thinking
Evaluate
- Have a volunteer read aloud the bracketed passage.
- Then, **ask** students: Do you think the fisherman, upon hearing that the jinnee intends to kill him, responds appropriately? Why or why not?
  Possible response: The fisherman's response is inappropriate because he does not humble himself before the jinnee. Instead, the fisherman provokes the jinnee by calling the giant an "ungrateful wretch."

9 Reading Strategy
Summarizing
- Have students read the second bracketed passage to themselves.
- Point out that the jinnee here is actually telling a very short story within the story.
- Have students **respond** to the Reading Strategy item: Summarize the story the jinnee tells about his past.
  Answer: The jinnee was one of several who rebelled against King Solomon but was defeated by Solomon's Vizier. When the jinnee refused to pledge Solomon obedience, Solomon had him imprisoned in a bottle that was tossed into the sea. At first, the jinnee vowed to bestow riches on whoever released him, but he was imprisoned so long that he grew angry and vowed to kill whoever released him.

7 "There is no god but Allah and Solomon is His Prophet!" cried the jinnee. Then, addressing himself to the fisherman, he said: "I pray you, mighty Prophet, do not kill me! I swear never again to defy your will or violate your laws!"

"Blasphemous giant," cried the fisherman, "do you presume to call Solomon the Prophet of Allah? Solomon has been dead these eighteen hundred years, and we are now approaching the end of Time. But what is your history, pray, and how came you to be imprisoned in this bottle?"

On hearing these words the jinnee replied sarcastically: "Well, then; there is no god but Allah! Fisherman, I bring you good news."

"What news?" asked the old man.

"News of your death, horrible and prompt!" replied the jinnee.

8 "Then may heaven's wrath be upon you, ungrateful wretch!" cried the fisherman. "Why do you wish my death, and what have I done to deserve it? Have I not brought you up from the depths of the sea and released you from your imprisonment?"

But the jinnee answered: "Choose the manner of your death and the way that I shall kill you. Come, waste no time!"

"But what crime have I committed?" cried the fisherman.

"Listen to my story, and you shall know," replied the jinnee.

"Be brief, then, I pray you," said the fisherman, "for you have wrung my soul with terror."

9 "Know," began the giant, "that I am one of the rebel jinn who, together with Sakhr the Jinnee, mutinied against Solomon son of David. Solomon sent against me his Vizier,[4] Asaf ben Berakhya, who vanquished me despite my supernatural power and led me captive before his master. Invoking the name of Allah, Solomon adjured me to embrace his faith and pledge him absolute obedience. I refused, and he imprisoned me in this bottle, upon which he set a seal of lead bearing the Name of the Most High. Then he sent for several of his faithful jinn, who carried me away and cast me into the middle of the sea. In the ocean depths I vowed: 'I will bestow eternal riches on him who sets me free!' But a hundred years passed away and no one freed me. In the second hundred years of my imprisonment I said: 'For him who frees me I will open up the buried treasures of the earth!' And yet no one freed me. Whereupon I flew into a rage and swore: 'I will kill the man who sets me free, allowing him only to choose the manner of his death!' Now it was you who set me free; therefore prepare to die and choose the way that I shall kill you."

"O wretched luck, that it should have fallen to my lot to free you!" exclaimed the fisherman. "Spare me, mighty jinnee, and Allah will spare you; kill me, and so shall Allah destroy you!"

"You have freed me," repeated the jinnee. "Therefore you must die."

"Chief of the jinn," cried the fisherman, "will you thus requite[5] good with evil?"

Vocabulary Builder
blasphemous (blas′ fə məs) *adj.* showing disrespect toward God or religious teachings

Vocabulary Builder
adjured (a joord′) *v.* ordered solemnly

Reading Strategy
Summarizing Summarize the story the jinnee tells about his past.

4. **Vizier** (vi zir′) high officer in the government; a minister.
5. **requite** (ri kwīt′) *v.* make return or repayment for.

Enrichment
The Fishing Industry
Tell students that fishing today is a highly complex modern industry. Those in the industry may work in one of several different settings.

Many work on boats that travel coastal waters, where most fish are caught. These fishers lay and haul nets or set out lines with multiple hooks to catch thousands of tons of fish each day. Their boats can be quite large, even equipped with freezing plants to store the fish.

Other fishers, such as those who catch lobsters, lay baskets and traps. These people return regularly to check, empty, and rebait their traps.

Others in the industry may work on fish farms, where fish are raised in captivity. They work building pens, monitoring the hatching of fish eggs, and raising the fish until they can be sold. Some are involved in preparing fish for market as well, working at processes such as freezing and drying.

"Enough of this talk!" roared the jinnee. "Kill you I must."

At this point the fisherman thought to himself: "Though I am but a man and he is a jinnee, my cunning may yet overreach his malice." Then, turning to his adversary, he said: "Before you kill me, I beg you in the Name of the Most High engraved on Solomon's seal to answer me one question truthfully."

The jinnee trembled at the mention of the Name, and, when he had promised to answer truthfully, the fisherman asked: "How could this bottle, which is scarcely large enough to hold your hand or foot, ever contain your entire body?"

"Do you dare doubt that?" roared the jinnee indignantly.

"I will never believe it," replied the fisherman, "until I see you enter this bottle with my own eyes!"

Upon this the jinnee trembled from head to foot and dissolved into a column of smoke, which gradually wound itself into the bottle and disappeared inside. At once the fisherman snatched up the leaden stopper and thrust it into the mouth of the bottle. Then he called out to the jinnee: "Choose the manner of your death and the way that I shall kill you! By Allah, I will throw you back into the sea, and keep watch on this shore to warn all men of your treachery!"

Illustration from *Arabian Nights,* for the story "The Fisherman and the Genie," Edmund Dulac

When he heard the fisherman's words, the jinnee struggled desperately to escape from the bottle, but was prevented by the magic seal. He now altered his tone and, assuming a submissive air, assured the fisherman that he had been jesting with him and implored him to let him out. But the fisherman paid no heed to the jinnee's entreaties,[6] and resolutely carried the bottle down to the sea.

"What are you doing with me?" whimpered the jinnee helplessly.

"I am going to throw you back into the sea!" replied the fisherman. "You have lain in the depths eighteen hundred years, and there you shall remain till the Last Judgment![7] Did I not beg you to spare me so

6. **entreaties** (en trēt′ ēz) *n.* earnest requests.
7. **Last Judgment** the final judgment of humankind at the end of the world.

11 ▲ **Critical Viewing**
Is the jinnee pictured menacing or comical? Explain. **[Make a Judgment]**

Vocabulary Builder
indignantly (in dig′ nənt lē) *adv.* in a way showing righteous anger or scorn
resolutely (rez′ ə lo͞ot′ lē) *adv.* in a determined way

12 

Reading Check
What name causes the jinnee to tremble?

10 Humanities

Illustration from *Arabian Nights,* for the story "The Fisherman and the Genie," by Edmund Dulac

The French illustrator Edmund Dulac (1882–1953) illustrated many literary classics, including *The Thousand and One Nights, The Rubáiyát,* and the works of Shakespeare.

The editions of *The Thousand and One Nights* containing Dulac's illustrations are among the most popular versions of this work. The romantic, dreamlike atmosphere of his illustrations helped shape the common Western impression of Persia and Arabia. In addition, his illustrations helped popularize such characters as Aladdin, Ali Baba, and the genie (or "jinnee").

In this illustration, the giant genie (jinnee) assumes form above the horrified fisherman. Although both characters are depicted in almost cartoonlike form, Dulac succeeds in giving his picture a fanciful air by filling it with exploding lines, billowing clouds, and dramatic sea currents.

Use the following questions for discussion:

- How do the arms of the jinnee and the fisherman accent their situations?
  Possible response: The jinnee's long arms emphasize his power. The fisherman's right arm is stretched up as if to ward off the jinnee, expressing the fisherman's shock and fear.
- Do the details of this correspond to the details of the story? Explain.
  Possible response: They basically correspond; however, the fisherman in the story stands rooted to the ground, but here he is knocked over. The jinnee in the story has his feet planted on the sand, he is not coming out of a vessel.

11 Critical Viewing

Possible response: Students who find the jinnee menacing may point to his great size and grotesque expression. Those who find the jinnee comical may say that he looks like a cartoon character.

12 Reading Check

Answer: The jinnee trembles at the Name of the Most High.

Differentiated Instruction
Solutions for All Learners

Strategy for Less Proficient Readers
Ask students to read the paragraph beginning with "When he heard." Have students compare the behavior of the fisherman and the jinnee in this passage with their behavior earlier in the story.

Strategy for Gifted/Talented Students
Suggest that students prepare arguments for a debate on the issues central to the story. Have them develop a position on the role of compassion and forgiveness in the administration of justice. Challenge students to use real-life examples as supporting evidence.

Strategy for Advanced Readers
Call students' attention to the fact that the fisherman asked the jinnee the same question when the jinnee was about to kill him. Have students explain the significance of this parallel. What predictions can they make about the fates of the doctor and the king?

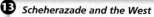

13 Themes in World Literature

Scheherazade and the West
Alfred, Lord Tennyson, published a poem called "Recollections of the *Arabian Nights*" in his 1830 volume *Poems, Chiefly Lyrical.* Fifteen years later, Edgar Allan Poe parodied *The Thousand and One Nights* in "The Thousand-and-Second Tale of Scheherazade," which pretends to explain what became of Scheherazade when her storytelling ended. Charles Dickens alludes to the Arabian classic in his 1850 tale "A Christmas Tree." Robert Louis Stevenson called his 1882 story collection *The New Arabian Nights.*

The Thousand and One Nights has continued to influence writers. Argentina's Jorge Luís Borges penned several tributes in the twentieth century; Italy's Italo Calvino borrowed the work's structure for his 1979 collection *If on a Winter's Night a Traveller.*

Connect to the Literature
Encourage students to name at least three qualities.
Possible responses: Qualities are the story-within-a-story structure that creates suspense over whether justice will prevail, the valuable reminder that rash actions can cause regret, and the magical elements used to teach a lesson about the struggle between good and evil.

14 Reading Strategy

Summarizing

- Have students pause after reading the first two paragraphs of "The Tale of King Yunan and Duban the Doctor."
- Have students **respond** to the Reading Strategy item.
  Answer: Duban is an elderly, respected doctor, knowledgeable in all the sciences. On hearing of King Yunan's leprosy, he dresses finely and goes to the palace to offer help.

➤ **Monitor Progress** Display the graphic organizer from p. 85, and have students complete it with the title of the second story.

➤ **Reteach** **Ask** a volunteer to explain how to summarize the two paragraphs.
Answer: Identify key ideas and details in the paragraphs, and then organize them into concise statements.

that Allah might spare you? But you took no pity on me, and He has now delivered you into my hands."

"Let me out," cried the jinnee in despair, "and I will give you fabulous riches!"

"Perfidious[8] jinnee," retorted the fisherman, "you justly deserve the fate of the King in the tale of 'Yunan and the Doctor'."

"What tale is that?" asked the jinnee.

The Tale of King Yunan and Duban the Doctor

It is related (began the fisherman) that once upon a time there reigned in the land of Persia a rich and mighty king called Yunan. He commanded great armies and had a numerous retinue of followers and courtiers. But he was afflicted with a leprosy[9] which baffled his physicians and defied all cures.

14 One day a venerable[10] old doctor named Duban came to the King's capital. He had studied books written in Greek, Persian, Latin, Arabic, and Syriac, and was deeply versed in the wisdom of the ancients. He was master of many sciences, knew the properties of plants and herbs, and was above all skilled in astrology and medicine. When this physician heard of the leprosy with which Allah had plagued the King and of his doctors' vain endeavors to cure him, he put on his finest robes and betook himself to the royal palace. After he had kissed the ground before the King and called down blessings upon him, he told him who he was and said: "Great king, I have heard about the illness with which you are afflicted and have come to heal you. Yet will I give you no potion to drink, nor any ointment to rub upon your body."

The King was astonished at the doctor's words, and asked: "How will you do that? By Allah, if you cure me I will heap riches upon you and your children's children after you. Anything you wish for shall be yours and you shall be my companion and my friend."

Then the King gave him a robe of honor and other presents, and asked: "Is it really true that you can heal me without draft or ointment? When is it to be? What day, what hour?"

"Tomorrow, if the King wishes," he replied.

15 He took leave of the King, and hastening to the center of the town rented for himself a house, to which he carried his books, his drugs, and his other medicaments. Then he distilled balsams and elixirs,[11] and these he poured into a hollow polo-stick.

Next morning he went to the royal palace, and, kissing the ground

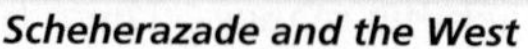

13 ***Scheherazade and the West***
From the time it was translated into French in 1704, *The Thousand and One Nights* has captured the imagination of many European writers. For example, William Wordsworth (1770–1850), father of English Romantic poetry, refers to the work in his long autobiographical poem *The Prelude.* Other European and American authors who were inspired by the book and who incorporated some of its ideas or imagery into their own works include Robert Louis Stevenson, Charles Dickens, Edgar Allan Poe, and Alfred, Lord Tennyson. In more recent times, numerous Hollywood filmmakers have adapted *The Thousand and One Nights* into successful movies, both live action and animated.

Connect to the Literature

What qualities of *The Thousand and One Nights* have kept it interesting for so many centuries?

Reading Strategy
Summarizing Summarize the doctor's background and his actions up to this point in the tale.

8. **perfidious** (pər fid′ ē əs) *adj.* treacherous.
9. **leprosy** (lep′ rə sē) *n.* chronic infectious disease that attacks the skin, flesh, and nerves.
10. **venerable** (ven′ ər ə bəl) *adj.* worthy of respect by reason of age and dignity or character.
11. **balsams** (bôl′ səmz) **and elixirs** (i lik′ sərz) two potions with supposed healing powers.

Enrichment

Leprosy
Explain to students that leprosy occurs chiefly among people who live in tropical climates. Today, most cases are found in Africa, Asia, the Pacific Islands, and South America. As the disease attacks the body, victims develop lesions on the skin and nerves. These lesions can lead to disfiguring destruction of body tissues. Although leprosy can now be treated with medication, it was once a disease that was highly feared.

Contrary to what many people believe, leprosy is not a highly infectious disease. However, throughout most of history, people who had the disease were isolated in special hospitals called leprosariums. Have interested students learn more about leprosy by researching the infectious organisms that cause the disease, the drugs used to treat it, and its historical significance.

15 before the King, requested him to ride to the field and play a game of polo with his friends. The King rode out with his viziers and his chamberlains,[12] and when he had entered the playing-field the doctor handed him the hollow club and said: "Take this and grasp it firmly. Strike the ball with all your might until the palm of your hand and the rest of your body begin to perspire. The cure will penetrate your palm and course through the veins and arteries of your body. When it has done its work, return to the palace, wash yourself, and go to sleep. Thus shall you be cured; and peace be with you."

The King took hold of the club and, gripping it firmly, struck the ball and galloped after it with the other players. Harder and harder he struck the ball as he dashed up and down the field, until his palm and all his body perspired. When the doctor saw that the cure had begun its work, he ordered the King to return to the palace. The slaves hastened to make ready the royal bath and prepare the linens and the towels. The King bathed, put on his night-clothes, and went to sleep.

Next morning the physician went to the palace. When he was admitted to the King's presence he kissed the ground before him and wished him peace. The King hastily rose to receive him; he threw his arms around his neck and seated him by his side.

For when the King had left the bath the previous evening, he looked upon his body and rejoiced to find no trace of the leprosy: his skin had become as pure as virgin silver.

The King regaled the physician sumptuously all day. He bestowed on him robes of honor and other gifts and, when evening came, gave him two thousand pieces of gold and mounted him on his own favorite horse. So enraptured was the King by the consummate skill of his doctor that he kept repeating to himself: "This wise physician has cured me without draft or ointment. By Allah, I will load him with honors and he shall henceforth be my companion and trusted friend." And that night the King lay down to sleep in perfect bliss, knowing that he was clean in body and rid at last of his disease.

Next morning, as soon as the King sat down upon his throne, with the officers of his court standing before him and his lieutenants and viziers seated on his right and left, he called for the physician, who went up to him and kissed the ground before him. The King rose and seated the doctor by his side. He feasted him all day, gave him a thousand pieces of gold and more robes of honor, and conversed with him till nightfall.

16 Now among the King's viziers there was a man of repellent aspect, an envious, black-souled villain, full of spite and cunning. When this Vizier saw that the King had made the physician his friend and lavished on him high dignities and favors, he became jealous and began to plot the doctor's downfall. Does not the proverb say: "All men envy, the strong openly, the weak in secret"?

12. **chamberlains** (chām′ bər linz) *n.* high officials in the king's court.

Literary Analysis
Folk Tales In what ways do the doctor's actions and instructions to the King seem magical or supernatural? Explain.

Vocabulary Builder
enraptured (en rap′ chərd) *adj.* completely delighted; spellbound

Literary Analysis
Folk Tales Which details in the description of the King's Vizier suggest the stark separation of good and evil that is common to folk tales? Explain.

17 
Reading Check
What does the doctor pour into the hollow polo-stick?

15 Literary Analysis
Folk Tales
- **Ask** students why they think the doctor suggests that the King take the cure while playing polo.
  Possible response: The King enjoys polo. It may be one of the few things the King does in which he holds something suitable to administer the cure and also exerts himself enough to perspire.
- **Ask** students the first Literary Analysis question: In what ways do the doctor's actions and instructions to the King seem magical or supernatural? Explain.
  Possible response: The doctor's balsams and elixirs seem to offer a magical cure, and his use of the polo club seems an almost magical way of administering them.

16 Literary Analysis
Folk Tales
- Have students read aloud the bracketed passage.
- Review with students the characteristics of folk tales. Point out that in addition to oral transmission and unknown authorship, folk tales usually contain magical elements, characters with one or two main traits, clear separation of good and evil, and lessons about life.
- **Ask** students the second Literary Analysis question: Which details in the description of the King's Vizier suggest the stark separation of good and evil that is common to folk tales? Explain.
  Possible response: The Vizier is depicted as a villain who is jealous of the doctor and plots his downfall. He seems motivated by evil; the doctor, by pure good.

Monitor Progress **Ask** how the story thus far illustrates other qualities of folk tales.
Answer: Characters display one or two main traits. The doctor's cure of the King seems magical or supernatural. The tale teaches a lesson about good and evil.

17 Reading Check
Answer: The doctor pours balsams and elixirs into the polo-stick to cure the king of leprosy.

Differentiated Instruction Solutions for All Learners

Strategy for Special Needs Students
Point out the titles of the stories within stories—"The Tale of King Yunan and Duban the Doctor" on p. 90 and "The Tale of King Sindbad and the Falcon" on p. 92. Ask students to pause and write a brief summary of events at the end of each story within a story. Make sure students recognize that they have made a transition from one tale into another and that a character from one tale has become the narrator of the next tale.

Support for English Learners
Students may better understand the roles of the doctor and the evil Vizier in "The Tale of King Yuban and the Doctor" if they read along with the recording on **Listening to Literature Audio CDs**. After they listen, encourage students to discuss how the characters illustrate the struggle between good and evil. Ask them to explain what motivates the evil Vizier. Make sure that they understand that the King's response to the Vizier results in the next story.

18 Literary Analysis

Folk Tales

- Have a student read aloud the King's response to the Vizier in the bracketed passage.
- **Ask** students to explain what character traits or qualities motivate the Vizier.
  Answer: The Vizier is motivated by jealousy, spite, and ambition to remain the King's powerful favorite.
- **Ask** students how they know that the Vizier is not actually concerned about the King's safety, as he says.
  Answer: The narrator tells us that the Vizier is a "black-souled villain, full of spite and cunning."
- **Ask** students the Literary Analysis question: What motivates the King to tell the story of King Sindbad and the falcon?
  Possible response: The King wants to teach a lesson about the dangers of acting rashly and living to regret it; he wants to show the Vizier the consequences of ungrateful behavior.

19 Critical Thinking

Analyze Causes and Effects

- Have students read the second bracketed passage on the page.
- **Ask** them what King Sindbad says he will do to whoever lets the gazelle escape.
  Answer: King Sindbad says that he will kill the person who lets the gazelle escape.
- **Ask:** Who is responsible for the gazelle's escape?
  Answer: King Sindbad is responsible.
- Have students **explain** precisely why the King's courtiers are winking at one another.
  Answer: The courtiers see ironic humor in the fact that King Sindbad says that he will kill whoever let the gazelle escape when in the end, it is the King himself who is responsible for the escape.
- **Ask** what this incident suggests about the King's personality and perhaps about the way he governs.
  Possible response: The King is rash in his pronouncements. He is harsh in meting out punishments and hypocritical in punishing others for faults he also has. He probably governs rashly and tyrannically.

So, on the following day, when the King entered the council-chamber and was about to call for the physician, the Vizier kissed the ground before him and said: "My bounteous master, whose munificence extends to all men, my duty prompts me to forewarn you against an evil which threatens your life; nor would I be anything but a base-born wretch were I to conceal it from you."

Perturbed at these ominous words, the King ordered him to explain his meaning.

"Your majesty," resumed the Vizier, "there is an old proverb which says: 'He who does not weigh the consequences of his acts shall never prosper.' Now I have seen the King bestow favors and shower honors upon his enemy, on an assassin who cunningly seeks to destroy him. I fear for the King's safety."

"Who is this man whom you suppose to be my enemy?" asked the King, turning pale.

"If you are asleep, your majesty," replied the Vizier, "I beg you to awake. I speak of Duban, the doctor."

18 "He is my friend," replied the King angrily, "dearer to me than all my courtiers; for he has cured me of my leprosy, an evil which my physicians had failed to remove. Surely there is no other physician like him in the whole world, from East to West. How can you say these monstrous things of him? From this day I will appoint him my personal physician, and give him every month a thousand pieces of gold. Were I to bestow on him the half of my kingdom, it would be but a small reward for his service. Your counsel, my Vizier, is the prompting of jealousy and envy. Would you have me kill my benefactor and repent of my rashness, as King Sindbad repented after he had killed his falcon?"

The Tale of King Sindbad and the Falcon

19 Once upon a time (went on King Yunan) there was a Persian King who was a great lover of riding and hunting. He had a falcon which he himself had trained with loving care and which never left his side for a moment; for even at night-time he carried it perched upon his fist, and when he went hunting took it with him. Hanging from the bird's neck was a little bowl of gold from which it drank. One day the King ordered his men to make ready for a hunting expedition and, taking with him his falcon, rode out with his courtiers. At length they came to a valley where they laid the hunting nets. Presently a gazelle fell into the snare, and the King said: "I will kill the man who lets her escape!"

They drew the nets closer and closer round the beast. On seeing the King the gazelle stood on her haunches and raised her forelegs to her head as if she wished to salute him. But as he bent forward to lay hold of her she leapt over his head and fled across the field. Looking round, the King saw his courtiers winking at one another.

"Why are they winking?" he asked his Vizier.

"Perhaps because you let the beast escape," ventured the other, smiling.

Vocabulary Builder

munificence (myo͞o nif′ ə səns) *n.* great generosity

ominous (äm′ ə nəs) *adj.* hinting at bad things to come

Literary Analysis

Folk Tales What motivates the King to tell the story of Sindbad and the falcon?

Enrichment

Music and Dance Inspired by *The Thousand and One Nights*

Scheherazade has served as an inspiration for a number of composers and choreographers. Among these is the celebrated Russian composer Nikolai Rimsky-Korsakov (1844–1908), whose free-flowing symphonic suite *Scheherazade* parallels *The Thousand and One Nights* in structure. The French composer Maurice Ravel (1875–1937) also wrote a piece entitled *Scheherazade* that was inspired by the princess and her situation.

Both Rimsky-Korsakov's and Ravel's compositions have been used as the music for ballets about Scheherazade. Rimsky-Korsakov's piece was used for a ballet choreographed by Michel Fokine, which was first performed in 1910. Ravel's piece was used for a ballet choreographed by George Balanchine, which was performed in 1975 by the New York City Ballet.

22 "On my life," cried the King, "I will chase this gazelle and bring her back!"

At once he galloped off in pursuit of the fleeing animal, and when he had caught up with her, his falcon swooped upon the gazelle, blinding her with his beak, and the King struck her down with a blow of his sword. Then dismounting he flayed the animal and hung the carcass on his saddle-bow.

It was a hot day and the King, who by this time had become faint with thirst, went to search for water. Presently, however, he saw a huge tree, down the trunk of which water was trickling in great drops. He took the little bowl from the falcon's neck and, filling it with this water, placed it before the bird. But the falcon knocked the bowl with its beak and toppled it over. The king once again filled the bowl and placed it before the falcon, but the bird knocked it over a second time. Upon this the King became very angry, and, filling the bowl a third time, set it down before his horse. But the falcon sprang forward and knocked it over with its wings.

"Allah curse you for a bird of ill omen!" cried the King. "You have prevented yourself from drinking and the horse also."

So saying, he struck the falcon with his sword and cut off both its wings. But the bird lifted its head as if to say: "Look into the tree!" The King raised his eyes and saw in the tree an enormous serpent spitting its venom down the trunk.

The King was deeply grieved at what he had done, and, mounting his horse, hurried back to the palace. He threw his kill to the cook, and no sooner had he sat down, with the falcon still perched on his fist, than the bird gave a convulsive gasp and dropped down dead.

The King was stricken with sorrow and remorse for having so rashly killed the bird which had saved his life.

When the Vizier heard the tale of King Yunan, he said: "I assure your majesty that my counsel is prompted by no other motive than my devotion to you and my concern for your safety. I beg leave to warn you that, if you put your trust in this physician, it is certain that he will destroy you. Has he not cured you by a device held in the hand? And might he not cause your death by another such device?"

"You have spoken wisely, my faithful Vizier," replied the King. "Indeed, it is quite probable that this physician has come to my court

20

21 **Critical Viewing**
Which details in this image illustrate moments from "The Fisherman and the Jinnee"? **[Analyze]**

Reading Strategy
Summarizing Which are the most important events and details in the tale of King Sindbad and the falcon? Explain.

Reading Check 23
What animal becomes trapped in the King's nets?

20 Humanities

This painting by George Hood shows a bearded magician or holy man pouring out a smoky potion while standing before a city atop a mountain.

Use the following question for discussion:

How does the illustration convey the mood of *The Thousand and One Nights?*
Possible response: The smoke, clouds, and mountaintop perch give it a fantastic quality that is in keeping with the tales.

21 Critical Viewing

Possible response: Details include the palace, which could be the king's residence; the bearded man performing the magic, who is something like the doctor; and the magic itself, which relates to all three stories including the smoke out of which the jinnee appears.

22 Reading Strategy

Summarizing

- Have students continue reading until the end of the bracketed passage, where the story of King Sindbad and the falcon ends.
- Make sure students understand that falcons are birds of prey that can be trained to help a hunter find and kill animals.
- Have students **respond** to the Reading Strategy question: Which are the most important events and details in the tale of King Sindbad and the falcon? Explain.
  Answer: King Sindbad is hunting with his falcon; he is thirsty; he sees what he thinks is water trickling down a tree trunk and gathers it in a water bowl; his falcon knocks the water bowl from his hands three times; in his fury, the King lops off the falcon's wings; the dying falcon indicates that the tree contains a snake spitting venom, not water, down the trunk; the King deeply regrets his hasty act.

23 Reading Check

Answer: A gazelle becomes trapped in the king's nets.

Differentiated Instruction Solutions for All Learners

Strategy for Less Proficient Readers
Students may have difficulty understanding the chain of events in "The Tale of King Sindbad and the Falcon." Have students work in small groups to create comic strips of scenes showing the main events in the story. Ask them to include speech bubbles with dialogue modified from that of the tale. They also might add simple remarks to clarify a scene; for example, King Sindbad might say, "I'm thirsty."

Strategy for Advanced Readers
Ask students to write a set of guidelines on good and bad leadership based on the events and characters in "The Tale of King Sindbad and the Falcon." For each guideline, they should explain how King Sindbad's behavior meets the guideline. For example, if a student were to write "Do not act rashly," he or she might add, "as King Sindbad did when he killed the falcon for knocking over the water bowl, when in fact the falcon did so to save his life."

24 **Literary Analysis**

Folk Tales

- Have students read the bracketed passage.
- **Ask** to what lesson about life the doctor's final question points.
  Possible response: It is wrong to repay good with evil; when one person is good to another, that person should be good in return.
- **Ask** students the Literary Analysis question: In what ways do the Vizier's words and the doctor's response emphasize the separation of good and evil?
  Possible response: The evil Vizier suggests that the King execute the doctor who has saved his life. The good doctor points out that such an execution would be an evil act and that goodness should be repaid with goodness.

25 **Humanities**

The caricatures of palace servants were illustrated by Edmund Dulac, the same artist who rendered the fisherman and the jinnee on p. 89.

Use the following questions for discussion:

- What does the art on these pages have in common with the illustration of the fisherman and the jinnee on p. 89?
  Possible response: All the illustrations are cartoonish and comical.
- Do you think the two kings were likely to have palace servants who behaved like the ones pictured on this page and the next? Why?
  Possible response: Yes; the kings are arrogant, harsh, and tyrannical, and these servants look as though they are harried by a difficult master.

26 **Critical Thinking**

Compare and Contrast

- **Ask** students what the doctor's earlier motive had been in coming to the King.
  Answer: The doctor wanted to save the King's life.
- **Ask** students how the doctor's attitude toward the King changes here.
  Answer: The doctor feels bitter about the effort he has made to help the King and wishes he had never done so.

as a spy to destroy me. And since he cured my illness by a thing held in the hand, he might as cunningly poison me with the scent of a perfume. What should I do, my Vizier?"

"Send for him at once," replied the other, "and when he comes, strike off his head. Only thus shall you be secure from his perfidy."

Thereupon the King sent for the doctor, who hastened to the palace with a joyful heart, not knowing what lay in store for him.

25

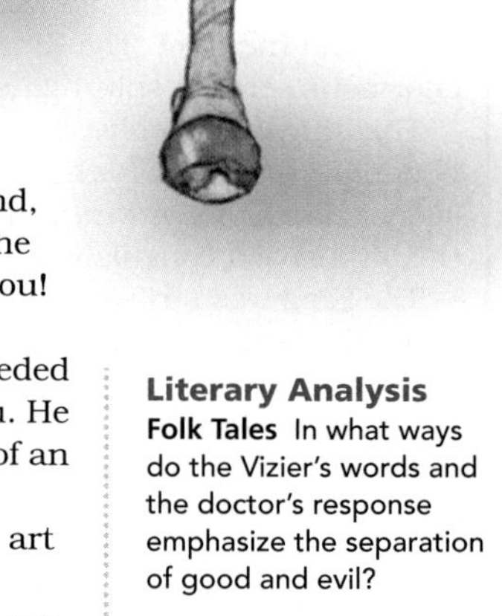

"Do you know why I have sent for you?" asked the King.

"Allah alone knows the unspoken thoughts of men," replied the physician.

"I have brought you here to kill you," said the King.

The physician was thunderstruck at these words, and cried: "But why should you wish to kill me? What crime have I committed?"

24 "It has come to my knowledge," replied the King, "that you are a spy sent here to cause my death. But you shall be the first to die."

Then he called out to the executioner, saying: "Strike off the head of this traitor!"

"Spare me, and Allah will spare you!" cried the unfortunate doctor. "Kill me, and so shall Allah kill you!"

But the King gave no heed to his entreaties. "Never will I have peace again," he cried, "until I see you dead. For if you cured me by a thing held in the hand, you will doubtless kill me by the scent of a perfume, or by some other foul device."

"Is it thus that you repay me?" asked the doctor. "Will you thus requite good with evil?"

But the King said: "You must die; nothing can now save you."

26 When he saw that the King was determined to put him to death, the physician wept, and bitterly repented the service he had done him. Then the executioner came forward, blindfolded the doctor and, drawing his sword, held it in readiness for the King's signal. But the doctor continued to wail, crying: "Spare me, and Allah will spare you! Kill me, and so shall Allah kill you!"

Moved by the old man's lamentations, one of the courtiers interceded for him with the King, saying: "Spare the life of this man, I pray you. He has committed no crime against you, but rather has he cured you of an illness which your physicians have failed to remedy."

"If I spare this doctor," replied the King, "he will use his devilish art to kill me. Therefore he must die."

27 Again the doctor cried: "Spare me, and Allah will spare you! Kill me, and so shall Allah kill you!" But when at last he saw that the King was fixed in his resolve, he said: "Your majesty, if you needs must kill me, I

Literary Analysis

Folk Tales In what ways do the Vizier's words and the doctor's response emphasize the separation of good and evil?

27 beg you to grant me a day's delay, so that I may go to my house and wind up my affairs. I wish to say farewell to my family and my neighbors, and instruct them to arrange for my burial. I must also give away my books of medicine, of which there is one, a work of unparalleled virtue, which I would offer to you as a parting gift, that you may preserve it among the treasures of your kingdom."

"What may this book be?" asked the King.

"It holds secrets and devices without number, the least of them being this: that if, after you have struck off my head, you turn over three leaves of this book and read the first three lines upon the left-hand page, my severed head will speak and answer any questions you may ask it."

The King was astonished to hear this, and at once ordered his guards to escort the physician to his house. That day the doctor put his affairs in order, and next morning returned to the King's palace. There had already assembled the viziers, the chamberlains, the nabobs,[13] and all the chief officers of the realm, so that with their colored robes the court seemed like a garden full of flowers.

The doctor bowed low before the King; in one hand he held an ancient book, and in the other a little bowl filled with a strange powder. Then he sat down and said: "Bring me a platter!" A platter was instantly brought in, and the doctor sprinkled the powder on it, smoothing it over with his fingers. After that he handed the book to the King and said: "Take this book and set it down before you. When my head has been cut off, place it upon the powder to stanch the bleeding. Then open the book."

The King ordered the executioner to behead the physician. He did so.

13. **nabobs** (nā bäbz) *n.* very rich or important people; aristocrats.

Literary Analysis
Folk Tales and Narrative Structure In what ways do the doctor's words echo those of the fisherman in the first story?

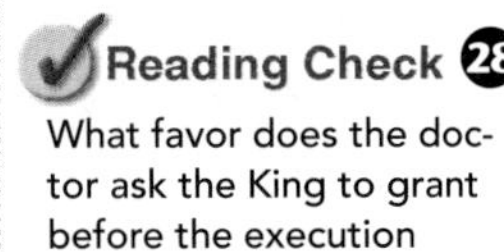

Reading Check 28
What favor does the doctor ask the King to grant before the execution takes place?

29 ◀ **Critical Viewing**
What might the facial expressions and the general energy of these caricatures convey about life as a palace servant for the kings in these tales? **[Hypothesize]**

27 Literary Analysis
Folk Tales and Narrative Structure

- Have students read aloud the bracketed passage on these pages.
- Ask students to go back and reread the portion of the first interrelated story that discusses the encounter between the fisherman and the jinnee (pp. 88–90).
- **Ask** students the Literary Analysis question: In what ways do the doctor's words echo those of the fisherman in the first story?
  Possible response: Like the fisherman, the doctor tells someone bent on harming him, "Spare me, and Allah will spare you! Kill me, and so shall Allah kill you!"
- Have students **explain** how the doctor's situation is similar to the fisherman's.
  Possible response: Like the fisherman, the doctor has done something beneficial, only to be repaid by cruelty from the one he aided. Like the fisherman, the doctor is being punished for a crime or bad act that he never committed.

28 Reading Check

Answer: The doctor asks for a day's delay so that he can say farewell to his family and neighbors, instruct them about his burial, and give away his valuable books of medicine, one of which he offers to the King as a parting gift.

29 Critical Viewing

Possible response: The facial expressions and general energy suggest harried servants who work hard and receive harsh treatment.

Differentiated Instruction
Solutions for All Learners

Support for Special Needs Students
Students may have difficulty following the arguments in "The Tale of King Yunan and Duban the Doctor." To increase their understanding, have them read along with the recording on **Listening to Literature Audio CDs.** After they have listened, encourage students to restate in their own words the argument that the Vizier makes for killing the doctor.

Enrichment for Advanced Readers
Have students debate the following question: *Did the Vizier give the King any real cause to change his opinion of the doctor?* Encourage students to plan their arguments with strong supporting evidence from the text. They may use outside evidence as well as logical argument. Have students debate the question for the rest of the class, with the audience deciding who has won the debate.

30 Critical Thinking

Make a Judgment

- Remind students that when making a judgment about a character's actions, a reader must evaluate the character's behavior against moral or other criteria.
- Read aloud the bracketed passage.
- **Use** the following question to guide students as they make judgments about the action described in the passage: Is the physician's trick defensible? Why or why not? **Possible response:** Yes; the physician's trick is justified because the King is putting him to death. No; the physician becomes like the evil King.

ASSESS

Answers

1. **Possible response:** Yes; the connections are clever. No; they are forced or confusing.
2. (a) The fisherman asks, "How could this bottle, which is scarcely large enough to hold your hand or foot, ever contain your entire body?" (b) He is indignant and goes back into the bottle to prove that he can. (c) The jinnee is arrogant and gullible.
3. (a) The King refuses to believe the Vizier. (b) The Vizier presents a clever argument. (c) He is foolish, gullible, unappreciative, arrogant, and violent.
4. (a) The falcon prevents the King from drinking the poison. (b) He realizes that the bird he killed was trying to save his life. (c) The story suggests that unrestrained anger may have unanticipated consequences.
5. The jinnee returns to the bottle and is imprisoned again. King Yunan kills the doctor and takes his poisoned medical book. King Sindbad kills the falcon, only to learn that the falcon had saved his life.
6. **Possible response:** Yes; communicating a moral lesson in the story makes it more memorable. No; the moral gets lost in the story.

Then the King opened the book, and, finding the pages stuck together, put his finger to his mouth and turned over the first leaf. After much difficulty he turned over the second and the third, moistening his finger with his spittle at every page, and tried to read. But he could find no writing there.

30 "There is nothing written in this book," cried the King.

"Go on turning," replied the severed head.

The King had not turned six pages when poison (for the leaves of the book had been treated with venom) began to work in his body. He fell backward in an agony of pain, crying: "Poisoned! Poisoned!" and in a few moments breathed his last.

"Now, treacherous jinnee," continued the fisherman, "had the King spared the physician, he in turn would have been spared by Allah. But he refused, and Allah brought about the King's destruction. And as for you, if you had been willing to spare me, Allah would have been merciful to you, and I would have spared your life. But you sought to kill me; therefore I will throw you back into the sea and leave you to perish in this bottle!". . .

Critical Reading

1. **Respond:** Did you enjoy the tales-within-tales format? Why or why not?
2. **(a) Recall:** What question does the fisherman ask the jinnee "in the name of the Most High"? **(b) Analyze Cause and Effect:** How does the jinnee respond? **(c) Analyze:** Which character trait in the jinnee allows the fisherman to defeat him? Explain.
3. **(a) Recall:** How does King Yunan react when the Vizier first denounces Duban the Doctor? **(b) Interpret:** Why does he change his mind? **(c) Generalize:** What does Yunan's willingness to believe the Vizier suggest about his character? Explain.
4. **(a) Recall:** In the story of King Sindbad and the falcon, how does the falcon save the King's life? **(b) Analyze Cause and Effect:** Why is the King later stricken with sorrow and remorse? **(c) Interpret:** What does this story suggest about the dangers of unrestrained anger?
5. **Apply:** The evil Vizier tells King Yunan, "He who does not weigh the consequences of his acts shall never prosper." In what ways might this statement apply to the jinnee, King Yunan, and King Sindbad? Explain.
6. **Take a Position:** Are stories such as these an effective vehicle for teaching moral lessons? Why or why not?

Apply the Skills

from *The Thousand and One Nights: The Fisherman and the Jinnee*

Literary Analysis

Folk Tales

1. Identify the magical or supernatural element in each of these interlocking **folk tales.**
2. Use a chart like the one shown to identify the main personality traits of the fisherman, the jinnee, King Yunan, Duban the Doctor, the Vizier, the falcon, and King Sindbad. Note the details that support your answers.

Character	Main Personality Trait	Supporting Details

3. **(a)** Which characters are seemingly weak or powerless? Explain. **(b)** Which seemingly powerless characters use cunning or trickery to achieve their goals? Explain.
4. Are any of these characters purely good or purely evil? Explain.

Connecting Literary Elements

5. **(a)** Describe the **narrative structure** of "The Fisherman and the Jinnee" by explaining who narrates each interlocking tale. **(b)** What motivates each narrator to tell each story?
6. **(a)** In what ways are the tales connected by theme or message? **(b)** How does the ending of the tale of King Sindbad and the falcon differ from the endings of the other two stories?

Reading Strategy

Summarizing

7. **(a)** Which main events and key details would you include in a **summary** of the main story about the fisherman and the jinnee? Explain. **(b)** Write a summary of that story.
8. In what ways might the use of summaries help a reader who is struggling with the narrative structure of interlocking stories? Explain.

Extend Understanding

9. **History Connection:** What do these tales reveal about the daily life and culture of the medieval Muslim world? Explain your response, citing examples.

QuickReview

Folk tales are stories that have been passed down by word of mouth from generation to generation.

Narrative structure refers to the way in which a work of fiction is organized.

To **summarize,** briefly state main ideas or events and key details in your own words.

For: Self-test
Visit: www.PHSchool.com
Web Code: eta-6108

Answers

1. Supernatural elements include the jinnee, the falcon's human behavior, and the doctor's severed head speaking.
2. **Fisherman:** clever; tricks the jinnee into the bottle; **Jinnee:** cruel; wants to kill the person who frees him; **Yunan:** gullible; falls for the Vizier's trick; **Duban:** learned; cures the king; **Vizier:** jealous; accuses an innocent man; **Falcon:** observant; sees the poison; **Sindbad:** impetuous; kills the bird.
Another sample answer can be found on **Literary Analysis Graphic Organizer B,** p. 20 in ***Graphic Organizer Transparencies.***
3. (a) The fisherman has no magical powers. The doctor and falcon seem weak because of their kings. (b) The fisherman tricks the jinnee. The doctor dies but takes Yunan with him.
4. The falcon is purely good. The fisherman is good because he stops the jinnee. The jinnee and the Vizier demonstrate only evil in their actions.
5. (a) Scheherazade tells the story of the fisherman and the jinnee. Within that story, the fisherman tells of Yunan and the doctor. Within that story, Yunan tells of Sindbad and the falcon.
(b) Scheherazade tells her story to save her life. The fisherman tells his story to show the consequence of treating people unfairly. Yunan tells his story to show the evil of rash punishment.
6. (a) All focus on whether the powerful will treat others fairly. They also show that the less powerful can be clever. (b) The falcon does not get revenge.
7. (a) Main events are releasing the jinnee, the jinnee's threats, and the fisherman's outsmarting him. Details include the jinnee's vow to kill whoever releases him and how the fisherman tricks the jinnee.
(b) A fisherman nets a bottle containing a jinnee who has vowed to kill whoever releases him. The fisherman says that the jinnee cannot fit in the bottle. The jinnee returns to the bottle to demonstrate; the fisherman corks it and threatens to throw it into the sea.
8. A summary identifies the narrators and follows the action.

Answers continued

9. The tales reveal a hierarchic society ruled by harsh monarchs; specialized government jobs; the existence of physicians; polo and falcon hunting for sport.

Go Online Assessment Students may use the **Self-test** to prepare for **Selection Test A** or **Selection Test B.**

Answers

❶ Vocabulary Lesson

Word Analysis: Latin Root *-vert-*

1. convert: to turn something from one thing into another
2. revert: to return something to its former state
3. diverted: turned away from a particular action or direction

Spelling Strategy

The physician was baffled by the fisherman's affliction.

Vocabulary Builder: Synonyms

1. a
2. c
3. b
4. a
5. c
6. c
7. c
8. b

❷ Grammar and Style Lesson

1. appeared: linking
2. broke: action
3. seemed: linking
4. felt: action
5. tricked: action

Writing Application

Possible response:

King Yunan was very ill with leprosy. (linking)

Duban the Doctor cured the King. (action)

At first the King planned a reward for the doctor. (action)

Later, he became suspicious of Duban's motives. (linking)

Writing and Grammar Platinum Level

For support in teaching the Grammar and Style Lesson, use Chapter 16, Section 3.

Build Language Skills

❶ Vocabulary Lesson

Word Analysis: Latin Root *-vert-*

The Latin root *-vert-* means "turn." *Inverted* means "turned upside down." Using your understanding of the root *-vert-*, write a brief definition of the italicized word in each of the following sentences.

1. We can *convert* this old theater into a store.
2. If the new system does not work, we will *revert* to the old one.
3. The plane was *diverted* to another airport.

Spelling Strategy

The *f* sound is sometimes spelled *ph*, as in *blasphemous*. More often, it is spelled *f* or *ff*: *fish, staff.* Rewrite the following sentence, correcting the misspelled words in italics:

The *fysician* was *bafled* by the *ffisherman's afliction.*

Vocabulary Builder: Synonyms

Select the letter of the word that is closest in meaning to the first word.

1. inverted: (a) reversed, (b) wicked, (c) shy
2. blasphemous: (a) loud, (b) unwise, (c) sinful
3. adjured: (a) disliked, (b) commanded, (c) healed
4. indignantly: (a) angrily, (b) noisily, (c) slyly
5. resolutely: (a) weakly, (b) helpfully, (c) stubbornly
6. enraptured: (a) puzzled, (b) repressed, (c) charmed
7. munificence: (a) poverty, (b) violence, (c) generosity
8. ominous: (a) shining, (b) threatening, (c) open

❷ Grammar and Style Lesson

Action and Linking Verbs

Action verbs, such as *saw, thought,* and *went,* express physical or mental action. **Linking verbs,** such as *was, felt,* and *became,* express a state of being. Linking verbs are followed by a noun or pronoun that renames the subject or by an adjective that describes it.

Some linking verbs can also function as action verbs. If you can replace the verb with a form of *be*—such as *is, are, was,* or *were*—and still express a similar meaning, the verb is a linking verb.

Action: The fisherman *looked* in the bottle. We *tasted* the food.

Linking: The jinnee *looked* monstrous. (was) The food *tasted* good. (was)

Practice Identify the verb in each sentence below as an action verb or a linking verb.

1. The bottle appeared heavy.
2. The fisherman broke the seal.
3. Once outside, the jinnee seemed like a powerful giant.
4. The fisherman felt enormous fear.
5. The fisherman tricked the jinnee in the end.

Writing Application Write four sentences about a character in "The Fisherman and the Jinnee." Use at least two action verbs and two linking verbs in your writing.

Prentice Hall Writing and Grammar Connection: Platinum Level, Chapter 16, Section 3

Assessment Practice

Using Context Clues to Determine Meaning

(For more practice, see *Test Preparation Workbook*, p. 6.)

Many tests require students to use context clues to determine meaning. Use the following sample item to help students practice this skill.

"Is it thus that you repay me?" asked the doctor.

"Will you thus requite good with evil?"

—"The Fisherman and the Jinnee"

According to this passage, the word *requite* means—

A heal.
B explain.
C return.
D ignore.

A and *B* can be eliminated as illogical because evil does not heal or explain good. *D* can be eliminated because *ignore* does not make sense in the context of the sentence. The correct answer is C.

❸ Writing Lesson

Timed Writing: Critique of a Work

The interlocking stories that make up "The Fisherman and the Jinnee" have been told and retold for centuries. Write a brief critique that attempts to account for the enduring popularity of these tales. *(40 minutes)*

Prewriting (*10 minutes*) Reread "The Fisherman and the Jinnee," noting details that could appeal to readers of different cultures in different times. Then, list those details that you think give the stories universal appeal.

Drafting (*20 minutes*) Begin your critique with a statement about the enduring appeal of "The Fisherman and the Jinnee." Then, provide examples to support that statement. Dedicate one paragraph to each story.

Revising (*10 minutes*) As you review your draft, study the cause-and-effect relationships you have proposed. Add transitions like *therefore* and *as a result* to make your reasoning clear.

Model: Revising to Show Cause and Effect

The fisherman is a poor man with little power or influence. ~~E~~As a result, everyday people hearing or reading his story can identify with him.

Transitional terms like *as a result* help clarify cause-and-effect relationships.

Prentice Hall Writing and Grammar Connection: Platinum Level, Chapter 9, Section 4

❹ Extend Your Learning

Research and Technology Conduct research to find out more about jinns and their role in Persian and Middle Eastern folklore. Use a variety of sources such as the following:

- encyclopedias
- handbooks of literature or folklore
- reliable Internet Web sites with information on Persian or Arabic literature

Present your findings in a written **report.**

Listening and Speaking Listen to Nikolai Rimsky-Korsakov's orchestral work *Scheherazade,* a musical interpretation of *The Thousand and One Nights.* Then, hold a **panel discussion** to determine how well the music captures the mood of *The Thousand and One Nights,* based on the tales you have read from it. Present your findings to your class. **[Group Activity]**

For: An additional research activity
Visit: www.PHSchool.com
Web Code: etd-7107

Assessment Resources

The following resources can be used to assess students' knowledge and skills.

Unit 1 Resources
- **Selection Test A,** pp. 86–88
- **Selection Test B,** pp. 89–91
- **Benchmark Test 1,** pp. 92–97

General Resources
- **Rubrics for Exposition: Cause-and-Effect Essay,** pp. 61–62
- **Rubrics for Research: Research Report,** pp. 51–52

Go Online Assessment Students may use the **Self-test** to prepare for **Selection Test A** or **Selection Test B.**

Benchmark

Administer **Benchmark Test 1.** If some students need further work, use the **Interpretation Guide** to determine the appropriate reteaching page in the **Reading Kit** and on **Success Tracker.**

❸ Writing Lesson

You may use this Writing Lesson as a timed-writing practice, or you may allow students to develop the Critique of a Work as a writing assignment over several days.

- Have students use **Support for Writing Lesson,** page 83 in ***Unit 1 Resources,*** to organize their critiques.
- Tell students that a critique explains or analyzes a situation by offering facts and opinions.
- Make sure that students include a general statement about the enduring appeal of "The Fisherman and the Jinnee." Students should include a paragraph dedicated to each of the three interlocking stories. These paragraphs will contain cause-and-effect relationships in offering examples from the stories to explain the tales' popularity.
- Use the Exposition: Cause-and-Effect Essay rubrics in ***General Resources,*** on pp. 61–62, to evaluate students' work.

Writing and Grammar Platinum Level

To give students further instruction for writing a critique, use Chapter 9, Section 4.

❹ Research and Technology

- Note that the term *jinnee* is rendered phonetically as *genie* and *jinni* and that the plural *jinn* is used. When students conduct their research, remind them to look under variant spellings.
- Remind students that although *The Thousand and One Nights* is an Arabic-language work, it also draws heavily on Persian-language literature.
- Use the Research: Research Report rubrics in ***General Resources,*** pp. 51–52, to evaluate students' reports.
- The **Support for Extend Your Learning** page (***Unit 1 Resources,*** p. 84) provides guided note-taking opportunities to help students complete the Extend Your Learning activities.

Go Online Research Have students type in the Web Code for another research activity.

Standard Course of Study

Goal 1: WRITTEN LANGUAGE

- **WL.1.03.3** Provide textual evidence to support understanding and response to personal reflection.
- **WL.1.03.7** Analyze influences, contexts, or biases in personal reflection.

Goal 5: LITERATURE

- **LT.5.01.3** Analyze literary devices and explain their effect on the work.
- **LT.5.03.9** Analyze and evaluate the effects of author's craft and style in world literature.

Goal 6: GRAMMAR AND USAGE

- **GU.6.01.1** Employ varying sentence structures and sentence types.
- **GU.6.02.4** Edit for clichés/trite expressions.

Step-by-Step Teaching Guide	Pacing Guide
PRETEACH	
• Administer Vocabulary and Reading Warm-ups as necessary.	5 min.
• Engage students' interest with the motivation activity.	5 min.
• Read and discuss author and background features. **FT**	10 min.
• Introduce the Literary Analysis Skill: Didactic Literature. **FT**	5 min.
• Introduce the Reading Strategy: Breaking Down Long Sentences.	10 min.
• Prepare students to read by teaching the selection vocabulary. **FT**	
TEACH	
• Informally monitor comprehension while students read independently or in groups. **FT**	30 min.
• Monitor students' comprehension with the Reading Check notes.	as students read
• Reinforce vocabulary with Vocabulary Builder notes.	as students read
• Develop students' understanding of didactic literature with the Literary Analysis annotations. **FT**	5 min.
• Develop students' ability to break down long sentences with the Reading Strategy annotations. **FT**	5 min.
ASSESS/EXTEND	
• Assess students' comprehension and mastery of the Literary Analysis and Reading Strategy by having them answer the Apply the Skills questions. **FT**	15 min.
• Have students complete the Vocabulary Lesson and the Grammar and Style Lesson. **FT**	15 min.
• Apply students' ability to revise to ensure a strong conclusion by using the Writing Lesson. **FT**	45 min. or homework
• Apply students' understanding by using one or more of the Extend Your Learning activities.	20–90 min. or homework
• Administer Selection Test A or Selection Test B. **FT**	15 min.

Resources

Print

Unit 1 Resources

Transparency

Graphic Organizer Transparencies

Print

Reader's Notebook [L2]

Reader's Notebook: Adapted Version [L1]

Reader's Notebook: English Learner's Version [EL]

Unit 1 Resources

Technology

Listening to Literature Audio CDs [L2, EL]

Print

Unit 1 Resources

General Resources

Technology

Go Online: Research [**L3**]
Go Online: Self-test [**L3**]
ExamView®, **Test Bank** [**L3**]

Choosing Resources for Differentiated Instruction

[**L1**] Special Needs Students
[**L2**] Below-Level Students
[**L3**] All Students
[**L4**] Advanced Students
[**EL**] English Learners

For Vocabulary and Reading Warm-ups and for Selection Tests, **A** signifies "less challenging" and **B** "more challenging." For Graphic Organizer transparencies, **A** signifies "not filled in" and **B** "filled in."

FT Fast Track Instruction: To move the lesson more quickly, use the strategies and activities identified with **FT**.

Scaffolding for Less Proficient and Advanced Students

The leveled Critical Thinking questions after selections progress in the levels of thinking required to answer them. To address the needs of your different students, you may use the (a) level questions for your less proficient students and the (b) level questions with your on-level and advanced students. The occasional (c) level questions are appropriate for your advanced students.

Use this complete suite of powerful teaching tools to make lesson planning and testing quicker and easier.

PRENTICE HALL
StudentEXPRESS™
Learn · Study · Succeed

Use the interactive textbook (online and on CD-ROM) to make selections and activities come alive with audio and video support and interactive questions.

Monitoring Progress

Before students read the excerpt from *The Rubáiyát,* administer **Diagnostic Test 2 (*Unit 1 Resources,* pp. 98–100).** This test will determine students' level of readiness for the reading and vocabulary skills.

For: Information about Lexiles
Visit: www.PHSchool.com
Web Code: eue-1111

PREACH

Motivation

Ask students what statement they have heard or read—such as a line from a popular song, a proverb, or the moral of a story—that best expresses their views of life. After volunteers offer examples, tell students that they are now going to read some centuries-old poetry that offers similar sorts of advice about living.

❶ Background

More About the Authors

Omar Khayyám's poetry was not well-known in his native land, but his achievements in math and science were widely recognized. In addition to reforming the Persian calendar, Khayyám built an observatory in the city of Isfahan in collaboration with other astronomers. He also taught science, philosophy, and mathematics; at times, he even worked as a fortuneteller.

Sa'di was educated in Baghdad, which was the capital of the Islamic world until it was sacked by Mongols in 1258. During his thirty years of traveling, Sa'di visited Asia Minor, Syria, India, and Egypt and made a pilgrimage to Mecca.

Geography Note

Draw students' attention to the map at the top of the page. Note that it highlights Iran, formerly called Persia, and adjoining regions where Persian influence extended.

Build Skills Poem • Fable

from The Rubáiyát • *from the* Gulistan ❶

Omar Khayyám (1048–1131)

A Persian poet, scientist, and mathematician, Omar Khayyám (ō′ mär kī yäm′) is probably the best-known Islamic poet in the West, where his poems, called rubáiyát because of their stanza structure, have been read and appreciated for centuries.

Khayyám was born in Persia (now Iran) in the city of Nishapur (nē′ shä po͝or), a major center of art and learning in the Middle Ages. He quickly earned a reputation as a mathematician and as a scholar of philosophy, history, law, and astrology. Despite his accomplishments in all these fields, he wrote very little, focusing mostly on scholarly writings about mathematics.

Khayyám's Poetry In recent times, Omar Khayyám's reputation as a poet has eclipsed his scientific fame. A collection of poetry called *The Rubáiyát* is attributed to him, although it is now known that Khayyám did not write the majority of the poems in the collection. Over the years, many poems written by other authors have been added to *The Rubáiyát* and ascribed to Khayyám. The question of authorship, however, is of little concern to Omar Khayyám's admirers, who read and enjoy *The Rubáiyát* to this day.

Why So Well Known? The success of the Rubáiyát is largely the result of an English translation published in 1859 by the noted English scholar Edward FitzGerald (1809–1883). In his translation, FitzGerald was less concerned with textual accuracy than with capturing the spirit of the original poems as he interpreted them. As he adapted, Fitzgerald created a series of lyrical and energetic poems that are often quite different in content from the originals. Despite their inaccuracy, FitzGerald's rubáiyát are widely recognized for their beauty and have enjoyed enormous popularity throughout the English-speaking world.

Sa'di (c.1213–1291)

Sa'di (sä′ dē) is revered for his wit, learning, and elegant style of writing. Persian-speaking people of all ages still read his works for enjoyment and ethical guidance in their lives.

Born in the Persian city of Shiraz, Sa'di, whose real name was Muslihuddin (mo͞os lə ho͞o dēn′), adopted the pseudonym Sa'di to show his appreciation for his royal patron, a local ruler named Sa'd bin Zangi (säd′ bēn zäŋ gē′).

Education and Travel Sa'di was educated in Baghdad, which was the capital of the Islamic world until it was sacked by the Mongols in 1258. In addition to studying at a major university, he was a disciple of several famous religious and mystical teachers. After devoting the first three decades of his life to his education, Sa'di spent approximately thirty years traveling and composing poetry. Then, he spent another three decades in religious seclusion, devoting much of his time and energy to revising his poems. During the last ten years of his life, Sa'di focused on teaching the ways of Islamic mysticism and taking care of the needy.

Fables and Poems As a writer, Sa'di is known mainly for three major works: the *Bustan,* or "Garden," which is a collection of religious and ethical poems; the *Gulistan,* or "Rose Garden," which is a book of fables; and the *Divan,* or "Collection of Poems," which contains a large number of odes, along with a variety of light, humorous poems.

The *Gulistan* has crossed easily from one culture to another. Its speculations on life and its guidelines for moral behavior are so accessible to Westerners that it has been repeatedly translated since 1787.

Preview

Connecting to the Literature

Fairy tales, fables, and other teaching stories often try to guide readers toward proper and humane behavior. Consider what such stories have in common with the selections you are about to read.

NC Standard Course of Study

- Analyze literary devices and explain their effect on the work. (LT.5.01.3)

❷ Literary Analysis

Didactic Literature

Didactic literature teaches lessons on ethics, or principles regarding right and wrong conduct, and it often reflects the values of the society that produces it. This literature usually presents specific situations or details from which a more general lesson, or **moral,** may be drawn. Look for the moral within each of these didactic works.

Comparing Literary Works

To better teach its lessons, didactic literature uses literary tools such as the following:

- **Aphorisms**—short, pointed statements expressing a truth about human experience.
- **Personification**—a technique that gives human qualities to nonhuman things.
- **Metaphor**—a figure of speech in which one thing is spoken of as though it were something else.

Although these devices appear in all of the selections you are about to read, each selection uses them in different ways. As you read, look for these tools of didactic literature and compare the differing ways each one is used.

❸ Reading Strategy

Breaking Down Long Sentences

Analyze meaning by **breaking down long sentences** and considering what they say, one section at a time. Separate a sentence's key parts (the *who* and the *what*) from the difficult language to get to the main idea. Use a diagram like the one shown to analyze long sentences.

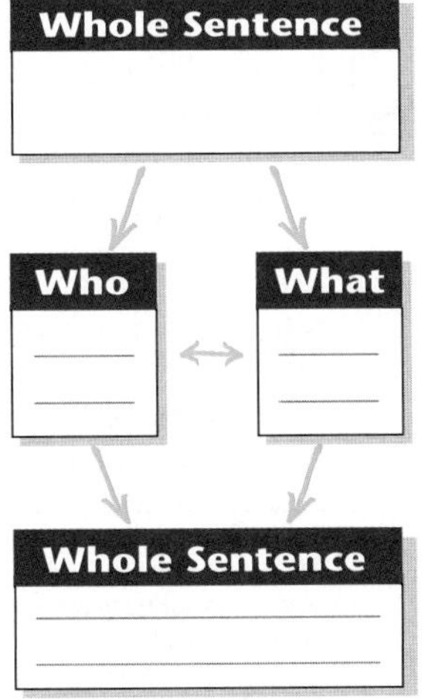

Vocabulary Builder

repentance (ri pen′ təns) *n.* sorrow for wrongdoing; remorse (p. 102)

pomp (pämp) *n.* ceremonial splendor; magnificence (p. 103)

myriads (mir′ ē ədz) *n.* great numbers of persons or things (p. 105)

piety (pī′ ə tē) *n.* devotion to religious duties or practices (p. 105)

beneficent (bə nef′ ə sənt) *adj.* charitable (p. 106)

extortions (eks tôr′ shənz) *n.* acts of obtaining money or something else through threats, violence, or misuse of authority (p. 108)

❷ Literary Analysis

Didactic Literature

- Have students read the information about didactic literature in the Literary Analysis feature.
- Explain that the word *didactic* comes from the Greek for "teaching" and literally means "instructional" or "used for teaching."
- Discuss some common examples of didactic literature, such as Aesop's fables. Note that fables that guide human behavior are a type of didactic literature.

❸ Reading Strategy

Breaking Down Long Sentences

- Have students read the Reading Strategy instructions.
- Write this sample sentence on the board: *It is narrated that a king of Persia had stretched forth his tyrannical hand and oppressed his subjects most violently.* **Ask** students what they would put in the *Who* and *What* boxes to break this sentence into parts.
  Possible responses: Who: king of Persia; **What:** stretched forth his hand and oppressed his subjects
- Give students a copy of **Reading Strategy Graphic Organizer A** in *Graphic Organizer Transparencies,* p. 21, to help them break down long sentences in the selection.

Vocabulary Builder

- Pronounce each vocabulary word for students, and read the definitions as a class. Have students identify any words with which they are already familiar.

Differentiated Instruction Solutions for All Learners

Support for Special Needs Students
Have students complete the **Preview** and **Build Skills** pages for these selections in the ***Reader's Notebook: Adapted Version.*** These pages provide a selection summary, an abbreviated presentation of the reading and literary skills, and the graphic organizer on the **Build Skills** page in the student book.

Support for Less Proficient Readers
Have students complete the **Preview** and **Build Skills** pages for these selections in the ***Reader's Notebook.*** These pages provide a selection summary, an abbreviated presentation of the reading and literary skills, and the graphic organizer on the **Build Skills** page in the student book.

Support for English Learners
Have students complete the **Preview** and **Build Skills** pages for these selections in the ***Reader's Notebook: English Learner's Version.*** These pages provide a selection summary, an abbreviated presentation of the skills, additional contextual vocabulary, and the graphic organizer on the **Build Skills** page in the student book.

Facilitate Understanding

Have students take turns reading the poems aloud. Encourage students to identify connections between the individual poems and consider what the poems suggest about Omar Khayyám's attitudes and beliefs.

❶ About the Translation

Edward FitzGerald (1809—1883) was a nineteenth-century English poet. Yet, his translation of *The Rubáiyát* is far more famous than his own poems.

Despite its success, FitzGerald's *The Rubáiyát* has aroused controversy and raised questions about the relative importance of literal accuracy in the art of translation. In translating *The Rubáiyát*, FitzGerald clearly paid much more attention to capturing the form and spirit of the original poems than he did to literal accuracy. As a result, while the beauty of his translation is widely recognized, some scholars have criticized the translation and suggested that it should be regarded as *The Rubáiyát* of FitzGerald rather than *The Rubáiyát* of Khayyám. Even FitzGerald himself admitted that his translations were not altogether accurate, commenting, "I suppose few people have ever taken such pains in translation as I have, though certainly not to be literal."

❷ Literary Analysis

Didactic Literature

- Ask a volunteer to read poem VII aloud.
- Remind students that a *moral* is a lesson about life.
- **Ask** students the Literary Analysis question: Which lines or phrases in poem VII might serve as a moral in a didactic story?
  Possible response: "The Bird of Time has but a little way/To flutter—and the Bird is/on the Wing" might serve as the moral.

from The Rubáiyát ❶

Omar Khayyám *translated by* Edward FitzGerald

Background In the eleventh century, Seljuk Turks took over the Persian Empire, imposing authoritarian government and strict religious practices on the population. Many believe that Omar Khayyám wrote his poems as a quiet protest against Seljuk rule. The poems, unpublished in his lifetime, offer an alternative philosophy that stresses enjoying life in the here and now. This philosophy is often expressed as *carpe diem,* Latin for "seize the day." Figuratively, the phrase expresses the principle "Enjoy life fully while you can."

I

Wake! For the Sun, who scatter'd into flight
The Stars before him from the Field of Night,
  Drives Night along with them from Heav'n, and strikes
The Sultán's Turret[1] with a Shaft of Light.

VII

❷ Come, fill the Cup, and in the fire of Spring
Your Winter-garment of Repentance fling:
  The Bird of Time has but a little way
To flutter—and the Bird is on the Wing.

VIII

Whether at Naishápúr or Babylon,[2]
Whether the Cup with sweet or bitter run,
  The Wine of Life keeps oozing drop by drop,
The Leaves of Life keep falling one by one.

Literary Analysis
Didactic Literature Which lines or phrases in poem VII might serve as a moral in a didactic story?

Vocabulary Builder
repentance (ri pen′ təns) *n.* sorrow for wrongdoing; remorse

1. **turret** (tur′ it) *n.* small tower projecting from a large building.
2. **Naishápúr** (nä shä poor′) . . . **Babylon** (bab′ ə lən) Naishápúr, also known as Neyshabur, is a city in northeastern Iran. It was one of the foremost cities of the Persian Empire and was the birthplace of Omar Khayyám. Babylon, an ancient city that was famous for its wealth, luxury, and wickedness, was the capital of the Babylonian Empire, which flourished from 2100 to 689 B.C.

Differentiated Instruction Solutions for All Learners

Accessibility at a Glance

	from The Rubáiyát	*from the* Gulistan: *from* The Manners of Kings
Context	11th Century Persia	Traditions of Islamic Sufism
Language	Poetic with several exclamatory sentences	Persian or Arabic terms are explained in side notes and footnotes.
Concept Level	Accessible (Enjoy life fully while you can.)	Accessible (Leaders should be moral and compassionate.)
Literary Merit	Ancient didactic poetry	Fable
Lexile	NP	1030L
Other	Quatrains of iambic pentameter with *aaba* rhyme; personification	Aphorisms and metaphors; verse passages stating morals highlight narrative prose
Overall Rating	Challenging	Average

XII

A Book of Verses underneath the Bough,
A Jug of Wine, a Loaf of Bread—and Thou
Beside me singing in the Wilderness—
Oh, Wilderness were Paradise enow![3]

XIII

Some for the Glories of This World; and some
Sigh for the Prophet's Paradise to come;
Ah, take the Cash, and let the Credit go,
Nor heed the rumble of a distant Drum!

XVI

The Worldly Hope men set their Hearts upon
Turns Ashes—or it prospers; and anon,[4]
Like Snow upon the Desert's dusty Face,
Lighting a little hour or two—is gone.

XVII

Think, in this batter'd Caravanserai[5]
Whose Portals are alternate Night and Day,
How Sultán after Sultán with his Pomp
Abode[6] his destined Hour, and went his way.

XXVII

Myself when young did eagerly frequent
Doctor and Saint, and heard great argument
About it and about: but evermore
Came out by the same door where in I went.

XXVIII

With them the seed of Wisdom did I sow,
And with mine own hand wrought to make it grow;
And this was all the Harvest that I reap'd—
"I came like Water, and like Wind I go."

XLVII

5 When You and I behind the Veil are past,
Oh, but the long, long while the World shall last,
Which of our Coming and Departure heeds
As the Sea's self should heed a pebble-cast.

3 

Rubáiyát of Omar Khayyám, Edmund Dulac

4 ▲ **Critical Viewing**
In what ways does the setting in this illustration capture the imaginary quality in Khayyám's poetry? **[Analyze]**

Vocabulary Builder
pomp (pämp) *n.* ceremonial splendor; magnificence

Literary Analysis
Didactic Literature and Metaphor For what condition is "behind the Veil" a metaphor?

6 **Reading Check**
In poem XXVIII, what seeds did the speaker sow?

3. **enow** (i nou′) *adj.* enough.
4. **anon** (ə nän′) *adv.* immediately; at once.
5. **caravanserai** (kar′ ə van′ sə rī) *n.* inn with a large central court.
6. **abode** (ə bōd′) *v.* awaited.

Differentiated Instruction Solutions for All Learners

Strategy for English Learners
Vocabulary may be more comprehensible if students look for cognates, words that they recognize because of similarities with words in their native languages. Note that Latin-based cognates are used more frequently in higher-level English vocabulary, so students whose native tongue derives from Latin will not find a cognate in the simple English word *doors* but are likely to find one in the less common word *portals,* which appears in Poem XVII of *The Rubáiyát.* Have students list cognates as they read.

Enrichment for Advanced Readers
Have students find different translations of *The Rubáiyát* in print or online. Ask them to compare and contrast some of the poems in different translations, focusing on the poems that appear in their textbook and including FitzGerald's translations in their discussion. Among the elements students might examine are diction, imagery, figurative language, mood, tone, rhythm, and rhyme.

3 Humanities

Rubáiyát of Omar Khayyám,
by Edmund Dulac

In his classic illustrations for the 1909 edition of *The Rubáiyát of Omar Khayyám,* French artist Edmund Dulac (1882–1953) blended Middle Eastern costumes and the traditional flower-strewn landscape of Persian miniatures with the flowing lines and romantic aura of the French art of his day.

Use the following question for discussion:

Where does Dulac contrast straight lines and curves? How do these contrasts affect the viewer?
Possible response: Rounded forms include the lily pond, lily pads, cactus, treetop, and daisylike flowers. Straighter lines include the figures, the man's cloak, the tree boughs, the plant to the left of the woman, and the aloelike plant in the lower right. The contrasts suggest both a connection and a difference between humans and nature.

4 Critical Viewing

Possible response: It shows a romantic scene in an exquisite Persian setting of natural beauty, stressing the glories of this world that the poet also stresses.

5 Literary Analysis

Didactic Literature and Metaphor

- **Ask** what figurative comparison poem XLVII uses to show the world's attitude toward the speaker and his beloved and what the comparison means.
Answer: The world pays as much heed to their coming and departure as the sea pays to a pebble cast into it. It means that the world pays little heed to their lives and deaths.
- **Ask** students the Literary Analysis question: For what condition is "behind the Veil" a metaphor?
Answer: It is a metaphor for passing from life to death.

6 Reading Check

Answer: The speaker sows the seed of wisdom.

❼ Humanities

Rubáiyát of Omar Khayyám,
by Edmund Dulac

The art on this page is another of Edmund Dulac's illustrations for the 1909 edition of *The Rubáiyát of Omar Khayyám.*

Use the following question for discussion:

How does the couple shown on this page differ from the couple in the illustration on p. 103?
Possible response: They seem more dreamy and contemplative. They are relaxing rather than declaring their love.

❽ Critical Viewing

Possible response: It best illustrates poem XII. It shows a man who we assume is the speaker, with a poetry book in his hand. He is sitting in an idyllic wilderness with bread and wine resting on the grass beside him and his beloved leaning on a tree branch.

❾ Background

Rubái

A quatrain, or four-line poem or stanza, is called a *rubái* in Arabic and Persian literature. Each of the poems by Omar Khayyám is a *rubái.* The word *rubáiyát,* applied to translator Edward FitzGerald's compilation of the poems, is simply the plural of *rubái.* Each quatrain uses lines of iambic pentameter (five stresses and ten syllables per line) in which the first, second, and fourth lines rhyme *(aaba).* FitzGerald's translation became so famous that in English poetry ever since, stanzas with this pattern of meter and rhyme are known as *Rubáiyát* stanzas.

❿ Critical Thinking

Analyze

- Have a volunteer **read** aloud poem LXXI and **paraphrase** what the Moving Finger does.
  Answer: It writes and moves on and cannot be called back to change even half a line.
- **Ask** students what the figurative language stresses about fate and human power.
  Possible response: Human beings are powerless to change fate or understand God's plan.

❼

Rubáiyát of Omar Khayyám, Edmund Dulac

❽ ▲ Critical Viewing
Which of Khayyám's poems does this scene best illustrate? Explain. **[Interpret]**

XLVIII

❾
A Moment's Halt—a momentary taste
Of BEING from the Well amid the Waste—
 And Lo!—the phantom Caravan has reach'd
The NOTHING it set out from—Oh, make haste!

Enrichment

Caravans

Note that Omar Khayyám's poems frequently use the image of a caravan, often as a metaphor for an individual life or the path taken in life. Make sure students are aware that a *caravan* is a company of travelers, usually merchants or pilgrims. Because of the harsh, desert climate of so much of the Middle East, people were forced to travel in caravans for safety. Caravan leaders generally were drawn from the nomadic herdsmen of the desert—people who knew the routes and the terrain. The most popular beasts of burden were camels, which could carry good-sized loads and go for long stretches with minimal food and water.

The word *caravan* is of Persian origin. The *caravanserai* (also spelled *caravansary*) mentioned in poem XVII was an inn used by travelers in caravans as well as others seeking shelter.

LXIV

Strange, is it not? that of the myriads who
Before us pass'd the door of Darkness through,
Not one returns to tell us of the Road,
Which to discover we must travel too.

Vocabulary Builder
myriads (mir′ ē ədz) *n.* great numbers of persons or things

LXXI

10

The Moving Finger writes; and, having writ,
Moves on: nor all your Piety nor Wit
Shall lure it back to cancel half a Line,
Nor all your Tears wash out a Word of it.

Vocabulary Builder
piety (pī′ ə tē) *n.* devotion to religious duties or practices

XCIX

Ah, Love! could you and I with Him conspire
To grasp this sorry Scheme of Things entire,
Would not we shatter it to bits—and then
Remold it nearer to the Heart's Desire!

Critical Reading

1. **Respond:** Which images did you find especially vivid and powerful? Why?
2. **(a) Recall:** In line 3 of poem VIII, what image describes life? **(b) Infer:** What does the imagery in the next line suggest life is like? **(c) Connect:** What do the images in both lines stress about life? Explain.
3. **(a) Recall:** According to poem XII, what four things does the speaker need to enjoy paradise? **(b) Infer:** Who might "Thou" be? **(c) Make a Judgment:** Do you think the speaker requires a great deal to be happy? Explain.
4. **(a) Recall:** What two possibilities does poem XVI offer regarding human hopes? **(b) Relate:** How does the description of the Sultan in poem XVII relate to one of these two possibilities? **(c) Speculate:** What does the speaker suggest about the lives of both the least and greatest of people?
5. **(a) Evaluate:** What do you think of the speaker's view of life and how to spend it? **(b) Criticize:** Do you find inconsistencies in his ideas? Explain.
6. **Relate:** In what ways is *carpe diem* still a relevant philosophy for people today?

For: More about Omar Khayyám
Visit: www.PHSchool.com
Web Code: ete-9102

ASSESS

Answers

1. Some readers may cite images with strong sensory appeal, such as "The Wine of Life keeps oozing drop by drop," or that seem unusual, such as "Your Winter-garment of Repentance fling."
2. (a) Life is described as wine. (b) It is like a tree or another plant with falling leaves. (c) They stress its transience.
3. (a) He needs a book of verses (underneath a tree bough), a jug of wine, a loaf of bread, and "Thou." (b) It is probably the speaker's beloved. (c) No; his needs seem simple.
4. (a) They may turn to ashes or may prosper briefly until the person involved is gone. (b) They illustrate the second option—each Sultan prospered briefly as Sultan but then died. (c) There is no difference between their lives.
5. (a) **Possible response:** The speaker's view of life as short and his *carpe diem* philosophy are probably appealing to most teenagers. (b) **Possible response:** It is inconsistent to urge enjoyment of the delights of life and then refer cynically to life as "this sorry Scheme of Things" that might best be shattered and then remolded.
6. **Possible response:** The *carpe diem* philosophy still appeals to modern audiences as evidenced by the popularity of such films as *Dead Poets Society* and *The Fast and the Furious.* Such a philosophy negates the belief that one should worry about the past or the future.

Go Online Author Link For additional information about Omar Khayyám, have students type in the Web Code, select *K* from the alphabet, and then select Omar Khayyám.

Differentiated Instruction
Solutions for All Learners

Support for Special Needs Students

Students may have difficulty following the syntax in several of the poems. Help them restate the clauses in a more familiar way by rearranging the words in a standard subject-verb-object order. For example, "Your Winter-garment of Repentance fling" in poem VII would be restated as "fling your Winter-garment of Repentance," and "could you and I with Him conspire" in poem XCIX would be restated as "could you and I conspire with Him."

Enrichment for Gifted/Talented Students

Have interested students prepare a choral reading of the poems from *The Rubáiyát.* Students should decide which lines should be spoken by individual students and which by several voices or the group as a whole. They should consider including suitable background music for their performance. After rehearsing, students might give their final performances to classmates or in a school assembly.

Facilitate Understanding

Explain to students that the central messages or morals in these short tales by Sa'di are stated in passages of verse.

11 About the Selection

In these short didactic tales sprinkled with poems and aphorisms, Sa'di offers humane moral guidance for rulers—guidance that often applies to the behavior of other people as well.

12 Critical Thinking

Analyze Cause and Effect

- Have students read the bracketed material at the start of story 1.
  Ask what has caused the prisoner to insult the king.
  Answer: The king has ordered his execution.
- Have a student **paraphrase** the aphorism beginning "Who washes his hands" and **identify** the cause and effect it contains.
  Answer: Someone is about to die (the cause), so the person speaks his or her true feelings (the effect).
- **Ask** students whether they agree with this observation and whether they think the prisoner behaves wisely.
  Possible response: Those who agree may say that deathbed confessions are true. Those who do not agree may point out that someone dying may still lie to protect others left behind. They may say that the prisoner is foolish to insult the ruler who still has the power to pardon him.
- Have a student **paraphrase** the aphorism beginning "When a man is in despair" and **identify** the cause and effect it contains.
  Answer: Someone has lost all hope (the cause), so the person speaks without restraint, lashing out at perceived enemies (the effect).
- Have a student **paraphrase** the aphorism beginning "In time of need" and **explain** how it applies to the prisoner.
  Answer: Someone knows defeat is inescapable (the cause), so he or she behaves self-destructively (the effect). The prisoner lashes out at the king who ordered his execution.

11 *from the* Gulistan

Sa'di *translated by* Edward Rehatsek

Background Sa'di was a mystic, or dervish, in the Islamic sect of Sufism, which stresses the importance of freeing oneself from material desires and living a simple life of prayer and meditation. Like many Sufi mystics, Sa'di often used literature to convey his moral convictions. His *Gulistan* comprises fables—such as "The Manners of Kings"— that offer moral guidance through simple, didactic stories sprinkled with poems and aphorisms. The following sections from "The Manners of Kings" offer moral guidance to rulers.

from The Manners of Kings

1

12 I heard a padshah[1] giving orders to kill a prisoner. The helpless fellow began to insult the king on that occasion of despair, with the tongue he had, and to use foul expressions according to the saying:

> Who washes his hands of life
> Says whatever he has in his heart.

When a man is in despair his tongue becomes long and he is like a vanquished cat assailing a dog.

> In time of need, when flight is no more possible,
> The hand grasps the point of the sharp sword.

13 When the king asked what he was saying, a good-natured vizier[2] replied: "My lord, he says: *Those who bridle their anger and forgive men; for Allah loveth the beneficent.*"[3]

The king, moved with pity, forbore taking his life, but another vizier, the antagonist of the former, said: "Men of our rank ought to speak nothing but the truth in the presence of padshahs. This fellow has insulted the king and spoken unbecomingly." The king, being

Vocabulary Builder
beneficent (bə nef′ ə sənt) *adj.* charitable

1. **padshah** (päd′ shä) king.
2. **vizier** (vi zir′) high officer in the government; a minister.
3. **Those who bridle . . . beneficent** passage from the Qur'an. The beneficent are those who are kind and charitable.

Enrichment

The Role of Love in Sufi Belief and Poetry

Many Sufis believe that the best way to reach God is through love. This is not the romantic love of one person for another but divine love, which is the love of a human being for God. When a person truly loves God, Sufis believe, this love fills the person completely and produces a sense of joy and contentment. In addition, Sufis believe that their love for God causes God to love them in return. As a consequence of this mutual love, the Sufi is drawn to God and eventually becomes united with Him. Having become united with God, the person then loses a sense of his or her individuality.

In shedding their sense of individuality, Sufis develop a strong desire to describe their feelings of love to the general public in order to induce other people to join them in their union with God. Generally the Sufis consider poetry the best means for conveying their divine love.

13 displeased with these words, said: "That lie was more acceptable to me than this truth thou hast uttered because the former proceeded from a conciliatory disposition and the latter from malignity;[4] and wise men have said: 'A falsehood resulting in conciliation is better than a truth producing trouble.'"

He whom the shah follows in what he says,
It is a pity if he speaks anything but what is good.

The following inscription was upon the portico of the hall of Feridun:[5]

O brother, the world remains with no one,
Bind the heart to the Creator, it is enough.

4. **malignity** (mə lig′ nə tē) *n.* persistent or intense ill will or desire to do harm to others.
5. **Feridun** (fer ə dōn′) legendary Persian king whose life is recorded in Firdawsi's *Shah-nama.* Feridun's three sons all died as a result of their dispute concerning who should succeed their father.

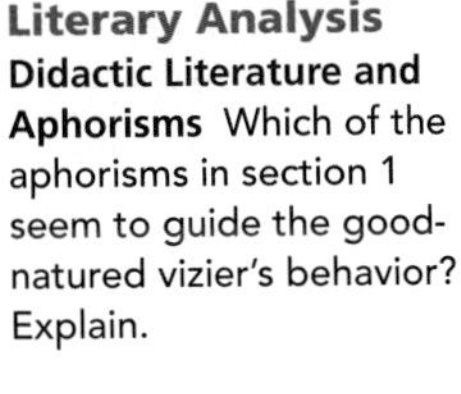

Literary Analysis
Didactic Literature and Aphorisms Which of the aphorisms in section 1 seem to guide the good-natured vizier's behavior? Explain.

14  **Reading Check**
What decision does the king make regarding the desperate prisoner?

15 

16 **Critical Viewing**
Which details in this portrait suggest that this grand vizier is a respected member of society? **[Interpret]**

13 Literary Analysis
Didactic Literature and Aphorisms

- Have students **identify** three aphorisms in the bracketed passage beginning on p. 106.
  Answer: The aphorisms are the statements beginning "Those who bridle. . .," "A falsehood resulting. . .," and "He whom the shah follows. . . ."
- **Ask** students the Literary Analysis question: Which of the aphorisms in section 1 seem to guide the good-natured vizier's behavior? Explain.
  Answer: "He whom the shah follows in what he says, / It is a pity if he speaks anything but what is good." The vizier is more concerned with speaking words that soothe than with words that injure, regardless of their truth.

Monitor Progress **Ask** a student to define an aphorism.
Answer: An aphorism is a short, pointed statement that expresses a truth about human experience.

14 Reading Check
Answer: The king stays the execution.

15 Humanities
A Grand Vizir,
by Jean-Étienne Liotard

This portrait, titled *A Grand Vizir* (an alternate spelling of *vizier*), is displayed in the National Gallery in London, England. Many scholars, however, believe that it simply portrays someone in a grand vizier's costume, possibly even the artist himself.

Use the following question for discussion:

What seems to be the artist's view of grand viziers?
Possible response: He seems impressed with their magnificence.

16 Critical Viewing
Possible response: The Vizier's elegant headwear, his opulent robes, his impressive beard, and his calm, direct expression suggest he is respected.

Differentiated Instruction
Solutions for All Learners

Support for Special Needs Students
Students may have difficulty following the lines of verse within Sa'di's tales. To increase their understanding, have them read along with the recording on **Listening to Literature Audio CDs**. After they have listened, encourage students to restate the verses in their own words.

Strategy for Advanced Readers
Have students list on the board the various messages of Sa'di's tales. Then, ask students to discuss what the messages suggest about Sa'di's attitudes and beliefs. Finally, have students share their ideas in response to these questions: In what ways are Sa'di's attitudes and beliefs similar to and different from your own? What do you believe you learn about Persian culture and moral attitudes by reading Sa'di's tales?

17 **Vocabulary Builder**

Latin Root *-tort-*

- Call students' attention to the word *extortions* and its definition.
- Tell students that the Latin root for *-tort-* means "twist."
- **Ask** students to name and define other words that incorporate the Latin root *-tort-*.
Possible response: *Tortellini, tortile,* or *torture* are possible choices.

18 **Literary Analysis**

Didactic Literature

- Ask students to focus on the second bracketed passage on this page.
- **Ask** students the Literary Analysis question: What lesson does the vizier attempt to teach the king?
Possible response: A tyrant cannot govern effectively because he destroys his support base.

Monitor Progress Have students **identify** aphorisms that express the main ethical lesson the vizier wants to teach.
Answer: "A tyrannic man cannot be a sultan / As a wolf cannot be a shepherd" and "A padshah who establishes oppression / Destroys the basis of the wall of his own reign."

Reteach Elicit from students that didactic literature is literature that teaches ethics, or lessons in right and wrong. Remind students that the ethical lessons of didactic literature may be expressed in aphorisms.

19 **Reading Strategy**

Breaking Down Long Sentences

- Have a student read aloud the third bracketed passage.
- Have students **complete** the Reading Strategy activity: Break down the last sentence of this paragraph to determine the order of events within the sentence.
Answer: First, the oppressed population assembled and supported the king's cousins; then, the king lost control of the government; and finally, the cousins and their supporters took control of it.

Rely not upon possessions and this world
Because it has cherished many like thee and slain them.
When the pure soul is about to depart,
What boots it if one dies on a throne or on the ground?

6

17 It is narrated that one of the kings of Persia had stretched forth his tyrannical hand to the possessions of his subjects and had begun to oppress them so violently that in consequence of his fraudulent extortions they dispersed in the world and chose exile on account of the affliction entailed by his violence. When the population had diminished, the prosperity of the country suffered, the treasury remained empty and on every side enemies committed violence.

Who desires succor in the day of calamity,
Say to him: "Be generous in times of prosperity."
The slave with a ring in his ear, if not cherished will depart.
Be kind because then a stranger will become thy slave.

18 One day the *Shah-namah* was read in his assembly, the subject being the ruin of the dominion of Zohak[6] and the reign of Feridun. The vizier asked the king how it came to pass that Feridun, who possessed neither treasure nor land nor a retinue, established himself upon the throne. He replied: "As thou hast heard, the population enthusiastically gathered around him and supported him so that he attained royalty." The vizier said: "As the gathering around of the population is the cause of royalty, then why dispersest thou the population? Perhaps thou hast no desire for royalty?"

It is best to cherish the army as thy life
Because a sultan reigns by means of his troops.

The king asked: "What is the reason for the gathering around of the troops and the population?" He replied: "A padshah must practice justice that they may gather around him and clemency that they may dwell in safety under the shadow of his government; but thou possessest neither of these qualities."

A tyrannic man cannot be a sultan
As a wolf cannot be a shepherd.
A padshah who establishes oppression
Destroys the basis of the wall of his own reign.

The king, displeased with the advice of his censorious vizier, sent him to prison. Shortly afterward the sons of the king's uncle rose in rebellion, desirous of recovering the kingdom of their father. The population, which
19 had been reduced to the last extremity by the king's oppression and scattered, now assembled around them and supported them, till he lost control of the government and they took possession of it.

Vocabulary Builder
extortions (eks tôr´ shənz) *n.* acts of obtaining money or something else through threats, violence, or misuse of authority

Literary Analysis
Didactic Literature What lesson does the vizier attempt to teach the king?

Reading Strategy
Breaking Down Long Sentences Break down the last sentence of this paragraph to determine the order of events within the sentence.

6. **Zohak** (zä´ hăk) legendary and tyrannical Persian king who was dethroned by Feridun.

Enrichment

The *Shah-namah*

Note that story 6 refers to the *Shah-namah,* the great Persian epic attributed to the poet Firdawsi (c. 935–c. 1020). The *Shah-namah,* which chronicles early Persian history, is so important to the culture that it is sometimes called the Persian Qur'an. It focuses on the stories of Persian kings; in fact, the Persian word *shah* means "ruler or king," and the *Shah-namah* is also called the *Book of Kings.* (The selection word *padshah,* also spelled *padishah,* is a related word for the Persian ruler.)

Have students learn more about the *Shah-namah* and present their findings in oral or written reports. They might research and report on famous specific legends in the *Shah-namah,* like that of Rustam and Suhrab; on early illuminated manuscripts of the *Shah-namah;* or on the importance of the *Shah-namah* in Persian culture. Remind students that names may be transliterated in different ways; for instance, *Firdawsi* is also spelled *Firdausi* and *Ferdowsi; Shah-namah* is also spelled *Shahnameh.*

A padshah who allows his subjects to be oppressed
Will in his day of calamity become a violent foe.
Be at peace with subjects and sit safe from attacks of foes
Because his subjects are the army of a just shahanshah.[7]

7

A padshah was in the same boat with a Persian slave who had never before been at sea and experienced the inconvenience of a vessel. He began to cry and to tremble to such a degree that he could not be pacified by kindness, so that at last the king became displeased as the matter could not be remedied. In that boat there happened to be a philosopher, who said: "With thy permission I shall quiet him." The padshah replied: "It will be a great favor." 22 The philosopher ordered the slave to be thrown into the water so that he swallowed some of it, whereon he was caught and pulled by his hair to the boat, to the stern of which he clung with both his hands. Then he sat down in a corner and became quiet. This appeared strange to the king who knew not what wisdom there was in the proceeding and asked for it. The philosopher replied: "Before he had tasted the calamity of being drowned, he knew not the safety of the boat; thus also a man does not appreciate the value of immunity from a misfortune until it has befallen him."

20

O thou full man, barley-bread pleases thee not.
She is my sweetheart who appears ugly to thee.
To the huris[8] of paradise purgatory seems hell.
Ask the denizens[9] of hell. To them purgatory is paradise.

There is a difference between him whose friend is in his arms
And him whose eyes of expectation are upon the door.

7. **shahanshah** (shä´ hän shä) emperor or King of kings, usually referred to as a *shah.*
8. **huris** (ho͞o´ rēs) dark-eyed women who, in Islamic legend, live with the blessed in paradise.
9. **denizens** (den´ i zənz) *n.* Inhabitants or occupants.

21 ▼ **Critical Viewing**
Which of the men pictured is a visiting ambassador, and which is a sultan? Which details helped you determine your answer? **[Speculate]**

Literary Analysis
Didactic Literature and Aphorisms What modern aphorism might be a good substitute for the philosopher's words?

23 **Reading Check**
In story 6, what punishment is given to the vizier who displeases his king?

20 Humanities

This illustration from a sixteenth-century Turkish manuscript shows a Persian ambassador visiting a sultan's palace.

Use the following questions for discussion:

- What are some reasons that the ambassador might visit the sultan?
  Possible response: He might want to present credentials, flatter the sultan for a favor, or negotiate to prevent a war.
- What does the picture show about interior decor in Persian palaces?
  Possible response: It was plush; carpets and wall hangings were used as ornamentation; ornamental designs were abstract; people sat on elegant stools.

21 Critical Viewing

Possible response: The man in the center is the sultan because he is sitting on a throne at the center of activity. The man on the right is the ambassador because he is kneeling and has his hands out in petition.

22 Literary Analysis

Didactic Literature and Aphorisms

- Have students focus on the bracketed passage.
- Tell students to consider the basic message of all the philosopher's advice in this passage. Then, **ask** students the Literary Analysis question: What modern aphorism might be a good substitute for the philosopher's words?
  Possible response: Everything is relative; things can always be worse; you never appreciate something until it is gone.

23 Reading Check

Answer: The vizier is sent to prison.

Differentiated Instruction
Solutions for All Learners

Support for English Learners
To avoid confusion, explain to English learners that a number of Persian or Arabic terms are used in these selections. These words include *padshah, vizier, shahanshah, huri,* and *dinar.* Remind students that it is important for them to read the footnote that accompanies each of these words.

Enrichment for Advanced Readers
Remind students that the title *Gulistan* means "Rose Garden." Then, have them imagine that they are writing a blurb for the book jacket or back cover of Sa'di's *Gulistan.* Like all good blurbs, theirs is designed to sell the book by giving readers information about it. Ask students to use punchy, appealing language in composing a one- or two-paragraph blurb that mentions who Sa'di was, sums up the kind of writing the book contains, and suggests in what way the book is like a rose garden.

㉔ Critical Thinking

Interpret

- Direct students' attention to the dialogue and closing verses of the bracketed tale.
- Have a student **explain** the narrator's misconception about why one brother was not saved.
  Answer: The narrator thinks the brother perished because of fate alone; the sailor explains that when he could not save both brothers, he chose to save the one who had not mistreated him.
- Have students **think** of an aphorism or quotation that sums up the main message of this story.
  Possible response: "Do unto others as you would have them do unto you"; "what goes around comes around."

ASSESS

Answers

1. **Possible response:** A falsehood resulting in conciliation is better than a truth producing trouble. The statement justifies "white lies," which are often important among friends.
2. (a) He insults the king. (b) The vizier wants the king to be merciful. He follows the maxim that someone advising a ruler should speak what is good.
3. (a) The king is an oppressive and violent tyrant who drives so many people from the kingdom that the revenues drop. (b) He is ineffective because he is a tyrant. (c) He is a tyrant who failed in his leadership. His subjects have left their homes and will tell their stories.
4. (a) He turns to a philosopher. (b) He is a good ruler, modest and wise enough to seek advice from those wiser than he.
5. (a) The choices we make in our behavior can affect our fate. (b) Rulers should treat others compassionately so that they will receive support in return.
6. **Possible response:** People in power, regardless of how they come to power, would benefit from advice about how to behave in order to rule successfully. Wisdom and compassion are valuable attributes in modern rulers.

35

I was sitting in a vessel with a company of great men when a boat which contained two brothers happened to sink near us. One of the great men promised a hundred dinars[10] to a sailor if he could save them both. Whilst however the sailor was pulling out one, the other perished. I said: "He had no longer to live and therefore delay took place in rescuing him." The sailor smiled and replied: "What thou hast said is certain. Moreover, I preferred to save this one because, when I once happened to lag behind in the desert, he seated me on his camel, whereas I had received a whipping by the hands of the other. When I was a boy I recited: *He, who doth right, doth it to his own soul and he, who doth evil, doth against the same.*"[11] ㉔

> As long as thou canst, scratch the interior[12] of no one
> Because there are thorns on this road.
> Be helpful in the affairs of a dervish[13]
> Because thou also hast affairs.

---

10. **dinars** (di närz´) *n.* gold coins used in a number of Islamic countries.
11. **He, who doth right . . . the same** passage from the Qur'an.
12. **scratch the interior** injure the feelings.
13. **dervish** (dur´ vish) Muslim dedicated to a life of poverty and chastity.

Critical Reading

1. **Respond:** Which of the lessons from the *Gulistan* would you share with a friend? Why?
2. **(a) Recall:** In story 1, what kinds of comments does the prisoner direct toward the king? **(b) Analyze Cause and Effect:** Why does the vizier lie on the prisoner's behalf?
3. **(a) Recall:** In story 6, why does the economy of the kingdom fail? **(b) Draw Conclusions:** What do the details of the fable reveal about the effectiveness of the king's rule? **(c) Hypothesize:** What do you think history will remember about this king? Explain.
4. **(a) Recall:** To whom does the padshah, or king, turn for help in story 7? **(b) Infer:** What do his actions reveal about the kind of ruler the padshah is?
5. **(a) Interpret:** What does the incident in story 35 suggest about the effect of individual human choice? **(b) Speculate:** In what way might this story be relevant to kings or rulers, even though none appear in it?
6. **Evaluate:** In what ways do you think the fables in "The Manner of Kings" might be relevant to leaders today?

Go Online
Author Link
For: More about Sa'di
Visit: www.PHSchool.com
Web Code: ete-9103

Go Online Author Link For additional information about Sa'di, have students type in the Web Code, select *S* from the alphabet, and then select Sa'di.

Apply the Skills

from *The Rubáiyát* • from the *Gulistan*

Literary Analysis

Didactic Literature

1. In what ways does *The Rubáiyát* qualify as **didactic literature**?
2. **(a)** What behavior does Sa'di encourage in the four sections from "The Manners of Kings"? **(b)** Why might these behaviors be particularly important for kings?
3. State in your own words the most important lesson in "The Manners of Kings."

Comparing Literary Works

4. **(a)** Which three **metaphors** represent life in poem VIII of *The Rubáiyát*? **(b)** Which use of metaphor do you think is most effective? Explain.
5. **(a)** On a chart like the one shown, list two **aphorisms** from each selection. **(b)** In the circles, list those qualities the aphorisms share and identify ways in which they differ.

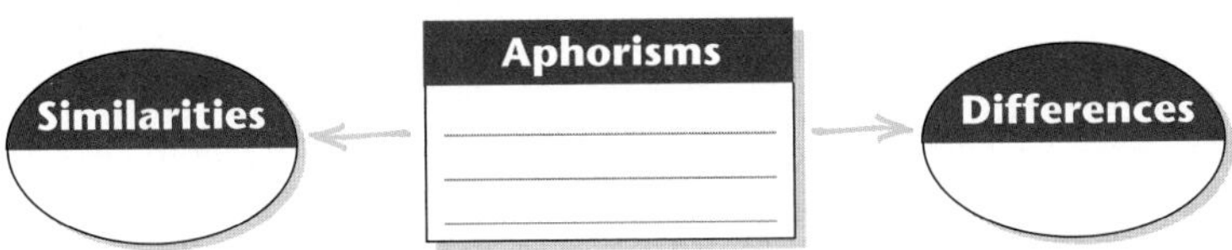

6. **(a)** In what way does the use of **personification** in *The Rubáiyát* make the verse more appealing? **(b)** Why do you think didactic literature often uses personification?

Reading Strategy

Breaking Down Long Sentences

7. **Break down the long sentence** in poem I of *The Rubáiyát*. **(a)** Who performs the main action? **(b)** What action is performed?
8. **(a)** In section 7 of "The Manner of Kings," what actions suggested by the philosopher finally calm the distraught slave? **(b)** In what way does breaking down a long sentence help you determine the answer to this question?

Extend Understanding

9. **Cultural Connection:** Based on the selections, what can you conclude about the relationship, centuries ago, between a good padshah and his vizier?

QuickReview

Didactic literature teaches lessons on ethics, or principles regarding right and wrong conduct.

Common tools of didactic literature include **aphorisms, personification,** and **metaphors.**

To **break down a long sentence,** separate the key parts (the ***who*** and the ***what***) from the difficult language to get to the main idea.

Go Online Assessment
For: Self-test
Visit: www.PHSchool.com
Web Code: eta-6109

Go Online Assessment Students may use the **Self-test** to prepare for **Selection Test A** or **Selection Test B.**

Answers

1. It teaches a philosophy of life and offers guidance about how human beings should and should not behave.
2. (a) He encourages compassion, fairness, and understanding.
   (b) Most kings need to govern mercifully and fairly in order to maintain support and be successful rulers.
3. A ruler must be compassionate in order to rule effectively.
4. (a) Metaphors include the cup, the wine, and the leaves.
   (b) **Possible response:** The cup, which represents a life full of misery or sweetness, is probably the most effective metaphor. It is still in use today in "The cup runneth over."
5. (a) **Possible response:**
   Aphorisms: *The Rubáiyát:* "I came like Water, and like Wind I go" and "The Moving Finger writes; and, having writ, moves on." **"The Manners of Kings":** "Who washes his hands of life / Says whatever he has in his heart" and "Allah loveth the beneficent."
   (b) **Possible response:** Shared qualities might relate to conciseness, diction, and imagery. Differences might relate to content or message.
   Another sample answer can be found on **Literary Analysis Graphic Organizer B,** p. 24 in ***Graphic Organizer Transparencies.***
6. (a) **Possible response:** In *The Rubáiyát,* personification is used to create appealing images and communicate ideas. (b) **Possible response:** Learning a moral from nonhumans is less threatening to the human ego.
7. (a) The sun performs the main action. (b) The sun drives off the night.
8. (a) Throwing him in the water and hauling him back into the boat calm the slave. (b) Breaking down a long sentence helps the reader identify key actions.
9. **Possible response:** A good padshah respected his vizier and took his advice. The vizier was philosophical and pious and understood life and morality.

Answers

❶ Vocabulary Lesson

Word Analysis: Latin Root *-tort-*

1. A *contortion* is a movement in which the body twists.
2. To *distort* is to twist out of shape.
3. *Tortuous* means twisted and hard to follow.

Spelling Strategy

1. magnificence
2. defiant
3. competence
4. repugnant

Vocabulary Builder: Sentence Completions

1. pomp
2. Myriads
3. beneficent
4. piety
5. repentance
6. extortions

❷ Grammar and Style Lesson

1. Hey, I finally got my copy of *The Rubáiyát.* Hurray!
2. Oh, I just read it!
3. Well, did you like it? Huh?
4. Wow! It was really good.
5. The *Gulistan* still has not arrived, alas.

Writing Application

Possible response:

Gee, those padshahs were powerful.

Hey, the philosophers who guided them were powerful, too.

Wow! Were they really?

Well, the good padshahs listened to the advice of the philosophers.

WG Writing and Grammar Platinum Level

For support in teaching the Grammar and Style Lesson, use Chapter 18, Section 2.

Build Language Skills

❶ Vocabulary Lesson

Word Analysis: Latin Root *-tort-*

The word *extortions* contains the Latin root *-tort-*, which means "twist." *Extortions* are acts that wring money or valuables from others through threats, violence, or the misuse of power. Explain how the words below reflect the meaning of the root *-tort-*.

1. contortion **2.** distort **3.** tortuous

Spelling Strategy

Nouns ending in *ance* usually end in *ant* in their adjective forms: *repentance* becomes *repentant.* Nouns ending in *ence* usually end in *ent* in their adjective forms.

1. Write the noun form of *magnificent.*

2. Write the adjective form of *defiance.*

3. Write the noun form of *competent.*

4. Write the adjective form of *repugnance.*

Vocabulary Builder: Sentence Completions

Review the vocabulary list on page 101. Then, fill in each blank below with an appropriate word from that list.

1. For the celebration, the queen appeared in all her __?__.

2. __?__ of stars shine in the nighttime sky.

3. Because she was rich, she could afford to be __?__.

4. He was a holy man praised for his __?__.

5. After doing wrong, she said a prayer as an act of __?__.

6. The criminal used threats and violence to back up his __?__.

❷ Grammar and Style Lesson

Interjections

An **interjection** is a word that expresses emotion and functions independently of a sentence. Interjections express sentiments such as happiness, fear, anger, frustration, and surprise. Use a comma to punctuate an interjection that expresses mild emotion, and use an exclamation point for interjections expressing strong emotions.

Examples:

Lo! The phantom caravan has returned.

Oh, make haste!

Ah, my Love!

Practice Correctly punctuate the interjections in each item below. Add capital letters and end punctuation where necessary.

1. Hey I finally got my copy of *The Rubáiyát* hurray.

2. Oh I just read it.

3. Well did you like it? Huh.

4. Wow it was really good.

5. The *Gulistan* still has not arrived alas.

Writing Application Write four sentences about the lessons in one of the selections. Include correctly punctuated interjections with each sentence.

WG Prentice Hall Writing and Grammar Connection: Platinum Level, Chapter 18, Section 2

❸ Writing Lesson

Fable

"The Manners of Kings" qualifies as a fable, a simple didactic story in which each character usually has just one flaw or virtue. Often the characters are animals that behave like people. Write a fable aimed at a modern-day leader or role model.

Prewriting Consider the issues modern-day leaders or role models face, and choose a lesson to address that issue. Then, brainstorm for the plot of a simple story. Finally, list each character, animal or human, and indicate a chief flaw or virtue next to each one.

Drafting Use your lists to guide you in writing your fable. Include dialogue to make the events livelier. Make sure that you have a strong conclusion that states the moral clearly, either through a character or within the narrative.

Model: Drafting a Strong Conclusion

In the next election, the greedy politician was finally voted from office. And so he learned that his desire for money had cost him the trust of the community.

A strong conclusion transforms the moral of didactic literature into a simple lesson that all readers can understand.

Revising Reread your draft, making sure that the characters are clearly drawn and that the events of the story lead to the moral. Check that the moral is a message your readers can relate to their own lives.

WG *Prentice Hall Writing and Grammar Connection: Platinum Level, Chapter 5, Section 2*

❹ Extend Your Learning

Research and Technology In *The Rubáiyát*, Omar Khayyám expresses a philosophy of life known as *carpe diem*, Latin for "seize the day." Using library and Internet resources, create an **annotated anthology** of poems that express the *carpe diem* philosophy of life. Keep these tips in mind:

- Include poems from the past and the present.
- For each poem, provide a brief comment.
- Create a cover illustration and design.

Share your anthology with the class. If possible, post it on your school's Web site.

Listening and Speaking With a group, hold a **panel discussion** about one of the aphorisms, philosophies, or moral lessons presented in *The Rubáiyát* or "The Manners of Kings." Focus your discussion on whether this principle or lesson applies to contemporary life. **[Group Activity]**

For: An additional research activity
Visit: www.PHSchool.com
Web Code: etd-7108

Assessment Resources

The following resources can be used to assess students' knowledge and skills.

Unit 1 Resources
Selection Test A, pp. 112–114
Selection Test B, pp. 115–117

General Resources
Rubrics for Narration: Short Story, pp. 63–64

Go Online Assessment: Students may use the **Self-test** to prepare for **Selection Test A** or **Selection Test B.**

❸ Writing Lesson

Fable

You may use this Writing Lesson as timed-writing practice, or you may allow students to develop the fable as a writing assignment over several days.

- To give students help with this Writing Lesson, give them the **Support for Writing Lesson** page in ***Unit 1 Resources***, p. 109.
- Remind students that a fable teaches a moral lesson that is often stated near the end of the tale.
- Have students work in pairs or small groups to brainstorm the plots of their fables. Then, have them write the fables individually.
- Encourage students to share their fables with classmates and perhaps to gather some or all of them into a class book of fables. Artistically gifted students could create cover art and illustrations.
- Use the Narration: Short Story rubrics in ***General Resources***, pp. 63–64, to evaluate students' work.

WG **Writing and Grammar Platinum Level**

To give students further instruction for writing a fable, use Chapter 5, Section 2.

❹ Speaking and Listening

- Encourage students to work in pairs and translate into their own words the aphorisms, philosophies, and morals they find. Then have students choose the item they wish to discuss.
- Have students who made the same choice form a group and decide how they will persuade others that their choice applies to contemporary life.
- Remind students to use courteous language and not to interrupt another speaker.
- The **Support for Extend Your Learning** page (***Unit 1 Resources***, p. 110) provides guided note-taking opportunities to help students complete the Extend Your Learning activities.

Go Online Research: Have students type in the Web Code for another research activity.

Standard Course of Study

Goal 1: WRITTEN LANGUAGE

- **WL.1.03.6** Make inferences and draw conclusions based on personal reflection.

Goal 3: FOUNDATIONS OF ARGUMENT

- **FA.3.04.9** Analyze and evaluate the effects of author's craft and style in argument.

Goal 4: CRITICAL THINKING

- **CT.4.01.1** Interpret and make generalizations about events supported by specific references.
- **CT.4.02.3** Examine how elements such as irony and symbolism impact theme.

Goal 5: LITERATURE

- **LT.5.01.3** Analyze literary devices and explain their effect on the work of world literature.

Goal 6: GRAMMAR AND USAGE

- **GU.6.02.1** Edit for agreement, tense choice, pronouns, antecedents, case, and complete sentences.
- **GU.6.02.4** Edit for clichés/trite expressions.

Step-by-Step Teaching Guide	Pacing Guide
PRETEACH	
• Administer Vocabulary and Reading Warm-ups as necessary.	5 min.
• Engage students' interest with the motivation activity.	5 min.
• Read and discuss author and background features. **FT**	10 min.
• Introduce the Literary Analysis Skill: Analogy. **FT**	5 min.
• Introduce the Reading Strategy: Making Generalizations. **FT**	10 min.
• Prepare students to read by teaching the selection vocabulary. **FT**	
TEACH	
• Informally monitor comprehension while students read independently or in groups. **FT**	30 min.
• Monitor students' comprehension with the Reading Check notes.	as students read
• Reinforce vocabulary with Vocabulary Builder notes.	as students read
• Develop students' understanding of analogy with the Literary Analysis annotations. **FT**	5 min.
• Develop students' ability to make generalizations with the Reading Strategy annotations. **FT**	5 min.
ASSESS/EXTEND	
• Assess students' comprehension and mastery of the Literary Analysis and Reading Strategy by having them answer the Apply the Skills questions. **FT**	15 min.
• Have students complete the Vocabulary Lesson and the Grammar and Style Lesson. **FT**	15 min.
• Apply students' ability to use imagery, rhythm, and other poetic devices by using the Writing Lesson. **FT**	45 min. or homework
• Apply students' understanding by using one or more of the Extend Your Learning activities. **FT**	20–90 min. or homework
• Administer Selection Test A or Selection Test B. **FT**	15 min.

Resources

Print

Unit 1 Resources

- Vocabulary Warm-up Word Lists **[L1, L2, EL]** .... p. 120
- Vocabulary Warm-up Practice **[L1, L2, EL]** .... p. 121
- Reading Warm-up A **[L1, L2, EL]** .... p. 122
- Reading Warm-up B **[L1, L2, L3]** .... p. 123

Transparency

Graphic Organizer Transparencies

- Literary Analysis Graphic Organizer A **[L3]** .... p. 27
- Literary Analysis Graphic Organizer B **[L1, L2, EL]** .... p. 28
- Reading Strategy Graphic Organizer A **[L3]** .... p. 25
- Reading Strategy Graphic Organizer B **[L1, L2, EL]** .... p. 26

Print

Reader's Notebook [L2]

Reader's Notebook: Adapted Version [L1]

Reader's Notebook: English Learner's Version [EL]

Unit 1 Resources

- Literary Analysis **[L3]** .... p. 124
- Reading Strategy **[L3]** .... p. 125
- Vocabulary Builder **[L3]** .... p. 126

Technology

Listening to Literature Audio CDs [L2, EL]

Reader's Notebook: Adapted Version Audio CD [L1, L2]

Print

Unit 1 Resources

- Grammar and Style **[L3]** .... p. 127
- Support for Writing Lesson **[L3]** .... p. 128
- Support for Extend Your Learning **[L3]** .... p. 129
- Enrichment **[L4]** .... p. 130
- Selection Test A **[L1, L2, EL]** .... pp. 131–133
- Selection Test B **[L3, L4]** .... pp. 134–136

General Resources

- Rubrics for Poem (Rhyming) **[L3]** .... pp. 73–74

Technology

- **Go Online**: Research **[L3]**
- **Go Online**: Self-test **[L3]**
- *ExamView®*, **Test Bank [L3]**

Choosing Resources for Differentiated Instruction

[**L1**] Special Needs Students

[**L2**] Below-Level Students

[**L3**] All Students

[**L4**] Advanced Students

[**EL**] English Learners

For Vocabulary and Reading Warm-ups and for Selection Tests, **A** signifies "less challenging" and **B** "more challenging." For Graphic Organizer transparencies, **A** signifies "not filled in" and **B** "filled in."

FT Fast Track Instruction: To move the lesson more quickly, use the strategies and activities identified with **FT**.

Scaffolding for Less Proficient and Advanced Students

The leveled Critical Thinking questions after selections progress in the levels of thinking required to answer them. To address the needs of your different students, you may use the (a) level questions for your less proficient students and the (b) level questions with your on-level and advanced students. The occasional (c) level questions are appropriate for your advanced students.

PRENTICE HALL **TeacherEXPRESS™** Plan · Teach · Assess Use this complete suite of powerful teaching tools to make lesson planning and testing quicker and easier.

PRENTICE HALL **StudentEXPRESS™** Learn · Study · Succeed Use the interactive textbook (online and on CD-ROM) to make selections and activities come alive with audio and video support and interactive questions.

For: Information about Lexiles
Visit: www.PHSchool.com
Web Code: eue-1111

 From the Translator's Desk

Coleman Barks

- You might wish to have students reread Coleman Barks's introduction to the unit on pages 2–3.
- Show Segment 2 on Coleman Barks on *From the Author's Desk DVD* to provide insight into Rumi's poetry. After students have watched the segment, **ask:** Why do you think Rumi's poetry is popular today?
  Answer: Rumi writes about universal themes that are relevant today, such as unity, peace, and love—things we want in society and for ourselves.
- Have students read Barks's comments on these pages.
- Ask a student to summarize how Barks became involved in translating Rumi's poetry. Then **ask:** What did Robert Bly want Barks to do with Rumi's poetry?
  Answer: Bly wanted Barks to release Rumi's poems from their "cages."
- **Ask:** What did you think that Bly meant when he said that Rumi's poems "need to be released from their cages"?
  Answer: The scholarly translations of Rumi's work were like cages that imprisoned the beauty and power of Rumi's poetry. Bly wanted Barks to use a contemporary free verse translation and to make Rumi's poetry more accessible to non-scholars.

Critical Viewing

Possible response: Yes. The bird looks as though it were just released from captivity and is beginning to soar.

From the Translator's Desk

COLEMAN BARKS INTRODUCES *The Poetry of Rumi*

The poet Coleman Barks is famous for his translations of the Persian poet Rumi, including *The Essential Rumi* and *The Soul of Rumi*.

How I Got Into This

I knew nothing of the thirteenth-century Persian poet Rumi until I was thirty-nine. That was in 1976, when my friend, the poet Robert Bly, handed me a book of scholarly translations of Rumi and said, "These poems need to be released from their cages." I was teaching university classes in American literature at the time. In the late afternoon after teaching, I'd go to the Bluebird Restaurant in downtown Athens, Georgia, have some hot tea, and work on freeing a Rumi poem from its cage. I would read it through in a scholarly, word-for-word English translation and try to sense what came through in the original moment, in the thirteenth century. What I felt in the Bluebird was a new freedom and spaciousness of movement. Here was poetry that could not be *explicated*—fully explained. It felt more like play than work.

I Am What I Don't Know There is another connection to Rumi in my life. I grew up on the campus of a private school, where my father was the headmaster. At six years old I was a geography freak. Strange child. I memorized all the capitals of all the countries in the 1943 Rand McNally atlas. As I walked across the quadrangle to the dining hall, people would call out countries, and I'd yell back the capital. I never missed. It got to be a thing. Bulgaria! *Sofia!* Uruguay! *Montevideo!* says the little smart aleck.

Then the Latin teacher found a country that didn't seem to have a capital, at least on his map. Cappodocia! The look on my stumped face named me. I was "Cappadocia" from then on, or "Capp." It turns out that the central city of Cappadocia was Iconium, later Konya,

▶ **Critical Viewing**
Do you think that the bird in this painting suggests the kind of freedom that Barks is trying to achieve in his translations? Explain. **[Connect]**

Teaching Resources

The following resources can be used to enrich or extend the instruction for From the Translator's Desk.

Unit 1 Resources
- **Support for Penguin Essay,** p. 118
- **Listening and Viewing,** p. 119

From the Author's Desk DVD
- **Coleman Barks,** Segment 2

where Rumi lived and is buried. The universe played a little joke on me, and I finally got it. I am what I don't know.

How I Do What I Do Here's an example of how I collaborate with Persian (Farsi) scholars to create a contemporary free verse translation: In the scholarly version of the poem "Two Kinds of Intelligence" (page 120), the phrase for the second knowledge was "a fountain in the midst of the soul gushing from the house of the heart." I edited that to "A spring overflowing its springbox. A freshness / in the center of the chest. . . / It's fluid, that second knowing." I try to make the idea more accessible without dumbing it down.

When I translate, I don't always leave out God-words *(soul, spirit, heart, bliss),* but I often find ways to make them more alive to myself, to bring across my own sense of the sacred. Springs are sacred. The word *fountain* is artificial.

Rumi has supposedly become the most read poet in the United States. If that's true, then he must be serving this innate, sweet springwater of the soul.

▲ Critical Viewing
This painting shows whirling dervishes, members of the spiritual community that Rumi founded. What connection do you see between whirling, hypnotic dance and the kind of knowledge that Rumi (in Barks's translation) describes as "A freshness in the center of the chest"? **[Connect]**

Thinking About the Commentary

1. **(a) Recall:** How did Coleman Barks become interested in the poet Rumi? **(b) Speculate:** Why do you think Barks's translating felt more like play than work to him?
2. **(a) Recall:** What is Barks's goal as he translates? **(b) Connect:** Why do you think this goal might produce a particularly effective translation?

As You Read the Poetry of Rumi . . .

3. Think about how Barks's translations of Rumi reveal his passion for the poems.
4. Consider the ways in which reading this commentary helped you understand Rumi's poems.

How I Do What I Do

- Have students explain the differences between the scholarly translation of the example and Barks's free verse translation of it. **Ask:** Why might Barks consider a fountain more artificial than a spring?
Answer: Springs are found in nature, whereas fountains are human constructions.

Critical Viewing

Possible response: The connection between whirling, hypnotic dance, and the second kind of knowledge that Rumi describes is *motion:* all three are dynamic, active, and unfettered.

ASSESS

Answers

1. (a) Barks became interested in the poet Rumi when his friend, poet Robert Bly, asked him to release Rumi's poems from their cages. (b) **Possible response:** Barks could translate the poetry more freely and try to catch the essence of the poems rather than translate them word for word.
2. (a) Barks tries to sense the meaning that Rumi expressed and then tries to make this meaning accessible to non-scholars, maintaining the fresh spirit of the poem. (b) **Possible response:** Writing the poem's original meaning into a free verse English translation would help relate the feeling that Rumi was trying to express, not simply relate Rumi's words.
3. **Possible response:** By not translating rigidly, Barks's work shows that he wants to express the spirit of Rumi's poetry. He also makes the poetry seem contemporary, as if it were a conversation.
4. **Possible response:** Students might respond that the commentary helped them understand the background of Rumi's poetry and why Barks translated it as free verse.

PREACH

Motivation

The musings on life written hundreds of years ago in Turkey still strike a note of familiarity with readers today. The ideas and questions about which Rumi wrote in his poetry are very similar to questions students may ask. His poem "Elephant in the Dark," for example, questions how we understand the reality or essence of something. Ask students what types of questions are universal to all people. Have students brainstorm for a list of universal questions on paper, and then have them share their ideas.

❶ Background

More About the Author

The threat of an invasion of the Mongols probably prompted Rumi's family to move from Balkh to Konya. At the time, the Mongols were in the process of establishing a massive empire that included almost all of Asia.

After his death in 1273, Rumi was buried in Konya beside his father. Although Konya is now part of the secular Turkish state, Rumi's burial place, preserved to this day, has been visited by thousands of Muslims who have traveled great distances to pay homage to Rumi.

Build Skills | *Poems*

❶ Elephant in the Dark • Two Kinds of Intelligence • The Guest House • Which Is Worth More?

Rumi (1207–1273)

Rumi (rü´ mē) was born in the central Asian city of Balkh—now part of Afghanistan—but lived most of his life in Anatolia, which is now Turkey. The poet's full name was Jalal ad-Din; he later acquired the nickname "Rumi" from the word for the region where his family settled. In Anatolia, the family made its home in Konya, which was the capital of the Seljuk Empire. There, Rumi's father served as a teacher in *a madrasah,* or Islamic religious school.

Early Adulthood When Rumi's father died in 1231, Rumi assumed his father's position as a teacher of religion, quickly developing into a famous Sufi master with a large circle of disciples. Sufism was a movement within Islam that developed in the late tenth century and stressed the immediate, personal union of the human soul with God. Some Sufi orders embraced mysticism, while others stressed ascetic practices of self-denial. Through contacts with religious teachers in Iran and Syria, especially a wandering mystic named Shams ad-Din ("Sun of Religion"), Rumi grew increasingly committed to Sufi philosophy and theology.

Rumi himself was the founder of the Sufi order known as the "Whirling Dervishes," whose hypnotic dancing was the means to spiritual enlightenment. According to legend, Rumi began his ecstatic dance when he heard the rhythmic sounds of a goldsmith's hammer in the bazaar, or marketplace, of Konya.

The *Masnavi* Rumi is regarded as not only one of the finest Persian mystical poets but also one of the finest poets the world has ever known. His most famous work is the *Masnavi,* a long poem written in Persian in rhymed couplets at the suggestion of one of his students and intended to provide guidance for his disciples and for future generations. In the *Masnavi,* Rumi uses a wide variety of literary forms—including fables, short stories, allegories, and proverbs—to illustrate all the aspects of Sufism in his own era. The *Masnavi* has stood through time as one of the most important Sufi works ever written. It has been translated into many languages and analyzed by countless religious and literary scholars.

Rumi's Influence Rumi is believed to have completed the *Masnavi* shortly before his death. Although he seems to have had a turbulent family life, he remained highly respected in Konya throughout his lifetime, and government officials as well as Christian monks sought his advice. Various disciples succeeded him in turn as the master of his Sufi circle. One of these followers, Rumi's son Sultan Walad, formally organized the Whirling Dervishes, whose dances may be seen in Konya to this day. Muslims from all over the world now follow the teachings that Rumi presented in his verse, and his philosophical insights have also had great appeal to millions of non-Muslim readers. The English translations of Rumi's poetry by Coleman Barks, for example, have been bestsellers.

Preview

Connecting to the Literature

Many different types of literature guide readers toward ethical and humane behavior. The poems you are about to read contain gentle advice that is presented in some unexpected ways. As you read each poem, think about the way its message applies to your own life or the lives of people you know.

NC Standard Course of Study

- Interpret and make generalizations supported by specific references. (CT.4.01.1)
- Analyze and evaluate the effects of author's craft and style in world literature. (LT.5.03.9)

❷ Literary Analysis

Analogy

An **analogy** is an explanation of how two things are similar. Analogies are usually extended comparisons that explain something unfamiliar by showing how it is like something familiar. They frequently use figurative language such as similes and metaphors. Unlike these figures of speech, however, analogies are essentially explanations or arguments. The assumption that often underlies an analogy is that if two things are alike in one or more ways, they are probably also alike in other ways.

Comparing Literary Works

A **metaphor** is a figure of speech that compares two apparently unlike things without using the words *like* or *as*. **Direct metaphors** connect the two terms directly, while **implied metaphors** suggest the comparison. Look for examples like the ones shown as you read the poems of Rumi.

Direct Metaphor: This being human is a guest house.

Implied Metaphor: . . . getting always more / marks on your preserving tablets.

❸ Reading Strategy

Making Generalizations

Apply the ideas and themes of your reading by making generalizations. A **generalization** is a broad statement that applies to many situations and is supported by details or evidence. As you read, use the details in Rumi's poems to make generalizations about the author's beliefs, philosophy, and main ideas or messages. Test the validity of each generalization by applying it to multiple elements of the poem or to real-life situations. You may find it helpful to use a diagram like the one shown.

Detail	Detail
Generalization	

Vocabulary Builder

competence (käm′ pə təns) *n.* ability (p. 121)

conduits (kän do͞o itz) *n.* channels or pipes (p. 121)

malice (mal′ is) *n.* ill will; evil intent (p. 122)

solitude (säl ə to͞od) *n.* isolation (p. 124)

Differentiated Instruction — Solutions for All Learners

Support for Special Needs Students

Have students use the support pages for these selections in the ***Reader's Notebooks, Adapted Version.*** Completing these pages will prepare students to read the selections in the Student Edition.

Support for Less Proficient Readers

Have students use the support pages for these selections in the ***Reader's Notebooks.*** After students finish the pages in the Reader's Notebooks, have them complete the questions and activities in the Student Edition.

Support for English Learners

Have students use the support pages for these selections in the ***Reader's Notebooks: English Learner's Version.*** Completing these pages will prepare students to read the selections in the Student Edition.

❷ Literary Analysis

Analogy

- Explain that students will focus on analogies as they read the four selections in this lesson.
- Read the instruction about analogies as students read silently. Draw students' attention to the description of analogies and how they explain something unfamiliar by showing how it is like something familiar.
  Ask students to fill in this analogy: Weight lifting is to strengthening the body as studying is to _____.
  Answer: strengthening the mind
- As they read each selection, have students look for elements of figurative language that help to compare the familiar with the unfamiliar. Point out that the poetry of Rumi uses figurative language extensively in order to create analogies.

❸ Reading Strategy

Making Generalizations

- Ask a student to state facts or details about your classroom, and list this information on the board. Then have students look at the list and make a generalization about the classroom. Point out that they can only make generalizations based on the facts and details.
- Pick a topic, and engage students in a discussion about how many facts and details they need to know about the topic in order to make an accurate generalization about it. Then ask students whether they have ever made a generalization based on insufficient evidence and have learned that their generalization was wrong.
- Give students a copy of the **Reading Strategy Graphic Organizer A,** p. 25 in ***Graphic Organizer Transparencies.*** As they read the selections in this grouping, urge students to use the details or evidence that they find to make generalizations about Rumi's main ideas.

Vocabulary Builder

- Pronounce each vocabulary word for students, and read the definitions as a class. Have students identify any words with which they are already familiar.

Learning Modalities
Mathematical/Logical Learners
Because many of these students will not have a natural affinity for poetry, with its metaphors and rhyming schemes, Coleman Barks's free verse translating style may enable mathematical/logical learners to appreciate the poetry of Rumi. After students read a poem, ask them to take a conceptual step back from the words and identify the lesson or point that Rumi is trying to make.

❶ About the Selection

In this poem, Rumi reflects on the way that people tend to look at a part of a thing rather than working together to see the whole. Using an elephant as a symbol for what people wish to understand, he explains how they distort the elephant if each person works individually in the dark. He points out that such people never see the whole.

❷ Critical Viewing

Possible response: No single image in the poem matches the elephant in the painting; each image in the poem shows only a part of the elephant.

❸ Translator's Insight

- **Ask**: What is the mystery that the scene implies?
  Answer: The mystery that the people are trying to know and name is how the parts of the elephant fit together and what they form.
- Point out to students that the mystery can function on two levels: a literal level (the elephant) and a symbolic level. **Ask** students what the elephant might symbolize in the poem?
  Possible responses: The elephant might symbolize truth, God, the essence of things, or wisdom.

❶ Elephant in the Dark

Rumi

translated by Coleman Barks

❷ ◀ **Critical Viewing**
Which image in the poem best matches this painting of an elephant? Explain your choice. **[Connect]**

Differentiated Instruction Solutions for All Learners

Accessibility at a Glance

	Elephant in the Dark	Two Kinds of Intelligence	The Guest House	Which is Worth More
Context	Analogy	Acquired vs. spontaneous intelligence	The experience of powerful emotions	Power vs. solitude
Language	Accessible vocabulary	Syntax complicated	Accessible vocabulary and syntax	Direct and simple
Concept Level	Accessible (Describing an elephant, based on touching it)	Average (the value of studied vs. natural intelligence)	Accessible (the value of learning from bad times)	Accessible (very direct and clear)
Literary Merit	Classic	Classic	Classic	Classic
Lexile	NP	NP	NP	NP
Overall Rating	More accessible	Average	Average	More accessible

Background About 1250, when he was living in the city of Konya in what is now Turkey, Rumi began to compose his greatest work, the *Masnavi.* He was inspired by a friend and disciple, Husam ad-Din Chelebi. Hasam ad-Din urged Rumi to follow Persian models of long poems written during the preceding centuries. Those works expressed mystical teachings through a varied assortment of anecdotes, fables, stories, proverbs, and allegories. In the years that followed, Rumi composed over 25,000 rhymed couplets. According to legend, the poet recited his verses in public while Husam ad-Din committed them to writing.

"Elephant in the Dark," "Two Kinds of Intelligence," and "The Guest House" come from the *Masnavi.* "Which is Worth More?" is drawn from Rumi's *rubaiyat*, a large collection of quatrains, or four-line stanzas.

Some Hindus have an elephant to show.
No one here has ever seen an elephant.
They bring it at night to a dark room.

One by one, we go in the dark and come out
saying how we experience the animal.

One of us happens to touch the trunk.
"A water-pipe kind of creature."

Another, the ear. "A very strong, always moving
back and forth, fan-animal."

Another, the leg. "I find it still,
like a column on a temple."

Another touches the curved back.
"A leathery throne."

Another, the cleverest, feels the tusk.
"A rounded sword made of porcelain."
He's proud of his description.

Each of us touches one place
and understands the whole in that way.

The palm and the fingers feeling in the dark are
how the senses explore the reality of the elephant.

If each of us held a candle there,
and if we went in together,
we could see it.

Coleman Barks
Translator's Insight
The scene implies that there is some mystery we are trying to know and *name* using the five senses (the hand).

Reading Strategy
Making Generalizations On the basis of the evidence so far, what generalization might you make?

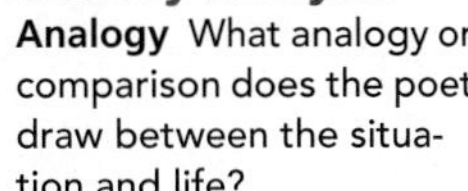

Literary Analysis
Analogy What analogy or comparison does the poet draw between the situation and life?

4 Reading Strategy
Making Generalizations

- Have a volunteer read aloud the first eleven lines as the rest of the class follows in the text. **Ask:** In the first eleven lines, how have the people experienced the elephant?
  Answer: The people have experienced the elephant as a "water-pipe kind of creature," a "fan-animal," and a "column on a temple."
- Then, **ask** students the Reading Strategy question: On the basis of the evidence so far, what generalization might you make?
  Possible response: Students might say that each one who goes into the dark experiences a different part of the animal, and no one really knows what it is.

5 Literary Analysis
Analogy

- Have students scan the entire poem. Then ask a volunteer to read the bracketed passage aloud for the class.
- **Ask** the Literary Analysis question: What analogy or comparison does the poet draw between the situation and life?
  Answer: The poet says that if the people would work together to find out what the animal is, they would come to know the whole elephant. The poem suggests that no one can attain full knowledge on his or her own.

Differentiated Instruction Solutions for All Learners

Strategy for Less Proficient Learners
To help students understand the futility of looking only at a part of something and trying to understand the whole, either cut a picture in pieces and give each student a different piece or place parts of an object, such as a disassembled toy truck, into separate paper bags. By looking at separate parts of the picture or by each student feeling a separate part of the truck, have students work together to try to combine each of the separate parts into the idea of a whole. The difficulty that each student experiences from seeing only a part will help students understand Rumi's point in the poem.

Strategy for Advanced Learners
Blindfold students, and pass around a large stuffed animal or other object. Allow students to touch only one part of the object, and have each of them touch a different part. Afterwards, have each student write a description of the part that he or she touched, and have students work together to describe what the object is. Then tell students to draw a conclusion about the effectiveness of that method for trying to describe something. Point out that this method of learning about something is similar to what Rumi describes in the poem.

❻ About the Selection

In this poem, Rumi contrasts a type of intellectual intelligence that the world admires and that accumulates in us to an innately internal intelligence. He says that the innate intelligence creates a freshness in people and is a fountainhead within them. This type of intelligence never stagnates, and it moves from inside people to the outside—not from the outside in.

❼ Critical Viewing

Possible response: The illuminated manuscript represents both kinds of intelligence. The words represent the facts and concepts characteristic of the first kind of intelligence; the art surrounding the words represents the creativity and dynamism characteristic of the second kind of intelligence.

❽ Reading Strategy

Making Generalizations

- Ask a student volunteer to read aloud lines 1–11 of the poem.
- **Ask** students what descriptions Rumi uses to indicate acquired intelligence.
  Answer: He refers to it as memorized, collected, getting marks, and causing a person to rise in the world's esteem.
- Then **ask** students the Reading Strategy question: What generalization can you make about acquired intelligence?
  Possible response: It is artificial and is there to help a person in a career, but it is unrelated to human meaning.

❾ Translator's Insight

- Point out Coleman Barks's comment that the first kind of intelligence is mental or intellectual, but the second kind is different.
- **Ask** students: What things might demonstrate the kind of intelligence that flows from the inside out?
  Possible responses: Intelligence that flows from the inside out may be characterized by the capacity to feel joy at a sunrise; kindness; a good sense of values; or wisdom.

❻ Two Kinds of Intelligence

Rumi

translated by Coleman Barks

❼ ▲ **Critical Viewing** Which kind of intelligence do you think this illuminated manuscript represents? Why? **[Interpret]**

Enrichment

Didactic Literature

Didactic literature is central to many religions. It imparts moral lessons through simple stories that may take the form of short tales or fables. The word *didactic* comes from a Greek word meaning "to teach."

The purpose of didactic literature is not to reveal psychological truths but to define the values of a society. It is not to entertain or to raise questions, but to establish codes of behavior. Therefore, didactic literature often contains aphorisms, or short pointed statements expressing human truths. The stories themselves often end with morals, or principles regarding right and wrong conduct.

There are two kinds of intelligence: one acquired,
as a child in school memorizes facts and concepts
from books and from what the teacher says,
collecting information from the traditional sciences
as well as from the new sciences.

8 With such intelligence you rise in the world.
You get ranked ahead or behind others
in regard to your <u>competence</u> in retaining
information. You stroll with this intelligence
in and out of fields of knowledge, getting always more
marks on your preserving tablets.

There is another kind of tablet, one
already completed and preserved inside you.
A spring overflowing its springbox. A freshness
in the center of the chest. This other intelligence
9 does not turn yellow or stagnate. It's fluid,
and it doesn't move from outside to inside
through the <u>conduits</u> of plumbing-learning.

This second knowing is a fountainhead
from within you, moving out.

Reading Strategy
Making Generalizations
What generalization can you make about acquired intelligence?

Vocabulary Builder

competence (käm′ pə təns) *n.* ability

conduits (kän′ do͞o itz) *n.* channels or pipes

Coleman Barks
Translator's Insight
The first sort of intelligence is all too familiar—the information that comes from the outside in. The second kind is not *mental.* It flows from the inside out. That's the joy of it.

Critical Reading

1. **Respond:** Do you agree with the ideas expressed in these poems? Why or why not?
2. **(a) Recall:** In "Elephant in the Dark," what conclusion does the person draw about the elephant after touching its trunk? **(b) Analyze:** What circumstances may explain this mistaken conclusion?
3. **(a) Recall:** What does the fifth person call the elephant's tusk in lines 15–16 of "Elephant in the Dark"? **(b) Infer:** Why do you think Rumi calls this person "the cleverest"?
4. **(a) Recall:** In "Two Kinds of Intelligence," what does the schoolchild do in lines 2–5? **(b) Interpret:** What kind of person does the schoolchild grow up to be in lines 6–11?
5. **(a) Recall:** Which adjectives does the poet use to describe the second kind of intelligence? **(b) Interpret:** Basing your opinion on these words, explain which kind of intelligence you think Rumi valued.

Author Link
For: More about Rumi
Visit: www.PHSchool.com
Web Code: ete-9104

ASSESS

Answers

1. Students may agree or disagree. Make sure that they support their positions with sound reasoning and that their position shows an understanding of the poems.
2. (a) This person calls it "a water-pipe kind of creature." (b) The elephant's trunk is hollow and is used to suck water in or blow it out.
3. (a) The fifth person calls it "a rounded sword made of porcelain." (b) Students may say that Rumi calls this person the cleverest because he or she offers a creative description or because Rumi is mocking the person's self-assurance and pride.
4. (a) The child memorizes facts and concepts and learns old and new information in school. (b) The child grows up to be someone whose value is measured by the ability to do well on tests.
5. (a) Rumi uses *completed, preserved, overflowing, fluid, within you, moving out.* (b) These words indicate that Rumi valued the inner intelligence.

Go Online Author Link For additional information about Rumi, have students type in the Web code and then select Rumi.

⓾ About the Selection

This poem compares being human to a guest house. Rumi says that all types of visitors may enter people's lives, and people need to welcome them all, regardless of the pain and difficulty they may bring. He says that these "unexpected visitors" will teach and guide the one who accepts them and help the individual to understand life.

⑪ Translator's Insight

- Have students read the Translator's Insight.
- Explain that a human tendency is for people to confuse their emotions with personhood; some people think that they *are* their emotions. **Ask** students to provide evidence from "The Guest House" to refute this idea.
  Possible response: In "The Guest House," Rumi separates a person (the guest house) from his or her emotions (unexpected guests).

⑫ Literary Analysis

Analogy

- Point out that although analogies show similarities between two things, they do not say that one thing is equal to another.
- Read aloud for students the first six lines of the poem, and have students name what visitors come into the poem's "guest house," how they act, and what they bring with them.
- **Ask** students the Literary Analysis question: What extended comparison does the poet develop in this analogy?
  Answer: The poet compares a person's awareness of unexpected emotions to the arrival of guests in a guest house.
- **Ask:** Why do you suppose that Rumi counsels acceptance of negative emotions?
  Possible response: Suppressing negative emotions only makes them stronger; accepting the presence of negative emotions gives a person the freedom to decide how to act on them.

⓾ The Guest House

Rumi

translated by Coleman Barks

This being human is a guest house.
Every morning a new arrival.

A joy, a depression, a meanness,
some momentary awareness comes
as an unexpected visitor.

Welcome and entertain them all!
Even if they're a crowd of sorrows,
who violently sweep your house
empty of its furniture,
still, treat each guest honorably.
He may be clearing you out
for some new delight.

The dark thought, the shame, the malice,
meet them at the door laughing,
and invite them in.

Be grateful for whoever comes,
because each has been sent
as a guide from beyond.

Coleman Barks
Translator's Insight
So we are *not* the various emotions, moods, and compulsions that come to visit us, those clowns. What are we, then?

Literary Analysis
Analogy What extended comparison does the poet develop in this analogy?

Vocabulary Builder
malice (mal′ is) *n.* ill will; evil intent

Reading Strategy
Making Generalizations What generalization sums up this poem's message about life?

⑭ ▶ **Critical Viewing** What details in this painting suggest that the man walking through the door is an "unexpected visitor"? **[Interpret]**

Enrichment

Love

The driving force in Rumi's life was his overflowing love for God. This type of sentiment is typical of the Sufis in general. As the literary scholar Peter Avery has commented, "Sufism's motive force is love. This love cannot be equated with agape. Nor is it simply eros. The dichotomy between these two does not seem to have been present in the Persian mind. What the Persians call *'Ishq,* the passion of love, was directed in Sufism solely toward God the Creator."

⓭ Reading Strategy

Making Generalizations

- Have students follow along as a student volunteer reads the poem. **Ask** students what people can learn from unpleasant emotions. **Possible response:** Students might say that people can learn patience, strength, courage, emotional depth, that they need friends, and so forth.
- **Ask** students the Reading Strategy question: What generalization sums up this poem's message about life? **Possible response:** Students may respond that the poem is telling people to learn from all the visiting emotions as these emotions will help them to learn about themselves and about life.

⓮ Critical Viewing

Possible response: The man walking through the door appears to be entering the house quickly, as if he is barging in the house. The man on the right turns his head, as if the visitor surprises him.

Differentiated Instruction Solutions for All Learners

Strategy for Less Proficient Learners
Have students list the "guests" that Rumi includes in the poem, and write them on the board. Have students discuss how each of these "guests" might affect the "owner" of the guest house. Ask students to describe experiences that characters from television, film, or literature may have had with these kinds of emotions. Then ask students to explain how the individuals handled the situation and how they changed from the experience. Have students write a response to Rumi's poem, agreeing or disagreeing with his final stanza.

Strategy for English Learners
Have students go through the poem and list any words that they do not understand. Clarify as necessary any confusing concepts. Then have students list the "guests" that Rumi includes in the poem and give an example of an event or situation that could represent that type of guest. For example, a "joy" could be a goal that they had reached. As they list each emotion, have them explain what they might learn from each of these "guests."

15 About the Selection

Rumi compares popularity to solitude and power to freedom in this poem. Solitude, he suggests, is worth more than anything else and enables freedom, something that power cannot provide.

16 Translator's Insight

- After students have read the Translator's Insight, point out that Rumi seems to have little regard for "a crowd of thousands" and "power over an entire nation." **Ask** students why it can be dangerous to have "a crowd of thousands" flock around them or to have "power over an entire nation."
  Possible responses: Having crowds of people flock around a person can lead that person to become inflated with pride; having power over a nation can trap a person in games of power and rob them of solitude.

17 Literary Analysis

Analogy

- Point out that to some people solitude means isolation and loneliness, but to others, solitude means a chance to be away from the noise and chaos of the world; to relax, to think, and to refresh oneself.
- After students have read the poem, **ask** them the Literary Analysis question: How might solitude and freedom be similar?
  Possible response: When someone is alone, he or she has freedom from the demands and traps that exercising power brings.

18 Critical Viewing

Answer: The poem's theme is the inestimable value of solitude. The painting depicts a man in solitude, sitting alone in his room.

15 Which Is Worth More?

Rumi

translated by Coleman Barks

16

Which is worth more, a crowd of thousands,
or your own genuine solitude?
Freedom, or power over an entire nation?

A little while alone in your room
will prove more valuable than anything else
that could ever be given you.

Vocabulary Builder
solitude (säl′ ə to͞od′) *n.* isolation

17 ***Coleman Barks***
Translator's Insight
Rumi's radical statement here is that time by yourself is better than any power or popularity game.

Literary Analysis
Analogy How might solitude and freedom be similar?

18 ◄ **Critical Viewing**
What details in this painting reflect the theme of Rumi's poem? Explain. **[Connect]**

Critical Reading

1. **Respond:** Which of these two poems appeals to you more? Explain.
2. **(a) Recall:** What two things does Rumi compare in the first two lines of "The Guest House"? **(b) Analyze:** What do the visitors in lines 2–5 have in common?
3. **(a) Recall:** In lines 6–12 of "The Guest House," what advice does Rumi give his readers? **(b) Interpret:** What makes this advice unexpected? **(c) Apply:** How might you apply the message of the poem to everyday life?
4. **(a) Recall:** In "Which Is Worth More?" what choice does Rumi identify in lines 1–3? **(b) Explain:** Why is solitude so valuable, according to Rumi?
5. **(a) Recall:** In what ways are Rumi's insights still relevant today?

Go Online
Author Link
For: More about Rumi
Visit: www.PHSchool.com
Web Code: ete-9104

ASSESS

Answers

1. Students may choose either poem, but have them support their choice with examples from the text.
2. (a) He compares being human to a guest house. (b) All of the visitors are emotions that come unexpectedly.

Answers continued

3. (a) He advises them to welcome and learn from all of the emotions. (b) This is unexpected because these emotions may be painful. (c) This message encourages people to accept whatever comes and learn from it, even if it is painful.
4. (a) He identifies choosing between popularity and solitude and between freedom and exercising power. (b) Solitude is so valuable because it provides freedom.
5. Rumi's insights are still relevant because people still deal with unexpected and negative emotions, the need for solitude, and the temptations of popularity and power.

Go Online Author Link For additional information about Rumi, have students type in the Web Code, then select *R* from the alphabet, and then select Rumi.

Apply the Skills

Elephant in the Dark • Two Kinds of Intelligence • The Guest House • Which Is Worth More?

Literary Analysis

Analogy

1. **(a)** In "Elephant in the Dark," what **analogy** does Rumi use to highlight a contrast between ignorance and wisdom? **(b)** What do the last lines suggest about overcoming such ignorance?
2. **(a)** Using a chart like the one shown, explore the analogy Rumi develops in "Two Kinds of Intelligence."

First Kind of Intelligence	Second Kind of Intelligence
Key Theme:	

   (b) What insight does the poet convey through this analogy?
3. **(a)** According to "The Guest House," what aspects of being human are like running a guest house? **(b)** What does the analogy show about the way Rumi wants his readers to face misfortunes or sorrows?
4. In "Which Is Worth More?" Rumi contrasts power with freedom. In what ways might power be like a trap or prison?

Comparing Literary Works

5. In "Two Kinds of Intelligence," what does the **implied metaphor** (lines 10–11) say about how people gain knowledge?
6. What does the **direct metaphor** in lines 19–20 say about the power and source of the second kind of knowledge?
7. In "The Guest House," what do the implied metaphors in lines 7–12 say about the power of emotion? Explain.

Reading Strategy

Making Generalizations

8. What **generalizations** can you draw from "Elephant in the Dark" about human beings' ability to discover reality and truth?
9. From your reading of "The Guest House," what **generalizations** can you make about Rumi's philosophy of life ?

Extend Understanding

10. **Cultural Connection:** From the selections, what can you conclude about the poet's role in Sufi society?

QuickReview

An **analogy** is an explanation of how two things are similar.

A **metaphor** compares two apparently unlike things without the use of words such as *like* or *as*. A **direct metaphor** connects the two terms directly, while an **implied metaphor** suggests the comparison.

When you **make a generalization,** you use details or examples to develop a broad statement that applies to many situations.

For: Self-test
Visit: www.PHSchool.com
Web Code: eta-6111

Go Online Assessment Students may use the **Self-test** to prepare for **Selection Test A** or **Selection Test B.**

Answers

1. (a) Rumi compares ignorance to knowing only part of an elephant rather than seeing the whole animal. (b) The lines suggest that people need to work together to gain true knowledge or wisdom.
2. (a) **First Kind of Intelligence:** acquired, memorized, collecting information, ranking of competence, gaining marks, moves from outside to inside; **Second Kind of Intelligence:** already within you, completed, freshness inside, fountainhead within you, never stagnates, moves from inside of you to outside; **Key Theme:** The innate intelligence within someone goes from inside the person out to the world. (b) He indicates that the internal intelligence is more important and will never stagnate. Another sample answer can be found on **Literary Analysis Graphic Organizer B,** p. 28 in ***Graphic Organizer Transparencies.***
3. (a) Life sends unexpected—and sometimes unpleasant—"visitors" to both; the host has no choice of who or what comes. (b) He wants his readers to accept everything that comes in life because it all has a purpose, no matter how painful.
4. **Possible response:** Students may say that leadership is a trap or prison because the responsibilities that accompany leadership limit one's free time.
5. The comparison says that people gain knowledge through formal instruction.
6. This metaphor indicates that the second kind of knowledge is powerful—like an overflowing spring, and its source is within a person.
7. The metaphors say that powerful emotions can be helpful if they are respected and not rejected.
8. A person's ability to discover reality and truth is limited to what he or she can conclude from the senses. People need to work together to discover reality and truth.
9. Rumi believes that all of life must be accepted as it instructs people in the way to live their lives.
10. **Possible response:** Students may say that the poet's job was to instruct, to speculate on the philosophical questions of life, and to act as a counselor for people during difficult times.

EXTEND/ASSESS

Answers

1 Vocabulary Lesson

Word Analysis: Latin Prefix *com–* or *con–*

1. *conduct;* to lead or guide people or events; the prefix adds "together" to –duct, which means "to lead."
2. *consolidate;* combine; the prefix adds "together" to –solidate, which comes from a root that means "to make solid."
3. *compact;* closely and firmly united; the prefix adds "with" to –pact, which comes from a root that means "to fasten."

Spelling Strategy

1. -ance	4. -ence
2. -ance	5. -ance
3. -ence	6. -ence

Vocabulary Builder: Fluency

1. True; *competence* means the ability to do something.
2. True; a *conduit* is a channel or pipe that joins two things together.
3. False; *malice* means a desire to harm others and does not elicit love from people.
4. False; *solitude* means being alone, which does not happen with friends.

2 Grammar and Style Lesson

1. Rumi believes that each of our experiences may contain its own lessons.
2. No one in the dark room thought that his or her explanation of the elephant was wrong.
3. No one values wisdom more than Rumi.
4. Correct

Writing Application

Students' sentences should contain correct subject-verb agreement and pronoun-antecedent agreement.

WG Writing and Grammar Platinum Level

For support in teaching the Grammar and Style Lesson, use Chapter 24, Sections 1 and 2.

Build Language Skills

1 Vocabulary Lesson

Word Analysis: Latin Prefix *com-* or *con-*

The Latin prefix *com-* or *con-* means "with" or "together." For example, a *conduit* is a channel or pipe that joins two things together. Add the prefix *com-* or *con-* to the word roots below. Then, define each word and explain how the prefix contributes to its meaning. Use a dictionary to check your definition.

1. -duct **2.** -solidate **3.** -pact

Spelling Strategy

Nouns ending in *-ence* and *-ance* are spelled with the same vowel as their adjective forms. For example, the noun *competence* and the adjective *competent* both use an *e*. The noun *elegance* and the adjective *elegant* both use an *a*. Complete the spelling of the following nouns.

1. reli________	**3.** independ___	**5.** signific_____
2. compli_____	**4.** differ_____	**6.** intellig_____

Vocabulary Builder: Fluency

Review the vocabulary list on page 117, and notice the way each word is used in the context of the selections. Then, using your knowledge of the italicized word, decide whether each statement is true or false. Explain your answers.

1. His *competence* made everyone trust him with the money.
2. The plumber built a new *conduit* for the wastewater from the washing machine.
3. His *malice* toward neighbors made everyone love him.
4. During the long car trip with her friends, Andrea enjoyed the *solitude*.

2 Grammar and Style Lesson

The Pronouns *each* and *no one*

The indefinite pronouns *each* and *no one* are always singular. Study the following examples of subject-verb and pronoun-antecedent agreement.

SUBJECT VERB
No one here has ever seen an elephant.

SUBJECT VERB
Each of us touches one place.

ANTECEDENT PRONOUN
Treat each honorably; he may be preparing some new delight for you.

ANTECEDENT PRONOUNS
No one can predict the unexpected turns of his or her life.

Practice Rewrite the following sentences, correcting all errors in agreement. If a sentence does not contain an error, write *Correct*.

1. Rumi believes that each of our experiences may contain their own lessons.
2. No one in the dark room thought that their explanation of the elephant was wrong.
3. No one valued wisdom more than Rumi.
4. Each one of the poems contains an analogy.

Writing Application Write five sentences describing scenes in nature. In each sentence, use the pronouns *each* or *no one*, and correct subject-verb agreement and pronoun-antecedent agreement.

WG *Prentice Hall Writing and Grammar Connection: Platinum Level, Chapter 24, Sections 1 and 2*

Assessment Practice

Analogies **(For more practice, see *Standardized Test Preparation Workbook*, p. 7)**

Many tests require students to answer vocabulary questions that ask them to complete analogies. Use the following sample item to demonstrate.

Choose the pair of words with the relationship most like the relationship of the words in capital letters.

TYRANNICAL: RULER

A paradise: wilderness
B wanderer: exile
C wise: philosopher
D harsh: judge

The words in *A* and *B* are antonyms and synonyms. *C* is similar but more positive. *D* is the best answer.

❸ Writing Lesson

Poem With an Insight

Write a poem modeled after the style and content of Rumi's works. In your poem, convey an insight or a message about life. Make sure that each detail of your poem supports your central theme and creates an overall mood that helps convey that theme.

Prewriting Brainstorm for a list of insights, messages, or life lessons. Then, choose your best insight and generate ideas about how to develop it through an analogy, a central metaphor, or a striking image.

Drafting Remember that you are writing a poem, not a sermon or a speech. Look for ways to use imagery, rhythm, alliteration, onomatopoeia, word choice, and other poetic devices to convey your idea concisely and poetically.

Revising Read your poem aloud. Cross out repetitive words or phrases that may contain clichés, or overused language. Make sure that you have not accidentally created a *mixed metaphor* by combining metaphors that do not work well together.

Model: Revising to Remove Repetition, Clichés, or Mixed Metaphors

Friendship is ~~the sturdy~~ lifeline ~~knitting~~ binding us together on ~~the~~ our journey ~~of life~~.

With these revisions, the writer deletes repetitive language and clichés.

Prentice Hall Writing and Grammar Connection: Platinum Level, Chapter 10, Section 4

❹ Extend Your Learning

Research and Technology Write a brief **research report** on Sufism and whirling dervishes, including the order that Rumi founded. Sources for your report might include some of the following:

- print or online reference works on Sufism and Rumi
- Web sites about Sufism or Rumi
- interviews with people who practice Sufism
- nonfiction books about Sufism or Rumi

Include a list of your sources in your finished work.

Listening and Speaking In a small group, listen to a brief selection from a contemporary English-language recording of Rumi's works. Then, hold a **group discussion** to share your responses to the recording. **[Group Activity]**

For: An additional research activity
Visit: www.PHSchool.com
Web Code: etd-7110

❸ Writing Lesson

- To give students guidance for writing this poem with an insight, give them the **Support for Writing Lesson** p. 128 in ***Unit 1 Resources.***
- Students' poems should clearly express insights on life's lessons. Students should be sure to use poetic devices to create and develop their poetry.
- Students may wish to begin free writing to create images and get ideas on paper. Then students can look for the most effective images and figurative language to help convey their messages or insights about life.
- Use the Poem (Rhyming) rubrics in ***General Resources,*** p. 73–74, to evaluate students' poems with an insight.

❹ Listening and Speaking

- Have students listen to the recording of Rumi's poetry several times, jotting down their responses and noting instances of how the speaker uses tone to highlight parts of the poems.
- Allow time for students to write their responses to a poem and discuss it before playing the recording of the next poem. When students have discussed all of Rumi's poetry, have them identify themes that run throughout his poetry.
- The **Support for Extend Your Learning** page (***Unit 1 Resources,*** p. 129) provides guided note-taking opportunities to help students complete the Extend Your Learning activities.

Go Online Research Have students type in the Web Code for another research activity.

Assessment Resources

The following resources can be used to assess students' knowledge and skills.

Unit 1 Resources
- **Selection Test A,** pp. 131–133
- **Selection Test B,** pp. 134–136

General Resources
- **Rubric for Poem (Rhyming),** p. 73–74

Go Online Assessment Students may use the **Self-test** to prepare for **Selection Test A** or **Selection Test B.**

Standard Course of Study

Goal 1: WRITTEN LANGUAGE

WL.1.03.1 Select, monitor, and modify reading strategies appropriate to personal reflection.

WL.1.03.10 Analyze connections between ideas, concepts, characters and experiences in reflection.

Goal 3: FOUNDATIONS OF ARGUMENT

FA.3.04.5 Summarize key events and/or points from argumentative text.

Goal 5: LITERATURE

LT.5.01.1 Use strategies for preparation, engagement, and reflection on world literature.

LT.5.03.4 Demonstrate comprehension of main idea and supporting details in world literature.

Goal 6: GRAMMAR AND USAGE

GU.6.01.2 Analyze author's use of language to demonstrate understanding of expression.

Step-by-Step Teaching Guide	Pacing Guide
PRETEACH	
• Administer Vocabulary and Reading Warm-ups as necessary.	5 min.
• Engage students' interest with the motivation activity.	5 min.
• Read and discuss author and background features. **FT**	10 min.
• Introduce the Literary Analysis Skill: Epic Conflict. **FT**	5 min.
• Introduce the Reading Strategy: Rereading for Clarification. **FT**	10 min.
• Prepare students to read by teaching the selection vocabulary. **FT**	
TEACH	
• Informally monitor comprehension while students read independently or in groups. **FT**	30 min.
• Monitor students' comprehension with the Reading Check notes.	as students read
• Reinforce vocabulary with Vocabulary Builder notes.	as students read
• Develop students' understanding of epic conflict with the Literary Analysis annotations. **FT**	5 min.
• Develop students' ability to reread for clarification with the Reading Strategy annotations. **FT**	5 min.
ASSESS/EXTEND	
• Assess students' comprehension and mastery of the Literary Analysis and Reading Strategy by having them answer the Apply the Skills questions. **FT**	15 min.
• Have students complete the Vocabulary Lesson and the Grammar and Style Lesson. **FT**	15 min.
• Apply students' ability to gather details about characters and events by using the Writing Lesson. **FT**	45 min. or homework
• Apply students' understanding by using one or more of the Extend Your Learning activities. **FT**	20–90 min. or homework
• Administer Selection Test A or Selection Test B. **FT**	15 min.

Resources

Print

Unit 1 Resources

Transparency

Graphic Organizer Transparencies

Print

Reader's Notebook [L2]

Reader's Notebook: Adapted Version [L1]

Reader's Notebook: English Learner's Version [EL]

Unit 1 Resources

Technology

Listening to Literature Audio CDs [L2, EL]

Print

Unit 1 Resources

General Resources

Technology

Go Online: Research [**L3**]
Go Online: Self-test [**L3**]
***ExamView®*, Test Bank [L3]**

Choosing Resources for Differentiated Instruction

[**L1**] Special Needs Students
[**L2**] Below-Level Students
[**L3**] All Students
[**L4**] Advanced Students
[**EL**] English Learners

For Vocabulary and Reading Warm-ups and for Selection Tests, **A** signifies "less challenging" and **B** "more challenging." For Graphic Organizer transparencies, **A** signifies "not filled in" and **B** "filled in."

FT Fast Track Instruction: To move the lesson more quickly, use the strategies and activities identified with **FT**.

Scaffolding for Less Proficient and Advanced Students

The leveled Critical Thinking questions after selections progress in the levels of thinking required to answer them. To address the needs of your different students, you may use the (a) level questions for your less proficient students and the (b) level questions with your on-level and advanced students. The occasional (c) level questions are appropriate for your advanced students.

Use this complete suite of powerful teaching tools to make lesson planning and testing quicker and easier.

Use the interactive textbook (online and on CD-ROM) to make selections and activities come alive with audio and video support and interactive questions.

Go Online Professional Development
For: Information about Lexiles
Visit: www.PHSchool.com
Web Code: eue-1111

PRETEACH

Motivation

Have students recall some of the proverbs that they have heard, such as "A penny saved is a penny earned." Have students discuss each proverb, responding to some or all of the following questions: What main point does the proverb make? Does that point seem valid? If so, to what situations would the proverb apply? How do the language and imagery of the proverb make it effective? After all suggestions are discussed, have students consider which they find the wisest or most interesting. Then, tell students that they are about to read a group of proverbs from Africa. After that, they will read part of a famous African epic, or hero poem, that contains several proverbs.

❶ Background

More About the Selections

Explain that in the past, much of African society was hierarchical, with social roles based on the family into which one was born. The profession of *griot* was generally held by members of one family, passed down from parent to child over the generations, just as the griots' stories were. Officially appointed by their monarchs, griots were highly respected as tribal historians. Kings often called on them for advice and to tutor the royal children, including future kings.

Geography Note

Draw students' attention to the map on this page. The proverbs students are to read come from different places on the African continent: from South Africa in the south to Uganda, Tanzania, and Kenya in the east to Liberia, Ghana, and Nigeria in the west. The *Sundiata* epic is a product of the ancient kingdom of Mali, also in western Africa.

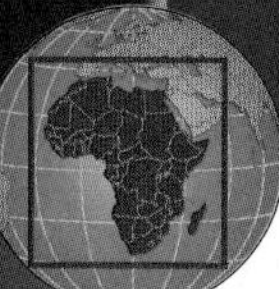

Build Skills | *Proverbs • Epic*

African Proverbs • *from* Sundiata ❶

African Proverbs and *Sundiata*

Much of West Africa's rich history is not found on paper. Instead, the history is preserved in the elaborate recountings of the oral historians known as *griots* (grē´ ōz). Griots serve as a kind of living library for their communities. As a combined historian, storyteller, and teacher, a griot travels from village to village, retelling ancestral histories and legends. Griots think of themselves as the memory of their people, and many African ethnic groups rely on the memories of their griots to preserve a record of the past.

The Power of Proverbs

Embedded within the stories of the griots are many proverbs, or concise sayings, that reveal a truth about human experience. Proverbs play an important role in cultures with a strong oral tradition. They are the distillation of the culture's common wisdom. Because proverbs often use fresh or surprising metaphors, they can communicate a complicated idea in a clear, artful, and often diplomatic way. In many African cultures, these sayings have been used for centuries to teach children, settle arguments, and offer advice. Furthermore, using them deftly is often seen as a sign of the speaker's eloquence and intellect. (A collection of proverbs from several African ethnic groups appears on pp. 130–131).

Sundiata, An Unlikely Hero A griot tale that combines the instructive role of proverbs with an entertaining story is the epic of *Sundiata*. In the thirteenth century, Sundiata was a legendary hero-king who ruled a region that included most of what is now the West African republic of Mali. Initially, Sundiata seems an unlikely hero, one who might be considered an "underdog" today. As the story progresses, however, Sundiata's early childhood struggles lead to later dramatic successes in battle.

For those looking for factual accuracy, it is difficult to tell how much of the original story of Sundiata has been preserved. Over the centuries, Sundiata's story has become so embellished that it is perhaps just as much fiction as fact. Because the epic is told to instruct and entertain, individual griots have adapted the tale to emphasize particular lessons or details. Sundiata's story, in particular, was often told to warriors before battle to spur them to greater feats than they thought possible. Like other oral tales told by griots, *Sundiata* recounts the positive or negative results of its hero's actions in order to instruct listeners in appropriate behavior.

From Griot's Story to the Printed Page

Folklorist D. T. Niane wrote *Sundiata: An Epic of Old Mali* in his Malinke language after listening to the stories told by Mamadou Kouyate (mä´ mä do͞o ko͞o yä´ te), a griot of the Keita clan. Niane's work was then translated into English and other languages, enabling the griot's wisdom to reach the farthest corners of the globe. In fact, Niane's own ancestors were griots, and his documentation of ancient oral histories is a direct continuation of their work. In addition to *Sundiata*, he has collected and retold many other legends of Mali.

Preview

Connecting to the Literature

If someone has ever made fun of you—even over something trivial—you know that the temptation to strike back can be very strong. Sundiata finds a noble way to stop ridicule and, in the process, becomes a hero.

2 Literary Analysis

Epic Conflict

An **epic** is a narrative or narrative poem that focuses on the deeds of heroes. At its heart is an **epic conflict,** a challenge in which the hero struggles against an obstacle or a series of obstacles and usually emerges triumphant. The obstacles may include the following:

- menacing enemies
- natural dangers
- moral dilemmas
- problems with society
- difficulties with fate
- challenging decisions

As you read *Sundiata*, notice the conflict that drives the epic's action.

Comparing Literary Works

While epic poems are among the longest literary genres, proverbs are among the shortest. **Proverbs** are sayings that offer cultural wisdom and practical truths about life. Both literary forms express key cultural values by offering suggestions about living correctly. As you read the African proverbs presented here, consider the ways in which the details apply to human experiences. Then, look for the proverbs contained within *Sundiata.* Notice the way these proverbs flavor the epic and direct the characters' actions. Then, consider the view of African culture that both selections provide.

3 Reading Strategy

Rereading for Clarification

Rereading passages can often help clarify characters' identities, the relationships among characters, the sequence of events, and even puzzling language. Sometimes, earlier passages provide the key to understanding information that seems confusing or unclear. Use a diagram like the one shown to clarify difficult passages that you encounter.

Vocabulary Builder

fathom (fa*th*′ əm) *v.* probe the depths of; understand (p. 133)

taciturn (tas′ ə tʉrn) *adj.* not given to talking (p. 133)

malicious (mə lish′ əs) *adj.* intending harm; spiteful (p. 134)

infirmity (in fʉr′ mə tē) *n.* weakness; illness (p. 135)

innuendo (in′ yo͞o en′ dō) *n.* indirect remark or gesture that hints at something bad; sly suggestion (p. 135)

diabolical (dī ə bäl′ ik əl) *adj.* devilish; wicked (p. 135)

estranged (e strānjd′) *adj.* isolated and unfriendly; alienated (p. 135)

NC Standard Course of Study

- Make connections between historical and contemporary issues in world literature. (LT.5.01.6)
- Explore a range of works which relate to an issue, author, or theme. (LT.5.02.1)
- Demonstrate comprehension of main idea and supporting details. (LT.5.03.4)

Passage

With the help of Sassouma Bérété's intrigues, Dankaran Touman was proclaimed king.

Reread Earlier Passage

Dankaran Touman, the son of Sassouma Bérété, was now a fine youth.

Clarification

Dankaran Touman is Sassouma Bérété's son.

2 Literary Analysis

Epic Conflict

- Have students recall powerful heroes in adventure fiction that they have read or viewed. Ask them to provide details about the particular problems these heroes faced and overcame.
- Then, have students read the Literary Analysis instruction. Ask them to match the problems they mentioned with the obstacles listed here.
- If students have read the selection from *Gilgamesh* earlier in this book, have them apply the explanation of epic conflicts to that selection. Students should recognize that although Gilgamesh overcomes menacing enemies like Humbaba and the Bull of Heaven, he does not overcome his difficulty with fate, for he is unsuccessful in his quest for the secret of immortality.

3 Reading Strategy

Rereading for Clarification

- Direct students to read the Reading Strategy instruction.
- Stress that the strategy means going back over material already read in order to gain an understanding of something that is confusing or unclear.
- Review the graphic organizer in the right column, which illustrates the process of rereading for clarification. Give students a copy of **Reading Strategy Graphic Organizer A** in ***Graphic Organizer Transparencies,*** p. 29, to use when they reread to clarify information.

Vocabulary Builder

- Pronounce each vocabulary word for students, and read the definitions as a class. Have students identify any words with which they are already familiar.

Differentiated Instruction Solutions for All Learners

Support for Special Needs Students
Have students complete the **Preview** and **Build Skills** pages for these selections in the ***Reader's Notebook: Adapted Version.*** These pages provide a selection summary, an abbreviated presentation of the reading and literary skills, and the graphic organizer on the **Build Skills** page in the student book.

Support for Less Proficient Readers
Have students complete the **Preview** and **Build Skills** pages for these selections in the ***Reader's Notebook.*** These pages provide a selection summary, an abbreviated presentation of the reading and literary skills, and the graphic organizer on the **Build Skills** page in the student book.

Support for English Learners
Have students complete the **Preview** and **Build Skills** pages for these selections in the ***Reader's Notebook: English Learner's Version.*** These pages provide a selection summary, an abbreviated presentation of the skills, additional contextual vocabulary, and the graphic organizer on the **Build Skills** page in the student book.

TEACH

Facilitate Understanding

Tell students that a proverb often makes its point using figurative language. For instance, instead of saying "Catching things early saves time later," a famous proverb says "A stitch in time saves nine." The figurative language may be more puzzling, but it is also more imaginative and memorable.

❶ About the Selections

These proverbs come from the literature of several African peoples. Many of the sayings reflect the African landscape, using imagery from nature to convey truths about human nature.

❷ Humanities

This wooden sculpture comes from the Mbala people of Zaire, who are known for carvings representing drummers. This particular piece is of the sort kept in chiefs' houses as symbols of authority.

Use the following question for discussion:

What characteristics suggest that this sculpture depicts a symbol of authority?
Possible response: The sculpture is formal and solid. It may represent someone leading others.

❸ Reading Strategy

Rereading for Clarification

- Have a student read aloud the bracketed proverb. Mention these meanings of *fell:* "lost balance," "cut down," "turn over a seam and sew it flat," and "rocky hill."
- Have students **respond** to the Reading Strategy question: Reread the Zulu proverb about trees. Based on the context, what does the word *fell* seem to mean here?
Answer: *Fell* means "cut down."

❶ African Proverbs ❷

Background Proverbs, or wise sayings, are an important part of the folk literature of many African peoples. Though they may appear to be the shortest of all literary forms, proverbs and the wisdom they convey can be found in lengthy epic works such as *Sundiata*. The proverbs presented here reflect the cultures of six different tribes, representing nations from all parts of the African continent.

Uganda: The Baganda

A small deed out of friendship is worth more than a great service that is forced.
One who loves you, warns you.
The one who has not made the journey calls it an easy one.
Where there are no dogs, the wild cats move about freely.
Words are easy, but friendship is difficult.

Liberia: The Jabo

One who cannot pick up an ant and wants to pick up an elephant will someday see his folly.
The butterfly that flies among the thorns will tear its wings.
A man's ways are good in his own eyes.
Daring talk is not strength.
Children are the wisdom of the nation.
The one who listens is the one who understands.

South Africa: The Zulu

Do not speak of a rhinoceros if there is no tree nearby.
The one offended never forgets; it is the offender who forgets.
It never dawns in the same way.
❸ Look as you fell a tree.
Eyes do not see all.
You cannot chase two gazelles.
What has happened before happens again.
No dew ever competed with the sun.
There is no foot which does not stumble.

Reading Strategy Rereading for Clarification Reread the Zulu proverb about trees. Based on the context, what does the word *fell* seem to mean here?

Differentiated Instruction Solutions for All Learners

Accessibility at a Glance

	African Proverbs	*from* Sundiata
Context	Reflections of tribes in six African countries	Ancient kingdom of Mali, West Africa, in the 1200s
Language	Syntax: short declarative sentences with simple vocabulary	Challenging pronunciation of African names and nicknames
Concept Level	Accessible (The truth of human experiences speaks to all cultures.)	Accessible (One can overcome physical weakness and the scorn of others.)
Literary Merit	African Proverbs	Epic
Lexile	NP	940L
Overall Rating	Average	More accessible

Ghana: The Ashanti

Rain beats a leopard's skin, but it does not wash out the spots.
If you are in hiding, don't light a fire.
One falsehood spoils a thousand truths.
No one tests the depth of a river with both feet.

Nigeria: The Yoruba

The day on which one starts out is not the time to start one's preparations.
He who is being carried does not realize how far the town is.
Time destroys all things.
Little is better than nothing.

Tanzania and Kenya: The Masai

The hyena said, "It is not only that I have luck, but my leg is strong."
Baboons do not go far from the place of their birth.
We begin by being foolish and we become wise by experience.
The zebra cannot do away with his stripes.
Do not repair another man's fence until you have seen to your own.
It is better to be poor and live long than rich and die young.
Do not say the first thing that comes to your mind.

Critical Reading

1. **Respond:** Of the proverbs presented here, which one did you find the most thought-provoking or relevant to today's world? Why?
2. **(a) Recall:** What does a Baganda proverb say about a person who has not made the journey? **(b) Infer:** Does the proverb imply that the journey is actually easy? Explain. **(c) Generalize:** What does the proverb say about human experience in general?
3. **(a) Recall:** What does a Jabo proverb say about daring talk? **(b) Compare and Contrast:** What is similar about the messages in that proverb and the proverb about lifting ants and elephants? **(c) Connect:** Describe a situation in which one of these proverbs might apply.
4. **(a) Recall:** What does a Masai proverb say about baboons? **(b) Interpret:** What lesson do you think this proverb teaches?
5. **(a) Compare and Contrast:** Give examples of sayings you know that have messages similar to those in some of these African proverbs, explaining what these proverbs have in common. **(b) Generalize:** Why do you think proverbs like these can transcend their culture? Explain.

ASSESS

Answers

1. **Possible response:** The proverb "Daring talk is not strength" is relevant to today's world. Many world leaders want to exert control through the use of threatening words, but such words do not demonstrate the true wisdom of strength.
2. (a) The person calls the journey easy. (b) No; it implies the opposite—that someone who has actually made the journey knows its difficulties. (c) **Possible response:** People who do not perform or experience something difficult do not appreciate its difficulties; people who do not experience something do not understand it.
3. (a) Daring talk is not strength. (b) Both proverbs suggest that people may think they can do more than they actually can do. (c) **Possible response:** Either proverb may apply when someone is boasting about the ability to do something difficult that he or she clearly cannot do. For example, a child who cannot ride a horse might insist that he or she can ride a bucking bronco.
4. (a) Baboons do not go far from the place of their birth. (b) **Possible response:** The proverb may mean that people do not go far from their roots.
5. (a) **Possible response:** The second Jabo proverb is similar to the metaphor of a moth flying too close to a flame. Both proverbs suggest that a creature who does not respect danger will be destroyed. The first Ashanti proverb and the fourth Masai proverb are similar to the common saying "A leopard cannot change his spots." Each proverb suggests that people do not change. (b) **Possible response:** Proverbs often communicate truths about human experiences that cross cultures.

Differentiated Instruction Solutions for All Learners

Strategy for Special Needs Students

Point out to students that each proverb is stated in one sentence. Ask them how many Zulu proverbs there are. *(nine)* Then have students work in pairs to determine the meaning of the proverbs. Suggest that they pause after reading each proverb and talk through what it would be like to be in each situation. Have students share their interpretations and get input from other classmates. Finally, encourage them to create a poster for their favorite proverb.

Enrichment for Gifted/Talented Students

Point out that many of the proverbs draw on the African landscape and closeness with nature. Have students choose ten such proverbs and rewrite them to seem more like the product of an urban environment. Note that each rewritten proverb should still have the same basic message. As an example, point to the sixth Zulu proverb: Instead of "You cannot chase two gazelles," students might say, "You cannot answer two phone calls at the same time."

Facilitate Understanding

Point out that political leaders often use negotiation to solve problems. In contrast, action heroes often rely on their brawn, or physical strength. Ask students for examples of each—politicians who use their mental talents, and action heroes who use their extraordinary physical talents. Then, explain that the heroes of many epics are both political leaders and action heroes. Tell students, as they read, to think about the combination of skills that the hero of *Sundiata* will need to rule.

4 About the Selection

In this selection from *Sundiata,* future king Mari Djata (also known as Sogolon Djata and Sundiata) seems a most unlikely hero, with his huge head and inability to stand upright. How Mari Djata overcomes his physical weaknesses and regains his honor is an inspiring and instructive tale.

5 Background

The Mandingo Royal Family

Have students read the Background section and the list of characters. Reiterate that Mari Djata was a member of the Keita clan of the Mandingo people. Note that many of the Mandingo, who came to Mali from the East, were adherents of the Islamic faith, which at that time and in that region allowed men to take up to four wives at a time. A king in particular was likely to have several wives because multiple marriages could help cement political alliances. Naré Maghan, Sundiata's father (also called Maghan Kon Fatta, though not in this portion of *Sundiata*), had three wives: his first wife Sassouma (also called Sassouma Bérété); Sundiata's mother Sogolon (also called Sogolon Kedjou); and a third wife called Namandjé.

FROM SUNDIATA:

4 An Epic of Old Mali

D. T. Niane

5 **Background** Nearly one thousand years ago, the region of West Africa that included what is now Ghana and Mali was caught up in turmoil as rival kings fought for control of the profitable salt and gold trade. In the Keita clan of the Mandingo, there arose a heroic leader named Mari, or Sogolon, Djata, who united his people, fought off their rivals, and ushered in a glorious period of peace and prosperity. (In the rapidly spoken Mandingo language, "Sogolon Djata" became "Sundiata.") In this epic, Sogolon Djata's battle for strength echoes the Mandingos' struggle for survival.

CHARACTERS IN *SUNDIATA*

BALLA FASSÉKÉ (bä′ lä fä sā′ kā): Griot and counselor of Sundiata.

BOUKARI (bo͞o kä′ rē): Son of the king and Namandjé, one of his wives; also called Manding (män′ diŋ) Boukari.

DANKARAN TOUMAN (dän′ kä rän to͞o män): Son of the king and his first wife, Sassouma, who is also called Sassouma Bérété.

DJAKMAROU (jä mä′ ro͞o): Daughter of the king and Sogolon; sister of Sundiata and Kolonkan.

FARAKOUROU (fä rä ko͞o′ ro͞o): Master of the forges.

GNANKOUMAN DOUA (nän ko͞o′ män do͞o′ ə): The king's griot; also called simply Doua.

KOLONKAN (kō lōn′ kən): Sundiata's elder sister.

NAMANDJÉ (nä män′ jā): One of the king's wives.

NARE MAGHAN (nä′ rā mäg′ hän): Sundiata's father.

NOUNFAÏRI (no͞on′ fä ē′ rē): Soothsayer and smith; father of Farakourou.

SASSOUMA BÉRÉTÉ (sä so͞o′ mä bā rā′ tā): The king's first wife.

SOGOLON (sô gô lōn′): Sundiata's mother; also called Sogolon Kedjou (ked′ jo͞o).

SUNDIATA (so͞on dyä′ tä): Legendary king of Mali; referred to as Djata (dyä′ tä) and Sogolon Djata, which means son of Sogolon. Also called Mari (mä′ rē) Djata.

Enrichment

Mali

Tell students that the empire of Mali, which Sundiata formed in the thirteenth century, is in the region now known as the Republic of Mali. It is the largest country in West Africa.

This empire was a very rich state and one of the world's major producers of gold, but it has a history of instability. It was taken over in the fifteenth century by the Songhai empire, but that empire declined rapidly, and the region became a jumble of small states. In the nineteenth century, Mali became part of the French empire. It broke from the French in 1960 under the leadership of Modibo Keita, a man from the same Keita clan as Sundiata. Keita became the first president of the republic, but he was overthrown in 1968 by General Moussa Traoré, who in turn was overthrown in 1991.

Childhood

God has his mysteries which none can fathom. You, perhaps, will be a king. You can do nothing about it. You, on the other hand, will be unlucky, but you can do nothing about that either. Each man finds his way already marked out for him and he can change nothing of it.

Sogolon's son had a slow and difficult childhood. At the age of three he still crawled along on all-fours while children of the same age were already walking. He had nothing of the great beauty of his father Naré Maghan. He had a head so big that he seemed unable to support it; he also had large eyes which would open wide whenever anyone entered his mother's house. He was taciturn and used to spend the whole day just sitting in the middle of the house. Whenever his mother went out he would crawl on all-fours to rummage about in the calabashes[1] in search of food, for he was very greedy.

1. **calabashes** (kal′ ə bash′ iz) *n.* dried, hollow shells of gourds, used as bowls.

Vocabulary Builder

fathom (fath′ əm) *v.* probe the depths of; understand

taciturn (tas′ ə tʉrn) *adj.* not given to talking

Reading Check 6

What effect does Sogolon's son's illness have on his childhood?

7

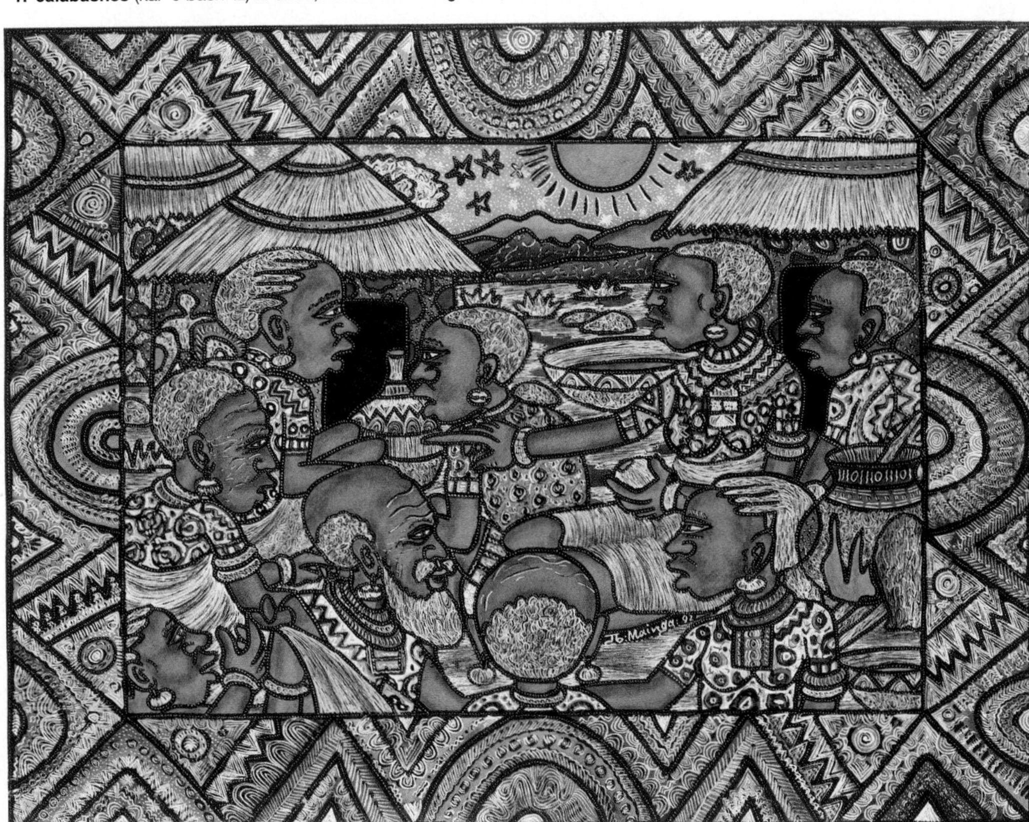

8 ▲ **Critical Viewing** In many cultures, storytellers narrate tales about their community's history. Which details in this tapestry suggest such an activity? **[Interpret]**

6 Reading Check

Possible response: It keeps him crawling around on all fours when he is three and other children of the same age are already walking; makes him taciturn; and prompts him to spend a great deal of time indoors.

7 Humanities

Evening Storytelling, by John Mainga

This painting on leather by Nigerian artist John Mainga is in the Gallery of Contemporary African Art. It shows a traditional scene of a group of Africans socializing with one another as they listen to a storyteller.

Use the following questions for discussion.

- Which details in the picture suggest that it is evening?
  Possible response: The simultaneous appearance of stars and the sun happens only in the evening or the first thing in the morning. But storytelling is likely to occur in the evening, when people have finished a day's work.
- Which person seems most likely to be the storyteller? Why?
  Possible response: The bearded man seems most likely to be the storyteller because the other people are arranged in a circle around him.

8 Critical Viewing

Possible response: The storyteller appears older than his listeners, and the listeners seem to be examining tribal artifacts.

Differentiated Instruction Solutions for All Learners

Support for Special Needs Students

Students may have trouble keeping track of the characters' relationships and the different names and nicknames used for the same characters. Go over the list of characters with students, helping them with the pronunciations of names as well as their relationships. Write the names on the board as students say them. Stress that the hero, Sundiata, is also called Sogolon's son, Sogolon Djata, and Mari Djata.

Strategy for Less Proficient Readers

Have students create a modified family tree for the characters in *Sundiata.* Students should start with the king. They should draw lines to three boxes, each containing the name of one of the king's wives. From each of those boxes another line should branch down to the names of the offspring. When characters have alternate names, students should include those in parentheses.

9 Critical Thinking

Compare and Contrast

- Direct students' attention to the bracketed passage.
- Have a student read aloud the three questions. **Ask** what these rhetorical questions imply about the typical three-year-old child.
  Answer: A three-year-old child can walk; would be the despair of his or her parents through his whims and shifts of mood; and would bring his or her parents joy as he or she learned to speak.
- Have students name three ways in which Mari Djata differs from a typical three-year-old child.
  Answer: Mari Djata is not walking. He speaks very little, and he does not smile.

10 Humanities

British-born artist David Wisniewski created this vivid cut-paper illustration for the cover of the 1992 book *Sundiata.* Trained at Ringling Brothers and Barnum & Bailey Clown College, Wisniewski worked for three years as a clown, designing and creating his own props and costumes. His striking cut-paper illustrations stem from his years of designing for an award-winning puppet theater in the Baltimore-Washington area, Clarion Shadow Theater, in which he and his wife performed.

Use the following questions for discussion:

- Which details in the illustration suggest that the book will feature an action hero?
  Possible response: Details include the spear about to be launched and the horse rearing up, perhaps about to charge.
- What adjectives describe the figure on the horse?
  Possible response: Adjectives include *courageous, bold, heroic, impressive,* and *colorful.*

11 Critical Viewing

Possible response: The image shows a heroic leader charging into battle—an image of the man Sogolon probably hopes her ailing son will become.

9 Malicious tongues began to blab. What three-year-old has not yet taken his first steps? What three-year-old is not the despair of his parents through his whims and shifts of mood? What three-year-old is not the joy of his circle through his backwardness in talking? Sogolon Djata (for it was thus that they called him, prefixing his mother's name to his), Sogolon Djata, then, was very different from others of his own age. He spoke little and his severe face never relaxed into a smile. You would have thought that he was already thinking, and what amused children of his age bored him. Often Sogolon would make some of them come to him to keep him company. These children were already walking and she hoped that Djata, seeing his companions walking, would be tempted to do likewise. But nothing came of it. Besides, Sogolon Djata would brain the poor little things with his already strong arms and none of them would come near him any more.

Vocabulary Builder
malicious (mə lish′ əs) *adj.* intending harm; spiteful

10

11 ▲ **Critical Viewing** In what ways might this image represent the hope Sogolon held for her son? **[Speculate]**

Enrichment

Oral Tradition

Explain that long before there were books and libraries, people shared their history and stories through oral literature. Information was passed from generation to generation in song, poem, or story form. These oral histories recounted the culture of a people through plots and characters that everyone could understand and remember. The themes of oral literature centered on the beginning of the world, on love, and on tragedy. Oral histories included epic tales of heroism, ballads, folk tales, fables, and proverbs. These oral tales often followed people as they moved from place to place, telling stories they knew. That is why we find stories of a great flood in the literature of many different cultures and why certain fairy tales with the same character(s) reappear. Much later, when written works became more common, many oral tales were recorded in writing. That is how the epic of Gilgamesh, Greek myths, the *Ramayana,* and *Sundiata* have come down to us today.

12 The king's first wife was the first to rejoice at Sogolon Djata's infirmity. Her own son, Dankaran Touman, was already eleven. He was a fine and lively boy, who spent the day running about the village with those of his own age. He had even begun his initiation in the bush.[2] The king had had a bow made for him and he used to go behind the town to practice archery with his companions. Sassouma was quite happy and snapped her fingers at Sogolon, whose child was still crawling on the ground. Whenever the latter happened to pass by her house, she would say, "Come, my son, walk, jump, leap about. The jinn[3] didn't promise you anything out of the ordinary, but I prefer a son who walks on his two legs to a lion that crawls on the ground." She spoke thus whenever Sogolon went by her door. The innuendo would go straight home and then she would burst into laughter, that diabolical laughter which a jealous woman knows how to use so well.

Her son's infirmity weighed heavily upon Sogolon Kedjou; she had resorted to all her talent as a sorceress to give strength to her son's legs, but the rarest herbs had been useless. The king himself lost hope.

How impatient man is! Naré Maghan became imperceptibly estranged but Gnankouman Doua never ceased reminding him of the hunter's words. Sogolon became pregnant again. The king hoped for a son, but it was a daughter called Kolonkan. She resembled her mother and had nothing of her father's beauty. The disheartened king debarred Sogolon from his house and she lived in semi-disgrace for a while. Naré Maghan married the daughter of one of his allies, the king of the Kamaras. She was called Namandjé and her beauty was legendary. A year later she brought a boy into the world. When the king consulted soothsayers[4] on the destiny of this son he received the reply that Namandjé's child would be the right hand of some mighty king. The king gave the newly-born the name of Boukari. He was to be called Manding Boukari or Manding Bory later on.

Naré Maghan was very perplexed. Could it be that the stiff-jointed son of Sogolon was the one the hunter soothsayer had foretold?

13 "The Almighty has his mysteries," Gnankouman Doua would say and, taking up the hunter's words, added, "The silk cotton tree emerges from a tiny seed."

One day Naré Maghan came along to the house of Nounfaïri, the blacksmith seer of Niani. He was an old, blind man. He received the king in the anteroom which served as his workshop. To the king's question he replied, "When the seed germinates growth is not always easy; great trees grow slowly but they plunge their roots deep into the ground."

2. **initiation in the bush** education in tribal lore given to twelve-year-old West African boys so they can become full members of the tribe.
3. **jinn** (jin) *n.* supernatural beings that influence human affairs; their promise was that the son of Sogolon would make Mali a great empire.
4. **soothsayers** (so͞oth′ sā ərz) *n.* people who can foretell the future.

Vocabulary Builder
infirmity (in fʉr′ mə tē) *n.* weakness; illness

Vocabulary Builder
innuendo (in′ yo͞o en′ dō) *n.* indirect remark or gesture that hints at something bad; sly suggestion
diabolical (dī ə bäl′ ik əl) *adj.* devilish; wicked
estranged (e strānjd′) *adj.* isolated and unfriendly; alienated

Literary Analysis
Epic Conflict and Proverbs What does the proverb about the silk cotton tree suggest will be the outcome of Mari Djata's childhood conflict?

14 **Reading Check**
What special talent does Sogolon use to try to heal her son?

Differentiated Instruction Solutions for All Learners

Support for Special Needs Students
Students may have difficulty following the narrative and dialogue. To increase their understanding, have them read along with the recording on **Listening to Literature CDs.** After they have listened, encourage students to restate each section in their own words.

Strategy for Less Proficient Readers
Have students pause at the end of each page to ask themselves: "What is Mari Djata's (Sogolon's son's) problem?" Then, have them predict how these problems may be solved. When they finish reading, have students go back and review their predictions to see which were most nearly correct.

12 Vocabulary Builder
Latin Root *-firm-*
- Call students' attention to the word *infirmity* and its definition.
- Explain that *infirmity* includes the prefix *in-*, meaning "not"; the Latin root *-firm-*, meaning "strengthen" or "strong"; and the suffix *-ity*, meaning "the state or condition." An *infirmity* literally is "a condition that is not strong"—that is, an illness or a weakness.
- **Ask** students to use their knowledge of the root to explain what confirming a statement does.
  Answer: *Confirming* strengthens or reinforces a statement.
- **Ask** students for more examples and definitions of words with the root *-firm-*.
  Possible response: Words include *affirm, confirmation, infirmary,* and *reaffirm.*

13 Literary Analysis
Epic Conflict and Proverbs
- Have a student read aloud Gnankouman Doua's bracketed words.
- Point out that the griot's first statement would qualify as a proverb and is similar to the well-known saying "The Lord works in mysterious ways."
- Have a student **state** Mari Djata's childhood conflict.
  Answer: The conflict is Mari Djata's struggle to overcome his physical infirmity and the low regard of others and to emerge strong and triumphant.
- **Ask** students the Literary Analysis question: What does the proverb about the silk cotton tree suggest will be the outcome of Mari Djata's childhood conflict?
  Answer: The proverb suggests that something large and impressive can emerge from something weak and small. The parallel is that Mari Djata, though weak and puny now, will be large and impressive.
- Elicit that this proverb is similar to the English proverb "Great oaks from little acorns grow."

14 Reading Check
Answer: Sogolon resorts to her sorcery, using rare herbs to strengthen her son's legs.

15 Reading Strategy

Rereading for Clarification

- **Direct** students to reread the previous page to clarify the identity of Naré Maghan and his relationship to Mari Djata.
  Answer: Naré Maghan is the king, Mari Djata's father.
- Direct students to the bracketed passage, and have them **respond** to the Reading Strategy item: Reread to clarify the way in which lineage plays a part in being a griot.
  Answer: The job of griot to the king is passed down from father to son. Doua's father was the king's father's griot; Doua is the king's griot, and Doua's son will be Mari Djata's griot.

16 Critical Viewing

Possible response: The baobab has an odd appearance, just like the young Sogolon Djata. It has its roots and trunk planted firmly in the African soil, signifying an African heritage also associated with Sogolon Djata. It is leafless for a long period but then grows leaves, just as Sogolon Djata is a late bloomer but eventually shows his strength and skill. It supplies food, medicine, and other valuable products, just as Sogolon is a benefactor to his people. Its thick trunk is often home to many wild animals, just as Sogolon Djata offers protection to his subjects.

17 Literary Analysis

Epic Conflict

- Have a volunteer read aloud the bracketed passage. Discuss with students the characters who have helped Mari Djata and the characters who have behaved more like his enemies.
- **Ask** students the Literary Analysis question: Which three events succeed in shifting more power to Mari Djata's enemies?
  Answer: The three events are the death of Mari Djata's father, the succession of Dankaran Touman to the throne and the enhanced power of his mother on the regency council; and the death of Doua the griot.

"But has the seed really germinated?" said the king.

"Of course," replied the blind seer. "Only the growth is not as quick as you would like it; how impatient man is."

This interview and Doua's confidence gave the king some assurance. To the great displeasure of Sassouma Bérété the king restored Sogolon to favor and soon another daughter was born to her. She was given the name of Djamarou.

However, all Niani talked of nothing else but the stiff-legged son of Sogolon. He was now seven and he still crawled to get about. In spite of all the king's affection, Sogolon was in despair. Naré Maghan aged and he felt his time coming to an end. Dankaran Touman, the son of Sassouma Bérété, was now a fine youth.

15 One day Naré Maghan made Mari Djata come to him and he spoke to the child as one speaks to an adult. "Mari Djata, I am growing old and soon I shall be no more among you, but before death takes me off I am going to give you the present each king gives his successor. In Mali every prince has his own griot. Doua's father was my father's griot, Doua is mine and the son of Doua, Balla Fasséké here, will be your griot. Be inseparable friends from this day forward. From his mouth you will hear the history of your ancestors, you will learn the art of governing Mali according to the principles which our ancestors have bequeathed to us. I have served my term and done my duty too. I have done everything which a king of Mali ought to do. I am handing an enlarged kingdom over to you and I leave you sure allies. May your destiny be accomplished, but never forget that Niani is your capital and Mali the cradle of your ancestors."

The child, as if he had understood the whole meaning of the king's words, beckoned Balla Fasséké to approach. He made room for him on the hide he was sitting on and then said, "Balla, you will be my griot."

"Yes, son of Sogolon, if it pleases God," replied Balla Fasséké.

The king and Doua exchanged glances that radiated confidence.

Reading Strategy
Rereading for Clarification Reread to clarify the way in which lineage plays a part in being a griot.

16 ▶ Critical Viewing A mature baobab's trunk can measure 30 feet in diameter. In what ways might the baobab, like the one pictured, represent Sogolon Djata? **[Infer]**

The Lion's Awakening

17 A short while after this interview between Naré Maghan and his son the king died. Sogolon's son was no more than seven years old. The council of elders met in the king's palace. It was no use Doua's defending the king's will which reserved the throne for Mari Djata, for the council took no account of Naré Maghan's wish. With the help of Sassouma Bérété's intrigues, Dankaran Touman was proclaimed king and a regency council was formed in which the queen mother was all-powerful. A short time after, Doua died.

18 As men have short memories, Sogolon's son was spoken of with nothing but irony and scorn. People had seen one-eyed kings, one-armed kings, and lame kings, but a stiff-legged king had never been heard tell of. No matter how great the destiny promised for Mari Djata might be, the throne could not be given to someone who had no power in his legs; if the jinn loved him, let them begin by giving him the use of

Literary Analysis
Epic Conflict Which three events succeed in shifting more power to Mari Djata's enemies? Explain.

Enrichment

The Baobab

Before students respond to the Critical Viewing question on this page, explain that the baobab is one of the world's longest-lived trees, living several thousand years. Impressively tall, it also increases in girth as it ages—of all the world's trees, only the sequoia has a thicker trunk. Found in hot and rocky areas of Africa and India, the baobab has adapted to a climate with a rainy period followed by many months of dry weather.

Because the baobab grows so tall and is leafless for such long stretches, its branches form an intricate pattern against the sky. The leafless limbs look much more like roots than like the leafy branches of other trees. As a result, the baobab is sometimes called "the upside-down tree." Folklore tells how the baobab, created before other trees, was jealous of each new tree that came along. Angered by its perpetual jealousy, the gods pulled it up by the roots and replanted it upside down to keep it quiet.

18 his legs. Such were the remarks that Sogolon heard every day. The queen mother, Sassouma Bérété, was the source of all this gossip.

Having become all-powerful, Sassouma Bérété persecuted Sogolon because the late Naré Maghan had preferred her. She banished Sogolon and her son to a back yard of the palace. Mari Djata's mother now occupied an old hut which had served as a lumber-room of Sassouma's.

The wicked queen mother allowed free passage to all those inquisitive people who wanted to see the child that still crawled at the age of seven. Nearly all the inhabitants of Niani filed into the palace and the poor Sogolon wept to see herself thus given over to public ridicule. Mari Djata took on a ferocious look in front of the crowd of sightseers. Sogolon found a little consolation only in the love of her eldest daughter, Kolonkan. She was four and she could walk. She seemed to understand all her mother's miseries and already she helped her with the housework. Sometimes, when Sogolon was attending to the chores, it was she who stayed beside her sister Djamarou, quite small as yet.

Sogolon Kedjou and her children lived on the queen mother's leftovers, but she kept a little garden in the open ground behind the village. It was there that she passed her brightest moments looking after her onions and gnougous.[5] One day she happened to be short of condiments and went to the queen mother to beg a little baobab leaf.[6]

"Look you," said the malicious Sassouma, "I have a calabash full. Help yourself, you poor woman. As for me, my son knew how to walk at seven and it was he who went and picked these baobab leaves. Take them then, since your son is unequal to mine." Then she laughed derisively with that fierce laughter which cuts through your flesh and penetrates right to the bone. 19

5. **gnougous** (nōō´ gōōz) *n.* root vegetables.
6. **baobab** (bā´ ō bab´) **leaf** *n.* The baobab is a thick-trunked tree; its leaves are used to flavor foods.

Literary Analysis
Epic Conflict In what way is the young Mari Djata in conflict with his own society?

Reading Check
How old is Sogolon Djata when Dankaran Touman is pronounced king?

18 Literary Analysis

Epic Conflict

- Have students read the bracketed passage that begins on p. 136.
- **Ask** students the Literary Analysis question: In what way is the young Mari Djata in conflict with his own society?
  Possible response: Mari Djata must overcome the contempt with which he is treated and the exile into which he and his mother are forced. He struggles against those who have gained power and rule his society.

➤ **Monitor Progress** **Ask** students to describe how Mari Djata's conflict involves obstacles of epic conflicts beyond problems with society.
Possible response: Mari Djata's struggle with Sassouma Bérété and her son, Dankaran Touman, might qualify as a struggle with menacing enemies; he faces the natural danger or problem of a physical infirmity with which he was born; he has difficulties with fate, which predicts his future in puzzling ways; and he faces a challenging decision when he tries to overcome the other obstacles.

➤ **Reteach** Review the definition of an epic conflict on p. 129, and then **ask** students to identify the six common obstacles that heroes often face in such conflicts.
Answer: The common obstacles are menacing enemies, natural dangers, moral dilemmas, problems with society, difficulties with fate, and challenging decisions.

19 Reading Check

Answer: Sogolon Djata is seven.

Differentiated Instruction Solutions for All Learners

Support for English Learners
Students may have difficulty with the metaphor in the title of this episode. Ask a volunteer to read aloud the title of this episode and describe the characteristics of a typical lion. Then remind students that a metaphor is a figure of speech in which one thing is spoken of as though it were something else. Ask who they think the lion might be. As they read the episode, tell students to watch for actions that show why Mari Djata realizes that he must change his ways and how he overcomes his obstacles with the strength of a lion.

Enrichment for Advanced Readers
Have students compare and contrast *Sundiata* with another epic in this unit, *Gilgamesh*. Have students compare the two works and write essays that focus on which work contains the grandest conflicts and the boldest hero. Ask students to share their essays with the class.

20 Literary Analysis

Epic Conflict

- **Ask** students what Mari Djata has done up to this point regarding the conflict.
  Answer: Mari Djata has done nothing; he has accepted things as they are.
- **Ask** students why they think Mari Djata has done nothing to overcome his problems until now.
  Possible response: Until now, Mari Djata was biding his time, waiting to have the strength and wisdom to take his place in society.
- Direct students to read the first bracketed passage on the page.
- **Ask** students the Literary Analysis question: In what way does this event contribute to the epic conflict?
  Possible response: Mari Djata's decision to overcome his infirmity and show his strength is a turning point in his epic conflict.

➤ **Reteach** Have a student once again **reiterate** Mari Djata's epic conflict.
Answer: Mari Djata struggles to overcome his physical infirmity and the malicious way his society treats him because of it.

21 Reading Strategy

Rereading for Clarification

- Have students focus on the second bracketed passage.
- **Ask** students to complete the first part of the Reading Strategy item: Reread to find out who Balla Fasséké is.
  Answer: Balla Fasséké is Mari Djata's griot, the son of Doua, Mari Djata's father's griot.
- Then, **ask** students the second part of the Reading Strategy question: Where do you locate information about Nounfaïri's connection to Mari Djata?
  Answer: The information to reread is in the last paragraph on p. 135.

Sogolon Kedjou was dumbfounded. She had never imagined that hate could be so strong in a human being. With a lump in her throat she left Sassouma's. Outside her hut Mari Djata, sitting on his useless legs, was blandly eating out of a calabash. Unable to contain herself any longer, Sogolon burst into sobs and seizing a piece of wood, hit her son.

"Oh son of misfortune, will you never walk? Through your fault I have just suffered the greatest affront of my life! What have I done, God, for you to punish me in this way?"

Mari Djata seized the piece of wood and, looking at his mother, said, "Mother, what's the matter?"

"Shut up, nothing can ever wash me clean of this insult."

"But what then?"

"Sassouma has just humiliated me over a matter of a baobab leaf. At your age her own son could walk and used to bring his mother baobab leaves."

"Cheer up, Mother, cheer up."

"No. It's too much. I can't."

"Very well then, I am going to walk today," said Mari Djata. "Go and
20 tell my father's smiths to make me the heaviest possible iron rod. Mother, do you want just the leaves of the baobab or would you rather I brought you the whole tree?"

"Ah, my son, to wipe out this insult I want the tree and its roots at my feet outside my hut."

Balla Fasséké, who was present, ran to the master smith, Farakourou, to order an iron rod.

Sogolon had sat down in front of her hut. She was weeping softly and holding her head between her two hands. Mari Djata went calmly back to his calabash of rice and began eating again as if nothing had happened. From time to time he looked up discreetly at his mother, who was murmuring in a low voice, "I want the whole tree, in front of my hut, the whole tree."

All of a sudden a voice burst into laughter behind the hut. It was the wicked Sassouma telling one of her serving women about the scene of humiliation and she was laughing loudly so that Sogolon could hear. Sogolon fled into the hut and hid her face under the blankets so as not to have before her eyes this heedless boy, who was more preoccupied with eating than with anything else. With her head buried in the bedclothes Sogolon wept and her body shook violently. Her daughter, Sogolon Djamarou, had come and sat down beside her and she said, "Mother, Mother, don't cry. Why are you crying?"

Mari Djata had finished eating and, dragging himself along on his legs, he came and sat under the wall of the hut for the sun was scorching. What was he thinking about? He alone knew.

The royal forges were situated outside the walls and over a hundred smiths worked there. The bows, spears, arrows and shields of Niani's
 warriors came from there. When Balla Fasséké came to order the iron rod, Farakourou said to him, "The great day has arrived then?"

Literary Analysis
Epic Conflict In what way does this event contribute to the epic conflict?

Reading Strategy
Rereading for Clarification Reread to find out who Balla Fasséké is. Where do you locate information about Nounfaïri's connection to Mari Djata?

"Yes. Today is a day like any other, but it will see what no other day has seen."

The master of the forges, Farakourou, was the son of the old Nounfaïri, and he was a soothsayer like his father. In his workshops there was an enormous iron bar wrought by his father, Nounfaïri. Everybody wondered what this bar was destined to be used for. Farakourou called six of his apprentices and told them to carry the iron bar to Sogolon's house.

When the smiths put the gigantic iron bar down in front of the hut the noise was so frightening that Sogolon, who was lying down, jumped up with a start. Then Balla Fasséké, son of Gnankouman Doua, spoke.

"Here is the great day, Mari Djata. I am speaking to you, Maghan, son of Sogolon. The waters of the Niger can efface the stain from the body, but they cannot wipe out an insult. Arise, young lion, roar, and may the bush know that from henceforth it has a master."

The apprentice smiths were still there, Sogolon had come out, and everyone was watching Mari Djata. He crept on all-fours and came to the iron bar. Supporting himself on his knees and one hand, with the other hand he picked up the iron bar without any effort and stood it up vertically. Now he was resting on nothing but his knees and held the bar with both his hands. A deathly silence had gripped all those present. Sogolon Djata closed his eyes, held tight, the muscles in his arms tensed. With a violent jerk he threw his weight on to it and his knees left the ground. Sogolon Kedjou was all eyes and watched her son's legs which were trembling as though from an electric shock. Djata was sweating and the sweat ran from his brow. In a great

23 effort he straightened up and was on his feet at one go—but the great bar of iron was twisted and had taken the form of a bow!

Then Balla Fasséké sang out the "Hymn to the Bow," striking up with his powerful voice:

"Take your bow, Simbon,
Take your bow and let us go.
Take your bow, Sogolon Djata."

When Sogolon saw her son standing she stood dumb for a moment, then suddenly she sang these words of thanks to God, who had given her son the use of his legs:

"Oh day, what a beautiful day,
Oh day, day of joy;
Allah[7] Almighty, you never created a finer day.
So my son is going to walk!"

7. **Allah** (al′ ə) Muslim name for God.

Themes in World Masterpieces

22 *The Trials of an Epic Hero*

The literature of vastly different times and cultures portrays epic heroes who face great struggles or conflicts. Such heroes always display superhuman bravery, strength, or perseverance during their struggles, and their success often affects the fate of others—a tribe, a nation, or even all of humankind. In the Sumerian epic *Gilgamesh* (page 18), for example, the hero struggles to defeat evil Humbaba and find the secret of eternal life. In the ancient Greek epic the *Odyssey*, Odysseus struggles against many perils on his long journey home from the Trojan War. In the early English epic *Beowulf*, Beowulf struggles against three monsters that threaten his community as well as his own weakness in old age. In his struggle for respect and recognition, Sundiata is part of a great tradition in world literature.

Connect to the Literature

What epic heroes of today—from books or movies—remind you of Djata? Why?

Literary Analysis
Epic Conflict Why might the iron bar take the shape of a bow?

24  **Reading Check**

What does Farakourou use to help Sogolon Djata stand?

Differentiated Instruction
Solutions for All Learners

Enrichment for Gifted/Talented Students

Students might enjoy creating fictionalized epics about an actual world leader of more recent times. Have students write epics patterned after *Sundiata* involving a hero based on a modern person who faces a challenge, supporting characters who create obstacles to the hero's success, and a hero who is able to overcome those obstacles.

Enrichment for Advanced Readers

Point out that today we would call Mari Djata an *underdog,* someone who seems outmatched and unlikely to triumph but who nevertheless often does. Point out that the underdog is a common hero in modern times. Have students give examples of underdog heroes that they have encountered in films, TV shows, books, and stories. Then, encourage them to discuss the reasons for the wide appeal of underdogs.

22 Themes in World Literature

The Trials of an Epic Hero In the Roman epic the *Aeneid,* which parallels elements of the *Odyssey,* the hero Aeneas overcomes many dangers as he journeys from ancient Troy to Italy. In the *Ramayana,* a great epic of India, a princely hero named Rama faces problems similar to Sundiata's when one of his father's wives plots his exile so that he will not inherit the throne. In the French national epic *The Song of Roland,* Roland bravely battles the Saracens until he eventually perishes. In the German epic *The Nibelungenlied,* a prince named Siegfried displays amazing powers of invisibility and near invulnerability in his battles with the Nibelungs.

Connect to the Literature
Encourage students to give at least two examples and their reasons for each choice.

Possible responses: The Irish writer and artist Christy Brown was born with cerebral palsy and could not control his limbs or speak. However, Brown overcame these limits and used his left foot to paint and write. His book *My Left Foot* became a movie. In the movie "Star Wars," the hero Luke Skywalker, overcomes many obstacles and fights evils.

23 Literary Analysis

Epic Conflict

- Have students read the bracketed passage.
- **Ask** students the Literary Analysis question: Why might the iron bar take the shape of a bow?
  Possible response: The drawn bow is a weapon ready to be fired, stressing the new powers that Sogolon Djata displays. Dankaran Touman was previously described as being old enough to have a bow and use it to hunt in the bush; because Mari Djata now has a bow, he too now seems mature enough to claim his destiny.
- **Ask** what actions or qualities Balla Fasséké's song stresses about the bow and how it can be used.
  Answer: The song stresses the use of the bow for hunting or fighting and the importance of a weapon to a warrior.

24 Reading Check

Answer: Farakourou uses an iron bar that Nounfaïri has forged.

ASSESS

Answers

1. **Possible response:** Seeing Mari Djata triumph was satisfying because of the hardships he endured early in life.
2. (a) The community treated Mari Djata scornfully and unfairly. (b) He was odd looking and unable to walk even at the age of seven. (c) **Possible response:** Those who are different are often scorned or treated unfairly. A person's physical appearance is often given more weight than it deserves.
3. (a) The king keeps faith in Mari Djata because he believes the predictions that indicate the boy will one day be a great leader. (b) **Possible response:** Society scorns Mari Djata and does not think someone with his weaknesses should be king; they prefer Sassouma Bérété's son, who is older and seems more physically suited for the role.
4. (a) Sassouma Bérété taunts Sogolon about her son's inability to bring the leaves that Sassouma's own son brings. (b) Sogolon wants her son to be accepted; although she loves him and wants what is best for him, she is also a bit ashamed of his infirmity and angry that he does nothing to overcome it.
5. (a) Mari Djata makes up his mind to walk, uses an iron bar to help him stand, manages to reach a baobab tree, and pulls out the whole tree to bring his mother the leaves. (b) **Possible response:** The community was likely impressed.
6. (a) Mari Djata will be a great king. (b) **Possible response:** Do not prejudge a seemingly weak person's ability to achieve greatness.
7. **Possible response:** Men could have more than one wife at the same time. People believed in the Islamic faith but also in soothsayers' predictions. Sons often followed their fathers' professions.

Standing in the position of a soldier at ease, Sogolon Djata, supported by his enormous rod, was sweating great beads of sweat. Balla Fasséké's song had alerted the whole palace and people came running from all over to see what had happened, and each stood bewildered before Sogolon's son. The queen mother had rushed there and when she saw Mari Djata standing up she trembled from head to foot. After recovering his breath Sogolon's son dropped the bar and the crowd stood to one side. His first steps were those of a giant. Balla Fasséké fell into step and pointing his finger at Djata, he cried:

"Room, room, make room!
The lion has walked;
Hide antelopes,
Get out of his way."

Behind Niani there was a young baobab tree and it was there that the children of the town came to pick leaves for their mothers. With all his might the son of Sogolon tore up the tree and put it on his shoulders and went back to his mother. He threw the tree in front of the hut and said, "Mother, here are some baobab leaves for you. From henceforth it will be outside your hut that the women of Niani will come to stock up."

Critical Reading

1. **Respond:** How did you feel about Mari Djata's feat at the end of the selection? Why?
2. **(a) Recall:** Up to that point, how did most of the community treat Mari Djata? **(b) Infer:** Why was he treated that way? **(c) Generalize:** What does this treatment show about human nature?
3. **(a) Analyze Cause and Effect:** How do the soothsayers' predictions affect the king's view of Mari Djata? **(b) Infer:** After the king dies, why do you think his wishes for Mari Djata are not followed?
4. **(a) Recall:** What happens that causes Sogolon to want her son to bring her baobab leaves? **(b) Infer:** How has pressure from Sassouma Bérété and the rest of the community affected Sogolon?
5. **(a) Summarize:** What does Mari Djata do to get the baobab leaves and bring them to his mother? **(b) Speculate:** How do you think the community reacted to this act?
6. **(a) Connect:** Based on the Background on page 132 and the soothsayer's predictions, what rank will Mari Djata eventually achieve in his community? **(b) Draw Conclusions:** Considering Mari Djata's past infirmity, what lesson might readers draw from this outcome?
7. **Apply:** What does the selection show about customs and traditions in Old Mali? Explain.

Apply the Skills

African Proverbs • from *Sundiata*

Literary Analysis

Epic Conflict

1. Think about the **epic conflict** that Mari Djata faces in this part of *Sundiata.* **(a)** In what sense is it a conflict with nature? **(b)** In what sense is it a conflict with society? **(c)** In what sense is it an internal conflict that takes place within Mari Djata himself?
2. What role do Sassouma Bérété and Sogolon play in Mari Djata's childhood conflict? Explain.
3. **(a)** How could the Zulu proverb about feet that do not stumble apply to Mari Djata and his conflict? **(b)** How does the Jabo proverb about lifting ants and elephants contrast with or contradict Mari Djata's experiences?

Comparing Literary Works

4. On a chart like the one below, list and explain at least two of the **proverbs** that appear in *Sundiata.* Also, indicate how they apply to Mari Djata and his situation.

Proverb	General Meaning	How It Applies

5. Choose three African proverbs about nature that you find the most thought-provoking or perceptive. Explain how the lessons they draw from nature apply to human experience.

Reading Strategy

Rereading for Clarification

6. The first paragraph of "The Lion's Awakening" reveals that the king's will reserved the throne for Mari Djata. **Reread** the first two paragraphs of that section. Which details explain why the king left Mari Djata the throne?
7. **(a)** In the final paragraph of *Sundiata,* why does Mari Djata tear out the whole baobab tree? **(b)** Identify the passages that helped you answer this question.

Extend Understanding

8. **Science Link:** What do *Sundiata* and the African proverbs suggest about the traditional African knowledge of nature? Explain.

QuickReview

An **epic conflict** is the hero's struggle, or series of struggles, around which an epic centers.

A **proverb** is a wise saying that has been passed down by word of mouth for generations before being written down.

Rereading passages can often help clarify characters' identities and relationships, the sequence or cause of events, and puzzling language.

For: Self-test
Visit: www.PHSchool.com
Web Code: eta-6110

Go Online Assessment Students may use the **Self-test** to prepare for **Selection Test A** or **Selection Test B.**

Answers

1. (a) Mari Djata must overcome his physical condition. (b) He must prove that he is a strong and capable leader. (c) He must have the mental strength to overcome his infirmity, and to prove he is no weakling.
2. Sassouma makes much of Mari Djata's handicap and helps keep him from taking the place that is his. Sogolon is so troubled by his condition that Djata overcomes his handicap to make her happy.
3. (a) The proverb indicates that everyone is weak sometimes and suggests that people should not mock Mari Djata's infirmity.
(b) The proverb would seem to predict that Mari Djata will be unable to pull out the tree, because he has never even walked.
4. **Possible response: Proverb:** The silk cotton tree emerges from a tiny seed. **General Meaning:** Something impressive may come from something insignificant. **How It Applies:** Mari Djata seems small and weak but becomes a great leader. **Proverb:** Great trees grow slowly but they plunge their roots deep into the ground. **General Meaning:** Those who reach greatness slowly have a solid foundation. **How It Applies:** Mari Djata reaches greatness slowly but has a foundation of valuable experiences. Another sample answer can be found on **Literary Analysis Graphic Organizer B,** p. 32 in ***Graphic Organizer Transparencies.***
5. **Possible response:** "You cannot chase two gazelles" means that a person who does not focus on a single task will not perform any task well. "Baboons do not go far from the place of their birth" means that foolish people are afraid to stray from the familiar. "The zebra cannot do away with his stripes" means that a person cannot change his or her true nature.
6. The soothsayer predicted greatness for Mari Djata.
7. (a) Mari Djata's bringing the whole tree will wipe out the insult. (b) The passages appear in the middle of p. 138 with a short paragraph beginning "Ah, my son."
8. Africans' knowledge of nature is extensive; they apply lessons from nature to their own lives.

EXTEND/ASSESS

Answers

❶ Vocabulary Lesson

Word Analysis: Latin Root *-firm-*

1. to strengthen by proving
2. a place where those who are not strong are treated
3. to strengthen by agreeing

Spelling Strategy

1. delicious
2. courteous
3. envious
4. beauteous

Vocabulary Builder

1. False; a *malicious* person is bent on doing harm.
2. False; a *taciturn* person speaks little.
3. True; an *infirmity* may be a physical weakness or an illness.
4. True; an *innuendo* suggests something without stating it.
5. False; a *diabolical* smile is devilish.
6. True; an *estranged* couple has grown unfriendly.
7. True; a mystery is something many do not understand.

❷ Grammar and Style Lesson

1. Although he was now seven, the stiff-legged boy still crawled.
2. Futilely, Sogolon tried to heal her son using potions and herbs.
3. In her actions, the queen mother was very wicked and cruel.
4. Burying her head in the bedclothes, Sogolon wept.
5. From the ground, the young prince slowly straightened up and was on his feet.

Writing Application

Possible response: When he was young, Mari Djata suffered from a severe physical infirmity. Finally, he overcame his infirmity. In time, he would become a great leader of his people.

Build Language Skills

❶ Vocabulary Lesson

Word Analysis: Latin Root *-firm-*

The word *infirmity* contains the prefix *in-*, meaning "not," and the Latin root *-firm-*, meaning "strengthen" or "strong." Sundiata's *infirmity* is "a condition that is not strong" or "a weakness; an illness." Explain how the meaning of *-firm-* figures into the meanings of these words.

1. confirm **2.** infirmary **3.** affirm

Spelling Strategy

Many adjectives end in the suffix *-ious: malicious, previous.* Sometimes, after an *n* or a *t*, this suffix is spelled *eous: instantaneous, righteous.* Complete each word below with the correct spelling of the suffix. Check your answers in a dictionary.

1. delic_?_ous
2. court_?_ous
3. env_?_ous
4. beaut_?_ous

Vocabulary Builder: True/False

Use the meanings of the italicized words to decide whether each statement below is true or false. Be prepared to explain your responses.

1. You can rely on the kindness of a *malicious* person.
2. A *taciturn* person talks a lot.
3. A chronic illness can be an *infirmity*.
4. An *innuendo* hints at something instead of saying it directly.
5. A *diabolical* smile is sweet and innocent.
6. A couple who become *estranged* probably will stop dating.
7. A mystery is something most people find hard to *fathom*.

❷ Grammar and Style Lesson

Sentence Variety

Many sentences begin with a subject and a verb, but **sentence variety** keeps writing interesting. Writers can add variety by using different sentence beginnings:

Adverb: *Now* he was resting on nothing but his own two feet.

Prepositional Phrase: *With a lump in her throat*, she left Sassouma's.

Participial Phrase: *Having become all-powerful*, Sassouma Bérété persecuted Sogolon.

Subordinate Clause: *When the seed germinates*, growth is not always easy.

Practice Revise the following sentences using the sentence beginnings suggested in parentheses. Add new words wherever necessary.

1. The stiff-legged boy still crawled although he was now seven. (*subordinate clause*)
2. Sogolon tried to heal her son using potions and herbs. (*adverb*)
3. The queen mother was very wicked and cruel. (*prepositional phrase*)
4. Sogolon wept with her head buried in the bedclothes. (*participial phrase*)
5. The young prince slowly straightened up and stood on his feet. (*prepositional phrase*)

Writing Application Write a paragraph predicting what will happen to Mari Djata. Use at least three different sentence beginnings in your writing.

Prentice Hall Writing and Grammar Connection: Platinum Level, Chapter 21, Section 3

Assessment Practice

Recognize Facts and Details **(For more practice, see *Test Preparation Workbook*, p. 8.)**

Many tests require students to recognize facts and details. Use this sample test item to demonstrate the skill.

When the king consulted soothsayers on the destiny of this son, he received the reply that Namandjé's child would be the right hand of some mighty king.

According to this passage, Namandjé's child is—

A a boy destined to be a great king.
B a girl destined to be queen.
C a troublemaker who will rebel against the king.
D a boy destined to support a king.

Note that *B* can be eliminated because Namandjé's child is a son. *A* and *C* can be eliminated because the details indicate the boy will be "the right hand of some mighty king." The correct choice is *D*.

❸ Writing Lesson

Storytelling Notes

Although the griots of Old Mali presented epics from memory, a modern storyteller might want to work from a good set of notes. Create notes in outline form for a retelling of a story you know.

Prewriting On a chart like the one shown, list the characters and events in your story, and jot down details you think should be included to make the retelling clear and interesting.

Model: Gathering Details

Character	Character Details
Event	**Event Details**

Drafting Drawing on the details in your chart, create a set of notes in outline form. Under important headings such as *background*, *conflict*, *complications*, *climax*, and *resolution*, jot down phrases that will prompt your memory during your performance.

Revising Review your notes and make sure that you have included enough information for a good retelling. Add any background detail or action that makes your story complete.

WG *Prentice Hall Writing and Grammar Connection: Platinum Level, Chapter 5, Section 3*

❹ Extend Your Learning

Listening and Speaking Practice and perform an **oral retelling** of the selection from *Sundiata*. Follow these guidelines:

- Take notes on the details that are important to include in your retelling.
- Use your notes as you practice. Work on achieving the right tone of voice for each character.
- Practice before performing. Do not read your notes; use them as a guide.

Retell the story to classmates. Afterward, invite feedback from your listeners.

Research and Technology Working in a group, create a **booklet of proverbs** from around the world. Students who gather the proverbs might consult books of quotations, proverbs, and folk literature. Other students should work on the editing and organization of the booklet, as well as its production, including typing, printing, binding, and illustrating it. **[Group Activity]**

For: An additional research activity
Visit: www.PHSchool.com
Web Code: etd-7109

Assessment Resources

The following resources can be used to assess students' knowledge and skills.

Unit 1 Resources
- **Selection Test A,** pp. 148–150
- **Selection Test B,** pp. 151–153

General Resources
- **Rubrics for Narration: Short Story,** pp. 63–64
- **Rubric for Speaking: Narrative Account,** p. 88

Go Online Assessment — Students may use the **Self-test** to prepare for **Selection Test A** or **Selection Test B.**

❸ Writing Lesson

Storytelling Notes

- Have students use the **Support for Writing Lesson** page in ***Unit 1 Resources,*** p. 145, to plan their outlines.
- Tell students that the story they retell can be based on real events or entirely fictional.
- Have students use a chart like the one on the page to gather details about characters and events.
- If necessary, go over outline form using **Writing and Grammar,** Platinum Level, p. 228, or by demonstrating at the board.
- Use the Narration: Short Story rubrics in ***General Resources,*** pp. 63–64, to evaluate students' work.

WG **Writing and Grammar Platinum Level**

To give students further instruction for this writing lesson, use Chapter 5, Section 2.

❹ Listening and Speaking

- Tell students to focus on key information and on details they think are the most interesting.
- Encourage students to work in pairs to practice their retellings. After each student practices his or her retelling, tell the partner to suggest ways to improve it.
- Use the Speaking: Narrative Account rubric in ***General Resources,*** p. 88, to evaluate students' work.
- The **Support for Extend Your Learning** page (***Unit 1 Resources,*** p. 146) provides guided note-taking opportunities to help students complete the Extend Your Learning activities.

Go Online Research — Have students type in the Web Code for another research activity.

Standard Course of Study

IR.2.01.5 Summarize key events and/or points from research text.

FA.3.02.2 Provide relevant, reliable support in editorials.

CT.4.05.1 Select, monitor, and modify reading strategies appropriate to critical interpretation.

See Teacher Express™/Lesson View for a detailed lesson for Reading Informational Material.

About Brochures

- Have students read "About Brochures" independently. Then, discuss the bulleted elements that may be included in a brochure. Also, point out that students should look for a persuasive message included in the brochure; then, **ask** students why this message might be included.
  Possible response: The persuasive message is included to encourage people to visit the attraction or place of interest.
- **Ask** students how a brochure can be helpful to a traveler or to someone unfamiliar with an area or an attraction.
  Possible response: Information about the cost, location, hours, and where to find additional information is very helpful to potential visitors.

Reading Strategy

Adjusting Your Reading Rate

- Have students read the Reading Strategy instruction.
- Explain to students that when reading, people often look for only the information they need. For example, if people are reading the classified section of the newspaper for jobs, they do not read every advertisement. Instead, they skim the columns, looking for headings that interest them or that apply to their abilities and skills.
- Draw students' attention to the chart describing how to skim and scan.

Reading Informational Materials

Brochures

About Brochures

A **brochure** is a pamphlet that combines information and advertising to highlight an attraction or a place of interest. Brochures usually contain some of the following elements:

- Historical background
- Details about the attraction
- Images that highlight the attraction
- Map to guide visitors
- Hours of operation
- Ticket and contact information

A brochure may also contain a persuasive message that supports the goals, mission, or political perspective of the sponsoring organization or company. As you read this brochure about an exhibit on ancient Egyptian civilization at the Museum of Science in Boston, note which of these elements it contains.

Reading Strategy

Adjusting Your Reading Rate

Brochures often include more information than you want or need. To find the specific information that you want, **adjust your reading rate.** Using the techniques of skimming and scanning will help you locate information quickly and efficiently. The chart shown gives instructions for skimming and scanning.

Obtaining Information Quickly

To Skim	• Read quickly across a page, without reading word for word. • Stop at headlines, italics, and other text features if the words are related to what you want to know. • Once you have located these features, begin reading more carefully.
To Scan	• Run your eyes across and down the page. • Scan headlines, bold type, italics, and other text features to locate information quickly.

As you read this brochure about the exhibit on ancient Egyptian civilization, adjust your reading rate by skimming and scanning the material to learn as much as you can about the exhibit.

Differentiated Instruction Solutions for All Learners

Reading Support

Give students reading support with the appropriate version of the **Reader's Notebooks:**

Reader's Notebook: [L2, L3]
Reader's Notebook: Adapted Version [L1, L2]
Reader's Notebook: English Learner's Version [EL]

THE QUEST for IMMORTALITY

Treasures of Ancient Egypt

Confronting the mystery of death is a fundamental human endeavor. The ancient Egyptians believed they could ensure their continued existence after death, and they devoted tremendous energy and resources to achieving this goal. The pursuit of immortality was the central feature of a complex, evolving set of beliefs that characterized Egyptian civilization throughout its first 3,000 years of history.

For modern archaeologists, Egyptian tombs are treasure houses—not of objects, but of evidence. It is through examination and excavation of tombs and their furnishings that archaeologists have begun to understand the remarkably complex religion of ancient Egypt. This exhibition explores Egyptians' quest for immortality from the Old Kingdom (2686–2125 BCE*) through the Late Period (664–332 BCE). It also tells the story of archaeologists' 200-year quest to understand the thought and practices of an accomplished and intricate culture.

*Before Common Era

The Afterlife

The boat is a recurring image in Egyptian funerary art. It is a reminder of Egypt's reliance on the Nile River, the country's life giver and major artery. For the Egyptians, the Nile was the center of the world. It was also a metaphor for the soul's journey through the netherworld: sailing in a solar boat, the sun god Re travels through the hours of night to be reborn with each dawn. In imitation of the gods, pharaohs hoped to secure their own immortality. While some rituals seemed to have been reserved exclusively for the pharaohs, the quest was shared by all Egyptians. Scribes and maids, mayors and generals all sought to deny the impermanence of the body. Through the material remains of their endeavors, their names and histories live again—immortality of a sort.

...to-...ohs of ...se arti-...s from ...exhibit ...vide a ...view for ...ders.

This cover image of a sphinx attracts readers' interest and gives the brochure visual appeal.

This page of the brochure provides historical background information.

Reading Brochures

- Have students reread the first paragraph. **Ask** them what information they gained from this paragraph and why this information is important to the exhibit.
  Possible response: This paragraph explains the title of the exhibit and the beliefs that characterized ancient Egyptian civilization.
- Tell students to review the historical background information under the heading The Afterlife. **Ask** them what other information about the ancient Egyptians and the exhibit is included on this page.
  Possible response: The exhibit explores the ancient Egyptians' search for immortality, as well as the archaeological quest to understand the practices of the culture. The brochure also provides background on the symbols and rituals of the period.
- Have students read the first call-out note. **Ask** them to explain why photographs are included in brochures.
  Possible response: Photographs catch the reader's attention and provide some idea of what the attraction or place of interest features.
- Draw students' attention to the second call-out note. **Ask** students why the creators of the brochure may have included the image of a sphinx.
  Possible response: This image helps potential visitors connect to something familiar.
- Call students' attention to the last call-out note. **Ask** students why historical information is important in this brochure.
  Answer: Historical background helps the reader understand the subject of the exhibit and appreciate the society from which the exhibit's artifacts were culled.

continued on page 146

Differentiated Instruction Solutions for All Learners

Strategy for Special Needs Students
Ask students to bring to class brochures from attractions in your area or state. Use the bulleted items to create a checklist, and have students work in pairs to skim the brochures for that information. Then, have students use their checklists to find and list any similarities among the various brochures.

Strategy for English Learners
Provide students with several brochures. Have them skim each brochure, looking for the information they might need if they were to visit each attraction. Ask students to explain how skimming helps them find the information they need without having to read all of the other information in the brochure.

Enrichment for Advanced Readers
Have students compare a brochure with a television commercial about an attraction. Have students evaluate which of the two provides more information and what the purpose of the commercial might be. Then, have students complete a written evaluation of the effectiveness of each medium.

Reading Brochures *(cont.)*

- Explain to students that the exhibition information provides details about exhibition hours, tickets and reservations, event options, the exhibition Web site, and museum membership.
- **Ask** students to identify features that make the text easier to skim or scan.
  Answer: The use of bold type, capital letters, headings, and columns make the text easier to skim or scan.
- **Ask** students how the accessibility of the information would change if the exhibition information had been written in paragraph form.
  Possible response: The information would be far more difficult to scan if it were written in paragraph form.
- Have students read the call-out note at the bottom of the page. Then, **ask** them why a map might be included in a brochure.
  Possible response: A map provides some idea of the size of the exhibit and the topics covered in the display, as well as the location of the different areas.

Reading Informational Materials

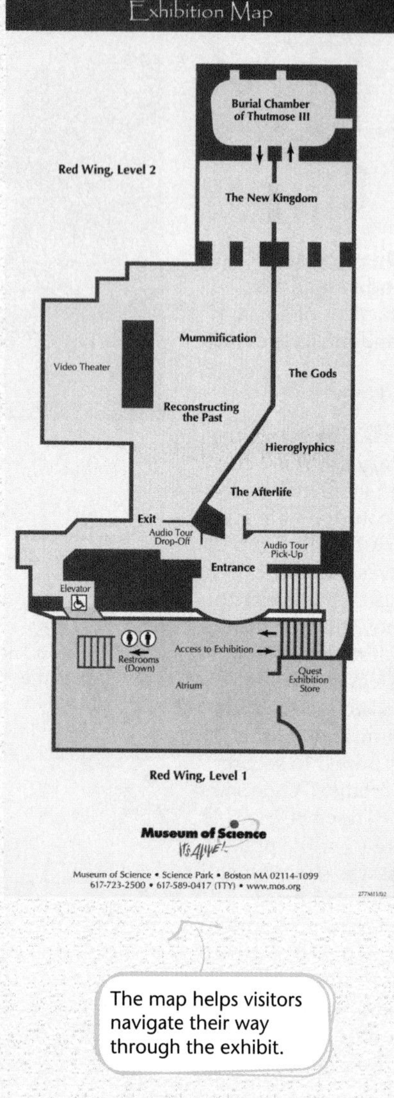

The map helps visitors navigate their way through the exhibit.

EXHIBITION INFORMATION

EXHIBITION AMENITIES

- Audio tour provided by Antenna Audio.
- Exhibition store featuring Egypt-inspired gifts and merchandise, including the beautifully illustrated catalog.
- Science Street Café on Thursday and Friday evenings, offering cocktails, gourmet appetizers, and special desserts, 6–10 p.m.

EXHIBITION HOURS

The Quest for Immortality gallery will be open during regular Exhibit Halls hours, plus special extended hours on Thursday evening, just for adults. Timed ticket entry.

- **Saturday–Wednesday: 9 a.m.–5 p.m.**
- **Thursday–Friday: 9 a.m.–9 p.m.**

TICKETING INFORMATION AND RESERVATIONS

Full-price admission to *The Quest for Immortality* includes a separate ticket for general admission to the Exhibit Halls that may be used on the same day or on another day within six months.

Individual & Group
Reserve by Phone
(daily 9 a.m.–5 p.m.)
617-723-2500
617-589-0417 (TTY)

Event Options
Reserve by Phone
(Mon.–Fri. 9 a.m.–5 p.m.)
617-589-0125
617-589-0417 (TTY)

Individual tickets may also be reserved online at www.mos.org/quest

WWW.MOS.ORG/QUEST

Find out more about ancient Egypt, explore a 3-D mummy, or learn how to play the ancient game of senet. This site also offers the latest information about *The Quest for Immortality* exhibition and related Museum attractions, tickets, events, lectures, hotel packages, special offers, shopping, visiting tips, and directions.

MUSEUM MEMBERSHIP

Becoming a member is the best way to receive priority treatment for *The Quest for Immortality* and enjoy the Museum all year long. Hold on to your Exhibit Halls ticket vouchers—we will apply a portion of your ticket price toward the cost of any membership level. **For details,** visit the Membership Booth or contact us at 617-589-0180, membership@mos.org.

The Quest for Immortality is organized by the United Exhibits Group™, Denmark, and the National Gallery of Art, Washington, in association with the Supreme Council of Antiquities, Cairo.

Monitor Your Progress

Assessment Practice

Reading: Adjusting Your Reading Rate

Directions: *Choose the letter of the best answer to each question about the brochure.*

1. Which heads are used in the Exhibition Information section of the brochure to help you locate information when you skim?
   A Ticket Vouchers, General Admission, Cafe
   B Exhibition Amenities, Exhibition Hours, Ticketing Information and Reservations
   C Afterlife, Museum Membership, Quest
   D Event Options, Reserve by Phone, 3-D Mummy
2. Scan the first page of the brochure to find the dates of the period covered by the exhibition.
   A 2686–2125 BCE
   B 2686–332 BCE
   C 2125–664 BCE
   D 664–332 BCE
3. Which headline signals that you should read closely if you are looking for information about admission to the museum?
   A Museum Membership
   B Exhibition Amenities
   C Ticketing Information and Reservations
   D Treasures of Ancient Egypt

Reading: Comprehension and Interpretation

Directions: *Write your answers on a separate sheet of paper.*

4. Describe the ancient Egyptians' perception of the Nile.
5. Using the map, identify the first three parts of the exhibition that visitors see.

Timed Writing: Persuasion

Write a persuasive letter encouraging people to visit this exhibition. Your audience is the general public. In your letter, include informative details about the exhibition that will spark your readers' interest. Also include specific reasons to support the argument that this show is worth seeing. ***(20 minutes)***

ASSESS

Answers

Reading: Adjusting Your Reading Rate

1. B
2. B
3. C

Reading: Comprehension and Interpretation

4. **Possible response:** The Ancient Egyptians considered the Nile River the center of the world, a life-giver, and a main artery. In Egyptian funerary art, the image of a boat represents the Egyptians' dependence on the Nile River and also functions as a metaphor for the soul's journey through the netherworld.
5. **Possible response:** When they enter the exhibit, visitors will first see The Afterlife, Hieroglyphics, and The Gods.

Timed Writing
Persuasion

- Remind students that the proper form for a letter includes a date, a salutation, the body, and a closing.
- Encourage students to use persuasive language to engage the audience's interest and to convince them of the worth of this exhibit.
- Suggest that students plan their time to give 5 minutes to planning, 10 minutes to writing, and 5 minutes to revising and editing.

Extend the Lesson

Designing a Brochure

To give students further practice with brochures, have each student design a brochure for an event in school or an attraction in town. Students should use a local newspaper, the library, or the Internet to find information about the town or event. They might also consult the group or school official who is sponsoring the school event. Encourage students to use notecards first to organize details for their brochures. Then have them use headlines, text, graphics, maps, or lists and organize their brochures to promote the event and interest readers.

Point out also that the use of color and photos will attract the reader's attention. Students should provide background information about the event and include a persuasive message to attract visitors. When students have finished their brochures, display their work on a class bulletin board.

Standard Course of Study

WL.1.03.7 Analyze influences, contexts, or biases in personal reflection.

LT.5.01.5 Analyze archetypal characters, themes, and settings in world literature.

LT.5.02.1 Explore works which relate to an issue, author, or theme and show increasing comprehension.

Prewriting

- Have students review selections in this unit that they particularly enjoyed reading. Ask them to write a sentence about a theme found in each selection. Then, have students circle the "value words" in each stated theme—for example, *bravery, justice,* or *loyalty.*
- As students work to narrow their choices, have them consider how each selection expresses a universal value. Does one express the value directly, through a character's or narrator's words? Does another express the value indirectly, through events, images, or symbols? Students should choose works that express values in strikingly different ways.

Tips for Test Taking

A writing prompt on the SAT or ACT test may assess students' abilities to analyze a topic, state a point of view regarding a topic, and support the point of view with evidence. When writing under timed circumstances, students will need to clarify quickly a point of view (the thesis statement) and the evidence that supports it. Because they will not be able to refer to a text, their evidence must be based on their own experiences, readings, or observations.

Analyze Literary Periods

In the ancient world, life was short and often brutal, dependent on ill-understood and unpredictable natural forces and events. Much of the literature of ancient times was morally instructive, providing a pattern for life in a chaotic world. The Bible, for example, transmitted the core religious values of Judaism and Christianity, just as the Qur'an transmitted the values of Islam.

Examine the literary works in this unit to discover the values expressed in them. Note especially the values that seem most universal. Then, write an essay that describes some of these shared values, using specific examples from the literature to support your ideas. Consult the box at the right for details of this assignment.

Assignment: Shared Values in the Literature of the Ancient World

Write an analytical essay that explores the shared values expressed in two or more of the excerpts from the literature of the ancient world that you have read in this unit.

Criteria:
- Include a thesis statement drawn from your analysis of the literature.
- Support your thesis with detailed analyses of at least two of the selections.
- Cite several examples from each work you explore.
- Approximate length: 700 words

Prewriting

Review the selections. List the values that the writers of the selections express directly or indirectly. You may use the following questions as a guide:

- What is the theme of the selection?
- How do the actions and statements of the main character express and amplify the theme?
- What societal values does that theme reflect?
- Which other selections reflect similar values?

Review at least five of the selections. Take notes using a chart similar to the one below. Then, review your chart and select two or more works that express common values.

Model: Listing to Find Values

Selection	Value	Example	Page #
The Epic of Gilgamesh	bravery	"If your heart is fearful throw away fear . . ."	18

Gather examples. Return to the works that you have selected and, using your chart, gather additional examples reflecting the values they share. In addition to direct statements about right and wrong in the works, consider what characters' actions, motives, and fates may imply.

Write a working thesis. After you have gathered examples, write a working thesis. Introduce the values you will discuss and explain the way in which they are central to the selections.

Read to Write
As you reread the texts, pay special attention to the main characters' actions and speech. What values do these words and deeds demonstrate?

Teaching Resources

The following resources can be used to extend or enrich the instruction for Writing About Literature.

General Resources
- **Response to Literature rubrics,** pp. 55–56

Graphic Organizer Transparencies
- **Outline Organizer,** p. 248

Drafting

Organize logically. A logical organization makes your ideas clear to readers. After you introduce your thesis, you may want to write a paragraph for each value you discuss and include examples from each of the selections. If the paragraphs seem too long using this method of organization, you may decide to write a separate paragraph for each selection.

Model: Use a Logical Organization

I Value 1
- Selection 1
- Selection 2
- Selection 3

II Value 2
- Selection 1
- Selection 2
- Selection 3

Provide examples. Illustrate the values you cite with specific examples from the selections, such as direct value statements by the author or a character or values you infer from the behavior of the characters and the twists and turns of the plot.

Write to Learn
As you write your first draft, you may notice that some examples you have chosen do not adequately support the values you are discussing. Be flexible and willing to reexamine the literature to choose other examples or to revise your thesis.

Write to Explain
Remember that your reader may not be as familiar with the selections as you are. Provide enough context so that the examples you cite make sense and support your thesis persuasively.

Revising and Editing

Review content: Check the validity of your connections. Make sure that the examples you have chosen clearly and unambiguously illustrate the values you are discussing. Add transition sentences as necessary to make those connections clear.

Review style: Rephrase for clarity. Reword sentences to make your intended meaning as clear as possible.

Original: Psalm 8 expresses the belief that humans are close to God. So are angels, but the Psalm expresses the belief that humans are better than other animals.

Revised: Psalm 8 expresses the belief that humans are close to God. In their position as God's favorites—just a little lower than the angels—humans rule over the rest of creation.

Publishing and Presenting

Write and present a summary. Gather with classmates who wrote about some of the same selections you did. Compare your group's reactions to the literature. Summarize the discussion in writing, and share your summary with the rest of the class.

WG *Writing and Grammar Connection: Diamond Level, Chapter 14*

Drafting

- As you discuss the model, point out that each selection could be addressed in a separate paragraph. Have a volunteer write on the board an alternative model for organizing.
- Have students write one or two possible outlines for their essays. Ask them to include a third tier containing relevant details and examples.

Revising and Editing

- Have each student check the validity of his or her thesis statement. Does it reflect and sum up the body of the essay? If not, encourage students to revise as needed.
- If any evidence seems weak or irrelevant, have students return to the selection to find stronger evidence.

Publishing and Presenting

- Students should include in their summaries points about which students disagree as well as agree.
- After all students have presented their summaries, work together to draw conclusions about the shared values of ancient societies.

WG Writing and Grammar Platinum Level
Students will find additional instruction on writing an analytical essay in Chapter 14.

Six Traits Focus

✓	Ideas	✓	Word Choice
✓	Organization		Sentence Fluency
	Voice	✓	Conventions

Assessing the Essay

- Have students use the Response to Literature rubrics in ***General Resources,*** pp. 55–56, to evaluate each other's work.

Differentiated Instruction
Solutions for All Learners

Strategy for Less Proficient Writers
As students identify values expressed by each selection, have them focus on main characters. Ask them to write three words that describe each character. Then, help them change each adjective into a value word—for example, *courageous* would become *courage.*

Strategy for English Learners
Make sure that students understand the meaning of the word *value* in this context. Explain that a *societal value* is an idea or a trait that is considered important by most of the people in a society. Give examples, such as honesty and fairness, and have students provide examples of their own.

Strategy for Advanced Writers
Have students draw conclusions about the values they discuss in their essays. Ask them to include in their essays a paragraph answering the following questions: Are the values in the essay universal—do they span all times and cultures? Or are they particular to certain societies?

PRETEACH

Writing Workshop

Standard Course of Study

WL.1.01.2 Explain the significance of a reminiscence.

WL.1.01.3 Move effectively between past and present in a reminiscence.

WL.1.01.4 Produce reminiscences that recreate the mood felt during the experience.

 **From the Translator's Desk**

Coleman Barks

Show students Segment 3 on Coleman Barks on ***From the Author's Desk DVD.*** Discuss how he prepares to translate and the research that he does for a translation. Tell students that one's personal and educational history play a role in producing creative work. Even in the work of translating Rumi, for instance, readers can detect Coleman Barks's own style.

Writing Genres

Using the Form Point out to students that autobiographical narration is often incorporated into other types of writing. Point out these examples:

- Personal letters often contain descriptions of autobiographical events.
- Elements of autobiographical narrative are sometimes used in persuasive essays, as in a letter to the editor in which a writer draws on his or her personal experience as support for an opinion.
- Autobiographical narrative may be the core of a reflective essay or a journal entry.

 **Online Essay Scorer**

A writing prompt for this mode of writing can be found on the ***PH Online Essay Scorer*** at PHSuccessNet.com.

Narration: Autobiographical Narrative

"This really happened to me." "This is a true story." Everyone's life is made up of many "true stories." They take us deeper into the actual world we inhabit, revealing the lives behind the faces we see on the street. Such stories are called **autobiographical narratives.** Follow the steps explained in this workshop to write your own autobiographical narrative.

Assignment Write an autobiographical narrative about an experience that was significant to you, that helped you grow, or that changed your outlook.

What to Include Your autobiographical narrative should feature the following elements:

- well-established characters, including the writer as the main character
- an organized sequence of events with a significance that is clearly communicated
- action that incorporates shifts in time and mood
- conflict or tension between characters or between a character and another force
- insights that the writer has gained from the experience

To preview the criteria on which your autobiographical narrative may be assessed, see the rubric on page 157.

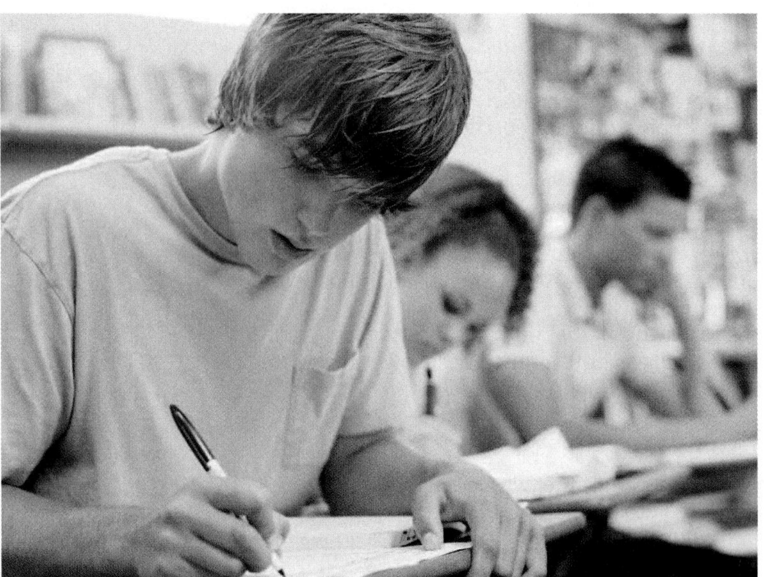

 **Standard Course of Study**

- Explain the significance of a reminiscence. (WL.1.01.2)
- Move effectively between past and present in a reminiscence. (WL.1.01.3)
- Produce reminiscences that recreate the mood felt during the experience. (WL.1.01.4)

Using the Form

You may use elements of autobiographical narrative in these writing situations:

- personal letters
- college application essays
- journal entries
- reflective essays

To get a feel for the form, read the excerpt from the writings of Galileo on page 758.

Teaching Resources

The following resources can be used to enrich or extend the instruction for the Writing Workshop.

Unit 1 Resources
Writing Workshop: Autobiographical Narrative, pp. 156–157

General Resources
Rubric for Narration: Autobiographical Narrative, pp. 43–44

Graphic Organizer Transparencies
Rubric for Self-Assessment, p. 33

From the Author's Desk DVD
Coleman Barks, Segments 3 and 4

Prewriting

Choosing Your Topic

Select an experience that is important to you. For example, you might write about a difficult decision or a discovery that changed you. To help you find a topic, use one of the following strategies:

- **Freewriting** Write for five minutes, using any or all of the following **sentence starters:**

  I really learned what being responsible means when I____.

  A day that turned out just the opposite from what I expected was____.

  I discovered something about myself the day I____.

- **Descriptive Prompting** Write adjectives such as *exciting, funny, surprising, puzzling, moving, challenging,* and *sad* on different slips of paper. On the other side of each slip, jot down moments in your life that match the term. Review your work and choose a topic.
- **Blueprint/Map** Draw a floor plan or a map of a significant place in your life, such as a house or your elementary school. Label the rooms or areas, and, if you like, sketch in details like furniture or trees. Then, list the words or phrases that come to mind as you "walk through" this special place. Choose a topic based on this experience.

Narrowing Your Topic

After you have chosen the basic topic for your narrative, think about what you want to say about it—what point you want to make, what specific moments you will discuss, what people and places you will describe. For example, in writing about your experiences as an athlete, you could focus on the first time you realized that you had a special talent.

Gathering Details

Interview yourself. As the writer of an autobiographical narrative, you have an advantage: an intimate knowledge of your subject. To gather vivid details, make a list of interview questions like the ones shown, and answer them in writing in detail. Refer to your responses as you draft.

Self-Interview

1. What makes this experience/event/person special to you?
2. What is the one word you would choose to describe this experience/event/person?
3. Who else shared in this experience or event? Does he or she share your feelings? Why or why not?
4. Did you change in any way because of this experience/event/person? Explain.
5. What did you learn from this experience/event/person?

Tips for Using Rubrics

- Before students begin work on this assignment, have them preview the Rubric for Self-Assessment, p. 157, to know what is expected.
- Review the Assessment criteria in class. Before students use the Rubric for Self-Assessment, work with them to rate the student model by applying one or two criteria to it.
- If you wish to assess students' autobiographical narratives with a 4-point, a 5-point, or a 6-point scoring rubric, see ***General Resources,*** pp. 43 and 44.

TEACH

Prewriting

- Give students support for prewriting and drafting with p. 156 from ***Unit 1 Resources.***
- Help students get started with their freewriting by having volunteers suggest ideas to complete each of the sentence starters. Encourage students to talk about what ideas these prompts start them thinking about.
- After developing ideas through descriptive prompting, suggest that students meet with partners and discuss some of their ideas. Partners should ask questions and help each other dig deeper into their ideas.
- As students draw their blueprint/map and imagine themselves walking through the place, urge them to try to think about what they see, hear, smell, taste, and feel.
- Suggest that students develop a cluster diagram as a way of narrowing their topics. They can write their basic topic in the center and related ideas in the surrounding circles. This process may help students decide that one of the related topics is more limited and better suited to the requirements of their autobiographical narrative.
- Suggest that students use the *Who? What? When? Where? Why?* and *How?* questions to generate ideas for their self-interview.

Six Traits Focus

✓	Ideas	✓	Word Choice
	Organization		Sentence Fluency
	Voice		Conventions

WG Writing and Grammar Platinum Level

Students will find additional instruction on prewriting for an autobiographical narrative in Chapter 4, Section 2.

Writing and Grammar Interactive Textbook CD-ROM

Students can use the following tools as they complete their autobiographical essays:

- Self-Interview
- Cluster Diagram
- Story Map
- Editing

Drafting

- If students are still struggling to select a topic about which they will write, allow some time for students to free write about an event or situation in which they are currently involved or concerned about. Have them use this event or situation as the topic for their story maps. Alternatively, have students begin their story maps using an idea or event that has captured their attention from a movie that they have seen recently.
- Explain that of the three plot enhancements, interior monologue is the most crucial in an autobiographical narrative. Require students to use interior monologue at least once in their writing, in addition to one of the other two enhancements.
- Help students to elaborate by telling them to think about a single event they have described in a paragraph and then to brainstorm or freewrite about it. They should write every idea or thought that comes to mind. After a couple of minutes, they should pause and evaluate the ideas they have identified.
- After students have practiced "exploding the moment," remind them that when they write the final draft, they should include only details that are pertinent to their story. If a detail does not directly explain or highlight something related to the story, it should not be included.

Six Traits Focus

✓	Ideas	✓	Word Choice
✓	Organization		Sentence Fluency
	Voice		Conventions

Writing and Grammar Platinum Level
Students will find additional instruction on drafting an autobiographical narrative in Chapter 4, Section 3.

Drafting

Shaping Your Writing

Make a story map. Map the events of your story in the order in which they originally occurred. Write a sentence stating the central conflict, change, or insight that you want to portray. Decide how you want to begin your story and end. Then, to maintain an appropriate pacing, refer to your story map as you go along. Also keep your sentence in mind as you draft your narrative so that your story remains focused on the central conflict or insight that you have identified.

Add interest plot enhancements. To make your narrative more interesting, try one or more of these techniques:

- **Foreshadowing** Give a hint early in the story of what is to come.
- **Flashback** Go back in time to relate an incident that has a bearing on your story.
- **Interior monologue** Re-create the thoughts that occurred to you while events were taking place.

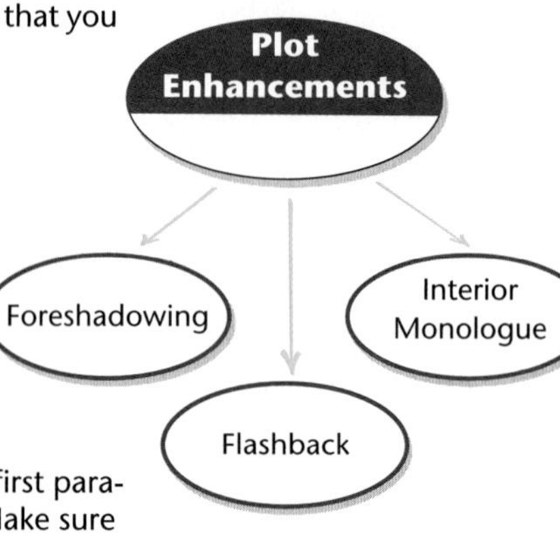

Providing Elaboration

Flesh out your opening paragraph. After you have drafted your first paragraph, look for ways to flesh it out to hook the reader's interest. Make sure you have established the time and place of the events. Also make sure you have introduced yourself and perhaps one or two of the other significant people in your narrative. Think about adding a few key details that will make the setting and personalities come alive.

Explode a moment. You can "explode a moment" by telling more about what happened, what something looked like, or how people reacted. As you draft, follow these steps:

1. Cut several "explosion" shapes from construction paper.
2. As you write each paragraph, look for ways to "explode amoment" by expanding a description or elaborating on what happened.
3. Write the details that you want to add on the construction paper shapes, and then tape or lightly glue them to your draft.

When it is time to write your final draft, incorporate these details.

Student Model: Elaborating by Exploding a Moment

A few years ago, when I was fourteen, I got stuck in a hole that my cousin and I dug. It was the middle of summer in beautiful Mancelona, Michigan. Woodpeckers were yammering away, and my cousin and I were out exploding the woods.

the dogs were chasing chipmunks

thirty-two acres of

These details "explode the moment" by elaborating on the descriptions.

Tips for Using Technology in Writing

After drafting, have students type their narrative into a word processing software program. Direct them to double-space the document as they type. Double-spacing helps students see their words clearly on the screen and on the printout. It also provides space for students to enter new text or notes to themselves.

After creating the draft, tell students to save the text as "Draft." After marking up the drafts and adding elaboration, students can enter the changes and save the document again. Later, when they revise, they may want to save changes as "Revision 1," "Revision 2," and so on. By saving each version of their narrative, students can look back at changes that they have made and, if they have second thoughts about a change, they can return to a version of the earlier text.

Coleman Barks

From the Translator's Desk
Coleman Barks on Word Choice

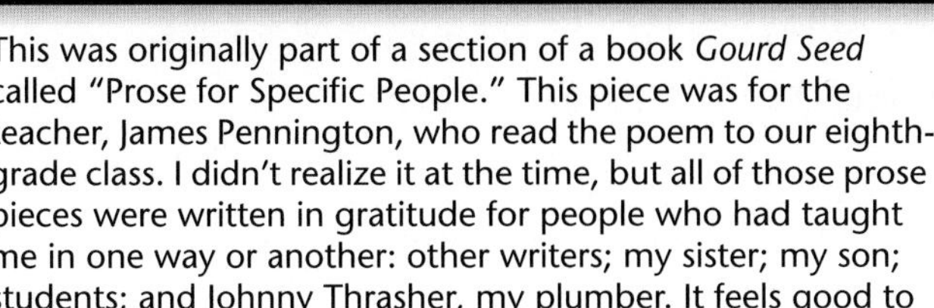

This was originally part of a section of a book *Gourd Seed* called "Prose for Specific People." This piece was for the teacher, James Pennington, who read the poem to our eighth-grade class. I didn't realize it at the time, but all of those prose pieces were written in gratitude for people who had taught me in one way or another: other writers; my sister; my son; students; and Johnny Thrasher, my plumber. It feels good to be specific about, and openly grateful to, those who teach us.

> *"I like that long string of five adjectives . . ."*
> —Coleman Barks

Professional Model:

from Gourd Seed

I was fourteen, sitting in an eighth-grade classroom, when I heard a teacher read aloud the last two stanzas of a poem, Edna St. Vincent Millay's "Afternoon on a Hill":

I will look at cliffs and clouds
With quiet eyes.
Watch the wind bow down the grass
And the grass rise.

And when lights begin to show
Up from the the town,
I will mark which must be mine,
And then start down.

It's the first poem I ever *got.* I felt it in my bones. I had done that joyful, solitary, purposeless, afternoon, after-school wandering. I had felt the spacious aloneness and the quiet inwardness that being outdoors can bring. As afternoon turned to evening and the lights in the houses began to come on, I had felt the necessary descent back into a family residence, a community. It is a simple, almost transparent poem, but I heard it on a deep level. Language and my most private way of being came together in a moment of recognition. I still look for and enjoy the delight of that entangling, when words and the world, or my experience of it, find a voice.

I like that long string of five adjectives because it participates in the expansive feeling of that time of day.

I first wrote about this memory using the term *hieros gamos,* Greek for "sacred marriage," a psychological phrase for the peak experience of feeling at one—married—with one's soul. I like the account better without that fancy trimming.

I like saving the central word, the whole point of the shift I felt in my listening, for last: *voice.*

From the Translator's Desk
Coleman Barks

- Show students Segment 4 on Coleman Barks on ***From the Author's Desk DVD.*** Discuss the contributions that writing can make to society and the rewards that writing can bring to writers. Also discuss how Barks emphasizes that good writing involves taking personal risks and challenges writers to tell the truth, even if it is uncomfortable.
- Point out that Coleman Barks writes from his own experience. Tell students that when they write honestly from their experience, their writing has authenticity and, therefore, has the capacity to touch others' lives.
- Review Coleman Barks's comments about the effect that "Afternoon on a Hill" had on him as a young man. Ask students to explain what Barks means when he describes the "entangling" of words and personal experience.

Writing Workshop

Revising

Revising Your Overall Structure

Use dialogue. In narrative writing, conversation, called **dialogue,** helps you create realistic characters because it captures the way people actually speak. Dialogue is also a great way to bring a moment to vivid life. To add dialogue, follow these steps:

1. Highlight passages in which your charaters' emotions are most intense.
2. Also highlight points in the narrative at which the addition of dialogue might help reveal the personality or motivation of a character.
3. Instead of summarizing or restating what people said, revise to recreate the words they actually used.
4. Use active verbs and vivid adverbs to describe the way people speak the dialogue.
5. Use a new paragraph for each new speaker.

Model: Revising to Add Dialogue

When Mom saw my predicament, she started to laugh ~~and.~~ "I should have brought the camera."

~~wish she'd had a camera.~~ "I would burn the picture!" I sobbed.

Adding dialogue makes the passage more vivid and interesting to read.

Revising Your Sentences

Revise for unnecessary tense changes. Although your narrative may move back and forth in time, check to make sure that you have not changed verb tenses unnecessarily. For example, look for passages in which you have moved from past to present within the same sentence or nearby sentences for no reason.

Example: It *was* an hour after closing time, and I *am* still waiting for my mom.

Corrected: It *was* an hour after closing time, and I *was* still waiting for my mom.

Peer Review: Have a partner review your draft, underlining places where you have switched tenses within a sentence or from one sentence to the next. Check to see whether these tense changes are necessary. If not, revise your verbs to be consistent in tense.

Revising

- Encourage students to write dialogue that captures the way that the people in their narrative actually speak. They should include appropriate slang, colloquialisms, and even dialect if it is fitting.
- After students have written dialogue, have them work with partners and read the sentences aloud. Tell students to listen for lines that do not sound like natural speech.
- Some students' experiences may have involved only one person and contain little or no dialogue. Explain that in these cases, students need not insert dialogue where it does not naturally belong. Encourage them instead to revise their work to add more interior monologue or descriptive language.
- After you have discussed unnecessary tense changes and have reviewed the models, write the following sentences on the board. Have students identify and correct errors.

1. I sat down on the soft, warm sand and think, "This is a perfect day."
2. My brother had left an hour ago, and he still hasn't returned.
3. When Greta asks me to hold her backpack, I wasn't prepared for what would happen next.

Answers

1. I sat down on the soft, warm sand and thought, "This is a perfect day."
2. My brother left an hour ago, and he still hasn't returned.
3. When Greta asked me to hold her backpack, I wasn't prepared for what would happen next.

Six Traits Focus

✓	Ideas	✓	Word Choice
	Organization	✓	Sentence Fluency
✓	Voice		Conventions

WG Writing and Grammar Platinum Level

Students will find additional instruction on revising an autobiographical narrative in Chapter 4, Section 4.

Tips for Using Technology in Writing

Point out to students that there are several ways to highlight text and incorporate comments when working with their essays on a computer. Both of the following features are available on the toolbars of common word processing programs:

- Students can highlight a passage with their mouse and then choose a different color type for that passage. They might use this feature to highlight passages in which emotions are most intense, sentences that they want to revise for stronger word choice, or passages that peer reviewers have questioned.
- Students can also use the feature on many word processing programs that inserts comments, ideas, or even changes at specific parts in their drafts. They can then continue with their drafting and revising and return to these points later on to decide whether to make changes or revert to the original text.

Developing Your Style

Vivid Word Choice

Word Choice Mark Twain once said, "The difference between the almost right word and the right word is the difference between the lightning bug and the lightning." In narrating an experience, you are trying to re-create reality by using nothing but *words*. Fortunately, the English language is full of juicy, quirky, luminous, and pinpoint-exact words. Take the time to find them, instead of settling for words that vaguely sketch your meaning.

Vague and dull: The dog chased her tennis ball behind the sofa and brought it out.

Specific and colorful: The terrier scurried behind the sofa and emerged with a frayed tennis ball wedged between her jaws.

Finding More Active Verbs You will take your biggest step toward improving your word choice if you make an effort to use more precise, vivid, and active verbs. Some writers use "general" verbs such as *walk, run, do, say,* and *is*. Whenever you find such a verb in one of your sentences, replace it with a verb that creates a clearer picture or expresses a stronger attitude.

Look for verbs that . . .	Dull, general verbs	Livelier/sharper verbs
→ create a picture	ran	*hurtled, bolted, scurried, dashed, scooted*
→ express an attitude or emotion	say	*complain, assert, argue, retort, whisper, holler*

Find It in Your Reading Read or review the selection from *Sundiata: An Epic of Old Mali* on page 132.

1. Find three sentences that describe the Sundiata in precise terms. Identify the words that strike you as most vivid in these sentences.
2. Choose the section of the story that you find most memorable, and point out three examples of words that appeal to your senses.

Apply It to Your Writing Review the draft of your autobiographical narrative. For each paragraph in your draft, follow these steps:

1. Underline sentences that describe scenes, people, and actions.
2. Circle any words in these sentences that strike you as lively and exact.
3. Look at the underlined sentences with *no* circled words. Improve them by replacing vague or colorless words with more vivid expressions. Set a goal to have at least one circled word in every descriptive sentence.

WG *Prentice Hall Writing and Grammar Connection: Platinum Level, Chapter 1.*

Developing Your Style

- Give students some additional examples of sentences in which vague and dull words have been replaced with specific and colorful ones. Here are some examples:
  - 1a. On a hot day in July, the man walked slowly down the sidewalk.
  - 1b. On a scorching July day, Mr. Stevens strolled down the sidewalk.
  - 2a. Julie angrily pushed the paper toward me.
  - 2b. Julie furiously shoved the paper toward me.
  - 3a. The flooding river ran through the town.
  - 3b. The rampaging river gushed through the town.

  Encourage students to suggest other vivid words.
- Emphasize to students that the most intense word is not necessarily the best choice. Students must find words that accurately reflect the shade of meaning that their writing needs. Although a thesaurus can be helpful in choosing more precise, vivid words, emphasize the importance of checking a dictionary before using an unfamiliar word to ensure that it is an appropriate choice.
- If students are having difficulty writing with vivid words and active verbs, have them work on **Find It in Your Reading** in small groups or as a whole class. Tell students to pay special attention to the underlined words in the selection, such as *fathom, taciturn,* and *malicious.*

WG Writing and Grammar Platinum Level

Students will find additional instruction on vivid word choices in Chapter 8, Section 4.

Differentiated Instruction
Solutions for All Learners

Strategies for Special Needs Students

Review with students how verbs function and how to identify them in sentences. You might use the example sentences in the notes above. Then ask students to make up sentences. Help them identify the verbs. Point out overused verbs, discuss why they are vague or dull, and show students how to use a thesaurus to find more precise and vivid words. Then, have students work in pairs to review their narratives and to find and replace dull and vague verbs.

Strategies for English Learners

Invite volunteers to provide sample sentences from their narratives. Discuss the word choices, pointing out dull and vague words. Then, guide students in using a thesaurus to find alternative words that are precise and vivid. Explain that although the thesaurus lists synonyms of words, the meanings are not exactly the same, and often the connotations suggest a different feeling or idea. Emphasize that students need to check the definitions of possible words in a dictionary to make sure they are entirely appropriate for the context.

Student Model

- Explain that the student model is a sample and that narratives may be longer.
- After students have read the model, point out that Sarah has centered her narrative on an event that happened during a summer excursion. This may give students ideas for topics of their own.
- Have students identify the details Sarah uses to set the scene. Then, have them list specific details regarding time and place for their own narratives.
- Point out that Sarah uses clear and precise language to describe how she became stuck. Explain that this language helps Sarah express the frustration she felt at the time.
- **Ask** students how the exchange between Sarah and her mother enriches the story.
  Possible response: The dialogue helps the reader become more involved in the story's events and the characters' feelings.
- Help students recognize that in the final lines, Sarah recalls the purpose of the story—to describe a lesson learned—and summarizes this lesson in simple yet poignant language.

Writing Genres

Autobiographical Narratives in the Real World Explain that college applications frequently request personal essays that are autobiographical in nature. Tell students that speakers, authors, and other professionals are often asked to provide autobiographical sketches for use in spoken introductions and in written materials such as book jackets, Web sites, or company brochures.

Writing Workshop

Student Model: Sarah Beck, Harrison, TN

My Underground Experience

A few years ago, when I was fourteen, I got stuck in a hole that my cousin and I dug. It was the middle of summer in beautiful Mancelona, Michigan. Woodpeckers were yammering away, the dogs were chasing chipmunks, and my cousin and I were out exploring thiry-two acres of woods.

Sarah provides specific details that establish the time and place of the incident she is describing.

Ashley and I had come upon a fox den, not uncommon in the area. Somehow, we got it into our heads to build an "underground house" of our own, in a clearing near the house. For a good half-hour or more we dug, every now and then testing its depth. First it was up to our knees, then our waists, and finally our chests. I was a bit jealous that Ashley could crawl in backward and pull her knees up to her chest and then get out again.

I crawled in and tried to pull my knees up, but I could not. I crawled in again, this time with my knees already up, and I slid right in. I then attempted to crawl back out, to no avail. I tried moving my knees to inch out, but I was stuck. I tried pushing on the side of the hill, but still nothing happened.

Sarah creates a clear sequence relating how she became stuck.

"Ash, help me. Get me out!" I yelled, half-angrily. She grabbed my wrists and began to pull her hardest, while I tried to make myself smaller. I was still stuck fast. I yelled for her to get my mom, fast.

One minute, then two, passed. Ashley reappeared with Mom walking slowly behind, carrying a wooden spoon and a shovel. When Mom saw my predicament, she started to laugh. "I should have brought the camera."

"I would burn the picture!" I sobbed. "Just get me out of here."

Sarah adds dialogue to capture both the humor and frustration of the moment.

Mom tried to pull me out. One knee almost slid out, but my left leg was still stuck. It felt as though my joints would pop. My grandmother volunteered to get our neighbor, Dan, who lived almost a quarter mile away. Mom grabbed the shovel and told me to cover my head while she used it. It was then that I realized that I was sliding farther into the hole.

Mom began shoveling out a ramp for my knees. Just as I was finally pulled out, Dan walked up. The first words out of his mouth were, "Sarah, this is the stupidest thing I've ever seen you do." He had known me for a long time. I tried standing up but fell right back down. I had little circulation in my legs for more than thirty minutes. Grandmother and Mom helped me get to the porch until I could stand.

Mom told me to thank Dan for coming anyway, so I wobbled over to give him my thanks. "Thank goodness you didn't go in head first," he replied. His eyes said, "You're welcome." Mom then told me to fill in the hole. I did this very well. For a while, I was in pain and afraid to go to sleep. What did I learn? Never dig a hole and climb in after.

Sarah concludes her narrative with a terse statement of what she has learned.

Editing and Proofreading

Read your narrative and correct errors in grammar, usage, punctuation, and spelling.

Focus on Proofreading: Read your revised version line by line. Use a ruler or a sheet of paper to help you focus on one line at a time. Mark any errors you find in a different color from the one you used in writing. Make any corrections neatly. If you are working with a word processor, print a clean final copy.

Publishing and Presenting

Consider the following activities to share your writing with a wider audience:

Make an oral presentation. Before you read your work aloud, mark up a copy of it, underlining words to be emphasized and starring points at which you will pause or change your tone of voice.

Create an illustrated anthology. Combine your narrative with those of several classmates. Put them in a single binder. Illustrate each narrative with artwork or photographs that capture the mood of the written work.

Reflecting on Your Writing

Writer's Journal Write a few notes describing the experience of writing an autobiographical narrative. Begin by answering the following questions:

- What did you learn from the experience itself? What did you learn from writing about the experience?
- If you could turn your nonfiction narrative into a work of fiction or a movie, what would you change?

WG *Prentice Hall Writing and Grammar Connection: Platinum Level, Chapter 4*

Rubric for Self-Assessment

Evaluate your autobiographical narrative *using the following criteria and rating scale, or, with your classmates, determine your own reasonable evaluation criteria.*

NC Criteria	Rating Scale				
	not very				*very*
Focus: How clearly do you establish yourself as the main character?	1	2	3	4	5
Organization: How well is the sequence of events organized?	1	2	3	4	5
Support/Elaboration: How well do you use specific details to communicate the significance of your experience?	1	2	3	4	5
Style: How well do you use dialogue to establish characters?	1	2	3	4	5
Conventions: How correct is your use of grammar and spelling?	1	2	3	4	5

Tips for Test Taking

Remind students that when they take a test that calls for narrative writing, they will be scored on how well they execute several basic elements.

First, narratives will be scored on organization. Because narrative writing tells a story, it should be organized chronologically and use clear transitions that show the relationship between events over time.

Second, narratives may be scored on whether students provide sufficient background information about the characters and setting.

Third, narratives will be assessed on how well they focus on and develop a central conflict that leads to a climax and a resolution.

Encourage students to create mnemonic devices to help them remember the basic elements of narrative writing. Here is an example: *Clouds Tend to Bring in Cold, Chilly Rain* (chronological, transitions, background information, conflict, climax, resolution).

Editing and Proofreading

- List common errors that students should look for as they proofread, such as incorrect verb tense, incorrectly punctuated dialogue, and dull language. Work with students to devise a checklist for grammar, usage, punctuation, and spelling.
- Tell students to proofread by reading sentence by sentence from the end of the paper to the beginning. This strategy forces them to focus on the grammar rather than the meaning of the paper.

Six Traits Focus

	Ideas	✓	Word Choice
	Organization	✓	Sentence Fluency
	Voice	✓	Conventions

ASSESS

Publishing and Presenting

- Encourage students to create visual images, such as a mural or illustrations, to use to help them set the scene for their oral presentations. They might also play recorded music that helps create an appropriate mood and tone.
- If students do not have photographs of the actual events described in their narratives, they can create illustrations of scenes that symbolize important story elements.

Reflecting on Your Writing

- Invite students to explore other reactions to the writing process. Ask, What part of writing an autobiographical narrative was most challenging for you? What part was most rewarding?

WG **Writing and Grammar Platinum Level**

Students will find additional instruction on editing and proofreading and publishing and presenting an autobiographical narrative in Chapter 4, Sections 5 and 6.

Standard Course of Study

GU.6.01.2 Analyze author's use of language to demonstrate understanding.

GU.6.02.2 Edit for appropriate and correct mechanics.

Know Your Terms: Recalling Information

Explain that the terms listed under Terms to Learn will be used in standardized-testing situations when students are asked to recall information from a reading passage.

Terms to Learn

- Review *define* and *definition.* Tell students that a definition is the essential meaning. When defining a term, suggest that students ask themselves, "What is . . . ?" For example, "What is indirect characterization?" or "What is an archetype?" The reading passage on which they base their definition may provide many details; point out that students need to focus on the essential meaning, not the details.
- Review *identify.* Point out to students that identification is a process of pointing out or selecting. When students are asked to identify an error in usage or identify a character or other textual feature, they are being asked to point out something specific.

ASSESS

Answers

1. *Oral tradition* means handing down literature by word of mouth.
2. Three types of oral traditions in Africa can include any of these forms: epic narratives, jokes, proverbs, riddles, praise poems, genealogies, oratory, and healing chants.
3. A "griot" is a storyteller.
4. *were* should be *was*
5. B

SAT® PREP ACT

Vocabulary Workshop

High-Frequency Academic Words

High-frequency academic words are words that appear often in textbooks and on standardized tests. Although you may already know the meaning of many of these words, they usually have a more specific meaning when they are used in textbooks and on tests.

Standard Course of Study

- Analyze author's use of language to demonstrate understanding. (GU.6.01.2)
- Edit for agreement, tense choice, pronouns, antecedents, case, and complete sentences. (GU.6.02.1)

Know Your Terms: Recalling Information

Each of the following words is a verb that tells you to show that you remember and understand the significance of the information in the text. These words indicate the type of information you should provide in your answer.

Terms to Learn

Define Tell the specific qualities or features that make something what it is.

Sample test item: ***Define*** indirect characterization.

Sample test item: What is the ***definition*** of archetype?

Identify Name or show that you recognize something.

Sample test item: In the following sentence, ***identify*** the error in usage.

Practice

Directions: *Read the following passage. Items 1–3 refer to this passage.*

Africa has a rich oral tradition, in which a broad array of literary forms have been handed down by word of mouth from generation to generation. Oral literature in Africa runs the gamut from epic narratives to jokes, riddles, praise poems, genealogies, oratory, healing chants, and—that most concise, epigrammatic form of all—proverbs. A key figure in the oral tradition of many societies is the griot (grē′ ō). The griot, or storyteller, traditionally holds a place of honor in the culture, for it is he who is charged with the official retelling of events from history, with the praises of the ruler, and with the skillful retelling of poems, riddles, proverbs, and folk tales.

1. On a separate piece of paper, *define* "oral tradition," basing your response on information in the passage.
2. *Identify* three types of literature in the oral tradition in Africa.
3. On a separate piece of paper, *define* "griot."
4. Read the following sentence, and *identify* the usage error.

   Control of the profitable salt and gold trade were the main focus of struggles among rival kings nearly one thousand years ago in the West African region.

5. The usage error in the sentence is

   A trade **C** focus
   B were **D** among

Tips for Test Taking

- When students are asked to choose the best definition of a term on multiple-choice tests, they may find that the best definition synthesizes information. Students should examine the possible answers for the one that most clearly and concisely includes all the essential elements of the meaning.
- Also, tell students that the definition they choose should correspond to the part of speech of the word being defined.
- If asked to identify an error in usage, students may wish to read the sentences aloud quietly and try to hear what sounds incorrect or does not make sense.

Go Online Vocabulary **For:** An Interactive Crossword Puzzle
Visit: www.PHSchool.com
Web Code: etj-5101

This crossword puzzle contains vocabulary that reflects the concepts in Unit 1. After students have completed Unit 1, give students the Web Code and have them complete the crossword puzzle.

Critical Reading: Conventions of Grammar and Language Usage

On the writing sections of some tests, you may be required to show your knowledge of the conventions of standard written English. Use the following strategies to help you answer test questions about punctuation, grammar, usage, and sentence structure.

- Identify errors in a sentence by quietly reading the sentence aloud. Mistakes that you might not notice when you read a sentence silently will often sound wrong when you hear them.
- Be alert to common mistakes, such as confusing *its* and *it's* or *who* and *whom.* Make sure that verbs agree with their subjects. Watch for unclear antecedents for pronouns.
- Learn to recognize and avoid structural errors, such as run-on sentences, sentence fragments, and misplaced modifiers.

 **Standard Course of Study**

- GU.6.01.1
- GU.6.02.1
- GU.6.02.2

Practice

A. Directions: *Read the sentence, and then choose the letter of the best answer to the question.*

The Romans adopted many of the Greek gods, they changed the names.

1. Which of the following choices is the best revision of the underlined words?

A gods. They changed the names.

B gods, but they changed the names.

C gods, and they changed the names.

D correct as is

B. Directions: *Read the passage, and then choose the letter of the best answer to the question.*

(1) Like giants, pygmies, and griffins, centaurs were monsters of Greek myth. (2) A centaur was a man from head through torso, and a horse in the lower part of his body. (3) Because the Greeks admired horses, they assigned centaurs many admirable traits, and unlike the other monsters in Greek myth, centaurs were often admitted to the company of humans. (4) When Chiron, the wisest of the centaurs, died, Zeus placed him in the constellation Sagittarius.

2. Which sentence contains an error in punctuation?

A 1 **C** 3

B 2 **D** 4

Test-Taking Strategies

- When you need to identify errors in a passage, remember that there may be more than one error in each item.
- Choose the answer that corrects *all* of the errors in an item.

 **Standard Course of Study**

GU.6.01.1 Employ varying sentence structures and sentence types.

GU.6.02.1 Edit for agreement, tense choice, pronouns, antecedents, case, and complete sentences.

GU.6.02.2 Edit for appropriate and correct mechanics.

Critical Reading

- Remind students to be cautious as they read to see whether a sentence sounds correct. Sometimes overfamiliarity with nonstandard forms may make a sentence sound correct when it is really incorrect.
- Remind students that *its* is possessive and *it's* is a contraction for *it is.* If they can substitute *it is* in place of the word, they should use the contraction. Also remind them that English does not contain the construction *its'.*
- Although it is probably clear to many students that *who* is subjective and *whom* is objective, point out this one confusing instance: "The board members will award scholarships to *whoever* they think merits them." Explain that despite following the preposition *to, whoever* is the subject of the dependent clause and therefore should not be changed to *whomever.* The entire clause, not the pronoun alone, is the object of the preposition
- Point out that every sentence should make sense. If a sentence lacks a subject or a verb or is not a complete thought, it contains an error.
- After students have read the practice passages and have answered the questions, point out that in question 1, A, B, and C are correct sentences, but B is the best answer because it shows the relationship between both parts of the sentence.
- Point out that in question 2, B is the correct answer. Sentence 2 does not need the comma because the sentence is not a compound sentence.

Tips for Test Taking

Remind students that although several answer choices on a standardized test may be technically correct, they must select the best choice. In such instances, tell them that they have to go beyond mere correctness and look for the answer that contains the most accurate relationship between the sentence parts. Tell them also that even though they may be used to placing extra commas in their writing, a comma that divides the two parts of a compound subject, verb, or object is considered incorrect usage.

ASSESS

Answers

1. B
2. B

Standard Course of Study

IR.2.01.11 Identify and analyze information in light of purpose, audience, and context.

IR.2.02.3 Use transitions to make logical connections.

Organizing Content

- Remind students that the goal of a speech is to communicate a main idea to the audience. Encourage students to identify their main ideas early in the speech-writing process and then state these main ideas at least twice during the speech.
- Draw students' attention to the sample index cards on p. 160. Explain that the index cards utilize an outline format in which each main idea is discussed on a separate card.
- Point out that some audiences require more background information than others. For example, if a student is speaking to classmates about a childhood experience at Nannie's house, the audience will need to be told who Nannie is. If the speech were being given at a family wedding, the audience would know Nannie's identity.
- Remind students to keep the audience in mind as they organize and pace their speeches and as they fine-tune their word choices.

Giving the Speech

- Have students rehearse their speeches with partners. Ask partners to provide positive and negative feedback. After students make adjustments, have partners give "dress rehearsals" for each other before the actual event.
- Tell students to become so familiar with their speeches that their index cards serve as safety nets rather than crutches. Emphasize the importance of eye contact.

Assess the Activity

To evaluate students' delivery, use the Peer Assessment: Speech rubric, p. 129 in ***General Resources.***

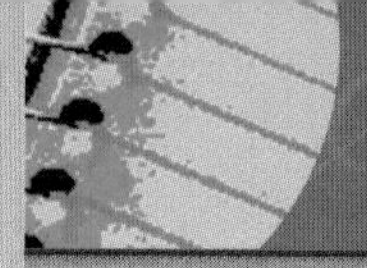

Delivering a Speech

Whether you are comparing translations of *The Epic of Gilgamesh,* recounting an anecdote from your childhood, or persuading your peers to get involved in a political campaign, giving a speech can be an effective way to share your ideas. Whatever the topic or goal, follow these strategies to **organize and deliver an effective speech.**

Standard Course of Study

- Identify and analyze information in light of purpose, audience, and context. (IR.2.01.11)
- Use transitions to make logical connections. (IR.2.02.3)

Organizing Content

Take time to develop and organize the content of your speech.

Focus on purpose. Ask yourself what your goal is in giving the speech—whether to persuade, to entertain, or to inform. Formulate your purpose clearly and in detail. Keep this all-important purpose in mind as you organize the structure and content of your speech.

Consider your audience. Be aware of the background and interests of your audience as you develop your speech. A speech about the future of computers, for example, would be very different for a general audience than it would be for an audience of computer programmers. Your style and tone, your word choice and details, and the examples you choose will vary depending on the audience. If you are discussing a topic that may be intimidating, consider beginning with an anecdote or a joke.

Craft the speech. Organize your speech. Use an informal outline, perhaps by writing your main ideas on numbered index cards. Rewrite until you are satisfied that your speech is engaging and clear.

I. Need for a Student Cafeteria Committee
A. Purpose
B. Needs
C. Examples from other schools

II. Benefits of a Cafeteria Committee
A. Advantages for students
B. Advantages for cafeteria management
C. Possible complications

III. Establishing the Committee
A. Election of members
B. Responsibilities
C. Coordinating with cafeteria management

Giving the Speech

Effective speakers know what they want to say and how to say it.

- Rehearse aloud and listen to your words; revise awkward language. Become familiar with any visual aids that you plan to use.
- Memorize the main ideas of your speech. Refer as little as possible to your notes so that you can make eye contact with your audience.
- Make sure that your listeners can hear you, and don't race through your speech. If you think you may be talking too fast, you probably are.

Activity *Prepare and Deliver a Speech* Prepare, rehearse, and deliver a three-minute speech on a topic and for a purpose and an audience of your choice. Ask your classmates for feedback to improve your performance, and respond to any questions they might have.

Differentiated Instruction Solutions for All Learners

Strategy for Less Proficient Readers
Provide students with a tape recorder and cassette tape. After students finish writing their speeches, have them take turns recording their own speeches. As they hear themselves speaking on tape, tell students to listen for places where they had difficulty reading their work. Have them record themselves again as needed, in order to focus on speaking smoothly and clearly. Ask partners to also listen to the tapes and give feedback.

Strategy for English Learners
Explain to students that they do not need to memorize their speeches; they can refer to their index cards as they speak. Remind students that speaking slowly and clearly is the best way for all speakers to ensure their audience's understanding. Have students take turns reading their speeches to partners. Partners should provide feedback that helps students present clear, precise speeches.

Suggestions for Further Reading

Featured Titles:

The Bible's Greatest Stories

Paul Roche, *translator and reteller, Signet Classic, 2001*

Scripture The stories of Noah and the flood and of Ruth's loyalty to Naomi are only two of the many classic Bible tales related in this comprehensive collection. In this publication, translator and reteller Paul Roche includes maps of Palestine and the Greco-Roman world to help readers place major events that occur in the stories. Introductory material links related tales while, at the same time, making them accessible to today's readers. All the themes of great literature can be found in these stories: love, honor, war, pride, celebration, and death. These themes emerge in dramatic episodes—such as the birth of Moses or the story of Joseph's coat of many colors—gathered from such biblical books as Genesis, the four Gospels, and Acts of the Apostles.

Tales of Ancient Egypt

Selected and retold by Roger Lancelyn Green, *Puffin Classic, 1996*

Fables Ancient Egypt is a land of fables. In *Tales of Ancient Egypt,* Roger Lancelyn Green retells twenty of these stories. Some are as close to us as our own childhoods—"The Girl with the Red-Rose Slippers," for instance, is the earliest version of the Cinderella story. Others, such as the story of how the goddess Isis tricked the god Ra, give glimpses of faraway ancient beliefs—beliefs in the power of names and in a person's immortal double. Discovered carved in temple walls or written on papyrus scrolls, some of these tales explain why a particular monument was built. Others tell of life's fundamentals—of love, of the desire to be remembered, of the struggle for justice. In these tales, readers will encounter some familiar themes; they may also rediscover the strange scent of mystery that makes tales from the past so fascinating.

Work Presented in Unit One:

If sampling a portion of the following text has built your interest, treat yourself to the full work.

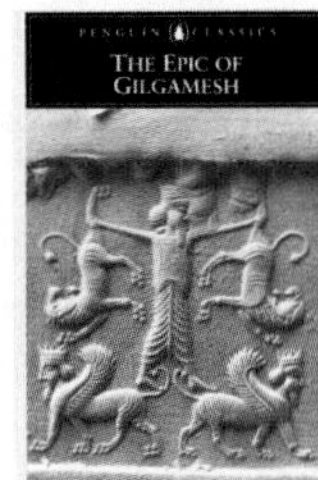

The Epic of Gilgamesh

Anonymous, *translated by N. K. Sandars, Penguin Classic, 1960*

Related British Literature:

Early Irish Myths and Sagas

Anonymous, *translated by Jeffrey Gantz, Penguin Classic, 1982*

Mythology The Celtic people who told the stirring tales in this book lived at about the same time as the ancient Mesopotamians, Egyptians, and Hebrews.

Related American Literature:

The Conquest of New Spain

Bernal Díaz del Castillo, *translated by J. M. Cohen, Penguin Classic, 1963*

Historical Nonfiction The author provides a vivid firsthand account of how the Spaniard Hernán Cortés conquered the Aztecs, one of the ancient people of Mexico.

***Many of these titles are available in the* Prentice Hall/Penguin Literature Library.**
Consult your teacher before choosing one.

Planning Students' Further Reading

Discussions of literature can raise sensitive and often controversial issues. Before you recommend further reading to your students, consider the values and sensitivities of your community as well as the age, ability, and sophistication of your students. It is also good policy to preview literature before you recommend it to students. The notes below offer some guidance on specific titles.

The Bible's Greatest Stories, translated by Paul Roche

These tales include depictions of violence, portray subjugated women and peoples, and refer to rape and incest. To prepare students to read these tales, discuss their setting and didactic purpose.

Lexile: Appropriate for high school students

Tales of Ancient Egypt

These tales include brief depictions of violence and magic, as well as references to drunkenness and to wine and beer. Religiously ordained marriages between brother and sister gods or rulers are also mentioned.

Lexile: Appropriate for high school students

The Epic of Gilgamesh

Battle scenes are graphically described, and, in one case, men attempt to appease Gilgamesh by "giving" him a woman.

Lexile: 1100L

Early Irish Myths and Sages

These myths and sagas include graphic descriptions of violence. They also include references to sexual relations, intimate body parts, pregnancy, incest, and drunkenness, as well as to the magic of druids.

Lexile: Appropriate for high school students

The Conquest of New Spain, by Bernal Díaz del Castillo

This classic record of cultural encounter includes accounts of human sacrifice and ritual cannibalism, as well as violence, torture, slavery, and prejudice. To prepare students to understand these elements, discuss the historical and cultural context.

Lexile: Appropriate for high school students

Standard Course of Study

- **WL.1.01.3** Move effectively between past and present in a reminiscence.
- **WL.1.02.5** Demonstrate an understanding of media's impact on analyses and personal reflection.
- **IR.2.01.7** Analyze influences, contexts, or biases in research texts.
- **CT.4.03.2** Analyze how writers choose and incorporate significant, supporting, details.

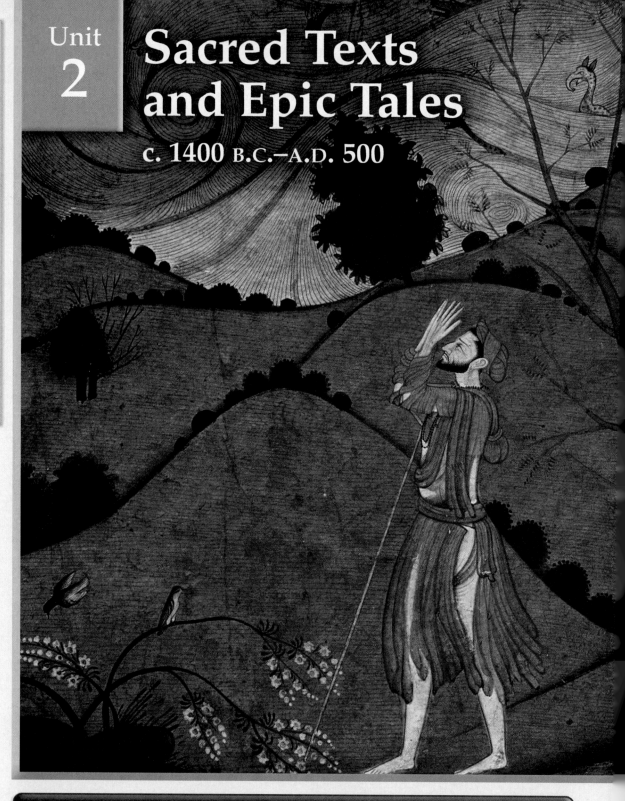

Unit 2 Sacred Texts and Epic Tales

c. 1400 B.C.–A.D. 500

Unit Instructional Resources

In *Unit 2 Resources,* you will find materials to support students in developing and mastering the unit skills and to help you assess their progress.

Vocabulary and Reading

Additional vocabulary and reading support, based on Lexile scores of vocabulary words, is provided for each selection or grouping.

- **Word Lists A and B** and **Practices A and B** provide vocabulary-building activities for students reading two grades or one grade below level, respectively.
- **Reading Warm-ups A and B,** for students reading two grades or one grade below level, respectively, consist of short readings and activities that provide a context and practice for newly learned vocabulary.

Selection Support

- Reading Strategy
- Literary Analysis
- Vocabulary Builder
- Grammar and Style
- Support for Writing
- Support for Extend Your Learning
- Enrichment

You may also access these resources at TeacherExpress.

Assessment Resources

Listed below are the resources available to assess and measure students' progress in meeting the unit objectives and your state standards.

Skills Assessment

Unit 2 Resources
- Selection Tests A and B

TeacherExpress™
- *ExamView®* Test Bank Software

Adequate Yearly Progress Assessment

Unit 2 Resources
- Benchmark Test 2

Standardized Assessment

Standardized Test Preparation Workbook

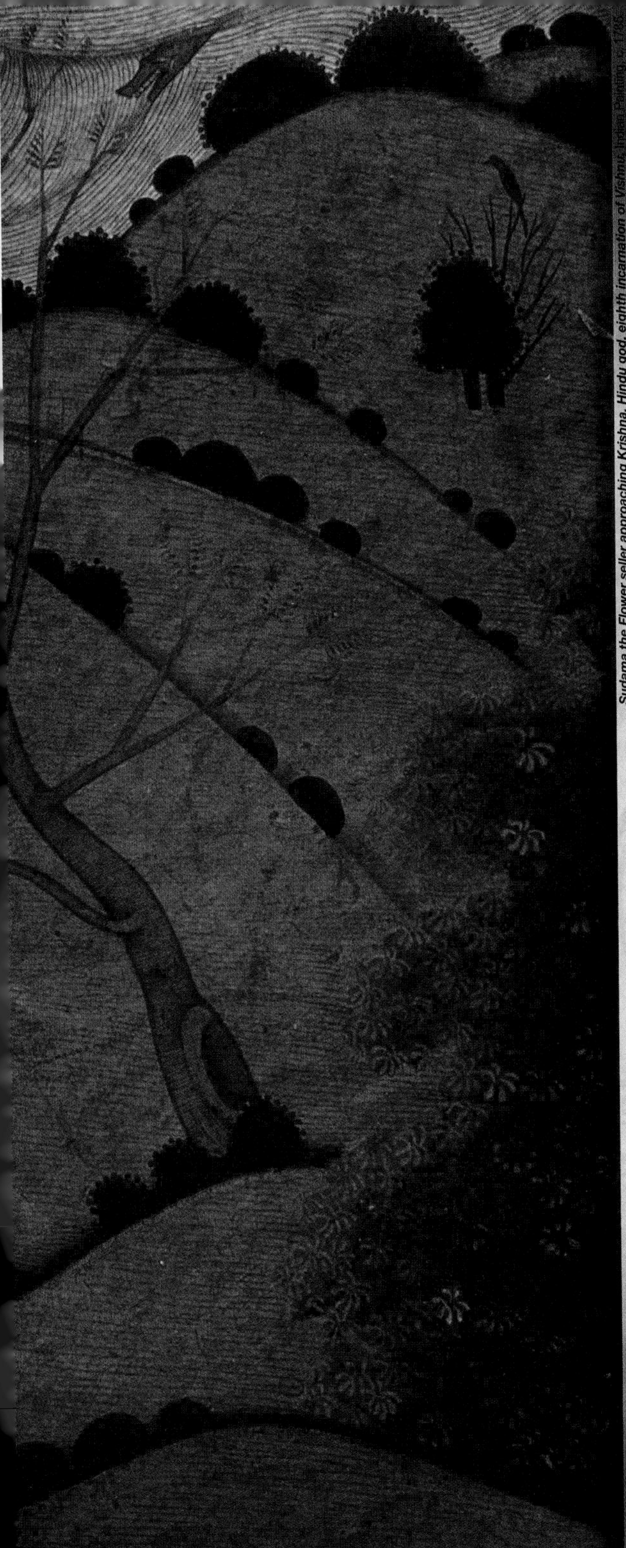

Sudama the Flower seller approaching Krishna, Hindu god, eighth incarnation of Vishnu, Indian Painting, c. 1785

Indian Literature

Standard Course of Study
In This Unit You Will

- Produce reminiscences that use specific and sensory details with purpose. (WL.1.01.1)
- Explain how culture affects personal responses. (WL.1.02.4)
- Prioritize and organize information to construct an explanation to answer a question. (IR.2.03.2)
- Build knowledge of literary genres, and explore how characteristics apply to literature of world cultures. (LT.5.01.2)
- Analyze literary devices and explain their effect on the work. (LT.5.01.3)
- Analyze archetypal characters, themes, and settings in world literature. (LT.5.01.5)
- Understand the cultural and historical impact on text. (LT.5.01.7)
- Use language effectively to create mood and tone. (GU.6.01.7)

◄ This painting shows Sudama, a school friend of the Hindu god Krishna, who took human form. In Hinduism, the story of Sudama and Krishna is often used to illustrate Krishna's loyalty and unconditional love.

Introduce Unit 2

- Direct students' attention to the title and time period of this unit. Have a student read the quotation. **Ask** students: What does this quotation suggest about Indian literature?
  Possible response: The quotation suggests that Indian literature contains masterpieces whose influence extended to people across time and culture.
- Have students look at the art. Read the Humanities note to them, and ask the discussion question.
- Then **ask:** What kinds of literature or themes in literature do you think might come out of this period of Indian history?
  Possible response: The literature may include stories about Hindu deities and how these deities interact with people.

Humanities

Indian Painting

Painted about 1785, this image depicts a scene from a Hindu folk tale. According to the folk tale, Sudama and Krishna were best friends as children. Sudama, now a poor man, approaches the grand palace of Krishna, now a king, to ask his old friend for help to support his family. Krishna is one of the most popular and widely worshipped Hindu gods, and is known for his love and compassion for poor and suffering people.

Use the following question for discussion:

What role does the sky play in this painting?
Possible response: The pink sky and swirling clouds are filled with animals, who appear to be facing toward the palace. This may suggest that Sudama is entering into the realm of the divine and that something special awaits Sudama.

Unit Features

Wendy Doniger

Each unit features commentary by a contemporary writer or scholar under the heading "From the Translator's Desk." Scholar Wendy Doniger introduces Unit 2 in Setting the Scene, in which she discusses the influence that ancient Indian literature has had on her life and basic human questions addressed in this literature to which all people can relate. Later in the unit, she introduces selections from the *Rig Veda.* In the Writing Workshop, she discusses how she uses word choice to emphasize a serious point in her writing.

Connections

Every unit contains a feature that connects literature to a related topic, such as art, science, or history. In this unit, students will read James Thurber's "The Tiger Who Would Be King" on p. 230.

Use the information and questions on the Connections pages to help students enrich their understanding of the selections presented within the unit.

Reading Informational Materials

These selections will help students learn to analyze and evaluate informational texts, such as workplace documents, technical directions, and consumer materials. They will expose students to the organization and features unique to nonnarrative texts.

In this unit, the focus is on atlases and maps. A map of India appears on p. 234.

From the Translator's Desk

Introduce Wendy Doniger

- Wendy Doniger, an expert in mythology, world religion, and Hindu literature, introduces the unit and provides insight into the literature of early India. Her commentary about her translation of the *Rig Veda* appears later in the unit on pages 176–177.
- Have students read the introductory paragraph about Wendy Doniger. Tell them that, in addition to translating the *Rig Veda,* she translated 395 French articles called *Mythologies.*
- Use the ***From the Author's Desk DVD*** to introduce Wendy Doniger. Show Segment 1 to provide insight into her scholarly career. After students have watched the segment, **ask:** What other types of writing has Doniger done besides translating? **Answer:** She has written articles and is working on a novel.

Ancient Indian Literature

- Have students read Doniger's commentary on why she was drawn to ancient Indian literature. Point out that all major world religions address similar metaphysical questions to the ones that haunted Doniger as an adolescent. **Ask:** Why do you think that humans feel the need to answer such questions? **Possible response:** Like Doniger, people feel a need to make sense out of their lives and their experiences especially experiences that shape or define human life.
- Tell students that they will also read Wendy Doniger's introduction to the selections from her translation of the *Rig Veda* later in this unit. Doniger will explain the difficulty of translating a hymn from the *Rig Veda.*

Critical Viewing

Answer: In both cases, Arjuna appears calm as he goes into battle, and Arjuna's army is shown in the background. In the painting on this page of the student book, Krishna and the horses appear to be charging into battle; in the other painting, Krishna and the horses appear as calm as Arjuna does. In the painting on this page of the student book, the only soldiers shown are Arjuna's; the other painting shows the opposing soldiers.

Setting the Scene

Unit 2 features writing from India's earliest literary tradition. In the following essay, scholar and translator Wendy Doniger talks about how she became interested in Indian literature—and in particular, a collection of ancient Hindu writings called the *Rig Veda.* As you read her essay, the unit introduction that follows, and the literature in Unit 2, enjoy the richness of Indian culture and the beauty of these texts.

From the Translator's Desk
Wendy Doniger Talks About the Time Period

Wendy Doniger

Introducing Wendy Doniger (b. 1940) Born in New York, Doniger is an expert on mythology, world religion, and Hindu literature, with a special interest in the role that gender plays. She is not only a scholar but also a translator of mythological texts.

Why I Was Drawn to Ancient Indian Literature

I first became fascinated by ancient Indian literature when I read a book of Hindu philosophical texts called the Upanishads when I was about fifteen, in 1955. As the child of relentlessly secular[1] Jewish refugees who had come to America to escape the pogroms in Russia[2] and the Nazis in Vienna, I wasn't allowed to be interested in religion. But I *was,* sneaking out to hang out in churches the way other kids snuck out to commit the more traditional sins of adolescence.

▼ Critical Viewing
Compare and contrast this painting with the one on page 202, which shows the same scene from the *Mahabharata.* **[Compare and Contrast]**

Discussing Unanswerable Questions
I was haunted by the great metaphysical questions: How did the universe begin? Why are we here? What is the purpose of human life? When I discovered the Upanishads, I felt that I had come home (although to someone else's home), that here was a religion that had what I longed for—a discussion of the unanswerable questions that

1. **secular** (sek′ yə lər) *adj.* not religious.
2. **pogroms** (pō grämz′) *n.* mob attacks, either sponsored or condoned by the authorities, against religious or other minorities. The term is generally used to refer to the numerous attacks against Jews in Russia and Poland during the late nineteenth and early twentieth centuries.

Teaching Resources

The following resources can be used to enrich or extend the instruction for Unit 2 Introduction.

From the Author's Desk DVD
- **Wendy Doniger**, Segment 1

Unit 2 Resources
- **Unit Introduction: Names and Terms to Know,** p. 2
- **Unit Introduction: Focus Questions,** p. 3
- **Listening and Viewing,** p. 5

were already beginning to haunt me. I was hooked, and when I went off to Radcliffe College as a seventeen-year-old freshman, I majored in Sanskrit, the ancient language in which the classical Hindu texts are written. The rest is history—of religions, that is, the subject I have studied and taught ever since.

Finding Meaning Without Baggage Along the way I learned that many Americans, from the great nineteenth-century Transcendentalist philosophers Ralph Waldo Emerson and Henry Thoreau to the students in my classes, have found meaning in these texts, in part simply because they are *not* our own texts, do not have our own baggage, and in part because they say many wonderful things that our own texts do not say—or do not say in a way that is so startling and therefore so thought-provoking for us.

Recognizing Our Own Assumptions The ancient Hindu texts were composed on the other side of the world, from about 1000 B.C.E. (the *Rig Veda*) through about 400 C.E. (the *Mahabharata*), and though many of their assumptions are very different from ours—ideas about reincarnation, about the relationship between many gods and One God, about the class system (and the far more detailed caste system, which divides human beings into thousands of carefully ranked social groups)—we have much in common with them: the fear of death and the hope of knowing what happens to us when we die; a vision of the order and majesty of the universe; a need to be reassured that there is a plan and a purpose to human life on earth.

One certainly does not have to be a Hindu or believe what Hindus believe to learn something of value from these poems and prose passages—or to understand our own assumptions better by realizing what does not make sense to us in the Hindu conceptual world.

Author Link

For: An online video
Visit: www.PHSchool.com
Web Code: ete-8201

For: More about Wendy Doniger
Visit: www.PHSchool.com
Web Code: ete-9201

Reading the Unit Introduction

Reading for Information and Insight Use the following terms and questions to guide your reading of the unit introduction on pages 168–175.

Names and Terms to Know
Indus Valley
Aryans
Dravidians
Hinduism
Buddhism
Jainism
Sanskrit
Sikh

Focus Questions As you read this introduction, use what you learn to answer these questions:
- Which religions began on the Indian subcontinent?
- In what way is Hinduism a social system?
- List two or more achievements of Indian painters, sculptors, and architects.
- In what way is the concept of memory important in the literature of India?

Reading the Unit Introduction

Tell students that the terms and questions listed here are the key points in this introductory material. This information provides a context for the selections in this unit. Students should use the terms and questions as a guide to focus their reading of the unit introduction. When students have completed the unit introduction, they should be able to identify or explain each of these terms and answer or discuss the Focus Questions.

Concept Connector

After students have read the unit introduction, return to the Focus Questions to review the main points. For key points, see p. 175.

Go Online **Author Link** Typing in the Web Codes when prompted will bring students to a video clip and more information on Wendy Doniger.

Using the Timeline

The Timeline can serve a number of instructional purposes, as follows:

Getting an Overview

Use the Timeline to help students get a quick overview of themes and events of the period. This approach will benefit all students but may be especially helpful for Visual/Spatial Learners, English Learners, and Less Proficient Readers. (For strategies in using the Timeline as an overview, see the bottom of this page.)

Thinking Critically

Questions are provided on the facing page. Use these questions to have students review the events, discuss their significance, and examine the "so what" behind the "what happened."

Connecting to Selections

Have students refer to the Timeline when they begin to read individual selections. By consulting the Timeline regularly, they will gain a better sense of the period's chronology. In addition, they will appreciate world events that gave rise to these works of literature.

Projects

Students can use the Timeline as a launching pad for projects like these:

- **Literary Timeline** Have students create a timeline of both Indian and world events relating to the creation and compilation of literary texts. Then, have students look for parallels among the literary developments in various countries during the same periods.
- **Journal Entry** Have students look through the Timeline for Indian advances that have influenced the world of mathematics. Have them research the influence each advance has had. Then, ask each student to write a journal entry explaining how Indian mathematicians have had an impact on the world of mathematics.

Indian and World Events

1400 B.C. 1000 B.C. 600 B.C.

INDIAN EVENTS

- 1400 Indus Valley civilization had ended by this date.
- 1400 The Aryan migration began about 1,000 years earlier.
- c. 1000 A compilation of the Vedic hymns is made. ▼

- c. 700 This is the final date for the composition of the *Brahmanas*, texts that discuss religious rituals.
- c. 600s This is the earliest possible period for the founding of Jainism. ▼

- c. 500s This is the earliest possible period for the founding of Buddhism. ▶
- 400s Panini describes and standardizes Sanskrit in an important grammar text.
- 327 Alexander the Great invades India.
- c. 321–185 This is the period during which the Maurya emperors ruled much of India.
- c. 300 This is the earliest possible date for the composition of the *Ramayana*.
- c. 272 The Maurya emperor Asoka comes to power and rules for almost 40 years.

Buddha Standing, bronze, first half of 7th century, The Metropolitan Museum of Art

WORLD EVENTS

- 1353–1336 **(Egypt)** Akhenaton reigns and establishes the monotheistic worship of the sun-god Aton. ▶
- c. 1150 **(Mexico)** Olmecs, first major culture in Americas, are active.

- 1000–800 **(Greece)** Tribes evolve into city-states.
- mid-900s **(Israel)** King Solomon reigns over a united country.
- 800s or 700s **(Greece)** The legendary poet Homer composes the *Iliad* and the *Odyssey*. ▶
- mid-600s **(Italy)** Most of the major Etruscan towns have been established.
- 509 **(Rome)** The Roman republic is founded.
- c. 500 **(China)** The *Shih Ching* ("Classic of Poetry"), classic anthology of psalms and folk songs, is compiled.
- c. 495 **(Greece)** The great Athenian statesman Pericles is born.
- 492–449 **(Greece)** Greeks triumph in a series of wars fought against the Persian Empire.
- 479 **(China)** The philosopher Confucius dies.

Getting an Overview of the Period

Introduction To give students an overview of the period, have them indicate the span of dates in the title of the Timeline. Next, point out that the Timeline is divided into Indian Events (on the top) and World Events (on the bottom). Have students scan the Timeline, looking at both the Indian Events and the World Events. Finally, point out that the events in the Timeline often represent beginnings, turning points, and endings (for example, the earliest possible date for the composition of the *Ramayana* is 300 B.C.)

Key Events Have students identify key events in Indian literature from 1000 B.C. through A.D. 200.
Possible response: The *Brahmanas, Ramayana, Panchatantra, Bhagavad-Gita,* and *Mahabharata* were all composed during this period.

Why might the description and categorization of Sanskrit be important for Indian literature?
Possible response: Standardized written language would make it easier to compile and record literature.

200 B.C. 200 A.D. 500 A.D.

- 100 B.C. This is the earliest possible date for the composition of the *Panchatantra.*
- 100–0 B.C. The *Bhagavad-Gita* ("Divine Song") is composed; it is part of the *Mahabharata.*

- 100–0 B.C. Early Indian sculpture decorates the gateways of the Buddhist relic mound called the Great Stupa.
- 100–0 B.C. Work on the Ajanta caves begins; construction continues through the seventh century A.D. ▲

- early 300s–late 500s The Gupta dynasty rules an empire that includes northern sections of western and central India.
- late 300s–early 400s The Hindu author of an astronomical handbook tabulates the sine function.
- c. 400 The Pillar of Delhi, a solid metal column 23 feet tall and weighing more than 6 tons, is constructed.
- c. 400 The final compilation of the *Mahabharata* is made. ▼
- 400s and 500s Using the concept of zero, Indian mathematicians develop the decimal system.

- 27 B.C. **(Rome)** The Roman Empire is established.
- c. A.D. 30 **(ancient Palestine)** Jesus Christ is crucified.
- A.D. 43–85 **(Britain)** Romans conquer Britain.
- A.D. 70 **(ancient Palestine)** The temple at Jerusalem is destroyed, ending the sacrificial rituals called for in the Old Testament.
- A.D. 75–100 **(Roman Empire)** The four Gospels, which describe the life of Jesus Christ, are written; they become a significant part of the New Testament.

- 220 **(China)** Warlords overthrow the last Han emperor; Han dynasty helped establish basis for Chinese culture.
- 250 **(Mexico and Central America)** Rise of Mayan civilization begins; classic period lasts until about 900.
- c. 300 **(Africa)** Ghana emerges as a state. ▶
- c. 320 **(Rome)** From this time, Christianity is supported by the Roman Empire.
- 395 **(Rome)** The Roman Empire divides into Eastern and Western empires.
- 476 **(Rome)** The Western Roman Empire falls.

Analyzing the Timeline

1. (a) When were Jainism and Buddhism founded? (b) What might the founding of new religions suggest about people's attitudes toward Hinduism? **[Infer]**
   Answers: (a) Jainism was founded no earlier than c. 600s B.C., and Buddhism was founded no earlier than c. 500s B.C. (b) Some people might have been looking for a world view different from the one provided by Hinduism.
2. (a) When did Alexander the Great invade India? (b) What influence might this invasion have had on India? **[Analyze Causes and Effects]**
   Answers: (a) Alexander the Great invaded India in 327 B.C. (b) Alexander the Great might have brought a Greek influence to the culture and art of India.
3. (a) What cultural events took place around 100 B.C.? (b) What can you deduce about Indian society at this time, given these events? **[Deduce]**
   Answers: (a) The *Panchatantra* and the *Bhagavad-Gita* were completed, early Indian sculpture decorated the Great Stupa, and work on the Ajanta caves began. (b) These events indicate that Indian culture was beginning to develop in new directions.
4. (a) When did the Gupta dynasty reign in India? (b) What can you infer about the intellectual climate during the Gupta dynasty? **[Infer]**
   Answers: (a) The Gupta dynasty reigned from the early 300s to the late 500s. (b) The dynasty encouraged learning and thinking, especially in mathematics.
5. (a) What great Greek epic poems were composed during the 800s or 700s B.C.? (b) What conclusions can you draw about literature on the basis of what is happening throughout the world before 0 B.C.? **[Draw Conclusions]**
   Answers: (a) Homer composed the *Iliad* and the *Odyssey.* (b) Many civilizations were developing and compiling their literature.

Critical Viewing

1. Why might the Hindu artist have surrounded Vishnu with other deities (1000 B.C.)? **[Speculate]**
   Possible response: Vishnu is one of the main deities in Hinduism.
2. Compare and contrast the statue of Buddha (c. 500s B.C.) with the portrait of Vishnu (c. 1000 B.C.). **[Compare and Contrast]**
   Possible response: The portrait of the Buddha is much less ornate. Nothing detracts from him, and he does not appear to be the center of anything.
3. What does the African carving (c. 300) suggest about the culture that created it? **[Infer]**
   Possible response: The culture that created the carving valued attention to detail and skilled craftsmanship.

Literature of the Period

- In the "Creation Hymn" and "Night," pp. 180–182, students will experience the devotion and piety found in the *Rig Veda.*
- Sacrifices to the gods are described in India's epic poems, the *Mahabharata* and the *Ramayana,* found on pp. 192 and 208.
- Animal fables are also part of the Indian literature of this period. "Numskull and the Rabbit" from the *Panchatantra* appears on p. 222.

Humanities

Show students Art Transparency 23: *Autumn Leaves, No. 2,* in the **Fine Art Transparencies** booklet. Have students discuss what O'Keeffe's painting shares with the philosophies presented in the *Rig Veda.*

Themes in World Literature

Point/Counterpoint

Was There an Aryan Invasion of India? Point out to students that because of a lack of historical records, historians must sometimes use artifacts and linguistic evidence to draw conclusions about a particular time.

1. What do these two viewpoints have in common?
   Possible response: Both mention that the Aryans intermingled with the indigenous populations.
2. In what ways do these viewpoints differ?
   Possible response: Basham believes that the Aryans tamed horses and migrated westward, southward, and eastward to conquer the inhabitants of India. Kak believes that this idea was invented in the nineteenth century to reinforce racial attitudes of the time and to credit the Vedas with being in India before the Aryans.
3. Can you think of any current debates about who was responsible for a particular event or how that event took place?
   Possible response: The origin of macaroni and cheese is a matter of culinary debate. The dish may have first been prepared in the kitchens of the ancient Romans, Etruscans, Chinese, or Koreans.

Indian Literature

Historical Background

The modern nation of India has existed since 1947. Through most of history, though, the term *India* has been used to describe the entire subcontinent that is also called South Asia. Surrounded by oceans and by the forbidding Himalayan Mountains, India remained isolated for long periods of its history. This isolation was broken periodically by invasions. Often, however, invading peoples became cut off from their original homelands and then were gradually absorbed into the Indian population.

The Indus Valley, Aryans, and Dravidians Some early settlers developed an impressive civilization in the northwest, where modern Pakistan and western India are located. This culture—the Indus Valley civilization, named for the river that runs through the region—was urban and highly sophisticated. The Indus Valley civilization mysteriously ended around 1500 B.C. At about the same time, people who called themselves Aryans (ar′ ē ənz)—from the word *arya,* meaning "noble"—migrated into India from the north and west. The Aryans brought with them the hymns of the *Rig Veda,* which expressed their religious ideas.

Another cultural group, the Dravidians (drə vid′ ē ənz), inhabited southern India in ancient times. We do not know much about the earliest history of these dark-skinned, small-framed people, but we do know that they developed a thriving culture sometime during the first millennium B.C.

Themes in World Masterpieces — Point/Counterpoint

Was There an Aryan Invasion of India?

Two scholars express opposing points of view.

Yes! About 2000 B.C. the great steppeland which stretches from Poland to Central Asia was inhabited by semi-nomadic barbarians, who were tall, comparatively fair, and mostly long-headed. They had tamed the horse, which they harnessed to light chariots. . . . In the early part of the 2nd millennium, . . . [t]hey migrated in bands westwards, southwards and eastwards, conquering local populations, and intermarrying with them to form a ruling class.

—from *The Wonder That Was India,* by A. L. Basham

No! The concept of invading hordes of Aryans conquering northern India around 1500 B.C. arose in the nineteenth century for a variety of reasons. . . .

Although . . . there was little supporting evidence, the reason this theory became popular was that it . . . reinforced the racial attitudes popular in the nineteenth century so that the highly regarded Vedas [collections of hymns] could be assigned to a time before the Aryans in India mixed with the indigenous races.

—from *"The Aryans and Ancient Indian History,"* by Subhash Kak

Enrichment

The Indus Valley Civilization

Tell students that the Indus Valley civilization, also known as the Harappa Culture, extended for about 1,000 miles north and south along the Indus River. This civilization was so well organized that even the bricks used in widely separated towns were the same size. Each city had a fortified citadel, and the streets were laid out in a regular plan. In fact, the same street plans were followed for almost 1,000 years.

One of the most impressive achievements of this civilization was its drainage system. Each house had a bathroom, and the water from the bathroom drained into sewers beneath the main streets and then into pits. Scholars guess that such an elaborate system must have required a centralized authority to maintain it. Of all ancient peoples, only the Minoans and Romans had comparable drainage systems.

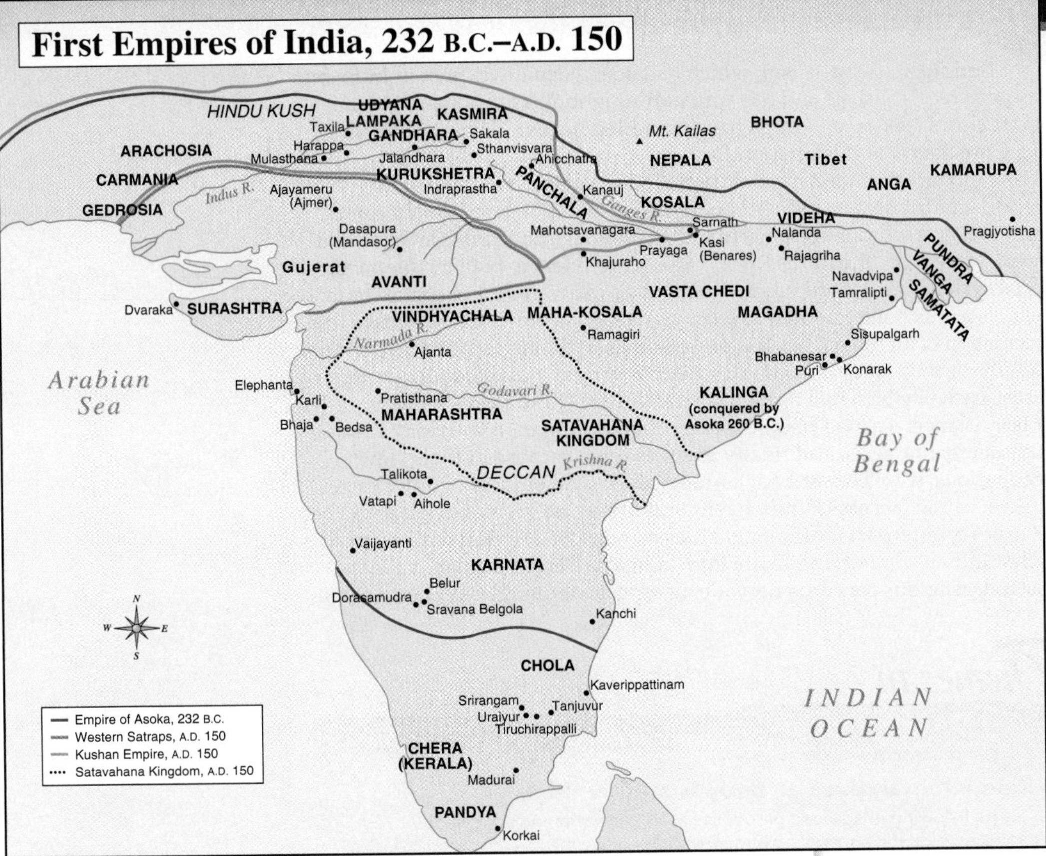

A Political Checkerboard The map of India's political history is a checkerboard of continually changing boundaries between kingdoms that do battle, absorb one another, and then split into new divisions. There were many empires in India's history (see the map above). Perhaps the greatest was that carved out by Candragupta Maurya (chän drə gōōp′ tə mä oor yə), ruled by his son Bindusāra and expanded by his grandson Asoka. Much later, in the sixteenth century A.D., the Moguls (mō′ gulz), Islamic rulers who were descendants of Genghis Khan, established a great empire in north India.

The subcontinent, however, was never united under any single political administration until the British succeeded in making India a colony. While the British did leave a significant mark on the region, we must also remember that their rule of nearly the entire subcontinent lasted for a relatively short period, from the early 1800s to 1947. For most of its history, India has been a collection of kingdoms with ever-changing boundaries.

Religious Thought Indian creativity is especially evident in the field of religion. The subcontinent was the birthplace of many important faiths: Hinduism (hin′ dōō′ iz əm), the dominant religion of India;

▲ Critical Viewing
Asoka (ə sō′ kə), who reigned in the third century B.C., was one of India's greatest kings and embraced the compassionate teachings of Buddhism. What evidence from this map supports A. L. Basham's assertion that after Asoka, "the political . . . unity of India was lost for nearly two thousand years"? Explain. **[Read a Map]**

Background

Asoka

Asoka, who reigned over the Mauryan dynasty from about 270 to 232 B.C., was not only a powerful emperor but a wise and humane one as well. In the following edict, he asserts his intentions toward the people who live beyond the borders of his empire following an earlier apology for the Kalinga war (see the map on p. 169):

> The people of the unconquered territories beyond the borders might think: "What is the king's intentions towards us?" My only intention is that they live without fear of me, that they may trust me and that I may give them happiness not sorrow. Furthermore, they should understand that the king will forgive those who can be forgiven, and that he wishes to encourage them to practice Dhamma so that they may attain happiness in this world and the next . . . assure them that "The king is like a father. He feels towards us as he feels towards himself. We are to him like his own children."

Critical Viewing

Possible response: The key to the map indicates that much of India was united under Asoka. However, the map also shows the three divisions of India in A.D. 150, indicating that the political unity of India was lost.

Differentiated Instruction

Solutions for All Learners

Strategy for Less Proficient Readers
To help students understand the Historical Background and Literature of the period, have them use information from the text to make a timeline that integrates the major world events and the events taking place in India. Have them list the world events above the line and the Indian events below the line.

Strategy for English Learners
Students may have a difficult time with the types of literature such as *hymn, epic,* and *fable.* Have students work with native English speakers to define these terms and to find similar types of literature in their first language or from their own experiences to use as examples as they read further.

Enrichment for Advanced Readers
As students read, have them take notes on the type of literature that was developing and on the other cultural and historical events that were occurring. Then, have students draw parallels between what was happening in India and what was happening in other areas of the world.

Background
Hindu Temples

The standard Hindu temple was not much different from that of the ancient Greeks. The chief icon was in the heart of the temple, a small, dark shrine-room that opened onto a hall for worshipers. The temple carvings show a deep appreciation of the human form and are characterized by their expressiveness.

Background
Karma

The Indians regard karma as actual matter, invisible to the human eye. Bright souls become dulled and clouded over by karmic matter just as dust dulls a bright, oily surface. Activity causes karma to adhere to the soul, and all activities, of good and evil natures alike, induce karma.

Background
Shiva

Shiva, one of the three most important divinities in Hinduism, is called the Destroyer. As the counterpart of Vishnu, Shiva periodically destroys the world in order to re-create it, according to Hindu belief. Despite his fearsome characteristics, Shiva's followers believe that he is a merciful god. Hindus depict Shiva in many forms, one of which is Nataraja, or Lord of the Cosmic Dance. In this form, the four-armed Shiva dances on a prostrate demon.

Themes in World Literature
Close-up on Culture

Point out to students that although Indian religions view life on Earth as suffering, their religious belief about the life of the soul is uniquely creative.

- **Ask:** In this religious thought, why is the body viewed as an old shirt?
  Answer: The religious belief is that after the death of a human body, the soul can be reborn as another human body, an animal, or an insect.
- **Ask:** What determines how a soul will be reborn?
  Answer: Indians believe that their good deeds become good karma that guarantees the soul's rebirth into better circumstances. Bad karma, which is caused by evil deeds, punishes the soul, which is then reborn into worse circumstances.

Buddhism (bood′ iz′ əm), which had been virtually extinct in India but has been reestablished and has spread throughout Asia; Jainism (jīn′ iz′ əm); and Sikhism (sēk′ iz′ əm). India has also added its own flavor to religions like Christianity and Islam.

The mixture of three early cultures—Indus Valley, Dravidian, and Aryan—contributed to India's Hindu civilization. The word *Hindu* comes from *sindhu*, a word in the ancient Indian language Sanskrit (san′ skrit′) that means "river" or "the Indus River." This word refers to both a religion and a social system. The Hindu religion recognizes many gods, but central to its belief is a final reality known as *brahman* (brä′ mən). Not only is *brahman* the foundation of all things, but it is present in every living being as its essential identity, or *atman* (ät′ mən). Hindu society was rigidly divided into groups, or castes, each of which had its own special duties. These castes were, in order of importance, learned people and priests (Brahmans); warriors; farmers and merchants; serfs; and finally, menials who, because of their "low" occupations, were considered "untouchable" by members of other castes.

A revealing fact about Indian religious life is that no Indian language has an exact counterpart for the English word *religion*. The explanation for this is that Indians do not divide life into "religious" and "secular" spheres. Instead, religious concerns pervade all aspects of thought in Hindu India.

Themes in World Masterpieces
Close-up on Culture

Religion in India: The Body Is an Old Shirt

The following images are part of the kaleidoscope of Indian religious practices: gigantic bonfires consuming effigies of ten-headed demons; sacred texts that are chanted without interruption for a month at a time; naked ascetics smeared with ashes from sacred fires; and monks absorbed in silent meditation.

As the richness of these images suggests, few places on Earth have devoted more creative energy to religious expression than has India. The best-known religious belief to come out of India—one shared by Hindus, Jains, and Buddhists—is the notion that the soul is repeatedly reborn into this world. As the body is cast off like an old shirt, the soul can go to heaven for a period of time or it can be reborn in a human body, an animal, or even an insect.

Whether a soul is reborn in better circumstances depends on a person's deeds, the totality of which is known as karma (kär′ mə). A good and virtuous person, with good karma, will be reborn as a higher-ranking person; for example, an honorable merchant may become a warrior. However, the texts record unpleasant punishments for those with bad karma. A person who steals grain, for instance, will be reborn as a rat.

Indian religions tend to view this life as a place of impermanence and inevitable disappointment. Continual rebirth, therefore, can result only in continual suffering. The way to avoid such suffering is to escape from the process of death and rebirth.

Enrichment
Buddha or Siddhartha Gautama

Buddha, or Siddhartha Gautama, is the founder of Buddhism. *Buddha* means "enlightened one." Buddhists believe that they are in a continuous cycle of death and rebirth. People who have attained enlightenment, however, will reach nirvana, or the final death, thereby breaking the cycle of rebirth. Buddha is one such person. To distinguish Buddha from mortals, artists use established symbols to depict him and his achievements. At the top of Buddha's head is a bump that signifies his special knowledge.

His short, curly hair represents a time when Buddha gave up his princely life to devote himself to a new disciplined life. The dot between his eyes symbolizes his special wisdom. His elongated earlobes refer to the time before his enlightenment. According to tradition, when he was a wealthy prince, Buddha wore heavy gold jewelry that stretched his earlobes. Finally, his webbed fingers are believed to be a net by which Buddha gathers his followers.

Religions Other Than Hinduism Jainism (7th–5th century B.C.) and Buddhism (6th–4th century B.C.) arose in protest against certain Hindu beliefs and complex rituals of sacrifice. Jains—a name that derives from the Sanskrit for "saint," *jina*—renounced earthly pleasures and devoted themselves to protecting all forms of life.

Buddhism was founded by Siddhartha Gautama (sid där′ tə gout′ ə mə), an Indian prince. When he left the palace grounds and learned about suffering and death for the first time, he was so affected by this experience that he renounced luxury and became a wandering religious man. After years of fasting and intense study, he achieved *nirvana* (nir vä′ nə). This Sanskrit word refers to a state of being in which the desire for earthly things has been quenched and the soul therefore need not be reborn. Gautama was given the name Buddha, Sanskrit for "enlightened one," to honor his achievement.

The Sikh religion developed in northern India about two thousand years after the origins of Buddhism and Jainism. Like these two religions, Sikhism rejected the caste system and rituals of Hinduism; however, the Sikhs' belief in a single god set them apart.

Seagoing Arab traders brought the Muslim religion to western India in the eighth century. Later, Muslim armies invaded India from the north and established the Mogul empire. Under the Mogul emperors (1526–1857), Islamic and Indian traditions mingled to produce a distinctive style of art and architecture. The most famous example of this style is the Taj Mahal, built by a Muslim emperor after the death of his favorite wife.

Mathematics Some of India's cultural achievements are so much a part of our everyday lives that they have lost their identity as Indian discoveries. Among these is our number system. The numerals that we use come from India; they are called Arabic numerals because Arab traders brought them

▲ Critical Viewing

Do these pictures of the wall of a Hindu temple (left) and the Taj Mahal (right) suggest the Hindu belief in many gods and the Islamic belief in one God? Why or why not? **[Compare and Contrast]**

Background

The Taj Mahal

The emperor Shah Jahan ordered the building of the Taj Mahal at Agra as a memorial to his favorite wife, Mumtaz Mahal, who died in 1631. The building of the Taj Mahal began in 1632 and was completed in 1648. One of the most resplendent mausoleums in India, the Taj Mahal was probably designed by Ustad Ahmad Lahawri, an Indian of Persian descent. The exterior of the tomb is white marble inlaid with semiprecious stones.

Critical Viewing

Possible response: The interior of the Hindu temple reflects the view of many gods in that more than one god appears in the picture. The Taj Mahal is shaped more like a mosque than a Hindu temple and thus might reflect the Islamic belief in one God.

Critical Viewing

Possible response: The concept of zero probably continues to fascinate artists and thinkers because it represents nonexistence and is therefore known only by what it is not.

Historical Background

Comprehension Check

1. Name the two main groups that made up the population of India after the end of the Indus Valley civilization.
   Answer: The Aryans and the Dravidians made up the population of India at that time.
2. When did India unite under a single political administration?
   Answer: India was united under a single political administration when the British made India a colony in the early 1800s.
3. What contributed to India's Hindu civilization, and to what does the word *Hindu* refer?
   Answer: The mixture of the Indus Valley, Aryan, and Dravidian cultures contributed to India's Hindu civilization. *Hindu* refers to a religion and a social system.
4. What aspects of Hinduism did Sikhism, Buddhism, and Jainism reject?
   Answer: These religions rejected the caste system and the rituals.
5. Indian cultural discoveries have become part of our everyday lives. Name some of these discoveries.
   Answer: Indians invented the concept of zero and are responsible for our number system. In medicine they were able to set broken bones, knew to keep wounds clean, and developed plastic surgery.

from India to Europe. In addition, ancient Indian mathematicians are responsible for the invention of the zero and the decimal notation that this discovery made possible.

A Link Between Religion and Mathematics Scholars speculate that philosophical and religious ideas may have led Indian mathematicians to invent the zero and develop other advanced concepts. For example, in the religious writings of Hindus and Jains, time and space were regarded as limitless. It is not surprising, therefore, that mathematicians familiar with these beliefs would study the problems of defining infinite numbers and distinguishing between various types of infinity. Similarly, the Buddhist belief in nirvana and philosophical ideas about emptiness and the void may have prompted mathematicians to develop the concept of zero.

Technology and Medicine Indians also excelled in metalworking. A monument that testifies to their skill is the Iron Pillar of Delhi, a solid metal column that measures more than 23 feet tall and weighs more than 6 tons. It was erected c. A.D. 400 by the ruler Kumāra Gupta I in honor of his father.

Medicine was another field in which Indians distinguished themselves. Ancient Indian physicians were able to set broken bones, knew the importance of keeping wounds clean, and developed plastic surgery long before it was practiced in Europe.

Painting, Sculpture, and Architecture Indian painters and sculptors were patronized by kings and wealthy merchants. As artists traveled from kingdom to kingdom to show their work, they spread the inventions and secrets of their craft. For the most part, they depicted religious themes. However, their work also reveals the daily life, dress, and pastimes of ancient India, so it is a valuable record for us today.

Among the most notable achievements of Indian art are the frescoes, or wall paintings, in caves near the village of Ajanta in western India. These caves were created by Buddhist monks during the period from the first century B.C. to the seventh century A.D. The vibrant and colorful paintings on their walls depict Buddhist themes. (See Timeline, page 167.)

The artificial caves at Ajanta and elsewhere in western India are also great architectural achievements. Their interiors were designed to imitate the brightly colored halls in which Buddhist monks gathered during the rainy season to recite texts and debate religious questions. Some of the cave temples are also Hindu or Jain. The Hindu cave-temple Kailasa at Ellora was carved downward from a basaltic hillside. It is about 164 feet long, 108 feet wide, and 100 feet high.

▲ **Critical Viewing** The contemporary artist Robert Indiana created this sculpture of the numeral zero. Why do you think the concept of zero, first developed by Indian mathematicians, continues to fascinate artists and thinkers? **[Speculate]**

Enrichment

Ahimsa

Ahimsa, or non-injury, has long been considered a basic philosophy in Hinduism. *Ahimsa* refers to the "absence of the desire to harm." Killing in war or capital punishment was accepted by many in ancient India, as was animal sacrifice. Those who accepted killing often still did not eat meat.

The desire to preserve animals, which was present in both ahimsa and vegetarianism, did lead to protecting and honoring cattle. Cows are seen as providing food (milk) without being eaten. Even though ahimsa is considered a basic of Hindu belief, many Hindus do eat beef, and violence is still present in Hindu society.

Literature

The Sacredness of Language The universal concern with religious values in Hindu life explains the lack of a clear separation between religion and literature. In fact, language itself—the sound of words—was regarded as sacred. An example of this belief is the practice of repeating the word *om* (ōm) during Hindu prayers. The repetition of this word is a religious act, a means of saying "yes" to the universe. While all language was considered sacred, the ancient Indian language Sanskrit was considered to be the perfect language. It ceased being a spoken language many hundreds of years ago, but all of the selections in this unit were written in Sanskrit. (Today, we recognize that Sanskrit is related to other ancient Indo-European languages like Latin and Greek.)

Because they believed that language was holy, Indians speculated a great deal about its power to convey ideas and emotions. This speculation led to a greater understanding about how language works. The Sanskrit grammars written by Panini in the sixth century B.C. are still admired by modern linguists.

Ancient Hymns and Epics The earliest surviving record of Indian religious thought, and the basis of Hinduism, is the collection of hymns known as the *Rig Veda* (rig′ vä′ də). These hymns do not set forth religious ideas in a systematic manner. Their homage to the gods of nature, however, sets a tone of devotion and piety that carries down to the present day.

These ancient hymns accompanied elaborate sacrifices to the gods, some of which lasted as long as a year! The writings that were developed to describe the details of these sacrifices had a profound effect on the way that Hindus thought. This influence is apparent, for example, in the structure of India's longest epic poem, the *Mahabharata* (mə hä′ bä′ rə tə), which means "Great Epic of the Bharata Dynasty." Just as a sacrificial ritual was divided into many small parts, the *Mahabharata* was divided into many small episodes told by different narrators.

Still another ancient epic is the *Ramayana* (rä mä′yə nə), which means "Romance of Rama." The hero, Rama, is one of the forms of the Hindu god Vishnu, and the high point of the epic is the battle between Rama and the evil demon Ravana (rə vä′ nə). An army of monkeys led by the monkey-general Hanuman (hän′ oo män′) assists Rama in this battle.

Rama and Lakshman Confer with the Animal Armies, from the *Adventures of Rama*, Courtesy of the Freer Gallery of Art, Smithsonian Institution, Washington, D.C.

▲ **Critical Viewing**
This picture illustrates a scene from the *Ramayana*. Which details suggest that the *Ramayana* is a fantastic—not realistic—tale? Explain. **[Infer]**

Critical Viewing

Possible response: The presence of the animals in conference with the armies of Rama is a fantastic element. Also, the clothing is not consistent with battle.

Background

Sanskrit

Ancient Indian thinkers began to study phonetics and grammar in order to preserve the original pronunciations and meanings of words in the *Rig Veda*. They believed that these words had to be pronounced properly or they would not be effective in bringing divine blessings. Also, they were aware that Sanskrit was changing; its grammar was being simplified, certain word endings were disappearing, and older words were falling out of use.

Background

The Power of *Om*

Ancient Indians came to associate the brahmans' power with the words they spoke. Individual letters of the alphabet were thought of as gods. Given this orientation, it is not surprising that a special holiness was later attributed to certain sounds like *om* (ah-OOM).

Critical Thinking

1. Why might India have had difficulty uniting as a single political unit before the early 1800s? **[Speculate]**
   Possible response: Some areas of India were susceptible to invasions, and India lacked a common language. Also, India covers a very large area, and before the 1800s, communication and transportation were poor.
2. What elements in the Hindu religion may have resulted in the word *Hindu* referring to both a religion and a social system? **[Draw Conclusions]**
   Possible response: The religious belief sets up the basis for society and provides consequences for those who violate that social order.
3. How can you support the idea that the concept of zero was a natural outcome of the religious and philosophical ideas in India? **[Support]**
   Possible response: The idea of the escape from the cycle of rebirth might lead to the idea of zero or nothing. Also, because people could be reborn multiple times, ideas of infinity would be part of religion and philosophy.

Critical Viewing

Possible response: Both pictures show action, but neither is frantic. Both appear to be peaceful but animated, and in both, the figures are highly ornate and decorated.

Background

The *Ramayana*

The *Ramayana* tells of the royal birth of Rama, his training, and his ability to bend Shiva's bow, winning the hand of Sita, the daughter of King Janaka. When Sita is taken from him, Rama fights to rescue her and defeats Ravana, the demon king.

The Ram-Lila, an annual pageant in North India, is based on the events of the *Ramayana;* in South India, the kathakali dance-drama of Malabar is based on the *Ramayana* and the *Mahabharata.*

Literature of the Period

Comprehension Check

1. How did the Hindus regard language?
   Answer: The Hindus regarded language and the sounds of the words as sacred. Of all languages, the Hindus considered Sanskrit to be the most sacred.
2. What is the earliest surviving record of Indian religious thought, and what does it tell us about the early Hindus?
   Answer: The *Rig Veda* is the earliest surviving record of Indian religious thought. These hymns show a devotion and piety still observed today.
3. Which American authors did the earliest Indian literature inspire?
   Answer: Early Indian literature inspired Emerson and Thoreau.

Epics and Storytelling Both the *Mahabharata* and the *Ramayana* are extremely popular in India and in Southeast Asia. People dramatize events from these poems in colorful pageants, dance performances, and puppet shows. Also, storytellers recount the tales of epic heroes in villages across India. The modern writer R. K. Narayan, for example, describes the typical village storyteller, who knows "by heart all the . . . 100,000 stanzas of the *Mahabharata,*" beginning an evening session:

> . . . the storyteller will dress himself for the part by smearing sacred ash on his forehead and wrapping himself in a green shawl, while his helpers set up a framed picture of some god on a pedestal in the veranda, decorate it with jasmine garlands, and light incense to it. After these preparations, when the storyteller enters to seat himself in front of the lamps, he looks imperious and in complete control of the situation. He begins the session with a prayer, prolonging it until the others join and the valleys echo with the chants, drowning the cry of jackals."

▲ **Critical Viewing** This photograph shows an Indian dancer performing a peacock dance. Compare and contrast the colors, gestures, and mood of the dancer with those of the characters in the *Ramayana* illustration, page 173. **[Compare and Contrast]**

The Importance of Memory As the recitation of the storyteller suggests, Indians placed great importance on memory, more so perhaps than did other ancient cultures. The traditional way of studying a subject in India was to memorize—completely and perfectly—the *entire* text and then to hear the teacher explain it. In the case of a sacred text like the *Rig Veda,* every syllable, every accent, every pause in the recitation had to be correct; otherwise, when these hymns were recited during a sacrifice, their power would be lost.

Students of the *Rig Veda* were first taught to memorize all 1,028 hymns in the normal way. One hymn, for example, begins, "I pray to the God of Fire, the household priest. . . . " After memorizing this hymn, each student would be assigned another way to memorize it—for example, "I pray I to pray the to God the of God Fire of the Fire household the priest household. . . ." This second version of the hymn was purposely nonsensical so that the student's act of memory would not be dependent on meaning. These incredible feats of memory took years, of course, and they seem utterly impossible to us. Yet it was just such dedication that preserved the hymns unchanged from 1500 B.C. to the present.

Texts were also written down in ancient India, but Hindus believed that trusting to the written medium involved too great a risk. A written copy could be lost or damaged. Strange as it may seem to us, a person's memory was regarded as a far safer means of preserving a text.

Enrichment

The *Mahabharata*

Both religious inspiration and high-quality literature can be found in the *Mahabharata,* making it one of the most highly regarded of the Indian epics. The *Mahabharata* contains the *Bhagavad-Gita,* the most important text in Hindu religious literature. The *Mahabharata* also provides important information on the development of Hinduism from 400 B.C. to A.D. 200.

The *Mahabharata* is very long. It contains nearly 100,000 couplets and is about seven times as long as the combined length of the *Iliad* and the *Odyssey,* the famous Greek epics attributed to Homer. The *Mahabharata* is divided into eighteen sections and explains the conduct expected of kings, warriors, people living in troubled times, and those seeking to escape the cycle of rebirth.

The Evolution of Sanskrit Literature Ancient Indians had no literary genres like the novel or the short story. Except for poetry and drama, most Sanskrit texts imitated the *Rig Veda* in attempting to convey general and timeless truths. Even the myths that tell the story of the god Krishna—another form of Vishnu, one of the three most important Indian deities—deal with abstract principles. The same is true of the animal fables of the *Panchatantra* (pun′ chə tun′ trə). They use vivid language and are disarmingly naïve, but their purpose is to enable people to fulfill their *dharma* (dur′ mə), or unique obligations in life.

Indian poetry and drama did not come into their own until centuries after the *Rig Veda* was compiled. The greatest Indian poet was Kalidasa (see below). His plays and epic poems set the standards for those two genres.

The Continuing Influence of Indian Literature The selections in this unit come from the earliest products of India's literary tradition. Despite the fact that some of these works are 3,500 years old, however, their influence continues to be felt in modern times. They inspired the American authors Emerson and Thoreau, the Indian writer Rabindranath Tagore (see page 1160), and the Indian leader who pioneered the methods of nonviolent protest, Mohandas K. Gandhi.

Themes in World Masterpieces — A Writer's Voice

Kalidasa, The Sanskrit Shakespeare

Kalidasa (kä′ lē dä′ sä), who is as important in Indian literature as Shakespeare is in English literature, wrote verse dramas, love lyrics, and verse epics. His birth and death dates are unknown, but the sophistication of his work leads many scholars to link him with the sparkling court of Candragupta II (reigned c. A.D. 380–c. 415). As a court poet, Kalidasa wrote in Sanskrit, the ancient Indian tongue that by his day had become a literary rather than a spoken language.

One of his dramas, *Vikramorvasiya* ("Urvashi Won by Valor"), tells about a king's love for the goddess Urvashi. In this excerpt from the drama (translated by John Brough), the jealous goddess has fled to the forest and the grief-crazed king is searching for her:

. . . The woods are desolate, who will tell me of my beloved? There, on top of that massive rock which breathes out steam after the rain-storm,
A peacock perches,
While east-wind gusts ruff every tail-fan feather,
And stretches
His shriek-filled throat, eyeing the rain-cloud weather.
[He goes up to it.] I can at least ask.
In this wild woodland, bird of lovely blue,
Saw you my wife whose love is true?
How could your white-flecked eyes have failed to mark
A face so fair, slant-eyes so dark?

Themes in World Literature

A Writer's Voice

Remind students that Sanskrit, once the spoken language in ancient India, ceased to be spoken hundreds of years ago.

- **Ask** students why Kalidasa is compared with Shakespeare.
  Answer: Kalidasa is as important to Indian literature as Shakespeare is to English literature. Both were poets and dramatists.
- **Ask** why the grieving king approaches the bird.
  Answer: The king believes that the bird might have seen the beautiful Urvashi.

Critical Thinking

- Do you believe the Indians were wise to trust their memories, or would they have been wiser to write down their early epics? Support your view. **[Support]**
  Possible response: Memory was better than a written record because no one could secretly alter or destroy it; all would have access to memory whether they could read or not; and committing something to memory guaranteed that all would know it. However, a written record would have provided more consistency and guaranteed that it did not vary from place to place.

Concept Connector

Have students discuss the Focus Questions on p. 165. Students' discussions should include the following points:

Religions that began in the Indian subcontinent:
- Hinduism began in India and is the dominant religion.
- Buddhism, Jainism, and Sikhism also originated there.

Hinduism as a social system:
- Hindu society was divided into social groups, or castes.
- The languages of India do not have a word for "religion." There is no separation between "religious" and "secular."

Achievements of Indian artists:
- Between the first century B.C. and 800 A.D., Buddhist monks painted frescoes of religious themes on the caves near Ajanta.
- Architects carved caves into hillsides to imitate the brightly colored halls of Buddhist monks.

Memory and Indian literature:
- Students memorized entire texts as a way to begin studying them.
- Written copies of stories could be damaged or lost; memory was a safer means by which to preserve stories.

 From the Translator's Desk

Wendy Doniger

- You might wish to have students reread Wendy Doniger's introduction to the unit on pages 164–165.
- Show Segment 2 on Wendy Doniger on ***From the Author's Desk DVD*** to provide insight into the importance of oral tradition. After students have watched the segment, **ask:** How important is the oral tradition in Indian culture?
Answer: In the past, oral tradition was crucial to Indian culture; it preserved the ancient texts until modern times, but now oral tradition has practically died out.

The Easiest and the Hardest Text

- After students have read these pages, **ask** a volunteer to summarize Doniger's comments about the characteristics of the "Creation Hymn" from the *Rig Veda.*
Answer: The "Creation Hymn" uses simple language that is expressed through double negatives to convey profound ideas about existence. The text admits that it does not have all of the answers about the origins of creation.
- Point out to students that the *Rig Veda* is a collection of hymns passed down orally in Indian tradition.

Critical Viewing

Answer: Vishnu's four arms suggest that he is a god in human form. Three of the arms extend out, making symbolic gestures.

From the Translator's Desk

WENDY DONIGER INTRODUCES *"Creation Hymn" and "Night" from the* Rig Veda

Wendy Doniger

Wendy Doniger is an expert on mythology, religion, and Hindu literature. She is the author of *Other People's Myths: The Cave of Echoes* and the translator of the *Rig Veda.*

The Easiest and the Hardest Text to Translate

"Creation Hymn" from the *Rig Veda* is both one of the easiest and one of the hardest pieces I've ever tried to translate from Sanskrit to English. It's easy because the words are, for the most part, simple. The first three words are the straightforward Sanskrit words for "not" [*na*] and "was" [*asit*], giving us "was not," plus the word for "non-existence" or "non-being" [*asat*]. Easy as pie: "Not non-existence was" or "Non-existence was not" [*na asat asit*]. And then the second phrase just takes away the "non" [*a*] and adds an "and" [*u*] and says it all again: "and existence was not" [*na u sat asit*].

Double Negatives Fine, great. The hymn is actually known in India as the "Not Non-existence" hymn (the *Na-asat-iya* or *Nasadiya*). But then, think about what it says. Can you get your head around the double negatives to actually *think* the idea that there was not non-existence? I can't. And if there was no non-existence, how could there also be no existence? Or for that matter, how could there be "neither death nor immortality," as the hymn states a few lines later? Doesn't the absence of one require the presence of the other?

So that is why this hymn is one of the hardest texts I've ever tried to translate. Thinking about it all these years, I've come to respect it more than any of the hundreds of texts about creation that I know in several different religions—because it dares to admit that it doesn't have all the answers. And when we take that open-mindedness about not having all the answers and apply it to the opening lines, we realize that the hymn is saying that we don't even have the *questions* about the original creation of the universe—that we cannot really even imagine it. An amazing text.

◀ Critical Viewing
This sculpture, shows the Hindu god Vishna, who took the form of a man to conquer an evil giant. What details in the sculpture suggest that Vishnu is a god in mortal form? **[Analyze]**

Teaching Resources

The following resources can be used to enrich or extend the instruction for From the Author's Desk.

Unit 2 Resources
Support for Penguin Essay, p. 4
Listening and Viewing, p. 5

From the Author's Desk DVD
Wendy Doniger, Segment 2

The World at Night, Going Home to Rest

What I like best about "Night," another hymn from the *Rig Veda*, is that it is not really about night at all. It is dedicated to the night as a kind of goddess, and it thinks of her as a woman who has a sister, the twilight, whom she is pushing aside. But most of the hymn is about the world on earth, the world of humans and animals.

Vivid Imagery This short hymn packs into a small space an amazing amount of vivid information about the lives of people in India in 1000 B.C.E., in part through poetic images and figures of speech and in part through the scenes it visualizes as taking place at night. The poet compares himself to a herdsman driving cows, or a man making a song to praise a conqueror, and he likens the people to birds settling in trees. The poet shows us people, hawks, and wolves—all going home to rest at night. This vivid imagery helps us imagine how we might feel if we were living in India three thousand years ago, watching the night come on.

▲ Critical Viewing
This sculpture, carved into a cave, shows Indra, who was king of the gods in the *Rig Veda*. What elements of the sculpture and its setting create a sense of grandeur? **[Respond]**

Thinking About the Commentary

1. **(a) Recall:** What characteristics of "Creation Hymn" make Wendy Doniger say that it is easy to translate from Sanskrit? **(b) Recall:** Why does Doniger go on to say that translating "Creation Hymn" is difficult? **(c) Speculate:** How do you think this combination of easy and hard contributes to Doniger's fascination with this hymn?
2. **(a) Recall:** What does Doniger like best about "Night"? **(b) Infer:** Why do you think it is important for a translator to make a personal connection with the work she is translating?

As You Read "Creation Hymn" and "Night" . . .

3. Think about the ways in which Doniger's translations reveal her love for the poems.
4. Consider the ways in which reading this commentary enriched your understanding of these poems.

The World at Night

- **Ask:** What vivid imagery about the lives of the people in India in 1000 B.C.E. does Doniger point out in the hymn "Night"?
  Answer: The poet uses poetic images and figures of speech. For instance, the poet compares himself to a herdsman driving cows, and he compares people going home for the night to birds settling in trees as night approaches.

ASSESS

Answers

1. (a) Simple Sanskrit words make the hymn easy to translate. (b) The hymn uses double negatives, such as *not non-existence was,* which are difficult to fathom. (c) **Possible response:** Students may say that it causes her to think a great deal about the poem and question its real meaning.
2. (a) What Doniger likes best about "Night" is that it is not about night. It is dedicated to the night as a kind of goddess that pushes her sister, twilight, away. (b) **Possible response:** Students may say that if a translator makes a personal connection with the work, she will care more about making the translation capture the nuances of the original.
3. **Possible response:** Doniger is in awe of the unknowability of the origins of the universe; her translation of "Creation Hymn" expresses this sense of awe. In "Night," the care and sensitivity with which she chooses her words show her love for the poem.
4. **Possible response:** Reading this commentary helped me to appreciate that simple, short words can effect profound nuances of meaning.

Standard Course of Study

Goal 1: WRITTEN LANGUAGE

WL.1.02.2 Show awareness of culture in personal reflections.

Goal 3: FOUNDATIONS OF ARGUMENT

FA.3.01.1 Share and evaluate initial personal response to a controversial issue.

Goal 5: LITERATURE

LT.5.01.3 Analyze literary devices and explain their effect on the work.

LT.5.03.5 Summarize key events and points from the text.

Goal 6: GRAMMAR AND USAGE

GU.6.01.3 Use recognition strategies to understand vocabulary and exact word choice.

Step-by-Step Teaching Guide	Pacing Guide
PRETEACH	
• Administer Vocabulary and Reading Warm-ups as necessary.	5 min.
• Engage students' interest with the motivation activity.	5 min.
• Read and discuss author and background features. **FT**	10 min.
• Introduce the Literary Analysis Skill: Vedic Hymn. **FT**	5 min.
• Introduce the Reading Strategy: Paraphrasing. **FT**	10 min.
• Prepare students to read by teaching the selection vocabulary. **FT**	
TEACH	
• Informally monitor comprehension while students read independently or in groups. **FT**	30 min.
• Monitor students' comprehension with the Reading Check notes.	as students read
• Reinforce vocabulary with Vocabulary Builder notes.	as students read
• Develop students' understanding of Vedic hymn with the Literary Analysis annotations. **FT**	5 min.
• Develop students' ability to paraphrase with the Reading Strategy annotations. **FT**	5 min.
ASSESS/EXTEND	
• Assess students' comprehension and mastery of the Literary Analysis and Reading Strategy by having them answer the Apply the Skills questions. **FT**	15 min.
• Have students complete the Vocabulary Lesson and the Grammar and Style Lesson. **FT**	15 min.
• Apply students' ability to compare and contrast by using the Writing Lesson. **FT**	45 min. or homework
• Apply students' understanding by using one or more of the Extend Your Learning activities.	20–90 min. or homework
• Administer Selection Test A or Selection Test B. **FT**	15 min.

Resources

Print

Unit 2 Resources

- Vocabulary Warm-up Word Lists **[L1, L2, EL]** .... p. 6
- Vocabulary Warm-up Practice **[L1, L2, EL]** .... p. 7
- Reading Warm-up A **[L1, L2, EL]** .... p. 8
- Reading Warm-up B **[L1, L2, L3]** .... p. 9

Transparency

Graphic Organizer Transparencies

- Literary Analysis Graphic Organizer A **[L3]** .... p. 36
- Literary Analysis Graphic Organizer B **[L1, L2, EL]** .... p. 37
- Reading Strategy Graphic Organizer A **[L3]** .... p. 34
- Reading Strategy Graphic Organizer B **[L1, L2, EL]** .... p. 35

Print

Reader's Notebook [L2]

Reader's Notebook: Adapted Version [L1]

Reader's Notebook: English Learner's Version [EL]

Unit 2 Resources

- Literary Analysis **[L3]** .... p. 10
- Reading Strategy **[L3]** .... p. 11
- Vocabulary Builder **[L3]** .... p. 12

Technology

Listening to Literature Audio CDs [L2, EL]

Reader's Notebook: Adapted Version Audio CD [L1, L2]

Print

Unit 2 Resources

- Grammar and Style **[L3]** .... p. 13
- Support for Writing Lesson **[L3]** .... p. 14
- Support for Extend Your Learning **[L3]** .... p. 15
- Enrichment **[L4]** .... p. 16
- Selection Test A **[L1, L2, EL]** .... pp. 17–19
- Selection Test B **[L3, L4]** .... pp. 20–22

General Resources

- Rubrics for Exposition: Comparison-and-Contrast Essay **[L3]** .... pp. 53–54
- Rubric for Peer Assessment: Oral Interpretation .... p. 130

Technology

- **Go Online:** Research **[L3]**
- **Go Online:** Self-test **[L3]**
- ***ExamView®*, Test Bank [L3]**

Choosing Resources for Differentiated Instruction

[L1] Special Needs Students

[L2] Below-Level Students

[L3] All Students

[L4] Advanced Students

[EL] English Learners

For Vocabulary and Reading Warm-ups and for Selection Tests, **A** signifies "less challenging" and **B** "more challenging." For Graphic Organizer transparencies, **A** signifies "not filled in" and **B** "filled in."

FT Fast Track Instruction: To move the lesson more quickly, use the strategies and activities identified with **FT**.

Scaffolding for Less Proficient and Advanced Students

The leveled Critical Thinking questions after selections progress in the levels of thinking required to answer them. To address the needs of your different students, you may use the (a) level questions for your less proficient students and the (b) level questions with your on-level and advanced students. The occasional (c) level questions are appropriate for your advanced students.

PRENTICE HALL **TeacherEXPRESS™** Plan · Teach · Assess Use this complete suite of powerful teaching tools to make lesson planning and testing quicker and easier.

PRENTICE HALL **StudentEXPRESS™** Learn · Study · Succeed Use the interactive textbook (online and on CD-ROM) to make selections and activities come alive with audio and video support and interactive questions.

Go Online Professional Development **For:** Information about Lexiles **Visit:** www.PHSchool.com **Web Code: eue-1111**

PRETEACH

Motivation

Explain to students that Vedic poets are in awe of nature but that they also desire to control and understand it. By endowing natural forces with the qualities of humans and animals, they make it easier to approach, flatter, and manage these forces. Such attempts at control lead to thoughts about the workings and origins of the world, speculations that will become even more important in later Hindu texts. Ask students to share and discuss creation or nature myths and legends with which they are familiar.

❶ Background

More About the Selections

The Aryans, whose culture gave birth to the *Rig Veda,* invaded India from the northwest, coming through passes in the Hindu Kush mountain range and then crossing the Indus River. This onslaught was not a single occurrence but a series of invasions.

The Indus Valley civilization lay directly along this invasion route. The enemies to whom the Aryans refer in the Vedic hymns—and the references are naturally uncomplimentary—are the survivors of this civilization. In contrast to these city dwellers, the Aryans were fierce, nomadic people organized in tribes led by rajahs.

Geography Note

Draw students' attention to the map on this page. Explain that India and its neighbors make up a distinct region large enough to be called a subcontinent. Surrounded by oceans and by the forbidding Himalaya Mountains, India's isolation was broken periodically by invasions. Often, however, invading peoples like the Aryans who brought with them the hymns of the *Rig Veda* became isolated from their original homelands and were gradually absorbed into the Indian population.

Build Skills | *Hymns*

from the Rig Veda ❶

About the *Rig Veda*

The earliest surviving record of Indian religious thought, and the basis of Hinduism, is the sacred text known as the *Rig Veda*. Compiled around 1400 B.C., the *Rig Veda* is a collection of 1,028 hymns composed by different authors at different times. These hymns do not set forth religious ideas in a systematic manner. However, their homage to the gods of nature sets a tone of devotion and piety that carries down to the present day.

The Authors of the *Rig Veda* The identity of the hymns' authors remains a mystery. We know only that they were part of the Indo-European race that gradually migrated into the Indian subcontinent from central Europe via what are now Iran and Afghanistan. These Indo-Europeans, who also migrated throughout Europe, referred to themselves as Aryans, a name that in Sanskrit means "noble" and that distinguished the migrants from the native peoples. Traces of the word *Aryan* can still be found in the names of countries like *Ireland* and *Iran*.

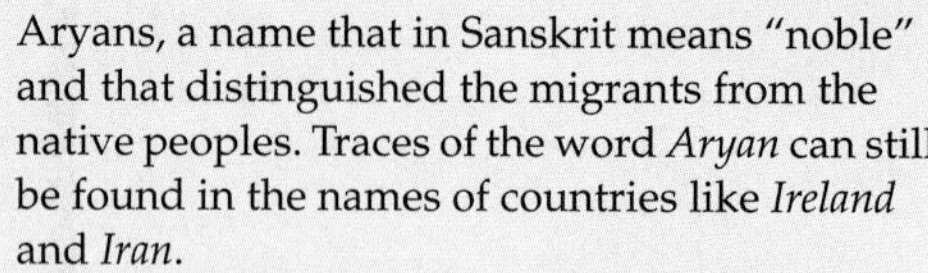

Wherever they traveled, Indo-Europeans naturally took their language with them. Over a long period of time, modern languages as diverse as English, Greek, French, Polish, Bengali, and Albanian evolved from Indo-European. (Most dictionaries and encyclopedias have a chart of Indo-European languages.) Sanskrit, the language of the *Rig Veda,* is one of the oldest Indo-European tongues.

The Religion of the *Rig Veda* The poets of the *Rig Veda* were awed by the forces of nature. In many hymns, they portray natural phenomena— the sun, the moon, rain, night, wind, storms—as godlike beings. The authors praise these gods for their power and beauty and for the benefits they bring to humankind.

Because the hymns were composed at different times, they indicate different stages of religious thought. There is, however, a general interest in prosperity and comfort. The gods are invoked for protection and sustenance. Unlike later Hindu writings, the hymns place little emphasis on doing good for its own sake. They reflect the concerns of an agricultural people who needed rain for their crops, protection from storms, and a feeling of security in the night. Hymns that appear later in the *Rig Veda* diverge from this pattern by speculating about the purpose and creation of the universe.

Sacrifice and the *Rig Veda* The *Rig Veda* describes a world in which the forces of nature are both benevolent and threatening. Rain, which is necessary for crops, can also bring catastrophe if it comes at the wrong time. The hymns were therefore recited at sacrificial offerings intended to win the favor of the gods and to ward off natural disturbances and chaos.

The earliest Vedic poets sought to please the gods through offerings of food and drink. They thought that such gifts would incline the forces of nature to perform beneficially for humans. The idea gradually evolved, however, that sacrifice is not only helpful to the gods, since it provides them with sustenance and praise, but is actually necessary for them. Eventually, the notion emerged that sacrifice *controls* the gods and the order of the universe. This belief gave the priests, who supervised the sacrifice, enormous power and influence.

The ancient practice of Vedic sacrifice is slowly dying out in modern India and is being replaced by other religious rituals based on the *Rig Veda*.

Preview

Connecting to the Literature

The *Rig Veda* offers clues to an ancient civilization yet also reflects timeless concerns. Like the speaker in the hymn "Night," we too have nighttime fears, despite all our modern protections. Also, like the speaker in "Creation Hymn," we wonder about the origin of the universe.

NC Standard Course of Study

- Analyze literary devices and explain their effect on the work. (LT.5.01.3)
- Summarize key events and points from the text. (LT.5.03.5)

2 Literary Analysis

Vedic Hymn

A hymn is a poem or song of praise. **Vedic hymns** emphasize the importance of gods and nature in Indian life and ponder timeless questions, such as the origin of the universe. These hymns were originally meant to be chanted, and they were passed down through the ages by word of mouth before they were written. While reading, look for devices that reflect this oral tradition, such as the repetition of words or of grammatical structure.

Comparing Literary Works

"Creation Hymn" and "Night" both involve mysteries of nature, but they approach their uncertainties from different angles. "Night" uses concrete language and familiar terms to make the unknown easier to comprehend. For example, the speaker uses **personification,** a description of something nonhuman as if it were human, to make the night seem less foreboding. The speaker also addresses the night directly, as in the following passage:

> As you came near to us today, we turned homeward to rest,
> as birds go to their home in a tree.

"Creation Hymn," in contrast, confronts the unknown on an abstract level. The hymn speaks of concepts such as existence and immortality and leaves many questions purposely unanswered.

As you read these hymns, think about the ways in which "Night" tries to remove nature's mystery while "Creation Hymn" embraces it.

3 Reading Strategy

Paraphrasing

Poets use concise language, compressing a wealth of meaning into just a few words. To unpack this meaning, pause occasionally as you read, and **paraphrase** the hymns, restating in your own words what each line says. Use a chart like the one shown to paraphrase passages from the hymns.

Poet's Words

The goddess Night has drawn near, looking about on many sides with her eyes. She has put on all her glories.

Paraphrase

It is dusk. The stars have begun to come out.

Vocabulary Builder

immortality (im′ môr tal′ i tē) *n.* quality or state of being exempt from death; unending existence (p. 181)

distinguishing (di stiŋ′ gwish iŋ) *adj.* serving to mark as separate or different (p. 181)

stems (stemz) *v.* stops or dams up (as a river) (p. 182)

palpable (pal′ pə bəl) *adj.* able to be touched, felt, or handled (p. 182)

2 Literary Analysis

Vedic Hymn

- Read the description of Vedic hymns with the class. Tell students that the Vedic poets use figurative language to create memorable images and to capture their audience's imagination.
- Explain, in addition, that the use of personification and simile makes an often mysterious, even dangerous, world seem familiar and understandable.

3 Reading Strategy

Paraphrasing

- Explain to students that paraphrasing poetry can be especially challenging because it is often dense with meaning.
- Direct students' attention to the paraphrased text in the graphic organizer. Point out that the paraphrase uses more accessible language and makes the passage's meaning easier to understand.
- Remind students that paraphrasing and summarizing are not the same. A paraphrase restates the original idea without omitting any details.
- Explain the use of the graphic organizer. Then give students a copy of **Reading Strategy Graphic Organizer A** in ***Graphic Organizer Transparencies,*** p. 34, to use as they read the hymns.

Vocabulary Builder

- Pronounce each vocabulary word for students, and read the definitions as a class. Have students identify any words with which they are already familiar.

Differentiated Instruction Solutions for All Learners

Support for Special Needs Students
Have students read the adapted version of excerpts from the *Rig Veda* in the ***Reader's Notebook: Adapted Version.*** This version provides basic-level instruction in an interactive format with questions and write-on lines. Completing these pages will prepare students to read the selection in the Student Edition.

Support for Less Proficient Readers
Have students read the excerpts from the *Rig Veda* in the ***Reader's Notebook.*** This version provides basic-level instruction in an interactive format with questions and write-on lines. After students finish the selection in the ***Reader's Notebook,*** have them complete the questions and activities in the Student Edition.

Support for English Learners
Have students read the excerpts from the *Rig Veda* in the ***Reader's Notebook: English Learner's Version.*** This version provides basic-level instruction in an interactive format with questions and write-on lines. Completing these pages will prepare students to read the selection in the Student Edition.

Facilitate Understanding

Because the "Creation Hymn" is abstract, it may prove difficult for some students. In order to prepare students for the hymn, read it aloud first. Encourage students to relax and listen without trying to analyze its meaning.

Before reading "Night," remind students that personification assigns human characteristics to a nonhuman subject in order to make a description more vivid or accessible. Before they read, have students scan the hymn for examples of personification.

1 About the Selections

Both of these selections are from the *Rig Veda,* a collection of hymns expressing the knowledge and wisdom of the Hindu religion. In "Creation Hymn," the speaker speculates on the origin of the world. "Night" is an appeal to the goddess of the night to give protection against dangers in the dark.

2 Background

Culture

Portions of the *Rig Veda,* such as "Night," are an appeal to the natural forces to maintain their order. Part of Vedic belief held that the universe was in constant peril of being overrun by chaos and that rituals of human appeal could preserve order.

from the 1 2 Rig Veda

translated by Wendy Doniger

Differentiated Instruction Solutions for All Learners

Accessibility at a Glance

	Creation Hymn	Night
Context	Hindu speculations about the world's origin	Hindu belief in nature's protective forces
Language	Abstract nouns and several series of short questions	Concrete nouns and different personal pronouns referring to a goddess
Concept Level	Accessible (The origin of the world is mysterious.)	Accessible (Think of night as a protective goddess.)
Literary Merit	Vedic hymn from the *Rig Veda*	Vedic hymn from the *Rig Veda*
Lexile	590L	590L
Overall Rating	Average	Average

Background Vedic poets are in awe of nature, but they also desire to control and understand it. By endowing natural forces with the qualities of humans and animals, as in "Night," Vedic poets make it easier to approach, flatter, and manage these forces. Such attempts at control lead to thoughts about the workings and origin of the world, speculations that will become even more important in later Hindu texts. Of all the Vedic poems, the "Creation Hymn" represents the most self-conscious effort to fathom the world's mysteries.

Creation Hymn

1 There was neither non-existence nor existence then; there was neither the realm of space nor the sky which is beyond. What stirred? Where? In whose protection? Was there water, bottomlessly deep?

2 There was neither death nor immortality then. There was no distinguishing sign of night nor of day. That one breathed, windless, by its own impulse. Other than that there was nothing beyond.

3 Darkness was hidden by darkness in the beginning; with no distinguishing sign, all this was water. The life force that was covered with emptiness, that one arose through the power of heat.

4 Desire came upon that one in the beginning; that was the first seed of mind. Poets seeking in their heart with wisdom found the bond of existence in non-existence.

5 Their cord was extended across. Was there below? Was there above? There were seed-placers; there were powers. There was impulse beneath; there was giving-forth above.

6 Who really knows? Who will here proclaim it? Whence was it produced? Whence is this creation? The gods came afterwards, with the creation of this universe. Who then knows whence it has arisen?

7 Whence this creation has arisen—perhaps it formed itself, or perhaps it did not—the one who looks down on it, in the highest heaven, only he knows—or perhaps he does not know.

Vocabulary Builder

immortality (im′môr tal′ i tē) *n.* quality or state of being exempt from death; unending existence

distinguishing (di stiŋ′gwish iŋ) *adj.* serving to mark as separate or different

Reading Check 4

According to the speaker, why wouldn't the gods know how the universe was created?

3 Vocabulary Builder

Latin Prefix *im-* / *in-*

- Draw students' attention to the word *immortality.* Ask a volunteer to read the word and its definition.
- Have students **suggest** other words containing the prefix *im-* or *in-*, and write the suggestions on the board.
  Possible response: *Inactive, improper,* or *inadequate* are some suggestions.
- Break each suggested word down into its base word plus prefix. For example, *inactive* becomes *in-* + *active.* On the basis of these words, have students **infer** the meaning of the prefix *im-* or *in-*.
  Answer: The prefix *im-* or *in-* means "not."

4 Reading Check

Answer: The gods came after the creation.

Differentiated Instruction Solutions for All Learners

Enrichment for Gifted/Talented Students

Tell students that many different cultures have myths and legends that explain the origin of the world. Have students work independently to research creation myths and to select one to present to the class. Students' presentations can take the form of dramatic adaptations, musical performances, artwork, or written retellings. Ask students to share their presentations with the class, discussing their artistic interpretations and intent.

Enrichment for Advanced Readers

Call students' attention to the questions posed in stanzas 1, 5, and 6. Have students discuss how the speaker's questions are another device for expressing the inexpressible. Then, point out that in the end, the speaker states that even the highest power may share in the speaker's uncertainty. Ask students to consider whether this admission makes the questions more or less effective as techniques for communicating the inexpressible. Students can share their thoughts in a panel discussion.

❺ Literary Analysis

Vedic Hymn

- Remind students that nature inspired the Vedic poets' awe.
- Then, **ask** students the Literary Analysis question: In what ways does portraying night as a goddess make it more familiar and reassuring?
  Possible response: Gods and goddesses usually assume human form, so this personification of night makes it familiar to the human audience.

ASSESS

Answers

1. **Possible response:** Abstract thinkers might prefer "Creation Hymn" because it makes them think about the uncertain origin of the world. Others might prefer "Night" because it is more concrete and presents reassuring images.
2. (a) The world neither exists nor fails to exist. (b) Describing what was not suggests that no words can describe what was. This device allows the reader to experience the mystery of creation.
3. (a) The poet wants to know what was active ("what stirred?") when the world began and who was responsible for it ("In whose protection?"). (b) The gods came after the creation of the world and therefore cannot answer these questions. (c) If the gods are unable to answer these questions, humans will surely be unable to provide answers.
4. (a) The speaker asks the goddess to ward off wolves and thieves. (b) The speaker and audience will feel safer knowing that the goddess will ward off these evils.
5. **Possible response:** Both are successful. The descriptions of what does not exist and the use of unanswerable questions effectively portray the mysteries of the universe in "Creation Hymn." The personification of night as a protective and helpful goddess in "Night" alleviates the audience's fears about the dark.

Night

1 The goddess Night has drawn near, looking about on many sides with her eyes. She has put on all her glories.

❺ 2 The immortal goddess has filled the wide space, the depths and the heights. She stems the tide of darkness with her light.

3 The goddess has drawn near, pushing aside her sister the twilight. Darkness, too, will give way.

4 As you came near to us today, we turned homeward to rest, as birds go to their home in a tree.

5 People who live in villages have gone home to rest, and animals with feet, and animals with wings, even the ever-searching hawks.

6 Ward off the she-wolf and the wolf; ward off the thief. O night full of waves, be easy for us to cross over.

7 Darkness—palpable, black, and painted—has come upon me. O Dawn, banish it like a debt.

8 I have driven this hymn to you as the herdsman drives cows. Choose and accept it, O Night, daughter of the sky, like a song of praise to a conqueror.

Literary Analysis
Vedic Hymn In what ways does portraying night as a goddess make it more familiar and reassuring?

Vocabulary Builder
stems (stemz) *v.* stops or dams up (as a river)

Vocabulary Builder
palpable (pal′pə bəl) *adj.* able to be touched, felt, or handled

Critical Reading

1. **Respond:** To which of the hymns did you relate more, "Creation Hymn" or "Night"? Explain.
2. **(a) Recall:** How is the world described in the first two lines of "Creation Hymn"? **(b) Infer:** Why does the hymn say what was *not* rather than what was?
3. **(a) Recall:** Identify two specific questions the poet wants answered in "Creation Hymn." **(b) Infer:** Why can't the gods answer these questions? **(c) Deduce:** What does the gods' inability to answer suggest about the questions themselves?
4. **(a) Recall:** In "Night," what does the speaker ask the goddess Night to do? **(b) Analyze:** How might this request help the speaker and audience of this hymn feel safer in the darkness?
5. **Evaluate:** How successful are these hymns at expressing their central ideas? Explain.

Apply the Skills

from the *Rig Veda*

Literary Analysis

Vedic Hymn

1. Complete a chart like the one shown to identify two devices in the opening verses of "Creation Hymn" that suggest the oral tradition of **Vedic hymns**.

Device	Examples

2. **(a)** What eternal question does "Creation Hymn" explore? **(b)** What conclusion, if any, does the hymn reach with regard to this question?
3. Explain how the hymn "Night" reflects the Vedic sense of awe and respect for the forces of nature.

Comparing Literary Works

4. Why do you think "Creation Hymn" avoids using concrete language, such as **personification**, in questioning the origin of the universe?
5. **(a)** Which three natural phenomena are personified in "Night"? **(b)** In what way does personification support the hymn's purpose?
6. Why do you think the speaker of "Night" refers to the night using the concrete terms "tide of darkness" and "night full of waves"?

Reading Strategy

Paraphrasing

7. Reread the seventh verse of "Creation Hymn" and provide a **paraphrase** of that verse.
8. The fifth verse of "Night" is made up of one long sentence. Paraphrase this verse by breaking it down into several sentences.

Extend Understanding

9. **Science Connection:** According to "Creation Hymn," water existed before anything else. Many Native American creation myths also assert that water was the first element to exist. Why do you think many different peoples have imagined that the world began with water?

QuickReview

A **Vedic hymn** is an ancient Indian religious poem originally intended as a chant. Vedic hymns reflect a sense of awe toward nature.

Personification is the description of something nonhuman as if it were human.

When you **paraphrase,** you restate something in your own words.

For: Self-test
Visit: www.PHSchool.com
Web Code: eta-6201

Answers

1. **Device:** Repetition of words **Example:** "*There was neither* nonexistence nor existence then: *there was neither* the realm of space nor the sky which is beyond."
   Device: Repetition of grammatical structure **Example:** "What stirred? Where?"
   Another sample answer can be found on **Literary Analysis Graphic Organizer B,** p. 37, in ***Graphic Organizer Transparencies.***
2. (a) "Creation Hymn" explores the origin of the world. (b) The conclusion is that perhaps no one knows how or when the world was created.
3. By personifying night as a goddess, the hymn suggests that nature is a force worthy of worship, to which humans must appeal for protection.
4. Using personification or other concrete language would suggest that the beginning of the world can be clearly grasped or visualized. Abstract language reveals that the world's origins are mysterious.
5. (a) Night, twilight, and darkness are personified in "Night." (b) The personification allows the speaker to address these natural occurrences as concrete, rational beings as the speaker requests protection.
6. The speaker draws a comparison between the general idea of night and concrete details of water to make a general idea vivid. The audience is familiar with both the dangers of the night and the dangers water can hold.
7. **Possible response:** Where did Creation come from: Creation may have arisen with or without a creator; the highest god may or may not know the origin of creation.
8. **Possible response:** The villagers have gone home to sleep. The animals and birds have also returned home. Even the hawks have returned home.
9. **Possible response:** Water is necessary for life to exist, so it seems natural that life would have originated from water.

Go Online Assessment Students may use the **Self-test** to prepare for **Selection Test A** or **Selection Test B.**

EXTEND/ASSESS

Answers

❶ Vocabulary Lesson

Word Analysis: Latin Prefix *im- / in-*

1. infinite
2. imperfection
3. informal
4. impure
5. inflexible
6. immobile

Vocabulary Builder

1. c 2. d 3. a 4. b

Spelling Strategy

1. innumerable
2. immodest
3. immature
4. inadequate

❷ Grammar and Style Lesson

1. protection
2. (water)
3. death; immortality
4. (hymn); (herdsman); (cows)
5. (sun); (warmth); hope; (darkness)

Writing Application

Possible response: The little girls (concrete) wrap themselves in the quilts (concrete). They stand at the door (concrete) and plead with desire (abstract), "Take us to go see the moon!" (concrete). When we clear the trees (concrete), one child (concrete) follows my pointing finger (concrete). The moon, aware of its charm, (abstract) winks at us. The girl's breath (concrete) stops for a moment (abstract) before she turns to me and smiles.

Writing and Grammar Platinum Level

For support in teaching the Grammar and Style Lesson, use Chapter 16, Section 1.

Build Language Skills

❶ Vocabulary Lesson

Word Analysis: Latin Prefix *im- / in-*

The Latin prefix *im- / in-* means "not." The word *impossible* means "not possible." Consider the meaning of the prefix *im- / in-* as you choose the word from the following list that best completes each sentence below.

informal	immobile	infinite
impure	imperfection	inflexible

1. There are no limits to what you can achieve; the possibilities are ___.
2. The diamond was flawless, without a single ___.
3. Do not dress up for this event; it's ___.
4. Smoke from the factory made the air ___.
5. We tried to convince him to change his mind, but his will was ___.
6. The doctor said that the broken arm could heal only if it remained ___.

Vocabulary Builder: Synonyms

Match each vocabulary word on the left with its synonym, or word with a similar meaning, on the right.

1. distinguishing
2. immortality
3. palpable
4. stems

a. touchable
b. stops
c. differentiating
d. deathlessness

Spelling Strategy

When you add a prefix to a word, keep all the letters of the original word. For example, *im-* + *mortality* = *immortality.* Add the prefix *im- / in-* to each word listed below to create a new word.

1. numerable
2. modest
3. mature
4. adequate

❷ Grammar and Style Lesson

Concrete and Abstract Nouns

A **noun** is the name of a person, place, or thing. A **concrete noun** names something that you can physically see, touch, hear, or smell. An **abstract noun** names something that is nonphysical, or that you cannot readily perceive through any of your five senses.

Concrete: eyes, tree, wolf
Abstract: existence, desire, wisdom

Practice Copy each item, circling all *concrete* nouns and underlining all *abstract* nouns.

1. What stirred? Where? In whose protection?
2. Was there water, bottomlessly deep?
3. There was neither death nor immortality then.
4. I have driven this hymn to you as the herdsman drives cows.
5. The rising sun brings warmth and hope to those who fear darkness.

Writing Application Write five sentences about some aspect of nature that inspires a sense of awe in you. For example, you might describe a thunder-storm or sunset. Underline at least three nouns in your writing, and indicate whether each one is concrete or abstract.

Prentice Hall Writing and Grammar Connection: Platinum Level, Chapter 16, Section 1

Assessment Practice

Recognize Details **(For more practice, see *Standardized Test Preparation Workbook*, p. 9)**

Many tests require students to recognize facts, details, and sequence. Use the following test item to demonstrate.

1. The goddess Night has drawn near, looking about on many sides with her eyes. She has put on all her glories.
2. The immortal goddess has filled the wide space, the depths and the heights. She stems the tide of darkness with her light.

Choose the detail that best supports this main idea: *Night is a watchful goddess that fills the sky.*

A The goddess Night draws near.
B The goddess Night stems the tide of darkness.
C The goddess Night is frightening.
D The goddess Night brings rainfall.

Neither *C* nor *D* appears in the text. *A* appears in the text but does not support the main idea. Therefore, the correct answer is C.

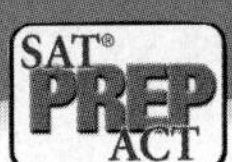

❸ Writing Lesson

Timed Writing: Comparison-and-Contrast Essay

"Creation Hymn" and "Night" both express awe about nature, but they differ in their treatment of it. In a **comparison-and-contrast** essay, examine the similarities and differences in how these hymns approach natural mysteries. ***(40 minutes)***

Prewriting *(10 minutes)* Review the hymns to consider how each one attempts to comprehend the workings of nature. Use a Venn diagram, like the one shown, to identify points to compare and contrast. Then, gather details and passages that support the points you have noted.

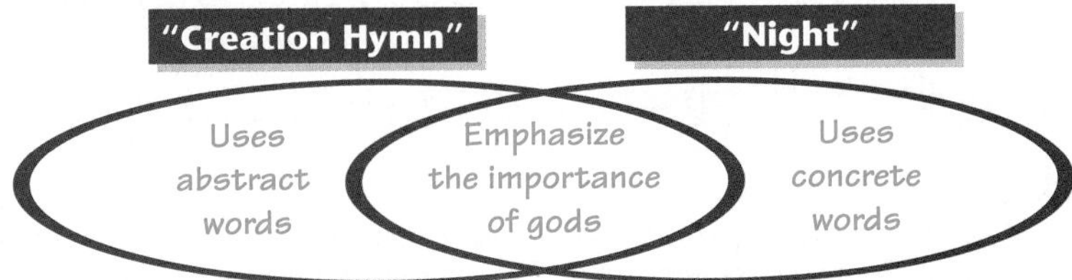

Drafting *(20 minutes)* Decide how to organize your essay. One possibility is to discuss each point in turn, using examples from both hymns. You could also discuss all aspects of one hymn first and then all aspects of the second hymn. Cite passages and details from the hymns to support your points.

Revising *(10 minutes)* Review your work to be sure that you have supported your main points. You might also ask the following questions and revise accordingly: *Have I organized points logically? Have I used transitions to show comparisons?*

WG *Prentice Hall Writing and Grammar Connection: Platinum Level, Chapter 9, Section 3*

❹ Extend Your Learning

Listening and Speaking With a small group, give an **oral interpretation** of one of the hymns. To prepare, consider these questions:

- What is the mood of the hymn?
- What ideas are being expressed?
- Which words and phrases best capture these elements?

Have each member of the group practice reading a verse aloud. Then, perform your reading for the class. **[Group Activity]**

Research and Technology The *Rig Veda* reflects religious ideas of the Aryans, a people who migrated to India around 1400 B.C. Research the Aryans using library resources, such as encyclopedias and other print materials. Then, create a **culture spreadsheet** summarizing the information and the data you find.

For: An additional research activity
Visit: www.PHSchool.com
Web Code: etd-7203

❸ Writing Lesson

You may use this Writing Lesson as a timed-writing practice, or you may allow students to develop the comparison-and-contrast essay as a writing assignment over several days.

- To give students guidance in writing this comparison-and-contrast essay, give them **Support for Writing Lesson**, p. 14 in ***Unit 2 Resources.***
- Before students complete their Venn diagrams, encourage them to formulate a main idea about the way each poem approaches the subject of natural mysteries.
- Use the Exposition: Comparison-and-Contrast rubrics in ***General Resources***, pp. 53–54, to evaluate students' work.

WG **Writing and Grammar Platinum Level**

For support in teaching the Writing Lesson, use Chapter 9, Section 3.

❹ Listening and Speaking

- Have each group answer the bulleted questions to determine the appropriate mood to convey and to identify words and phrases to emphasize.
- As students practice their oral interpretations, encourage the other members of the groups to provide feedback that presenters can incorporate into their final presentations.
- The **Support for Extend Your Learning** page (***Unit 2 Resources,*** p. 15) provides guided note-taking opportunities to help students complete the Extend Your Learning activities.
- Use the rubric for Peer Assessment: Oral Interpretation, p. 130 in ***General Resources,*** to evaluate student work.

Go Online Research Have students type in the Web Code for another research activity.

Assessment Resources

The following resources can be used to assess students' knowledge and skills.

Unit 2 Resources
- **Selection Test A**, pp. 17–19
- **Selection Test B**, pp. 20–22

General Resources
- **Rubrics for Exposition: Comparison-and-Contrast Essay**, pp. 53–54
- **Rubric for Peer Assessment: Oral Interpretation**, p. 130

Go Online Assessment Students may use the **Self-test** to prepare for **Selection Test A** or **Selection Test B.**

PREPREACH/TEACH

Standard Course of Study

LT.5.01.2	Build knowledge of literary genres and explore how characteristics apply to literature of world cultures.
LT.5.01.3	Analyze literary devices and explain their effect on the work of world literature.

❶ Types of Wisdom Literature

- Tell students that they will study wisdom literature in Unit 2. **Ask** students: What examples of literature that you know might fall in the category of wisdom literature?
  Possible responses: Students may mention the Bible, the Qur'an, Poor Richard's Almanack, myths, fables, and other philosophical or religious writings.
- Review the types of wisdom literature with students.
- Have students read the Yiddish proverb on this page. Then have students **discuss** the wisdom that the quotation offers.
  Answer: Real understanding is not superficial, and words cannot be accepted at face value. A wise person sees things in different ways.
- Point out to students that not all wisdom literature is ancient. Although some wisdom literature is thousands of years old, other examples of wisdom literature are only a century or two old.

❷ Features of Wisdom Literature

- **Ask** students why they think much wisdom literature is aphoristic and uses figurative language.
  Possible response: Many examples came from the oral tradition, which uses short sayings and figurative language.
- As you review the features of wisdom literature, ask students to recall any aphorisms with which they are familiar, such as A *rolling stone gathers no moss.* List the aphorisms on the board, and ask students to explain the wisdom that each aphorism imparts.

Unit 2

Focus on Literary Forms: Wisdom Literature

Defining Wisdom Literature

Wisdom literature consists of oral and written works that focus on the search for understanding, meaning, and enlightenment. This type of literature is concerned with profound questions about human existence. More specifically, it tends to focus on human conduct and morality: how we should live and how we should treat others.

A WISE MAN HEARS ONE WORD AND UNDERSTANDS TWO. — *Yiddish Proverb*

❶ Types of Wisdom Literature

Wisdom literature encompasses a wide range of forms, many of which overlap. Some works are part of the oral tradition—moral and spiritual insights that were originally handed down by word of mouth. Others are attributed to a specific author or philosophical teacher, whose words may have been written down by a follower. Some works are considered sacred texts that are the foundation of a religion.

The chart to the right lists some of the most important types of wisdom literature.

Types of Wisdom Literature	Examples
A **myth** is an anonymous tale that explains the actions of gods or the causes of natural phenomena.	• the *Rig Veda,* p. 180 • the *Mahabharata,* p. 192 • Ovid's *Metamorphoses,* p. 550
A **fable** is a brief story that teaches a moral or practical lesson about life and usually features animal characters.	• Sa'di's *Gulistan,* p. 106 • the *Panchatantra,* p. 222 • Jean de La Fontaine's fables
A **parable** is a brief story that teaches a moral or religious lesson and usually features human characters.	• Jesus' parables in the New Testament of the Bible • Zen parables, p. 320
A **proverb, a maxim,** or an **aphorism** is a wise saying that offers practical wisdom about life. Such sayings are often included within larger works.	• African proverbs, p. 130 • Sa'di's *Manners of Kings,* p. 10[illegible] • Lao Tzu's *Tao Te Ching,* p. 266 • Confucius' *Analects,* p. 268
A **sacred text** is the foundation of a religion. A **spiritual** or **philosophical text** teaches moral conduct or explores questions about the meaning of life. It may be the foundation of a system of spiritual beliefs.	• the Bible, pp. 38, 60, and 67 • the Qur'an, p. 78 • the *Rig Veda,* p. 180 • the Upanishads, p. 188 • Lao Tzu's *Tao Te Ching,* p. 266 • Confucius' *Analects,* p. 268 • Plato's *Apology,* p. 440

❷ Features of Wisdom Literature

- Wisdom literature often uses an **aphoristic style.** An **aphorism** is a brief, memorable, and often witty saying that expresses a truth about life—as in a proverb or the moral at the end

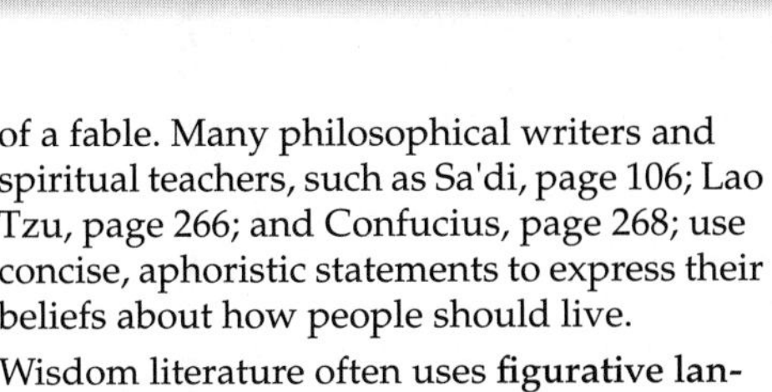

of a fable. Many philosophical writers and spiritual teachers, such as Sa'di, page 106; Lao Tzu, page 266; and Confucius, page 268; use concise, aphoristic statements to express their beliefs about how people should live.

- Wisdom literature often uses **figurative language** and **symbolism** to express meaning. **Figurative language** is language that is not meant to be understood literally. Instead, it expresses an imaginative connection. A **symbol** is an object, a person, an animal, a place, or an image that represents both itself and something larger in meaning—usually an abstract idea. For example, in the African proverb "The zebra cannot do away with his stripes," the zebra stands for unchangeable human nature.
- Sometimes the symbolism of wisdom literature rises to the level of **allegory**. An allegory is a literary work with two levels of meaning. Every element has both a literal and a symbolic meaning, with specific characters standing for abstract qualities. Fables and parables are considered types of allegory. Dante's *Divine Comedy*, p. 658, is a famous example of a book-length allegory in which a literal journey represents a man's struggle for redemption.
- Wisdom literature is usually **didactic** in its purpose—that is, it is meant to teach a moral or ethical lesson about life. This lesson may be taught directly, as in a fable, or indirectly, as in a parable, in which the moral is not explicitly stated. Although wisdom literature may use wit and even humor to convey its message, its purpose is nevertheless to instruct rather than simply to entertain.

▲ **Critical Viewing** 4
This painting is an illustration for the fable "The Fox and the Crow." Based on the illustration, what do you think is the moral of the fable? **[Infer]**

3 Strategies for Reading Wisdom Literature

Use these strategies as you read wisdom literature.

Read the Text Aloud Because wisdom literature often developed within the oral tradition, reading the work aloud will usually deepen your appreciation of its beauty and meaning. As you read, consider how the sound of the language affects you on an emotional or even spiritual level.

Read Between the Lines Sometimes, the wisdom in a work of wisdom literature is directly stated. In other texts, however, you may need to interpret details to draw inferences about the moral or theme. As you read, consider whether there are characters, images, or statements that are not meant to be understood literally. Then, think about what these elements may represent on a figurative, a symbolic, or even an allegorical level.

3 Strategies for Reading Wisdom Literature

- Provide students with a copy of the two-column chart from ***Graphic Organizer Transparencies***, p. 285. Then, read aloud a short selection of wisdom literature, and ask students to use the chart to identify the form of the work and its characteristic features. Then have students identify language that should be interpreted literally, figuratively, or both.
- Have students read silently a short selection of poetry from wisdom literature. Then, ask a volunteer to read aloud the same poem. Elicit responses from students on the ways in which the poem affected them when it was read aloud versus when they read it silently to themselves.

4 Critical Viewing

Possible response: The moral of the story is to not trust flatterers. However, students may suggest the moral is that arguments are futile or that one should be cautious of strangers.

Differentiated Instruction
Solutions for All Learners

Strategy for Less Proficient Readers
Remind students that the *Rig Veda* is an example of the type of wisdom literature known as a sacred text. Review the features of wisdom literature with students. Then, have pairs of students return to the *Rig Veda* and look for an example of each of the following features of wisdom literature: figurative language, symbol, and moral or ethical lesson. Have students make a chart that shows the feature, the text from the *Rig Veda* that exemplifies the feature, and a brief explanation of why the text is an example of the feature. Have students present their findings to the group.

Strategy for English Learners
Ask students to recall some of the wisdom literature from their native cultures. Have them select one piece and write a paragraph that identifies and explains any two features of wisdom literature, such as aphoristic style, question-and-answer format, examples of figurative language, symbolism, or allegory, and a moral or ethical lesson. Invite students to present their paragraphs to the class.

Standard Course of Study

WL.1.03.10 Analyze connections between ideas, concepts, characters and experiences in reflection.

CT.4.01.1 Interpret and make generalizations about events supported by specific references.

Critical Thinking

1. Consider the progression of things on which Bhrigu's father tells him to meditate. Why are the different items—food, life, mind, reason, joy—mentioned in this order? **[Analyze]**
   Possible response: The progression of items indicates a pattern of eliminating what Brahman is not, moving from the specific to the general, the material to the spiritual.
2. Why do you think Bhrigu's father does not recommend scientific investigation as a means of knowing Brahman? **[Generalize]**
   Possible response: Scientific investigation leads to one definitive, indisputable answer. Varuna knows that one must investigate Brahman individually, exploring it in terms of what one can discover and understand for oneself.

Critical Viewing

Possible response: The students are sitting near the teacher to learn from him. The meditative pose of the students suggests that they are pondering Brahman.

A Closer Look

The Mystery of Brahman, *translated* by Juan Mascaró

Once Bhrigu Varuni went to his father Varuna and said: "Father, explain to me the mystery of Brahman."

Then his father spoke to him of the food of the earth, of the breath of life, of the one who sees, of the one who hears, of the mind that knows, and of the one who speaks. And he further said to him: "Seek to know him from whom all beings have come, by whom they all live, and unto whom these all return. He is Brahman."

So Bhrigu went and practiced *tapas*, spiritual prayer. Then he thought that Brahman was the food of the earth: for from earth all beings have come, by food of the earth they all live, and unto the earth they all return.

After this he went again to his father Varuna and said: "Father, explain further to me the mystery of Brahman." To him his father answered: "Seek to know Brahman by *tapas*, by prayer, because Brahman is prayer."

So Bhrigu went and practiced *tapas*, spiritual prayer. Then he thought that Brahman was life: for from life all beings have come, by life they all live, and unto life they all return.

After this he went again to his father Varuna and said: "Father, explain further to me the mystery of Brahman." To him his father answered: "Seek to know Brahman by *tapas*, by prayer, because Brahman is prayer."

So Bhrigu went and practiced *tapas*, spiritual prayer. Then he thought that Brahman was mind: for from mind all beings have come, by mind they all live, and unto mind they all return.

After this he went again to his father Varuna and said: "Father, explain further to me the mystery of Brahman." To him his father answered: "Seek to know Brahman by *tapas*, by prayer, because Brahman is prayer."

So Bhrigu went and practiced *tapas*, spiritual prayer. Then he thought that Brahman was reason: for from reason all beings have come, by reason they all live, and unto reason they all return.

He went again to his father, asked the same question, and received the same answer.

So Bhrigu went and practiced *tapas*, spiritual prayer. And then he saw that Brahman is joy: for FROM JOY ALL BEINGS HAVE COME, BY JOY THEY ALL LIVE, AND UNTO JOY THEY ALL RETURN.

This was the vision of Bhrigu Varuni which came from the Highest: and he who sees this vision lives in the Highest.

▲ **Critical Viewing** How does this painting reflect the philosophy of the Upanishads? **[Connect]**

Enrichment

The Influence of the Upanishads

Despite their status as secret books, the Upanishads have had a strong influence on Indian philosophy. In the eighth century A.D., for example, one of India's greatest thinkers, Shankara, developed a system of thought based on the Upanishads. He believed that everything we see, hear, and feel derives from a single ultimate reality. Shankara's philosophy was so popular in India that it became the standard against which all other philosophies were measured.

The Upanishads also have had a great influence beyond the borders of India. When they were translated into European languages in the 1800s, their teachings contributed to the Western philosophical tradition.

The Upanishads: Teaching Philosophy

Indian philosophers pursued the answers to questions about the meaning of life in texts called the Upanishads (o͞o pan' i shadz'), which were written by many different authors from 1000 to 600 B.C.

To Sit Nearby Upanishad in the Indian language Sanskrit means "to sit nearby," in the sense of sitting near a teacher to learn from him. The Upanishads often present complicated subjects, such as the nature of reality, in dialogues between teachers and students. The Upanishads are the final stage in the development of sacred books called the Vedas (vā' dəz), which include the *Rig Veda* (page 206). The Upanishads pursue philosophical questions about the meaning of life.

> *"Upanishad in the Indian language Sanskrit means "to sit nearby," in the sense of sitting near a teacher to learn from him."*

Brahman, "the Absolute" The central concept of the Upanishads is the idea of Brahman (brä mən). This term has been rendered in English as "the one, universal Soul," and "the Absolute," but not as "God." Brahman is neither a god nor an object of worship. As the reality that underlies all appearances, Brahman is the subject of meditation, a kind of prayerlike thought.

Peeling the Onion Brahman is a difficult concept to grasp. It can best be defined by stating what it is not. Like peeling the layers of an onion, when everything that is mere appearance has been stripped away, the remaining core will be Brahman. In the Upanishads, this type of description is called "not this, not that." The excerpt on page 290 illustrates how these sacred books use the "not this, not that" method to arrive at truth.

Secret and Dangerous Books In ancient India, scholars secretly studied the Upanishads, because these books focused on Brahman rather than the Hindu gods. Yet this literature influenced many great thinkers, including Ralph Waldo Emerson in nineteenth-century America.

Activity

The Quest for Meaning

With a group, discuss the different ways modern people seek meaning in their lives. Use these questions to guide your discussion:

- What, if anything, can people in the twenty-first century learn from ancient philosophical texts such as the Upanishads? Explain.
- Do philosophical questions about the meaning of life and the nature of reality have any application to your own life? Why or why not?

Choose a point person to share your ideas with the class.

Background

The Authors of the Upanishads

The Upanishads themselves are attributed to certain sages who were divorced from society and living in the forest. These authors defied the ritualistic practices of the Vedic cult, yet they incorporated much of the ritual imagery into their literary style, which indicated a move toward inward contemplation and self-realization. The specific writer of the excerpt is not known.

Background

The Indian Oral Tradition

Indian literature, such as the Upanishads, is grounded in oral tradition. Not only was individual religious instruction conducted orally, but the majority of knowledge was also transmitted in this way from generation to generation. Even in recent years, much of India's population has been illiterate, thus allowing the oral tradition to continue as a primary means of education.

Activity

Form students into groups, and advise them to listen courteously to one another's opinions. Suggest that individuals in each group take responsibility for different aspects of the topic, such as which spiritual texts people rely on and why, and whether people seek spiritual advice from religious leaders or self-help assistance from therapists or philosophy teachers. Have students take notes as they discuss these topics. Then have group members pool their ideas and organize them on index cards for the point person to use in a presentation to the class.

Standard Course of Study

Goal 1: WRITTEN LANGUAGE

WL.1.02.4 Explain how culture affects personal responses.

Goal 3: FOUNDATIONS OF ARGUMENT

FA.3.02.2 Provide relevant, reliable support in editorials.

Goal 4: CRITICAL THINKING

CT.4.05.6 Make inferences and draw conclusions based on critical text.

CT.4.05.9 Analyze and evaluate the effects of craft and style in critical text.

Goal 5: LITERATURE

LT.5.01.5 Analyze archetypal characters, themes, and settings in world literature.

LT.5.01.7 Understand the cultural and historical impact on text.

Step-by-Step Teaching Guide	Pacing Guide
PRETEACH	
• Administer Vocabulary and Reading Warm-ups as necessary.	5 min.
• Engage students' interest with the motivation activity.	5 min.
• Read and discuss author and background features. **FT**	10 min.
• Introduce the Literary Analysis Skill: The Indian Epic. **FT**	5 min.
• Introduce the Reading Strategy: Inferring Beliefs of the Period. **FT**	10 min.
• Prepare students to read by teaching the selection vocabulary. **FT**	
TEACH	
• Informally monitor comprehension while students read independently or in groups. **FT**	30 min.
• Monitor students' comprehension with the Reading Check notes.	as students read
• Reinforce vocabulary with Vocabulary Builder notes.	as students read
• Develop students' understanding of the Indian epic with the Literary Analysis annotations. **FT**	5 min.
• Develop students' ability to infer beliefs of the period with the Reading Strategy annotations. **FT**	5 min.
ASSESS/EXTEND	
• Assess students' comprehension and mastery of the Literary Analysis and Reading Strategy by having them answer the Apply the Skills questions. **FT**	15 min.
• Have students complete the Vocabulary Lesson and the Grammar and Style Lesson. **FT**	15 min.
• Apply students' ability to revise for the connotations of words by using the Writing Lesson. **FT**	45 min. or homework
• Apply students' understanding by using one or more of the Extend Your Learning activities.	20–90 min. or homework
• Administer Selection Test A or Selection Test B. **FT**	15 min.

Resources

Print

Unit 2 Resources

- Vocabulary Warm-up Word Lists **[L1, L2, EL]** .... p. 23
- Vocabulary Warm-up Practice **[L1, L2, EL]** .... p. 24
- Reading Warm-up A **[L1, L2, EL]** .... p. 25
- Reading Warm-up B **[L1, L2, L3]** .... p. 26

Transparency

Graphic Organizer Transparencies

- Literary Analysis Graphic Organizer A **[L3]** .... p. 38
- Literary Analysis Graphic Organizer B **[L1, L2, EL]** .... p. 39
- Reading Strategy Graphic Organizer A **[L3]** .... p. 40
- Reading Strategy Graphic Organizer B **[L1, L2, EL]** .... p. 41
- Outline **[L3]** .... p. 279

Print

Reader's Notebook [L2]

Reader's Notebook: Adapted Version [L1]

Reader's Notebook: English Learner's Version [EL]

Unit 2 Resources

- Literary Analysis **[L3]** .... p. 27
- Reading Strategy **[L3]** .... p. 28
- Vocabulary Builder **[L3]** .... p. 29

Technology

Listening to Literature Audio CDs [L2, EL]

Print

Unit 2 Resources

- Grammar and Style **[L3]** .... p. 30
- Support for Writing Lesson **[L3]** .... p. 31
- Support for Extend Your Learning **[L3]** .... p. 32
- Enrichment **[L4]** .... p. 33
- Selection Test A **[L1, L2, EL]** .... pp. 34–36
- Selection Test B **[L3, L4]** .... pp. 37–39

General Resources

- Rubrics for Persuasion: Persuasive Essay **[L3]** .... pp. 47–48
- Rubric for Speaking: Delivering an Oral Response to Literature **[L3]** ...... p. 91

Technology

- **Go Online:** Research **[L3]**
- **Go Online:** Self-test **[L3]**
- ***ExamView®*, Test Bank [L3]**

Choosing Resources for Differentiated Instruction

[L1] Special Needs Students

[L2] Below-Level Students

[L3] All Students

[L4] Advanced Students

[EL] English Learners

For Vocabulary and Reading Warm-ups and for Selection Tests, **A** signifies "less challenging" and **B** "more challenging." For Graphic Organizer transparencies, **A** signifies "not filled in" and **B** "filled in."

FT Fast Track Instruction: To move the lesson more quickly, use the strategies and activities identified with **FT**.

Scaffolding for Less Proficient and Advanced Students

The leveled Critical Thinking questions after selections progress in the levels of thinking required to answer them. To address the needs of your different students, you may use the (a) level questions for your less proficient students and the (b) level questions with your on-level and advanced students. The occasional (c) level questions are appropriate for your advanced students.

PRENTICE HALL **TeacherEXPRESS™** Plan · Teach · Assess Use this complete suite of powerful teaching tools to make lesson planning and testing quicker and easier.

PRENTICE HALL **StudentEXPRESS™** Learn · Study · Succeed Use the interactive textbook (online and on CD-ROM) to make selections and activities come alive with audio and video support and interactive questions.

For: Information about Lexiles
Visit: www.PHSchool.com
Web Code: eue-1111

PREETEACH

Motivation

Have students imagine what it would be like if everyone believed that all living beings, from insects through elephants, contributed to the well-being of the universe. In what ways might the world be different if all people shared this belief? Would people behave differently? Why or why not?

❶ Background

More About the Selections

The *Mahabharata* plays an important role in contemporary Indian society. Many of the episodes in the *Mahabharata* are recited by Indian parents to their children.

Supposedly written by the same author as the *Mahabharata,* the *Bhagavad-Gita* is a dialogue between Lord Krishna and his prince disciple Arjuna. The dialogue is witnessed by Sanjaya (san ja´ ya), a personal messenger who relates the entire text to the blind Dhrtarastra (dre´ tə räsh´ trə) via a kind of mystical, closed-circuit television.

The writer R. K. Narayan cites the importance of oral literature in traditional Indian society: "The storyteller who has studied the epics, the *Ramayana* and the *Mahabharata,* may take up any of the thousand episodes in them, create a narrative with his individual stamp on it, and hold the attention of an audience, numbering thousands, for hours."

Geography Note

Draw students' attention to the map on this page. Point out that India, the setting for the following selections, has experienced the rise and fall of several powerful empires over many centuries.

Build Skills Epics

from the Mahabharata • *from the* Bhagavad-Gita • ❶ *from the* Ramayana

About the *Mahabharata*

The *Mahabharata* (mə hä´ bä´ rə tə) is the world's longest epic. Although it was compiled sometime between 200 B.C. and A.D. 200, Indian storytellers who have memorized it still entertain and instruct their village audiences with recitations from this epic poem.

The myths and tales of the *Mahabharata* are woven into the fabric of its main story: the account of a fight over the rights to a kingdom. Two branches of a family, the Pandavas and the Kauravas, are involved in this dispute.

Many of these myths and tales concern the Indian concept of **dharma** (där´ mə), the unique obligations that each person must fulfill in order to maintain harmony in the universe. The stories reflect the belief that unrighteous behavior leads one astray, while righteous behavior will eventually be rewarded.

About the *Bhagavad-Gita*

The *Bhagavad-Gita* (bug´ ə vəd gē´ tä), which means "Song of the Lord," has been one of the most important texts in the Hindu tradition. It has been translated more often and into more languages than any other Sanskrit text, and many Hindu religious teachers have written commentaries on it. This ancient Sanskrit book has also played a role in modern politics. During the struggle for his country's independence, the Indian leader Mohandas Gandhi turned to the *Gita* for inspiration almost daily.

Although it can be read as a self-contained book, the *Bhagavad-Gita* is actually a small part in the middle of the *Mahabharata.* As in the *Mahabharata,* the main story in the *Bhagavad-Gita* is the conflict between the Pandavas and the Kauravas.

About the *Ramayana*

Written by the poet Valmiki, the great Indian epic the *Ramayana* (rä mä´ yə nə) consists of 24,000 couplets, parts of which date from 300 B.C. The *Ramayana* tells the story of Prince Rama. It is divided into seven sections, or *kandas*, each focusing on a different period of Rama's life. The purpose of the *Ramayana* is to spread the teaching of the Vedas, the sacred texts of Hinduism, in an entertaining and easy-to-understand manner through stories that focus on themes of duty and morality. Like the *Bhagavad-Gita*, the *Ramayana* teaches the ideal way to live and reinforces the theory that good prevails over evil.

The main villain in the *Ramayana* is Ravana, an evil giant with ten heads and twenty arms. Ravana believed himself to be immortal because no god had the power to slay him. When Ravana began to persecute both gods and men, the Indian god Vishnu took the form of a man in order to conquer Ravana and put an end to his destruction. Vishnu's mortal form was Rama. Rama, who grew up to be brave and honorable, was the favorite son of King Dasharatha (dä sä rä´ tä), who upon retiring decided to make Rama king. However, just as Rama was about to assume the throne, Dasharatha was tricked into banishing him for 14 years. The *Ramayana* chronicles Rama's efforts during his exile to fulfill his dharma (his unique duties in life) by killing Ravana and reclaiming the throne.

Preview

Connecting to the Literature

Mythical heroes from all times and cultures—from King Arthur to Luke Skywalker—possess certain traits in common. Notice how the heroes in these selections display such characteristics as bravery, loyalty, and integrity.

❷ Literary Analysis

The Indian Epic

An **Indian epic** is a long narrative—often a poem—about the deeds and adventures of an Indian hero. It usually tells a story that bears great religious significance and can include elements of myth, legend, and history. In the *Mahabharata,* the *Bhagavad-Gita,* and the *Ramayana,* the actions of the heroes reflect the values of Hinduism and Indian society. As you read each selection, note the personal qualities and actions of its epic hero.

Comparing Literary Works

An **epic hero** is the central figure of an epic, possessing such qualities as

- courage
- loyalty
- great physical strength

This larger-than-life hero usually faces some challenge in which he must prove his heroic qualities and achieve something of great value to his society. Use a chart like the one shown to compare the qualities of the epic heroes in these selections.

❸ Reading Strategy

Inferring Beliefs of the Period

By paying close attention to the ideas expressed in these selections, you can **infer beliefs of the period** in which they were written. For example, Sri Krishna's discussion of the Atman in the *Bhagavad-Gita* reveals the ancient Indian belief in an eternal soul. As you read, look for words and actions that reflect the values and beliefs of ancient India.

Vocabulary Builder

mitigated (mit′ ə gāt′ id) *v.* moderated; eased (p. 192)

caricature (kar′ i kə chər) *n.* likeness or imitation that is so distorted or inferior as to seem ridiculous (p. 193)

scruples (skro͞o′ pəlz) *n.* feelings of doubt over what is ethical (p. 200)

pervades (pər vādz′) *v.* spreads throughout (p. 201)

manifested (man′ ə fest′ id) *v.* proved or revealed (p. 203)

dispel (di spel′) *v.* cause to vanish (p. 209)

invoked (in vōkt′) *v.* called on for help (p. 215)

pristine (pris′ tēn′) *adj.* unspoiled; uncorrupted (p. 215)

NC Standard Course of Study

- Analyze archetypal characters, themes, and settings in world literature. (LT.5.01.5)
- Understand the cultural and historical impact on text. (LT.5.01.7)

Epic Hero	Heroic Traits
Sibi	
Arjuna	
Rama	

❷ Literary Analysis

The Indian Epic

- Read with the class the characteristics of an Indian epic and the qualities of an epic hero. Then, point out that an epic hero is usually based on a legendary or historic person. A typical hero travels on a long and challenging journey.
- Direct students' attention to the graphic organizer. Then give them a copy of **Literary Analysis Graphic Organizer A** in ***Graphic Organizer Transparencies,*** p. 38. Have them use it to record each character's heroic qualities.
- Tell students that they can compare the traits displayed by the heroes of Indian epics with those of other epic heroes to gain insight into universal heroic traits.

❸ Reading Strategy

Inferring Beliefs of the Period

- Remind students that we often draw inferences about an individual's beliefs or behavior. Use this example: "Net in hand, a person slowly and quietly approaches a trash can. What might you infer about the person's behavior?"
  Answer: The person believes there is an animal in or near the trash can.
- Explain that, similarly, readers must infer a society's beliefs when reading a work from that society. Readers must note cultural details and apply details from their own background and experiences.
- As they read the selections, have students record words, actions, and other details that reflect the values and beliefs of ancient India.

Vocabulary Builder

- Pronounce each vocabulary word for students, and read the definitions as a class. Have students identify any words with which they are already familiar.

Differentiated Instruction Solutions for All Learners

Support for Special Needs Students
Have students complete the **Preview** and **Build Skills** pages for these selections in the ***Reader's Notebook: Adapted Version.*** These pages provide a selection summary, an abbreviated presentation of the reading and literary skills, and the graphic organizer on the **Build Skills** page in the student book.

Support for Less Proficient Readers
Have students complete the **Preview** and **Build Skills** pages for these selections in the ***Reader's Notebook.*** These pages provide a selection summary, an abbreviated presentation of the reading and literary skills, and the graphic organizer on the **Build Skills** page in the student book.

Support for English Learners
Have students complete the **Preview** and **Build Skills** pages for these selections in the ***Reader's Notebook: English Learner's Version.*** These pages provide a selection summary, an abbreviated presentation of the skills, additional contextual vocabulary, and the graphic organizer on the **Build Skills** page in the student book.

TEACH

Facilitate Understanding

"Sibi" is an accessible and entertaining story. To ensure that students do not have any difficulties, however, read this selection together as a class, with student volunteers taking turns reading aloud. Encourage students to raise any questions that arise as the text is being read.

1 About the Selection

This selection explores the Indian notion of duty by recounting the tale of Sibi, a king who protects a dove from a hawk. When the hawk wants the dove as food for his family, the king is willing to give his own flesh to protect the dove. Sibi, above all a man of his word, knows that he must fulfill this duty or face a terrible punishment when his soul is reborn. So, Sibi suffers dire consequences, but not in vain; his heroic qualities are rewarded in the end.

2 Literary Analysis

The Indian Epic

- Remind students that the actions of the Indian epic hero reflect the values of Hinduism and Indian society.
- Have students read the bracketed passage, and discuss how the king treats his guests.
- Then, **ask** students the Literary Analysis question: What values does the king's behavior toward his guests reflect?
  Possible response: By ensuring his guests' comfort, the king demonstrates the value of placing others' needs before one's own.

1 FROM THE MAHABHARATA

retold by R. K. Narayan

Background The *Mahabharata* has been handed down orally from generation to generation, and its stories are still told today. Indian writer and translator R. K. Narayan describes the typical village storyteller beginning an evening session: ". . . the storyteller will dress himself for the part by smearing sacred ash on his forehead and wrapping himself in a green shawl, while his helpers set up a framed picture of some god on a pedestal in the veranda, decorate it with jasmine garlands, and light incense to it. . . . He begins the session with a prayer, prolonging it until the others join and the valleys echo with the chants, drowning the cry of jackals."

SIBI

There is a half-moon in the sky today which will disappear shortly after midnight, said the storyteller. I'll select a tale which will end before the moon sets, so that you may all go home when there is still a little light.

2 The tale concerns a king and two birds. The king was Sibi, who had just performed a holy sacrifice on the banks of the Jumna.[1] The guests were resting in the tree shade after partaking of a feast. The air was charged with the scent of flowers and incense. Sibi went round to make sure that everyone was comfortable. A cool breeze blew from the south, patches of clouds mitigated the severity of the sun in the blue sky, the embers of the holy fire subsided into a soft glow under the ash.

The king, satisfied that all his guests were happy, dismissed his attendants and proceeded to his own corner of the camp to rest under a canopy. He had closed his eyes, half in sleep and half in prayer, when he felt a gust of air hitting him in the face and some object suddenly dropping on his lap. He awoke and noticed a dove, white and soft,

Vocabulary Builder
mitigated (mit´ ə gāt´ id) *v.* moderated; eased

Literary Analysis
The Indian Epic What values does the king's behavior toward his guests reflect?

1. **Jumna** (jum´ nə) river in northern India, flowing from the Himalayas southwest into the Ganges.

Differentiated Instruction Solutions for All Learners

Accessibility at a Glance

	SIBI	The Yoga of Knowledge	Rama and Ravana in Battle
Context	Dharma of India	Karma and duty	Hindu values
Language	Syntax: compound-complex sentences and dialogue	Formal dialogue in prose and verse	Words describing battle and destruction
Concept Level	Accessible (Every person has duties.)	Accessible (Focus on duties, not on rewards.)	Accessible (Good prevails over evil.)
Literary Merit	Ancient Indian Epic	Ancient Indian Epic	Ancient Indian Epic
Lexile	950L	950L	1070L
Overall Rating	Average	Average	Average

nestling in his lap. Its feathers were ruffled in terror and its eyes were shut. It looked so limp that he thought it was dead, but then he noticed a slight flutter of breath. He sat still in order not to frighten away the bird, and looked about for a servant.

3

Just then a hawk whirled down in pursuit, and perched itself on a low branch of the tree beside the canopy. The hawk exclaimed, "Ah, at last! What a game of hide and seek!"

"What do you want?" asked the king.

"I am addressing myself to that creature on your lap! Never been so much tricked in my life! If every mouthful of food has to be got after such a trial, a nice outlook indeed for the so-called king of birds! As one king to another, let me tell you, the dove nestling in your lap is mine. Throw it back to me."

The king thought over the statement of the hawk and said, "I am indeed honored by a visit from the king of birds, although I had thought till now that the eagle was the king!"

"I am a hawk, not a kite.[2] Know you that the hawk belongs to the kingly race while the kite is a mere caricature of our family, pursuing a career of deception by seeming no bigger than its victim and then attacking it. How often one mistakes a kite for a dove!"

Vocabulary Builder
caricature (kar′ i kə chər) *n.* likeness or imitation that is so distorted or inferior as to seem ridiculous

Sibi wanted to divert the attention of the hawk from the subject of the dove and so said, "The kite also goes out of sight when it flies, so don't be offended if we land-bound creatures imagine that the kite floats in the same heaven as the hawk."

The hawk sharpened his beak on the tree-trunk and lifted one leg to display his talons and said, "I'm sorry to see the mistakes you human beings make. The kite no doubt flies—but not beyond the back of the lowest cloud. And you think that it sports in the heavens itself! The only common element between us is that we both have pointed, curved beaks, that's all; but the kite has a taste for helpless little creatures such as mice and sparrows—creatures which we would not care to notice."

The king realized that the subject was once more drifting towards food and diverted the hawk's attention again by saying, "The general notion is that the eagle is the king of birds."

4

The hawk chuckled cynically. "Ignorant mankind! How the eagle came to be so much respected, I shall never understand; what is there to commend the eagle? Its wingspread? You people are too easily carried away by appearances! Do you know that the hawk can fly just as high as the eagle? And yet you have no regard for us!"

Sibi said, "You can't blame us, we take things as they seem from here! I now know better."

The hawk looked pleased at this concession and said, "Have you ever seen a mountain eagle walk on the ground? Is there anything more

5

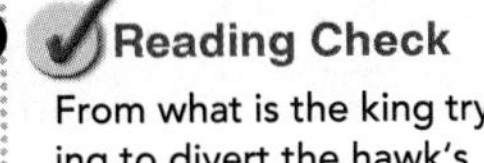

Reading Check

From what is the king trying to divert the hawk's attention?

2. **kite** any of various birds, including the hawk, that prey on insects, reptiles, and small mammals. The hawk is haughtily distinguishing himself from his smaller, less significant relatives.

3 Background

King Sibi's Duty

King Sibi's dharma (set of obligations particular to him) requires him to protect all of his subjects. Because animals are believed to have an *atman,* or eternal spirit, the king must protect them as well as human beings. According to the law of karma, the type of body that an atman incarnates into is determined by its past deeds or misdeeds. Occasionally, however, because of a slight infraction of dharma, a saintly person or king may take an animal body for a single lifetime as punishment. At the conclusion of this time, the atman will then be restored to either a human body or a higher position as a demigod in heaven. Aware that the dove may once have been a noble person, Sibi takes great pains to protect it in order to avoid the possibility of his own suffering in a future lifetime.

4 Critical Thinking

Cause and Effect

- Ask a volunteer to read the bracketed passage aloud.
- Then, **ask** students: What does the king tell the hawk in this passage?
  Answer: The king says that most people believe the eagle, not the hawk, is the king of birds.
- Then, **ask:** What effect does this statement have on the hawk?
  Answer: This statement stings the hawk's ego and distracts him from pursuing the dove.

5 Reading Check

Answer: The king is trying to divert the hawk's attention from the dove.

Differentiated Instruction Solutions for All Learners

Support for Less Proficient Readers
Preview the selections, using the footnotes and phonetic spellings to pronounce the following Indian words and names: *Jumna, Vishnu, maharaja, Indra, Arjuna, Sri Krishna, Atman, Shiva, rakshasas, Hanuman, Lakshmana, Veena, Lanka, asthras,* and *mantra.*

Support for English Learners
Have students follow along in their texts as they listen to the recorded versions on the **Listening to Literature Audio CDs.** Also, have students work in pairs to create a list of questions about each character's words and actions. These lists can form the basis of a class discussion.

Strategy for Advanced Readers
In addition to examining the selections to find evidence of the values of Hinduism and Indian society, students might preview the text to note examples of figurative language and poetic devices. Encourage students to list these elements and to analyze, as they read, the purpose of each.

❻ Reading Strategy
Inferring Beliefs of the Period

- Review with students the concept of atman, defined in the ATE Background note on p. 193, and lead them in a discussion about how the concept of atman might affect people's behavior toward animals.
- Then, read aloud the bracketed passage. **Ask** the Reading Strategy question: What does the king's statement reveal about ancient Indian beliefs concerning animals?
Answer: The king's statement reveals the ancient Indian belief that humans have duties toward animals and that animals should be protected.

❼ Critical Viewing

Possible response: This image clearly depicts an eagle-like being, Garuda, as the bearer of Vishnu, a privileged role that shows the eagle is kingly.

grotesque? Don't you agree that the first requirement for kingliness would be grace of movement? Only we hawks have it."

"True, true," said the king. "When I move from my bed to the bathroom, even if alone at night, I catch myself strutting along as in a parade, I suppose!" The king laughed, to entertain the hawk; he thought it might please the bird to be treated as a fellow king. The hawk looked pleased, and the king hoped that it would take itself off after these pleasantries.

The dove slightly stirred on his lap, and he hastened to draw over it his silk scarf. The hawk noticed this and bluntly said, "King, what is the use of your covering the dove? I will not forget that my food, which I have earned by honest chase, is there, unfairly held by you."

❻ The king said, "This bird has come to me for asylum; it is my duty to protect it."

"I may brave your sword and swoop on my prey, and if I die in the attempt the spirits of my ancestors will bless me. We have known no fear for one thousand generations, what should we fear when the back of our prime ancestor serves as the vehicle of the great god Vishnu?"[3]

Reading Strategy
Inferring Beliefs of the Period What does the king's statement reveal about ancient Indian beliefs concerning animals?

3. **Vishnu** (vish´ no̅o̅) Hindu god known as the Preserver because he became a human being on nine separate occasions to save humanity from destruction.

Vishnu and Lakshmi Riding on Garuda, Ann & Bury Peerless Picture Library

❼ ▲ Critical Viewing This image depicts Garuda, half-man and half-eagle, carrying the god Vishnu and Vishnu's wife. What does the image suggest about the claim that the hawk, not the eagle, is the king of birds? **[Analyze]**

Enrichment

India Today

What is life like in India today? The contemporary writer Santha Rama Rau gives us a view of an Indian bazaar:

> To me an Indian bazaar is a source of endless delight and excitement. It is usually a series of plain wooden stalls on which are piled, with unconscious artistry, brightly colored fruits, vegetables, spices, gleaming silver jewelry, brilliant silks and cottons, or charming, grotesque painted wooden toys. The vendors who can't afford a stall sit on the sidewalk outside the market, their baskets stacked behind them, their wives in vivid cotton saris crouching in the shade, and in front of them are spread carpets of scarlet chilies drying in the sun, small hills of saffron, tumeric, coriander, ginger, cinnamon—all the magical names from the old days of the spice trade with the Indies. With a worn stone mortar and pestle the vendor or his wife will grind your spices for you, blending them according to your particular taste, and weigh them in tiny brass scales strung on twine and balanced delicately in one hand. . . .

Again the king was on the point of correcting him, that it was a golden eagle that Vishnu rode, not a hawk, but he checked himself.

The bird emphasized his own status again. "You who are reputed to be wise, O king, don't confuse me with the carrion[4] birds wheeling over your head. I know where I stand," said the bird, preening its feathers.

The king felt it was time to say something agreeable himself, secretly worrying that he was reaching the limits of his wit. The dove nestled within the silk scarf. There was an uneasy pause while the king dreaded what might be coming next.

8 The hawk suddenly said, "All the world speaks of you as one who has the finest discrimination between right and wrong. And so you have a serious responsibility at this moment. You must not do anything that goes contrary to your reputation. Remember, I am in the agonies of hunger, and you refuse me my legitimate diet. By your act you cause me suffering, you injure me every second that you keep your hold on that parcel of meat. You have attained immeasurable spiritual merit by your deeds of perfection; now this single selfish act of yours will drain away all your merit and you will probably go to hell."

"O infinitely wise bird, does it seem to you that I am holding this dove out of selfishness so that I may eat it myself?"

"I am not so simple-minded," said the bird haughtily. "By selfish I meant that you were thinking of your own feelings, totally ignoring my viewpoint."

"When I recollect the terror in its eye as it fell on my lap, I feel nothing ever matters except affording it protection."

"O prince among princes, food is life, out of food all things exist and stir. Between life and death stands what? Food! I am faint with hunger. If you deny me my food any longer I may die. In a cranny of yonder rock my wife has hatched four eggs, the little ones are guarded by their mother, and all of them await my return home. If I die here of hunger, they will keep peeping out for my return home until they perish of the same hunger. And the sin of ending six lives will be on you. O maharaja,[5] consider well whether you want to save one doubtful life, which is probably half gone already, or six lives. Let not the performance of what seems to you a rightful act conflict with bigger issues. You know all this, king, but choose to ignore the issues. And all this talking only fatigues me and takes me nearer to death. So please spare me further argument."

9 Sibi said, "I notice that you are an extraordinary bird. You talk wisely, knowledgeably; there is nothing that you do not know. Your mind journeys with ease at subtle heights of thought. But, bird, tell me, how is it that you fail to notice the sheer duty I owe a creature that cries for protection? As a king is it not my duty?"

"I am only asking for food; food is to life what oil is to a lamp."

4. **carrion** (kar′ ē ən) *adj.* feeding on the dead.
5. **maharaja** (mä hə rä′ jə) prince ruling over one of the native states in India; here, king.

Literary Analysis
The Indian Epic and the Epic Hero In what ways do the hawk's words reinforce Sibi's heroic status?

Literary Analysis
The Indian Epic What ancient Indian values does Sibi express in this paragraph?

10 
Reading Check
What does the hawk say will happen if Sibi does not give him the dove?

8 Literary Analysis
The Indian Epic and the Epic Hero

- Direct students' attention to the bracketed passage. Have a volunteer read the passage aloud.
- To ensure comprehension, **ask** students to paraphrase the hawk's words.
  Answer: The hawk says that Sibi, who is known for his strong sense of right and wrong and his adherence to his dharma, is acting uncharacteristically by denying the hawk his meal. The hawk says that Sibi may go to hell for indulging in this one selfish act.
- Then, **ask** students the first Literary Analysis question: In what ways do the hawk's words reinforce Sibi's heroic status?
  Possible response: The hawk emphasizes Sibi's heroic status by acknowledging the king's moral fortitude and selflessness.

9 Literary Analysis
The Indian Epic

- Review with students the concept of dharma, defined on p. 190. Tell students that, according to this concept, by fulfilling their specific duties, people contribute to the sustenance of the world.
- Have students read the bracketed passage independently. Then, **ask:** What question does Sibi ask the hawk?
  Answer: Sibi asks why the hawk does not acknowledge the king's duty to protect the dove.
- **Ask** students the second Literary Analysis question: What ancient Indian values does Sibi express in this paragraph?
  Possible response: Sibi expresses the importance of wisdom and duty, especially a king's duty to protect his subjects, human or animal, who ask for his protection.

10 Reading Check

Answer: The hawk says that Sibi will be saddled with the sin of ending six lives. For denying the hawk his meal, Sibi also may go to hell.

Differentiated Instruction
Solutions for All Learners

Strategy for Special Needs Students
Have students create a two-column chart, labeling the first column *Hawk* and the second column *King Sibi.* Then, guide students to use the chart to summarize and record the main ideas expressed by both characters on on these two pages.

Strategy for English Learners
Draw students' attention to the analogy at the bottom of this page: "I am only asking for food; food is to life what oil is to a lamp." Have students look up the various meanings of the words *lamp* and *oil* in a dictionary. Tell students that in ancient India, oil was the primary fuel for lamps.

Enrichment for Gifted/Talented Students
Have students discuss what the dove's reaction might be to the discussion between King Sibi and the hawk. Then, ask students to work in pairs to write the dove's reaction to the arguments each character sets forth. Each student pair can present its reaction as a dramatic reading for the class.

⓫ Literary Analysis

The Indian Epic and the Epic Hero

- Read the bracketed line aloud. Then, have students **discuss** which of the hawk's arguments prompt Sibi's statement.
  Answer: The hawk argues that Sibi is interfering with God's plan by denying the hawk the dove.

Monitor Progress **Ask** students: To what heroic quality of Sibi's does the hawk appeal by accusing Sibi of interfering with God's plan?
Answer: The hawk is appealing to the king's devoutness by suggesting that Sibi is going against what has been ordained.

Reteach If students are having difficulty with the Literary Analysis strategy, use the **Literary Analysis** support, p. 27 in ***Unit 2 Resources.***

- **Ask** students the Literary Analysis question: What personal quality does Sibi demonstrate by claiming not to know God's plan?
  Possible response: Sibi demonstrates humility, piety, wisdom, and cleverness.

⓬ Reading Strategy

Inferring Beliefs of the Period

- Have a volunteer read the bracketed passage aloud. Then, have students offer their reactions to the idea of a king's sacrificing his own flesh to protect one of his subjects.
- **Ask** students why Sibi must consider which part of his flesh to take.
  Answer: He wants to select a part of his body that, if sacrificed, will still allow him to live.
- **Ask** students the Reading Strategy question: In explaining why he must stay alive, what belief does Sibi reveal regarding a ruler's responsibilities?
  Answer: Sibi reveals the belief that a ruler cannot make the choice to die because his people are dependent on him. The ruler's duty is to live.

"Very well. You see all these people lying around, they have all rested after a feast in which nothing was lacking to satisfy the sixfold demands of the palate. Tell me what you want, and I will spread a feast before you in no time."

"King, the nature of food differs with different creatures. What you call a feast seems to me just so much trash. We observe from our heights all the activity that goes on in your royal kitchen and ever wonder why you take all that trouble with spice, salt, and fire to ruin the taste of God-given stuff. King, I do not want to speak at length. I am famished and I feel my eyes dimming. Have consideration for me too."

"If it is flesh you want, I will ask them to get it for you."

The hawk gave an ironical laugh at this. "See where all this leads you! How are you going to get flesh without killing something else? When you interfere with what God has ordained, you complicate everything."

⓫ "What is God's plan, actually? Please enlighten me."

"The dove is intended for me; God has no other purpose in creating it and letting it multiply so profusely. Are you not aware of the ancient saying that hawks eat doves?"

The king thought it over and said, "If you spare this dove, I'll guarantee you food every day in my palace all your life."

"I have already told you, my lord, that your food is inedible. Your assurance of daily feeding does not appeal to me. I hunt for food when I want it. I do not see why I should bother about tomorrow. Hoarding for generations ahead is a human failing, a practice unknown to us. I repeat the ancient saying that hawks eat doves."

The king brooded over the words of the hawk for a moment. "Ask for anything, except this little bird on my lap. I won't give it up, whichever way you may argue."

The hawk tilted its head, rolled its eyes, and said, "So be it. I will ask for the next best thing. I want warm flesh, with warm blood dripping, equal in weight to the dove. We are used to eating only fresh meat, we are not carrion birds, let me remind you. You will have to cut it out of your own body, as I know you will not choose to kill another creature for it."

⓬ The king brooded over this. "Yes, but I must consider which part of my body will yield the flesh you want without destroying my life. Give me a little time. Bear your hunger for a moment." And he added, "A ruler has no liberty to die. Many depend on him."

"In the same way as my family," said the hawk.

The king beckoned to an attendant. "Bring a pair of weighing scales."

The attendant was nonplussed. "Your Majesty, how can we find one here, in this remote place?"

The king repeated, "I want a pair of scales for accurate weighing."

"May I send a messenger to fetch one from the city?"

"How long will he take?" asked the king.

The courtier made a swift reckoning and declared, "If he rides a galloping horse, he should be back tomorrow at dawn."

Literary Analysis
The Indian Epic and the Epic Hero What personal quality does Sibi demonstrate by claiming not to know God's plan?

Reading Strategy
Inferring Beliefs of the Period In explaining why he must stay alive, what belief does Sibi reveal regarding a ruler's responsibilities?

Enrichment

Dharma

King Sibi, as a heroic character, understands that the only means to escape rebirth is to perform one's dharma, or the duties and responsibilities unique to every individual. As Indian society dictates, individuals are required to accept their dharma, even if they consider it to be inappropriate or unjust. If they refuse, it is believed that the Hindu gods will force them to do so. The worst thing a person can do is to try to perform someone else's duty. A famous verse in the *Bhagavad-Gita* says:

> It is better to do one's own duty badly than to do another's well. Death in one's own duty is preferable to another's duty which is fraught with danger.

Because King Sibi functions as a vehicle for the values of Hinduism and Indian society, he is depicted as willing to perform his duty, even in the face of great adversity.

The king looked at the hawk, who already seemed to droop. He did not want to hear again about his family on the mountain. It was also time to clear up all this situation and feed the refugee on his lap. He said to the courtier, "Construct a balance immediately with whatever is available here. I'll give you ten minutes!"

"Whoever fails will have his head cut off, I suppose?" sneered the hawk. "That would be truly kinglike, but let me tell you straight away that I am not interested in a cut-off head."

"You shall have my flesh and nothing less," said the king.

They bustled about. By now the whole camp was astir, watching this incredible duel between the king and the hawk. They managed to dangle a beam from the branch of a tree. Suspended from either end was a plate from the kitchen; a pointer, also improvised, marked the dead center of the beam.

The king looked at the hawk and said, "This is the best we can manage."

"I understand. A little fluctuation should not matter in the least. Only I do not want you to lose more flesh than is necessary to balance the dove."

The king did not let the bird finish his sentence, but rose, bearing the dove in his hand. He walked up to the crude scales in order to test them. He addressed the hawk, "Will you step nearer?"

"I can watch quite well from here. Also I can trust you."

The king placed the dove on the right-hand side of the scale pan, which immediately went down, making the king wonder how a little bird which had lain so lightly on his lap could weigh down the balance in this manner.

He wasted no further time in speculation. He sat on the ground, stretched out his leg, and after a brief prayer, incised his thigh with a sharp knife. The courtiers and guests assembled groaned at the sight of the blood. The king gritted his teeth and tore out a handful of flesh and dropped it on the scale.

The pan became bloodstained but the pointer did not move. Someone cursed the dove, "It has the weight of an abandoned corpse. It looks dead, see if it is dead."

Another added, "Just pick it up and fling it to that hawk and be done with it, the miserable creature."

The king was too faint to talk; he gestured to them to stop commenting. He had now only the skin on his right thigh. Still the scales were

13

A Hawk, Indian Mughal, 18th century miniature, Victoria and Albert Museum

14 ▲ Critical Viewing

Does the hawk in this painting convey a mood that is similar to that of the hawk in the story? Explain. **[Compare and Contrast]**

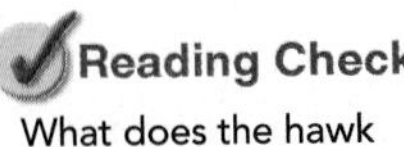

Reading Check 15

What does the hawk agree to take in place of the dove?

13 Humanities

A Hawk

This miniature eighteenth-century Indian painting reflects the influence of a seventeenth-century Indian emperor named Jahangir, who was both a nature lover and a patron of the arts. An avid bird watcher, he set his artists to work depicting the species of birds known to the court. The artists created dozens of paintings of birds for Jahangir, all using the detailed, lifelike style shown here.

Use the following questions for discussion:

- What impression of the hawk does this painting convey?
  Possible response: The hawk is depicted as formidable and noble. However, the fact that the hawk is tethered shows the bird's subservience and lack of freedom.
- Is this an appropriate illustration for the story? Why or why not?
  Possible response: This illustration is appropriate because the hawk's haughty, intelligent, and intimidating expression in the painting mirrors the attitude of the hawk in the story. However, the hawk in the painting is tethered to a perch, so he lacks the freedom that the hawk in the story exhibits.

14 Critical Viewing

Possible response: Both hawks share an angry yet determined attitude.

15 Reading Check

Answer: The hawk agrees to take an equal amount of Sibi's flesh in lieu of the dove.

Differentiated Instruction Solutions for All Learners

Enrichment for Gifted/Talented Students

Have students draw, paint, or sculpt their own depictions of the hawk. First, have each student list descriptive details from the story. Then, have students research and discuss the physical characteristics that the story does not provide. Make sure that the necessary art materials are available, and allow students ample time to complete their depictions. When students have finished, encourage them to display their work in the classroom.

Enrichment for Advanced Readers

Organize students into pairs, and have them use reference materials or the Internet to research balances. Encourage students to discover the origin of balances, how they work, and how they have been used throughout history to settle disputes. Then, challenge students to learn how a balance came to represent justice in American society. After completing their research, students should compose oral reports on their findings and present the reports to the class.

16 Critical Thinking

Infer

- After students read the bracketed passage independently, **ask:** Why do you think Sibi is willing to continue with the sacrifice? **Possible response:** Sibi believes that he must complete his duty.
- **Ask** students what they can infer about Sibi from this action. **Possible response:** Sibi is a devout man of integrity and will complete his duty even if it costs him his life and his salvation.

17 Humanities

King Sibi's Sacrifice to the God Indra

This stone carving is an example of second century Ghandaran art, a term used to describe the sculptures produced by a school of artists from the northwestern Indus Valley during the first centuries A.D. These sculptures are noted for their finely proportioned bodies and classically styled portrait heads. Although the Ghandaran artists were heavily influenced by Greek sculpture, they typically focused on distinctively Indian subjects. This sculpture, for example, depicts the story of King Sibi from the *Mahabharata.*

Use the following items for discussion:

- Describe what is happening in the sculpture. **Answer:** One of the king's subjects supports Sibi as flesh is removed from Sibi's leg and is placed on the balance. The dove rests by Sibi's feet while the hawk appears to hover above the scene. Several subjects watch.
- What do you find most interesting about the sculpture? **Possible response:** It is interesting to note that the dove is not sitting on the other side of the balance.

18 Critical Viewing

Possible response: King Sibi appears very weak and needs to be supported by those around him.

unbalanced. The king went on to scoop the flesh from his other leg; the pointer was still down.

People averted their eyes from the gory spectacle. The hawk watched him critically.

"O hawk, take all that meat and begone!" they said.

"I have been promised the exact equal weight of the dove," insisted the hawk, at which all those assembled cursed the hawk and drew their swords. The king was faint with pain now, but mustered the last ounce of his strength to command his followers to keep away.

16 He beckoned to his chief minister to come nearer. "One has no right to end one's life, but this is unforeseen. Even if this means hell to me, I have to face it," he said. Everyone looked at the dove with distaste. "My brother shall be the regent[6] till the prince comes of age."

With this he struggled onto his feet and stepped on the flesh-filled pan. At once the other pan went up and equalized.

The hawk now flitted nearer and said, "This is more than a mouthful for me and my family. How am I to carry you to the mountain?"

6. **regent** (rē′ jənt) *n.* person appointed to rule when the king is too young to rule himself.

17

King Sibi's Sacrifice to the God Indra, Gandharan Art, c. 2nd century, Courtesy of the Trustees of the British Museum

18 ▲ Critical Viewing In this depiction of Sibi's sacrifice, how does Sibi appear to have been affected by the experience? **[Infer]**

Enrichment

The Story of Yudhishthira

"Sibi" parallels another story from the *Mahabarata* about a king named Yudhishthira. After reaching the end of his life on Earth, Yudisthira reaches the gates of heaven and is greeted by the great god Indra. Yudhishthira requests that his loyal dog be allowed to accompany him through the gates. Indra responds, "In paradise there is no place for men with dogs," and demands that Yudhishthira renounce the dog.

Yet, Yudhishthira refuses to do so, declaring that he would rather sacrifice his own pleasure than renounce the dog. As it turns out, however, the dog is not an ordinary dog but is rather the God Dharma himself. In the end, Dharma reveals himself to Yudhishthira and leads him into paradise. Like Sibi, Yudhishthira has been put to a test, and he has passed.

The king mumbled feebly, "I did not think of that problem," and added, "You wouldn't have been able to lift the dove either! So bring your family here."

The hawk flapped its wings and rose in the air and swooped down as if to peck at the king's flesh. People shut their eyes, unable to bear the spectacle. But presently they heard divine instruments filling the skies with music. The hawk was gone, but in its place they found Indra,[7] the god with the dazzling crown, armed with the diamond spear, seizing Sibi's hand and helping him down off the weighing scales. A flame rose where the dove had lain, and from the heart of it emerged the God of Fire.

They said, "O king, we put you to a severe test. We challenged your integrity; and we happily accept defeat. You are indeed blessed, and as long as human beings recollect your tale, they will partake of the spiritual merit that you have yourself acquired"—and vanished. The king recovered his energy in a moment, while the pieces of flesh in the scale pan turned to fragrant flowers.

---

7. **Indra** (in´ drə) chief god of the early Hindu religion, often depicted wielding a thunderbolt.

Critical Reading

1. **Respond:** Do you think that Sibi was foolish to keep his promise to the dove regardless of the consequences? Why or why not?
2. **(a) Recall:** Explain the duties of Sibi and the hawk.
   (b) Analyze: How do their duties conflict?
3. **(a) Recall:** How does Sibi first attempt to resolve his conflict with the hawk? **(b) Infer:** What does this strategy reveal about his attitude toward the painful sacrifice he later undertakes?
4. **(a) Recall:** What arrangement finally satisfies the hawk's demand for food?
   (b) Analyze: Why do you think the king agrees to this plan?
5. **(a) Recall:** What happens after Sibi steps onto the scale?
   (b) Interpret: What is the meaning of this event?
6. **(a) Interpret:** What values do Sibi's actions demonstrate?
   (b) Infer: What do these values suggest about the purpose of this story?
7. **Apply:** How does the importance that ancient Indians placed on keeping one's word compare with attitudes toward honesty and duty in the modern world? Explain.

ASSESS

Answers

1. **Possible response:** Sibi behaved foolishly by risking his life. If he had died, he would not have fulfilled his dharma as ruler. However, a wise ruler must find a way to keep resources and fulfill his duties.
2. (a) Sibi's duty is to protect the dove. The hawk's duty is to feed its family. (b) **Possible response:** By protecting the dove, Sibi prevents the hawk from feeding its family.
3. (a) Sibi tries to divert the hawk's attention from the dove.
   (b) **Possible response:** Sibi is not eager to make the painful sacrifice that he later undertakes.
4. (a) The hawk is finally satisfied when Sibi offers his own flesh to replace the dove. (b) **Possible response:** The king agrees to this plan because it is the only way he can protect the dove and not destroy other lives, such as those of the hawk and its family.
5. (a) After Sibi steps on the scale, the hawk rises in the air and dives down to claim Sibi's flesh. Before the hawk is able to do this, the air fills with music and Indra appears, helping Sibi down from the scales.
   (b) **Possible response:** The gods are testing Sibi, and he will be rewarded for maintaining his integrity.
6. (a) Sibi's actions demonstrate duty, integrity, and self-sacrifice.
   (b) **Possible response:** These values suggest that the purpose of the story is to instruct people to follow the king's example. If they do, they will be rewarded for completing their own personal duties.
7. **Possible response:** Our society is fairly lenient toward those who do not keep their word because modern society does not emphasize the importance of honesty and duty.

Differentiated Instruction Solutions for All Learners

Strategy for Special Needs Students

Organize students into small groups to answer the questions. Each group can then report its answers to the entire class. If there is significant disagreement, have students identify words, phrases, and lines from the story that support their interpretations.

Enrichment for Advanced Readers

Tell students that Mohandas Gandhi (1869–1948), the celebrated Indian nationalist and reformer, possessed many of the traits that the Indian hero King Sibi exhibits. Ask students to research the life of Mohandas Gandhi, noting his deeds and behaviors. Then, have students use the information they have gathered to write an essay that contrasts Mohandas Gandhi with King Sibi. Encourage students to field questions from the student audience about their essays.

Facilitate Understanding

Ask students to offer definitions of the word *soul* as they understand the use of the term. Encourage students to share and discuss their definitions. Then, help students understand the abstract idea of Atman by means of the poem on pp. 201–203.

19 About the Translation

The translators of this selection are the well-known novelist Christopher Isherwood and Swami Prabhavananda, the founder of the Vedanta Society of Southern California. In this partnership, Isherwood provided an expert knowledge of English and the Swami contributed a knowledge of Hinduism and of the Sanskrit verse in which the original text was written. Isherwood, however, was far more than a hired consultant. He himself was a believer in Indian Vedanta, a philosophy based on the Vedas, and a follower of the Swami.

In a brief preface, the translators indicate the balance they wanted to achieve in their version of the *Bhagavad-Gita.* On the one hand, they wanted to remain faithful to Hindu beliefs by using Sanskrit terms such as *Brahman, Atman,* and *gunas,* terms for which there are no exact English words. (For explanations of these Hindu terms, see the footnotes to the selection.) On the other hand, they wanted to make the religious beliefs of the *Bhagavad-Gita* accessible to readers of English by translating some of the Sanskrit poetry of the original into more expansive and welcoming English prose.

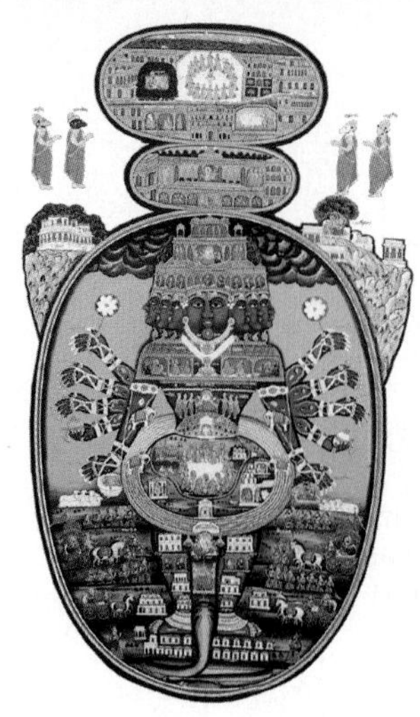

from the

Bhagavad-Gita

19 ***translated by*** **Swami Prabhavananda and Christopher Isherwood**

Background Arjuna (är′ jo͞o nə), a Pandava, has chosen his brother-in-law, Krishna (krish′ nə), as his charioteer and trusted advisor for the coming battle with the Kauravas. At this early point in the story, Arjuna knows only that Krishna is a special person. He does not yet realize that Krishna is a god. As the poem begins, Arjuna faces a dilemma: He knows it is wrong to kill his cousins and uncles who are on the opposing side, but he also knows that it is his duty to fight. In the first chapter of the *Gita*, he refuses to take part in the battle; dropping his bow, he asks Krishna for advice. The great warrior Arjuna appears here in Chapter 2, weeping with frustration and confusion.

One of the main themes of the *Bhagavad-Gita* is the concept of **nonattached work,** the performance of one's duty without concern for the results. This idea is tied to both the structure of Indian society and the Indian belief in reincarnation. Indian society was rigidly divided into social classes, or **castes** (kasts), each of which had its own special duties. In this selection, narrated by a character named Sanjaya, Krishna reminds Arjuna that as a member of the warrior caste, he is obligated to fight. He reminds him that the Atman, or soul, is eternal; it can be reborn into countless bodies.

The Yoga of Knowledge

SANJAYA: Then his eyes filled with tears, and his heart grieved and was bewildered with pity. And Sri Krishna spoke to him, saying:

SRI KRISHNA: Arjuna, is this hour of battle the time for scruples and fancies? Are they worthy of you, who seek enlightenment? Any brave man who merely hopes for fame or heaven would despise them.

What is this weakness? It is beneath you. Is it for nothing men call you the foe-consumer? Shake off this cowardice, Arjuna. Stand up.

Vocabulary Builder
scruples (skro͞o′ pəlz) *n.* feelings of doubt over what is ethical

Enrichment

Indian Thought and the *Bhagavad-Gita*

"The Yoga of Knowledge" propounds the basic philosophy of reincarnation that pervades nearly all Indian thought. Krishna presents the standard definitions of the soul and its relationship to the body as accepted by Hindu belief. He proceeds to reveal himself as the ultimate source of everything and as the object of personal faith and devotion who awards ultimate liberation from the cycle of birth and death described here. As God is detached from the universe yet involved in its creation, maintenance, and destruction, similarly, human beings must also be detached from their work. Thus, the essence of Krishna's teaching here is "Believe in and imitate me."

ARJUNA: Bhisma and Drona are noble and ancient, worthy of the deepest reverence. How can I greet them with arrows, in battle? If I kill them, how can I ever enjoy my wealth, or any other pleasure? It will be cursed with blood-guilt. I would much rather spare them, and eat the bread of a beggar.

Which will be worse, to win this war, or to lose it? I scarcely know. Even the sons of Dhritarashtra stand in the enemy ranks. If we kill them, none of us will wish to live.

20 Is this real compassion that I feel, or only a delusion? My mind gropes about in darkness. I cannot see where my duty lies. Krishna, I beg you, tell me frankly and clearly what I ought to do. I am your disciple. I put myself into your hands. Show me the way.

Not this world's kingdom,
Supreme, unchallenged,
No, nor the throne
Of the gods in heaven,
Could ease this sorrow
That numbs my senses!

SANJAYA: When Arjuna, the foe-consuming, the never-slothful, had spoken thus to Govinda, ruler of the senses, he added: "I will not fight," and was silent.

Then to him who thus sorrowed between the two armies, the ruler of the senses spoke, smiling:

SRI KRISHNA: Your words are wise, Arjuna, but your sorrow is for nothing. The truly wise mourn neither for the living nor for the dead.

There was never a time when I did not exist, nor you, nor any of these kings. Nor is there any future in which we shall cease to be.

Just as the dweller in this body passes through childhood, youth and old age, so at death he merely passes into another kind of body. The wise are not deceived by that.

Feelings of heat and cold, pleasure and pain, are caused by the contact of the senses with their objects. They come and they go, never lasting long. You must accept them.

A serene spirit accepts pleasure and pain with an even mind, and is unmoved by either. He alone is worthy of immortality.

That which is non-existent can never come into being, and that which is can never cease to be. Those who have known the inmost Reality know also the nature of *is* and *is not.*

That Reality which pervades the universe is indestructible. No one has power to change the Changeless.

Bodies are said to die, but That which possesses the body is eternal. It cannot be limited, or destroyed. Therefore you must fight.

Some say this Atman[1]
Is slain, and others

1. **Atman** (ät′ mən) universal soul; source of all individual souls.

Literary Analysis
The Indian Epic What ancient Indian values does Arjuna express in this passage?

Vocabulary Builder
pervades (pər vādz′) *v.* spreads throughout

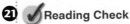

21  **Reading Check**
According to Sri Krishna, how should one accept both pleasure and pain?

20 Literary Analysis

The Indian Epic

- Have a volunteer read aloud the bracketed text.
- Review with students Arjuna's dilemma by rereading the Background text. **Ask** students to paraphrase Arjuna's choice.
  Answer: Arjuna must decide between completing his duty to fight, which involves killing members of his family, or not fighting, thus shirking his duty.
- Then, **ask** students the Literary Analysis question: What ancient Indian values does Arjuna express in this passage?
  Possible response: Arjuna's expression of concern indicates that Indian society values an adherence to one's duty and a loyalty to one's family.

21 Reading Check

Answer: Sri Krishna says that pleasure and pain are fleeting and that one must accept calmly both sensations.

Differentiated Instruction
Solutions for All Learners

Support for Special Needs Students
Students may find the ideas on these pages difficult to follow. Ask: If Arjuna is a trained warrior, why is he hesitating about going into battle? Have students reread to find the answer to this question. Then, explain that Arjuna's dilemma involves choosing between what he sees as two evils. Sri Krishna tries to show him that one of these "evils" is not an evil and that Arjuna's dilemma is based on an illusion.

Support for English Learners
It may be beneficial to students to review the rules of capitalization. Then, discuss the capitalization of words in this selection, such as *It, That, Reality,* and *Changeless.* Remind students that the translators of this *Gita* used capitalization freely, unlike the way capitalization is used in standard English. Encourage students to find other examples of capitalization as they read and to consider whether these words reflect capitalization rules they have learned.

22 Reading Strategy

Inferring Beliefs of the Period

- Have students read the bracketed passage. **Ask** students to summarize what Sri Krishna says.
  Answer: Sri Krishna says that the soul continues on after death.
- **Ask** students the Reading Strategy question: In what way does this passage reflect ancient Indian beliefs about the spirit?
  Answer: The passage reflects the belief in reincarnation and the notion that the soul is eternal.

23 Humanities

Arjuna and Krishna in the Chariot, Between the Two Armies

An artist who wanted to continue the Indian tradition of picturing well-known Hindu legends painted this modern version of a scene from the *Bhagavad-Gita.*

Use the following questions for discussion:

- Do you think it is possible to fully capture or re-create an event from an earlier period using a modern artistic style?
  Possible responses: No; a historical event depicted in a modern style will not "feel" like an event from the past. Yes; an artist can successfully capture the spirit of a past event using a modern style.
- Is the painting on this page successful in capturing the legend about which you are reading?
  Possible response: The painting captures the warriors in detail, but the mood of the painting is almost festive; it does not capture the horrors of war or Arjuna's torment as he faces his dilemma.

24 Critical Viewing

Possible response: The painting shows heavy forces on both sides. Because Arjuna is shown leading forces into battle, he is unlikely to escape unharmed.

Call It the slayer:
They know nothing.
How can It slay
Or who shall slay It?

22 Know this Atman
Unborn, undying,
Never ceasing,
Never beginning,
Deathless, birthless,
Unchanging for ever.
How can It die
The death of the body?

Knowing It birthless,
Knowing It deathless,
Knowing It endless,
For ever unchanging,
Dream not you do
The deed of the killer,
Dream not the power
Is yours to command it.

Worn-out garments
Are shed by the body:
Worn-out bodies
Are shed by the dweller
Within the body.
New bodies are donned
By the dweller, like garments.

Reading Strategy
Inferring Beliefs of the Period In what way does this passage reflect ancient Indian beliefs about the spirit?

24 ▼ **Critical Viewing** What does this painting suggest about the danger Arjuna would face going into battle? **[Infer]**

23

Arjuna and Krishna in the Chariot, Between the Two Armies, Illustration from *Bhagavad-Gita*

Enrichment

"Song of Myself"

Indian thought has had a profound influence on American writers, specifically Emerson and Thoreau who, in turn, exerted their influence on Walt Whitman. The following excerpt from Whitman's "Song of Myself" reflects especially the Indian reincarnation philosophy and, like the *Bhagavad-Gita,* suggests that the soul is involved in a cycle of birth and death:

"What do you think has become of the young and old men? / And what do you think has become of the women and children? / They are alive and well somewhere, / The smallest sprout shows there is really no death, / And if ever there was it led forward life, and does not wait at the end to arrest it, / And ceas'd the moment life appear'd. / All goes onward and outward, nothing collapses, / And to die is different from what anyone supposed, and luckier."

Not wounded by weapons,
Not burned by fire,
Not dried by the wind,
Not wetted by water:
Such is the Atman,
Not dried, not wetted,
Not burned, not wounded,
Innermost element,
Everywhere, always,
Being of beings,
Changeless, eternal,
For ever and ever.

This Atman cannot be manifested to the senses, or thought about by the mind. It is not subject to modification. Since you know this, you should not grieve.

But if you should suppose this Atman to be subject to constant birth and death, even then you ought not to be sorry.

Death is certain for the born. Rebirth is certain for the dead. You should not grieve for what is unavoidable.

Before birth, beings are not manifest to our human senses. In the interim between birth and death, they are manifest. At death they return to the unmanifest again. What is there in all this to grieve over?

There are some who have actually looked upon the Atman, and understood It, in all Its wonder. Others can only speak of It as wonderful beyond their understanding. Others know of Its wonder by hearsay. And there are others who are told about It and do not understand a word.

He Who dwells within all living bodies remains for ever indestructible. Therefore, you should never mourn for any one.

Even if you consider this from the standpoint of your own caste-duty, you ought not to hesitate; for, to a warrior, there is nothing nobler than a righteous war. Happy are the warriors to whom a battle such as this comes: it opens a door to heaven.

But if you refuse to fight this righteous war, you will be turning aside from your duty. You will be a sinner, and disgraced. People will speak ill of you throughout the ages. To a man who values his honor, that is surely worse than death. The warrior-chiefs will believe it was fear that drove you from the battle; you will be despised by those who have admired you so
25 long. Your enemies, also, will slander your courage. They will use the words which should never be spoken. What could be harder to bear than that?

Die, and you win heaven. Conquer, and you enjoy the earth. Stand up now, son of Kunti, and resolve to fight. Realize that pleasure and pain, gain and loss, victory and defeat, are all one and the same: then go into battle. Do this and you cannot commit any sin.

I have explained to you the true nature of the Atman. Now listen to the method of Karma Yoga.[2] If you can understand and follow it, you

Vocabulary Builder
manifested (man´ ə fest´ id) *v.* proved or revealed

Reading Strategy
Inferring Beliefs of the Period What do Krishna's words regarding Arjuna's duty reveal about the importance of honor in ancient India?

Reading Check 26
According to Sri Krishna, how will others view Arjuna if he does not fight?

2. **Karma Yoga** the path of selfless, God-dedicated action.

25 Reading Strategy
Inferring Beliefs of the Period

- Remind students that dharma refers to the sum of a person's obligations, or duty. Completing these obligations contributes to the well-being of the entire universe. Then, have students read the bracketed passage independently.

Monitor Progress **Ask** students to explain the lines "New bodies are donned / By the dweller, like garments."
Answer: After death, the soul is reborn into another body, an animal, or an insect and takes on the appearance of that new body accordingly.

Reteach If students are having difficulty with the Reading Strategy, use the **Reading Strategy** support, p. 28 in ***Unit 2 Resources.***

- **Ask** students the Reading Strategy question: What do Krishna's words regarding Arjuna's duty reveal about the importance of honor in ancient India?
Answer: Krishna's words reveal that honor is extremely important —those who do not behave with honor will be disgraced; those who do will be rewarded.

26 Reading Check
Answer: Others will see Arjuna as a coward and a sinner. He will be disgraced.

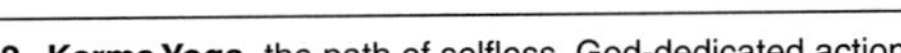

Differentiated Instruction Solutions for All Learners

Strategy for Advanced Readers
Have students reread the bracketed passage beginning with "But if you refuse . . ." Tell students that Krishna's argument suggests that Arjuna will suffer long-term social consequences if he pays too much attention to short-term consequences.

Ask students to compare the long- and short-term consequences of an action, such as cheating on a test. Then, have students discuss the similarities and differences between the situation in "The Yoga of Knowledge" and this comparable situation.

27 Background

The "Terrible Wheel"

The "terrible wheel" is the Wheel of Life, the endless cycle of birth, life, death, and rebirth of the soul. Its symbol, the mandala, also represents the universe—the physical plane within which the soul can remain trapped by its karma, or burden of past actions.

28 Literary Analysis

The Indian Epic and the Epic Hero

- Have students read the bracketed passage. Then, **ask** students: What does the phrase "fruits of work" mean?
  Answer: "Fruits of work" means the results of or reward for work.
- To review with students the concept of the Indian hero, direct them back to the Literary Analysis instruction on p. 191. Remind students that the list of heroic characteristics is not comprehensive and that heroes can exhibit any quality that a society values.
- **Ask** students the Literary Analysis question: What does Krishna's statement about "the fruits of work" reveal about the Indian idea of heroism?
  Possible response: Krishna's statement reveals that a hero does not work for material gain or to garner accolades. A true hero focuses on the work, not on what it earns him or her.

will be able to break the chains of desire which bind you to your actions.

27 In this yoga, even the abortive attempt is not wasted. Nor can it produce a contrary result. Even a little practice of this yoga will save you from the terrible wheel of rebirth and death.

In this yoga, the will is directed singly toward one ideal. When a man lacks this discrimination, his will wanders in all directions, after innumerable aims. Those who lack discrimination may quote the letter of the scripture, but they are really denying its inner truth. They are full of worldly desires, and hungry for the rewards of heaven. They use beautiful figures of speech. They teach elaborate rituals which are supposed to obtain pleasure and power for those who perform them. But, actually, they understand nothing except the law of Karma,[3] that chains men to rebirth.

Those whose discrimination is stolen away by such talk grow deeply attached to pleasure and power. And so they are unable to develop that concentration of the will which leads a man to absorption in God.

The Vedas[4] teach us about the three gunas[5] and their functions. You, Arjuna, must overcome the three gunas. You must be free from the pairs of opposites.[6] Poise your mind in tranquillity. Take care neither to acquire nor to hoard. Be established in the consciousness of the Atman, always.

When the whole country is flooded, the reservoir becomes superfluous. So, to the illumined seer, the Vedas are all superfluous.

28 You have the right to work, but for the work's sake only. You have no right to the fruits of work. Desire for the fruits of work must never be your motive in working. Never give way to laziness, either.

Literary Analysis
The Indian Epic and the Epic Hero What does Krishna's statement about "the fruits of work" reveal about the Indian idea of heroism?

Perform every action with your heart fixed on the Supreme Lord. Renounce attachment to the fruits. Be even-tempered in success and failure; for it is this evenness of temper which is meant by yoga.

Work done with anxiety about results is far inferior to work done without such anxiety, in the calm of self-surrender. Seek refuge in the knowledge of Brahman.[7] They who work selfishly for results are miserable.

In the calm of self-surrender you can free yourself from the bondage of virtue and vice during this very life. Devote yourself, therefore, to reaching union with Brahman. To unite the heart with Brahman and then to act: that is the secret of non-attached work. In the calm of self-surrender, the seers renounce the fruits of their actions, and so reach enlightenment. Then they are free from the bondage of rebirth, and pass to that state which is beyond all evil.

---

3. **the law of Karma** Hindus believe that everyone is reborn many times and that one's actions in each life determine one's fate in future lives.
4. **Vedas** sacred books of the Hindus.
5. **the three gunas** (gōōn´əz) qualities of nature: passion, dullness or inertia, and goodness or purity.
6. **opposites** The world that seems real is composed of illusory opposites like heat and cold.
7. **Brahman** the oversoul of which each individual's Atman is a part.

When your intellect has cleared itself of its delusions, you will become indifferent to the results of all action, present or future. At present, your intellect is bewildered by conflicting interpretations of the scriptures. When it can rest, steady and undistracted, in contemplation of the Atman, then you will reach union with the Atman.

29

ARJUNA: Krishna, how can one identify a man who is firmly established and absorbed in Brahman? In what manner does an illumined soul speak? How does he sit? How does he walk?

SRI KRISHNA:
He knows bliss in the Atman
And wants nothing else.
Cravings torment the heart:
He renounces cravings.
I call him illumined.

Not shaken by adversity,
Not hankering after happiness:
Free from fear, free from anger,
Free from the things of desire.
I call him a seer, and illumined.
The bonds of his flesh are broken.
He is lucky, and does not rejoice:
He is unlucky, and does not weep.
I call him illumined.

The tortoise can draw in his legs:
The seer can draw in his senses.
I call him illumined.

The abstinent[8] run away from what they desire
But carry their desires with them:
When a man enters Reality,
He leaves his desires behind him.

30 **▲ Critical Viewing**
In what way does this painting suggest the kind of serenity that Sri Krishna describes? **[Interpret]**

31 **Reading Check**
In what knowledge does Sri Krishna advise Arjuna to seek refuge?

8. **The abstinent** (ab′ stə nənt) those who voluntarily do without food, drink, or other pleasures.

29 Humanities

Point out that this piece was painted long after the *Bhagavad-Gita* was completed, c. 1700. The painting shows Krishna, typically identified by his blue face, and his brother in the forest with cow herds. Many of the legends associated with Krishna depict him as an amorous cow herd who could charm animals. Cows and bulls are sacred animals in India in honor of Nandin the Bull, who carried the god Shiva. Even today, many Indians neither eat beef nor sanction the killing of cows or bulls. The forest is symbolic of an enchanted world where Krishna invites humans to abandon earthly pursuits and experience the joys of religion.

Use this question for discussion:

How do the cow herds respond to Krishna's visit?
Possible response: Two of the cow herds seem appreciative and respectful of Krishna's visit. One bows to him, and another gestures toward Krishna with clasped hands. However, one cow herd either looks away from Krishna or has not yet seen him.

30 Critical Viewing

Possible response: The peaceful pastoral scene does not depict cravings, fear, or anger, which are also absent from the serenity Sri Krishna describes.

31 Reading Check

Answer: Sri Krishna advises Arjuna to seek refuge in the contemplation of the Atman.

Differentiated Instruction Solutions for All Learners

Support for Less Proficient Readers

Read the following line: "They who work selfishly for results are miserable." Guide students to elaborate by discussing why people who work only to meet a goal, only to achieve self-satisfaction, or only to please others might be miserable. Suggest that perhaps such an approach precludes satisfaction in the work itself. Some students might note that playing a sport hard for the sake of playing well offers a satisfaction different from the satisfactions of scoring or receiving praise.

Support for English Learners

Tell students that the phrase "fruits of work" means the same as the phrase "fruits of labor." Explain that both are figures of speech—specifically metaphors—in which one thing is spoken of as though it were something else. A metaphor suggests a comparison between the two things that are identified. Point out to students that in this example, the rewards of work are being compared to fruit. Then, lead students in a discussion about why this comparison is appropriate and effective.

32 Reading Strategy

Inferring Beliefs of the Period

- **Ask** students to define the word *materialism.*
  Answer: *Materialism* is a preoccupation with amassing things or material goods.
- Then, **ask** students the Reading Strategy question: What ancient Indian ideas about materialism does this stanza reveal?
  Answer: This stanza reveals the idea that materialism triggers a chain of events and psychological reactions that ultimately makes one miss one's life's purpose.
- Extend the discussion by asking students to consider how materialism has affected contemporary society.

33 Literary Analysis

The Indian Epic

- Have students read aloud the bracketed passage. Make sure that students understand the meaning of the word *meditation.*
- Then, have students **summarize** the passage.
  Answer: By focusing on things, the mind becomes "uncontrolled," or occupied, and thus cannot focus on the eternal soul. Without a focus on the eternal soul, deep and continuous thought is impossible, making peace and happiness unattainable.
- **Ask** students the Literary Analysis question: What Indian values does this verse convey?
  Possible response: This verse conveys the importance of acknowledging the eternal soul in order to achieve meditation, peace, and happiness.

Even a mind that knows the path
Can be dragged from the path:
The senses are so unruly.
But he controls the senses
And recollects the mind
And fixes it on me.
I call him illumined.

32
Thinking about sense-objects
Will attach you to sense-objects;
Grow attached, and you become addicted;
Thwart your addiction, it turns to anger;
Be angry, and you confuse your mind;
Confuse your mind, you forget the lesson of experience;
Forget experience, you lose discrimination;
Lose discrimination, and you miss life's only purpose.

When he has no lust, no hatred,
A man walks safely among the things of lust and hatred.
To obey the Atman
Is his peaceful joy:
Sorrow melts
Into that clear peace:
His quiet mind
Is soon established in peace.

33
The uncontrolled mind
Does not guess that the Atman is present:
How can it meditate?[9]
Without meditation, where is peace?
Without peace, where is happiness?

The wind turns a ship
From its course upon the waters:
The wandering winds of the senses
Cast man's mind adrift
And turn his better judgment from its course.
When a man can still the senses
I call him illumined.
The recollected mind is awake
In the knowledge of the Atman
Which is dark night to the ignorant:
The ignorant are awake in their sense-life
Which they think is daylight:
To the seer it is darkness.

Reading Strategy
Inferring Beliefs of the Period What ancient Indian ideas about materialism does this stanza reveal?

Literary Analysis
The Indian Epic What Indian values does this verse convey?

9. **meditate** (med′ ə tāt′) *v.* to think deeply and continuously.

Enrichment

Nonattached Work

Nonattached work is the performance of one's caste-duty in a spirit of "calm" and "self-surrender." This calmness comes from the insight that the body and the world are unimportant, but the Atman, or soul, is eternal. It is therefore unnecessary, and even harmful, to strive for worldly success and rewards.

Krishna teaches these ideas to Arjuna in two ways. Speaking directly, he provides a poetic and philosophical explanation of terms like the Atman: "Not dried by the wind, / Not wetted by water: / Such is the Atman. . . ." However, he also explains these ideas indirectly by telling Arjuna how the person who understands them will behave: "Free from fear, free from anger / Free from the things of desire."

Water flows continually into the ocean
But the ocean is never disturbed:
Desire flows into the mind of the seer
But he is never disturbed.
The seer knows peace:
The man who stirs up his own lusts
Can never know peace.
He knows peace who has forgotten desire.
He lives without craving:
Free from ego, free from pride.

This is the state of enlightenment in Brahman:
A man does not fall back from it
Into delusion.
Even at the moment of death
He is alive in that enlightenment:
Brahman and he are one.

Critical Reading

1. **Respond:** Do you agree with Sri Krishna's advice to Arjuna? Why or why not?
2. **(a) Recall:** When Arjuna is distraught at the beginning of the selection, whom does he ask for advice? **(b) Analyze Causes and Effects:** What is the cause of his confusion?
3. **(a) Recall:** What does Krishna explain to Arjuna about the Atman? **(b) Infer:** Why might that knowledge comfort Arjuna?
4. **(a) Recall:** What action does Krishna advise Arjuna to take? **(b) Analyze:** Does Arjuna have a choice? Why or why not?
5. **(a) Recall:** In what manner does Krishna advise Arjuna to fight? **(b) Deduce:** What will Arjuna ultimately gain from acting this way?
6. **(a) Analyze:** What do Krishna's statements about the Atman suggest about the relationship between knowledge and action? **(b) Draw Conclusions:** Is one element in this relationship more important than the other? Explain.
7. **(a) Deduce:** What three Hindu beliefs does the dialogue between Krishna and Arjuna promote? **(b) Connect:** How do these concepts relate to each other?
8. **Apply:** What advice might Krishna give to people in modern society who believe that wealth is the measure of success?

ASSESS

Answers

1. **Possible response:** No; Arjuna should ignore his duty to fight because the safety of his family is more important.
2. (a) Arjuna asks Sri Krishna, his charioteer and advisor, for advice. (b) **Possible response:** The cause of Arjuna's confusion is his desire to adhere to his duty to fight and his reluctance to injure or kill in battle members of his family.
3. (a) Krishna explains that the Atman is unchanging; it cannot be slain and never ceases. (b) **Possible response:** That knowledge might comfort Arjuna because even if he kills others or is killed, the Atman will endure.
4. (a) Krishna advises Arjuna to follow his duty and fight. (b) **Possible response:** Arjuna has a choice; but if he chooses not to fight, he will lose his honor and commit a sin.
5. (a) By schooling Arjuna in the qualities of the Atman, Krishna hopes Arjuna will understand the nature of the eternal soul, will realize that in killing his enemies he is not destroying what is of highest value, and will embrace his duty to fight. (b) **Possible response:** Arjuna will win heaven if he dies and enjoy the earth if he defeats the enemy.
6. (a) Krishna's words suggest that knowledge of the Atman will enable a person to act correctly. (b) **Possible response:** Knowledge and action are equally important. Knowledge can manifest itself only through action. Action taken without knowledge may be rash or foolish.
7. (a) The interaction between Krishna and Arjuna promotes the concept of dharma (one's unique duties), nonattached action, and the eternal unchangingness of the Atman (the soul). (b) **Possible response:** To act only in order to fulfill one's dharma, without thought for the "fruits of the work" (results), is to act in a nonattached manner. By acting in a nonattached manner, free of fear and craving, one affirms the eternity and unchangingness of the Atman within oneself.

Answers continued

8. **Possible response:** Krishna would advise people who are occupied with obtaining material things to control their senses and to focus on the soul. This focus, or careful thought, is the only road to peace and happiness.

Facilitate Understanding

Have students work in pairs to brainstorm a list of heroic qualities. Then, ask each pair to share its list, and record students' suggestions on the board. Encourage students to keep these heroic characteristics in mind as they read the excerpt from the Indian epic the *Ramayana*.

34 About the Selection

This selection from the great Indian epic the *Ramayana* details Prince Rama's quest to rescue his wife, Sita, from the evil giant, Ravana. The story opens as the battle between Rama and Ravana's forces rages. When Ravana decides to enter the battle, the gods intervene in favor of Rama, sending Rama Indra's chariot and charioteer. The battle soon escalates, and each side thwarts the other with supernatural weapons. Soon, Ravana is weakened, but Rama proves himself a fair and noble man by refusing to attack Ravana when he is incapacitated. In the end, despite Ravana's tricks, Rama defeats the giant, sending him to his death.

35 Critical Thinking

Define

- Read aloud the bracketed passage.
- Then, draw students' attention to the word *accouterments.* **Ask** students to offer definitions of this word.
  Answer: The word *accouterments* means "equipment" or "accessories."
- Have students **identify** the words in the passage that suggest this definition.
  Answer: The words *sword-belt, attached, protection,* and *decoration* indicate that *accouterments* refers to the trappings that Ravana is donning before battle.

34 

retold by R. K. Narayan

Background As an adult, Rama is about to inherit the throne from his father when evil plots result in his banishment from the kingdom. For fourteen years, he wanders in exile with his wife, Sita, and his brother, Lakshmana. During this time, Sita is kidnapped by the evil giant Ravana, whose name means "He who makes the universe scream." Rama sets out to rescue Sita with the help of Hanuman, the monkey god, and a huge battle ensues. This selection opens as the battle is reaching its climax.

Rama and Ravana in Battle

Every moment, news came to Ravana of fresh disasters in his camp. One by one, most of his commanders were lost. No one who went forth with battle cries was heard of again. Cries and shouts and the wailings of the widows of warriors came over the chants and songs of triumph that his courtiers arranged to keep up at a loud pitch in his assembly hall. Ravana became restless and abruptly left the hall and went up on a tower, from which he could obtain a full view of the city. He surveyed the scene below but could not stand it. One who had spent a lifetime in destruction, now found the gory spectacle intolerable. Groans and wailings reached his ears with deadly clarity; and he noticed how the monkey hordes[1] reveled in their bloody handiwork. This was too much for him. He felt a terrific rage rising within him, mixed with some admiration for Rama's valor. He told himself, "The time has come for me to act by myself again."

He hurried down the steps of the tower, returned to his chamber, and prepared himself for the battle. He had a ritual bath and performed special prayers to gain the benediction of Shiva;[2] donned his battle dress, matchless armor, armlets, and crowns. He had on a pro-
 tective armor for every inch of his body. He girt his sword-belt and attached to his body his accouterments[3] for protection and decoration.

When he emerged from his chamber, his heroic appearance was breathtaking. He summoned his chariot, which could be drawn by

1. **monkey hordes** Rama's army, the result of his alliance with Sugriva, the monkey king.
2. **Shiva** (shē´ və) Hindu god of destruction and reproduction.
3. **accouterments** (ə ko͞ot´ ər mənts) *n.* soldier's equipment, other than clothes and weapons.

Enrichment

Vishnu

Along with Shiva, the Hindu god of destruction and reproduction, and Brahma, the creator, Vishnu, called the Preserver, is one of the three most important divinities in Hinduism. Hindus believe that Vishnu, with his everlasting power and constant presence, ensures the welfare of humanity. According to tradition, Vishnu periodically descends from heaven to Earth in an avatar, or physical form. Vishnu is said to have appeared nine times in different avatars, including once as the prince Rama (the hero of the *Ramayana)* and once as the god Krishna, one of the principal characters in the *Bhagavad-Gita.* Hindus believe that Vishnu will return again to destroy all evil and begin a new Golden Age of humanity.

horses or move on its own if the horses were hurt or killed. People stood aside when he came out of the palace and entered his chariot. "This is my resolve," he said to himself: "Either that woman Sita, or my wife Mandodari, will soon have cause to cry and roll in the dust in grief. Surely, before this day is done, one of them will be a widow."

36 The gods in heaven noticed Ravana's determined move and felt that Rama would need all the support they could muster. They requested Indra[4] to send down his special chariot for Rama's use. When the chariot appeared at his camp, Rama was deeply impressed with the magnitude and brilliance of the vehicle. "How has this come to be here?" he asked.

"Sir," the charioteer answered, "my name is Matali. I have the honor of being the charioteer of Indra. Brahma, the four-faced god and the creator of the Universe, and Shiva, whose power has emboldened Ravana now to challenge you, have commanded me to bring it here for your use. It can fly swifter than air over all obstacles, over any mountain, sea, or sky, and will help you to emerge victorious in this battle."

Rama reflected aloud, "It may be that the rakshasas[5] have created this illusion for me. It may be a trap. I don't know how to view it." Whereupon Matali spoke convincingly to dispel the doubt in Rama's mind. Rama, still hesitant, though partially convinced, looked at Hanuman[6] and Lakshmana[7] and asked, "What do you think of it?" Both answered, "We feel no doubt that this chariot is Indra's; it is not an illusory creation."

Rama fastened his sword, slung two quivers full of rare arrows over his shoulders, and climbed into the chariot.

The beat of war drums, the challenging cries of soldiers, the trumpets, and the rolling chariots speeding along to confront each other, created a deafening mixture of noise. While Ravana had instructed his charioteer to speed ahead, Rama very gently ordered his chariot driver, "Ravana is in a rage; let him perform all the antics he desires and exhaust himself. Until then be calm; we don't have to hurry forward. Move slowly and calmly, and you must strictly follow my instructions; I will tell you when to drive faster."

Ravana's assistant and one of his staunchest supporters, Mahodara—the giant among giants in his physical appearance—begged Ravana, "Let me not be a mere spectator when you confront Rama. Let me have the honor of grappling with him. Permit me to attack Rama."

"Rama is my sole concern," Ravana replied. "If you wish to engage yourself in a fight, you may fight his brother Lakshmana."

Noticing Mahodara's purpose, Rama steered his chariot across his path in order to prevent Mahodara from reaching Lakshmana.

Literary Analysis
The Indian Epic How do the gods help Rama as he is about to face Ravana?

Vocabulary Builder
dispel (di spel′) *v.* cause to vanish

37 **Reading Check**
For whom do Hanuman and the monkeys fight in the battle?

4. **Indra** (in′ drə) Hindu god of rain and thunder; chief god in early Hinduism.
5. **rakshasas** (räk′ shə səz) demons that can change form at will.
6. **Hanuman** (hun′ o͞o män′) leader of Rama's army of monkeys.
7. **Lakshmana** (läk shmä′ nə) Rama's half-brother and loyal companion.

36 Literary Analysis

The Indian Epic

- Remind students that an epic hero usually encounters several challenges, by which he demonstrates his heroic qualities. Then, **ask:** What challenges is Rama facing?
  Answer: Rama must contend with the giant Ravana and must rescue his wife, Sita.
- After students read the bracketed passage independently, **ask** the Literary Analysis question: How do the gods help Rama as he is about to face Ravana?
  Answer: Indra sends his special chariot and driver for Rama's use.

➤ **Monitor Progress** To help students understand Rama's status as a hero, **ask:** Why do the gods probably prefer to help Rama instead of Ravana?
Possible response: The gods want to help Rama because he is a heroic character who has been unfairly banished from his kingdom. Ravana, on the other hand, is an evil, destructive giant.

➤ **Reteach** Direct students' attention to the Literary Analysis instruction on p. 191. Have them share the heroic qualities of Rama that they have inserted in their graphic organizers.

37 Reading Check

Answer: Hanuman and the monkeys fight for Rama.

Differentiated Instruction Solutions for All Learners

Strategy for Special Needs Students
On the board or a wall, have students create a timeline that documents the events described in "Rama and Ravana in Battle." Begin the timeline with the events described in the Background text, beginning with Rama's banishment. As students read, have them record events in the order in which they occur. Suggest that students add events after they finish reading each page. Then, have students add their own drawings or magazine pictures to the timeline to illustrate events further.

Strategy for Less Proficient Readers
Students may have difficulty with words such as *valor, resolve, muster, emboldened, antics,* and *staunchest.* Encourage students to use thesauruses to find synonyms for these words. Then, have students read the sentence in which each word appears, substituting the synonym for the original word. For example, students could substitute the word *bravery* for *valor* in the sentence: "He felt a terrific rage rising within him, mixed with some admiration for Rama's valor."

38 Critical Thinking

Infer

- Remind students that readers can use information from a text and information they already know to make inferences.
- Have a volunteer read aloud the bracketed passage. Then, **ask** students: What qualities does Ravana possess that cause him to disregard the omens?
Possible response: He is easily angered and quick to react, without thinking about the consequences.

39 Literary Analysis

The Indian Epic and the Epic Hero

- Direct students' attention back to p. 191, and review the qualities of an epic hero.
- Then, have students discuss what they know about Rama so far.
- Read the bracketed passage aloud, and **ask** the Literary Analysis question: What heroic trait does Rama demonstrate with the strategy he employs in this passage?
Possible response: Rama's strategy reveals his heroic concern for others. Even though Ravana is his enemy, Rama still gives Ravana an opportunity to stop his rampage.

Whereupon Mahodara ordered his chariot driver, "Now dash straight ahead, directly into Rama's chariot."

The charioteer, more practical-minded, advised him, "I would not go near Rama. Let us keep away." But Mahodara, obstinate and intoxicated with war fever, made straight for Rama. He wanted to have the honor of a direct encounter with Rama himself in spite of Ravana's advice; and for this honor he paid a heavy price, as it was a moment's work for Rama to destroy him, and leave him lifeless and shapeless on the field. Noticing this, Ravana's anger mounted further. He commanded his driver, "You will not slacken now. Go." Many ominous signs were seen now—his bowstrings suddenly snapped; the mountains shook; thunders rumbled in the skies; tears flowed from the horses' eyes; elephants with decorated foreheads moved along dejectedly. Ravana, noticing them, hesitated only for a second, saying, "I don't care. This mere mortal Rama is of no account, and these omens do not concern me at all." 38 Meanwhile, Rama paused for a moment to consider his next step; and suddenly turned towards the armies supporting Ravana, which stretched away to the horizon, and destroyed them. He felt that this might be one way of saving Ravana. 39 With his armies gone, it was possible that Ravana might have a change of heart. But it had only the effect of spurring Ravana on; he plunged forward and kept coming nearer Rama and his own doom.

Literary Analysis
The Indian Epic and the Epic Hero What heroic trait does Rama demonstrate with the strategy he employs in this passage?

Rama's army cleared and made way for Ravana's chariot, unable to stand the force of his approach. Ravana blew his conch[8] and its shrill challenge reverberated through space. Following it another conch, called "Panchajanya," which belonged to Mahavishnu (Rama's original form before his present incarnation), sounded of its own accord in answer to the challenge, agitating the universe with its vibrations. And then Matali picked up another conch, which was Indra's, and blew it. This was the signal indicating the commencement of the actual battle. Presently Ravana sent a shower of arrows on Rama; and Rama's followers, unable to bear the sight of his body being studded with arrows, averted their heads. Then the chariot horses of Ravana and Rama glared at each other in hostility, and the flags topping the chariots—Ravana's ensign of the Veena[9] and Rama's with the whole universe on it—clashed, and one heard the stringing and twanging of bow-strings on both sides, overpowering in volume all other sound. Then followed a shower of arrows from Rama's own bow. Ravana stood gazing at the chariot sent by Indra and swore, "These gods, instead of supporting me, have gone to the support of this petty human being. I will teach them a lesson. He is not fit to be killed with my arrows but I shall seize him and his chariot together and fling them into high heaven and dash them to destruction." Despite his oath, he still strung his bow and sent a shower of arrows at Rama, raining in thousands, but they were all invariably shattered and neutralized by the arrows from Rama's bow, which met arrow for arrow. Ultimately

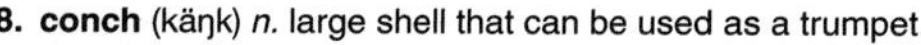

8. **conch** (käŋk) *n.* large shell that can be used as a trumpet.
9. **Veena** (vē´ nä´) *n.* stringed musical instrument.

Enrichment

Indian Classical Music

Draw students' attention to the word *Veena* and its definition. Tell students that unlike western music, which features harmony and development of themes, Indian classical music focuses on melodic ideas and rhythm. The music is built around a drone, a continual pitch heard throughout a piece; a raga, or melodic structure that serves as the basis for improvisation; and a tala, or rhythmic structure. Suggest that students listen to several works performed by Indian sitar player Ravi Shankar.

Then, have students research Indian melodic instruments, such as the bansuri, bin, santur, sarangi, sarod, shehnai, sitar, and surbahar; as well as the rhythm instruments dholak, pakhawaj, and tabla; and the drone instruments tamboura and swarpeti.

Ravana, instead of using one bow, used ten with his twenty arms, multiplying his attack tenfold; but Rama stood unhurt.

Ravana suddenly realized that he should change his tactics and ordered his charioteer to fly the chariot up in the skies. From there he attacked and destroyed a great many of the monkey army supporting Rama. Rama ordered Matali, "Go up in the air. Our young soldiers are being attacked from the sky. Follow Ravana, and don't slacken."

There followed an aerial pursuit at dizzying speed across the dome of the sky and rim of the earth. Ravana's arrows came down like rain; he was bent upon destroying everything in the world. But Rama's arrows diverted, broke, or neutralized Ravana's. Terror-stricken, the gods watched this pursuit. Presently Ravana's arrows struck Rama's horses and pierced the heart of Matali himself. The charioteer fell. Rama paused for a while in grief, undecided as to his next step. Then he recovered and resumed his offensive. At that moment the divine eagle Garuda was seen perched on Rama's flag-post, and the gods who were watching felt that this could be an auspicious sign.

After circling the globe several times, the dueling chariots returned, and the fight continued over Lanka.[10] It was impossible to be very clear about the location of the battleground as the fight occured here, there, and everywhere. Rama's arrows pierced Ravana's armor and made him wince. Ravana was so insensible to pain and impervious to attack that for him to wince was a good sign, and the gods hoped that this was a turn for the better. But at this moment, Ravana suddenly changed his tactics. Instead of merely shooting his arrows, which were powerful in themselves, he also invoked several supernatural forces to create strange effects: He was an adept in the use of various asthras[11] which could be made dynamic with special incantations. At this point, the

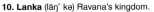

41 ▲ Critical Viewing
Which details in this depiction of Hanuman suggest that he is an ally of the hero and not an evil character? **[Infer]**

42 Reading Check
Why does Ravana order his charioteer to fly the chariot up in the skies?

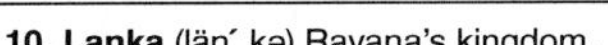

10. **Lanka** (läŋ´ kə) Ravana's kingdom.
11. **asthras** (äs´ trəz) *n.* weapons with supernatural powers.

40 Humanities

Hanuman, Monkey God of Rama's Army

The leader of the monkey army, Hanuman, carries a crown. He fights on the side of Rama against Ravena in "Rama and Ravena in Battle." The monkey leader is dressed as a human, adorned with clothing and jewelry. Point out that he does not place the crown on his own head but extends it to an unseen individual.

Use this question for discussion:

How does the artist humanize Hanuman, the monkey leader?
Possible response: Hanuman's clothing, his jewelry, his extended hand, his recognition of authority, and his intelligent face are human characteristics.

41 Critical Viewing

Possible response: Hanuman has a pleasant expression and is shown with hands uplifted, not brandishing weapons.

42 Reading Check

Answer: Ravana takes to the air to gain a vantage point from which he can destroy many of the monkey soldiers.

Differentiated Instruction Solutions for All Learners

Strategy for Less Proficient Readers

Suggest that as students read independently, they use self-sticking notes to mark any passages that present them with confusing ideas or vocabulary. Tell students that when they encounter such passages, they should not stop reading. Sustained reading like this may clarify many ambiguous points. If students remain confused about certain passages, they can use the self-sticking notes to return to these pages and to ask questions during class discussion.

Support for English Learners

Some students may have difficulty applying the Literary Analysis strategy to this epic. To provide students with a model for recognizing heroic qualities in characters, give them a copy of **Literary Analysis Graphic Organizer B,** p. 39 in ***Graphic Organizer Transparencies.*** The completed graphic organizer will give students insight into the process of recognizing the qualities of an epic hero. They can use it as a model to help them identify Rama's heroic qualities.

43 Literature in Context

Hindu Gods

Many of the Hindu gods either are represented as animals or actually are animals.

For example, the snake deities are often represented as upright stone figures of cobras. In Karnataka state, all families have a snake deity that is thought to be necessary for their welfare. Manasa, a snake goddess worshiped in Assam and Bengal, is believed to fend off snake bites and bring about prosperity.

The significance of animals is also due in part to the Hindu doctrine of reincarnation in which a person's soul never dies but can be reborn in an animal: The less worthy the soul, the more lowly the animal.

Connect to the Literature
Ask students to give two examples of Rama's godlike qualities.
Possible response: Rama was godlike when he used his mantra to destroy Ravana's trident and later when he refused to attack the incapacitated Ravana. He then used "Brahmasthra" to defeat the monstrous Ravana.

44 Literary Analysis

The Indian Epic

- Have students discuss the weapons Rama and Ravana use during battle. Remind them that asthras have supernatural powers.
- Then, **ask** students the Literary Analysis item: Explain how Rama and Ravana's use of asthras reinforces their roles in this epic.
  Possible response: Rama's weapons reflect knowledge and piety and thus reinforce his role as the hero of the epic. He uses his weapons only to deflect attack. Ravana, as the attacker, uses weapons of destruction and chaos, which reinforce his role as the antagonist.

Monitor Progress **Ask** students what type of weapon an epic hero would be expected to use if he or she were engaged in a battle he or she did not start.
Possible response: A hero would probably select weapons that would stave off an attack.

fight became one of attack with supernatural powers, and parrying of such an attack with other supernatural powers.

Ravana realized that the mere aiming of shafts with ten or twenty of his arms would be of no avail because the mortal whom he had so contemptuously thought of destroying with a slight effort was proving formidable, and his arrows were beginning to pierce and cause pain. Among the asthras sent by Ravana was one called "Danda," a special gift from Shiva, capable of pursuing and pulverizing its target. When it came flaming along, the gods were struck with fear. But Rama's arrow neutralized it.

Now Ravana said to himself, "These are all petty weapons. I should really get down to proper business." And he invoked the one called "Maya"—a weapon which created illusions and confused the enemy.

With proper incantations and worship, he sent off this weapon and it created an illusion of reviving all the armies and its leaders—Kumbakarna and Indrajit and the others—and bringing them back to the battlefield. Presently Rama found all those who, he thought, were no more, coming on with battle cries and surrounding him. Every man in the enemy's army was again up in arms. They seemed to fall on Rama with victorious cries. This was very confusing and Rama asked Matali, whom he had by now revived, "What is happening now? How are all these coming back? They were dead." Matali explained, "In your original identity you are the creator of illusions in this universe. Please know that Ravana has created phantoms to confuse you. If you make up your mind, you can dispel them immediately." Matali's explanation was a great help. Rama at once invoked a weapon called "Gnana"—which means "wisdom" or "perception." This was a very rare weapon, and he sent it forth. And all the terrifying armies who seemed to have come on in such a great mass suddenly evaporated into thin air.

44 Ravana then shot an asthra called "Thama," whose nature was to create total darkness in all the worlds. The arrows came with heads exposing frightening eyes and fangs, and fiery tongues. End to end the earth was enveloped in total darkness and the whole of creation was paralyzed. This asthra also created a deluge of rain on one side, a rain of stones on the other, a hailstorm showering down intermittently, and a tornado sweeping the earth. Ravana was sure that this would arrest Rama's enterprise. But Rama was able to meet it with what was named "Shivasthra." He understood the nature of the phenomenon and the cause of it and chose the appropriate asthra for counteracting it.

Literature in Context

43 Religion Connection

Hindu Gods

Hindus worship thousands of gods. Each god is part of a single supreme force called Brahman, which only a few sages can truly understand. The three main gods of Hinduism are *Brahma*, the creator of the world; *Vishnu*, the preserver, who restores moral order; and *Shiva*, the destroyer, who regularly destroys the world in order to re-create it. Rama, the epic hero, is believed to be an incarnation of Vishnu, who combines qualities of both a man and a god.

Statue of Shiva

Connect to the Literature

What godlike characteristics does Rama have?

Literary Analysis
The Indian Epic Explain how Rama's and Ravana's use of asthras reinforces their roles in this epic.

Enrichment

Sanskrit

The *Ramayana* is one of the most important works of classical Sanskrit. The Sanskrit language is considered part of the Indo-European family of languages, which includes English, German, Latin, and Farsi (spoken in ancient Persia, now modern Iran). The beginnings of Sanskrit can be traced to approximately 1500 B.C., when the Aryans invaded India, bringing their language with them. This language evolved into Vedic Sanskrit, the language of the Indian upper classes. Gradually, Vedic Sanskrit fell out of use as a spoken language but became a standard form of written language, referred to now as classical Sanskrit. The Sanskrit literature began orally and was passed down through many generations before the stories were recorded.

Ravana now shot off what he considered his deadliest weapon—a trident endowed with extraordinary destructive power, once gifted to Ravana by the gods. When it started on its journey there was real panic all round. It came on flaming toward Rama, its speed or course unaffected by the arrows he flung at it.

44 When Rama noticed his arrows falling down ineffectively while the trident sailed towards him, for a moment he lost heart. When it came quite near, he uttered a certain mantra[12] from the depth of his being and while he was breathing out that incantation, an esoteric syllable in perfect timing, the trident collapsed. Ravana, who had been so certain of vanquishing Rama with his trident, was astonished to see it fall down within an inch of him, and for a minute wondered if his adversary might not after all be a divine being although he looked like a mortal. Ravana thought to himself, "This is, perhaps, the highest God. Who could he be? Not Shiva, for Shiva is my supporter; he could not be Brahma, who is four faced; could not be Vishnu, because of my immunity from the weapons of the whole trinity. Perhaps this man is the primordial being, the cause behind the whole universe. But whoever he may be, I will not stop my fight until I defeat and crush him or at least take him prisoner."

With this resolve, Ravana next sent a weapon which issued forth monstrous serpents vomiting fire and venom, with enormous fangs and red eyes. They came darting in from all directions.

Rama now selected an asthra called "Garuda" (which meant "eagle"). Very soon thousands of eagles were aloft, and they picked off the serpents with their claws and beaks and destroyed them. Seeing this also fail, Ravana's anger was roused to a mad pitch and he blindly emptied a quiverful of arrows in Rama's direction. Rama's arrows met them half way and turned them round so that they went back and their sharp points embedded themselves in Ravana's own chest.

Ravana was weakening in spirit. He realized that he was at the end of his resources. All his learning and equipment in weaponry were of no avail and he had practically come to

12. **mantra** (män′ trə) *n.* hymn or portion of text that is chanted or spoken as a prayer or incantation.

▼ Critical Viewing 46
How does this depiction of the battle between Rama and Ravana compare to the way the battle is described in the *Ramayana*? **[Compare and Contrast]**

45

Rama and Lakshmana shooting arrows at the demon Ravana, © Victoria and Albert Museum

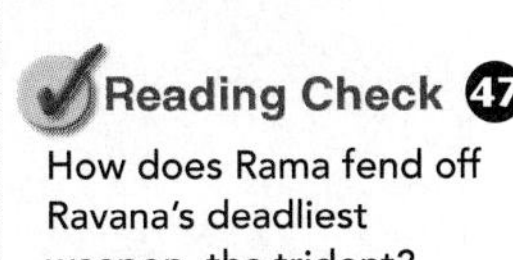

Reading Check 47
How does Rama fend off Ravana's deadliest weapon, the trident?

45 Humanities

Rama and Lakshmana shooting arrows at the demon Ravana

Like many historic and contemporaneous works, this picture's theme is warfare. But Indian art does not typically reflect violence and war. On the contrary, most Indian art depicts pleasurable events and fanciful scenes—art is not meant to imitate reality.

Use this question for discussion:

What does this picture suggest about the battle between Rama and Ravana?
Possible response: Ravana is superhuman. He is larger than his attackers, possessing ten heads and twenty arms. Ravana stands as an army of one, while Rama and his warriors are human and therefore must fight Ravana as a force. However, regardless of their apparent human weaknesses, Rama and his men approach Ravana without fear.

46 Critical Viewing

Possible response: This depiction of the battle does not capture the scale and action of the scene described in the *Ramayana*.

47 Reading Check

Answer: Rama utters a mantra from the depths of his being that causes Ravana's trident to collapse.

Differentiated Instruction Solutions for All Learners

Support for Less Proficient Readers
To help students create rounded pictures of Rama and Ravana, have them create a web for each character. On the board, demonstrate how to create such a web by placing Rama's name in the center cell and creating outer cells labeled to describe Rama's views, actions, and words.

Enrichment for Gifted/Talented Students
Have students write a monologue in which Ravana explains why he is so bitter and angry. Before students begin writing, encourage them to note details from the story that will support Ravana's explanation. Then, have students draft their monologues. Invite volunteers to perform their monologues for the class.

Enrichment for Advanced Readers
Have students select and read another story from the *Ramayana,* such as "Rama's Initiation." Then, have students write an essay in which they compare and contrast the two stories in regard to the heroic deeds of Rama and the lessons each story teaches. Make sure that students use the revision process.

48 Critical Thinking

Connect

- Tell students that while reading, it is often necessary to connect events with other significant events that occurred earlier in a selection.
- Have a volunteer read aloud the bracketed passage.
- Remind students that on p. 211, one of Ravana's arrows pierces the heart of Rama's charioteer, Matali. Then, **ask:** How does it happen that Matali is still alive?
  Answer: On p. 212, we read that Rama has revived Matali.

49 Humanities

Ravana is again pictured as superhuman. His jeweled armor and his physical size depict his wealth and power. The horsemen and soldiers are remarkably small and seemingly weak by comparison. Point out that the battle appears to be taking place in the air above the kingdom.

Use this question for discussion:

How do depictions of Ravana such as this help reinforce the heroic status of Rama?
Possible response: Rama must be fearless and steadfast in his resolve to attack and defeat such a powerful and monstrous demon.

50 Critical Viewing

Possible response: Ravana is shown as extremely large, an appropriate depiction, for he is a giant. The representation also shows him as aggressive, as he is in the story.

the end of his special gifts of destruction. While he was going down thus, Rama's own spirit was soaring up. The combatants were now near enough to grapple with each other and Rama realized that this was the best moment to cut off Ravana's heads.[13] He sent a crescent-shaped arrow which sliced off one of Ravana's heads and flung it far into the sea, and this process continued; but every time a head was cut off, Ravana had the benediction of having another one grown in its place. Rama's crescent-shaped weapon was continuously busy as Ravana's heads kept cropping up. Rama lopped off his arms but they grew again and every lopped-off arm hit Matali and the chariot and tried to cause destruction by itself, and the tongue in a new head wagged, uttered challenges, and cursed Rama. On the cast-off heads of Ravana devils and minor demons, who had all along been in terror of Ravana and had obeyed and pleased him, executed a dance of death and feasted on the flesh.

Ravana was now desperate. Rama's arrows embedded themselves in a hundred places on his body and weakened him. Presently he collapsed in a faint on the floor of his chariot. Noticing his state, his charioteer
48 pulled back and drew the chariot aside. Matali whispered to Rama, "This is the time to finish off that demon. He is in a faint. Go on. Go on."

50 ▼ Critical Viewing
In what way is this depiction of Ravana appropriate for this story? **[Connect]**

13. **Ravana's heads** Ravana is usually depicted as having ten heads and twenty arms.

49

51 But Rama put away his bow and said, "It is not fair warfare to attack a man who is in a faint. I will wait. Let him recover," and waited.

When Ravana revived, he was angry with his charioteer for withdrawing, and took out his sword, crying, "You have disgraced me. Those who look on will think I have retreated." But his charioteer explained how Rama suspended the fight and forebore to attack when he was in a faint. Somehow, Ravana appreciated his explanation and patted his back and resumed his attacks. Having exhausted his special weapons, in desperation Ravana began to throw on Rama all sorts of things such as staves, cast-iron balls, heavy rocks, and oddments he could lay hands on. None of them touched Rama, but glanced off and fell ineffectually. Rama went on shooting his arrows. There seemed to be no end of this struggle in sight.

Now Rama had to pause to consider what final measure he should take to bring this campaign to an end. After much thought, he decided to use "Brahmasthra," a weapon specially designed by the Creator Brahma on a former occasion, when he had to provide one for Shiva to destroy Tripura, the old monster who assumed the forms of flying mountains and settled down on habitations and cities, seeking to destroy the world. The Brahmasthra was a special gift to be used only
52 when all other means had failed. Now Rama, with prayers and worship, invoked its fullest power and sent it in Ravana's direction, aiming at his heart rather than his head; Ravana being vulnerable at heart. While he had prayed for indestructibility of his several heads and arms, he had forgotten to strengthen his heart, where the Brahmasthra entered and ended his career.

Rama watched him fall headlong from his chariot face down onto the earth, and that was the end of the great campaign. Now one noticed Ravana's face aglow with a new quality. Rama's arrows had burnt off the layers of dross, the anger, conceit, cruelty, lust, and egotism which had encrusted his real self, and now his personality came through in its pristine form—of one who was devout and capable of tremendous attainments. His constant meditation on Rama, although as an adversary, now seemed to bear fruit, as his face shone with serenity and peace. Rama noticed it from his chariot above and commanded Matali, "Set me down on the ground." When the chariot descended and came to rest on its wheels, Rama got down and commanded Matali, "I am grateful for your services to me. You may now take the chariot back to Indra."

Surrounded by his brother Lakshmana and Hanuman and all his other war chiefs, Rama approached Ravana's body, and stood gazing on it. He noted his crowns and jewelry scattered piecemeal on the ground. The decorations and the extraordinary workmanship of the armor on his chest were blood-covered. Rama sighed as if to say, "What might he not have achieved but for the evil stirring within him!"

At this moment, as they readjusted Ravana's blood-stained body, Rama noticed to his great shock a scar on Ravana's back and said with a smile, "Perhaps this is not an episode of glory for me as I seem

Literary Analysis
The Indian Epic and the Epic Hero What heroic qualities does Rama display through his actions when Ravana is in a faint?

Vocabulary Builder
invoked (in vōkt′) *v.* called on for help

Vocabulary Builder
pristine (pris′ tēn′) *adj.* unspoiled; uncorrupted

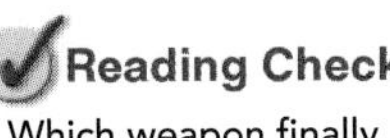
Reading Check 53
Which weapon finally brings the battle to an end?

51 Literary Analysis
The Indian Epic and the Epic Hero

- Direct students' attention to the qualities of an epic hero listed on p. 191.
- Then, have students read the bracketed passage independently.
- Lead students in a discussion of what they might do if they were faced with a similar situation.
- Then, **ask** students the Literary Analysis question: What heroic qualities does Rama display through his actions when Ravana is in a faint? **Possible response:** Rama displays fairness, honor, respect, and patience.

52 Vocabulary Builder
Latin roots *-voc-/-vok-*

- Call students' attention to the word *invoked* and its definition. Let students know that the roots *-voc-* and *-vok-* come from the Latin word *vox,* meaning "voice."
- Have students write short explanations of how the idea of voice influenced the formation of the word *invoke.*
- **Ask** students to suggest and define any other words they may know that incorporate these word roots. **Possible response:** *Vocalize, vociferous,* and *provoke* are possible suggestions.

53 Reading Check

Answer: "Brahmasthra," a special asthra, brings the battle to an end.

Differentiated Instruction Solutions for All Learners

Enrichment for Gifted/Talented Students
Tell students that "Rama and Ravana in Battle" has all the ingredients for a summer blockbuster—an exotic setting, a fearless superhero, and a dastardly villain. Encourage students to write a script treatment outlining how they would tell the story, cast the film, and use special effects and music to create a box-office success. Volunteers can present their script treatments for the class. Invite students to discuss which treatment would draw the largest audience and why.

Enrichment for Advanced Readers
Tell students that the *Ramayana,* like Homer's epic poems, was recited from memory for centuries before being written down. Organize students into pairs, and have each pair select a passage from this prose translation to render into verse. Suggest that students search for passages that they can change easily. Then, have each pair read or recite from memory their verse for the class. Encourage students to use appropriate gestures and an animated speaking voice in their performances.

ASSESS

Answers

1. **Possible response:** Rama's humility and fairness in battle, his persistence, and his determination and ingenuity are admirable qualities. Ravana's determination is admirable.
2. (a) Ravana resolves that either he or Rama will die in battle. (b) **Possible response:** This reveals that Ravana is determined to accomplish what he sets out to do, regardless of the cost.
3. (a) Indra sends Rama his special chariot and charioteer. (b) **Possible response:** Ravana is the source of the conflict, and Rama is a humble and fair man. The gods think that Rama needs help to win the battle.
4. (a) Ravana decides to act on his own and ignores the omens that foretell trouble. Rama is skeptical of the aid from the gods, he is cautious, and he protects his young soldiers and his half-brother. He also suspends the battle when he knows that Ravana has fainted and cannot defend himself. (b) **Possible response:** Ravana's actions reveal him to be angry and vengeful. Rama's actions reveal a man who is concerned for others and who fights honorably and fairly.
5. (a) Rama's victory indicates that patience and strength of character will be rewarded. Ravana's defeat indicates that wrath and destructiveness will be punished. (b) **Possible response:** Ancient Indians believed that justice would be done. (c) **Possible response:** The message probably influenced people's behavior and values by encouraging them to emulate Rama.
6. (a) **Possible response:** Rama, like Superman, is powerful and righteous. (b) **Possible response:** Rama is the more heroic figure because he is fair in battle and shows pity for his opponent.

to have killed an enemy who was turning his back and retreating. Perhaps I was wrong in shooting the Brahmasthra into him." He looked so concerned at this supposed lapse on his part that Vibishana, Ravana's brother, came forward to explain. "What you have achieved is unique. I say so although it meant the death of my brother."

"But I have attacked a man who had turned his back," Rama said. "See that scar."

Vibishana explained, "It is an old scar. In ancient days, when he paraded his strength around the globe, once he tried to attack the divine elephants that guard the four directions. When he tried to catch them, he was gored in the back by one of the tuskers and that is the scar you see now; it is not a fresh one though fresh blood is flowing on it."

Rama accepted the explanation. "Honor him and cherish his memory so that his spirit may go to heaven, where he has his place. And now I will leave you to attend to his funeral arrangements, befitting his grandeur."

Critical Reading

1. **Respond:** What did you most admire about Rama? What did you most admire about Ravana?
2. **(a) Recall:** What does Ravana resolve as he prepares to go into battle? **(b) Infer:** What does this resolution reveal about his character?
3. **(a) Recall:** What does Indra send to Rama before Rama goes into battle? **(b) Infer:** Why do you think the gods want to help Rama win?
4. **(a) Compare and Contrast:** How does Rama's approach to the battle differ from Ravana's? **(b) Infer:** What do their actions reveal about their characters?
5. **(a) Infer:** What message is revealed by Rama's defeat of Ravana? **(b) Draw Conclusions:** What does this message suggest about the ancient Indian attitude toward justice? **(c) Speculate:** What effect might the message of this story have had on ancient Indian society?
6. **(a) Connect:** How does Rama compare with modern super-heroes, such as Superman? **(b) Take a Position:** Who would you say is the more heroic figure—Rama or Superman? Explain your answer.

Apply the Skills

from the *Mahabharata* • from the *Bhagavad-Gita* • from the *Ramayana*

Literary Analysis

Indian Epic

1. **(a)** What purpose do **Indian epics** serve in Indian culture? **(b)** What message do "Sibi," "The Yoga of Knowledge," and "Rama and Ravana in Battle" each attempt to convey?
2. **(a)** In the *Mahabharata*, what values does Sibi represent? **(b)** What details of his character or actions support your answer?
3. Identify an ancient Indian religious idea that is conveyed by "The Yoga of Knowledge."

Comparing Literary Works

4. Explain how the heroic traits of each **epic hero** are demonstrated in these selections.
5. What message can be inferred from the gods' willingness to assist the hero in each of these epics?
6. **(a)** What challenge must each hero face and overcome in order to fulfill his sacred duty? **(b)** Who do you think has the most difficult challenge? Explain.

Reading Strategy

Inferring Beliefs of the Period

7. Use a chart like the one shown to **infer beliefs** of ancient Indian culture. Provide a detail from each of the epics, and explain what it suggests about ancient Indian beliefs.

Epic	Detail	Belief It Suggests

8. Which of these selections reinforces most strongly the ancient Indian belief in nonattached work? Explain.

Extend Understanding

9. **Social Studies Connection:** Which modern leaders have made major sacrifices for their people? Explain.

QuickReview

An **Indian epic** is a long narrative about the adventures of an Indian hero.

An **epic hero** is a larger-than-life figure possessing such qualities as courage, strength, and loyalty.

If you pay close attention to the ideas expressed in a literary work, you can **infer beliefs of the period** in which it was written.

For: Self-test
Visit: www.PHSchool.com
Web Code: eta-6202

Answers

1. (a) Epics relay social values through narrative. (b) "Sibi" stresses the importance of duty. "The Yoga of Knowledge" teaches that the Atman is unchanging and eternal, so an individual should pursue duty without regarding earthly consequences. "Rama and Ravana in Battle" teaches that righteous, patient, and humble behavior will be rewarded.
2. (a) **Possible response:** Sibi represents duty, selflessness, and piety. (b) Sibi's concern for his guests and protection of the dove show his selflessness. Keeping his word to the hawk shows piety and a sense of duty.
3. **Possible response:** The Atman as the eternal and unchanging universal soul is conveyed in this work.
4. **Possible response:** Sibi protects the dove by sacrificing his own body. Arjuna's concern for his family and desire to complete his dharma reveal him as heroic. Rama is patient in battle and pities Ravana.
5. **Possible response:** The gods are interested in humans and their deeds and help those who do their duty.
6. (a) Sibi must determine how to protect his subjects without sacrificing his own body. Arjuna must decide between fighting or sparing his family. Rama must rescue his wife and defeat Ravana. (b) **Possible response:** Those who see physical fighting as more of a challenge will say Rama. Those who understand a "catch-22" will say Arjuna. Those who sympathize with refusal to compromise may say Sibi.
7. **Epic:** "Sibi;" **Detail:** Sibi protects the dove; **Belief It Suggests:** Leaders must protect their subjects. **Epic:** "Yoga of Knowledge;" **Detail:** Krishna states that everyone must follow his or her duty; **Belief It Suggests:** Completing one's duty contributes to the universal soul. **Epic:** "Rama and Ravana in Battle;" **Detail:** Indra sends his chariot and charioteer to Rama; **Belief It Suggests:** The gods help those who pursue their duty.

Answers continued

8. **Possible response:** "The Yoga of Knowledge" develops the idea at great length; "Sibi" also illustrates the idea in dramatic terms.
9. **Possible response:** Mohandas Gandhi was imprisoned for leading the Indian struggle for independence from Britain.

Go Online Assessment: Students may use the **Self-test** to prepare for **Selection Test A** or **Selection Test B.**

EXTEND/ASSESS

Answers

❶ Vocabulary Lesson

Word Analysis: Latin Root *-voc-/-vok-*

1. *Vocal* means "of or relating to the voice."
2. *Provoke* means "to call forth," as one might by speaking.
3. *Vociferous* means "making a noisy and vehement outcry," as when speaking in a loud voice.

Spelling Strategy

1. departure
2. legislature
3. forfeiture

Vocabulary Builder

1. synonyms
2. synonyms
3. synonyms
4. antonyms
5. antonyms
6. synonyms
7. synonyms
8. antonyms

❷ Grammar and Style Lesson

1. abandoned; modifies *corpse*
2. dazzling; modifies *crown*
3. illumined; modifies *soul*
4. recollected; modifies *mind*
5. determined; modifies *move*

Writing Application

Possible response: One's duties must be performed regardless of an abandoned body, a bewildered mind, or a dueling soul. Duty must prevail. For without duty, there is chaos.

Writing and Grammar Platinum Level

For support in teaching the Grammar and Style Lesson, use Chapter 20, Section 1.

Build Language Skills

❶ Vocabulary Lesson

Word Analysis: Latin Root *-voc- / -vok-*

The Latin root *-voc-/-vok-* means "speak" or "say." It derives from the Latin word *vox*, meaning "voice." For example, notice how the root *-vok-* influences the meaning of the word *invoke*. Explain how each of the following words is related to "speaking" or "saying." If necessary, use a dictionary to check word origins.

1. vocal **2.** provoke **3.** vociferous

Spelling Strategy

The *chur* sound is spelled *ture* at the ends of words with Latin origins, like *caricature* and *miniature*. For each of the following verbs, write its noun form ending in *ture*.

1. depart **2.** legislate **3.** forfeit

Vocabulary Builder: Synonyms and Antonyms

Review each of the following items, and indicate whether the paired words are synonyms—words with similar meanings—or antonyms—words with opposite meanings.

1. mitigated, lessened
2. caricature, mockery
3. scruples, doubts
4. pervades, vacates
5. manifested, concealed
6. dispel, disperse
7. invoked, summoned
8. pristine, tarnished

❷ Grammar and Style Lesson

Participles as Adjectives

A **participle** is a verb form that can be used as an adjective. Participles usually end in *-ing* or *-ed*. A participle used as an adjective answers the question *What kind?* or *Which one?* about the noun or pronoun it modifies.

Examples: The bewildered warrior sought advice from his friend. (modifies *warrior*)

After circling the globe several times, the dueling chariots returned. (modifies *chariots*)

Practice Identify the participle in each item that follows, as well as the noun or pronoun each participle modifies.

1. It has the weight of an abandoned corpse.
2. In the hawk's place, they found Indra, the god with the dazzling crown.
3. In what manner does an illumined soul speak?
4. The recollected mind is awake / In the knowledge of the Atman.
5. The gods in heaven noticed Ravana's determined move.

Writing Application Write a paragraph on the importance of performing one's duties. Use at least three participles as adjectives in your writing.

Prentice Hall Writing and Grammar Connection: Platinum Level, Chapter 20, Section 1

Assessment Practice

Recognize Facts, Details, and Sequence

(For more practice, see *Test Preparation Workbook*, p. 10.)

Many tests require students to identify logical sequence. Use the following passage and sample item to show students how to identify the most logical sequence of ideas.

(1) Ravana then decides that he must go out and fight the battle himself. (2) Ravana sees that his men are suffering many defeats. (3) After Ravana has dressed in his battle dress and put on his armor, he is ready for battle. (4) Ravana prepares for battle with a ritual bath and prayers to Shiva for protection.

Which of the following reflects the most logical sentence sequence?

A 1, 3, 4, 2
B 2, 1, 4, 3
C 3, 2, 1, 4
D 4, 2, 1, 3

Guide students to see that the correct answer is *B*. The sentences should be arranged chronologically.

❸ Writing Lesson

Timed Writing: Editorial

These selections explore ancient Indian ideas such as *dharma* and nonattachment. Consider which of these ideas might be beneficial when applied to a modern issue. Write an editorial to argue your point of view persuasively. ***(40 minutes)***

Prewriting ***(10 minutes)*** Choose a topic that is important to you and that can be discussed in a brief paper. Then, make notes to clarify how ancient Hindu wisdom could address this problem.

Drafting ***(20 minutes)*** Begin with an introduction that outlines your point of view. Then, construct a persuasive argument, and support it with examples. Use engaging language to convey your idea's appeal.

Revising ***(10 minutes)*** Reread your editorial, and evaluate its language for connotations—the ideas and feelings associated with words. Make sure that you have chosen words that convey the meaning you intend.

Model: Revise for Connotations of Words

People would not be motivated by worldly success and rewards but by the sincere desire to do good. The ~~crime~~ corruption that robs ~~citizens~~ taxpayers of their hard-earned ~~money~~ dollars would disappear, and in its place . . .

Precise language helps support the main points of an editorial.

Prentice Hall Writing and Grammar Connection: Platinum Level, Chapter 7, Section 3

❹ Extend Your Learning

Listening and Speaking Work in a group to write and "broadcast" a **TV news report** on the battle between Rama and Ravana. Remember to answer these questions:

- *Who?*
- *Where?*
- *Why?*
- *What?*
- *When?*
- *How?*

You might consider having one student act as anchor, while others give live reports. Rehearse until you are ready to deliver your news report to the class. **[Group Activity]**

Research and Technology The ideas of *dharma* and nonattached work had a profound influence on Dr. Martin Luther King, Jr. Use the Internet and other resources to prepare an **oral presentation** on the influence of these ideas on Dr. King and the civil rights movement in the United States.

For: An additional research activity
Visit: www.PHSchool.com
Web Code: etd-7201

Assessment Resources

The following resources can be used to assess students' knowledge and skills.

Unit 2 Resources
- **Selection Test A**, pp. 34–36
- **Selection Test B**, pp. 37–39

General Resources
- **Rubrics for Persuasion: Persuasive Essay,** pp. 47–48
- **Rubric for Speaking: Delivering an Oral Response to Literature**, p. 91

Go Online Assessment Students may use the **Self-test** to prepare for **Selection Test A** or **Selection Test B.**

❸ Writing Lesson

You may use this Writing Lesson as a timed-writing practice, or you may allow students to develop the editorial as a writing assignment over several days.

- To give students guidance in writing this editorial, give them the **Support for Writing Lesson,** p. 31 in ***Unit 2 Resources.***
- Tell students that an editorial is a type of persuasive writing. To persuade, a writer must build an argument and support main ideas with evidence, such as facts, statistics, examples, and statements from experts.
- Before students begin writing, have them work in small groups to brainstorm possible modern issues.
- Use the Persuasion: Persuasive Essay rubrics in ***General Resources,*** pp. 47–48, to evaluate students' work.

Writing and Grammar Platinum Level
For support in teaching the Writing Lesson, use Chapter 7, Section 3.

❹ Research and Technology

- Help students brainstorm a list of key words to use for a library catalog or Internet search.
- Give students a copy of the **Outline Graphic Organizer** in ***Graphic Organizer Transparencies,*** p. 279, to outline their presentations.
- Encourage students to write main ideas and supporting details on separate index cards. Students should use these cards as they give their oral presentations.
- The **Support for Extend Your Learning** page (***Unit 2 Resources,*** p. 32) provides guided note-taking opportunities to help students complete the Extend Your Learning activities.
- Use the Rubric for Speaking: Delivering an Oral Response to Literature, p. 91 in ***General Resources,*** to evaluate students' presentations.

Go Online Research Have students type in the Web Code for another research activity.

Standard Course of Study

Goal 1: WRITTEN LANGUAGE

- **WL.1.03.1** Select, monitor, and modify reading strategies appropriate to personal reflection.

Goal 4: CRITICAL THINKING

- **CT.4.03.2** Analyze how writers choose and incorporate significant, supporting, details.
- **CT.4.05.4** Comprehend main idea and supporting details in critical text.
- **CT.4.05.9** Analyze and evaluate the effects of craft and style in critical text.

Goal 5: LITERATURE

- **LT.5.01.2** Build knowledge of literary genres, and explore how characteristics apply to literature of world cultures.

Goal 6: GRAMMAR AND USAGE

- **GU.6.01.7** Use language effectively to create mood and tone.

Step-by-Step Teaching Guide	Pacing Guide
PRETEACH	
• Administer Vocabulary and Reading Warm-ups as necessary.	5 min.
• Engage students' interest with the motivation activity.	5 min.
• Read and discuss author and background features. **FT**	10 min.
• Introduce the Literary Analysis Skill: Indian Fable. **FT**	5 min.
• Introduce the Reading Strategy: Reread for Clarification. **FT**	10 min.
• Prepare students to read by teaching the selection vocabulary. **FT**	
TEACH	
• Informally monitor comprehension while students read independently or in groups. **FT**	30 min.
• Monitor students' comprehension with the Reading Check notes.	as students read
• Reinforce vocabulary with Vocabulary Builder notes.	as students read
• Develop students' understanding of Indian fables with the Literary Analysis annotations. **FT**	5 min.
• Develop students' ability to reread for clarification with the Reading Strategy annotations. **FT**	5 min.
ASSESS/EXTEND	
• Assess students' comprehension and mastery of the Literary Analysis and Reading Strategy by having them answer the Apply the Skills questions. **FT**	15 min.
• Have students complete the Vocabulary Lesson and the Grammar and Style Lesson. **FT**	15 min.
• Apply students' ability to respond to peer reviews by using the Writing Lesson. **FT**	45 min. or homework
• Apply students' understanding by using one or more of the Extend Your Learning activities.	20–90 min. or homework
• Administer Selection Test A or Selection Test B. **FT**	15 min.

Resources

Print

Unit 2 Resources

Vocabulary Warm-up Word Lists **[L1, L2, EL]** . . . . . . p. 40
Vocabulary Warm-up Practice **[L1, L2, EL]** . . . . . . p. 41
Reading Warm-up A **[L1, L2, EL]** . . . . . . p. 42
Reading Warm-up B **[L1, L2, L3]** . . . . . . p. 43

Transparency

Graphic Organizer Transparencies

Literary Analysis Graphic Organizer A **[L3]** . . . . . . p. 42
Literary Analysis Graphic Organizer B **[L1, L2, EL]** . . . . . . p. 43
Reading Strategy Graphic Organizer A **[L3]** . . . . . . p. 44
Reading Strategy Graphic Organizer B **[L1, L2, EL]** . . . . . . p. 45

Print

Reader's Notebook [L2]
Reader's Notebook: Adapted Version [L1]
Reader's Notebook: English Learner's Version [EL]

Unit 2 Resources

Literary Analysis **[L3]** . . . . . . p. 44
Reading Strategy **[L3]** . . . . . . p. 45
Vocabulary Builder **[L3]** . . . . . . p. 46

Technology

Listening to Literature Audio CDs [L2, EL]
Reader's Notebook: Adapted Version Audio CD [L1, L2]

Print

Unit 2 Resources

Grammar and Style **[L3]** . . . . . . p. 47
Support for Writing Lesson **[L3]** . . . . . . p. 48
Support for Extend Your Learning **[L3]** . . . . . . p. 49
Enrichment **[L4]** . . . . . . p. 50
Selection Test A **[L1, L2, EL]** . . . . . . pp. 51–53
Selection Test B **[L3, L4]** . . . . . . pp. 54–56

General Resources

Rubrics for Narration: Short Story **[L3]** . . . . . . pp. 63–64
Rubrics for Multimedia Report **[L3]** . . . . . . pp. 57–58

Technology

Go Online: Research **[L3]**
Go Online: Self-test **[L3]**
***ExamView®*, Test Bank [L3]**

Choosing Resources for Differentiated Instruction

[L1] Special Needs Students
[L2] Below-Level Students
[L3] All Students
[L4] Advanced Students
[EL] English Learners

For Vocabulary and Reading Warm-ups and for Selection Tests, **A** signifies "less challenging" and **B** "more challenging." For Graphic Organizer transparencies, **A** signifies "not filled in" and **B** "filled in."

FT Fast Track Instruction: To move the lesson more quickly, use the strategies and activities identified with **FT**.

Scaffolding for Less Proficient and Advanced Students

The leveled Critical Thinking questions after selections progress in the levels of thinking required to answer them. To address the needs of your different students, you may use the (a) level questions for your less proficient students and the (b) level questions with your on-level and advanced students. The occasional (c) level questions are appropriate for your advanced students.

PRENTICE HALL **TeacherEXPRESS™** Plan · Teach · Assess — Use this complete suite of powerful teaching tools to make lesson planning and testing quicker and easier.

PRENTICE HALL **StudentEXPRESS™** Learn · Study · Succeed — Use the interactive textbook (online and on CD-ROM) to make selections and activities come alive with audio and video support and interactive questions.

Benchmark

After students have completed reading the excerpt from *The Panchatantra,* administer **Benchmark Test 2 (*Unit 2 Resources* pp. 64–69).** If the Benchmark Test reveals that some of the students need further work, use the **Interpretation Guide** to determine the appropriate reteaching page in the **Reading Kit** and on **Success Tracker.**

For: Information about Lexiles
Visit: www.PHSchool.com
Web Code: eue-1111

PRETEACH

Motivation

Ask students to check the bestseller list and point out which books on the list are self-help books—books that show readers how to adapt their behavior to succeed. Have students discuss why this type of book is so popular. Then, explain that the *Panchatantra* is the ancient Indian equivalent of a self-help book—one intended for princes.

❶ Background

More About the Author

The *Panchatantra* consists of five books containing stories compiled by Vishnusharman (vish' no o- -shar' man). This learned priest-scholar was told by his king to educate the princes who someday would have to rule. Vishnusharman's original Sanskrit versions of the stories that he composed have been lost, but an Arabic version of the work has survived.

Many of these didactic tales contain animal characters that act out human situations. Similar stories that use the same devices, are Aesop's fables, the Uncle Remus stories, *Alice in Wonderland,* and *Animal Farm.*

Geography Note

Draw students' attention to the map on this page. Tell them that India is the world's second-largest country in population. In fact, nearly one of every six people in the world lives in India! A country of vast differences, India includes in its lands a desert, jungles, broad plains, the tallest mountain system in the world, and one of the world's rainiest areas. The people of India belong to different ethnic groups, religions, and castes—or social classes. They speak sixteen major languages and more than one thousand minor languages and dialects.

Build Skills | Fable

from the Panchatantra ❶

About the Panchatantra

The *Panchatantra* (pun′ chə tun′ trə), which simply means "a treatise in five chapters," is a collection of Indian animal fables that was intended to teach Indian princes how to govern a kingdom. These entertaining stories give advice related to political matters and to interpersonal relationships in general.

For example, a fable called "The Jackal Who Killed No Elephants" taught princes the importance of knowing themselves and others. This fable tells about a baby jackal that is brought up in a family of lions. Everything goes well until, one day, the jackal's two lion cub brothers want to attack an elephant. The jackal dissuades them. Later, in the family circle, the lion cubs tease the jackal about his cowardice, and he becomes furious. The mother lion calms him down, but when he insists on his courage, she gives him this humorous warning:

> Handsome you are,
> and valorous;
> You have a scholar's
> brain:
> But in your family, my boy,
> No elephants are slain.

Taking the hint in good grace, the jackal departs before his brothers grow up, realize he is not a lion, and turn on him.

The moral of the fable is that one must appreciate human limitations and capacities—in oneself and in others. Just as jackals and lions have different strengths and weaknesses, so do human beings. Fables like this one typically convey their moral in a graceful and entertaining verse. By memorizing the verse quoted above, a young prince would have quick access to this fable's important lesson.

Animal Stories: A Long Tradition The use of animal stories to teach moral lessons is familiar to many people in the West because of Aesop's fables from ancient Greece. However, such instructive stories are also an ancient tradition in India: They are found in both the *Rig Veda* and the Upanishads. Buddhists, too, used these kinds of animal fables to depict previous lives of the Buddha and to teach the principles of compassion and mercy, which are so important to the Buddhist tradition.

An Ancient and Influential Book It is uncertain exactly when the *Panchatantra* was written, but scholars estimate that it was sometime between 200 B.C. and A.D. 500. What is known, however, is that the *Panchatantra* has had a wide-ranging influence. In the sixth century A.D., for example, it was translated into Pahlavi, a language of ancient Iran. There are old Syrian and Arabic versions of the fables, as well.

An Unknown Author Little is known about the author of these instructive tales. The collection is attributed to a man named Vishnusharman, who was charged with the responsibility of instructing the sons of a king named Amarashakti. The author's name indicates that he was a Brahman and a devotee of the god Vishnu. However, no record of his life has survived.

From the fables themselves, one can infer that the author was an artist of considerable accomplishment. The tales are woven together ingeniously, and they combine prose with poetry in a way that is fluid and natural. Realizing that poetry is easier to remember than prose, the author includes instructive verses designed to help students recall key points. The fact that the *Panchatantra* is still read today attests to the timeless wisdom of these fables and the narrative skill of their author.

Preview

Connecting to the Literature

Many self-help titles teach such skills as how to dress or how to succeed in business. The *Panchatantra* is an ancient Indian equivalent of these books. This story from the *Panchatantra* teaches a lesson about the interaction between a king and his subjects.

NC Standard Course of Study

- Build knowledge of literary genres, and explore characteristics. (LT.5.01.2)
- Analyze archetypal characters, themes, and settings in world literature. (LT.5.01.5)

2 Literary Analysis

Indian Fable

An **Indian fable** is a brief, simple tale that teaches a lesson about conduct in Indian culture. These fables often feature animal characters who behave like humans. Events in the fable point to a lesson called a **moral.** The moral may be stated directly or merely implied.

Use an organizer like the one shown to help you determine the moral that this fable from the *Panchatantra* teaches.

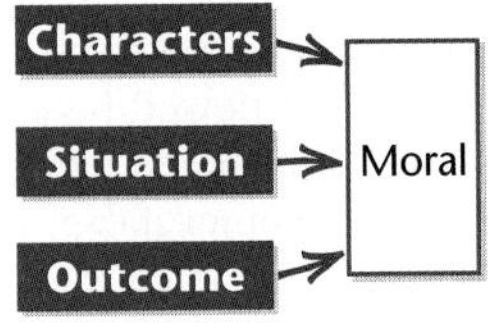

Connecting Literary Elements

The rabbit in this fable is an example of a type of character well known in folklore, the **trickster.** This character uses wit to overcome the greater strength of others. In African folklore, for instance, the spider Anansi often deceives larger animals like the leopard.

In this fable from the *Panchatantra,* the rabbit expresses the credo of all tricksters—"brains over brawn"—in a small poem:

> In what can wisdom not prevail?
> In what can resolution fail?
> What cannot flattery subdue?
> What cannot enterprise put through?

Notice how the rabbit's success highlights the weaknesses of the lion.

3 Reading Strategy

Reread for Clarification

To avoid misunderstanding a literature selection, **reread to clarify** any parts that you find unclear or confusing. For example, you might want to review details of the setting or of a key event. Also, remember to review footnotes for important information.

Vocabulary Builder

obsequiously (əb sē′ kwē əs lē) *adj.* in a manner that shows too great a willingness to serve (p. 222)

rank (raŋk) *adj.* foul; odorous (p. 222)

elixir (ē liks′ ir) *n.* magical potion that cures all ailments (p. 222)

accrue (ə kro͞o′) *v.* come to as an advantage or a right (p. 223)

tardily (tär′ də lē) *adv.* late (p. 224)

reprobate (rep′ rə bāt′) *n.* scoundrel (p. 224)

extirpate (ek′ stər pāt′) *v.* exterminate; destroy or remove completely (p. 224)

skulks (skulks) *v.* lurks in a cowardly way (p. 225)

2 Literary Analysis

Indian Fable

- Read the discussion of the characteristics of Indian fables together with the class. Point out that many cultures have fables. Ask students to share fables they know, and discuss what lessons these fables teach.
- Point out the prevalence of trickster characters in fables from Br'er Rabbit to the cartoon character Roadrunner to Anansi the Spider. Explain that such characters often demonstrate the superiority of intelligence over strength and of humor over a narrow, literal-minded focus.
- Explain the use of the graphic organizer. Then give students a copy of **Literary Analysis Graphic Organizer A** in ***Graphic Organizer Transparencies,*** p. 42, to use as they read the selection.

3 Reading Strategy

Reread for Clarification

- Point out that good readers frequently reread text to make sure that they understand difficult or unfamiliar concepts or to review content.
- Remind students to stop and reread any sections of the selection that are unclear. Encourage students to review earlier sections of the work to clarify the events that follow.

Vocabulary Builder

- Pronounce each vocabulary word for students, and read the definitions as a class. Have students identify any words with which they are already familiar.

Differentiated Instruction Solutions for All Learners

Support for Special Needs Students
Have students read the adapted version of "Numskull and the Rabbit" in the ***Reader's Notebook: Adapted Version.*** This version provides basic-level instruction in an interactive format with questions and write-on lines. Completing these pages will prepare students to read the selection in the Student Edition.

Support for Less Proficient Readers
Have students read "Numskull and the Rabbit" in the ***Reader's Notebook.*** This version provides basic-level instruction in an interactive format with questions and write-on lines. After students finish the selection in the ***Reader's Notebook,*** have them complete the questions and activities in the Student Edition.

Support for English Learners
Have students read "Numskull and the Rabbit" in the ***Reader's Notebook: English Learner's Version.*** This version provides basic-level instruction in an interactive format with questions and write-on lines. Completing these pages will prepare students to read the selection in the Student Edition.

TEACH

Facilitate Understanding

Explain to students how difficult it can be to decide on a method for teaching a particular idea or skill. Ask students to think of a time when they had to teach a friend or sibling. Invite students to share teaching strategies they may have used, including explanation, repetition, and memorable comparisons. Tell students that "Numskull and the Rabbit" is a fable that could be used to teach the powers of intelligence.

❶ About the Selection

This fable tells about a forest terrorized by a proud and greedy lion. The forest creatures petition the lion to eat only one animal each day instead of killing everything he sees. When it is the rabbit's turn to be the lion's dinner, the rabbit uses his own cleverness and the lion's pride to send the lion to his death and to free the forest from his tyranny.

❷ Literary Analysis

Fable

- Review with students the characteristics of Indian fables on p. 221, and emphasize the role that a moral plays in a fable's meaning.
- Then, have a volunteer read the bracketed paragraphs aloud. **Ask** students to predict what the moral of this story will be.
  Possible response: The character of the lion probably will be used to teach the reader a moral about pride and greed.
- Have students **respond** to the Literary Analysis item: Identify elements of a fable in the opening paragraphs of the story.
  Answer: The opening paragraphs feature animal characters that act as humans. The paragraphs also introduce the dilemma that will lead to a moral.

from the Panchatantra

translated by Arthur W. Ryder

❶ Numskull and the Rabbit

In a part of a forest was a lion drunk with pride, and his name was Numskull. He slaughtered the animals without ceasing. If he saw an animal, he could not spare him.

❷ So all the natives of the forest—deer, boars, buffaloes, wild oxen, rabbits, and others—came together, and with woe-begone countenances,[1] bowed heads, and knees clinging to the ground, they undertook to beseech obsequiously the king of beasts: "Have done, O King, with this merciless, meaningless slaughter of all creatures. It is hostile to happiness in the other world. For the Scripture says:

A thousand future lives
  Will pass in wretchedness
For sins a fool commits
  His present life to bless.

Again:

What wisdom in a deed
  That brings dishonor fell,
That causes loss of trust,
  That paves the way to hell?

And yet again:

The ungrateful body, frail
  And rank with filth within,
Is such that only fools
  For its sake sink in sin.

"Consider these facts, and cease, we pray, to slaughter our generations. For if the master will remain at home, we will of our own motion send him each day for his daily food one animal of the forest. In this way neither the royal sustenance nor our families will be cut short. In this way let the king's duty be performed. For the proverb says:

The king who tastes his kingdom like
  Elixir, bit by bit,
Who does not overtax its life,
  Will fully relish it.

1. **countenances** (koun′ tə nən səz) *n.* faces.

Vocabulary Builder
obsequiously (əb sē′ kwē əs lē) *adv.* in a manner that shows too great a willingness to serve

Literary Analysis
Indian Fable Identify elements of a fable in the opening paragraphs of the story.

Vocabulary Builder
rank (raŋk) *adj.* foul; odorous

Vocabulary Builder
elixir (ē liks′ ir) *n.* magical potion that cures all ailments

Differentiated Instruction — Solutions for All Learners

Accessibility at a Glance

	from the Panchatantra, "Numskull and the Rabbit"
Context	Didactic tales of Ancient India
Language	Complex syntax: narrated dialogue with embedded quotations
Concept Level	Accessible (The powers of intelligence can triumph over the powers of brute strength.)
Literary Merit	Ancient Indian animal fable with a moral lesson that still has meaning
Lexile	840L
Overall Rating	Average

The king who madly butchers men,
Their lives as little reckoned
As lives of goats, has one square meal,
But never has a second.

A king desiring profit, guards
His world from evil chance;
With gifts and honors waters it
As florists water plants.

Guard subjects like a cow, nor ask
For milk each passing hour:
A vine must first be sprinkled, then
It ripens fruit and flower.

The monarch-lamp from subjects draws
Tax-oil to keep it bright:
Has any ever noticed kings
That shone by inner light?

A seedling is a tender thing,
And yet, if not neglected,
It comes in time to bearing fruit:
So subjects well protected.

Their subjects form the only source
From which accrue to kings
Their gold, grain, gems, and varied drinks,
And many other things.

The kings who serve the common weal,
Luxuriantly sprout;
The common loss is kingly loss,
Without a shade of doubt."

After listening to this address, Numskull said: "Well, gentlemen, you are quite convincing. But if an animal does not come to me every day as I sit here, I promise you I will eat you all." To this they assented with much relief, and fearlessly roamed the wood. Each day at noon one of them appeared as his dinner, each species taking its turn and providing an individual grown old, or religious, or grief-smitten, or fearful of the loss of son or wife.

One day a rabbit's turn came, it being rabbit-day. And when all the thronging animals had given him directions, he reflected: "How is it possible to kill this lion—curse him! Yet after all,

❹ Critical Viewing Does the lion in this painting convey the image of "king of the jungle"? Explain. **[Make a Judgment]**

❸

A Lion at Rest, The Metropolitan Museum of Art

Vocabulary Builder
accrue (ə kro͞o') *v.* come to as an advantage or a right

❺  **Reading Check**
What are the animals trying to convince Numskull to do?

❸ Humanities

A Lion at Rest

Depictions of lions, such as the one shown here, are common in many cultures. Throughout the world, the lion has been associated with royalty and divinity since before the sixth century B.C. In India specifically, the lion has an important history as a religious symbol. Often, Buddha is depicted as seated on a lion throne. In his fourth avatar, Lord Vishnu emerges as Narasimah, the Hindu god who is half lion and half man. The lion, previously known as *simham* in Sanskrit, is now called *singh* in northern India. During the late-seventeenth century merge of Hinduism and Islam that became known as Sikhism, many Sikhs took *singh* as a surname.

Use the following items for discussion.

- Describe the relationship between the lion and the other animals in this image.
  Possible response: He appears to have a harmonious relationship with the other animals and with his natural environment.
- How does this relationship differ from the relationship between the lion the animals in the story?
  Possible response: Unlike the lion in the story, the lion in the illustration is not terrorizing the other animals.

❹ Critical Viewing

Possible response: No; with his tongue out and hind feet in air, the lion looks relaxed and playful, not regal.

❺ Reading Check

Answer: The animals are trying to convince the lion to stop slaughtering them pointlessly.

Differentiated Instruction Solutions for All Learners

Support for Special Needs Students

Tell students that this fable makes use of several proverbs, or popular sayings that express general truths or common observations. Explain that proverbs are often metaphorical, meaning that they present one thing as though it were something else. Draw students' attention to the fourth proverb above. Help students identify the metaphors of the lamp and oil, and discuss how these figures of speech reveal a king's relationship to his subjects.

Support for Less Proficient Readers

Students may have difficulty with the large number of proverbs in this selection. Have students read aloud each proverb, and guide them to summarize each proverb's meaning. Tell students that changing the word order may help them as they develop their summaries. For example, a summary of the sixth proverb above might read: "Kings gather their riches and other advantageous items from their subjects."

❻ Literary Analysis

Fable and the Trickster

- Remind students that actions of a trickster character often highlight weaknesses of another character.
- **Ask** students the first Literary Analysis question: How does the choice of a rabbit as the trickster emphasize the importance of cleverness over strength?
Answer: The rabbit may not be able to conquer the lion physically, but the lion's strength may turn out to be no match for the rabbit's cunning.

❼ Vocabulary Builder

Latin Prefix *ex-*

- Explain to students that the Latin prefix *ex-* means "out."
- Have students **use** dictionaries to research the etymology of the word *extirpate.*
Answer: *Extirpate* contains the Latin base word *stirps,* meaning "trunk, root." Adding the prefix *ex-* to this base word produces the meaning "pull out by the roots," that is, "exterminate; destroy or remove completely."

❽ Literary Analysis

Fable

- Read the second bracketed passage aloud.
- **Ask** students the second Literary Analysis question: What human flaws does Numskull show in this passage?
Possible response: The lion shows impatience, pride, and anger.

Monitor Progress **Ask** students for what moral Numskull's conduct might prepare the reader.
Answer: The fable may show that acting from pride and arrogance will lead to one's downfall.

Reteach Direct students' attention to the Literary Analysis instruction on p. 221. Suggest that students use their copy of the graphic organizer to help them determine the moral of this fable.

---

❻

In what can wisdom not prevail?
In what can resolution fail?
What cannot flattery subdue?
What cannot enterprise put through?

I can kill even a lion."

So he went very slowly, planning to arrive tardily, and meditating with troubled spirit on a means of killing him. Late in the day he came into the presence of the lion, whose throat was pinched by hunger in consequence of the delay, and who angrily thought as he licked his chops: "Aha! I must kill all the animals the first thing in the morning."

While he was thinking, the rabbit slowly drew near, bowed low, and stood before him. But when the lion saw that he was tardy and too small at that for a meal, his soul flamed with wrath, and he taunted the rabbit, saying: "You reprobate! First, you are too small for a meal. Second, you are tardy. Because of this wickedness I am going to kill you, and tomorrow morning I shall extirpate every species of animal." ❼

Then the rabbit bowed low and said with deference: "Master, the wickedness is not mine, nor the other animals'. Pray hear the cause of it." And the lion answered: "Well, tell it quick, before you are between my fangs."

"Master," said the rabbit, "all the animals recognized today that the rabbits' turn had come, and because I was quite small, they dispatched me with five other rabbits. But in mid-journey there issued from a great hole in the ground a lion who said: 'Where are *you* bound? Pray to your favorite god.' Then I said: 'We are traveling as the dinner of lion Numskull, our master, according to agreement.' 'Is that so?' said he. 'This forest belongs to me. So all the animals, without exception, must deal with me—according to agreement. This Numskull is a sneak thief. Call him out and bring him here at once. Then whichever of us proves stronger, shall be king and shall eat all these animals.' At his command, master, I have come to you. This is the cause of my tardiness. For the rest, my master is the sole judge."

❽

After listening to this, Numskull said: "Well, well, my good fellow, show me that sneak thief of a lion, and be quick about it. I cannot find peace of mind until I have vented on him my anger against the animals. He should have remembered the saying:

Land and friends and gold at most
Have been won when battles cease;
If but one of these should fail,
Do not think of breaking peace.

Where no great reward is won,
Where defeat is nearly sure,
Never stir a quarrel, but
Find it wiser to endure."

Literary Analysis
Indian Fable and the Trickster How does the choice of a rabbit as the trickster emphasize the importance of cleverness over strength?

Vocabulary Builder
tardily (tär′ də lē) *adv.* late
reprobate (rep′ rə bāt′) *n.* scoundrel
extirpate (ek′ stər pāt) *v.* exterminate; destroy or remove completely

Literary Analysis
Indian Fable What human flaws does Numskull show in this passage?

Enrichment

Aesop

Like the stories in the *Panchatantra,* the ancient Greek fables attributed to Aesop feature animals as characters. Aesop's fables have been enjoyed for centuries. However, we know very little about their origin—including who actually wrote them. Aesop, supposed to have lived in the sixth century B.C., may have been a slave who lived on the Greek island of Samos, a spokesman who defended criminals in court, or an advisor or a riddle-solver for one of the Greek kings. The most widely held theory, however, is that Aesop was not an actual person at all. Rather, because certain stories in ancient Greece were told over and over, people invented an imaginary author for them. Encourage students to read several of Aesop's fables, such as "The Lion and the Statue," "The Fox and the Crow," and "The Lion and the Bull."

9 "Quite so, master," said the rabbit. "Warriors fight for their country when they are insulted. But this fellow skulks in a fortress. You know he came out of a fortress when he held us up. And an enemy in a fortress is hard to handle. As the saying goes:

A single royal fortress adds
More military force
Than do a thousand elephants,
A hundred thousand horse.

A single archer from a wall
A hundred foes forfends;
And so the military art
A fortress recommends.

God Indra used the wit and skill
Of gods in days of old,
When Devil Gold-mat plagued the world,
To build a fortress-hold.

And he decreed that any king
Who built a fortress sound,
Should conquer foemen. This is why
Such fortresses abound."

When he heard this, Numskull said: "My good fellow, show me that thief. Even if he is hiding in a fortress, I will kill him. For the proverb says:

The strongest man who fails to crush
At birth, disease or foe,
Will later be destroyed by that
Which he permits to grow.

And again:

The man who reckons well his power,
Nor pride nor vigor lacks,
May single-handed smite his foes
Like Rama-with-the-ax.[2]

"Very true," said the rabbit. "But after all it was a mighty lion that I saw. So the master should not set out without realizing the enemy's capacity. As the saying runs:

2. **Rama-with-the-ax** the sixth incarnation of the Hindu god Vishnu. He became angry with the warrior caste and killed them all with his ax. (Rama of the *Ramayana* was the seventh incarnation of Vishnu.)

Themes in World Masterpieces

10 ***Animal Fables***

Animal fables can be found in cultures around the world and throughout history. They have 11 influenced Western society largely through the ancient Greek fables attributed to Aesop. Other important fables are those of Horace, the early Roman poet who relates the story of the city mouse and the country mouse, and those of the fourteenth-century English author Geoffrey Chaucer, who incorporated the tale of Chanticleer and the fox into his famous *Canterbury Tales.* In the 1600s, the French poet Jean de La Fontaine further popularized the form when he used retellings of ancient fables to satirize his own society. Because they are entertaining and easily understood by youngsters, fables remain a staple of children's literature today.

Connect to the Literature

What characteristics of the animal fable *Numskull and the Rabbit* have helped the fable survive for centuries?

Vocabulary Builder

skulks (skulks) *v.* lurks in a cowardly way

12  **Reading Check**

What does Numskull plan to do to the other lion described by the rabbit?

9 Critical Thinking

Analyze

- Have a volunteer read the bracketed passage aloud. Then, **ask:** How does the rabbit further incite and distract Numskull in this passage?
Answer: The rabbit's warnings imply that Numskull may not be able to defeat an enemy in a fortress. This strategy touches the lion's pride. The lion wants to show that he will confront his challenger, fortress or no fortress.

10 Themes in World Literature

Animal Fables

It may seem unusual that it is the tiny rabbit, rather than the bear or ox, who decides to challenge the lion. This choice serves to emphasize the importance of cleverness over brute strength. The supposedly timid rabbit is often used in animal tales to play a surprising role. Even in American cartoons, Bugs Bunny has been outwitting Elmer Fudd for years.

Connect to the Literature **Ask** students to contribute at least two characteristics that helped this fable survive for centuries.

Possible response: The rabbit trickster in this fable is very clever and proves the power of intelligence in an entertaining manner. This fable also teaches lessons that are still meaningful: (a) A leader who mistreats his subjects robs himself of future benefits. (b) Pride and vanity are one's own worst enemies.

11 Background

Literature

The *Panchatantra* has been translated into many languages and distributed widely around the world. Although it is similar in nature to Aesop's *Fables,* scholars have not been able to demonstrate any direct connection between the two. Some experts, however, have argued convincingly that both Chaucer and Shakespeare were influenced to some extent by the *Panchatantra* in one of its many forms.

12 Reading Check

Answer: Numskull plans to kill the other lion.

Differentiated Instruction Solutions for All Learners

Enrichment for Gifted/Talented Students

Challenge students to use "Numskull and the Rabbit" as the basis for a play about a modern issue. Have students write a script, using as many of the proverbs as possible, and assign parts. Then, have students present their modern fable for the class. Suggest that at the end of the play, the narrator summarize the fable and give the moral for the modern world.

Enrichment for Advanced Readers

Have students locate and read several of the fables of Aesop, Horace, and La Fontaine. Ask students to read closely, noting similarities in characters, settings, situations, and morals. Then, ask students to write brief essays comparing and contrasting two or more fables. Students can present to the class oral retellings of the fables they analyze along with their essays.

⓭ Reading Strategy

Reread for Clarification

- Remind students that they may have to reread parts of a selection to clarify events or meaning.
- Then, have students read the bracketed passage. **Ask** them which earlier passage they might need to reread to understand how the lion meets his fate.
  Possible response: The previous paragraph, in which the rabbit claims that the well is the lion's "fortress," may need to be reread.

ASSESS

Answers

1. **Possible response:** Some readers may agree because they see the solution as the only way to deal with the lion. Others may say that the rabbit is a dishonest trickster.
2. (a) The animals' moral reason is that such behavior will bring the lion unhappiness in the next world. Their political reason is that a king who depletes his kingdom robs himself of future benefits. (b) The animals are trying to appeal to the lion's desire for happiness in the next life and his desire for a steady source of food in this life.
3. (a) The lion says he will do as they ask as long as an animal sacrifices itself each day for the lion's meal. (b) The lion's response indicates that he is willing to negotiate only if the result is in his favor.
4. (a) The rabbit says that he was stopped by a lion who said that he controlled the forest. This lion called Numskull a thief and challenged him. (b) The rabbit expects Numskull to want to meet and defeat the other lion.
5. (a) The lion's eagerness for a fight, coming from his pride and desire for power, keeps him from recognizing his own reflection. (b) The lion is his own worst enemy.
6. **Possible response:** Greed and pride will cause an individual's downfall. Cunning is more important than strength.

A warrior failing to compare
　　Two hosts, in mad desire
For battle, plunges like a moth
　　Headforemost into fire.

And again:

The weak who challenge mighty foes
　　A battle to abide,
Like elephants with broken tusks,
　　Return with drooping pride."

But Numskull said: "What business is it of yours? Show him to me, even in his fortress." "Very well," said the rabbit. "Follow me, master." And he led the way to a well, where he said to the lion: "Master, who can endure your majesty? The moment he saw you, that thief crawled clear into his hole. Come, I will show him to you." "Be quick about it, my good fellow," said Numskull.

⓭ So the rabbit showed him the well. And the lion, being a dreadful fool, saw his own reflection in the water, and gave voice to a great roar. Then from the well issued a roar twice as loud, because of the echo. This the lion heard, decided that his rival was very powerful, hurled himself down, and met his death. Thereupon the rabbit cheerfully carried the glad news to all the animals, received their compliments, and lived there contentedly in the forest.

Critical Reading

1. **Respond:** Do you agree with the rabbit's solution to the problem? Why or why not?
2. **(a) Recall:** What moral and political reasons do the animals give Numskull for stopping the slaughter? **(b) Deduce:** To what instinct are the animals hoping to appeal?
3. **(a) Recall:** How does the lion respond to the animals' plea? **(b) Analyze:** What does his response reveal about his character?
4. **(a) Recall:** What explanation does the rabbit give for his tardiness? **(b) Infer:** How does the rabbit expect Numskull to react to this information?
5. **(a) Infer:** What prevents the lion from recognizing his own reflection when he looks into the well? **(b) Draw Conclusions:** What does the rabbit's trick suggest about who is the lion's greatest enemy?
6. **Apply:** What moral or morals do you think this fable teaches?

Apply the Skills

from the *Panchatantra*

Literary Analysis

Indian Fable

1. **(a)** What does this **Indian fable** suggest about the qualities that ancient Indians admired in their rulers? **(b)** Which details in the fable reflect those values?
2. Which actions of the characters support the fable's **moral**(s)?
3. In what ways might this fable be instructive to princes or other political leaders?

Connecting Literary Elements

4. Which of the rabbit's behaviors identify him as the fable's **trickster**?
5. **(a)** What human weaknesses does Numskull display over the course of the story? **(b)** What human strengths does the rabbit display?
6. Why does the rabbit use the image of another fierce lion to trick Numskull?
7. Would you say that the rabbit is a virtuous character? Explain.

Reading Strategy

Reread for Clarification

8. Complete a chart like this one to show how the character traits of Numskull and the rabbit are revealed. First, identify a trait of one of the characters. Then, **reread** to identify the earliest details in the story that **clarify** that information.

Character	Character Traits	Clarifying Details
Numskull		
Rabbit		

9. If a reader does not know whether the rabbit is lying when he tells Numskull about the other lion, what earlier passage would clarify this point?

Extend Understanding

10. **Social Studies Connection:** Do you think that political cartoons and comic strips perform the same function in our society as the *Panchatantra* did in ancient India? Explain.

QuickReview

A **fable** is a simple tale—often featuring animal characters—that teaches a lesson about human conduct.

A **trickster** is a character who uses wit to overcome the greater strength of others.

When you come to a confusing passage in a selection, go back to earlier passages and **reread for clarification.**

For: Self-test
Visit: www.PHSchool.com
Web Code: eta-6203

Go Online Assessment Students may use the **Self-test** to prepare for **Selection Test A** or **Selection Test B.**

Answers

1. (a) This fable suggests that leaders should exhibit concern for their subjects, wisdom, and self-restraint, not arrogance. (b) The fact that the rabbit is able to trick Numskull into self-destruction through Numskull's arrogance and lack of self-restraint demonstrates these values.
2. Numskull's arrogance, the animal's speech concerning the virtue of restraint, and Numskull's death support the fable's moral.
3. The fable suggests to leaders that they should recognize the importance of their subjects and use temperance when ruling. It emphasizes that a leader who rules harshly will be punished.
4. The rabbit's lie to Numskull about his reason for being tardy and his cunning appeal to Numskull's pride identify the rabbit as the fable's trickster.
5. (a) Numskull displays self-centeredness, selfishness, recklessness, and arrogance. (b) The rabbit displays cunning and intelligence.
6. Numskull is arrogant and believes that he is the strongest animal in the jungle. The rabbit knows that for these reasons Numskull will want to defeat the fierce lion.
7. **Possible response:** Some may say that the rabbit is not virtuous because he deceives Numskull. Others may argue that the rabbit does what is necessary to right a serious wrong.
8. **Numskull—Character Traits:** selfishness, arrogance; **Clarifying Details:** slaughters animals at will; says that animals must feed him. **Rabbit—Character Traits:** cleverness; insight; **Clarifying Details:** devises plan to destroy Numskull; appeals to Numskull's pride and arrogance.
9. The rabbit's speech on the day his turn comes, in which he says, "I can kill even a lion," indicates that he will try to trick Numskull.
10. **Possible response:** Political cartoons and comic strips do not instruct leaders about how they should lead, but these satires do point out the folly of a leader's conduct in a specific case.

EXTEND/ASSESS

Answers

❶ Vocabulary Lesson

Word Analysis: Latin Prefix *ex-*

1. c 2. a 3. b

Spelling Strategy

1. dutiful
2. copier
3. easily

Vocabulary Builder

1. e
2. h
3. b
4. f
5. g
6. a
7. d
8. c

❷ Grammar and Style Lesson

1. who madly butchers men; *king*
2. which included all the animals; *forest*
3. whose throat was pinched by hunger; *lion*
4. who refused to surrender to the lion; *animal*
5. that saved the rabbit's life; *ingenuity*

Writing Application

Possible response: This fable tells about a *forest* that is terrorized by a proud and greedy lion. The forest *creatures* who petition the lion ask that he eat only one animal each day. When it is the rabbit's turn to be the lion's dinner, the *rabbit,* who is clever, uses the lion's pride against him, sending the lion to his death.

WG Writing and Grammar Platinum Level

For support in teaching the Grammar and Style Lesson, use Chapter 20, Section 2.

Build Language Skills

❶ Vocabulary Lesson

Word Analysis: Latin Prefix *ex-*

The Latin prefix *ex-* means "out," as in *extend,* which means "to stretch out." Consider how the prefix *ex-* influences the meaning of the words in the left column, and then match each word with its definition on the right.

1. extract	**a.** leave out
2. exclude	**b.** speak out strongly
3. exclaim	**c.** pull or draw out

Spelling Strategy

When a word ends in *y* preceded by a consonant, change the *y* to *i* before adding most suffixes. For example, *happy + -ness = happiness.* Combine each word below with its suffix.

1. duty +*-ful* **2.** copy + *-er* **3.** easy + *-ly*

Vocabulary Builder: Antonyms

Review the vocabulary words on page 221. Then, complete the following activity by matching each vocabulary word on the left with its antonym, or a word with the opposite meaning, on the right.

1. obsequiously	**a.** gentleman
2. rank	**b.** toxin
3. elixir	**c.** swaggers
4. accrue	**d.** restore
5. tardily	**e.** arrogantly
6. reprobate	**f.** dissipate
7. extirpate	**g.** punctually
8. skulks	**h.** fragrant

❷ Grammar and Style Lesson

Adjective Clauses

An **adjective clause** is a subordinate clause that modifies a noun or a pronoun. The clause usually begins with a relative pronoun—such as *that, which, who, whom,* or *whose*—that acts as a subject, and it always includes a verb.

> The king who tastes his kingdom like Elixir . . . will fully relish it. (modifies *king*)

Practice Identify the adjective clause in each sentence that follows, and name the noun or pronoun that the clause modifies.

1. The king who madly butchers men . . . has one square meal, but never has a second.
2. Numskull claimed to be king of the forest, which included all the animals.
3. The rabbit came into the presence of the lion, whose throat was pinched by hunger.
4. The rabbit was the only animal in the forest who refused to surrender to the lion.
5. It was ingenuity that saved the rabbit's life.

Writing Application Write a one-paragraph plot summary of "Numskull and the Rabbit." Use at least three adjective clauses in your summary, and indicate the noun or pronoun that each clause modifies.

WG *Prentice Hall Writing and Grammar Connection: Platinum Level, Chapter 20, Section 2*

Assessment Practice

Recognize Details **(For more practice, see *Test Preparation Workbook*, p. 11.)**

Many tests require students to recognize the significance of details within a passage. Use the following sample passage to give students practice in this skill:

> So all the natives of the forest—deer, boars, buffaloes, wild oxen, rabbits, and others—came together, and with woe-begone countenances, bowed heads, and knees clinging to the ground, they undertook to beseech obsequiously the king of beasts. . . .
>
> —from the *Panchatantra*

The details in the description of the animals approaching the lion suggest that the animals are—

A servile.
B angry.
C arrogant.
D careless.

The correct answer is *A*. Details in the description indicate that the animals are humbling themselves before the lion, whom they fear.

❸ Writing Lesson

Animal Fable

Basing your work on what you have learned about fables, write a brief fable of your own, using animal characters to teach a lesson about human behavior. Close your fable with a moral that flows logically from the events in the narrative.

Prewriting List sayings that offer rules or observations about human behavior, and choose one of them to be the moral of your fable. Jot down ideas for animal characters and a plot related to your moral. Then, narrow and organize those ideas into a rough outline of the story you will tell.

Drafting Write a fable based on your rough outline. Keep your moral in mind as you write, and choose details that help point to it.

Revising Share your draft with classmates, inviting them to use the questions below as a checklist. Consider their responses as you revise your work.

Fable Checklist for Peer Review

- ☐ Are my characters related to the qualities treated in my moral? For example, if my moral is about greed, is at least one of my characters greedy?
- ☐ Does the outcome of my fable illustrate my moral? For example, if my moral says that greed is bad, does the greedy behavior in my fable lead to an unhappy outcome?
- ☐ If the moral is stated within my fable, is the statement brief and clear?

WG *Prentice Hall Writing and Grammar Connection: Platinum Level, Chapter 5, Section 2*

❹ Extend Your Learning

Listening and Speaking Prepare a **retelling** of "Numskull and the Rabbit." Imagine that you are Vishnusharman telling the fable to the sons of the king, and use these tips to guide your retelling:

- Speak expressively, using tones appropriate for each character.
- Vary the pace and intensity of your speaking according to the action in the story.
- Speak clearly so that your audience understands you.

Perform your retelling for an audience of younger students.

Research and Technology Work with a small group of classmates to prepare a **multimedia report** on the role of the trickster in folklore. For example, you might prepare a slide show pairing images of tricksters from different cultures with excerpts from corresponding fables. **[Group Activity]**

For: An additional research activity
Visit: www.PHSchool.com
Web Code: etd-7202

Assessment Resources

The following resources can be used to assess students' knowledge and skills.

Unit 1 Resources
- **Selection Test A,** pp. 51–53
- **Selection Test B,** pp. 54–56
- **Benchmark Test 2,** pp. 64–69

General Resources
- **Rubric for Narration: Short Story,** pp. 63–64
- **Rubrics for Multimedia Report,** pp. 57–58

Go Online Assessment Students may use the **Self-test** to prepare for **Selection Test A** or **Selection Test B.**

Benchmark
Administer **Benchmark Test 2.** If some students need further work, use the **Interpretation Guide** to determine the appropriate reteaching page in the **Reading Kit** and on **Success Tracker.**

❸ Writing Lesson

- To give students guidance in writing this fable, give them the **Support for Writing Lesson,** p. 48 in ***Unit 2 Resources.***
- Remind students that fables are short, instructive stories that provide stated or unstated suggestions about appropriate behaviors.
- Organize students into small groups, and have each group brainstorm a list of morals or common sayings about human behavior. Then, have each student select a moral or saying to illustrate with his or her fable.
- Encourage students to revise their fables by adding dialogue and details to make the characters seem human.
- Use the Narration: Short Story rubrics in ***General Resources,*** pp. 63–64, to evaluate students' work.

WG **Writing and Grammar Platinum Level**
For support in teaching the Writing Lesson, use Chapter 5, Section 2.

❹ Research and Technology

- Suggest that students work in small groups to research other trickster tales in folklore. Each group member should check at least one source for information.
- Use the Multimedia Report rubric in ***General Resources,*** pp. 57–58, to assess students' presentations.
- The **Support for Extend Your Learning** page (***Unit 2 Resources,*** p. 49) provides guided note-taking opportunities to help students complete the Extend Your Learning activities.

Go Online Research Have students type in the Web Code for another research activity.

Standard Course of Study

CT.4.05.8	Make connections between works, self and related topics in critical texts.
LT.5.01.6	Make connections between historical and contemporary issues in world literature.
LT.5.01.7	Understand the cultural and historical impact on world literature texts.

Connections

American Literature

Tell students that ancient Indian writers used fables to teach universal lessons about life and that modern writers still use them for the same purpose. Have students reread the fable "Numskull and the Rabbit" on pp. 222–226. Then, ask them to read "The Tiger Who Would Be King." Ask students: What similarities and differences can you note between the two fables?

Fables

- Tell students that in both ancient and modern fables, the animal characters behave like human beings. Their experiences point to a lesson about human behavior called a *moral.* The moral can be stated directly or implied.
- **Ask** students to offer examples of human behavior demonstrated by the characters of "The Tiger Who Would Be King" and "Numskull and the Rabbit."
  Possible response: In "The Tiger Who Would Be King," the tiger's behavior is human-like in that he shows pride, greed, and impatience. Similarly, the other animals take sides and fight without specific reasons as humans sometimes do. In "Numskull and the Rabbit," the lion's desire for power and extreme arrogance are human-like. In the end, the lion is punished for exhibiting these behaviors.
- Then, have students discuss the moral of each fable and determine whether the moral of "Numskull and the Rabbit" applies to today's world.
- If possible, read several other ancient and modern fables. Encourage students to note the lessons offered about human behavior.

CONNECTIONS

American Literature

Fables

The fable of "Numskull and the Rabbit" in this unit comes from the *Panchatantra,* a kind of ancient Indian "how-to" book for young princes. Like fables from other cultures and time periods, it uses animal characters to teach universal lessons about life. While offering entertainment and amusement, it provides insights into human weaknesses and strengths.

Because fables tell amusing tales about animals, they have a real advantage as moral teaching. Readers can enjoy them on one level as funny stories but, at another level, absorb the moral lesson effortlessly and connect it to their own lives.

A Twentieth-Century Fable "Numskull and the Rabbit" was written thousands of years ago—sometime between 200 B.C. and A.D. 500—but you will notice that it has quite a bit in common with the following twentieth-century fable by James Thurber. Both "Numskull and the Rabbit" and "The Tiger Who Would Be King" use animal characters with human characteristics and have simple plots with humorous twists at the end. They both also contain devastating and dramatic conflicts, and each teaches a timeless lesson that the reader can take away from the tale.

The Tiger Who Would Be King

James Thurber

Enrichment

Fabulists

The fable is a popular mainstay of literature. Permeating all levels of writing, it has influenced Western society through the works of Aesop and his Roman collector, Phaedrus, before being retold in the writings of French author Jean de La Fontaine. Other important fabulists, or creators or writers of fables, include Horace, the Roman poet who relates the story of the city mouse and the country mouse; Geoffrey Chaucer, who incorporates the tale of Chanticleer and the fox in his *Canterbury Tales;* Rudyard Kipling, the author of *The Jungle Books* and *Just So Stories;* and Joel Chandler Harris, whose Uncle Remus stories emphasize the wisdom of the weaker animals who must survive the attacks of stronger, more ferocious beasts.

One morning the tiger woke up in the jungle and told his mate that he was king of beasts.

"Leo, the lion, is king of beasts," she said.

"We need a change," said the tiger. "The creatures are crying for a change."

The tigress listened but she could hear no crying, except that of her cubs.

"I'll be king of beasts by the time the moon rises," said the tiger. "It will be a yellow moon with black stripes, in my honor."

"Oh, sure," said the tigress as she went to look after her young, one of whom, a male, very like his father, had got an imaginary thorn in his paw.

The tiger prowled through the jungle till he came to the lion's den. "Come out," he roared, "and greet the king of beasts! The king is dead, long live the king!"

Inside the den, the lioness woke her mate. "The king is here to see you," she said.

"What king?" he inquired, sleepily.

"The king of beasts," she said.

"I am the king of beasts," roared Leo, and he charged out of the den to defend his crown against the pretender.

It was a terrible fight, and it lasted until the setting of the sun. All the animals of the jungle joined in, some taking the side of the tiger and others the side of the lion. Every creature from the aardvark to the zebra took part in the struggle to overthrow the lion or to repulse the tiger, and some did not know which they were fighting for, and some fought for both, and some fought whoever was nearest, and some fought for the sake of fighting.

"What are we fighting for?" someone asked the aardvark.

"The old order," said the aardvark.

"What are we dying for?" someone asked the zebra.

"The new order," said the zebra.

When the moon rose, fevered and gibbous,[1] it shone upon a jungle in which nothing stirred except a macaw[2] and a cockatoo,[3] screaming in horror. All the beasts were dead except the tiger, and his days were numbered and his time was ticking away. He was monarch of all he surveyed, but it didn't seem to mean anything.

MORAL: You can't very well be king of beasts if there aren't any.

---

1. **gibbous** (gib′ əs) *adj.* more than half but less than completely illuminated.
2. **macaw** (mə kô′) *n.* large parrot of Central or South America with bright colors and a harsh voice.
3. **cockatoo** (käk′ ə to͞o′) *n.* crested parrot with white plumage tinged with yellow or pink.

Connecting American Literature

1. **(a)** In what ways is the tiger in "The Tiger Who Would Be King" like the lion in "Numskull and the Rabbit"? **(b)** In what ways are the two characters different?
2. Which fable is more relevant to today's world? Explain.

CONNECTIONS

Vocabulary Builder
repulse (ri puls′) *v.* drive back; repel, as an attack

James Thurber (1894–1961)

James Thurber left college to become a clerk in the U.S. State Department, but he soon left this serious position to pursue writing and cartooning. Much of his early work appeared in *The New Yorker* magazine. When failing eyesight forced him to give up drawing, Thurber kept making people laugh with his writing. Many of his funny stories, like "The Tiger Who Would Be King," have a serious message behind the humor.

Background
Parable

A parable, like a fable, is a type of allegorical writing which has an underlying meaning that focuses on an idea rather than an event. A fable uses animals to point out human weakness, whereas a parable focuses on humans to show the differences between what a specific human does and human behavior in general. Both fables and parables are simple stories, but parables often teach spiritual values.

Background
Modern Fables

Americans adopted both printed and animated sources for their modern fables. Walt Disney's characters of Mickey Mouse, Donald Duck, Pluto, and Dumbo act in ways that humans might act, often producing comic results. In the middle of the twentieth century, Americans encountered puns and satires in the form of newspaper comic strips. Many comic strips today, with animal characters such as Garfield, Pogo, and Snoopy, give us fables for modern times.

ASSESS
Answers

1. (a) Both the tiger in "The Tiger Who Would Be King" and the lion in "Numskull and the Rabbit" are consumed with power and greed and blinded by pride and arrogance. (b) The lion in "Numskull and the Rabbit" has been in power and feels threatened by an imaginary usurper, while the tiger in "The Tiger Who Would Be King" wants to appropriate power from the legitimate king. Also, the lion in "Numskull and the Rabbit" meets his fate because of his behavior; the tiger survives but loses his would-be subjects.
2. **Possible response:** Both fables address the consequences of engaging in timeless and universal human behaviors, such as pride, arrogance, and recklessness; therefore, both fables are relevant to today's society.

Differentiated Instruction
Solutions for All Learners

Strategy for Less Proficient Readers
Have students write short and simple fables based on either incidents in their lives or on current events. Students might find it helpful to create their moral statements first and then think of experiences or events that support that moral. Ask volunteers to share their fables with the class.

Strategy for English Learners
Organize students into small groups, and have them discuss fables from their native countries. Have students discuss common animals, behaviors, or morals that appear in the fables. You might want to discuss the significance of particular animals in certain cultures.

Enrichment for Advanced Learners
Organize students into pairs, and have each pair research ancient and modern fables. Ask each pair to select two fables—one ancient fable and one modern fable—to compare and contrast. Each pair should write a brief essay that addresses the similarities and differences of the two fables.

Standard Course of Study

IR.2.01.8	Make connections between works, self and related topics in research texts.
IR.2.02.4	Develop appropriate strategies to illustrate points about cause/effect relationships.
FA.3.03.1	Gather information to prove a point about issues in literature.

*See **Teacher Express**™**/Lesson View** for a detailed lesson for Reading Informational Material.*

About Atlases and Maps

- **Ask** students to read the "About Atlases and Maps" instruction and to offer examples of how people use maps today.
  Answer: People use maps to locate geographical places and to get directions from one place to another.
- Use a wall map or a transparency to show students the components of a map: the legend or key, the scale, and the compass rose.
- Ask students to look at the map and locate geographical features such as countries, cities, towns, lakes, rivers, oceans, and mountains.

Reading Strategy

Locating Information Using Atlases and Maps

- Have students read the "Locating Information Using Atlases and Maps" instruction. Use a map and an atlas to show students examples of heads, color variations, legends, and scales.
- Review the steps to locate information in an atlas by **asking** students to explain how they would go about the process.
  Answer: First, students must decide what category of information they need. Then, they must use the headings on the atlas pages, the colors of the map, or the legend or scale to find information.
- Draw students' attention to the graphic organizer. Use the Dorling Kindersley atlas to show students where the information in the example entries appears.

Atlases and Maps

About Atlases and Maps

An **atlas** is a book of maps showing physical information about the world, such as cities, mountains, rivers, and roads. Some atlases also include facts and statistics about the places depicted. The pages from the modern Dorling Kindersley atlas shown here include the following additional information:

- Climate
- People and Society
- Government
- Economy

The general purpose of a **map** is to present geographical information in a convenient graphic form. To use a map effectively, you should be familiar with the following components of most maps:

- A *legend* or *key* defines the symbols used on the map.
- A *scale* shows the ratio between distances on the map and actual distances on Earth.
- A *compass rose* shows directions (north, south, east, and west).

Reading Strategy

Locating Information Using Atlases and Maps

Atlases and maps provide a variety of information, some as text and some as visual images. To **locate the information** you need, follow these steps:

1. Decide what category of information you need. Keep in mind that an atlas or a map will provide statistics and basic facts rather than detailed background.
2. Use the heads on the atlas pages, the colors of the map, or the legend or scale to locate the category of information.

Use a graphic organizer like the one shown to record the kind of information that you can find on the pages of the Dorling Kindersley atlas. One example is given.

Location of Information in an Atlas

Category	Location	Information
Population	Fact File box	953 million

Differentiated Instruction Solutions for All Learners

Reading Support

Give students reading support with the appropriate version of the **Reader's Notebooks:**

Reader's Notebook: [L2, L3]
Reader's Notebook: Adapted Version [L1, L2]
Reader's Notebook: English Learner's Version [EL]

INDIA

Separated from the rest of Asia by the Himalayan mountain range, India forms a subcontinent. It is the world's second most populous country.

GEOGRAPHY

Three main regions: Himalayan Mountains; northern plain between Himalayas and Vindhya Mountains; southern Deccan plateau. The Ghats are smaller mountain ranges on the east and west coasts.

CLIMATE

Varies greatly according to latitude, altitude, and season. Most of India has three seasons: hot, wet, and cool. In summer, the north is usually hotter than the south, with temperatures often over 104°F (40°C).

PEOPLE AND SOCIETY

Cultural and religious pressures encourage large families. Today, nationwide awareness campaigns aim to promote the idea of smaller families. Most Indians are Hindu. Each Hindu is born into one of thousands of castes and subcasts, which determine their future status and occupation. Middle class enjoys a very comfortable lifestyle, but at least 30% of Indians live in extreme poverty. In Bombay alone, over 100,000 people live on the streets.

THE ECONOMY

Undergoing radical changes from protectionist mixed economy to free market. Increasing foreign investment. New high-tech industries. Principal exports are clothing, jewelry, gems, and engineering products.

◆ *INSIGHT India's national animal, the tiger, was chosen by the Mohenjo-Daro civilization as its emblem, 4,000 years ago*

FACT FILE

OFFICIAL NAME: Republic of India
DATE OF FORMATION: 1947 / 1961
CAPITAL: New Delhi
POPULATION: 953 million
TOTAL AREA: 1,269,338 sq miles (3,287,590 sq km)
DENSITY: 751 people per sq mile
LANGUAGES: Hindi, English, other
RELIGIONS: Hindu 83%, Muslim 11%, Christian 2%, Sikh 2%, other 2%
ETHNIC MIX: Indo-Aryan 72%, Dravidian 25%, Mongoloid and other 3%
GOVERNMENT: Multiparty republic
CURRENCY: Rupee = 100 paisa

Clearly marked sections of the atlas entry provide important information.

Essential information about India is set off in a separate box.

Reading Atlases and Maps

- Have students read the atlas material. Explain that students will find similar information in most atlases. Then, discuss how the material is presented on the page.
- Point out the first call-out note. **Ask** students why the page is divided into four main sections.
  Answer: It is easy to locate information by heading, and these headings are general enough to apply to any country in the atlas.
- Direct students' attention to the second call-out note. **Ask** students why this information about India might be set off in a separate "Fact File" box.
  Answer: The "Fact File" box contains crucial information about India. This is information to which readers need quick access.
- Explain to students that the page is arranged by levels of information. General information is at the top of the page, and more detailed information is at the bottom of the page.

continued on page 234

Differentiated Instruction Solutions for All Learners

Enrichment for Less Proficient Readers
Have students work in a group to create an informational state poster. Instruct them to look up their state in an atlas. Then, have them find the capital, the population, and the total area of their state and create a fact file similar to the one above. Have students display their work.

Enrichment for English Learners
Have each student use an atlas to look up his or her native country, find the official name, the date of formation, the capital, the population, and the total area. Then, have them report their findings to the class. Instruct students to make posters with a map or outline of the country and display them in the classroom.

Enrichment for Advanced Readers
Have students use atlases to write reports on the geography, climate, economy, and society of the countries of their choice. Remind them to cite their sources when they turn in their reports. Provide a space for students to display the reports in the classroom for others to read.

Reading Atlases and Maps *(cont.)*

- Point out to students the first call-out note. **Ask** them what the color-coded boxes of the key represent.
  Answer: The color-coded boxes represent different elevations. The elevations are provided in both meters and feet.
- Direct students' attention to the second call-out note. **Ask** students what kinds of geographical information the map provides.
  Answer: The map shows bodies of water such as oceans, rivers, and bays, and the elevations of regions within India. It also shows names of cities, towns, and bordering countries.
- As a class, discuss other features of the map: the grid that shows the longitude and latitude, notations on the map about political and geographical boundaries, outlying islands, and the scale of the map.

Reading Informational Materials

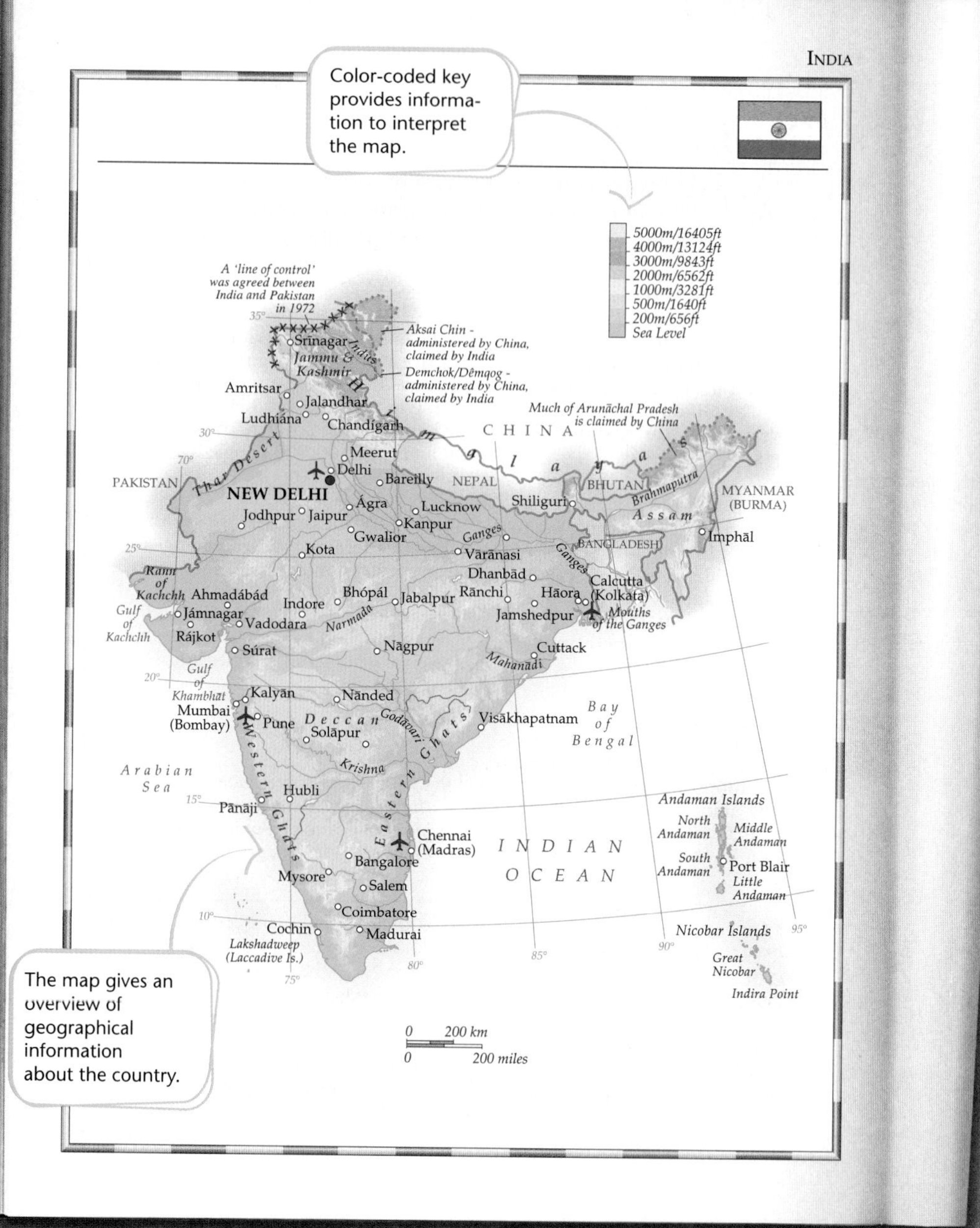

234 ■ *Indian Literature*

Monitor Your Progress

Assessment Practice

Reading: Locating Information Using Atlases and Maps

Directions: *Choose the letter of the best answer to each question about the atlas and the map.*

1. Which of the following is one of the three main regions of India?
   - A New Delhi
   - B the Ghats
   - C the Himalayas
   - D Bangladesh
2. What is the largest religious group in India?
   - A Muslims
   - B Sikhs
   - C Christians
   - D Hindus
3. Which of the following is the *best* way to determine the total area of India, using either the atlas or the map?
   - A Use the map scale to measure.
   - B Read the atlas "Fact File."
   - C Count squares on the map.
   - D Estimate a figure based on population density.
4. Approximately how far is New Delhi from Bombay?
   - A 600 miles
   - B 600 kilometers
   - C 900 kilometers
   - D 1,000 miles

Reading: Comprehension and Interpretation

Directions: *Write your answers on a separate sheet of paper.*

5. According to the atlas, what are two ways in which India's economy is changing?
6. What are two major problems facing India's people and society?
7. Do you think that changes to India's economy will solve some of its social problems? Why or why not?

Timed Writing: Explanation

Using the information in the atlas and the map, write a letter to a friend explaining why you have decided to visit India. In your letter, include descriptions of India's geography, climate, economy, people, and society. Be sure to specify which regions and cities you plan to visit, and why. Also include any topics, questions, or areas of interest that you would like to explore during your visit. ***(20 minutes)***

ASSESS

Answers

Reading: Locating Information Using Atlases and Maps

1. C
2. D
3. B
4. A

Reading: Comprehension and Interpretation

5. India now has a free-market economy with increasing foreign investment and new high-tech industries.
6. Poverty and overpopulation are two main problems that India faces.
7. Yes. More jobs will help many homeless people get off the streets.

Timed Writing Explanation

- Suggest that students plan their time to give 5 minutes to planning, 10 minutes to writing, and 5 minutes to revising and editing.
- Point out to students that their friendly letters should follow the appropriate form with a date, salutation, body, and closing.

Extend the Lesson

Understanding Atlas Entries

Have students help one another assess how well they understand the atlas entry about India. Tell them to write several questions based on information on the map and in the text. Students will then challenge their classmates to answer, using the atlas entry. Advise students that before they begin their challenge, they must provide both questions and answers from the map. They should write their questions, edit them for clarity, and verify that the answers are on the map. Before students challenge their classmates, you may want to review their questions and answers for accuracy.

Standard Course of Study

LT.5.01.3 Analyze literary devices and explain their effect on the work of world literature.

LT.5.01.5 Analyze archetypal characters, themes, and settings in world literature.

LT.5.02.1 Explore works which relate to an issue, author, or theme and show increasing comprehension.

Prewriting

- After students read the assignment, discuss and clarify each of the criteria listed in the "Assignment: Appearance Versus Reality" box. Have students recall the selections in this unit and share their initial reactions to those selections.
- Discuss the contrasts at the heart of this assignment—that of appearance versus reality or self-interest versus universal truth. Stimulate the discussion by inviting students to respond orally to the bulleted questions.
- Review and model the use of the chart. Ask volunteers to read aloud each entry and explain how it reflects the heading. Remind students as they complete the chart to support their ideas with specific examples.

Tips for Test Taking

A writing prompt on the SAT or ACT test may assess students' ability to analyze a literary theme, state a point of view regarding how this theme is expressed in different literary selections, and support the point of view with evidence. When writing under timed circumstances, students will need to clarify quickly a point of view (their thesis statement) and the evidence that supports it. Because students will not be able to refer to a text, their evidence must be based on their own readings and observations.

Writing About Literature

Analyze Literary Themes

The core texts of ancient Indian literature in this unit—the *Rig Veda,* the Upanishads, and the *Mahabharata*—explore the basic questions of religion: How did this world come to be? How can we lead righteous lives? What happens after we die? The answers are perhaps uniquely Indian. They develop from a perception of a deep difference between the tumultuous world of the senses and the unchanging, unified truth that manifests in that world.

To explore this theme in greater depth, write an essay that analyzes its treatment in the works. Refer to the box at right for details.

Assignment: Appearance Versus Reality

Write an analytical essay exploring the contrast that the works in this unit present between the world of appearances or of individual existence and an underlying universal truth.

Criteria:
- Include a thesis statement that defines the theme and explains the specific contrasts through which this theme is expressed in two or three of the selections.
- Support your analysis of the theme with examples from the selections.
- Discuss the likenesses and differences between the treatments of the theme in the selections.
- Approximate length: 700 words

Prewriting

Review selections. Review the selections in this unit, taking notes on the theme of appearance versus reality in each. To guide your review, ask yourself the following questions:

- Does the work present the world as divided into distinct, individual beings, or does it present a different idea?
- What attitudes do characters in the selection take toward their own passions or self-interests?
- What truths are contrasted with passion or self-interest?

Use your notes to fill out a chart like the one shown.

Model: Charting to Analyze Theme

Selection	Underlying Reality/ Universal Principle	Appearance/ Desire
"Creation Hymn"	In the beginning, all is "water," indistinct.	"Desire" creates differences; individual things emerge.
"Sibi"	Sibi must fulfill his dharma.	Sibi should protect his own life.

Choose selections. Review your chart, and choose the two or three selections that suggest rich ideas on the theme of appearance versus reality. To help you make your choice, look for contrasts as well as similarities.

Focus your analysis. Write a sentence or two defining which aspects of your chosen works express the theme—whether the theme appears in the philosophical statements of a character or in the transformation that characters undergo. When you begin drafting, keep your focus in mind.

Read to Write

As you reread the texts, note both significant statements by characters and their actions and transformations. Both are likely to convey the theme.

Teaching Resources

The following resources can be used to extend or enrich the instruction for Writing About Literature.

General Resources

Rubrics for Response to Literature, pp. 55–56

Drafting

Organize your ideas. Decide how best to organize your ideas before you begin to write your essay. Use one of the following strategies:

- **Organize by work.** Discuss each work in turn, analyzing its use of the theme. Then, sum up the similarities and differences.
- **Discuss how and then why.** Compare the means that each work uses to present the theme, and then sum up the conclusions or questions suggested by each work's presentation of the theme.

Revising and Editing

Review content: Check for sufficient support. Circle each main point in your draft, and then draw an arrow to the quotation, paraphrase, or reference to the text that supports the point. If you do not find such a supporting reference, consider adding one or deleting the point.

Model: Revising for Support

"Creation Hymn" expresses the theme of appearance versus reality by contrasting the world before creation with the world we live in. The poet writes, "Darkness was hidden by darkness in the beginning: with no distinguishing sign, all this was water," suggesting that the world at creation was formless, without distinctions among individual things.

Review style: Replace pronouns that have unclear antecedents. Reread your essay. Make sure that each pronoun has a single, clear antecedent (the noun or noun phrase that names the thing to which the pronoun refers).

Vague Antecedent: Many epics, such as the *Mahabharata,* were written by several poets. That is why *they* include such a variety of voices.

Clarification: Many epics, such as the *Mahabharata,* were written by several poets. That is why *these epics* include such a variety of voices.

Publishing and Presenting

Present a theme map. Create a map or other graphic representation of the ideas in your essay. Your map should be large enough to display to a group. Then, "walk" classmates through your map, explaining each point.

WG *Writing and Grammar Connection: Diamond Level, Chapter 14*

Write to Learn
As you analyze some of the questions ancient Indian literature poses, you may begin to relate these questions to your own life and to other works you have read.

Write to Explain
As you draft, put yourself in the reader's place. Spell out each step in your analysis. The reader can see only what is on the paper, not what is in your mind.

Differentiated Instruction Solutions for All Learners

Support for Less Proficient Writers
Elaborate on the theme of appearance versus reality. Ask students how figures in the media, such as athletes or actors, appear to them. Then, ask what students think are the celebrities' actual thoughts and feelings about certain topics. Help students understand that appearances do not always reflect reality.

Support for English Learners
Discuss with students how the media bring the lives of public figures—or at least the appearance of these lives—into our living rooms. Ask students whether they think other cultures are less focused on appearances and why a lesser focus may exist. Discuss how a focus on appearances can blur reality.

Strategy for Advanced Writers
Challenge students to include in their essays all three major works listed at the top of p. 236. Suggest that they use the "organize by work" structure to keep the comparison and contrast clear for readers. Remind students to finish with a strong conclusion that links the three works to the overall focus of the analysis.

Drafting

- Review the bulleted organizational approaches to make sure that students understand how to use them.
- Have students briefly outline their essays, with page references indicating the sources of supporting examples. Take time to review outlining for any students who are having difficulty.

Revising and Editing

- Stress the importance of leading the reader through the analysis in a navigable fashion. For example, students should make a clear connection between their main point and supporting text and should add necessary transition words to make the connection clear.
- Have each student exchange papers with a partner for an additional content review. Students should look for sufficient supporting evidence and a clear chain of analysis.

Publishing and Presenting

- Encourage students to experiment with the graphic or drawing tools commonly found in word processing computer software.
- When conducting their presentations, students should use appropriate gestures and tone of voice.

WG **Writing and Grammar Platinum Level**
Students will find additional instruction on writing an analytical essay in Chapter 14.

Writing and Grammar Interactive Textbook CD-ROM
Students can use the following tools as they complete their analytical essays:

- Editing
- Comparitives

Six Traits Focus

✓	Ideas	✓	Word Choice
✓	Organization		Sentence Fluency
	Voice	✓	Conventions

Assessing the Essay

To evaluate students' essays, use the Response to Literature rubrics, in *General Resources,* pp. 55–56.

PRETEACH

Standard Course of Study

- **CT.4.04.2** Apply criteria to evaluate others using reasoning and substantiation.
- **LT.5.01.1** Use strategies for preparation, engagement, and reflection on world literature.
- **LT.5.03.3** Provide textual evidence to support understanding of and response to world literature.

From the Translator's Desk

Wendy Doniger

Show students Segment 3 on Wendy Doniger on ***From the Author's Desk DVD.*** Discuss the research she does in prewriting, how she translates material when she is drafting, how she revises or checks her writing, and how she shares her knowledge and work.

Writing Genres

Using the Form Point out to students that reflective essays are often used in the real world. Point out these examples:

- Reflective essays are a common type of writing that students do in college.
- Personal letters may reflect on an experience that both the sender and receiver have shared.
- A supervisor or employer may request that an employee write a short reflective essay as part of the application process or a performance review.
- Brief versions of reflective essays may appear as details or examples in professional speeches.

Online Essay Scorer

A writing prompt for this mode of writing can be found on the *PH Online Essay Scorer* at PHSuccessNet.com.

Writing Workshop

Narration: Reflective Essay

Essays provide opportunities for writers to discuss their experiences and to offer insights into intriguing issues such as friendship, family, and society. Writers of **reflective essays** do more than report events; they interpret them and consider their larger meaning. Follow the steps outlined in this workshop to write your own reflective essay.

Assignment Write a reflective essay exploring a broader insight that you have gained from one or more experiences.

What to Include Your reflective essay should feature the following elements:

- a statement of a belief or an insight that you have gained from experience
- a narrative of the events that led to the belief or insight
- a balance between narration of incidents and statements of general ideas
- an organization that shows clear connections between insights and events
- a consistent and appropriate tone

To preview the criteria on which your reflective essay may be assessed, see the rubric on page 245.

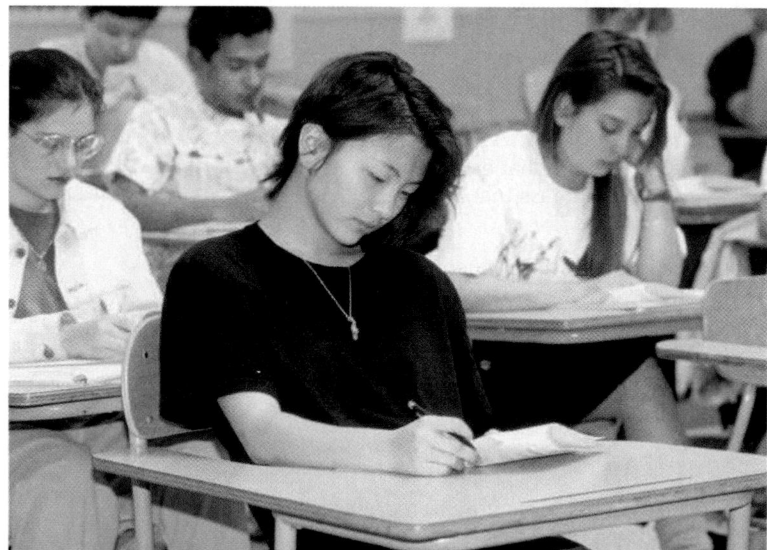

Standard Course of Study

- Produce reminiscences that use specific and sensory details with purpose. (WL.1.01.1)
- Explain how culture affects personal responses. (WL.1.02.4)
- Use language effectively to create mood and tone. (GU.6.01.7)

Using the Form

You may use elements of a reflective essay in these types of writing:

- letters to friends
- journal entries
- college application essays
- autobiographical narratives

To get a feel for reflective writing, read "Freedom to Breathe" by Alexander Solzhenitsyn, page 1290.

Teaching Resources

The following resources can be used to enrich or extend the instruction for the Writing Workshop.

Unit 2 Resources
- **Writing Workshop: Reflective Essay,** pp. 59–60

General Resources
- **Rubrics for Reflective Essay,** pp. 45–46

Graphic Organizer Transparencies
- **Rubric for Self-Assessment,** p. 46
- **Two-column Chart,** p. 254

From the Author's Desk DVD
- **Wendy Doniger,** Segments 3 and 4

Prewriting

Choosing Your Topic

To write a strong reflective essay, you need to discover a theme, or central meaning, in experiences that you have had. Use any or all of the following strategies to discover potential topics:

- **Make a timeline.** Create a timeline of the past four or five years of your life, noting several memorable experiences. Look for events that changed you or taught you something. Include both happy and sad experiences, successes and failures. Circle the ones that meant the most to you, and list the reasons they affected you so much.
- **Freewrite about your beliefs.** Finish the following statements by freewriting for three minutes about each one. Then, list the experiences in your life that led you to each belief, and choose the one that appeals to you the most as your topic.
    - The best thing about being part of a family is . . .
    - The most valuable qualities in a friend are . . .
    - In the future, I hope . . .
    - I could not do without . . .

Narrowing Your Topic

Review your notes, identifying the strongest insights, values, or beliefs that emerge. Look for connections between the events of your life and any broader insights or themes. Then, write one sentence that identifies the event or events you have chosen as your topic and the lesson they taught you. As you prepare to draft, focus your attention on two things: the events and the lesson.

Gathering Details

Provide specific support. Use a chart like the one shown to gather specific ideas and details to develop your topic. Include events that you listed in your earlier prewriting activities. Then, connect those events to the general insights, themes, or lessons you gained from the experiences. Use your chart as a resource as you draft your essay.

General Belief: People use words in deceptive and damaging ways.	
Incident	**What It Showed**
Watching Lila talk her way onto the team	People talk to be accepted by others.
Listening to Sam convince Mrs. Day that he was really smart	People talk to impress others.
What happened when I tried tricks like these with Evie	Insincerity can destroy friendships.

Tips for Using Rubrics

- Before students begin work on this assignment, have them preview the Rubric for Self-Assessment, p. 46, to know what is expected.
- Review the Assessment criteria in class. Before students use the Rubric for Self-Assessment, work with them to rate the student model by applying one or two criteria to it.
- If you wish to assess students' reflective essays, with either a 4-point, 5-point, or 6-point scoring rubric, see ***General Resources,*** pp. 45–46.

TEACH

Prewriting

- Point out that although the selections in Unit 2 are not reflective essays, they do lead readers to speculate about broader meanings. In particular, the *Panchatantra,* the *Bhagavad-Gita,* and the *Mahabharata* offer important lessons to readers. Suggest that students consider writing about something in one of these texts that has impacted their lives or that parallels an experience that they have had.
- Have students choose topics either from their Work-in-Progress ideas or by using the timeline or freewriting strategies.
- Use the Writing Workshop support, pp. 59–60 from ***Unit 2 Resources,*** as students write their reflective essays.
- Direct students to review their ideas from the Work in Progress assignment and from the timeline and freewriting activities. Have students circle any thoughts or ideas that repeat or overlap. These may be feelings, descriptive words, or actual facts. Observing repeated thoughts or ideas will help highlight connections between events and beliefs.

Six Traits Focus

✓	Ideas		Word Choice
✓	Organization		Sentence Fluency
	Voice		Conventions

Writing and Grammar Platinum Level

Students will find additional instruction on prewriting for a reflective essay in Chapter 4, Section 2.

Writing and Grammar Interactive Textbook CD-ROM

Students can use the following tools as they complete their reflective essays:

- Timeline
- Self-Interview
- Descriptive Word Bin
- Transition Words Revising Tool

Drafting

- Point out to students that making a simple outline, such as the graphic organizer on this page, will help them stay focused on their topics and organize their thoughts.
- Tell students that a powerful image or engaging hook can offer a strong opening. Have them consider opening with a powerful, short quotation, with dialogue, or with a general or concise description of the situation.
- Remind students that when they elaborate on their experiences, they must relate the experiences by making them as real as possible to readers. To help students achieve this, encourage them to use vivid language, vary sentence length, and use dialogue to describe people's appearances and characteristics and to balance the amount of detail and reflection in the essay.
- Suggest that students work with partners to experiment with tone. Have partners recount aloud part of their experience. As they speak, a tone will naturally emerge from the topic and from their feelings about it. Partners can help each other hear and identify that tone.
- Tell students that if they need more details as they write, they can return again to the prewriting stage and freewrite about the experience. This process may remind them of forgotten details that will help flesh out their essays.

Six Traits Focus

✓	Ideas	✓	Word Choice
✓	Organization		Sentence Fluency
	Voice		Conventions

WG Writing and Grammar Platinum Level

Students will find additional instruction on drafting a reflective essay in Chapter 4, Section 3.

Drafting

Shaping Your Writing

Use an outline to stay on track. Consider using a short outline to help you connect your accounts of specific experiences with the general insight you have drawn from them. Use an outline like the one shown here as a model.

Write a strong opening. A reflective essay invites readers to see and understand your own thoughts and to hear about the discoveries that have made you who you are. Set the scene in your opening paragraph. Re-create the spirit of your discoveries—whether that spirit is wonder, regret, or powerful conviction. In a one-sentence statement of your main idea, or a thesis statement, indicate just how these experiences have changed you.

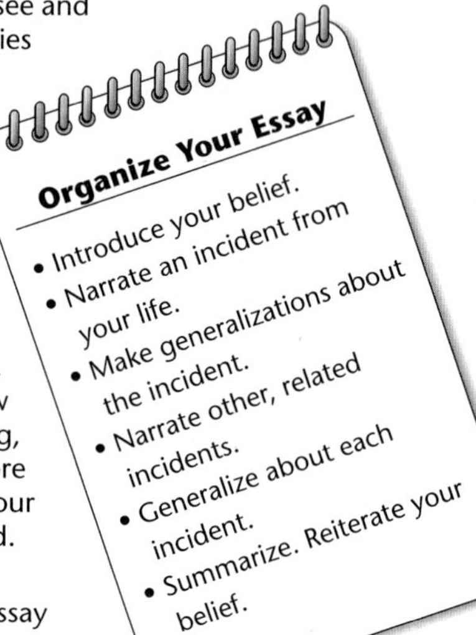
Organize Your Essay
• Introduce your belief.
• Narrate an incident from your life.
• Make generalizations about the incident.
• Narrate other, related incidents.
• Generalize about each incident.
• Summarize. Reiterate your belief.

Providing Elaboration

Establish a tone. As you invite readers into your thoughts and feelings, find a tone of voice that feels comfortable to you. For example, a serious, straightforward tone would show how you value your insights. If some of your examples are amusing, however, you might be more comfortable using a lighter, more humorous tone. Similarly, an ironic tone is a good choice if your examples show that things don't always work out as intended. Whatever tone you strike, be consistent.

Maintain a strong framework. A well-organized reflective essay weaves together incidents from your life with the insights or lessons that you have drawn from them. Keep in mind that you are moving back and forth between the specific—the events of your life, and the general—the broader meaning of these events. As you draft your essay, flesh out your narrative and your reflective insights by incorporating the ideas and details you gathered earlier, as well as any new ideas that come to mind as you write.

Reading Writing
Connection

To read the complete student model, see page 244.

Student Model: Adding Ideas to Flesh Out Connections

Even today, my conservative Indian parents still want me to live by the customs they observed as children. And so I live in a home where I am "AH-Kahr." Yet by day, I am "Uh-Car." The battle over the sounding of my name was the first symbol I recognized of the rift that existed between my Indian heritage and the American culture in which I will spend my future.

Akar adds a statement that fleshes out the connection between the specific incident and its larger significance in his life.

Tips for Test Taking

Point out to students that when they are asked to write during a standardized-test situation they need to read the question carefully, quickly jot down their ideas, formulate their thesis, and create a brief outline. The use of a brief outline will help them focus their thoughts and quickly begin writing productively. Remind students that in test situations, especially, their outlines do not have to follow any particular pattern; the outlines should keep them from straying off their topics and including irrelevant or unimportant information that will divert their time and attention.

From the Translator's Desk
Wendy Doniger on Word Choice

Wendy Doniger

I am a writer as well as a translator. This is the final paragraph in my book *The Woman Who Pretended to Be Who She Was.* The book argues that we are always pretending to be who we want to be, wearing the masks of people we want others to think we are. But, the conclusion suggests, we wear many masks, which are not false but real, in order to discover the many people that we are or can be.

> *"I worried that the pun would make readers laugh, or groan . . ."*
> —— Wendy Doniger

Professional Model:

from The Woman Who Pretended to Be Who She Was

Putting on a mask gets us closer to one self and farther from another, and so does taking off the mask. Since every lie covers up a truth, a series of masks passes through a series of lies and truths. Perhaps, then, the best bet is to wear as many as possible, and realize that we are wearing them, and try to find out what each one conceals and reveals. As we strip away masks, or faces, each time we see more in the hall of looking-glasses. If we just stand there with our unconscious masks on our faces, like egg in the saying, we never learn anything about the selves. Though few of us actually put on masks that replicate our faces, it is not uncommon for us to become unrecognizable travesties of ourselves, particularly as we age and change. For the ultimate mask is the body itself. And so, we look into the mirror and say to the stranger we see there, "Another gray hair; shall I dye it?" "Another five pounds; shall I diet?" But the falling away of the final, unaccented syllable reveals the submerged, suppressed question: "Shall I die?" And then, "Who is this I who will die?" These realizations constantly open up for us the possibility of multiple selves and the infinite regress of self-discovery.

At first I wrote "hall of mirrors," a stock phrase, but "looking-glasses" resonated more with Alice in Wonderland and fairy tales.

I worried that the pun would make readers laugh, or groan, but hoped the contrasting moods would give the final, serious lines more punch.

Infinite regress—one text or mask leading to another and so on without end—is a recurrent theme in the book.

From the Translator's Desk
Wendy Doniger

- Show students Segment 4 on Wendy Doniger on ***From the Author's Desk DVD.*** Ask students to explain how Doniger has helped create connections between distant social worlds and how that process has provided personal rewards.
- Point out that Doniger uses a pun to make her readers laugh but also as a transition to introduce a very serious human concern: death. Urge students to be mindful of the power that selecting the right word can bring to their essays.
- Review Wendy Doniger's comments about her choice of words in *from The Woman Who Pretended to Be Who She Was.* Ask students to evaluate how her word choice increases the effectiveness of her writing.

Tips for Improving Word Choice

Give students these suggestions for revising for word choice:

1. Look for clichés or stock phrases, and replace them with original phrases that express your thoughts more clearly. If you cannot think of original phrases, use conventional language and avoid often-repeated catch phrases or figures of speech.
2. Circle "to be" verbs such as *am, is, are, was, were, be, being,* and *been.* Substitute them for action or descriptive verbs. By using more precise and lively verbs, you will probably have to change the structure of some of your sentences and therefore end up with a livelier essay.
3. Avoid useless adverbs and adjectives. Try to rely on strong verbs and the active voice to carry your message.

Revising

- Encourage students to use oral reading as a tool. Have them read their essays aloud, listening for awkward transitions or wordy sections as well as for a balance between incidents and commentary. A reflective essay should read smoothly, as in an experience recounted for a friend.
- You might provide colored pencils or highlighters so that students can mark troublesome passages. Have students mark narration with one color and commentary with a second color. This strategy will help them visualize their balance between the two elements.
- As students read, encourage them to use self-stick notes to record additional comments or suggestions.
- Direct students to the Transition Words Revising Tool on the **Writing and Grammar Interactive Textbook CD-ROM** for help as they revise to strengthen connections.
- During the peer review process, have classmates use pencil or self-stick notes to identify the places that need improved connections. This strategy will help the writer distinguish between his or her own markings and the markings of peers.

Six Traits Focus

✓	Ideas	✓	Word Choice
✓	Organization		Sentence Fluency
	Voice	✓	Conventions

WG Writing and Grammar Platinum Level

Students will find additional guidance for revising a reflective essay in Chapter 4, Section 4.

Revising

Revising Your Overall Structure

Balance narration with reflection. In your reflective essay, maintain a balance between the incidents you relate and your reflections about them. A reflective essay full of incidents but with too little commentary may be chatty and lively, but it will seem to have no point. On the other hand, a reflective essay that is mostly reflection with few incidents will feel too general, with little grounding in real life.

Follow these steps to make sure that you have balanced the narration of your experiences with reflections about them:

1. Circle any sections that offer general insights.
2. Place a check mark next to any insights that stray from your main idea or that do not illuminate a specific incident.
3. Put an *X* next to any experiences that do not seem connected to the insights you are presenting.
4. Rewrite, adding commentary and experiences as needed. Be prepared to cut both commentary and experiences that stray from your main focus.

Student Model: Revising for Balance

in his strongly accented English.

My father hated the idea. "Why must you change yourself to help the Americans? Anyone can pronounce anything perfectly, unless he doesn't try," he said. Yet it is a known fact that if your language does not include a given sound, you will have trouble pronouncing foreign words using that sound. Besides, my father himself tends to pronounce English *v's* as *w's*.

Akar deleted the circled general sentences, which strayed from his point. He rewrote one humorous detail as a brief phrase.

Revising Your Sentences

Strengthen connections. A reflective essay moves back and forth between experiences and reflection. It is important to keep your audience on track each time you shift from one to the other. Review passages in which you go from narrating an event to generalizing about its meaning. Wherever necessary, rewrite to reinforce the connections between specific experiences and general insights about them. Add appropriate explanatory sentences and transitional phrases:

Afterward . . .	I finally realized . . .
As a result . . .	These experiences showed me that . . .

Peer Review: Have a group of three or four classmates read your writing. Ask them to identify places in your draft where you can improve the connections between your ideas.

To read the complete student model, see page 244.

Tips for Using Technology in Writing

When they reach the revision stage, students working with word processing software may wish to use the Find or Find/Replace feature to avoid repetition. If an initial reading indicates overuse of particular words, students can search for these words using the Find feature. Then they can use the Thesaurus function to identify possible synonyms. Remind students to check that all synonyms make sense in the context of the sentence and to use a dictionary to check the meaning of unfamiliar synonyms.

Developing Your Style

Voice and Tone

Create a personal voice. One of the greatest joys of writing is finding a way to make people "hear" your voice as they read your words. These tips will help you create a comfortable but distinctive voice when you write:

- **Talk directly to your reader.** Start by imagining that your readers are sitting right in front of you. Treat them as people you know—your older brother, your lab partner, a family friend.
- **Limit your use of fancy vocabulary words.** Avoid *clichés*, which are trite, overused words and expressions, and *jargon*, which is specialized vocabulary used by those in a particular profession. Use words that you are comfortable saying but that are precise enough to express your meaning.

Use an appropriate tone. Your **tone** is your attitude toward your reader and your subject. Maintain a consistent tone throughout your essay. For example, if you narrate your experiences in a simple, direct tone, do not shift into a more pompous tone when you reflect on them.

Inconsistent tone: I'll never forget the day my little brother began to grow up. His pet hamster had died, and Evan came to me crying, "Something's wrong with Boxer!" Instantaneously, I empathized with the child, for I recalled that I too had endured a similar loss at his age.

Consistent tone: I'll never forget the day my little brother began to grow up. His pet hamster had died, and Evan came to me crying, "Something's wrong with Boxer!" Right away, I knew what he felt, because I could remember when I had lost my cat at his age.

Find It in Your Reading Read or review the selection from the *Mahabharata* on page 192.

1. Choose three sentences spoken by the hawk, and describe the tone you hear the hawk taking. Identify the words that create this tone.
2. Choose three sentences that narrate actions in the story, and describe their tone. Identify the words that create the tone, and evaluate the ways the narrator's tone is different from the hawk's tone.

Apply It To Your Writing Review the draft of your reflective essay. For each paragraph in your draft, follow these steps:

1. Locate sentences or phrases that reveal your voice. If your essay lacks a detectable personal voice, revise, as necessary, to create writing that sounds more like you.
2. Read your draft aloud to hear the words that suggest the tone. Revise, as necessary, to create a consistent tone that is appropriate for both your reflections and your larger themes.

WG *Prentice Hall Writing and Grammar Connection: Platinum Level, Chapter 3, Section 3*

Differentiated Instruction Solutions for All Learners

Support for Special Needs Students

Point out to students that people use tone in everyday speech. Ask students how they can tell when a family member or a teacher is pleased with them or how they can tell when someone is in trouble for something that may have upset someone else. Have them focus not on the tone of voice but on the words the person uses. Have students list the verbal clues that indicate tone.

Strategy for English Learners

Have students look at sentence length to provide clues regarding tone. Point out to students that lengthy sentences often indicate a more formal tone, while short, more clipped sentences may indicate a more informal tone. Have students write short paragraphs using different tones. Suggest that they write on the same topic in a tone of boredom, a tone of enthusiasm, and a tone of anxiety.

Developing Your Style

- Point out to students that voice in writing is similar to a writer's "personality" in that piece of writing; voice differentiates one writer's work from another's work. The details that writers include and how they describe these details reflect their voice.
- Have students think about an incident that was serious at the time it happened but has become humorous when they look back on it. Then have them reflect how their attitude toward the incident has changed and how they describe the incident now compared to when it occurred. Point out that the tone they use to tell it has changed.
- Explain that a helpful strategy for checking for inconsistent tone is to ask whether the same narrator seems to be telling the entire story. If the narrator sounds the same, the tone will mostly likely be consistent; if the narrator sounds different in parts, students need to revise.
- Help students understand tone and how to identify it in a selection by assigning pairs of students to work on **Find It in Your Reading.** **Model answer:** 1. ". . . the kite is a mere caricature of our family"; haughty tone; *mere caricature;* 2. "The hawk chuckled cynically"; descriptive and uninvolved tone; the hawk is self-important while the narrator merely observes events.
- Have students work on **Apply It To Your Writing.** Students may find it helpful to read their essays to a partner. Have the partner listen to the essay and then provide feedback on personal voice.

WG Writing and Grammar Platinum Level

Students will find additional instruction on crafting voice and tone in Chapter 3, Section 3.

Student Model

- Explain that the Student Model is a sample and that students' own essays may be longer. Also remind students that the model shows only one approach to the assignment. Students' own essays may focus on a less personal experience or may use a more serious tone.
- After students have read the model, point out that the writer, Akar, is the main character. Tell students that this is typical, though not required, in a reflective essay.
- Have a volunteer read aloud the specific example Akar gives in the second paragraph. Point out how Akar uses phonetic respellings and familiar English words to bring the sounds of his dilemma to readers' ears.
- Point out the irony in Akar's description of his father's response in accented English. **Ask** students how this irony strengthens the essay. **Possible response:** The irony strengthens the essay by helping readers imagine the situation more vividly while making Akar's father seem more like a real person.
- Point out to students how Akar makes the transition from the specific story about his name to the more general issue on which he wished to reflect. This is an example of how a writer can move from specific and personal thoughts or events to a more general idea or theme.
- Point out the speculation with which Akar ends his essay. Clarify that this ending leaves readers with something to think about and an opportunity to imagine Akar in the future.

Writing Genres

Reflective Writing on Applications

Explain that students may be asked to write about an experience that has strongly shaped their lives. Point out that a reflective essay is often ideal for this purpose. Discuss why a school or company might ask a potential student or employee to write about an experience that shaped his or her life. Then, ask students to think about what experience they would write about if they were applying for admission to college or for a job. Why would they choose this experience? If appropriate, ask volunteers to share their ideas.

Student Model: Akar Bharadvaj, Monroe, Louisiana

The Sound of My Name

When I was a young child, my parents encouraged me not to give up my Indian heritage for the strange American culture of blue jeans and rock music. For the first five years of my life, I was familiar with no Americans save the mailman and the garbage man. I simply stayed at home, learning Gujarati and a little bit of English. When I first went out in public life, I encountered problems.

Akar is the main character in his reflective essay.

On my first day of preschool, I was scared by the number of Americans around me. All these white faces were Johnnys, Rosies, and Matthews—not a single Varendra or Vikram in the entire bunch. When I told my classmates my name was Akar, they all looked at me strangely. They had lived their entire five years never having to make the *aardh* sound; their small tongues had slowly molded into an American shape. As a result, my classmates called me "aye-KAR" or "Acre" or "Acorn" or "Achy-Breaky." They could never get it right.

Specific examples contribute interest and authenticity to Akar's essay.

In the midst of my confusion, someone called me "A-Car." I liked the way that sounded, and I had a brilliant idea. I simply met people halfway by calling myself "Uh-Car." The simplified name could be pronounced easily. Everyone knew what a car was; they just had to get used to the idea that this was a person, not a thing. Even allowing for some inevitable corny "A Boat, A Truck, A . . ." jokes, it was the perfect idea.

My father hated the idea. "Why must you change yourself to help the Americans? Anyone can pronounce anything perfectly, unless he doesn't try," he said in his strongly accented English.

Akar's description of his father's accented English adds humor to the essay.

The battle over the sounding of my name was the first symbol I recognized of the rift that existed between my Indian heritage and the American culture in which I will spend my future. Even today, my conservative Indian parents still want me to live by the customs they observed as children. And so I live in a home where I am "AH-Kahr." Yet by day, I am "Uh-Car." My mask is that of a left-brained devout Hindu vegetarian who studies hard and does well in mathematics and science. My face is that of an American teenager who wears blue jeans and listens to the music of his era. My parents cannot fathom my preferences for bread over chapati, guitars over sitars, or American action movies over tedious Bollywood films. They see my brown Indian skin, not the quick American spirit yearning to be set free.

Akar develops incidents about the sound of his name into a generalization about his two cultural identities.

The sound of my name is a trigger. When I hear "Uh-Car," I am myself, an American with Indian parents. When I hear "AH-Kahr," I don the mask of the Indian boy my father was. The sounds tell me who I must be. As I look to the future, I wonder whether my face will not outgrow and so crack the mask.

Still poised between his two identities, Akar ends his reflective essay with a speculation.

Differentiated Instruction
Solutions for All Learners

Strategy for Less Proficient Writers

Have students work in pairs to share ideas for their essays. Ask students to talk about their beliefs or about important experiences in their lives. Hearing each other's ideas might be a good anchor for students as they approach the assignment. Students should write down any ideas that come to mind as their partners share. Be sure that students are not led or instructed to write about anything that they find too personal.

Strategy for Advanced Writers

Have students explain how Akar's closing speculation adds great dimension to his essay. Make sure that students notice how it takes the essay beyond the personal by linking it to the universal theme of individuation and applying its meaning across time. Challenge students to find ways throughout their essays to draw links to universal themes and experiences. Tell them that their essays, too, should transcend the personal.

Editing and Proofreading

Review your essay to eliminate errors in grammar, spelling, or punctuation.

Focus on Errors: An intimate, reflective tone may tempt you to use sentence fragments or run-on sentences for effect. Review your work, revising any fragment by joining it with another sentence or adding the missing subject or verb. Then, correct all run-ons by splitting them into two or more sentences.

Publishing and Presenting

Consider one of the following ways to share your reflective essay:

Read to a discussion group. Read your reflective essay to a small group of classmates who all share their work. Discuss the range of topics covered by the group and the insights developed by the various essays.

Make a formal oral presentation. Use your reflective essay as the basis of a formal oral presentation to your class. As you speak, *summarize* incidents or events, rather than reading them word for word from your essay.

Reflecting on Your Writing

Writer's Journal Jot down your thoughts on the experience of writing a reflective essay. Begin by answering these questions:

- What have you learned about moving from narrating an incident to reflecting on it and back again in your writing?
- In what ways did writing your essay help you see your experiences differently? Explain.

WG *Prentice Hall Writing and Grammar Connection: Platinum Level, Chapter 21, Section 4*

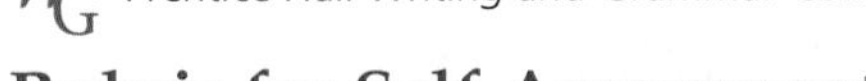

Rubric for Self-Assessment

Evaluate your reflective essay *using the following criteria and rating scale, or, with your classmates, determine your own reasonable evaluation criteria.*

NC Criteria	Rating Scale (not very – very)				
Focus: How clearly do you state the belief or insight that you gained through experience?	1	2	3	4	5
Organization: How well does your organization connect insights and events?	1	2	3	4	5
Support/Elaboration: How well do you use details to describe the incidents that led to your belief or insight?	1	2	3	4	5
Style: How well do you establish your tone through word choice?	1	2	3	4	5
Conventions: How well do you avoid sentence fragments and run-on sentences?	1	2	3	4	5

Tips for Test Taking

Tell students that many standardized tests include writing prompts. It is critical that test-takers remember the timed aspect of the task. Students should set a time limit for each phase of the writing process, calculated from the overall available time. For example, if the test allows thirty minutes to write the essay, students should spend no more than five minutes choosing a topic and five minutes organizing their ideas.

Editing and Proofreading

- Point out that a sentence fragment or run-on sentence can ruin the tone or voice that students have worked hard to develop.
- Point out to students that reading each sentence aloud beginning with the end of the essay and going backwards may help them find fragments and run-on sentences.

Six Traits Focus

	Ideas		Word Choice
	Organization		Sentence Fluency
	Voice	✓	Conventions

ASSESS

Publishing and Presenting

- Invite all of the discussion groups to share the common insights that they discovered among their essays. As a class, explore why these insights might appear repeatedly in human experience.
- Before students give their formal presentations, encourage them to "tell" their experiences as if sharing them with a close friend or relative. Reading the incident or event word for word can cause listeners to lose interest. Urge students to use gestures and a sense of drama to bring their experiences to life.

Reflecting on Your Writing

- To help students understand the rubric, point out ways that it could be applied to Akar's essay. Review each criterion, and remind students to consider these same points as they revise their essays.
- Have students write journal entries, reflecting on what they did well in their essays and how they would revise them if they were to use them for college applications.

WG **Writing and Grammar Platinum Level**

Students will find additional guidance for editing and proofreading, publishing and presenting, and reflecting on a reflective essay in Chapter 4, Sections 5 and 6.

Standard Course of Study

LT.5.03.5 Summarize key events and points from the text.

GU.6.01.3 Use recognition strategies to understand vocabulary and exact word choice.

Know Your Terms: Recalling Information

Explain that the terms listed under Terms to Learn will be used in standardized-test situations when students are asked to recall information from a reading passage.

Terms to Learn

- Review *recall.* Tell students that *to recall* means "to remember details or specific information from the text." Have students ask themselves, "Who?" "What?" "When?" "Where?" "Why?" and "How?" to help recall information. Tell students that when they write responses, they should include only the details asked for in the question.
- Review *summarize.* Point out that *to summarize* means "to write a brief version of a text, including only the main ideas of the text." Tell students that summaries should be short and to the point.

ASSESS

Answers

1. People saw the hawk begin to attack the king. Then they heard divine music and saw Indra take the hawk's place.
2. The gods said that they had tested the king and challenged his integrity. The king was blessed, and from telling his tale, people will gain from his spiritual merit.
3. Sibi, the king, was about to be attacked by a hawk, but it was really the god Indra, who helped Sibi down from the scale. The gods challenged his integrity and told of his spiritual merit.
4. The people closed their eyes, unable to watch their king suffer.

SAT® PREP ACT

Vocabulary Workshop

High-Frequency Academic Words

High-frequency academic words are words that appear often in textbooks and on standardized tests. Though you may already know the meaning of many of these words, they usually have a more specific meaning when they are used in textbooks and on tests.

Know Your Terms: Recalling Information

Each of the words listed is a verb that tells you to show that you understand the significance of the information in the text. The words indicate the kinds of details and information you should provide in your answer.

Standard Course of Study

- Use recognition strategies to understand vocabulary and exact word choice. (GU.6.01.3)

Terms to Learn

Recall Remember and retell details from the text.

Sample test item: ***Recall*** the setting of the *Bhagavad-Gita.*

Summarize Briefly state the most important information and ideas in the text.

Sample test item: ***Summarize*** the fable "Numskull and the Rabbit" in your own words.

Practice

Directions: *Read the following passage from the Indian epic the* Mahabharata. *Then, on a separate piece of paper, answer questions 1–4.*

The hawk flapped its wings and rose in the air and swooped down as if to peck at the king's flesh. People shut their eyes, unable to bear the spectacle. But presently they heard divine instruments filling the skies with music. The hawk was gone, but in its place they found Indra, the god with dazzling crown, armed with the diamond spear, seizing Sibi's hand and helping him down off the weighing scales. A flame rose where the dove had lain, and from the heart of it emerged the God of Fire.

They said, "O king, we put you to a severe test. We challenged your integrity, and we happily accept defeat. You are indeed blessed, and as long as human beings recollect your tale, they will partake of the spiritual merit that you have yourself acquired"—and vanished. The king recovered his energy in a moment, while the pieces of flesh in the scale pan turned to fragrant flowers.

1. *Recall* what the people heard and saw. Who took the place of the hawk?
2. *Recall* the words addressed to Sibi, the king.
3. *Summarize* the tale told in this passage.
4. *Summarize* the people's reaction to their king's test.

Tips for Test Taking

When students are asked to recall information on a standardized test, the questions will usually ask about details directly stated in a passage; these questions usually do not require students to interpret information. Therefore, remind students that when they are asked to recall information they should select an answer that supplies literal information. If asked to select the best summary for a text selection, students should focus only on the main ideas of the selection. Answers that contain details are not accurate summaries.

Go Online Vocabulary **For:** An Interactive Crossword Puzzle
Visit: www.PHSchool.com
Web Code: etj-5201

This crossword puzzle contains vocabulary that reflects the concepts in Unit 2. After students have completed Unit 2, give students the Web Code and have them complete the crossword puzzle.

Critical Reading: Sequential Order

Standard Course of Study

- IR.2.02.1
- IR.2.02.2
- IR.2.02.3

In the reading sections of some tests, you may be required to answer questions on the order of events in a passage. Use the following strategies to help you answer such questions:

- To help clarify sequential order, determine the logical relation between causes and effects.
- Take note of words signaling sequence, such as *first, next, then, after that, last,* and *finally.*
- Distinguish the order of the statements (what is *stated* first) from the order of events (what *happens* first). If in doubt, summarize the main events in chronological or time order.

Practice

Directions: *Read the passages below, and answer the questions that follow:*

Passage A. Thanks for offering to give my dog Juno a bath, but it won't be easy! First, gather the supplies—bucket, shampoo, and old towels—and put them outside beside the hose. Then, put on Juno's collar and leash and lead her outside. Stand on her leash and use the hose to wet her down. Next, apply plenty of shampoo and massage the shampoo into her fur. Be sure to remove all the shampoo. Finally, dry her with the towels.

Passage B. Confucius was an influential thinker who led an eventful life. During his difficult childhood, it is said, he began to wonder why there was so much pain in the world. As Confucius grew older, he decided the answer to this question lay in respect for *li,* or rituals and rules of courtesy. Confucius began to share his views, and he gradually attracted followers. Eventually, he became an official of the Kingdom of Lu. In this post, he applied his ideas of *li* and of virtue to politics and diplomacy. Confucius, however, fell victim to the power struggles that swirled around the king of Lu. Confucius resigned, and he and some followers traveled through various kingdoms of China looking for a great king to serve.

1. In Passage A, what should you do immediately before you wet down the dog?

A shampoo her
B gather the supplies
C stand on the leash
D towel her off

2. According to Passage B, when did Confucius wander through various kingdoms of China looking for a king to serve?

A before he gained followers
B when he was an official of Lu
C before developing his idea of *li*
D after he resigned as an official of Lu

Test-Taking Strategies

- As you read a text passage, number the events in order, indicating which one happened first, which next, and which last.

Standard Course of Study

IR.2.02.1	Summarize situations to examine cause/effect relationships.
IR.2.02.2	Show clear, logical connection among cause/effect events.
IR.2.02.3	Logically organize cause/effect connections through transitions.

Critical Reading

- Point out that a situation or event may have more than one cause and/or effect. Also, remind students that a passage may have a causal chain in which one cause leads to an effect, and then that effect becomes the cause for the next effect.
- Have students name other words that signal sequence.
- Remind students of the word *summarize* that they learned in the Vocabulary Workshop for Unit 2, p. 246. If the events of a passage are not in chronological order and seem confusing, students may need to summarize to help them determine the sequence of events.
- After students have read the Practice passage and have answered the questions, point out that for question 1, both B and C must be done before wetting down the dog. However, the question asks what needs to be done *immediately* before wetting down the dog, so the correct answer is C.
- Point out that D is the only possible answer for Passage 2.

ASSESS

Answers

1. C
2. D

Tips for Test Taking

Remind students to read test questions carefully. Although more than one answer may seem correct for a question, many times the question will have a word that limits the answer to only one choice. Explain to students that by reading the question carefully, they have a better chance of avoiding the "post hoc" fallacy: one event following another does not mean that the first event caused the second.

Standard Course of Study

IR.2.03.1	Access cultural information from media sources.
IR.2.03.2	Prioritize and organize information to construct an explanation to answer a question.
CT.4.05.11	Identify and analyze elements of critical environment.

Preparing for an Interview

- Tell students that they can expect to have to interview for a job.
- Encourage students to use the Internet for interview preparation. A company's Web site may list a staff directory, for example, which enables an applicant to learn the chain of command and identify the role of the person conducting the interview.
- Explain that although interview questions should always be respectfully presented, job applicants should take the opportunity to learn about the company and any of its potential weaknesses.

Participating in an Interview

- Students might practice their interviewing skills with a friend or family member. They can wear their interview clothing to make sure that it is comfortable but professional.
- Make sure that students are comfortable with the courtesies involved in interviewing. For example, a handshake should be firm and include eye contact with the other party.
- Emphasize that one of the most important things an applicant can bring to an interview is a strong sense of interest. People in any conversation want to believe that others are listening and responding.
- Encourage students to make and use a list of their questions and discussion points. It is entirely appropriate to refer to such prepared notes in an interview.

Assess the Activity

To evaluate students' role-plays, use the Peer Assessment: Speech rubric, p. 129 in ***General Resources.***

Interviewing Techniques

Standard Course of Study

- Access cultural information from media sources. (IR.2.03.1)
- Prioritize and organize information. (IR.2.03.2)

Obtaining a job requires going on an interview with an employer. Your best chances of obtaining a job will come if you apply specific skills for **interviewing.** Follow the strategies below to prepare for and participate in job interviews. To help you practice, complete the Activity that follows.

Preparing for an Interview

Preparing properly is the first step in a successful job interview. Follow these steps before an interview:

- **Research the job and the company.** Find out all you can in advance about the company and the job for which you will interview. Speak to friends, neighbors, and family members who may know the company. Also, consult library and Internet sources.
- **Prepare questions and talking points.** As you do your research, jot down any questions about the company that come to mind. At the same time, take notes on how your experiences, skills, and ambitions could fit in with the work done by the company.

Feedback Form for an Interview

Rating System
+ = Excellent ✓= Average – = Weak

Preparation
Knowledge of company ______
Knowledge of job requirements ______
List of questions ______

Interview
Appropriate language ______
Demonstration of knowledge of company ______
Ability to highlight skills ______

Post-Interview
Which of my questions about the company were answered?
What will I write in a follow-up letter?
What will I do differently in my next interview?

Participating in an Interview

Make sure that you present yourself at your best for a job interview, dressing suitably and grooming yourself properly. During the interview, sit up straight and meet the interviewer's look without shyness or fear. Keep these interviewing tips in mind:

- **Speak clearly.** Use Standard English and speak at a comfortable volume, avoiding "space fillers" such as *like, umm,* and *well.* Do not use slang or jargon.
- **Relax and listen.** By staying relaxed, you ensure that you are listening carefully to what the interviewer is saying. Make sure that you understand each question, requesting a clarification if you do not.
- **Take the time you need to respond.** Organize your thoughts before you answer a question. If you have more than one point to make, mentally count off points as you respond. Avoid repeating yourself, and stay on the subject of the question.
- **Draw on your prepared questions and talking points.** Ask informed questions about the company and the position, drawing on the research you have conducted. At appropriate points in the discussion, explain which special skills or interests qualify you for the job.

Activity *Role-Play in Interview* Working with a partner, select a job and take turns role-playing an interview for it. Use a Feedback Form like the one shown to evaluate each other's interviews.

Differentiated Instruction Solutions for All Learners

Strategies for Special Needs Students

Have students share some of their strengths and then discuss ways to present any weaknesses in a positive light. For example, students who have organizational difficulties are often extremely creative idea generators. Focusing on the positive creates a strong picture for the interviewer. Remind students, however, never to present a false picture and to acknowledge any specific disabilities if directly asked.

Strategies for English Learners

Remind students that much of the language in an interview is body language. Although they may feel unsure of their use of English, they can be sure of their body language. Have students work with an English-speaking partner to practice and become familiar with body language customs in America. Practice will increase students' comfort with American customs and therefore their effectiveness in interviews.

Suggestions for Further Reading

Featured Titles:

A Tiger for Malgudi

R. K. Narayan, *Penguin Classic, 1994*

Fiction This novel by one of India's most celebrated authors features an unusual first-person narrator: a tiger. Set in the fictional South-Indian territory of Malgudi, *A Tiger for Malgudi* traces the life of a tiger named Raja from his days as a cub in the jungle to his misery as a circus animal to his eventual happiness in the care of a kind master. As the old tiger—now living in a zoo—reflects on his life and his experiences, readers gain a glimpse into Indian culture and even learn some Hindu philosophy. Raja also points out how absurd some human behaviors can seem when viewed through the eyes of a wild animal.

The Penguin Gandhi Reader

Mohandas K. Gandhi, *Penguin, 1995*

Philosophical Text Gandhi was one of the most important political leaders of the twentieth century. His method of uncompromising yet peaceful protest helped gain India's freedom from British rule and inspired the world. This reader presents many of Gandhi's most important writings. The book is divided into sections, focusing on the following themes that occupied Gandhi's work and life: his criticism of modern culture and rejection of materialism; the principles of *swaraj* (independence, or self-rule) and *swadeshi* (responsibility to one's immediate community); the doctrine of nonviolence; his participation in mass protest movements; his opinions about the role of women; his arguments against the Indian caste system; his thoughts on economic and social systems; his belief in religious tolerance; his commitment to a united India; and his struggle for Indian independence.

Work Presented in Unit Two:

If sampling a portion of the following text has built your interest, treat yourself to the full work.

The Ramayana

R. K. Narayan, editor and reteller, *Penguin Classic, 1972*

Related British Literature:

Kim

Rudyard Kipling, *Penguin Classic, 1987*

This novel by a Nobel Prize-winning British author tells how a young boy learns the deadly game of espionage in nineteenth-century India.

Related American Literature:

Why We Can't Wait

Martin Luther King, Jr., *Signet Classic, 2000*

Dr. King describes his use of nonviolent action, a principle he learned from the life and writings of Indian leader Mohandas K. Gandhi.

Many of these titles are available in the* Prentice Hall/Penguin Literature Library. *Consult your teacher before choosing one.

Planning Students' Further Reading

Discussions of literature can raise sensitive and often controversial issues. Before you recommend further reading to your students, consider the values and sensitivities of your community as well as the age, ability, and sophistication of your students. It is also good policy to preview literature before you recommend it to students. The notes below offer some guidance on specific titles.

A Tiger for Malgudi by R.K. Narayan

The story's narrator, a tiger, kills animals and, in one case, a human. The book also makes references to smoking, guns, cruelty to animals, and drinking. A major character leaves his wife and children.

Lexile: Appropriate for high school students

The Penguin Gandhi Reader by Mohandas K. Gandhi

Gandhi expresses a belief in the "intrinsic superiority of India to the West." He also comments on gambling, the use of alcohol and tobacco, and the subjugation of women.

Lexile: Appropriate for high school students

The Ramayana edited and retold by R.K. Narayan

The Ramayana contains sexual references and several scenes of graphic violence, as well as references to suicide. To prepare students, discuss ways in which epics map a culture's experience from the depths to the heights.

Lexile: 1060L

Kim by Rudyard Kipling

This panoramic novel of India under British rule includes occasional stereotyping generalizations about Asian people, as well as references to magic and prostitution. There are allusions to drink, drugs, and intoxication, and a hill woman attempts, unsuccessfully, to seduce Kim.

Lexile: Appropriate for high school students

Why We Can't Wait by Martin Luther King, Jr.

Care and sensitivity should be exercised in discussing issues of racial oppression and blame.

Lexile: 1200L

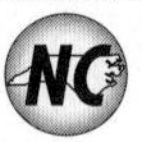

NC	Standard Course of Study
WL.1.03.6	Make inferences and draw conclusions based on personal reflection.
IR.2.02.1	Summarize situations to examine cause/effect relationships.
FA.3.04.7	Identify and analyze influences, contexts, or biases in argument.
CT.4.02.3	Examine how elements such as irony and symbolism impact theme.
LT.5.01.4	Analyze the importance of tone and mood in world literature.

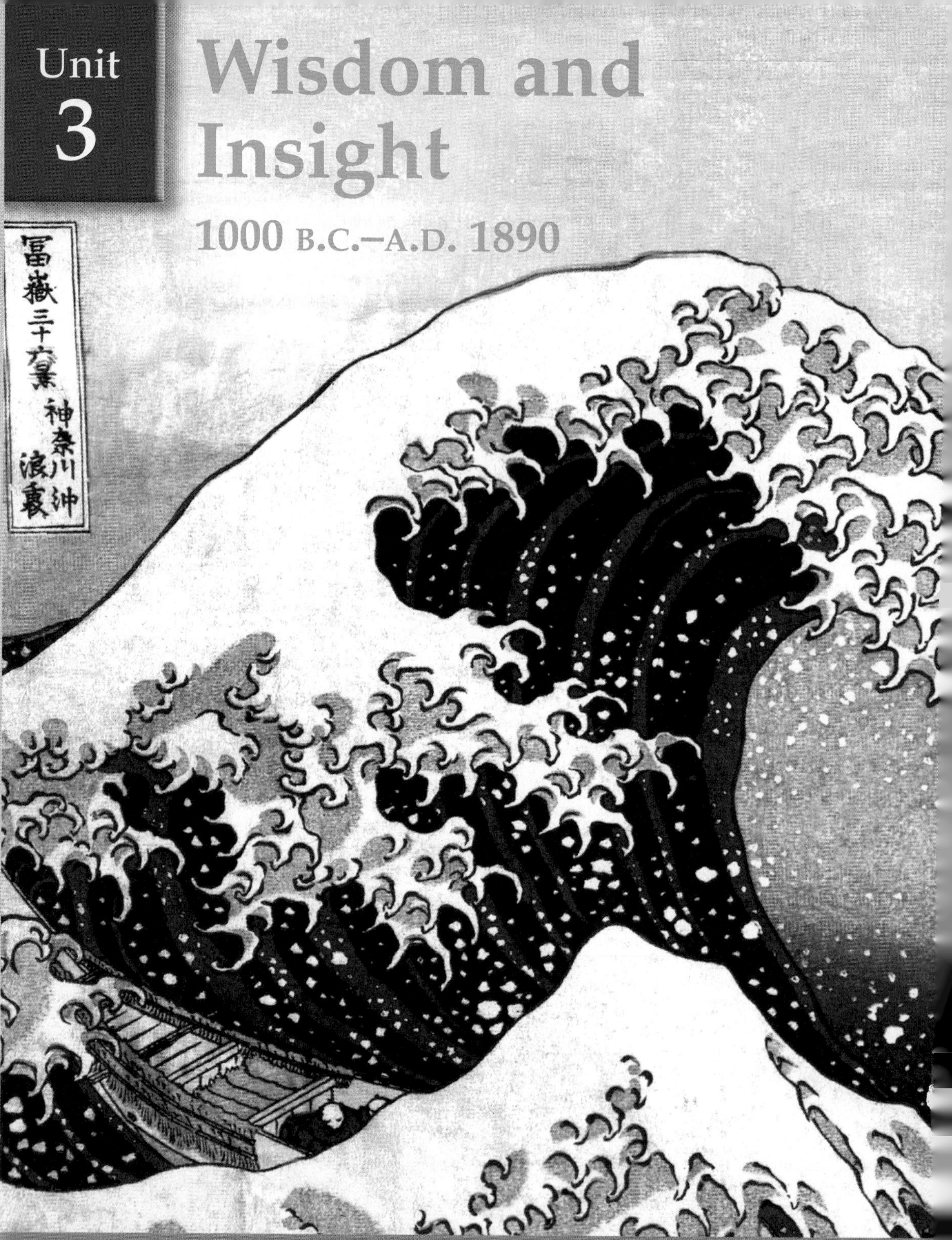

Unit Instructional Resources

In *Unit 3 Resources,* you will find materials to support students in developing and mastering the unit skills and to help you assess their progress.

▶ **Vocabulary and Reading**

Additional vocabulary and reading support, based on Lexile scores of vocabulary words, is provided for each selection or grouping.

- **Word Lists A and B** and **Practices A and B** provide vocabulary-building activities for students reading two grades or one grade below level, respectively.
- **Reading Warm-ups A and B,** for students reading two grades or one grade below level, respectively, consist of short readings and activities that provide a context and practice for newly learned vocabulary.

▶ **Selection Support** Practice and reinforcement pages support each selection:

- Reading Strategy
- Literary Analysis
- Vocabulary Builder
- Grammar and Style
- Support for Writing
- Support for Extend Your Learning
- Enrichment

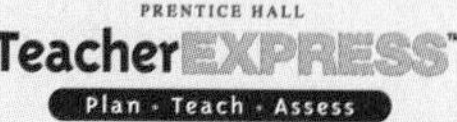

PRENTICE HALL **TeacherEXPRESS™** Plan · Teach · Assess You may also access these resources at TeacherExpress.

Unit 3 Wisdom and Insight

1000 B.C.–A.D. 1890

Assessment Resources

Listed below are the resources available to assess and measure students' progress in meeting the unit objectives and your state standards.

Skills Assessment

Unit 3 Resources
Selection Tests A and B

TeacherExpress™
ExamView® Test Bank Software

Adequate Yearly Progress Assessment

Unit 3 Resources
Diagnostic Test 3
Benchmark Test 3

Standardized Assessment

Standardized Test Preparation Workbook

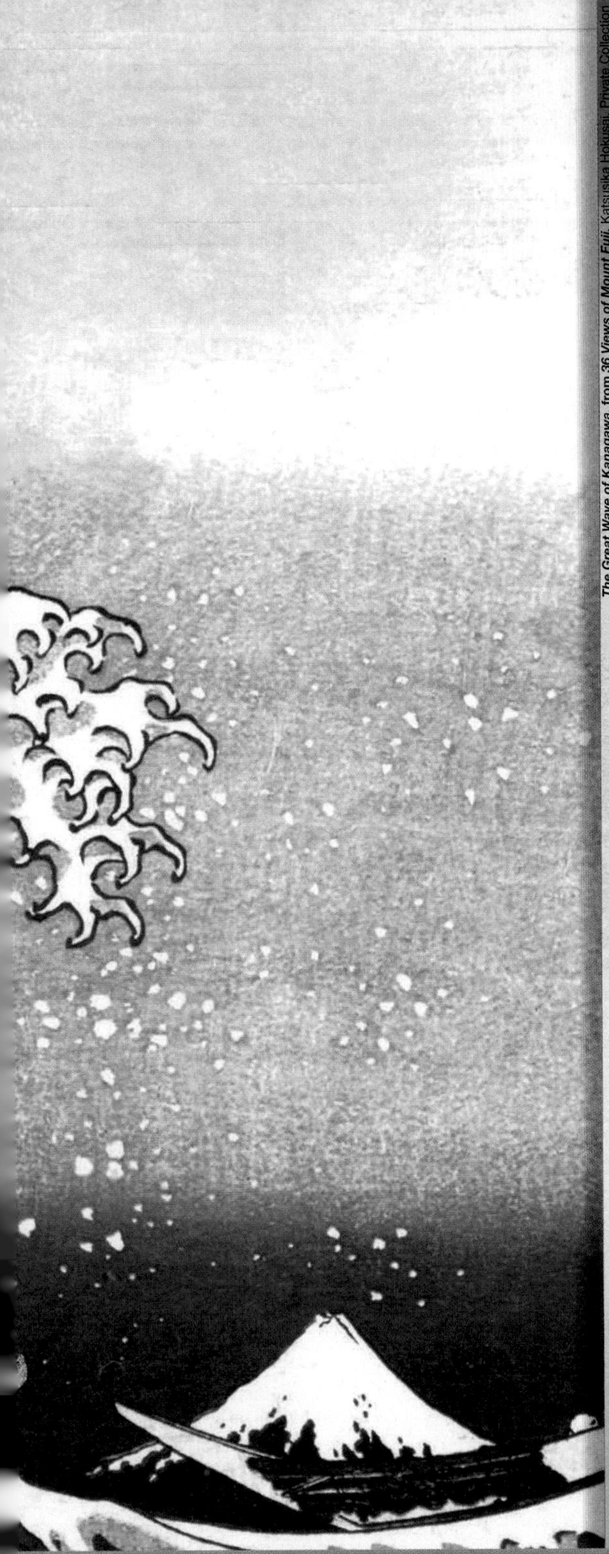

Chinese and Japanese Literature

Standard Course of Study
In This Unit You Will

- Make inferences and draw conclusions based on personal reflection. (WL.1.03.6)
- Summarize situations to examine cause/effect relationships. (IR.2.02.1)
- Analyze elements of argumentative environment. (FA.3.04.11)
- Examine how elements such as irony and symbolism impact theme. (CT.4.02.3)
- Analyze literary devices and explain their effect on the work of world literature. (LT.5.01.3)
- Analyze the importance of tone and mood in world literature. (LT.5.01.4)
- Provide textual evidence to support understanding of and response to world literature. (LT.5.03.3)
- Make inferences, predictions, and draw conclusions based on world literature. (LT.5.03.6)

◀ This woodblock by the Japanese printmaker Katsushika Hokusai is one of the most famous images in Japanese art.

Introduce Unit 3

- Direct students' attention to the title and time period of this unit. Have a student read the quotations. **Ask** them: What idea do the two quotations have in common? **Possible response:** Both quotes suggest that the physical world is always changing.
- Have students look at the art. Read the Humanities note to them, and ask the discussion question.
- Then **ask:** What kinds of literature or themes in literature do you think might come out of this period in Chinese and Japanese history? **Possible response:** Themes in literature might include humans' experiences with the natural world, the violent capacity of nature, the transitory nature of humans' lives, and relationships among humans.

Humanities

The Great Wave off Kanagawa,
by Katsushika Hokusai

The Japanese printmaker Hokusai (1760–1840) was a foremost designer of a type of print known as *ukiyo-e* ("the floating world"). Part of a series entitled *36 Views of Mount Fuji,* the print shown here is one of his best-known.

Use the following question for discussion:

What impression does the small boat convey about the relationship between humanity and nature? **Possible response:** The boat's presence emphasizes the power of nature and suggests that human beings are at the mercy of nature.

Unit Features

Royall Tyler

Each unit features commentary by a contemporary writer or scholar under the heading "From the Author's Desk." Scholar Royall Tyler introduces Unit 3 in Setting the Scene, in which he discusses Japanese women's literature. Later in the unit, he introduces Japanese tanka and haiku. He also contributes his insights on using precise words to create the desired image in readers' minds in the Writing Workshop.

Connections

Every unit contains a feature that connects literature to a related topic, such as art, science, or history. In this unit, students will read: Benjamin Franklin: from ***Poor Richard's Almanack*** on p. 275.

Use the information and questions on the Connections pages to help students enrich their understanding of the selections presented within the unit.

Reading Informational Materials

These selections will help students learn to analyze and evaluate informational texts, such as workplace documents, technical directions, and consumer materials. They will expose students to the organization and features unique to nonnarrative texts.

In this unit, the focus is on Reference Materials. **The Origins of Origami** is on pp. 326–331.

From the Scholar's Desk

Introduce Royall Tyler

- Royall Tyler, who has taught Japanese literature, language, and culture at many universities, introduces the unit and provides insight into the golden age of women's literature in Japan. His insights about Japanese tanka and haiku appear later in the unit on pages 294–295.
- Have students read the introductory paragraph about Royall Tyler. Tell them that he has studied Japanese throughout his life and has translated many Japanese works.
- Use the *From the Author's Desk DVD* to introduce Royall Tyler. Show Segment 1 to provide insight into his scholarly career. After students have watched the segment, **ask:** When did Royall Tyler begin translating Japanese literature?
  Answer: He began translating it in graduate school when he translated plays of the Noh theater.

Private Lives a Thousand Years Ago

- Have students read Tyler's commentary on Japanese literature written by women a thousand years ago.
- Tyler explains the importance of the written Japanese language in the development of Japanese women's literature.
  Ask: How did the development of the written Japanese language affect the writing of women?
  Answer: Japanese was a language that was accessible to women, who were not trained in Chinese, the official written language of the time. Therefore, Japanese became the vehicle for women to record their observations about life and their private lives.
- Tell students that they will also read Royall Tyler's introduction to Japanese tanka and haiku later in this unit. Tyler will also explain the importance of poetry in Japanese society.

Critical Viewing

Possible response: She may be thinking about the beauty of the trees and the mountains. She may be thinking about the scroll on the table.

Setting the Scene

Unit 3 features Chinese and Japanese literature from 1000 B.C. to A.D. 1890. The following essay by Royall Tyler introduces you to a golden age of women's literature in Japan, beginning around A.D. 1000. As you read his essay, the unit introduction that follows, and the literature in Unit 3, immerse yourself in the remarkable literary history of these two cultures.

From the Scholar's Desk
Royall Tyler Talks About the Time Period

Royall Tyler

Introducing Royall Tyler (b. 1936) Born in London, Tyler has taught Japanese literature, language, and culture at Ohio State University, Harvard University, and the Australian National University. His acclaimed translations include *Japanese Tales* and *The Tale of Genji,* which is widely recognized as the world's first novel. Now retired, Tyler lives in Australia and raises alpacas as a hobby.

Private Lives a Thousand Years Ago

> There I was, she thought, as miserable as I could be, and he, simple pastime or not, was sharing his love with somebody else! Well, I'm me! She turned away and sighed, as though to herself, "And we were once so happy together!"
>
> —Murasaki Shikibu, *The Tale of Genji*

This passage is from a novel written in Japan a thousand years ago. The heroine's husband has just returned from years of exile. She loves him very much, but she knows he was unfaithful to her while he was gone. She is jealous and hurt. We understand exactly how she feels.

Creating a New Literature The novel's author, a great writer, was a woman. Other women of her time were writing, too. They were creating a new literature, one focused not on public events but on private lives. Moreover, in an age when men wrote in Chinese, these women were doing so in Japanese, their own language. It happened this way.

In the year 1000, the Japanese were a minor people on the fringes of Asia. China was important to them, but few Japanese people actually traveled there. They had heard of India, the birthplace of their Buddhist faith, and they had a dim notion of a few other lands beyond India—for example, Persia (Iran)—but the rest was a blank. No one living anywhere on earth at this time had a full picture of the world.

▼ **Critical Viewing**
What do you imagine this woman is thinking about in this painting? **[Speculate]**

Teaching Resources

The following resources can be used to enrich or extend the instruction for Unit 3 Introduction.

Unit 3 Resources
- **Names and Terms to Know,** p. 5
- **Focus Questions,** p. 6
- **Listening and Viewing,** p. 42

From the Author's Desk DVD
- **Royall Tyler,** Segment 1

Writing in a Language All Their Own Centuries earlier, the Japanese had learned writing from the Chinese, and by the year 1000 they had turned Chinese characters into a phonetic writing system suitable for their own radically different language. Yet Chinese remained the language of public life. Chinese philosophy and culture remained basic to education, at least for men. Well-born Japanese men served in the government, and for formal purposes they wrote in Chinese, although they did not speak it.

The "important" matters men wrote about were not supposed to concern women any more than women in nineteenth-century America were expected to think about public affairs. The men's domain was "public," the women's "private" and personal. Few women studied Chinese, and the rare woman who could read it kept her knowledge to herself.

Japanese men seldom wrote good Chinese, however, and their subjects were dull. Meanwhile, Japanese women had their native language more or less to themselves and wrote about things that were attractive to anyone. The women who lived around the year 1000 were exceptionally gifted at this type of personal, intimate writing.

How Did She Know? These women's great forerunner in the previous generation was a writer known only as "Michitsuna's Mother." She so resented her husband's neglect that she devoted a book, *The Kagerō Diary*, to describing what life was like for her. No one had done that kind of writing before.

The women of the next generation made their time a literary golden age. Sei Shōnagon's witty *Pillow Book* is full of fresh perceptions and amusing scenes of court life. "I put down things exactly as they came to me," she wrote at the end, "but readers have declared that I can be proud of my work." Murasaki Shikibu, a true genius, wrote *The Tale of Genji*, a masterpiece of Japanese literature and a major world classic. Rich in its understanding of life, her writing often rings so true that you wonder as you read, "How did she know?"

Author Link
For: An online video
Visit: www.PHSchool.com
Web Code: ete-8301

For: More about Royall Tyler
Visit: www.PHSchool.com
Web Code: ete-9301

Reading the Unit Introduction

Reading for Information and Insight Use the following terms and questions to guide your reading of the unit introduction on pages 256–263.

Names and Terms to Know
Confucianism
Taoism
Buddhism
Shogun
Shintoism
Zen
Tanka
Haiku

Focus Questions As you read this introduction, use what you learn to answer these questions:

- Why did Japan shut itself off from the world in the seventeenth century?
- In what ways does early Chinese poetry reflect the culture's philosophy?
- What role did the poetry contest play in developing standards for Japanese poetry?

Reading the Unit Introduction

Tell students that the terms and questions listed here are the key points in this introductory material. This information provides a context for the selections in this unit. Students should use the terms and questions as a guide to focus their reading of the unit introduction. When students have completed the unit introduction, they should be able to identify or explain each of these terms and answer or discuss the Focus Questions.

Concept Connector

After students have read the unit introduction, return to the Focus Questions to review the main points. For key points, see p. 263.

Go Online Author Link Typing in the Web Code when prompted will bring students to a video clip and more information on Royall Tyler.

Using the Timeline

The Timeline can serve a number of instructional purposes, as follows:

Getting an Overview

Use the Timeline to help students get a quick overview of themes and events of the period. This approach will benefit all students but may be especially helpful for Visual/Spatial Learners, English Learners, and Less Proficient Readers. (For strategies in using the Timeline as an overview, see the bottom of this page.)

Thinking Critically

Questions are provided on the facing page. Use these questions to have students review the events, discuss their significance, and examine the "so what" behind the "what happened."

Connecting to Selections

Have students refer to the Timeline when they begin to read individual selections. By consulting the Timeline regularly, students will gain a better sense of the period's chronology. In addition, they will appreciate world events that gave rise to these works of literature.

Projects

Students can use the Timeline as a launching pad for projects like these:

- **Focused Timeline** Have students choose one of the Chinese dynasties identified on the Timeline for further research. Students should then create a smaller, more focused timeline covering the rise, reign, and decline of the dynasty they have chosen. Focused Timelines should include political events and cultural developments.
- **Oral Report** Have students search the Timeline for key events in the development of Japanese literature. Students should then compare this information with the overview of Japanese literature on pp. 261–263. Finally, have students summarize their findings for the class in an oral report.

Chinese, Japanese, and World Events

1000 B.C. 500 B.C. 0

CHINESE AND JAPANESE EVENTS

- **1000 B.C. (China)** The Shang dynasty fell about 100 years earlier.
- **551 (China)** Confucius is born. ▼

- **c. 500s (China)** *The Book of Songs* is compiled.
- **256/255 B.C. (China)** The Chou dynasty is overthrown.
- **221–206 (China)** The Ch'in dynasty reigns. ▼

- **206 (China)** The Han dynasty takes power.
- **200 (Japan)** By this date, the Japanese cultivate irrigated rice.
- **c. 100s A.D. (China)** Buddhism begins to take hold.
- **220 (China)** The Han dynasty is deposed.
- **300s (Japan)** The Yamato emerge as the most powerful clan, opening the way to Chinese cultural influences.
- **365–427 (China)** T'ao Ch'ien, one of China's greatest poets, lives.

WORLD EVENTS

- **c. 1000 B.C. (India)** The Vedic hymns are compiled.
- **1000–800 (Greece)** Tribes evolve into city-states.
- **mid-900s (Israel)** King Solomon reigns over a united country.
- **800s or 700s (Greece)** Homer composes the *Iliad* and the *Odyssey*.
- **600s (India)** Hindu sages flourish in India, recording their thoughts in the Upanishads.
- **400s (Greece)** Sophocles writes *Oedipus the King*.
- **431–404 B.C. (Greece)** Sparta defeats Athens in the Peloponnesian War.
- **330 (Persian Empire)** An inscription recognizes Alexander the Great as lord of the Persian Empire.
- **320 (India)** Chandragupta begins the Maurya dynasty.
- **c. 300 (southern Mexico/Central America)** The Mayas begin to build elaborate cities. ▼

- **392 (Roman empire)** Christianity becomes the official religion of the empire.

Getting an Overview of the Period

Introduction To give an overview of the period, have students indicate the span of dates in the title of the Timeline. Next, point out that the Timeline is divided into Chinese and Japanese Events (on the top) and World Events (on the bottom). Have students scan the Timeline, looking at both the Chinese and Japanese Events and the World Events. Finally, point out that the events in the Timeline often represent beginnings, turning points, and endings (for example, the Han dynasty in China was deposed in A.D. 220).

Key Events Ask students to identify key events that suggest Japanese isolation.
Possible response: The Tokugawa closure in 1639 suggests Japanese isolation.
Ask students to identify one key event that shows a relationship between Japan's isolation and its cultural development.
Possible response: The first Japanese poetry anthology appeared in the 700s, some 1,200 years after *The Book of Song* in China.

A.D. 500 A.D. 1000 A.D. 1500 A.D. 1890

- 618–907 **(China)** The T'ang dynasty rules.
- early 700s **(Japan)** The first works of Japanese prose appear.
- 762 **(China)** The great T'ang poet Li Po dies.
- 770 **(China)** The great T'ang poet Tu Fu dies.
- 794 **(Japan)** A new imperial capital is built at Heian (Kyoto). ◀
- 700s **(Japan)** "Collection of Ten Thousand Leaves," an early poetry anthology, appears.
- 960 **(China)** The Sung dynasty begins.
- c. 1000 **(Japan)** Lady Murasaki Shikibu writes *The Tale of Genji*.
- 1192 **(Japan)** Yoritomo founds the shogunate, a system of rule that continues for 700 years.
- 1279 **(China)** The Sung dynasty ends.
- 1279–1368 **(China)** The Yuan dynasty, founded by Mongols, rules all of China.
- 1300s **(Japan)** First Nō dramas emerge.
- 1368 **(China)** The Ming dynasty reestablishes Chinese rule.

- 1639 **(Japan)** The Tokugawas close Japan to the rest of the world.
- 1644 **(China)** The Ming dynasty is overthrown by armies from Manchuria.
- 1763–1828 **(Japan)** The haiku poet Kobayashi Issa lives.
- 1842 **(China)** China is forced to sign treaties with Western nations.
- 1853 **(Japan)** Commander Perry opens Japan to the world. ▲

- 527 **(Turkey)** Justinian begins to rule the Byzantine empire.
- 500s **(Western Europe)** German tribes like the Franks dominate the region.
- 600s **(Africa)** Islam spreads to North Africa.
- 622 **(Arabian Peninsula)** Muhammad journeys from Mecca to Yathrib, an event that marks the rise of Islam.
- 711 **(Spain)** Muslims enter Spain.
- 800 **(France)** King Charlemagne is crowned emperor by the pope.
- c. 1100 **(France)** The *Song of Roland* is composed.
- 1215 **(England)** King John signs the Magna Carta, limiting royal power.
- 1321 **(Italy)** Dante completes *The Divine Comedy*.
- 1492 **(Americas)** Christopher Columbus reaches the New World. ▶

- 1503–1506 **(Italy)** Leonardo da Vinci paints the *Mona Lisa*.
- 1508–1512 **(Italy)** Michelangelo paints the Sistine Chapel ceiling.
- 1517 **(Germany)** The Reformation begins as Martin Luther posts his Ninety-Five Theses.
- 1558–1603 **(England)** Queen Elizabeth I reigns.

Analyzing the Timeline

1. (a) How many Chinese dynasties are cited on the Timeline? (b) What does this number of dynasties suggest about Chinese society between 1000 B.C. and A.D. 1890? **[Draw Conclusions]**
   Answer: (a) Eight Chinese dynasties appear on the Timeline. (b) Chinese society was fairly stable.
2. (a) What is the earliest development in Japan listed on the Timeline? (b) What does the date of this event suggest about the growth of Japanese civilization? **[Speculate]**
   Answer: (a) The earliest Japanese development is the cultivation of irrigated rice by 200 B.C. (b) The date of this development suggests that Japanese civilization began to develop much later than Chinese civilization.
3. (a) When did the earliest Chinese and Japanese literatures appear? (b) What impact might the development of Chinese literature have had on Japanese literature? **[Analyze Causes and Effects]**
   Answer: (a) The earliest Chinese literature appeared c. 500s B.C.; the earliest Japanese literature appeared in the early A.D. 700s. (b) Chinese literature may have influenced the growth of Japanese literature.
4. (a) In what period did the Yüan dynasty rule China? (b) What was especially significant about the Yüan dynasty? **[Synthesize]**
   Answer: (a) The Yüan dynasty ruled from A.D. 1279–1368. (b) The Yüan dynasty was the first foreign dynasty to rule China.
5. (a) When did the shogunate system of rule emerge in Japan? (b) What event do you think had the most influence on the collapse of the shogunate? **[Speculate]**
   Answer: (a) The shogunate began in Japan in A.D. 1192. (b) The opening of Japan to the world in 1853 probably had the greatest influence on the collapse of the shogunate.

Critical Viewing

1. What does the portrait of Confucius (551 B.C.) suggest about his character? **[Infer]**
   Possible response: The portrait makes Confucius appear wise, authoritative, and benevolent.
2. Consider the architecture of the imperial capital built at Heian, Japan (A.D. 794). What type of government do you think would hold court in this building? **[Speculate]**
   Possible response: The building, with its detailed traditional features, probably would serve as a meeting place for a court concerned with ritual and ceremony.
3. Compare and contrast the appearance of Commander Perry and of the Japanese officials who greet him in the illustration of their meeting (1853). **[Compare and Contrast]**
   Possible response: The dress of Perry and the Japanese officials is markedly different; however, many of the men carry swords and wear hats to indicate rank. Additionally, Perry is physically larger than the Japanese officials.

Literature of the Period

- Poetry is an essential element of Chinese culture. Examples of Chinese poetry, including poems from *The Book of Songs* and poetry by T'ao Ch'ien, Li Po, and Tu Fu, pp. 280–290, offer students a glimpse of this vital cultural force.
- Poetry is no less important in Japanese culture. As students read examples of tanka, pp. 298–299, they will discover the brevity and suggestiveness that characterize Japanese poetry.
- Japanese haiku relies even more on suggestion than does tanka. Students will learn about this form as they read the poetry of Matsuo Bashō, Yosa Buson, and Kobayashi Issa, pp. 300–302.

Themes in World Literature

Close-up on Culture

- Point out that even though the Chinese government has changed radically since 1912, these three schools of thought continue to influence the way of life in China and in many other cultures.
- Have students offer an example of how one of these doctrines affects Chinese culture.
  Possible responses: **Confucianism:** It emphasizes the need to respect authority, so the Chinese honor and obey parents, elders, teachers, and government officials. **Taoism:** It links people with all other forms of life, and teaches that a simple and solitary life is best. **Buddhism:** It is a religion that emphasizes the suffering and sorrows of earthly existence.

Humanities

After students read the Close-up on Culture feature, display Art Transparency 3: The Flight of Emperor Ming Huan to Shu in the **Fine Art Transparencies** booklet. Tell students that painters of the T'ang Dynasty were influenced by Buddhist teachings about harmony and balance in nature. Buddhists believed mountains and water to be two opposing elements of spirituality. Landscapes held a sense of calm and beauty in the face of insignificant human concerns. Encourage students to discuss how Buddhist teachings may have influenced this painting.

Historical Background

China: A Long Line of Dynasties Chinese civilization, which has endured for about 3,500 years, is the world's oldest surviving civilization. It began in the Yellow River basin in northern China when the people who lived there established permanent farming villages. By 1600 B.C., they had developed a complex social and economic system. At about this time, an elite group of kings established authority over northern China and founded the Shang dynasty, the first in a long series of Chinese dynasties.

The Mandate of Heaven The Chinese came to believe that heaven granted each dynastic ruler a mandate, or right to rule. In return for good government, the people owed the ruler complete obedience. If the ruler failed to maintain order, however, the people had the right to rebel. Following are some highlights from China's dynastic history.

The Chou Dynasty (1122–256/255 B.C.) The Shang dynasty was overthrown by a Central Asian people known as the Chou (Zhou), who established the longest of all the Chinese dynasties. Despite political turmoil, the final centuries of the Chou dynasty saw major advances in Chinese philosophy with the founding of Taoism (dou′ iz′ əm) and Confucianism (kən fyoo′ shən iz′ əm) (see box).

Themes in World Masterpieces — Close-up on Culture

Confucianism, Taoism, and Buddhism in Chinese Culture

Chinese culture has been dominated by three schools of thought—Confucianism, Taoism, and Buddhism (bood′ iz əm). Through the centuries, elements of all these schools have influenced the way in which Chinese people live.

Confucianism, the official Chinese state doctrine for over two thousand years, is more of a social philosophy than a religion. Founded by Confucius (kən fyoo′ shəs) (551–479 B.C.), it is primarily concerned with the moral nature of social relationships. It emphasizes the need to respect and obey people in authority, such as heads of households and government officials.

By contrast, Taoism, founded by the legendary Lao Tzu (Lao Zi) (lou′ dzu′), is more concerned with the relation of humanity to the larger world of nature. In the classical Taoist view, human beings are perceived as being merely one of the many manifestations of nature, on an equal level with all other creatures. Taoism teaches that people should withdraw from society and strive to live a simple life.

The third school of thought, Buddhism, began to take hold in China in the second century A.D. during the period of disunity that followed the decline of the Han dynasty. Because Buddhism taught that life on Earth is filled with suffering and is characterized by illusion, it was appealing during a chaotic era.

▼ Language Note
One system of spelling Chinese names in English is called Wade-Giles, and the other is called Pinyin. The following chart shows examples of these two systems.

Wade-Giles	Pinyin
Chou dynasty	Zhou dynasty
Lao Tzu	Lao Zi
Ch'in dynasty	Qin dynasty

In this introduction, the Pinyin spelling appears in parentheses next to the first mention of the Wade-Giles version.

Enrichment

China's Emperors

At the head of each of China's dynasties were its emperors. Emperors ruled China until 1912. The Chinese believed that the emperor was more than human; he was the mediator between heaven and earth. They called the emperor the "son of Heaven" who ruled the "central country."

The emperor lived in the Forbidden City in Beijing with his family and servants. Because the emperor was more than human, almost every detail of his life emphasized his uniqueness and superiority over other humans. Yellow, for example, was the imperial color, and the emperor was the only one allowed to write in red. Each emperor also had an official seal that only he used, and the written character representing the emperor's name was banned from use except by the emperor himself.

The Ch'in Dynasty (221–206 B.C.) By 221 B.C., the feudal state of Ch'in (Qin) had succeeded in unifying China. The Ch'in dynasty was overthrown within fifteen years. Yet it managed to build a system of roads, establish an administrative system that lasted for 2,000 years, and patch together defensive walls on the northern border to form the Great Wall of China. Eventually this wall would stretch for about 4,500 miles!

The Han Dynasty (206 B.C.–A.D. 220) The next dynasty, the Han, produced one of the most glorious eras in Chinese history. During this period, China established trade with Europe and western Asia. One significant effect of increased foreign contacts was the introduction of the Buddhist religion from India (see page 256).

The T'ang Dynasty (618–907) The T'ang (Tang) dynasty is regarded as the Golden Age of Chinese civilization. T'ang rulers created an empire that extended from the Pacific Ocean to the borders of Persia and India, and they established the world's most effective system of government. Major technological advances of the time included the invention of gunpowder and block printing.

The Sung Dynasty (960–1279) Reacting against Buddhist influence, Sung (Song) philosophers created a new school of thought called Neo-Confucianism—a school that would dominate Chinese intellectual life for the next thousand years. Neo-Confucianists unconsciously borrowed from Buddhism, however, in seeking enlightenment through a combination of meditation and moral action.

The Yüan Dynasty (1206–1368) During the late twelfth and early thirteenth centuries, northern China was overrun by Mongol invaders led by Genghis Khan (geŋ′ gis kän′). He established the Yüan (Yuan) dynasty, the first foreign dynasty in China's history. The Sung dynasty, however, ruled in southern China until 1279. One of the many traders to visit China during this period was the Venetian Marco Polo.

The Ming Dynasty (1368–1644) Chinese rule was reestablished with the foundation of the Ming dynasty. Because of lingering resentment from the Mongol conquest, the Ming emperors tried to avoid foreign influence.

The Ch'ing Dynasty (1644–1911/1912) Armies from Manchuria conquered China and established a second foreign dynasty, the Ch'ing (Qing). The country prospered during the early years of the Ch'ing dynasty. Yet unrest ultimately toppled this dynasty and put an end to imperial rule.

Traditional Chinese Government By the time the Ch'ing dynasty was overthrown, imperial rule had lasted in China for thousands of years. Throughout most of this period, the Chinese government was organized into a pyramid-shaped hierarchy. At the top of this hierarchy was an all-powerful emperor, and beneath him were numerous officials.

▲ **Critical Viewing**
The first Ch'in emperor began the Great Wall in the third century B.C., but it was worked on throughout Chinese history. What do you think it reveals about Chinese civilization? Explain. **[Infer]**

Background
Buddhism in China

Buddhism began in India with the thinking and experiences of Siddhartha Gautama. Born around 563 B.C., Gautama was a prince who abandoned his life of privilege and committed himself to the search for enlightenment. He came to be known as the Buddha ("Enlightened One"). Buddhism grew from the Buddha's teachings. The religion spread rapidly throughout India and soon began to move into the rest of Asia along trade routes. Buddhism may have reached China as early as the first century A.D., although it did not take hold until the second century. Although Chinese Buddhism experienced periods of oppression, it remained an important part of Chinese culture.

Background
Marco Polo

Marco Polo (c. 1254–1324) was an Italian trader and writer. In 1271, when Polo was seventeen, he began his journey to China. He reached Kublai Khan's palace three years later. The Khan employed Polo on business in central and northern China and in Southeast Asia, including India. In addition, Polo served as a government official in the Chinese city of Yanghouz for three years. In 1292, Polo began his return to Italy, acting as escort for the wife of the Khan of Persia. After his return in 1295, Polo joined the Venetian forces fighting Genoa and was soon taken prisoner. During his two-year captivity, Polo recorded information about his travels to China and other lands in *Descriptions of the World.* Scholars copied Polo's book, and it soon became the most widely read book in Europe. Historians believe that Polo's recorded travels may have influenced other explorers, including Christopher Columbus.

Critical Viewing

Possible response: The size of the wall and the fact that it was worked on throughout China's history suggest that fear of invasion was a central element in Chinese civilization.

Differentiated Instruction
Solutions for All Learners

Support for Less Proficient Readers
Students may have difficulty grasping the differences between Chinese and American governments. Work with students to prepare a poster-sized Venn diagram in which they compare the Chinese dynasties described with American government. Then, have students present their diagram to the class.

Strategy for English Learners
Direct student groups to draw a timeline for the Chinese dynasties described. Under each dynasty entry, students should include a bulleted list of significant contributions. Ask students to include at least one illustration for each dynasty.

Enrichment for Advanced Readers
Ask students to research the two foreign Chinese dynasties: the Yüan and the Ch'ing. Direct students to focus their research on the effect of foreign rule in China as contrasted with Chinese rule. Student groups can prepare poster-sized Venn diagrams that cite similarities and differences. Ask students to present their diagrams to the class.

Literature Connection

- In the excerpts from *The Pillow Book* by Sei Shōnagon, pp. 308–312, students will find a highly personal depiction of life in the Heian imperial court.
- Students will gain insight into the Zen Buddhist philosophy of life as they read the *Zen Parables*, pp. 320–322.

Critical Viewing

Possible response: The sutra's elegance suggests the refined and ritualized life of the imperial courtiers of Japan's Heian Age.

Humanities

Samurai Commander with War Fan

The painting shows a samurai warrior charging on a horse. He brandishes a fan and a bow as his cape billows out behind.

Use the following question for discussion:

What details in this painting contribute to the depiction of the samurai as a fierce warrior?
Possible response: The samurai's determined expression, confident posture, and formidable armor and accessories create an image of fierceness.

China and the West While China pursued isolation, Europe expanded. In 1793, the Ch'ing emperor refused Britain's request for trading rights, calling the British "barbarians." In 1842, however, China was forced to sign treaties with Westerners when British "barbarians" on warships destroyed the outdated Chinese fleet. By 1900, European powers and Japan had carved China into spheres of influence for themselves.

Japan: Beginnings of Civilization Little is known about the first inhabitants of the Japanese islands, who arrived there several thousand years ago. By 200 B.C., however, the Japanese people had begun to practice farming, using irrigation to cultivate rice. At the same time, a steady flow of immigrants began to arrive from Korea and other regions of continental Asia. This influx of people lasted for centuries and gradually led to the emergence of a distinct Japanese culture.

Yet the nation was not politically unified. Japanese society was divided into tribal organizations called *uji*, or clans, which were dominated by aristocrats and also included warriors and spiritual leaders. Because the islands' mountainous terrain forced settlements in scattered coastal plains or in narrow valleys divided by sharply rising slopes, the clans were able to remain relatively independent.

The Yamato Clan and Chinese Influence During the fourth century A.D., the Yamato emerged as the nation's most powerful clan. Forging a relationship with the Chinese, the Yamato brought many Chinese beliefs to Japanese society, including those associated with Buddhism and Confucianism. The Japanese copied Chinese architectural and artistic forms and clothing styles, and they adapted the Chinese system of writing to the Japanese language. Yamato leaders also reformed the Japanese political structure by using the Chinese system of central imperial rule as a model.

The Heian Age The central government retained its authority for only a brief period. In 794, a new imperial capital was built at Heian (hā′ än′), which is now Kyoto (kē′ ōt′ ō). There, courtiers lived a refined life devoted to elaborate ceremonies and festivals, but the emperor's power began to diminish. The real political authority had slipped into the hands of the powerful, aristocratic Fujiwara family.

Meanwhile, ambitious aristocrats who were not part of the Fujiwara family settled in the countryside, beyond the reach of the central government. There, they established huge estates and assembled bands of warriors, hoping to challenge the authority of the Fujiwaras.

Feudal Japan As rural lords grew more powerful, Japan became a feudal society that was similar in some ways to that of Western Europe. Feudal Japan was dominated by the *samurai* (sam′ ə rī′) class, which included lords, or *daimyo*, and their *samurai* soldiers. Each *samurai* carried

▼ **Critical Viewing**
Which qualities of this fan-shaped sutra, or section of Buddhist scripture, suggest that it belongs to the Heian Age? Explain. **[Connect]**

Enrichment

Art and Architecture of the Heian Age

The fan-shaped sutra shown on p. 258 is an example of Heian art. Its elegance reflects the refined life of courtiers at the new capital of Heian. However, the art of the period was not always so elegant. In the early part of the Heian age, more austere religious art was produced, and Buddhist temples, built in the mountains above the capital, had wooden floors and roofs made of bark rather than tile.

Art of the later Heian period—beginning around 900—embodied the elegance and aesthetic tastes of the capital's courtiers. Late Heian temples were mansion-like structures full of elaborate decorations. Illustrated scrolls known as *emaki* also became popular in this period. The *emaki* combined narrative text and painting. One of the finest *emaki* was a twelfth-century edition of *The Tale of Genji.*

a pair of swords and followed a code of conduct that emphasized bravery, loyalty, and honor.

In 1185, the *daimyo* Minamoto Yoritomo became the most powerful figure in Japan. Later, he accepted the title of *shogun* (shō′ gun′), or chief general. Other shoguns who followed him, however, had trouble unifying the country, and Japan experienced feudal warfare for centuries.

Japan Shuts Out the World In the 1600s, the Tokugawa shoguns created a peaceful, orderly society; strengthened the central government; and built a new capital at Edo (Tokyo). The Tokugawas, however, felt threatened by the arrival of European traders and missionaries. Finally, in 1639, they closed Japan to the world.

▲ Critical Viewing
How is this *samurai* warrior similar to and different from a medieval European knight? **[Compare and Contrast]**

Perry Opens the Door In 1853, a United States fleet under Commander Perry arrived in Edo (Tokyo) Bay, intent on ending Japanese isolation. Japanese leaders, realizing that their weapons were no match for American cannon, granted limited trading rights to Americans. Before long, the United States and other Western nations won additional rights.

Fourteen years after Perry's visit, the Tokugawa shogunate ended. The new emperor called his reign Meiji (mā′ jē′), or "enlightened rule." During the Meiji restoration, many Japanese studied western ways, and by 1900, Japan had become a modern industrial nation.

Japanese Religious Traditions Two major religious faiths, Shintoism (shin′ tō iz′ əm) and Buddhism, were important in Japanese society. By the 500s A.D., the practice of nature worship became known as *Shintoism*, "the way of the gods," to distinguish it from Buddhism. Central to Shintoism was the belief that elements of nature were inhabited by spirits called *kami*. For this reason, a waterfall, a gnarled tree, or a full moon could inspire reverence.

Though popular, Buddhism did not compete with Shintoism. Instead, the Japanese embraced both religions. They looked to Buddhism, which empha-sized life's impermanence, to overcome the sorrows of earthly existence. Military aristocrats favored a form of Buddhism known as Zen. In contrast to other Buddhist sects, Zen rejects the notion that salvation is attained outside of life. Instead, Zen emphasizes the attainment of tranquillity and insight through mental and physical discipline. Both the rituals of the tea ceremony and the rigors of samurai training reflect Zen values.

Critical Viewing

Possible response: The samurai's code of conduct is similar to the chivalric values of a medieval European knight. However, the appearance of the samurai is different from that of a knight.

Historical Background

Comprehension Check

1. What distinguishes Chinese civilization from all other civilizations?
Answer: Chinese civilization is the world's oldest surviving civilization.
2. What factors made the T'ang dynasty the Golden Age of Chinese civilization?
Answer: The T'ang dynasty founded an expansive empire and established the world's most effective system of government. Major technological advances were also made during the T'ang dynasty.
3. What kept Japan from becoming politically unified until the fourth century A.D.?
Answer: Japan's geography—especially its mountains—kept its clans separate and independent.
4. Why did the Tokugawa shoguns close Japan to the outside world in 1639? What event reopened Japan?
Answer: The Tokugawa shoguns felt threatened by European traders and missionaries. Japan was reopened by the arrival of Commander Perry of the United States in 1853.
5. How did Japan and China interact with the West in the second half of the 1800s?
Answer: China was forced to submit to the influences of Europe, and Japan negotiated treaties with the West and emerged as a modern nation.

Critical Thinking

1. What place did the "Mandate of Heaven" hold in the long dynastic history of China? **[Connect]**
Possible response: The "Mandate of Heaven," the common belief that an emperor had a divine right to rule the nation, made it possible for China to remain under the control of imperial dynasties for many centuries.

Answers continued

2. Compare and contrast Buddhism in Chinese and Japanese societies. How did the religion's role in the two nations differ? **[Compare and Contrast]**
Possible response: Buddhism in China offered comfort during the chaotic period at the end of the Han dynasty, but it came into conflict with Neo-Confucianism during the Sung dynasty. Although Buddhism came to Japan via China, the religion was able to comfortably coexist with Shintoism.
3. Why do you think China and Japan responded so differently to the West in the second half of the nineteenth century? **[Speculate]**
Possible response: China's struggles against foreign dominance in the 1300s and 1600s did not prepare it to adapt to the West. However, Japan's early acceptance of influence from China allowed it to adapt more readily to the West, despite Japan's period of isolation from 1639 to 1853.

Background

Chinese Classics

The Book of Songs, or the *Shih Ching,* is indeed the oldest collection of Chinese poetry. But it is only one of a series of books endorsed by Confucius for the training of future leaders of China. Along with *The Book of Songs,* Confucius named the *Book of Changes* or *I Ching,* a book of philosophy; the *Book of History,* which focuses on government; the *Book of Ritual,* which instructed courtiers how to behave; the *Spring and Autumn Annals,* a book of history; and the *Book of Music.* Together, they became known as the Confucian Classics, or *Jing.* For centuries thereafter, students who hoped to gain government positions studied the *Jing.*

Background

T'ao Ch'ien

T'ao Ch'ien (A.D. 365–427), also known as T'ao Yuan-ming, was born into a family of government officials. He began a career in government service. At thirty-five, however, he resigned from his post and settled on a farm on the outskirts of a village. There T'ao Ch'ien spent the rest of his life as a semi-recluse. During his later years, T'ao Ch'ien wrote poetry that expressed his philosophy of living tranquilly. His poetry also exhibits his fondness for a few of his favorite activities, including farming and playing the zither, a stringed instrument similar to a dulcimer.

Critical Viewing

Possible response: Li Po's apparent admiration of the waterfall in the picture suggests that nature was a major inspiration for his poetry.

Literature

China: Philosophy Along with poetry, the most highly valued Chinese literary works are philosophical texts. Of these books, the most notable are *The Analects* of Confucius and the *Tao Te Ching* of Lao Tzu—the principal works of Confucianism and Taoism, respectively (see page 256).

Chinese Poetry As is suggested by the content of civil-service examinations, poetry has always held an especially important place in Chinese culture. Even after the current Communist regime came into power in the mid-twentieth century, poetry continued to be highly valued. In fact, Mao Tse-tung (Mao Zedong; 1893–1976), the leader of the Communist Revolution, was himself a gifted poet.

The oldest collection of Chinese poetry is *The Book of Songs,* or the *Shih Ching.* Compiled around the sixth century B.C., this collection consists of 305 poems, many of which were originally folk songs, focusing on such themes as farming, love, and war. Throughout Chinese history, *The Book of Songs* has retained an honored status in Chinese society, and students have been expected to memorize it.

Despite the importance of *The Book of Songs,* most great Chinese poetry was written after the fall of the Han dynasty. At about the same time that the Han collapsed, poets began writing beautiful, emotive verses using a fairly rigid poetic form known as the *shih* (shə). One of the first masters of the *shih* form, T'ao Ch'ien (Tao Qian) (dou′ chē′ en), is still ranked as one of the finest Chinese poets.

The *shih* form was raised to its greatest heights, however, by the poets of the T'ang dynasty. Among the many talented poets of this period, Li Po (Li Bo) (lē′ bō′) and Tu Fu (Du Fu) (do͞o′ fo͞o′) are highly regarded. Many of Li Po's verses are best described as romantic, imaginative, or playful. Tu Fu, on the other hand, is known for his superb craftsmanship and his command of the language.

Chinese poetry continued to flourish in later ages, and new poetic forms, such as the lyrical *tz'u* form, emerged. Yet the T'ang era, with its many fine poets, has come to be universally acknowledged as the golden age of Chinese poetry.

Chinese Drama and Fiction For the most part, the Chinese have always regarded drama and fiction as

The Poet Li Po Admiring a Waterfall, Hokusai, Honolulu Academy of Arts

▼ **Critical Viewing** What does this picture of the Chinese poet Li Po suggest about the source of inspiration for his poetry? Explain. **[Infer]**

Enrichment

Poetic Songs

The word *tz'u* means "words" or "lyrics." As this name suggests, *tz'u* poems are written to be set to music. The form first came into being in the eighth century A.D., when poets began composing new lyrics for popular songs. Because the length of lines in the original songs varied greatly to fit the twists and rhythms of the melodies, the lines of the new lyrics also varied in length. As a result, the *tz'u* form is often referred to as "long and short lines," in contrast to the *shih,* in which every line of a given poem has the same number of words.

Themes in World Masterpieces — A Living Tradition

Bertolt Brecht and Chinese Drama

The German playwright Bertolt Brecht (ber´ tôlt brekt´) (1898–1956) was one of the most innovative dramatists of the modern age. Rejecting the traditional Western approach to theater, he established a new type of drama known as "epic theater." In doing so, he was heavily influenced by traditional Chinese theater.

A fervent political activist, Brecht used his plays to convey political and social messages. He felt that audiences would not grasp his messages, however, if they became emotionally involved in the stage action. As a result, his epic theater employs techniques to distance the audience from the characters and action.

Many of Brecht's distancing techniques reflect the influence of traditional Chinese theater. As in Chinese dramas, the actors in Brecht's plays express an awareness that they are being watched and at times address the audience directly. In addition, rather than submerging themselves in the emotions of their characters, the actors merely demonstrate these emotions. An actor might demonstrate fear by simply rubbing white makeup on his or her face.

Another similarity between Brecht's plays and the Chinese theater is the exaggerated, highly stylized manner in which the actors move. Still another similarity is that both types of drama generally blend dialogue with singing and dancing, performed to the accompaniment of musicians who sit in full view.

Two of Brecht's plays that most clearly exhibit the influence of Chinese theater are *The Good Woman of Setzuan* (1943) and *The Caucasian Chalk Circle* (1948). The first is set in China, and the second was inspired by a thirteenth-century Chinese play.

inferior to poetry. Despite this fact, however, the Chinese have produced a number of notable dramas and works of fiction.

The golden age of Chinese drama occurred during the Yuan dynasty. By this time, the Chinese already had a longstanding tradition of dramatic entertainments involving singing and dancing. Like these earlier spectacles, the plays produced during the Yuan dynasty combined singing and dancing with dialogue, but they differed from their predecessors in that they had a consistent plot. Among the most famous plays written during this period are *The Romance of the Western Chamber* by Wang Shih-fu (Wang Shi-fu) and *Injustice Suffered by Tou-o* by Kuan Han-ch'ing (Guan Han-qing).

Although the Chinese had a rich oral tradition that included countless legends and folk tales, Chinese fiction did not come into its own until the Ming and Ch'ing dynasties. The most famous Chinese novel, *Dream of the Red Chamber* by Ts'ao Chan (Cao Zhan), was written in the eighteenth century. A long, complicated work filled with penetrating psychological insights, this novel chronicles the decline of a prominent aristocratic family.

Japan: Poetry Poetry is one of the oldest and most popular means of expression and communication in Japanese culture. Although poetry had already existed for centuries as part of an oral tradition, the first anthology of Japanese poetry, the *Man'yoshu*, or "Collection of Ten Thousand Leaves,"

Themes in World Literature

A Living Tradition

- Point out to students that classic literary traditions stretch across time and culture.
- **Ask:** Why was Bertolt Brecht attracted to the techniques of Chinese drama?
  Possible response: Brecht was a political activist who wanted to communicate political and social messages rather than create characters that would distract his audience from his messages. Similarly, Chinese dramatic techniques kept audiences at a distance from emotional involvement with characters.
- **Ask** students to give an example of a Chinese dramatic technique that distances the audience.
  Possible response: Rather than assuming the emotions of a character, an actor steps outside of the character, lets the audience know that he or she is being watched, and often speaks directly to the audience.

Background

The Evolution of Chinese Fiction

Dream of the Red Chamber is still considered China's greatest novel. Chinese fiction evolved dramatically in the four centuries before Ts'ao Chan wrote his masterpiece. Through the T'ang dynasty, Chinese fiction focused primarily on adventure, love, and the supernatural, rather than on the psychological realities of *Dream of the Red Chamber.* More importantly, the earlier Chinese fiction was written in an elevated, literary language that greatly limited its audience.

Things started to change during the Yuan dynasty. Commercial printers in China began printing novels for a mass market. The language of fiction shifted to vernacular Chinese. Fiction continued to address adventure, although most popular novels of the fourteenth and fifteenth centuries dealt with historical subjects. In the sixteenth century, however, more complex subject matter began to appear. Novels began to explore religion, social manners, and domestic life. Finally, in the eighteenth century, Ts'ao Chan's novel set the standard for Chinese fiction.

Themes in World Literature

A Writer's Voice

The Humanity of Kakinomoto Hitomaro

Hitomaro's poetry has earned him a reputation as one of the finest writers in the Japanese poetic tradition. He was one of the main contributors to the poetic collection *Collection of Ten Thousand Leaves.* In both his public and his personal poems, Hitomaro conveys a sense of optimism; an awareness of human concerns, motivations, and limitations; and a belief in the unity of humanity and nature.

Themes in World Literature

A Writer's Voice

- Point out that, while Hitomaro was a voice for three Japanese emperors, he still wrote poems using emotionally moving words about his personal experiences. Have a student read aloud the excerpt.
- **Ask:** What figure of speech does the poet use to describe his dead wife?
  Answer: He uses the simile of a soaring morning bird.
- **Ask:** How does the poet express sorrow?
  Possible response: He mentions that the bird is hidden from "our world" and also describes their hungry, whimpering child whom he can comfort and help only by holding him in his arms.
- **Ask:** Why doesn't the poet feed his hungry son?
  Answer: He cannot find food to give him.

Background

Lady Murasaki Shikibu

Japanese novelist and diarist Lady Murasaki Shikibu (c. 978–c. 1014) is the celebrated author of *The Tale of Genji.* This tale of adventure and courtly love is undisputedly one of the greatest works of Japanese prose literature. The book details the life of Genji, or "the Shining One," as he was called. Genji was a prince known for his physical attractiveness. This novel is particularly renowned for its beautiful descriptions of nature and of life in a Japanese court. Some historians consider *Genji* the first novel ever written. Although the exact date of its writing is uncertain, some scholars believe it was completed by 1010.

did not appear until the eighth century. Containing more than four thousand poems, the anthology includes works by poets from a wide range of social classes. The anthology makes it clear that poetry was an integral part of daily life in ancient Japanese society.

Poetry Contests In the centuries that followed, Japanese emperors and their courts became increasingly interested in and supportive of the efforts of poets. The court held regular poetry contests and published a series of poetry anthologies that included the best poems of the time.

Nearly all the poems in these anthologies were written in tanka form, consisting of five lines of five, seven, five, seven, and seven syllables. In previous centuries, the choka, consisting of an unlimited number of alternating lines of five and seven syllables, had rivaled the tanka in popularity. However, as the court began playing an active role in establishing poetic standards, an increasing emphasis was placed on brevity, and the choka form was almost completely abandoned.

The Haiku During the age of Japanese feudalism, groups of poets worked together to write chains of interlocking tanka, known as renga. Each tanka within a renga was divided into verses of seventeen and fourteen syllables, composed by different poets.

Themes in World Masterpieces — A Writer's Voice

The Humanity of Kakinomoto Hitomaro

Little is known about the life of poet Kakinomoto Hitomaro (kä´ kē´ nä´ mō´ tō´ hē´ tō´ mä´ rō´), who lived during the late seventh and early eighth centuries A.D. Yet from his poetry we can infer that he was extremely dignified, genuine, and perceptive.

Hitomaro served as the court poet for three Japanese emperors and wrote a number of poems extolling the causes of the rulers he served. In other poems, he relates his personal experiences, both triumphs and tragedies, in a style that enables readers to share those experiences. For example, in "I Loved Her Like the Leaves" (translated by Geoffrey Bownas), he expresses deep sorrow for the death of his wife:

. . . To the wide fields where the heat haze shimmers,
Hidden in a white cloud,
White as white mulberry scarf,
She soared like the morning bird
Hidden from our world like the setting sun.
The child she left as token
Whimpers, begs for food; but always
Finding nothing that I might give,
Like birds that gather rice-heads in their beaks,
I pick him up and clasp him in my arms. . . .

Enrichment

The Influence of Nō Theater

Although Nō theater is vastly different from traditional Western drama, it has influenced Western literature. Along with other Asian literary forms, Nō plays showed writers in America and Europe a style based on suggestion, image, and strict formal conventions. These aspects of Nō had a great impact on two of the twentieth century's most important poets.

The American poet Ezra Pound discovered Nō in 1913, when he received manuscript translations of Chinese and Japanese literature. Pound completed the translations and published Nō plays. Like haiku, Nō helped Pound shape such poetic ideas as Imagism.

Pound also introduced the Irish poet William Butler Yeats to Nō. Impressed by its form and content, Yeats wrote his own Nō-like *Four Plays for Dancers.* Yeats hoped to create a new type of theater using elements from Nō and other sources. Yeats wrote, "I have invented a new form of drama, distinguished, indirect, and symbolic. . . . ."

Eventually, the opening verse of a renga, known as the hokku, developed into a distinct literary form, consisting of three lines of five, seven, and five syllables. The haiku (hī′ ko͞o′), the name by which this verse form came to be known, soon became more popular than the tanka.

Three famous haiku masters were Matsuo Bashō (mä′ tzo͞o′ ō bä′ shō′), Yosa Buson (yō′ sä′ bo͞o′ sän′), and Kobayashi Issa (kō′ bä′ yä′ shē′ ē′ sä′).

Japanese Prose Appearing early in the eighth century, the first works of Japanese prose, the *Kojiki*, or "Record of Ancient Matters," and *Nihon shoki*, or "Chronicles of Japan," focused on Japanese history.

Among the court ladies who vividly captured the lives of the Heian aristocracy in prose were Murasaki Shikibu (mo͞o′ rä sä′ kē shē′ kē bo͞o′) and Sei Shōnagon (sā′ shō′ nä′ gōn′). Aside from Lady Murasaki Shikibu's novel *The Tale of Genji*, the most famous early Japanese prose work may be *The Tale of the Heike*. Written by an unknown author during the thirteenth century, this work presents a striking portrait of war-torn Japan during the early stages of the age of feudalism. Another important work of prose produced during the age of feudalism is *Essays in Idleness*, a loosely organized collection of insights, reflections, and observations written by a Buddhist priest named Kenko.

Japanese Drama Nō plays, the earliest surviving form of Japanese drama, emerged during the fourteenth century. In some respects, the Nō theater is like the drama of ancient Greece: The plays are performed on an almost-bare stage by a small but elaborately costumed cast of actors wearing masks; the actors are accompanied by a chorus; and the plays are written either in verse or in highly poetic prose. Yet the dramas themselves are decidedly Japanese, reflecting many Shinto and Buddhist beliefs.

▲ **Critical Viewing**
This illustration comes from an edition of *The Tale of Genji*, the great Japanese novel by Lady Murasaki Shikibu. Judging by this picture, what would you expect to find in the novel? Why? **[Speculate]**

Critical Viewing

Possible response: The delicately beautiful branches, leaves, and flowers encourage expectations of extensive descriptions of nature's beauty.

Literature of the Period

Comprehension Check

1. What two literary forms were most highly valued in China?
   Answer: Poetry and philosophical texts were the most highly valued Chinese literary forms.
2. What era is considered the golden age of Chinese poetry?
   Answer: The T'ang era is the golden age of Chinese poetry.
3. Name two women of the Japanese court who portrayed in prose the lives of the Heian aristocracy.
   Answer: Both Murasaki Shikibu and Sei Shōnagon wrote prose about the lives of the Heian aristocracy.

Critical Thinking

1. What indicates the importance of poetry in Chinese and Japanese societies? Explain. **[Analyze]**
   Possible response: Such details as the presence of poetry in Chinese civil service examinations, the study of *The Book of Songs* by Chinese students, and the sponsoring of poetry contests by the Japanese court all suggest that poetry was valued highly at all levels of both societies.
2. What do the range of styles of the Chinese poets T'ao Ch'ien, Li Po, and Tu Fu suggest about the *shih* form in which they all wrote? **[Infer]**
   Possible response: Although *shih* is a rigid form, it allows for a wide range of styles.
3. The Japanese poetic forms of tanka and haiku are both characterized by brevity. What does that brevity suggest about writing in these forms? **[Analyze]**
   Possible response: The extreme brevity of tanka and haiku requires poets to use clear images and suggestion to get the maximum effect from each word.

Concept Connector

Have students discuss the Focus Questions on p. 253. Students' discussion should include the following points:

Reasons Japan isolated itself:
- Tokugawa shoguns created peaceful, orderly society.
- Tokugawa felt threatened by the arrival of European traders and missionaries and closed Japan to the world in 1639.

Ways that early Chinese poetry reflects the culture's philosophy:
- Confucianism, which began in the sixth century B.C., emphasized social relationships and obeying authority.
- *The Book of Songs* was highly influential, and students were expected to memorize it.
- Poetry was included in Chinese civil service examinations.

Role of the Japanese poetry contest:
- Japanese royal court held poetry contests and began establishing poetic standards.
- The court preferred brevity. The shorter form, tanka, replaced the much longer form, choka.

Standard Course of Study

Goal 2: INFORMATIONAL READING

IR.2.02.1	Summarize situations to examine cause/effect relationships.
IR.2.02.2	Show clear, logical connection among cause/effect events.
IR.2.03.2	Prioritize and organize information to construct an explanation to answer a question.

Goal 4: CRITICAL THINKING

CT.4.04.1	Identify clear criteria for evaluation of work of others.
CT.4.04.2	Apply criteria to evaluate others using reasoning and substantiation.

Goal 6: GRAMMAR AND USAGE

GU.6.01.2	Analyze author's use of language to demonstrate understanding of expression.
GU.6.02.1	Edit for agreement, tense choice, pronouns, antecedents, case, and complete sentences.

Step-by-Step Teaching Guide	Pacing Guide
PRETEACH	
• Administer Vocabulary and Reading Warm-ups as necessary.	5 min.
• Engage students' interest with the motivation activity.	5 min.
• Read and discuss author and background features. **FT**	10 min.
• Introduce the Literary Analysis Skill: Aphorisms. **FT**	5 min.
• Introduce the Reading Strategy: Questioning Causes and Effects. **FT**	10 min.
• Prepare students to read by teaching the selection vocabulary. **FT**	
TEACH	
• Informally monitor comprehension while students read independently or in groups. **FT**	30 min.
• Monitor students' comprehension with the Reading Check notes.	as students read
• Reinforce vocabulary with Vocabulary Builder notes.	as students read
• Develop students' understanding of aphorisms with the Literary Analysis annotations. **FT**	5 min.
• Develop students' ability to question causes and effects with the Reading Strategy annotations. **FT**	5 min.
ASSESS/EXTEND	
• Assess students' comprehension and mastery of the Literary Analysis and Reading Strategy by having them answer the Apply the Skills questions. **FT**	15 min.
• Have students complete the Vocabulary Lesson and the Grammar and Style Lesson. **FT**	15 min.
• Apply students' ability to show connections between ideas by using the Writing Lesson. **FT**	45 min. or homework
• Apply students' understanding by using one or more of the Extend Your Learning activities.	20–90 min. or homework
• Administer Selection Test A or Selection Test B. **FT**	15 min.

Resources

Print

Unit 3 Resources

Transparency

Graphic Organizer Transparencies

Print

Reader's Notebook [L2]

Reader's Notebook: Adapted Version [L1]

Reader's Notebook: English Learner's Version [EL]

Unit 3 Resources

Technology

Listening to Literature Audio CDs [L2, EL]

Reader's Notebook: Adapted Version Audio CD [L1, L2]

Print

Unit 3 Resources

General Resources

Technology

Go Online: Research [**L3**]
Go Online: Self-test [**L3**]
ExamView®, **Test Bank [L3]**

Choosing Resources for Differentiated Instruction

[**L1**] Special Needs Students
[**L2**] Below-Level Students
[**L3**] All Students
[**L4**] Advanced Students
[**EL**] English Learners

For Vocabulary and Reading Warm-ups and for Selection Tests, **A** signifies "less challenging" and **B** "more challenging." For Graphic Organizer transparencies, **A** signifies "not filled in" and **B** "filled in."

FT Fast Track Instruction: To move the lesson more quickly, use the strategies and activities identified with **FT**.

Scaffolding for Less Proficient and Advanced Students

The leveled Critical Thinking questions after selections progress in the levels of thinking required to answer them. To address the needs of your different students, you may use the (a) level questions for your less proficient students and the (b) level questions with your on-level and advanced students. The occasional (c) level questions are appropriate for your advanced students.

PRENTICE HALL **TeacherEXPRESS**™ Plan · Teach · Assess Use this complete suite of powerful teaching tools to make lesson planning and testing quicker and easier.

PRENTICE HALL **StudentEXPRESS**™ Learn · Study · Succeed Use the interactive textbook (online and on CD-ROM) to make selections and activities come alive with audio and video support and interactive questions.

Monitoring Progress

Before students read these selections, administer **Diagnostic Test 3 (*Unit 3 Resources*, pp. 2–4).** This test will determine students' level of readiness for the reading and vocabulary skills.

Go Online Professional Development **For:** Information about Lexiles
Visit: www.PHSchool.com
Web Code: eue-1111

PRETEACH

Motivation

To engage students' interest in the selections, bring one fortune cookie to class for each student. Lead students in a discussion about the appeal of fortune cookies. Tell students that the words of wisdom in the *Tao Te Ching* and *The Analects* are concentrated into pithy verses, models for the messages inside many fortune cookies, although fortune cookies were invented in the United States.

1 Background

More About the Authors

Both Lao Tzu and Confucius lived during a time of political turmoil and intellectual ferment known as the period of the Warring States. Both authors lamented the breakdown of moral and social order that characterized this tragic period of Chinese history.

Lao Tzu's response to the tragedy of his times can be seen in Taoism's emphasis on understanding the universe as a means for self-preservation. However, while Lao Tzu looked to the mysteries of nature, Confucius looked to humanity itself for solutions to China's crisis.

Geography Note

Draw students' attention to the map on this page. Point out that China encompasses an enormous land mass; and yet the philosophies of two men, Lao Tzu and Confucius, influenced people all across China.

Build Skills | Philosophical Texts

1 *from the* Tao Te Ching • *from* The Analects

Lao Tzu
(c. sixth century B.C.)

Lao Tzu (lou′ dzu′), which means "Old Master" or "Ancient One," is the name given to the author of a book called the *Tao Te Ching*, one of the two basic texts of Taoist philosophy.

The Legend of Lao Tzu No one knows exactly who the "Old Master" was or when he lived, though it seems most likely that he lived during the sixth century B.C. According to legend, he remained in his mother's womb for sixty-two years before birth and emerged as a white-haired old man. He then served as Keeper of the Archives in the ancient Chinese kingdom of Chou. Unhappy with the political situation of his day, he mounted a black ox and headed for a western pass, hoping to leave the chaos in China. As he approached the pass, the gate-keeper recognized him as a sage and refused to let him through unless he wrote down some words of wisdom. Lao Tzu proceeded to write the 5,000-word *Tao Te Ching* and was allowed to depart through the pass. Some say he was 160 years old when he departed, while others put his age at 200.

The Philosophy of Lao Tzu *Tao Te Ching* is translated into English as *The Way and Its Power.* In writing this book, Lao Tzu had two primary concerns: understanding the way of the universe and using that understanding for self-preservation. He was not interested in how to win fame, glory, honor, or wealth, but rather in how to survive. Some of the passages of the *Tao Te Ching* seem to be addressed to a ruler, advising how to ensure the survival of a kingdom in a time of political upheaval. Others are addressed to anyone who wishes to understand the fundamental principles of existence and to use them to preserve himself or herself in a chaotic world.

Confucius
(551–479 B.C.)

The ideas of Confucius (kən fyo͞o′ shəs) have shaped the pattern of Chinese life for over two thousand years, yet the details of Confucius's life remain a mystery. No writings from his own hand are known to exist. *The Analects*, or collected sayings of Confucius, were compiled long after his death by disciples of his disciples.

A Transmitter of Truth Confucius was a scholar from the state of Lu, now part of the Shantung province in northeast China. Confucius wished to be an adviser to kings but never achieved that goal. Instead, he made his living by wandering from place to place instructing any young men who appeared to have talent for learning. He considered himself to be a transmitter of ancient truths and believed that the values of the ancient golden age were generally ignored by his generation. In his opinion, his generation cared more about appearances than about the soul.

In all of his teachings, Confucius emphasized the importance of moral conduct. He believed that people in positions of authority, such as political officials, should maintain high standards for themselves, even when out of office.

A Teacher of Tradition Confucius lived at a time when corruption and civil strife raged in China. He taught that by following tradition and authority with the proper spirit of reverence, the country's moral health could be restored.

The words of one who warned of the decline of tradition became a tradition in their own right. Starting in the second century B.C., under the Han emperors, Confucianism became an official state doctrine and its study was required of all who served in government.

Preview

Connecting to the Literature

Have you ever heard the expression "Sometimes, less is more"? Often, the best way to say something is also the simplest way. The *Tao Te Ching* and *The Analects* both illustrate this principle, conveying profound ideas in short, simple statements.

NC Standard Course of Study

- Summarize situations to examine cause/effect relationships. (IR.2.02.1)
- Make inferences, predictions, and draw conclusions based on world literature. (LT.5.03.6)

❷ Literary Analysis

Aphorisms

Aphorisms, sometimes called maxims or proverbs, are short statements expressing general truths or principles. Here are two famous aphorisms:

- "A penny saved is a penny earned." (Benjamin Franklin)
- "Look before you leap." (John Heywood)

The *Tao Te Ching* and *The Analects* are collections of philosophical aphorisms that express universal truths about life. They are not fully reasoned explanations; instead, these selections provide a hint of truth to get readers thinking and leave them to draw conclusions.

Comparing Literary Works

Lao Tzu and Confucius both embrace the idea of a Tao, a "way" that refers to the force that controls the universe. Confucius speaks of this "way" as a "moral force" with which people should align their behavior, but Lao Tzu teaches that the Tao is a natural order with which people should not interfere. As you read, notice the examples each philosopher uses to illustrate and support his essential ideas.

❸ Reading Strategy

Questioning Causes and Effects

These selections offer lessons by showing causes and effects. For example, Lao Tzu says, "Not to honor men of worth will keep the people from contention." However, Lao Tzu does not explain why this statement is true. When you **question causes and effects,** you can fully understand the author's message. Use a chart like the one shown to analyze cause-and-effect relationships and to identify the principles they demonstrate.

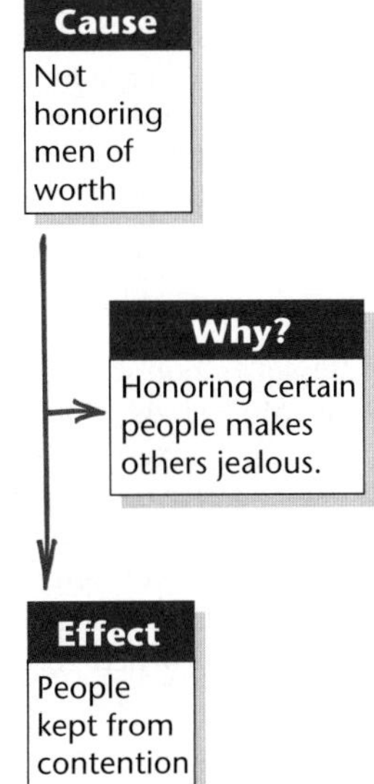

Vocabulary Builder

manifestations (man′ ə fes tā′ shənz) *n.* material forms (p. 266)

contention (kən ten′ shən) *n.* disputing; quarreling (p. 266)

calamity (kə lam′ ə tē) *n.* deep trouble (p. 267)

submissive (sub mis′ iv) *adj.* yielding; giving in without resistance (p. 267)

homage (häm′ ij) *n.* act of reverence and respect (p. 269)

chastisements (chas′ tiz mənts) *n.* punishments (p. 269)

ritual (rich′ o͞o əl) *n.* observance of prescribed rules (p. 269)

bias (bī′əs) *n.* prejudice; partiality (p. 269)

Differentiated Instruction — Solutions for All Learners

Support for Special Needs Students
Have students read the adapted version of *The Analects* in the ***Reader's Notebook: Adapted Version.*** This version provides basic-level instruction in an interactive format with questions and write-on lines. Completing these pages will prepare students to read the selection in the Student Edition.

Support for Less Proficient Readers
Have students read *The Analects* in the ***Reader's Notebook.*** This version provides basic-level instruction in an interactive format with questions and write-on lines. After students finish the selection in the ***Reader's Notebook,*** have them complete the questions and activities in the Student Edition.

Support for English Learners
Have students read *The Analects* in the ***Reader's Notebook: English Learner's Version.*** This version provides basic-level instruction in an interactive format with questions and write-on lines. Completing these pages will prepare students to read the selection in the Student Edition.

❷ Literary Analysis

Aphorisms

- Explain to students that aphorisms are well suited to conveying universal messages because they are brief and well phrased.
- Discuss with students the meanings of these examples from *Poor Richard's Almanack:* "Be slow in choosing a friend, slower in changing;" "Early to bed, early to rise, makes a man healthy, wealthy, and wise."
- Point out that Franklin's aphorisms reflect American values. Encourage students to look for insights about ancient Chinese culture in these selections.

❸ Reading Strategy

Questioning Causes and Effects

- Make sure that students recognize the cause-and-effect relationship in "Not to honor men of worth will keep the people from contention": Lao Tzu implies that honoring important men will cause contention. Review the graphic organizer.
- Give students a copy of **Reading Strategy Graphic Organizer A** in ***Graphic Organizer Transparencies,*** p. 47. Help students use the organizer to explain the cause-and-effect relationship in this aphorism: "Not to value goods which are hard to come by will keep them from theft." **Answer: Cause:** Not valuing goods which are hard to obtain; **Why:** Valuing rare goods creates jealousy. **Effect:** People will not steal the goods.
- Encourage students to identify and evaluate the cause-and-effect relationships described in these selections.

Vocabulary Builder

- Pronounce each vocabulary word for students, and read the definitions as a class. Have students identify any words with which they are already familiar.

TEACH

Facilitate Understanding

For the *Tao Te Ching,* remind students about Thomas Jefferson's statement that the government that governs least governs best. Have students compare Lao Tzu's philosophy of government with Jefferson's philosophy and with modern American government.

For *The Analects,* have students imagine Confucius as a parent. Discuss how a Confucian family would differ from modern families. Of what aspects of modern life might Confucius approve or disapprove?

1 About the Selection

This selection exemplifies the Taoist belief that life is a mystery that cannot be understood or even described by conventional means. Acceptance of the mystery of life gives the verse its air of contradiction and rejection of everyday logic. Behind the words, however, lies a philosophy based on aligning oneself with the universe. Explain to students that when Lao Tzu advocates "no action," he does not mean simply doing nothing. He means doing nothing that is contrary to the natural course of the universe or society.

2 Reading Strategy

Questioning Causes and Effects

- Read aloud the first section of the *Tao Te Ching* with students. Ask them to recall other theories of the origin of the universe.
- **Ask** students: How does Lao Tzu propose that one can understand cause and effect in the universe?
  Answer: Lao Tzu suggests that one must rid oneself of desire to observe secrets, or causes, in the universe. Simultaneously, one must allow desire to observe manifestations, or effects.
- **Ask** students the Reading Strategy question.
  Answer: A wise leader has intimidated the clever so that they will not disrupt the natural course of the universe and society. The effect is order.

1 from the Tao Te Ching

Lao Tzu *translated by* D. C. Lau

Background Early Taoists and Confucianists both believed the Tao was the force that controlled the universe. However, as these selections demonstrate, Taoists differed from Confucianists in that they did not ascribe human moral qualities to the Tao. They considered it as being beyond the scope of human concerns, but they believed that people could see its workings by observing nature.

I

The way that can be spoken of
Is not the constant way;
The name that can be named
Is not the constant name.
The nameless was the beginning of heaven and earth;
The named was the mother of the myriad creatures.
2 Hence always rid yourself of desires in order to observe its secrets;
But always allow yourself to have desires in order to observe its
manifestations.
These two are the same
But diverge in name as they issue forth.
Being the same they are called mysteries,
Mystery upon mystery—
The gateway of the manifold secrets.

Vocabulary Builder
manifestations (man′ ə fes tā′ shən) *n.* material forms

III

Not to honor men of worth will keep the people from contention; not to value goods which are hard to come by will keep them from theft; not to display what is desirable will keep them from being unsettled of mind.

Therefore in governing the people, the sage empties their minds but fills their bellies, weakens their wills but strengthens their bones. He always keeps them innocent of knowledge and free from desire, and ensures that the clever never dare to act.

Do that which consists in taking no action, and order will prevail.

Vocabulary Builder
contention (kən ten′ shən) *n.* disputing; quarreling

Reading Strategy
Questioning Causes and Effects What causes the clever not to act, and what is the effect of this inaction?

Differentiated Instruction Solutions for All Learners

Accessibility at a Glance

	from the Tao Te Ching	*from* The Analects
Context	Early Chinese Taoist philosophy	The philosophy of Confucianism
Language	Syntax: many infinitive phrases	Each aphorism starts with the clause "The Master said, . . ."
Concept Level	Accessible (Respect the order of the universe.)	Accessible (Keep your promises.)
Literary Merit	Challenging Taoist aphorisms	Meaningful Confucian aphorisms
Lexile	1080L	1110L
Overall Rating	More Challenging	Average

Poet on a Mountain Top, Shen Chou, The Nelson-Atkins Museum of Art, Kansas City, Missouri

❸

IX

Rather than fill it to the brim by keeping it upright
Better to have stopped in time;[1]
Hammer it to a point
And the sharpness cannot be preserved for ever;

There may be gold and jade to fill a hall
But there is none who can keep them.
❺ To be overbearing when one has wealth and position
Is to bring <u>calamity</u> upon oneself.
To retire when the task is accomplished

Is the way of heaven.

XLIII

The most <u>submissive</u> thing in the world can ride roughshod over the hardest in the world—that which is without substance entering that which has no crevices.

That is why I know the benefit of resorting to no action. The teaching that uses no words, the benefit of resorting to no action, these are beyond the understanding of all but a very few in the world.

1. **Rather than . . . in time** These lines refer to a container that stands in position when empty but overturns when full.

❹ **Critical Viewing**
Which elements in this painting support the ideas expressed in the Tao Te Ching? **[Connect]**

Vocabulary Builder
calamity (kə lam′ ə tē) *n.* deep trouble

Vocabulary Builder
submissive (sub mis′ iv) *adj.* yielding; giving in without resistance

❻  **Reading Check**
What does Lao Tzu say is "the way of heaven"?

❸ Humanities

Poet on a Mountain Top,
by Shen Chou (Chen Zhou)

Shen Chou (1427–1509) was an extraordinarily versatile Chinese painter of the Ming dynasty. He was among the most important painters of the Wu school, a group of *wenren*—amateur painters whose work stood apart from the accepted courtly styles of the time. Shen Chou's work demonstrates his interest in the many aspects of nature and is characterized by confidence, calm, and warmth.

Use the following question for discussion:

How does this painting depict the relationship between humanity and nature?
Possible response: The only human elements in the painting—a small house partially obscured by rocks and trees and a tiny figure—are less striking than the cliffs and waves.

❹ Critical Viewing

Possible response: The emphasis on the power of nature supports ideas in the *Tao Te Ching.* The figure, far less significant than the landscape, appears inactive in the face of natural forces.

❺ Critical Thinking

Relate

- Ask a volunteer to read the bracketed passage.
- **Invite** students to name examples of people who have brought calamity upon themselves by going too far.
  Possible responses: Napoleon, Macbeth and Baron Frankenstein are possible suggestions.

❻ Reading Check

Answer: "The way of heaven" is to retire when the job is done.

Differentiated Instruction
Solutions for All Learners

Support for Less Proficient Readers

Some students may have difficulty with the metaphors in section *IX.* Point out that in this poem one's life is compared to a container. Ask students why the container of life should not be filled. Then explain that the hammer metaphor compares one's compulsive effort to improve one's life. Ask students why such an effort is pointless.

Support for English Learners

Explain the sentence structure in section *III.* Remind students that an infinitive is a verb form that usually appears with the word *to* and can be joined with other words to form a phrase that act as a single part of speech. Point out that the infinitive phrase *Not to honor men of worth* is the subject of the verb *will keep.*

Support for Advanced Readers

Direct students to research an incident of extreme pollution or a political plan to exploit the environment. Then have them write an essay in which they analyze the validity of the Taoist philosophical statement, "Do that which consists in taking no action, and order will prevail" as it applies to the situation they have researched.

❼ About the Selection

Unlike Taoism, Confucianism is a social philosophy concerned with the moral nature of social relationships. In this selection from *The Analects,* Confucius instructs his students to respect authority, and he urges society's directors to demonstrate moral leadership.

❽ Humanities

Old Trees by Cold Waterfall, by Wen Zhengming

Wen Zhengming (1470–1559) was a Ming dynasty painter who was revered as the ideal scholar-artist. After a career as a government official and historian, he abandoned his city position and returned to the country. For the last thirty years of his life, he devoted himself to painting, poetry, and calligraphy.

Among China's most revered figures were scholar-artists like Wen Zhengming. Many of their paintings either convey a truth about humans' relationship to nature or reflect the changing seasons.

Use the following questions for discussion:

- What "truths" do you think the artist expresses in this painting? **Possible response:** The painting expresses the true beauty and wonder of nature. It also reveals the balance between humanity and nature; although the human figures are in the foreground, they seem far less significant than the natural landscape.
- Why do you think the title refers to the landscape and not to the two people in the foreground? **Possible response:** The artist considers the landscape the true subject of the painting, not the two people.

❾ Critical Viewing

Answer: By de-emphasizing people, the artist presents them as deferring to the moral power and authority of nature.

❼ from The Analects

CONFUCIUS
translated by Arthur Waley

❽

Old Trees by Cold Waterfall, 1470–1559, Wen Zhengming, The Los Angeles County Museum of Art

Background Confucius lived in a chaotic period in Chinese history. Responding to such upheaval in society, he taught the value and importance of tradition and social order. Unlike Taoism, which advocates submission and taking no action, Confucianism focuses on moral behavior, duty, and education.

Confucianism deals with all types of social units, from the most basic (the family) to the largest (the state). In the Confucian system, social relations are based on a system of subordination, with younger family members subordinate to older members and subjects subordinate to government officials. However, all must be governed by the concept of *ren*, or benevolence.

In addition to obeying those of superior status, people are expected to conduct themselves in a virtuous manner. Confucianists believe that Heaven is the supreme moral authority that dictates an ethical code by which all people, including rulers, must live. People in positions of authority are expected to serve as models of virtue for their subordinates.

The Master[1] said, To learn and at due times to repeat what one has learnt, is that not after all[2] a pleasure? That friends should come to one from afar, is this not after all delightful? To remain unsoured even though one's merits are unrecognized by others, is that not after all what is expected of a gentleman?

▲ Critical Viewing ❾ What Confucian ideas are reflected in the fact that the people are de-emphasized in this painting? **[Apply]**

1. **The Master** Confucius.
2. **after all** even though one does not hold public office.

Enrichment

The Reach of Confucian Thought

Confucius himself probably never imagined the extent to which his ideas would spread and the impact they would have on Chinese society. Thanks to the efforts of some of his later disciples—primarily Mencius, or Meng-tzu, and Hsun Tzu—Confucius' teachings were developed into a philosophy that has had an unparalleled impact on life in China and other countries in East Asia.

Confucianism became the dominant ethical, social, and political philosophy in China. It was even official state doctrine from as early as the second century B.C. to 1911.

The Analects is one of the most important books of philosophy and literature in China and throughout most of East Asia. According to sinologist Burton Watson, "*The Analects,* along with the *Five Classics,* had always been read and studied by educated Chinese, and from the Han dynasty on we find constant allusions to or echoes of its phraseology in literary works of all kinds."

The Master said, A young man's duty is to behave well to his parents at home and to his elders abroad, to be cautious in giving promises and punctual in keeping them, to have kindly feelings towards everyone, but seek the intimacy of the Good. If, when all that is done, he has any energy to spare, then let him study the polite arts.[3]

The Master said, (the good man) does not grieve that other people do not recognize his merits. His only anxiety is lest he should fail to recognize theirs.

10 The Master said, He who rules by moral force is like the pole-star,[4] which remains in its place while all the lesser stars do homage to it.

The Master said, If out of three hundred *Songs*[5] I had to take one phrase to cover all my teaching, I would say, "Let there be no evil in your thoughts."

11 The Master said, Govern the people by regulations, keep order among them by chastisements, and they will flee from you, and lose all self-respect. Govern them by moral force, keep order among them by ritual and they will keep their self-respect and come to you of their own accord.

Mêng Wu Po[6] asked about the treatment of parents. The Master said, Behave in such a way that your father and mother have no anxiety about you, except concerning your health.

The Master said, A gentleman can see a question from all sides without bias. The small man is biased and can see a question only from one side.

The Master said, Yu,[7] shall I teach you what knowledge is? When you know a thing, to recognize that you know it, and when you do not know a thing, to recognize that you do not know it. That is knowledge.

The Master said, High office filled by men of narrow views, ritual performed without reverence, the forms of mourning observed without grief—these are things I cannot bear to see!

The Master said, In the presence of a good man, think all the time how you may learn to equal him. In the presence of a bad man, turn your gaze within!

The Master said, In old days a man kept a hold on his words, fearing the disgrace that would ensue should he himself fail to keep pace with them.

3. **the polite arts** such activities as reciting from *The Book of Songs*, practicing archery, and learning proper behavior.
4. **pole-star** Polaris, the North Star.
5. **three hundred *Songs*** poems in *The Book of Songs*.
6. **Mêng Wu Po** (muŋ wo͞o bō) the son of one of Confucius's disciples.
7. **Yu** (yo͞o) Tzu-lu, one of Confucius's disciples.

Vocabulary Builder
homage (häm′ ij) *n.* act of reverence and respect

Vocabulary Builder
chastisements (chas′ tiz mənts) *n.* punishments
ritual (rich′ o͞o əl) *n.* observance of prescribed rules
bias (bī′ əs) *n.* prejudice; partiality

12  **Reading Check**
What is a young man's duty, according to Confucius?

10 Literary Analysis

Aphorisms

- Read aloud the first bracketed passage.
- **Ask** students to restate this aphorism in their own words, identifying the truth or principle it expresses.
  Possible response: "A true leader" sets a moral example that everyone will respect. The pole-star is an image of ideal moral leadership, which inspires reverence.

Monitor Progress Ask students to offer a definition of *aphorism* and offer examples of such statements.

Reteach If students have difficulty understanding or interpreting aphorisms, review the Literary Analysis instruction on p. 265.

11 Vocabulary Builder

Latin Suffix *-ment*

- Call students' attention to the word *chastisements* and its definition. Tell students that the Latin suffix *-ment* means "action or process" or "result of an action or process."
- Have students **suggest** and **define** other words that contain this suffix. List suggestions on the board.
  Possible responses: *Government, appeasement, movement,* or *agreement* are possible suggestions.
- Direct students to use the suggested words to write original aphorisms. Remind students that their aphorisms must contain a general truth or principle.

12 Reading Check

Answer: According to Confucius, a young man has several duties; some are "to behave well" toward his parents and elders; to make promises with "caution" and then keep them; to be kind; and to "seek the intimacy of the Good."

Differentiated Instruction Solutions for All Learners

Support for Special Needs Students
Students might find Confucius' language extremely challenging. Yet, some of the aphorisms have meanings that they can easily understand. Help students decode some of these aphorisms. For example, the second aphorism above has a very simple message. Have students identify the meanings of *grieve, merits,* and *anxiety.* Then, have students use these definitions to paraphrase the aphorism in their own words. Students can repeat this process with other aphorisms in the selection.

Enrichment for Gifted/Talented Students
The connection between Confucius' ideas and the themes of Chinese art may be especially apparent to students. Encourage them to find visual representations for at least three of Confucius' aphorisms. Suggest that students use the Internet or library resources to locate the art. Students should begin with the Chinese art from Unit 3 of ***World Masterpieces.*** Students may locate other classical Chinese art. For each aphorism, students should present an artwork to the class and explain how it illustrates Confucius' meaning.

⓭ Literary Analysis

Aphorisms

- Have students read the bracketed passage.
- **Ask** students the Literary Analysis question: In what way might a ruler interpret the lesson of this aphorism about words and deeds?
  Possible response: A ruler would learn that it is desirous to be known as one who is not too quick to make promises and as a keeper of promises.

ASSESS

Answers

1. **Possible response:** Happiness may lie in recognizing the natural course of the universe and acting in accordance with it so as not to expend one's energy fighting what cannot be changed.
2. (a) Lao Tzu advises readers to get rid of desire to observe the secrets of the universe but to allow desire to observe manifestations of the universe. (b) **Possible response:** When a person can achieve a fusion of opposites, he or she is at one with natural order.
3. (a) The images are a container, a hammer, and gold and jade. (b) Wealth may be accumulated but must not be a means of oppression. (c) Lao Tzu advises his readers to achieve a balance between having and lacking.
4. (a) Confucius advises caution and punctuality. (b) **Possible response:** Confucius believes that moral order is based on integrity.
5. (a) Confucius compares the leader to the North Star. (b) He believes moral and natural forces are aligned.
6. (a) One's words should not "outrun" one's deeds. (b) **Possible response:** This advice underscores Confucius' position that promises should be made carefully so that they can be kept.
7. (a) **Possible responses:** Confucius might have had a dim view of democracy. (b) Confucius' ideas about respect and morality might ensure the health of a democracy.

⓭ The Master said, A gentleman covets the reputation of being slow in word but prompt in deed.

The Master said, In old days men studied for the sake of self-improvement; nowadays men study in order to impress other people.

The Master said, A gentleman is ashamed to let his words outrun his deeds.

The Master said, He who will not worry about what is far off will soon find something worse than worry close at hand.

The Master said, To demand much from oneself and little from others is the way (for a ruler) to banish discontent.

Literary Analysis
Aphorisms In what way might a ruler interpret the lesson of this aphorism about words and deeds?

Critical Reading

1. **Respond:** Do you agree with Lao Tzu's basic philosophy that the way to achieve happiness is to take no action? Explain your answer.
2. **(a) Recall:** In section I of the *Tao Te Ching*, what advice does Lao Tzu give with regard to desires? **(b) Connect:** In what way does this advice relate to his overall philosophy of the natural order?
3. **(a) Analyze:** What three images does Lao Tzu present in the first six lines of section IX? **(b) Interpret:** In what way do these images illustrate Lao Tzu's message about wealth in the last four lines of the selection? **(c) Connect:** Explain how this message relates to Lao Tzu's earlier statements about desires.
4. **(a) Recall:** What advice does Confucius give regarding promises? **(b) Infer:** Why is this principle important to Confucius and to his philosophy?
5. **(a) Recall:** To what does Confucius compare a leader who rules by "moral force"? **(b) Interpret:** Based on this comparison, describe Confucius's belief about the power of "moral force."
6. **(a) Recall:** According to Confucius, how should one's words relate to one's deeds? **(b) Connect:** In what way does this advice support Confucius's earlier statements about promises?
7. **(a) Speculate:** How do you think Confucius would view the concept of democracy? **(b) Apply:** Do you think Confucius's ideas can be applied to a democratic society? Explain.

For: More about Lao Tzu and Confucius
Visit: www.PHSchool.com
Web Code: ete-9301

Go Online Author Link For additional information about Lao Tzu or Confucius, have students type in the Web Code, then select the first letter of the author's last name from the alphabet, and then select the author's name.

Apply the Skills

from the *Tao Te Ching* • from *The Analects*

Literary Analysis

Aphorisms

1. **(a)** In the **aphorism** that concludes section IX of the *Tao Te Ching*, what does Lao Tzu say that one should do when a task is accomplished? **(b)** What kind of behavior does he mean to discourage?
2. Explain how the aphorism form supports Lao Tzu's philosophy of the Tao, as expressed in the *Tao Te Ching*.
3. In what way is Confucius's use of aphorisms in *The Analects* consistent with his belief that a gentleman "is ashamed to let his words outrun his deeds"?

Comparing Literary Works

4. **(a)** In what way do Lao Tzu and Confucius differ on the subject of education? **(b)** Explain how this contrast reflects each philosopher's essential ideas.
5. **(a)** Use a Venn diagram like the one shown to compare and contrast the two philosophies of government presented by Lao Tzu and Confucius. **(b)** Do you find these two philosophers to be in disagreement with each other? Why or why not?

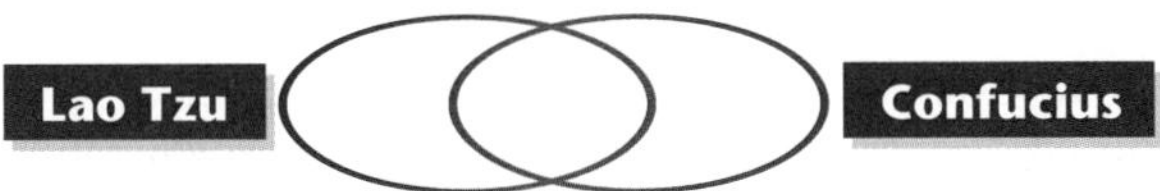

Reading Strategy

Questioning Causes and Effects

6. **(a)** According to Lao Tzu, what is the effect of being "overbearing when one has wealth and position"? **(b)** How might Lao Tzu explain this **cause-and-effect** relationship?
7. **(a)** What does Confucius say will happen to a person "who will not worry about what is far off"? **(b)** Do you think this is a valid cause-and-effect relationship? Why or why not?

Extend Understanding

8. **Social Studies Connection:** Compare the philosophies of Taoism and Confucianism with the principle of nonviolent protest, demonstrated by marches, sit-ins, and boycotts. What does this approach share with both Taoism and Confucianism?

QuickReview

Aphorisms are short statements expressing general truths or principles.

By **questioning causes and effects**, you can discover the principle underlying an author's message.

Go Online Assessment

For: Self-test
Visit: www.PHSchool.com
Web Code: eta-6301

Go Online Assessment Students may use the **Self-test** to prepare for **Selection Test A** or **Selection Test B.**

Answers

1. (a) One should "retire." (b) Lao Tzu is discouraging people from pursuing accomplishments to gain excessive rewards.
2. **Possible response:** Lao Tzu's aphorisms set thought in motion, encouraging the contemplation of nature and the universe.
3. **Possible response:** By using aphorisms, Confucius remains focused on specific principles of behavior.
4. (a) Lao Tzu believes that the masses should not be educated; Confucius believes that education is a pleasure that gentlemen pursue for self-improvement.
   (b) **Possible response:** Lao Tzu's ideas reflect his understanding natural order for the sake of self-preservation; Confucius' views are in keeping with his beliefs about social subordination.
5. (a) **Possible response: Lao Tzu:** A wise ruler empties the minds of the people but fills bellies, weakens wills but strengthens bones, frees them from desire, and ensures that the clever are afraid to act. If the ruler does not act against nature, then order will prevail. **Confucius:** A leader should rule by moral force and reverence for ritual. **Overlap:** Both advocate reverence for forces outside the self. (b) The philosophies are not contradictory. However, Confucius' connection between moral and natural forces disagrees with Lao Tzu's belief that natural forces exist without morality.
   Another sample answer can be found on **Literary Analysis Graphic Organizer B**, p. 50, in ***Graphic Organizer Transparencies.***
6. (a) The effect is "to bring calamity upon oneself." (b) **Possible response:** To be overbearing with wealth and position may cause others to act from envy, thus bringing calamity.
7. (a) The person will find something worse than worry. (b) **Possible response:** Yes; refusing to plan the future may lead to trouble.
8. **Possible response:** Nonviolent resistance is similar to Lao Tzu's statement: That which yields can be more powerful than that which does not yield.

EXTEND/ASSESS

Answers

❶ Vocabulary Lesson

Word Analysis: Latin Suffix *-ment*

1. Winning first prize was a great *achievement* for me.
2. After hours of debate, we finally reached an *agreement.*
3. She pursued her dreams for many years before finding *fulfillment.*

Spelling Strategy

1. appeasement
2. immediately
3. advancement
4. graceful

Vocabulary Builder: Analogies

1. submissive
2. ritual
3. bias
4. contention
5. homage
6. chastisements
7. manifestations
8. calamity

❷ Grammar and Style Lesson

1. To demand much from oneself and little from others (noun); to banish discontent (adjective)
2. To be overbearing (noun); to bring calamity (noun)
3. To retire (noun)
4. To impress other people (adverb)
5. To learn (noun); to repeat what one has learnt (noun)

Writing Application

Possible response: *To undertake more than you can accomplish* is the path to ruin. *To be lazy* is a path to disaster. True love seems impossible *to find* until it suddenly appears.

WG Writing and Grammar Platinum Level

For support in teaching the Grammar and Style Lesson, use Chapter 20, Section 1.

Build Language Skills

❶ Vocabulary Lesson

Word Analysis: Latin Suffix *-ment*

When added to a verb, the Latin suffix *-ment* forms a noun. Adding *-ment* to the verb *chastise,* which means "to punish," forms the noun *chastisement,* "an act of punishing." Change the following verbs to nouns by adding the suffix *-ment*. Then, use each new word in a sentence.

1. achieve **2.** agree **3.** fulfill

Spelling Strategy

When you add a suffix that begins with a consonant to a word ending in *e,* do not drop the *e: chastise + -ment = chastisement.* Combine each of these words with its suffix to form a new word.

1. appease + *-ment*

2. immediate + *-ly*

3. advance + *-ment*

4. grace + *-ful*

Vocabulary Builder: Analogies

Study the relationship presented in each first pair. Then, complete each analogy with a vocabulary word from the list on page 265 to make a word pair expressing the same relationship.

1. active : passive :: aggressive : ______

2. improvisation : spontaneous :: ______ : planned

3. narrowness : broadness :: ______ : open-mindedness

4. peace : calm :: war : ______

5. respect : irreverence :: ______ : ridicule

6. admirer : compliments :: accuser : ______

7. plans : actions :: abstractions : ______

8. health : wellness :: disaster : ______

❷ Grammar and Style Lesson

Infinitives and Infinitive Phrases

An **infinitive** is the base form of a verb, usually preceded by *to*. It can be used as a noun, an adjective, or an adverb. An **infinitive phrase** is an infinitive with modifiers or complements, words that complete the meaning of the verb, all acting together as one part of speech. In each example below, the infinitive or infinitive phrase is underlined.

As a noun: Lao Tzu's advice in the *Tao Te Ching* is <u>to take no action</u>.

As an adverb: This advice may be difficult <u>to understand</u>.

As an adjective: One must have a willingness <u>to consider new ideas</u>.

Practice Identify each infinitive or infinitive phrase below and indicate whether it is acting as a noun, an adjective, or an adverb.

1. To demand much from oneself and little from others is the way . . . to banish discontent.

2. To be overbearing when one has wealth and position/Is to bring calamity upon oneself.

3. To retire when the task is accomplished/Is the way of heaven.

4. . . . nowadays men study in order to impress other people.

5. To learn and at due times to repeat what one has learnt, is that not after all a pleasure?

Writing Application Write three aphorisms of your own, using at least one infinitive or infinitive phrase in each.

WG *Prentice Hall Writing and Grammar Connection: Platinum Level, Chapter 20, Section 1*

Assessment Practice

Recognize Details **(For more practice, see *Test Preparation Workbook,* p. 12.)**

Use the following sample test item to give students practice in recognizing details.

Founded early in China's history, Taoism stresses freedom, simplicity, and the contemplation of nature. Taoist philosophy encourages its followers to embrace a simple lifestyle as part of the quest to understand the Tao, or "Way," of life.

Why does Taoist philosophy encourage its followers to embrace a simple lifestyle?

A to study Chinese history
B to practice freedom
C to understand the *Tao*
D to contemplate nature

Although Chinese history, freedom, and the contemplation of nature are all cited in the passage, they are not named as the primary reasons Taoists are encouraged to practice a simple lifestyle, so *A, B,* and *D* are not the best answers. C is the correct answer: to understand the *Tao.*

❸ Writing Lesson

Timed Writing: Critical Comparison

The *Tao Te Ching* and *The Analects* offer differing philosophies on how people should live. Yet, there are many ideas that the two works share. In an essay, compare and evaluate the validity of the main ideas in these two selections. ***(40 minutes)***

Prewriting *(10 minutes)* Create a two-column chart, labeling one column *Tao Te Ching* and the other *The Analects*. Review the selections, using the chart to note key ideas and identify similarities and differences among them.

Drafting *(20 minutes)* Choose an organization before you begin drafting. In a subject-by-subject organization, address all the points for the *Tao Te Ching* first, then address *The Analects*. In a point-by-point organization, move between the selections as you discuss each point of comparison.

Revising *(10 minutes)* Reread your essay to be sure that you have shown connections between ideas when making comparisons. Consider adding transitional words and phrases to clarify relationships between points.

Model: Revising to Show Connections Between Ideas

Lao Tzu believed that order comes about when individuals take no action. ^In contrast, Confucius taught that people must take action to create order.

Transitional phrases like *In contrast* strengthen the connection between two points.

WG Prentice Hall Writing and Grammar Connection: Platinum Level, Chapter 9, Section 4

❹ Extend Your Learning

Listening and Speaking With a group, hold a **philosophical debate** on Taoism and Confucianism. One team should argue for Taoism; the other, for Confucianism. Each team should prepare to answer these questions:

- What are the strengths of each philosophy?
- What are the weaknesses of each?
- Which philosophy is more applicable in today's world?

Present the debate to an audience of classmates. **[Group Activity]**

Research and Technology The teachings of Confucius influenced Chinese government from the days of ancient emperors to the era of Mao Zedong. Using print and electronic sources, make a **research presentation** explaining that influence. Include visual aids with your presentation.

For: An additional research activity
Visit: www.PHSchool.com
Web Code: etd-7301

Assessment Resources

The following resources can be used to assess students' knowledge and skills.

Unit 3 Resources
Selection Test A, pp. 18–20
Selection Test B, pp. 21–23

General Resources
Rubrics for Exposition: Comparison-and-Contrast Essay, pp. 53–54

Go Online Assessment Students may use the **Self-test** to prepare for **Selection Test A** or **Selection Test B.**

❸ Writing Lesson

You may use this Writing Lesson as a timed-writing practice, or you may allow students to develop the critical comparison essay as a writing assignment over several days.

- To give students guidance in writing this critical comparison essay, give them the **Support for Writing Lesson**, p. 15, in ***Unit 3 Resources.***
- Instruct students to identify key ideas in both the *Tao Te Ching* and *The Analects* and to explain how the positions Lao Tzu and Confucius take are similar or different. Explain that this approach can be applied to either subject-by-subject or point-by-point organization.
- Use the Exposition: Comparison-and-Contrast rubric in ***General Resources,*** pp. 53–54, to evaluate students' work.

WG Writing and Grammar Platinum Level
For support in teaching the Writing Lesson, use Chapter 9, Section 4.

❹ Listening and Speaking

- Instruct students to review the selections and work in teams to identify major strengths and weaknesses of Taoism and Confucianism.
- Have students find examples in the selections that support the strengths and weaknesses they have identified. Encourage each student to focus on making and supporting one argument in favor of Taoism or Confucianism.
- The **Support for Extend Your Learning** page ***(Unit 3 Resources,*** p. 16) provides guided note-taking opportunities to help students complete the Extend Your Learning activities.

Go Online Research Have students type in the Web Code for another research activity.

Standard Course of Study

FA.3.04.11	Analyze elements of argumentative environment.
CT.4.02.1	Show an understanding of cultural context in analyzing thematic connections.
CT.4.03.5	Analyze how writers achieve a sense of completeness and closure.

Connections

American Literature

Aphorisms, or short statements that express universal truths about life, provide useful guidance for the Chinese. Americans also find the aphorisms of Benjamin Franklin useful. Have students reread the aphorisms by Lao Tzu and Confucius on pp. 266–270 after they have read Benjamin Franklin's work. Ask students what similarities and differences they note between the values of the two cultures.

Voices of Wisdom

- Remind students that Benjamin Franklin wrote *Poor Richard's Almanack* before the American Revolutionary War, when the colonies were developing an American culture that was distinct from British and European culture.
- Point out that the aphorisms of Lao Tzu and Confucius prescribe how to live life according to Chinese cultural values.
- Have students select one aphorism from each writer. Then, direct students to draw three graphic organizers, each consisting of one circle, an equal sign, another circle, an arrow, and a third circle. Tell students to label the first circle "Aphorism," the second circle "Cultural Value," and the third circle "Explanation." Have students write one aphorism in each of the three circles labeled "Aphorism." Help students identify the cultural value each aphorism reflects and record it in the circle labeled "Cultural Value." Tell students to write an explanation of each aphorism in the circle labeled "Explanation."

Critical Viewing

Answer: *Philomath* means "a lover of learning" or "a scholar."

American Literature

Voices of Wisdom

Advice columns, self-help books, and motivational speakers recommending specific behaviors are found everywhere today. Centuries ago, however, Confucius and Lao Tzu were masters of aphorisms, or short statements that express universal truths about life. *The Analects*, a summary of the doctrines of Confucius, provides guidelines to his code of conduct, and the *Tao Te Ching* by Lao Tzu helps readers remember the basic principles of existence in a chaotic world.

Later, in eighteenth-century America, a group of revolutionaries founded an entirely new nation. In the process, they worked diligently to define the culture of that nation and to determine the characteristics of a good citizen. One of their most eminent statesmen, Benjamin Franklin, was influential in the building of the new culture, asserting in *Poor Richard's Almanack* and other writings the importance of hard work, discipline, and appropriate behavior.

Proverbs to Live By Franklin adapted traditional proverbs and folk sayings into aphorisms of his own. Believing that clarity and brevity are two of the most important characteristics of good prose, Franklin rewrote many proverbs to create short, witty sayings that teach a lesson. Franklin's aphorisms, like Confucius' and Lao Tzu's, reflect his culture's views of the world. As memorable bits of wisdom that have survived for centuries, the words of Confucius, Lao Tzu, and Benjamin Franklin reflect unchanging truths about human nature.

Poor Richard, 1733.

AN

Almanack

For the Year of Chriſt

1733,

Being the Firſt after LEAP YEAR:

And makes ſince the Creation	Years
By the Account of the Eaſtern *Greeks*	7241
By the Latin Church, when ☉ ent. ♈	6932
By the Computation of *W.W.*	5742
By the *Roman* Chronology	5682
By the *Jewiſh* Rabbies	5494

Wherein is contained

The Lunations, Eclipſes, Judgment of the Weather, Spring Tides, Planets Motions & mutual Aſpects, Sun and Moon's Riſing and Setting, Length of Days, Time of High Water, Fairs, Courts, and obſervable Days.

Fitted to the Latitude of Forty Degrees, and a Meridian of Five Hours Weſt from *London*, but may without ſenſible Error, ſerve all the adjacent Places, even from *Newfoundland* to *South-Carolina*.

By *RICHARD SAUNDERS*, Philom.

PHILADELPHIA:

Printed and ſold by *B. FRANKLIN*, at the New Printing-Office near the Market.

▶ **Critical Viewing** The abbreviation "Philom.," short for *philomath*, follows Franklin's pseudonym, Richard Saunders. Can you guess the meaning of the word *philomath*? **[Speculate]**

Enrichment

Man of Science

No other colonial American represented the promise of America more than Benjamin Franklin. Through hard work, dedication, and ingenuity, Franklin rose out of poverty to become a wealthy, famous, and influential person. Franklin made important contributions in literature, journalism, and education. He also made important scientific inventions, including the lightning rod, bifocals, and a new type of stove. Ask students to research one of Franklin's inventions and trace its evolution to modern times. Students can display their research in the form of an illustrated and annotated timeline.

from *Poor Richard's Almanack*

BENJAMIN FRANKLIN

- Fools make feasts, and wise men eat them.
- Be slow in choosing a friend, slower in changing.
- Keep thy shop, and thy shop will keep thee.
- Early to bed, early to rise, makes a man healthy, wealthy, and wise.
- Three may keep a secret if two of them are dead.
- God helps them that help themselves.
- The rotten apple spoils his companions.
- An open foe may prove a curse; but a pretended friend is worse.
- Have you somewhat to do tomorrow, do it today.
- A true friend is the best possession.
- A small leak will sink a great ship.
- No gains without pains.
- ''Tis easier to prevent bad habits than to break them.
- Well done is better than well said.
- Dost thou love life? Then do not squander time; for that's the stuff life is made of.
- Write injuries in dust, benefits in marble.
- A slip of the foot you may soon recover, but a slip of the tongue you may never get over.
- If your head is wax, don't walk in the sun.
- A good example is the best sermon.
- Hunger is the best pickle.
- Genius without education is like silver in the mine.
- For want of a nail the shoe is lost; for want of a shoe the horse is lost; for want of a horse the rider is lost.
- Haste makes waste.
- The doors of wisdom are never shut.
- Love your neighbor; yet don't pull down your hedge.
- He that lives upon hope will die fasting.

Vocabulary Builder

squander (skwän′ dər) *v.* spend or use wastefully

fasting (fast′ iŋ) *v.* eating very little or nothing

CONNECTIONS

Benjamin Franklin (1706–1790)

After moving from Boston to Philadelphia at seventeen, Benjamin Franklin began publishing *Poor Richard's Almanack,* an annual publication containing information, observations, and advice. When he retired, Franklin devoted himself to science. In spite of his many scientific achievements, Franklin is best remembered as a statesman. He played an important role in drafting the Declaration of Independence and the United States Constitution, and in his later years, he was ambassador to England and then France.

Connecting American Literature

1. Which of Benjamin Franklin's aphorisms is your favorite? Why?
2. What beliefs about human nature do you think Benjamin Franklin shares with Confucius and Lao Tzu? Explain.
3. Do you agree that there are certain truths about human nature that do not change from century to century or from culture to culture? Explain.

Background
The "Write" Reputation

When he was seventeen, Franklin left Boston and traveled to Philadelphia, intending to open his own print shop. This move gave birth to *Poor Richard's Almanack.* Franklin created for the *Almanack* a fictitious author/editor, the chatty Richard Saunders (and his wife, Bridget). Although Poor Richard's early appearances in the *Almanack* present him as a dull and foolish astronomer, his character developed over the years, becoming more thoughtful, pious, and humorous.

ASSESS
Answers

1. **Possible response:** "Three may keep a secret if two of them are dead" is a favorite aphorism because it inspires laughter through a shrewd assessment of human nature: the inability to keep a secret.
2. **Possible response:** All three writers view human nature as inherently ridiculous and in need of direction. Many of their aphorisms expose human frailties and provide instruction to prevent people from making foolish mistakes.
3. **Possible response:** Yes; People are people, no matter when or where they live. Because of their commonality, people consistently need the same types of instruction to avoid making the mistakes that others before them have made.

Differentiated Instruction
Solutions for All Learners

Support for Less Proficient Readers
Give students a contemporary aphorism, such as "Life is like a box of chocolates." Discuss its meaning to help students recognize metaphoric comparisons as they read Franklin's aphorisms. Ask volunteers to give an example of a "chocolate" in their box of life. Then have pairs discuss which of Franklin's aphorisms apply to their lives.

Strategy for English Learners
Have students select one of Franklin's aphorisms. Ask students to create a pictogram with captions to illustrate both the literal and figurative meaning of the aphorism. Direct students to post their work in class and share it with classmates.

Enrichment for Advanced Readers
Challenge students to distill the meaning of Franklin's aphorisms. Then, have them write their own aphorisms, in which they convey their personal philosophies about life. Direct students to display their favorite original aphorisms as bumper stickers on their backpacks or book covers.

PRETEACH/TEACH

Standard Course of Study

LT.5.01.3	Analyze literary devices and explain their effect on the work.
LT.5.03.9	Analyze and evaluate the effects of author's craft and style in world literature.
LT.5.03.11	Analyze elements of literary environment in world literature.

❶ Types of Poetry

- Tell students that they will be focusing on certain types of poetry. **Ask** students these questions: What types of poetry have you studied in the past? How are poems similar to and different from other genres of literature?
  Possible answers: Students may say that they have studied limericks or acrostics. Rhymed poetry is different from prose, which is written in everyday speech.
- After reviewing the types of poetry with students, have students read Robert Frost's quotation. **Ask:** What do you think that Frost means?
  Possible response: Before a poet begins writing, he or she must have deep feelings for the topic or theme of the poem.
- Ask students to imagine reading a poem by someone who cared little for the poem's theme and content or for poetry in general. **Ask:** How good of a poem would it be?
  Possible response: It would probably be boring and poorly written. People usually do their best work when they care about what they do.

❷ Elements of Poetry

- Review the elements of poetry. Clarify the information on these pages, and suggest that students use these pages as a reference as they read poetry in Unit 3 and in other units.
- **Ask** students: How do the sound devices help poetry sound like music lyrics?
  Answer: Lyrics often depend on rhyme, consonance, and assonance, as well as other sound devices.

Unit 3 **Focus on Literary Forms**

Defining Poetry

Poetry is one of the three major genres, or forms, of literature, along with prose and drama. Poetry usually contains concise, musical language that differs from that of everyday speech. A poem is often arranged in lines and groups of lines that form stanzas.

❶ Types of Poetry

There are three broad categories of poetry:

- Narrative poetry tells a story. Narrative poetry includes ballads, epics, and verse romances.
- Lyric poetry expresses the thoughts and feelings of a single speaker. Lyric poetry includes sonnets, odes, elegies, and haiku.
- Dramatic poetry uses the techniques of drama to present the speech of one or more characters.

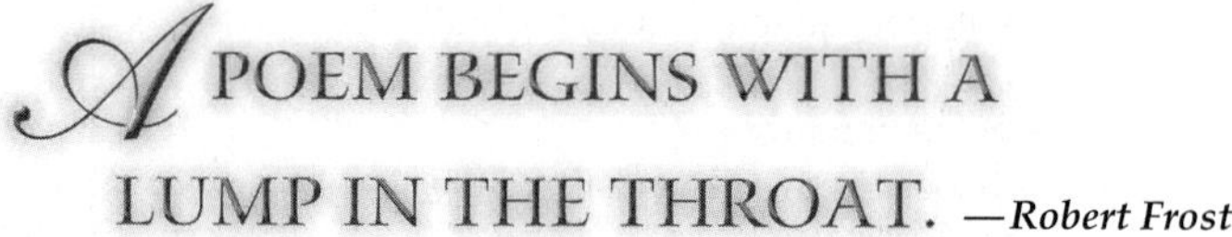
A POEM BEGINS WITH A
LUMP IN THE THROAT. —Robert Frost

❷ Elements of Poetry

Here are some of the most common elements of poetry.

Meter and Rhythm

Meter is the regular pattern of stressed (/) and unstressed (˘) syllables in each poetic line. A poem's meter is often described according to its main type of **foot,** or unit of rhythm. These are the most common English feet:

- iamb (˘/) as in *again*
- trochee (/˘) as in *wonder*
- dactyl (/˘ ˘) as in *utterly*
- anapest (˘ ˘ /) as in *disbelief*
- spondee (//) as in *go home*

You can also describe meter according to the number of feet per line:

- monometer (one foot)
- dimeter (two feet)
- trimeter (three feet)
- tetrameter (four feet)
- pentameter (five feet)
- hexameter (six feet)

A complete description of a poem's meter tells its main foot and number of feet per line. The most common meter in English is **iambic pentameter.**

> "That then I scorn to change my state with kings."
> (Shakespeare, Sonnet 29)

Poetry that does not use a regular meter is called **free verse.** The poet instead recreates the natural **rhythm** of everyday speech or any suitable rhythm.

Extend the Lesson

Activity

- Have students read the quotation from Shakespeare's "Sonnet 29" aloud and tap their desks each time they read an accented syllable.
- Then write the line on the board and demonstrate how to mark the accented and unaccented syllables. You might read the line again, showing how incorrectly stressed syllables affect the sound and meaning of the passage.

Stanzas

Poems are often divided into groups of lines called **stanzas**, which are usually defined by the number of lines they contain.

- couplets (two lines)
- tercets (three lines)
- quatrains (four lines)
- sestets (six lines)

Sound Devices

Sound devices are elements that enhance a poem's meaning by adding a musical quality:

- rhyme: repetition of sounds at the ends of words, as in *side* and *tide*
- alliteration: repetition of initial consonant sounds, as in *wild wind*
- consonance: repetition of final consonant sounds, as in *stroke* and *luck*
- assonance: repetition of similar vowel sounds, as in *blue moon*
- onomatopeoia: a word that sounds like what it means, as in *buzz*

Imagery and Figurative Language

Imagery is language that uses **images:** words or phrases that appeal to one or more of the senses of sight, hearing, touch, taste, or smell. **Figurative language** is language that is used imaginatively instead of literally and includes one or more **figures of speech:**

A simile is a figure of speech that compares two apparently unlike things by using *like* or *as,* as in *eyes like burning coals.*

- A metaphor is a figure of speech that compares two apparently unlike things without using *like* or *as,* as in *my life is a roller coaster.*
- Personification is a figure of speech that gives human traits to something nonhuman, as in *the wind sang a sad song.*
- An oxymoron is a figure of speech that combines two contradictory words, as in *a fine mess.*

3 Strategies for Reading Poetry

Use these strategies as you read poetry.

Read the Poem Aloud Sound effects and rhythm are important to a poem's overall meaning and emotional effect. To fully understand and appreciate a poem, read it aloud and listen to the way it sounds.

Focus on Imagery As you read a poem, identify language that appeals to the senses. Allow yourself to experience the vivid sensations and emotions that these images evoke.

3 Strategies for Reading Poetry

- Tell students that poetry is read differently from prose. Point out to students that as they read poetry, they must pay particular attention to the punctuation. Emphasize that when they read a poem, they should look at the punctuation first, not the line breaks. Reading according to punctuation rather than line breaks will help readers understand the meaning of the poem.
- Tell students that a good strategy for reading poetry aloud is first to skim the poem to find out where the pauses and breaks lie.
- Remind students that the speaker is not necessarily the poet. Poets can take on whatever voice they want to use in a poem. Even when a poet writes in the first person, tell students that "I" may or may not be the poet speaking.

Standard Course of Study

Goal 3: FOUNDATIONS OF ARGUMENT

FA.3.02.1 State position or proposed solution in an editorial or response.

Goal 4: CRITICAL THINKING

CT.4.05.3 Provide evidence to support understanding of and response to critical interpretation.

Goal 5: LITERATURE

LT.5.01.2 Build knowledge of literary genres, and explore how characteristics apply to literature of world cultures.

LT.5.01.4 Analyze the importance of tone and mood in world literature.

Goal 6: GRAMMAR AND USAGE

GU.6.01.2 Analyze author's use of language to demonstrate understanding.

GU.6.02.1 Edit for agreement, tense choice, pronouns, antecedents, case, and complete sentences.

Step-by-Step Teaching Guide	Pacing Guide
PRETEACH	
• Administer Vocabulary and Reading Warm-ups as necessary.	5 min.
• Engage students' interest with the motivation activity.	5 min.
• Read and discuss author and background features. **FT**	10 min.
• Introduce the Literary Analysis Skill: Chinese Poetic Forms. **FT**	5 min.
• Introduce the Reading Strategy: Responding. **FT**	10 min.
• Prepare students to read by teaching the selection vocabulary. **FT**	
TEACH	
• Informally monitor comprehension while students read independently or in groups. **FT**	30 min.
• Monitor students' comprehension with the Reading Check notes.	as students read
• Reinforce vocabulary with Vocabulary Builder notes.	as students read
• Develop students' understanding of Chinese poetic forms with the Literary Analysis annotations. **FT**	5 min.
• Develop students' ability to respond with the Reading Strategy annotations. **FT**	5 min.
ASSESS/EXTEND	
• Assess students' comprehension and mastery of the Literary Analysis and Reading Strategy by having them answer the Apply the Skills questions. **FT**	15 min.
• Have students complete the Vocabulary Lesson and the Grammar and Style Lesson. **FT**	15 min.
• Apply students' ability to include supporting quotations by using the Writing Lesson. **FT**	45 min. or homework
• Apply students' understanding by using one or more of the Extend Your Learning activities.	20–90 min. or homework
• Administer Selection Test A or Selection Test B. **FT**	15 min.

Resources

Print

Unit 3 Resources

Transparency

Graphic Organizer Transparencies

Print

Reader's Notebook [L2]

Reader's Notebook: Adapted Version [L1]

Reader's Notebook: English Learner's Version [EL]

Unit 3 Resources

Technology

Listening to Literature Audio CDs [L2, EL]

Print

Unit 3 Resources

General Resources

Technology

Go Online: Research [**L3**]
Go Online: Self-test [**L3**]
***ExamView®*, Test Bank [L3]**

Choosing Resources for Differentiated Instruction

[**L1**] Special Needs Students
[**L2**] Below-Level Students
[**L3**] All Students
[**L4**] Advanced Students
[**EL**] English Learners

For Vocabulary and Reading Warm-ups and for Selection Tests, **A** signifies "less challenging" and **B** "more challenging." For Graphic Organizer transparencies, **A** signifies "not filled in" and **B** "filled in."

FT Fast Track Instruction: To move the lesson more quickly, use the strategies and activities identified with **FT**.

Scaffolding for Less Proficient and Advanced Students

The leveled Critical Thinking questions after selections progress in the levels of thinking required to answer them. To address the needs of your different students, you may use the (a) level questions for your less proficient students and the (b) level questions with your on-level and advanced students. The occasional (c) level questions are appropriate for your advanced students.

Use this complete suite of powerful teaching tools to make lesson planning and testing quicker and easier.

PRENTICE HALL **StudentEXPRESS™** Learn · Study · Succeed

Use the interactive textbook (online and on CD-ROM) to make selections and activities come alive with audio and video support and interactive questions.

For: Information about Lexiles
Visit: www.PHSchool.com
Web Code: eue-1111

PREETEACH

Motivation

Play examples of contemporary love songs to stimulate a discussion about love poetry. Record on the board students' answers to these questions: What feelings are expressed in love poetry? Why is love poetry so powerful? Why is it found in literature from around the world? Then, tell students that *The Book of Songs* contains love poems.

❶ Background

More About the Works and the Authors

The Book of Songs covers centuries of Chinese culture and a range of literary styles and poets. The majority of the poems in the book are simple folk songs that describe the daily lives of the people.

T'ao Ch'ien is known for his simple and direct style, yet he experienced the tumult of a divided China that was partly under foreign rule. His poetry, however, expresses his vision of how to live tranquilly in a chaotic world.

Li Po lived extravagantly, indulging his love of wine, women, and song. He was heavily influenced by Taoist thought and often wrote about nature.

Tu Fu was a younger contemporary of Li Po. Tu Fu's poetry reveals much about his character—his love for nature and his family and friends, his frustration at living in poverty, and his disappointment over a lackluster political career.

Geography Note

Draw students' attention to the map of China on this page. Explain that although T'ao Ch'ien wrote much of his poetry while living in one place, Li Po and Tu Fu traveled extensively throughout China. The poems from *The Book of Songs* also come from all over China.

Build Skills | Poems

❶ Chinese Poetry

The Book of Songs (c. sixth century B.C.)

The Book of Songs, also known as *The Book of Odes*, is an anthology of 305 ancient Chinese poems. According to tradition, Confucius (see p. 264) chose the poems to be included. It is doubtful that Confucius actually selected the poems, but he did know them well and recommended their study.

Because of the book's honored status and its association with Confucius, traditional Chinese interpreters of the poems have stressed their political and social importance. These interpreters have sometimes gone to great lengths to find hidden meanings in what appear to be simple love songs. In recent years, however, scholars have begun to interpret the ancient songs more literally, appreciating them for their simplicity and directness and using them as a window into the lives of the early Chinese people.

T'ao Ch'ien (A.D. 365–427)

T'ao Ch'ien (dou´ chē´ en´) was born into a family of prominent but impoverished government officials. As an adult, T'ao Ch'ien himself began a career in government service, but he found it difficult to behave in the subservient manner required of lower-ranking officials. When he was about thirty-five, he resigned from office and retired to a farm on the outskirts of a rural village.

In his later years, T'ao Ch'ien devoted most of his energy to writing poetry. Inspired by the serenity of his life in the countryside, T'ao Ch'ien wrote many poems about the simple beauty of the landscapes surrounding farms and villages. In addition to showing his love for nature, T'ao Ch'ien's poetry reveals his passion for some of his favorite activities—farming, spending time with his family, and writing poetry.

Li Po (701–762)

Along with Tu Fu, Li Po (lē´ bō´) is considered one of the supreme masters of Chinese poetry. The details of Li Po's early life are not clear, but he probably grew up in southwestern China, in the region that is now Szechuan province. During his mid-twenties, he moved to eastern China, and throughout the remainder of his life he moved from place to place.

Li Po is known for his free-spirited, graceful, and lyrical style. His poetry frequently conveys a love of freedom and a sense of harmony with nature. These qualities, along with Li Po's vivid imagery and timeless insights, have earned his poems a secure place among China's finest works of literature.

Tu Fu (712–770)

Tu Fu (do͞o´ fo͞o´) is regarded as the supreme craftsman of Chinese *shih* (shi) poetry. In all of his poetry—poems dealing with social issues and those that focus on his personal experiences—Tu Fu shows a command of language and a mastery of the *shih* form. As a result, his poems are admired as much for their form as for their content.

Early in Tu Fu's career, China was relatively peaceful and prosperous, but later the poet witnessed a major rebellion, the destruction of the capital city, and an invasion by tribes from the northwest. In his poems, Tu Fu gives some of the most vivid accounts of war and destruction in all of Chinese literature. He also harshly criticizes the nobility's extravagance in the face of extreme poverty among the common people.

Preview

Connecting to the Literature

If you have ever reflected on life, love, or nature, then you already have something in common with the poets whose work follows. Look for universal themes in these poems, and compare the poets' reflections with your own.

❷ Literary Analysis

Chinese Poetic Forms

You may be familiar with certain European forms of poetry, such as the sonnet, but Chinese literature has its own poetic forms.

- *Shih* **poems** are poems that, in the original Chinese, have an even number of lines, each with the same number of words. Old-style *shih* poems, like those of T'ao Ch'ien, can be of any length. The new style, the one used by Tu Fu, has strict rules about length and form.
- **Songs** are poems that were originally set to music and have strong, regular rhythms. Songs may also include **refrains**—words or phrases repeated at regular intervals. "Indeed I am afraid" is a refrain in "I Beg of You, Chung Tzu." If one or two words within a refrain are varied in successive stanzas, this technique is called **incremental variation.**
- **Ballads** are songs that tell stories. "The River-Merchant's Wife: A Letter" is an example of a ballad.

As you read these poems, notice the ways in which their forms are both similar to and different from poems that you have read from other cultures.

Comparing Literary Works

Each speaker in these poems has a unique **tone,** or attitude, toward his or her subject or audience. Tone is revealed by the speaker's **diction**, or word choice. It can be described using words like *friendly, distant, serious,* or *playful.* Use a chart like the one shown to identify key words and phrases from each poem and to compare the tones of the varied speakers in these poems.

❸ Reading Strategy

Responding

When you **respond** to a poem, you reflect on the poet's message and how that message relates to your own life. As you read these selections, take time to respond to them. Note the emotions you feel and the images each work prompts in your imagination.

Vocabulary Builder

bashful (bash′ fəl) *adj.* shy (p. 286)

eddies (ed′ ēz) *n.* waters moving in circles against the main current (p. 286)

scurry (skur′ ē) *v.* to run hastily; to scamper (p. 289)

pathos (pā′ thäs′) *n.* quality in something that evokes sorrow or compassion (p. 289)

imperceptibly (im′ pər sep′ tə blē) *adv.* without being noticed (p. 289)

NC Standard Course of Study

- Analyze the importance of tone and mood in world literature. (LT.5.01.4)
- Analyze author's use of language to demonstrate understanding. (GU.6.01.2)

Poem
"Addressed Humorously to Tu Fu"
Representative Diction
"You must have been suffering from poetry again."
Speaker's Tone
playful, ironic

❷ Literary Analysis

Chinese Poetic Forms

- Use popular folk and rock-and-roll songs to help students recognize examples of the following terms: *song, ballad, refrain,* and *incremental variation.* Then, lead students in a discussion of similarities and differences among the three Chinese poetic forms.
- Give students a copy of **Literary Analysis Graphic Organizer A,** p. 51, in ***Graphic Organizer Transparencies.*** Have them use it to identify the speaker's tone in each poem.

❸ Reading Strategy

Responding

- Explain that these poems from ancient China can have personal meaning for students today.
- As they read, ask students to pay close attention to the emotions and memories that each poem evokes.
- Encourage students to keep reading journals in which they note their emotional responses to each of the poems and the relevance of each poem to their lives.

Vocabulary Builder

- Pronounce each vocabulary word for students, and read the definitions as a class. Have students identify any words with which they are already familiar.

Differentiated Instruction Solutions for All Learners

Support for Special Needs Students
Have students complete the **Preview** and **Build Skills** pages for these selections in the ***Reader's Notebook: Adapted Version.*** These pages provide a selection summary, an abbreviated presentation of the reading and literary skills, and the graphic organizer on the **Build Skills** page in the student book.

Support for Less Proficient Readers
Have students complete the **Preview** and **Build Skills** pages for these selections in the ***Reader's Notebook.*** These pages provide a selection summary, an abbreviated presentation of the reading and literary skills, and the graphic organizer on the **Build Skills** page in the student book.

Support for English Learners
Have students complete the **Preview** and **Build Skills** pages for these selections in the ***Reader's Notebook: English Learner's Version.*** These pages provide a selection summary, an abbreviated presentation of the skills, additional contextual vocabulary, and the graphic organizer on the **Build Skills** page in the student book.

TEACH

Facilitate Understanding

Ask students to set the poems from *The Book of Songs* to music. They may simply establish rhythm with percussion or create a melody.

❶ About the Selections

In "I Beg of You, Chung Tzu," the speaker worries about how her family and community will feel about her beloved Chung Tzu. In contrast, the speaker of "Thick Grow the Rush Leaves" must overcome natural obstacles to find her beloved.

❷ Literary Analysis

Chinese Poetic Forms

- Remind students that many songs have refrains.
- Have students read the bracketed stanza. Then, **ask** them to respond to the Literary Analysis item. **Possible response:** Refrains in this stanza include "I beg of you, Chung Tzu" and "Indeed I am afraid."

❸ Reading Strategy

Responding

- **Ask** students: Have you ever befriended someone of whom your family did not approve? How did you feel about your family's disapproval?
- Read aloud the bracketed passage. Then, **ask** students the Reading Strategy question. **Possible response:** The speaker is torn between wanting Chung Tzu to visit her and fears of her family's rejection.

from

❶ The Book of Songs

translated by Arthur Waley

Background The poems in *The Book of Songs* come from many different regions of China. Most of them were originally folk songs describing people's daily activities, such as farming, fishing, or gathering herbs. Others focus on love or courtship. The book also contains a group of poems written by courtiers in praise of kings, describing banquets and court ceremonies.

All of the songs were originally set to music. Some, especially the songs of the court, may have been accompanied by dancing and by musical instruments, such as bells and drums. The tunes are long lost, but the songs' powerful rhythms are preserved in their four-beat lines.

I Beg of You, Chung Tzu

I beg of you, Chung Tzu,
Do not climb into our homestead,
Do not break the willows we have planted.
Not that I mind about the willows,
But I am afraid of my father and mother.
Chung Tzu I dearly love;
But of what my father and mother say
Indeed I am afraid.

❷
I beg of you, Chung Tzu,
Do not climb over our wall,
Do not break the mulberry trees we have planted.
Not that I mind about the mulberry trees,
But I am afraid of my brothers.
Chung Tzu I dearly love;
But of what my brothers say
Indeed I am afraid.

I beg of you, Chung Tzu,
Do not climb into our garden,
Do not break the hardwood we have planted.
Not that I mind about the hardwood,
❸
But I am afraid of what people will say.
Chung Tzu I dearly love;
But of all that people will say
Indeed I am afraid.

Literary Analysis
Chinese Poetic Forms Find two refrains in this stanza that identify the poem as a song.

Reading Strategy
Responding What is your response to the speaker's fears? Explain.

Differentiated Instruction

Solutions for All Learners

Accessibility at a Glance

	The Book of Songs	Form, Shadow, Spirit	I Built My House . . .	A Letter	Jade Flower Palace	Poems of Li Po and Tu Fu
Language	Clauses in rhythmic refrains	Abstract words in two-line verses	Written in first person	Syntax: participial phrases	Vivid verbs and colorful adjectives	Humorous, friendly diction
Concept Level	Accessible (Feelings of young love)	Accessible (Beauty of nature)	Accessible (Comfort of solitude)	Accessible (Loss of love)	Accessible (Impermanence of power)	Accessible (Strength of friendship)
Literary Merit	Chinese love songs	Old style Shih poems	Shih poem	Classic Chinese Ballad	Shih poem in the new style	Poems strong in humor
Lexile	NP	NP	NP	NP	NP	NP
Overall Rating	Average	Average	More Accessible	Average	Average	Average

Thick Grow the Rush Leaves

Thick grow the rush leaves;
Their white dew turns to frost.
He whom I love
Must be somewhere along this stream.
I went up the river to look for him,
But the way was difficult and long.
I went down the stream to look for him,
And there in mid-water
Sure enough, it's he!

Close grow the rush leaves,
Their white dew not yet dry.
He whom I love
Is at the water's side.
Up stream I sought him;
But the way was difficult and steep.
Down stream I sought him,
And away in mid-water
There on a ledge, that's he!

Very fresh are the rush leaves;
The white dew still falls.
He whom I love
Is at the water's edge.
Up stream I followed him;
But the way was hard and long.
Down stream I followed him,
And away in mid-water
There on the shoals is he!

❹

❺ ▲ Critical Viewing Judging from this painting, why might it be difficult to search for someone on a river, as the speaker does in "Thick Grow the Rush Leaves"? Explain. **[Apply]**

Critical Reading

1. **(a) Recall:** In "I Beg of You, Chung Tzu," what are the speaker's fears? **(b) Analyze:** What conflicting feelings does she have?
2. **(a) Recall:** In "Thick Grow the Rush Leaves," what words describe the rush leaves and their growth? **(b) Interpret:** In what way might the rush leaves be symbolic of the speaker's feelings?
3. **(a) Compare:** In terms of their subjects, how are these two poems similar? **(b) Contrast:** What makes them different?

❹ Humanities

Fishing Village in the Wind and Rain,
by Li K'e-jan

Li K'e-jan (1907–1989), a major Chinese artist of the twentieth century, was dedicated to changing traditional Chinese landscape painting. He literally painted what he heard and saw, and he believed that painting should be appreciated by the people. He combined elements of traditional Chinese art with a solid grounding in Western techniques. This synthesis can be seen in *Fishing Village in the Wind and Rain.*

Use the following question for discussion:

What qualities does this painting share with these poems from *The Book of Songs?*
Possible response: The painting depicts the life of common people in China, just as the poems do.

❺ Critical Viewing

Possible response: The tightly packed houses and dense vegetation might make the search difficult.

ASSESS

Answers

1. (a) The speaker fears that her family and community members will disapprove of Chung Tzu. (b) The speaker is in conflict over her feelings for Chung Tzu and her desire to have familial approval.
2. (a) "Thick," "close," and "very fresh" describe the rush leaves. (b) **Possible response:** The rush leaves symbolize the speaker's growing and vibrant love.
3. (a) **Possible response:** Both poems address young love. Both appear to express a female speaker's feelings toward a male beloved. Also, both use some natural details. (b) In "I Beg of You, Chung Tzu," the speaker's conflict remains unresolved, but the speaker of "Thick Grow the Rush Leaves" finds her beloved.

Differentiated Instruction Solutions for All Learners

Support for Special Needs Students

Students may benefit from having a clear sense of the rhythms of the poems from *The Book of Songs.* First, make sure students understand that the poems are songs: They were originally set to music. Next, have students read the poems as they listen to the **Listening to Literature Audio CDs.** Make sure students understand that the elements of the songs, such as refrains, add to their rhythms.

Enrichment for Gifted/Talented Students

Point out to students that just like the writers of *The Book of Songs,* modern folk singers write songs about everyday activities. Organize students in groups, and have each group write a folk song that uses refrains and incremental variations. Have groups brainstorm song ideas. Explain that after students write one stanza, they should vary the lines slightly for the remaining stanzas.

6 About the Selections

The simple elements of these poems by T'ao Ch'ien—the beauty of nature and the spirit's contemplation of life's mysteries—reflect the Taoist appreciation of the mysterious universe. They exemplify the belief that life cannot be understood or even described using conventional methods.

7 Reading Strategy

Responding

- Remind students that they can respond to a poem by relating its meaning to their own lives.
- Have students read and **summarize** the argument Form makes in "Form Addresses Shadow."
  Answer: In contrast to heaven and earth, Form points out that people live only a short time and vanish entirely when they die, save for the rare memories of loved ones. Having decided that death is the absolute end, Form concludes that there is no point in forsaking worldly pleasures.
- Ask students to use specific examples from their own lives to write a response to Form before they read "Shadow Replies." Invite volunteers to read aloud their responses to classmates.
- **Ask** students the Reading Strategy question: How does your response to the argument made in lines 7–15 compare with Form's conclusion in lines 15–16?
  Possible response: There is no physical evidence to contradict Form's argument, so one might do well to experience pleasure while in human form. However, what one does with one's life may have an impact on how the person is remembered.

▶ Monitor Progress Encourage students to compare their responses with Shadow's reply. Venn diagrams might assist students with their comparisons.

▶ Reteach If students are having difficulty responding to the poem, suggest they use ***Literary Analysis,*** p. 28, in ***Unit 3 Resources.***

FORM, SHADOW, SPIRIT

6 T'ao Ch'ien *translated by* David Hinton

Background T'ao Ch'ien was among the finest "old style" *shih* poets. In classical Chinese, each line of a *shih* poem has the same number of syllables, words, and characters. Classical Chinese is not written with letters; instead, characters stand for words. For example, the character 木 means "tree" or "wood." T'ao Ch'ien's simple, direct style is easy to enjoy in translation, but his carefully formed structure, unfortunately, is not preserved.

Rich or poor, wise or foolish, people are all busy clinging jealously to their lives. And it's such delusion. So, I've presented as clearly as I could the sorrows of Form and Shadow. Then, to dispel those sorrows, Spirit explains occurrence coming naturally of itself. Anyone who's interested in such things will see what I mean.

1 Form Addresses Shadow

Heaven and earth last. They'll never end.
Mountains and rivers know no seasons,

and there's a timeless law plants and trees
follow: frost then dew, vigor then ruin.

They call us earth's most divine and wise
things, but we alone are never as we are

again. One moment we appear in this world,
and the next, we vanish, never to return.

And who notices one person less? Family?
Friends? They only remember when some

7 everyday little thing you've left behind
pushes grief up to their eyes in tears.

I'm no immortal. I can't just soar away
beyond change. There's no doubt about it,

death's death. Once you see that, you'll
see that turning down drinks is for fools.

Reading Strategy
Responding How does your response to the argument made in lines 7–15 compare with Form's conclusion in lines 15–16?

Enrichment

Chinese Characters and *Shih* Poetry

Shih was the dominant Chinese poetic form from the second through the twelfth centuries A.D. Generally, *shih* lines have five or seven words. Rhymes occur at the end of even-numbered lines. *Shih* also frequently uses parallelism—couplets that are similar in structure and meaning, enhancing rhythm and emphasizing key ideas.

To fully appreciate the *shih* form, one needs a basic understanding of the classical Chinese language. As explained in the Background note on p. 282, Chinese is written with ideograms, characters that represent individual words. In classical Chinese, each ideogram represents a word and is pronounced as one syllable. This gives a classic *shih* poem its structure, with the same number of words, ideograms, and syllables in each line. Most of these qualities are lost when the poems are translated, but the parallelism of the couplets often survives.

8

9 ◀ Critical Viewing
In what way does this painting suggest the timelessness of nature that Form describes? **[Connect]**

2 Shadow Replies

Who can speak of immortality when simply
staying alive makes such sad fools of us?

We long for those peaks of the immortals,
but they're far-off, and roads trail away

early. Coming and going together, we've
always shared the same joys and sorrows.

Resting in shade, we may seem unrelated,
but living out in the sun, we never part.

10

This togetherness isn't forever, though.
Soon, we'll smother in darkness. The body

can't last, and all memory of us also ends.
It sears the five feelings. But in our

good works, we bequeath our love through
generations. How can you spare any effort?

Though it may be true wine dispels sorrow,
how can such trifles ever compare to this?

Reading Strategy
Responding Do you think Shadow's argument is more valid than Form's? Why or why not?

11  Reading Check
To whom or to what does Shadow reply?

Differentiated Instruction Solutions for All Learners

Support for Less Proficient Readers
Read aloud the introduction and section titles of "Form, Shadow, Spirit." On the basis of this information, have students speculate about the poems' form. Lead them to understand that it is a discussion between three entities: Form, which represents earthly life; Shadow, which represents the mind or soul; and Spirit, which represents the spiritual realm beyond human understanding.

Enrichment for Advanced Readers
Encourage students to expand on the arguments that Form, Shadow, and Spirit make in the poem. Students may want to conduct further research on Taoist perspectives on the nature of life. Have students work in groups of three to present the characters and arguments of Form, Shadow, and Spirit. Alternatively, two students can debate as Form and Shadow while a third moderates as Spirit.

8 Humanities

A Myriad of Trees on Strange Peaks,
by Yen Wen-kuei

Yen Wen-kuei was a well-known Sung dynasty (A.D. 960–1279) painter who worked primarily in ink on silk. This picture, which is part of a fan-shaped album page, is typical of Sung landscape art. It possesses the characteristic fusion of mystery and poetry. As in so many Sung paintings, distance and space are indefinite, leaving viewers lost in the expanse of the painting.

Use the following question for discussion:

What scenes do you imagine lie beyond the mists?
Possible response: Scenes of magical splendor lie beyond the mists, including strange beasts and kingdoms.

9 Critical Viewing

Possible response: The indefinite distance and form in the painting make the landscape look unending and timeless, just as Form describes heaven and earth.

10 Reading Strategy

Responding

- Have students read and **summarize** the argument Shadow makes in "Shadow Replies."
  Answer: Shadow acknowledges the impermanence of body and memory but suggests that the soul, which is light and love, is immortal.
- **Ask** students the Reading Strategy question: Do you think Shadow's argument is more valid than Form's? Why or why not?
  Possible response: Shadow's argument is more valid because it recognizes a spiritual dimension to life beyond the body.

11 Reading Check

- **Answer:** Shadow is responding to the arguments made by Form in the preceding poem.

⓬ Critical Thinking

Analyze

- Ask a volunteer to read aloud the bracketed passage. Then, draw students' attention to lines 45–47.
- **Ask:** What do the lines, "Young and old die the same death. When it / comes, the difference between sage and fool / vanishes" mean?
  Answer: These lines mean that death is the great equalizer. The status enjoyed during life means nothing at the moment of death.

⓭ Literary Analysis

Chinese Poetic Forms

- Remind students that T'ao Ch'ien wrote *shih* poetry—a Chinese poetic form with structural requirements based on the Chinese language.
- Have students read the poem in its entirety. Suggest that they count the number of lines and the number of words per line in the bracketed passage.
- Then, **ask** the Literary Analysis question: In what way does this poem, even in translation, follow the *shih* form?
  Answer: The poem has an even number of lines, and all the lines are approximately the same length.

3 Spirit Answers

The Great Potter[1] never hands out favors.
These ten thousand things thrive each

of themselves alone. If humans rank with
heaven and earth, isn't it because of me?

And though we're different sorts of things
entirely, we've been inseparable since

birth, together through better and worse,
and I've always told you what I thought.

The Three Emperors[2] were the wisest of
men,
but where are they now? And loving his

eight-hundred-year life, old P'eng-tsu[3]
12 wanted to stay on here, but he too set out.

13 Young and old die the same death. When it
comes, the difference between sage and fool

vanishes. Drinking every day may help you
forget, but won't it bring an early grave?

And though good works may bring lasting
joy, who will sing your praise? Listen—

it's never-ending analysis that wounds us.
Why not circle away in the seasons, adrift

on the Great Transformation, riding its vast
swells without fear or delight? Once your

time comes to an end, you end: not another
moment lost to all those lonely worries.

Literary Analysis
Chinese Poetic Forms In what way does this poem, even in translation, follow the *shih* form?

1. **The Great Potter** the force that gives things their form, sometimes translated as *God.*
2. **The Three Emperors** three mythical rulers of ancient times.
3. **P'eng-tsu** the archetypal Chinese aged man.

I BUILT MY HOUSE NEAR WHERE OTHERS DWELL

T'ao Ch'ien

translated by William Acker

14

The River and Mountains in Autumn Color, 1120–1182, Zhao Boju, Imperial Palace Museum, Beijing, China

I built my house near where others dwell,
And yet there is no clamor of carriages and
 horses.
You ask of me "How can this be so?"
"When the heart is far the place of itself is distant."
I pluck chrysanthemums under the eastern hedge,
And gaze afar towards the southern mountains.
The mountain air is fine at evening of the day
And flying birds return together homewards.
Within these things there is a hint of Truth,
But when I start to tell it, I cannot find the words.

15 ▲ Critical Viewing

What qualities does the setting of this painting share with the setting of this poem? **[Connect]**

Critical Reading

1. **Respond:** Do you agree that "When the heart is far the place of itself is distant"? Why or why not?
2. **(a) Recall:** In lines 1–8 of "Form, Shadow, Spirit," what key difference does Form identify between humans and mountains, rivers, plants, and trees? **(b) Connect:** In what way does this contrast support Form's conclusion in lines 15–16?
3. **(a) Infer:** What attitude toward nature does the speaker reveal in lines 5–8 of "I Built My House Near Where Others Dwell"? **(b) Connect:** What lines in "Form, Shadow, Spirit" reflect a similar attitude toward nature?
4. **Take a Position:** Considering the ideas he expresses in these poems, how do you think T'ao Ch'ien would respond to living in a modern industrial city? Explain.

For: More about T'ao Ch'ien
Visit: www.PHSchool.com
Web Code: ete-9303

14 Humanities

River and Mountains in Autumn Color, by Zhao Boju

When the Sung dynasty established its court at Hangchou in 1127, it became a center for artists who relished its civilized environment and natural beauty. Among those working at the court was Zhao Boju (c. 1120–c. 1173), a descendant of the first Sung emperor.

Use this item for discussion:

Describe the relationship the painting suggests between human beings and their environment. **Possible response:** The tiny people in the foreground are dwarfed by the landscape, suggesting that they are far less important than their environment.

15 Critical Viewing

Possible response: The poem and the painting both contain mountain settings. Like the house described in the poem, the house in the foreground of the painting is near other houses yet secluded.

ASSESS

Answers

1. **Possible response:** Yes; one can achieve solitude in a physically crowded place within one's heart.
2. (a) Mountains, rivers, plants, and trees are eternal—they "never end"—but humans are ephemeral. (b) **Possible response:** Form suggests that human impermanence makes all pursuits beyond earthly pleasure meaningless.
3. (a) **Possible response:** The speaker shows a deep admiration and love for nature and suggests that universal Truth resides in nature. (b) Lines 1–4 of "Form, Shadow, Spirit" reflect a similar attitude toward nature.
4. **Possible response:** T'ao Ch'ien probably would have rejected the modern industrial city and moved to the country to lead an isolated, rustic life.

Go Online Author Link For additional information about T'ao Ch'ien, have students type in the Web Code, then select *C* from the alphabet, and then select T'ao Ch'ien.

Differentiated Instruction Solutions for All Learners

Support for Special Needs Students

To help improve students' understanding of T'ao Ch'ien's poetry, have them read the poems as they listen to the **Listening to Literature Audio CDs.** Next, discuss the poems with students. Then, have them read the poems again with the class.

Support for English Learners

Students may have difficulty with some unfamiliar words in the poem on this page. Post the meanings of *dwell, clamor, pluck, gaze,* and *afar.* Then tell students to rewrite the poem, substituting familiar terms for these words.

Enrichment for Gifted/Talented Students

Much of the power of "I Built My House Near Where Others Dwell" comes from its use of imagery, language that appeals to the five senses. Encourage students to create illustrations for the poem that capture its sensual imagery. Students may use any medium they choose.

THE RIVER-MERCHANT'S WIFE: A Letter

LI PO *translated by* EZRA POUND (16)

Background Li Po and Tu Fu first met in 744 and formed a lasting friendship. The two poets greatly admired each other's work but were very different people. Li Po was known to be free-spirited, while Tu Fu was more serious-minded. The poetry of Li Po and Tu Fu reflects the differences in their personalities. In "Addressed Humorously to Tu Fu," Li Po teases his somber young friend, who seems to be "suffering from poetry again."

While my hair was still cut straight across my forehead
I played about the front gate, pulling flowers.
You came by on bamboo stilts, playing horse,
(17) You walked about my seat, playing with blue plums.
And we went on living in the village of Chōkan:[1]
Two small people, without dislike or suspicion.

At fourteen I married My Lord you.
I never laughed, being <u>bashful</u>.
Lowering my head, I looked at the wall.
Called to, a thousand times, I never looked back.

(18) At fifteen I stopped scowling,
I desired my dust to be mingled with yours
Forever and forever and forever.
Why should I climb the look out?

At sixteen you departed,
You went into far Ku-tō-en,[2] by the river of swirling <u>eddies</u>,
And you have been gone five months.

Reading Strategy
Responding What memories or feelings about the past do these lines evoke in you?

Vocabulary Builder
bashful (bash′ fəl) *adj.* shy

Literary Analysis
Chinese Poetic Forms In what way does the first line of each stanza help to tell the story of this ballad?

Vocabulary Builder
eddies (ed′ ēz) *n.* waters moving in circles against the main current

1. **Chōkan** (chō′ kän′) Japanese name for Ch'ang-kan (chäŋ′ gän), a village in eastern China.
2. **Ku-tō-en** (ko͞o′ tō′ yen′) Japanese name for Ch'ü-t'ang-yen (cho͞o′ taŋ′ yen′), the shoals at the mouth of the dangerous Yangtze (yäŋk′ sē) Gorges, in the upper reaches of the Yangtze River.

(16) About the Translation

Although it deviates from the literal meaning in places, Ezra Pound's translation of "The River-Merchant's Wife" is deservedly famous. An example of Pound's deviation from the literal is his reference to "blue plums" in line 4. Arthur Cooper's more faithful translation refers to "green plums," whose color symbolizes youth. Also, Cooper uses Chinese place names, while Pound uses Japanese versions of those names. Finally, Cooper's translation runs 30 lines, while Pound's is slightly briefer. Note, however, the way in which Pound's abbreviations make the poem more powerful in English. Cooper's lines 25–26 read "And what I feel hurts me in my heart, /Sadness to make a pretty face old . . ." Pound brilliantly compresses these two lines into one (the initial pronoun refers to "The paired butterflies"): "They hurt me. I grow older." He moves directly from the image to the pain, knowing that an explanation is unnecessary.

(17) Reading Strategy

Responding

- Ask a volunteer to read aloud the bracketed lines. Then, **ask** the Reading Strategy question: What memories or feelings about the past do these lines evoke in you?
  Possible reponse: These lines evoke a nostalgia for childhood—a time of innocent games and friends.
- Encourage students to use personal connections as a means of responding to all forms of literature.

(18) Literary Analysis

Chinese Poetic Forms

- **Ask** students to summarize the story in the ballad "The River-Merchant's Wife: A Letter."
  Answer: The ballad tells the story of the speaker's love for her husband, a love that has evolved over a number of years. She laments the present absence of her husband.
- Have students independently read the bracketed lines. Then, **ask** the Literary Analysis question: In what way does the first line of each stanza help tell the story of this ballad?
  Answer: The first line of each stanza moves the plot forward in time. It identifies the speaker's age at a particular stage of her relationship with the river-merchant.

Enrichment

Images in the Work of Ezra Pound

Ezra Pound was one of the most influential poets of the early twentieth century, and Chinese poets such as Li Po appear to have influenced his work.

Pound believed that American poetry often lacked clarity and concentration. Li Po, however, used clear, concrete images. For Pound, an image was "an intellectual and emotional complex in an instant of time." With a single specific image, a poet could instantly communicate ideas, emotions, and physical experience.

Influenced also by Japanese haiku (examples of which can be found on pp. 300–302), Pound strived to focus his poetry on images. A famous example is "In a Station of the Metro":

The apparition of these faces in the crowd,
Petals on a wet, black bough.

The monkeys make sorrowful noise overhead.
You dragged your feet when you went out.
By the gate now, the moss is grown, the different mosses,
Too deep to clear them away!
The leaves fall early this autumn, in wind.
The paired butterflies are already yellow with August
Over the grass in the West garden;
They hurt me. I grow older.
If you are coming down through the narrows of the river Kiang,[3]
Please let me know beforehand,
And I will come out to meet you
As far as Chō-fū-Sa.[4]

19 Reading Check

How old was the speaker when her husband went away?

3. **the river Kiang** (kyaŋ) the Yangtze River.
4. **Chō-fū-Sa** (chō′ fōō′ sä′) Japanese name for Chang-feng Sha (chaŋ′ fuŋ′ shä′), a village on the Yangtze River, about 200 miles upstream from Chōkan.

20

River Village in a Rainstorm, Hanging scroll, Lü Wenying, The Cleveland Museum of Art

21 ◀ Critical Viewing

Why might an image like this one make the poem's speaker fearful about her husband's safety? **[Connect]**

19 Reading Check

Answer: The speaker was sixteen when her husband went away.

20 Humanities

River Village in a Rainstorm,
by Lu Wen-ying

Lu Wen-ying lived during the late fifteenth-century Ming dynasty. This silk-scroll painting depicts a popular subject of landscape artists—the changing seasons and the weather.

Use the following question for discussion:

Does this painting elicit the same mood that the poem conveys?
Possible response: The dark, sweeping browns used to represent the rainstorm in the painting create a sense of imbalance or uncertainty that mirror the speaker's mood at the end of the poem.

21 Critical Viewing

Possible response: The river looks like a dangerous place to travel and conduct business, especially during such a violent storm.

Differentiated Instruction
Solutions for All Learners

Strategy for Less Proficient Readers

Students may have difficulty moving beyond literal meanings. Ask: What does it mean that butterflies are "yellow with August"? Organize students into groups, and have them label two circles with the word *yellow* and the word *August*. Tell students to brainstorm and record around each circle all the words they associate with *yellow* and *August*. Ask students to use these associations to explain the meaning of "yellow with August."

Enrichment for Gifted/Talented Students

Encourage students to use "The River-Merchant's Wife: A Letter" as a model for an original ballad. Tell students to give themselves a descriptive identifier for the title of their ballads: "The Teacher's Daughter: A Letter." Students should write in the first person, identify the recipient of the "letter," tell a story that covers a span of time, and use sensory images and setting as integral elements of the story.

㉒ About the Selections

Invite students to imagine the tone of a friendly e-mail exchange between two rival poets—witty, possibly flattering, probably sharpened with a sly put-down or two. Then, tell them that the poems "Addressed Humorously to Tu Fu" and "Sent to Li Po as a Gift" (p. 290) might be compared to such an exchange of friendly put-downs. By contrast, "Jade Flower Palace" is a lyric poem that expresses the speaker's feelings about the impermanence of human power.

ASSESS

Answers

1. **Possible response:** Li Po illustrates his affection for Tu Fu by including the word "humorously" in the title so that Tu Fu knows the mood of the poem before reading it.
2. (a) The speaker says that she was without laughter and bashful. (b) **Possible responses:** Although she felt obligated to her husband at first, the speaker was detached, shy, and even uncomfortable with him. (c) The speaker's feelings change to real love and ultimately to loneliness in his absence.
3. (a) The butterflies are in pairs, and they "are already yellow with August," meaning that they are near the end of their lives. (b) **Possible response:** The butterflies seem to have grown old together while the speaker and her beloved husband are apart.
4. (a) The speaker says that Tu Fu wears a "huge hat" and is "wretchedly thin." (b) **Possible response:** The speaker's manner suggests that he has a close and open relationship with Tu Fu.
5. (a) The speaker concludes that Tu Fu "must have been suffering from poetry again." (b) **Possible response:** Li Po worries that Tu Fu's serious, socially conscious poetry is affecting Tu Fu's judgment and his health.
6. **Possible response:** Tu Fu would be pleased by Li Po's attention and affection for him and might chuckle at the poem's gentle chiding.

㉒ Addressed Humorously to Tu Fu

Li Po *translated by* **Shigeyoshi Obata**

Here! is this you on top of Fan-ko Mountain,
Wearing a huge hat in the noonday sun?
How thin, how wretchedly thin, you have grown!
You must have been suffering from poetry again.

Critical Reading

1. **Respond:** Based on his poem "Addressed Humorously to Tu Fu," do you think Li Po is a good friend to Tu Fu? Why or why not?
2. **(a) Recall:** In "The River-Merchant's Wife: A Letter," how does the speaker describe her behavior when she first married her husband? **(b) Infer:** How did the speaker feel about her marriage at first? **(c) Analyze:** How does her attitude change over time?
3. **(a) Recall:** How does the speaker of "The River-Merchant's Wife: A Letter" describe the butterflies she sees? **(b) Interpret:** Why do you think the butterflies "hurt" the speaker?
4. **(a) Recall:** In "Addressed Humorously to Tu Fu," how does the speaker describe Tu Fu's appearance? **(b) Infer:** What does the manner in which the speaker addresses Tu Fu suggest about their relationship?
5. **(a) Recall:** In "Addressed Humorously to Tu Fu," what does the speaker conclude about Tu Fu's condition? **(b) Interpret:** What do you think the speaker means by this comment?
6. **Speculate:** How do you think Tu Fu would have responded to "Addressed Humorously to Tu Fu"?

Go Online
Author Link
For: More about Li Po
Visit: www.PHSchool.com
Web Code: ete-9304

Go Online Author Link For additional information about Li Po, have students type in the Web Code, then select *P* from the alphabet, and then select Li Po.

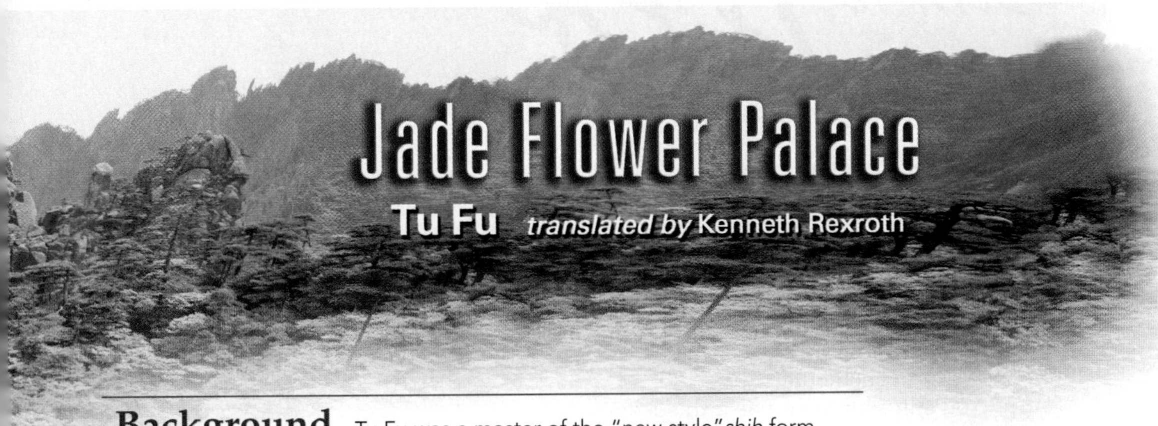

Jade Flower Palace

Tu Fu *translated by* Kenneth Rexroth

Background Tu Fu was a master of the "new style" *shih* form. New style *shih* poetry has very strict rules that dictate the number of lines, the number of words per line, and the rhyme scheme. Even within these restrictions, Tu Fu established his own style.

Unfortunately, Tu Fu's stylistic achievements cannot be appreciated in translation. In the original Chinese, new style *shih* poems have a blocklike structure; each line is made up of the same number of one-syllable characters. For example, Tu Fu's "Sent to Li Po as a Gift" is four lines long and each line has seven characters. The translation on page 290 has eleven lines of varying lengths.

The stream swirls. The wind moans in
The pines. Gray rats scurry over
Broken tiles. What prince, long ago,
Built this palace, standing in
Ruins beside the cliffs? There are
Green ghost fires in the black rooms.
The shattered pavements are all
Washed away. Ten thousand organ
Pipes whistle and roar. The storm
Scatters the red autumn leaves.
His dancing girls are yellow dust.
Their painted cheeks have crumbled
Away. His gold chariots
And courtiers are gone. Only
A stone horse is left of his
Glory. I sit on the grass and
23 Start a poem, but the pathos of
It overcomes me. The future
Slips imperceptibly away.
Who can say what the years will bring?

Vocabulary Builder
scurry (skʉr′ ē) *v.* to run hastily; to scamper

Vocabulary Builder
pathos (pā′ thäs′) *n.* quality in something that evokes sorrow or compassion

imperceptibly (im′ pər sep′ tə blē) *adv.* without being noticed

Reading Check
What feeling overcomes the speaker of "Jade Flower Palace"?

23 Vocabulary Builder

Greek Root *-path-*

- Call students' attention to the word *pathos* and its definition. Tell students that the Greek root *-path-* means "feeling" or "suffering."
- Have students **suggest** words that contain this root. List their suggestions on the board.
  Possible response: *Apathy, pathetic,* and *sympathy* contain the root *-path-*.
- Allow students to use dictionaries to look up the meanings of these words.
- Then, direct them to write short poems about suffering that include some of these vocabulary words. Invite volunteers to read their poems to the class.

24 Reading Check

Answer: The speaker is overcome by pathos, meaning compassion or sorrow.

Differentiated Instruction Solutions for All Learners

Strategy for Less Proficient Readers
Provide each student with a copy of "Jade Flower Palace," and invite students to highlight the details in the poem that describe the palace. Instruct each student to use these details to draw an image of the palace, exactly as Tu Fu describes it in the poem.

Strategy for English Learners
To help students understand the descriptive details of "Jade Flower Palace," have them work in pairs to write prose descriptions of the poem. Tell students that like the poem, their descriptions should convey a melancholy mood.

Enrichment for Advanced Readers
Have students read "The Fall of the House of Usher" by Edgar Allan Poe and use the author's descriptions to draw an image of the house. Tell students to do the same with "Jade Flower Palace." Then, have students compare and contrast the literature and the two drawings: What is each author saying about humanity?

25 Literary Analysis

Chinese Poetic Forms and Tone

- Remind students that tone is the attitude of the speaker of a poem toward his or her subject. Explain to students that tone is revealed by diction, or the choice of words the poet gives to the speaker. In "To Li Po as a Gift," the tone is the speaker's attitude toward the poet Li Po.
- Have students read the bracketed lines. Ask them to pay close attention to the speaker's diction.
- **Ask** students the Literary Analysis question: How would you describe the speaker's tone in lines 6–8?
  Possible response: The speaker is friendly toward Li Po yet worried about, and even critical of, his extravagant excess.

ASSESS

Answers

1. **Possible response:** The ruins of a building might evoke feelings of loss and loneliness.
2. (a) All that remains is a "stone horse." (b) **Possible responses:** The palace is much less rich and splendid than what the speaker says used to be there. (c) The speaker is pointing out the futility of earthly glory, given the fleeting nature of human life.
3. (a) The speaker says that Li Po's "nature is a spreading fire" that is "swift and strenuous."
   (b) **Possible response:** The speaker means that Li Po is passionate, free-spirited, and living outside the bounds of conventional behavior.
4. (a) **Possible responses:** The poem is a gift because it is meant to incite Li Po to self-reflection and improvement. (b) **Possible response:** The speaker is gently teasing Li Po for his wild character. At the same time, he is critical of Li Po's lifestyle, questioning the older poet's values and beliefs.

Sent to Li Po as a Gift

Tu Fu

translated by
Florence Ayscough and Amy Lowell

Autumn comes,
We meet each other.
You still whirl about as a thistledown in the wind.
Your Elixir of Immortality[1] is not yet perfected
And, remembering Ko Hung,[2] you are ashamed.
You drink a great deal,
25 You sing wild songs,
Your days pass in emptiness.
Your nature is a spreading fire,
It is swift and strenuous.
But what does all this bravery amount to?

1. **Elixir** (ē liks´ ir) **of Immortality** hypothetical substance, sought by alchemists in the Middle Ages, believed to prolong life indefinitely.
2. **Ko Hung** (kō´ ho͞oŋ) Chinese philosopher and alchemist who tried to create an Elixir of Immortality.

Literary Analysis
Chinese Poetic Forms and Tone How would you describe the speaker's tone in lines 6–8?

Critical Reading

1. **Respond:** What feelings does seeing the ruins of a building like the one in "Jade Flower Palace" evoke in you?
2. **(a) Recall:** In "Jade Flower Palace," what remains of the long-gone prince's "glory"? **(b) Connect:** In what way does this image contrast with the speaker's description of what used to be in the palace?
   (c) Draw Conclusions: What point do you think the speaker is making through this contrast?
3. **Recall:** What does the speaker of "Sent to Li Po as a Gift" say about Li Po's "nature"? **(b) Interpret:** What do you think the speaker means by this comparison?
4. **(a) Analyze:** Why do you think Tu Fu considers "Sent to Li Po as a Gift" to be a gift? **(b) Make a Judgment:** Do you think the speaker is criticizing Li Po or simply teasing him? Explain your answer.

Go Online
Author Link
For: More about Tu Fu
Visit: www.PHSchool.com
Web Code: ete-9305

Go Online Author Link For additional information about Tu Fu, have students type in the Web Code, then select *T* from the alphabet, and then select Tu Fu.

Apply the Skills

Chinese Poetry

Literary Analysis

Chinese Poetic Forms

1. **(a)** Identify a **refrain** in the **song** "I Beg of You, Chung Tzu." **(b)** Identify a refrain with **incremental variation** in "Thick Grow the Rush Leaves." **(c)** Explain the effect of refrains in each poem.
2. **(a)** What feature of "The River-Merchant's Wife: A Letter" indicates that it is a **ballad**? **(b)** In what way does each of the poem's four stanzas reveal a part of the ballad's subject?
3. In what way do the structures of these translations of "Form, Shadow, Spirit" and "I Built My House Near Where Others Dwell" reflect the original Chinese structure of these ***shih* poems**?

Comparing Literary Works

4. **(a)** How would you describe the speaker's **tone** in "Thick Grow the Rush Leaves"? **(b)** What words and phrases reveal the speaker's tone?
5. What do the contrasting tones of "Addressed Humorously to Tu Fu" and "Sent to Li Po as a Gift" suggest about each poet?

Reading Strategy

Responding

6. Which of these poems evoked your strongest emotional **response**?
7. **(a)** Using a chart like the one shown, note your response to each stanza of "The River-Merchant's Wife: A Letter," as well as to the poem as a whole, by jotting down words and phrases that describe the feelings evoked by the poem. **(b)** Did your response to the poem change between the beginning and the end of the poem? Explain.

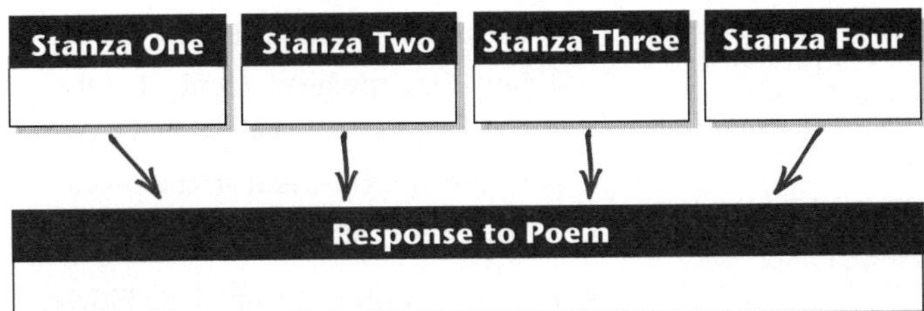

Extend Understanding

8. **Philosophy Connection:** Which of these poems most reflects the Taoist idea that one should submit oneself to the way of the universe and not interfere with the natural order? Explain.

QuickReview

A **song** is a poem originally set to music.

A **refrain** is a word or phrase repeated regularly in a song. If one or two words within a refrain are varied in successive stanzas, this technique is called **incremental variation.**

A **ballad** is a song that tells a story.

A ***shih* poem** is a poem that, in the original Chinese, has an even number of lines of equal length.

Tone is the speaker's attitude toward his or her subject or audience. To **respond** to a poem, reflect on the poet's message and how it relates to your own life.

Go Online Assessment

For: Self-test
Visit: www.PHSchool.com
Web Code: eta-6302

Answers

1. (a) **Possible response:** One refrain is "I beg of you, Chung Tzu." (b) A refrain with incremental variation is "Thick grow [Close grow, Very fresh are] the rush leaves" and "Their [The] white dew turns to frost [not yet dry, still falls]." (c) The refrains enhance rhythm and underscore the simple themes of the poems.
2. (a) The poem tells a story of a husband and wife. (b) Each stanza reveals a different stage of the speaker's life and a change in the feelings she has for her husband.
3. Both translations have an even number of lines that are roughly equal in length. Many lines in the poems are paired, and the poems include the parallelism that is typical of *shih* poetry.
4. (a) **Possible response:** The tone is one of romantic yearning and ultimately celebration. (b) **Possible response:** "Difficult and steep" reveal a yearning tone, and "it's he!", "that's he!", and "is he!" reveal a celebratory tone.
5. **Possible response:** The contrasting tones suggest that Li Po has a relaxed, carefree attitude about poetry, while Tu Fu views poetry as a serious undertaking.
6. **Possible response:** The poems from *The Book of Songs* evoke the strongest emotional response.
7. (a) **Possible response: Stanza One:** innocent pleasures of childhood; **Stanza Two:** pain and awkwardness of adolescence; **Stanza Three:** blossoming of true love; **Stanza Four:** loneliness, abandonment, the slipping away of time; **Response to Poem:** The poem is melancholy because it suggests that the period of innocence and joy in which most teenagers are caught will end with loneliness, abandonment, and the passage of time. (b) The reader's feelings, along with the speaker's, mutate from fond remembrance to joy to sorrow.
Another sample answer can be found on **Reading Strategy Graphic Organizer B**, p. 54 in ***Graphic Organizer Transparencies.***

Answers continued

8. **Possible response:** "Form, Shadow, Spirit" most reflects the Taoist ideal of natural order and inaction. Spirit advocates that humans stop questioning the ways of the universe and accept the experience of the journey.

Go Online Assessment Students may use the **Self-test** to prepare for **Selection Test A** or **Selection Test B.**

EXTEND/ASSESS

Answers

❶ Vocabulary Lesson

Word Analysis: Greek Root *-path-*

1. d
2. e
3. c
4. b
5. a

Vocabulary Builder: Sentence Completion

1. imperceptibly
2. scurry
3. bashful
4. pathos
5. eddies

Spelling Strategy

1. hopeful
2. respectful
3. forceful
4. pitiful

❷ Grammar and Style Lesson

1. of you; **Object:** you; **Related to:** beg
2. at the wall; **Object:** wall; **Related to:** looked
3. over broken tiles; **Object:** tiles; **Related to:** scurry
4. on the grass; **Object:** grass; **Related to:** sit
5. in emptiness; **Object:** emptiness; **Related to:** pass

Writing Application

Possible response:

I stood outside the gate
Of a factory in a quiet town,
Watching walls crumble in the gloom,
Old bricks falling into the weeds.

Writing and Grammar Platinum Level

For support in teaching the Grammar and Style Lesson, use Chapter 18, Section 1.

Build Language Skills

❶ Vocabulary Lesson

Word Analysis: Greek root *-path-*

Pathos is a Greek word whose root, *-path-*, means "feeling" or "suffering." The word *pathos* refers to the quality in something experienced or observed that arouses feelings of pity or sympathy. However, the root *-path-* appears in other words that are related in different ways to feeling or suffering. The root *-path-* can also mean "disease."

Use your understanding of this word root to match each word on the left with its definition on the right.

1. pathetic	**a.** to share the feelings of another
2. apathy	**b.** the study of disease
3. pathogen	**c.** disease-causing agent
4. pathology	**d.** evoking compassion, as for suffering; pitiful
5. sympathize	**e.** lack of feeling or concern

Vocabulary Builder: Sentence Completion

Choose the vocabulary word from the list on page 279 that best completes each sentence below.

1. He moved slowly, almost ____.
2. We saw a chipmunk ___ across the trail.
3. The kitten was ____ around people.
4. The ____ of her story brought us to tears.
5. Leaves swirled in the ____ of the stream.

Spelling Strategy

Adjectives with endings that sound like *full* and that name a quality, like *bashful*, end with one *l*, not two. For each quality described below, provide the appropriate word that ends with the *full* sound.

1. full of hope
2. showing respect
3. having force
4. evoking pity

❷ Grammar and Style Lesson

Prepositional Phrases

A preposition shows the relationship between a noun or pronoun—called the object of the preposition—and another word in the sentence. A **prepositional phrase** is a group of words that includes a preposition and a noun or pronoun. Prepositional phrases never include the subject or verb of the sentence.

Do not climb into our homestead. — OP (relates to *climb*)

I went down the stream. — OP (relates to *went*)

He . . . is at the water's edge. — OP (relates to *is*)

Practice For each item below, identify the prepositional phrase, the object of the preposition, and the word to which the object is related.

1. I beg of you, Chung Tzu . . .
2. Lowering my head, I looked at the wall.
3. Gray rats scurry over broken tiles.
4. I sit on the grass and start a poem.
5. Your days pass in emptiness.

Writing Application Using "Jade Flower Palace" as inspiration, write a short poem reflecting on the ruins of an old building. Your poem should have at least four lines, each containing at least one prepositional phrase.

Prentice Hall Writing and Grammar Connection: Platinum Level, Chapter 18, Section 1

Assessment Practice

Recognize Facts and Details **(For more practice, see *Test Preparation Workbook*, p. 13.)**

Many standardized tests require students to recognize facts and details in works of literature. Use the following sample test item to give students practice with the skill.

Very fresh are the rush leaves;
The white dew still falls.
—from "Thick Grow the Rush Leaves"

What do the details in this passage add to the poem?

A a sense of the fragility of love
B a sense of the freshness of nature
C a sense of the speaker's fear
D a sense of the coldness of the spring

There is no mention of love, fear, or cold in the passage, so *A, C,* and *D* are not the best answers. *Fresh* and *dew* both suggest freshness. The correct answer is *B*.

3 Writing Lesson

Timed Writing: Response to Criticism

Critic Herbert A. Giles wrote, "Brevity is indeed the soul of a Chinese poem, which is valued not so much for what it says as for what it suggests." In an essay, use evidence from the poems you have read to support or refute Giles's statement. ***(40 minutes)***

Prewriting *(10 minutes)* In each poem, note passages that clearly "say" or express something, as well as passages in which an idea is merely suggested or implied. Then, decide whether you agree or disagree with Giles's thesis.

Drafting *(20 minutes)* As you draft, use examples from the poems to support your position. Quote passages that demonstrate that the effect of a poem is the result of either what is expressed or what is implied.

Model: Using Quotations as Evidence

Chinese poems suggest, rather than express, their themes. For example, T'ao Ch'ien conveys a sense of harmony with nature through small details: "The mountain air is fine at evening of the day / And flying birds return together homewards."

Quotations provide concrete examples that strengthen an argument.

Revising *(10 minutes)* Reread your essay to be sure that all of the quotations are needed to support your argument. If you have more than two quotations per paragraph, eliminate all but the strongest examples.

Prentice Hall Writing and Grammar Connection: Platinum Level, Chapter 12, Section 3

4 Extend Your Learning

5 Research and Technology Li Po and Tu Fu lived during the T'ang Dynasty, which lasted from c. 600 to c. 900. This was widely seen as the Golden Age of China. With a group, make a **poster** illustrating the structure of T'ang society.

- Use print and electronic resources to research the different classes in T'ang society, including the role played by poets.
- Organize the information and design graphics to illustrate facts and statistics.

Present your poster in class. **[Group Activity]**

Listening and Speaking Prepare and present an **oral report** on the life and times of T'ao Ch'ien, Li Po, or Tu Fu. Choose a poet and research his life, as well as the historical period in which he lived. In your report, explain how the poet's life and times affected his poetry.

For: An additional research activity
Visit: www.PHSchool.com
Web Code: etd-7302

Assessment Resources

The following resources can be used to assess students' knowledge and skills.

Unit 3 Resources
- **Selection Test A**, pp. 35–37
- **Selection Test B**, pp. 38–40

General Resources
- **Rubrics for Response to Literature,** pp. 55–56
- **Rubrics for Research: Research Report,** pp. 51–52

Go Online Assessment Students may use the **Self-test** to prepare for **Selection Test A** or **Selection Test B.**

3 Writing Lesson

You may use this Writing Lesson as a timed-writing practice, or you may allow students to develop the response to criticism essay as a writing assignment over several days.

- To give students guidance in writing this response to criticism essay, give them the **Support for Writing Lesson**, p. 32, in ***Unit 3 Resources.***
- Read the statement by Herbert A. Giles with the class. Make sure students understand that Giles means that Chinese poetry is spare and suggestive and that it forces the reader to *think* rather than telling the reader *what* to think.
- Explain to students that their responses must be their own. They should not overwhelm their arguments with quotations.
- Use the Response to Literature rubric in ***General Resources,*** pp. 55–56, to evaluate students' work.

Writing and Grammar Platinum Level

For support in teaching the Writing Lesson, use Chapter 12, Section 3.

4 Extend Your Learning

- The **Support for Extend Your Learning** page ***(Unit 3 Resources,*** p. 33) provides guided note-taking opportunities to help students complete the Extend Your Learning activities.

5 Research and Technology

- Encourage each student in a group to focus on one element of T'ang society, such as government, social structure, or the role of poets.
- Have groups present their posters to the class. Encourage students to discuss the posters by asking each group one or two questions.
- Use the Research: Research Report rubrics in ***General Resources,*** pp. 51–52, to evaluate students' research.

Go Online Research Have students type in the Web Code for another research activity.

Standard Course of Study

Goal 1: WRITTEN LANGUAGE

WL.1.03.9 Analyze effects of author's craft and style in reflection.

Goal 5: LITERATURE

LT.5.01.2 Build knowledge of literary genres, and explore how characteristics apply to literature of world cultures.

LT.5.01.3 Analyze literary devices and explain their effect on the work of world literature.

Goal 6: GRAMMAR AND USAGE

GU.6.01.3 Use recognition strategies to understand vocabulary and exact word choice.

Step-by-Step Teaching Guide	Pacing Guide
PRETEACH	
• Administer Vocabulary and Reading Warm-ups as necessary.	5 min.
• Engage students' interest with the motivation activity.	5 min.
• Read and discuss author, background, and From the Scholar's Desk features. **FT**	10 min.
• Introduce the Literary Analysis Skill: Japanese Poetic Forms. **FT**	5 min.
• Introduce the Reading Strategy: Picturing Imagery. **FT**	10 min.
• Prepare students to read by teaching the selection vocabulary. **FT**	
TEACH	
• Informally monitor comprehension while students read independently or in groups. **FT**	30 min.
• Monitor students' comprehension with the Reading Check notes.	as students read
• Reinforce vocabulary with Vocabulary Builder notes.	as students read
• Develop students' understanding of Japanese poetic forms with the Literary Analysis annotations. **FT**	5 min.
• Develop students' ability to picture imagery with the Reading Strategy annotations. **FT**	5 min.
ASSESS/EXTEND	
• Assess students' comprehension and mastery of the Literary Analysis and Reading Strategy by having them answer the Apply the Skills questions. **FT**	15 min.
• Have students complete the Vocabulary Lesson and the Grammar and Style Lesson. **FT**	15 min.
• Apply students' ability to choose words to create tone by using the Writing Lesson. **FT**	45 min. or homework
• Apply students' understanding by using one or more of the Extend Your Learning activities.	20–90 min. or homework
• Administer Selection Test A or Selection Test B. **FT**	15 min.

Resources

Print

Unit 3 Resources

Support for Penguin Essay . . . . p. 41
Listening and Viewing . . . . p. 42
Vocabulary Warm-up Word Lists **[L1, L2, EL]** . . . . p. 43
Vocabulary Warm-up Practice **[L1, L2, EL]** . . . . p. 44
Reading Warm-up A **[L1, L2, EL]** . . . . p. 45
Reading Warm-up B **[L1, L2, L3]** . . . . p. 46

Transparency

Graphic Organizer Transparencies

Literary Analysis Graphic Organizer A **[L3]** . . . . p. 57
Literary Analysis Graphic Organizer B **[L1, L2, EL]** . . . . p. 58
Reading Strategy Graphic Organizer A **[L3]** . . . . p. 55
Reading Strategy Graphic Organizer B **[L1, L2, EL]** . . . . p. 56

Technology

From the Scholar's Desk DVD . . . . Royall Tyler, Segment 2

Print

Reader's Notebook [L2]
Reader's Notebook: Adapted Version [L1]
Reader's Notebook: English Learner's Version [EL]

Unit 3 Resources

Literary Analysis **[L3]** . . . . p. 47
Reading Strategy **[L3]** . . . . p. 48
Vocabulary Builder **[L3]** . . . . p. 49

Technology

Listening to Literature Audio CDs [L2, EL]
Reader's Notebook: Adapted Version Audio CD [L1, L2]

Print

Unit 3 Resources

Grammar and Style **[L3]** . . . . p. 50
Support for Writing Lesson **[L3]** . . . . p. 51
Support for Extend Your Learning **[L3]** . . . . p. 52
Enrichment **[L4]** . . . . p. 53
Selection Test A **[L1, L2, EL]** . . . . pp. 54–56
Selection Test B **[L3, L4]** . . . . pp. 57–59

General Resources

Rubrics for Narration: Short Story **[L3]** . . . . pp. 63–64
Rubrics for Multimedia Report **[L3]** . . . . pp. 57–58

Technology

Go Online: Research **[L3]**
Go Online: Self-test **[L3]**
***ExamView®*, Test Bank [L3]**

Choosing Resources for Differentiated Instruction

[L1] Special Needs Students
[L2] Below-Level Students
[L3] All Students
[L4] Advanced Students
[EL] English Learners

For Vocabulary and Reading Warm-ups and for Selection Tests, **A** signifies "less challenging" and **B** "more challenging." For Graphic Organizer transparencies, **A** signifies "not filled in" and **B** "filled in."

FT Fast Track Instruction: To move the lesson more quickly, use the strategies and activities identified with **FT**.

Scaffolding for Less Proficient and Advanced Students

The leveled Critical Thinking questions after selections progress in the levels of thinking required to answer them. To address the needs of your different students, you may use the (a) level questions for your less proficient students and the (b) level questions with your on-level and advanced students. The occasional (c) level questions are appropriate for your advanced students.

PRENTICE HALL **TeacherEXPRESS™** Plan · Teach · Assess — Use this complete suite of powerful teaching tools to make lesson planning and testing quicker and easier.

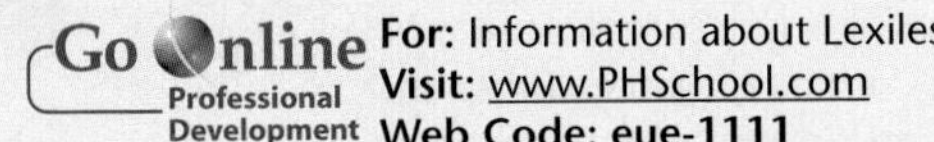

Use the interactive textbook (online and on CD-ROM) to make selections and activities come alive with audio and video support and interactive questions.

Go Online Professional Development — **For:** Information about Lexiles
Visit: www.PHSchool.com
Web Code: eue-1111

 From the Scholar's Desk

Royall Tyler

- You might wish to have students reread Royall Tyler's introduction to the unit on pages 252–253.
- Show Segment 2 on Royall Tyler on *From the Author's Desk DVD* to provide insight into Japanese poetry and translation. After students have watched the segment, **ask:** Why is studying a second language valuable for students?
  Answer: Knowledge of a second language strengthens reading and writing skills and allows students to understand a text as it was originally written.
- Have students read Tyler's comments on these pages.
- **Ask:** What were the purposes of poetry in early Japanese society?
  Answer: Poetry was used to express responses to sights, sounds, and feelings, and for social needs, obligations, and pastimes.

Poetry as Social Interaction

- Point out that social interaction was much different before the advent of electronic media and technologies. Although some people today attend poetry readings in bookstores or coffee shops, music brings many more people together. The poetry that structures the lyrics, however, continues to resonate with people.
- **Ask** students to name the ways in which lyrical music functions as a form of social interaction today.
  Answer: People gather together to enjoy the following musical activities that involve lyrics: rock concerts, opera, karaoke, dance clubs, and televised singing competitions.

From the Scholar's Desk

ROYALL TYLER INTRODUCES *Japanese Tanka and Haiku*

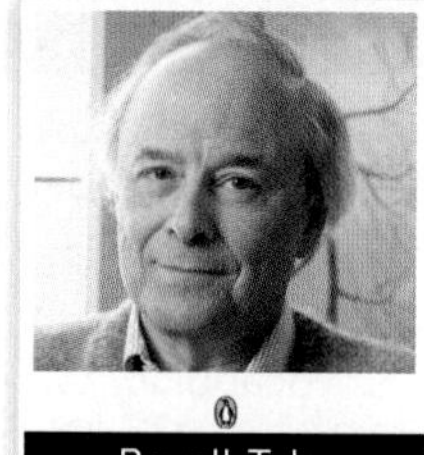
Royall Tyler

Royall Tyler is an expert on Japanese literature and the acclaimed translator of *The Tale of Genji, Japanese Tales,* and *Japanese Nōh Dramas.*

When Poetry Could Move Heaven and Earth

In the Japan of centuries past, you needed no special calling to be a poet. Verse, whether oral or written, was common in everyday life. An essay from the year 905 talks about how poetry springs naturally from the heart in response to sights, sounds, and feelings. Poetry, it says, can "move heaven and earth, smooth the relations between men and women, and calm the fiercest warrior." In short, poetry makes a difference. It works. Stories tell how an apt poem could save a man's life, for example, or win him favor with his beloved.

◀ **Critical Viewing** How would you describe the mood of this landscape painting? **[Interpret]**

Poetry as Social Interaction These powerful poems were *tanka,* a short verse form that began early in Japanese history and still survives today. Nowadays, we associate poetry with individual creativity, but for most Japanese people then, it had more to do with social needs, obligations, and pastimes. If someone sent you a poem (a tanka), you either sent one back or else, socially, you had cut that person dead. A courting couple exchanged poems often, and many other social situations also called for the writing of poetry.

There were even festive poetry contests, like contemporary poetry slams or rap contests. Lack of talent was no excuse. You just did your best, and some people were very good indeed. Poetic skill was highly prized, and everyone agreed that poetry was the noblest of the arts.

Teaching Resources

The following resources can be used to enrich or extend the instruction for From the Scholar's Desk.

Unit 3 Resources
- **From the Scholar's Desk,** p. 41
- **Listening and Viewing,** p. 42

From the Author's Desk DVD
- **Royall Tyler,** Segment 2

Counting Syllables What makes a tanka a poem? Neither rhyme, since rhyme in Japanese is no challenge, nor meter, since the language flows too evenly for that. Instead, the defining feature is syllable count. A tanka consists of thirty-one syllables in five segments: five, seven, five, seven, seven. These segments stand out clearly in Japanese, although they are not necessarily divided into separate lines.

This is about as close as you can get to the structure of a Japanese tanka in an English translation: *Snow upon the hills, // ice along frozen rivers: // these for you I trod, // yet for all that never lost // the way to be lost in you.* Count the syllables: they are all there. A young man in a classic novel, *The Tale of Genji,* sends this tanka to his girlfriend after a winter journey home from her house. She, of course, answers with a tanka of her own.

Going Solo Three or four centuries ago, a new, even shorter Japanese verse form developed: the *haiku.* Consisting of only seventeen syllables (five, seven, five—the first half of a tanka), the haiku started out not as a solo poem, but as the opening of a chain of "linked verse." A few people would get together and, turn by turn, put together a sequence of verses, in a process comparable to jazz improvisation, when one musician elaborates on the ideas of other band members. Composing linked verse was a hugely popular pastime throughout Japan for several hundred years. Then, the haiku went independent, so to speak, becoming a separate verse form that eventually eclipsed the tanka in popularity.

Today, the haiku is one of the world's most famous and recognizable verse forms, and people write haiku—or haiku-like poems—in a variety of languages. Japanese poetry has become international.

Thinking About the Commentary

1. **(a) Recall:** What was the function of poetry in early Japan?
   (b) Compare and Contrast: In what way is that function different from the role of poetry in contemporary American life?
2. **(a) Recall:** What is the key feature of a tanka? **(b) Speculate:** What challenges might a translator of tanka encounter?
3. **(a) Recall:** How did haiku develop as a poetic form? **(b) Infer:** Why do you think haiku became more popular than tanka?

As You Read Tanka and Haiku . . .

4. Consider the social occasions that may have inspired the poets to compose tanka and haiku.
5. Think about the ways in which these poetic forms are both similar to and different from other types of poetry that you have read.

ASSESS

Answers

1. (a) In early Japan, poetry was used for social purposes such as smoothing the relations between men and women and calming warriors. Social situations required the writing of poetry. (b) Poetry is not a key element in everyday social interactions. However, some forms of poetry, such as greeting card verse, serve a similar function of smoothing relations and conveying feelings. Poetry also is used in the lyrics of contemporary music, especially love songs, to express relations between men and women.
2. (a) The key feature of a tanka is the sequence of 31 syllables that are divided into five segments of five, seven, five, seven, and seven syllables. (b) **Possible answer:** It may be difficult to be faithful to the meaning of the original language and still maintain the tanka syllable structure.
3. (a) As a poetic form, haiku developed as the opening of a chain of linked verse. (b) Because haiku was shorter and was divided into lines, it was probably easier to write and thus became more popular.
4. **Possible answer:** The social occasions might have included courtship and travel.
5. **Possible answer:** Students may mention that Tanka and Haiku are similar to poetry by Emily Dickinson because she frequently wrote poetry about nature, used very short lines, and rarely rhymed her lines. Tanka and Haiku are different from poetry such as Geoffrey Chaucer's. He valued rhyme and wrote little about nature, choosing instead to focus on the details of human nature.

Motivation

To prepare students to appreciate imagery, hang posters or magazine photos depicting seasons and moods of nature. Also, play an audiotape of natural sounds like wind, water, or bird songs. Have students discuss feelings and memories they have when they see each photo and hear each sound.

❶ Background

More About the Authors

During the period when Ki Tsurayuki, Ono Komachi, and Priest Jakuren lived and wrote, male scholars and poets wrote primarily in Chinese. Yet only a small percentage of Japan's population could read Chinese, and women were permitted to read and write only Japanese. However, men used poetry to court women, so male poets wrote love poems in Japanese, usually in the Tanka form.

Matsuo Bashō is known for his travel writings as well as his haiku. Yosa Buson, however, believed that poetry should be an expression of beauty, not a depiction of the poet's experiences. For him, life and art were separate entities. An interesting aspect of Kobayashi Issa's life is its eerie similarity to that of Edgar Allan Poe. Both endured unhappy childhoods, suffered the losses of beloved wives, lived in poverty, and gained recognition only after their deaths.

Geography Note

Draw students' attention to the map above. Point out that although China is bigger than the United States, Japan is about the size of Montana.

❶ Tanka • Haiku

Ki Tsurayuki (died c. 945)

The chief aid of Emperor Daigo (dī´ gō´), Ki Tsurayuki (kē´ tso͞or´ ī´ o͞o´ kē´) was one of the leading poets, critics, and diarists of his time. Tsurayuki deserves much of the credit for assembling the *Kokinshu* (kō´ kēn´ sho͞o´), an anthology of over eleven hundred poems of the Heian (hā´ än´) Age. In addition, his *Tosa Diary* helped to establish the Japanese tradition of the literary diary. This tradition includes some of Japan's finest works of literature, one of the most famous being Sei Shōnagon's *Pillow Book*.

Ono Komachi (833–857)

A great beauty with a strong personality, Ono Komachi (ō´ nō´ kō´ mä´ chē´) was an early tanka (täŋ´ kə) poet whose poems are characterized by their passion and energy. Few details of Ono Komachi's life are known. However, there are a vast number of legends about her, and these legends serve as the basis for a well-known series of plays.

Priest Jakuren (1139?–1202)

Jakuren (jä´ ko͞o´ ren´) was a Buddhist priest and prominent tanka poet whose poems are filled with beautiful yet melancholic imagery. After entering the priesthood at the age of twenty-three, Jakuren spent much of his time traveling the Japanese countryside, writing poetry and seeking spiritual fulfillment. In addition to contributing poems to the *Senzaishu* (sen´ zē´ sho͞o´), a court anthology, he produced *Jakuren Hoshi Shu* (hō´ shē´ sho͞o´), a personal collection of poetry.

Matsuo Bashō (1644–1694)

Generally regarded as the greatest Japanese haiku poet, Matsuo Bashō (mä´ tzo͞o´ ō´ bä´ shō´) began studying and writing poetry at an early age. As an adult, he became a Zen Buddhist and lived the life of a hermit, supporting himself by teaching and judging poetry contests. When he traveled, he did so with only the barest essentials and relied on the hospitality of temples and fellow poets. Bashō's poems reflect the natural beauty he observed in his travels, as well as the simplicity encouraged by his faith.

Yosa Buson (1716–1784)

Although Yosa Buson (yō´ sä´ bo͞o´ sän´) is widely regarded as the second-greatest Japanese haiku poet, little is known about him. It is known that, in addition to being a celebrated poet, he was one of the finest painters of his time. In both his paintings and his poetry, Buson presents a romantic view of the Japanese landscape that captures the wonder and mystery of nature.

Kobayashi Issa (1763–1828)

Although his talent was not widely recognized until after his death, Kobayashi Issa (kō´ bä´ yä´ shē´ ē´ sä´) is now considered to be on the same poetic level as Bashō and Buson. Born into poverty, Issa wrote haiku that reflect an appreciation for the hardships faced by the common people. His poems capture the essence of daily life in Japan and convey his compassion for the less fortunate.

Preview

Connecting to the Literature

Have you ever had an experience that seemed unimportant on the surface but had great emotional impact? These very short poems each capture a single, simple image or moment, yet each one has great depth of meaning.

Standard Course of Study

- Analyze effects of author's craft and style in reflection. (WL.1.03.9)
- Analyze literary devices and explain their effect on the work. (LT.5.01.3)

2 Literary Analysis

Japanese Poetic Forms

The **tanka** is the most prevalent verse form in traditional Japanese literature. In the original Japanese, each short poem consists of five lines of five, seven, five, seven, and seven syllables. Most tanka include at least one *caesura* (si zyo͞or′ ə), or pause, often indicated by punctuation in English translations. Tanka usually tell a brief story or express a single thought or insight, often about love or nature.

A **haiku** consists of three lines of five, seven, and five syllables in the original Japanese. Haiku typically focus on some aspect of nature and often include a *kigo*, or seasonal word such as "snow" or "cherry blossom," that indicates the time of year being described. Most haiku present a comparison or contrast of two images, actions, or states of being, as in this poem by Bashō:

Summer grasses—
All that remains
Of soldiers' visions.

As you read each of these simple poems, consider what deeper meaning the poet might be suggesting.

Comparing Literary Works

Tanka and haiku poets convey a great deal of meaning in a small number of words by using vivid **imagery,** language that appeals to the senses. For example, "summer grasses" appeals to the senses of sight, touch, and smell by evoking the sight of a green field, the feeling of warm air, and the smell of fragrant grass. As you read, note the different senses to which these poems' nature imagery appeals.

3 Reading Strategy

Picturing Imagery

A tanka or haiku often presents two images that imply a contrast. To fully appreciate this contrast, try to **picture** the imagery. Use your memory and imagination to see, feel, hear, smell, or taste what the poet describes. In a chart like the one shown, list associations that help you see pairs of images, and then note the contrast implied by each pair.

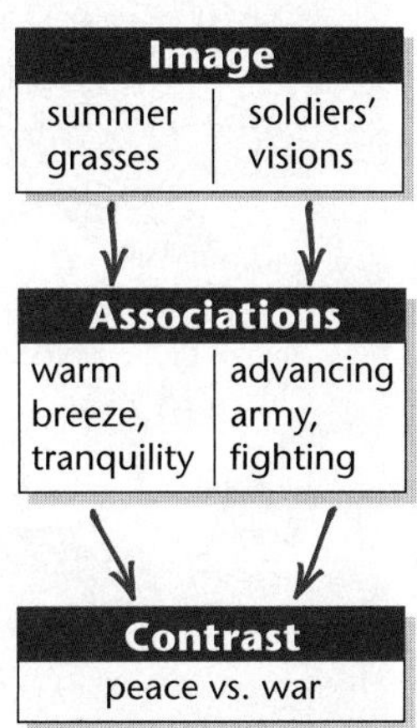

Vocabulary Builder

veiled (vāld) *v.* covered (p. 300)
bland (bland) *adj.* mild (p. 302)
serenity (sə ren′ ə tē) *n.* peace; tranquillity (p. 302)

2 Literary Analysis

Japanese Poetic Forms

- Read the definitions of tanka and haiku with the class. Make sure students understand that tanka tell brief stories or express single thoughts and that haiku generally compare two images.
- Using the haiku in the Reading Strategy activity below, **ask** students to identify sensory words or phrases. Underline students' suggestions, and write the sense to the side of the poem.
  Possible response: Students may suggest clouds/sight; rest/touch; and moon/sight.

3 Reading Strategy

Picturing Imagery

- Tell students that an image is a picture a poem creates in the reader's mind. Poets use words that appeal to the five senses.
- Write the following haiku on the board, and **ask** students to complete a graphic organizer like the one on the page for the poem:

  Clouds come from time to time—
  and bring to men a chance to rest
  from looking at the moon.

  Possible response: Image: sky: clouds/moon; resting men; **Associations:** distance, dreams, future, goals; interruptions, fatigue, reality; **Contrast:** dreams vs. reality
- Give students a copy of **Reading Strategy Graphic Organizer A** in *Graphic Organizer Transparencies,* p. 55, to use to compare imagery in the poems as they read.

Vocabulary Builder

- Pronounce each vocabulary word for students, and read the definitions as a class. Have students identify any words with which they are already familiar.

Differentiated Instruction
Solutions for All Learners

Support for Special Needs Students
Have students complete the **Preview** and **Build Skills** pages for these selections in the ***Reader's Notebook: Adapted Version.*** These pages provide a selection summary, an abbreviated presentation of the reading and literary skills, and the graphic organizer on the **Build Skills** page in the student book.

Support for Less Proficient Readers
Have students complete the **Preview** and **Build Skills** pages for these selections in the ***Reader's Notebook.*** These pages provide a selection summary, an abbreviated presentation of the reading and literary skills, and the graphic organizer on the **Build Skills** page in the student book.

Support for English Learners
Have students complete the **Preview** and **Build Skills** pages for these selections in the ***Reader's Notebook: English Learner's Version.*** These pages provide a selection summary, an abbreviated presentation of the skills, additional contextual vocabulary, and the graphic organizer on the **Build Skills** page in the student book.

TEACH

Facilitate Understanding

Have students focus on content rather than form in both tanka and haiku.

❶ About the Selections

These tanka use clear images and simple language to evoke strong emotion. Ki Tsurayuki and Ono Komachi focus on love, whereas Priest Jakuren contemplates loneliness.

❷ Reading Strategy

Picturing Imagery

- **Ask** the Reading Strategy question. **Possible response:** The words call to mind a cold, star-filled night.

❸ Humanities

Snow at Senso-ji Temple in Asakusa, by Utagawa Kuniyoshi

Kuniyoshi (1798–1861) was a member of the *ukiyo-e* school of Japanese art. Wood-block prints like this one were highly popular. **Ask:** What is the relationship between nature and humanity in this print?

Possible response: The relationship appears to be one of balance.

❹ Critical Viewing

Possible response: The scene in the print seems less cold and lonely than the night in the poem.

Tanka

❶ **Background** When tanka are translated into English, the translator often must alter the syllabic structure of the poem and, in some cases, also change the number of lines. Therefore, when reading a tanka in translation, it is more important to focus on the imagery used and the emotions evoked than on the poem's form.

Ki Tsurayuki translated by Geoffrey Bownas

When I went to visit
The girl I love so much,
❷ That winter night
The river blew so cold
That the plovers[1] were crying.

Reading Strategy
Picturing Imagery What feelings and associations do the words *winter night* call to mind?

1. **plovers** (pluv´ ərz) *n.* wading shorebirds with short tails, long, pointed wings, and short, stout beaks.

❸

Snow at Senso-ji Temple in Asakusa, Victoria and Albert Museum, London

◀ **Critical Viewing** ❹
How does this winter scene compare with the one described in Ki Tsurayuki's tanka? Explain. **[Compare and Contrast]**

Differentiated Instruction Solutions for All Learners

Accessibility at a Glance

	Tanka	Tanka	Tanka	Haiku	Haiku	Haiku
Language	Evocative	Evocative	Evocative	Concrete words	Concrete words	Concrete words
Concept Level	Accessible (Loss of love)	Accessible (Dreams of love)	Accessible (Origins of Loneliness)	Accessible (Wisdom of nature)	Accessible (Melancholy of rain)	Accessible (Contrasts in nature)
Literary Merit	Clear images	Evokes feelings	Sensory images	Contrasting images	Contrasting images	Contrasting images
Lexile	NP	NP	NP	NP	NP	NP
Overall Rating	More Accessible	More Accessible	More Accessible	More Accessible	More Accessible	More Accessible

Ono Komachi translated by *Geoffrey Bownas*

Was it that I went to sleep
Thinking of him,
That he came in my dreams? | 5
Had I known it a dream
I should not have wakened.

Literary Analysis
Japanese Poetic Forms
Where does the caesura occur in this tanka?

Priest Jakuren translated by *Geoffrey Bownas*

One cannot ask loneliness
How or where it starts.
On the cypress-mountain,[2]
Autumn evening.

2. **cypress-mountain** Cypress trees are cone-bearing evergreen trees, native to North America, Europe, and Asia.

Critical Reading

1. **Respond:** To which of these tanka could you relate most? Explain your answer.
2. **(a) Recall:** What is the setting of Tsurayuki's tanka? **(b) Infer:** What does the speaker's willingness to face that setting suggest about the depth of his love? **(c) Interpret:** What does the setting suggest about the outcome of his visit?
3. **(a) Recall:** What question does the speaker of Ono Komachi's tanka ask? **(b) Infer:** What do her question and her response to that question suggest about her feelings toward the man in her dreams?
4. **Make a Judgment:** Do you think a poem is more effective when it suggests a feeling or when it describes the feeling in detail? Explain.

For: More about Ki Tsurayuki, Ono Komachi, and Priest Jakuren
Visit: www.PHSchool.com
Web Code: ete-9306

5 Literary Analysis
Japanese Poetic Forms

- Explain that most tanka include a caesura, or pause. In English translations, caesuras are often indicated by end punctuation such as semicolons, periods, and question marks.
- **Ask** the Literary Analysis question: **Answer:** The caesura occurs at the end of the third line. It is represented by a question mark.
- **Ask** students to describe the effect the caesura has on the poem. **Possible response:** The caesura divides the poem into two sections. The first questions the nature of dreams; the second laments the weakness of human knowledge in the face of such dreaming.

ASSESS
Answers

1. **Possible response:** Ki Tsurayuki's or Ono Komachi's tanka will probably appeal to teenagers because each uses spare, evocative language to express love and longing.
2. (a) The setting is a bitter winter night. (b) The speaker's willingness indicates his deep love. (c) The cold suggests that the speaker's beloved has rejected him.
3. (a) The speaker asks whether she dreamed about a man because she was "thinking of him" when she went to sleep. (b) **Possible response:** She has strong feelings.
4. **Possible response:** More effective poems suggest a feeling, thereby evoking a personal response.

Go Online Author Link For additional information about Ki Tsurayuki, Ono Komachi, or Priest Jakuren, have students type in the Web Code, then select the first letter of the author's last name from the alphabet, and then select the author's name.

Differentiated Instruction
Solutions for All Learners

Support for Special Needs Students
Tanka may offer students a strong opportunity to respond to poetry. To overcome any intimidation, remind them that tanka are very brief, simple poems that use few details to suggest universal emotions. Then, have them read the poems along with **Listening to Literature Audio CDs.**

Enrichment for Gifted/Talented Students
The spare, evocative detail of tanka may be enhanced by music. Encourage students to find music that complements these poems. Then, have students perform a reading set to music. Students may use recordings or may compose their own music to accompany the tanka.

Enrichment for Advanced Readers
Students may wish to try their hands at writing their own tanka. Students' tanka should be five lines long, include one caesura, and tell a very brief story or express a single thought or insight. Ask students to use lines of five, seven, five, seven, and seven syllables.

❻ About the Selections

Using vivid, fleeting images from nature, the haiku reflect a traditional Buddhist emphasis on the contemplation of nature as a path to wisdom and understanding.

❼ Literary Analysis

Japanese Poetic Forms

- Explain that the *kigo,* or seasonal reference, is characteristic of haiku.
- Have students read the bracketed haiku by Bashō. Then, **ask** the Literary Analysis question.
  Answer: The *kigo* is *May.*

❽ Vocabulary Builder

Connotations and Denotations

- Draw student attention to *veiled* and its denotation, and **invite** students to discuss its connotations.
  Possible response: "Hazy," "hidden," or "marital" are connotations.

❾ Humanities

The Monkey Bridge in Koshu Province, by Ando Hiroshige

Hiroshige (1797–1858) was a renowned Japanese painter and print maker. He was known for his delicate colors and ability to suggest vast landscapes with just a few brushstrokes.

Use this question for discussion:

How does the artist convey a sense of harmony between the bridge and the surrounding landscape?
Answer: The trees that surround the bridge obscure its ends.

❿ Critical Viewing

Possible response: The spare use of detail is characteristic of haiku. The juxtaposition of the bridge and landscape is similar to a haiku's comparison of images.

❻ Haiku

Matsuo Bashō

translated by Harold G. Henderson (first 2) and Geoffrey Bownas (last 3)

Background The haiku evolved from a form of collaborative poetry known as *renga.* At festive poetry contests during the Middle Ages, groups of writers would gather to create interlocking groups of renga verses, which consisted of seventeen and fourteen syllables. The results were judged by a poetry master. Listeners who attended the contests developed a love for this simple yet profound poetic form. Eventually, the *hokku,* the opening verse of a renga, developed into a distinct literary form known as haiku.

❾ 

The Monkey Bridge in Koshu Province, 1841, Hiroshige Hitsu, Christie's, New York

❼ The sun's way:
hollyhocks turn toward it
through all the rain of May.

Clouds come from time to time—
and bring to men a chance to rest
from looking at the moon.

The cuckoo—
Its call stretching
Over the water.

❽ Seven sights were veiled
In mist—then I heard
Mii Temple's bell.[1]

Summer grasses—
All that remains
Of soldiers' visions.

Literary Analysis
Japanese Poetic Forms
What is the *kigo* in the third line of this haiku?

Vocabulary Builder
veiled (vāld) *v.* covered

❿ **Critical Viewing**
Which characteristics of haiku are also evident in this painting? **[Connect]**

1. **Mii** (mē´ ē´) **Temple's bell** The bell at Mii Temple is known for its extremely beautiful sound. The temple is located near Otsu, a city in southern Japan.

Enrichment

Japanese Visual Arts

During Japan's feudal period, the visual arts reflected the Zen values of self-discipline, simplicity, and closeness to nature. Painters learned to suggest an idea or a feeling with a minimum of detail. A few bold lines might be enough to convey an impression of a mountain. In much the same way, Japanese tanka and haiku poets evoked images and emotion with only a word or two. Zen also influenced such crafts as landscape gardening and flower arranging.

As the Tokugawa period of Japanese history began around the turn of the seventeenth century, new art styles emerged. These new styles reflected the tastes of the growing middle class. Among the best-known works of this period are brilliantly colored wood-block prints called *ukiyo-e*—"pictures of the floating world." City life was a popular *ukiyo-e* subject, as were beautiful women, famous actors, and legendary heroes.

Ando Hiroshige, whose prints appear on pp. 300–301, was a part of the *ukiyo-e* school.

Haiku

Yosa Buson
translated by Geoffrey Bownas

Spring rain:
Telling a tale as they go,
Straw cape, umbrella.

Spring rain:
In our sedan
Your soft whispers.

Spring rain:
A man lives here—
Smoke through the wall.

Spring rain:
Soaking on the roof
A child's rag ball.

⓫

Sudden Shower on Ohashi Bridge, Hiroshige

⓬ ▲ Critical Viewing
Which of the four haiku by Yosa Buson would you choose to accompany this painting? Why? **[Connect]**

⓫ Humanities

Sudden Shower on Ohashi Bridge, by Ando Hiroshige

Among Japanese artists, Hiroshige (1797–1858) was second in stature only to Katsushika Hokusai, whose work appears on pp. 250-251. From a series entitled *One Hundred Views of Edo,* this print is among the artist's most ingenious and subtle compositions, with its delicately graded colors, fine lines, and balanced design.

Japanese prints like this one were a major influence on European artists of the nineteenth century. The works of Japanese artists such as Hiroshige and Hokusai were first introduced to the Western world at a Japanese exhibition in Paris. The Western painters who viewed this exhibition were exposed to the asymmetrical arrangement of space and the balancing of light and dark colors. As a result, some Western artists tried printmaking, and others incorporated the Japanese ideas into their painting. Vincent Van Gogh even made a copy of this particular print.

Use the following questions for discussion:

- What details in the print indicate that it is raining?
  Possible response: The vertical lines indicate rain. Also, the efforts the people on the bridge take to cover themselves suggest rain.
- How would you describe the mood, or atmosphere, of this print? How is the mood established?
  Possible response: The mood is melancholy and somber. The rain is the major element in creating the mood. The darkness of the sky, the deep blue of the water, and the hurrying of the people across the bridge also contribute to the mood.

⓬ Critical Viewing

Possible response: The first haiku is the best accompaniment for the painting because it cites the details "Straw cape, umbrella" to create a picture of people hurrying through the rain—much like the scene in the painting.

Differentiated Instruction
Solutions for All Learners

Support for Less Proficient Readers

Students may benefit from extra assistance with the Reading Strategy, Picturing Imagery. Give students a copy of **Reading Strategy Graphic Organizer B**, p. 56, in ***Graphic Organizer Transparencies.*** Then help students describe and explain the imagery in each of Yosa Buson's haiku on this page.

Strategy for English Learners

Translators must remain true to the original language by selecting English words with similar connotations. Provide students with a short poem in a non-English language familiar to the students. Then, pair students with an English speaker, and challenge them to negotiate an English translation of the poem.

Enrichment for Gifted/Talented Students

Encourage students to write several haiku in which they relay their own observations of nature. Students may want to follow Buson's lead and write a series of poems about the same subject. Take students outside to observe and write about nature. Challenge students to capture their observations in the traditional haiku form.

13 Literary Analysis

Japanese Poetic Forms

- Remind students that in its three lines, haiku generally present a comparison or contrast between two images.
- **Ask** the Literary Analysis question: What two images are being contrasted in this haiku?
  Answer: The haiku contrasts the mountain peaks and a dragonfly.

Monitor Progress **Ask** students to read the fourth haiku and compare its use of imagery with that of the second haiku. Students may wish to use a Venn diagram for this comparison.
Possible response: Mountain Peaks: insect, mountain, passive; **Center:** structure, comparison between life and nature, message; **Serenity:** animal, hills, emotion, action.

Reteach Encourage students to read the haiku in the selection and mark each pair of images.

ASSESS

Answers

1. **Possible response:** "The sun's way," "Clouds come from time to time," all four of the "Spring Rain" haiku, and "Far-off mountain peaks" are especially evocative. Concrete words and phrases create strong mental images.
2. (a) Clouds are contrasted with resting men. (b) **Possible response:** Men looking at the moon are searching for universal truth that is beyond human understanding. Nature occasionally sends clouds, giving the people time to rest.
3. (a) **Possible response:** Haiku rely more on suggestion and evocation than Western poetry does.
   (b) **Possible response:** Western poets might make their poems more concise and evocative.

Haiku

Kobayashi Issa

translated by Geoffrey Bownas

Beautiful, seen through holes
Made in a paper screen:
The Milky Way.

Far-off mountain peaks
Reflected in its eyes:
The dragonfly.

A world of dew:
Yet within the dewdrops—
Quarrels.

With bland serenity
Gazing at the far hills:
A tiny frog.

Literary Analysis
Japanese Poetic Forms
What two images are being contrasted in this haiku?

Vocabulary Builder
bland (bland) *adj.* mild
serenity (sə ren′ ə tē) *n.* peace; tranquillity

Critical Reading

1. **Respond:** Which haiku created the strongest mental images for you? Why?
2. **(a) Recall:** In "Clouds come from time to time," with what is the image of clouds contrasted? **(b) Interpret:** What does this contrast suggest about humanity's relationship with nature?
3. **(a) Compare and Contrast:** In what ways are these haiku similar to and different from traditional Western nature poems that you have read? **(b) Evaluate:** What do you think a traditional Western poet could learn from haiku poems?

Go Online
Author Link
For: More about Matsuo Bashō, Yosa Buson, and Kobayashi Issa
Visit: www.PHSchool.com
Web Code: ete-9309

Go Online Author Link For additional information about Matsuo Bashō, Yosa Buson, or Kobayashi Issa, have students type in the Web Code, then select the first letter of the author's last name from the alphabet, and then select the author's name.

Apply the Skills

Tanka • Haiku

Literary Analysis

Japanese Poetic Forms

1. **(a)** What brief story is told in the **tanka** by Ki Tsurayuki? **(b)** How would you describe the emotion conveyed by this poem?
2. **(a)** Where does the **caesura** occur in the tanka by Priest Jakuren? **(b)** What effect does this pause create?
3. **(a)** What contrasting images are presented in the **haiku** "Seven sights were veiled"? **(b)** What is the effect of this contrast?
4. **(a)** Identify the *kigo* in the haiku "Summer grasses—." **(b)** In what way does this *kigo* help create a contrast between the first and third lines of the poem?

Comparing Literary Works

5. **(a)** Identify the nature **imagery** in the tanka by Priest Jakuren. **(b)** To what sense or senses does this imagery appeal?
6. **(a)** Use a Venn diagram like the one shown to compare and contrast the nature imagery in the tanka by Ki Tsurayuki and the Bashō haiku "The sun's way." **(b)** In what way do these poems present two different views of nature?

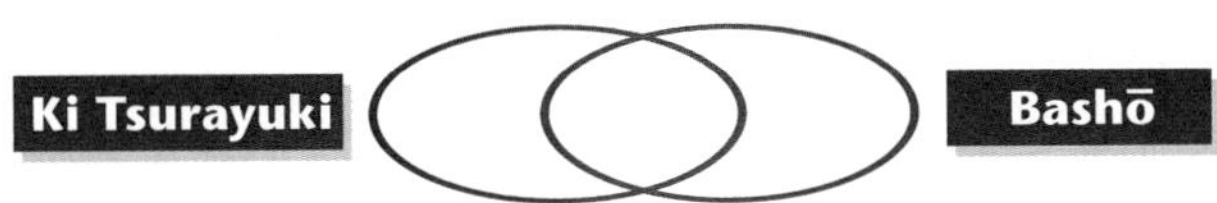

Reading Strategy

Picturing Imagery

7. **(a)** Which words help you **picture the imagery** in the four haiku by Yosa Buson? **(b)** What other images do you associate with these words or phrases that help you see the images in the poem?
8. **(a)** Which haiku or tanka created the strongest mental picture for you? **(b)** Identify the words or phrases in the poem that created this effect.

Extend Understanding

9. **Humanities Connection:** The process by which renga poetry is created has been compared to the artistic collaboration seen in jazz music. To what kind of music or visual art form or style would you compare tanka and haiku? Give examples to support your answer.

QuickReview

A **tanka** is a poem that, in the original Japanese, has five lines of five, seven, five, seven, and seven syllables.

A **caesura** is a pause in a poem.

A **haiku** is a poem that, in the original Japanese, has three lines of five, seven, and five syllables.

A ***kigo*** is a word indicating the season that is being described.

Imagery is language that appeals to the senses.

When you **picture imagery,** you use your memory and imagination to mentally see, hear, smell, taste, or touch what the poet describes.

For: Self-test
Visit: www.PHSchool.com
Web Code: eta-6303

Go Online Assessment Students may use the **Self-test** to prepare for **Selection Test A** or **Selection Test B.**

Answers

1. (a) The tanka by Ki Tsurayuki tells the story of a man visiting his beloved on a bitter winter night. (b) **Possible response:** It conveys sorrow over a lost love.
2. (a) The caesura appears at the end of the second line. (b) The pause divides the poem in two.
3. (a) The contrast is between a visual image and an auditory image. It is also a contrast between mist, an undefined image and the bell, a specific one. (b) **Possible response:** The contrast shifts from the vague and mysterious to the clearly defined sound of the bell.
4. (a) The *kigo* is *Summer.* (b) Summer is associated with sun and idleness and contrasts with the imagery evoked by "soldiers' visions."
5. (a) The imagery is an autumn evening on a mountain covered with cypress trees. (b) It appeals to sight, touch, and smell.
6. (a) **Possible response: Ki Tsurayuki:** winter night, river blew cold, plovers crying; **Center:** *kigo,* nature images; **Bashō:** sun, hollyhocks, rain of May (b) The tanka depicts nature as harsh and bitter; the haiku portrays it as warm and welcoming.

   Another sample answer can be found on **Literary Analysis Graphic Organizer B,** p. 58, in ***Graphic Organizer Transparencies.***
7. (a) **Possible response:** "Cape, umbrella, sedan, Smoke, roof," and "rag ball" convey images. (b) They call to mind images of city or small-town life.
8. (a) **Possible response:** The haiku of Yosa Buson is image-centered. (b) Repeating *kigo,* such as "Spring rain," create a strong mental image.
9. **Possible response:** Tanka and haiku might be compared to Japanese painting because their minimal lines suggest rather than depict.

EXTEND/ASSESS

Answers

❶ Vocabulary Lesson

Connotations and Denotations

1. *solitude* or *isolation*
2. *night, twilight,* or *dusk*
3. *story, narrative, myth, legend,* or *yarn*

Vocabulary Builder: Analogies

1. bland
2. veiled
3. serenity

Spelling Strategy

1. electricity
2. propriety
3. intensity
4. activity

❷ Grammar and Style Lesson

1. *Thinking* of him; modifies *I*
2. *stretching* over the water; modifies *call*
3. *Soaking* on the roof; modifies *ball*
4. *Reflected* in its eyes; modifies *peaks*
5. *Telling* a tale; modifies *cape, umbrella*

Writing Application

Possible response:

Through summer stillness
I ran—
Expecting joy.

The heavy snow
Falling like a blanket;
Cozy fire.

Early evening
In early June—
Bringing darkness.

Writing and Grammar Platinum Level

For support in teaching the Grammar and Style Lesson, use Chapter 20, Section 1.

Build Language Skills

❶ Vocabulary Lesson

Connotations and Denotations

A word's **denotation** is its direct, literal meaning. For example, the denotation of *spring* is "the season that follows winter." The **connotations** of a word are the ideas associated with it. *Spring*'s connotations include warmth and rebirth.

Writers and translators have connotations in mind when they choose words. For example, one might use the word *gazing* instead of *looking* in order to imply "looking thoughtfully," rather than simply "directing one's eyes." Connotations are especially important in tanka and haiku. Because these poems contain so few words, each word must convey a great deal of meaning.

For each of the following words, provide another word that has the same denotation but different connotations.

1. loneliness **2.** evening **3.** tale

Vocabulary Builder: Analogies

Complete the following analogies using the words from the vocabulary list on page 297.

1. jagged : smooth :: harsh : _____
2. uncovered : exposed :: _____ : concealed
3. volcano : turmoil :: flower : _____

Spelling Strategy

The suffixes *-ity* and *-ety* are both used to form nouns from adjectives. The suffix *-ity* is more common, but the suffix *-ety* is used for a few adjectives that end in *e* or *i: safe/safety; various/variety.* Add the correct suffix, *-ity* or *-ety,* to each of the following roots.

1. electric-
2. propri-
3. intens-
4. activ-

❷ Grammar and Style Lesson

Participial Phrases

Participles are forms of verbs that can act as adjectives. Participles usually end in *-ing* or *-ed*. A **participial phrase** is a participle that is modified by an adverb or adverb phrase or accompanied by a complement. The entire participial phrase functions as an adjective. Participles and participial phrases answer the question *Which one?* or *What kind?* and can either precede or follow the words they modify.

> **Participle:** exciting news
>
> **Participial Phrase:** The runners, exhausted from the race, rested on the grass. (modifies *runners*)

Practice Identify the participles and participial phrases in these items. Indicate which word or words each one modifies.

1. Was it that I went to sleep / Thinking of him,
2. Its call stretching / Over the water.
3. Soaking on the roof / A child's rag ball.
4. Far-off mountain peaks / Reflected in its eyes:
5. Telling a tale as they go, / Straw cape, umbrella.

Writing Application Write three haiku of your own. In each one, use at least one participial phrase to convey the same sort of concise imagery found in the haiku and tanka you have read.

Prentice Hall Writing and Grammar Connection: Platinum Level, Chapter 20, Section 2

Assessment Practice

Recognize Facts, Details, and Sequence

(For more practice, see *Test Preparation Workbook*, p. 14.)

The reading sections of standardized tests often require students to identify details. To give students practice with this skill, have them answer this sample test item.

> Every year, at New Year's, a poetry exhibition called the *utakai* is held in Japan. Thousands of people, from the emperor on down, submit poems that are then read before a national television audience.

Who participates in the *utakai?*

A the emperor and other government officials
B people from all over the world
C everyone from the emperor on down
D a world-wide television audience

The passage does not suggest that people outside of Japan participate in the *utakai*, so answers *B* and *D* are not correct. While answer *A* is partially correct, it is too limited to be the correct answer. Answer *C* is a detail in the passage, so it is the correct answer.

❸ Writing Lesson

Short Story

In just a few short lines, a tanka or haiku can provide a glimpse into an entire world. Yet, there is more that could be said about that world. Write a short story that expands on the scene described in one of the tanka or haiku you have read.

Prewriting Choose a poem on which to base your story. Also, decide what kind of tone you would like your story to have. For example, it can be happy or sad, humorous or serious.

Drafting Begin your story by describing the characters and setting. Then, describe an incident that introduces an element of conflict—a struggle between opposing forces. This conflict should build to a climax, or high point of tension, before being resolved.

Revising Reread your draft to be sure that you have used words that create the right tone. If you find words that do not suit the tone you intended, replace them with more appropriate ones.

Model: Choosing Words to Create Tone

The frog looked ~~apathetic~~ carefree as he ~~abandoned~~ sprang from his lily pad. He swam through the ~~cold~~ cool water to the shore of the pond.

Words with positive associations create a cheerful tone.

Prentice Hall Writing and Grammar Connection: Platinum Level, Chapter 6, Section 4

❹ Extend Your Learning

Listening and Speaking With a small group of classmates, hold a **poetry reading.** Consult poetry anthologies to find more haiku. Then, have each member of the group read at least four favorite haiku. Consider enhancing the reading in the following ways:

- Select and play appropriate music to accompany each poem.
- Make a backdrop with seasonal colors.

Rehearse your reading as a group, and then perform it for the class. **[Group Activity]**

Research and Technology Research Japan's weather, landscape, and seasons, and present a **climate report.** Be sure to note aspects of the landscape and climate that are reflected in the haiku you have read, such as hollyhocks and spring rain. Include photographs of Japanese landscapes and graphics to explain climate data in your report.

For: An additional research activity
Visit: www.PHSchool.com
Web Code: etd-7303

❸ Writing Lesson

You may use this Writing Lesson as timed-writing practice, or you may allow students to develop the short story as a writing assignment over several days.

- To give students guidance in writing this short story, give them the **Support for Writing Lesson,** p. 51, in ***Unit 3 Resources.***
- Before students begin drafting, review conflict, climax, and resolution with the class.
- After students complete drafts, have them revise for tone. Encourage them to use precise words to establish the proper tone.
- Use the Narration: Short Story rubric in ***General Resources,*** pp. 63–64, to evaluate students' work.

Writing and Grammar Platinum Level
For support in teaching the Writing Lesson, use Chapter 6, Section 4.

❹ Listening and Speaking

- Have students practice evocative readings of the haiku as a group before presenting them.
- Use the Multimedia Report rubrics in ***General Resources,*** pp. 57–58, to evaluate students' work.
- The **Support for Extend Your Learning** page (***Unit 3 Resources,*** p. 52) provides guided note-taking opportunities to help students complete the Extend Your Learning activities.

Go Online Research Have students type in the Web Code for another research activity.

Assessment Resources

The following resources can be used to assess students' knowledge and skills.

Unit 3 Resources
- **Selection Test A,** pp. 54–56
- **Selection Test B,** pp. 57–59

General Resources
- **Rubrics for Narration: Short Story,** pp. 63–64
- **Rubrics for Multimedia Report,** pp. 57–58

Go Online Assessment Students may use the **Self-test** to prepare for **Selection Test A** or **Selection Test B.**

Standard Course of Study

Goal 1: WRITTEN LANGUAGE

- **WL.1.02.1** Relate personal knowledge to textual information in a written reflection.
- **WL.1.03.6** Make inferences and draw conclusions based on personal reflection.
- **WL.1.03.7** Analyze influences, contexts, or biases in personal reflection.
- **WL.1.03.10** Analyze connections between ideas, concepts, characters and experiences in reflection.

Goal 5: LITERATURE

- **LT.5.01.1** Use strategies for preparation, engagement, and reflection on world literature.

Goal 6: GRAMMAR AND USAGE

- **GU.6.02.1** Edit for agreement, tense choice, pronouns, antecedents, case, and complete sentences.

Step-by-Step Teaching Guide	Pacing Guide
PRETEACH	
• Administer Vocabulary and Reading Warm-ups as necessary.	5 min.
• Engage students' interest with the motivation activity.	5 min.
• Read and discuss author and background features. **FT**	10 min.
• Introduce the Literary Analysis Skill: Journal. **FT**	5 min.
• Introduce the Reading Strategy: Relating to Your Own Experiences. **FT**	10 min.
• Prepare students to read by teaching the selection vocabulary. **FT**	
TEACH	
• Informally monitor comprehension while students read independently or in groups. **FT**	30 min.
• Monitor students' comprehension with the Reading Check notes.	as students read
• Reinforce vocabulary with Vocabulary Builder notes.	as students read
• Develop students' understanding of journals with the Literary Analysis annotations. **FT**	5 min.
• Develop students' ability to relate to their own experiences with the Reading Strategy annotations. **FT**	5 min.
ASSESS/EXTEND	
• Assess students' comprehension and mastery of the Literary Analysis and Reading Strategy by having them answer the Apply the Skills questions. **FT**	15 min.
• Have students complete the Vocabulary Lesson and the Grammar and Style Lesson. **FT**	15 min.
• Apply students' ability to gather details by using the Writing Lesson. **FT**	45 min. or homework
• Apply students' understanding by using one or more of the Extend Your Learning activities.	20–90 min. or homework
• Administer Selection Test A or Selection Test B. **FT**	15 min.

Resources

Print

Unit 3 Resources

- Vocabulary Warm-up Word Lists **[L1, L2, EL]** . . . p. 60
- Vocabulary Warm-up Practice **[L1, L2, EL]** . . . p. 61
- Reading Warm-up A **[L1, L2, EL]** . . . p. 62
- Reading Warm-up B **[L1, L2, L3]** . . . p. 63

Transparency

Graphic Organizer Transparencies

- Literary Analysis Graphic Organizer A **[L3]** . . . p. 59
- Literary Analysis Graphic Organizer B **[L1, L2, EL]** . . . p. 60
- Reading Strategy Graphic Organizer A **[L3]** . . . p. 61
- Reading Strategy Graphic Organizer B **[L1, L2, EL]** . . . p. 62

Print

Reader's Notebook [L2]

Reader's Notebook: Adapted Version [L1]

Reader's Notebook: English Learner's Version [EL]

Unit 3 Resources

- Literary Analysis **[L3]** . . . p. 64
- Reading Strategy **[L3]** . . . p. 65
- Vocabulary Builder **[L3]** . . . p. 66

Technology

Listening to Literature Audio CDs [L2, EL]

Reader's Notebook: Adapted Version Audio CD [L1, L2]

Print

Unit 3 Resources

- Grammar and Style **[L3]** . . . p. 67
- Support for Writing Lesson **[L3]** . . . p. 68
- Support for Extend Your Learning **[L3]** . . . p. 69
- Enrichment **[L4]** . . . p. 70
- Selection Test A **[L1, L2, EL]** . . . pp. 71–73
- Selection Test B **[L3, L4]** . . . pp. 74–76

General Resources

- Rubrics for Narration: Autobiographical Narrative **[L3]** . . . pp. 43–44

Technology

- **Go Online:** Research **[L3]**
- **Go Online:** Self-test **[L3]**
- ***ExamView®*, Test Bank [L3]**

Choosing Resources for Differentiated Instruction

[L1] Special Needs Students

[L2] Below-Level Students

[L3] All Students

[L4] Advanced Students

[EL] English Learners

For Vocabulary and Reading Warm-ups and for Selection Tests, **A** signifies "less challenging" and **B** "more challenging." For Graphic Organizer transparencies, **A** signifies "not filled in" and **B** "filled in."

FT Fast Track Instruction: To move the lesson more quickly, use the strategies and activities identified with **FT**.

Scaffolding for Less Proficient and Advanced Students

The leveled Critical Thinking questions after selections progress in the levels of thinking required to answer them. To address the needs of your different students, you may use the (a) level questions for your less proficient students and the (b) level questions with your on-level and advanced students. The occasional (c) level questions are appropriate for your advanced students.

PRENTICE HALL **TeacherEXPRESS™** Plan · Teach · Assess Use this complete suite of powerful teaching tools to make lesson planning and testing quicker and easier.

PRENTICE HALL **StudentEXPRESS™** Learn · Study · Succeed Use the interactive textbook (online and on CD-ROM) to make selections and activities come alive with audio and video support and interactive questions.

For: Information about Lexiles
Visit: www.PHSchool.com
Web Code: eue-1111

PREТEACH

Motivation

Direct students to write freely for five minutes on one of the following topics: seasons/nature, pets, or memories. Tell students not to put their names on their papers. Collect and redistribute the papers to student groups. Direct students to read the entries and record and discuss what they reveal about life in the United States. Explain that in *The Pillow Book,* Sei Shōnagon describes her life in the Imperial Court of tenth-century Japan. By reading her journal, we can learn what that life was like.

❶ Background

More About the Author

The word *shōnagon* means "minor counselor." The author of *The Pillow Book,* whose real name is believed to be Najiko, was called Shōnagon because of her service to the empress.

In the final entry of *The Pillow Book,* Sei Shōnagon offers insight into the origin of her work.

"One day Lord Koerchika, the Minister of the Center, brought the Empress a bundle of notebooks. 'What shall we do with them?' Her Majesty asked me. . . .

"'Let me make them into a pillow,' I said.

"'Very well,' said Her Majesty. 'You may have them.'

"I now had a vast quantity of paper at my disposal, and I set about filling the notebooks with odd facts, stories from the past, and all sorts of other things."

Geography Note

Draw students' attention to the map above. When she composed *The Pillow Book,* Sei Shōnagon was a lady in waiting in the imperial court at the capital city, Heian, now Kyoto, Japan.

Build Skills | Primary Source

❶ *from* The Pillow Book

Sei Shōnagon (c. tenth century A.D.)

Sei Shōnagon (sä´ shō´ nä´ gōn´) is responsible for providing us with a detailed portrait of upper-class life in Japan during the Heian (hā´ än´) Age, which lasted from 794 to 1185 A.D. Her *The Pillow Book,* a collection of personal notes written during her ten years of court service, is filled with character sketches, descriptions, anecdotes, lists, and witty insights. A precursor of the Japanese literary form *zuihitsu,* or "occasional writings," *The Pillow Book* is widely recognized as one of the finest works of Japanese prose.

A Complex Figure Sei Shōnagon was the daughter of a provincial official who was also a noted scholar and poet. She was a lady-in-waiting for the Empress Sadako (sä´ dä´ kō´) during the last decade of the tenth century, and she may have been married briefly to a government official. Aside from what *The Pillow Book* reveals about her years of court service, however, little is known about Sei Shōnagon. In fact, her life following her court service remains a mystery.

Although few details are known about Sei Shōnagon's life, *The Pillow Book* offers a wealth of insights into her personality. The 185 sections of the book reveal her to be an intelligent, observant, and quick-witted woman. While she had a tremendous amount of admiration for the imperial family, she seems to have had little respect for the lower social orders. Sei Shōnagon's scorn for the less fortunate, her judgmental nature, her competitive attitude toward men, and her lack of restraint have angered some scholars and critics—even some of her contemporaries. The great Japanese novelist Murasaki Shikibu (mōō´ rä´ sä´ kē´shē´ kē´ bōō´) wrote, "Sei Shōnagon has the most extraordinary air of self-satisfaction. . . . Someone who makes such an effort to be different from others is bound to fall in people's esteem, and I can only think that her future will be a hard one. She is a gifted woman, to be sure. Yet, if one gives free rein to one's emotions even under the most inappropriate circumstances, if one has to sample each interesting thing that comes along, people are bound to regard one as frivolous. And how can things turn out well for such a woman?" However, it should be remembered that these two women were not only contemporaries—they were rivals, as well.

An Uncontested Classic Despite the criticism Sei Shōnagon has received, it is impossible to deny the literary and historical value of her book. Filled with vivid and evocative language, *The Pillow Book* is clearly the work of an extremely gifted writer. When evaluating Japanese works of prose, many critics rank *The Pillow Book* above Murasaki Shikibu's *The Tale of Genji,* which is widely regarded as the greatest Japanese novel. Among these critics is Arthur Waley, who wrote, "As a writer [Sei Shōnagon] is incomparably the best poet of her time, a fact which is apparent only in her prose. . . . Passages such as that about the stormy lake or the few lines about crossing a moonlit river show a beauty of phrasing that Murasaki, a much more deliberate writer, certainly never surpassed."

The Language of Literature One might wonder how it is possible that two of the most important writers of the Heian court were women. During this time, boys at court were trained to write in Chinese, much as monks in medieval Europe were trained to write in Latin. Girls, on the other hand, were taught to write in low Japanese because Chinese was considered to be beyond their ability. This discrimination backfired, however, because more people were able to read low Japanese than Chinese. As a result, works written by women were widely read, and their place in Japanese literary history was assured.

Preview

Connecting to the Literature

If you have ever kept a diary, you probably know that it is easier to write openly and honestly when your only audience is yourself. This kind of free expression can be found in *The Pillow Book,* which Sei Shōnagon says she wrote "entirely for my own amusement."

Standard Course of Study

- Relate personal knowledge to textual information in a written reflection. (WL.1.02.1)
- Make inferences and draw conclusions based on personal reflection. (WL.1.03.6)
- Analyze connections between ideas, concepts, characters and experiences in reflection. (WL.1.03.10)

❷ Literary Analysis

Journal

A **journal** is a day-by-day account of the writer's thoughts and experiences. By reading a journal from the past, one can gain a unique perspective on the culture and the historical period in which the journal was written. A journal can also reveal a great deal about its author's personality, as this example from *The Pillow Book* shows:

> ". . . it strikes me as a strange and moving scene; when people talk to me about it, I start crying myself."

As you read Sei Shōnagon's observations and reflections, look for details that reveal information about the author's personality and her life in the Heian court.

Connecting Literary Elements

In *The Pillow Book,* many of the author's observations take the form of **anecdotes,** short accounts of amusing or interesting events. Anecdotes can be told purely for entertainment, but they are often used to illustrate a point or to share insight that the author gained from an experience. Use a chart like the one shown to note the insights Sei Shōnagon offers in her anecdotes.

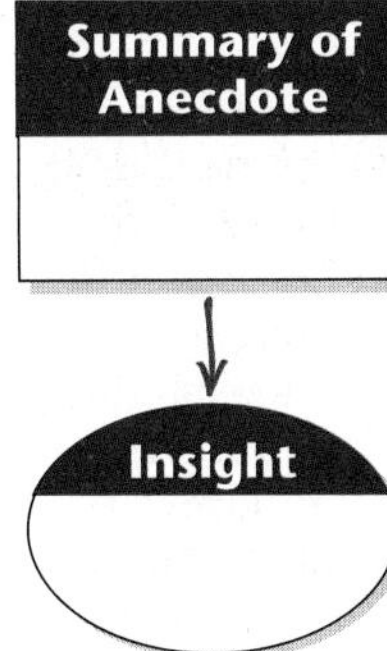

❸ Reading Strategy

Relating to Your Own Experiences

Sei Shōnagon lived and wrote centuries ago, yet you may find that you share some of the feelings she expresses. For example, just as finding an old letter arouses a fond memory of the past for the author, finding an old photograph may arouse fond memories for you. **Relating to your own experiences** will increase your understanding and enjoyment of Sei Shōnagon's observations. As you read, note similarities between your own feelings and experiences and those that the author describes.

Vocabulary Builder

earnest (ʉr′ nist) *adj.* serious; not joking (p. 309)

chastised (chas′ tīzd) *v.* punished (p. 309)

loathsome (lōth′ səm) *adj.* detestable (p. 310)

indefinitely (in def′ ə nit lē) *adv.* without a specified limit (p. 311)

❷ Literary Analysis

Journal

- Read aloud the Literary Analysis instruction. Point out to students that a journal, as a personal record of a writer's thoughts, can also give readers a view into the author's personality.
- Read aloud the first paragraph from *The Pillow Book* on p. 308. Then, **ask** what the reader learns about the writer from this paragraph.
  Possible response: The writer is observant and appreciates nature.
- Tell students that journals are often full of anecdotes, short stories used to illustrate an insight about life.
- Give students a copy of **Literary Analysis Graphic Organizer A** in ***Graphic Organizer Transparencies,*** p. 59. Have them use it to analyze each of the anecdotes in *The Pillow Book.*

❸ Reading Strategy

Relating to Your Own Experiences

- Have students read the Reading Strategy.
- Tell students that they can relate the literature they read—even literature from a culture as different as Sei Shōnagon's—to their own experiences.

Vocabulary Builder

- Pronounce each vocabulary word for students, and read the definitions as a class. Have students identify any words with which they are already familiar.

Differentiated Instruction — Solutions for All Learners

Support for Special Needs Students
Have students read the adapted version of *The Pillow Book* in the ***Reader's Notebook: Adapted Version.*** This version provides basic-level instruction in an interactive format with questions and write-on lines. Completing these pages will prepare students to read the selection in the Student Edition.

Support for Less Proficient Readers
Have students read *The Pillow Book* in the ***Reader's Notebook.*** This version provides basic-level instruction in an interactive format with questions and write-on lines. After students finish the selection in the ***Reader's Notebook,*** have them complete the questions and activities in the Student Edition.

Support for English Learners
Have students read *The Pillow Book* in the ***Reader's Notebook: English Learner's Version.*** This version provides basic-level instruction in an interactive format with questions and write-on lines. Completing these pages will prepare students to read the selection in the Student Edition.

Facilitate Understanding

Tell students that *The Pillow Book* is filled with Sei Shōnagon's observations, insights, and opinions. Some of Sei Shōnagon's entries are sarcastic or humorous and others are serious. Lead students in a discussion about journal writing. Invite students who keep diaries or journals to share some of their insights about the form. Use these questions to stimulate discussion: What types of observations or opinions might be kept in a journal? What types of experiences would be described in a journal? Should journals be read by an outside audience?

1 About the Selection

The title of *The Pillow Book* is derived from the wooden pillow box in which Sei Shōnagon probably kept her notebooks. At the time, most Japanese women slept on wooden pillows, because these pillows helped keep their hairdos neatly arranged. The pillows were hollow, and men and women occasionally kept notebooks in the pillow-box drawers. In these selections from *The Pillow Book,* readers learn about two pampered pets as well as the author's feelings about the relative beauty of different seasons.

2 Literary Analysis

Journal

- Remind students that a journal is a day-by-day account of the writer's thoughts and experiences.
- Have students read the bracketed passage independently. Then, **ask** the Literary Analysis question: What do these observations reveal about the author's personality?
  Possible response: Sei Shōnagon has a personal connection with nature, belongs to a privileged class, and is prone to complaining.

1 *from* The Pillow Book

Sei Shōnagon *translated by* Ivan Morris

Background During Sei Shōnagon's time, Japan was dominated by the powerful Fujiwara family. The leader of the family was the true ruler of Japan; the emperor was merely a figurehead. In addition, other members of the family usurped the power of officials in the various national and provincial offices. As a result, many of the people referred to by title in *The Pillow Book* had few official responsibilities.

Despite the essentially ceremonial nature of the positions, members of the Japanese aristocracy placed a great deal of importance on obtaining a government post. The offices were closely tied to social rank; holders of rank were often given land or servants and were entitled to a variety of privileges, including exemption from military service.

In Spring It Is the Dawn

In spring it is the dawn that is most beautiful. As the light creeps over the hills, their outlines are dyed a faint red and wisps of purplish cloud trail over them.

In summer the nights. Not only when the moon shines, but on dark nights too, as the fireflies flit to and fro, and even when it rains, how beautiful it is!

In autumn the evenings, when the glittering sun sinks close to the edge of the hills and the crows fly back to their nests in threes and
2 fours and twos; more charming still is a file of wild geese, like specks in the distant sky. When the sun has set, one's heart is moved by the sound of the wind and the hum of the insects.

In winter the early mornings. It is beautiful indeed when snow has fallen during the night, but splendid too when the ground is white with frost; or even when there is no snow or frost, but it is simply very cold and the attendants hurry from room to room stirring up the fires and bringing charcoal, how well this fits the season's mood! But as noon approaches and the cold wears off, no one bothers to keep the braziers[1] alight, and soon nothing remains but piles of white ashes.

Literary Analysis
Journal What do these observations reveal about the author's personality?

1. braziers (brā´ zhərz) n. metal pans or bowls used to hold burning coals or charcoal.

Differentiated Instruction Solutions for All Learners

Accessibility at a Glance

	From The Pillow Book
Context	Palace life in tenth-century Japan
Language	• Personal observations using sensory details • Syntax: some sentence fragments
Concept Level	Accessible (Respect animal sensitivities as well as people's.)
Literary Merit	Famous insightful journal about Japanese aristocracy
Lexile	860L
Overall Rating	Average

The Cat Who Lived in the Palace ❸

The cat who lived in the Palace had been awarded the headdress of nobility and was called Lady Myobu. She was a very pretty cat, and His Majesty saw to it that she was treated with the greatest care.

One day she wandered on to the veranda, and Lady Uma, the nurse in charge of her, called out, "Oh, you naughty thing! Please come inside at once." But the cat paid no attention and went on basking sleepily in the sun. Intending to give her a scare, the nurse called for the dog, Okinamaro.

"Okinamaro, where are you?" she cried. "Come here and bite Lady Myobu!" The foolish Okinamaro, believing that the nurse was in earnest, rushed at the cat, who, startled and terrified, ran behind the blind in the Imperial Dining Room, where the Emperor happened to be sitting. Greatly surprised, His Majesty picked up the cat and held her in his arms. He summoned his gentlemen-in-waiting. When Tadataka, the Chamberlain,[2] appeared, His Majesty ordered that Okinamaro be chastised and banished to Dog Island. The attendants all started to chase the dog amid great confusion. His Majesty also reproached Lady Uma. "We shall have to find a new nurse for our cat," he told her. "I no longer feel I can count on you to look after her." Lady Uma bowed; thereafter she no longer appeared in the Emperor's presence.

The Imperial Guards quickly succeeded in catching Okinamaro and drove him out of the Palace grounds. Poor dog! He used to swagger about so happily. Recently, on the third day of the Third Month,[3] when the Controller First Secretary paraded him through the Palace grounds, Okinamaro was adorned with garlands of willow leaves, peach blossoms on his head, and cherry blossoms round his body. How could the dog have imagined that this would be his fate? We all felt sorry for him. "When Her Majesty was having her meals," recalled one of the ladies-in-waiting, "Okinamaro always used to be in attendance and sit opposite us. How I miss him!"

6 It was about noon, a few days after Okinamaro's banishment, that we heard a dog howling fearfully. How could any dog possibly cry so long? All the other dogs rushed out in excitement to see what was happening. Meanwhile a woman who served as a cleaner in the Palace latrines[4] ran up to us. "It's terrible," she said. "Two of the Chamberlains are flogging a dog. They'll surely kill him. He's being punished for

Triptych of Snow, Moon, and Flower, (center panel), c.1780s, Shunsho, Museum of Art, Tami, Japan

❹ ▲ Critical Viewing
How does this painting compare with your mental image of Sei Shōnagon writing *The Pillow Book*? Explain. **[Compare and Contrast]**

Vocabulary Builder

earnest (ʉr′ nist) *adj.* serious; not joking

chastised (chas′ tīzd′) *v.* punished

❺ Reading Check
Why does the Emperor banish Okinamaro?

2. **Chamberlain** (chām′ bər lin) *n.* high official in the emperor's court.
3. **the third day of the Third Month** the day of the Jōmi Festival, an event during which the dogs in the palace were often decorated with flowers.
4. **latrines** (lə trēnz′) *n.* lavatories.

❸ Humanities

***Triptych of Snow, Moon, and Flower* (center panel),** by Shunsho

Shunsho (1726–1792) was a painter and woodblock artist noted for his unusual compositions, fine brushwork, and portrayals of beautiful women and famous actors.

This picture is from a three-panel painted screen. The woman depicted is the famous novelist Murasaki Shikibu, who wrote *The Tale of Genji*, often considered the world's first novel. Shikibu is shown deep in thought, contemplating her next line. Her chamber is illuminated by the moonlight streaming in through the window. Because of the artist's use of angular, overlapping shapes, it is difficult to tell where the walls of the chamber begin or end. This gives the picture a mysterious quality that is heightened by the lack of shadows in the painting.

Use the following questions for discussion:

- What impression of Lady Murasaki does the artist convey? What details contribute to this impression?
  Possible response: Because of such details as her expression, the careful arrangement of items on her desk, and the elegant decoration of her room, she appears thoughtful but also highly organized and possessed of exceptional taste.
- Explain the ways in which this painting is and is not an appropriate illustration for *The Pillow Book*.
  Possible response: The painting is an appropriate illustration because it reflects Sei Shōnagon's sensibilities and writing. However, because Lady Murasaki and Sei Shōnagon were rivals, and because Murasaki seems more thoughtful and less self-absorbed than Sei Shōnagon, the illustration is not entirely appropriate.

❹ Critical Viewing

Possible response: The title suggests that Sei Shōnagon wrote in her journal before going to bed. Students may envision her writing at night in her sleeping chamber and wearing her night clothes.

❺ Reading Check

Answer: The Emperor banishes Okinamaro because he chases Lady Myōbu, the cat who lives in the palace.

Differentiated Instruction — Solutions for All Learners

Background for Less Proficient Readers

Lead students in a discussion about the relationship between owners and their pets. Encourage students to share their own experiences with owning and caring for animals. Then, remind students that while the Empress is fond of the dog, the Emperor favors the cat.

Support for English Learners

Help students recognize that writers use sensory details to describe what they see, hear, taste, smell, and feel. Tell students that "As the light creeps over the hill" is an example of a visual detail, while the "hum of the insects" describes a sound. Encourage students to be aware of such sensory details and list them as they read.

Enrichment for Advanced Readers

Direct students to research the symbolism of cats and dogs in Japanese culture. Remind students that while the Empress is especially fond of the dog, the emperor clearly favors the cat. Instruct students to create character analysis maps in which they analyze the Empress and Emperor on the basis of their research.

6 Critical Thinking

Infer

- Have students read the bracketed passage, beginning on p. 309.
- **Ask** students to discuss what the brutality of the Chamberlains suggests about the political and social atmosphere in Japan.
  Possible response: Such brutality suggests a displacement of anger on the part of the servants and a tolerance of cruelty toward the weak.

7 Literary Analysis

Journal and Anecdote

- Point out that much of *The Pillow Book* consists of anecdotes. **Ask** students whether they can identify an anecdote in the selection.
  Answer: "The Cat Who Lived in the Palace" is a long anecdote.
- Have students read the bracketed passage. Then, **ask** the Literary Analysis question: What insight does the Emperor express in this paragraph?
  Possible response: The Emperor is surprised to find that even dogs have deep feelings. The subtextual meaning is that even a creature without any social rank at all possesses human characteristics.

▶ **Monitor Progress** **Ask** students to evaluate the effect of this insight on the characters in the story.
Possible response: The insight is lost on the characters. The world of the court is restored to its former state at the story's end.

▶ **Reteach** If students have difficulty with anecdotes, encourage them to reread the Connecting Literary Elements section on p. 307 and to use the graphic organizer as they reread "The Cat Who Lived in the Palace."

8 Critical Viewing

Possible response: The painting conveys an impression of Sei Shōnagon as a flamboyant, colorful woman with dramatic flair.

---

6 having come back after he was banished. It's Tadataka and Sanefusa who are beating him." Obviously the victim was Okinamaro. I was absolutely wretched and sent a servant to ask the men to stop; but just then the howling finally ceased. "He's dead," one of the servants informed me. "They've thrown his body outside the gate."

That evening, while we were sitting in the Palace bemoaning Okinamaro's fate, a wretched-looking dog walked in; he was trembling all over, and his body was fearfully swollen.

"Oh dear," said one of the ladies-in-waiting. "Can this be Okinamaro? We haven't seen any other dog like him recently, have we?"

We called to him by name, but the dog did not respond. Some of us insisted that it was Okinamaro, others that it was not. "Please send for Lady Ukon,"[5] said the Empress, hearing our discussion. "She will certainly be able to tell." We immediately went to Ukon's room and told her she was wanted on an urgent matter.

"Is this Okinamaro?" the Empress asked her, pointing to the dog.

"Well," said Ukon, "it certainly looks like him, but I cannot believe that this loathsome creature is really our Okinamaro. When I called Okinamaro, he always used to come to me, wagging his tail. But this dog does not react at all. No, it cannot be the same one. And besides, wasn't Okinamaro beaten to death and his body thrown away? How could any dog be alive after being flogged by two strong men?" Hearing this, Her Majesty was very unhappy.

Vocabulary Builder
loathsome (lōth′ səm) *adj.* detestable

When it got dark, we gave the dog something to eat; but he refused it, and we finally decided that this could not be Okinamaro.

On the following morning I went to attend the Empress while her hair was being dressed and she was performing her ablutions.[6] I was holding up the mirror for her when the dog we had seen on the previous evening slunk into the room and crouched next to one of the pillars. "Poor Okinamaro!" I said. "He had such a dreadful beating yesterday. How sad to think he is dead! I wonder what body he has been born into this time. Oh, how he must have suffered!"

At that moment the dog lying by the pillar started to shake and tremble, and shed a flood of tears. It was astounding. So this really was Okinamaro! On the previous night it was to avoid betraying himself that he had refused to answer to his name. We were immensely moved and pleased. "Well, well, Okinamaro!" I said, putting down the mirror. The dog stretched himself flat on the floor and yelped loudly, so that the Empress beamed with delight. All the ladies gathered round, and Her Majesty summoned Lady Ukon. When the Empress explained what had happened, everyone talked and laughed with great excitement.

7 The news reached His Majesty, and he too came to the Empress's room. "It's amazing," he said with a smile. "To think that even a dog

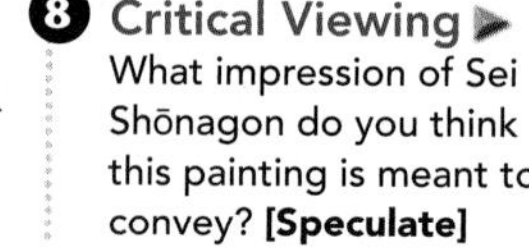
8 Critical Viewing ▶ What impression of Sei Shōnagon do you think this painting is meant to convey? **[Speculate]**

5. **Lady Ukon** (o͞o′ kôn′) one of the ladies in the Palace Attendants' Office, a bureau of female officials who waited on the emperor.
6. **ablutions** (ab lo͞o′ shənz) *n.* washings of the body.

Enrichment

Ceremony in Japanese Culture

The Pillow Book reveals how important ritual and ceremony were in the imperial court of Heian Japan. Ceremony remains important at all levels of Japanese society. A variety of ceremonies play a role in Japanese life and culture today.

There are ceremonies for every stage of life. Children in Japan are named at a ceremony that takes place when they are about three days old. Friends and relatives attend, bringing gifts for the child. At the age of about one month, the child is taken to the nearest Shinto shrine. There, the priest records the name and birthday, and the child formally becomes a member of the community.

A Japanese man's entry into old age is marked with a special ceremony that occurs between his fifty-ninth and sixtieth birthdays. At that time, he dons a red kimono, a color not usually worn by adult males, to signify that he has shed the responsibilities of maturity.

7 has such deep feelings!" When the Emperor's ladies-in-waiting heard the story, they too came along in a great crowd. "Okinamaro!" we called, and this time the dog rose and limped about the room with his swollen face. "He must have a meal prepared for him," I said. "Yes," said the Empress, laughing happily, "now that Okinamaro has finally told us who he is."

The Chamberlain, Tadataka, was informed, and he hurried along from the Table Room. "Is it really true?" he asked. "Please let me see for myself." I sent a maid to him with the following reply: "Alas, I am afraid that this is not the same dog after all." "Well," answered Tadataka, "whatever you say, I shall sooner or later have occasion to see the
9 animal. You won't be able to hide him from me indefinitely."

Before long, Okinamaro was granted an Imperial pardon and returned to his former happy state. Yet even now, when I remember how he whimpered and trembled in response to our sympathy, it strikes me as a strange and moving scene; when people talk to me about it, I start crying myself.

Literary Analysis
Journal and Anecdote
What insight does the Emperor express in this paragraph?

Vocabulary Builder
indefinitely (in def´ə nit lē) *adv.* without a specified limit

10 **Reading Check**
What does Okinamaro do that reveals his identity when everyone believes he has died?

11

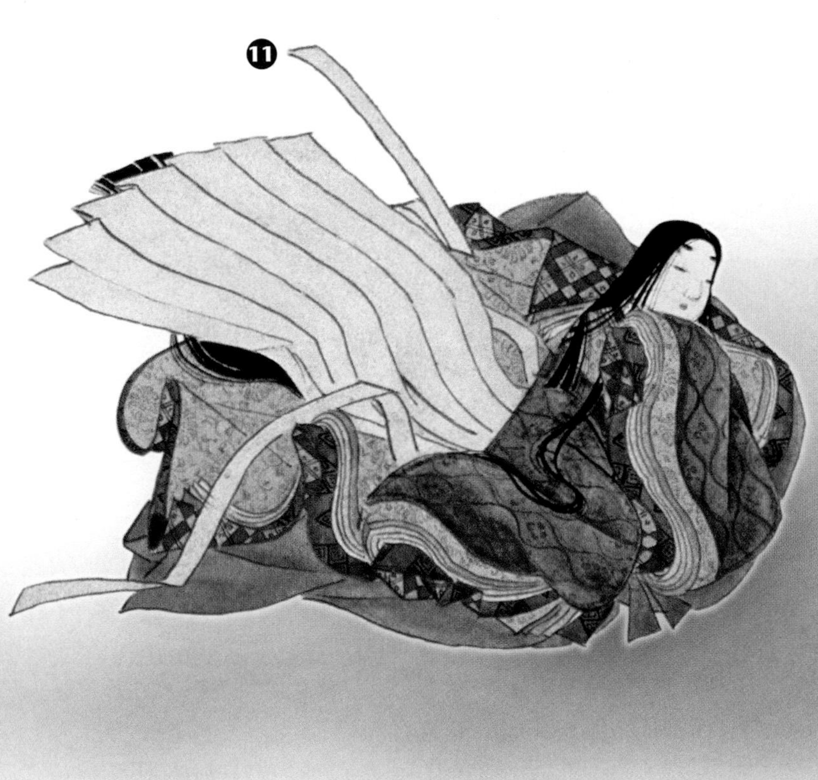

9 Vocabulary Builder

Latin Prefix *in-*

- Call students' attention to the word *indefinitely* and its definition. Tell students that the Latin prefix *in-* usually means "not."
- Have students **suggest** other words that contain this prefix. List the suggestions on the board.
  Possible responses: *Insecure, insensitive,* and *inactive* are possible suggestions.
- Next, have students define these words.
- Finally, direct students to write journal entries about favorite animals or pets that include some of these vocabulary words.

10 Reading Check

Answer: Okinamaro shakes and weeps when Sei Shōnagon says out loud how it saddens her to think that he is dead.

11 Humanities

The colorful portrait of Sei Shōnagon presents the writer as a woman of style. Although the artist and date of the portrait are not known, it may be an example of Heian era painting. During the Heian period, Japanese art began to look beyond Buddhist subjects to elements of Japanese life. Within this movement, painting reflected two distinct styles: *otoko-e* ("men's painting") and *onna-e* ("women's painting"). In otoko-e paintings, color was less important than bold line.

Use the following question for discussion:

How does the artist use color in this portrait?
Possible response: Bold, rich color dominates the portrait.

Differentiated Instruction
Solutions for All Learners

Support for Special Needs Students
Reread with students "The Cat Who Lived in the Palace." Pause after the partial paragraph at the top of p. 310. Help students understand that after Okinamaro has been beaten outside the palace, Sei Shōnagon is told that the dog is dead. Pause again after the sixth full paragraph on p. 310, and help students understand that a beaten dog that looks like Okinamaro has come to the palace but does not answer to Okinamaro's name.

Enrichment for Gifted/Talented Students
As a first-hand account of life at the Heian court, *The Pillow Book* includes a great deal of visual detail. Students may be interested in creating artwork that draws on that detail. Encourage students to create illustrations for scenes from *The Pillow Book.* Have them display their work for the class.

⓬ Background

Culture

The material that Sei Shōnagon refers to in the third sentence of "Things That Arouse a Fond Memory of the Past" would have come from a costume worn years earlier at a festival.

⓭ Reading Strategy

Relating to Your Own Experiences

- Ask a volunteer to read aloud "Things That Arouse a Fond Memory of the Past."
- Invite students to share some examples of things they have saved from a previous time in their lives. For each example, ask the student to explain why he or she saved this item.

ASSESS

Answers

1. **Possible response:** Yes; Sei Shōnagon's description of dawn in Spring is lovely.
2. (a) Sei Shōnagon finds evenings the most beautiful. (b) **Possible response:** Her description reveals sensitivity to the beauty of nature and a strong sense of detail. She connects her emotions to her observations.
3. (a) Sei Shōnagon's list includes dried hollyhocks, material pressed in a notebook, an old love letter, a paper fan, and a moonlit night. (b) **Possible response:** She prefers suggestion to evoke memories.
4. (a) **Possible response:** For contemporary readers, Sei Shōnagon herself may be more amusing or interesting than her subject matter.
5. (a) **Possible response:** Members of the court were petty and foolish, interested more in their daily affairs than with national concerns. (b) **Possible response:** The anecdote shows the nobility to be irresponsible and ineffective, doing nothing for Japanese citizens.

Things That Arouse a Fond Memory of the Past

⓬ Dried hollyhock. The objects used during the Display of Dolls. To find a piece of deep violet or grape-colored material that has been pressed between the pages of a notebook.

It is a rainy day and one is feeling bored. To pass the time, one starts looking through some old papers. And then one comes across the letters of a man one used to love. ⓭

Last year's paper fan. A night with a clear moon.

Reading Strategy Relating to Your Own Experiences Identify a time when an object reminded you of an experience in your past.

I Remember a Clear Morning

I remember a clear morning in the Ninth Month when it had been raining all night. Despite the bright sun, dew was still dripping from the chrysanthemums in the garden. On the bamboo fences and the criss-cross hedges I saw tatters of spider webs; and where the threads were broken the raindrops hung on them like strings of white pearls. I was greatly moved and delighted.

As it became sunnier, the dew gradually vanished from the clover and the other plants where it had lain so heavily; the branches began to stir, then suddenly sprang up of their own accord. Later I described to people how beautiful it all was. What most impressed me was that they were not at all impressed.

Critical Reading

1. **Respond:** Do you agree with the author about springtime dawn? Why or why not?
2. **(a) Recall:** In "In Spring It Is the Dawn," what time of day does Sei Shōnagon say she finds most beautiful during autumn?
   (b) Generalize: What does Sei Shōnagon's description of this time of day reveal about her sense of detail?
3. **(a) Recall:** What items does Sei Shōnagon list in "Things That Arouse a Fond Memory of the Past"? **(b) Interpret:** Why do you think she avoids sharing the fond memories that these items evoke?
4. **Evaluate:** Do you think Sei Shōnagon succeeds in conveying what is amusing or interesting about what she observes? Why or why not?
5. **(a) Generalize:** Based on the events described in "The Cat Who Lived in the Palace," how would you describe the life of the upper class in Japan during the Heian Age? **(b) Criticize:** Do you think the anecdote shows the Japanese nobility to be responsible, effective leaders? Explain.

Go Online Author Link
For: More about Sei Shōnagon
Visit: www.PHSchool.com
Web Code: ete-9312

Go Online Author Link For additional information about Sei Shōnagon, have students type in the Web Code, then select *S* from the alphabet, and then select Sei Shōnagon.

Apply the Skills

from *The Pillow Book*

Literary Analysis

Journal

1. In the final paragraph of the **journal** entry "In Spring It Is the Dawn," what detail of day-to-day court life does Sei Shōnagon describe?
2. In "The Cat Who Lived in the Palace," what does the cat's name suggest about certain animals' status in the emperor's court during Sei Shōnagon's time?
3. Which aspects of her personality does Sei Shōnagon reveal in her journal entry "Things That Arouse a Fond Memory of the Past"? Explain.

Connecting Literary Elements

4. What would you identify as the main insight or point of interest in the **anecdote** "The Cat Who Lived in the Palace"? Explain.
5. **(a)** What impresses Sei Shōnagon the most about the scene she describes in "I Remember a Clear Morning"? **(b)** Summarize the insight she gains from other people's reactions to her description of the scene.

Reading Strategy

Relating to Your Own Experiences

6. Use a chart like the one shown to note the relationships you can find between Sei Shōnagon's observations in *The Pillow Book* and your own experiences.

Writer's Experience	My Experience	How They Relate

7. Which of Sei Shōnagon's experiences or reflections could you most easily relate to your own? Why?

Extend Understanding

8. **Cultural Connection:** Which of Sei Shōnagon's reflections seem to have universal meaning? Which ones seem to apply only to Sei Shonagon's own life and times? Explain.

QuickReview

A **journal** is a day-by-day account of one's thoughts and experiences.

An **anecdote** is a short account of an amusing or interesting event.

To **relate to your own experiences,** look for similarities between your own feelings and experiences and those described by the author.

For: Self-test
Visit: www.PHSchool.com
Web Code: eta-6304

Go Online Assessment Students may use the **Self-test** to prepare for **Selection Test A** or **Selection Test B.**

Answers

1. **Possible response:** Sei Shōnagon reveals that attendants carry out such duties as making sure that each room in the court is properly heated.
2. **Possible response:** The cat's name, Lady Myōbu, suggests that a favored court pet could be granted a much higher status than many—or even most—human beings. Sei Shōnagon seems to have less status than the noble cat.
3. **Possible response:** Sei Shōnagon reveals her keen sense of detail and her ability to draw strong emotions from the things she observes.
4. **Possible response:** The main insight for contemporary readers may be that the Heian court was so ineffectual that its courtiers could devote days to the affairs of palace pets.
5. (a) Sei Shōnagon is "most impressed" by people's indifference to the beautiful scene.
(b) **Possible response:** She gains the insight that other people are insensitive to beauty.
6. **Possible response: Writer's Experience:** Sei Shōnagon is moved by a clear, sunny morning after a rainy night; **My Experience:** A brilliant, clear morning made me feel happy and optimistic; **How They Relate:** Both Sei Shōnagon and I were moved by the natural beauty of a clear, sunny morning. Another sample answer can be found in **Reading Strategy Graphic Organizer B,** p. 62, in ***Graphic Organizer Transparencies.***
7. **Possible response:** "Things That Arouse a Fond Memory of the Past" evokes the universal need to preserve experiences and memories of the people we treasure.
8. **Possible response:** "In the Spring It Is the Dawn," "Things That Arouse a Fond Memory of the Past," and "I Remember a Clear Morning" have universal meaning because all deal with the ways in which ordinary experiences evoke emotions. "The Cat Who Lived in the Palace" may be the only entry that applies to Sei Shōnagon's own life and times, because it deals with the peculiarities of the Heian court.

EXTEND/ASSESS

Answers

1 Vocabulary Lesson

Word Analysis: Latin Prefix *in-*

1. not complete; not finished
2. not distinct; vague; not clear
3. not significant; not important
4. not tolerable; not able to be tolerated

Spelling Strategy

1. illogical
2. irresponsible
3. immodest

Vocabulary Builder: Words in Context

1. indefinitely
2. chastised
3. earnest
4. loathsome

2 Grammar and Style Lesson

1. that this would be his fate; direct object
2. that he was innocent; predicate nominative
3. What amazed us; subject
4. what we saw; object of a preposition
5. what we were saying; direct object

Writing Application

Possible response: I looked out the window and saw <u>that it was snowing</u>. The white flakes were beautiful to me. I told my dad to look. He said <u>that the snow was nothing but trouble</u>. My mom said the same thing. <u>What I thought</u>, though, was <u>that the snow was the most beautiful thing</u> I'd ever seen.

Writing and Grammar Platinum Level
For support in teaching the Grammar and Style Lesson, use Chapter 20, Section 2.

Build Language Skills

1 Vocabulary Lesson

Word Analysis: Latin Prefix *in-*

The Latin prefix *in-* usually means "not," as in *indefinitely,* which can be defined as "not definitely." Use this knowledge to define the following words:

1. incomplete
2. indistinct
3. insignificant
4. intolerable

Spelling Strategy

The negative prefix *in-* is spelled differently depending on the letter it precedes. It becomes

- *im-* before *m*, as in *immortal*, and before *b* or *p*, as in *improper.*
- *il-* before *l*, as in *illegal*.
- *ir-* before *r*, as in *irrelevant*.

Add the correct prefix to each word below to create a word with the opposite meaning.

1. logical 2. responsible 3. modest

Vocabulary Builder: Words in Context

Review the vocabulary list on page 307 and consider the context in which each word is used in *The Pillow Book.* Then, choose the word from the vocabulary list that best completes each sentence below.

1. Due to a shortage of funds, the concert organizers have decided to postpone the event __?__.
2. The coach __?__ the team and made them run extra laps.
3. Tim is a very __?__ person who seldom makes jokes.
4. Many people who love cats find dogs to be __?__.

2 Grammar and Style Lesson

Noun Clauses

A **noun clause** is a subordinate clause that acts as a noun. It can be used as a subject, a predicate nominative, a direct object, an indirect object, or the object of a preposition. Noun clauses are commonly introduced by words such as *that, which, where, what, who, whatever, whoever,* and *why.*

Subject: *What most impressed me* was that . . .

Predicate Nominative: That is *what I heard.*

Direct Object: We finally decided *that this could not be Okinamaro.*

Object of a Preposition: No one was impressed by *what I described.*

Practice Identify the noun clause in each item and explain the clause's function.

1. How could the dog have imagined that this would be his fate?
2. The saddest part is that he was innocent.
3. What amazed us was his reaction.
4. We couldn't stop talking about what we saw.
5. People did not believe what we were saying.

Writing Application In a paragraph, describe an experience of finding something beautiful that others did not. Use at least three noun clauses in your writing.

WG Prentice Hall Writing and Grammar Connection: Platinum Level, Chapter 20, Section 2

Assessment Practice

Recognize Details

(For more practice, see *Test Preparation Workbook*, p. 15.)

Standardized tests often require students to recognize details that support the main idea in written texts. Use this sample passage from *The Pillow Book* to help students recognize details.

> In winter the early mornings. It is beautiful indeed when snow has fallen during the night, but splendid too when the ground is white with frost; or even when there is no snow or frost, but it is simply very cold and the attendants hurry from room to room stirring up the fires and bringing charcoal.

Which is NOT a detail supporting the author's belief that the early morning is the most beautiful time of day in the winter?

A snow has fallen during the night
B the ground is white with frost
C In winter it is the early mornings
D it is simply very cold

A, B, and *D* are all details that support the main idea. The answer is C, which is the main idea rather than a detail.

❸ Writing Lesson

Journal Entry

"The Cat Who Lived in the Palace" tells the story of Okinamaro from the perspective of Sei Shōnagon. Using the author's account as inspiration, write a journal entry describing the same events from the perspective of the Empress.

Prewriting Decide on an appropriate "voice" in which to write the Empress's journal entry. Review "The Cat Who Lived in the Palace" and gather details that reveal the Empress's personality.

Model: Using a Cluster Diagram to Gather Details

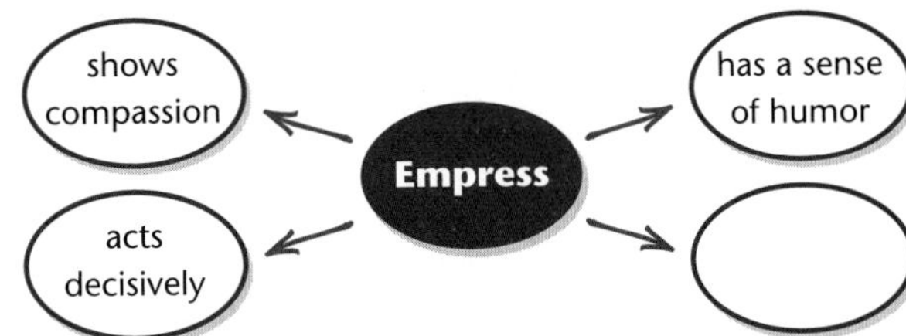

Drafting Refer to your notes about the Empress's personality and begin to draft your journal entry. As you write, consider how the Empress might have reacted to the events Sei Shōnagon describes.

Revising Reread your journal entry to be sure that the voice you developed is consistent with the character of the Empress in "The Cat Who Lived in the Palace." Revise or delete sentences that do not suit the Empress's personality.

WG *Prentice Hall Writing and Grammar Connection: Platinum Level, Chapter 5, Section 4*

❹ Extend Your Learning

Research and Technology Conduct a poll among your classmates to determine some of the things that evoke fond memories for them. Then, create a **graphic presentation of poll results** to illustrate your findings. You might represent the most popular responses in one of the following forms:

- bar graph
- pie chart
- illustrated table

Display your graphic presentation and explain the results of the poll to the class.

Listening and Speaking With a group of classmates, research and prepare an **oral report** on Japanese court life during the Heian Age. Each member of the group should focus on a specific aspect of court life, such as the roles of officials or how people dressed. Present your report to the class. **[Group Activity]**

For: An additional research activity
Visit: www.PHSchool.com
Web Code: etd-7304

Assessment Resources

The following resources can be used to assess students' knowledge and skills.

Unit 3 Resources
Selection Test A, pp. 71–73
Selection Test B, pp. 74–76

General Resources
Rubrics for Narration: Autobiographical Narrative, pp. 43–44

Go Online Assessment Students may use the **Self-test** to prepare for **Selection Test A** or **Selection Test B.**

❸ Writing Lesson

You may use this Writing Lesson as timed-writing practice, or you may allow students to develop the journal entry as a writing assignment over several days.

- To give students guidance in writing this journal entry, give them the **Support for Writing Lesson,** p. 68, in ***Unit 3 Resources.***
- Make sure students understand that they will be writing in the voice of the Empress. Suggest that they prepare by gathering details about the Empress from Sei Shōnagon's own entry. Model this strategy for students using a cluster diagram like the one on the page.
- Explain to students that their journal entries should reflect the personality of the Empress. Ask them to consider what the Empress is like. Does she show compassion? Does she act decisively? Does she have a sense of humor? Students should revise their entries to reflect her personality.
- Use the Narration: Autobiographical Narrative rubrics in ***General Resources,*** pp. 43–44, to evaluate students' work.

WG **Writing and Grammar Platinum Level**

For support in teaching the Writing Lesson, use Chapter 5, Section 4.

❹ Research and Technology

- Make sure students write poll questions that will be easily understood.
- Encourage students to design a graphic presentation that is appropriate for their results. If poll results are divided among many responses, for example, a pie chart might be more appropriate than an illustrated table. Students should also consider categorizing the responses.
- The **Support for Extend Your Learning** page (***Unit 3 Resources,*** p. 69) provides guided note-taking opportunities to help students complete the Extend Your Learning activities.

Go Online Research Have students type in the Web Code for another research activity.

Standard Course of Study

CT.4.05.6	Make inferences and draw conclusions based on critical text.
LT.5.01.6	Make connections between historical and contemporary issues in world literature.
LT.5.03.8	Make connections between works, self and related topics in world literature.

Background

Lady Otomo

Lady Otomo was born into a powerful Japanese family that was known in both political and literary circles. As a young woman, she lived with her brother and taught his son, Yakamochi. After the death of her brother, Lady Otomo remained in his house to care for Yakamochi and to continue fostering her nephew's interest in poetry. She later married and had a daughter, whom Yakamochi married in 740. When Yakamochi prepared the anthology *Manyoshu,* he included seventy-nine of his aunt's poems in the collection.

Humanities

The Celebrated Beauty of the Teahouse, Kagiya, at Kasamori Shrine, **by Suzuki Harunobu**

This woodblock print is by one of the most famous Japanese artists of the eighteenth century, Suzuki Harunobu. Harunobu's favorite subjects were beautiful women. In this print, he depicts a celebrated beauty of the time named Osin, who is shown sweeping up love letters and placing them into two large baskets on the back of an ox.

Use the following questions for discussion:

- Which details in the print indicate that the woman depicted is greatly admired?
  Answer: The woman is so admired that she needs an ox to carry the love letters addressed to her. The cargo is so great that letters have spilled onto the ground.
- How does the artist capture the delicate beauty of the woman?
  Possible response: The artist draws the woman's neck and face with elegant curves. Her hands, feet, and features are small.

A Closer Look

Women Writers in Japan

During Japan's Nara period (710–784) and Heian Age (794–1185), most women were not allowed to speak or write Chinese, the language of scholars and serious literature. Paradoxically, the restrictions that kept women from learning Chinese left them free to write in Japanese, the spoken language that had, at that time, no clear literary form. In so doing, they became pioneers in the creation of Japan's distinctive literature, especially diaries, poetry, and romances. Here are just a few of the women writers who created the foundations of Japanese literature.

> *"Paradoxically, the restrictions that kept women from learning Chinese left them free to write in Japanese, the spoken language that had, at the time, no clear literary form."*

Poet: Lady Otomo *Manyoshu*, which means *Collection of 10,000 Leaves*, is an anthology of Japanese poetry that was compiled sometime after 760. The volume contains more than 4,500 poems, one third of them written by women. A number of these poems are by Lady Otomo, who stands at the beginning of a long line of talented Japanese women. She wrote about nature, the small details of daily life, her daughters, and the promises and the heartaches of love:

You come no more, who came so often,
Nor yet arrives a messenger with your letter.
There is—alas!—nothing I can do.
Though I sorrow the black night through
And all day till the red sun sinks,
It avails me nothing. Though I pine,
I know not how to soothe my heart's pain.

—from "Love's Complaint"

Novelist: Lady Murasaki Shikibu Many scholars consider Lady Murasaki Shikibu's novel The Tale of Genji the single greatest work of Japanese literature. Like the works of Homer, Milton, Dante, and Shakespeare in the Western literary tradition, *The Tale of Genji* has provided a rich source of characters and themes that have been reworked by Japanese writers for nearly a thousand years. It is a seminal work that has defined Japan's national identity. Extremely long and complex, *The Tale of Genji* is filled with profound insights and beautiful prose. Note the intimacy and precision in this description of the emperor's reaction to the death of his beloved:

Critical Viewing

Possible response: On the basis of this print, it appears that Japanese women devoted a good deal of time to elaborate hairstyles and clothing. Women were probably admired. This woman is apparently literate and engages in correspondence with admirers.

But when he thought of the lost lady's Voice and form, he could find neither in The beauty of flowers nor in the song of Birds any fit comparison. Continually he Pined that fate should not have allowed Them to fulfill the vow which morning and Evening was ever talked of between them —the vow that their lives should be as the twin birds that share a wing, the twin trees that share a bough. The rustling of the wind, the chirping of an insect would cast him into the deepest melancholy . . .

The Celebrated Beauty of the Teahouse, Kagiya, at Kasamori Shrine, Suzuki Harunobu, 18th century, The Metropolitan Museum of Art

▲ Critical Viewing
Which details in this painting reflect the realities of life for Japanese women in the Nara and Heian periods? Explain. **[Interpret]**

Women Writers and Diaries Lady Murasaki Shikibu, like most notable Japanese writers, was a member of the imperial court. In addition to writing *The Tale of Genji,* Murasaki produced a diary that offers vivid insights into court life during the Heian Age. Diaries like Lady Murasaki's allowed women of the court to express their most intimate thoughts. Many of these diaries exhibit a level of literary sophistication that has earned them a place among the great works of Japanese literature.

Brilliant Stylist: Sei Shōnagon Another woman of the Heian court, Sei Shōnagon, wrote *The Pillow Book,* a loosely organized collection of about 320 pieces that include reminiscences, character sketches, descriptions, opinions, anecdotes, witty insights, and lists. Scholars celebrate Shōnagon's pure gift with language, and many regard *The Pillow Book* as an even greater work than *The Tale of Genji.*

Today, the voices of these and other Japanese women writers still speak to the modern reader. They show that even when it is restricted or confined, the human need for self-expression will find a way to free itself.

Activity

Freedom of Expression

The notion that creativity will always find an outlet, as grass pushes through a crack in the pavement, is as relevant today as it was in Japan a thousand years ago. With a group, discuss the ways in which modern artists, writers, and musicians find outlets for self-expression. Use these questions to guide your discussion:

- What types of restrictions might affect creative expression? What is the effect of such restrictions on creativity?
- Brainstorm for a list of examples of "outlaw" artistic genres that eventually became mainstream. Why have these forms become popular?

Choose a point person to share your ideas with the class.

Background

Murasaki Shikibu and Sei Shōnagon

Many scholars consider Lady Murasaki Shikibu and Sei Shōnagon contemporaries who occupied opposite ends of the personality spectrum. Shikibu was introverted, and her writing reflects an ironic, dark outlook. Shōnagon, on the other hand, was outgoing and daring.

Some scholars attribute the difference in the women's personalities and work to a change in political climate that occurred during the few years separating the women's service in the imperial court. During Sei Shōnagon's service as a lady-in-waiting for Empress Sadako from about 993 to 1000, a relaxed attitude and general openness characterized the court. Just a few years later, however, during Murasaki Shikibu's service to Empress Akiko (1005–1013), an oppressive and powerful ruler curtailed the freedoms of the earlier court. Naturally, the writings of the two authors reflected the two different environments in which they lived.

Critical Thinking

1. Most notable Japanese women writers were members of the imperial court. What impact do you think this membership had on women's literary pursuits? **[Speculate]**
   Possible response: Members of the imperial court might have received more education than did those outside the court. In addition, court members probably had more leisure time to devote to writing.
2. How does the role of women in the Japanese literary tradition compare with the role of women in other literary traditions with which you are familiar? **[Compare and Contrast]**
   Possible response: The role of women in the Japanese literary tradition is much the same as that of women in other literary traditions. Typically, women wrote diaries, journals, and poetry in nonacademic languages. These works were not generally recognized as literature during the time period in which they were written. Such recognition and study often occurred much later.

Activity

Form students into groups. Lead a discussion about restrictions on creativity, such as writer's block, and provide an example of an author who suffered from this problem (Mark Twain, while writing *The Adventures of Huckleberry Finn*). Other examples of such restrictions are lack of funds for independent work, governmental sanctions, and family, religious, and social disapproval.

Suggest that individuals take responsibility for different aspects of creativity: modern artists, writers, and musicians. Direct students to use newspapers and the Internet to research examples of local and national cultural events that provide outlets for creative expression. Then have students do research on "outlaw" genres that eventually became mainstream and lead a discussion on why these became popular. Finally, have students pool and organize their information for the presentation.

Zen Parables

Standard Course of Study

Goal 1: WRITTEN LANGUAGE

WL.1.03.6 Make inferences and draw conclusions based on personal reflection.

Goal 4: CRITICAL THINKING

CT.4.03.3 Analyze how writers relate the organization to the ideas.

Goal 5: LITERATURE

LT.5.03.2 Analyze text components and evaluate impact on world literature.

LT.5.03.3 Provide textual evidence to support understanding of and response to world literature.

LT.5.03.9 Analyze and evaluate the effects of author's craft and style in world literature.

Goal 6: GRAMMAR AND USAGE

GU.6.01.3 Use recognition strategies to understand vocabulary and exact word choice.

Step-by-Step Teaching Guide	Pacing Guide
PRETEACH	
• Administer Vocabulary and Reading Warm-ups as necessary.	5 min.
• Engage students' interest with the motivation activity.	5 min.
• Read and discuss author and background features. **FT**	10 min.
• Introduce the Literary Analysis Skill: Zen Parables. **FT**	5 min.
• Introduce the Reading Strategy: Interpreting Paradox. **FT**	10 min.
• Prepare students to read by teaching the selection vocabulary. **FT**	
TEACH	
• Informally monitor comprehension while students read independently or in groups. **FT**	30 min.
• Monitor students' comprehension with the Reading Check notes.	as students read
• Reinforce vocabulary with Vocabulary Builder notes.	as students read
• Develop students' understanding of Zen parables with the Literary Analysis annotations. **FT**	5 min.
• Develop students' ability to interpret paradox with the Reading Strategy annotations. **FT**	5 min.
ASSESS/EXTEND	
• Assess students' comprehension and mastery of the Literary Analysis and Reading Strategy by having them answer the Apply the Skills questions. **FT**	15 min.
• Have students complete the Vocabulary Lesson and the Grammar and Style Lesson. **FT**	15 min.
• Apply students' ability to cite sources by using the Writing Lesson. **FT**	45 min. or homework
• Apply students' understanding by using one or more of the Extend Your Learning activities.	20–90 min. or homework
• Administer Selection Test A or Selection Test B. **FT**	15 min.

Resources

Print

Unit 3 Resources

- Vocabulary Warm-up Word Lists **[L1, L2, EL]** .... p. 77
- Vocabulary Warm-up Practice **[L1, L2, EL]** .... p. 78
- Reading Warm-up A **[L1, L2, EL]** .... p. 79
- Reading Warm-up B **[L1, L2, L3]** .... p. 80

Transparency

Graphic Organizer Transparencies

- Literary Analysis Graphic Organizer A **[L3]** .... p. 65
- Literary Analysis Graphic Organizer B **[L1, L2, EL]** .... p. 66
- Reading Strategy Graphic Organizer A **[L3]** .... p. 63
- Reading Strategy Graphic Organizer B **[L1, L2, EL]** .... p. 64

Print

Reader's Notebook [L2]

Reader's Notebook: Adapted Version [L1]

Reader's Notebook: English Learner's Version [EL]

Unit 3 Resources

- Literary Analysis **[L3]** .... p. 81
- Reading Strategy **[L3]** .... p. 82
- Vocabulary Builder **[L3]** .... p. 83

Technology

Listening to Literature Audio CDs [L2, EL]

Print

Unit 3 Resources

- Grammar and Style **[L3]** .... p. 84
- Support for Writing Lesson **[L3]** .... p. 85
- Support for Extend Your Learning **[L3]** .... p. 86
- Enrichment **[L4]** .... p. 87
- Selection Test A **[L1, L2, EL]** .... p. 88–90
- Selection Test B **[L3, L4]** .... p. 91–93

General Resources

- Rubrics for Research: Research Report **[L3]** .... pp. 51–52

Technology

- **Go Online:** Research **[L3]**
- **Go Online:** Self-test **[L3]**
- ***ExamView®*, Test Bank [L3]**

Choosing Resources for Differentiated Instruction

[L1] Special Needs Students

[L2] Below-Level Students

[L3] All Students

[L4] Advanced Students

[EL] English Learners

For Vocabulary and Reading Warm-ups and for Selection Tests, **A** signifies "less challenging" and **B** "more challenging." For Graphic Organizer transparencies, **A** signifies "not filled in" and **B** "filled in."

FT Fast Track Instruction: To move the lesson more quickly, use the strategies and activities identified with **FT**.

Scaffolding for Less Proficient and Advanced Students

The leveled Critical Thinking questions after selections progress in the levels of thinking required to answer them. To address the needs of your different students, you may use the (a) level questions for your less proficient students and the (b) level questions with your on-level and advanced students. The occasional (c) level questions are appropriate for your advanced students.

PRENTICE HALL **TeacherEXPRESS™** Plan · Teach · Assess — Use this complete suite of powerful teaching tools to make lesson planning and testing quicker and easier.

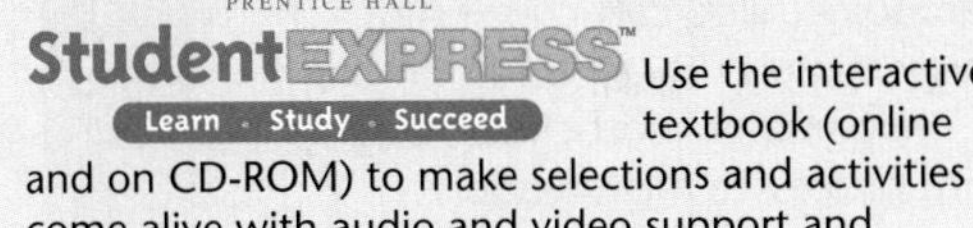

PRENTICE HALL **StudentEXPRESS™** Learn · Study · Succeed — Use the interactive textbook (online and on CD-ROM) to make selections and activities come alive with audio and video support and interactive questions.

Benchmark

After students have completed reading *The Zen Parables,* administer **Benchmark Test 3 (*Unit 3 Resources,* pp. 101–106).** If the Benchmark Test reveals that some of the students need further work, use the **Interpretation Guide** to determine the appropriate reteaching page in the **Reading Kit** and on **Success Tracker.**

For: Information about Lexiles
Visit: www.PHSchool.com
Web Code: eue-1111

PRETEACH

Motivation

Prepare students for a quiz, instructing them to answer the following questions that you write on the board: *If a tree falls in the forest when no one is there, does it make a sound? What did your face look like before you were born?* and *Which came first, the chicken or the egg?* Explain that Zen masters used seemingly nonsensical questions like these to prepare students to learn about Zen Buddhism. Tell students that Zen parables, or short, moral stories, may appear illogical and confusing but convey meaning through paradoxes, or statements that convey truth through seeming contradiction.

❶ Background

More About the Selection

Unlike other forms of Buddhism, in which adherents seek to attain salvation beyond the material world, Zen aims for enlightenment within this world. Zen Buddhists use meditation and physical discipline to overcome obstacles to enlightenment, such as the strictures of rational thought. Zen parables, like the puzzling koans, are a tool in this process. The koans are riddles that Zen masters offer directly to their students, whereas the parables are brief stories that teach the nature of Zen. At the heart of the parables are paradoxes, illogical actions that defy expectations. By focusing on paradox, the parables short-circuit the thought processes most readers would consider "normal," thus opening the mind for a sudden burst of enlightenment.

Geography Note

Draw students' attention to the map above. Point out the relative proximity of Japan to China. Make sure students understand that Zen Buddhism originated in China. Japanese monks went to China to study Buddhism and brought Zen to Japan in the twelfth and thirteenth centuries.

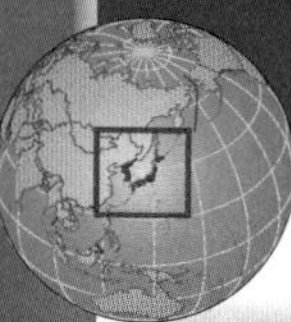

Build Skills | Parables

Zen Parables ❶

About Zen Buddhism

In a famous saying of Zen Buddhism, a monk is asked to discard everything. "But I have nothing!" the monk exclaims, to which his master responds, "Discard that too!" This puzzling exchange illustrates the basic outlook of Zen Buddhism. Falling somewhere between religion and philosophy, Zen Buddhism seeks to leap over everyday logic and reach enlightenment through intuition.

From China to Japan Zen is a branch of Buddhism that arose in sixth-century China, where Buddhist ideas intermingled with the Taoist philosophy of Lao Tzu. From China, Zen Buddhism traveled to Japan, where it continued to evolve and to flourish, eventually spreading to Korea and Vietnam, as well.

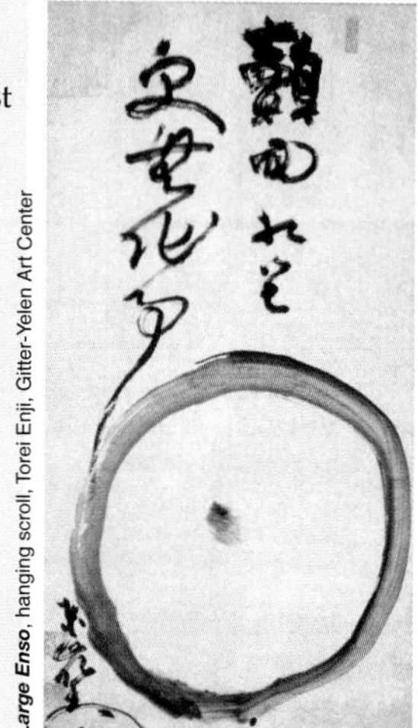

Large Enso, hanging scroll, Torei Enji, Gitter-Yelen Art Center

Defining Zen Buddhism Stressing neither worship nor scripture nor good deeds, as other religions do, Zen instead focuses on a sudden breakthrough to enlightenment, which is achieved through meditation, or deep thought. In fact, the word *Zen* comes from the Chinese *ch'an*, which means "meditation." According to Zen teachings, every human being has the potential to achieve this state. Qualities of the enlightened state include mental tranquillity, spontaneity, and fearlessness.

Zen Buddhism does not have the same kind of communal worship found in other religions. Instead, it emphasizes individual enlightenment passed down personally from master to student. The master cannot teach enlightenment; rather, the master must prompt the student on his or her own personal journey.

Zen Training The path to enlightenment varies with different Zen sects. The Rinzai sect, for example, stresses enlightenment through focus on puzzling, riddlelike questions called *koans* (kō′ änz′). The Soto sect, in contrast, focuses on meditation. In the Obaku sect, the student meditates on a particular phrase paying homage to Buddha. In all cases, the person abandons his or her sense of self and breaks through everyday, logical thought to reach an enlightened state. Enlightenment may also be achieved by self-disciplined focus on a ritualized everyday activity, like chopping wood, or on one of the Zen arts—archery, for example, or swordsmanship. Tutored by a master, the Zen student practices over and over until one day enlightenment comes with complete spontaneity, fusing the mind, body, and spirit so that performer and activity are one.

Impact of Zen Swordsmanship and the Zen qualities of mental tranquillity, spontaneity, self-discipline, and fearlessness proved particularly valuable to samurai warriors of medieval Japan, who were among those who practiced Zen. Japanese painting also began to reflect Zen influence, as pen-and-ink drawing is another of the ritualized Zen arts. Indeed, by the sixteenth century, Zen influenced almost all aspects of Japanese culture.

Zen Today Zen Buddhism continues to be an influential school of thought. People often study it along with the martial arts. Many business people find it helps them to focus and relax. Books like *Zen in the Art of Archery* have exposed Western readers to Zen teachings and have become bestsellers. Zen thinking is even evident in the *Star Wars* films, which feature an order of knights—the Jedi (je′ dī′)—whose beliefs, conduct, and societal role bear striking similarities to those of the samurai warriors of feudal Japan.

Preview

Connecting to the Literature

Some stories entertain, while others teach a lesson. Zen parables do both and more: They allow readers to contemplate a subject that, according to Zen masters, will help them achieve enlightenment.

NC Standard Course of Study

- Examine how elements such as irony and symbolism impact theme. (CT.4.02.3)
- Provide textual evidence to support understanding of and response to world literature. (LT.5.03.3)

2 Literary Analysis

Zen Parables

A **parable** is a short story that teaches a moral or spiritual lesson. **Zen parables** teach the principles of Zen Buddhism. They do so by inspiring contemplation rather than by expressing a clear moral. As you read each of these enlightening tales, notice the absence of a statement summarizing the parable's lesson.

Comparing Literary Works

Zen parables often are based on a **paradox**—a statement or situation that seems contradictory but actually presents a truth. For example, "The more things change, the more they stay the same" is a paradoxical statement. Some Zen parables contain paradoxical statements, but others present situations that are paradoxical because they contradict logic or expectation, as in this exchange:

> "If I become your devoted servant, how long might it be [before I am a master swordsman]?"
> "Oh, maybe ten years," Banzo relented.
> ". . . If I studied far more intensively, how long would it take me?"
> "Oh, maybe thirty years," said Banzo.

As you read each parable, note whether it presents ideas that contradict each other or ideas that contradict your expectations.

3 Reading Strategy

Interpreting Paradox

To **interpret** the paradox in a Zen parable, identify the contradiction—the statements, images, or ideas that do not logically go together. Then, draw a conclusion about what point the contradiction forces you to consider. Use a chart like the one shown to help you interpret these stories' paradoxes.

Situation
man facing certain doom pauses to enjoy a strawberry

↓

Contradiction
gravity of situation vs. enjoyment of food

↓

Point to Consider
When worrying won't help, why not enjoy?

Vocabulary Builder

sustained (sə stānd′) *v.* maintained; supported (p. 320)

epidemic (ep′ ə dem′ ik) *n.* rapidly and widely spreading disease (p. 321)

mediocre (mē′ dē ō′ kər) *adj.* not good enough; inferior (p. 321)

anticipate (an tis′ ə pāt′) *v.* expect (p. 321)

rebuked (ri byo͞okt′) *v.* scolded sharply (p. 322)

2 Literary Analysis

Zen Parables

- Read aloud the Literary Analysis instruction.
- **Ask** students this question: *If a tree falls in the forest when no one is there, does it make a sound?* Instead of asking students what the question means or what the answer to the question might be, ask them what the question inspires them to contemplate.
  Possible response: Is existence dependent on a human witness?
- When students attack the question this way, they might have a sudden insight: It may be ridiculous, as well as arrogant, to think that all existence is dependent on human witnesses.
- Have students use **Literary Analysis,** p. 81, in ***Unit 3 Resources,*** to build their understanding of parables.

3 Reading Strategy

Interpreting Paradox

- Have a volunteer read aloud the Reading Strategy instruction.
- Review the graphic organizer. Make sure that students understand what the paradox is and how it can draw attention to the point of the parable.
- Give students a copy of **Reading Strategy Graphic Organizer A,** p. 63, in ***Graphic Organizer Transparencies.*** Have them use it to interpret paradoxes as they read.

Vocabulary Builder

- Pronounce each vocabulary word for students, and read the definitions as a class. Have students identify any words with which they are already familiar.

Differentiated Instruction Solutions for All Learners

Support for Special Needs Students
Have students complete the **Preview** and **Build Skills** pages for these selections in the ***Reader's Notebook: Adapted Version.*** These pages provide a selection summary, an abbreviated presentation of the reading and literary skills, and the graphic organizer on the **Build Skills** page in the student book.

Support for Less Proficient Readers
Have students complete the **Preview** and **Build Skills** pages for these selections in the ***Reader's Notebook.*** These pages provide a selection summary, an abbreviated presentation of the reading and literary skills, and the graphic organizer on the **Build Skills** page in the student book.

Support for English Learners
Have students complete the **Preview** and **Build Skills** pages for these selections in the ***Reader's Notebook: English Learner's Version.*** These pages provide a selection summary, an abbreviated presentation of the skills, additional contextual vocabulary, and the graphic organizer on the **Build Skills** page in the student book.

TEACH

Facilitate Understanding

Explain that Zen masters used paradoxical behavior and koans to open students' minds to Buddhism. Lead a discussion with students comparing the relationship between Zen masters and their students and teaching and learning in the United States today.

❶ About the Selection

The three parables in this selection use paradox, illogical actions, and unexpected twists to teach lessons about the nature of Zen Buddhism. In the most striking parable, a man facing certain death takes a moment to enjoy a strawberry. In another, a Zen devotee shows his love of the sutras. In the last, a student is challenged by his master.

❷ Reading Strategy

Interpreting Paradox

- Explain to students the Japanese and Buddhist symbolism behind some of the details in the parable: The tiger is a symbol of courage; the vine is a symbol of desire; black is a symbol of bondage; and white is a symbol of self-mastery.
- Use the graphic organizer on p. 319 to help students analyze the parable.
- **Ask** students to explain the meaning of the parable.
  Possible response: The man does not show courage when he runs from the tiger. He clings to a vine, which symbolizes a desire for life. Two mice begin to gnaw at the man's lifeline, one black, a symbol of bondage to desire, and another white, a symbol for self-mastery. The man achieves enlightenment, or self-mastery, when he begins to let go of the vine and reaches for the strawberry. In so doing, the man releases his desire for material life and demonstrates courage. He enjoys the moment without bondage to desire or fear.
- By paradoxically defying expectations, the parable forces the reader to adapt to a Zen view of life.

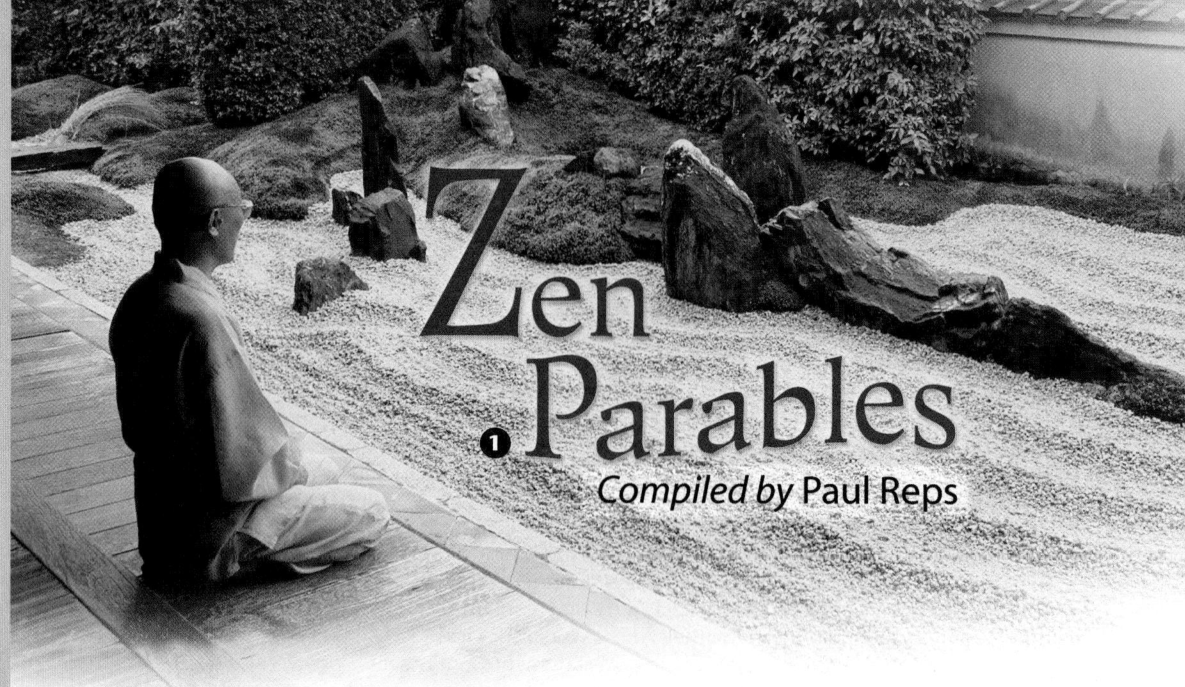

Zen ❶ Parables

Compiled by Paul Reps

Background "A Parable" begins with a reference to the Buddha. *Buddha* means "Enlightened One" and refers to Siddhartha Gautama (sid där′ tə gout′ ə mə) (563?–483? B.C.), the Hindu prince who founded Buddhism. Although Gautama is considered *the* Buddha, the term *buddha* can also refer to any Buddhist who has attained full *prajna* (pruj′ nyə), or enlightenment.

A Parable

Buddha told a parable in a sutra:[1]

❷ A man traveling across a field encountered a tiger. He fled, the tiger after him. Coming to a precipice, he caught hold of the root of a wild vine and swung himself down over the edge. The tiger sniffed at him from above. Trembling, the man looked down to where, far below, another tiger was waiting to eat him. Only the vine sustained him.

Two mice, one white and one black, little by little started to gnaw away the vine. The man saw a luscious strawberry near him. Grasping the vine with one hand, he plucked the strawberry with the other. How sweet it tasted!

Vocabulary Builder
sustained (sə stānd′) *v.* maintained; supported

1. **sutra** (so͞o′ trə) Buddhist scriptural narrative.

Differentiated Instruction Solutions for All Learners

Accessibility at a Glance

	A Parable	Publishing the Sutras	The Taste of Banzo's Sword
Context	Zen Buddhist view of life	Zen Buddhist views on humanitarianism	Zen Buddhist lesson on learning
Language	Simple words with symbolic meanings	Syntax: Compound and complex sentences	Dialogue with some casual diction
Concept Level	Accessible (Enjoy life while you can.)	Accessible (Practice charity to others.)	Accessible (Patience helps one learn.)
Literary Merit	Classic parable	Classic parable	Classic parable
Lexile	800L	890L	790L
Overall Rating	Average	Average	Average

Publishing the Sutras

Tetsugen, a devotee of Zen in Japan, decided to publish the sutras, which at that time were available only in Chinese. The books were to be printed with wood blocks in an edition of seven thousand copies, a tremendous undertaking.

Tetsugen began by traveling and collecting donations for this purpose. A few sympathizers would give him a hundred pieces of gold, but most of the time he received only small coins. He thanked each donor with equal gratitude. After ten years Tetsugen had enough money to begin his task.

It happened that at that time the Uji River[2] overflowed. Famine followed. Tetsugen took the funds he had collected for the books and spent them to save others from starvation. Then he began again his work of collecting.

Several years afterwards an epidemic spread over the country. Tetsugen again gave away what he had collected, to help his people.

For a third time he started his work, and after twenty years his wish was fulfilled. The printing blocks which produced the first edition of sutras can be seen today in the Obaku monastery in Kyoto.

The Japanese tell their children that Tetsugen made three sets of sutras, and that the first two invisible sets surpass even the last.

The Taste of Banzo's Sword

4 Matajuro Yagyu was the son of a famous swordsman. His father, believing that his son's work was too mediocre to anticipate mastership, disowned him.

So Matajuro went to Mount Futara and there found the famous swordsman Banzo. But Banzo confirmed the father's judgment. "You wish to learn swordsmanship under my guidance?" asked Banzo. "You cannot fulfill the requirements."

"But if I work hard, how many years will it take me to become a master?" persisted the youth.

"The rest of your life," replied Banzo.

"I cannot wait that long," explained Matajuro. "I am willing to pass through any hardship if only you will teach me. If I become your devoted servant, how long might it be?"

"Oh, maybe ten years," Banzo relented.

"My father is getting old, and soon I must take care of him," continued Matajuro. "If I work far more intensively, how long would it take me?"

2. **Uji** (ōō´ jē) **River** river near the city of Kyoto (kyō´ tō) in central Japan.

3 

Parables and Paradox

Religions around the world use parables to teach lessons. One Christian parable is "The Parable of the Prodigal Son." In this story, a young man leaves home and squanders his inheritance. He returns in disgrace and tells his father that he is no longer worthy of being called his son. Instead of punishing his son, the father calls for a celebration. The parable is meant to teach forgiveness.

Like many parables, "The Parable of the Prodigal Son" is based on a paradox. One might have expected that the father would punish his son, but he does the opposite—he rewards him. The paradox suggests a contrast between a natural behavior and the correct behavior—between wrong and right. A successful parable helps the reader know what to do when presented with a similar choice.

With a partner, discuss the use of paradox in these Zen parables.

Vocabulary Builder

epidemic (ep´ ə dem´ ik) *n.* rapidly and widely spreading disease

mediocre (mē´ dē ō´ kər) *adj.* not good enough; inferior

anticipate (an tis´ ə pāt´) *v.* expect

5 **Reading Check**

Why has Matajuro's father disowned him?

Differentiated Instruction Solutions for All Learners

Support for Special Needs Students
To help build understanding, have students read the selections while listening to the recordings on **Listening to Literature Audio CDs.** Encourage students to ask questions about difficult parts of the parables. Then, have students reread the parables on their own.

Support for Less Proficient Readers
Write this Zen koan on the board: *"When I hear I see, when I see I hear."* Ask students how it is possible to "see" while hearing. Record their responses on the board. Then, ask students how it is possible to "hear" while seeing. Record their responses. Students should see that the senses of sight and hearing are connected.

Enrichment for Advanced Readers
Tell students to select one of these Zen sayings: *"If you do not get it from yourself, where will you go for it?"* or *"Where there is great doubt, there will be great awakening; small doubt, small awakening; no doubt, no awakening."* Direct each student to write a children's story that illuminates the Zen saying he or she selected.

3 Themes in World Literature

Parables and Paradox "The Parable of the Prodigal Son" places greater emphasis on its lesson than do Zen parables. Some Biblical scholars believe that the parable is really more about the older brother than about the prodigal son. When the prodigal son's older brother comes home to find a celebration honoring his brother's return, he is angry. His brother has done nothing but bring disgrace on the family. The father urges his older son not to be jealous. The father forgives both of his sons' transgressions. The lesson is not one of entitlement for work but one of forgiveness.

Connect to the Literature Have students work in pairs to identify the paradox in each parable and determine its meaning. Ask a volunteer to select a parable with the most meaningful paradox and explain it.
Possible response: A *Parable* has the most meaningful paradox, which is a situation where, despite facing his death, a man enjoys the taste of a strawberry. Since he cannot do anything to alter his fate, he refuses to worry.

4 Vocabulary Builder

Latin Prefix *ante-/anti-*

- Call students' attention to the word *anticipate* and its definition. Tell students that the Latin prefix *anti-* is a variant of *ante-*. The prefix means "before" or "preceding in time." Make sure that students do not confuse it with the Latin prefix *anti-*, meaning "opposed to."
- Have students **suggest** words that contain this prefix. List the suggestions on the board.
  Possible responses: *Anterior, antebellum,* and *antedate* all contain the prefix.
- Next, have students define the suggested words.

5 Reading Check

Answer: Matajuro's father, a famous swordsman, disowns his son because he believes that his son's swordsmanship is mediocre.

❻ Literary Analysis

Zen Parables

- Have students read the bracketed passage.
- **Ask** the Literary Analysis question: What Zen principles does the master seem to be teaching Matajuro?
Possible response: The master is teaching Matajuro that mastery of a subject comes from necessity, not direct instruction.

▶ **Monitor Progress** **Ask** students to describe the role of paradox in Banzo's teaching.
Answer: Banzo teaches by refusing to teach.

▶ **Reteach** If students have difficulty with the concept of paradox, review with them the Literary Analysis instruction on p. 319.

ASSESS

Answers

1. **Possible response:** Students feeling pressure may appreciate the lesson of enjoying the strawberry.
2. (a) The man is clinging to a vine on the edge of a cliff, a tiger above and below him and mice chewing on the vine. (b) **Possible response:** Because the situation is desperate, it is surprising for the man to enjoy the fruit rather than save himself.
3. (a) Both efforts end when Tetsugen spends the money he has raised to help victims of famine and illness. (b) **Possible response:** The "invisible" editions are greater because they represent Zen Buddhism's humanitarian spirit.
4. (a) Matajuro wants to earn his father's respect. (b) Banzo makes Matajuro work as a servant and then suddenly attacks him. Matajuro must defend himself. (c) **Possible response:** The years of delay clear Matajuro's mind of impatience. The barrage of surprise attacks forces Matajuro to become an expert swordsman.
5. **Possible response:** Banzo's cruelty may not justify the end. However, Banzo fulfils his student's desires.

"Oh, maybe thirty years," said Banzo.

"Why is that?" asked Matajuro. "First you say ten and now thirty years. I will undergo any hardship to master this art in the shortest time!"

"Well," said Banzo, "in that case you will have to remain with me for seventy years. A man in such a hurry as you are to get results seldom learns quickly."

"Very well," declared the youth, understanding at last that he was being rebuked for impatience, "I agree."

Matajuro was told never to speak of fencing and never to touch a sword. He cooked for his master, washed the dishes, made his bed, cleaned the yard, cared for the garden, all without a word of swordsmanship.

Three years passed. Still Matajuro labored on. Thinking of his future, he was sad. He had not even begun to learn the art to which he had devoted his life.

But one day Banzo crept up behind him and gave him a terrific blow with a wooden sword.

The following day, when Matajuro was cooking rice, Banzo again sprang upon him unexpectedly.

❻ After that, day and night, Matajuro had to defend himself from unexpected thrusts. Not a moment passed in any day that he did not have to think of the taste of Banzo's sword.

He learned so rapidly he brought smiles to the face of his master. Matajuro became the greatest swordsman in the land.

Vocabulary Builder
rebuked (ri byo͞okt′) *v.* scolded sharply

Literary Analysis
Zen Parables What Zen principles does the master seem to be teaching Matajuro?

Critical Reading

1. **Respond:** Of the lessons these Zen parables teach, which one is most applicable to your own life? Explain.
2. **(a) Recall:** In what situation does the man in "A Parable" find himself? **(b) Analyze:** Given his situation, why is it surprising when he decides to enjoy a strawberry?
3. **(a) Recall:** In "Publishing the Sutras," what happens the first two times Tetsugen attempts to publish the sutras? **(b) Interpret:** What do you think the Japanese mean when they tell their children that "the first two invisible sets surpass even the last"?
4. **(a) Recall:** In "The Taste of Banzo's Sword," why is Matajuro so eager to learn swordsmanship from Banzo? **(b) Recall:** How does Banzo train Matajuro? **(c) Draw Conclusions:** Why do you think Banzo's instruction is so successful?
5. **Make a Judgment:** Do you agree with the methods that Banzo uses to train Matajuro in "The Taste of Banzo's Sword"? Why or why not?

Apply the Skills

Zen Parables

Literary Analysis

Zen Parables

1. **(a)** What lesson or outlook on life is illustrated in "A Parable"? **(b)** In what way does this **Zen parable** reflect Zen beliefs about the qualities of an enlightened mind?
2. In one or two sentences, state the moral of the story in "Publishing the Sutras."
3. **(a)** What principles of Zen philosophy are illustrated by "The Taste of Banzo's Sword"? **(b)** Do you think the lessons of this parable are more or less apparent than those of the other two? Explain.

Comparing Literary Works

4. **(a)** What is the **paradox** of the last sentence in "Publishing the Sutras"? **(b)** In what way does this paradox help convey the parable's lesson?
5. **(a)** Use a chart like the one shown to indicate whether "A Parable" and "Publishing the Sutras" make their points by presenting paradoxical statements or paradoxical situations. **(b)** Which parable do you think uses paradox more effectively to convey its message?

Parable	Paradox	Statement or Situation
"A Parable"		
"Publishing the Sutras"		

Reading Strategy

Interpreting Paradox

6. **(a)** Identify a pair of contradictory statements, images, or ideas in "The Taste of Banzo's Sword" that represent a paradox. **(b)** Explain why these statements, images, or ideas do not logically go together. **(c)** What point does this paradox force you to consider?

Extend Understanding

7. **Cultural Connection: (a)** Based on "The Taste of Banzo's Sword," how would you describe the relationship between teacher and student in feudal Japan? **(b)** How does this relationship compare to the teacher/student relationship in modern America? Explain.

QuickReview

Zen parables are short stories that teach the principles of Zen Buddhism.

A **paradox** is a statement or situation that seems contradictory but actually presents a truth.

To **interpret** a paradox, identify the contradiction, then draw a conclusion about the point the paradox forces you to consider.

For: Self-test
Visit: www.PHSchool.com
Web Code: eta-6305

Go Online Assessment Students may use the **Self-test** to prepare for **Selection Test A** or **Selection Test B.**

Answers

1. (a) **Possible response:** Life is short and death is inevitable, so one should enjoy pleasure rather than struggle against death.
   (b) **Possible response:** An enlightened mind is not distracted by the futile struggle against the inevitable.
2. **Possible response:** A true devotee of Zen will sacrifice resources to help people in need and thus glorify Zen.
3. (a) **Possible response:** The parable illustrates that students must give up impatience and preconceptions in order to learn.
   (b) **Possible response:** The lessons are more apparent because "The Taste of Banzo's Sword" contains more plot development.
4. (a) **Possible response:** It is paradoxical to view the "invisible" sutras as greater than the sutras that actually exist. (b) The paradox exemplifies the value Zen Buddhism places on charity.
5. (a) **Possible responses: A Parable:** A man facing certain death takes time to enjoy a strawberry; situation; **Publishing the Sutras:** The "invisible" sutras are said to surpass the real one; statement. (b) **Possible response:** "A Parable" uses paradox more effectively because the paradoxical situation subverts expectations so dramatically that it focuses the reader's attention on the message.
   Another sample answer can be found on **Literary Analysis Graphic Organizer B**, p. 66, in ***Graphic Organizer Transparencies.***
6. (a) **Possible response:** Banzo says that it will take Matajuro ten years to master swordsmanship; when Matajuro promises to work harder, Banzo says it will take thirty years. (b) The harder Matajuro works, the less time it should take him to learn. (c) It forces the reader to consider the negative impact of impatience and preconceived notions regarding learning.
7. (a) **Possible response:** In feudal Japan, teachers are masters of their subjects, and students must request permission to study with them. (b) **Possible response:** In America, students are legally required to attend school and are assigned to teachers.

EXTEND/ASSESS

Answers

❶ Vocabulary Lesson

Word Analysis: Latin Prefix *ante-/anti-*

1. b 2. a 3. d 4. c

Vocabulary Builder: Synonyms or Antonyms?

1. antonyms
2. synonyms
3. antonyms
4. synonyms
5. antonyms

Spelling Strategy

1. antedate
2. antechamber
3. ante-Roman

❷ Grammar and Style Lesson

1. If I work hard; modifies *will take*
2. as quickly as I need to learn; modifies *will learn*
3. so that Matajuro would learn to be patient; modifies *slowly*
4. when Matajuro was cooking rice; modifies *sprang*
5. when he did not expect it; modifies *attacking*

Writing Application

Possible response:

While two friends were walking through a park, one noticed a woman's wallet fall out of her purse. He could see from *where he stood* that there was money in the wallet. *As the woman walked away,* he asked his friend, "Should we take the money?"

The other responded by picking up the wallet and returning it to the woman.

WG Writing and Grammar Platinum Level

For support in teaching the Grammar and Style Lesson, use Chapter 20, Section 2.

Build Language Skills

❶ Vocabulary Lesson

Word Analysis: Latin Prefix *ante- / anti-*

The Latin prefix *anti-*, as in *anticipate*, is a variant of the prefix *ante-*, which means "before" or "preceding in time." It should not be confused with the Greek prefix *anti-*, which appears in words like *antipathy* and *anticlimactic* and which means "opposed to."

Using your understanding of the Latin prefix *ante-/anti-*, match each of the following words on the left with its definition on the right.

1. antebellum	a. early history, before the Middle Ages
2. antiquity	b. before the war
3. antecedent	c. earlier form
4. antetype	d. something prior to another

Vocabulary Builder: Synonyms or Antonyms?

Decide whether the words in each pair below are antonyms (*opposites*) or synonyms (*similar*).

1. sustained, released
2. epidemic, plague
3. mediocre, superior
4. anticipate, foresee
5. rebuked, praised

Spelling Strategy

When adding a prefix like *ante-* or *post-* to a word part that is a proper adjective, also add a hyphen: *post-Confucian.* Otherwise, a hyphen is usually not needed. Add the prefix *ante-* to each word root below, including a hyphen if needed.

1. date 2. chamber 3. Roman

❷ Grammar and Style Lesson

Adverb Clauses

Subordinate clauses contain subjects and verbs but do not express a complete idea. An **adverb clause** is a subordinate clause that modifies a verb, an adjective, or an adverb. Adverb clauses explain *how, where, when, why, to what extent,* or *under what circumstances.*

Under What Circumstances:

I am willing to pass through any hardship *if only you will teach me.* (modifies *willing*)

Practice Identify the adverb clause and the word it modifies in each of the following items.

1. If I work hard, how long will it take me?
2. I will learn as quickly as I need to learn.
3. Banzo taught slowly so that Matajuro would learn to be patient.
4. The following day, when Matajuro was cooking rice, Banzo again sprang upon him unexpectedly.
5. Banzo kept attacking Matajuro when he did not expect it.

Writing Application Write a short parable of your own with a lesson that can be applied to everyday life. Use at least three adverb clauses in your writing.

WG Prentice Hall Writing and Grammar Connection: Platinum Level, Chapter 20, Section 2

Assessment Practice

Stated and Implied Main Ideas **(For more practice, see *Test Preparation Workbook*, p. 16.)**

Students will encounter questions on standardized tests that will require the ability to identify both stated and implied main ideas. For practice, have students reread "A Parable" on p. 320 and answer the following sample.

What is the implied main idea of "A Parable"?

A Watch out for tigers and for mice.
B Strawberries taste better when you are in grave danger.
C Never travel across a field.
D Enjoy life while you can.

A, B, and *C* each refer to details from the parable, not to the implied main idea. The correct answer is *D*.

❸ Writing Lesson

Annotated Bibliography

These parables are just a few of the writings relating to Zen Buddhism that are available. Compile an annotated bibliography—a bibliography with descriptions and evaluations of sources—on Zen practice and ideas.

Prewriting Use print materials and the Internet to develop your bibliography. Consult style guides to determine a style for citing the sources you find—for example, MLA style.

Drafting Prepare your bibliography, writing annotations that show why each source is unique and valuable. Each annotation should be only a few sentences long.

Revising Review your bibliography to make sure that you have cited each source according to the style you have chosen. Correct any omissions or inconsistencies you find.

Model: Citing Sources Using MLA Style

"Zen." *Britannica Student Encyclopedia.* 2003.

Encyclopædia Britannica Online. ^16 Apr. 2003

<http://search.eb.com/ebi/article?eu=298026>

MLA style includes the date that the Web site was accessed.

WG Prentice Hall Writing and Grammar Connection: Platinum Level, Chapter 12, Section 5

❹ Extend Your Learning

Research and Technology Research and present a **multimedia report** that shows the influence of Zen thought on Japanese architecture and landscaping. You might use the following media in your presentation:

- music
- photographs
- models of buildings or gardens

Rehearse your presentation to make sure that it flows smoothly. When you are ready, share your report with the class.

Listening and Speaking With several classmates, hold a **panel discussion** on the application of Zen ideas and practices in such fields as business and professional sports. Consider this question: *Are these applications valid, or do they distort the message of Zen?* Hold your panel discussion in class. **[Group Activity]**

For: An additional research activity
Visit: www.PHSchool.com
Web Code: etd-7305

Assessment Resources

The following resources can be used to assess students' knowledge and skills.

Unit 3 Resources
- **Selection Test A,** pp. 88–90
- **Selection Test B,** pp. 91–93
- **Benchmark Test 3,** pp. 101–106

General Resources
- **Rubrics for Research: Research Report,** pp. 51–52
- **Rubrics for Multimedia Report,** pp. 57–58

Go Online Assessment Students may use the **Self-test** to prepare for **Selection Test A** or **Selection Test B.**

Benchmark

Administer **Benchmark Test 3.** If some students need further work, use the **Interpretation Guide** to determine the appropriate reteaching page in the **Reading Kit** and on **Success Tracker**.

❸ Writing Lesson

You may use this Writing Lesson as timed-writing practice, or you may allow students to develop the annotated bibliography as a writing assignment over several days.

- To give students guidance in writing this annotated bibliography, give them the **Support for Writing Lesson,** p. 85, in ***Unit 3 Resources.***
- Tell students that their annotated bibliographies should list useful sources of information on Zen Buddhism in alphabetical order. The list should describe and evaluate each source.
- Direct students to consult **Writing and Grammar,** Platinum Level, pp. 848–853, to find a citation style. Recommend or require students to use MLA style documentation.
- Remind students to make bibliography cards and note cards on each source as they conduct their research. Students should use their cards as they draft their bibliographies.
- Use the Research: Research Report rubrics in ***General Resources,*** pp. 51–52, to evaluate students' work.

WG Writing and Grammar Platinum Level

For support in teaching the Writing Lesson, use Chapter 12, Section 5.

❹ Research and Technology

- Direct students to gather not only information but also images and music that they can use in their reports.
- Be prepared to assist students in obtaining, setting up, and using audio-visual equipment during their presentations.
- The **Support for Extend Your Learning** page (***Unit 3 Resources,*** p. 86) provides guided note-taking opportunities to help students complete the Extend Your Learning activities.

Go Online Research Have students type in the Web Code for another research activity.

Standard Course of Study

IR.2.01.1	Select, monitor, and modify reading strategies appropriate to research question.
IR.2.02.3	Logically organize cause/effect connections through transitions.
IR.2.03.1	Access cultural information from media sources.

*See **Teacher Express™/Lesson View** for a detailed lesson for Reading Informational Material.*

About Reference Materials

- Read aloud the "About Reference Materials" information. For each of the reference materials listed, ask students to describe a recent situation in which they used each source. Ask students to explain why they needed the source, where they found it, and how they located information within it.
- **Ask** students to name other reference materials they have used. **Possible response:** Other reference materials include the *Readers' Guide to Periodical Literature,* annotated bibliographies, atlases, travel guides, or study guides for standardized tests.

Reading Strategy
Following Directions

- Have students read the Reading Strategy instruction independently.
- Then, **ask:** How do directions help people accomplish tasks? **Possible response:** Directions help people save time and achieve successful results.
- Draw students' attention to the chart, "Tips for Following Directions." **Ask** why each of the first three steps is important. **Possible response:** Reading the directions before beginning a project provides the reader with an overall understanding of the process. Following each step carefully ensures that small details are not overlooked. Studying diagrams provides visual learners with another means of understanding the process and the final product.

Reading Informational Materials

Reference Materials
About Reference Materials

When you need to find information about a certain topic, learn how to do something, or check the spelling of a word, you might use a reference book. **Reference materials** are sources of information on specific topics. They are available in libraries and media centers, in both print and electronic form. Here are examples of common reference materials:

- A **dictionary** lists word pronunciations, origins, and definitions.
- A **thesaurus** contains synonyms and antonyms.
- An **encyclopedia** provides comprehensive information on all branches of knowledge, including history, science, and literature.
- An **almanac** contains information about such topics as weather forecasts; astronomical data; and statistics about people, places, and events.
- A **how-to book** gives practical and detailed instruction on making or doing something.

Reading Strategy
Following Directions

Whether you are taking a test or assembling a tent, your ability to **follow directions** is an important life skill. Directions may contain simple or complex instructions, but you must follow them carefully to ensure success. The chart shown provides helpful tips for following directions:

Tips for Following Directions
1. Read the directions thoroughly before beginning the task.
2. As you work through the task, do not skip any steps.
3. Study diagrams or illustrations.
4. Consider whether your finished product is what you expected it to be.
5. If there are problems with your finished product, review the directions and diagrams to determine where you went wrong. Make adjustments as necessary.

The reference material you are about to read gives information about the Japanese art of origami. As you read the directions for making a paper dove, notice the text elements, such as illustrations and headings, that make the instructions clear.

Differentiated Instruction Solutions for All Learners

Reading Support

Give students reading support with the appropriate version of the **Reader's Notebooks:**

Reader's Notebook: [L2, L3]
Reader's Notebook: Adapted Version [L1, L2]
Reader's Notebook: English Learner's Version [EL]

The Origins Of Origami

Steve and Megumi Biddle

The development of paper folding in the West can be traced back to a company of Japanese jugglers who visited Europe in the 1860s, at the time when the Japanese were beginning to make contact with other cultures. The jugglers brought with them the method for folding the "flapping bird." Soon directions for this and other folds were appearing in various European publications. Magicians, including Harry Houdini, were especially interested in paper folding, attesting to the association between origami and magic, which continues today.

The photographs help readers understand the information about paper folding.

Paper folding, of course, had begun long before—in fact nearly two thousand years before, with the invention of paper in China in 105 A.D. Paper documents were usually rolled and their ends tied. There is a long tradition in China of folding paper into decorative shapes that are tossed onto coffins as symbols of objects for the departed to take with them into the next world.

Like many paragraphs in reference materials, this one provides historical information.

For more than five hundred years, the Chinese kept the paper-making process a secret. Then in the eighth century, Chinese invaders captured in Arabia were forced to reveal the technique. Eventually the process reached southern Europe.

Documents show that the Spanish symbol of paper folding, the *pajarita*, or "little bird," existed in the seventeenth century. Elsewhere in Europe, the art of paper folding was echoed in decorative napkin folds. At a banquet given by the sixteenth-century pope Gregory XIII, the setting included a table "decorated with wonderfully folded napkins." And the English diarist Samuel Pepys wrote in March 1668, "Thence home and there find one laying napkins against tomorrow in figures of all sorts."

The Japanese tradition of folding paper is a long and continuous one. It probably began in the sixth century, when a Buddhist priest brought paper-making methods to Japan from China by way of Korea. At that time, paper was a rare and precious commodity, and a formal kind of paper folding developed for use in both religious and secular life. There is perhaps another reason for

Reading Reference Materials

The Origins of Origami

- Explain to students that they may encounter an article like this one when reading a reference book about Asian or Japanese art or a how-to book about paper crafts.
- Before students read the article, explain the importance of understanding how an article is organized. Have students preview the entire article. Then, **ask:** What kinds of information does the article contain?
  Answer: The article contains historical information about origami, helpful tips for creating origami models, and step-by-step directions for making an origami dove.
- Direct students' attention to the first call-out note. Then, **ask:** Why might the writer combine historical information with directional information?
  Possible response: The writer's intended audience is someone who is unfamiliar with origami. Before the reader begins to practice this art form, the writer provides origami's historical context, which enables the reader to appreciate origami more than she or he might have without such information.
- Ask students to look at the illustrations on this page, and direct their attention to the second call-out note. **Ask:** How do the illustrations assist the reader in understanding the text?
  Possible response: The illustrations provide a visual example of what may be an unfamiliar art form.

continued on p. 328

Differentiated Instruction Solutions for All Learners

Strategy for Less Proficient Readers
Before each student begins reading, have him or her make a four-column chart with the following headings: *China, Japan, Arabia, Europe.* As students read, have them record the facts about the history of origami in the appropriate columns.

Strategy for English Learners
Before each student begins reading, have him or her make a four-column chart with the following headings: *China, Japan, Arabia, Europe.* As students read, have them record the facts about the history of origami in the appropriate columns. Students may also benefit from annotating each column with the definitions of unfamiliar words.

Enrichment for Advanced Readers
Direct students to use the origami article as a model for writing directions for a task of their choosing. Students should include historical information and illustrations in their articles. After students have written their first drafts, suggest that they ask a classmate to follow the directions and note where steps need clarification.

Reading Reference Materials *(cont.)*

The Origins of Origami

- Have students finish reading the historical information independently, stopping at "Helpful Tips." Then, **ask** students to supply three details from the text that support the following statement: *Origami has served several functions in Japanese society.*
  Possible response: Origami was developed for use in religious life; origami became a form of entertainment; origami is used as a teaching tool for young children.
- Draw students' attention to the first call-out box. Then, **ask:** Why might the authors have included in this article more recent information along with historical information?
  Possible response: By including more recent information, the authors help the reader recognize connections between the past and present. This information also emphasizes the continued relevance of origami.
- Invite a volunteer to read aloud "Helpful Tips." Then, **ask** what new information about origami the tips provide.
  Possible response: The tips explain that the shape of the paper is important; that practitioners should fold paper on a flat surface and press folds with their thumbnails; and that origami takes time and practice.
- Draw students' attention to the second call-out box. Point out that the authors used bullets to organize this section. **Ask** students why the authors might have chosen to do this.
  Possible response: The authors probably used bullets to separate each tip for the reader.

continued on p. 329

importance of paper in Japanese life. The Japanese word *kami* can mean "paper" as well as "God," even though they are written differently. This has given rise to the belief that paper is sacred. It has long been associated with the Shinto religion and the folding of human figures (*hitogata*) that are blessed by God.

During Japan's Edo period (1600–1868), a time of development in the arts, paper became inexpensive enough to be used by everyone, and origami became a form of entertainment. Japanese woodblock prints from this period show origami models, people folding paper, and origami in kimono patterns.

In the 1890s, the Japanese government introduced a widespread system of preschool education, and origami was introduced as a tool for bringing minds and hands into coordination. It is still taught to young children today.

Since the 1950s, interest in origami has proliferated in the United States and Great Britain as well as Japan, resulting in a variety of books and articles on the subject and in the founding of many origami societies worldwide.

Despite its popularity, for many years origami generated only a dozen or so noteworthy creations, such as the flapping bird and jumping frog.

This paragraph provides more recent information to complement the historical facts.

Today, however, it seems there is no shape that cannot be folded. And it can be tremendously exciting to see a flat piece of paper become transformed into a three-dimensional object. Learning how to fold new models is thrilling: Enjoy the one you encounter on the next page.

Helpful Tips

This section provides helpful tips that will make the project easier.

- Before you start, make sure your paper is the correct shape.
- Fold on a smooth, flat surface, such as a table or a book. Make your folds neat and accurate.
- Press your folds into place by running your thumbnail along them. Do not panic if your first few attempts at folding are not very successful. With practice you will come to understand the ways a piece of paper behaves when it is folded.
- Look at each diagram carefully, read the instructions, then look ahead to the next diagram to see what shape should be created when you have completed the step you are working on.
- Above all, if a fold or whole model does not work out, do not give up hope. Go through all the illustrations one by one, checking that you have read the instructions correctly and have not missed an important word or overlooked a symbol. If you are still unable to complete the model, put it to one side and come back to it another day with a fresh mind.

328 ■ *Chinese and Japanese Literature*

Dove Hato

A passage from the eighth-century chronicle the *Kojiki* describes the mournful sound of the dove like this:

Hasa no yama no hato no shitanaki ni nauku.

I weep with the murmuring sound of doves crying at Mount Hasa.

Making an Origami Dove

Try changing the angle of the head and wings each time you fold this model to see how many different doves you can create. Use a square piece of paper, white side up.

1. Begin with a diaper fold. Fold and unfold it in half from side to side.

2. Valley fold the top points down two thirds of the way as shown.

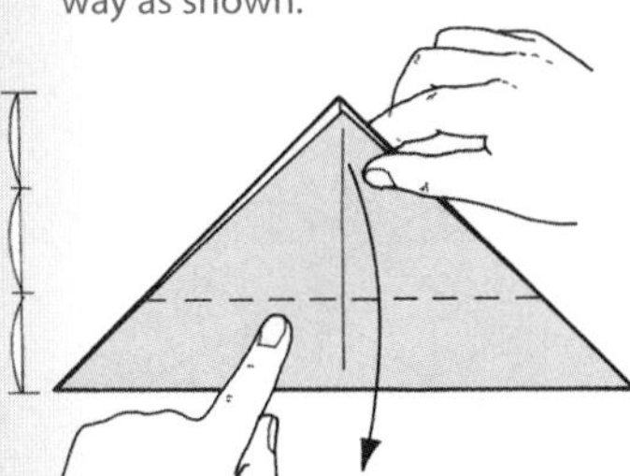

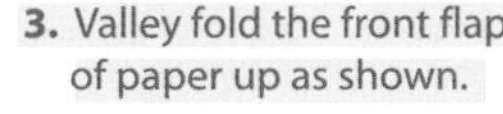

3. Valley fold the front flap of paper up as shown.

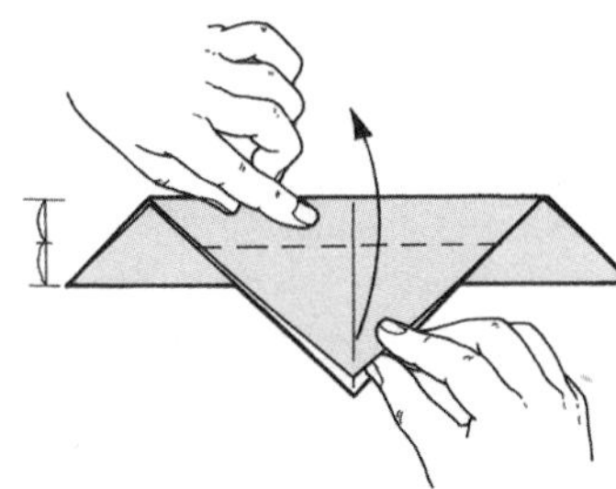

4. To make the wings, valley fold the paper in half from right to left.

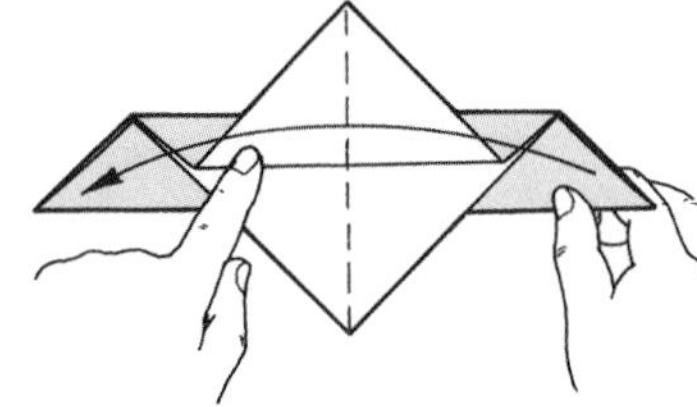

Step-by-step directions guide the process and make it easier to complete the activity.

Diagrams provide visual assistance to help clarify the directions.

Reading Reference Materials *(cont.)*

The Origins of Origami

- Provide students with square sheets of paper so that they can follow the directions for making an origami dove.
- Have students read the excerpt from the *Kojiki* at the top of the page. **Ask** them why the authors may have included this verse.
  Possible response: The authors may have wanted to remind readers of the sacred nature of origami and to illustrate that origami is connected to the natural world and human emotions.
- Before students read and execute the first four steps of the directions, draw their attention to the two call-out notes. Then, remind them to read all the directions thoroughly. They should complete every step and study the illustrations carefully.
- To convey the importance of the illustrations, ask students to close their books and complete the steps as you read the directions aloud. Ask students to share their experiences with this exercise and to discuss the advantages of illustrated instructions.

continued on p. 330

Differentiated Instruction Solutions for All Learners

Support for Special Needs Students

Work through the origami directions with students. Have a volunteer read a step aloud. Then, complete the step yourself so that students can model their process after yours. Next, give students some time to complete each step. As you fold your paper, share your thinking process aloud with students. For example, "I see, a 'valley fold' must be any fold that makes a V-shape in the paper."

Enrichment for Gifted/Talented Students

Students who easily master the directions for making an origami dove may enjoy crafting more intricate models. Obtain several origami reference books from the library and keep these books on hand for students who complete the dove quickly or who express interest in learning more about this art form. Encourage students to display the origami models in the classroom.

Reading Reference Materials *(cont.)*

The Origins of Origami

- As students work on steps 5 and 6, explain that they must follow the directions in both steps to make an *inside reverse fold.* After they complete the fold, **ask** students to explain which illustration they find more helpful.
  Possible responses: The first illustration is more helpful because it shows precisely where on the paper the fold should occur; the second illustration is more helpful because it shows a three-dimensional close-up of the fold.
- After students complete steps 7, 8, and 9, ask them to compare the product to the final illustration. Students whose doves do not resemble the illustration should reread the directions to see where they might have gone astray. While these students remake their doves, other students can make new doves to experiment with head and wing angles.

5. Now inside reverse fold the top point. This is what you do:

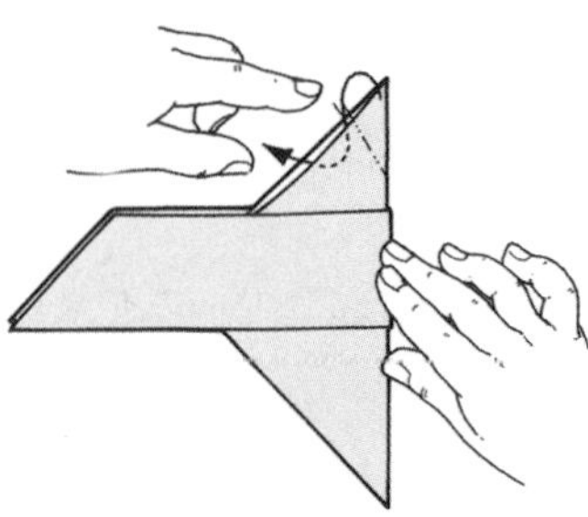

6. Place your thumb into the point's groove and, with your forefinger on top, pull the point down inside itself. To make the head and beak, press the paper flat.

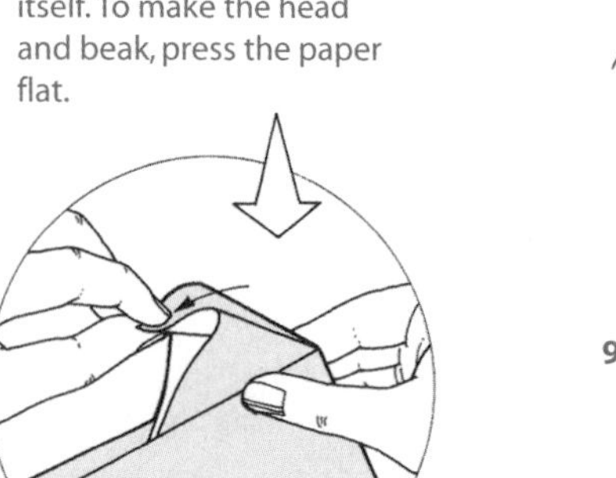

The illustrations clarify the directions by using arrows and showing exactly what your hands should do.

7. Valley fold the front wing over as shown. Repeat behind.

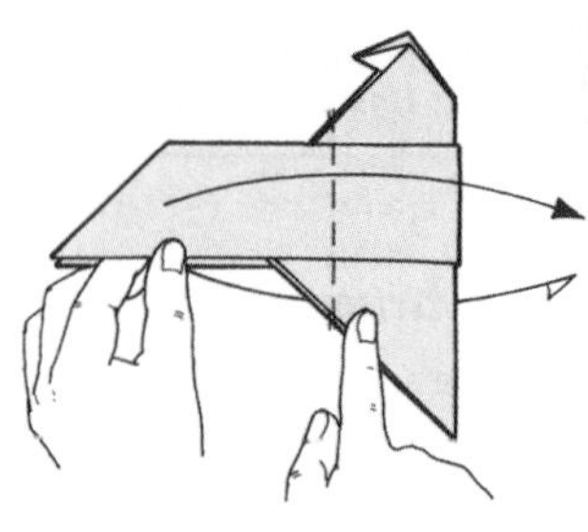

8. Open out the wings slightly.

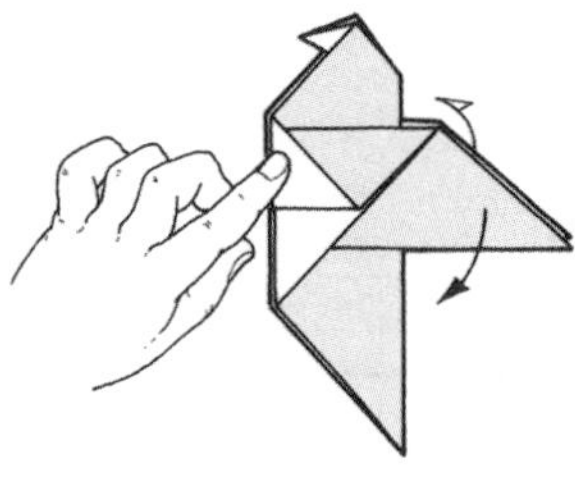

9. To complete the dove, turn the paper around.

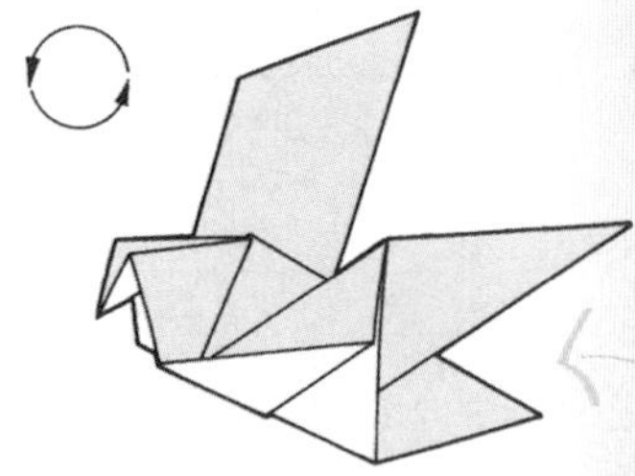

The final illustration shows what the finished product should look like.

330 ■ *Chinese and Japanese Literature*

Assessment Practice

Reading: Following Directions

Directions: *Choose the letter of the best answer to each question about the origami reference materials.*

1. Which element makes it easier to follow the directions?
   A the historical information about paper folding
   B the poem describing a dove
   C the diagrams
   D the photographs of completed origami animals
2. Of the steps listed here, what is the first direction you must follow to do origami correctly?
   A Make sure the paper is the right shape.
   B Check the illustrations for missed steps.
   C Press the fold into the paper with your thumbnail.
   D Begin with a diaper fold.
3. How do the arrows in the diagrams help you follow the directions?
   A They tell which step to complete first.
   B The tell what kind of paper to use.
   C They show the finished product.
   D They show which way to fold the paper.
4. Which type of fold divides the square into a triangle?
   A valley fold
   B diaper fold
   C inside reverse fold
   D outside reverse fold

Reading: Comprehension and Interpretation

Directions: *Write your answers on a separate sheet of paper.*

5. Describe the origins of paper folding, and explain how the art reached the West.
6. **(a)** In the late nineteenth century, why did the Japanese government decide to include origami in the preschool curriculum? **(b)** In what innovative way did the Europeans use the art of paper folding?
7. Explain how each diagram helps you complete the step described above it.

Timed Writing: Explanation

Using the reference materials on origami as a model, write step-by-step instructions for making something or completing a simple task. For example, you might write instructions for playing a game or directions for getting from one part of your school to another. Draw at least one diagram to clarify the steps the reader needs to follow. If you are explaining how to make something, include a list of materials. ***(30 minutes)***

ASSESS

Answers

Reading: Following Directions

1. C
2. A
3. D
4. B

Reading: Comprehension and Interpretation

5. Paper folding began in Japan in about the sixth century A.D., though the Chinese had a tradition of paper folding that may date back to the origins of paper itself in the second century A.D. The art reached the West when Japanese jugglers visited Europe in the 1860s.
6. (a) The Japanese government included Origami in the preschool curriculum as a teaching tool for bringing children's minds and hands into coordination. (b) The Europeans used paper folding techniques to make decorative napkin folds.
7. Each diagram in the directions shows you a picture of the results of the previous step. If you completed the previous step correctly, that will show in the diagram for the next step.

Timed Writing Explanation

- Suggest that students plan their time to give 5 minutes to planning, 10 minutes to writing, 10 minutes to drawing a diagram, and 5 minutes to revising and editing.
- Point out to students that successful instructions depend on a clear step-by-step organization.

Extend the Lesson

Writing Directions

Have students write step-by-step directions for going from your classroom to the cafeteria. Direct them to draw a diagram to clarify the steps and include these details along the route: specific hallways, left or right turns, up and down staircases, and landmarks, such as offices. When they have finished, tell students to give their directions to a classmate to review.

Each student's written directions and diagram should clearly and accurately lead a pedestrian from the classroom to the cafeteria. Ask each student to note steps or portions of the directions and diagram that need clarification. Students can then revise their work accordingly.

Standard Course of Study

LT.5.01.5 Analyze archetypal characters, themes, and settings in world literature.

LT.5.02.1 Explore works which relate to an issue, author, or theme and show increasing comprehension.

LT.5.03.10 Analyze connections between ideas, concepts, characters and experiences in world literature.

Prewriting

- After students select a philosophical school of thought and a theme, recommend that they photocopy the corresponding philosophical reading. Suggest that they highlight references to their chosen theme and make marginal notes about each reference.
- Suggest that students use a chart like the model to organize the highlighted text and marginal notes.
- Have each student use his or her chart to draft a working thesis statement. Explain that the thesis statement should clearly connect the philosophical school of thought to the literary selection.
- Have students craft a thesis statement such as the following: The Taoist belief in the power and harmony of nature is reflected in T'ao Chien's poem "I Built My House Near Where Others Dwell."

Tips for Test Taking

A writing prompt on a standardized test may assess students' ability to analyze a particular literary trend, state a point of view regarding the literary impact of this trend, and support the point of view with evidence. When writing under timed circumstances, students will need to quickly clarify a point of view (their thesis statement) and the evidence that supports it. Since they will not be able to refer to a text, their evidence must be based on their own readings and observations.

Writing About Literature

Analyze Literary Trends

Taoism, Confucianism, and Buddhism are three of the world's major systems of belief. In this unit, you can find texts teaching basic insights of each: the *Tao Te Ching* for Taoism; *The Analects* for Confucianism; and Zen parables for Zen, a Japanese school of Buddhism. You can also find literary texts showing the influence of each system of belief. For instance, the Confucian tradition in China, in which poetry was a part of civic life, might help you understand an exchange of poems between friends. To trace the literary impact of one of these schools, complete the assignment outlined in the box at the right.

Assignment: The Influence of Taoism, Confucianism, or Buddhism

Write an analytical essay that first analyzes a core Taoist, Confucian, or Buddhist belief in a philosophical work in this unit and then shows the impact of that belief on another work in this unit.

Criteria:

- Include a thesis statement that explains the impact of a Taoist, Confucian, or Buddhist belief on a specific literary work.
- Show how this belief is presented in the *Tao Te Ching, The Analects,* or the Zen parables.
- Support your thesis with a detailed analysis of your selected literary work, showing the influence of the belief.
- Approximate length: 700 words

Prewriting

Identify core themes. Select the teachings of one of the three schools of thought—the *Tao Te Ching* for Taoism, *The Analects* for Confucianism, or the Zen parables for Buddhism. As you review these teachings, take notes on passages that explore the following themes:

- Taoism: the harmony of nature; nature's mysterious, inexpressible essence; the virtue of quiet contemplation
- Confucianism: the power of a virtuous character; the importance of social relations, such as family duty, friendship, and leadership
- Buddhism: the illusions and suffering caused by reason and desire; the virtue of quiet contemplation; the concept of nothingness

Choose a literary work. To find a literary work influenced by your chosen school of thought, review the Unit Introduction, pages 256–263, and the biographies accompanying the selections. Reread the works of writers who lived in the right time and place to have been influenced by the school. Complete a chart similar to the one shown, and select a work based on the connections you uncover.

Read to Write

As you reread texts, note any emphasis on social and family relationships (Confucianism), nature (Taoism), or the illusions created by desire (Zen).

Model: Listing to Trace Beliefs

Selection	Connection	Theme/Evidence
T'ao Chien, "I Built My House Near Where Others Dwell"	T'ao Chien wrote in China when Taoism was well established.	Power and harmony in nature: "The mountain air is fine at evening of the day. . . ."

Review the work. Reread the work, taking notes on passages that reflect the influence of your selected school of thought.

Teaching Resources

The following resources can be used to extend or enrich the instruction for Writing About Literature.

Unit 3 Resources

Writing About Literature, pp. 94–95

General Resources

Rubrics for Response to Literature, pp. 55–56

Drafting

Organize using an outline. Use an outline similar to the one below to organize your thoughts logically. Don't lock yourself rigidly into your outline, though. If you gain new insights as you write, insert additional information where it makes sense.

Model: Create an Informal Outline

I. **Introduction:** Zen Buddhist idea that care creates illusions influences Bashō's haiku.

II. **Buddhist Idea of Illusion:** Parable of the man trapped between two tigers—rather than worrying about what has not yet happened (illusion), he enjoys a strawberry

III. **Bashō's Relationship to Buddhism:** Bashō became a Zen Buddhist later in his life.

IV. **Examples:** "Clouds Come From Time to Time": moon might symbolize hopes, dreams—clouds interrupt the illusion; moon might symbolize truth—clouds of illusion interfere

V. **Conclusion:** Bashō's haiku, like Zen parables, can create a moment of sudden illumination through contrast.

Frame your ideas. Write an engaging introduction to your essay. Consider beginning with a telling detail, a quotation, or an anecdote. Conclude your paper by summing up or extending your argument.

Revising and Editing

Review content: Check the relevance of details. Review your essay paragraph by paragraph to evaluate the connection between each main idea and the supporting details. Delete any details, no matter how interesting, that don't support the points you are making in a paragraph.

Review style: Revise to eliminate wordiness. Reread your paper, underlining any words that do not add to or clarify your meaning. Replace any unclear expressions with precise phrases.

Publishing and Presenting

Present an oral summary. Give a brief oral summary of the main points in your paper to your class. Then, encourage your classmates to ask questions to clarify their understanding of your summary.

WG *Writing and Grammar Connection: Platinum Level, Chapter 13*

Write to Learn

As you write your first draft, strive to be as specific as possible. Make sure that you include examples to support any global statements you make.

Write to Explain

Make sure that paraphrases and quotations in your paper illuminate the points you are trying to make. Be as specific as possible in making each connection clear to readers.

Differentiated Instruction Solutions for All Learners

Strategy for Less Proficient Writers

Have students begin drafting their thesis statements with a question such as, "What do T'ao Chien's poem 'I Built My House Near Where Others Dwell' and Taoism have in common?" Tell students that they can write a thesis statement by rephrasing and answering the question.

Strategy for English Learners

In addition to using the questioning strategy already discussed, provide students with several models of possible thesis statement constructions: ________ [Insert author and title of poem] and ________ [insert school of thought] share a common interest in ________ [insert theme].

Strategy for Advanced Writers

Encourage students to construct more sophisticated thesis statements. Ask them to analyze how a philosophical school of thought is reflected in several literary works by the same author. Encourage students to write about instances in which more than one philosophy is present in the literary works of an author.

Drafting

- Explain to students that an informal outline provides a way to organize information.
- **Ask** students to write thesis statements for the model outline.
  Possible response: Bashō's haiku "Clouds Come From Time to Time" reflects the Zen Buddhist idea that care creates illusions

Revising and Editing

- Draw students' attention to the Write to Explain note. Have students exchange drafts with one another. Ask students to pause after reading each paragraph to write a sentence that explains the connection between the thesis statement and the supporting details. Have students revise any paragraphs that readers could not clearly connect to thesis statements.

Publishing and Presenting

- Suggest that students prepare for their oral presentations by making note cards. When conducting their presentations, students should use their note cards as reminders and references rather than reading from them verbatim.

Writing and Grammar Platinum Level

Students will find additional instruction on writing an analytical essay in Chapter 13.

Writing and Grammar Interactive Textbook CD-ROM

Students can use the following tools as they complete their analytical essays:

- Comparitives
- Transition Words
- Editing

Six Traits Focus

✓	Ideas	✓	Word Choice
✓	Organization	✓	Sentence Fluency
	Voice		Conventions

Assessing the Essay

To evaluate students' essays, use the Response to Literature rubrics, pp. 55–56 in *General Resources.*

Standard Course of Study

FA.3.01.5	Present data about controversial issues in multiple forms.
FA.3.02.2	Provide relevant, reliable support in editorials.
FA.3.04.11	Analyze elements of argumentative environment.
GU.6.02.3	Edit for parallel structure.

 **From the Scholar's Desk**

Royall Tyler

Show students Segment 3 on Royall Tyler on ***From the Author's Desk DVD.*** Discuss how he prepares to translate and what background he likes to have. Also, discuss how he views translation and what he shares with his audiences as he lectures. Point out that Royall Tyler writes persuasive lectures and speaks persuasively about Japanese culture and literature, urging students to explore this culture and learn from it.

Writing Genres

Using the Form Tell students that they will encounter persuasion in many areas outside of school. Point out these examples in addition to the forms mentioned in the student edition.

- An editorial is a persuasive essay that journalists write to convince people to think in a certain way or to take action.
- People in the workplace may need to write persuasively to try to change a policy or to request new equipment—or even to ask for a raise in pay.
- Public relations specialists may use persuasive writing to convince the public that their company is doing or has done the right thing.

 **Online Essay Scorer**

A writing prompt for this mode of writing can be found on the ***PH Online Essay Scorer*** at PHSuccessNet.com.

Writing Workshop

Persuasion:
Persuasive Essay

You persuade people all the time—or at least, you try. You coax your parents to let you go to a concert, you apply to a college to admit you, or you ask a friend to borrow a CD. In addition, you yourself are barraged by all kinds of persuasive appeals: television commercials, newspaper editorials, friends asking to borrow *your* CDs. That means you are familiar with what persuasion looks and sounds like—and are probably skillful at it yourself. Writing a persuasive essay gives you the opportunity to use that awareness and skill to make a case for your interests and perhaps change a few minds in the process. Follow the steps outlined in this workshop to write your own persuasive essay.

Assignment Write an essay persuading your readers to accept your viewpoint about a controversial issue and to take action on that issue.

What to Include Your persuasive essay should feature the following elements:

- a focus on a controversial issue that is important to you and that has at least two sides
- a clear statement of your opinion on the issue and the action you support
- clearly organized support suited to the intended audience
- effective rhetorical devices such as charged language, vivid images, and dramatic analogies

To preview the criteria on which your persuasive essay may be assessed, see the rubric on page 341.

NC Standard Course of Study

- Present data about controversial issues in multiple forms. (FA.3.01.5)
- Provide relevant, reliable support in editorials. (FA.3.02.2)
- Analyze elements of argumentative environment. (FA.3.04.11)

Using the Form

You may use elements of a persuasive essay in these writing situations:

- business memos
- letters to the editor
- college applications
- speeches

To get a feel for persuasive writing, read the critical reviews of *A Doll House,* page 1029.

Teaching Resources

The following resources can be used to enrich or extend the instruction for the Writing Workshop.

Unit 3 Resources
- **Writing Workshop: Persuasive Essay,** pp. 96–97

General Resources
- **Rubrics for Persuasion: Persuasive Essay,** pp. 47–48

From the Author's Desk, DVD
- **Royall Tyler,** Segments 3 and 4

Graphic Organizer Transparencies
- **Two-column Chart,** p. 254

Prewriting

Choosing Your Topic

To choose an issue for your persuasive essay, use one of these strategies:

- **Freewriting** Write for five minutes using **sentence starters** like the ones shown. Then, review your writing to choose a topic.

  The United States has an obligation to _______________.

  Television would be much better if _______________.

  If I became (school principal/mayor/President), the first thing I would do is _______________.

- **Scanning the News** Read and listen to news media to learn more about current local and national controversies. List issues that interest you, and choose one on which you can take a clear, supportable position.

Narrowing Your Topic

When you have a general topic, focus it by **looping.** Write freely about the topic for five minutes. Then, read what you wrote and circle the most important idea. Write about that idea for five minutes, and circle the best idea. Repeat the process until you find an issue narrow enough to address satisfactorily in a persuasive essay. Your topic should meet these criteria:

- It must be an issue with more than one side.
- It should be an issue about which you have a strong opinion.
- It must be an issue that can be supported with logical arguments.

Gathering Details

Check for controversy. Make sure that your topic is one that stirs up disagreement. You want an issue that is a matter of opinion, not fact.

- A **fact** is a statement that can be verified by records, experimentation, or personal observation.
- An **opinion** is a belief or judgment that cannot be proved true.

Consider your audience. Gather arguments tailored to your audience. If your audience is the school board, for example, your arguments will be different from those you would use with students. Use a chart like the one shown to identify arguments for and against your position.

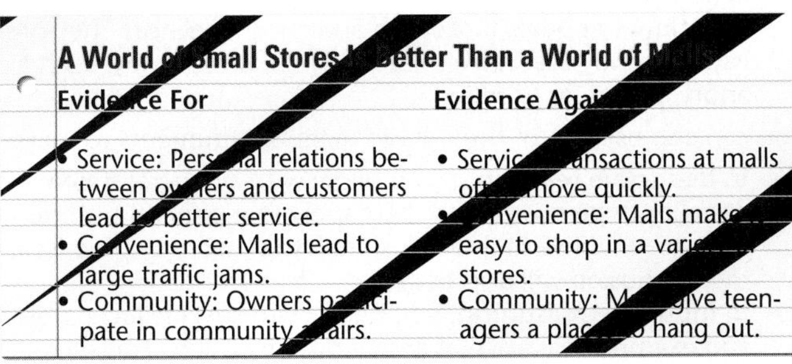

A World of Small Stores Is Better Than a World of Malls

Evidence For	Evidence Against
• Service: Personal relations between owners and customers lead to better service.	• Service: Transactions at malls often move quickly.
• Convenience: Malls lead to large traffic jams.	• Convenience: Malls make it easy to shop in a variety of stores.
• Community: Owners participate in community affairs.	• Community: Malls give teenagers a place to hang out.

TEACH

Prewriting

- Give students support for prewriting and drafting with p. 96 from ***Unit 3 Resources.***
- After students have generated a number of topics, ask them to circle the three topics on the list about which they feel most strongly. Organize students into small groups, and instruct them to share their circled topics with group members. Ask group members to provide feedback about the topics, such as whether the issue has two sides that can be argued.
- After students have selected topics, ask them to consider potential audiences. Help students design charts with columns for each potential audience. Under each heading, tell students to brainstorm for a list of audience characteristics that address these questions: What are the interests of this audience? Which arguments would convince this audience? Why might this audience object to my position? How will I address objections?

Six Traits Focus

✓	Ideas		Word Choice
✓	Organization		Sentence Fluency
	Voice		Conventions

WG Writing and Grammar Platinum Level

Students will find additional instruction on prewriting for a persuasive essay in Chapter 7, Section 2.

Writing and Grammar Interactive Textbook CD-ROM

Students can use the following tools as they complete their persuasive essays:

- Pros and Cons Chart Organizer
- Transition Word Bin
- Unity and Coherence Revising Tool

Tips for Using Rubrics

- Before students begin work on this assignment, have them preview the Rubric for Self-Assessment, p. 341, to know what is expected.
- Review the Assessment criteria in class. Before students use the Rubric for Self-Assessment, work with them to rate the student model by applying one or two criteria to it.
- If you wish to assess students' persuasive essays with either a 4-point, 5-point, or 6-point scoring rubric, see ***General Resources,*** pp. 47 and 48.

Drafting

- Point out to students that stating their position up front helps the audience stay focused as they read.
- Mention, too, that if students ignore opposing arguments, readers may perceive the essay as especially biased or the argument as carelessly researched.
- Remind students that readers will likely remember what they read last. Tell students that this is why writers often conclude with their calls to action or most persuasive points.
- Explain that students need to tailor their persuasive techniques to their topics and audience. Suggest that students list their main points in the left column of a chart and then create three additional columns with the headings *Logical, Ethical,* and *Emotional.* Direct students to create an appeal for each point in the left column and then select the most effective appeals for their audiences.
- Tell students that persuasive arguments should try to move people to take action. Therefore, the final paragraph should instruct or encourage readers to act.

Six Traits Focus

✓	Ideas	✓	Word Choice
✓	Organization		Sentence Fluency
	Voice		Conventions

WG Writing and Grammar Platinum Level
Students will find additional instruction on drafting a persuasive essay in Chapter 7, Section 3.

Writing Workshop

Drafting

Shaping Your Writing

State your position up front. State your opinion in the first paragraph of your essay. Present it in a clearly worded **thesis statement.** Build up to it with dramatic facts, or announce your viewpoint in the very first sentence. Wherever you place your thesis statement, make sure it creates maximum impact by being clear, specific, and forceful.

Weak: I dislike having to wait for parking at the mall.
Strong: The growth of a "mall society" has led to standardization of styles, less personal attention to customers, and many inconveniences.

Organize to emphasize the strongest support. Make your case by presenting your arguments in favor of it. Acknowledge good arguments on the other side of the issue, but then show why your position is better. The organization shown here is one way to make your case forcefully.

The Body of a Persuasive Essay

- Start with your second-best argument.
- State and then argue against an opposing view.
- Organize the rest of your argument to lead up to your conclusion.
- Present your strongest argument last.

Providing Elaboration

Cite evidence for and against your opinion. Marshall the facts, details, examples, and arguments you will need to convince people of your opinion.

- Use unbiased research. Your opinion will be easier to defend if it is based on solid evidence. Include objective facts and statistics, concrete examples, and expert opinions.
- Be aware of evidence opposing your viewpoint. Answering objections to your opinion will make your points more compelling.

Use effective arguing techniques. Consider using appeals of the following kinds to make your points:

- **Logical appeals** are assertions that appeal to reason.
- **Ethical appeals** make the point that it is morally right that a particular action be taken.
- **Emotional appeals** target the audience's feelings. They present the issue in a way that makes readers feel a certain way, such as happy, angry, proud, or horrified.

You can also use one of these basic types of arguments to make your case:

- In **deductive reasoning,** you begin with a general statement of truth—a theory or premise—and then apply that general truth to a specific example to arrive at a conclusion. If the theory or premise is true, then the conclusion will also be true.
- In **inductive reasoning,** you begin with specific facts, observations, and examples to arrive at a general conclusion. This type of reasoning is the basis of the scientific method.

Tips for Improving Word Choice

1. Look for places in your writing where a more precise detail can bring the passage to life.
2. Look for the repetition of the same sentence structures and rewrite these using a mixture of sentences types. For example, avoid a series of simple or compound sentences.
3. Wherever possible, use "surprising" language that describes what you are trying to say, such as "delicious stories."

From the Scholar's Desk
Royall Tyler on Capturing the Reader's Interest

Royall Tyler

Years ago, I translated a book of French folktales. In my introduction, I wanted to make the reader keen to savor these wonderful stories, so I drew on personal experience to convey the feeling of sitting down to a friendly, delicious meal. The great house was my father's. The old man, Paul Delleniaux, had fascinated me for hours with his talk of the old days. He died just two years later.

"Find your own words, but choose them well."
—Royall Tyler

Professional Model:
from *French Folktales*

An old man I know, past eighty now, lives in a hamlet in Burgundy. Admirers call him "le sage du village," which rhymes much better than "the village sage." He remembers the time when in all that countryside only the schoolmaster had a bicycle. No one had been to Paris then. People seldom got to the county seat, either, since the walk there and back took all day. The language they spoke was not exactly French, and the dialect two and a half kilometers away in the neighboring hamlet was recognizably different. In those days, each village had a mole catcher and a blacksmith, just as the villages in these stories do; and, just as in these stories, you ate your dinner with your knife. One summer day in 1988, the village sage graced with his presence a festive meal in the great house nearby, amid polished furniture and fine china. At first he tried out the silver knife and fork. Then, being among friends, he gave up and finished the meal comfortably with his Swiss army knife. These are stories to eat with your pocket knife, among friends. They are delicious, and the days they taste of will never come again.

I wanted the reader to see in Paul a wise, living link with the past described in the folktales.

The world of the tales was like this, too—so different from ours, but not so long ago.

This description contrasts folktale simplicity with fancier, more "sophisticated" ways. *Graced* and *festive*, though, suggest that the two share common ground.

Dear reader (I meant), these stories are not foreign to you. You will find that they speak directly to your heart.

From the Scholar's Desk

Royall Tyler

- Show students Segment 4 on Royall Tyler on **From the Author's Desk DVD.** Discuss the importance of translating and reading literature from other cultures. Also discuss the challenges he faced and the help he received in translating Japanese works.
- Point out that Tyler selected language that created a particular picture of the "le sage du village." Tell students that authors work hard to capture the reader's interest by creating the precise image that they want their readers to envision.
- Review Royall Tyler's comment about finding your own words. Ask students how his comments about his word choice in ***from* French Folktales** reflects his statement. Point out that Tyler used persuasive writing in the introduction to his translation of folktales, drawing on his personal experience to try "to make the reader keen to savor these stories."

Differentiated Instruction
Solutions for All Learners

Support for Less Proficient Writers
Explain that one strategy for capturing reader's interest and making an argument more persuasive is to use the active voice. Review the difference between active and passive voice, and emphasize that the active voice presents arguments strongly and authoritatively. Have students review their papers and circle instances of passive voice. Then, group students in pairs and have them work together to transform instances of passive voice into active voice. Provide students with a thesaurus to consult for more colorful and persuasive words.

Strategy for Advanced Writers
Explain that students can capture their reader's interest with strong research as well as with examples from personal experience. Give students the example from the student model in which Maggie collects research about the correlation between healthy eating and illness in order to make a distinction between hereditary and diet-related illnesses. Suggest that students find other opinions that agree with theirs and factual information that supports these opinions.

Revising

- Review the flaws with students. Make sure that students can distinguish among them. Then ask volunteers to cite examples of each flaw from advertising or political rhetoric.
- Write several dull sentences on the board, and ask students to revise them by using stronger language that makes the sentence persuasive. For example: Voting is a nice thing for citizens to do.
  Possible response: The act of voting honors those who spilled their blood in the struggle for this right.
- Point out that, on the other hand, words that overstate a case create a loss of credibility for the author. An audience does not want to be manipulated, and overstating a case can lead readers to feel manipulated or to doubt the author's information.
- Tell students that to help create a persuasive tone, they should avoid expressions such as "I think" or "It seems." Such expressions indicate that writers are unsure of their positions.

Six Traits Focus

	Ideas	✓	Word Choice
	Organization	✓	Sentence Fluency
✓	Voice		Conventions

Writing and Grammar Platinum Level

Students will find additional guidance for revising a persuasive essay in Chapter 7, Section 4.

Writing Workshop

Revising

Revising Your Paragraphs

Eliminate flaws in your arguments. You may feel passionately about your viewpoint, but passion is no excuse for sloppy reasoning or mud-slinging. Revise your arguments to eliminate flaws like these:

Bandwagon Appeal: **"Everyone thinks this way."** The fact that most people hold an opinion does not make that opinion right. Also, it is easy to say, "Everyone thinks this way," but difficult to *prove* it.

Faulty Logic: **"This happened because that happened."** Be careful when you claim logical or factual connections between events. Just because Event B happened after Event A does not mean that A caused B.

Ad Hominem Attack: **"Those who disagree with me are fools."** Making fun of your opponents is childish and unconvincing. You will lose your audience the moment you start.

Revising Your Word Choice

Strengthen your language. Sharpen the language you use to state and support your opinions. Review your draft, following these steps:

1. Circle expressions that seem vague or unclear, and substitute more precise language.
2. Circle expressions that seem dull, and add more vivid words and phrases.
3. Look for absolute expressions such as "all," "never," "everyone," and "certainly." These words may overstate your case. Ask yourself whether such language can be justified.
4. Underline any charged words, vivid images, or dramatic comparisons in your writing. If you find a passage without any underlined expressions, look for opportunities to add livelier language.

To read the complete student model, see page 340.

Model: Revising to Strengthen Language

I would be very careful about assuming that "Barking dogs seldom bite." It takes only one ~~bad dog to change the rule.~~

biting, barking dog to leave a scar.

Scar creates a vivid image that drives home Maggie's point, while *biting, barking* are punchy modifiers used to make the point memorably.

Peer Review: Ask a classmate to read your draft, circling words and phrases that seem vague or overstated. Revise them to be more precise and vivid.

Tips for Using Technology in Writing

If students are using word processors, they might want to use boldface type or the highlight option to make their main ideas stand out. This strategy will make it easier for them to review their organization and to check for supporting details. In addition, they can use the computer's thesaurus to find different, more persuasive words. Make sure to emphasize the importance of checking a dictionary before using an unfamiliar word to ensure that it is an appropriate choice.

Developing Your Style

Using Parallelism

Check for parallelism. In persuasive writing, the power of your language is important. Parallel expressions create a compelling rhythm and help emphasize the connections or contrasts in a subtle way.

Not parallel: . . . a place *crammed* with people, *lit* with glaring lights, and that *offers* the same brands you can find in the mall.

Parallel: . . . a place *crammed* with people, *lit* with glaring lights, and *offering* the same brands you can find in the mall.

Review your draft to identify related or contrasting concepts. Consider expressing these concepts in parallel form—that is, phrasing the ideas using the same grammatical structure.

Find It in Your Reading Read or review "Zen Parables," on page 320.

1. Find three sentences with related or contrasting elements.
2. Write out the sentences, and underline the compound elements.
3. Explain how they use the same grammatical structure.

Apply It to Your Writing Review the draft of your persuasive essay. Look for opportunities to link or contrast ideas through parallelism. Then, correct any unparallel constructions. For each paragraph in your draft, follow these steps:

1. Look for writing that expresses related or contrasting concepts.
2. If these concepts are in the same sentence, make sure that they have the same grammatical structure.
3. If the concepts are in different sentences, use parallelism to combine them, as shown:

Without parallelism: Everyone can recall an emergency in which it was vitally important to "make haste" to resolve a medical problem. Leaking pipes can't wait. And what about trying to avoid an accident?

With parallelism: Everyone can recall an emergency in which it was important to "make haste" to resolve a medical problem, to fix a leak, or to avoid an accident.

WG *Prentice Hall Writing and Grammar Connection: Platinum Level, Chapter 7, Section 4*

Developing Your Style

- Review the examples of parallel and nonparallel text. **Ask** students what difference they see in the two examples.
  Answer: The modifiers in the nonparallel example include two participial phrases and a dependent clause. In the parallel example, all three modifiers are participial phrases.
- Point out to students that when they relate or contrast concepts, all items must have the same grammatical structure.
- Provide other examples of parallel structure, such as the following, including parallel prepositional phrases and gerunds: We went over the river, across the field, and down the lane. I enjoy running more than I enjoy skiing.
- Help students understand parallelism by having them work on **Find It in Your Reading** in small groups or as a whole class.
  Model possible response: "He cooked for his master, washed the dishes, made his bed, cleaned the yard, cared for the garden, all without a word of swordsmanship. Three years passed. Still Matajuro labored on." The verbs in these three sentences consistently use the past tense.
- Have students continue to work in groups. Ask group members to exchange drafts and look for at least one opportunity to correct or create parallel structure.

WG **Writing and Grammar Platinum Level**

Students will find additional instruction on parallel structure in Chapter 7, Section 4.

Student Model

- Explain that the Student Model is a sample and that essays may be longer.
- **Ask** students to identify Maggie's position, or thesis statement, in the introduction.
  Answer: Proverbs should never be applied uncritically to personal experience.
- Note that a personal experience causes Maggie to revise her opinion about proverbs. **Ask** students how that information strengthens her essay.
  Answer: Her experience shows that she has credibility on the subject.
- Point out that Maggie's progression of significant points includes the ideas that some proverbs are too obvious, some are contradictory, and some have exceptions.
- Direct students' attention to Maggie's inclusion of the opposing argument. **Ask** students: "Why is it important to include the opposing argument even if it is sometimes valid?"
  Possible response: The strongest arguments acknowledge and address opposing viewpoints. This technique shows the completeness of the speaker's thought process, which included a consideration of the opposing viewpoint.
- **Ask** students why Maggie's humorous reference provides a good conclusion to her argument.
  Possible response: Humor lightens the mood and creates a positive feeling in the audience.

Writing Genres

Persuasive Writing in the Workplace

Explain that persuasive writing is frequently used in the workplace to move someone to action. Point out that teachers, managers, and production workers might write persuasively to convince principals or supervisors to purchase new equipment or to change a policy. Then, have students imagine that they know how to improve a policy in school. Have them select a policy and write three paragraphs that attempt to persuade school administrators to change this policy. Tell students to describe the policy, its shortcomings, and a proposal for a better policy. Remind students to use sharp, vivid language and active verbs. Invite students to share their paragraphs.

Student Model: Maggie Korn, Hawthorne, New York

Proverbs: Believe Them or Not

A proverb is a short, pithy saying in widespread use that expresses a basic truth. However, what if these "basic truths" aren't always truthful? I have made an unpleasant discovery about the saying "An apple a day keeps the doctor away." As a result, I believe that proverbs should never be applied uncritically to personal experience.

In her introduction, Maggie clearly states her position, based on a personal experience.

When I was five, I took the "apple advice" quite literally because I hated doctor visits. However, daily apples did not save me from going to the doctor when I developed a bad cold. By sixteen, I was less gullible. I understood the apple proverb to mean that if you ate healthy foods, you would enjoy good health. Despite my healthy diet, I was diagnosed with a hereditary illness, ironically one that affects my digestive tract: Crohn's Disease. No matter how many apples I devoured, or how many hamburgers I declined, I would still have to live with my illness. This bitter taste of reality has made me think twice about old proverbs.

Maggie explains the experience that caused her to revise her opinion about proverbs.

Some proverbs are terribly lame truisms: "Nothing ventured, nothing gained," "Something is better than nothing," and my personal favorite, "There are only twenty-four hours in a day." These are so obvious that they are not worth remembering, much less heeding.

This paragraph begins a series of progressively more significant points in support of Maggie's opinion.

Sometimes proverbs are contradictory. "Haste makes waste," for example, can easily be contradicted by another proverb: "He who hesitates is lost." Another saying, "A stitch in time saves nine," also emphasizes the importance of taking immediate action. Everyone can recall an emergency in which it was vitally important to "make haste" to resolve a medical problem, to fix a leak, or to avoid an accident.

Some proverbs make generalizations that have painful exceptions. My unhappy experience with "apples" is one example, and because of that, I would be very careful about assuming that "Barking dogs seldom bite." It takes only one biting, barking dog to leave a scar. Forgive me if I *don't* assume that "Lightning never strikes twice in the same place."

My point is not that proverbs are useless. I believe that they do offer suggestions that may help you cope with life. However, proverbs should always be measured against your own common sense, your own experience, your own particular situation. Follow the advice of an older and wiser me—and take your proverbs with a "grain of salt." After all, an apple a day simply keeps the orchards in business!

Maggie's concession that proverbs have some usefulness adds credibility to her conclusion.

Maggie clinches her argument with a humorous reference.

Tips for Test Taking

Remind students that when they take a test with a persuasive writing prompt, they should gather and organize their ideas before they begin writing. In a test situation, there is generally time for only one draft; proper planning will ultimately save students time and ensure success. Suggest that students use two-column charts like the one on p. 285 in ***Graphic Organizer Transparencies*** to list quickly the evidence for and against a position. This exercise may help them decide which side of the argument they can better defend and will allow them more time to craft a persuasive opinion.

Editing and Proofreading

Review your persuasive essay to eliminate errors in grammar, spelling, and punctuation.

Focus on Capitalization: To make sure that your writing is error-free, review the capitalization in your draft. Check that all sentences, all proper nouns, and all proper adjectives begin with capital letters.

Publishing and Presenting

Consider one of the the following ways to share your persuasive essay:

Turn your essay into an editorial or a letter to the editor. If your essay concerns a school issue, submit it to your school newspaper. If your essay appeals to a wider audience, submit it as a letter to the editor or as an opinion column in the local newspaper.

Make a speech. Read your persuasive essay aloud to an appropriate audience. When you have finished, invite comments and questions.

Reflecting on Your Writing

Writer's Journal Write down your thoughts on the experience of writing a persuasive essay. Begin by answering these questions:

- Have you changed your mind about your topic since you wrote the essay?
- Has any action been taken about the issue you discussed as a result of your essay? Describe what has been done.

WG *Prentice Hall Writing and Grammar Connection: Platinum Level, Chapter 8*

Rubric for Self-Assessment

Evaluate your persuasive essay *using the following criteria and rating scale, or, with your classmates, determine your own reasonable evaluation criteria.*

NC Criteria	Rating Scale (not very — very)				
Focus: How clearly do you state your position?	1	2	3	4	5
Organization: How effectively do you organize your arguments?	1	2	3	4	5
Support/Elaboration: How well do you use vivid images and dramatic appeals to support your position?	1	2	3	4	5
Style: How well do you use convincing language that is appropriate for your audience?	1	2	3	4	5
Conventions: How correct is your grammar, especially your use of capitalization?	1	2	3	4	5

Differentiated Instruction — Solutions for All Learners

Strategy for English Learners
Students may struggle finding active, vigorous verbs, which increase the persuasiveness of their papers. To help students edit for persuasiveness, first have students circle all instances of "to be" verbs, such as *be, am, are, is, was, were,* and *will.* Next, group students in pairs, and provide each pair with a thesaurus. Then, have pairs read each sentence that contains a circled "to be" verb and determine the meaning of the sentence. Finally, have students use the thesaurus to find suitable verbs to replace the verb forms of "to be."

Strategy for Advanced Writers
Provide students with examples of persuasive writing from a recent editorial in your city or community newspaper, or select an editorial from a nationally known newspaper or news magazine. Have students read the editorial and circle words and phrases that contribute to the persuasive power of the argument. Afterwards, have students explain why they selected the words and phrases and how these words and phrases add persuasion to the editorial. Then have students review their papers, identify ways to increase the persuasive power of their writing, and revise accordingly.

Editing and Proofreading

- Point out that one effective method of proofreading for errors is to read sentence by sentence from the end of the paper to the beginning. This strategy forces students to focus on the grammar rather than the meaning of the paper and helps keep them from reading over errors because they have seen the material so many times before during revision.
- Point out to students that only the brand name of a product is capitalized, not the product itself. Remind students to capitalize street names, such as Maple Street

Six Traits Focus

	Ideas		Word Choice
	Organization		Sentence Fluency
	Voice	✓	Conventions

ASSESS

Publishing and Presenting

- As students write their essays as letters to the editor of their local newspapers, tell them to consider the needs of their new audiences.
- If possible, provide students with videotape equipment and encourage them to videotape themselves while they rehearse their presentations. Then, have them watch the tapes to evaluate their vocal expression and body language.

Reflecting on Your Writing

- As they make entries in their writer's journals, have students discuss what they learned about the process of persuasion.
- Review the assessment criteria.
- Ask students how they would score the essay in terms of the clarity of the stated position and why students would give the essay this score. Then have students assess their own papers.

WG **Writing and Grammar Platinum Level**
Students will find additional guidelines for editing and proofreading, publishing and presenting, and reflecting on a persuasive essay in Chapter 8.

Standard Course of Study

LT.5.03.6	Make inferences, predictions, and draw conclusions based on world literature.
LT.5.03.10	Analyze connections between ideas, concepts, characters and experiences in world literature.
GU.6.01.4	Use vocabulary strategies to determine meaning.

Know Your Terms: Making Connections

Explain that the terms listed under Terms to Learn will be used in standardized-test situations when students are asked to understand the significance of the text and to use it.

Terms to Learn

- Review *predict* and *prediction.* Tell students that *to predict* means "to make an educated guess about what will occur or about what the writer might say, based on the details and information in the text." When students have to predict, suggest that they ask themselves, "On the basis of what I know, what should I expect?" Then have students ask, "What information in the text leads me to that prediction?"
- Review *apply.* Point out to students that information becomes valuable only when they can apply or use it in a specific situation. For example, when students write an essay, they can apply their knowledge of punctuation.

ASSESS

Answers

1. Probably Lady Myobu will be allowed to do whatever she chooses. No one will do anything to her that will anger the Emperor.
2. When you have responsibility for something, you must be very careful how you treat it and how others perceive or interpret your actions. To apply the message of the passage to life today, clear communication and responsibility are important qualities for an employee.

Vocabulary Workshop

High-Frequency Academic Words

High-frequency academic words are words that appear often in textbooks and on standardized tests. Though you may already know the meaning of many of these words, they usually have a more specific meaning when they are used in textbooks and on tests.

Know Your Terms: Making Connections

Each of the words listed is a verb that tells you to show that you understand the significance of the information in the text and can use it. The words indicate the kind of information you should provide in your answer.

Standard Course of Study

- Make inferences, predictions, and draw conclusions based on world literature. (LT.5.03.6)
- Analyze connections between ideas, concepts, characters and experiences. (LT.5.03.10)
- Use vocabulary strategies to determine meaning. (GU.6.01.4)

Terms to Learn

Predict Tell what you think will happen based on the evidence.

Sample test item: Based on the events in the first chapter, what do you ***predict*** will happen to the main character?

Apply Tell how you use information in a specific situation.

Sample test item: ***Apply*** the information in the chart to explain the change in migration patterns.

Practice

Directions: *Read the following passage from* The Pillow Book *by Sei Shōnagon. Then, answer the questions that follow.*

The cat who lived in the Palace had been awarded the headdress of nobility and was called Lady Myobu. She was a very pretty cat, and His Majesty saw to it that she was treated with the greatest care.

One day she wandered on to the veranda, and Lady Uma, the nurse in charge of her, called out, "Oh, you naughty thing! Please come inside at once." But the cat paid no attention and went on basking sleepily in the sun. Intending to give her a scare, the nurse called for the dog, Okinamaro.

"Okinamaro, where are you?" she cried. "Come here and bite Lady Myobu!" The foolish Okinamaro, believing that the nurse was in earnest, rushed at the cat, who, startled and terrified, ran behind the blind to the Imperial Dining Room, where the Emperor happened to be sitting. Greatly surprised, His Majesty picked up the cat and held her in his arms. He summoned his gentlemen-in-waiting. When Tadataka, the Chamberlain, appeared, His Majesty ordered that Okinamaro be chastised and banished to Dog Island.

1. What kind of life do you *predict* for Lady Myobu from now on?
2. Identify the message of this passage and *apply* it to life today.

Tips for Test Taking

- When students are asked to make a prediction about information in a reading passage on a standardized test, their choice should be based on known information and realistic expectations. Remind students to look for the details that validate the prediction. The correct answer will reflect only those details present in the text.
- If students are asked to apply information on a standardized test, they need to use the information in the text to answer the question. They will take general information and ask themselves, "How does this information work in this particular case?"

Go Online Vocabulary **For:** An Interactive Crossword Puzzle
Visit: www.PHSchool.com
Web Code: etj-5301

This crossword puzzle contains vocabulary that reflects the concepts in Unit 3. After students have completed Unit 3, give students the Web Code and have them complete the crossword puzzle.

Assessment Workshop

Critical Reading: Cause-and-Effect Relationships

Standard Course of Study

- WL.1.02.1
- IR.2.01.6
- IR.2.02.2
- CT.4.01.1
- CT.4.05.10
- LT.5.03.5

In the reading sections of some tests, you may be required to recognize the cause-and-effect relationships described or implied in a passage. In addition, you may be asked to make predictions based on these relationships or to evaluate whether the cause-and-effect relationship is supported by enough evidence. Use the following strategies to answer such test questions:

- Recognize cause-and-effect relationships by first asking, *What happened?* (effect) and then asking, *Why did it happen?* (cause).
- Remember that a single cause can have many effects, and a single effect can have many causes.
- Remember that an event can be both an effect and a cause.

Practice

Directions: *Read the passages, and then answer the questions that follow.*

Passage A. What really happens to kids who play lots of video games—particularly violent video games? No one can say for sure. But seeing violent images regularly makes players more comfortable with such images. Does an increased comfort level lead to an increase in violent behavior? All the evidence is anecdotal. Long-term studies have yet to prove a connection between violence and video games.

Passage B. What sort of community does the traditional Amish way of life foster, and what are its strengths and weaknesses? Amish people who follow a traditional way of life strive to be as removed from the rest of the world as possible. To keep their communities cohesive, they adhere to strict codes of moral behavior with little tolerance for differences. The people conform, work hard, and seldom pursue formal higher education. As a result, Amish people enjoy stable, productive lives, sure of their place in the world because of their clear, and clearly valuable, roles in the community.

1. According to Passage A, what is one effect that violent video games have on those who play them?
   - A poor grades in school
   - B better hand-eye coordination
   - C violent behavior
   - D comfort with violent imagery

2. Which of the following does Passage B give as an effect of the cohesiveness of Amish communities?
   - A. strict moral codes
   - B conformism
   - C stable lives
   - D hard work

Test-Taking Strategies

- Look for words that signal cause-and-effect relationships, such as *because, therefore,* and *as a result.*
- Visualize the events as a *chain reaction* in which the occurrence of an important event relies on the occurrence of those that precede it. View each individual event—each link in the chain between the first and the last—as both a cause and an effect.

Standard Course of Study

IR.2.02.2	Show clear, logical connection among cause/effect events.
CT.4.05.10	Analyze connections between ideas, concepts, characters and experiences in critical text.
LT.5.03.5	Summarize key events and points from world literature.

Critical Reading

- Remind students that either causes or effects can appear first in a passage.
- Point out that when reading a cause-and-effect passage, students should look for all of the causes and effects, making sure not to miss any.
- Tell students that a cause can also be an effect; this relationship between causes and effects is called a causal chain. It provides a type of domino effect in which each event causes the next event.
- After students have read the Practice passages and have answered the questions, point out that in question 1, although students may believe that several of the answer choices are the result of playing violent video games, the only answer that is supported in the passage as a cause is D.
- Point out that although all of the answer choices in question 2 are included in the passage, the only choice that is an effect of the cohesiveness of Amish communities is C.

ASSESS

Answers

1. D
2. C

Tips for Test Taking

Remind students that in a cause-and-effect passage, they are looking for relationships between events. These relationships tie the passage together and help make sense out of the information. When faced with a standardized-test question about cause-and-effect relationships, students should ask themselves, "How are the elements in the passage tied together?" If they can determine the relationship of the elements, students will find the cause and its effect. However, remind students to be careful in deciding whether an event occurred *because* of something or merely *after* it.

Standard Course of Study

FA.3.01.1 Share and evaluate initial personal response to a controversial issue.

FA.3.01.4 Compile response and research data to organize argument about controversial issues.

Plan the Content

- Provide student groups with copies of outrageous articles from tabloid newspapers that feature sources that are clearly suspect. Direct students to evaluate the supporting material in these articles while leading a discussion about the value of reliable source material for persuasive arguments.
- After students have planned the content of their speeches, have them exchange their drafts with other students. Ask each student to provide feedback for his or her partner using the Feedback Form.

Focus on Delivery

- Bring to class several copies of a familiar children's book such as Dr. Seuss' *The Cat in the Hat.* Assign sequential portions of the book to different students for oral presentation. Secretly give each presenter a different set of instructions: read slowly, read quickly, stress key words and statements, speak quietly, speak loudly, take several steps while reading, stand still, use facial expressions, and use hand gestures. Give students a few minutes to practice before the presentation. Lead students in a discussion about the effect of pace, tone of voice, and body language in oral presentation.
- Have students use the delivery section of the Feedback Form as they prepare to present their arguments.

Assess the Activity

To evaluate students' delivery, use the Rubric for Effective Listening, p. 83 in ***General Resources.***

Delivering a Persuasive Argument

Standard Course of Study

- Share and evaluate response to a controversial issue. (FA.3.01.1)

A **persuasive argument** delivered in a speech is meant to convince an audience to believe something or to take a specific course of action. A good persuasive argument uses clear, logical reasoning and effective emotional appeals. (For a review of the characteristics of persuasive writing, see the Writing Workshop on pages 334–341.) Follow these strategies to deliver an effective persuasive argument.

Plan the Content

To begin, choose a debatable topic for your presentation—that is, one on which reasonable people disagree.

Research supporting material. Gather facts and statistics, examples, expert opinions, and other evidence that supports your position. Select the strongest facts and figures, and present them in your speech.

Use rhetorical techniques. To catch your audience's imagination, strengthen your argument with rhetorical devices, including the following:

- **Dramatic questions:** Consider posing your key issue in the form of a stirring question. (For example, "How long before parents, worried by aging swing sets, forbid their kids to play in the park?").
- **Analogies:** By comparing an abstract idea to a simple, familiar relationship, an analogy makes even a complicated idea easy to grasp. (For example, "Developing a new ball field without repairing the playground is like spending your money on a great haircut while walking around in torn-up shoes.")

Feedback Form for a Persuasive Argument

Rating System
+ = Excellent ✓= Average – = Weak

Content
Uses supporting evidence effectively________
Anticipates opposing arguments________

Uses rhetorical techniques to strengthen argument________

Which techniques?________

Delivery
Varies pace and tone________
Gestures effectively________
Makes eye contact________

Other comments on delivery:________

Focus on Delivery

Use these techniques to make your speech engaging:

- **Vary your pace and tone of voice.** Slow down to stress key statements, and speed up to convey emotion. Raising and lowering your voice can be a very effective way to build drama.
- **Be aware of body language.** Relax! Avoid a stiff, wooden posture. Gesturing occasionally for emphasis and taking a few steps from time to time will help you communicate with your audience effectively. Also be sure to make eye contact and to use appropriate facial expressions as you speak.

Activity *Presentation and Feedback* Prepare a persuasive speech on a controversial issue. Have a partner use the Feedback Form shown above to evaluate your presentation. Use the evaluation to improve your speech. Then, deliver it to your class.

Differentiated Instruction Solutions for All Learners

Strategy for English Learners
Show students the first few minutes of several videotaped speeches. Lead a discussion about each speaker's purpose for speaking, and help students identify techniques used to get the audience's attention. Encourage students to use similar techniques in preparing their speeches.

Strategy for Gifted/Talented Students
Have students create artwork such as logos and other graphics to enhance their speeches. Encourage students to display this work on the front of the podium or on an easel as they present their speeches. Then, have other students evaluate the effectiveness of each speaker's visual display.

Enrichment for Advanced Writers
Have students find transcripts of several victory and concession speeches. After reading the transcripts, have students perform the speeches with vocal inflection and body language that match the words. Then, have students watch videotapes of the actual speeches to determine how closely their interpretations echo the original versions.

Suggestions for Further Reading

Featured Titles:

Treason by the Book
Jonathan D. Spence, *Penguin, 2002*

Historical Fiction Part history and part mystery, *Treason by the Book* details a plot to overthrow Yongzheng, the Manchu emperor of China. This true story begins in 1728 when a treasonous letter addressed to the emperor is passed to one of the emperor's generals. After reading the letter, Yongzheng launches a massive investigation to find its author. When the guilty party is identified, Yongzheng does something quite unexpected. Inspired by Confucian ideas about leading by example, the emperor decides to engage in a public written dialogue with the letter's author in order to disprove his accusations and stem the tide of rebellion. *Treason by the Book* is a study not only of imperial power but also of the power of the written word.

The Narrow Road to the Deep North
Matsuo Bashō, *translated by Nobuyuki Yuasa, Penguin Classic, 1967*

Haiku As you read this book, you will be traveling through seventeenth-century Japan with an adventurous and sensitive companion, the poet Matsuo Bashō. He is more concerned with the spiritual benefits of his journey than he is with material comforts. Being poor, he cannot pay much for lodgings, but he is always ready to "pay" with a poem for the beauty he sees. For example, on finding a famous ruined castle, he sits on his hat, weeps, and writes, "A thicket of summer grass / Is all that remains / Of the dreams and ambitions / Of ancient warriors." Share sights and insights with this poet who, three hundred years before the highway adventures of America's beatniks, knew how to travel with an empty wallet and a full spirit.

Work Presented in Unit Three:

If sampling a portion of the following text has built your interest, treat yourself to the full work.

The Analects
Confucius, *translated by Arthur Waley, Penguin Classic, 1979*

Related British Literature:

Across the Nightingale Floor
Lian Hearn, *Riverhead, 2003*

This novel by a British author tells about an orphan boy and his magical destiny in medieval Japan.

Related American Literature:

The Joy Luck Club
Amy Tan, *Putnam, 1989*

In her celebrated first novel, Amy Tan weaves together the stories of Chinese Americans living in San Francisco.

***Many of these titles are available in the* Prentice Hall/Penguin Literature Library.**
Consult your teacher before choosing one.

Planning Students' Further Reading

Discussions of literature can raise sensitive and often controversial issues. Before you recommend further reading to your students, consider the values and sensitivities of your community as well as the age, ability, and sophistication of your students. It is also good policy to preview literature before you recommend it to students. The notes below offer some guidance on specific titles.

Treason by the Book by Jonathan D. Spence

This compelling narrative history contains references to torture, execution, drinking, abuse of women, and philosophies of racial or ethnic purity.

Lexile: Appropriate for high school students

The Narrow Road to the Deep North by Matsuo Bashō

Among the stories is the mention of "concubines" in a room next door. To prepare students to read, discuss Zen Buddhism and its didactic use of parables.

Lexile: Appropriate for high school students

The Analects by Confucius

This founding work of one of the world's great schools of thought refers to Confucius' birth as the result of an "illicit union."

Lexile: Appropriate for high school students

Across the Nightingale Floor by Lian Hearn

Set in a world of feudal warlords, this text includes descriptions of violence and references to the occult.
Lexile: 840L

The Joy Luck Club by Amy Tan
Multiple narrators discuss life in both the United States and China, touching on such sensitive issues as smoking and drinking, divorce, premarital sex, abortion, families with multiple wives and concubines, the horrors of famine and war, and loss of faith in God. In China, one narrator's mother kills herself by taking poison. The book also contain examples of profane language.
Lexile: 930L

Standard Course of Study

IR.2.01.3	Provide evidence to support understanding of and response to research text.
FA.3.02.1	State position or proposed solution in an editorial or response.
CT.4.02.3	Examine how elements such as irony and symbolism impact theme.
LT.5.03.9	Analyze and evaluate the effects of author's craft and style in world literature.

Unit 4 Classical Civilizations

c. 800 B.C.–A.D. 500

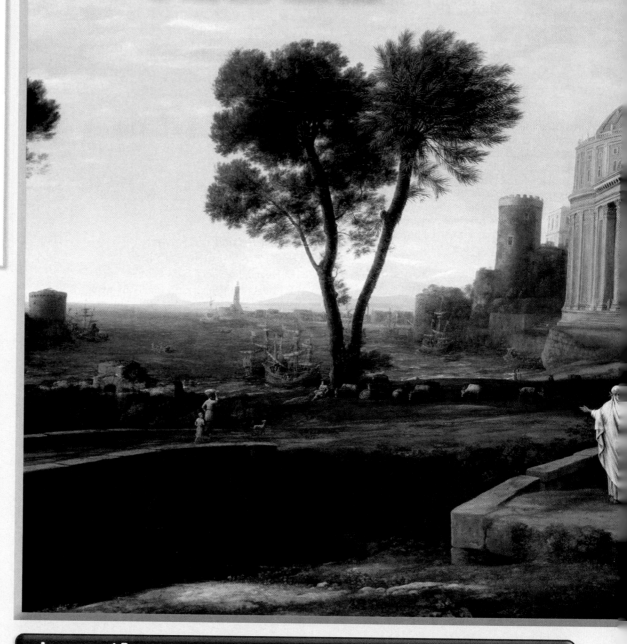

Unit Instructional Resources

In *Unit 4 Resources,* you will find materials to support students in developing and mastering the unit skills and to help you assess their progress.

Vocabulary and Reading

Additional vocabulary and reading support, based on Lexile scores of vocabulary words, is provided for each selection or grouping.

- **Word Lists A and B** and **Practices A and B** provide vocabulary-building activities for students reading two grades or one grade below level, respectively.
- **Reading Warm-ups A and B,** for students reading two grades or one grade below level, respectively, consist of short readings and activities that provide a context and practice for newly learned vocabulary.

Selection Support Practice and reinforcement pages support each selection:

- Reading Strategy
- Literary Analysis
- Vocabulary Builder
- Grammar and Style
- Support for Writing
- Support for Extend Your Learning
- Enrichment

You may also access these resources at TeacherExpress.

Assessment Resources

Listed below are the resources available to assess and measure students' progress in meeting the unit objectives and your state standards.

Skills Assessment

Unit 4 Resources
- Selection Tests A and B

TeacherExpress™
- *ExamView®* Test Bank Software

Adequate Yearly Progress Assessment

Unit 4 Resources
- Diagnostic Tests 4 and 5
- Benchmark Tests 4 and 5

Standardized Assessment

Standardized Test Preparation Workbook

Aeneas at Delos, Claude Lorrain, © National Gallery Collection; By kind permission of the Trustees of the National Gallery, Lond

Ancient Greece and Rome

Standard Course of Study
In This Unit You Will

- Make connections between works, self and related topics in response and reflection. (WL.1.03.8)
- State position or proposed solution in an editorial or response. (FA.3.02.1)
- Show an understanding of cultural context in analyzing thematic connections. (CT.4.02.1)
- Analyze how writers achieve a sense of completeness and closure. (CT.4.03.5)
- Build knowledge of literary genres, and explore how characteristics apply to literature of world cultures. (LT.5.01.2)
- Explore works which relate to an issue, author, or theme and show increasing comprehension. (LT.5.02.1)
- Analyze and evaluate the effects of author's craft and style in world literature. (LT.5.03.9)
- Analyze author's use of language to demonstrate understanding of expression. (GU.6.01.2)

◀ This painting shows Aeneas, the founder of Rome, and the hero of Virgil's epic the *Aeneid,* with his father, Anchises, and his son Ascanius. Anius, the king of Delos and a priest of Apollo, greets them.

Introduce Unit 4

- Direct students' attention to the title and time period of this unit. Have a student read the quotation. **Ask:** In what ways is this quotation a commentary on the painting?
  Possible response: The painting shows stately buildings, a beautiful stone bridge, ships at sea, and a serene environment—all the result of the wonders of human ingenuity.
- Have students look at the art. Read the Humanities note to them, and ask the discussion questions.
- Then **ask:** What kinds of literature or themes in literature do you think might come out of this period in literary history?
  Possible response: The quotation mentions the wonders of humanity, and the art shows examples of human ingenuity, so the literature might be about human abilities and limitations, understanding human nature, and humans' place in the world.

Humanities

Aeneas at Delos,
by Claude Lorrain

This landscape, created in 1672, shows Aeneas, the founder of Rome and the hero of Virgil's epic *Aeneid,* with his father, Anchises, and his son Ascanius. Anius, the king of Delos and a priest of Apollo, greets them.

Use the following questions for discussion:

1. Why do you think the artist includes the hero's father and son in this portrayal of Aeneas?
   Possible response: Claude Lorrain may wish to emphasize the continuity of generations.
2. How would you describe the mood of this scene?
   Possible response: The mood seems noble, dignified, and grand.

Unit Features

David Mamet

Each unit features commentary by a contemporary writer or scholar. Author David Mamet introduces Unit 4 in Setting the Scene, in which he discusses ancient Greek drama and tragedy. Later in the unit, he introduces *Oedipus the King,* by Sophocles. He also contributes his insights on writing dialogue in the Writing Workshop.

Connections

Every unit contains a feature that connects literature to a related topic, such as art, science, or history. In this unit, Abraham Lincoln's **Gettysburg Address** is on p. 437.

Use the information and questions on the Connections pages to help students enrich their understanding of the selections presented within the unit.

Reading Informational Materials

These selections will help students analyze and evaluate informational texts, such as workplace documents, technical directions, and consumer materials. They will expose students to the organization and features unique to nonnarrative texts.

In this unit, the focus is on the Web Research Sources. The **Perseus Digital Library** is on p. 529.

From the Scholar's Desk

Introduce David Mamet

- David Mamet, a playwright, director, and screenwriter, introduces the unit and provides insights into ancient Greek drama and its relevance for our world. His introduction to *Oedipus the King* appears later in this unit on pages 463–465.
- Have students read the introductory paragraph about David Mamet. Point out that he has won the Pulitzer Prize for Drama and the 2005 Screen Laurel Award from the Writers Guild of America.
- Use ***From the Author's Desk DVD*** to introduce David Mamet. Show Segment 1 to provide insight into his writing career. After students have watched the segment, **ask:** How did being born and raised in Chicago affect David Mamet's career?
Answer: In Chicago, playwrighting was a day-to-day skill, and community theaters were thriving, so he had the chance to try many different jobs in the theater. He was also influenced by the duality of the city and by Midwestern writers.

Ancient Drama

- After students have read Mamet's commentary on the development of ancient Greek drama, point out that the Greeks were aware of a human tendency for each person to believe that he or she is more important than anyone else is. This tendency can lead to conflicts that express the dramatic character of life, which the Greeks portrayed in their plays.
Ask: Why did drama develop?
Answer: People express the events in their lives dramatically, and the Greeks used drama to talk about an elevated person who is guilty either of offending the fates or excessive pride.
- **Ask:** How does Mamet explain the relevance of Greek drama today?
Answer: He says that everyone's life is dramatic and that Greek drama helps us understand how the world works.

Setting the Scene

Unit 4 features works of literature from ancient Greece and Rome that have had a profound impact on Western culture. In the following essay, playwright David Mamet analyzes the essential nature of ancient Greek drama and explains why it still relates to our everyday lives—even life in high school. As you read his essay, the unit introduction that follows, and the literature in Unit 4, think about why these classical civilizations continue to exert such a powerful cultural influence today.

From the Scholar's Desk
David Mamet Talks About the Time Period

David Mamet

Introducing David Mamet (b. 1947) Born in Chicago, David Mamet is a prize winning playwright, director, and screenwriter. The author of more than twenty plays, including *American Buffalo* and *Glengarry Glen Ross,* Mamet is known for gritty characters and rapid-fire dialogue that captures the fragmented rhythms of everyday speech. He has won the Pulitzer Prize and the 2005 Screen Laurel Award from the Writers Guild of America.

Ancient Drama

The ancient Greeks didn't *invent* drama. They were't sitting around one evening saying, "Let's invent drama tomorrow." They were expressing themselves the way that we humans express ourselves: dramatically. And we say, "Okay, there was this king." So of course we're going to say that *we* are the king—so that *we* are all-powerful. That's what being a king means: I'm all-powerful.

When Bad Things Happen to All-Powerful People But wait a second. The king is all-powerful, yet there is a plague in his country that he can't stop, as in Sophocles' *Oedipus the King.* How are we going to reconcile these two ideas: I'm all-powerful, yet something happens to me that I can't control? It's the same thing as saying, "I worked hard at work, yet my boss fired me." How can I live in a world where this greatest person to have lived, me, is subject to the vagaries of existence?

So we make up this drama where we're the good person, the elevated person, who always stands for us, yet who is subject to the vagaries of existence. The Greeks called these vagaries "gods," or they called what happens "offending the fates" or "having the sin of

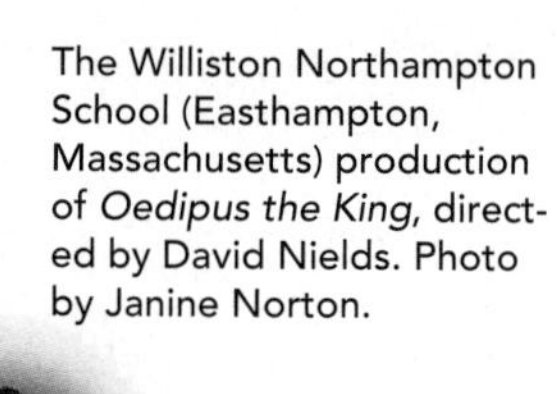

The Williston Northampton School (Easthampton, Massachusetts) production of *Oedipus the King*, directed by David Nields. Photo by Janine Norton.

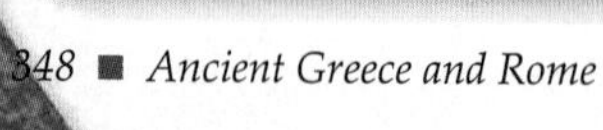

Teaching Resources

The following resources can be used to enrich or extend the instruction for Unit 4 Introduction.

Unit 4 Resources
- **Unit Introduction: Names and Terms to Know,** p. 5
- **Unit Introduction: Focus Questions,** p. 6
- **Listening and Viewing,** p. 101

From the Author's Desk DVD
- **David Mamet,** Segment 1

hubris," excessive pride. What happens at the end of the drama is that Oedipus, or any hero in any classical tragedy, finds that he isn't quite as powerful as these forces are. And yes, bad things do happen to us because of fate or because of an internal flaw in our character.

Everyone Is a Tragic Hero

The question is, "Why should people in high school want to read Greek tragedy?" And the answer is that life in high school is a tragedy, right? Everybody in high school is a tragic hero: nobody understands you. I was a tragic hero when I was in high school. I have teenaged daughters—they spend all their time talking on the phone with each other. And what they're doing is creating a drama, because their life is incredibly dramatic. They're full of energy; they're full of zeal. They don't know much about the way the world works, and they're trying to figure it out. That's exactly the same thing that a dramatist is doing.

So if I were going to teach high school drama, I would back into it. I would say, "Aha! You see what you did there, what I overheard you saying in the corridor? That's a perfect example of a dramatic scene. You said, "I got ready to have a surprise party for Johnny, but guess what. At the last minute, he went out on a date with Susie. What am I going to do?" So the answer to the question, "What am I going to do?" is the next scene. "What about if we blah, blah, blah?"

Everyday Drama That's the same thing that Sophocles was doing when he wrote *Oedipus:* I'm the king, I'm all-powerful, I'm going to find out why there is a plague on Thebes . . . Oh no! It seems that I've killed my father and married my mother! Just when everything was going so well . . . It's a little different from high school, but this is not some high-blown fantastical thing that you have to be an ancient Greek to do, but rather something that we all do. In this unit, you'll read an actual example of the same thing that you do everyday. It happens to be called *Oedipus the King*.

Critical Viewing
The photograph on page 348 shows a high school production of *Oedipus the King*. What is your response to the costumes and set design? **[Respond]**

Go Online Author Link
For: An online video
Visit: www.PHSchool.com
Web Code: ete-8401

For: More about David Mamet
Visit: www.PHSchool.com
Web Code: ete-9406

Reading the Unit Introduction

Reading for Information and Insight Use the following terms and questions to guide your reading of the unit introduction on pages 352–359.

Names and Terms to Know
- Trojan War
- Pericles
- Peloponnesian War
- Delphic Oracle
- Punic Wars
- Julius Caesar
- Augustus
- Roman Empire

Focus Questions As you read this introduction, use what you learn to answer these questions:
- What are some of the characteristics of the Golden Age of Athens under Pericles?
- What factors brought about the birth and downfall of the Roman Empire?
- What forms of literature flourished in ancient Greece and Rome? Why?

Reading the Unit Introduction

Tell students that the terms and questions listed here are the key points in this introductory material. This information provides a context for the selections in this unit. Students should use the terms and questions as a guide to focus their reading of the unit introduction. When students have completed the unit introduction, they should be able to identify or explain each of these terms and answer or discuss the Focus Questions.

Concept Connector

After students have read the unit introduction, return to the Focus Questions to review the main points. For key points, see p. 359.

Go Online Author Link Typing in the Web Codes when prompted will bring students to a video clip and more information on David Mamet.

Critical Viewing

Possible response: Students may say that the costumes, which are typical clothing that teens might wear, and the basic, contemporary set design suggest that the drama of *Oedipus the King* could be played out in people's lives even today.

Using the Timeline

The Timeline can serve a number of instructional purposes, as follows:

Getting an Overview

Use the Timeline to help students get a quick overview of themes and events of the period. This approach will benefit all students but may be especially helpful for Visual/Spatial Learners, English Learners, and Less Proficient Readers. (For strategies in using the Timeline as an overview, see the bottom of this page.)

Thinking Critically

Questions are provided on the facing page. Use these questions to have students review the events, discuss their significance, and examine the "so what" behind the "what happened."

Connecting to Selections

Have students refer to the Timeline when they begin to read individual selections. By consulting the Timeline regularly, students will gain a better sense of the period's chronology. In addition, they will appreciate world events that gave rise to these works of literature.

Projects

Students can use the Timeline as a launching pad for projects like these:

- **Customized Timeline** Have students choose either ancient Greece or ancient Rome and create period timelines in their notebooks, adding key details as they read new selections. They can use dates from this Timeline as a framework.
- **Special Report** Have students scan the Timeline for items that interest them, research these further, and report on them to the class. For example, a student group interested in architecture might present a comparative report on the Parthenon in Athens and the Colosseum in Rome.

Ancient Greek, Roman, and World Events

800 B.C. 540 B.C. 280 B.C.

ANCIENT GREEK AND ROMAN EVENTS

- 700s **(Greece)** It was likely during this period that the polis, or city-state, emerged.
- 700s **(Greece)** Probable era of the life of Homer, author of the *Iliad* and the *Odyssey*.
- 776 **(Greece)** The first Olympic games are held. ▼
- 753 **(Rome)** The city of Rome is founded.

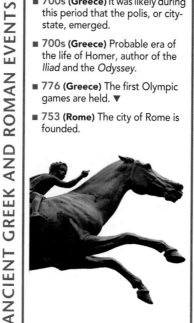

- 525/524 **(Greece)** The tragic dramatist Aeschylus is born.
- 509 **(Rome)** Rome becomes a republic.
- early 400s **(Greece)** Athens and Sparta are the most powerful city-states.
- c. 496 **(Greece)** The tragic dramatist Sophocles is born.
- 495–429 **(Greece)** Pericles, Athenian statesman, lives.
- 490–479 **(Greece)** Greco-Persian Wars are fought.
- c. 470–399 **(Greece)** The philosopher Socrates lives.
- 447 **(Greece)** Ordered by Pericles, work begins on the Parthenon, a great temple of Athena in Athens. ▲
- 431–404 **(Greece)** Athens is defeated by Sparta in the Peloponnesian War.

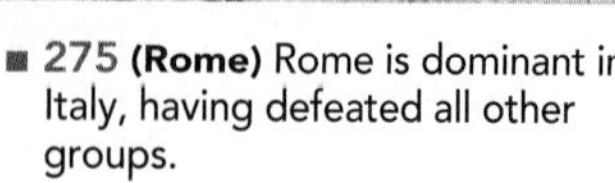

- 275 **(Rome)** Rome is dominant in Italy, having defeated all other groups.

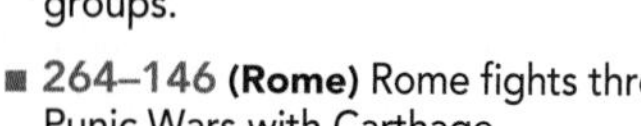

- 264–146 **(Rome)** Rome fights three Punic Wars with Carthage.
- 70–19 **(Rome)** Virgil, author of the *Aeneid*, lives.

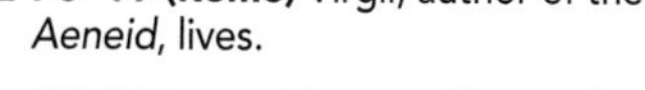

- 65–8 **(Rome)** The poet Horace lives.
- 63 **(Rome)** Augustus, first Roman emperor, is born.

WORLD EVENTS

- 721 **(ancient Israel)** The Assyrians conquer the northern kingdom of Israel.
- c. 700 **(India)** This is the final date for the composition of the *Brahmanas*, texts that discuss religious rituals.
- c. 628–c. 551 **(Persia)** Zoroaster, founder of Zoroastrianism, lives. ▶

- 515 **(ancient Israel)** The Second Temple is built in Jerusalem.
- 400s **(India)** Panini standardizes Sanskrit in an important grammar text.
- c. 330 **(Persian Empire)** Alexander the Great conquers the Persian Empire.

- 256/255 **(China)** The Chou dynasty is overthrown.
- 221–206 **(China)** The Ch'in dynasty reigns.
- 206 **(China)** The Han dynasty takes power. ▶
- 200 **(Japan)** By this date, the Japanese cultivate irrigated rice.
- 100–0 **(India)** Work on the Ajanta caves begins; construction continues through the 7th century A.D.

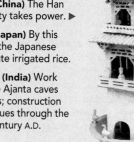

Getting an Overview of the Period

Introduction To give students an overview of the period, have them indicate the span of dates in the title of the Timeline. Next, point out that the Timeline is divided into Ancient Greek and Roman Events (on the top) and World Events (on the bottom). Have students scan the Timeline, looking at both Ancient Greek and Roman Events and World Events. Finally, point out that the events in the Timeline often represent beginnings, turning points, and endings (for example, c. 496 B.C., the tragic dramatist Sophocles is born).

Key Events Have students identify key political events, such as conquests.
Answer: In 721 B.C., the Assyrians conquered the northern kingdom of Israel; in 431–404 B.C., Athens was defeated by Sparta in the Peloponnesian War; c. 330 B.C., Alexander the Great conquered the Persian Empire.

Then, have students identify events that suggest religious upheaval.
Possible response: In A.D. 30, Jesus of Nazareth was crucified.

20 B.C. A.D. 240 A.D. 500

- A.D. 8 **(Rome)** The emperor Augustus banishes the poet Ovid to Tomis, near the Black Sea.
- 14 **(Rome)** Augustus, the first Roman Emperor, dies.
- 30 **(Roman Empire)** Jesus of Nazareth is crucified.
- 56–120 **(Rome)** The historian Tacitus lives.
- 70–72 **(Rome)** Construction of the Colosseum, a giant stadium for gladiatorial combats, begins. ▼

- c. 376 **(Roman Empire)** The fierce tribe known as the Huns reaches the frontier of the empire. ▶
- 379–395 **(Roman Empire)** Under the emperor Theodosius I, Christianity becomes essential to Roman citizenship.
- 391 **(Roman Empire)** The emperor Theodosius I ends all visits to the Oracle at Delphi.
- 410 **(Rome)** Rome is sacked by the Visigoths, a Germanic tribe.
- 476 **(Roman Empire)** The Western Roman Empire falls.

- c. A.D. 100s **(China)** Buddhism begins to take hold. ▼
- c. 200 **(Mexico/Central America)** Mayan villages have developed into cities.

- 300s **(Japan)** The Yamato emerge as the most powerful clan, opening the way to Chinese cultural influences.
- 365–427 **(China)** T'ao Ch'ien, one of China's greatest poets, lives.
- late 300s to early 400s **(India)** The Hindu author of an astronomical handbook tabulates the sine function.
- c. 400 **(India)** The Pillar of Delhi, a solid metal column over 23 feet tall and weighing more than 6 tons, is constructed.
- c. 400 **(India)** The final compilation of the *Mahabharata* is made.
- 476–750 **(France)** Merovingian kings rule the Franks.

Critical Viewing

1. What does the picture of the horse and rider (776 B.C.) suggest about the athletic skills that the Greeks valued at the Olympic Games? **[Infer]**
   Possible response: The Greeks most likely valued the skills of speed, agility, and endurance.
2. What does the image of the Parthenon (447 B.C.) suggest about the architectural elements that the Greeks admired? **[Infer]**
   Possible response: The Greeks probably admired symmetry, proportion, and harmony.
3. What does the picture of the gladiator (70–72 A.D.) suggest about the atmosphere during an event at the Colosseum? **[Apply]**
   Possible response: Combat between humans and wild beasts would likely have produced an excited, perhaps even bloodthirsty, atmosphere among the spectators.

Analyzing the Timeline

1. (a) Which two entries in the 700s B.C. show that historians must often deal with approximate dates? (b) How do historians go about making such estimates? **[Speculate]**
   Answer: (a) The emergence of the polis and the era of the lifetime of Homer are dated approximately. (b) Archaeological evidence and cultural, scientific, and sociopolitical references in ancient writings help historians assign approximate dates to events.
2. (a) How many years after the founding of Rome did the city become a republic? (b) How did Rome maintain its dominance for nearly 1,000 years? **[Infer]**
   Answer: (a) The republic began 244 years after the city was founded. (b) Rome maintained its dominance through warfare.
3. (a) Describe the growth of Rome in the 200s and 100s B.C. (b) What does this growth suggest about the Romans' long-term aspirations? **[Interpret]**
   Answer: (a) By 275 B.C., Rome had become dominant in Italy and then fought three wars with Carthage. (b) The entries suggest that Rome aspired to become not only the strongest power in Italy but also the dominant force in the Mediterranean region.
4. (a) Name two events on the Timeline related to Christianity. (b) What do these events suggest about the appeal of this religion in the Roman empire? **[Draw Conclusions]**
   Answer: (a) Two events are the crucifixion of Jesus and Theodosius' requirement that Roman citizens be Christian. (b) The events suggest that Christianity had such a strong appeal for government officials that it became the official religion of the empire.
5. (a) Name two events signaling the threat to Rome from tribes outside the empire in the A.D. 300s and 400s. (b) What may have been some of the causes of the Western empire's decline and fall in 476? **[Infer]**
   Answer: (a) Two events are the arrivals of the Huns and the Visigoths. (b) The decline of the Western empire may have been caused by military invasion and the introduction of a different religion in Rome.

Literature of the Period

- The excerpts from Homer's epic, the *Iliad,* will provide students with insight into the heroic code of ancient Greek warriors.
- The value of citizenship in ancient Greece is stressed in the selections from Thucydides' *History of the Peloponnesian War* and Plato's *Apology.*
- In Sophocles' *Oedipus the King,* first performed during the Golden Age of Athens, one of the most famous Greek myths becomes the source of shattering dramatic irony.
- Students will gain insight into Roman cultural and literary values as they read the selection from Virgil's *Aeneid,* the brief lyrics of Catullus and Horace, Ovid's retelling of the myth of Daedalus and Icarus, and the historian Tacitus' account of the great fire at Rome during the reign of the emperor Nero.

Historical Background

Ancient Greece: The Minoans The brilliant Minoan (mi nō′ ən) culture, named after the mythical king Minos (mī′ näs′), thrived on the island of Crete from about 3000 to 1100 B.C. The Minoans were sophisticated palace dwellers accustomed to comfort, luxury, and beauty. By about 1600 B.C., Minoan civilization was influencing the entire Greek world through trade and colonization.

Mycenean Civilization Minoan influence gave rise to the Mycenaean (mī′ sə nē′ ən) palace culture on the Greek mainland. The Mycenaeans' empire flourished in Greece from about 1600 B.C. to 1200 B.C. In about 1250 B.C., the Mycenaeans defeated the city of Troy in Asia Minor in a legendary struggle known as the Trojan War, but they made no other important conquests. By 1100 B.C., their network of imperial palaces had disappeared.

The Dark Age and After Because no written evidence survives, we call the approximately 300-year period after the collapse of Mycenaean civilization the Dark Age. During this era, a relatively primitive group called the Dorians invaded Greece.

Somewhat later, in the eighth century B.C., the Greeks established major colonies throughout Sicily and southern Italy. Greek traders voyaged and settled throughout the Mediterranean. This commerce brought the Greeks in contact with the Phoenicians (fi nish′ ənz), a trading people who lived in what is now Lebanon and Syria. The Greeks adapted the Phoenicians' written signs to create the first true alphabet, one that became the basis for our own. The use of this new alphabet explains why there is evidence of literacy everywhere in Greece by 750 B.C.

Literacy, new currents in art and intellectual history, colonization, and the creation of the polis (pō′ lis), or city-state, all resulted from thriving trade. City-states were small, independent cities that functioned as nations. It is no surprise that Greece, with its rugged mainland terrain and many islands, was not politically unified. True, the many different city-states had a common heritage, but differences in dialect, customs, and government fostered rivalries and prompted conflicts among these mini-nations.

The Greco-Persian Wars By the beginning of the fifth century B.C., Athens and Sparta had emerged as the two most powerful city-states. Together, they resisted the Persian invasions of Europe during the period 490–479 B.C. Success in defeating the Persians, however, was largely due to victories won by the Athenians at the Battle of Marathon and the naval Battle of Salamis.

Pericles and the Golden Age of Athens Athens' role in the war against Persia led to the rise of the Athenian Empire. At home, Athenian democracy was experiencing a golden age under the statesman Pericles (per′ i klēz′). He fostered the highest ideals of citizen participation and channeled

Enrichment

Minoan Art

After 2000 B.C., Cretan farmers were prosperous and civilized enough to build wealthy private villas or palaces such as Phaestos. As the power and wealth increased at Phaestos and other such villas, a palace bureaucracy grew and flourished. The introduction of the potter's wheel enabled artists to produce exquisite ceramics—called Kamares ware—which were decorated with abstract patterns. The abstract patterns later gave way to designs drawn from plant and animal life.

Wall paintings, statuettes, and other art works offer tantalizing glimpses of Minoan palace life: processions, graceful young athletes somersaulting over the horns of charging bulls, tame monkeys, and spectators at a contest. Women are depicted as handling snakes and having elaborate hairstyles and mascaraed eyes. These graceful and sophisticated palace dwellers prized comfort and beauty. Wall paintings are full of color and motion, depicting scenes from nature (blue dolphins cavorting in the waves) and daily life.

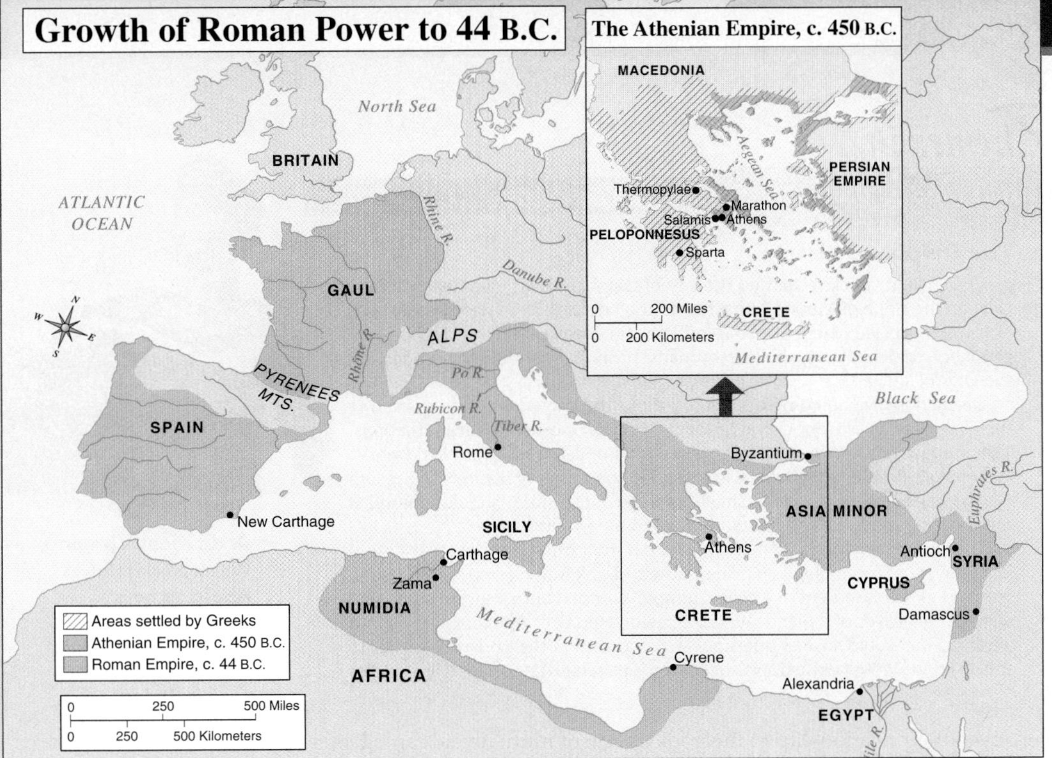

the city's prosperity into impressive new public architecture and art. Abroad, his hawkish foreign policy fostered the growth of an empire but also caused resentment among other city-states. (See the map above.)

One of Athens' greatest rivals was Sparta, a totalitarian society in which individuals were subordinate to the state. Spartan discipline contributed to the superiority of its army, and the army allowed Sparta to control most of the city-states in Peloponnesus (pel′ ə pə nē′ səs), a peninsula forming the southern part of the Greek mainland.

The Peloponnesian War Gradually, Greece became polarized between Athens and Sparta. These two city-states fought each other in a long conflict called the Peloponnesian War (431–404 B.C.), which Sparta won.

Alexander the Great After the defeat of Athens, however, Macedonia—not Sparta—emerged as a power. Macedonia was a kingdom in the northeastern part of the Greek peninsula. It was ruled by King Philip, whose son Alexander (356–323 B.C.) became known as "the Great" due to his military skills. Alexander's armies marched south and east, spreading Greek language and culture throughout what is today Egypt, Turkey, Iraq, Iran (Persia), and part of India.

Greek Religion: The Gods As personifications of war, plague, or earthquake, the Greek gods were formidable. Yet because they had human qualities and foibles, they were approachable and even comic. The Greeks

▲ Critical Viewing
The Romans greatly admired Greek culture. What does this map suggest about the role of the Roman Empire in spreading Greek thought and beliefs? Explain. **[Read a Map]**

Background

The Peloponnesian War

To its allies, Athens was not "the savior of Greece" but a tyrant city, whose armed forces mercilessly crushed any allies who were unwilling subjects. Greece became polarized between Athens and Sparta, and in 432 B.C., Sparta officially declared war on Athens.

In 430 B.C., Athens was decimated by a severe plague; one of the victims was Pericles. Still, Athens might have won the war had it not decided to fight on too many fronts. In 415 B.C., the Athenian fleet sailed against the rich Greek cities of Sicily, confident that they would gain wealth and natural resources to continue the war. The fleet suffered a disastrous defeat, however, and although the war dragged on, Athens was finally defeated in 404 B.C.

Critical Viewing

Possible response: The map suggests that Rome was extremely influential in the dissemination of Greek thought and beliefs through Roman power and colonization throughout western Europe, north Africa, Asia Minor, and the Middle East.

Differentiated Instruction
Solutions for All Learners

Background for Less Proficient Readers
Have students study the map with special care. Point out the geographical advantages that both Rome and Athens had in projecting into the Mediterranean Sea. Ask students to explain how the Mediterranean Sea aided the spread of Greek and Roman culture.

Background for English Learners
Lead a discussion in which students who are not native to the United States share their personal experiences with the blending of two cultures. Ask students to discuss what aspects of their home culture they value most and wish to maintain. What aspects of their new culture do students most welcome?

Enrichment for Advanced Readers
Suggest that students read some contemporary works of literature that center on cultural exchanges based on immigration or colonization such as Amy Tan's *The Joy Luck Club.* Ask students to keep journals as they read in order to record and respond to the works' cultural themes.

Background

Greek Gods

The Greek gods were organized in a patriarchal hierarchy with Zeus, "father of the gods and men," at the top. Zeus maintained the precarious balance of forces that, as the Greeks saw it, made the world possible. Without that balance, chaos (which in Greek means "gaping void") would have taken over. They perceived the universe as an orderly arrangement (cosmos) in which potentially warring forces were kept in harmony.

The gods intervened in the lives of mortals, but they never imposed on a mortal a fate not in keeping with his or her own character. For the Greeks, destiny was simply a recognition of the way things were. The gods did not make reality; they embodied it and were not to blame for human suffering. They gave true signs, but it was the nature of mortals to misinterpret those signs.

Themes in World Literature

Close-up on Culture

Tell students that the Delphic Oracle was a mouthpiece for Apollo. People were less intimidated by her than by the god himself.

- **Ask:** Why did the people seek out the Delphic Oracle?
  Answer: People believed that she would communicate Apollo's wisdom and knowledge to them and thus solve their problems.
- **Ask:** Why did the Oracle enter into a trance?
  Possible response: It was while in a trance that she heard the voice of Apollo, who inspired her to speak out and advise her audience.

Critical Viewing

Possible response: The qualities of youth, beauty, and grace suggest that Apollo is a god. In art, Apollo is typically portrayed as a beardless youth holding a bow or lyre.

Background

Art

Display **Art Transparency 1: The Charioteer of Delphi** in the **Fine Art Transparencies** booklet as another example of the classical ideals in Greek sculpture.

Themes in **World Masterpieces** — **Close-up on Culture**

The Delphic Oracle

The ancient Greeks regarded the city of Delphi (del′ fī), perched dramatically on the slope of Mount Parnassus, as the "navel," or center of the world. This was the place where Apollo (ə päl′ ō), the Greek god of music, poetry, prophecy, and medicine, spoke to humans through the mouth of his priestess, the Oracle.

Delegations would come from throughout the known world to question the Oracle, especially about the outcome of wars or other political situations. They hoped that Apollo would answer human uncertainties with his divine knowledge. Private individuals also attended the monthly sessions of the Oracle, in the hope of solving life's small but urgent dilemmas: Should I marry? Is this a good time to travel? Should I move to a new city?

The Oracle, an elderly woman, followed a strict ritual in order to give Apollo's answers to these questions. She bathed, drank from sacred waters, descended to the basement of Apollo's temple, climbed onto a sacred stool, and chewed the leaves of a plant, the laurel, associated with Apollo. Entering into a trance, she would answer questions with words that the god inspired her to speak. Priests would write down these words in verse that sounded like riddles.

▲ **Critical Viewing** Which qualities of Apollo, as he is portrayed in this famous statue, suggest that he is a god? Explain. **[Infer]**

perceived their relationship to the gods as one of mutually advantageous exchange. They often held religious festivals in honor of the gods, hoping that the gods would reward them. The most famous example of such a festival is the Olympic Games, first held in 776 B.C. in honor of Zeus (zyo͞os), the king of the gods. (For more on Greek and Roman gods, see page 355).

Rome: Earliest History Until Rome emerged as a power in the fourth century B.C., Italy was dominated by the Etruscans in the north and the Greeks in the south. Both these cultures enjoyed a level of civilization Rome would not achieve for centuries. Nevertheless, a distinct culture was emerging in the region of west-central Italy called Latium, a culture that would come to be known as "Roman."

The Rise of Rome Surrounded by Etruscan and Greek powers, early Latin settlements joined in self-defense. The strongest city in this group was Rome, which gave its name to the region's culture. Tradition assigns Rome's founding to 753 B.C. At first, Rome was ruled by kings, advised by a council of elders. Offices were held by members of the ruling class. In 509 B.C., however, Rome became a republic.

By 275 B.C., Rome had defeated all other Italian groups, as well as the Etruscans and the Greeks. African and Asian countries recognized Rome as a world power.

The Punic Wars In the Punic Wars (264–146 B.C.), Rome battled with Carthage, a prosperous city-state in North Africa. Rome's victories in each of these three conflicts mark key dates in its history. The initial victory, in 241 B.C., ushered in the first flowering of Roman literature and art. The second victory, in 201 B.C., signaled a turning point in Roman foreign policy. Rome went on to wage aggressive rather than defensive wars, conquering Macedonia and what is now Spain and Portugal. The third victory against Carthage, in 146 B.C., allowed Rome to seize its former trading rival as a province.

Civil Wars By the late second century B.C., Roman society was divided between a conservative, slave-owning senatorial aristocracy and more liberal senatorial aristocrats. Meanwhile, poorer citizens often rioted, and groups of slaves sometimes staged revolts. Attempts at reform did not take hold, and Rome experienced a series of bitter conflicts. During the period 49–45 B.C., Gaius Julius Caesar seized power. His brief dictatorship lasted until March 15, 44 B.C., when he was assassinated by a group of senators headed by Brutus and Cassius.

In the power struggles that followed, Caesar's grandnephew Octavius emerged victorious. Elected consul and given special emergency powers, Octavius was named *imperator*, the word from which we derive "emperor." He began using the name Augustus.

A selection of **Greek and Roman Gods**

God or Goddess		Powers and Relationships
Greek *Roman*	Zeus Jupiter	■ King of the gods ■ Husband of Hera; father of Ares, Athena, and Hephaestus, the blacksmith god; brother of Poseidon and Hades
Greek *Roman*	Poseidon Neptune	■ God of the sea ■ Brother of Zeus
Greek *Roman*	Hades Pluto	■ God of the underworld ■ Brother of Zeus
Greek *Roman*	Hera Juno	■ Queen of the gods ■ Wife of Zeus; mother of Ares and Hephaestus
Greek *Roman*	Athena Minerva	■ Goddess of war, crafts, and wisdom ■ Daughter of Zeus; sprang from his forehead
Greek *Roman*	Aphrodite Venus	■ Goddess of love ■ Born from the foam of the sea; wife of Hephaestus and lover of Ares
Greek *Roman*	Ares Mars	■ God of war ■ Son of Zeus and Hera

The Birth of the Empire Augustus' reign, the beginning of the Roman Empire, is marked by a flowering of literature and architecture. Although he ruled as an emperor, he declared that he was restoring the old republic. Also, he instituted religious and legal reforms that were meant to promote old-fashioned virtues. Augustus ruled skillfully for more than forty years. Many of his immediate successors, however, were cruel and inept, and the general quality of Roman emperors was uneven.

The Fall of the Empire As time went on, the empire came under stress both at home and abroad, with its very size making it vulnerable on its frontiers. The size of the empire also led to a split between the eastern and western parts. Eventually, these two parts came to be ruled by different emperors.

The eastern Roman Empire survived longer than did the western, which ended in A.D. 476 when Germanic tribes overran it and replaced it with a multitude of kingdoms.

Literature Connection

In the selections from the *Iliad* on pp. 363–408, students can read more about these Greek gods and goddesses:

Aphrodite
Apollo
Ares
Athena
Hades
Hera
Hermes
Thetis
Zeus

Background

Roman Religion

From the earliest period, religion played a central role in the organization of Rome. The leader of religious ceremonies, called the King of Sacred Rites, was aided by priestly colleges, all of whose members were patricians (belonging to the senatorial class). These were the *flamines* (burners of offerings), the *salii* (priests of the war-god Mars, in whose honor they danced in armor), the *luperci* (the wolf-brotherhood, who on certain holidays ran around the sacred boundary of the city to drive away evil spirits and ensure the fertility of women and flocks), and the *pontifices* (religious and ritual advisors to the king, guardians of religious and civil law, who made pronouncements or "pontificated" on critical matters). These last offices, the pontifices, were considered very important; therefore, emperors showed their own power by each assuming the title of Chief Pontifex.

Themes in World Literature

A Living Tradition

Point out to students that our nation's capital city, with all of its architectural grandeur, is actually a mirror of the ancient Roman and Greek republics.

- **Ask:** What is the Federal style of architecture?
  Answer: The Federal style is a product of architects Benjamin Latrobe and Thomas Jefferson, who designed Washington's buildings to mirror ancient Roman models. Therefore, Washington's monuments, museums, and some government buildings are graced with dignified columns and other classical features.

Critical Viewing

Possible response: The imposing marble columns, which suggest the structure and layout of an ancient temple, indicate a classical influence.

Historical Background

Comprehension Check

1. Why is the 300-year period after the collapse of Mycenaean civilization known as the Dark Age?
   Answer: No written evidence survives for this period of history.
2. Why did people from all over the ancient world travel to Delphi?
   Answer: Many wanted to consult the Oracle, who was believed to convey the knowledge and wisdom of the god Apollo.
3. What transition does the rule of Augustus mark in the history of Roman politics and government?
   Answer: Augustus' rule marks the transition from Roman republic to empire.
4. As the Roman empire declined, what happened to Christianity?
   Answer: Christianity grew stronger and more widespread, and by the end of the fourth century, belief in this religion was essential to Roman citizenship.

Religion: Rome Versus Greece Unlike the Greeks, the Romans were obsessed with correct ritual, and they had a practice, unknown to the Greeks, of beginning a public religious ceremony all over again if any detail went wrong. Also, Romans viewed fate as a command to be obeyed, while Greeks thought of it as an allotment, like a plot of land given to a person for cultivation.

Native Gods and Greek Influences The Romans were polytheistic, believing in many gods, and their native deities reveal the Romans' concern with home, cattle, and agriculture. The worship of the family *genius*, or ancestor of the clan, and the obedience owed a living father led Romans to view themselves as dutiful sons of a father-like emperor.

Through contact with Greek religion, literature, and art, the Romans came to see their own gods as corresponding to those of the Greeks. (For more on Greek and Roman gods, see the chart on page 355).

Christianity Christianity began under the Roman Empire as a first century A.D. movement within Judaism. Believing in the divinity of Jesus of Nazareth (c. 6–4 B.C.–A.D. 30), Christians soon developed a faith distinct from Judaism and were frequently persecuted by the Romans. Yet Christianity strengthened as the empire declined. Finally, the emperor Theodosius I (reigned A.D. 379–395) made belief in Christianity essential to Roman citizenship.

▼ **Critical Viewing**
In this picture taken at the Lincoln Memorial, which details reveal the influence of the classical world on Washington, D.C.? Why? **[Connect]**

Themes in World Masterpieces — A Living Tradition

Washington, D.C., and the Classical World

Benjamin Latrobe, the architect who oversaw the building of the Capitol in Washington, D.C., spoke of "the days of Greece. . . in the woods of America." Like many other late-eighteenth-century Americans, Latrobe hoped that the nation's new capital city would reflect the spirit of the ancient Greek and Roman republics.

This goal was not surprising, considering that America's founders were believers in the Enlightenment, an intellectual movement that praised reason and looked to the classical world for examples of reason in action—in science, law, and architecture.

Thomas Jefferson, one of the greatest Founding Fathers, was a friend of Latrobe's and a distinguished architect in his own right. Together, these two men pioneered the Federal style of architecture, which was based on ancient Roman models.

Today, visitors to the nation's capital can appreciate this new Athens or Rome on the Potomac. Surveyed by the African American mathematician Benjamin Banneker and planned by architect Pierre-Charles L'Enfant, the city consists of wide avenues that radiate diagonally from circles, interspersed with parks and squares for monuments. Imposing marble buildings with classical columns proclaim the nation's allegiance to reason and classical civilization.

Critical Thinking

1. How would you compare and contrast Athens with its chief rival, Sparta? **[Compare and Contrast]**
   Possible response: Athens was a democracy, in which citizens were encouraged to participate in government and to achieve individual and artistic expression. Sparta had a totalitarian government, in which individuals were subordinate to the state. Both city-states had expansionist foreign policies and came to dominate a number of other states.
2. Why do you think the Roman emperor Augustus was careful to claim that he was restoring the old republic? **[Infer]**
   Possible response: Such a claim would have made Augustus seem conservative and non-threatening to those who were repelled by the dictatorship of Gaius Julius Caesar.

Literature

Greek Literature: The Epic From the Dark Age of Greece came oral epic poetry that served as the raw material for Homer's sophisticated epics, the *Iliad* and the *Odyssey*. These two works deal, respectively, with the Greek conquest of Troy and the wanderings of the hero Odysseus (ō dis′ ē əs) after the Trojan War. The Homeric epics convey such values of ancient Greek culture as physical bravery, skill, honor, reverence for the gods, and intelligence.

Lyric Poetry Of all the genres of Greek literature, lyric poetry loses the most in translation. Specifically, it loses its musical quality—*lyric* originally meant "sung to the lyre." Nevertheless, Greek lyric poets like Sappho influenced the Roman poets and still influence today's writers.

Philosophy In the fifth century B.C., the philosopher Socrates (säk′ rə tēz′) developed a method of uncovering truth by asking probing questions. Socrates' most famous follower was Plato (plāt′ ō), who recorded the dialogues that show his master practicing the Socratic method. Plato's vision of a realm of changeless, perfect forms that are imperfectly reflected in this world attracted some of the finest minds of later generations. (See Music in the Historical Context on page 358). Aristotle, Plato's most famous student, pioneered in developing logic, zoology, psychology, and many other arts and sciences. His work was a dominant force in Western culture for almost 2,000 years and still influences philosophy.

The Romans admired Greek philosophy and helped make it the basis for Western thought. In fact, some scholars have half-humorously referred to the Western philosophical tradition as a 2500-year disagreement between Plato and Aristotle!

Tragedy Greek drama developed in connection with religious rituals and reached its peak in fifth-century Athens. Tragedies, which chronicled the downfall of a noble person, raised difficult questions about justice, evil, and the reasons for human suffering. In keeping with its religious origin, tragedy provided an emotional rather than a philosophical resolution for the questions it raised.

As a means of making the audience feel purged or cleansed, Greek tragedy aroused in them the powerful emotions of pity for the tragic hero and awe at his or her fate.

▼ Critical Viewing
The sorceress Circe both helps and hinders the hero Odysseus in the *Odyssey*. What can you tell about her from this picture? Explain. **[Infer]**

Circe Meanwhile Had Gone Her Ways . . ., 1924, From the ***Odyssey*** by Homer, William Russell Flint, Collection of the New York Public Library; Astor, Lenox and Tilden Foundations

Background

Greek Literature and Oral Culture

It is now widely accepted that Homer's *Iliad* and *Odyssey* were composed orally. That is, Homer did not create the plot or the characters of the epics ascribed to him; rather, he inherited the stories of those epics. Generations of Greeks had preserved orally the subject matter of Homer's epics—the story of the Trojan War and the heroic mythology that pervades both poems. As a result, Homer is the ultimate spokesperson of a long and rich tradition of oral poetry developed over centuries.

Critical Viewing

Possible response: Circe appears to control or lead animals.

Background

Diogenes

Stoicism, with its emphasis on peace of mind, moderation, and endurance became the Romans' most respectable and prestigious philosophy. Stoicism is so respectable that it is easy to forget its debt to the most colorful and outrageous figure among the ancient philosophers, Diogenes. Born in the Black Sea region, Diogenes "the Cynic" (400 B.C.–320 B.C.) was known to his contemporaries as "Socrates gone mad." He was a wealthy man who gave up everything to roam the world as a beggar, living as a "street person" and practicing what he preached—complete self-sufficiency. Seeing all human beings as alike in their animal nature, he found both national and class distinctions pointless and artificial. He called himself a "citizen of the universe," coining the term "cosmopolitan," and he cared nothing for status or power. When Alexander the Great found him sunning on a street corner and offered to grant him any wish, Diogenes replied, "Move out of the way, you're blocking the sun."

Background

Great Tragedians

Aeschylus wrote the Oresteia, the sequence of tragedies composed of *Agamemnon, The Libation Bearers,* and the *Eumenides;* Sophocles lived until the age of ninety, when he wrote his powerfully religious play, *Oedipus at Colonus;* Euripides is perhaps best known for *The Medea* and *The Bacchae.* Many tragedians wrote plays and won prizes, but we have the works of only these three, who were recognized as the three greatest. Even of their output, we have a very small percentage: The seven surviving tragedies of Aeschylus, for instance, represent not even a tenth of the tragedies he composed. All of the tragedians influenced one another, and each in his own way was daring and innovative.

Critical Viewing

Possible response: The harp and the Greek instrument are similar. They are both U-shaped, and both are played with the hands. However, the harp is larger than the Greek instrument and sits on the floor rather than being held.

Themes in World Literature

Music in the Historical Context

Tell students that the Greeks had a wide range of musical instruments but that three of them were especially important: the stringed lyre, the cithara, and a wind instrument called the aulos. The lyre and the cithara were popular with lyric poets; the aulos was popular with dramatists and in military and social life.

- **Ask:** Why did Plato prefer the Dorian musical mode to the Lydian mode?
  Answer: Plato thought that the strong, manly music of the Dorians had a positive effect on brave men, but that the Lydian mode made men "soft" and encouraged drinking.

Critical Viewing

Possible response: The elegant villas in a dramatic landscape suggest that upper-class Romans of the period enjoyed paintings that reflected their sophisticated tastes.

In order of birth, the three greatest Greek tragedians are Aeschylus (es′ ki ləs); Sophocles (säf′ ə klēz′), who wrote *Oedipus the King;* and Euripides (yoo rip′ ə dēz). Although the surviving Greek tragedies are among the best works of world literature, we have available only a small percentage of the dramas these men actually wrote.

History Two great historians of the fifth century B.C., like playwrights and philosophers, saw themselves as teachers: Herodotus (hə räd′ ə təs), who wrote on the Persian Wars, and Thucydides (thoo sid′ i dēz′), who wrote about the Peloponnesian War between Athens and Sparta.

Roman Literature: Epic and Drama Until Rome defeated Carthage in 241 B.C. and emerged as a world power, educated Romans still conducted foreign policy and read literature in Greek. After winning their victory, Romans began to create a national literature. One product of this era was the historical epic, a form that the first-century B.C. poet Virgil perfected in the *Aeneid* (ē nē′ id). This long narrative poem describes the fall of Troy and the founding of Rome by the legendary Trojan hero Aeneas.

▼ **Critical Viewing**
Compare and contrast the ancient Greek instrument shown in this illustration with a similar instrument in use today. Consider such factors as appearance, size, type, and manner of playing. **[Compare and Contrast]**

Themes in World Masterpieces — Music in the Historical Context

Ancient Greek Modes, or the Morality of Music

When rock-and-roll exploded onto the scene in the 1950s, some people claimed it was immoral and should be banned. They argued that the "wild" rhythms of rock would encourage wild behavior. A similar debate about the morality of music took place more than 2000 years ago in ancient Greece. This debate, however, focused on Greek musical scales, called modes, rather than on rhythms.

Scales and modes are sets of notes that are separated by definite intervals. Each Greek mode had seven notes. Also, the names of the modes were associated with groups and regions. The Dorian mode, for instance, was linked with the Dorians, a tribe that had conquered part of mainland Greece. The Lydian mode was linked with Lydia, a western kingdom in ancient Asia Minor.

These regions and the modes named for them had definite meanings for the Greeks. The Dorian mode, linked with a warlike area, was regarded as strong and manly. Songs composed in this mode were suitable for inspiring soldiers. By contrast, songs in the Lydian mode—named for Lydia, viewed as a corrupt place—were suitable for feasts.

In Book III of the Republic (c. 360 B.C.), the Greek philosopher Plato joined the debate about music. He warned against the influence of the Lydian mode, which seems to have been the rock music of its time. Plato banned these songs from his ideal republic because they made men "soft" and encouraged "drinking." He favored the Dorian mode, which was "warlike" and sounded "the note or accent which a brave man utters in the hour of danger. . . ."

If he were living today, what would Plato say about heavy metal, hip-hop, or rap?

Enrichment

Roman Voices

The truth of a civilization may be found in the voices of its people.

I came, I saw, I conquered. —Julius Caesar

What fools these mortals be. —Seneca

Absence makes the heart grow fonder. —Sextus Propertius

The greatest reverence is due the young. —Juvenal

Seize the day, put no trust in tomorrow. —Horace

All art is but an imitation of nature. —Seneca

I love treason but hate the traitor. —Julius Caesar

More worship the rising than the setting sun. —Pompey

Better late than never. —Livy

Drama also flourished after 241 B.C., with the state funding elaborate productions of tragedy and comedy. Two masters of Roman comedy from that time were Plautus (plôt′ əs) and Terence. Both these writers have influenced Western drama.

As drama gave way to the epic, two long works stand out in addition to Virgil's. Both are anti-epics, however, in the sense that they do not promote heroic values. The *Metamorphoses* by Ovid (äv′ id) contains a series of mythical stories involving changes of shape (*metamorphosis* means "transformation"). This poem angered the Emperor Augustus, who saw it as a sly attack on established religion and rulers. Later, Petronius (pi trō′ nē əs) Arbiter wrote the *Satyricon*, perhaps the first novel to describe the adventures of a wandering, mischievous hero.

History and Biography In works of history and biography, Romans examined major events and sought to find in great men's lives the causes of these events. The historian Tacitus (tas′ i təs), who lived from A.D. 56 to c. 120, was keenly analytical and included in his work examples of public oration as well as the biographies of public figures.

Lyric Poetry Lyric poetry for the Romans was an essentially derivative form, although the greatest poets transformed their models. For instance, Catullus (kə tul′ əs) and Horace, poets of the first century B.C., imitated Greek forms but created poems essentially Roman in their point of view.

Philosophy As philosophers, the Romans were masterful imitators rather than original thinkers. The major philosophical work in Latin literature is a poem by Lucretius (lo͞o krē′ shəs) entitled *On the Nature of Things*. In this work, he uses the atomic theory of Greek thinkers to present a world in which everything results from the random combination of particles rather than the actions of the gods. He urges a way of life that promotes freedom from violent emotion and irrational behavior.

▲ **Critical Viewing**
This ancient fresco, or wall painting, comes from a Roman villa in Pompeii, Italy. What does it suggest about the type of painting that upper-class Romans preferred? Explain. **[Infer]**

Literature of the Period

Comprehension Check

1. What values of ancient Greek culture do the Homeric epics convey?
Answer: The epics stress such values as physical bravery, skill, honor, piety, and intelligence.
2. Name three great philosophers in ancient Greece, and briefly characterize each one.
Answer: Socrates uncovered truth by asking probing questions; Plato envisioned a realm of changeless, perfect forms; and Aristotle pioneered such subjects as logic, zoology, and psychology.
3. What emotions did Greek tragedy arouse in its audience?
Answer: Tragedy aroused the emotions of pity for the tragic hero and awe for his or her fate.
4. When did the Romans begin to create a literature of their own, and with what literary form did they start?
Answer: The Romans began to create their own literature after they defeated Carthage in 241 B.C. One product of this era was the historical epic.
5. What is the importance of Lucretius in the history of Latin literature?
Answer: Lucretius wrote a major philosophical poem entitled *On the Nature of Things.*

Critical Thinking

1. Why might lyric poetry be especially difficult to translate? **[Analyze]**
Answer: Lyric poetry in translation loses its musical quality.
2. Why might Virgil's epic *Aeneid* have enjoyed enormous popularity in Augustan Rome? **[Infer]**
Answer: The *Aeneid* was regarded as a national epic because it recounted the founding of Rome.

Concept Connector

Have students return to the Focus Questions on p. 349. Ask them to summarize the main points in the Unit Introduction. Students' summaries should include the following:

Traits of the Golden Age of Athens:

- Pericles encouraged citizens to participate in the affairs of the city-state.
- Athenians poured money into public architecture and art.
- Pericles expanded the empire. This inspired resentment in other city-states.

Factors that brought about the birth and downfall of the Roman Empire:

- Under Augustus, the Roman Empire flourished. He encouraged literature and architecture and instituted legal and religious reforms.
- The vastness of the Roman Empire made it vulnerable to attack and led to a split between its eastern and western parts.

Forms of literature that flourished in ancient Greece and Rome:

- The *epic* flourished through the writings of Homer and expressed ancient Greek values such as physical bravery, honor, and reverence for the gods.
- *Tragic drama* raised difficult questions. Romans also produced comedy and drama.
- Romans contributed works of *history* and *biography.*

Standard Course of Study

Goal 4: CRITICAL THINKING

- **CT.4.02.2** Use specific references from texts to show theme.

Goal 5: LITERATURE

- **LT.5.01.5** Analyze archetypal characters, themes, and settings in world literature.
- **LT.5.03.9** Analyze and evaluate the effects of author's craft and style in world literature.

Goal 6: GRAMMAR AND USAGE

- **GU.6.01.2** Analyze author's use of language to demonstrate understanding of expression.
- **GU.6.01.4** Use vocabulary strategies to determine meaning.
- **GU.6.02.1** Edit for agreement, tense choice, pronouns, antecedents, case, and complete sentences.

Step-by-Step Teaching Guide	Pacing Guide
PRETEACH	
• Administer Vocabulary and Reading Warm-ups as necessary.	5 min.
• Engage students' interest with the motivation activity.	5 min.
• Read and discuss author and background features. **FT**	10 min.
• Introduce the Literary Analysis Skill: Theme. **FT**	5 min.
• Introduce the Reading Strategy: Analyzing Confusing Sentences. **FT**	10 min.
• Prepare students to read by teaching the selection vocabulary. **FT**	
TEACH	
• Informally monitor comprehension while students read independently or in groups. **FT**	30 min.
• Monitor students' comprehension with the Reading Check notes.	as students read
• Reinforce vocabulary with Vocabulary Builder notes.	as students read
• Develop students' understanding of theme with the Literary Analysis annotations. **FT**	5 min.
• Develop students' ability to analyze confusing sentences with the Reading Strategy annotations. **FT**	5 min.
ASSESS/EXTEND	
• Assess students' comprehension and mastery of the Literary Analysis and Reading Strategy by having them answer the Apply the Skills questions. **FT**	15 min.
• Have students complete the Vocabulary Lesson and the Grammar and Style Lesson. **FT**	15 min.
• Apply students' ability to recognize a code of conduct by using the Writing Lesson. **FT**	45 min. or homework
• Apply students' understanding by using one or more of the Extend Your Learning activities.	20–90 min. or homework
• Administer Selection Test A or Selection Test B. **FT**	15 min.

Resources

Print

Unit 4 Resources

Vocabulary Warm-up Word Lists [**L1, L2, EL**] . . . . p. 7
Vocabulary Warm-up Practice [**L1, L2, EL**] . . . . p. 8
Reading Warm-up A [**L1, L2, EL**] . . . . p. 9
Reading Warm-up B [**L1, L2, L3**] . . . . p. 10

Transparency

Graphic Organizer Transparencies

Literary Analysis Graphic Organizer A [**L3**] . . . . p. 70
Literary Analysis Graphic Organizer B [**L1, L2, EL**] . . . . p. 71
Reading Strategy Graphic Organizer A [**L3**] . . . . p. 68
Reading Strategy Graphic Organizer B [**L1, L2, EL**] . . . . p. 69

Print

Reader's Notebook [L2]
Reader's Notebook: Adapted Version [L1]
Reader's Notebook: English Learner's Version [EL]

Unit 4 Resources

Literary Analysis [**L3**] . . . . p. 11
Reading Strategy [**L3**] . . . . p. 12
Vocabulary Builder [**L3**] . . . . p. 13

Technology

Listening to Literature Audio CDs [L2, EL]

Print

Unit 4 Resources

Grammar and Style [**L3**] . . . . p. 14
Support for Extend Your Learning [**L3**] . . . . p. 15
Enrichment [**L4**] . . . . p. 16
Selection Test A [**L1, L2, EL**] . . . . pp. 17–19
Selection Test B [**L3, L4**] . . . . pp. 20–22

General Resources

Rubrics for Persuasion: Persuasive Essay [**L3**] . . . . pp. 47–48

Technology

Go Online: Research [**L3**]
Go Online: Self-test [**L3**]
***ExamView®*, Test Bank [L3]**

Choosing Resources for Differentiated Instruction

[**L1**] Special Needs Students
[**L2**] Below-Level Students
[**L3**] All Students
[**L4**] Advanced Students
[**EL**] English Learners

For Vocabulary and Reading Warm-ups and for Selection Tests, **A** signifies "less challenging" and **B** "more challenging." For Graphic Organizer transparencies, **A** signifies "not filled in" and **B** "filled in."

FT Fast Track Instruction: To move the lesson more quickly, use the strategies and activities identified with **FT**.

Scaffolding for Less Proficient and Advanced Students

The leveled Critical Thinking questions after selections progress in the levels of thinking required to answer them. To address the needs of your different students, you may use the (a) level questions for your less proficient students and the (b) level questions with your on-level and advanced students. The occasional (c) level questions are appropriate for your advanced students.

Use this complete suite of powerful teaching tools to make lesson planning and testing quicker and easier.

Use the interactive textbook (online and on CD-ROM) to make selections and activities come alive with audio and video support and interactive questions.

Monitoring Progress

Before students read the excerpts from the *Iliad,* administer **Diagnostic Test 4 (*Unit 4 Resources,* pp. 2–4)**. This test will determine students' level of readiness for the reading and vocabulary skills.

Go Online Professional Development
For: Information about Lexiles
Visit: www.PHSchool.com
Web Code: eue-1111

PRETEACH

Motivation

Invite students to share some of their favorite books, movies, television programs, comic books, and video games that center on epic battles. Then, ask: What makes these stories so appealing? Invite students to offer items for a list of qualities shared by the best "epic battle stories." Then, tell them that Homer created one of the first stories of this type, featuring superheroes aided by the gods, hand-to-hand combat, and a war that lasted ten years.

❶ Background

More About the Author

Whatever Homer's own history, the conditions of his poems reveal his unwavering commitment to humanity. He had a universal view of humankind, as his unbiased portrayal of the Greeks and the Trojans shows in the *Iliad.* He uses no ethnic descriptions; in fact, he bestows glorious epithets on both Greek and Trojan characters. According to his design, Greeks and Trojans are on the same human level. Homer's view of the essential quality of humans is perhaps far more humane than most of the world has achieved even now.

Geography Note

Draw students' attention to the map on this page. Point out Greece, the Aegean Sea, and the western coast of Asia Minor, where the historical Troy is believed to have been located. Remind students that the Greeks traveled by ship to lay siege to Troy.

Build Skills | Epic Poem

from the Iliad ❶

Homer (c. eighth century B.C.)

The ancient Greeks ascribed the *Iliad* and the *Odyssey,* their two oldest, monumental epic poems, to Homer, whom they called simply "The Poet." Nothing certain is known about Homer's life. His name, which means "hostage," gives no clue to his origins, since small wars and raids between neighboring towns were frequent in ancient Greece, and prisoners were routinely held for ransom or sold into slavery. Homer is commonly referred to as the "Ionian bard," or poet; more than likely, he came from Ionia in the eastern Mediterranean, where Eastern and Western cultures met and new intellectual currents were born. In support of that theory, the *Iliad* contains several accurate descriptions of the Ionian landscape and its natural features, whereas Homer's grasp of the geography of mainland Greece seems less authoritative.

A Sightless Visionary Legend has it that Homer was blind. This legend may have some basis in fact; if he lived to be an old man, he may simply have become blind. However, the idea of Homer's blindness may have arisen because of its symbolic implications. The Greeks contrasted inner vision with physical vision, as in the case of the blind seer Teiresias and of Oedipus himself, who becomes blind in *Oedipus the King.* Also, Homer's image—the blind bard singing the myths of his people—is a striking symbol for the beginning of Western literature.

Heroes and Legends Although it is not known for certain when Homer lived, the *Iliad* was almost certainly composed late in the eighth century B.C. Historically, however, both the *Iliad* and the *Odyssey* take place in a long-past heroic age known as the Late Bronze Age. One might wonder how Homer was able to depict an era five hundred years before his time. The answer is that Homer did not create the plot or characters of the epics he is credited with writing; rather, he inherited the stories of those epics. Generations of Greeks had preserved orally the subject matter of the *Iliad* and the *Odyssey*—the story of the Trojan War and the heroic mythology that pervades both poems. As a result, Homer is the ultimate spokesman of a long and rich tradition of oral poetry developed over centuries.

From generation to generation, ancient Greek poets transmitted tales of warriors' heroic deeds. Many of the stories were about those who fought in the war against Troy (twelfth or thirteenth century B.C.). A bard might choose to sing about the exploits of a particular war hero, at Troy or elsewhere, about his homecoming, and about his ancestors or his descendants. In the world of Homer's audience, the landed warrior aristocracy claimed descent from the heroes of legend and ultimately from the gods. For such a society, the legends about heroes formed a kind of tribal, and later national, family history.

A Culture's Identity The *Iliad* was, in fact, considered history; children in the fifth century B.C. memorized large sections of the poem and practiced the ethical codes that Homer presents. Athenians even claimed the Homeric gods and heroes as founders or champions of Athens and its people. Homer's epics also had a tremendous influence on later generations of Greek writers. Greek lyric poets, dramatists, and philosophers considered themselves Homer's heirs, drawing on his work either to imitate it or to argue with it. As Greek culture spread through the eastern Mediterranean and west to Italy, Homer's epics formed a common text for a large part of the Western world.

The Epic Form

Just as the oral tradition supplied Homer with a vast body of legend, it also provided him with the form and structure in which to express the legend. Although Homer was free to choose and shape the elements of the story according to his own vision, his language, meter, and style were formulaic. Over time, bards had developed a common fund of
2 expressions, phrases, and descriptions that fit the rhythms of the epic verse line. These conventions became the building blocks of the epic genre.

The Invocation *In Medias Res* Homer begins the *Iliad* powerfully by stating the epic's theme and invoking one of the Muses. The Muses are nine goddesses in Greek mythology who were believed to preside over all forms of art and science. The poet calls on the Muse to inspire him with the material he needs to tell his story. This type of opening is one of the defining features of a Homeric epic.

Homer observes another epic convention by beginning the story *in medias res,* which is Latin for "in the middle of things." Reading a Greek epic from the beginning is like tuning in to a story already in progress, in that many of the story's events have already taken place. Information about those events is revealed later in the poem through flashbacks and other narrative devices. Homer could begin his poems *in medias res* because the general outline of the plot and the main characters were already familiar to his audience. The *Iliad,* like
other epics, is a small fragment of a large body of 3
legendary material that formed the cultural and historical heritage of its society.

Homeric Epithets The particular demands of composing and listening to oral poetry gave rise to the use of stock descriptive words or phrases, such as "brilliant Achilles" or "Hector breaker of horses." These epithets, often compound adjectives like "blazing-eyed Athena," allowed the poet to describe an object or a character quickly and economically, in terms his audience would recognize. Homeric epithets and other formulaic language may have helped the poet shape his story and compose while reciting, and the repetition of familiar expressions also would have helped the audience follow the narrative.

How the War Began

The *Iliad* recounts only part of a long series of events in the Trojan War, which was fought, according to legend, because of a quarrel among gods and the resulting incidents of betrayal among mortals. How did the war start? King Peleus and the sea-goddess Thetis were the parents of Achilles, hero of the Iliad. When Peleus and Thetis were married, all the gods were invited except Eris, the goddess of discord. Angry at being excluded, Eris tossed a golden apple among the guests; on it was inscribed "for the fairest one." Hera, Athena, and Aphrodite each claimed the prize. They chose the Trojan prince Paris, a handsome and unworldly man, to decide which goddess was the fairest. Each goddess offered him a bribe, and Paris chose Aphrodite's: She promised to give him the most beautiful woman alive, Helen, who was already married to Menelaus, king of Sparta.

Paris violated the sacred bond of hospitality when he went to Menelaus' court as a guest and abducted the host's wife. Menelaus sought the help of his brother Agamemnon, king of Mycenae and the most powerful ruler of his time. Together with other kings, they mounted an expedition against Troy, to reclaim Helen and to sack a city famed for its opulence. The war lasted for ten years until Troy was finally taken.

Out of a vast body of material that his audience knew, Homer chose to focus on a period of less than two months in the tenth year of the war. Homer did not concentrate on the war as such, but on the Greek warrior Achilles and the consequences of his rage.

Enrichment

The Story of Achilles

The *Iliad* is the story of Achilles, or, as it is often called, the tragedy of Achilles and how he brings disaster upon himself through his anger. Although parts of the *Iliad* have nothing to do with Achilles, he is the central figure, the medium through which Homer conveys the poem's theme. As Homer shows Achilles coming face to face with his own humanity, he takes his audience on a moral journey. This is perhaps the main reason the *Iliad* transcends the limits of time, place, and gender to speak to all human beings, who must come to terms with how and why to live and how to face death.

2 Background

The Epic Form

The lengthy, formal speech is another typical element of the Homeric epic form. Homer's characters commonly express their thoughts and feelings by delivering long speeches addressed to other characters. In addition, especially at moments of crisis, they deliver long monologues in which they address their own souls or inner spirits. Homer's characters, however, neither speculate about their emotions nor analyze their thought processes; nor does the poet directly reveal the characters' inner workings to his audience. Later Greek and Roman authors, like modern writers, give us access to a character's thoughts and feelings through interior monologues and soliloquies. Both of these forms are modeled on the long Homeric speech.

3 Background

Homer and Later Epics

The building blocks of the epic genre—the invocation *in medias res,* stock epithets, fixed formulas, and long speeches—were commonly used by the bards of oral tradition. However, because Homer was so influential in Western literature, these same features were imitated in later epics, even though they no longer served the same purposes. Among the greatest epic poets who adopted Homer as a model were the Roman writer Virgil (see p. 532), the Florentine medieval poet Dante Alighieri, and the seventeenth-century English poet John Milton.

❹ Literary Analysis

Theme

- Tell students that as they read the excerpts from Homer's *Iliad,* they will focus on theme, an important insight into life that is usually conveyed indirectly in a literary work.
- Read aloud the instruction on theme. Draw students' attention to the ways in which theme can be implied by various story elements, including characters, plot events, and images.
- Use the instruction for Connecting Literary Elements to help students recognize instances of foreshadowing that may suggest theme. Ask students to offer ideas about what consequences might result from Achilles' rage.

❺ Reading Strategy

Analyze Confusing Sentences

- Remind students that breaking down and analyzing long or confusing sentences will help them understand the meaning of Homer's complex verse.
- Tell students that it may be helpful to break down extremely long sentences into a series of shorter sentences.
- Draw students' attention to the graphic organizer. Then, give them a copy of **Reading Strategy Graphic Organizer A,** p. 68 in ***Graphic Organizer Transparencies.*** Have students use the organizer to break down long sentences as they read.

Vocabulary Builder

- Pronounce each vocabulary word for students, and read the definitions as a class. Have students identify any words with which they are already familiar.

Preview

Connecting to the Literature

When you read the epics of Homer, you take part in a cultural tradition that spans more than two thousand years. Generations of writers, from Shakespeare to Sting, have been inspired by and have alluded to Homer. The warriors in the *Iliad* are from a distant time and culture, yet many of their basic concerns will be familiar to you.

NC Standard Course of Study

- Use specific references from texts to show themes. (CT.4.02.2)
- Analyze and evaluate the effects of author's craft and style in world literature. (LT.5.03.9)
- Analyze author's use of language to demonstrate understanding of expression. (GU.6.01.2)

❹ Literary Analysis

Theme

The **theme** of a literary work is its central idea, concern, or message. Long works, such as novels and epics, often contain more than one major theme. For example, the theme stated at the beginning of the *Iliad* is "the rage of Peleus' son Achilles" and its consequences, but the poem also contains profound insights about war and peace, honor, duty, compassion, and life and death. Among the means Homer uses to reveal these themes are the following:

- characters' statements and actions
- events in the plot
- images and their associations

As you read, note the ideas and insights that the poem conveys.

Connecting Literary Elements

The *Iliad*'s opening statement of theme is also its first instance of **foreshadowing,** the use of clues to suggest future events in a literary work. This technique creates suspense by building the audience's anticipation. For example, the *Iliad*'s opening lines leave the reader wondering why Achilles is enraged and what consequences might follow. Look for other examples of foreshadowing as you read, and consider what effect the poet is trying to create.

❺ Reading Strategy

Analyze Confusing Sentences

Homer wove lines dense with images and other details. To **analyze confusing sentences,** consider one section at a time. Look at a complex sentence, and separate its essential parts (the *who* and *what*) from the difficult language until you get to the main idea. As you read, use a chart like the one shown to help you analyze and interpret the meaning of difficult sentences.

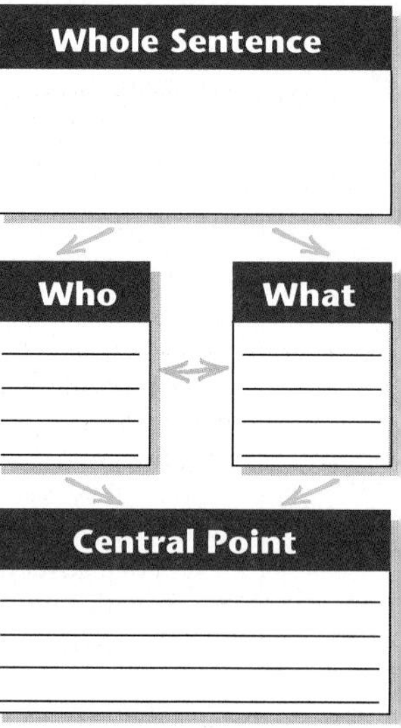

Vocabulary Builder

incensed (in senst′) *adj.* very angry; enraged (p. 364)

plunder (plun′ dər) *v.* to rob by force in warfare (p. 364)

sacrosanct (sak′ rō saŋkt′) *adj.* very holy; sacred (p. 365)

brazen (brā′ zən) *adj.* literally, of brass; shamelessly bold (p. 372)

harrowed (har′ ōd) *v.* distressed; tormented (p. 372)

bereft (bē reft′) *adj.* deprived or robbed (p. 375)

Differentiated Instruction — Solutions for All Learners

Support for Special Needs Students
Have students complete the **Preview** and **Build Skills** pages for the selections from the *Iliad* in the ***Reader's Notebook: Adapted Version.*** These pages provide a selection summary, an abbreviated presentation of the reading and literary skills, and the graphic organizer on the **Build Skills** page in the student book.

Support for Less Proficient Readers
Have students complete the **Preview** and **Build Skills** pages for the selections from the *Iliad* in the ***Reader's Notebook.*** These pages provide a selection summary, an abbreviated presentation of the reading and literary skills, and the graphic organizer on the **Build Skills** page in the student book.

Support for English Learners
Have students complete the **Preview** and **Build Skills** pages for the selections from the *Iliad* in the ***Reader's Notebook: English Learner's Version.*** These pages provide a selection summary, an abbreviated presentation of the reading and literary skills, additional contextual vocabulary, and the graphic organizer on the **Build Skills** page in the student book.

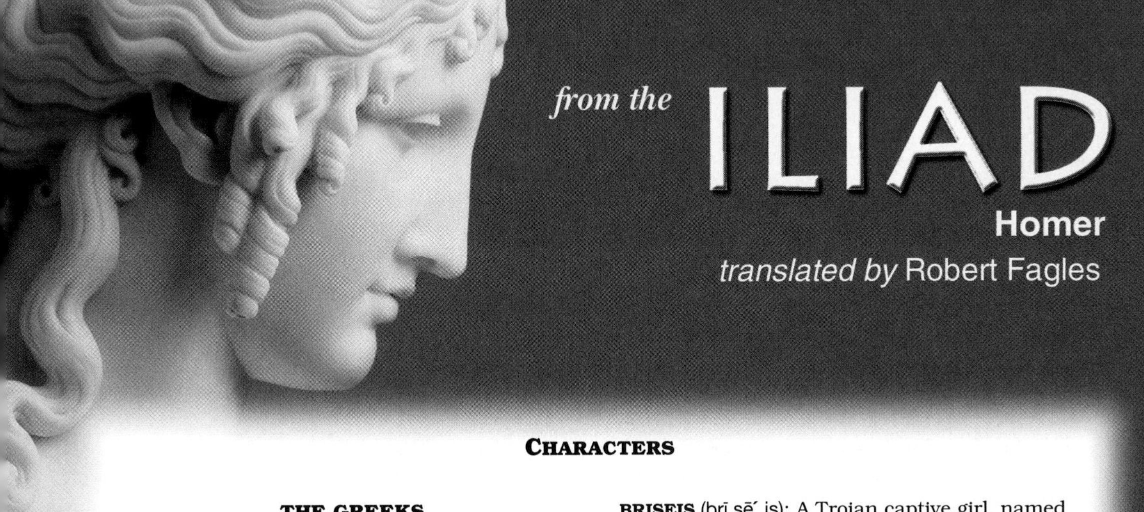

from the ILIAD

Homer

translated by Robert Fagles

CHARACTERS

THE GREEKS

❶ (ALSO CALLED ACHAEANS, DANAANS, AND ARGIVES)

❷ ACHILLES (ə kil′ ēz): Son of Peleus, a mortal king, and the sea-goddess Thetis. The best warrior among the Achaeans; leader of the Myrmidons. Other names: Pelides, Aeacides.

AGAMEMNON (ag′ ə mem′ nän): King of Mycenae; husband of Clytemnestra; brother of Menelaus. Leader of the Greek expeditionary force. Other name: Atrides.

AJAX (ā′ jaks): The strongest warrior on the Greek side after Achilles.

HELEN (hel′ ən): Wife of Menelaus, king of Sparta.

CLYTEMNESTRA (klī′ təm nes′ trə): Wife of Agamemnon, sister of Helen.

MENELAUS (men′ ə lā′ əs): King of Sparta and the surrounding area (Lacedaemon). Son of Atreus, brother of Agamemnon, husband of Helen.

NESTOR (nes′ tər): King of Pylos, belonging to an older generation than the other Greek warriors. He serves as a wise old counselor.

ODYSSEUS (ō dis′ yo͞os′): King of Ithaca. The smoothest talker and wiliest thinker among the Greeks; a favorite of the goddess Athena.

PATROCLUS (pə träk′ ləs): Son of Menoetius, a companion and henchman to Achilles.

PELEUS (pēl′ yo͞os): Father of Achilles; husband of the goddess Thetis.

THE TROJANS

(ALSO CALLED DARDANIANS AND PHRYGIANS)

ANDROMACHE (an dräm′ ə kē): Wife of Hector.

ASTYANAX (ə stī′ ə naks): Infant son of Hector and Andromache. Other name: Scamandrius.

BRISEIS (brī sē′ is): A Trojan captive girl, named after her father Briseus, given as a prize to Achilles.

CHRYSEIS (krī sē′ is): The daughter of Chryses, priest of Apollo. A captive girl given to Agamemnon as his prize.

HECTOR (hek′ tər): Son of Priam; leader of the Trojans and their greatest fighter.

PARIS (par′ is): Son of Priam.

PRIAM (prī′ əm): King of Troy; husband of Hecuba, father of Hector and Paris.

❸ IMMORTALS

APHRODITE (af′ rō dī′ tē): Goddess of love, beauty; protects Helen and Paris and favors the Trojans. Other name: Lady of Cyprus.

APOLLO (ə päl′ ō): The archer god; a god of light and of healing. Apollo not only heals, he visits pestilence on men. He favors and protects the Trojans. Other names: Phoebus, Smintheus.

ARES (a′ rēz): God of war; favors the Trojans.

ATHENA (ə thē′ nə): Daughter of Zeus only (she has no mother). She emerged from her father's head fully armed and is associated with victory in war and clever thinking and speaking. She protects the Greeks. Other names: Pallas and Tritogenia.

HADES (hā′ dēz): Ruler of the dead and the underworld; brother of Zeus.

HERA (her′ ə): Sister and wife of Zeus; favors the Greeks.

HERMES (hʉr′ mēz′): Messenger god; son of Zeus.

THETIS (thet′ is): Sea goddess; wife of the mortal Peleus and mother of Achilles.

ZEUS (zo͞os): The most powerful of the gods, known as "father of men and gods."

TEACH

❶ Background

History

Achaeans refers to the inhabitants of either of the two Greek regions known as Achaea. However, Homer applies the term *Achaeans* to all of the Greek forces in the Trojan War; he never calls them Greeks, as we do.

The Trojans are the inhabitants of the walled Phrygian city of Troy, also called Ilium. Although we are reasonably certain that Troy existed, its mythical history is unclear. One theory suggests that the Trojans were a group of tribes that had formed a federation to share the great walled city of Troy.

❷ Background

Achilles

An epithet applied to Achilles is "godlike Achilles"; indeed, he is of semidivine origin. However, unlike the gods, Achilles is not invulnerable. At his birth, his mother, Thetis, held him by his heel and dipped his body in the river Styx in an attempt to make him invulnerable, as she herself was. However, when it came time for Achilles' fated death, the hero was lethally wounded in his heel.

Achilles is also vulnerable in non-physical ways. He experiences human emotions—grief, fear, and, above all, anger. As they read, ask students to think about how Achilles and the other characters embody aspects of human nature.

❸ Background

The Gods

Athena and Hera despised the Trojans because of Paris, who chose Aphrodite over both Hera and Athena as "the fairest one" at the wedding of Peleus and Thetis. Thus, the two goddesses favor the Greeks.

Differentiated Instruction Solutions for All Learners

Accessibility at a Glance

	from the Iliad, *from* Book 1 The Rage of Achilles	*from the* Iliad, *from* Book 6 Hector Returns to Troy
Context	The Trojan War	The Trojan War
Language	Challenging syntax: long sentences with embedded clauses	Challenging syntax: long sentences with embedded clauses
Concept Level	Accessible (Consequences of greed and rage)	Accessible (Honor versus family love)
Literary Merit	Ancient Homeric epic	Ancient Homeric epic
Lexile	NP	NP
Overall Rating	Challenging	Challenging

Facilitate Understanding

Students might be interested in discussing mythological elements in the *Iliad.* Have students volunteer what they know about the myths associated with the immortals listed on the previous page.

❹ About the Selection

As is typical of the *Iliad,* these excerpts are full of interesting contradictions. Although Homer is himself a Greek, he portrays both sides in the war as equally likely to include heroes, villains, and scoundrels. Moreover, even a hero like Achilles can behave badly, first sulking in his tent and then needlessly desecrating the memory of Hector by dragging his slain enemy's body through the dust. Our sympathies are mixed: we feel for Achilles, who has lost his friend Patroclus, but we also pity Andromache when she loses her husband. The Homeric gods take both sides and interfere with humans in ways that sometimes seem helpful and sometimes unfair. In Homer's world, there are many heroic deeds but few easy answers.

❺ Literary Analysis

Theme

- Direct students to read the bracketed passage and then to paraphrase its main idea.
- Have students notice the prominent placement of the word *rage* in line 1, as well as the word's repetition in that line.
- **Ask** students the Literary Analysis question: In these opening lines, what does the poet single out as his major theme?
  Answer: The poet singles out Achilles' rage as his major theme.

from BOOK 1: ❹ THE RAGE OF ACHILLES

Background At the time of the Trojan War, Greece was not a unified nation. The Greek campaign against the Trojans was led by a loose group of independent tribal lords, or kings, who commanded their own soldiers. Leaders like Achilles and Agamemnon did not owe each other unconditional allegiance.

❺
Rage—Goddess, sing[1] the rage of Peleus' son Achilles,
murderous, doomed, that cost the Achaeans[2] countless losses,
hurling down to the House of Death so many sturdy souls,
great fighters' souls, but made their bodies carrion,
feasts for the dogs and birds,
and the will of Zeus was moving toward its end.
Begin, Muse, when the two first broke and clashed,
Agamemnon lord of men and brilliant Achilles.

What god drove them to fight with such a fury?
Apollo the son of Zeus and Leto. Incensed at the king
he swept a fatal plague through the army—men were dying
and all because Agamemnon spurned Apollo's priest.
Yes, Chryses approached the Achaeans' fast ships
to win his daughter back, bringing a priceless ransom
and bearing high in hand, wound on a golden staff,
the wreaths of the god, the distant deadly Archer.
He begged the whole Achaean army but most of all
the two supreme commanders, Atreus' two sons,
"Agamemnon, Menelaus—all Argives geared for war!
May the gods who hold the halls of Olympus[3] give you
Priam's city[4] to plunder, then safe passage home.

Literary Analysis
Theme In these opening lines, what does the poet single out as his major theme?

Vocabulary Builder
incensed (in senst′) *adj.* very angry; enraged

Vocabulary Builder
plunder (plun′ dər) *v.* rob by force in warfare

1. **Goddess, sing** conventional epic opening whereby the narrator invites a goddess called a Muse to inspire in him the epic's story.
2. **Achaeans** (ə kē′ ənz) tribal name for the Greeks.
3. **Olympus** (ō lim′ pəs) mountain in Greece between Thessaly and Macedonia; mythological home of the gods.
4. **Priam's city** Troy.

Enrichment

Tolstoy's Evaluation of Homer

The great Russian novelist Leo Tolstoy (1828–1910) said, "However distant Homer is from us we can still without the slightest effort transport ourselves into the life he describes. And we are thus transported chiefly because, however alien to us may be the events Homer describes, he believes in what he says and speaks seriously of what he is describing, and therefore he never exaggerates and the sense of measure never deserts him."

Just set my daughter free, my dear one . . . here,
accept these gifts, this ransom. Honor the god
who strikes from worlds away—the son of Zeus, Apollo!"

And all ranks of Achaeans cried out their assent:
"Respect the priest, accept the shining ransom!"
But it brought no joy to the heart of Agamemnon.
The king dismissed the priest with a brutal order
ringing in his ears: "Never again, old man,
let me catch sight of you by the hollow ships!
Not loitering now, not slinking back tomorrow.
The staff and the wreaths of god will never save you then.
The girl—I won't give up the girl. Long before that,
old age will overtake her in *my* house, in Argos,[5]
far from her fatherland, slaving back and forth
at the loom, forced to share my bed!
Now go,
don't tempt my wrath—and you may depart alive."

The old man was terrified. He obeyed the order,
turning, trailing away in silence down the shore
where the battle lines of breakers crash and drag.
And moving off to a safe distance, over and over
the old priest prayed to the son of sleek-haired Leto,
lord Apollo, "Hear me, Apollo! God of the silver bow
who strides the walls of Chryse and Cilla sacrosanct—
lord in power of Tenedos[6]—Smintheus,[7] god of the plague!
If I ever roofed a shrine to please your heart,
ever burned the long rich bones of bulls and goats
on your holy altar, now, now bring my prayer to pass.
Pay the Danaans back—your arrows for my tears!"

His prayer went up and Phoebus Apollo heard him.
Down he strode from Olympus' peaks, storming at heart
with his bow and hooded quiver slung across his shoulders.
The arrows clanged at his back as the god quaked with rage,
the god himself on the march and down he came like night.
Over against the ships he dropped to a knee, let fly a shaft

Vocabulary Builder
sacrosanct (sak´ rō saŋkt´) *adj.* very holy; sacred

8 **Critical Viewing** What are the advantages and disadvantages of armor like that worn by Achilles, who is depicted here? **[Analyze]**

Reading Check 9
What does the priest Chryses ask the Achaeans to do?

5. **Argos** (är´ gäs´) city in the northwest of Peloponnese.
6. **Tenedos** (ten´ ə däs) island off the coast of Troad, the name given to the country of the Trojans.
7. **Smintheus** (smin´ thyo͞os) another name for Apollo; Smintheus means "rat/mouse god," an appropriate name for him as the god of plague.

6 Vocabulary Builder

Latin Root *-sacr-*

- Draw students' attention to the word *sacrosanct* and its definition.
- Tell students that the Latin root *-sacr-* means "sacred" or "holy."
- Write the words *sacrilege* and *sacrifice* on the board. Then, **ask** students to relate the root *-sacr-* to the definition of each of these words.

7 Humanities

Achille en Habit Militaire, c. 1802

In this illustration, Achilles is shown as a proud warrior, decked in the typical garb of a Greek soldier. The protective armor—including a cuirass covering the torso and greaves covering the legs below the knee—would have deflected the weapons used in combat.

Use the following questions for discussion:

- How does this image of Achilles compare with the description of him in lines 1–8?
  Possible response: In lines 1–8, Achilles is described as a fierce killing machine. The illustration, by contrast, shows Achilles as calm and noble, the epitome of an epic hero not currently engaged in battle.
- How do the colors of this illustration contribute to the depiction of Achilles as somewhat sedate?
  Possible response: The artist has used pastels instead of the bright, vivid colors often associated with battle. These muted tones reflect the disposition of the composed Achilles shown here.

8 Critical Viewing

Answer: Advantages include protection for the most vulnerable parts of the body, including the head, chest, and legs. Disadvantages include loss of mobility.

9 Reading Check

Answer: Chryses asks the Achaeans to set his daughter free.

Differentiated Instruction

Solutions for All Learners

Strategy for Less Proficient Readers

Have students participate in a choral reading of Agamemnon's speech (lines 29–37) and of Chryses' prayer to Apollo (lines 43–49). Then, invite students to form groups to discuss the tone or mood of each speech. Ask students what the words of each speaker reveal about his character.

Strategy for Advanced Readers

Have students examine the emotionally charged words used by Agamemnon in his speech (lines 29–37) and by Chryses in his prayer (lines 43–49). Ask students to discuss the connotations of each speaker's highly emotional language. Also have students note each speaker's use of compression and implication in the final line of his speech. For example, Agamemnon implies that the penalty for testing his wrath will be death.

10 Critical Thinking

Analyze Cause and Effect

- Have students read the bracketed passage. Then, ask them to paraphrase the lines.
- **Ask** students what they think Achilles' motivations may have been in calling the assembly.
  Possible response: Achilles is said to have been motivated by the goddess Hera, who grieved for the death of so many Greek warriors. In addition, Achilles might have been motivated by his own suspicion that the plague was a sign of divine wrath at Agamemnon's selfish, stubborn refusal to honor the priest Chryses.

11 Humanities

The Anger of Achilles,
by Jacques-Louis David

The French artist Jacques-Louis David (1748–1825) was one of the most important painters of the neoclassical style that flourished in the eighteenth century. In 1784, David was elected to the prestigious Académie Royale (Royal Academy). His masterworks include two paintings from 1784: *Andromache Mourning Hector* and *The Oath of the Horatii,* based on an event from Roman history. The patriotism and sacrifice of the Horatius brothers helped turn David into a cultural hero of the French Revolution. David was politically active during the revolution, imprisoned for a time at the end of the Reign of Terror. Later, David served as an official government painter under Napoleon. In *The Anger of Achilles* (1819), Achilles' sword balances Agamemnon's scepter at the moment of Athena's intervention in typical neoclassical fashion.

Use this question for discussion:

How does the artist contrast Achilles (left) with Agamemnon (right)?
Possible response: Achilles' facial expression and stance suggest passion and impulsiveness, whereas Agamemnon looks cool and almost dismissively arrogant.

12 Critical Viewing

Answer: Achilles' helmet and armor hint that he is a soldier; Agamemnon's scepter hints that he is a king.

and a terrifying clash rang out from the great silver bow.
First he went for the mules and circling dogs but then,
launching a piercing shaft at the men themselves,
he cut them down in droves—
and the corpse-fires burned on, night and day, no end in sight.

10

Nine days the arrows of god swept through the army.
On the tenth Achilles called all ranks to muster—
the impulse seized him, sent by white-armed Hera
grieving to see Achaean fighters drop and die.
Once they'd gathered, crowding the meeting grounds,
the swift runner Achilles rose and spoke among them:
"Son of Atreus, now we are beaten back, I fear,
the long campaign is lost. So home we sail . . .
if we can escape our death—if war and plague
are joining forces now to crush the Argives.
But wait: let us question a holy man,
a prophet, even a man skilled with dreams—
dreams as well can come our way from Zeus—
come, someone to tell us why Apollo rages so,
whether he blames us for a vow we failed, or sacrifice.
If only the god would share the smoky savor of lambs

12 ▼ Critical Viewing
Which details in this painting indicate that Achilles (left) is a soldier and Agamemnon (right) is a king? **[Infer]**

11

Enrichment

Greek Ritual Sacrifice

Ritual sacrifice of animals was common practice in ancient Greece. Normally, only certain parts of the slaughtered animals were burned. Among these were the fatty parts that make aromatic smoke sacrificers hoped would reach the gods; the remaining meat was shared among the people. When the entire animal was burned, the sacrifice was called a holocaust, which means "wholly burned" in Greek.

Calchas clarifies the severity of Apollo's anger by explaining that to propitiate, or appease, the angered archer god, the Greeks must not only return Chryseis but also perform a hecatomb. A hecatomb is the sacrifice of one hundred animals (typically oxen, sheep, or goats), although the term may be used to refer to any large sacrifice.

and full-grown goats, Apollo might be willing, still,
somehow, to save us from this plague."
So he proposed
and down he sat again as Calchas rose among them,
Thestor's son, the clearest by far of all the seers
who scan the flight of birds.[8] He knew all things that are,
all things that are past and all that are to come,
the seer who had led the Argive ships to Troy
with the second sight that god Apollo gave him.
For the armies' good the seer began to speak:

"Achilles, dear to Zeus . . .
you order me to explain Apollo's anger,
the distant deadly Archer? I will tell it all.
But strike a pact with me, swear you will defend me
with all your heart, with words and strength of hand.
13 For there is a man I will enrage—I see it now—
a powerful man who lords it over all the Argives,
one the Achaeans must obey . . . A mighty king,
raging against an inferior, is too strong.
Even if he can swallow down his wrath today,
still he will nurse the burning in his chest
until, sooner or later, he sends it bursting forth.
Consider it closely, Achilles. Will you save me?"

And the matchless runner reassured him: "Courage!
Out with it now, Calchas. Reveal the will of god,
whatever you may know. And I swear by Apollo
dear to Zeus, the power you pray to, Calchas,
when you reveal god's will to the Argives—no one,
14 not while I am alive and see the light on earth, no one
will lay his heavy hands on you by the hollow ships.
None among all the armies. Not even if you mean
Agamemnon here who now claims to be, by far,
the best of the Achaeans."
The seer took heart
and this time he spoke out, bravely: "Beware—
he casts no blame for a vow we failed, a sacrifice.
The god's enraged because Agamemnon spurned his priest,
he refused to free his daughter, he refused the ransom.
That's why the Archer sends us pains and he will send us more
and never drive this shameful destruction from the Argives,
not till we give back the girl with sparkling eyes
to her loving father—no price, no ransom paid—
and carry a sacred hundred bulls to Chryse town.
Then we can calm the god, and only then appease him."

8. **seers . . . birds** people who read omens that are believed to be carried by certain birds.

Literary Analysis
Theme and Foreshadowing To whom do you think Calchas is referring when he speaks of the "wrath" of a "mighty king"? How do you know?

Reading Strategy
Analyze Confusing Sentences What is the central point of what Achilles says to Calchas in these lines?

15 
Reading Check
According to Calchas, why is Apollo enraged?

13 Literary Analysis

Theme and Foreshadowing

- Have students read Calchas' words in the bracketed passage.
- Ask students to recall Agamemnon's brutal treatment and public humiliation of Chryses.
- **Ask** students the Literary Analysis question: To whom do you think Calchas is referring when he speaks of the "wrath" of a "mighty king"? How do you know?
  Answer: Calchas is referring to Agamemnon. Clues to his meaning are Agamemnon's role as supreme commander of the Greeks and the king's harsh treatment of Chryses, which has incurred Apollo's wrath.
- Have students predict what may happen if Achilles takes Calchas' side against Agamemnon.

14 Reading Strategy

Analyze Confusing Sentences

- Have students read the bracketed passage. Note Achilles' long sentence in lines 101–105.
- Have students break down the sentence into parts, separating the subordinate clauses "when you reveal . . ." and "not while I am alive. . . ."
- **Ask** students the Reading Strategy question: What is the central point of what Achilles says to Calchas in these lines?
  Answer: The central point is that Achilles will protect Chryseis at all costs.

15 Reading Check

Answer: Apollo is enraged because Agamemnon has dishonored the god's priest, Chryses, and has refused to release Chryseis, the priest's daughter.

Differentiated Instruction Solutions for All Learners

Strategy for Special Needs Students

As students read the dialogue between Achilles and Calchas, help them focus on the text by using a graphic organizer to list especially vivid or striking phrases. Have student pairs take turns reading the speeches aloud and listing such phrases as "distant deadly Archer," "swallow down his wrath," "nurse the burning in his chest," "heavy hands," and "the girl with sparkling eyes."

Strategy for Gifted/Talented Students

Have students practice a dramatic reading of Calchas' speech in lines 86–98. Encourage students to focus on pitch, volume, pacing, emphasis, gesture, and facial expression. After each dramatic reading, allow the audience time for discussion and constructive criticism.

⓰ Background

The Sacrifice of Iphigeneia

Agamemnon interprets Calchas' prophesies as always bringing him hardship. In these lines, Agamemnon refers to an earlier incident at Aulis, where the fleet was kept from sailing to Troy because Artemis was angered and had stopped the winds. On that occasion, Calchas explained that to propitiate the goddess, Agamemnon had to sacrifice his daughter Iphigeneia. Homer thus hints that there has been a longstanding personal quarrel between the king and the prophet.

⓱ Literary Analysis

Theme

- Have students reread Agamemnon's words about prizes in the bracketed passage.
- Then, have students review Achilles' remarks about treasure and booty in lines 142–148.
- Ask students to consider how material possessions, both in Homer's era and ours, may be considered a sign of worth, dignity, power, or achievement.
- Then, **ask** students the Literary Analysis question: What does Agamemnon's insistence on having a prize imply about the values of Homeric warriors?
  Answer: Homeric warriors considered prizes and war booty an outward sign or symbol of their heroism and military achievement.

So he declared and sat down. But among them rose
the fighting son of Atreus, lord of the far-flung kingdoms,
Agamemnon—furious, his dark heart filled to the brim,
blazing with anger now, his eyes like searing fire.
With a sudden, killing look he wheeled on Calchas first:
"Seer of misery! Never a word that works to my advantage!
⓰ Always misery warms your heart, your prophecies—
never a word of profit said or brought to pass.
Now, again, you divine[9] god's will for the armies,
bruit it about, as fact, why the deadly Archer
multiplies our pains: because I, I refused
that glittering price for the young girl Chryseis.
Indeed, I prefer *her* by far, the girl herself,
I want her mine in my own house! I rank her higher
than Clytemnestra, my wedded wife—she's nothing less
in build or breeding, in mind or works of hand.
But I am willing to give her back, even so,
if that is best for all. What I really want
is to keep my people safe, not see them dying.
But fetch me another prize, and straight off too,
else I alone of the Argives go without my honor.
That would be a disgrace. You are all witness,
look—*my* prize is snatched away!"
But the swift runner
Achilles answered him at once, "Just how, Agamemnon,
great field marshal . . . most grasping man alive,
how can the generous Argives give you prizes now?
I know of no troves of treasure, piled, lying idle,
anywhere. Whatever we dragged from towns we plundered,
all's been portioned out. But collect it, call it back
from the rank and file? *That* would be the disgrace.
So return the girl to the god, at least for now.
We Achaeans will pay you back, three, four times over,
if Zeus will grant us the gift, somehow, someday,
to raze Troy's massive ramparts to the ground."

But King Agamemnon countered, "Not so quickly,
brave as you are, godlike Achilles—trying to cheat *me*.
Oh no, you won't get past me, take me in that way!
What do you want? To cling to your own prize
⓱ while I sit calmly by—empty-handed here?
Is that why you order me to give her back?
No—if our generous Argives *will* give me a prize,
a match for my desires, equal to what I've lost,
well and good. But if they give me nothing
I will take a prize myself—your own, or Ajax'

Literary Analysis
Theme What does Agamemnon's insistence on having a prize imply about the values of Homeric warriors?

9. **divine** (də vīn′) *v.* conjecture; guess.

Enrichment

Reciprocal Exchange in Ancient Greece

Throughout the *Iliad,* reciprocity and exchange are the glue that holds a society together, mending the cracks that would split it apart. Exchanging gifts and services is the way *xenia* works, the guest-host relationship in ancient Greece that binds together people not related by blood or clan.

Early in the sixth book of the *Iliad,* the heroes Glaucus and Diomedes come together to fight. Before engaging in battle, each ascertains the other's identity. The two men discover that their ancestors had established a bond of *xenia.* Realizing that they are bound to uphold this ancestral bond, the two warriors vow not to fight each other and exchange armor as a gesture of friendship. This symbolic act of reciprocity is based on a fiction of equal exchange. Refusing to take part in the system, as Agamemnon does when he rejects Chryses and as Achilles does later in the poem, threatens the foundations of civilized community.

(17) ↑
or Odysseus' prize—I'll commandeer her myself
and let that man I go to visit choke with rage!
Enough. We'll deal with all this later, in due time.
Now come, we haul a black ship down to the bright sea,
gather a decent number of oarsmen along her locks
and put aboard a sacrifice, and Chryseis herself,
in all her beauty . . . we embark her too.
Let one of the leading captains take command.
Ajax, Idomeneus, trusty Odysseus or you, Achilles,
you—the most violent man alive—so you can perform
the rites for us and calm the god yourself."
A dark glance
and the headstrong runner answered him in kind: "Shameless—
armored in shamelessness—always shrewd with greed!
How could any Argive soldier obey your orders,
freely and gladly do your sailing for you
or fight your enemies, full force? Not I, no.
It wasn't Trojan spearmen who brought me here to
fight.
The Trojans never did *me* damage, not in the least,
they never stole my cattle or my horses, never
in Phthia[10] where the rich soil breeds strong men
did they lay waste my crops. How could they?
Look at the endless miles that lie between us . . .
shadowy mountain ranges, seas that surge and thunder.
No, you colossal, shameless—we all followed you,
to please you, to fight for you, to win your honor
back from the Trojans—Menelaus and you, you dog-face!
What do *you* care? Nothing. You don't look right or left.
And now you threaten to strip me of my prize in person—
the one I fought for long and hard, and sons of Achaea
handed her to me.
My honors never equal yours,
whenever we sack some wealthy Trojan stronghold—
my arms bear the brunt of the raw, savage fighting,
(20) true, but when it comes to dividing up the plunder
the lion's share is yours, and back I go to my ships,
clutching some scrap, some pittance that I love,
when I have fought to exhaustion.
No more now—
back I go to Phthia. Better that way by far,
to journey home in the beaked ships of war.
I have no mind to linger here disgraced,
brimming your cup and piling up your plunder."

But the lord of men Agamemnon shot back,

10. **Phthia** (fthī´ ə) Achilles' home in northern Greece.

(18)

(19) ▲ **Critical Viewing**
This mask, thought to be one of Agamemnon, is made of solid gold. What does this fact suggest about Agamemnon's status in society? **[Infer]**

(21) **Reading Check**
Why does Achilles threaten to leave the battle?

(18) Humanities

Mask of Agamemnon

German-American archaeologist Heinrich Schliemann unearthed this solid gold funerary mask during an excavation in Mycenae. Convinced that he had discovered the grave of Agamemnon, Schliemann attributed the mask to the great Greek leader, even though the mask predates the proposed date of the Trojan War by at least 300 years.

Use the following question to initiate discussion:

What details of this mask indicate that the wearer might have been a nobleman?
Possible response: The elegant features give the mask a refined quality that one might associate with royalty.

(19) Critical Viewing

Answer: The gold mask suggests that Agamemnon was a king or supreme commander.

(20) Background

The Spoils of War

Customarily, the foremost fighter, by virtue of how hard and how well he fights, is formally recognized by the booty distributed to him. Stripping Achilles of his prize is like stripping him of a medal of honor and, in turn, threatens his stature as the greatest warrior. Achilles' complaint that his rewards should equal, if not surpass, Agamemnon's prizes reveals his desire for power. The fact that Agamemnon has the authority to revoke the prize frustrates and angers Achilles. Rather than accept his status as inferior in power to Agamemnon, Achilles withdraws from the war.

(21) Reading Check

Answer: Achilles threatens to leave because he believes Agamemnon has gravely insulted him by threatening to confiscate his prize. Achilles also believes that the war is futile.

Differentiated Instruction Solutions for All Learners

Strategy for Less Proficient Readers

Have students set up a talk show segment in which they portray Achilles and Agamemnon as guests. Make sure that the "host" and audience members ask questions that highlight the men's viewpoints, motivation, and temperaments. Then, have each student make a Venn diagram to compare and contrast the two characters.

Strategy for English Learners

Pair each student with a native English speaker and have the pairs review the speeches and actions of Agamemnon and Achilles so far in Book 1. Then, have each pair develop a two-column chart in which they use appropriate words and phrases to describe the character traits of both warriors.

Strategy for Advanced Readers

Have students discuss the escalation of the quarrel between Agamemnon and Achilles. Ask them to explain the character traits of each hero that lend an air of inevitability to their quarrel. Then, discuss how Homer establishes and maintains suspense in this narrative.

22 Humanities

Minerva Restrains Achilles from Killing Agamemnon, by Giovanni Battista Tiepolo

This fresco of Minerva (the Roman counterpart of the Greek Athena) restraining Achilles is one of many executed in 1757 by Tiepolo (1696–1770) for Count Valmarana's palazzo in Vicenza. The artist's technique of using a light-washed background with indistinct details provides a dramatic setting for the action in the foreground. Here he has abandoned his palette of bright and cheerful colors for more somber earth tones that bring a subtle feeling of melancholy to the scene.

Tiepolo worked closely on the project with famed rococo painter Girolamo Mengozzi Colonna. The relaxed, expansive quality of Tiepolo's compositions is perfectly suited to architecture of this style.

Use the following questions for discussion:

- What do the stance and expression of Agamemnon convey?
  Possible response: The stance and expression convey sternness, anger, and perhaps apprehension.
- Is Achilles' anger accurately portrayed in this painting? Explain.
  Possible response: The hero's anger is accurately portrayed, as evidenced by such details as his wide staring eyes, his aggressive stance, and his drawn sword.

23 Critical Viewing

Answer: Achilles would have used his sword to kill or wound Agamemnon.

22

23 ▲ **Critical Viewing** This painting depicts Athena restraining Achilles from attacking Agamemnon. Based on the painting, what do you think would have happened if Athena had not intervened? **[Speculate]**

Enrichment

Achilles

Achilles is greater than a mere mortal because of his divine mother but at the same time bereft of much of the comfort associated with being human. Thetis' immortality and invulnerability distance her from her mortal son, no matter how much she loves him or how deeply his death distresses her. In *On the Iliad,* Rachel Bespaloff writes of the bond between Thetis and Achilles:

Thetis keeps watch over her son, and her vigilance never sleeps. . . . The anxious love that has taught her the lesson of human distress has also taught her to despise her immortal status. . . . Outside of Patroklos (Patroclus), the only being that Achilles is capable of affection for is Thetis. . . . For Achilles, self is at the center of love.

"*Desert*, by all means—if the spirit drives you home!
I will never beg you to stay, not on *my* account.
Never—others will take my side and do me honor,
Zeus above all, whose wisdom rules the world.
You—I hate you most of all the warlords
loved by the gods. Always dear to your heart,
strife, yes, and battles, the bloody grind of war.
What if you are a great soldier? That's just a gift of god.
Go home with your ships and comrades, lord it over
your Myrmidons![11]
You *are* nothing to me—you and your overweening anger!
[24] But let this be my warning on your way:
since Apollo insists on taking my Chryseis,
I'll send her back in my own ships with *my* crew.
But I, I will be there in person at your tents
to take Briseis in all her beauty, your own prize—
so you can learn just how much greater I am than you
and the next man up may shrink from matching words with me,
from hoping to rival Agamemnon strength for strength!"

He broke off and anguish gripped Achilles.
The heart in his rugged chest was pounding, torn . . .
Should he draw the long sharp sword at his hip,
thrust through the ranks and kill Agamemnon now?—
or check his rage and beat his fury down?
As his racing spirit veered back and forth,
just as he drew his huge blade from its sheath,
down from the vaulting heavens swept Athena,
the white-armed goddess Hera sped her down:
Hera loved both men and cared for both alike.
Rearing behind him Pallas seized his fiery hair—
only Achilles saw her, none of the other fighters—
struck with wonder he spun around, he knew her at once,
Pallas Athena! the terrible blazing of those eyes,
and his winged words went flying: "Why, why now?
Child of Zeus with the shield of thunder, why come now?
To witness the outrage Agamemnon just committed?
I tell you this, and so help me it's the truth—
he'll soon pay for his arrogance with his life!"

Her gray eyes clear, the goddess Athena answered,
"Down from the skies I come to check your rage
if only you will yield.
[25] The white-armed goddess Hera sped me down:
she loves you both, she cares for you both alike.
Stop this fighting, now. Don't lay hand to sword.
Lash him with threats of the price that he will face.

11. **Myrmidons** (mur´ mə dänz´) Achilles' warriors from his home in northern Greece.

[26]  **Reading Check**

Whom does Agamemnon claim as his prize in place of Chryseis?

[24] Background

Culture

A king with the best interests in mind would not want to humiliate the most valuable warrior. By humiliating Achilles, Agamemnon preserves his status as the most powerful king, who commands absolute obedience from even his most essential warrior.

[25] Literary Analysis

Theme and Foreshadowing

- Have students read Athena's words in the bracketed passage.
- Ask students to recall the importance Homeric warriors attached to prizes, gifts, and other material possessions.
- Make sure students understand that Athena, as an immortal, is endowed with foreknowledge. Then, **ask** students: What event do you think Athena foreshadows in this passage? **Possible response:** The poet foreshadows the grave need for Achilles that will cause the Greeks—and, in particular, Agamemnon—to entreat him with gifts to return to the war.

[26] Reading Check

Answer: Agamemnon claims Briseis, the captive who was awarded to Achilles.

Differentiated Instruction

Solutions for All Learners

Strategy for Less Proficient Readers

Encourage students to use dictionaries to find the meanings of words such as *strife* (line 210), *comrades* (line 212), *vaulting* (line 229) and *rearing* (line 232). Then, suggest synonyms with which they are more familiar.

Support for English Learners

Point out the words *grind* (line 210) and *lord* (line 212). Explain that in this passage, *grind* is used as a noun to mean "monotonous labor or routine." *Lord* is used as a verb to mean "to act like a lord," or "to put on airs." Have students write four sentences, using each word in both its noun and verb form.

Enrichment for Gifted/Talented Students

Have students create drawings, paintings, sculptures, or collages depicting the scene in which Athena restrains Achilles from killing Agamemnon. Before students begin, encourage them to reread lines 222–251, noting sensory details that will aid them in creating their artistic interpretations.

27 Critical Thinking

Infer

- Read aloud the bracketed passage. Ask students what these lines mean.
- Then, **ask** students what kind of relationship between men and gods does Achilles' statement imply.
  Answer: Achilles' words imply a reciprocal relationship. Because gods are stronger than men and are immortal, human beings must obey the divinities. In return, however, the gods listen to the prayers of obedient men.

28 Humanities

Ancient Greek stone carving

This triangular stone features Achilles riding a chariot drawn by two horses. As spectators (or gods) look on, the hero brandishes a weapon and a shield against an unseen foe.

Use the following question for discussion:

What details suggest that Achilles is a confident warrior?
Possible response: Achilles stands erect in the chariot, holding his weapon and shield aloft. Instead of facing forward, he looks back to confront his attacker.

29 Critical Viewing

Possible response: The carving conveys the hero's godlike qualities by emphasizing his strength, bravery, and military skill. He appears invincible.

25
And I tell you this—and I *know* it is the truth—
one day glittering gifts will lie before you,
three times over to pay for all his outrage.
Hold back now. Obey us both."
So she urged
and the swift runner complied at once: "I must—
when the two of you hand down commands, Goddess,
a man submits though his heart breaks with fury.
27
Better for him by far. If a man obeys the gods
they're quick to hear his prayers."
And with that
Achilles stayed his burly hand on the silver hilt
and slid the huge blade back in its sheath.
He would not fight the orders of Athena.
Soaring home to Olympus, she rejoined the gods
aloft in the halls of Zeus whose shield is thunder.

But Achilles rounded on Agamemnon once again,
lashing out at him, not relaxing his anger for a moment:
"Staggering drunk, with your dog's eyes, your fawn's heart!
Never once did you arm with the troops and go to battle
or risk an ambush packed with Achaea's picked men—
you lack the courage, you can see death coming.
Safer by far, you find, to foray all through camp,
commandeering the prize of any man who speaks against you.
King who devours his people! Worthless husks, the men you rule—
if not, Atrides,[12] this outrage would have been your last.
I tell you this, and I swear a mighty oath upon it . . .
by this, this scepter, look,
that never again will put forth crown and branches,
now it's left its stump on the mountain ridge forever,
nor will it sprout new green again, now the brazen ax
has stripped its bark and leaves, and now the sons of Achaea
pass it back and forth as they hand their judgments down,
upholding the honored customs whenever Zeus commands—
This scepter will be the mighty force behind my oath:
someday, I swear, a yearning for Achilles will strike
Achaea's sons and all your armies! But then, Atrides,
harrowed as you will be, *nothing* you do can save you—
not when your hordes of fighters drop and die,
cut down by the hands of man-killing Hector! Then—
then you will tear your heart out, desperate, raging
that you disgraced the best of the Achaeans!"

12. Atrides (ə trī′ dēz) literally, son of Atreus; another name for Agamemnon.

28

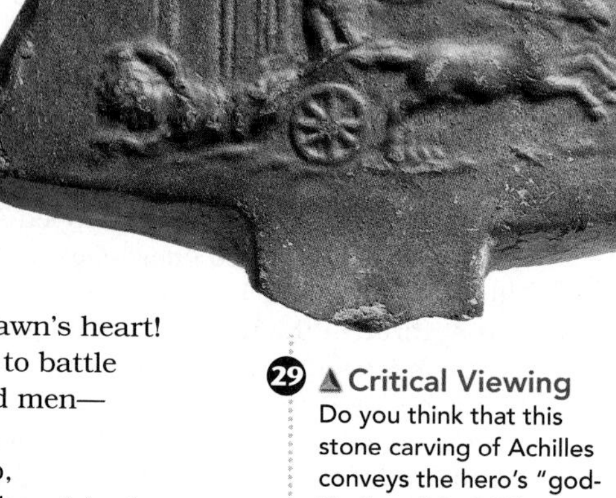

29 ▲ Critical Viewing
Do you think that this stone carving of Achilles conveys the hero's "god-like" qualities? Why or why not? **[Evaluate]**

Vocabulary Builder
brazen (brā′ zən) *adj.* literally, of brass; shamelessly bold

Vocabulary Builder
harrowed (har′ ōd) *v.* distressed; tormented

Enrichment

Oaths in Ancient Greece

In ancient Greece, oaths were sworn to solemnize promises or threats and to formalize official relationships between individuals, clans, or states. The gods were called on to witness the intentions of the speaker; if the speaker violated his oath, the gods would punish him. Achilles can swear by the scepter because it is unchanging—no longer a living tree, but a symbol of justice.

Nestor, one of the wisest Greek commanders and counselors, advises Agamemnon and Achilles to concede to each other; both men refuse. To appease the gods and spare the Achaeans further annihilation, Agamemnon orders Odysseus to return Chryseis. As compensation for his lost war prize, Agamemnon abducts Achilles' Briseis. Dishonored, Achilles swears that never again will he join the Achaeans in fighting against the Trojans. He convinces Thetis to persuade Zeus to help the Trojans defeat the Achaeans.

30
But *he* raged on, grimly camped by his fast fleet,
the royal son of Peleus, the swift runner Achilles.
Now he no longer haunted the meeting grounds
where men win glory, now he no longer went to war
but day after day he ground his heart out, waiting there,
yearning, always yearning for battle cries and combat.

But now as the twelfth dawn after this shone clear
the gods who live forever marched home to Olympus,
all in a long cortege, and Zeus led them on.
And Thetis did not forget her son's appeals.
She broke from a cresting wave at first light
and soaring up to the broad sky and Mount Olympus,
found the son of Cronus gazing down on the world,
peaks apart from the other gods and seated high
on the topmost crown of rugged ridged Olympus.
And crouching down at his feet,
quickly grasping his knees with her left hand,
her right hand holding him underneath the chin,
she prayed to the lord god Zeus, the son of Cronus:
"Zeus, Father Zeus! If I ever served you well
among the deathless gods with a word or action,
bring this prayer to pass: honor my son Achilles!—
doomed to the shortest life of any man on earth.
And now the lord of men Agamemnon has disgraced him,
seizes and keeps his prize, tears her away himself. But you—
exalt him, Olympian Zeus: your urgings rule the world!
Come, grant the Trojans victory after victory
till the Achaean armies pay my dear son back,
building higher the honor he deserves!"

Literary Analysis
Theme In what way does this passage reinforce the theme stated at the opening of the *Iliad*?

31  **Reading Check**
Whose help does Thetis seek on behalf of her son, Achilles?

30 Literary Analysis

Theme

- Read aloud the bracketed passage. Then, invite volunteers to comment on emotionally charged words and phrases such as "raged," "grimly," "no longer . . .," "ground his heart out," and "yearning." Point out the repetition of "no longer" and "yearning."
- Remind students of Homer's invocation to the muse in lines 1–8, and to note the poet's stress on the wrath of Achilles.
- **Ask** students the Literary Analysis question: In what way does this passage reinforce the theme stated at the opening of the *Iliad*?
  Answer: The passage echoes Homer's emphasis on Achilles' fateful rage at the beginning of the epic.

Monitor Progress **Ask** students to explain the causes for the conflict between Achilles and Agamemnon.
Answer: The conflict originates in Agamemnon's refusal to surrender Chryseis, which precipitates the plague. Achilles' challenge to Agamemnon's overall authority then causes Agamemnon to threaten to confiscate Achilles' prize, an action that deeply insults Achilles.

Reteach To assist students with the themes in Homer, use **Literary Analysis,** p. 11 in ***Unit 4 Resources.***

31 Reading Check

Answer: Thetis seeks the help of Zeus, king of the gods.

Differentiated Instruction Solutions for All Learners

Strategy for Less Proficient Readers
Work with students to develop a comprehension check for the events mentioned in the italicized prose passage at the top of this page. Ask students to create sequence charts, listing the major events in chronological order.

Strategy for English Learners
Have students refer to p. 363 to identify and describe the following characters: Nestor, Odysseus, and Thetis. Then, have them identify the major events in Book I of the *Iliad* with which these characters are associated.

Enrichment for Advanced Readers
Challenge students to select one of the scenes briefly summarized in the italicized prose passage: for example, the speech of Nestor to Agamemnon and Achilles, the return of Chryseis, or the abduction of Briseis. Have students write or stage a dramatic version of the selected scene.

32 Background

Repetition in Homeric Verse

Call students' attention to the repetition in lines 16–18 of details from lines 11–13. Remind students that the repetition of lines and, in some cases, of entire passages, is a feature of orally composed traditional literature such as the *Iliad*. In Homer's epic, the poet often uses repetition to preserve the rhythm of the poem; repetition also reinforces important information for the listening audience.

33 Critical Thinking

Speculate

- Ask a volunteer to read aloud the bracketed passage. Then, **ask** where Andromache has gone.
  Answer: Andromache has gone to the gate-tower of Troy with her servant and child.
- **Ask** students to speculate on why Andromache has gone to the gate.
  Possible response: Andromache is concerned about Hector's welfare as Troy's forces are being driven back.

from BOOK 6: HECTOR RETURNS TO TROY

At Thetis' request, Zeus intervenes to help the Trojans defeat the Achaeans. Bitter fighting resumes, causing massive casualties on both sides. Although the Achaeans suffer a disadvantage from Achilles' absence, they manage to subdue the Trojans. Under the leadership of Diomedes, the Achaeans drive the Trojans back into temporary retreat behind the city gates. Realizing the gravity of the Trojan cause, Hector and his men go to Priam's palace to urge the gods to take pity on Troy. Hector also tries to persuade his brother Paris, who caused the war by abducting Helen, to fight. Finally, Hector goes in search of his wife, Andromache.

A flash of his helmet
and off he strode and quickly reached his sturdy,
well-built house. But white-armed Andromache—
Hector could not find her in the halls.
She and the boy and a servant finely gowned
were standing watch on the tower, sobbing, grieving.
When Hector saw no sign of his loyal wife inside
he went to the doorway, stopped and asked the servants,
"Come, please, tell me the truth now, women.
Where's Andromache gone? To my sisters' house?
To my brothers' wives with their long flowing robes?
Or Athena's shrine where the noble Trojan women
gather to win the great grim goddess over?"

32

A busy, willing servant answered quickly,
"Hector, seeing you want to know the truth,
she hasn't gone to your sisters, brothers' wives
or Athena's shrine where the noble Trojan women
gather to win the great grim goddess over.
Up to the huge gate-tower of Troy she's gone
because she heard our men are so hard-pressed,
33 the Achaean fighters coming on in so much force.
She sped to the wall in panic, like a madwoman—
the nurse went with her, carrying your child."

At that, Hector spun and rushed from his house,
back by the same way down the wide, well-paved streets
throughout the city until he reached the Scaean Gates,[1]
the last point he would pass to gain the field of battle.
There his warm, generous wife came running up to meet him,
34 Andromache the daughter of gallant-hearted Eetion[2]
who had lived below Mount Placos[3] rich with timber,
in Thebe below the peaks, and ruled Cilicia's people.[4]
His daughter had married Hector helmed in bronze.
She joined him now, and following in her steps
a servant holding the boy against her breast,
in the first flush of life, only a baby,
Hector's son, the darling of his eyes
and radiant as a star . . .
Hector would always call the boy Scamandrius,
townsmen called him Astyanax, Lord of the City,
since Hector was the lone defense of Troy.
The great man of war breaking into a broad smile,
his gaze fixed on his son, in silence. Andromache,
pressing close beside him and weeping freely now,
clung to his hand, urged him, called him: "Reckless one,
my Hector—your own fiery courage will destroy you!
Have you no pity for *him*, our helpless son? Or me,
and the destiny that weighs me down, your widow,
now so soon? Yes, soon they will kill you off,
all the Achaean forces massed for assault, and then,
bereft of you, better for me to sink beneath the earth.
What other warmth, what comfort's left for me,
once you have met your doom? Nothing but torment!
I have lost my father. Mother's gone as well.
Father . . . the brilliant Achilles laid him low
when he stormed Cilicia's city filled with people,
Thebe with her towering gates. He killed Eetion,
35 not that he stripped his gear—he'd some respect at least—
for he burned his corpse in all his blazoned bronze,
then heaped a grave-mound high above the ashes
and nymphs[5] of the mountain planted elms around it,
daughters of Zeus whose shield is storm and thunder.
And the seven brothers I had within our halls . . .
all in the same day went down to the House of Death,
the great godlike runner Achilles butchered them all,
tending their shambling oxen, shining flocks.

Reading Strategy
Analyze Confusing Sentences Which details in lines 28–31 are not essential to the central point of the sentence?

Vocabulary Builder
bereft (bē reft′) *adj.* deprived or robbed

36  **Reading Check**
Who does Andromache say killed her father, Eetion?

1. **Scaean** (sē′ ən) **Gates** northwest gates of Troy.
2. **Eetion** (ē ē′ tē än′) king of Thebe, a city near Troy.
3. **Mount Placos** (pla′ käs) mountain dominating Thebe.
4. **Cilicia's** (sə li′ shəz) **people** people of a region in southeast Asia Minor.
5. **nymphs** (nimfs) goddesses of nature.

34 Reading Strategy
Analyze Confusing Sentences

- Have students read aloud lines 28–31, carefully observing the punctuation.
- Lead students to recognize that the main idea of the passage is that Andromache runs to meet her husband.
- **Ask** students the Reading Strategy question: Which details in lines 28–31 are not essential to the central point of the sentence? **Answer:** Nonessential details include Eetion as the father of Andromache, Eetion's residence in Thebe below Mount Placos, the fact that Mount Placos is rich in timber, and Eetion's ruling over the people of Cilicia.

➤ **Reteach** Illustrate the answer to the Reading Strategy question by analyzing lines 28–31 with the chart on p. 362.

35 Background
Ancient Code of Ethics

Embedded in Andromache's recital of Achilles' brutality is proof of his capacity for human compassion. In observance of the ancient code of ethics, for example, Achilles killed Andromache's father, but out of respect for the dead man, he burned him in his armor and gave him his rite of burning.

36 Reading Check

Answer: Andromache says Achilles killed Eetion.

Differentiated Instruction Solutions for All Learners

Strategy for Less Proficient Readers

Encourage students to break down Andromache's longer, highly emotional sentences to clarify their meanings. Ask students to list events and details that Andromache mentions in each segment of the sentence:

- They (the enemy) will soon kill you.
- The Achaian forces are massed for assault.
- I will be bereft of you.
- It would be better for me to be dead.

Enrichment for Gifted/Talented Students

Remind students that the audiences for oral epic listened to a dramatic performance by an epic bard. Encourage students to develop and rehearse a dramatic reading of Andromache's emotional speech in lines 44–82. Ask students to focus on tone, pacing, variation, volume, and pitch. As students give their presentations, allow time for discussion and reactions from the listening audience.

37 Literary Analysis

Theme and Foreshadowing

- Have students note Andromache's words "orphan," "son," and "widow" (line 74).
- Point out that Andromache hints at the city's vulnerability when she mentions the place where it "lies most open to assault" (line 76).
- **Ask** students the Literary Analysis question: What do Andromache's comments in this passage suggest about the fate of Hector, his family, and the city of Troy?
  Possible response: Andromache's comments suggest that Hector is fated to be killed by the enemy. After Troy's fall to the Greeks, the hero's family will be enslaved or destroyed.

38 Critical Thinking

Analyze

- Have students read the bracketed passage. Ask them to analyze Hector's response to Andromache.
- **Ask** students what role shame has in Hector's decision to fight?
  Possible response: Hector's fear that he will be shamed if he does not fight compels him.
- **Ask** students to find words that suggest Hector has no choice but to fight.
  Possible response: Hector's "spirit urges" him not "to shrink from battle." Also, he feels fighting is something that will bring "great glory" to his father and himself.

39 Critical Viewing

Possible response: The image captures the urgency and poignancy of the couple's farewell.

And mother,
who ruled under the timberline of woody Placos once—
he no sooner haled her here with his other plunder
than he took a priceless ransom, set her free
and home she went to her father's royal halls
where Artemis,[6] showering arrows, shot her down.
You, Hector—you are my father now, my noble mother,
a brother too, and you are my husband, young and warm
and strong!
Pity me, please! Take your stand on the rampart here,
before you orphan your son and make your wife a widow.
Draw your armies up where the wild fig tree stands,
there, where the city lies most open to assault,
the walls lower, easily overrun. Three times
they have tried that point, hoping to storm Troy,
their best fighters led by the Great and Little Ajax,[7]
famous Idomeneus,[8] Atreus' sons, valiant Diomedes.[9]
Perhaps a skilled prophet revealed the spot—
or their own fury whips them on to attack."

And tall Hector nodded, his helmet flashing:
"All this weighs on my mind too, dear woman.
But I would die of shame to face the men of Troy
and the Trojan women trailing their long robes
if I would shrink from battle now, a coward.
Nor does the spirit urge me on that way.
I've learned it all too well. To stand up bravely,
always to fight in the front ranks of Trojan soldiers,
winning my father great glory, glory for myself.
For in my heart and soul I also know this well:
the day will come when sacred Troy must die,
Priam must die and all his people with him,
Priam who hurls the strong ash spear . . .
Even so,
it is less the pain of the Trojans still to come
that weighs me down, not even of Hecuba[10] herself
or King Priam, or the thought that my own brothers
in all their numbers, all their gallant courage,
may tumble in the dust, crushed by enemies—
That is nothing, nothing beside your agony
when some brazen Argive hales you off in tears,
wrenching away your day of light and freedom!

Literary Analysis
Theme and Foreshadowing What do Andromache's comments in this passage suggest about the fate of Hector, his family, and the city of Troy?

39 Critical Viewing ▶ How well do you think this painting captures the mood of Hector's farewell to his family? Explain. **[Evaluate]**

6. **Artemis** (är′ tə mis) goddess of the hunt and of the moon; daughter of Zeus and Leto; sister of Apollo.
7. **Great and Little Ajax** Ajax of Salamis, son of Telamon, and Ajax of Locris, son of Oileus.
8. **Idomeneus** (ī′ dä′ men yo͞os) commander of the Achaean forces from Crete; son of Deucalion.
9. **Diomedes** (dī′ ə mē′ dēz) son of Tydeus, king of Argos.
10. **Hecuba** (hek′ yo͞o bə) queen of Troy; wife of Priam; mother of Hector.

Enrichment

Divided Loyalties

The farewell of Hector and Andromache in Book 6 eloquently dramatizes Hector's conflict between loyalty to his family and loyalty to his city. As a husband and father, he is responsible for caring for his wife and child, but as a man and hero, he belongs on the battlefield, fighting for Troy with his fellow Trojans. In his response to Andromache's plea that he remain within the safety of the city walls, Hector articulates how acutely he feels the conflict. Significantly, the city walls will play a prominent role in Homer's narrative of the final confrontation between Hector and Achilles in Book 22. Achilles will pursue the Trojan champion around the walls, slay him within sight of the Trojan onlookers, and then degrade his body by dragging it in the dust.

Achaeans off the battlefield back to their ships. To prevent the Achaeans from sailing away, the Trojans light watchfires and camp on the plain overnight, ready to attack in the morning. The demoralized Achaean army feels handicapped by Achilles' absence. To persuade their most valuable fighter to reconsider and join the battle, Agamemnon sends Ajax and Odysseus on an embassy to Achilles.

In his speech to Achilles, Odysseus reminds him of his father's advice. Peleus had told Achilles that the Argives would hold him in higher honor if he did not let the anger of his proud heart get the best of him. Odysseus adds that if Achilles gives up his anger and joins the Achaeans in battle, Agamemnon has promised to give Achilles numerous war prizes, including the prize he stole: Briseis. Finally, Odysseus pleads with Achilles to fight, if not in acceptance of Agamemnon's offer, at least for the afflicted Achaeans who will honor Achilles as a god. Agamemnon's offer serves only to drive Achilles deeper into his pride. Hurt, dishonored, and, above all, angry, he refuses to help the Greeks defeat Hector and the Trojans. Odysseus and Ajax return to Agamemnon with the news of their unsuccessful embassy.

44

Odysseus' Mission to Achilles, Cleophrades Painter, Staatliche Antikensammlungen und Glyptothek, Munich

45 ▲ Critical Viewing
This urn depicts Ajax's and Odysseus' embassy to Achilles. Why do you think the ancient Greeks depicted scenes from the *Iliad* in various art forms? **[Infer]**

Critical Reading

1. **Respond:** With whom would you side in the argument between Achilles and Agamemnon in Book 1? Why?
2. **(a) Recall:** As the *Iliad* begins, what problem confronts the Greeks? **(b) Infer:** Why is the problem of such importance to the soldiers and their campaign?
3. **(a) Recall:** Why does Agamemnon claim Briseis as his prize? **(b) Analyze Causes and Effects:** How does this action relate to Achilles' decision to withdraw from battle?
4. **(a) Recall:** In Book 6, what prediction does Hector make about Troy's destiny? **(b) Compare and Contrast:** In light of this prediction, compare and contrast the poem's portrayals of Achilles and Hector as heroes so far.
5. **(a) Generalize:** What does the concept of honor seem to mean in the Homeric world? Explain. **(b) Take a Position:** Do you agree with this notion of honor? Why or why not?

Author Link
For: More about Homer
Visit: www.PHSchool.com
Web Code: ete-9401

Assessment Practice

Stated and Implied Main Ideas **(For more practice, see *Test Preparation Workbook,* p. 17.)**

Many tests require students to identify stated and implied main ideas. Use the following for practice.

Achilles called all ranks to muster— / the impulse seized him, sent by white-armed Hera / grieving to see Achaean fighters drop and die. / Once they'd gathered, crowding the meeting grounds, / the swift runner Achilles rose and spoke among them: / "Son of Atreus, now we are beaten back, I fear, / the long campaign is lost."

—from the *Iliad,* Book 1, lines 62–68

The main idea of this passage is—

A Achilles gathers his defeated troops.
B Achilles is embarrassed to be the leader.
C Achilles is the best speaker among them.
D Achilles is angry at the god Apollo.

The correct answer is *A*; Achilles has gathered his troops after they have been defeated.

44 Humanities

Odysseus' Mission to Achilles, by the Cleophrades Painter

This three-handled water jar was painted by one of the greatest artists of the Late Archaic period, the Cleophrades painter (active from 500 B.C. to 475 B.C.). He worked in the "red-figure" style, characterized by blacking out the background and allowing the natural red of the clay to serve as the color of the figures.

Ask the following question.

What can you tell from the posture of Achilles?
Answer: Achilles is angry.

45 Critical Viewing

Answer: The *Iliad* was integral to ancient Greek culture; its scenes were depicted in a variety of art forms.

ASSESS

Answers

1. **Possible responses:** Achilles bravely objects to Agamemnon's arbitrary and destructive decisions; Agamemnon is the expedition leader and should be obeyed in the interests of unity.
2. (a) Agamemnon's refusal to ransom the captive Chryseis angers Apollo, who sends a deadly plague. (b) The Greeks are dying, and their ten-year effort to take Troy may end in disaster.
3. (a) Claiming her as a substitute prize also embarrasses Achilles. (b) This action confirms Achilles' decision.
4. (a) The Greeks will destroy Troy. (b) Achilles seems self-centered and focused on material possessions and honor, whereas Hector seems torn between duty and love for his family. Each figure is heroic in his own way.
5. (a) Honor seems to mean loyalty, courage, military glory, public reputation, and outward recognition of a hero's merit through awards. (b) **Possible responses:** Honor deserves tangible recognition; honor is too connected to materialism.

Go Online Author Link For additional information about Homer, have students type in the Web Code, then select *H* from the alphabet, and then select Homer.

Answers

1. The theme revealed by the quarrel is the conflict between Achilles' claim to premier status as the most accomplished warrior and Agamemnon's claim to overlordship and supreme authority as the leader of the expedition.
2. (a) He is torn between his quest for glory and the desire for tangible recognition of his achievements. (b) The dilemma helps convey the theme of a lack of balance between merit and external recognition.
3. (a) **Achilles War:** He experiences internal conflicts about the purpose and validity of the war; **Duty:** he does not believe that duty constrains him to fight at the expense of honor; **Heroism:** he believes that heroism is symbolized by tangible prizes. **Hector War:** The war directly threatens his city; **Duty:** his duty is to fight, even though he may be doomed to defeat; **Heroism:** heroism consists of intangible loyalty to family and city, as well as martial valor. (b) The similarities and differences highlight the theme of the split between achievement and honor. Another sample answer can be found on **Literary Analysis Graphic Organizer B,** p. 71 in ***Graphic Organizer Transparencies.***
4. Thetis foreshadows Achilles' destiny to lead a short life.
5. The foreshadowing of Troy's fall creates a poignant, melancholy tone.
6. The words are not essential; the main idea of the sentence is that it will be helpful to consult a prophet.
7. **Possible response:** She came out of the sea, soared up to Mount Olympus, and found Zeus seated alone, gazing down on the world.
8. **Possible response:** In both worlds, material possessions are important. However, the acknowledgment of materialistic motives is perhaps more open in the Homeric world. In the modern world, material possessions might be more closely associated with power than with honor.

Apply the Skills

from the *Iliad,* Books 1 and 6

Literary Analysis

Theme

1. What **theme** does the quarrel between Agamemnon and Achilles reveal regarding the nature of honor and status in Homeric society?
2. **(a)** What conflicting feelings does Achilles experience as a result of his decision to withdraw from battle? **(b)** What theme of the poem does this dilemma help convey?
3. **(a)** Using a chart like the one shown, compare and contrast Hector's outlook on war, duty, and heroism with that of Achilles.

	Achilles' Outlook	Hector's Outlook
War		
Duty		
Heroism		

(b) What themes are highlighted by the similarities or differences in the two characters' outlooks on each of these subjects?

Connecting Literary Elements

4. In her speech to Zeus in Book 1, what fact about Achilles' destiny does his mother Thetis **foreshadow**?
5. Considering that Homer's audience knew the Greeks would ultimately defeat the Trojans, what effect do you think the foreshadowing in Book 6 is meant to have? Explain.

Reading Strategy

Analyze Confusing Sentences

6. Are the words *"dreams as well can come our way from Zeus"* essential to the main idea of the sentence beginning on line 71 of Book 1? Why or why not?
7. Identify the main idea of the sentence that begins on line 298 of Book 1 by rewriting it to include only essential information.

Extend Understanding

8. **Cultural Connection:** Do the characters in the *Iliad* place greater value on prizes and material possessions than do people in contemporary American society? Explain your answer.

QuickReview

The **theme** of a literary work is its central idea, concern, or message.

Foreshadowing is the use of clues to suggest future events.

To **analyze confusing sentences,** determine the main ideas by considering one section at a time and identifying the essential parts.

For: Self-test
Visit: www.PHSchool.com
Web Code: eta-6401

Go Online Assessment Students may use the **Self-test** to prepare for **Selection Test A** or **Selection Test B.**

Build Language Skills

Vocabulary Lesson

Word Analysis: Latin Root *-sacr-*

The word *sacrosanct* contains the Latin root *-sacr-*, which means "sacred or holy." Add the root *-sacr-* to the following word parts. Then, write a brief definition of each word.

1. -ed **2.** -ilege **3.** -ifice

Spelling Strategy

In American English, words ending in the sound *ens* are usually spelled with *ence*, as in *reverence.* However, there are some that end with *ense*, such as *incense.* Complete each word below with the correct spelling of the *ens* sound.

1. nons- **2.** pres- **3.** int-

Vocabulary Builder: Synonyms

Select the letter of the word that is closest in meaning to the first word.

1. incensed: **(a)** eager, **(b)** angry, **(c)** anxious
2. plunder: **(a)** flatter, **(b)** rebuild, **(c)** ransack
3. sacrosanct: **(a)** abundant, **(b)** empty, **(c)** respected
4. harrowed: **(a)** troubled, **(b)** relieved, **(c)** denounced
5. bereft: **(a)** joyful, **(b)** deprived, **(c)** humbled
6. brazen: **(a)** impudent, **(b)** ashamed, **(c)** mournful

Grammar and Style Lesson

Compound Adjectives

An adjective modifies or clarifies the meaning of a noun or pronoun. A **compound adjective** is an adjective made up of two or more words. Most are hyphenated; others are combined into one word.

Hyphenated: *well-built* house
full-grown goats
Combined: *godlike* Achilles
topmost crown

Practice Use the italicized words to form compound adjectives in the following sentences.

1. The old priest prayed to the son of *sleek haired* Leto, lord Apollo.
2. Among them rose Agamemnon, lord of the *far flung* kingdoms.
3. The *head strong* runner answered him in kind.
4. Andromache was the daughter of *gallant hearted* Eetion.
5. She was *heart broken* when Hector went off to battle.

Writing Application In a paragraph, describe what you think will happen when Hector enters the battle. Use four compound adjectives in your writing: two with hyphens and two without.

WG Prentice Hall Writing and Grammar Connection: Platinum Level, Chapter 17, Section 1

Extend Your Learning

Writing Take an event from your daily life and write an **everyday epic** version of it. Use Homeric techniques to make your characters and events seem larger than life.

Research and Technology With classmates, create a **multimedia map** of the region in which the *Iliad* takes place. Include pictures, recordings, and references to the poem. **[Group Activity]**

Assessment Resources

The following resources can be used to assess students' knowledge and skills.

Unit 4 Resources
Selection Test A, pp. 17–19
Selection Test B, pp. 20–22

Go Online **Assessment** Students may use the **Self-test** to prepare for **Selection Test A** or **Selection Test B.**

EXTEND/ASSESS

Answers

1 Vocabulary Lesson

Word Analysis: Latin Root *-sacr-*

1. sacred; holy
2. sacrilege; violation of the sacred
3. sacrifice; something offered

Spelling Strategy

1. nonsense 3. intense
2. presence

Vocabulary Builder

1. b 3. c 5. b
2. c 4. a 6. a

2 Grammar and Style Lesson

1. sleek-haired 4. gallant-hearted
2. far-flung 5. heartbroken
3. headstrong

Writing Application

Possible response: Hector will be open-minded about fighting beside Paris. The two will make level-headed decisions regarding battle strategy. The homesick Achaeans will leave Troy feeling downtrodden.

WG Writing and Grammar Platinum Level
For support in teaching the Grammar and Style Lesson, use Chapter 17, Section 1.

3 Writing

- Have students review some conventions of epic form found on p. 361.
- The **Support for Extend Your Learning** page (*Unit 4 Resources*, p. 15) provides guided note-taking opportunities to help students complete the Extend Your Learning activities.

Standard Course of Study

Goal 1: WRITTEN LANGUAGE

- **WL.1.03.2** Identify and analyze text components and evaluate impact on personal reflection.
- **WL.1.03.9** Analyze effects of author's craft and style in reflection.

Goal 3: FOUNDATIONS OF ARGUMENT

- **FA.3.02.2** Provide relevant, reliable support in editorials.

Goal 5: LITERATURE

- **LT.5.01.3** Analyze literary devices and explain their effect on the work of world literature.

Goal 6: GRAMMAR AND USAGE

- **GU.6.01.3** Use recognition strategies to understand vocabulary and exact word choice.
- **GU.6.02.2** Edit for appropriate and correct mechanics.

Step-by-Step Teaching Guide	Pacing Guide
PRETEACH	
• Administer Vocabulary and Reading Warm-ups as necessary.	5 min.
• Engage students' interest with the motivation activity.	5 min.
• Read and discuss background features. **FT**	10 min.
• Introduce the Literary Analysis Skill: Imagery. **FT**	5 min.
• Introduce the Reading Strategy: Picture the Action. **FT**	10 min.
• Prepare students to read by teaching the selection vocabulary. **FT**	
TEACH	
• Informally monitor comprehension while students read independently or in groups. **FT**	30 min.
• Monitor students' comprehension with the Reading Check notes.	as students read
• Reinforce vocabulary with Vocabulary Builder notes.	as students read
• Develop students' understanding of imagery with the Literary Analysis annotations. **FT**	5 min.
• Develop students' ability to picture the action with the Reading Strategy annotations. **FT**	5 min.
ASSESS/EXTEND	
• Assess students' comprehension and mastery of the Literary Analysis and Reading Strategy by having them answer the Apply the Skills questions. **FT**	15 min.
• Have students complete the Vocabulary Lesson and the Grammar and Style Lesson. **FT**	15 min.
• Apply students' ability to revise for persuasive language by using the Writing Lesson. **FT**	45 min. or homework
• Apply students' understanding by using one or more of the Extend Your Learning activities.	20–90 min. or homework
• Administer Selection Test A or Selection Test B. **FT**	15 min.

Resources

Print

Unit 4 Resources

- Vocabulary Warm-up Word Lists **[L1, L2, EL]** . . . . p. 23
- Vocabulary Warm-up Practice **[L1, L2, EL]** . . . . p. 24
- Reading Warm-up A **[L1, L2, EL]** . . . . p. 25
- Reading Warm-up B **[L1, L2, L3]** . . . . p. 26

Transparency

Graphic Organizer Transparencies

- Literary Analysis Graphic Organizer A **[L3]** . . . . p. 72, 74
- Literary Analysis Graphic Organizer B **[L1, L2, EL]** . . . . p. 73, 75

Print

Reader's Notebook [L2]

Reader's Notebook: Adapted Version [L1]

Reader's Notebook: English Learner's Version [EL]

Unit 4 Resources

- Literary Analysis **[L3]** . . . . p. 27
- Reading Strategy **[L3]** . . . . p. 28
- Vocabulary Builder **[L3]** . . . . p. 29

Technology

Listening to Literature Audio CDs [L2, EL]

Print

Unit 4 Resources

- Grammar and Style **[L3]** . . . . p. 30
- Support for Writing Lesson **[L3]** . . . . p. 31
- Support for Extend Your Learning **[L3]** . . . . p. 32
- Enrichment **[L4]** . . . . p. 33
- Selection Test A **[L1, L2, EL]** . . . . pp. 34–36
- Selection Test B **[L3, L4]** . . . . pp. 37–39

General Resources

- Rubrics for Persuasion: Persuasive Essay **[L3]** . . . . pp. 47–48

Technology

- **Go Online:** Research **[L3]**
- **Go Online:** Self-test **[L3]**
- ***ExamView®*, Test Bank [L3]**

Choosing Resources for Differentiated Instruction

[L1] Special Needs Students

[L2] Below-Level Students

[L3] All Students

[L4] Advanced Students

[EL] English Learners

For Vocabulary and Reading Warm-ups and for Selection Tests, **A** signifies "less challenging" and **B** "more challenging." For Graphic Organizer transparencies, **A** signifies "not filled in" and **B** "filled in."

FT Fast Track Instruction: To move the lesson more quickly, use the strategies and activities identified with **FT**.

Scaffolding for Less Proficient and Advanced Students

The leveled Critical Thinking questions after selections progress in the levels of thinking required to answer them. To address the needs of your different students, you may use the (a) level questions for your less proficient students and the (b) level questions with your on-level and advanced students. The occasional (c) level questions are appropriate for your advanced students.

PRENTICE HALL **TeacherEXPRESS™** Plan · Teach · Assess

Use this complete suite of powerful teaching tools to make lesson planning and testing quicker and easier.

PRENTICE HALL **StudentEXPRESS™** Learn · Study · Succeed

Use the interactive textbook (online and on CD-ROM) to make selections and activities come alive with audio and video support and interactive questions.

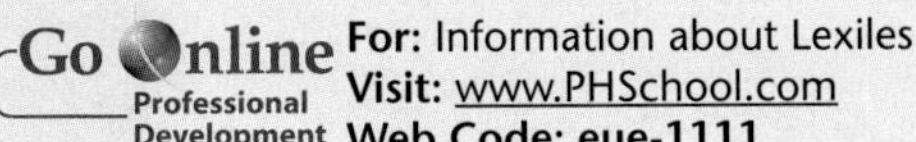

For: Information about Lexiles
Visit: www.PHSchool.com
Web Code: eue-1111

PRETEACH

❶ Literary Analysis

Imagery

- Tell students that as they read the excerpts from Books 22 and 24 of the *Iliad,* they will focus on imagery, or descriptive language that writers use to make sensory experiences vivid.
- Read aloud the instruction on imagery. Draw students' attention to the various ways in which imagery can enrich a passage.
- Give students a copy of **Literary Analysis Graphic Organizer A,** p. 72 in ***Graphic Organizer Transparencies.*** Have them use the organizer to link single images or patterns of imagery with the poem's main ideas or themes.
- Use the instruction for Connecting Literary Elements to help students recognize examples of epic similes.

❷ Reading Strategy

Picture the Action

- Explain to students that picturing the action in a literary work can bring the work to life for a reader, enhancing its power.
- Point out to students that these excerpts from the epic contain vivid details that can help students visualize what Homer describes.

Vocabulary Builder

- Pronounce each vocabulary word for students, and read the definitions as a class. Have students identify any words with which they are already familiar.

Build Skills | *Epic Poem*

from the Iliad, Books 22 and 24

Standard Course of Study

- Analyze literary devices and explain their effect on the work of world literature. (LT.5.01.3)

❶ Literary Analysis

Imagery

Imagery is the descriptive language that writers use to re-create sensory experiences. It is what helps you see, hear, feel, smell, and taste what is being described. Imagery can enrich a passage by making it more vivid, by setting a tone, by suggesting emotions, or by guiding a reader's reactions. In the *Iliad,* certain recurring images also help establish and reinforce the poem's themes. As you read, use a chart like the one shown to link patterns of images with the poem's central ideas.

Connecting Literary Elements

Among the most vivid images in the *Iliad* are those in Homer's **epic similes.** An epic simile, also called a Homeric or an extended simile, is a lengthy comparison of two dissimilar things introduced by the word *like* or *as.* Unlike a simple simile, which involves a single, distinct image, an epic simile is longer and more elaborate. It might recall an entire place or story.

Notice how this description of Hector heightens the suspense of his battle with Achilles:

> . . . like a soaring eagle
> launching down from the dark clouds to earth
> to snatch some helpless lamb or trembling hare.
> So Hector swooped now, swinging his whetted sword

Look for other epic similes as you read, and consider how they enrich the story.

❷ Reading Strategy

Picture the Action

To keep track of the fast-paced action and fully appreciate Homer's verse, pause occasionally to **picture the action.** Use the details and descriptions to help you form a mental image of what you are reading. These mental pictures will help the poem come alive.

Vocabulary Builder

implore (im plôr′) *v.* beg (p. 384)

marshals (mär′ shəlz) *v.* arranges in order; commands (p. 386)

whetted (wet′ id) *adj.* sharpened (p. 389)

brandished (bran′ disht) *v.* waved or shook in a threatening manner (p. 389)

stinted (stint′ id) *v.* limited to a certain quantity (p. 399)

lustrous (lus′ trəs) *adj.* shining (p. 403)

gaunt (gônt) *adj.* thin and bony; haggard (p. 404)

illustrious (i lus′ trē əs) *adj.* distinguished; famous (p. 408)

Differentiated Instruction Solutions for All Learners

Support for Special Needs Students
Have students complete the **Preview** and **Build Skills** pages for these selections from the *Iliad* in the ***Reader's Notebook: Adapted Version.*** These pages provide a selection summary, an abbreviated presentation of the reading and literary skills, and the graphic organizer on the **Build Skills** page in the student book.

Support for Less Proficient Readers
Have students complete the **Preview** and **Build Skills** pages for these selections from the *Iliad* in the ***Reader's Notebook.*** These pages provide a selection summary, an abbreviated presentation of the reading and literary skills, and the graphic organizer on the **Build Skills** page in the student book.

Support for English Learners
Have students complete the **Preview** and **Build Skills** pages for these selections from the *Iliad* in the ***Reader's Notebook: English Learner's Version.*** These pages provide a selection summary, an abbreviated presentation of the skills, additional contextual vocabulary, and the graphic organizer on the **Build Skills** page in the student book.

from BOOK 22:

THE DEATH OF HECTOR

Review and Anticipate

As Book 1 opens, the Greek army besieging Troy is stricken by a plague, sent by the god Apollo to punish Agamemnon's refusal to ransom a captive girl, Chryseis. Agamemnon reluctantly returns the girl to her father, but he replaces her with another female captive, Briseis, who is Achilles' prize. The two warriors quarrel, and Achilles withdraws from the battle in protest.

The tide of battle then turns in favor of Hector and the Trojans. Achilles refuses Agamemnon's offer of compensation for returning to battle, and the Greeks suffer heavy losses. Achilles finally agrees to allow his friend Patroclus to fight wearing Achilles' armor. Patroclus manages to drive the Trojans back to the city walls, but Apollo intervenes, allowing Hector to slay Patroclus and strip the body of its armor. Almost mad with grief, Achilles re-enters the battle wearing new armor made for him by the god Hephaestus. The confrontation in Book 22 between Achilles and Hector, so long delayed, is the dramatic climax of the epic.

Clad in his divine armor, Achilles re-enters the war to avenge Patroclus' death. He kills every Trojan in his path. During Achilles' combat with Hector's half-brother Agenor, Apollo assumes Agenor's shape and diverts Achilles from Troy, allowing the Trojan troops to take refuge in the city. Priam and Hecuba try unsuccessfully to convince Hector to stay within the walls, safe from Achilles.

So they wept, the two of them crying out
to their dear son, both pleading time and again
but they could not shake the fixed resolve of Hector.
No, he waited Achilles, coming on, gigantic in power.
As a snake in the hills, guarding his hole, awaits a man—
bloated with poison, deadly hatred seething inside him,
glances flashing fire as he coils round his lair . . .
so Hector, nursing his quenchless fury, gave no ground,
leaning his burnished shield against a jutting wall,
but harried still, he probed his own brave heart:
"No way out. If I slip inside the gates and walls,
Polydamas[1] will be first to heap disgrace on me—

Literary Analysis
Imagery What emotions does the image in these lines convey?

1. **Polydamas** (pə lid′ ə məs) Trojan commander who frequently opposed Hector's recklessness.

Differentiated Instruction

Solutions for All Learners

Accessibility at a Glance

	from the Iliad, *from* Book 22 The Death of Hector	*from the* Iliad, *from* Book 24 Achilles and Priam
Context	Achilles confronts Hector	Priam meets with Achilles
Language	Syntax: Long sentences with Homeric epic similes	Syntax: Long sentences with Homeric epic similes
Concept Level	Accessible (Pointlessness of vengeful cruelty)	Accessible (Virtue of compassion and mercy)
Literary Merit	Classic Homeric epic	Classic Homeric epic
Lexile	NP	NP
Overall Rating	Challenging	Challenging

TEACH

Facilitate Understanding

Have students think about other stories they have encountered in which a human figure meets a superhuman one. How often does the little person win, and in what kind of genre? In folk tales, science fiction, romance epics, and many other genres, the underdog, because of his or her very humanity, may vanquish the troll, the bully, or the "system." Readers generally root for the sympathetic underdog and are saddened if he or she is defeated—as often happens in "real life." Invite students to suggest and discuss examples, such as David vs. Goliath.

1 About the Selection

Tell students that in Book 22, as in Book 6, Hector is presented as very human in contrast to Achilles. In the books just prior to Book 22, Achilles has been characterized as a terrifying natural force—fighting gods, glutting the river with corpses, and destroying all in front of him like uncontrolled fire.

2 Literary Analysis

Imagery

- Call on a volunteer to read aloud the epic simile in lines 5–8.
- Make sure students understand that the comparison equates the snake with Hector.
- Have students note charged words in the passage, such as "guarding his hole," "bloated with poison, deadly hatred seething inside him," and "glances flashing fire."
- Then, **ask** students the Literary Analysis question: What emotions does the image in these lines convey?
  Possible response: The simile suggests hatred and fury. Just as the snake defends its lair against the intruder, Hector prepares to defend Troy at any cost, including his own death.

❸ Reading Strategy

Picture the Action

- Call on a volunteer to read lines 25–37 aloud.
- As students picture the hypothetical meeting between Hector and Achilles, **ask** them whether they think Hector's alternative of a peace agreement is realistic, given the Trojan leader's current situation and Achilles' grim determination to avenge Patroclus' death at the hands of Hector.
  Possible response: Considering Achilles' quest for vengeance, the offer to return Helen, as well as to surrender all the wealth Troy holds, will probably mean little to Achilles. Hector recognizes the futility of this alternative when he forecasts Achilles' probable reaction in lines 40–43.

he was the one who urged me to lead our Trojans
back to Ilium just last night, the disastrous night
Achilles rose in arms like a god. But did I give way?
Not at all. And how much better it would have been!
Now my army's ruined, thanks to my own reckless pride,
I would die of shame to face the men of Troy
and the Trojan women trailing their long robes . . .
Someone less of a man than I will say, 'Our Hector—
staking all on his own strength, he destroyed his army!'
So they will mutter. So now, better by far for me
to stand up to Achilles, kill him, come home alive
or die at his hands in glory out before the walls.
But wait—what if I put down my studded shield
and heavy helmet, prop my spear on the rampart
and go forth, just as I am, to meet Achilles,
noble Prince Achilles . . .
why, I could promise to give back Helen, yes,
and all her treasures with her, all those riches
Paris once hauled home to Troy in the hollow ships—
and they were the cause of all our endless fighting—
Yes, yes, return it all to the sons of Atreus now
to haul away, and then, at the same time, divide
the rest with all the Argives, all the city holds,
and then I'd take an oath for the Trojan royal council
that we will hide nothing! Share and share alike the hoards
our handsome citadel stores within its depths and—
Why debate, my friend? Why thrash things out?
I must not go and implore him. He'll show no mercy,
no respect for me, my rights—he'll cut me down
straight off—stripped of defenses like a woman
once I have loosed the armor off my body.
No way to parley with that man—not now—
not from behind some oak or rock to whisper,
like a boy and a young girl, lovers' secrets
a boy and girl might whisper to each other . . .
Better to clash in battle, now, at once—
see which fighter Zeus awards the glory!"
So he wavered,
waiting there, but Achilles was closing on him now
like the god of war, the fighter's helmet flashing,
over his right shoulder shaking the Pelian[2] ash spear,
that terror, and the bronze around his body flared
like a raging fire or the rising, blazing sun.
Hector looked up, saw him, started to tremble,
nerve gone, he could hold his ground no longer,

Vocabulary Builder
implore (im plôr′) *v.* beg

2. **Pelian** (pēl′ ē ən) of Achilles' spear, which was made on Pelion, a mountain in Magnesia.

Enrichment

The Real Trojan War

For years, scholars were skeptical about the existence of an actual city of Troy. Then, the German archaeologist Heinrich Schliemann (1822–1890) discovered the ruins of four cities, one on top of the other, which were indeed Troy, also known as Ilion. The city was located on a mound known as Hissarlik, located in modern-day Asian Turkey. Eventually, Troy was established as a city whose culture dated back to the Bronze Age (3500 B.C.). Scholars now believe that the events in Homer's epic reflect an actual war that took place about 1200 B.C., over control of trade in the Dardanelles, a long, narrow body of water known in ancient times as the Hellespont, which links the Sea of Marmara to the Mediterranean Sea. Schliemann also engaged in excavations at Mycenae, Ithaca (home of the Homeric hero Odysseus), and Tiryns. Students might enjoy learning more about Schliemann's life and his discoveries concerning the true story behind Homer's epic.

he left the gates behind and away he fled in fear—
and Achilles went for him, fast, sure of his speed
as the wild mountain hawk, the quickest thing on wings,
launching smoothly, swooping down on a cringing dove
and the dove flits out from under, the hawk screaming
over the quarry, plunging over and over, his fury
driving him down to beak and tear his kill—
so Achilles flew at him, breakneck on in fury
with Hector fleeing along the walls of Troy,
fast as his legs would go. On and on they raced,
passing the lookout point, passing the wild fig tree
tossed by the wind, always out from under the ramparts
down the wagon trail they careered until they reached
the clear running springs where whirling Scamander
rises up from its double wellsprings bubbling strong—
and one runs hot and the steam goes up around it,
drifting thick as if fire burned at its core
but the other even in summer gushes cold
as hail or freezing snow or water chilled to ice . . .
And here, close to the springs, lie washing-pools
scooped out in the hollow rocks and broad and smooth
where the wives of Troy and all their lovely daughters
would wash their glistening robes in the old days,
the days of peace before the sons of Achaea came . . .
Past these they raced, one escaping, one in pursuit
and the one who fled was great but the one pursuing
greater, even greater—their pace mounting in speed
since both men strove, not for a sacrificial beast
or oxhide trophy, prizes runners fight for, no,
they raced for the life of Hector breaker of horses.
Like powerful stallions sweeping round the post for trophies,
galloping full stretch with some fine prize at stake,
a tripod, say, or woman offered up at funeral games
for some brave hero fallen—so the two of them
whirled three times around the city of Priam,
sprinting at top speed while all the gods gazed down,
and the father of men and gods broke forth among them now:
"Unbearable—a man I love, hunted round his own city walls
and right before my eyes. My heart grieves for Hector.
Hector who burned so many oxen in my honor, rich cuts,
now on the rugged crests of Ida,[3] now on Ilium's heights.
But now, look, brilliant Achilles courses him round
the city of Priam in all his savage, lethal speed.
Come, you immortals, think this through. Decide.
Either we pluck the man from death and save his life

3. **Ida** (īd´ ə) central mountain and range of Troad; favored seat of Zeus.

Literary Analysis
Imagery and Epic Simile What does this epic simile suggest about the character of Achilles?

Reading Strategy
Picture the Action In what way does the image of Trojan women at the washing-pools enrich the battle scene?

6 **Reading Check**
Why does Hector rule out the idea of approaching Achilles peacefully?

4 Literary Analysis

Imagery and Epic Simile

- Have students reread the simile in lines 59–64 carefully.
- Remind students that whereas a simple simile contains a single, distinct image, an epic simile typically presents a longer, more elaborate scene that may contain multiple images. In lines 59–64, have students **identify** the series of images in the comparison.
  Answer: The series includes the swooping hawk, the flitting dove that tries to escape, and the final capture of the prey.
- Make sure students recognize that, in context, the hawk is equated with Achilles, whereas the dove is equated with Hector.
- Then, **ask** students the Literary Analysis question: What does this epic simile suggest about the character of Achilles?
  Possible response: The simile suggests that Achilles is relentless in his fury and determination.
- Encourage students to examine the vivid verbs in the comparison: for example, *swooping, cringing, screaming, plunging,* and *driving.* **Ask** students to describe the connotations of such language.
  Possible response: The words suggest power, violent attack, or emotional reactions to such an attack.

5 Reading Strategy

Picture the Action

- Have students reread the vivid description of the washing-pools in lines 76–80.
- Make sure students recognize that the washing-pools were used in peacetime, before the war became an everyday reality for the Trojans.
- **Ask** students the Reading Strategy question: In what way does the image of Trojan women at the washing-pools enrich the battle scene?
  Answer: The description of a tranquil, peacetime scene contrasts with the chaos and grief of war and with the urgency of this particular battle scene.

6 Reading Check

Answer: Hector realizes that Achilles will show him no mercy.

Differentiated Instruction

Solutions for All Learners

Support for Less Proficient Students
To help students picture the action, read aloud lines 49–57. Then help students create a list of details that describe Hector, such as *so he wavered, waiting there, looked up, saw him, started to tremble, left the gates behind and away he fled.* Encourage students to look for action verbs and list such details of the characters' actions as they continue to read.

Support for English Learners
Picturing the action may be challenging for students. To assist them, use **Reading Strategy,** p. 28 in ***Unit 4 Resources.*** Explain that this will help them visualize what is happening. Then encourage them to work with a partner and list details of the action in the race between Achilles and Hector.

Strategy for Advanced Readers
To challenge students, suggest that they move beyond picturing only the action. Encourage them to picture the emotional responses of the characters. What might their facial expressions and body language reveal? Have students write a paragraph or two summarizing how they visualize specific scenes in the narrative.

❼ Humanities

Head of Bronze Statue of Apollo from Pompeii (first century A.D.)

Working in a variety of media, including bronze, clay, marble, and precious metals, Roman sculptors blended Etruscan and Greek elements in order to create a distinctive style. As with this statue of the god Apollo, sculptures generally portrayed gods or important military or political leaders in full figure.

Use the following questions for discussion.

- Why do you think Apollo is portrayed with his head slightly bent downward?
  Possible response: The god looks down benevolently from the sky on mortals, wishing to protect or aid them.
- What qualities of Apollo does the sculpture suggest or emphasize?
  Possible response: The sculpture suggests or emphasizes Apollo's strength, power, and beauty.

❽ Critical Viewing

Answer: In the sculpture, Apollo is presented as meditative and serene. As he is presented in the *Iliad,* however, Apollo can be aggressive and hostile: witness, for example, his instigation of the plague on the Greeks in Book 1.

❾ Literary Analysis

Imagery and Epic Simile

- Have students read lines 117–129 carefully and locate the part of the text that constitutes the epic simile (lines 118–122).
- Focus students' attention on the final words of the simile: *until he lands his kill* (line 122).
- **Ask** students in what way this epic simile foreshadows the outcome of the battle between the two warriors.
  Answer: By mentioning that the hound (Achilles) manages to kill the fawn (Hector), the simile foreshadows Hector's death.

or strike him down at last, here at Achilles' hands—
for all his fighting heart."
                    But immortal Athena,
her gray eyes wide, protested strongly: "Father!
Lord of the lightning, king of the black cloud,
what are you saying? A man, a mere mortal,
his doom sealed long ago? You'd set him free
from all the pains of death?
                    Do as you please—
but none of the deathless gods will ever praise you."

And Zeus who marshals the thunderheads replied,
"Courage, Athena, third-born of the gods, dear child.
Nothing I said was meant in earnest, trust me,
I mean you all the good will in the world. Go.
Do as your own impulse bids you. Hold back no more."

So he launched Athena already poised for action—
down the goddess swept from Olympus' craggy peaks.

And swift Achilles kept on coursing Hector, nonstop
as a hound in the mountains starts a fawn from its lair,
hunting him down the gorges, down the narrow glens
and the fawn goes to ground, hiding deep in brush
but the hound comes racing fast, nosing him out
until he lands his kill. So Hector could never throw
Achilles off his trail, the swift racer Achilles—
time and again he'd make a dash for the Dardan Gates,
trying to rush beneath the rock-built ramparts, hoping
men on the heights might save him, somehow, raining spears
but time and again Achilles would intercept him quickly,
heading him off, forcing him out across the plain
and always sprinting along the city side himself—
endless as in a dream . . .
when a man can't catch another fleeing on ahead
and he can never escape nor his rival overtake him—
so the one could never run the other down in his speed
nor the other spring away. And how could Hector have fled
the fates of death so long? How unless one last time,
one final time Apollo had swept in close beside him,
driving strength in his legs and knees to race the wind?
And brilliant Achilles shook his head at the armies,
never letting them hurl their sharp spears at Hector—
someone might snatch the glory, Achilles come in second.
But once they reached the springs for the fourth time,
then Father Zeus held out his sacred golden scales:

in them he placed two fates of death that lays men low—

❽ ▲ **Critical Viewing**
How does this sculpture of Apollo compare with the way the god is presented in the *Iliad*? **[Compare and Contrast]**

Vocabulary Builder
marshals (mär′ shəlz) *v.* arranges in order; commands

Enrichment

The Rage of Achilles

In the preceding books of the epic, Achilles' superhuman (or subhuman) fury after the death of Patroclus has led to the threat of chaos. The gods have been fighting bitterly among themselves on the battlefield; the river Scamander, glutted with corpses, has risen up in fury to fight Achilles' fire with water; Hades, lord of the underworld, has shrieked in terror. Achilles has seen war in all its horror, personified. The Trojans have been portrayed as helpless in the face of Achilles' ferocity.

Now, in Book 22, Zeus' threat of sparing Hector may plunge the universe into disorder. Students may wish to research the role of Zeus in ancient Greek society.

one for Achilles, one for Hector breaker of horses—
and gripping the beam mid-haft the Father raised it high
and down went Hector's day of doom, dragging him down
to the strong House of Death—and god Apollo left him.
Athena rushed to Achilles, her bright eyes gleaming,
standing shoulder-to-shoulder, winging orders now:
"At last our hopes run high, my brilliant Achilles—
Father Zeus must love you—
we'll sweep great glory back to Achaea's fleet,
we'll kill this Hector, mad as he is for battle!
No way for him to escape us now, no longer—
not even if Phoebus the distant deadly Archer
goes through torments, pleading for Hector's life,
groveling over and over before our storming Father Zeus.
But you, you hold your ground and catch your breath
while I run Hector down and persuade the man
to fight you face-to-face."
So Athena commanded
and he obeyed, rejoicing at heart—Achilles stopped,
leaning against his ashen spearshaft barbed in bronze.
And Athena left him there, caught up with Hector at once,
and taking the build and vibrant voice of Deiphobus[4]
stood shoulder-to-shoulder with him, winging orders:
"Dear brother, how brutally swift Achilles hunts you—
coursing you round the city of Priam in all his lethal speed!
Come, let us stand our ground together—beat him back."

"Deiphobus!"—Hector, his helmet flashing, called out to her—
"dearest of all my brothers, all these warring years,
of all the sons that Priam and Hecuba produced!
Now I'm determined to praise you all the more,
you who dared—seeing me in these straits—
to venture out from the walls, all for *my* sake,
while the others stay inside and cling to safety."

The goddess answered quickly, her eyes blazing,
"True, dear brother—how your father and mother both
implored me, time and again, clutching my knees,
and the comrades round me begging me to stay!
Such was the fear that broke them, man for man,
but the heart within me broke with grief for you.
Now headlong on and fight! No letup, no lance spared!
So now, now we'll *see* if Achilles kills us both
and hauls our bloody armor back to the beaked ships
or *he* goes down in pain beneath your spear."

4. **Deiphobus** (dē ĭ′ fə bəs) son of Priam; powerful Trojan warrior.

Reading Strategy
Picture the Action What does the image of Zeus with his scales suggest about the role of the gods in the lives of mortals?

Reading Check
In whose form does Athena appear to Hector?

10 Reading Strategy
Picture the Action

- Have students reread lines 142–147 carefully.
- Ask students what associations they have with the "golden scales." Elicit from them that scales are a symbol for justice or fate.
- Make sure students recognize that the sinking of Hector's "day of doom" is a metaphor for his approaching death.
- **Ask** the Reading Strategy question: What does the image of Zeus with his scales suggest about the role of the gods in the lives of mortals?
  Possible response: The image implies that, in the end, the gods are responsible for the fate of mortals, judging who will die and who will triumph in battle.

11 Reading Strategy
Picture the Action

- Have students reread lines 163–170.
- **Ask** students what emotions Hector might feel at the "appearance" of Deiphobus.
  Possible response: Hector might feel amazement, relief, or sudden optimism.
- **Ask** students to describe the contrast between Hector's likely emotions and their own as they read the passage.
  Possible response: The reader, who knows that Hector is the victim of an illusion, may experience pity or fear.

12 Reading Check

Answer: Athena appears in the form of Deiphobus, Hector's brother.

Differentiated Instruction
Solutions for All Learners

Support for Special Needs Students
Direct students' attention to the epic simile in lines 117–122. Then, make sure that students recognize who is who in the comparison: the "fawn" is Hector, and the "hound" is Achilles. Invite students to give a choral reading of the lines.

Strategy for Gifted/Talented Students
Have students think about how the simile in lines 117–122 works. The simile vividly paints a scene presumably familiar to the original audience. Yet even while the determination of the hound in the simile mirrors Achilles' tenacity, the image of a startled fawn introduces a surprising contrast with the figure of Hector, a mighty warrior. Have students discuss ways in which the simile illuminates the action and, at the same time, competes with it for the reader's attention.

Literary Analysis

Imagery

- Invite students to share their associations with the image of a flashing helmet.
- Remind students of the scene in Book 6 in which Hector's helmet frightened the warrior's son, Astyanax.
- Then, **ask** students the Literary Analysis question: What theme is reinforced by the recurring image of a helmet flashing?
  Answer: The recurring image suggests the fury of warfare.

Athena luring him on with all her immortal cunning—
and now, at last, as the two came closing for the kill
it was tall Hector, helmet flashing, who led off:
"No more running from you in fear, Achilles!
Not as before. Three times I fled around
the great city of Priam—I lacked courage then
to stand your onslaught. Now my spirit stirs me
to meet you face-to-face. Now kill or be killed!
Come, we'll swear to the gods, the highest witnesses—
the gods will oversee our binding pacts. I swear
I will never mutilate you—merciless as you are—
if Zeus allows me to last it out and tear your life away.
But once I've stripped your glorious armor, Achilles,
I will give your body back to your loyal comrades.
Swear you'll do the same."
A swift dark glance
and the headstrong runner answered, "Hector, stop!
You unforgivable, you . . . don't talk to me of pacts.
There are no binding oaths between men and lions—
wolves and lambs can enjoy no meeting of the minds—
they are all bent on hating each other to the death.
So with you and me. No love between us. No truce
till one or the other falls and gluts with blood
Ares who hacks at men behind his rawhide shield.
Come, call up whatever courage you can muster.
Life or death—now prove yourself a spearman,
a daring man of war! No more escape for you—
Athena will kill you with my spear in just a moment.
Now you'll pay at a stroke for all my comrades' grief,
all you killed in the fury of your spear!"
With that,
shaft poised, he hurled and his spear's long shadow flew
but seeing it coming glorious Hector ducked away,
crouching down, watching the bronze tip fly past
and stab the earth—but Athena snatched it up
and passed it back to Achilles
and Hector the gallant captain never saw her.
He sounded out a challenge to Peleus' princely son:
"You missed, look—the great godlike Achilles!
So you knew nothing at all from Zeus about my death—
and yet how sure you were! All bluff, cunning with words,
that's all you are—trying to make me fear you,
lose my nerve, forget my fighting strength.

Well, you'll never plant your lance in my back
as I flee *you* in fear—plunge it through my chest
as I come charging in, if a god gives you the chance!
But now it's for you to dodge *my* brazen spear—
I wish you'd bury it in your body to the hilt.

Literary Analysis
Imagery What theme is reinforced by the recurring image of a helmet flashing?

Enrichment

Customs in Ancient Greek Warfare

As warfare is presented in the *Iliad,* there are several options in dealing with a dead opponent. The winner might strip the armor of the vanquished warrior and then return the body. Hector did strip Patroclus' armor but did not wish to return the corpse. The Greeks, however, were able to retrieve Patroclus' body by fighting. In lines 195–200, Hector, in effect, is asking Achilles to follow a more merciful course than Hector himself followed with Patroclus.

How much lighter the war would be for Trojans then
if you, their greatest scourge, were dead and gone!"

Shaft poised, he hurled and his spear's long shadow flew
and it struck Achilles' shield—a dead-center hit—
but off and away it glanced and Hector seethed,
his hurtling spear, his whole arm's power poured
in a wasted shot. He stood there, cast down . . .
he had no spear in reserve. So Hector shouted out
to Deiphobus bearing his white shield—with a ringing
shout he called for a heavy lance—
but the man was nowhere near him,
vanished—
yes and Hector knew the truth in his heart
and the fighter cried aloud, "My time has come!
At last the gods have called me down to death.
I thought he was at my side, the hero Deiphobus—
he's safe inside the walls, Athena's tricked me blind.
And now death, grim death is looming up beside me,
no longer far away. No way to escape it now. This,
this was their pleasure after all, sealed long ago—
Zeus and the son of Zeus, the distant deadly Archer—
though often before now they rushed to my defense.
So now I meet my doom. Well let me die—
but not without struggle, not without glory, no,
in some great clash of arms that even men to come
will hear of down the years!"
And on that resolve
he drew the whetted sword that hung at his side,
tempered, massive, and gathering all his force
he swooped like a soaring eagle
launching down from the dark clouds to earth
to snatch some helpless lamb or trembling hare.
So Hector swooped now, swinging his whetted sword
and Achilles charged too, bursting with rage, barbaric,
guarding his chest with the well-wrought blazoned shield,
head tossing his gleaming helmet, four horns strong
and the golden plumes shook that the god of fire
drove in bristling thick along its ridge.
Bright as that star amid the stars in the night sky,
star of the evening, brightest star that rides the heavens,
so fire flared from the sharp point of the spear Achilles
brandished high in his right hand, bent on Hector's death,
scanning his splendid body—where to pierce it best?
The rest of his flesh seemed all encased in armor,
burnished, brazen—*Achilles'* armor that Hector stripped

Themes in World Masterpieces

16 ***Homer and the Epic Tradition***

For centuries, Homer's *Iliad* and *Odyssey* had a huge influence on Greek culture and education. As children, the Greeks memorized the epics, and Homer's language shaped their words and the ways they thought.

In later ages, when epics were written rather than recited, the *Iliad* and *Odyssey* still served as models. Thus, the Roman poet Virgil loosely modeled the first six books of his *Aeneid* on the *Odyssey* and the last six books on the *Iliad*. Virgil retained many of the epic conventions of oral poetry, including an invocation of the Muse, lengthy speeches, and Homeric similes. Virgil fashioned a uniquely Roman national epic while upholding the Homeric tradition.

During the Middle Ages, Homer and Virgil served as inspiration for Dante Alighieri in the *Divine Comedy*. Homer also profoundly influenced the English epic tradition, notably in John Milton's *Paradise Lost* and in Alexander Pope's satirical mock-epic poems, *The Rape of the Lock* and *The Dunciad*.

Connect to the Literature

What characteristics of the *Iliad* do you think have made it so influential for centuries?

Vocabulary Builder

whetted (wet′ id) *adj.* sharpened

brandished (bran′ disht) *v.* waved or shook in a threatening manner

Reading Check

Whom does Athena support in the battle between Achilles and Hector?

Differentiated Instruction Solutions for All Learners

Strategy for Less Proficient Readers

Ask students to create a sequence chart to illustrate how the goddess Athena helps Achilles. Students should recognize that Athena impersonates Hector's brother Deiphobus, thus giving the Trojan Warrior false hope. They should also mention the action at lines 215–220, where Athena returns Achilles' spear and deserts Hector.

Strategy for Advanced Readers

Have students discuss Athena's helping Achilles. Does her intervention seem unfair? Could her intervention be another way of visualizing or expressing the way circumstances sometimes go wrong for individuals, as they do for Hector in his conflict with Achilles? Have students create a two-column chart citing both positive and negative reactions to this scene.

14 Critical Thinking

Compare and Contrast

- Have students review Hector's two speeches in lines 222–233 and 243–254.
- **Ask** students to compare and contrast these speeches with respect to mood and overall effect.
  Answer: The first speech is confident and aggressive; it even contains notes of mockery. The second speech is resigned and might be described as fatalistic.

15 Critical Thinking

Speculate

- Have students reread lines 261–266 carefully.
- **Ask** students to speculate on why at this decisive moment of the narrative Homer refers to "the god of fire" in line 265.
  Possible response: The reference reminds us that Achilles' new armor was fashioned by the god, Hephaestus. Because he is protected by armor made by the immortals, Achilles seems invulnerable, at least for the moment. Homer thus foreshadows that the encounter will be fatal for Hector.

16 Themes in World Literature

Homer and the Epic Tradition

Tell students that Virgil's hero Aeneas plays a relatively minor part in the *Iliad*. A Trojan warrior, Virgil meets Achilles in combat in Book 20 but is saved by divine intervention. After the fall of Troy, he escapes from the city and wanders the Mediterranean until he lands in Italy, where he founds the city of Rome. Virgil's epic the *Aeneid* thus links the history of Rome with Homer's Trojan War.

Connect to the Literature Ask students to suggest three characteristics of the *Iliad* that account for its influence through the centuries.

Possible response: Three characteristics are the Homeric similes that enhance the action; the intervention of the gods; and the universal themes, such as the cost of rage, honor and merit versus greed and arrogance, and the destruction of war.

17 Reading Check

Answer: Athena supports Achilles.

18 Critical Thinking

Infer

- Have students read the bracketed passage.
- **Ask** students what this speech of Achilles reveals about his character.
  Possible response: Achilles is preoccupied not only with avenging Patroclus but also with triumphing over Hector and mocking Hector in his defeat. Achilles is fiercely loyal but also arrogant and somewhat cruel.

19 Background

Greek Customs

Burial was extremely important to the Greeks. Achilles' threat to leave Hector's body for the dogs and the vultures is the greatest dishonor that a dying man could face.

20 Reading Strategy

Picture the Action

- Call on a volunteer to read Achilles' speech aloud (lines 299–310).
- **Ask** students to identify examples of hyperbole, or exaggeration for effect, in the speech.
  Answer: Examples are the image of Achilles eating raw, hacked flesh; the ransom increased twenty-fold; and the delivery of Hector's weight in gold.
- **Direct** students to respond to the Reading Strategy question: In what way does the image presented in these lines illustrate the extent of Achilles' rage?
  Answer: The imagery shows that Achilles' rage is superhuman and relentless.

from strong Patroclus when he killed him—true,
but one spot lay exposed,
where collarbones lift the neckbone off the shoulders,
the open throat, where the end of life comes quickest—*there*
as Hector charged in fury brilliant Achilles drove his spear
and the point went stabbing clean through the tender neck
but the heavy bronze weapon failed to slash the windpipe—
Hector could still gasp out some words, some last reply . . .
he crashed in the dust—
godlike Achilles gloried over him:
"Hector—surely you thought when you stripped Patroclus' armor
that you, you would be safe! Never a fear of me—
[18] far from the fighting as I was—you fool!
Left behind there, down by the beaked ships
his great avenger waited, a greater man by far—
[19] that man was I, and I smashed your strength! And you—
the dogs and birds will maul you, shame your corpse
while Achaeans bury my dear friend in glory!"

Struggling for breath, Hector, his helmet flashing,
said, "I beg you, beg you by your life, your parents—
don't let the dogs devour me by the Argive ships!
Wait, take the princely ransom of bronze and gold,
the gifts my father and noble mother will give you—
but give my body to friends to carry home again,
so Trojan men and Trojan women can do me honor
with fitting rites of fire once I am dead."

Staring grimly, the proud runner Achilles answered,
"Beg no more, you fawning dog—begging me by my parents!
Would to god my rage, my fury would drive me now
to hack your flesh away and eat you raw—
such agonies you have caused me! Ransom?
No man alive could keep the dog-packs off you,
[20] not if they haul in ten, twenty times that ransom
and pile it here before me and promise fortunes more—
no, not even if Dardan Priam should offer to weigh out
your bulk in gold! Not even then will your noble mother
lay you on your deathbed, mourn the son she bore . . .
The dogs and birds will rend you—blood and bone!"

At the point of death, Hector, his helmet flashing,
said, "I know you well—I see my fate before me.
Never a chance that I could win you over . . .
Iron inside your chest, that heart of yours.
But now beware, or my curse will draw god's wrath
upon your head, that day when Paris and lord Apollo—
for all your fighting heart—destroy you at the Scaean Gates!"

Reading Strategy
Picture the Action In what way does the image presented in these lines illustrate the extent of Achilles' rage?

Enrichment

Homeric Imagery

The evening star Hesperus, prominent in the simile in lines 267–270, is the brightest in the sky. At the same time, Hesperus is associated with the west, where the sun sets, and thus with Hades and death. Thus, on one level, the simile is appropriate in that it suggestively evokes the death of Hector. However, Hector is wearing Achilles' old armor, which was given to Peleus and then to Achilles, who lent it to Patroclus. Achilles eyes the armor for a weak spot through which to slay Hector. Although Achilles sees nothing in common between himself and Hector, the evening star simile may be suggesting the two warriors' common humanity.

By slaying Hector, Achilles comes one step closer to fulfilling his own destiny, which is to die at Troy. Hector himself confirms this note of foreshadowing in his dying words to his opponent in lines 315–317.

Students may wish to research more information about Greek views of Hades and the underworld.

Death cut him short. The end closed in around him.
Flying free of his limbs
his soul went winging down to the House of Death,
wailing his fate, leaving his manhood far behind,
his young and supple strength. But brilliant Achilles
taunted Hector's body, dead as he was, "Die, die!
For my own death, I'll meet it freely—whenever Zeus
and the other deathless gods would like to bring it on!"

With that he wrenched his bronze spear from the corpse,
laid it aside and ripped the bloody armor off the back.
And the other sons of Achaea, running up around him,
crowded closer, all of them gazing wonder-struck
at the build and marvelous, lithe beauty of Hector.
And not a man came forward who did not stab his body,
glancing toward a comrade, laughing: "Ah, look here—
how much softer he is to handle now, this Hector,
than when he gutted our ships with roaring fire!" ㉑

Standing over him, so they'd gloat and stab his body.
But once he had stripped the corpse the proud runner Achilles ㉒
took his stand in the midst of all the Argive troops
and urged them on with a flight of winging orders:
"Friends—lords of the Argives, O my captains!

Reading Check

What final request does Hector make before he dies?

Achilles defeating Hector, Peter Paul Rubens, Musée des Beaux-Arts, Giraudon

㉓

◀ **Critical Viewing** ㉔

Do you think this depiction of Hector's death is consistent with Homer's description of it? Why or why not? **[Evaluate]**

Differentiated Instruction Solutions for All Learners

Strategy for Less Proficient Readers

Have students use their own words to paraphrase Hector's dying speech in lines 312–317. Make sure that students recognize the two major elements of this passage: Hector's recognition of the inevitability of his fate and his prediction about Achilles' fate.

Strategy for English Learners

The syntax of Hector's speech in lines 312–317 may be challenging. At the end of each line, students should write down the line's meaning. Encourage them to supplement missing words: for example, in line 313, "[There was] never a chance that I could win you over." Also, help students recognize inverted word order, as in line 314.

Enrichment for Advanced Readers

Have students summarize Hector's speech in lines 312–317. Then, have them clarify Hector's foreshadowing of Achilles' fate by researching what eventually happens to Achilles by consulting classical dictionaries and encyclopedias. Have them report their findings to the class.

㉑ Critical Thinking

Infer

- Have students read lines 331–335.
- **Ask** students to explain what the treatment of Hector's corpse and the taunts uttered over him suggest about the Trojan hero's stature.
  Possible response: The actions and words of the Greeks suggest that Hector was a mighty champion.

㉒ Reading Check

Answer: Hector begs Achilles to allow his parents and friends to ransom his body so that they can bring it back to Troy for burial.

㉓ Humanities

Achilles Defeating Hector,
by Peter Paul Rubens

Throughout his career, Rubens (1577–1640) was fascinated with historical and classical subjects. The painting *Achilles Defeating Hector* pays homage to the works of Homer. The massive figures, locked in fatal combat, are painted with vigor and passion. The most striking quality of this work is the light that radiates throughout. The architectural frame of columns and the laurels enhance the classical theme.

Use the following questions for discussion.

- What is your emotional response to this painting?
  Possible response: Reactions might include awe, anxiety, or horror.
- Do the colors of the painting affect the emotional tone? Explain.
  Possible response: Yes; the reds, blacks, and browns heighten the tone of violence and fatality.

㉔ Critical Viewing

Possible response: The violence conveyed in the painting is consistent with Homer's narrative. In addition, Rubens depicts the goddess Athena as she helps Achilles slay his opponent.

25 Humanities

Achilles Deciding to Resume Fighting Upon the Death of Patroclus, by Dirck van Baburen

A member of the seventeenth-century Dutch school, van Baburen here presents a vivid interpretation of Homer's narrative in Book 18 of the *Iliad.* The Greeks, through hard fighting, have recovered Patroclus' body after Patroclus was slain by Hector. Hector's stripping of the armor (which Achilles had lent his friend) is reflected in the portrayal of the corpse. Achilles, pictured at the left, reinforces his solemn declaration to seek vengeance.

Use the following questions for discussion.

- What details in this painting indicate Achilles' determination?
  Possible response: Achilles' gesture to the heavens, upward glance, and clenched fist indicate the hero's resolve.
- What emotions does this painting evoke?
  Possible response: On the one hand, the pleading, sorrowful expressions of the men and the frail, vulnerable appearance of the corpse of Patroclus evoke feelings of sadness and resignation. On the other hand, the firm stance of Achilles evokes feelings of confidence and vindication.

26 Critical Viewing

Possible response: The other figures in the painting all appear to be listening or appealing to the figure on the left. Because this figure commands the attention of the other men, and because his posture is one of determination, the viewer can assume that this figure is Achilles.

Now that the gods have let me kill this man
who caused us agonies, loss on crushing loss—
more than the rest of all their men combined—
come, let us ring their walls in armor, test them,
see what recourse the Trojans still may have in mind.
Will they abandon the city heights with this man fallen?
Or brace for a last, dying stand though Hector's gone?
But wait—what am I saying? Why this deep debate?
Down by the ships a body lies unwept, unburied—
Patroclus . . . I will never forget him,
not as long as I'm still among the living
and my springing knees will lift and drive me on.
Though the dead forget their dead in the House of Death,
I will remember, even there, my dear companion.
Now,
come, you sons of Achaea, raise a song of triumph!
Down to the ships we march and bear this corpse on high—
we have won ourselves great glory. We have brought
magnificent Hector down, that man the Trojans
glorified in their city like a god!"

26 ▼ Critical Viewing This painting depicts Achilles and the Greeks with the body of Patroclus. What details indicate the figure of Achilles? **[Analyze]**

25

Enrichment

The Funeral Games of Patroclus

The funeral rites for the still unburied Patroclus take place in Book 23 of the *Iliad.* After the ritual burning of the corpse and the sacrifice of twelve youthful Trojan captives, Achilles presides over a series of funeral games: contests in chariot racing, boxing, wrestling, running, spear duels, weight throwing, archery, and javelin casting. This episode gives Homer the chance to bring all the major Greek heroes on stage once again before the close of the epic. Each event illustrates one or more of the main character traits of a hero. For example, the clever Odysseus manages to defeat the mighty Ajax in wrestling through the use of a clever trick, while wise Nestor coaches his son with sage advice about how to win the chariot race (advice that is, in the end, ignored).

Students may wish to read Book 23 of the *Iliad* in its entirety in order to learn more about the funeral games for Patroclus and the gradual diminution of Achilles' grief.

So he triumphed
and now he was bent on outrage, on shaming noble Hector.
Piercing the tendons, ankle to heel behind both feet,
he knotted straps of rawhide through them both,
lashed them to his chariot, left the head to drag
and mounting the car, hoisting the famous arms aboard,
he whipped his team to a run and breakneck on they flew,
holding nothing back. And a thick cloud of dust rose up
from the man they dragged, his dark hair swirling round
that head so handsome once, all tumbled low in the dust—
since Zeus had given him over to his enemies now
to be defiled in the land of his own fathers.

So his whole head was dragged down in the dust.
(27) And now his mother began to tear her hair . . .
she flung her shining veil to the ground and raised
a high, shattering scream, looking down at her son.
(28) Pitifully his loving father groaned and round the king
his people cried with grief and wailing seized the city—
for all the world as if all Troy were torched and smoldering
down from the looming brows of the citadel to her roots.
Priam's people could hardly hold the old man back,
frantic, mad to go rushing out the Dardan Gates.
He begged them all, groveling in the filth,
crying out to them, calling each man by name,
"Let go, my friends! Much as you care for me,
let me hurry out of the city, make my way,
all on my own, to Achaea's waiting ships!
I must implore that terrible, violent man . . .
Perhaps—who knows?—he may respect my age,
may pity an old man. He has a father too,
as old as I am—Peleus sired him once,
Peleus reared him to be the scourge of Troy
but most of all to me—he made my life a hell.
So many sons he slaughtered, just coming into bloom . . .
but grieving for all the rest, one breaks my heart the most
and stabbing grief for him will take me down to Death—
my Hector—would to god he had perished in my arms!
Then his mother who bore him—oh so doomed,
she and I could glut ourselves with grief."

(30) So the voice of the king rang out in tears,
the citizens wailed in answer, and noble Hecuba
led the wives of Troy in a throbbing chant of sorrow:
"O my child—my desolation! How can I go on living?
What agonies must I suffer now, now *you* are dead and gone?

Literary Analysis
Imagery To which senses does the imagery in lines 371–373 appeal?

(29) 
Reading Check
What do Achilles and the Greeks do with the body of Hector?

(27) Literary Analysis

Imagery

- Have students read lines 371–373 aloud.
- Draw students' attention to key sensory words and phrases: "tear her hair"; "shining veil"; and "high, shattering scream."
- Then, **ask** students the Literary Analysis question: To which senses does the imagery in lines 371–373 appeal?
  Answer: The imagery appeals to the senses of touch, sight, and hearing.

(28) Critical Thinking

Connect

- Have students review lines 374–377.
- **Ask** students to explain how the actions described here suggest that Hector's death is closely linked to the fall of Troy itself.
  Answer: Priam groans and the people around him cry with grief. General wailing seizes the city, as if it were burning from top to bottom. The comparison used by Homer strongly suggests that the death of Hector will lead directly to the collapse of the city.

(29) Reading Check

Answer: They desecrate the body, stabbing it repeatedly and then dragging it through the dust.

Differentiated Instruction Solutions for All Learners

Strategy for Less Proficient Readers

Have students recall their reading of Book 6 of the epic, in which Homer clearly identified the death of Hector with the destruction of Troy itself (see pp. 375–376). Then, have students reread lines 376–377 on this page. Have students make a two-column chart to compare details from Book 6 with details from Book 22. Preview with students the fact that Book 24, the final book of the epic, will deal with the ransoming of Hector's body and with his funeral at Troy.

Strategy for Advanced Readers

Have students discuss the ways in which Homer makes Priam's grief seem unique and particular. What does Priam's lament convey about Hector's relationship with his father? How might Priam's speech foreshadow the action of Book 24, in which Priam ventures to Achilles' tent to entreat the Greek hero to ransom Hector's body? Have students address these issues in a paragraph or two or in a brief oral report.

30 Literary Analysis

Imagery

- Have students examine the phrase "rang out in tears" in context (lines 397 and 407).
- Draw students' attention to the dramatic contrast between the loud laments of the hero's parents and the fact that Andromache, Hector's wife, "had not heard a thing" (line 408).
- Have students examine line 422, in which Andromache hears the keening voice of Hector's mother, Hecuba.
- Then, **ask** students the first Literary Analysis question: What theme is reinforced by the recurring image of voices ringing out in tears?
  Answer: The imagery accentuates the grief and despair that the Trojans experience at the death of Hector.

31 Literary Analysis

Imagery

- Call on a volunteer to read lines 443–453 aloud.
- Draw students' attention to phrases such as "flung to the winds," "stunned to the point of death," "struggling for breath," and "burst out in grief."
- Then, **ask** students the second Literary Analysis question: What word pictures in this passage show the state of Andromache's emotions?
  Answer: Word pictures that show the desperate state of Andromache's emotions describe her treatment of her headdress and ornaments, her inner state, her difficulty in breathing, and her sudden speech of lamentation.

You were my pride throughout the city night and day—
a blessing to us all, the men and women of Troy:
throughout the city they saluted you like a god.
You, you were their greatest glory while you lived—
now death and fate have seized you, dragged you down!"

Her voice rang out in tears, but the wife of Hector
had not heard a thing. No messenger brought the truth
of how her husband made his stand outside the gates.
She was weaving at her loom, deep in the high halls,
30 working flowered braiding into a dark red folding robe.
And she called her well-kempt women through the house
to set a large three-legged cauldron over the fire
so Hector could have his steaming hot bath
when he came home from battle—poor woman,
she never dreamed how far he was from bathing,
struck down at Achilles' hands by blazing-eyed Athena.
But she heard the groans and wails of grief from the rampart now
and her body shook, her shuttle dropped to the ground,
she called out to her lovely waiting women, "Quickly—
two of you follow me—I must see what's happened.
That cry—that was Hector's honored mother I heard!
My heart's pounding, leaping up in my throat,
the knees beneath me paralyzed—Oh I know it . . .
something terrible's coming down on Priam's children.
Pray god the news will never reach my ears!
Yes but I dread it so—what if great Achilles
has cut my Hector off from the city, daring Hector,
and driven him out across the plain, and all alone?—
He may have put an end to that fatal headstrong pride
that always seized my Hector—never hanging back
with the main force of men, always charging ahead,
giving ground to no man in his fury!"
So she cried,
dashing out of the royal halls like a madwoman,
her heart racing hard, her women close behind her.
But once she reached the tower where soldiers massed
she stopped on the rampart, looked down and saw it all—
saw him dragged before the city, stallions galloping,
dragging Hector back to Achaea's beaked warships—
ruthless work. The world went black as night
before her eyes, she fainted, falling backward,
gasping away her life breath . . .
She flung to the winds her glittering headdress,
the cap and the coronet, braided band and veil,
31 all the regalia golden Aphrodite gave her once,
the day that Hector, helmet aflash in sunlight,
led her home to Troy from her father's house

Literary Analysis
Imagery What theme is reinforced by the recurring image of voices ringing out in tears?

Literary Analysis
Imagery What word pictures in this passage show the state of Andromache's emotions?

Enrichment

Irony, Suspense, and Symbol

In a comparatively rare comment, the poet goes out of his way to emphasize Andromache's ignorance ("poor woman"). In the succeeding passage (lines 418–433), irony gives way to suspense, as Andromache hears the wails and groans from the walls and experiences a terrifying premonition.

Homer combines formulaic elements to achieve subtle and particular effects. For example, lines 440–441 contain a standard formula for death. In this case, Andromache is not actually dead, but the shock and grief she experiences are strong enough to simulate death symbolically. As she falls (lines 443–448), she loses her bridal headgear (gifts of Aphrodite and the mark of her status as Hector's wife), just as a warrior might be stripped of the armor that identifies him and marks his status. The imagery in these lines concisely and symbolically portrays Andromache in the role of widow.

Students may wish to research the position of widows in ancient Greek society.

31

with countless wedding gifts to win her heart.
But crowding round her now her husband's sisters
and brothers' wives supported her in their midst,
and she, terrified, stunned to the point of death,
struggling for breath now and coming back to life,
burst out in grief among the Trojan women: "O Hector—
I am destroyed! Both born to the same fate after all!
You, you at Troy in the halls of King Priam—
I at Thebes, under the timberline of Placos,
Eetion's house . . . He raised me as a child,
that man of doom, his daughter just as doomed—
would to god he'd never fathered *me*!
Now you go down

32 **Reading Check**
How does Andromache react to the sight of Hector's dead body?

Andromache and Astyanax, 1789, Richard Cosway, Courtesy of the Trustees of Sir John Soane's Museum, London

33

Critical Viewing 34
How well do you think this depiction of Andromache and Astyanax captures Andromache's feelings for her son? **[Evaluate]**

32 Reading Check

Answer: Andromache is horrified; she regards herself as destroyed.

33 Humanities

Andromache and Astyanax,
by Richard Cosway

Cosway (c. 1742–1821) was one of the best-known artists of his day. He created skillful miniatures, many of members of the royal family and other high-profile aristocrats. Cosway's works often feature short brush strokes and color washes on light-colored backgrounds.

Use the following question for discussion.

How would the tone or impact of this work change if it were in color?
Possible response: The black-and-neutral palette allows the viewer to appreciate the work's emotional intensity. The use of color might diffuse this intensity and distract the viewer.

34 Critical Viewing

Possible response: Andromache is shown embracing Astyanax, more to comfort herself than the child. It is clear that she treasures her son and wants to protect him from a fate similar to his father's.

Differentiated Instruction
Solutions for All Learners

Strategy for Special Needs Students
Help students understand Andromache's actions during this segment of the text. Have students list in order Andromache's actions from the time she leaves her house in line 417 through her speech lamenting what will happen to her son with his father dead.

Enrichment for Gifted/Talented Students
Organize students into small groups. Then, have them reread lines 417–481 and discuss how this scene might have taken place. Have each group write a script for these lines and practice the scene. Then, have students videotape the scene with improvised costumes, if possible.

Enrichment for Advanced Readers
Have students read lines 443–448. Then, have students research the marriage customs and the role of women in ancient Greece. Suggest that they use Internet sources or the library for their research. Then, have them report their findings to the class.

35 Literary Analysis

Imagery

- Have students reread line 469 in context.
- Invite students to speculate on how youngsters might act cruelly toward those whom they perceive to be outsiders or weaklings.
- Then, **ask** students the Literary Analysis question: What is the emotional effect of the image of cutting in line 469?
  Answer: The image of cutting reinforces the vulnerability and pathos of an orphan's lot in ancient Greek culture.

36 Literary Analysis

Imagery

- Have students reread lines 491–499.
- **Invite** students to discuss the striking contrasts created by the imagery in this passage. How are these contrasts appropriate for the mood of the speaker?
  Possible response: The imagery contrasts the richness of Troy's treasures with the nakedness and decomposition of the fallen hero's body. The violent juxtaposition is appropriate to Andromache's mood of despair.

to the House of Death, the dark depths of the earth,
and leave me here to waste away in grief, a widow
lost in the royal halls—and the boy only a baby,
the son we bore together, you and I so doomed.
Hector, what help are you to him, now you are dead?—
what help is he to you? Think, even if he escapes
the wrenching horrors of war against the Argives,
pain and labor will plague him all his days to come.
Strangers will mark his lands off, stealing his estates.
35 The day that orphans a youngster cuts him off from friends.
And he hangs his head low, humiliated in every way . . .
his cheeks stained with tears, and pressed by hunger
the boy goes up to his father's old companions,
tugging at one man's cloak, another's tunic,
and some will pity him, true,
and one will give him a little cup to drink,
enough to wet his lips, not quench his thirst.
But then some bully with both his parents living
beats him from the banquet, fists and abuses flying:
'You, get out—you've got no father feasting with us here!'
And the boy, sobbing, trails home to his widowed mother . . .
Astyanax!
And years ago, propped on his father's knee,
he would only eat the marrow, the richest cuts of lamb,
and when sleep came on him and he had quit his play,
cradled warm in his nurse's arms he'd drowse off,
snug in a soft bed, his heart brimmed with joy.
Now what suffering, now he's lost his father—
Astyanax!
The Lord of the City, so the Trojans called him,
because it was you, Hector, you and you alone
who shielded the gates and the long walls of Troy.
But now by the beaked ships, far from your parents,
glistening worms will wriggle through your flesh,
once the dogs have had their fill of your naked corpse—
though we have such stores of clothing laid up in the halls,

fine things, a joy to the eye, the work of women's hands.
Now, by god, I'll burn them all, blazing to the skies!
No use to you now, they'll never shroud your body—
but they will be your glory
burned by the Trojan men and women in your honor!"

Her voice rang out in tears and the women wailed in answer.

Literary Analysis
Imagery What is the emotional effect of the image of cutting in line 469?

Enrichment

Beyond the *Iliad*

The poem itself ends with the funeral of Hector and with ritual laments for him (see pp. 405–408). Here, the lament addressed to Hector focuses on one repercussion of his dying: what will happen to his son. For the listeners, Andromache's vivid evocation of Astyanax's fate is made even more poignant because the misfortune she envisions still assumes that Troy will not fall. But the poet knows that Troy will be sacked, and the Greeks will dash the boy to his death from the top of the walls.

from BOOK 24:

ACHILLES AND PRIAM

Achilles and the Greeks perform Patroclus' funeral rites. Following the funeral, they hold a feast. The next morning, in honor of Patroclus, the Greeks hold funeral games—chariot races, discus throwing, boxing, and wrestling.

"Achilles," detail from the fresco *Thetis Consoling Achilles*, Giovanni Battista Tiepolo, Scala

The games were over now. The gathered armies scattered,
each man to his fast ship, and fighters turned their minds
to thoughts of food and the sweet warm grip of sleep.
But Achilles kept on grieving for his friend,
the memory burning on . . .
and all-subduing sleep could not take him,
not now, he turned and twisted, side to side,
he longed for Patroclus' manhood, his gallant heart—
What rough campaigns they'd fought to an end together,
what hardships they had suffered, cleaving their way
through wars of men and pounding waves at sea.
The memories flooded over him, live tears flowing,
and now he'd lie on his side, now flat on his back,
now facedown again. At last he'd leap to his feet,
wander in anguish, aimless along the surf, and dawn on dawn
flaming over the sea and shore would find him pacing.
Then he'd yoke his racing team to the chariot-harness,
lash the corpse of Hector behind the car for dragging
and haul him three times round the dead Patroclus' tomb,
and then he'd rest again in his tents and leave the body
sprawled facedown in the dust. But Apollo pitied Hector—
dead man though he was—and warded all corruption off
from Hector's corpse and round him, head to foot,
the great god wrapped the golden shield of storm
so his skin would never rip as Achilles dragged him on.

And so he kept on raging, shaming noble Hector,
but the gods in bliss looked down and pitied Priam's son.

▲ **Critical Viewing**
What does this depiction of Achilles suggest about the way he is feeling at this point in the story? **[Infer]**

Reading Check
Which god pities Hector and prevents his body from being damaged?

37 About the Selection

Book 24 tells of an encounter between opponents who for a moment surpass their differences to find their common humanity.

38 Humanities

"Achilles," detail from fresco, *Thetis Consoling Achilles*,
by Giovanni Battista Tiepolo

The Italian artist Giovanni Battista Tiepolo (1696–1770) is considered a master of rococo fresco painting. In 1757, Count Valmarana commissioned him to execute fresco paintings in the Count's palazzo near Vicenza. With the assistance of his thirty-year-old son, he painted a series of frescoes on classical subjects considered to be among his finest work.

This detail of Achilles is from one of the frescoes devoted to scenes from the *Iliad.* It clearly demonstrates Tiepolo's skill and sensitivity when rendering human figures on so difficult a surface as wet plaster. This fine portrait captures the melancholic introspection of the grieving Achilles.

Use the following question for discussion:

What might Achilles be thinking, as he is portrayed here?
Possible response: He may still be thinking about Patroclus, or he may be meditating on his own destiny.

39 Critical Viewing

Possible response: It suggests that he is melancholy and brooding.

40 Reading Check

Answer: Apollo pities Hector and preserves the hero's body.

Differentiated Instruction
Solutions for All Learners

Strategy for Less Proficient Readers

Homer's use of metaphor may pose challenges for some students. Direct students' attention to phrases such as "the sweet warm grip of sleep" (line 3) and "the memories flooded over him" (line 12). Ask students to explain the comparison in each phrase. Have students list and discuss any phrases they find difficult.

Strategy for English Learners

Students may occasionally feel challenged by the syntax of the translation. Pick out some phrases such as the following: "the memory burning on" (line 5) and "dawn on dawn" (line 15). Have students work with native English-speaking students to paraphrase confusing phrases.

Strategy for Advanced Readers

Have students discuss Homer's psychological portrayal of Achilles in lines 4–21. Do students consider this portrait of grief realistic? Why or why not? What specific details does Homer use to compose a vivid picture of a man tormented by mourning? Have students present their findings in a brief oral report.

41 Literature in Context

Honor in Ancient Greece

As critic Bernard M. W. Knox has pointed out, Achilles became the model for heroes of Sophoclean tragedy such as Oedipus, Ajax, Antigone, and Philoctetes. These characters burn with a white-hot idealism whose intensity allows no compromise. Knox also notes that in the Archaic period of the seventh and sixth centuries B.C., Achilles served as a model for the aristocratic echelon of Greek society. Even Socrates, who lived in the period of Athenian democracy, cites Achilles as his model when he tells the judges at his trial that he prefers not to compromise his principles by admitting any shame or regret for his actions.

Connect to the Literature Tell students that as the tale unfolds, their reactions to Achilles may change. Ask them to share their impressions of him and Agamemnon at this point.
Possible response: Agamemnon is a greedy and arrogant ruler who thinks he is entitled to everything because of his status. Achilles is a complex person who, while loyal to his friend Patroclus, is brutal and out of control in his need to avenge his friend's death and the treatment of his body. He is unable to compromise his standards. Both men confuse honor and merit and are victims of their own arrogance and the expectations of society, the military, and the gods.

42 Literary Analysis

Imagery and Epic Simile

- Have students reread lines 47–51.
- Make sure students recognize that the passage contains an epic simile.
- Then, **ask** students to identify the image Apollo uses to describe Achilles. Is this image justified, in students' opinions?
  Possible response: Apollo describes Achilles in terms of a lion's brute force and predatory nature. At this point in the narrative, the image is justified, especially considering Achilles' desecration of Hector's body.

They kept on urging the sharp-eyed giant-killer Hermes
to go and steal the body, a plan that pleased them all
but not Hera, Poseidon or the girl with blazing eyes.[1]
They clung to their deathless hate of sacred Troy,
Priam and Priam's people, just as they had at first
when Paris in all his madness launched the war.
He offended Athena and Hera—both goddesses.
When they came to his shepherd's fold he favored Love
who dangled before his eyes the lust that loosed disaster.
But now, at the twelfth dawn since Hector's death,
lord Apollo rose and addressed the immortal powers:
"Hard-hearted you are, you gods, you live for cruelty!
Did Hector never burn in your honor thighs of oxen
and flawless, full-grown goats? Now you cannot
bring yourselves to save him—even his corpse—
so his wife can see him, his mother and his child,
his father Priam and Priam's people: how they'd rush
to burn his body on the pyre and give him royal rites!
But murderous Achilles—you gods, you *choose* to help
Achilles.
That man without a shred of decency in his heart . . .
his temper can never bend and change—like some lion
42 going his own barbaric way, giving in to his power,
his brute force and wild pride, as down he swoops
on the flocks of men to seize his savage feast.
Achilles has lost all pity! No shame in the man,
shame that does great harm or drives men on to good.
No doubt some mortal has suffered a dearer loss than this,
a brother born in the same womb, or even a son . . .
he grieves, he weeps, but then his tears are through.
The Fates have given mortals hearts that can endure.
But this Achilles—first he slaughters Hector,
he rips away the noble prince's life
then lashes him to his chariot, drags him round
his beloved comrade's tomb. But why, I ask you?
What good will it do him? What honor will he gain?
Let that man beware, or great and glorious as he is,
we mighty gods will wheel on him in anger—look,
he outrages the senseless clay in all his fury!"

But white-armed Hera flared at him in anger:
"Yes, there'd be some merit even in what *you* say,
lord of the silver bow—if all you gods, in fact,
would set Achilles and Hector high in equal honor.
But Hector is mortal. He sucked a woman's breast.[2]

1. **the girl with blazing eyes** Athena.
2. **sucked a woman's breast** was breast-fed as an infant by a mortal woman, not a goddess.

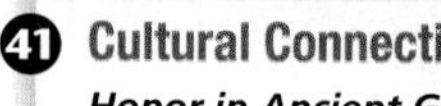

41 Cultural Connection

Honor in Ancient Greece

Honor was a fundamental part of the ancient Greek code of ethics. It was understood that a warrior fough for honor and that a glorious reput tion would outlive him. The tangibl expression of honor consisted of th prizes distributed to a warrior according to his rank, valor, and achievement. Thus, a warrior's shar of prizes was a visible symbol of hi merit and status. This is why, in the *Iliad*, Achilles and Agamemnon fee so shamed when they must forfeit their prizes and why such importan is placed on the treatment of faller soldiers' bodies. Ultimately, a herc honor depended on how the worlc saw him, not on how he saw himse

Connect to the Literature

In what way does the world see Achilles and Agamemnon based o the way Homer depicts them in the *Iliad*?

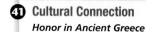

Achilles sprang from a goddess—one I reared myself:
I brought her up and gave her in marriage to a man,
to Peleus, dearest to all your hearts, you gods.
All you gods, you shared in the wedding rites,
and so did you, Apollo—there you sat at the feast
and struck your lyre. What company you keep now,
these wretched Trojans. You—forever faithless!"

But Zeus who marshals the storm clouds warned his queen,
"Now, Hera, don't fly into such a rage at fellow gods.
These two can never attain the same degree of honor.
Still, the immortals loved Prince Hector dearly,
best of all the mortals born in Troy . . .
so *I* loved him, at least:
he never stinted with gifts to please my heart.
Never once did my altar lack its share of victims,
winecups tipped and the deep smoky savor. These,
these are the gifts we claim—they are our rights.
But as for stealing courageous Hector's body,
we must abandon the idea—not a chance in the world
behind Achilles' back. For Thetis is always there,
his mother always hovering near him night and day.
Now, would one of you gods call Thetis to my presence?—
so I can declare to her my solemn, sound decree:
Achilles must receive a ransom from King Priam,
Achilles must give Hector's body back."

On Olympus, Zeus orders Thetis to tell Achilles to return Hector's body to Priam. Then Zeus commands Iris to tell Priam to ransom his son by bringing gifts to Achilles. Concerned for Priam's safety, Zeus tells Hermes to guide Priam through the hollow Achaean ships. Hermes assures Priam that the gods preserved Hector's body from defilement even while Achilles dragged the corpse for nine days.

With that urging
Hermes went his way to the steep heights of Olympus.
But Priam swung down to earth from the battle-car
and leaving Idaeus[3] there to rein in mules and team,
the old king went straight up to the lodge
where Achilles dear to Zeus would always sit.
Priam found the warrior there inside . . .
many captains sitting some way off, but two,
veteran Automedon and the fine fighter Alcimus

were busy serving him. He had just finished dinner,

3. **Idaeus** (ī dē´ əs) herald of Priam.

Vocabulary Builder
stinted (stint´ id) *v.* limited to a certain quantity

Literary Analysis
Imagery To what senses does Zeus' description of sacrifice appeal?

45 **Reading Check**
What decree does Zeus make regarding Hector's body?

43 Literary Analysis
Imagery
- Have students reread lines 85–87 carefully.
- Have students note sensory words and phrases, such as "altar," "winecups tipped,"and "smoky savor."
- Then, **ask** students the Literary Analysis question: To what senses does Zeus' description of sacrifice appeal?
  Answer: The description appeals to the senses of sight, taste, and smell.

44 Background
Etiquette
Achilles has eaten, so the food he offers Priam is not just an ordinary meal; it is part of the guest-host etiquette, *xenia,* a relationship that imposes at least the trust of hospitality and at best the duty of kinship between strangers or even enemies.

45 Reading Check
Answer: Zeus decrees that Achilles must return Hector's body to Priam for ransom.

Differentiated Instruction Solutions for All Learners

Strategy for Less Proficient Readers
Have students reread carefully the bridging passage on this page. Then, ask them to identify the principal events referred to in the passage, using chronological order. Ask students to list the major events on a sequence chart, and then have volunteers share and discuss their charts with the class.

Enrichment for Gifted/Talented Students
Have students read the bridging passage and briefly discuss the major events that are described. Then, organize students into small groups. Each group should select one of the events in the passage and make it the basis for an improvisation. Invite groups to perform their dramatic skits for the class as a whole.

46 Literary Analysis

Imagery and Epic Simile

- Have students reread the simile in lines 111–115.
- Ask students to discuss who is being equated with whom in the simile. Which details of the simile seem to correspond with the main action involving Achilles and Priam? Which details involve a reversal of expectation?
- Lead students to recognize that the feeling of wonder ("marvel" in lines 114 and "marveled" in lines 115–116) is a key concept that links the simile with the context. On the other hand, Priam, who is compared to the exile guilty of murder, is not guilty of a crime; rather, it is Achilles who has killed Priam's son in battle.
- Then, **ask** students the Literary Analysis question: Why do you think Homer describes Achilles' reaction to Priam the way that he does in lines 111–115?
  Possible response: Homer reverses expectations in the simile, perhaps to reinforce the chaos and upset that war creates.

47 Critical Viewing

Possible response: The Trojans might have felt embarrassed or shamed by seeing their king in a suppliant position.

44 ▲ eating, drinking, and the table still stood near.
The majestic king of Troy slipped past the rest
and kneeling down beside Achilles, clasped his knees
and kissed his hands, those terrible, man-killing hands
that had slaughtered Priam's many sons in battle.
Awesome—as when the grip of madness seizes one
who murders a man in his own fatherland and flees
46 abroad to foreign shores, to a wealthy, noble host,
and a sense of marvel runs through all who see him—
so Achilles marveled, beholding majestic Priam.
His men marveled too, trading startled glances.
But Priam prayed his heart out to Achilles:
"Remember your own father, great godlike Achilles—
as old as *I* am, past the threshold of deadly old age!
No doubt the countrymen round about him plague him now,
with no one there to defend him, beat away disaster.
No one—but at least he hears you're still alive
and his old heart rejoices, hopes rising, day by day,
to see his beloved son come sailing home from Troy.
But I—dear god, my life so cursed by fate . . .
I fathered hero sons in the wide realm of Troy
and now not a single one is left, I tell you.
Fifty sons I had when the sons of Achaea came,
nineteen born to me from a single mother's womb
and the rest by other women in the palace. Many,
most of them violent Ares cut the knees from under.
But one, one was left me, to guard my walls, my people—
the one you killed the other day, defending his fatherland,
my Hector! It's all for him I've come to the ships now,
to win him back from you—I bring a priceless ransom.
Revere the gods, Achilles! Pity me in my own right,
remember your own father! I deserve more pity . . .
I have endured what no one on earth has ever done before—
I put to my lips the hands of the man who killed my son."

Those words stirred within Achilles a deep desire
to grieve for his own father. Taking the old man's hand
he gently moved him back. And overpowered by memory
both men gave way to grief. Priam wept freely
for man-killing Hector, throbbing, crouching
before Achilles' feet as Achilles wept himself,
now for his father, now for Patroclus once again,
and their sobbing rose and fell throughout the house.
Then, when brilliant Achilles had had his fill of tears
and the longing for it had left his mind and body,
he rose from his seat, raised the old man by the hand
and filled with pity now for his gray head and gray beard,
he spoke out winging words, flying straight to the heart:

Literary Analysis
Imagery and Epic Simile Why do you think Homer describes Achilles' reaction to Priam the way that he does in lines 111–115?

47 **Critical Viewing ▶** This painting depicts Priam begging Achilles to return Hector's body to Troy. How might seeing their king in this position have affected the Trojans? **[Speculate]**

Enrichment

Ancient Greek Burial

Homer illustrates the need to bury the dead, and the gulf that separates them from the living, when Patroclus appears to Achilles in a dream in Book 23. Achilles has fallen asleep, exhausted from dragging Hector's corpse and obsessed with the memory of Patroclus. The apparition addresses him:

> "Sleeping, Achilles? You've forgotten me, my friend. You never neglected me in life, only now in death. Bury me, quickly—let me pass the Gates of Hades.
> They hold me off at a distance, all the souls, the shades of the burnt-out, breathless dead, never to let me cross the river, mingle with them . . .
> They leave me to wander up and down, abandoned, lost, at the House of Death with the all-embracing gates.
> Oh give me your hand—I beg you with my tears!
> Never, never again shall I return from Hades once you have given me the soothing rites of fire."

"Poor man, how much you've borne—pain to break the spirit!
What daring brought you down to the ships, all alone,
to face the glance of the man who killed your sons,
so many fine brave boys? You have a heart of iron.
Come, please, sit down on this chair here . . .
Let us put our griefs to rest in our own hearts,
rake them up no more, raw as we are with mourning.
What good's to be won from tears that chill the spirit?
So the immortals spun our lives that we, we wretched men
live on to bear such torments—the gods live free of sorrows.
There are two great jars that stand on the floor of Zeus's halls
and hold his gifts, our miseries one, the other blessings.
When Zeus who loves the lightning mixes gifts for a man,
now he meets with misfortune, now good times in turn.
When Zeus dispenses gifts from the jar of sorrows only,
he makes a man an outcast—brutal, ravenous hunger
drives him down the face of the shining earth,
stalking far and wide, cursed by gods and men.
So with my father, Peleus. What glittering gifts
the gods rained down from the day that he was born!
He excelled all men in wealth and pride of place,
he lorded the Myrmidons, and mortal that he was,
they gave the man an immortal goddess for a wife.

48  **Reading Check**
How does Achilles react when Priam reminds Achilles of his father?

49

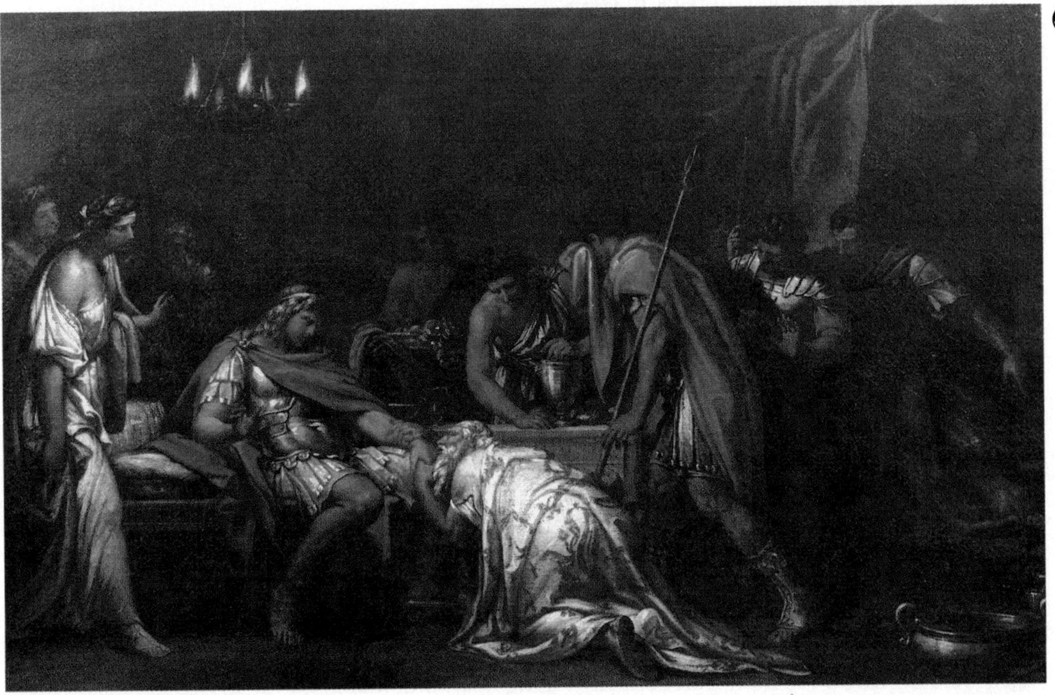

48 Reading Check

Answer: Achilles grieves for his own father, Peleus.

49 Humanities

Priam Pleading with Achilles for the Body of Hector, by Gavin Hamilton

The Scottish painter Gavin Hamilton (1723–1798) was born to a noble family. His financial independence allowed him the freedom to live and work in Rome for most of his life. Hamilton's neoclassical paintings reflect the genuine desire to re-create the art of ancient Greece and Rome.

Hamilton began painting large-scale illustrations of the story of the *Iliad* in the 1760s. His scholarly knowledge of Homer's work and his interest in accurate historical detail are apparent in the painting *Priam Pleading with Achilles for the Body of Hector.* The figures, painted life-size, have a shallow, frieze-like quality. The heavy color maintains the austere, formal quality of the painting.

Use the following questions for discussion.

- What is the atmosphere of the painting?
  Answer: The atmosphere seems melancholy or gloomy.
- How does the painting enhance your understanding of the scene depicted?
  Possible response: The painting graphically emphasizes the abasement that Priam forces himself to undergo as he entreats Achilles to accept a ransom for Hector's body.

Differentiated Instruction Solutions for All Learners

Support for Less Proficient Readers

Have a volunteer read aloud Priam's plea in lines 117–139. Then, read aloud lines 140–152, and ask another volunteer to read aloud Achilles' response in lines 153–175. Be sure that students understand that Achilles' expression of grief for his own father leads to his merciful reaction to Priam's grief.

Enrichment for Gifted/Talented Students

Have students reread lines 96–175. Then, have students create a live newscast of the meeting of these two leaders. Assign students to small groups. Have them select an anchor and reporters who will cover the meeting. They may also choose to interview Priam and Achilles about the meeting.

Enrichment for Advanced Readers

Have students reread lines 96–175. Then, assign them to groups and have them create the front page of a newspaper covering the meeting between Priam and Achilles. Remind students to include background information on both men as well as an obituary for Hector and the current status of the war.

50 Humanities

This cup depicts King Priam of Troy appealing to Achilles for the return of his son Hector's body.

Use the following question for discussion.

What lines of the narrative does the scene in the foreground illustrate?
Answer: The scene illustrates lines 107–110, in which Homer recounts Priam's supplication to Achilles. The aging Trojan king kneels before the youthful Greek warrior and kisses the hands that have slain his son.

51 Critical Viewing

Possible response: The depiction on the cup is consistent with what readers may have envisioned. The King kneels before Achilles and begs him for Hector's body. Achilles seems arrogant, and Priam seems desperate. However, students might have envisioned Achilles still wearing armor as in Hamilton's painting.

52 Reading Strategy

Picture the Action

- Have students reread lines 196–202 carefully, observing the punctuation.
- Have students discuss Priam's use of urgent imperatives in the passage: for example, "Don't make me sit . . .", "Give him back to me," "Accept the ransom," "Enjoy it," and "return to your own native land."
- Ask students to discuss what these imperative verbs suggest about Priam's tone of voice, posture, and gestures as he addresses Achilles.
- **Ask** students the Reading Strategy question: How do you think Priam might stand or gesture as he speaks these lines to Achilles?
Possible response: Priam might stand stiffly or restlessly; he might gesture to the ransom, as he urges Achilles to accept it.

Yes, but even on him the Father piled hardships,
no powerful race of princes born in his royal halls,
only a single son he fathered, doomed at birth,
cut off in the spring of life—
and I, I give the man no care as he grows old
since here I sit in Troy, far from my fatherland,
a grief to you, a grief to all your children . . .
And you too, old man, we hear you prospered once:
as far as Lesbos, Macar's kingdom, bounds to seaward,
Phrygia east and upland, the Hellespont vast and north—
that entire realm, they say, you lorded over once,
you excelled all men, old king, in sons and wealth.
But then the gods of heaven brought this agony on you—
ceaseless battles round your walls, your armies slaughtered.
You must bear up now. Enough of endless tears,
the pain that breaks the spirit.
Grief for your son will do no good at all.
You will never bring him back to life—
sooner you must suffer something worse."

52

But the old and noble Priam protested strongly:
"Don't make me sit on a chair, Achilles, Prince,
not while Hector lies uncared-for in your camp!
Give him back to me, now, no more delay—
I must see my son with my own eyes.
Accept the ransom I bring you, a king's ransom!
Enjoy it, all of it—return to your own native land,
safe and sound . . . since now you've spared my life."

A dark glance—and the headstrong runner answered,
"No more, old man, don't tempt my wrath, not now!
My own mind's made up to give you back your son.
A messenger brought me word from Zeus—my mother,
Thetis who bore me, the Old Man of the Sea's daughter.
And what's more, I can see through you, Priam—
no hiding the fact from me: one of the gods
has led you down to Achaea's fast ships.
No man alive, not even a rugged young fighter,
would dare to venture into our camp. Never—
how could he slip past the sentries unchallenged?
Or shoot back the bolt of my gates with so much ease?
So don't anger me now. Don't stir my raging heart still more.

51 ▼ Critical Viewing How does this depiction of Priam's plea for Hector's body compare with the way that you envision this scene? Explain. **[Compare and Contrast]**

50

Reading Strategy
Picture the Action How do you think Priam might stand or gesture as he speaks these lines to Achilles?

Or under my own roof I may not spare your life, old man—
suppliant that you are—may break the laws of Zeus!"

The old man was terrified. He obeyed the order.
53 But Achilles bounded out of doors like a lion—
not alone but flanked by his two aides-in-arms,
veteran Automedon and Alcimus, steady comrades,
Achilles' favorites next to the dead Patroclus.
They loosed from harness the horses and the mules,
they led the herald in, the old king's crier,
and sat him down on a bench. From the polished wagon
they lifted the priceless ransom brought for Hector's corpse
but they left behind two capes and a finely-woven shirt
to shroud the body well when Priam bore him home.
Then Achilles called the serving-women out:
"Bathe and anoint the body—
bear it aside first. Priam must not see his son."
He feared that, overwhelmed by the sight of Hector,
wild with grief, Priam might let his anger flare
and Achilles might fly into fresh rage himself,
cut the old man down and break the laws of Zeus.
So when the maids had bathed and anointed the body
54 sleek with olive oil and wrapped it round and round
in a braided battle-shirt and handsome battle-cape,
then Achilles lifted Hector up in his own arms
and laid him down on a bier, and comrades helped him
raise the bier and body onto the sturdy wagon . . .
Then with a groan he called his dear friend by name:
"Feel no anger at me, Patroclus, if you learn—
even there in the House of Death—I let his father
have Prince Hector back. He gave me worthy ransom
and you shall have your share from me, as always,
your fitting, lordly share."
So he vowed
and brilliant Achilles strode back to his shelter,
sat down on the well-carved chair that he had left,
at the far wall of the room, leaned toward Priam
and firmly spoke the words the king had come to hear:
"Your son is now set free, old man, as you requested.
Hector lies in state. With the first light of day
you will see for yourself as you convey him home.
Now, at last, let us turn our thoughts to supper.
Even Niobe[4] with her lustrous hair remembered food,
55 though she saw a dozen children killed in her own halls,
six daughters and six sons in the pride and prime of youth.
True, lord Apollo killed the sons with his silver bow

4. **Niobe** (nī´ ə bē).

Literary Analysis
Imagery What theme is supported by the comparison of Achilles to a lion?

Reading Strategy
Picture the Action Which details in lines 236–238 help you form a mental image of Hector's dead body?

Vocabulary Builder
lustrous (lus´ trəs) *adj.* shining

56 
Reading Check
How does Achilles respond to Priam's request for the return of Hector's body?

53 Literary Analysis

Imagery

- Ask a volunteer to read line 219 aloud.
- **Ask** students the Literary Analysis question: What theme is supported by the comparison of Achilles to a lion?
  Answer: The comparison supports the earlier characterization of Achilles as lacking humanity in his blood-thirsty quest for vengeance.

54 Reading Strategy

Picture the Action

- Have students reread lines 236–238 carefully.
- Have students discuss the body's probable condition. Remind students that many of the Greeks stabbed Hector after his death from Achilles' spear thrust in Book 22; also recall that Apollo is said to have preserved the body from corruption at the beginning of Book 24.
- **Direct** students to respond to the Reading Strategy question: Which details in lines 236–238 help you form a mental image of Hector's dead body?
  Answer: Details include the bathing, anointing, and wrapping of the body.

55 Vocabulary Builder

The Latin Root *-lustr-*

- Draw students' attention to the word *lustrous* and its definition.
- Tell students that the Latin root *-lustr-* means "shining."
- Write the words *luster* and *lackluster* on the board. Then, ask students to relate the root *-lustr-* to the definition of each of these words.

56 Reading Check

Answer: Achilles agrees to the request.

Differentiated Instruction Solutions for All Learners

Support for Special Needs Students

Remind students that for the ancient Greeks mythical stories served as guides for proper behavior. Go over the story of Niobe to make sure that students understand the basic parallel that Achilles presents: even at moments of extreme grief or stress, human beings must remember the basic necessities of life, such as food. Suggest that students write a brief summary of the myth of Niobe.

Enrichment for Advanced Readers

Remind students that characters may reshape a story to fit their own particular needs. Achilles is retelling the Niobe myth for his own purposes: to show that even the most extreme misfortune and the most extreme grief must be finite for human beings. Have students discuss whether Achilles expects Priam to stop grieving for Hector or simply to pause long enough to recognize that he is alive and needs to eat. Then, have students write a paragraph citing a recent example of grief being finite.

57 Literary Analysis

Imagery

- Have a volunteer read aloud the first bracketed passage.
- Then, **ask** the Literary Analysis question: What images in these lines recall earlier scenes in the *Iliad?*
  Possible response: Images of cutting and slaughter appear throughout the poem, contributing to its bloodiness. Achilles is featured throughout the poem cutting and piercing flesh, seeking to mutilate his enemies. With his friends, he cuts meat to feed them.
- **Ask** students how this scene recalls the death of Hector.
  Possible response: Hector was stabbed and stripped of his armor so violently as to evoke images of butchery. Achilles' slaughter and skinning of the sheep evokes the image of Achilles killing Hector and stripping his bloody armor.

58 Critical Thinking

Compare and Contrast

- Have a volunteer read lines 295–303 aloud.
- **Ask** students to discuss Priam's description of his own grief here and Achilles' earlier behavior as he mourned Patroclus' death.
  Possible response: Both Priam and Achilles remained sleepless. Their obsessive grief might be seen as a denial of the boundary that separates the living and the dead.

and Artemis showering arrows killed the daughters.
Both gods were enraged at Niobe. Time and again
she placed herself on a par with their own mother,
Leto in her immortal beauty—how she insulted Leto:
'All you have borne is two, but I have borne so many!'
So, two as they were, they slaughtered all her children.
Nine days they lay in their blood, no one to bury them—
Cronus' son had turned the people into stone . . .
then on the tenth the gods of heaven interred them.
And Niobe, gaunt, worn to the bone with weeping,
turned her thoughts to food. And now, somewhere,
lost on the crags, on the lonely mountain slopes,
on Sipylus[5] where, they say, the nymphs who live forever,
dancing along the Achelous River[6] run to beds of rest—
there, struck into stone, Niobe still broods
on the spate of griefs the gods poured out to her.

So come—we too, old king, must think of food.
Later you can mourn your beloved son once more,
when you bear him home to Troy, and you'll weep many tears."

57
Never pausing, the swift runner sprang to his feet
and slaughtered a white sheep as comrades moved in
to skin the carcass quickly, dress the quarters well.
Expertly they cut the meat in pieces, pierced them with spits,
roasted them to a turn and pulled them off the fire.
Automedon brought the bread, set it out on the board
in ample wicker baskets. Achilles served the meat.
They reached out for the good things that lay at hand
and when they had put aside desire for food and drink,
Priam the son of Dardanus gazed at Achilles, marveling
now at the man's beauty, his magnificent build—
face-to-face he seemed a deathless god . . .
and Achilles gazed and marveled at Dardan Priam,
beholding his noble looks, listening to his words.
But once they'd had their fill of gazing at each other,
the old majestic Priam broke the silence first:
58
"Put me to bed quickly, Achilles, Prince.
Time to rest, to enjoy the sweet relief of sleep.
Not once have my eyes closed shut beneath my lids
from the day my son went down beneath your hands . . .
day and night I groan, brooding over the countless griefs,
groveling in the dung that fills my walled-in court.
But now, at long last, I have tasted food again
and let some glistening wine go down my throat.
Before this hour I had tasted nothing."

Vocabulary Builder
gaunt (gônt) *adj.* thin and bony; haggard

Literary Analysis
Imagery What images in these lines recall earlier scenes in the *Iliad*?

5. **Sipylus** (sip′ i ləs) mountain in Asia Minor.
6. **Achelous River** (ak′ ə lō′ əs) river near Sipylus in Asia Minor, east of Troy.

Achilles calls a twelve-day truce while the Trojans perform Hector's funeral rites. Cassandra watches as her father Priam approaches Troy in his chariot. She sees her brother Hector's body drawn by the mules on a litter.

She [Cassandra] screamed and her scream rang out through all
Troy:
"Come, look down, you men of Troy, you Trojan women!
Behold Hector now—if you ever once rejoiced
to see him striding home, home alive from battle!
He was the greatest joy of Troy and all our people!"

Her cries plunged Troy into uncontrollable grief
and not a man or woman was left inside the walls.
They streamed out at the gates to meet Priam
bringing in the body of the dead. Hector—
his loving wife and noble mother were first
to fling themselves on the wagon rolling on,
the first to tear their hair, embrace his head
and a wailing throng of people milled around them.
And now, all day long till the setting sun went down
they would have wept for Hector there before the gates
if the old man, steering the car, had not commanded,
"Let me through with the mules! Soon, in a moment,
you can have your fill of tears—once I've brought him home."

So he called and the crowds fell back on either side,
making way for the wagon. Once they had borne him
59 into the famous halls, they laid his body down
on his large carved bed and set beside him singers
to lead off the laments, and their voices rose in grief—
they lifted the dirge high as the women wailed in answer.
And white-armed Andromache led their songs of sorrow,
cradling the head of Hector, man-killing Hector
gently in her arms: "O my husband . . .
cut off from life so young! You leave me a widow,
lost in the royal halls—and the boy only a baby,
the son we bore together, you and I so doomed.
I cannot think he will ever come to manhood.
Long before *that* the city will be sacked,
plundered top to bottom! Because you are dead,
her great guardian, you who always defended Troy,
who kept her loyal wives and helpless children safe,
all who will soon be carried off in the hollow ships
and I with them—
And you, my child, will follow me
61 to labor, somewhere, at harsh, degrading work,
slaving under some heartless master's eye—that,

60  **Reading Check**

What does Andromache believe will happen to Troy now that Hector is dead?

59 Critical Thinking

Apply

- Have students reread lines 322–327.
- **Ask** students how they think that formalized, ritual mourning that is led by professional mourners helps those who are having difficulty accepting their loss.
  Possible response: The presence of professional mourners may help objectify a sense of loss, thus helping people confront the reality of the death of a loved one.

60 Reading Check

Answer: Andromache thinks that Troy will fall now that Hector is dead.

Differentiated Instruction Solutions for All Learners

Strategy for Less Proficient Readers

Andromache's speech (lines 330–355) offers a good opportunity to explore with students the ways in which Homer uses foreshadowing and parallelism. Guide students in making a comparison of Andromache's lament here with the premonitions she voices in her speech in Book 6, lines 44–82. In that speech, Andromache had also lamented her husband's imminent fate, and she had predicted that the death of Hector would mean her own ruin, as well as the destruction of Troy itself.

Have students create a two-column chart for comparing the speeches of Andromache. Which details are repeated? Which elements are different? Invite students to sum up, either orally or in a few written sentences, their views on the overall effect of the parallel speeches.

61 Literary Analysis

Imagery

- Have students read lines 340–347.
- Ask students to identify graphic images and details in these lines having to do with war and its hardships.
- Then, **ask** students the first Literary Analysis question: Which details in this passage stress the violence and cruelty of war and its consequences?
Possible response: Details include harsh, degrading work; a heartless master; the child being seized and hurled down from the ramparts; and the Greeks gnawing the dust when they are crushed by Hector's hands.

62 Literary Analysis

Imagery

- Have students read lines 356–357 aloud.
- Draw students' attention to the following phrases: "her voice rang out in tears"; "the women wailed in answer"; and "a throbbing chant of sorrow."
- Then, **ask** students the second Literary Analysis question: To which sense does the imagery in lines 356 and 357 appeal most?
Answer: The images appeal to the sense of hearing.

or some Achaean marauder will seize you by the arm
and hurl you headlong down from the ramparts—horrible death—
enraged at *you* because Hector once cut down his brother,
his father or his son, yes, hundreds of armed Achaeans
gnawed the dust of the world, crushed by Hector's hands!
Your father, remember, was no man of mercy . . .
not in the horror of battle, and that is why
the whole city of Troy mourns you now, my Hector—
you've brought your parents accursed tears and grief
but to me most of all you've left the horror, the heartbreak!
For you never died in bed and stretched your arms to me
or said some last word from the heart I can remember,
always, weeping for you through all my nights and days!"

Her voice rang out in tears and the women wailed in answer
and Hecuba led them now in a throbbing chant of sorrow:
"Hector, dearest to me by far of all my sons . . .
and dear to the gods while we still shared this life—
and they cared about you still, I see, even after death.
Many the sons I had whom the swift runner Achilles
caught and shipped on the barren salt sea as slaves
to Samos, to Imbros, to Lemnos[7] shrouded deep in mist!
But you, once he slashed away your life with his brazen spear
he dragged you time and again around his comrade's tomb,
Patroclus whom you killed—not that he brought Patroclus
back to life by that. But I have you with me now . . .
fresh as the morning dew you lie in the royal halls
like one whom Apollo, lord of the silver bow,
has approached and shot to death with gentle shafts."

Her voice rang out in tears and an endless wail rose up
and Helen, the third in turn, led their songs of sorrow:
"Hector! Dearest to me of all my husband's brothers—
my husband, Paris, magnificent as a god . . .
he was the one who brought me here to Troy—
Oh how I wish I'd died before that day!
But this, now, is the twentieth year for me
since I sailed here and forsook my own native land,
yet never once did I hear from *you* a taunt, an insult.
But if someone else in the royal halls would curse me,
one of your brothers or sisters or brothers' wives
trailing their long robes, even your own mother—
not your father, always kind as my own father—
why, you'd restrain them with words, Hector,
you'd win them to my side . . .
you with your gentle temper, all your gentle words.

Literary Analysis
Imagery Which details in this passage stress the violence and cruelty of war and its consequences?

Literary Analysis
Imagery To which sense does the imagery in lines 356 and 357 appeal most?

---

7. **Samos** (sam´ äs) . . . **Imbros** (im´ bräs) . . . **Lemnos** (lem´ näs) islands in the Aegean Sea.

Enrichment

Ancient Greek Mourning

In the context of formal mourning in ancient Greece, only women sang dirges. Thus, Hecuba speaks here, but Priam does not. The king's silence suggests that he has accepted his traditional role in coming to terms with Hector's death. Hecuba expresses the wisdom that grief, mourning, and revenge cannot undo death. Her words also suggest that Achilles' vengeance is finally an ineffectual and meaningless way to exorcise his grief; only an acceptance of death and a respect for ritual can help.

63

Andromache mourning Hector, Jacques Louis David, photo by Peter Willi

And so in the same breath I mourn for you and me,
my doom-struck, harrowed heart! Now there is no one left
in the wide realm of Troy, no friend to treat me kindly—
all the countrymen cringe from me in loathing!"

Her voice rang out in tears and vast throngs wailed
and old King Priam rose and gave his people orders:
"Now, you men of Troy, haul timber into the city!
Have no fear of an Argive ambush packed with danger—
Achilles vowed, when he sent me home from the black ships,
not to do us harm till the twelfth dawn arrives."

At his command they harnessed oxen and mules to wagons,
they assembled before the city walls with all good speed
and for nine days hauled in a boundless store of timber.
But when the tenth Dawn brought light to the mortal world

64 ▲ **Critical Viewing**
Which details in this painting illustrate Andromache's grief over her husband's death and her concern for her child? **[Analyze]**

65 

Reading Check
Why does Andromache think that the Achaeans will be especially enraged at Astyanax?

63 Humanities

Andromache Mourning Hector,
by Jacques Louis David

French painter David (1748–1825) suffered many setbacks during his life. At nine years old, he experienced the death of his father and abandonment by his mother, who left her young son under the care of several uncles. As a fledgling artist, David attempted suicide after failing to win the much-coveted Prix de Rome several times. He finally won the award in 1774, but remained emotionally troubled throughout his life. David may have drawn on his own experiences to create the realistic and powerful depiction of grief in this painting.

Use the following questions for discussion.

- What is the mood of this painting?
  Possible response: The mood of this painting is one of sorrow.
- What juxtapositions in this painting strike you?
  Possible response: Hector's prone, vulnerable body is flanked by his helmet and sword, which symbolize strength and vigor in battle. The figure of Astyanax—representing youth and potential—emphasizes Hector's own youth and wasted life. Finally, Andromache's illuminated robe is presented in striking contrast to Hector's dim body.

64 Critical Viewing

Possible response: Andromache's pained expression and her gesture toward Hector's body make her appear as if she is appealing to or questioning the gods. She clings to Astyanax, perhaps recognizing the impact that Hector's death will have on their young son. Andromache is illuminated, and the contrast of her white, glowing robe against the dark and somber colors of the background and the other figures emphasizes her isolation.

65 Reading Check

Answer: Andromache fears the Achaeans will fault Astyanax for his father's offenses.

Differentiated Instruction Solutions for All Learners

Strategy for Less Proficient Readers
On a two-column chart, have students list the qualities they find in Andromache. Then, have them reread lines 371–390. Have them discuss how they picture Helen in this passage. Next, have them list Helen's qualities. Then, have students write a statement comparing the two women.

Enrichment for Gifted/Talented Students
Have students take the role of a servant in Priam's house. Then, have them write letters to relatives comparing the actions of Andromache and Helen. Suggest that in their letters they use quotations and examples of the behavior of both women.

Enrichment for Advanced Readers
Have students research Helen of Troy, exploring her personality and actions both before and during the Trojan War. Then, have students write a character sketch of Helen, using specific examples of her behavior and her reputation.

ASSESS

Answers

1. **Possible response:** Achilles' treatment of Hector after his death may inspire empathy. Achilles is consumed by grief, and his actions illustrate his frustration over the human inability to change fate, something most readers will recognize.
2. (a) Hector considers hiding inside the city, fighting Achilles, or negotiating with Achilles. (b) Hector decides to fight Achilles. (c) This decision is consistent because Hector has been portrayed as strongly committed to honor and duty; note his characterization in Book 6, for example.
3. (a) Hector pleads with Achilles to accept a ransom for Hector's body for proper burial. (b) Achilles is obsessed by cruelty and revenge for the death of Patroclus, whom Hector has slain.
4. (a) By experiencing compassion for Priam, Achilles is reintegrated into human society. His demonic obsession with revenge yields to empathy for a fellow human being. (b) Achilles' change of heart reinforces Homer's theme that human beings must cope with tragedy and loss, sustaining themselves through such virtues as loyalty, duty, love, respect, and compassion.
5. **Possible response:** Achilles' heroism is evident when he transcends his anger and returns Hector's body to Priam.

Go Online Author Link For additional information about Homer, have students type in the Web Code, then select *H* from the alphabet, and then select Homer.

they carried gallant Hector forth, weeping tears,
and they placed his corpse aloft the pyre's crest,
flung a torch and set it all aflame.
At last,
when young Dawn with her rose-red fingers shone once more,
the people massed around illustrious Hector's pyre . . .
And once they'd gathered, crowding the meeting grounds,
they first put out the fires with glistening wine,
wherever the flames still burned in all their fury.
Then they collected the white bones of Hector—
all his brothers, his friends-in-arms, mourning,
and warm tears came streaming down their cheeks.
They placed the bones they found in a golden chest,
shrouding them round and round in soft purple cloths.
They quickly lowered the chest in a deep, hollow grave
and over it piled a cope of huge stones closely set,
then hastily heaped a barrow, posted lookouts all around
for fear the Achaean combat troops would launch their attack
before the time agreed. And once they'd heaped the mound
they turned back home to Troy, and gathering once again
they shared a splendid funeral feast in Hector's honor,
held in the house of Priam, king by will of Zeus.

And so the Trojans buried Hector breaker of horses.

Vocabulary Builder
illustrious (i lus′ trē əs) *adj.* distinguished; famous

Critical Reading

1. **Respond:** Describe your reaction to Achilles' treatment of Hector after Hector's death.
2. **(a) Recall:** In Book 22, lines 11–49, what three courses of action does Hector consider? **(b) Recall:** What does Hector decide to do? **(c) Analyze:** In what way is this decision consistent with his character?
3. **(a) Recall:** After he has been fatally wounded, for what does Hector plead with Achilles? **(b) Analyze:** What does Achilles' response to Hector's dying wish suggest about him?
4. **(a) Infer:** In Book 24, what change does Homer portray in Achilles? **(b) Draw Conclusions:** What message do you think Homer meant to convey through this change?
5. **Evaluate:** Do you think that Achilles behaves heroically in the *Iliad?* Why or why not?

For: More about Homer
Visit: www.PHSchool.com
Web Code: ete-9401

Apply the Skills

from the *Iliad,* Books 22 and 24

Literary Analysis

Imagery

1. What theme or themes in the *Iliad* are reinforced by the recurring **imagery** of cutting?
2. **(a)** In line 3 of Book 24, to what senses does the imagery of "the sweet warm grip of sleep" appeal? **(b)** What is the effect of the contrast between this image and the description of Achilles in the following lines?
3. Two of the most striking images in Book 24 are those of Priam kissing the "man-killing hands" of Achilles and Achilles gazing in admiration at "majestic Priam." What message might Homer be trying to convey with these two images and with the ransoming scene as a whole?

Connecting Literary Elements

4. What is the effect of the **epic simile** in lines 5–8 of Book 22?
5. In what way does the epic simile in lines 267–270 of Book 22 convey the importance of that moment in the narrative?
6. **(a)** Complete a chart like the one shown to compare and contrast the epic simile describing Achilles in Book 22, lines 59–64, with the one describing Hector in lines 258–261. **(b)** In what way do the similarities and differences between these two similes reflect the qualities of each warrior?

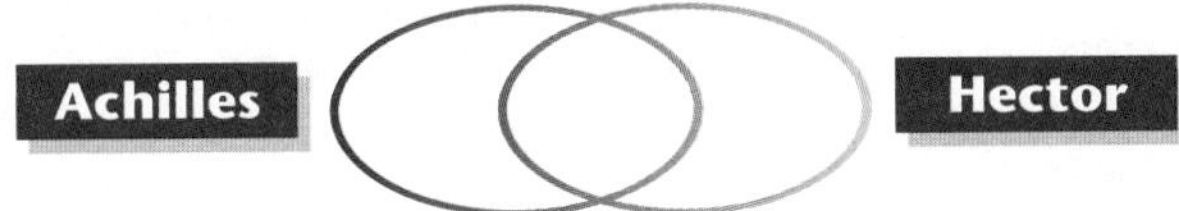

Reading Strategy

Picture the Action

7. **(a)** Identify three details that help you **picture the action** in the battle between Hector and Achilles. **(b)** Explain why you think these details make such a strong impression.
8. Of which character in Book 22 or 24 do you have the clearest mental picture? Explain your answer.

Extend Understanding

9. **Social Studies Connection:** What can Homer's *Iliad* tell readers about war that a history textbook might not?

QuickReview

Imagery is language that appeals to the senses.

An **epic simile** is a lengthy comparison of two dissimilar things using the word *like* or *as*.

To **picture the action** in a literary work, use details from the text to see the events in your mind.

Go Online Assessment
For: Self-test
Visit: www.PHSchool.com
Web Code: eta-6402

Answers

1. The imagery of cutting reinforces the themes of violent death, separation, and loss.
2. (a) The phrase appeals to the senses of taste and touch. (b) The contrast juxtaposes sleep's magnetic hold with Achilles' restlessness. The effect is to underline the deep trauma in Achilles' spirit.
3. The image of Priam kissing Achilles' hands might hint at the concept of shared mortality; the image of Achilles gazing in silent wonder at Priam might symbolize respect. The ransoming scene as a whole may convey the message of a return from obsession or extreme grief to the realm of shared humanity.
4. The simile emphasizes Hector's determination to defend Troy, even as it hints at the danger Achilles poses.
5. The simile comparing the point of Achilles' spear to the evening star makes Achilles seem more than human. The association of the evening star with death links the image to Hector's approaching doom.
6. (a) **Achilles:** Hawk; **Overlap:** Powerful birds of prey; **Hector:** Attacking eagle. (b) The simile for Achilles emphasizes ferocity whereas the simile for Hector is limited to an objective picture of predation in nature.
Another sample answer can be found on **Literary Analysis Graphic Organizer B**, p. 75 in ***Graphic Organizer Transparencies.***
7. (a) Details may include the following: the chase around the walls; Athena's misleading impersonation of Deiphobus; Achilles' refusal to agree to Hector's proposal of a surrender of the loser's body.
(b) Each of these details is linked with suspense in the epic's climactic scene; each detail deepens the characterization of the heroes.
8. Achilles, Hector, or Priam may be the most memorable characters in these books. Achilles undergoes a pronounced change, from vengeful obsession to mercy; Hector remains noble even as he faces great odds in battle; Priam steels himself to supplicate Achilles for the body of his son.

Answers continued

9. The epic presents the internal conflicts of the leading characters. A social studies textbook would probably present only external conflicts.

Go Online Assessment Students may use the **Self-test** to prepare for **Selection Test A** or **Selection Test B.**

EXTEND/ASSESS

Answers

❶ Vocabulary Lesson

Word Analysis: Latin Root *-lustr-*

1. glossy or shining appearance
2. mediocre; drab
3. picture; exemplify

Spelling Strategy

1. glorious
2. numerous
3. voluminous

Vocabulary Builder

1. synonym
2. antonym
3. synonym
4. synonym
5. synonym
6. antonym
7. antonym
8. synonym

❷ Grammar and Style Lesson

1. Hector begs Achilles, "Don't let the dogs devour me by the Argive ships!"
2. The phrase "breaker of horses" is used to describe Hector.
3. *Correct*
4. Before he dies, Hector predicts, "But now beware, or my curse will draw god's wrath upon your head."
5. *Correct*

Writing Application

Possible response: The funeral games for Patroclus end. Achilles fastens Hector's corpse to a chariot and drags the body "around the tomb of Menoitios' fallen son." However, Apollo pleads with the gods to preserve Hector's body, "Now did not Hector burn thigh pieces of oxen and unblemished goats in your honor?" Priam negotiates with Achilles over the return of Hector's body. Achilles agrees to return Hector's body. A twelve-day truce ensues so that the Trojans may bury Hector.

Build Language Skills

❶ Vocabulary Lesson

Word Analysis: Latin Root *-lustr-*

The words *lustrous* and *illustrious* both contain the Latin root *-lustr-*, which means "light" or "shine." Use your understanding of this root to write a brief definition of the words below. Use a dictionary to check your work.

1. luster **2.** lackluster **3.** illustrate

Spelling Strategy

When you use the suffix *-ous* to form an adjective, you may have to alter the ending of the base word. For example, the adjective *lustrous* comes from the noun *luster.* Use the suffix *-ous* to form an adjective from the following nouns.

1. glory **2.** number **3.** volume

Vocabulary Builder: Synonym or Antonym?

Review the vocabulary words on page 382. Then, indicate whether the word pairs below are synonyms—words with the same meaning—or antonyms—words with opposite meanings.

1. implore, plead
2. whetted, blunted
3. brandished, wielded
4. marshals, manages
5. stinted, limited
6. lustrous, dull
7. gaunt, robust
8. illustrious, eminent

❷ Grammar and Style Lesson

Commas With Quotations

Use a comma after short introductory expressions that precede direct quotations. Do not use a comma when you are only quoting a word, phrase, or fragment of a complete sentence.

Direct quotations:

. . . the fighter cried aloud, "My time has come!"

But Zeus who marshals the storm clouds warned his queen, "Now, Hera, don't fly into such a rage at fellow gods. . . ."

Partial quotations:

Homer refers to Achilles as "the swift runner."

The epithet "white-armed" is often used for the goddess Hera in the *Iliad.*

Practice Revise each sentence below as necessary for the correct use of commas. If a sentence requires no revision, write *Correct.*

1. Hector begs Achilles "Don't let the dogs devour me by the Argive ships!"
2. The phrase, "breaker of horses" is used to describe Hector.
3. Achilles replies, "Beg no more."
4. Before he dies, Hector predicts "But now beware, or my curse will draw god's wrath upon your head."
5. In a striking image, Homer speaks of "young Dawn with her rose-red fingers."

Writing Application Write a paragraph summarizing the action in Book 24. Include at least two direct quotations and one partial quotation in your writing.

WG Prentice Hall Writing and Grammar Connection: Platinum Level, Chapter 28, Section 2

Assessment Practice

Implied Main Ideas of Poetry **(For more practice, see *Test Preparation Workbook*, p. 18.)**

Use the following sample test item to give students practice identifying an implied main idea.

"Now my army's ruined, thanks to my own reckless pride. . . Someone less of a man than I will say, 'Our Hector—staking all on his own strength, he destroyed his army!' So they will mutter."

What does this passage suggest that Hector fears most?

A the destruction of the Trojan forces
B confronting Achilles outside the city walls
C an inferior's insult that has a grain of truth
D the grim future that awaits Andromache

Students should recognize that Choice *C* is the correct answer. Because much of the army has been destroyed, Choice *A* is wrong. Although Hector may fear Achilles, he decides to confront him anyway, so Choice *B* may be eliminated. Choice *D* touches on a topic broached elsewhere in the poem but is outside the scope of the context of this passage.

❸ Writing Lesson

Timed Writing: Editorial

Newspaper columnists often write persuasive editorials condemning or defending the conduct of prominent figures in society. Imagine that you are a columnist during the Trojan War. Write an editorial persuading your audience that Achilles does or does not conduct himself appropriately in the *Iliad*. ***(40 minutes)***

Prewriting *(10 minutes)* Review the *Iliad* and decide whether or not you think Achilles' actions and statements are honorable. Then, find quotations and examples that support your point of view.

Drafting *(20 minutes)* Begin your editorial by briefly describing what you think is appropriate behavior for a warrior in the time of the *Iliad*. Then, give a point-by-point explanation to show why Achilles meets or fails to meet that standard. Support your points with quotations and examples that portray Achilles either positively or negatively.

Revising *(10 minutes)* Review your draft, circling vague or general words and phrases. Replace these words and phrases with forceful, persuasive language.

Model: Revising for Persuasive Language

Achilles calls himself "the best of the Achaeans," but it is clear that this ~~headstrong~~ brutal and arrogant soldier fights only for himself.

A specific description using strong words adds persuasive force.

Prentice Hall Writing and Grammar Connection: Platinum Level, Chapter 8, Section 4

❹ Extend Your Learning

Listening and Speaking With a group of classmates, write and perform the narration for a **movie preview** of a film version of "The Death of Hector." Consider using the following features to enhance your preview:

- excerpts of dialogue from the poem
- background music
- sound effects

Rehearse and perform your preview for the class. **[Group Activity]**

Research and Technology Using library and Internet resources, explore the efforts of archaeologists over the past 150 years to identify and excavate the historical city of Troy. Prepare and present an **oral report** to summarize your findings.

For: An additional research activity
Visit: www.PHSchool.com
Web Code: etd-7401

Assessment Resources

The following resources can be used to assess students' knowledge and skills.

Unit 4 Resources
Selection Test A, pp. 34–36
Selection Test B, pp. 37–39

General Resources
Rubrics for Persuasion: Persuasive Essay, pp. 47–48

Go Online Assessment — Students may use the **Self-test** to prepare for **Selection Test A** or **Selection Test B.**

❸ Writing Lesson

You may use this Writing Lesson as a timed-writing practice, or you may allow students to develop the editorial as a writing assignment over several days.

- To give students guidance in writing this editorial, give them the **Support for Writing Lesson,** p. 31 in ***Unit 4 Resources.***
- Have students use the heroic code of warfare as Homer reveals it in these selections.
- Make sure editorials include examples of Achilles' statements or actions as portrayed in Books 1, 22, and 24 (and by implication in Book 6).
- Encourage students to give their editorials depth by comparing and contrasting Achilles with other characters, such as Hector and Agamemnon.
- Use the the Persuasive Essay rubrics in ***General Resources,*** pp. 47–48, to evaluate students' work.

Writing and Grammar Platinum Level
For support in teaching the Writing Lesson, use Chapter 8, Section 4.

❹ Research and Technology

- Share with students the note on p. 384 relating to the excavations of Schliemann at Troy and Mycenae.
- Encourage students to use a timeline to arrange the results of their research in chronological order.
- Urge students to illustrate their findings with color photographs from magazines or the Internet.
- The **Support for Extend Your Learning** page ***(Unit 4 Resources,*** p. 32) provides guided note-taking opportunities to help students complete the Extend Your Learning activities.

Go Online Research — Have students type in the Web Code for another research activity.

Standard Course of Study

Goal 1: WRITTEN LANGUAGE

WL.1.03.2 Identify and analyze text components, and evaluate impact on personal reflection.

WL.1.03.8 Make connections between works, self and related topics in response and reflection.

Goal 5: LITERATURE

LT.5.01.3 Analyze literary devices and explain their effect on the work of world literature.

LT.5.03.2 Analyze text structure and components and evaluate impact.

LT.5.03.8 Make connections between works, self and related topics in world literature.

Goal 6: GRAMMAR AND USAGE

GU.6.01.4 Use vocabulary strategies to determine meaning.

Step-by-Step Teaching Guide	Pacing Guide
PRETEACH	
• Administer Vocabulary and Reading Warm-ups as necessary.	5 min.
• Engage students' interest with the motivation activity.	5 min.
• Read and discuss author and background features. **FT**	10 min.
• Introduce the Literary Analysis Skill: Lyric Poetry. **FT**	5 min.
• Introduce the Reading Strategy: Responding to Imagery. **FT**	10 min.
• Prepare students to read by teaching the selection vocabulary. **FT**	
TEACH	
• Informally monitor comprehension while students read independently or in groups. **FT**	30 min.
• Monitor students' comprehension with the Reading Check notes.	as students read
• Reinforce vocabulary with Vocabulary Builder notes.	as students read
• Develop students' understanding of lyric poetry with the Literary Analysis annotations. **FT**	5 min.
• Develop students' ability to respond to imagery with the Reading Strategy annotations. **FT**	5 min.
ASSESS/EXTEND	
• Assess students' comprehension and mastery of the Literary Analysis and Reading Strategy by having them answer the Apply the Skills questions. **FT**	15 min.
• Have students complete the Vocabulary Lesson and the Grammar and Style Lesson. **FT**	15 min.
• Apply students' ability to organize to show comparisons by using the Writing Lesson. **FT**	45 min. or homework
• Apply students' understanding by using one or more of the Extend Your Learning activities.	20–90 min. or homework
• Administer Selection Test A or Selection Test B. **FT**	15 min.

Resources

Print

Unit 4 Resources

Transparency

Graphic Organizer Transparencies

Print

Reader's Notebook [L2]

Reader's Notebook: Adapted Version [L1]

Reader's Notebook: English Learner's Version [EL]

Unit 4 Resources

Technology

Listening to Literature Audio CDs [L2, EL]

Print

Unit 4 Resources

General Resources

Technology

Go Online: Research **[L3]**
Go Online: Self-test **[L3]**
ExamView®, **Test Bank [L3]**

Choosing Resources for Differentiated Instruction

[L1] Special Needs Students
[L2] Below-Level Students
[L3] All Students
[L4] Advanced Students
[EL] English Learners

For Vocabulary and Reading Warm-ups and for Selection Tests, **A** signifies "less challenging" and **B** "more challenging." For Graphic Organizer transparencies, **A** signifies "not filled in" and **B** "filled in."

FT Fast Track Instruction: To move the lesson more quickly, use the strategies and activities identified with **FT**.

Scaffolding for Less Proficient and Advanced Students

The leveled Critical Thinking questions after selections progress in the levels of thinking required to answer them. To address the needs of your different students, you may use the (a) level questions for your less proficient students and the (b) level questions with your on-level and advanced students. The occasional (c) level questions are appropriate for your advanced students.

Use this complete suite of powerful teaching tools to make lesson planning and testing quicker and easier.

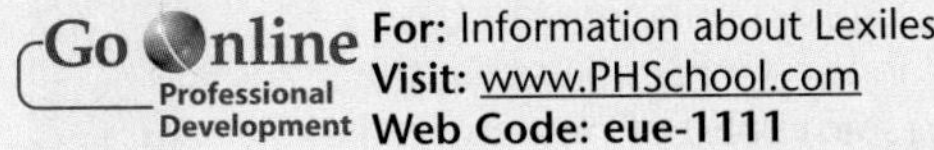

Use the interactive textbook (online and on CD-ROM) to make selections and activities come alive with audio and video support and interactive questions.

Go Online Professional Development
For: Information about Lexiles
Visit: www.PHSchool.com
Web Code: eue-1111

PREACH

Motivation

Tell students that in some ways both Sappho and Pindar invite the people to whom their poems are addressed into a distinctive, different world. Write some definitions of *invite* on the board: "to request the presence and participation of; to request formally; to welcome; to tend to bring on, provoke; to lure, entice." Ask students to think about how these definitions apply to Sappho's and Pindar's poems.

❶ Background

More About the Authors

Sappho's biography is difficult to disentangle from the legends that sprang up about her, many of them based on readings and misreadings of her poetry. She belonged to the aristocracy, and her family was involved in local politics. Along with many aristocrats, Sappho was exiled as a result of factional strife.

Pindar was intensely Theban—a member of a very conservative, tradition-bound aristocracy that still revered the values of the Homeric heroic world. In some ways, his education as a descendant of those old epic heroes—nobles who were constantly aware of how they were connected to the gods and to other nobles in distant communities—gave him the best preparation for becoming a panhellenic poet, one who celebrated victors in athletic contests that themselves look back to the world of Patroclus' funeral games.

Geography Note

Lesbos, Sappho's native island, is located in the Aegean Sea near the northwestern coast of modern Turkey. When Sappho was exiled, she emigrated to Sicily, far to the west. She was eventually allowed to return from exile.

Build Skills | *Poems*

You Know the Place: Then • ❶ He Is More Than a Hero • Olympia 11

Sappho (c. 630 B.C.– c. 570 B.C.)

Late in the seventh century B.C., the fame of earlier lyric poets was eclipsed by Sappho (saf´ ō) of Lesbos, one of the most prolific ancient lyricists. Sappho wrote nearly five hundred poems, only a small fraction of which remain, intact or in fragments. In most of her surviving poems, she addresses various girls of Lesbos, a group of female companions. Some critics believe that Sappho was the priestess of a *thiasos* (thī´ ə sōs), an organized group of women who worshipped Aphrodite. Recent scholars, however, maintain that the circle of girls evident in her poetry were students, or apprentices, who studied poetry and the lyre with Sappho.

Praise and Disapproval Sappho's poetry was admired in antiquity; Plato praised her, and the Roman poets Catullus, Horace, and Ovid alluded to her in their work. In fact, at least six Greek comedies parodied her on the late Greek comic stage. Those plays are now lost, but from them sprang a number of legends about Sappho that were the source of disapproval and, later, hatred of her and her work. For example, according to legend, she was short, dark, and ugly; she was a prostitute; and she committed suicide by throwing herself off a cliff after the ferryman Phaon did not return her love. Although these legends are now discredited, they led the Bishop of Constantinople to order all copies of Sappho's work burned early in the Middle Ages. As a result of the bishop's order and a general loss of classical manuscripts during the Middle Ages, no collection of Sappho's poetry survived the Medieval period.

Rebirth in the Renaissance Interest in Sappho revived during the Renaissance, when scholars used lines quoted by other Greek and Latin writers to reconstruct Sappho's work. Then, in 1879, an incredible discovery in an ancient Egyptian trash site uncovered additional poems by Sappho. Later archaeological digs in the 1890s brought to light shredded papyrus scrolls of Sappho's poetry; these scrolls had been used to wrap mummies and to stuff crocodiles.

Pindar (522 B.C.–440 B.C.)

Little information is available about the life of Pindar (pin´ dər), but it is known that he wrote in a century full of intellectual and political ferment. Although Pindar was born in Thebes, which stood outside the intellectual movements of the time, as a youth he spent a great deal of time away from his provincial birthplace. He may have studied music and poetry in Athens, the intellectual hub of classical Greece.

Odes for Athletes In his twenties, Pindar was commissioned by a great aristocratic family to write an ode in honor of their son's victory in the Olympic double footrace. Eventually, Pindar was commissioned to write for many athletic victors. He was sought after by powerful monarchs and nobles, and he spent time at the courts of the wealthy Sicilian tyrants. Like Sappho, the great fame he achieved in his lifetime lasted through antiquity. The Roman poet Horace, for example, considered Pindar to be a poet of unrivaled eloquence and originality.

Preview

Connecting to the Literature

Both Sappho and Pindar invite their readers into a unique poetic universe. As you read each poem, identify the characteristics of this new cosmos and compare it with the world you know.

Standard Course of Study

- Make connections between works, self and related topics in response and reflection. (WL.1.03.8)
- Analyze text structure and components and evaluate impact. (LT.5.03.2)

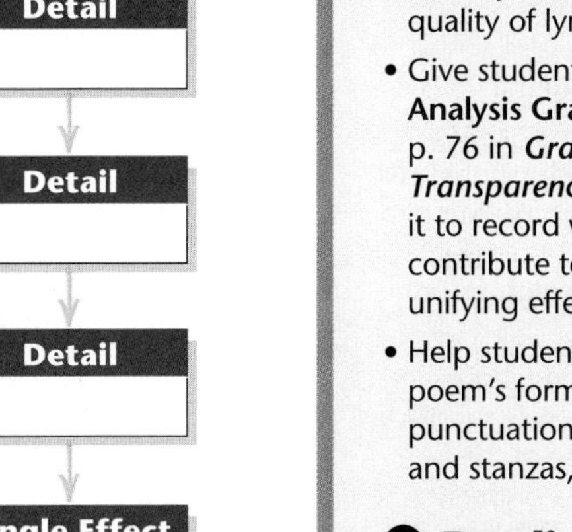

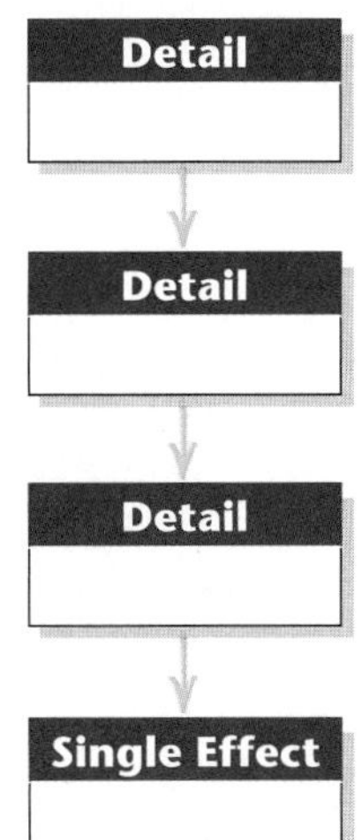

2 Literary Analysis

Lyric Poetry

Lyric poetry expresses the observations and feelings of a single speaker. Lyric poems were originally sung to the accompaniment of a stringed instrument called a lyre. Unlike narrative poems that tell stories, lyric poems focus on producing a single effect. In these lines from "He Is More Than a Hero," for example, the speaker emphasizes the powerful reaction she has to her hero:

> hearing only my own ears
> drumming, I drip with sweat;
> trembling shakes my body

As you read each poem, use a chart like the one shown to record the words and phrases that contribute to a single unifying effect.

Comparing Literary Works

The poems of Sappho and Pindar share the musical quality of lyric poems, but each poem's **form**—its organization and structure—creates a different poetic impression or emotional effect on the reader. Sappho's poems take the form of simple lyrics that are highly personal. In contrast, Pindar's poem, reflecting its purpose to honor winning athletes, uses a more complex and public form known as the **ode.** As you read, consider the ways in which your reaction is affected by each poem's form.

3 Reading Strategy

Responding to Imagery

Lyric poems nearly always use images of the senses—taste, touch, sight, hearing, and smell—to convey ideas and emotions. To **respond to imagery,**

- Identify the sensory word pictures in the poem.
- Take time to consider how these images relate to your own life.

As you read, connect your own experiences to the images and ideas that Sappho and Pindar present.

Vocabulary Builder

sleek (slēk) *adj.* smooth; glossy (p. 415)

murmur (mur′ mər) *n.* low, indistinct, continuous sound (p. 416)

tenuous (ten′ yo͞o əs) *adj.* slender or fine, as a fiber (p. 417)

suffuses (sə fyo͞o′ zəz) *v.* overspreads; fills with a glow (p. 417)

endeavor (en dev′ ər) *n.* earnest attempt at achievement (p. 418)

accordance (ə kôrd′ 'ns) *n.* agreement; harmony (p. 418)

2 Literary Analysis

Lyric Poetry

- Read aloud the Literary Analysis instruction.
- Tell students that the lyre is an ancestor of the guitar. Point out the lyres shown in the images on pp. 414 and 415. Explain that literary devices such as rhythm and repetition of sounds (alliteration and rhyme) enhance the musical quality of lyric poems.
- Give students a copy of **Literary Analysis Graphic Organizer A,** p. 76 in ***Graphic Organizer Transparencies.*** Have them use it to record words and phrases that contribute to each poem's single, unifying effect.
- Help students recognize that a poem's form relates to its use of punctuation, the length of its lines and stanzas, and so on.

3 Reading Strategy

Responding to Imagery

- Remind students that identifying and responding to images can help them understand poetry's deeper, often symbolic, meanings.
- Give students the image of a child attempting to ride a bike. Ask them to describe this image using sensory language (for example, the coldness of the handlebars, the sounds of a cheering parent, the vision of cracked pavement, the smell of falling autumn leaves, the metallic taste of fear).

Vocabulary Builder

- Pronounce each vocabulary word for students, and read the definitions as a class. Have students identify any words with which they are already familiar.

Differentiated Instruction Solutions for All Learners

Support for Special Needs Students

Have students complete the **Preview** and **Build Skills** pages for these poems in the ***Reader's Notebook: Adapted Version.*** These pages provide a selection summary, an abbreviated presentation of the reading and literary skills, and the graphic organizer on the **Build Skills** page in the student book.

Support for Less Proficient Readers

Have students complete the **Preview** and **Build Skills** pages for these poems in the ***Reader's Notebook.*** These pages provide a selection summary, an abbreviated presentation of the reading and literary skills, and the graphic organizer on the **Build Skills** page in the student book.

Support for English Learners

Have students complete the **Preview** and **Build Skills** pages for these poems in the ***Reader's Notebook: English Learner's Version.*** These pages provide a selection summary, an abbreviated presentation of the reading and literary skills, additional contextual vocabulary, and the graphic organizer on the **Build Skills** page in the student book.

TEACH

Facilitate Understanding

To enhance students' understanding of lyric poetry, have them suggest possible topics for lyrics. They may name subjects of lyrics they have already read or fresh subjects that they think would make topics for good lyric poems.

1 Humanities

Sappho and Alcaeus,
by Sir Lawrence Alma-Tadema

Sir Lawrence Alma-Tadema (1836–1912) was an Anglo-Dutch painter. His paintings of classical subjects won him admission to the Royal Academy in 1879 and earned him a knighthood in 1899.

The painting *Sappho and Alcaeus* demonstrates Alma-Tadema's sound archaeological knowledge of the ancient world in the dress of the figures and the details of their surroundings. This classical style of painting was admired in Victorian England.

Use the following questions to initiate discussion:

- What do you imagine is the occasion portrayed here?
  Possible response: Sappho is performing a lyric poem for her circle of students and friends.
- What do the listeners' expressions and postures reveal about their emotions?
  Possible response: The listeners appear to admire Sappho and to be enthralled by her performance.

Poetry of Sappho

1

Sappho and Alcaeus, Sir Lawrence Alma-Tadema, The Walters Art Museum, Baltimore

Differentiated Instruction Solutions for All Learners

Accessibility at a Glance

	You Know the Place: Then	He Is More Than a Hero	Olympia 11
Language	Evocative with sensory images	Vocabulary: echoic words	Formal with metaphors
Concept Level	Accessible (Yearning for love)	Accessible (Love's fearful emotions)	Accessible (Praises for athletic skills)
Literary Merit	Classic lyric poem	Classic lyric poem	Classic lyric poem
Lexile	NP	NP	NP
Overall Rating	Easy	Average	Average

❸

You Know the Place: Then ❷

Sappho

translated by Mary Barnard

Background Sappho wrote her poems for a group of female students who came to the famed poetess to learn the graceful arts of music, dance, and poetry. The school's patron deity was Aphrodite, the goddess of love. Ancient Greeks believed that under Aphrodite's influence the world thrived, flowered, and blossomed. In her poems, Sappho often calls on Aphrodite, who is called "Queen" and "Cyprian" in "You Know the Place: Then," to serve as an ally in love's turmoil.

You know the place: then

Leave Crete and come to us
waiting where the grove is
pleasantest, by precincts

sacred to you; incense
smokes on the altar, cold
streams murmur through the ❹

apple branches, a young
rose thicket shades the ground
and quivering leaves pour

down deep sleep; in meadows
where horses have grown sleek
among spring flowers, dill

❺ scents the air. Queen! Cyprian!
fill our gold cups with love
stirred into clear nectar

Vocabulary Builder
sleek (slēk) *adj.* smooth, glossy

Literary Analysis
Lyric Poetry What kind of musical accompaniment do you think would suit the final lines of this lyric? Explain.

❷ About the Selection

Many of Sappho's poems celebrate beauty and love. "You Know the Place: Then" is an invocation to Aphrodite.

❸ Humanities

Antique vase

This ancient Greek vase painting features a woman playing a lyre. The profile captures her sensitivity and personality. Her intent expression creates an aura of serenity.

Use the following question for discussion:

What conclusions can you draw about a society that features a female musician on a vase?
Possible response: Musical talent was a desirable quality in Greek women.

❹ Reading Strategy

Responding to Imagery

- Have students read the poem in its entirety. Then, **ask** them to identify the sensory images in the bracketed passage.
  Possible response: Sensory images include smoking incense, murmuring streams, a rose thicket, and quivering leaves that "pour down deep sleep."
- **Ask** students to describe the overall mood created by the images.
  Possible response: The mood is lush, sensuous, and peaceful.

❺ Literary Analysis

Lyric Poetry

- Have students read aloud the bracketed stanza.
- Then, **ask** the Literary Analysis question: What kind of musical accompaniment do you think would suit the final lines of this lyric? Explain.
  Possible response: The lines are a stirring invocation to Aphrodite, so they might be accompanied by a crescendo of sweeping strings.

Differentiated Instruction
Solutions for All Learners

Vocabulary for Special Needs Students
Students may be challenged by the words *precincts* (line 4), *quivering* (line 10), *sleek* (line 12), and *nectar* (line 16). Have students work in pairs to compile definitions for the words. When they finish, ask them to substitute new words in context: for example, *areas* for *precincts,* or *shaking* for *quivering.* Guide students to recognize how Sappho's vocabulary creates evocative shades of meaning.

Enrichment for Gifted/Talented Students
Have students prepare an oral reading of this poem, together with suitable musical accompaniment. First, have students practice reading the poem aloud, focusing on such factors as pitch, rate, volume, and emphasis. Then, tell them to find a suitable piece of background music that expresses or reflects the lyric's single, overall effect. After students have prepared their performance, have them deliver it to the class as a whole.

❻ About the Translations

In his first-century treatise *On the Sublime,* Longinus quotes what is apparently the complete text of Sappho's "He Is More Than a Hero." Thus, the text is more certain than that of Sappho's other poems.

Barnard's translations of Sappho have been praised for their "pungent downright plain style" (Dudley Fitts), and some scholars assert that Sappho's writing is more colloquial than literary. Lattimore's language, however, does seem literary. For example, compare his "underneath my breast all the heart is shaken" with Barnard's more natural "makes my own/heart beat fast."

Also, while Lattimore's translation has a breathless quality, Barnard's translation spills more delicately through its three-line stanzas. It is as if the speaker in this version is half-chastened by the awareness of her powerful emotions.

❼ Vocabulary Builder

Echoic Words

- Note the word *murmur,* its definition, and its use in the poem.
- Tell students that in an echoic word like *murmur,* the sound suggests the meaning: "a low, indistinct, continuous sound."
- Write *buzz, thump,* and *pop* on the board. Ask students to explain why each word is echoic.

❽ Reading Strategy

Responding to Imagery

- Ask students to read the first translation in its entirety.
- Discuss how the bracketed stanzas contain images of the senses. Then, **ask** the Reading Strategy question: To what emotions do these sensory images appeal?
  Answer: They appeal to helplessness and fear.
- **Ask:** What might cause the speaker to have these emotions?
  Possible response: The speaker is affected by powerful emotions she feels for the object of her love.

❻ He Is More Than a Hero

Sappho

Comparing Translations

Presented here are two translations of the same poem by Sappho, illustrating some of the choices that translators make when translating poetry. Beyond technical choices, such as whether or not to preserve the poem's original meter, a translator must also decide how—and how much—to interpret the poet's words. What translators do is attempt to re-create for readers the experience of reading a poem in its original language. However, as these two translations of "He Is More Than a Hero" demonstrate, the resulting translation is influenced greatly by the translator's own experience with the text.

translated by Mary Barnard

He is more than a hero

He is a god in my eyes—
the man who is allowed
to sit beside you—he

❼ who listens intimately
to the sweet murmur of
your voice, the enticing

laughter that makes my own
heart beat fast. If I meet
you suddenly, I can't

❽ speak—my tongue is broken;
a thin flame runs under
my skin; seeing nothing,

hearing only my own ears
drumming, I drip with sweat;
trembling shakes my body

and I turn paler than
dry grass. At such times
death isn't far from me

Vocabulary Builder
murmur (mʉr´ mər) *n.* low, indistinct, continuous sound

Reading Strategy
Responding to Imagery
To what emotions do these sensory images appeal?

Enrichment

Women in Ancient Greece

Sappho's status as an acclaimed and respected poet was rare for a woman in her time. Overall, women had far fewer rights and powers than men in ancient Greek society. The negative view of women in Greek culture was concisely summed up by the Athenian statesman Pericles, who stated in his *Funeral Oration* that good women were not talked about in the city, whether in praise or in blame.

In Greek society, women were expected to produce sons, or heirs, for their husbands. In order to prevent any possibility of premarital sex or adultery, daughters and wives were restricted in their movements, keeping mostly to their households.

However, in addition to Sappho, some women achieved distinction and fame, despite the constraints of the time period. Hypatia of Alexandria (died A.D. 415), for example, led a philosophical school and wrote treatises on astronomy.

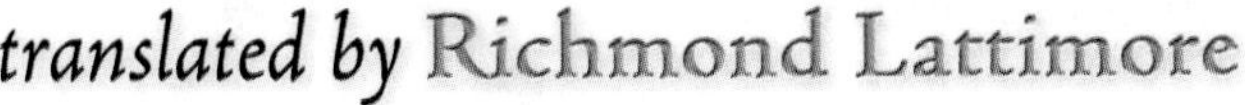

translated by Richmond Lattimore

Like the very gods in my sight is he who
sits where he can look in your eyes, who listens
close to you, to hear the soft voice, its sweetness
murmur in love and

laughter, all for him. But it breaks my spirit;
underneath my breast all the heart is shaken.
Let me only glance where you are, the voice dies,
I can say nothing,

but my lips are stricken to silence, underneath my skin the tenuous flame suffuses;
nothing shows in front of my eyes, my ears are
muted in thunder.

9 And the sweat breaks running upon me, fever
shakes my body, paler I turn than grass is;
I can feel that I have been changed, I feel that
death has come near me.

Vocabulary Builder
tenuous (ten′ yo͞o əs) *adj.* slender or fine, as a fiber
suffuses (sə fyo͞oz′ əz) *v.* overspreads; fills with a glow

Critical Reading

1. **Respond:** Which images in these two poems were most appealing to you? Why?
2. **(a) Recall:** What two requests does the speaker of "You Know the Place: Then" make of Aphrodite? **(b) Infer:** What does the speaker expect from Aphrodite?
3. **(a) Recall:** To what senses do the images in lines 9–18 of the Barnard translation of "He Is More Than a Hero" appeal? **(b) Interpret:** What is the overall effect of these images?
4. **(a) Recall:** At the end of "He Is More Than a Hero," what does the speaker say is close to her? **(b) Interpret:** What emotion does this figurative reference evoke?
5. In "He Is More Than a Hero," the speaker's emotions cloud her ability to think clearly. **(a) Apply:** What other emotions, such as fear, can cause emotions to interfere with reason? **(b) Generalize:** What can people do in these situations?

Go Online
Author Link
For: More about Sappho
Visit: www.PHSchool.com
Web Code: ete-9402

9 Literary Analysis

Lyric Poetry

- Have students reread the final stanza of Lattimore's translation.
- Discuss the atmosphere, or mood, created in these lines. Then, **ask:** What type of music would suitably accompany the poem's conclusion? Explain.
  Possible response: Suitable music might begin loudly, just as the speaker seems overcome by her feelings, and then it might gradually soften as the speaker is left exhausted.

Monitor Progress Ask students to explain why this poem is an example of lyric poetry.
Answer: The poem expresses the feelings of a single speaker, and it uses many images to create a single effect.

Reteach If students have difficulty recognizing the qualities of lyric poetry, have them use **Literary Analysis,** p. 44 in ***Unit 4 Resources.***

ASSESS

Answers

1. **Possible response:** The sacred precinct in "You Know the Place: Then" and love's physical symptoms in "He Is More Than a Hero" were most appealing because of their powerful descriptions.
2. (a) The speaker wants Aphrodite to join the throng of worshipers and give them the gift of love. (b) The speaker expects to receive love.
3. (a) They appeal to hearing, touch, and sight. (b) They express the speaker's trembling submission to love's power.
4. (a) Death is close to her. (b) It evokes fear.
5. (a) **Possible response:** Anger can interfere with reason. (b) **Possible response:** People should try to calm themselves and gain perspective on the situation.

Go Online Author Link For additional information about Sappho, have students type in the Web Code, then select *S* from the alphabet, and then select Sappho.

Differentiated Instruction Solutions for All Learners

Support for Less Proficient Readers
Point out examples of a simile *(like the very gods to my sight is he),* a metaphor *(ears muted in thunder),* and personification *(a thin flame runs under my skin).* Clarify that each contains an unexpected comparison of one thing to another. Ask students to identify the two things compared in each image.

Background for English Learners
Lead a discussion about the challenges that confront translators. Explain that translators must convey the meaning of an original text accurately, but they must also try to convey the spirit, or overall effect, of the text. Have students suggest how their own language might pose interesting problems for translators.

Enrichment for Advanced Readers
Mary Barnard and Richmond Lattimore have translated several of Sappho's poems. Invite students to compare their translations of other of Sappho's poems. Or, have them explore different translators, such as Anne Carson and Willis Barnstone. Have students write comparison-contrast essays on the basis of their research.

⑩ About the Selection

"Olympia 11" is Pindar's ode to a victorious young boxer named Agesidamos. In Pindar's day, victory odes were more than poems; they were celebratory processionals—a whole people joyfully united to pay homage to a young athletic hero.

⑪ Critical Thinking

Interpret

- Have a volunteer read aloud the bracketed passage.
- **Ask** students: What does the speaker mean by saying that "only by God's grace does a man blossom in accordance with his mind's wisdom"?
  Answer: God's grace gives the poet skill to find the right words for the thoughts or "wisdom" that are already in the mind.

ASSESS

Answers

1. (a) The speaker mentions wind and rain. (b) The references allow Pindar to introduce the theme of divine favor.
2. (a) "Soft-spoken songs" allow great deeds to be remembered by future generations. (b) The "great achievements" are athletic victories such as that of the young Agesidamos.
3. **Possible responses:** The poem is effective because the speaker eloquently compliments the young victor's fame and his lineage; the poem is not effective because the imagery and syntax are too dense to be understood readily by large numbers of people.

Go Online Author Link For additional information about Pindar, have students type in the Web Code, then select *P* from the alphabet, and then select Pindar.

⑩ Olympia 11

Pindar

translated by Richmond Lattimore

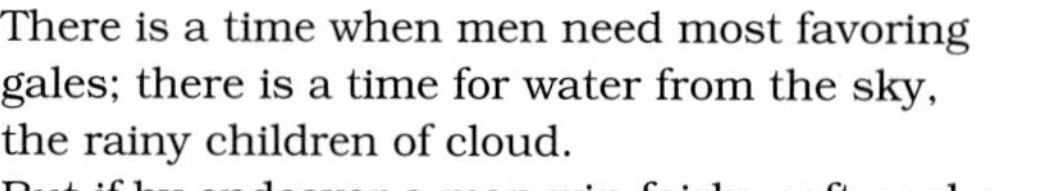

There is a time when men need most favoring
gales; there is a time for water from the sky,
the rainy children of cloud.
But if by endeavor a man win fairly, soft-spoken songs
are given, to be a beginning of men's
speech to come and a trusty pledge for great achievements.

Vocabulary Builder
endeavor (en dev′ ər) *n.* earnest attempt at achievement

⑪ Abundant is such praise laid up for Olympian
winners. My lips have good will
to marshal these words; yet only
by God's grace does a man blossom in accordance with his
mind's wisdom.
Son of Archestratos,[1] know
that for the sake, Agesidamos,[2] of your boxing

Vocabulary Builder
accordance (ə kôrd′ 'ns) *n.* agreement; harmony

I shall enchant in strain of song a glory upon
your olive wreath of gold
and bespeak the race of the West Wind Lokrians.[3]
There acclaim him; I warrant you,
Muses, you will visit no gathering cold to strangers
nor lost to lovely things
but deep to the heart in wisdom, and spearmen also. No
thing, neither hot-colored fox
nor loud lion, may change the nature born in his blood.

1. **Archestratos** (ärk ə strä′ tōs) **father of Agesidamos.**
2. **Agesidamos** (ə ges′ i dä′ mōs) victor in the boys' boxing competition in 476 B.C.
3. **West Wind Lokrians** (lō krē′ ənz) Lokris was a city on the Gulf of Corinth in Greece; "West Wind Lokrians" were Greek-speaking people from the colony of Lokris in southern Italy.

Critical Reading

1. **(a) Recall:** In the first stanza, what two natural forces does the speaker mention? **(b) Analyze:** Why do you think the speaker begins with these references to nature?
2. **(a) Recall:** According to lines 4–7, what is the function of "soft-spoken songs"? **(b) Infer:** To what "great achievements" do you think the speaker refers in line 7?
3. **(a) Evaluate:** In your opinion, is this poem an effective way to praise an athletic hero? Why or why not?

Go Online Author Link
For: More about Pindar
Visit: www.PHSchool.com
Web Code: ete-9403

Apply the Skills

You Know the Place: Then • He Is More Than a Hero • Olympia 11

Literary Analysis

Lyric Poetry

1. **(a)** Identify the observations and feelings of the speaker in the **lyric poem** "You Know the Place: Then." **(b)** What single, overall effect does the poem achieve?
2. In ancient Greece, lyrics were composed to be sung to musical accompaniment. In what ways might such music have reinforced the imagery and the overall effect in "He Is More Than a Hero"?
3. Which characteristics of lyric poetry are found in "Olympia 11"?

Comparing Literary Works

4. **(a)** Compare and contrast the **forms** of the lyrics of Sappho and Pindar. **(b)** How does each poem's form contribute to its effect?
5. In what ways might you describe Sappho's poems as "private" and Pindar's **ode** as "public"?

Reading Strategy

Responding to Imagery

6. **(a)** Use a chart like the one shown to list the **images** that are used to describe the precincts of Aphrodite in Crete in "You Know the Place: Then."

Images for Aphrodite in Crete

Image	Image	Image	Image

(b) What is your **response** to these images?

7. Describe a contemporary experience or event that relates to the images of a "strain of song" and an "olive wreath of gold" in lines 13–14 of "Olympia 11."

Extend Understanding

8. **Cultural Connection:** Pindar's odes celebrate the Olympic athletes of ancient Greece. In what ways are athletes honored in American culture?

QuickReview

Lyric poetry is melodic poetry that expresses the observations and feelings of a single speaker.

A poem's organization and structure, called its **form,** create a particular impression or emotional effect on the reader.

An **ode** is a complex and formal type of lyric that often honors a public figure.

To **respond to imagery,** think about the feelings and ideas that sensory word pictures evoke in you.

Go Online Assessment

For: Self-test
Visit: www.PHSchool.com
Web Code: eta-6403

Answers

1. (a) The speaker observes Aphrodite's sacred precinct, with its altar, streams, rose thicket, meadow, horses, and flowers. The speaker feels anticipation and excitement in awaiting the onset of love. (b) The poem conveys the delightful intensity with which a person anticipates love.
2. **Possible response:** Soft, alluring music might have reinforced the gentle imagery in the first half of "He Is More Than a Hero." Animated, discordant music might have reinforced the fearful and irrational images of the second half.
3. It contains vivid imagery, musical grace, observations and feelings of a single speaker, and an overall unifying effect.
4. (a) The lyrics of both poets are melodic and dense with imagery. However, Sappho's poems are briefer than Pindar's ode and more focused on the speaker's emotions. (b) Sappho's simpler form makes the poems direct and personal; the complex structure of Pindar's ode reflects its formal purpose.
5. **Possible response:** Sappho speaks intensely of private emotions, whereas Pindar publicly praises a young athlete.
6. (a) **Possible response: Image:** altars smoking with incense; **Image:** sleek horses in meadows; **Image:** the smell of dill; **Image:** gold cups filled with clear nectar (b) **Possible response:** The images may evoke a refreshing, emotional response. Another sample answer can be found on **Literary Analysis Graphic Organizer B,** p. 79 in ***Graphic Organizer Transparencies.***
7. **Possible response:** A contemporary example is an Olympic athlete being awarded a medal.
8. **Possible response:** Professional athletes in America receive high pay and celebrity status.

Go Online Assessment Students may use the **Self-test** to prepare for **Selection Test A** or **Selection Test B.**

EXTEND/ASSESS

Answers

❶ Vocabulary Lesson

Word Analysis: Echoic Words

1. to hum like a bee
2. to make a sudden, thudding noise
3. to make a slight, explosive sound
4. to talk continually
5. to bite or chew noisily
6. to make the sound of a prolonged *s*
7. to let fall in fine, mistlike drops
8. to utter a loud, harsh cry

Vocabulary Builder: Synonyms

1. b 3. c 5. b
2. a 4. a 6. b

Spelling Strategy

1. candor 3. conductor
2. humor

❷ Grammar and Style Lesson

1. Sappho, I call upon you as the tenth muse.
2. O moon! You far outshine the stars.
3. Agesidamos, future ages will remember your victory.
4. Aphrodite! Hear my prayer, I beg you.
5. You who sit nearby, remember these songs.

Writing Application

Possible response: Sappho, your poem "You Know the Place: Then" has lifted my spirits. I could almost smell the incense and hear the murmur of the stream. The world you described, Sappho, sounds like a beautiful and peaceful place.

Build Language Skills

❶ Vocabulary Lesson

Word Analysis: Echoic Words

Echoic is the term that dictionaries use to give the etymology, or origin and history, of words whose sound suggests their meaning. These words are called echoic because they echo, or imitate, the sounds that they name. The literary term to describe the use of such words is **onomatopeia.**

Murmur is an example of an echoic, or onomatopoetic, word. Pronounce *murmur* slowly and softly. Notice that the sound of the word suggests its meaning: a low, indistinct, continuous sound.

Pronounce each of the following words, paying close attention to the sound that each word seems to imitate. Then, use the sound of each word to write a brief definition.

1. buzz
2. thump
3. pop
4. chatter
5. crunch
6. hiss
7. drizzle
8. squawk

Vocabulary Builder: Synonyms

Select the letter of the word that is closest in meaning to the first word in each item below.

1. sleek: (a) sly, (b) glossy, (c) candid
2. murmur: (a) hum, (b) crash, (c) melody
3. tenuous: (a) tentative, (b) resigned, (c) slender
4. suffuses: (a) fills, (b) drains, (c) empties
5. endeavor: (a) failure, (b) attempt, (c) defeat
6. accordance: (a) insult, (b) harmony, (c) deprivation

Spelling Strategy

In nouns, the ending *-er* is more common than *-or.* Many nouns ending in *-or* name a quality or role. For each word root below, use *-er* or *-or* to add the proper suffix.

1. cand___ 2. hum___ 3. conduct___

❷ Grammar and Style Lesson

Direct Address

When the speaker in a poem talks directly to someone or something, the form of speech is called **direct address.** Nouns or pronouns of direct address may be followed either by a comma or by an exclamation mark, depending on the degree of emotion in the sentence.

Comma: *Son of Archestratos,* know that for the sake, *Agesidamos,* of your boxing . . .

Exclamation Mark: *Queen! Cyprian!* fill our gold cups with love . . .

Practice In each sentence below, insert a comma or an exclamation mark, as appropriate.

1. Sappho I call upon you as the tenth muse.
2. O moon You far outshine the stars.
3. Agesidamos future ages will remember your victory.
4. Aphrodite Hear my prayer, I beg you.
5. You who sit nearby remember these songs.

Writing Application Write a paragraph in which you address either Sappho or Pindar and give your reactions to a poem you have read and enjoyed. In your paragraph, use two examples of direct address.

WG *Prentice Hall Writing and Grammar Connection: Platinum Level, Chapter 28, Section 2*

Assessment Practice

Stated and Implied Main Ideas **(For more practice, see *Test Preparation Workbook*, p. 19.)**

In many tests, students will have to identify stated and implied main ideas by analyzing works of literature. Have students reread "Olympia 11" on p. 418 and then answer the following question.

Which of the following sentences best describes the dominant thought or feeling of "Olympia 11"?

A The poem is a tribute to the author's talents.
B The poem praises God's grace and wisdom.
C The poem honors a young athlete's victories.
D The poem pleads for the favors of the gods.

The main purpose of the poem is to honor the victories of the young boxer Agesidamos, choice C. The poem does not focus on the author's talents, so choice *A* is incorrect; God's grace is mentioned but is not the main idea of the poem, so choice *B* is incorrect; and choice *D* is not supported by the poem.

3 Writing Lesson

Timed Writing: Comparative Analysis of Translations

Translators of poems work hard to preserve the poem's original meaning and structure within the limits of a different language. Because translators' interpretations vary, translations sometimes differ dramatically. Write an analysis in which you compare and contrast the translations by Mary Barnard and Richmond Lattimore of Sappho's "He Is More Than a Hero." *(40 minutes)*

Prewriting *(10 minutes)* Read each version of the poem carefully. Note specific differences in words, phrases, and emphasis. Use a chart like the one shown to organize your observations.

Model: Comparing and Contrasting Translations

Barnard	Lattimore
Uses metaphor in line 2: "He is a god in my eyes"	Uses simile in line 1: "Like the very gods . . . is he"

Drafting *(20 minutes)* As you draft, choose an effective organization. Either discuss your observations point by point, or discuss your observations about one translation fully and then move on to the next.

Revising *(10 minutes)* Ask a partner to read your draft and help you identify any weak or vague comparisons or contrasts. Replace these points with specific examples.

WG *Prentice Hall Writing and Grammar Connection: Platinum Level, Chapter 9, Section 3*

4 Extend Your Learning

Listening and Speaking Memorize one of Sappho's poems. Then, rehearse a **recitation** of the poem. Use the following tips to enhance your interpretation:

- Adjust the pitch of your voice to echo the poem's tone.
- Change your rate of speaking to reflect the message of the poem.

Present your recitation to an audience of classmates or friends.

Research and Technology With a partner, use library and Internet resources to research the history of the lyre. Then, collect illustrations and notes on other stringed instruments from various cultures. Present your findings in an **illustrated report. [Group Activity]**

For: An additional research activity
Visit: www.PHSchool.com
Web Code: etd-7402

Assessment Resources

The following resources can be used to assess students' knowledge and skills.

Unit 4 Resources
Selection Test A, pp. 51–53
Selection Test B, pp. 54–56

General Resources
Rubrics for Exposition: Comparison-and-Contrast Essay, pp. 53–54

Go Online Assessment: Students may use the **Self-test** to prepare for **Selection Test A** or **Selection Test B.**

3 Writing Lesson

You may use this Writing Lesson as a timed-writing practice, or you may allow students to develop the comparison-and-contrast essay as a writing assignment over several days.

- To give students guidance in writing this comparison-and-contrast essay, give them **Support for Writing Lesson,** p. 48 in ***Unit 4 Resources.***
- Read aloud the Writing Lesson instruction on this page. Remind students that translators may choose different strategies to render the same original text.
- Suggest that students try reading aloud the two translations to compare their structure, diction, and sound effects.
- Use the Exposition: Comparison-and-Contrast Essay rubrics in ***General Resources,*** pp. 53–54, to evaluate students' essays.

WG **Writing and Grammar Platinum Level**

For support in teaching the Writing Lesson, use Chapter 9, Section 2.

4 Listening and Speaking

- Have students read the Listening and Speaking instruction on this page. Because Sappho's poems are brief, most students will find them easy to memorize.
- Remind students that tone is the writer's or speaker's attitude toward the subject matter. Encourage students to use context clues to determine the poem's tone.
- The **Support for Extend Your Learning** page (***Unit 4 Resources,*** p. 49) provides guided note-taking opportunities to help students complete the Extend Your Learning activities.

Go Online Research: Have students type in the Web Code for another research activity.

Standard Course of Study

Goal 1: WRITTEN LANGUAGE

WL.1.02.3 Exhibit an awareness of cultural context of text in a personal reflection.

Goal 3: FOUNDATIONS OF ARGUMENT

FA.3.02.1 State position or proposed solution in an editorial or response.

Goal 4: CRITICAL THINKING

CT.4.02.1 Show an understanding of cultural context in analyzing thematic connections.

CT.4.03.5 Analyze how writers achieve a sense of completeness and closure.

Goal 5: LITERATURE

LT.5.01.1 Use strategies for preparation, engagement, and reflection on world literature.

Goal 6: GRAMMAR AND USAGE

GU.6.01.5 Examine language for elements to apply effectively in own writing/speaking.

Step-by-Step Teaching Guide	Pacing Guide
PRETEACH	
• Administer Vocabulary and Reading Warm-ups as necessary.	5 min.
• Engage students' interest with the motivation activity.	5 min.
• Read and discuss author and background features. **FT**	10 min.
• Introduce the Literary Analysis Skill: Speech. **FT**	5 min.
• Introduce the Reading Strategy: Recognizing Cultural Attitudes. **FT**	10 min.
• Prepare students to read by teaching the selection vocabulary. **FT**	
TEACH	
• Informally monitor comprehension while students read independently or in groups. **FT**	30 min.
• Monitor students' comprehension with the Reading Check notes.	as students read
• Reinforce vocabulary with Vocabulary Builder notes.	as students read
• Develop students' understanding of speeches with the Literary Analysis annotations. **FT**	5 min.
• Develop students' ability to recognize cultural attitudes with the Reading Strategy annotations. **FT**	5 min.
ASSESS/EXTEND	
• Assess students' comprehension and mastery of the Literary Analysis and Reading Strategy by having them answer the Apply the Skills questions. **FT**	15 min.
• Have students complete the Vocabulary Lesson and the Grammar and Style Lesson. **FT**	15 min.
• Apply students' ability to use quotations to support main points by using the Writing Lesson. **FT**	45 min. or homework
• Apply students' understanding by using one or more of the Extend Your Learning activities.	20–90 min. or homework
• Administer Selection Test A or Selection Test B. **FT**	15 min.

Resources

Print

Unit 4 Resources

Transparency

Graphic Organizer Transparencies

Print

Reader's Notebook [L2]

Reader's Notebook: Adapted Version [L1]

Reader's Notebook: English Learner's Version [EL]

Unit 4 Resources

Technology

Listening to Literature Audio CDs [L2, EL]

Reader's Notebook: Adapted Version Audio CD [L1, L2]

Print

Unit 4 Resources

General Resources

Technology

Go Online: Research **[L3]**
Go Online: Self-test **[L3]**
***ExamView®*, Test Bank [L3]**

Choosing Resources for Differentiated Instruction

[L1] Special Needs Students
[L2] Below-Level Students
[L3] All Students
[L4] Advanced Students
[EL] English Learners

For Vocabulary and Reading Warm-ups and for Selection Tests, **A** signifies "less challenging" and **B** "more challenging." For Graphic Organizer transparencies, **A** signifies "not filled in" and **B** "filled in."

FT Fast Track Instruction: To move the lesson more quickly, use the strategies and activities identified with **FT**.

Scaffolding for Less Proficient and Advanced Students

The leveled Critical Thinking questions after selections progress in the levels of thinking required to answer them. To address the needs of your different students, you may use the (a) level questions for your less proficient students and the (b) level questions with your on-level and advanced students. The occasional (c) level questions are appropriate for your advanced students.

PRENTICE HALL **TeacherEXPRESS™** Plan · Teach · Assess Use this complete suite of powerful teaching tools to make lesson planning and testing quicker and easier.

PRENTICE HALL **StudentEXPRESS™** Learn · Study · Succeed Use the interactive textbook (online and on CD-ROM) to make selections and activities come alive with audio and video support and interactive questions.

Benchmark

After students have completed reading "Pericles' Funeral Oration," administer **Benchmark Test 4 *(Unit 4 Resources,* pp. 74–79).** If the Benchmark Test reveals that some of the students need further work, use the **Interpretation Guide** to determine the appropriate reteaching page in the **Reading Kit** and on **Success Tracker.**

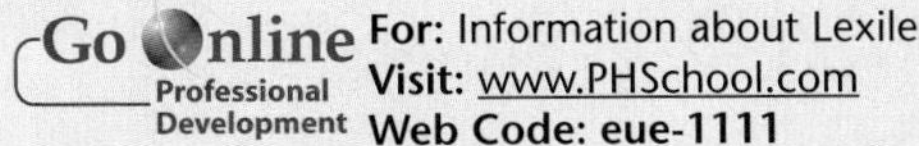

For: Information about Lexiles
Visit: www.PHSchool.com
Web Code: eue-1111

PRETEACH

Motivation

Although he is speaking in memory of the war dead of Athens, Pericles' true purpose is to inspire, challenge, and direct its living citizens. Ask students to cite well-known national orations. (Students may list speeches of Patrick Henry, Abraham Lincoln, John Kennedy, Martin Luther King, Jr., and more recent national leaders.) Ask: What cultural values or principles do these speeches express?

❶ Background

More About the Author

Although he was born in Thrace, Thucydides was connected with the old conservative nobility of Athens. His family's longstanding involvement in political life probably shaped his historical methods.

He examined the Peloponnesian War from a variety of angles. He was keenly interested in the politics of the war and attentive to the military aspects of a conflict between a powerful land force, Sparta, and a powerful naval force, Athens.

The primary aim of Thucydides, however, was to study human behavior in wartime. He was famous for his pessimism. The moral decline he noticed as the war dragged on caused him to predict the "inevitable corrosion of the human spirit."

Geography Note

Draw students' attention to the map on this page. Remind them that the Peloponnesian War was a conflict between the Greek cities of Athens, on the Ionian coast, and Sparta, an inland city-state that controlled most of the Peloponnese.

Build Skills | *Primary Source*

❶ Pericles' Funeral Oration *from* History of the Peloponnesian War

Thucydides (460 B.C.–404 B.C.)

The Athenian Thucydides (thōō sid′ i dēz′) is known as the greatest historian in antiquity and one of the most influential historians ever. No certain information about his life exists beyond what he reveals about himself in the course of his writing. However, his objective, scientific approach to history laid the foundation for modern historical methods.

Military Failure Thucydides was an important military magistrate in the Peloponnesian War, the long and bloody conflict between Athens and Sparta that ended with the fall of the Athenian empire. He appointed himself historian of the Peloponnesian War at its outset, and he called it the "greatest war of all." During his command of a fleet based at Thasos, he failed to protect the crucial Athenian colony of Amphipolis from a surprise Spartan attack. He went to trial for his military failure and was exiled for twenty years until the war ended.

Historical Success Exile provided Thucydides with the opportunity to observe the war from a distance. He took notes of events as they occurred, researched extensively, and recorded firsthand accounts of events told to him by Athenians and Spartans. Using the information he gathered, he wrote his historical masterpiece, the *History of the Peloponnesian War*.

In the first stages of his work, Thucydides took notes on events in which he participated or that he observed from a distance. Then, he rewrote and arranged his notes into a consecutive narrative. Finally, he elaborated the narrative so that it would not read as a mere chronicle of events. Unfortunately, he died before he could complete the *History*; it stops abruptly six years before the end of the war, though all the speeches are very polished. Thucydides is believed to have died suddenly in 404 B.C., shortly after Athens' defeat.

A Lasting Legacy Thucydides believed that history could be understood in terms of human behavior. Consequently, he presented character studies of leading Athenian and Spartan statesmen, in which he examined the human mind in wartime. Through the speeches included in the *History*, he articulated the motives and ambitions of both armies impartially. He aimed to teach people so that they would avoid making the same mistakes he witnessed in this war.

With a passion for truth, Thucydides refused to "accept all stories of ancient times in an uncritical way," and he adhered to rigorous standards of accuracy. Achieving accuracy was, by his own admission, difficult when he had to reconstruct speeches. Because he used speeches to paint a kind of moral portrait, he may have given himself freedom in shaping the speeches while maintaining their basic truth. In his words:

> I have found it difficult to remember the precise words used in the speeches which I listened to myself and my various informants have experienced the same difficulty; so my method has been, while keeping as closely as possible to the general sense of the words that were actually used, to make the speakers say what, in my opinion, was called for by each situation.

To what extent Thucydides relied on his opinion in reconstructing Pericles' funeral oration is uncertain, but he was a great admirer of Pericles, and he probably heard Pericles deliver the annual speech honoring the Athenian war dead in the winter of 430 B.C.

Preview

Connecting to the Literature

War always causes great loss of life, even for the winning side. In this speech, Pericles offers comfort to families of slain Athenian soldiers and inspires them to deal with their grief in positive ways.

❷ Literary Analysis

Speech

A **speech** is an oral presentation on an important issue. The speaker determines the content of the speech by considering the speech's *purpose*, the *occasion* for which it is being given, and the *audience* to whom it is addressed.

Speeches often include rhetorical techniques such as *restatement* (repeating an idea in different words) and *parallelism* (repeating grammatical structures).

Connecting Literary Elements

One form of speech is an **oration,** a formal address intended to inspire listeners and incite them to action. Orators deliver an impassioned appeal to the audience's religious, moral, or patriotic values. Classical orations like Pericles' have seven identifiable parts:

- an *opening,* intended to capture the audience's attention
- a *narration,* or recital of facts
- an *exposition,* or definition, of issues to be addressed
- a *proposition* to clarify the issues and state the speaker's purpose
- a *confirmation* to address arguments for and against the proposition
- a *confutation,* or refutation, to disprove opposing arguments
- a *conclusion,* or epilogue, to summarize arguments and stir listeners

Notice how Pericles develops his oration using these techniques.

❸ Reading Strategy

Recognizing Cultural Attitudes

Pericles' speech reveals the values and attitudes of Athenian society. For example, when he says that "the greatest glory of a woman is to be least talked about by men, whether they are praising you or criticizing you," he reveals women's inferior status in that society. Complete a chart like this one, listing and explaining passages that reveal Athenians' **cultural attitudes.**

Passage	Attitude It Reveals
______	______
______	______

Vocabulary Builder

incredulous (in krej′ oo ləs) *adj.* disbelieving; doubtful; skeptical (p. 425)

manifold (man′ ə fōld′) *adj.* many; various (p. 429)

tangible (tan′ jə bəl) *adj.* definite; objective (p. 429)

consummation (kän′ sə mā′ shən) *n.* state of supreme perfection, skillfulness, and expertise (p. 429)

culmination (kul′ mə nā′ shən) *n.* highest point or climax (p. 430)

commiserate (kə miz′ ər āt′) *v.* share grief or sorrow (p. 431)

NC Standard Course of Study

- Show an understanding of cultural context in analyzing thematic connections. (CT.4.02.1)
- Analyze how writers achieve a sense of completeness and closure. (CT.4.03.5)

❷ Literary Analysis

Speech

- Remind students that, although they will be reading a printed text, a speech is an oral form, meant to be spoken and heard.
- Read the instruction about speech together as a class. If you have not already done so, have students cite and discuss well-known historical or contemporary speeches.
- Use the instruction for Connecting Literary Elements to introduce students to the specific features of an oration. Encourage students to look for these elements as they read Pericles' speech.

❸ Reading Strategy

Recognizing Cultural Attitudes

- Point out that a speech may reveal more than a speaker actually intends, including cultural values, beliefs, and attitudes. For example, when he exhorts Athenians to have more children "to fill the empty places" left by war, Pericles is expressing a fairly coercive notion of civic duty.
- Give students a copy of **Reading Strategy Graphic Organizer A,** p. 80 in ***Graphic Organizer Transparencies.*** Have students use it to help them "read between the lines" for cultural attitudes in the oration.

Vocabulary Builder

- Pronounce each vocabulary word for students, and read the definitions as a class. Have students identify any words with which they are already familiar.

Differentiated Instruction — Solutions for All Learners

Support for Special Needs Students

Have students read the adapted version of *Pericles' Funeral Oration* in the ***Reader's Notebook: Adapted Version.*** This version provides basic-level instruction in an interactive format with questions and write-on lines. Completing these pages will prepare students to read the selection in the Student Edition.

Support for Less Proficient Readers

Have students read *Pericles' Funeral Oration* in the ***Reader's Notebook.*** This version provides basic-level instruction in an interactive format with questions and write-on lines. After students finish the selection in the ***Reader's Notebook,*** have them complete the questions and activities in the Student Edition.

Support for English Learners

Have students read *Pericles' Funeral Oration* in the ***Reader's Notebook: English Learner's Version.*** This version provides basic-level instruction in an interactive format with questions and write-on lines. Completing these pages will prepare students to read the selection in the Student Edition.

Facilitate Understanding

Tell students that they will be reading a public funeral oration. Help them think about what elements they might expect to find in a funeral speech of any sort, and list on the board key ideas they generate. Then, have students think about what would have to be different in an oration delivered in public. List these elements also, and encourage students to keep these expectations in mind as they read Pericles' speech.

❶ About the Selection

In his reconstruction of Pericles' speech, Thucydides presents two major concepts that weave through his *History:* the characteristics that have made Athens such a strong city-state economically and militarily and the ideals that the city represents. In its articulation of what Athenians were fighting for, Pericles' oration becomes one of the central artifacts of Hellenic culture and values.

1 PERICLES' FUNERAL ORATION

from HISTORY OF THE PELOPONNESIAN WAR

Thucydides

translated by Rex Warner

Background Pericles, a great statesman of ancient Greece, tried to unite his country under the leadership of his own city, Athens. He also promoted democracy in Athens. During his rule, which is sometimes called the Golden Age of Greece, many magnificent buildings, including the Parthenon, were built. Pericles was one of Athens' ten generals, or *strategoi* (strat´ ə goi), during the Peloponnesian War and is considered the greatest Athenian politician in the early days of that war. In isolation, his speech is a glowing account of Athens and of Athenian democracy, but it is not a complete picture of Athens as an imperial power. In fact, later in the war, Pericles was the target of angry criticism for his aggressive, expansionist policies.

In the same winter the Athenians, following their annual custom, gave a public funeral for those who had been the first to die in the war. These funerals are held in the following way: two days before the ceremony the bones of the fallen are brought and put in a tent which has been erected, and people make whatever offerings they wish to their own dead. Then there is a funeral procession in which coffins of cypress wood are carried on wagons. There is one coffin for each tribe, which contains the bones of members of that tribe. One empty bier is decorated and carried in the procession: this is for the missing, whose

Differentiated Instruction Solutions for All Learners

Accessibility at a Glance

	Pericles' Funeral Oration, *from* History of the Peloponnesian War
Context	Public funeral speech by General Pericles during the Peloponnesian War in Ancient Athens
Language	Challenging: rhetorical techniques include restatement and parallelism
Concept Level	Accessible (Value of happiness, freedom, courage, and honor)
Literary Merit	Classic oration of Hellenic culture and values
Lexile	1240L
Overall Rating	Challenging

bodies could not be recovered. Everyone who wishes to, both citizens and foreigners, can join in the procession, and the women who are related to the dead are there to make their laments at the tomb. The bones are laid in the public burial-place, which is in the most beautiful quarter outside the city walls. Here the Athenians always bury those who have fallen in war. The only exception is those who died at Marathon,[1] who, because their achievement was considered absolutely outstanding, were buried on the battlefield itself.

When the bones have been laid in the earth, a man chosen by the city for his intellectual gifts and for his general reputation makes an appropriate speech in praise of the dead, and after the speech all depart. This is the procedure at these burials, and all through the war, when the time came to do so, the Athenians fol-
2 lowed this ancient custom. Now, at the burial of those who were the first to fall in the war Pericles, the son of Xanthippus,[2] was chosen to make the speech. When the moment arrived, he came forward from the tomb and, standing on a high platform, so that he might be heard by as many people as possible in the crowd, he spoke as follows:

"Many of those who have spoken here in the past have praised the institution of this speech at the close of our ceremony. It seemed to them a mark of honor to our soldiers who have fallen in war that a speech should be made over them. I do not agree. These men have shown themselves valiant in action, and it would be enough, I think, for their glories to be proclaimed in action, as
3 you have just seen it done at this funeral organized by the state. Our belief in the courage and manliness of so many should not be hazarded on the goodness or badness of one man's speech. Then it is not easy to speak with a proper sense of balance, when a man's listeners find it difficult to believe in the truth of what one is saying. The man who knows the facts and loves the dead may well think that an oration tells less than what he knows and what he would like to hear: others who do not know so much may feel envy for the dead, and think the orator over-praises them, when he speaks of exploits that are beyond their own capacities. Praise of other people is tolerable only up to a certain point, the point where one still believes that one could do oneself some of the
4 things one is hearing about. Once you get beyond this point, you will find people becoming jealous and incredulous. However, the fact is that this institution was set up and approved by our forefathers, and it is my duty to follow the tradition and do my best to meet the wishes and the expectations of every one of you.

"I shall begin by speaking about our ancestors, since it is only right and proper on such an occasion to pay them the honor of

1. **Marathon** (mar′ ə thän′) ancient Greek village near Athens where the Athenians defeated the Persians in 490 B.C.
2. **Xanthippus** (zan′ thi pəs) victorious Athenian general in the war against Persia, and a member of one of the most illustrious noble families of Athens.

Literary Analysis
Speech According to Thucydides, what is the purpose of Pericles' speech?

Literary Analysis
Speech and Oration Why might Pericles open his oration by questioning the tradition of funeral orations?

Vocabulary Builder
incredulous (in krej′ oo ləs) *adj.* disbelieving; doubtful; skeptical

5 
Reading Check
Why does Pericles object to the tradition of a funeral oration for fallen Athenian soldiers?

Differentiated Instruction Solutions for All Learners

Strategy for Less Proficient Readers
Have students work in pairs to read through the speech, stopping at the end of each paragraph to consider any cultural attitudes expressed. Students can use their copy of the Literary Analysis graphic organizer to record their findings. Students should report to the class the cultural differences they find and discuss them.

Strategy for Advanced Readers
Point out the adroit maneuverings of Pericles' opening statement. He praises the heroism of the dead, defuses charges that he is exaggerating, recognizes the pitfalls of audience reaction, and reminds his listeners that he is only doing his duty. Have students rewrite this paragraph in their own words to clarify these details for the rest of the class.

2 Literary Analysis
Speech
- Remind students that a key element of a speech is its purpose. Ask students to review Pericles' opening statement to establish his purpose.
- **Ask** the first Literary Analysis question: According to Thucydides, what is the purpose of Pericles' speech?
  Answer: Thucydides says that the purpose of Pericles' speech is to honor the fallen soldiers. He will follow that tradition, even though he believes that the soldiers' glories are self-evident and that one man's words might not be properly balanced to give due honor.

3 Literary Analysis
Speech and Oration
- Have students read the second bracketed passage.
- Then, **ask** the second Literary Analysis question: Why might Pericles open his oration by questioning the tradition of funeral orations?
  Answer: The opening of a classical oration is meant to capture the audience's attention. Pericles' contrarian comments about the tradition would likely startle his audience and ensure their close attention.

4 Vocabulary Builder
Latin Root *-cred-*
- Call students' attention to the word *incredulous* and its definition. Tell them that the Latin root *-cred-* means "believe."
- Have students suggest other words that contain this root, and list them on the board.
  Possible response: Students may suggest *credible, incredible, credentials,* and *credit.*

5 Reading Check
Answer: The soldiers' deeds have already honored them more than any speech could, and their memory should not depend on the quality of one man's speech.

❻ Literary Analysis

Speech and Oration

- Point out that when Pericles states "I shall say nothing about" the heroism of Athenian soldiers, he is of course drawing attention to that very thing. This rhetorical ploy was so common in classical times that the Romans gave it a name: *praeteritio.*
- "Mentioning by not mentioning" is still common today both in public speeches and in ordinary conversation. ("I would never mention my opponent's recent arrest.") Ask students to recall or make up examples. ("I'm far too polite to point out your tardiness.")
- **Ask** the Literary Analysis question: Which of the seven parts of a classical oration is Pericles using in this paragraph?
  Answer: Pericles uses proposition here as he clarifies the issues and states his purpose.

❼ Reading Strategy

Recognizing Cultural Attitudes

- Point out to students that a speaker's cultural attitudes can be stated explicitly as well as implied. Have students review the bracketed passage for direct statements of cultural values.
- **Ask** the Reading Strategy question: What do Pericles' comments on public and private life show about the Athenian attitude toward tolerance of people's differences?
  Possible response: Athenians believe that tolerance is important, and in private life they respect individual differences. In public life, however, there seems to be less latitude, as evidenced by the statement "we keep to the law."

recalling what they did. In this land of ours there have always been the same people living from generation to generation up till now, and they, by their courage and their virtues, have handed it on to us, a free country. They certainly deserve our praise. Even more so do our fathers deserve it. For to the inheritance they had received they added all the empire we have now, and it was not without blood and toil that they handed it down to us of the present generation. And then we ourselves, assembled here today, who are mostly in the prime of life, have, in most directions, added to the power of our empire and have organized our State in such a way that it is perfectly well able to look after itself both in peace and in war.

❻ "I have no wish to make a long speech on subjects familiar to you all: so I shall say nothing about the warlike deeds by which we acquired our power or the battles in which we or our fathers gallantly resisted our enemies, Greek or foreign. What I want to do is, in the first place, to discuss the spirit in which we faced our trials and also our constitution and the way of life which has made us great. After that I shall speak in praise of the dead, believing that this kind of speech is not inappropriate to the present occasion, and that this whole assembly, of citizens and foreigners, may listen to it with advantage.

Literary Analysis
Speech and Oration Which of the seven parts of a classical oration is Pericles using in this paragraph?

"Let me say that our system of government does not copy the institutions of our neighbors. It is more the case of our being a model to others, than of our imitating anyone else. Our constitution is called a democracy because power is in the hands not of a minority but of the whole people. When it is a question of settling private disputes, everyone is equal before the law; when it is a question of putting one person before another in positions of public responsibility, what counts is not membership of a particular ❼ class, but the actual ability which the man possesses. No one, so long as he has it in him to be of service to the state, is kept in political obscurity because of poverty. And, just as our political life is free and open, so is our day-to-day life in our relations with each other. We do not get into a state with our next-door neighbor if he enjoys himself in his own way, nor do we give him the kind of black looks which, though they do no real harm, still do hurt people's feelings. We are free and tolerant in our private lives; but in public affairs we keep to the law. This is because it commands our deep respect.

Reading Strategy
Recognizing Cultural Attitudes What do Pericles' comments on public and private life show about the Athenian attitude toward tolerance of people's differences?

"We give our obedience to those whom we put in positions of authority, and we obey the laws themselves, especially those which are for the protection of the oppressed, and those unwritten laws which it is an acknowledged shame to break.

"And here is another point. When our work is over, we are in a position to enjoy all kinds of recreation for our spirits. There are various kinds of contests and sacrifices regularly throughout the year; in our own homes we find a beauty and a good taste

Enrichment

The Cost of Culture

There is no such thing as a free lunch—or a free Golden Age. The astounding half-century of Athenian achievement in art, architecture, philosophy, drama, and democracy was nourished in part by financial tributes from its allied city-states—monies intended for the common defense of the empire. While Athens was sated with cash and culture, Sparta and its allies gnawed on a meager diet of suspicion and resentment that eventually caused them to bring war to the gates of Athens. The Golden Age of Athens was ultimately paid for in coin of blood during the Peloponnesian War. Pericles died of plague during the siege of Athens, one year after his famous speech.

which delight us every day and which drive away our cares. Then the greatness of our city brings it about that all the good things from all over the world flow in to us, so that to us it seems just as natural to enjoy foreign goods as our own local products.

"Then there is a great difference between us and our opponents, in our attitude towards military security. Here are some examples: Our city is open to the world, and we have no periodical deportations[3] in order to prevent people observing or finding out secrets which might be of military advantage to the enemy. This is because we rely, not on secret weapons, but on our own real courage and loyalty. There is a difference, too, in our educational systems. The Spartans, from their earliest boyhood, are submitted to the most laborious training in courage; we pass our lives without all these restrictions, and yet are just as ready to face the same dangers as they are. Here is a proof of this: When the Spartans invade our land, they do not come by themselves, but bring all their allies with them; whereas we, when we launch an attack abroad, do the job by ourselves, and, though fighting on foreign soil, do not often fail to defeat opponents who are fighting

3. **deportations** (dē′ pôr tā′ shənz) *n.* orders that force people to leave the country.

9 ▲ Critical Viewing

What does the painting on this urn suggest about Athenians' attitude toward education? **[Infer]**

Reading Check 10

Name one way in which Pericles considers Athens superior to Sparta.

8 Humanities

Attic Red-figured Cup,
by Douris Painter

The Athenian vase decorator who signed his works "Douris made it" was one of the premier painters of the fifth century B.C. He was primarily a cup painter who produced over two hundred works that survive to the present day.

Pictured is a detail of a piece by Douris called the Schoolmaster Cup. A characteristic of this painter is the careful attention to the hands and drapery of each figure.

This urn is an example of the "red-figure" technique, in which a dark color is applied to the background, allowing the figures to appear in the natural red color of the clay.

Use the following questions for discussion:

- What physical objects do you notice in the painting on the urn?
  Possible response: Visible in the painting are musical instruments (a stringed instrument, a flute or pipes) and writing implements (a stylus or pen, a tablet).
- What activities do you see depicted on the cup?
  Possible response: The painting shows scenes of teaching, with adults seeming to demonstrate writing and music to individual students.

9 Critical Viewing

Possible response: The painting seems to glorify learning, suggesting that Athenians held education in high regard.

10 Reading Check

Possible response: The Spartans rely on foreign allies when attacking Athens. When the Athenians attack Sparta, they do so without foreign assistance.

Differentiated Instruction Solutions for All Learners

Enrichment for English Learners

Have students work in small groups to research traditions of honoring the dead. Ask them to find information about holidays such as Mexico's traditional Day of the Dead and about public events such as funeral orations for soldiers or firefighters who have died serving their country or community. Ask each group to present their findings in an oral report.

Enrichment for Gifted/Talented Students

Have students conduct research on Mexico's Day of the Dead and on public orations for those who have died serving their country or community. Ask students to find examples of clothing, memorial artwork, or other visual reminders of these events. Then, encourage students to create replicas of the items or make collages that feature images of the items. Students should present their work to the class along with background information.

⓫ Reading Strategy

Recognizing Cultural Attitudes

- Read aloud the bracketed passage.
- Have students **respond** to the first Reading Strategy item: Explain the Athenian attitude toward individual responsibility and duty.
  Answer: Athenians believe that it is the duty of citizens to be well informed about politics so that they can participate in decisions about the common good.
- Point out to students that Pericles seems to make political participation mandatory: "a man who takes no interest in politics . . . has no business here at all" (an Athenian version of "love it or leave it"). **Ask** students how this attitude relates to Pericles' earlier description of Athenian tolerance.
  Possible response: Pericles makes a distinction between the tolerance of "private life" and the sterner duties of "public affairs." This may account for the apparent paradox.

⓬ Reading Strategy

Recognizing Cultural Attitudes

- Have a volunteer read aloud the bracketed passage.
- **Ask** students the second Reading Strategy question: What do these lines about goodwill suggest about the Athenian attitude toward generosity?
  Answer: Athenians believe that one should be generous regardless of profit or loss.
- **Ask** students to consider how this picture of Athenian generosity relates to Pericles' account of a proud Athenian empire forcing "entry into every sea and land."
  Possible response: Students may find some inconsistency in these two aspects of Athens, which Pericles presents in virtually the same breath. It is possible that Pericles is again observing a distinction between the generosity of Athens in "private life" and the more self-aggrandizing "public" behavior of the dominant state.

for their own hearths and homes. As a matter of fact none of our enemies has ever yet been confronted with our total strength, because we have to divide our attention between our navy and the many missions on which our troops are sent on land. Yet, if our enemies engage a detachment[4] of our forces and defeat it, they give themselves credit for having thrown back our entire army; or, if they lose, they claim that they were beaten by us in full strength. There are certain advantages, I think, in our way of meeting danger voluntarily, with an easy mind, instead of with a laborious training, with natural rather than with state-induced courage. We do not have to spend our time practicing to meet sufferings which are still in the future; and when they are actually upon us we show ourselves just as brave as these others who are always in strict training. This is one point in which, I think, our city deserves to be admired. There are also others:

⓫ "Our love of what is beautiful does not lead to extravagance; our love of the things of the mind does not make us soft. We regard wealth as something to be properly used, rather than as something to boast about. As for poverty, no one need be ashamed to admit it: the real shame is in not taking practical measures to escape from it. Here each individual is interested not only in his own affairs but in the affairs of the state as well: even those who are mostly occupied with their own business are extremely well-informed on general politics—this is a peculiarity of ours: we do not say that a man who takes no interest in politics is a man who minds his own business; we say that he has no business here at all. We Athenians, in our own persons, take our decisions on policy or submit them to proper discussions: for we do not think that there is an incompatibility between words and deeds; the worst thing is to rush into action before the consequences have been properly debated. And this is another point where we differ from other people. We are capable at the same time of taking risks and of estimating them beforehand. Others are brave out of ignorance; and, when they stop to think, they begin to fear. But the man who can most truly be accounted brave is he who best knows the meaning of what is sweet in life and of what is terrible, and then goes out undeterred to meet what is to come.

⓬ "Again, in questions of general good feeling there is a great contrast between us and most other people. We make friends by doing good to others, not by receiving good from them. This makes our friendship all the more reliable, since we want to keep alive the gratitude of those who are in our debt by showing continued goodwill to them: whereas the feelings of one who owes us something lack the same enthusiasm, since he knows that, when he repays our kindness, it will be more like paying back a debt than giving something spontaneously. We are unique in this.

Reading Strategy
Recognizing Cultural Attitudes Explain the Athenian attitude toward individual responsibility and duty.

Reading Strategy
Recognizing Cultural Attitudes What do these lines about goodwill suggest about the Athenian attitude toward generosity?

4. **engage a detachment** enter into conflict with troops.

When we do kindnesses to others, we do not do them out of any calculations of profit or loss: we do them without afterthought, relying on our free liberality. Taking everything together then, I declare that our city is an education to Greece, and I declare that in my opinion each single one of our citizens, in all the manifold aspects of life, is able to show himself the rightful lord and owner of his own person, and do this, moreover, with exceptional grace and exceptional versatility. And to show that this is no empty boasting for the present occasion, but real tangible fact, you have only to consider the power which our city possesses and which has been won by those very qualities which I have mentioned. Athens, alone of the states we know, comes to her testing time in a greatness that surpasses what was imagined of her. In her case, and in her case alone, no invading enemy is ashamed at being defeated, and no subject can complain of being governed by people unfit for their responsibilities. Mighty indeed are the marks and monuments of our empire which we have left. Future ages will wonder at us, as the present age wonders at us now. We do not need the praises of a Homer, or of anyone else whose words may delight us for the moment, but whose estimation of facts will fall short of what is really true. For our adventurous spirit has forced an entry into every sea and into every land; and everywhere we have left behind us everlasting memorials of good done to our friends or suffering inflicted on our enemies.

"This, then, is the kind of city for which these men, who could not bear the thought of losing her, nobly fought and nobly died. It is only natural that every one of us who survive them should be willing to undergo hardships in her service. And it was for this reason that I have spoken at such length about our city, because I wanted to make it clear that for us there is more at stake than there is for others who lack our advantages; also I wanted my words of praise for the dead to be set in the bright light of evidence. And now the most important of these words has been spoken. I have sung the praises of our city; but it was the courage and gallantry of these men, and of people like them, which made her splendid. Nor would you find it true in the case of many of the Greeks, as it is true of them, that no words can do more than justice to their deeds.

14 "To me it seems that the consummation which has overtaken these men shows us the meaning of manliness in its first revelation and in its final proof. Some of them, no doubt, had their faults; but what we ought to remember first is their gallant conduct against the enemy in defense of their native land. They have blotted out evil with good, and done more service to the commonwealth than they ever did harm in their private lives. No one of these men weakened because he wanted to go on enjoying his wealth: no one put off the awful day in the hope that he might live to escape his poverty and grow rich. More to be desired than

Vocabulary Builder

manifold (man′ ə fōld′) *adj.* many; various

tangible (tan′ jə bəl) *adj.* definite; objective

13

Vocabulary Builder

consummation (kän′ sə mā′ shən) *n.* state of supreme perfection, skillfulness, and expertise

15  **Reading Check**

Why has Pericles spoken at such length about Athens?

13 Humanities

Warrior Draped in Cloak

In this bronze statue, the figure wears an unusual Corinthian-style helmet. The helmet and the artful shaping of the cloak produce an almost abstract image of soldiery.

Use the following question for discussion:

How is the warrior in this sculpture depersonalized?
Possible response: The helmet and cloak conceal individualizing characteristics. The rigid, unbending pose creates a forbidding aspect.

14 Literary Analysis

Speech

- Have a volunteer read aloud the bracketed passage, and then **ask:** According to Pericles, what can a heroic death accomplish for a man's reputation?
Answer: Pericles asserts that imperfect men have "blotted out" the wrongs they committed in life by gallant conduct on the battlefield.

➤ **Monitor Progress** Review with students the Literary Analysis instruction on p. 423. Then, have students **scan** the remainder of the selection, noting the use of rhetorical techniques such as restatement and parallelism.
Possible response: Examples of parallelism include the last complete sentence on this page ("No one . . . /no one . . ."). Examples of restatement include the last sentence in the first paragraph on p. 431 ("One's sense of honor . . .").

➤ **Reteach** If students have difficulty identifying rhetorical techniques, use **Literary Analysis** support page 61 in ***Unit 4 Resources.***

15 Reading Check

Answer: Pericles wants his audience to know what the soldiers died defending and also to understand that it is the courage of people like the soldiers that makes Athens great.

Differentiated Instruction Solutions for All Learners

Support for Less Proficient Readers

The style of the oration is dense and the arguments complicated. Point out that Pericles has two main aims: (1) to discuss the qualities that make Athens great and (2) to honor and praise those who died in battle. Encourage students to notice as they read how each passage relates to one of these two points. Help students outline the progression of Pericles' arguments.

Enrichment for Gifted/Talented Students

Invite students to prepare oral interpretations of passages from Pericles' oration. Have them consider various techniques for making the work accessible to an audience, such as appropriate gestures, speaking rate, volume, pitch, and tone. Remind students that all of these elements contribute to an effective delivery. Students may wish to select appropriate background music for their interpretations.

16 Themes in World Literature

History as Literature After reading and discussing "History as Literature," you may wish to invert the topic to discuss literature—and art—as history. Point out, for example, how Greek art conveys significant historical details about how Athenians looked and lived. Ask students to consider how their sense of American historical epochs has been shaped by novels and works of art, as well as by history books. Ask students to think about how history might be written a thousand years from now. What artifacts of the present time will survive to portray current events and culture?

Connect to the Literature Point out to students that many readers prefer historical novels and drama because they serve the double purpose of informing as well as entertaining.

- Ask students to share their ideas about what they might find entertaining in Thucydides' *History of the Peloponnesian War.* **Possible response:** It would be worthwhile to read this work to see what stories the author uses to reveal cultural attitudes about war and the enemy and attitudes toward women in Athenian society.

17 Critical Thinking

Analyze

- **Ask** students what concepts of patriotism they find in this passage. **Possible response:** Patriotism is often described in terms of duty or obligation that is owed to the country one inhabits. Pericles, by contrast, suggests that citizens "fall in love" with their country every day. This personal, constantly refreshed attachment should spring from a true appreciation of the greatness of Athens. Pericles might define patriotism as a loving allegiance to the essential nature of one's country.
- Point out to students that in his discussions of battlefield conduct, heroic sacrifice, citizenship, and memorials to the dead, Pericles conspicuously never mentions the gods or Greek religion. He deals with the issue of courage and heroic death consistently in human terms.

such things, they chose to check the enemy's pride. This, to them, was a risk most glorious, and they accepted it, willing to strike down the enemy and relinquish everything else. As for success or failure, they left that in the doubtful hands of Hope, and when the reality of battle was before their faces, they put their trust in their own selves. In the fighting, they thought it more honorable to stand their ground and suffer death than to give in and save their lives. So they fled from the reproaches of men, abiding with life and limb the brunt of battle; and, in a small moment of time, the climax of their lives, a culmination of glory, not of fear, were swept away from us.

17 "So and such they were, these men—worthy of their city. We who remain behind may hope to be spared their fate, but must resolve to keep the same daring spirit against the foe. It is not simply a question of estimating the advantages in theory. I could tell you a long story (and you know it as well as I do) about what is to be gained by beating the enemy back. What I would prefer is that you should fix your eyes every day on the greatness of Athens as she really is, and should fall in love with her. When you realize her greatness, then reflect that what made her great was men with a spirit of adventure, men who knew their duty, men who were ashamed to fall below a certain standard. If they ever failed in an enterprise, they made up their minds that at any rate the city should not find their courage lacking to her, and they gave to her the best contribution that they could. They gave her their lives, to her and to all of us, and for their own selves they won praises that never grow old, the most splendid of sepulchers[5]—not the sepulcher in which their bodies are laid, but where their glory remains eternal in men's minds, always there on the right occasion to stir others to speech or to action. For famous men have the whole earth as their memorial: it is not only the inscriptions on their graves in their own country that mark them out; no, in foreign lands also, not in any visible form but in people's hearts, their memory abides and grows. It is for you to try to be like them. Make up your minds that happiness depends on being free, and freedom depends on being courageous. Let there be no relaxation in face of the perils of the war. The people who have most excuse for despising death are not the wretched and unfortunate, who have no hope of doing well for themselves, but those who run the risk of a complete reversal in their lives, and who would feel the difference most intensely, if things went wrong for them. Any intelligent man would find a humiliation caused by his own slackness more painful to bear than death, when

5. **sepulchers** (sep′ əl kərz) *n.* graves.

16 History as Literature

Just as a great deal of history can be found in literature, many historical works can be read as literature. Thucydides' *History of the Peloponnesian War* is part of a long tradition of works that are informative enough to be read for historical purposes but compelling enough to be read for pure entertainment. Another example of this type of work is the *Annals* (c. 117) of Tacitus, which details the excesses of the Roman emperors who succeeded Augustus Caesar. *A Journal of the Plague Year* (1722) by Daniel Defoe, gives a fictional narrator's first-person account of the outbreak of bubonic plague in the 1660s. More than two centuries later, Mark Bowden's *Black Hawk Down* gives a gripping account of an American military mission gone awry. Published in 1999, Bowden's book was hailed by historians and literary critics alike proving that the tradition of history as literature is alive in modern times.

Connect to the Literature

What aspects of Thucydides' *History* do you think can be read for entertainment as well as for information?

Vocabulary Builder

culmination (kul′ mə nā′ shən) *n.* highest point or climax

Enrichment

Women in Athens

Pericles' words to Athenian women express succinctly the official view of their role. Athenian women could have no public role as citizens. They could not plead for themselves in court, nor could they hold office or control property. They were forever wards of a male kinsman and never treated as adults or as free agents. Their only public functions were religious; they were allowed special roles when it came to birth and death.

Ironically, Pericles' own partner in life, Aspasia, was famous for her education, charm, and wit. Pericles cherished her company and valued her advice; some political opponents claimed that she wrote Pericles' speeches.

death comes to him unperceived, in battle, and in the confidence of his patriotism.

"For these reasons I shall not commiserate with those parents of the dead, who are present here. Instead I shall try to comfort them. They are well aware that they have grown up in a world where there are many changes and chances. But this is good fortune—for men to end their lives with honor, as these have done, and for you honorably to lament them: their life was set to a measure where death and happiness went hand in hand. I know that it is difficult to convince you of this. When you see other people happy you will often be reminded of what used to make you happy too. One does not feel sad at not having some good thing which is outside one's experience: real grief is felt at the loss of something which one is used to. All the same, those of you who are of the right age must bear up and take comfort in the thought of having more children. In your own homes these new children will prevent you from brooding over those who are no
18 more, and they will be a help to the city, too, both in filling the empty places, and in assuring her security. For it is impossible for a man to put forward fair and honest views about our affairs if he has not, like everyone else, children whose lives may be at stake. As for those of you who are now too old to have children, I would ask you to count as gain the greater part of your life, in which you have been happy, and remember that what remains is not long, and let your hearts be lifted up at the thought of the fair fame of the dead. One's sense of honor is the only thing that does not grow old, and the last pleasure, when one is worn out with age, is not, as the poet said, making money, but having the respect of one's fellow men.

"As for those of you here who are sons or brothers of the dead, I can see a hard struggle in front of you. Everyone always speaks well of the dead, and, even if you rise to the greatest heights of heroism, it will be a hard thing for you to get the reputation of having come near, let alone equaled, their standard. When one is alive, one is always liable to the jealousy of one's competitors, but when one is out of the way, the honor one receives is sincere and unchallenged.

"Perhaps I should say a word or two on the duties of women to those among you who are now widowed. I can say all I have to say in a short word of advice. Your great glory is not to be inferior to what God has made you, and the greatest glory of a woman is to be least talked about by men, whether they are praising you or criticizing you. I have now, as the law demanded, said what I had

Vocabulary Builder
commiserate (kə miz′ ər āt′) *v.* share grief or sorrow

20 ▼ **Critical Viewing**
What does this vase painting suggest about how war was viewed in ancient Greece? **[Infer]**

19

21 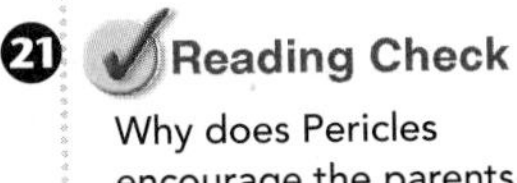 **Reading Check**
Why does Pericles encourage the parents of fallen soldiers to have more children?

18 Literary Analysis
Speech
- Have students read the bracketed passage independently, and then **ask:** What action does Pericles say he wants certain members of his audience to take?
  Answer: Pericles wants Athenian families to have more children.
- **Ask** students whether Pericles' request seems motivated more to help individual families or to help Athens in time of war.
  Possible response: Of Pericles' several reasons, one is clearly beneficial to bereaved families; three have benefits for Athens, including the calculation that having children at risk will increase a citizen's commitment to the war.

19 Humanities
Red-figured Volute Krater
The ancient Greeks used kraters, or mixing bowls, to blend wine and water. They are characterized by sturdy handles projecting from the neck and body of the bowl. The handles on this bowl resemble the volutes, or spirals, of an Ionic capital. This is another example of the red-figure technique in which color is applied to the background, leaving figures and objects in natural clay color.

Use the following question for discussion:

What scenes are depicted on this bowl?
Answer: The bowl displays scenes of battle.

20 Critical Viewing
Possible response: The painting suggests that the Greeks viewed war as something to be commemorated, but not necessarily celebrated. It suggests that people should remember the bravery of soldiers but also remember that war causes great suffering.

21 Reading Check
Answer: New children will prevent parents from brooding over the children they lost. More children will also make the city stronger.

Differentiated Instruction Solutions for All Learners

Enrichment for English Learners
Have students form groups to discuss societal rules about death and mourning in their native cultures. For example, have students compare timely burial customs, rules and norms for acceptable mourning periods, and ways in which the dead are remembered. Have each group present a brief oral summary to the class.

Enrichment for Advanced Readers
Have students form groups and select three ancient or modern cultures that interest them. Have groups research death customs in the cultures and write a brief report that compares and contrasts the burial customs and mourning periods of each. Ask groups to present their findings to the class.

ASSESS

Answers

1. **Possible response:** The freedom and tolerance in Athenian society is admirable; however, the culture's attitude toward women is not.
2. (a) Pericles says that the Athenian system is superior to other systems and that Athens is a model for other cities. (b) He is trying to arouse feelings of pride and honor.
3. (a) Pericles says that the Spartans must submit "to the most laborious training in courage," whereas the Athenians pass their lives "without all these restrictions."
(b) **Possible response:** He is suggesting that Athenians are naturally courageous.
4. (a) Pericles says that a man with no interest in politics has no business in Athens. (b) This suggests that the Athenians are so committed to democracy that they regard it a duty to participate in decision making.
5. (a) The war dead "blotted out evil with good" by serving the commonwealth and thus made Athens "splendid" with their "courage and gallantry." (b) **Possible response:** Because the war dead died with honor, they have the "most splendid of sepulchers"—they continue to inspire Athenians. They have "the whole earth as their memorial."
6. (a) According to Pericles, "Happiness depends on being free, and freedom depends on being courageous." (b) **Possible response:** Freedom is at the core of Pericles' statement; freedom is won with courage, and happiness comes with freedom.
7. (a) According to Pericles, it is fortunate to die with honor, so the survivors should take comfort in that. (b) **Possible response:** The Athenians believed that honor was extremely important and that it would be better to die with honor than to live in dishonor.
8. **Possible response:** During her campaign, a politician concluded a rousing speech by calling on the audience to vote for her party.

Go Online **Author Link** For additional information about Thucydides, have students type in the Web Code, then select *T* from the alphabet, and then select Thucydides.

to say. For the time being our offerings to the dead have been made, and for the future their children will be supported at the public expense by the city, until they come of age. This is the crown and prize which she offers, both to the dead and to their children, for the ordeals which they have faced. Where the rewards of valor are the greatest, there you will find also the best and bravest spirits among the people. And now, when you have mourned for your dear ones, you must depart."

Critical Reading

1. **Respond:** What do you admire most about Athenian society as described by Pericles in his funeral oration? What do you admire least?
2. **(a) Recall:** According to Pericles, how does the Athenian system of government compare to that of its neighbors? **(b) Deduce:** What emotions is Pericles trying to arouse in his listeners by making this comparison?
3. **(a) Recall:** What does Pericles say about the educational systems of Sparta and Athens with regard to courage? **(b) Infer:** What is Pericles suggesting about the nature of Athenians?
4. **(a) Recall:** What is Pericles' attitude toward a man who has no interest in politics? **(b) Infer:** What does this suggest about the Athenians' commitment to the principles of democracy?
5. **(a) Recall:** In honoring the war dead, Pericles says that their deaths accomplished two things. What are these two things? **(b) Analyze Causes and Effects:** Explain what each accomplishment has meant to the soldiers and to Athens.
6. **(a) Recall:** On what do happiness and freedom depend, according to Pericles? **(b) Interpret:** What values seem to be most important to Pericles?
7. **(a) Recall:** What comfort does Pericles offer to the parents of the dead? **(b) Draw Conclusions:** What does this tell you about the Athenian attitude toward honor?
8. **Apply:** Think about speeches you have heard given by political figures and community leaders, or even a pep talk given by a good coach. Then, give an example of how one of these speakers used elements of oration in his or her speech.

For: More about Thucydides
Visit: www.PHSchool.com
Web Code: ete-9404

Apply the Skills

Pericles' Funeral Oration

Literary Analysis

Speech

1. Complete a chart like this one to analyze the techniques Pericles uses in his **speech.**

	Example	Effect
Restatement		
Parallelism		

2. **(a)** Give one example of how Pericles appeals to his audience's sense of morality. **(b)** Why might this kind of appeal be particularly effective?
3. In your opinion, what is Pericles' most successful appeal to his audience's patriotism? Explain.

Connecting Literary Elements

4. **(a)** What is Pericles' proposition in this **oration**? **(b)** Where does he state his proposition most clearly?
5. List the arguments that Pericles presents in support of his proposition.
6. Explain how Pericles uses the example of the Spartans to address opposing viewpoints.
7. What is inspiring about the concluding paragraph of Pericles' oration?

Reading Strategy

Recognizing Cultural Attitudes

8. Explain the Athenian **cultural attitudes** toward wealth and poverty that are revealed in this selection.
9. Pericles says that a man achieves a position of public responsibility based on his actual ability, not on his social class. What does this say about the Athenian attitude toward the individual?

Extend Understanding

10. **Social Studies Connection:** In a time of mourning, crisis, or emergency, what effect can a speech like Pericles' have on those who hear it? Explain.

QuickReview

A **speech** is an oral presentation on an important issue. The speaker considers the speech's *purpose*, its *occasion*, and its *audience*. Speeches often include rhetorical techniques such as *restatement* and *parallelism*.

An **oration** is a formal speech intended to inspire listeners and incite them to action.

To **recognize cultural attitudes,** be aware of how literature reveals the values and attitudes of a society.

For: Self-test
Visit: www.PHSchool.com
Web Code: eta-6404

Answers

1. **Possible response:** **Example:** "What counts is not membership of a particular class, but the actual ability which the man possesses. No one, so long as he has it in him to be of service to the state, is kept in political obscurity because of poverty." **Effect:** This restatement of the same idea emphasizes its importance. **Example:** "Our love of what is beautiful does not lead to extravagance; our love of the things of the mind does not make us soft." **Effect:** The parallel structure makes the idea easy to remember.
   Another sample answer can be found on **Literary Analysis Graphic Organizer B** in ***Graphic Organizer Transparencies,*** p. 83.
2. (a) **Possible response:** Pericles' claim that Athenians "make friends by doing good to others, not by receiving good from them" is a moral appeal. (b) Athenians value morality.
3. **Possible response:** Pericles appeals to Athenian patriotism with: "our city is an education to Greece. . . ."
4. (a) Pericles' proposition is that he will honor the dead. (b) He states his proposition most clearly when he says, "What I want to do is . . . discuss the spirit in which we faced our trials and . . . the way of life which has made us great. After that I shall speak in praise of the dead . . ."
5. Pericles argues that Athens is a model of democracy and Athenians are naturally tolerant and law-abiding. He praises the dead for their sacrifice to preserve the Athenian way of life.
6. Pericles speaks in negative terms about the educational system and military tactics of Sparta.
7. **Possible response:** The paragraph concludes by invoking the "best and bravest spirits among the people."
8. Athenians look at wealth as something to be used but not flaunted. They see poverty as nothing to be ashamed of.
9. Athenians respect an individual's abilities; social class was neither a help nor a hindrance in gaining respect.

Answers continued

10. **Possible response:** Speeches like these can unite people in a common cause.

Go Online Assessment Students may use the **Self-test** to prepare for **Selection Test A** or **Selection Test B.**

EXTEND/ASSESS

Answers

1 Vocabulary Lesson

Word Analysis: Latin Root *-cred-*

1. b 2. c 3. a

Vocabulary Builder

1. f 3. a 5. c
2. e 4. b 6. d

Spelling Strategy

1. commiseration
2. consummation
3. fascination

2 Grammar and Style Lesson

1. Pericles spoke as follows:
2. Here are some examples:
3. This is a peculiarity of ours:
4. Several orators of the twentieth century come to mind: Winston Churchill, Franklin D. Roosevelt, and Martin Luther King, Jr.
5. Dear Sir or Madam: It has come to my attention . . .

Writing Application

Possible response: Before extended quotation: His words began in a memorable way: "Friends, Romans, countrymen . . ." **Before an explanation:** His excuse for being late was unacceptable: He had forgotten to set his alarm clock. **Before an example:** This recipe has one hard-to-find ingredient: crystallized ginger. **After the salutation in a business letter:** Dear Dr. Parker:

WG Writing and Grammar Platinum Level

For support in teaching the Grammar and Style Lesson, use Chapter 28, Section 3.

Build Language Skills

1 Vocabulary Lesson

Word Analysis: Latin Root *-cred-*

The word *incredulous* derives from the root *-cred-*, which comes from the Latin word *credere*, meaning "to believe." With the prefix *in-*, meaning "not," *incredulous* means "not believing." Use your understanding of the meaning of the root *-cred-* to choose the word from this list that best completes each sentence:

a. incredible **b.** discredit **c.** credence

1. The fact that he was a Spartan tended to __?__ him in Athens.
2. The general put great __?__ in the accuracy of the report.
3. The __?__ bravery of the soldier made him a hero.

Vocabulary Builder: Antonyms

Match each vocabulary word on the left with its antonym, or opposite, on the right.

1. commiserate — **a.** beginning
2. consummation — **b.** believing
3. culmination — **c.** few
4. incredulous — **d.** abstract
5. manifold — **e.** incompleteness
6. tangible — **f.** rejoice

Spelling Strategy

When adding the suffix *-tion* to a verb that ends in *-te*, first drop these letters. For example, *culminate* + *-tion* = *culmination*. For each of the following words, write its noun form ending in *-tion*.

1. commiserate **2.** consummate **3.** fascinate

2 Grammar and Style Lesson

Colons

A **colon** is a punctuation mark **(:)** used before an extended quotation, an explanation, an example, or a series, and after the salutation in a formal letter.

> These funerals are held in the following way: two days before the ceremony . . .

Practice Copy each item on a separate sheet of paper, inserting a colon where needed.

1. Pericles spoke as follows "Many of those who have spoken here in the past have praised the institution of this speech. . . ."
2. Here are some examples Our city is open to the world, and we have no periodical deportations. . . .
3. This is a peculiarity of ours We do not say that a man who takes no interest in politics is a man who minds his own business. . . .
4. Several orators of the twentieth century come to mind Winston Churchill, Franklin D. Roosevelt, and Martin Luther King, Jr.
5. Dear Sir or Madam
   It has come to my attention that there is a problem. . . .

Writing Application Write an example of each use of the colon: before an extended quotation, an explanation, an example, or a series, and after the salutation in a formal letter.

WG Prentice Hall Writing and Grammar Connection: Platinum Level, Chapter 28, Section 3

Assessment Practice

Stated and Implied Main Ideas **(For more practice, see *Test Preparation Workbook*, p. 20.)**

For practice, give students the following sample test question.

> "For these reasons I shall not commiserate with those parents of the dead, who are present here. Instead I shall try to comfort them. . . . But this is good fortune—for men to end their lives with honor, as these have done, and for you honorably to lament them: their life was set to a measure where death and happiness went hand in hand."
>
> —from Pericles' Funeral Oration

What is the implied main idea of this passage?

A Do not try to comfort grieving parents.
B Grieving parents should have more children.
C People honor the dead by living.
D Happiness and death mean the same thing.

A, B, and *D* each refer to details from the paragraph, not the implied main idea. The correct answer is *C*.

❸ Writing Lesson

Essay About Leadership

In his funeral oration, Pericles demonstrates why he is considered to have been the greatest Athenian statesman. Using details from his speech, write an essay in which you discuss qualities of leadership.

Prewriting Review the speech to identify qualities of leadership. Then, organize them into an outline of your essay.

Drafting Begin with an introduction in which you define leadership and discuss why it is important in wartime. Refer to Pericles' speech as you develop your essay, using examples of how Pericles demonstrates leadership.

Model: Using Quotations to Support Main Points

Realizing the importance of leadership even in mourning, Pericles offers comfort to the families of the fallen. "But this is a good fortune—for men to end their lives with honor, as these have done . . . ," he says, lightening the burden of the survivors.

Examples from the work help support the main points of an essay.

Revising Review your paper, making sure you have supported your main points. Consider color-coding to identify supporting details. Use a different color to highlight details that answer each of these questions: *Who? What? When? Where? Why?* If you find you have not included information that answers each question, revise your draft.

WG *Prentice Hall Writing and Grammar Connection: Platinum Level, Chapter 12, Section 3*

❹ Extend Your Learning

Listening and Speaking With a small group, present an **oral interpretation** of Pericles' oration. Take turns interpreting paragraphs, keeping in mind the following questions:

- What is Pericles saying?
- To what Athenian values is Pericles trying to appeal?

As you prepare your presentation, make sure that your interpretation suits the mood of the occasion. **[Group Activity]**

Research and Technology Pericles claims that everyone is equal under Athenian law. Evaluate the truth of this claim through research, including use of the Internet. Present your findings in the form of a **rights chart.** Your chart might include these headings: *men, women, slaves, boys, girls.* It also might include a list of rights and privileges, such as voting, owning property, and marrying.

For: An additional research activity
Visit: www.PHSchool.com
Web Code: etd-7403

Assessment Resources

The following resources can be used to assess students' knowledge and skills.

Unit 4 Resources
- **Selection Test A,** pp. 68–70
- **Selection Test B,** pp. 71–73
- **Benchmark Test 4,** pp. 74–79

General Resources
- **Rubrics for Response to Literature,** pp. 55–56

Go Online Assessment Students may use the **Self-test** to prepare for **Selection Test A** or **Selection Test B.**

Benchmark

Administer **Benchmark Test 4.** If some students need further work, use the **Interpretation Guide** to determine the appropriate reteaching page in the **Reading Kit** and on **Success Tracker.**

❸ Writing Lesson

- To give students guidance in writing this extended definition, give them **Support for Writing Lesson,** p. 65 in ***Unit 4 Resources.***
- Ask students to cite leaders whom they admire and to list specific words that exemplify their leadership qualities. Write these words on the board.
- As an alternative, ask: What emotions do citizens need to feel about their nation? How does Pericles achieve this?
- Use the Writing Lesson to guide students in developing their essays.
- Suggest that students trade drafts with partners to check support for their main points.
- Use the Response to Literature rubrics in ***General Resources,*** pp. 55–56, to evaluate students' work.

WG Writing and Grammar Platinum Level

For support in teaching the Writing Lesson, use Chapter 12, Section 3.

❹ Research and Technology

- Encourage students to avoid judging Athenian society against modern standards of social equality. Point out that at the time Thomas Jefferson was writing "All men are created equal," women in the American colonies had about the same political and legal status that Athenian women had 2,500 years before.
- Suggest that students add two columns to their charts: one for the modern United States and one for Sparta.
- Have students work in small groups to create their research charts and report their findings to the class.
- The **Support for Extend Your Learning** page (***Unit 4 Resources,*** p. 66) provides guided note-taking opportunities to help students complete the Extend Your Learning activities.

Go Online Research Have students type in the Web Code for another research activity.

Standard Course of Study

FA.3.03.3 Emphasize culturally significant events in editorials.

FA.3.04.7 Identify and analyze influences, contexts, or biases in argument.

LT.5.01.6 Make connections between historical and contemporary issues in world literature.

Connections

American Literature

Leaders throughout time have faced the difficult task of honoring fallen soldiers. In addition to explaining the deaths, leaders must also highlight and honor the causes for which soldiers have died. Both Pericles and Abraham Lincoln use great eloquence in addressing this challenge. Have students reread Pericles' Funeral Oration after they have read Lincoln's "Gettysburg Address." Challenge students to find similarities and differences between the two speeches.

Honoring the Dead

- Explain to students that Lincoln took the opportunity to speak at Gettysburg very seriously. Historians say that he was still revising the speech even as he spoke, for example, adding the phrase "under God" to describe the nation. An experienced speaker, Lincoln probably anticipated the positive effect this suggestion of divine approval of the United States and its goals of freedom would have on the audience.
- Invite volunteers to read aloud both speeches to underscore the eloquence of these great leaders. This will also help students identify overlapping ideas in the two texts.
- Point out that wartime leaders need to rally citizens around ideals such as liberty, justice, democracy, and so on. Both Pericles and Lincoln emphasize key ideals on which the futures of their societies rest.

CONNECTIONS

American Literature

Honoring the Dead

The battle of Gettysburg, Pennsylvania, fought in July 1863, was an important Union victory and marked a turning point in the Civil War in the United States. More than 50,000 Union and Confederate soldiers were killed or wounded in the battle. On November 19, 1863, while the war still raged, a military cemetery on the Gettysburg battlefield was dedicated. Unsure of President Lincoln's availability, the dedication organizers slated him as a secondary speaker, asking him to make only "a few appropriate remarks." In his brief address, Lincoln wanted to lead the 15,000 citizens attending the dedication through an emotional rite of passage. He also needed to gain continuing support for a bloody conflict that was far from over.

Timeless Praise for Fallen Soldiers Like Pericles in his *Funeral Oration*, Lincoln maintains in his address that a speech cannot really honor the soldiers who have died. Their brave actions have already brought them honor, and those actions will be remembered long after the speeches have ended. Centuries separate ancient Greece from nineteenth-century America, but Pericles and Lincoln speak with similar eloquence about their honored dead and the ideals for which they died. Though Lincoln's speech is much briefer than Pericles' oration—just 272 words—its reaffirmation of the democratic principles at the heart of American government is comparable to Pericles' pride in the democratic government of Athens.

◀ **Critical Viewing** What mood does the facial expression of this statue—the centerpiece of the Lincoln Memorial in Washington D.C.—convey? **[Analyze]**

Answers continued

- Explain that a wartime leader honoring the dead wants to comfort grieving families and secure support for a war effort. Have students preview the text and note that Lincoln accomplishes this with a speech of only 272 words. Have students compare this with Pericles' Funeral Oration and consider whether its greater length increases its effectiveness.

Critical Viewing

Possible response: Lincoln's facial expression can be described with words such as *grave, serious, resolute, concerned,* and *solemn.*

The Gettysburg Address

Abraham Lincoln

CONNECTIONS

Four score and seven years ago our fathers brought forth on this continent a new nation, conceived in Liberty, and dedicated to the proposition that all men are created equal.

Now we are engaged in a great civil war, testing whether that nation, or any nation so conceived and so dedicated, can long endure. We are met on a great battle-field of that war. We have come to dedicate a portion of that field, as a final resting place for those who here gave their lives that that nation might live. It is altogether fitting and proper that we should do this.

But, in a larger sense, we can not dedicate we can not consecrate[1]—we can not hallow[2]—this ground. The brave men, living and dead, who struggled here, have consecrated it, far above our poor power to add or detract. The world will little note, nor long remember what we say here, but it can never forget what they did here. It is for us the living, rather, to be dedicated here to the unfinished work which they who fought here have thus far so nobly advanced. It is rather for us to be here dedicated to the great task remaining before us that from these honored dead we take increased devotion to that cause for which they gave the last full measure of devotion hat we here highly resolve that these dead shall not have died in vain that this nation, under God, shall have a new birth of freedom and that government of the people, by the people, for the people, shall not perish from the earth.

1. **consecrate** (kän′ sə krāt′) *v.* cause to be revered or honored
2. **hallow** (hal′ ō) *v.* make holy or sacred

Abraham Lincoln (1809–1865)

Abraham Lincoln served in the Illinois state legislature and the United States Congress, where he earned a reputation as a champion of emancipation. He ran for the United States Senate in 1858. Lincoln lost the election, but his heated debates with Stephen Douglas brought him national recognition and helped him win the presidency in 1860.

Shortly after his election, the Civil War erupted. Throughout the war, Lincoln showed great strength and courage. He also demonstrated his gift for oratory, working diligently and thoughtfully to prepare effective messages. Lincoln was assassinated in 1865 while attending the theater with his wife.

Connecting American Literature

1. **(a)** Which speech is longer: Lincoln's address or Pericles' oration? **(b)** How does the length of a speech affect audience reaction?
2. How does the setting of a speech affect the way it is prepared and the way it is heard by an audience?
3. From each speech, give three examples of powerful language.
4. Which of these two speeches do you think would have been more interesting to hear? Explain.

Humanities

Lincoln Memorial,
by Henry Bacon, 1922

The Lincoln Memorial includes more than the statue designed by Daniel Chester French. Henry Bacon's memorial resembles a Greek temple with thirty-six columns. Each column represents one of the states in existence at the time of Lincoln's election. The walls surrounding the statue are inscribed with the words of Lincoln's "Gettysburg Address," his "Second Inaugural Address," and murals by Jules Guerin.

Use the following question for discussion:

Henry Bacon based his memorial on a Greek temple. What might this suggest about the relationship between American and ancient Greek ideals?
Answer: Americans value the same ideals as the ancient Greeks.

ASSESS

Answers

1. (a) Pericles' oration is longer than Lincoln's address. (b) A short speech keeps audiences attentive.
2. The setting may affect the way a speech is heard, such as with Lincoln's address at the Gettysburg cemetery; it was made more powerful by the surrounding graves.
3. **Possible responses:** Powerful language from Lincoln's speech includes "a great civil war," "the last full measure of devotion," and "these dead shall not have died in vain." Powerful language from Pericles' speech includes "Our love of what is beautiful does not lead us to extravagance," "So and such they were, these men—worthy of their city," and "Make up your minds that happiness depends on being free, and freedom depends on being courageous."
4. **Possible response:** Lincoln's speech would be more interesting because it pertains to American history.

Enrichment

Aaron Copland

At the outbreak of World War II, American composer Aaron Copland (1900–1990) received a letter from conductor Andre Kostelanetz, who asked him to contribute to a "musical portrait gallery of great Americans." In response, Copland chose Abraham Lincoln as his subject. "A Lincoln Portrait" blends original music with familiar American folk tunes to accompany a spare and dramatic script based on Lincoln's own words. In his notes about the work, Copland explained the structure he attempted to create: "In the opening section I wanted to suggest something of the mysterious sense of fatality that surrounds Lincoln's personality. . . . The quick middle section briefly sketches in the background of the times he lived in. This merges into the conclusion section where my sole purpose was to draw a simple but impressive frame about the words of Lincoln himself."

Invite students to listen to a recording of the piece and determine whether Copland succeeded in creating the effects he intended.

Standard Course of Study

Goal 3: FOUNDATIONS OF ARGUMENT

- **FA.3.01.3** Develop a framework in which to discuss controversial issues.
- **FA.3.02.1** State position or proposed solution in an editorial or response.

Goal 6: GRAMMAR AND USAGE

- **GU.6.01.3** Use recognition strategies to understand vocabulary and exact word choice.
- **GU.6.02.2** Edit for appropriate and correct mechanics.

Step-by-Step Teaching Guide	Pacing Guide
PRETEACH	
• Administer Vocabulary and Reading Warm-ups as necessary.	5 min.
• Engage students' interest with the motivation activity.	5 min.
• Read and discuss author and background features. **FT**	10 min.
• Introduce the Literary Analysis Skill: Monologue. **FT**	5 min.
• Introduce the Reading Strategy: Challenging the Text. **FT**	10 min.
• Prepare students to read by teaching the selection vocabulary. **FT**	
TEACH	
• Informally monitor comprehension while students read independently or in groups. **FT**	30 min.
• Monitor students' comprehension with the Reading Check notes.	as students read
• Reinforce vocabulary with Vocabulary Builder notes.	as students read
• Develop students' understanding of monologue with the Literary Analysis annotations. **FT**	5 min.
• Develop students' ability to challenge the text with the Reading Strategy annotations. **FT**	5 min.
ASSESS/EXTEND	
• Assess students' comprehension and mastery of the Literary Analysis and Reading Strategy by having them answer the Apply the Skills questions. **FT**	15 min.
• Have students complete the Vocabulary Lesson and the Grammar and Style Lesson. **FT**	15 min.
• Apply students' ability to gather details by using the Writing Lesson. **FT**	45 min. or homework
• Apply students' understanding by using one or more of the Extend Your Learning activities.	20–90 min. or homework
• Administer Selection Test A or Selection Test B. **FT**	15 min.

Resources

Print

Unit 4 Resources

Transparency

Graphic Organizer Transparencies

Print

Reader's Notebook [L2]

Reader's Notebook: Adapted Version [L1]

Reader's Notebook: English Learner's Version [EL]

Unit 4 Resources

Technology

Listening to Literature Audio CDs [L2, EL]

Print

Unit 4 Resources

General Resources

Technology

Go Online: Research **[L3]**
Go Online: Self-test **[L3]**
***ExamView®,* Test Bank [L3]**

Choosing Resources for Differentiated Instruction

[L1] Special Needs Students
[L2] Below-Level Students
[L3] All Students
[L4] Advanced Students
[EL] English Learners

For Vocabulary and Reading Warm-ups and for Selection Tests, **A** signifies "less challenging" and **B** "more challenging." For Graphic Organizer transparencies, **A** signifies "not filled in" and **B** "filled in."

FT Fast Track Instruction: To move the lesson more quickly, use the strategies and activities identified with **FT**.

Scaffolding for Less Proficient and Advanced Students

The leveled Critical Thinking questions after selections progress in the levels of thinking required to answer them. To address the needs of your different students, you may use the (a) level questions for your less proficient students and the (b) level questions with your on-level and advanced students. The occasional (c) level questions are appropriate for your advanced students.

Use this complete suite of powerful teaching tools to make lesson planning and testing quicker and easier.

PRENTICE HALL
StudentEXPRESS™
Learn · Study · Succeed
Use the interactive textbook (online and on CD-ROM) to make selections and activities come alive with audio and video support and interactive questions.

Monitoring Progress

Before students read the excerpt from *The Apology,* administer **Diagnostic Test 5 (*Unit 4 Resources,* pp. 80–82).** This test will determine students' level of readiness for the reading and vocabulary skills.

For: Information about Lexiles
Visit: www.PHSchool.com
Web Code: eue-1111

PRETEACH

Motivation

Write the term *apology* on the board, and ask students to offer scenarios in which one might apologize. Elicit from students that today's definition of the word implies regret and the seeking of forgiveness or pardon. Tell them that the original meaning of the Greek term *apology* had no such connotation; instead, it meant "a defense speech." Tell students that as they read, they should not expect Socrates to apologize for anything he has done, even though his life is at stake.

❶ Background

More About the Author

Legend has it that on his father's side, Plato could trace his descent from the old kings of Athens and the god Poseidon. Plato's mother was descended from old aristocratic stock, related to the lawgiver Solon. Her cousin Critias was a versatile author, one of the "beautiful people" of Athens in his youth, and the leader of the Thirty Tyrants who bathed the city in blood. Her brother Charmides was also disastrously involved in the repressive aristocratic politics of the Thirty. Both men appear in Plato's dialogues and were part of Socrates' circle. In other times, Plato would have become a leader of the democratic state; however, by the time he was a young adult, his uncles had distinguished themselves in infamy as destroyers of the democracy and leaders of a dictatorial regime.

Geography Note

Draw students' attention to the map on this page. Tell students that Socrates was tried in Athens, where he also taught other thinkers. Also point out the places to which Plato traveled after Socrates' dream: Italy, Sicily, and Egypt.

Build Skills | *Philosophical Text*

from the Apology ❶

Plato (429 B.C.–347 B.C.) Plato is considered the most influential thinker in the history of Western culture. So revered was Plato in his day and throughout history that his written work has survived practically undamaged and more completely than that of any other ancient Greek writer. Originally named Aristocles (ə ris′ tə klēz′), he took the nickname Plato, meaning "broad-shouldered." He was born during the Golden Age of Athens to a prominent family active in Athenian politics. Belonging to an aristocratic and influential family groomed him to be a political leader like Pericles, but the political corruption he observed in his youth led Plato to withdraw from political activity. However, his life changed and gained direction when he met the philosopher Socrates (säk′ rə tēz′): He turned his attention to philosophy, the love of wisdom.

The Influence of Socrates Although the Athens of Plato's youth was experiencing a period of cultural flowering, it was also engaged in a devastating war with Sparta. This war ended with Athens' defeat in 404 B.C. After the war, a repressive government called the Thirty Tyrants ruled Athens for a year until democracy was restored. At the same time, self-proclaimed thinkers called Sophists (from *sophia*, or wisdom) went about teaching Athenian youths the art of rhetoric, the ability to use language effectively and persuasively. Sophist teaching came to be considered empty, however, because it had little grounding in morals or values.

In the midst of this intellectual ferment, the philosopher Socrates wandered the streets, shabbily dressed and unbathed, questioning people about their ideas and values. He believed that the unexamined life was not worth living, and so he questioned daily the meaning of virtue, the value of knowledge, and the importance of truth. He compared himself to a gadfly because he knew he was an annoying presence, pressing others to think more clearly about their values and ideals.

In Socrates' view, a consistently thorough examination of beliefs was the path to wisdom and goodness. Plato was one of a group of young men who collected about Socrates, drawn to his magnetic personality. In fact, Plato is responsible for nearly all the information we have about Socrates.

The Dialogues Plato revealed his philosophy in the form of dialogues. Similar to works of drama, Plato's dialogues feature Socrates as a character engaging in philosophical discourse with various other characters. These dialogues constitute a portrait of Socrates: a representation of his interests, his methods, and his self-appointed mission to teach by questioning. Plato portrays Socrates as unwavering in his fidelity to the philosophic life.

The Academy After Socrates' death, Plato withdrew from Athens to travel in Italy, Cyrene, Sicily, and Egypt. Upon his return to Athens, he founded the Academy, the first European university and institution of pure research. Plato spent the next twenty years of his life directing the Academy, lecturing, and discussing philosophical and mathematical questions with members of the school.

Preview

Connecting to the Literature

At some time, most of us have had to defend or explain our actions. In this excerpt from the *Apology*, Socrates defends his philosophy in court. The stakes are high—if he fails to persuade the authorities that his ideas are not criminal, he could be sentenced to death.

❷ Literary Analysis

Monologue

A **monologue** is a long and revealing speech by one character. In this monologue from the *Apology*, Socrates explains and defends his philosophy and his life's mission, the pursuit of knowledge. This excerpt reveals Socrates' commitment to his beliefs:

> . . . a man who is good for anything ought not to calculate the chance of living or dying; he ought only to consider whether in doing anything he is doing right or wrong. . . .

As you read, look for other statements that reveal Socrates' character and philosophy.

Connecting Literary Elements

Socrates often makes his points through **analogy,** an extended comparison of relationships. An analogy shows how the relationship between one pair of things is like the relationship between another pair. Notice how Socrates compares himself to a gadfly and uses other comparisons to clarify his arguments.

❸ Reading Strategy

Challenging the Text

When reading a work that presents an argument, do not simply accept ideas—challenge them. To **challenge a text,** critically evaluate its assertions and reasoning. Compare the evidence and arguments with your own knowledge and experience or with other reading. Then, decide whether you agree or disagree with the ideas. Use a chart like the one shown to record your thinking.

Vocabulary Builder

eloquence (el′ ə kwəns) *n.* fluent, persuasive speech (p. 440)

affidavit (af′ ə dā′ vit) *n.* legal document containing sworn testimony (p. 442)

lamented (lə ment′ id) *v.* felt deep sorrow for (p. 444)

avenged (ə venjd′) *v.* took revenge on behalf of (p. 446)

exhorting (eg zôrt′ iŋ) *v.* urging (p. 447)

impudence (im′ pyo͞o dəns) *n.* rashness; boldness (p. 448)

indictment (in dīt′ mənt) *n.* formal accusation (p. 448)

piety (pī′ ə tē) *n.* respect for the gods (p. 450)

NC Standard Course of Study

- Develop a framework in which to discuss controversial issues. (FA.3.01.3)
- State position or proposed solution in an editorial or response. (FA.3.02.1)

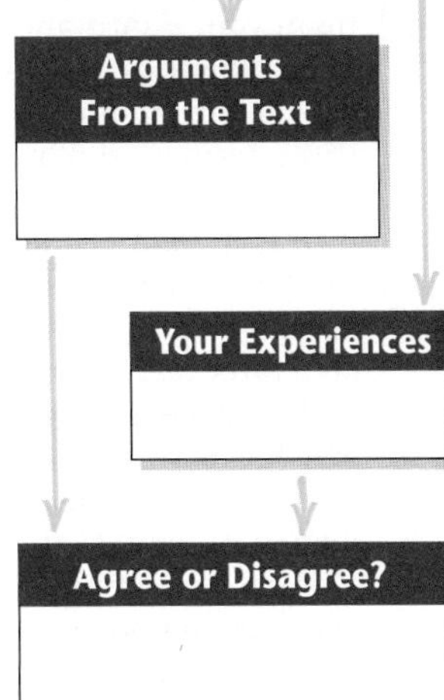

❷ Literary Analysis

Monologue

- Ask students to give examples of monologues, such as stand-up comedy performances and opening segments of talk shows.
- Tell students that although only one person speaks in a monologue, good speakers constantly interact with their audiences. **Ask** students to discuss the skills speakers need in order to do this.
  Possible response: Speakers observe the audience's nonverbal cues and tailor their remarks to this feedback.
- Tell students that Socrates' audience was a "tough crowd" in that many people were already in favor of putting him to death when he defended himself and his philosophy. Ask students to discuss the importance of Socrates' observing his audience as he makes his points.

❸ Reading Strategy

Challenging the Text

- Remind students to draw on their own logic and experiences as they read.
- Provide this example from the *Apology:* "A man who is good for anything ought not to calculate the chance of living or dying." Model ways to challenge the text, such as wondering aloud whether to interpret this statement as "live cautiously."
- Then, ask students whether living cautiously is generally considered "doing right."
- Give students a copy of **Reading Strategy Graphic Organizer A,** p. 84 in ***Graphic Organizer Transparencies,*** to use to challenge Plato's text.

Vocabulary Builder

- Pronounce each vocabulary word for students, and read the definitions as a class. Have students identify any words with which they are already familiar.

Differentiated Instruction
Solutions for All Learners

Support for Special Needs Students
Have students complete the **Preview** and **Build Skills** pages for the excerpt from the *Apology* in the ***Reader's Notebook: Adapted Version.*** These pages provide a selection summary, an abbreviated presentation of the reading and literary skills, and the graphic organizer on the **Build Skills** page in the student book.

Support for Less Proficient Readers
Have students complete the **Preview** and **Build Skills** pages for the excerpt from the *Apology* in the ***Reader's Notebook.*** These pages provide a selection summary, an abbreviated presentation of the reading and literary skills, and the graphic organizer on the **Build Skills** page in the student book.

Support for English Learners
Have students complete the **Preview** and **Build Skills** pages for the excerpt from the *Apology* in the ***Reader's Notebook: English Learner's Version.*** These pages provide a selection summary, an abbreviated presentation of the skills, additional contextual vocabulary, and the graphic organizer on the **Build Skills** page in the student book.

Facilitate Understanding

To help students arrive at their own definitions of wisdom, ask them to think about people whom they consider wise. They might name legendary or historical figures or people from their personal lives. Ask students what makes these people wise.

❶ About the Selection

The original speech, as delivered in court by Socrates in 399 B.C., was a public oration. In order to refute his opponents' accusations and public opinion in general, Socrates' aim was to persuade and teach by appealing to his audience's better sentiments. The stakes were high—his life. His speech, as we have it, is a text by Plato, written much later for a different audience. What Plato has produced is an oration in which Socrates presents a defense and an explanation of his life's mission, the pursuit of wisdom. Although it is difficult to distinguish between what Socrates actually said and what Plato presents as Socrates' words, scholars agree that the *Apology* provides a clear picture of the historical Socrates.

❷ Literary Analysis

Monologue

- Remind students that speakers of monologues need to work to keep their audience's attention.
- Have students read the bracketed passage, noting Socrates' mention of his accusers' having warned people of his "eloquence." **Ask** students why Socrates begins with this point.
  Possible response: Socrates anticipates what is on the minds of his listeners. He tries to win his audience over by implying that his accusers believe that the listeners do not have minds of their own.

from the APOLOGY

Plato

translated by Benjamin Jowett

Background Socrates was critical of local politicians and their ways of governing, and he advocated a moral code that was independent of religious dictates—one that would not change with the changing governments. In 399 B.C., prominent Athenians brought Socrates to trial for atheism (belief that no gods exist) and for corrupting Athenian youth. The *Apology* is Plato's account of what happened at Socrates' trial. In this excerpt, Socrates presents his defense.

❷ How you, O Athenians, have been affected by my accusers, I cannot tell; but I know that they almost made me forget who I was—so persuasively did they speak; and yet they have hardly uttered a word of truth. But of the many falsehoods told by them, there was one which quite amazed me;—I mean when they said that you should be upon your guard and not allow yourselves to be deceived by the force of my eloquence. To say this, when they were certain to be detected as soon as I opened my lips and proved myself to be anything but a great speaker, did indeed appear to me most shameless—unless by the force of eloquence they mean the force of truth; for if such is their meaning, I admit that I am eloquent. But in how different a way from theirs! Well, as I was saying, they have scarcely spoken the truth at all; but from me you shall hear the whole truth: not, however, delivered after their manner in a set oration duly ornamented with words and phrases. No, by heaven! but I shall use the words and arguments which occur to me at the moment; for I am confident in the justice of my cause: at my time of life I ought not to be appearing before you, O men of Athens, in the character of a juvenile orator—let no one expect it of me. And I must beg of you to grant me a favor:—If I defend myself in my accustomed manner, and you hear me using the words which

Vocabulary Builder
eloquence (elʹ ə kwəns) *n.* fluent, persuasive speech

Differentiated Instruction Solutions for All Learners

Accessibility at a Glance

	from the Apology
Context	399 B.C., Athenians' trial of Socrates for atheism
Language	Syntax: long sentences with embedded clauses, questions, and analogies
Concept Level	Accessible (Knowledge is knowing what you don't know.)
Literary Merit	Classic philosophical monologue
Lexile	1150L
Overall Rating	Challenging

3

I have been in the habit of using in the agora,[1] at the tables of the money-changers, or anywhere else, I would ask you not to be surprised, and not to interrupt me on this account. For I am more than seventy years of age, and appearing now for the first time in a court of law, I am quite a stranger to the language of the place; and therefore I would have you regard me as if I were really a stranger, whom you would excuse if he spoke in his native tongue, and after the fashion of his country:—Am I making an unfair request of you? Never mind the manner, which may or may not be good; but think only of the truth of my words, and give heed to that: let the speaker speak truly and the judge decide justly.

5 Well, then, I must make my defense, and endeavor to clear away in a short time, a slander which has lasted a long time. May I succeed, if to succeed be for my good and yours, or likely to avail me in my cause! The task is not an easy one; I quite understand the nature of it. And so leaving the event with God, in obedience to the law I will now make my defense.

1. **agora** (ag´ ə rə) *n.* ancient Greek marketplace.

4 ▲ Critical Viewing
Based on this depiction, how would you describe ancient Athens? **[Analyze]**

Literary Analysis
Monologue What attitudes does Socrates reveal in this paragraph?

6 

Reading Check
According to Socrates' accusers, why should Athenians be on guard while Socrates speaks?

3 Humanities

View of the Acropolis at Athens,
by Leo von Klenze (1784–1864)

The Acropolis (literally, "high city") represented both the practical and symbolic heart of ancient Athens. Many Greek cities developed around citadels built on high ground for defense in times of war. At Athens, the Acropolis became, over time, the center of a complex of temples and shrines.

Use the following question for discussion:

What emotions might an Athenian experience, looking up at the Acropolis from ground level?
Possible response: An Athenian might feel proud of the city and its culture or feel awe at the magnificence of the structures.

4 Critical Viewing

Possible response: The city's attractive buildings and temples seem permanent and appear to be the result of intelligent planning.

5 Literary Analysis

Monologue

- Have students read the bracketed passage. Then, **ask** them what Socrates accomplishes in introducing his defense.
  Possible response: Socrates notes that he will argue on behalf of the audience, which may make listeners more receptive to his argument. He also invokes the name of God, implying that the charge for which he is being tried—atheism—is unfounded.
- **Ask** students the Literary Analysis question: What attitudes does Socrates reveal in this paragraph?
  Answer: Socrates shows himself to be reasonable, ambitious, and concerned about others.

6 Reading Check

Answer: Socrates' accusers fear that his eloquent speech may dazzle people into believing what he says.

Differentiated Instruction Solutions for All Learners

Strategy for Special Needs Students

Help students understand that Socrates refers to different ways of speaking when he says that he will use his usual language in court. Remind students that the jargon associated with certain careers and the dialect spoken in small groups do not always "translate" well in all situations. Have students describe situations in which someone using the vocabulary and diction of a teacher or school administrator may find this mode of speaking ineffective.

Enrichment for Advanced Readers

Ask students to compare this excerpt from Socrates' oration to Abraham Lincoln's "Gettysburg Address" or Martin Luther King, Jr.'s "I Have a Dream" speech. Ask students to compare the speakers' techniques in addressing their audiences, using rhetorical devices, and incorporating details. Have students summarize their findings in brief oral reports that include excerpts from each speech to demonstrate their points.

7 Vocabulary Builder

Legal Terminology

- Draw students' attention to the word *affidavit* in the bracketed passage.
- Tell students that *affidavit* may be unfamiliar because it is a legal term meaning "a legal document containing sworn testimony."
- Explain that *affidavit* is a term used by attorneys, judges, and witnesses; if students watch courtroom dramas on television and film, they will likely hear this term frequently.

8 Humanities

Tholos Temple at Delphi

Delphi was the most important religious center in Greece. At Apollo's shrine at Delphi, his priestess, the Pyth, communicated his messages to visitors from throughout the ancient world. According to legend, the god himself built the shrine on the southern slopes of Mount Parnassus.

The Tholos Temple at Delphi probably dates from 380–360 B.C. The Doric columns that are still standing are three of twenty that once created a circular outer peristyle. Its design has been attributed to Theodorus of Phocaea.

Use the following questions for discussion:

- For what purpose might this temple have been built?
  Possible response: Devotions and sacrifices might have been made to the ancient Greek gods.
- Why might the Greeks have chosen this dramatic natural setting for the temple?
  Answer: The setting inspires awe and reverence.

9 Critical Thinking

Apply

- Ask students to read aloud the bracketed passage.
- **Ask** students why Socrates gives voice to the doubts many Athenians have about him.
  Possible response: This tactic demonstrates Socrates' respect for people who are not yet convinced that he is innocent.

I will begin at the beginning, and ask what is the accusation which has given rise to the slander of me, and in fact has encouraged Meletus to prefer[2] this charge against me. Well, what do the slanderers say? They shall be my prosecutors, and I will sum up their words in an affidavit: "Socrates is an evildoer, and a curious person, who searches into things under the earth and in heaven, and he makes the worse appear the better cause; and he teaches the aforesaid doctrines to others." Such is the nature of the accusation: it is just what you have yourselves seen in the comedy of Aristophanes,[3] who has introduced a man whom he calls Socrates, going about and saying that he walks in air, and talking a deal of nonsense concerning matters of which I do not pretend to know either much or little—not that I mean to speak disparagingly[4] of any one who is a student of natural philosophy. I should be very sorry if Meletus could bring so grave a charge against me. But the simple truth is, O Athenians, that I have nothing to do with physical speculations. Very many of those here present are witnesses to the truth of this, and to them I appeal. Speak then, you who have heard me, and tell your neighbors whether any of you have ever known me hold forth in few words or in many upon such matters. . . . You hear their answer. And from what they say of this part of the charge you will be able to judge of the truth of the rest.

I dare say, Athenians, that some one among you will reply, "Yes, Socrates, but what is the origin of these accusations which are brought against you; there must have been something strange which you have been doing? All these rumors and this talk about you would never have arisen if you had been like other men: tell us, then, what is the cause of them, for we should be sorry to judge hastily of you." Now, I regard this as a fair challenge, and I will endeavor to explain to you the reason why I am called wise and have such an evil fame.[5] Please to attend then. And although some of you may think that I am joking, I declare that I will tell you the entire truth. Men of Athens, this reputation of mine has come of a certain sort of wisdom which I possess. If

Vocabulary Builder
affidavit (af´ ə dā´ vit) *n.* legal document containing sworn testimony

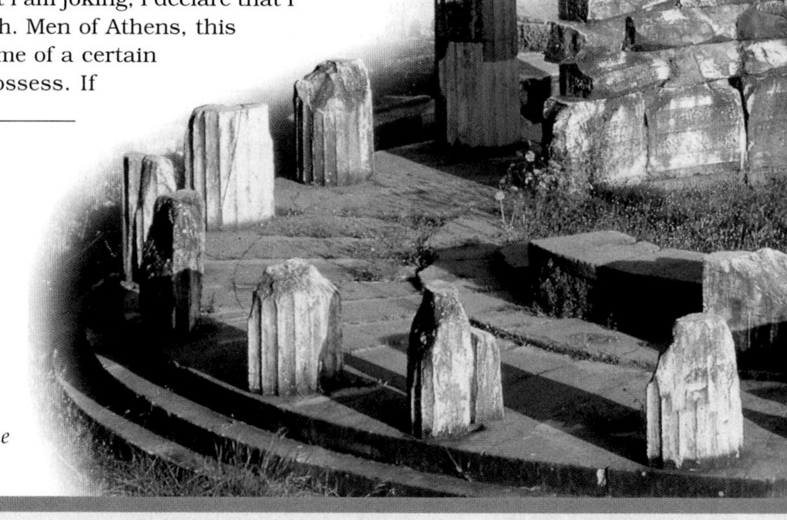

2. **prefer** (prē fʉr´) *v.* put before a magistrate or court.
3. **comedy of Aristophanes** (ar´ i stäf´ ə nēz) comic play *Clouds*, a satire on Socrates, written by Aristophanes, an ancient Greek playwright.
4. **disparagingly** (di spar´ ij iŋ lē) *adv.* disrespectfully; in a way that discredits or belittles.
5. **fame** reputation.

Enrichment

Socrates and Aristophanes

The dramatist Aristophanes (c. 445–385 B.C.) was one of the most important comic playwrights in Athens in the late fifth century. His plays address a broad array of issues of the day, including politics, literature, philosophy, the legal system, the Peloponnesian War, and the position of women in Athens. Aristophanes wrote in the tradition of Old Comedy, in which fantastic plots, topical subject matter, and the use of informal and even bawdy language were extremely popular.

In 423 B.C., Aristophanes presented his play *The Clouds,* which satirized the "new learning" popularized by the Sophists, itinerant philosophers who claimed to teach practical skills such as rhetoric. Although Socrates was very different from the Sophists—both in his approach to philosophy and in his refusal to take money for his teaching—Aristophanes included him as a character in his comedy.

you ask me what kind of wisdom, I reply, wisdom such as may perhaps be attained by man, for to that extent I am inclined to believe that I am wise; whereas the persons of whom I was speaking have a superhuman wisdom, which I may fail to describe, because I have it not myself; and he who says that I have, speaks falsely, and is taking away my character. And here, O men of Athens, I must beg you not to interrupt me, even if I seem to say something extravagant. For the word which I will speak is not mine. I will refer you to a witness who is worthy of credit; that witness shall be the god of Delphi[6]—he will tell you about my wisdom, if I have any, and of what sort it is. You
10 must have known Chaerephon; he was early a friend of mine, and also a friend of yours, for he shared in the recent exile of the people, and returned with you. Well, Chaerephon, as you know, was very impetuous in all his doings, and he went to Delphi and boldly asked the oracle to tell him whether—as I was saying, I must beg you not to interrupt—he asked the oracle to tell him whether any one was wiser than I was, and the Pythian prophetess answered, that there was no
11 man wiser. Chaerephon is dead himself; but his brother, who is in court, will confirm the truth of what I am saying.

Why do I mention this? Because I am going to explain to you why I have such an evil name. When I heard the answer, I said to myself, What can the god mean? and what is the interpretation of his riddle? for I know that I have no wisdom, small or great. What then can he mean when he says that I am the wisest of men? And yet he is a god, and cannot lie; that would be against his nature. After long consideration, I thought of a method of trying the question. I reflected that if I could only find a man wiser than myself, then I might go to
12 the god with a refutation[7] in my hand. I should say to him, "Here is a man who is wiser than I am; but you said that I was the wisest." Accordingly I went to one who had the reputation of wisdom, and observed him—his name I need not mention; he was a politician whom I selected for examination—and the result was as follows: When I began to talk with him, I could not help thinking that he was not

6. **god of Delphi** (del′ fī) Apollo.
7. **refutation** (ref′ yə tā′ shən) *n.* something that proves an argument false or wrong.

Reading Strategy
Challenging the Text Do you agree with the strategy that Socrates uses to refute the god's claim that Socrates is the wisest of all men? Why or why not?

Reading Check 13
What did Chaerephon ask the oracle at Delphi? What was the oracle's answer?

14 **Critical Viewing**
How might temples like the one shown have inspired respect for the gods of ancient Greece? **[Speculate]**

10 Background

Literature

Chaerephon was both a devoted disciple of Socrates and a well-known, ardent democrat who had been exiled for his beliefs. Socrates had never gone into exile and was viewed with suspicion by a jury of democrats who had suffered under the tyrants. Their leader had been Socrates' "pupil" Critias. By reminding the jury of Chaerephon, Socrates is in effect calling a political character witness.

11 Critical Thinking

Analyze

- Remind students that speakers of monologues stay aware of their audience's needs in order to hold their attention.
- Have students read the bracketed passage. Then, **ask** them why Socrates gives a detailed account of Chaerephon's visit to Delphi.
  Possible response: The account paves the way for Socrates to talk about his reaction to the oracle.

12 Reading Strategy

Challenging the Text

- Have students review the bracketed passage.
- Then, **ask** them the Reading Strategy question: Do you agree with the strategy that Socrates uses to refute the god's claim that Socrates is the wisest of all men? Why or why not?
  Possible responses: Yes; if Socrates can find a wiser person than himself, he will prove the oracle wrong. No; Socrates may overlook meeting someone who has more wisdom.

13 Reading Check

Answer: He asked whether anyone was wiser than Socrates. The oracle replied that no one was wiser.

14 Critical Viewing

Possible response: The stately, dignified design of the temple might have inspired respect.

Differentiated Instruction Solutions for All Learners

Strategy for Less Proficient Readers
Help students break down lengthy sentences to aid in understanding difficult syntax. On the board, write the sentence that begins "If you ask me what kind of wisdom . . ." (pp. 442–443). Explain that there are three main ideas separated by semicolons: 1. "If . . . wise"; 2. "Whereas . . . myself"; 3. "and . . . character." Read aloud and underline the embedded clauses in the first main idea: *(If you ask me what kind of wisdom,)* and *(that I am wise);* in the second main idea: *(of whom I was speaking), (which I may fail to describe),* and *(because I have it not myself);* and in the third main idea: *(who says)* and *(that I have).* Then, have students work in pairs to write a paraphrase of the sentence. Ask a few students to read aloud their paraphrases of the sentence.

Finally, discuss the kind of wisdom that Socrates believes he possesses versus "superhuman" wisdom, which he cannot identify in others because he does not have it himself.

⓯ Reading Strategy

Challenging the Text

- Ask students to read the bracketed passage. Point out Socrates' assertion that the poets he met seemed incompetent to discuss their own work.
- Then, **direct** students' attention to the Reading Strategy question: Do you agree with Socrates' assertion that poets write with "a sort of genius and inspiration"? Explain. **Possible responses:** Yes; poets must be creative in order to write original verse. Not necessarily; poets need dedication to their craft and advanced language skills.

⓰ Literary Analysis

Monologue

- Have students review the bracketed passage. Discuss how Socrates seems compelled by a supernatural force that he cannot resist.
- Then, **ask** students the Literary Analysis question: According to what he reveals in this passage, what is Socrates' mission in life? **Possible response:** Socrates' mission is to uncover the meaning of the oracle's statement and, in so doing, arrive at a true definition of wisdom.

really wise, although he was thought wise by many, and still wiser by himself; and thereupon I tried to explain to him that he thought himself wise, but was not really wise; and the consequence was that he hated me, and his enmity[8] was shared by several who were present and heard me. So I left him, saying to myself, as I went away: Well, although I do not suppose that either of us knows anything really beautiful and good, I am better off than he is,—for he knows nothing, and thinks that he knows; I neither know nor think that I know. In this latter particular, then, I seem to have slightly the advantage of him. Then I went to another who had still higher pretensions to wisdom, and my conclusion was exactly the same. Whereupon I made another enemy of him, and of many others besides him.

Then I went to one man after another, being not unconscious of the enmity which I provoked, and I lamented and feared this: but necessity was laid upon me,—the word of God, I thought, ought to be considered first. And I said to myself, Go I must to all who appear to know, and find out the meaning of the oracle. And I swear to you, Athenians, by the dog I swear!—for I must tell you the truth—the result of my mission was just this: I found that the men most in repute[9] were all but the most foolish; and that others less esteemed were really wiser and better. I will tell you the tale of my wanderings and of the "Herculean" labors,[10] as I may call them, which I endured only to find at last the oracle irrefutable. After the politicians, I went to the poets; tragic, dithyrambic,[11] and all sorts. And there, I said to myself, you will be instantly detected; now you will find out that you are more ignorant than they are. Accordingly I took them some of the most elaborate passages in their own writings, and asked what was the meaning of them—thinking that they would teach me something. Will you believe me? I am almost ashamed to confess the truth, but I must say that there is hardly a person present who would not have talked better about their poetry than they did themselves. Then I knew that not by wisdom do poets write poetry, but by a sort of genius and inspiration; they are like diviners[12] or soothsayers[13] who also say many fine things, but do not understand the meaning of them. The poets appeared to me to be much in the same case; and I further observed that upon the strength of their poetry they believed themselves to be the wisest of men in other things in which they were not wise. So I departed, conceiving myself to be superior to them for the same reason that I was superior to the politicians.

Vocabulary Builder
lamented (lə ment′ id) *v.* felt deep sorrow for

Reading Strategy
Challenging the Text Do you agree with Socrates' assertion that poets write with "a sort of genius and inspiration"? Explain.

Literary Analysis
Monologue According to what he reveals in this passage, what is Socrates' mission in life?

8. **enmity** (en′ mə tē) *n.* bitter attitude; hostility.
9. **in repute** (ri pyo͞ot′) here, regarded as being wise.
10. **Herculean** (hər kyo͞o′ lē ən) **labors** In a fit of madness, the hero Hercules killed his children. The Delphic oracle told him to perform twelve labors as punishment. Through these twelve feats of strength and courage, Hercules won immortality.
11. **dithyrambic** (dith′ ə ram′ bik) *adj.* in the style of impassioned, choric hymns that honor Dionysus, the god of wine.
12. **diviners** (də vin′ ərz) *n.* people who interpret divine omens.
13. **soothsayers** (so͞oth′ sā′ ərz) *n.* people who foretell the future.

Enrichment

The Labors of Hercules

Socrates' "Herculean labors" is a reference to Hercules, a figure from Greek mythology who was challenged by King Eurystheus of Tiryns to complete a number of seemingly impossible tasks. Hercules was obliged to kill or capture extremely ferocious, strong, or elusive animals. These included the Nemean lion, the Lernaean hydra (a monstrous water-serpent), the Cerynitian deer, the Erymanthian boar, the bull of Minos, the man-eating mares of Diomedes, and the cattle of Geryon. Other tasks required Hercules to travel great distances to find objects or talismans, such as the belt of the Amazonian queen Hippolyta and the golden apples of the Hesperides. King Eurystheus also asked Hercules to perform more than just feats of daring: he had to toil, cleaning the Augean stables and the filth created by the Stymphalian birds. Last on Hercules' "to-do list" was a trip to the underworld to retrieve Cerberus, the three-headed watchdog that guarded Hades.

At last I went to the artisans. I was conscious that I knew nothing at all, as I may say, and I was sure that they knew many fine things; and here I was not mistaken, for they did know many things of which I was ignorant, and in this they certainly were wiser than I was. But I observed that even the good artisans fell into the same error as the poets;—because they were good workmen they thought that they also knew all sorts of high matters, and this defect in them overshadowed their wisdom: and therefore I asked myself on behalf of the oracle, whether I would like to be as I was, neither having their knowledge nor their ignorance, or like them in both; and I made answer to myself and to the oracle that I was better off as I was.

This inquisition[14] has led to my having many enemies of the worst and most dangerous kind, and has given occasion also to many calumnies.[15] And I am called wise, for my hearers always imagine that I myself possess the wisdom which I find
18 wanting in others: but the truth is, O men of Athens, that God only is wise; and by his answer he intends to show that the wisdom of men is worth little or nothing; he is not speaking of Socrates, he is only using my name by way of illustration, as if he said, He, O men, is the wisest, who, like Socrates, knows that his wisdom is in truth worth nothing. And so I go about the world obedient to the god, and search and make enquiry into the wisdom of any one, whether citizen or stranger, who appears to be wise; and if he is not wise, then in vindication[16] of the oracle I show him that he is not wise; and my occupation quite absorbs me, and I have no time to give either to any public matter of interest or to any concern of my own, but I am in utter poverty by reason of my devotion to the god.

There is another thing:—young men of the richer classes, who have not much to do, come about me of their own accord; they like to hear the pretenders examined, and they often imitate me, and proceed to examine others; there are
19 plenty of persons, as they quickly discover, who think that they know something, but really know little or nothing; and then those who are examined by them instead of being angry with themselves are angry with me: This confounded Socrates, they say; this villainous misleader of youth!—and then if somebody asks them, Why, what evil does he practice or teach? they do not know, and cannot tell; but in order that they may not appear to be at a loss, they repeat the ready-made charges which are used against all philosophers about teaching things up in the clouds and under the earth, and having no

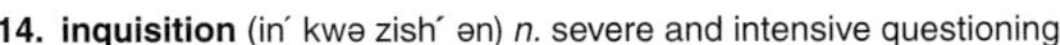

14. **inquisition** (in´ kwə zish´ ən) *n.* severe and intensive questioning.
15. **calumnies** (kal´ əm nēz) *n.* false, malicious statements meant to slander.
16. **vindication** (vin´ də kā´ shən) *n.* defense.

Literature in Context

17 Humanities Connection

The Socratic Method

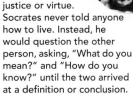

The Socratic method is a question-and-answer technique of philosophical dialogue that is used to arrive at a definition of some abstract idea, such as justice or virtue. Socrates never told anyone how to live. Instead, he would question the other person, asking, "What do you mean?" and "How do you know?" until the two arrived at a definition or conclusion.

Socrates would begin his inquiry with a hypothesis that seemed to be true, then question its consequences. For example, if justice means keeping promises and paying debts, what are some consequences of universally applying that principle of justice? If the consequences are true and consistent, then the hypothesis would be confirmed.

The Socratic method of establishing a working hypothesis and then testing it became central to Western thought and to science, in particular. It remains the foundation of the scientific method today.

Connect to the Literature

How might you use the Socratic method to question Socrates' accusers?

Reading Check 20

Why is Socrates in "utter poverty"?

Differentiated Instruction Solutions for All Learners

Support for Gifted/Talented Students

Model the Socratic method by sitting down with a small group of students and asking a question about an abstract idea, such as "What is justice?" or "What determines fairness?" Continue to ask questions to help students refine their definitions and clarify their ideas. Then, either open the conversation to other groups or arrange additional groups in which students take turns using the Socratic method, discussing other abstract ideas like freedom or wisdom.

Strategy for Advanced Readers

Have students read other works by Plato that present more of Socrates' ideas. In small groups, have students summarize a passage together and then use this summary to generate a discussion that employs the Socratic method. Tell students to take turns formulating questions and answers.

17 Literature in Context

The Socratic Method

The innovation of the Socratic method came about because Socrates preferred to exchange ideas with others, rather than to lecture as his Sophist contemporaries did. In Plato's dialogue *Protagoras,* Socrates discusses the nature of virtue and citizenship with Protagoras (485–415 B.C.), known for his doctrines on effective argument. Protagoras asserted that there are two opposing sides to any issue and that he could teach his pupils to make the weaker side seem more convincing than the stronger. Such rhetorical ingenuity differed markedly from Socrates' devotion to truth. Nevertheless, as the *Apology* shows, Socrates was charged with teaching the same distortion of rhetoric.

Connect to the Literature Remind students that the Socratic method is directed toward defining an abstract idea. Ask: How would you question Socrates' accusers?

Possible response: What is truth? Can any of you snap your fingers and find truth? Has Athens no room for the philosophical search for truth? Will the death of Socrates bring truth?

18 Background

Literature

"God only is wise" is a reaffirmation of profound, traditional piety. If the message, or truth, toward which Socrates has been building and which finally relieves the suspense is that "God only is wise," then Socrates is correct in distinguishing between human and divine wisdom.

19 Critical Thinking

Make Inferences

- Have students read the second bracketed passage.
- **Ask** why Socrates mentions "young men of the richer classes" who adopt his method of questioning.
  Possible response: The statement explains why those the young men interrogated blamed Socrates, not their interrogators.

20 Reading Check

Answer: His single-minded devotion to testing the truth of the oracle leaves no time to earn money.

㉑ Literary Analysis

Monologue and Analogy

- Have students independently read the bracketed passage. Then, ask a volunteer to read aloud the footnote explaining the three battles of the Peloponnesian War to which Socrates refers.
- **Ask** students the Literary Analysis question: What point does Socrates make by comparing his duty as a philosopher to his duty as a soldier? **Answer:** Socrates underscores the necessity of obeying the oracle in his philosophical mission. Just as patriotism and loyalty demand obedience in the military, piety and integrity demand obedience to the divine.

▶ **Monitor Progress:** Remind students that the success of a monologue depends on the speaker's ability to relate to his or her audience. **Ask** students to find examples here of Socrates' attempts to relate to his audience as he speaks. **Possible responses:** Socrates brings up a question he believes is on the minds of his listeners; he talks about mythological figures familiar to his audience to help explain his points about death and dishonor.

▶ **Reteach:** Help students recognize characteristics of a monologue by using **Literary Analysis** support, p. 87 in *Unit 4 Resources.*

㉒ Critical Thinking

Interpret

- Have students review the bracketed passage. Then, **ask** them to interpret Socrates' claim that the fear of death is "the pretense of wisdom." **Possible response:** People fear death even though they cannot know with certainty that death is a good or bad thing. Thus, fearing death fosters no wisdom.

gods, and making the worse appear the better cause; for they do not like to confess that their pretense of knowledge has been detected—which is the truth; and as they are numerous and ambitious and energetic, and are drawn up in battle array and have persuasive tongues, they have filled your ears with their loud and inveterate[17] calumnies.

Some one will say: And are you not ashamed, Socrates, of a course of life which is likely to bring you to an untimely end? To him I may fairly answer: There you are mistaken: a man who is good for anything ought not to calculate the chance of living or dying; he ought only to consider whether in doing anything he is doing right or wrong—acting the part of a good man or of a bad. Whereas, upon your view, the heroes who fell at Troy were not good for much, and the son of Thetis[18] above all, who altogether despised danger in comparison with disgrace; and when he was so eager to slay Hector, his goddess mother said to him, that if he avenged his companion Patroclus, and slew Hector, he would die himself—"Fate," she said, in these or the like words, "waits for you next after Hector"; he, receiving this warning, utterly despised danger and death, and instead of fearing them, feared rather to live in dishonor, and not to avenge his friend. "Let me die forthwith," he replies, "and be avenged of my enemy, rather than abide here by the beaked ships, a laughing stock and a burden of the earth." Had Achilles any thought of death and danger? For wherever a man's place is, whether the place which he has chosen or that in which he has been placed by a commander, there he ought to remain in the hour of danger; he should not think of death or of anything but of disgrace. And this, O men of Athens, is a true saying.

Vocabulary Builder
avenged (ə venjd′) *v.* took revenge on behalf of

Strange, indeed, would be my conduct, O men of Athens, if I, who, when I was ordered by the generals whom you chose to command me at Potidaea and Amphipolis and Delium,[19] remained where they placed me, like any other man, facing death—if now, when, as I conceive and imagine, God orders me to fulfil the philosopher's mission of searching into myself and other men, I were to desert my post

through fear of death, or any other fear; that would indeed be strange, and I might justly be arraigned in court for denying the existence

of the gods, if I disobeyed the oracle because I was afraid of death, fancying that I was wise when I was not wise. For the fear of death is indeed the pretense of wisdom, and not real wisdom, being a pretense of knowing the unknown; and no one knows whether death, which men in their fear apprehend to be the greatest evil, may not be the greatest good. Is not this ignorance of a disgraceful sort, the ignorance which is the conceit that a man knows what he does not know?

Literary Analysis
Monologue and Analogy What point does Socrates make by comparing his duty as a philosopher to his duty as a soldier?

17. **inveterate** (in vet′ ər it) *adj.* firmly established over time; deep rooted.
18. **son of Thetis** Achilles, epic hero of the *Iliad.*
19. **Potidaea** (pä ti dē′ ə) **and Amphipolis** (am fi′ pə lis) **and Delium** (dē′ lē əm) three of the battles in which Socrates fought in the Peloponnesian War.

Enrichment

Battles of the Peloponnesian War

As he mentions his own military service, Socrates refers to three important events in the first ten years of the Peloponnesian War. Potidaea was a Corinthian colony that joined the Delian League, the confederacy headed by Athens after the Persian Wars. Suspicious of the Potidaeans because of their connection to Corinth, an ally to Athens' adversary Sparta, Athens sharply increased Potidaea's annual tribute in 434 B.C. Two years later, the Potidaeans revolted in an action that helped start the Peloponnesian War. In 430 B.C., Athens succeeded in subduing its rebellious ally.

The campaigns at Amphipolis and Delium both resulted in Athenian defeats in 424 B.C. At Amphipolis, on the north Aegean coast, the brilliant Spartan general Brasidas took the city by surprise. Two years later, his forces decisively defeated the Athenians. At Delium, the Athenians attempted to overthrow their enemies the Boeotians, but they were defeated once more.

And in this respect only I believe myself to differ from men in general, and may perhaps claim to be wiser than they are:—that whereas I know but little of the world below, I do not suppose that I know: but I do know that injustice and disobedience to a better, whether God or man, is evil and dishonorable, and I will never fear or avoid a possible good rather than a certain evil. And therefore if you let me go now, and are not convinced by Anytus, who said that since I had been prosecuted I must be put to death; (or if not that I ought never to have been prosecuted at all); and that if I escape now, your sons will all be utterly ruined by listening to my words—if you say to me, Socrates, this time we will not mind Anytus, and you shall be let off, but upon one condition, that you are not to enquire and speculate in this way any more, and that if you are caught doing so again you shall die;—if this was the condition on which you let me go, I should reply: Men of Athens, I honor and love you; but I shall obey God rather than you, and while I have life and strength I shall never cease from the practice and teaching of philosophy, exhorting any one whom I meet and saying to him after my manner: You, my friend,— 24 a citizen of the great and mighty and wise city of Athens,—are you not ashamed of heaping up the greatest amount of money and honor and reputation, and caring so little about wisdom and truth and the greatest improvement of the soul, which you never regard or heed at all? And if the person with whom I am arguing, says: Yes, but I do care; then I do not leave him or let him go at once; but I proceed to interrogate and examine and cross-examine him, and if I think that he has no virtue in him, but only says that he has, I reproach him with undervaluing the greater, and overvaluing the less. And I shall repeat the same words to every one whom I meet, young and old, citizen and alien, but especially to the citizens, inasmuch as they are my brethren. For know that this is the command of God; and I believe that no greater good has ever happened in the State than my service to the God. For I do nothing but go about persuading you all, old and young alike, not to take thought for your persons or your properties, but first and chiefly to care about the greatest improvement of the soul. I tell you that virtue is not given by money, but that from virtue comes money and every other good of man, public as well as private. This is my teaching, and if this is the doctrine which corrupts the youth, I am a mischievous person. But if any one says that this is not my teaching, he is speaking an untruth. Wherefore, O men of Athens, I say to you do as Anytus bids or not as Anytus bids, and either acquit me or not; but whichever you do, understand that I shall never alter my ways, not even if I have to die many times.

Men of Athens, do not interrupt, but hear me; there was an understanding between us that you should hear me to the end: I have something more to say, at which you may be inclined to cry out; but I believe that to hear me will be good for you, and therefore I beg that you will not cry out. I would have you know, that if you kill such an one as I am, you will injure yourselves more than you will injure me.

Vocabulary Builder
exhorting (eg zôrt′ iŋ) v. urging

Reading Check 25

According to Socrates, what should be the primary concern of all Athenians?

23 Critical Thinking

Analyze

- Have a volunteer read aloud the bracketed passage. Then, **ask** students what role knowledge plays in Socrates' belief that he may be wiser than others.
  Possible response: It is awareness of the limits of one's knowledge that makes one wise, not one's body of knowledge.
- **Ask** students how Socrates links heroic courage, civic obedience, and obedience to God in this passage.
  Possible response: Socrates casts himself as heroic in his refusal to fear death and also in his respect for authority and sense of duty to the oracle.

24 Literary Analysis

Monologue

- Before reading the passage aloud, tell students to listen for the repetition of words and phrases that help them remember Socrates' points.
- **Ask** students how Socrates recognizes the needs of his listeners in this passage.
  Possible response: Repetition of the word *if* helps listeners follow Socrates' points; hypothetical dialogue between Socrates and a man whose values he questions gives the listeners a concrete example of his philosophical method.

25 Reading Check

Answer: The primary concern of Athenians should be the improvement of the soul.

26 Reading Strategy

Challenging the Text

- Read aloud the bracketed passage. Note the paradox of Socrates' statement, "Nothing will injure me," followed closely by mention of execution, exile, and deprivation.
- **Ask** students to explain what Socrates means in this passage. **Possible response:** Socrates believes that greater harm comes to the oppressor than to the unjustly oppressed. As a result, the harm done to the oppressed is negated.
- Discuss with students whether they agree or disagree with this statement. Use a chart like the one on p. 439 to show students how to challenge the text.

27 Vocabulary Builder

Legal Terminology

- Draw students' attention to the word *indictment* and its definition.
- Tell students that *indictment* is an example of legal terminology, or words that pertain to the law and to legal proceedings.
- Write the word *acquittal* on the board. **Ask** students to define this word and explain how it relates to the word *indictment.*
  Answer: After someone receives an indictment, he or she may be found innocent; if so, the person receives an acquittal.

28 Background

Philosophy

Socrates' "little divine voice" has fascinated readers for thousands of years. The most plausible view, in light of everything Plato has written, is that when a man has reached the stage of enlightenment and harmony with the immutable and divine that Socrates has attained, he can "hear" moral dissonance as other men cannot.

29 Critical Viewing

Answer: The balanced scales suggest that true justice is impartial.

Nothing will injure me, not Meletus nor yet Anytus—they cannot, for a bad man is not permitted to injure a better than himself. I do not deny that Anytus may, perhaps, kill him, or drive him into exile, or
26 deprive him of civil rights; and he may imagine, and others may imagine, that he is inflicting a great injury upon him: but there I do not agree. For the evil of doing as he is doing—the evil of unjustly taking away the life of another—is greater far.

And now, Athenians, I am not going to argue for my own sake, as you may think, but for yours, that you may not sin against the God by condemning me, who am his gift to you. For if you kill me you will not easily find a successor to me, who, if I may use such a ludicrous[20] figure of speech, am a sort of gadfly,[21] given to the State by God; and the State is a great and noble steed[22] who is tardy in his motions owing to his very size, and requires to be stirred into life. I am that gadfly which God has attached to the State, and all day long and in all places am always fastening upon you, arousing and persuading and reproaching you. You will not easily find another like me, and therefore I would advise you to spare me. I dare say that you may feel out of temper (like a person who is suddenly awakened from sleep), and you think that you might easily strike me dead as Anytus advises, and then you would sleep on for the remainder of your lives, unless God in his care of you sent you another gadfly. When I say that I am given to you by God, the proof of my mission is this:—if I had been like other men,I should not have neglected all my own concerns or patiently seen the neglect of them during all these years, and have been doing yours, coming to you individually like a father or elder brother, exhorting you to regard virtue; such conduct, I say, would be unlike human nature. If I had gained anything, or if my exhortations had been paid, there would have been some sense in my doing so; but now, as you will perceive, not even the impudence of my accusers dares to say that I have ever exacted or sought pay of any one; of that they have no witness. And I have a sufficient witness to the truth of what I say—my poverty.

Some one may wonder why I go about in private giving advice and busying myself with the concerns of others, but do not venture to come forward in public and advise the State. I will tell you why. You have heard me speak at sundry[23] times and in
27 diverse places of an oracle or sign which comes to me, and is the
28 divinity which Meletus ridicules in the indictment. This sign, which is a kind of voice, first began to come to me whenI was a child; it always

Vocabulary Builder
impudence (im′ pyo͞o dəns) *n.* rashness; boldness
indictment (in dīt′ mənt) *n.* formal accusation

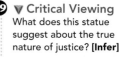

29 **▼ Critical Viewing** What does this statue suggest about the true nature of justice? **[Infer]**

20. **ludicrous** (lo͞o′ di krəs) *adj.* absurd; ridiculous.
21. **gadfly** (gad′ flī′) *n.* horsefly.
22. **steed** (stēd) *n.* horse.
23. **sundry** (sun′ drē) *adj.* various.

Enrichment

Plato's Major Dialogues

In his early works, Plato often depicts Socrates as searching for the essential meaning of a virtue or quality. For example, in the *Euthyphro,* Socrates investigates the true meaning of piety. In the *Charmides* the subject is self-discipline. The *Laches* focuses on courage; the *Lysis* explores the nature of friendship.

In Plato's middle period, a group of longer and more ambitious dialogues explores political and moral themes. The most famous work in this group is the *Republic,* which attempts to define justice and offer the best structure for the state, led ideally by a king who is also a philosopher. In the *Symposium,* Socrates and other thinkers discuss love.

Plato's later dialogues are more abstract. In the *Sophist,* for example, Socrates attempts to define the nature of definition. In the *Laws,* Plato returns to the practical consideration of how a state should be governed.

forbids but never commands me to do anything which I am going to
do. This is what deters me from being a politician. And rightly, as I
think. For I am certain, O men of Athens, that if I had engaged in
politics, I should have perished long ago, and done no good either to
you or to myself. And do not be offended at my telling you the truth:
30 for the truth is, that no man who goes to war with you or any other
multitude, honestly striving against the many lawless and unrighteous deeds which are done in a State, will save his life: he who will
fight for the right, if he would live even for a brief space, must have a
private station and not a public one.

Now, do you really imagine that I could have survived all these
years, if I had led a public life, supposing that like a good man I had
always maintained the right and had made justice, as I ought, the
first thing? No, indeed, men of Athens, neither I nor any other man.
But I have been always the same in all my actions, public as well as
private, and never have I yielded any base compliance[24] to those who
are slanderously termed my disciples, or to any other. Not that I have
any regular disciples. But if any one likes to come and hear me while
I am pursuing my mission, whether he be young or old, he is not
excluded. Nor do I converse only with those who pay; but any one,
whether he be rich or poor, may ask and answer me and listen to my
31 words; and whether he turns out to be a bad man or a good one, neither result can be justly imputed[25] to me; for I never taught or professed to teach him anything. And if any one says that he has ever
learned or heard anything from me in private which all the world has
not heard, let me tell you that he is lying.

Well, Athenians, this and the like of this is all the
defense which I have to offer. Yet a word more. Perhaps
there may be some one who is offended at me, when he
calls to mind how he himself on a similar, or even a less
serious occasion, prayed and entreated the judges
with many tears, and how he produced his children
in court, which was a moving spectacle, together with
a host of relations and friends; whereas I, who am
probably in danger of my life, will do none of these
things. The contrast may occur to his mind, and he may be set against
me, and vote in anger because he is displeased at me on this account.
Now, if there be such a person among you,—mind, I do not say that
there is,—to him I may fairly reply: My friend, I am a man, and like
33 other men, a creature of flesh and blood, and not "of wood or stone," as
Homer says; and I have a family, yes, and sons, O Athenians, three in

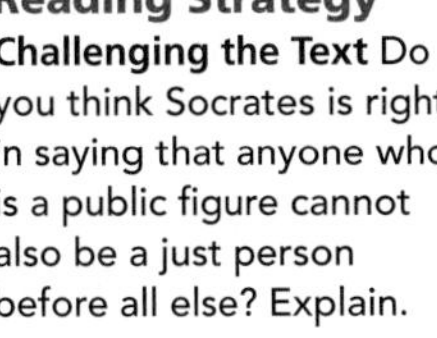

Reading Strategy
Challenging the Text Do you think Socrates is right in saying that anyone who is a public figure cannot also be a just person before all else? Explain.

Reading Check 32
Why has Socrates stayed out of politics?

24. **yielded any base compliance** given in to unjustified demands out of self-interest or cowardice.
25. **imputed** (im pyo͞ot′ id) *v.* attributed to; charged to.

30 Reading Strategy
Challenging the Text

- Have students read the bracketed passage. As they read, ask them to keep in mind Socrates' gadfly analogy.
- **Draw** students' attention to the Reading Strategy question: Do you think Socrates is right in saying that anyone who is a public figure cannot also be a just person before all else? Explain.
  Possible responses: Yes; one who holds political office must make many compromises. No; Socrates' outlook unreasonably and preemptively rules out free choice and integrity.

31 Critical Thinking
Evaluate

- As students read the bracketed passage, ask them to put themselves in the jurors' place.
- **Ask** students whether as jurors they would be put off by Socrates' defiance or impressed by his steadfast belief in himself.
  Possible response: Some students may argue that Socrates is needlessly defiant when he alludes to the inherent flaws in the political system; others may say that he needs to convince the jury that he is a man of integrity.

32 Reading Check

Answer: Socrates believes that he is able to do more good by avoiding public office.

Differentiated Instruction Solutions for All Learners

Strategy for Less Proficient Readers
Have students imagine that they are among the jurors at Socrates' trial. Ask them to compile charts that list the positive and negative qualities they have observed in Socrates so far in their reading. Among the positive qualities, students might note his displays of integrity, piety, consistency, patriotism, and logic. Negative qualities may include his defiance and his ironic attitude toward politicians, poets, and artisans.

Enrichment for Gifted/Talented Students
Invite students to choose a portion of the *Apology* and rehearse it for oral presentation. Remind students that Socrates had to keep his disruptive audience's attention as well as convince them to spare his life. As they rehearse, ask speakers to enhance the persuasiveness of the text with their volume, vocal inflection, posture, and gestures. Invite students to deliver their parts of the speech to the class. After each performance, encourage students to critique the delivery.

33 Literary Analysis
Monologue

- Have students read the bracketed passage that begins on p. 449.
- Discuss with students the contrast Socrates draws between himself and other courtroom defendants.
- Then, **ask** students the Literary Analysis question: What does Socrates reveal about himself by refusing to bring his children into court?
  Possible response: Socrates' remarks reveal his respect for the State and for his family and his disgust with the common practice of exploiting oneself and one's family in an attempt to win the mercy of the court.

34 Reading Strategy
Challenging the Text

- Have a student read aloud the bracketed passage.
- **Ask** students how Socrates' disdain for judges' "making a present of justice" fits his character.
  Possible response: Socrates' only interest is the truth, so it is no surprise that he abhors judges' practice of dispensing verdicts without employing true justice.
- **Direct** students' attention to the Reading Strategy question: Do you agree that bringing his children into court would demean Socrates? Explain.
  Possible responses: Yes; the presence of Socrates' children might make the jurors feel guilty about putting Socrates to death, distracting them from using the justice Socrates demands. No; it is common practice to bring the accused's children to court.

33 number, one almost a man, and two others who are still young; and yet I will not bring any of them hither in order to petition you for an acquittal. And why not? Not from any self-assertion or want of respect for you. Whether I am or am not afraid of death is another question, of which I will not now speak. But, having regard to public opinion, I feel that such conduct would be discreditable to myself, and to you, and to the whole State. One who has reached my years, and who has a name for wisdom, ought not to demean himself. Whether this opinion of me be deserved or not, at any rate the world has decided that Socrates is in some way superior to other men. And if those among you who are said to be superior in wisdom and courage, and any other virtue, demean themselves in this way, how shameful is their conduct! I have seen men of reputation, when they have been condemned, behaving in the strangest manner: they seemed to fancy that they were going to suffer something dreadful if they died, and that they could be immortal if you only allowed them to live; and I think that such are a dishonor to the State, and that any stranger coming in would have said of them that the most eminent men of Athens, to whom the Athenians themselves give honor and command, are no better than women. And 34 I say that these things ought not to be done by those of us who have a reputation; and if they are done, you ought not to permit them; you ought rather to show that you are far more disposed to condemn the man who gets up a doleful[26] scene and makes the city ridiculous, than him who holds his peace.

But, setting aside the question of public opinion, there seems to be something wrong in asking a favor of a judge, and thus procuring[27] an acquittal, instead of informing and convincing him. For his duty is, not to make a present of justice, but to give judgment; and he has sworn that he will judge according to the laws, and not according to his own good pleasure; and we ought not to encourage you, nor should you allow yourselves to be encouraged, in this habit of perjury[28]—there can be no piety in that. Do not then require me to do what I consider dishonorable and impious and wrong, especially now, when I am being tried for impiety on the indictment of Meletus. For if, O men of Athens, by force of persuasion and entreaty I could overpower your oaths, then I should be teaching you to believe that there are no gods, and in defending should simply convict myself of the charge of not believing in them. But that is not so—far otherwise. For I do believe that there are gods, and in a sense higher than that in which any of my accusers believe in them. And to you and to God I commit my cause, to be determined by you as is best for you and me.

There are many reasons why I am not grieved, O men of Athens, at the vote of condemnation. I expected it, and am only surprised that the votes are so nearly equal; for I had thought that the majority

Literary Analysis
Monologue What does Socrates reveal about himself by refusing to bring his children into court?

Reading Strategy
Challenging the Text Do you agree that bringing his children into court would demean Socrates? Explain.

Vocabulary Builder
piety (pī´ ē tē) *n.* respect for the gods

26. **doleful** (dōl´ fəl) *adj.* mournful; melancholy.
27. **procuring** (prō kyoor´ iŋ) *v.* securing; obtaining.
28. **perjury** (pur´ jə rē) *n.* act of lying while under lawful oath.

Enrichment

Athenian Courts and Juries

By the sixth century B.C., Athens had grown so large that it was nearly impossible for all citizens to hear every court case. Each year, 6,000 people were randomly chosen to be jurors on a variety of cases. The number of jurors needed ranged from 200 to over 1,000, depending on the type of case being tried. It is likely that Socrates faced a jury of about 500: evidence shows that the vote was about 280–220 to convict him.

No lawyers were in the Athenian courts. Each side presented its case directly, within a set time. Litigants could, however, employ a professional speechwriter, and they could ask friends to testify in their behalf. Juries did not take time for deliberation. After the litigants' presentation, jurors decided the case immediately. First, they voted for guilt or innocence. If the accused was found guilty, both sides then presented proposals for punishment before the jury chose the penalty.

against me would have been far larger; but now, had thirty votes gone over to the other side, I should have been acquitted. And I may say, I think, that I have escaped Meletus. I may say more; for without the assistance of Anytus and Lycon, any one may see that he would not have had a fifth part of the votes, as the law requires, in which case he would have incurred a fine of a thousand drachmae.

35

And so he proposes death as the penalty. And what shall I propose on my part, O men of Athens? Clearly that which is my due. And what is my due? What returns shall be made to the man who has never had the wit to be idle during his whole life; but has been careless of what the many care for—wealth, and family interests, and military offices, and speaking in the assembly, and magistracies, and plots, and parties. Reflecting that I was really too honest a man to be a politician and live, I did not go where I could do no good to you or to myself; but where I could do the greatest good privately to every one of you, thither I went, and sought to persuade every man among you that he must look to himself, and seek virtue and wisdom before he looks to his private interests, and look to the State before he looks to the interests of the State; and that this should be the order which he observes in all his actions. What shall be done to such an one? Doubtless some good thing, O men of Athens, if he has his reward; and the good should be of a kind suitable to him. What would be a reward suitable to a poor man who is your benefactor, and who desires leisure that he may instruct you? There can be no reward so fitting as maintenance in the Prytaneum,[29] O men of Athens, a reward which he deserves far more than the citizen who has won the prize at Olympia in the horse or chariot race, whether the chariots were drawn by two horses or by many. For I am in want, and he has enough; and he only gives you the appearance of happiness, and I give you the reality. And if I am to estimate the penalty fairly, I should say that maintenance in the Prytaneum is the just return. 37

Perhaps you think that I am braving you in what I am saying now, as in what I said before about the tears and prayers. But this is not so. I speak rather because I am convinced that I never intentionally wronged any one, although I cannot convince you—the time has been too short; if there were a law at Athens as there is in other cities, that a capital cause should not be decided in one day, then I believe that I should have convinced you. But I cannot in a moment refute great slanders; and, as I am convinced that I never wronged another, I will assuredly not wrong myself. I will not say of myself that I deserve any

36 ▲ Critical Viewing

Based on this depiction of the Academy, in what way does Plato seem to be continuing the work of Socrates? **[Analyze]**

38 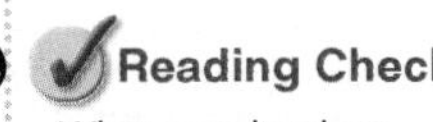 Reading Check

What penalty does Meletus propose for Socrates?

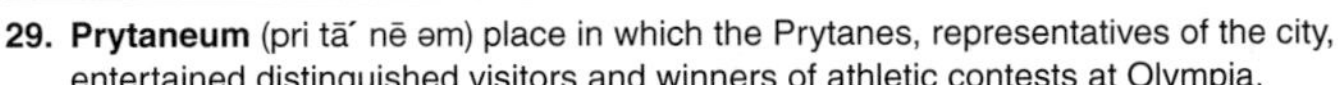

29. **Prytaneum** (pri tā´ nē əm) place in which the Prytanes, representatives of the city, entertained distinguished visitors and winners of athletic contests at Olympia.

35 Humanities

The School of Plato

This mosaic was taken from a Roman villa outside Pompeii. It shows a group of philosophers gathering beneath a tree to exchange ideas. In the upper right corner, the Acropolis and the Parthenon identify the location as Athens. The skill of the mosaicist is seen in the variety of expressions on the men's faces. Plato is identified as the third figure from the left. The scene is framed with an exquisitely crafted border of twined fruit, flowers, and masks.

Use the following questions for discussion:

- How would you describe this mosaic to a friend who has not seen it?
  Possible response: The mosaic looks almost like a painting in its use of color, shading, detail, and composition.
- What is the mood of this mosaic?
  Answer: The mood is meditative, relaxed, and serene.

36 Critical Viewing

Answer: Plato's position at the center of the group suggests that he has continued in Socrates' place, guiding dialogue by challenging the speakers.

37 Critical Thinking

Make Inferences

- Tell students that in the passage they will read, Socrates responds to the proposed penalty of death.
- **Ask** students why Socrates' counterproposal of maintenance in the Prytaneum may not be favored by the jury.
  Possible response: Allowing a condemned man to circulate among important Athenians and distinguished visitors probably did not seem like punishment.

38 Reading Check

Answer: He proposes death.

39 Literary Analysis
Monologue

- Draw students' attention to Socrates' rapid-fire series of questions in the bracketed passage. Have students consider what tone is created by these questions.
- Then, **ask** students whether they think this passage might have garnered jury sympathy.
  Possible responses: Yes; Socrates speaks specifically about the hardships exile will bring him. No; Socrates has forfeited his chances of winning the jurors' sympathy with his earlier suggestion that he be maintained at public expense.

40 Reading Strategy
Challenging the Text

- Have students read the bracketed passage. Tell them that they will encounter one of the most famous statements attributed to Socrates.
- Draw students' attention to the sentence that includes "the unexamined life is not worth living."
- **Ask** students whether they agree with Socrates' view about the importance of scrutiny and self-examination.
  Possible responses: Yes; people should be aware of their reasons for thinking and acting as they do. No; if taken to an extreme, scrutiny and self-examination can lead to self-consciousness and inactivity.

41 Critical Viewing

Answer: Socrates' followers are gripped by sadness and loss. Some of them turn away in grief or bury their faces in their hands.

42 Background
History

A mina is a very small sum and corresponds to what Socrates (who has said he is penniless) can afford himself. The jury would take his proposal as a joke in bad taste and an insult. The thirty minae he can offer with the help of his wealthy young friends is a much more reasonable sum. However, Socrates has already indicated in several ways that he does not think he should pay any fine.

evil, or propose any penalty. Why should I? Because I am afraid of
the penalty of death which Meletus proposes? When I do not know
whether death is a good or an evil, why should I propose a penalty
which would certainly be an evil? Shall I say imprisonment? And
why should I live in prison, and be the slave of the magistrate of the
year—of the Eleven?[30] Or shall the penalty be a fine, and imprisonment until the fine is paid? There is the same objection. I should
39 have to lie in prison, for money I have none, and cannot pay. And
if I say exile (and this may possibly be the penalty which you will
affix), I must indeed be blinded by the love of life, if I am so irrational
as to expect that when you, who are my own citizens, cannot endure
my discourses[31] and words, and have found them so grievous and
odious[32] that you will have no more of them, others are likely to
endure me. No, indeed, men of Athens, that is not very likely. And
what a life should I lead, at my age, wandering from city to city, ever
changing my place of exile, and always being driven out! For I am
quite sure that wherever I go, there, as here, the young men will flock
to me; and if I drive them away, their elders will drive me out at their
request; and if I let them come, their fathers and friends will drive me
out for their sakes.

Some one will say: Yes, Socrates, but cannot you hold your tongue,
and then you may go into a foreign city, and no one will interfere with
you? Now, I have great difficulty in making you understand my answer
to this. For if I tell you that to do as you say would be a disobedience
40 to the God, and therefore that I cannot hold my tongue, you will not
believe that I am serious; and if I say again that daily to discourse
about virtue, and of those other things about which you hear me
examining myself and others, is the greatest good of man, and that
the unexamined life is not worth living, you are still less likely to
believe me. Yet I say what is true, although a thing of which it is hard
for me to persuade you. Also, I have never been accustomed to think
that I deserve to suffer any harm. Had I money I might have estimated
the offense at what I was able to pay, and not have been much the
worse. But I have none, and therefore I must ask you to proportion the
fine to my means. Well, perhaps I could afford a mina,[33] and therefore I
propose that penalty: Plato, Crito, Critobulus, and Apollodorus, my
42 friends here, bid me say thirty minae, and they will be the sureties.[34]
Let thirty minae be the penalty; for which sum they will be ample
security to you.

Not much time will be gained, O Athenians, in return for the evil name which you will get from the detractors[35] of the city, who will

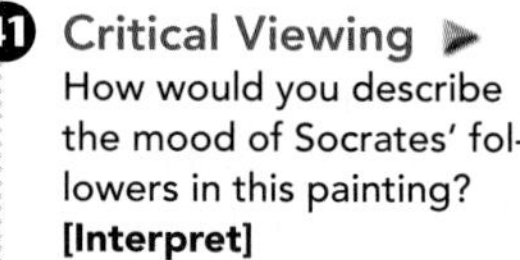
41 Critical Viewing ▶ How would you describe the mood of Socrates' followers in this painting? **[Interpret]**

30. **the Eleven** committee in charge of prisons and public executions.
31. **discourses** (dis´ kôrs´ iz) *n.* communications of ideas.
32. **odious** (ō´ dē əs) *adj.* disgusting; offensive.
33. **mina** (mī´ nə) very small sum of money.
34. **sureties** (shoor´ ə tēz) *n.* people who take responsibility for another person's debts.
35. **detractors** (dē trakt´ ərz) *n.* here, people who belittle.

43 say that you killed Socrates, a wise man; for they will call me wise, even although I am not wise, when they want to reproach you. If you had waited a little while, your desire would have been fulfilled in the course of nature. For I am far advanced in years, as you may perceive, and not far from death. I am speaking now not to all of you, but only to those who have condemned me to death. And I have another thing to say to them: You think that I was convicted because I had no words of the sort which would have procured my acquittal—I mean, if I had thought fit to leave nothing undone or unsaid. Not so; the deficiency which led to my conviction was not of words—certainly not. But I had not the boldness or impudence or inclination to address you as you would have liked me to do, weeping and wailing and lamenting, and saying and doing many things which you have been accustomed to hear from others, and which, as I maintain, are unworthy of me. I thought at the time that I ought not to do anything common or mean when in danger: nor do I now repent of the style of
44 my defense; I would rather die having spoken after my manner, than speak in your manner and live. For neither in war nor yet at law ought I or any man to use every way of escaping death. Often in battle there can be no doubt that if a man will throw away his arms, and fall on his knees before his pursuers, he may escape death; and in other dangers there are other ways of escaping death, if a man is willing to say and do anything. The difficulty, my friends, is not to avoid death, but to avoid unrighteousness; for that runs faster than death. I am old and move slowly, and the slower runner has overtaken me, and my accusers are keen and quick, and the faster runner, who is unrighteousness, has overtaken them. And now I depart

Reading Strategy
Challenging the Text Does Socrates truly believe that he is not wise, or is his humility false? Explain.

Literary Analysis
Monologue What does Socrates reveal in his statement, "I would rather die having spoken after my manner, than speak in your manner and live"?

45  **Reading Check**
Why does Socrates reject the idea of exile as his penalty?

46

The Death of Socrates, 1787, Jacques-Louis David, The Metropolitan Museum of Art, New York

43 Reading Strategy
Challenging the Text
- Call attention to the bracketed passage.
- **Ask** the Reading Strategy question: Does Socrates truly believe that he is not wise, or is his humility false? Explain.
  Possible response: Socrates' humility is false because he finds there is wisdom in being conscious of one's ignorance; to this end, he freely admits being wise.

44 Literary Analysis
Monologue
- Read aloud the bracketed text. Then, **ask** the Literary Analysis question: What does Socrates reveal in his statement, "I would rather die having spoken after my manner, than speak in your manner and live"?
  Possible response: Socrates reveals his consistency and integrity but also his stubbornness.

45 Reading Check
Answer: Socrates says that he is too old to move from place to place.

46 Humanities
The Death of Socrates,
by Jacques-Louis David

David (1748–1825) was an eminent historical painter and the leader of the Neoclassical movement in French art. David aspired in his paintings to represent events precisely and to render the personalities of the heroic past.

Use the following question for discussion:

What do the facial expressions of the figures in David's painting suggest?
Possible response: The expressions suggest grief and despair.

Differentiated Instruction
Solutions for All Learners

Strategy for Less Proficient Readers
Draw students' attention to Socrates' analogy on this page between his own situation in court and the situation of a soldier in battle. Assign different portions of this excerpt to students to scan for other references to soldiers and battles from well-known stories and from Socrates' military service in the Peloponnesian War. Record these references on the board, and then lead a discussion about the themes of honor and patriotism in the *Apology.*

Vocabulary for English Learners
Help students work in pairs to identify and define unfamiliar words or familiar words used in unexpected contexts on this page. Discuss the phrase *advanced in years,* in which the word *advanced* is used in the meaning of "far on in life" or "old." Ask students to find its context *(and not far from death).* Then tell students that the word *mean* is used in this context as "unworthy" or "base." Then explain the use of *runs* in the personification . . . *to avoid unrighteousness; for that runs faster than death.*

47 Themes in World Literature

Courtroom Drama Harper Lee's novel *To Kill a Mockingbird* was brought to film audiences in 1962. The film received three Oscars, including Best Actor for Gregory Peck's portrayal of Atticus Finch, the lawyer who, in a court case that throws the community into turmoil, defends a black man accused of raping a white woman.

Connect to the Literature Note that courtroom dramas are still popular in today's TV and film media. Ask students what they find dramatic in the *Apology.*

Possible response: Some dramatic moments occur when Socrates shows his disdain for the judges and says he is superior to politicians and when he takes on the role of a prophet and tells the judges that a terrible fate awaits them. His questions to the jury and his references to his belief in God also are dramatic.

48 Literary Analysis

Monologue

- Read aloud the bracketed passage. Ask students to listen for a heightened emotional quality in Socrates' words.
- Guide students to recognize that Socrates here places himself in the role of a prophet or seer.
- Then, **ask** students: What does Socrates reveal about himself when he forecasts such dire consequences for those who have voted to condemn him?
  Answer: Socrates reveals that he feels entitled to judge his jurors in turn. He calls them "murderers," rather than jurors, and professes confidence that his death will not be in vain.

49 Critical Thinking

Compare and Contrast

- Then, **ask** students to compare and contrast Socrates' tone in this paragraph with the tone of his remarks to those who condemned him.
  Possible response: Socrates uses a mild tone when he addresses the "friends" who would have acquitted him, saying that he can truly call them "judges." He is stern in addressing those who have condemned him, calling them "my murderers."

hence condemned by you to suffer the penalty of death,—they too go their ways condemned by the truth to suffer the penalty of villainy and wrong; and I must abide by my award—let them abide by theirs. I suppose that these things may be regarded as fated,—and I think that they are well.

48 And now, O men who have condemned me, I would fain prophesy to you; for I am about to die, and in the hour of death men are gifted with prophetic power. And I prophesy to you who are my murderers, that immediately after my departure punishment far heavier than you have inflicted on me will surely await you. Me you have killed because you wanted to escape the accuser, and not to give an account of your lives. But that will not be as you suppose: far otherwise. For I say that there will be more accusers of you than there are now; accusers whom hitherto I have restrained: and as they are younger they will be more inconsiderate with you, and you will be more offended at them. If you think that by killing men you can prevent some one from censuring your evil lives, you are mistaken; that is not a way of escape which is either possible or honorable; the easiest and the noblest way is not to be disabling others, but to be improving yourselves. This is the prophecy which I utter before my departure to the judges who have condemned me.

49 Friends, who would have acquitted me, I would like also to talk with you about the thing which has come to pass, while the magistrates are busy, and before I go to the place at which I must die. Stay then a little, for we may as well talk with one another while there is time. You are my friends, and I should like to show you the meaning of this event which has happened to me. O my judges—for you I may truly call judges—I should like to tell you of a wonderful circumstance. Hitherto the divine faculty of which the internal oracle is the source has constantly been in the habit of opposing me even about trifles, if I was going to make a slip or error in any matter; and now as you see there has come upon me that which may be thought, and is generally believed to be, the last and worst evil. But the oracle made no sign of opposition, either when I was leaving my house in the morning, or when I was on my way to the court, or while I was speaking, at anything which I was going to say; and yet I have often been stopped in the middle of a speech, but now in nothing I either said or did touching the matter in hand has the oracle opposed me. What do I take to be the explanation of this silence? I will tell you. It is an intimation[36] that what has happened to me is a good, and that those of us who think that death is an evil are

36. **intimation** (in′ tə mā′ shən) *n.* indirect suggestion.

47 Courtroom Drama

Some of the most dramatic and memorable moments in literature and film have taken place in the courtroom. Often the stakes are high, as in the *Apology*, when the accused's life hangs in the balance. Sometimes it is the deliberation of the judges or the jury that provides the drama.

In the film *Twelve Angry Men* (1957), for example, a young man is accused of murder and stands to lose his life if convicted. The jury is ready to convict until a lone juror persuades the others to re-examine the evidence. His persistence in calling for reasonable deliberation eventually leads to the young man's acquittal.

Startling revelations and climactic cross-examinations help make courtroom dramas among the most suspenseful and entertaining works in all of literature. From Harper Lee's novel *To Kill a Mockingbird* (1960) to Aaron Sorkin's play *A Few Good Men* (1989), literary works set in a courtroom have a way of keeping the audience on the edge of their seats, waiting eagerly to find out whether justice will be served.

Connect to the Literature

List some of the elements that provide drama in the *Apology*.

Enrichment

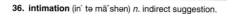

Socrates' Last Hours

After his trial, Socrates was executed by being compelled to drink a lethal dose of the poison hemlock. In two of his dialogues, Plato describes what happened immediately prior to the death of Socrates. In the *Crito,* named for one of Socrates' contemporaries and devoted friends, Crito lays plans for Socrates to escape from prison. The dialogue consists of Socrates' rationale in rejecting such a plan even though his sentence was unjust: He says that escape would constitute disobedience to the laws and would thus be morally harmful to him.

In the *Phaedo,* Socrates discusses his belief in the immortality of the soul. Socrates argues that the soul has many lives, which are independent of the life of the body, that the soul is analogous to the Forms, or abstract essences that have eternal existence, and that the soul's essence is life itself.

Students may wish to research one of these dialogues in more detail and to present their findings in brief oral or written reports.

in error. For the customary sign would surely have opposed me had I been going to evil and not to good.

Let us reflect in another way, and we shall see that there is great reason to hope that death is a good; for one of two things—either death is a state of nothingness and utter unconsciousness, or, as men say, there is a change and migration of the soul from this world to another. Now, if you suppose that there is no consciousness, but a sleep like the sleep of him who is undisturbed even by dreams, death
50 will be an unspeakable gain. For if a person were to select the night in which his sleep was undisturbed even by dreams, and were to compare with this the other days and nights of his life, and then were to tell us how many days and nights he had passed in the course of his life better and more pleasantly than this one, I think that any man, I will not say a private man, but even the great king will not find many such days or nights, when compared with the others. Now, if death be of such a nature, I say that to die is gain, for eternity is then only a single night. But if death is the journey to another place, and there, as men say, all the dead abide, what good, O my friends and judges, can be greater than this? If, indeed, when the pilgrim arrives in the world below, he is delivered from the professors of justice in this world, and finds the true judges who are said to give judgment there, Minos and Rhadamanthus and Aeacus and Triptolemus,[37] and other sons of God who were righteous in their own life, that pilgrimage will be worth
52 making. What would not a man give if he might converse with Orpheus and Musaeus and Hesiod[38] and Homer? Nay, if this be true, let me die again and again. I myself, too, shall have a wonderful interest in there meeting and conversing with Palamedes,[39] and Ajax[40] the son of Telamon, and any other ancient hero who has suffered death through an unjust judgment; and there will be no small pleasure, as I think, in comparing my own sufferings with theirs. Above all, I shall then be able to continue my search into true and false knowledge; as in this world, so also in the next; and I shall find out who is wise, and who pretends to be wise, and is not. What would not a man give, O judges, to be able to examine the leader of the great Trojan expedition, or Odysseus or Sisyphus,[41] or numberless others, men and women too! What infinite delight would there be in conversing with them and asking them questions! In another world they do not put a man to death for asking questions: assuredly not. For

51 Reading Strategy
Challenging the Text
What assumptions about dreams does Socrates make in this argument? Do you agree with this idea?

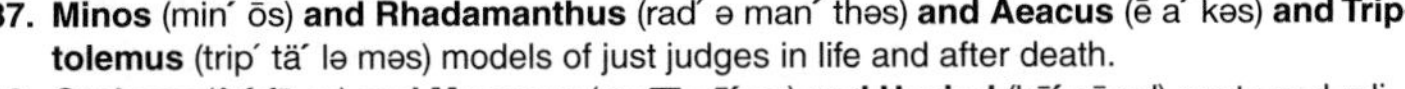

37. **Minos** (min´ ōs) **and Rhadamanthus** (rad´ ə man´ thəs) **and Aeacus** (ē a´ kəs) **and Triptolemus** (trip´ tä´ lə məs) models of just judges in life and after death.
38. **Orpheus** (ôr´ fē əs) **and Musaeus** (myo͞o zā´ əs) **and Hesiod** (hē´ sē əd) poets and religious teachers.
39. **Palamedes** (pal´ə mē´ dēz) one of the Greek chieftains at Troy who was unjustly executed for treason.
40. **Ajax** (ā´ jaks) Greek warrior who committed suicide after Achilles' arms were given to Odysseus as the bravest Greek warrior.
41. **Sisyphus** (sis´ ə fəs) in Greek mythology, a king of Corinth, famous for his cunning.

53 
Reading Check
What does Socrates honor about Palamedes, Ajax, and other ancient heroes?

50 Background

Culture

Here, Socrates is alluding to a belief widely held as early as the fifth century B.C., that the soul was immortal and suffered a variety of fates after death, depending on the individual's conduct in life. For Plato and others, this belief was linked with the belief in reincarnation, or the transmigration of souls.

51 Reading Strategy

Challenging the Text

- Have students read the bracketed passage, paying particular attention to Socrates' mentions of dreams.
- **Ask** students the Reading Strategy question: What assumptions about dreams does Socrates make in this argument? Do you agree with this idea?
  Possible response: Socrates mentions "sleep undisturbed by dreams" as extremely desirable, so he seems to suggest that dreams are undesirable. Students may disagree with this statement, believing that dreams help them sort out problems.

52 Literary Analysis

Monologue

- Have students read the lists of mythological, legendary, and historical people mentioned by Socrates in the bracketed passage. Remind them to use the footnotes to help identify the names.
- **Ask** students: What does Socrates reveal about himself as he gives this catalogue of some of the greatest figures of ancient Greek culture?
  Possible response: Socrates reveals a keen understanding of Greek mythology, history, and poetry. He also reveals that he places himself among these legendary figures.

53 Reading Check

Answer: These heroes suffered death unjustly.

54 Critical Thinking

Evaluate

- Have students read the bracketed passage. Tell them that they will encounter Socrates' final request.
- **Ask** students whether they believe that this passage is an effective conclusion to his speech.
  Possible responses: Yes; it demonstrates once again Socrates' devotion to justice and truth. No; it seems only tangentially related to the major issues of the speech as a whole.

ASSESS

Answers

1. **Possible responses:** Yes; it was an impassioned and consistent defense of Socrates' way of living and teaching. No; certain parts of the speech showed Socrates' arrogance.
2. (a) Socrates wants to test the validity of the oracle's assertion that no one is wiser than he. (b) Socrates angers them by unmasking their shortcomings.
3. (a) Socrates calls the fear of death "the pretense of wisdom." (b) He is wiser because he is conscious of his own ignorance. (c) The wisest person is one who knows that he or she does not possess any appreciable knowledge, especially in comparison with divine knowledge.
4. (a) Socrates believes that such a course would be impious and disrespectful to the God. (b) **Possible responses:** Yes; he must be true to himself. No; his extreme course of action will result in his death and the grief of his followers.
5. **Possible response:** Yes; a life lived without reflection might just as well not have been lived. Only by reflecting on life may a person learn from and then improve or enrich his or her life.

Go Online Author Link For additional information about Plato, have students type in the Web Code, then select *P* from the alphabet, and then select Plato.

besides being happier than we are, they will be immortal, if what is said is true.

Wherefore, O judges, be of good cheer about death, and know of a certainty, that no evil can happen to a good man, either in life or after death. He and his are not neglected by the gods; nor has my own approaching end happened by mere chance. But I see clearly that the time had arrived when it was better for me to die and be released from trouble; wherefore the oracle gave no sign. For which reason, also, I am not angry with my condemners, or with my accusers; they have done me no harm, although they did not mean to do me any good; and for this I may gently blame them.

54 Still, I have a favor to ask of them. When my sons are grown up, I would ask you, O my friends, to punish them; and I would have you trouble them, as I have troubled you, if they seem to care about riches, or anything, more than about virtue; or if they pretend to be something when they are really nothing,—then reprove[42] them, as I have reproved you, for not caring about that for which they ought to care, and thinking that they are something when they are really nothing. And if you do this, both I and my sons will have received justice at your hands.

The hour of departure has arrived, and we go our ways—I to die, and you to live. Which is better God only knows.

42. reprove (ri pro͞ov′) *v.* express disapproval of.

Critical Reading

1. **Respond:** Imagine yourself as a juror at Socrates' trial. Would his speech have moved you? Explain.
2. **(a) Recall:** According to Socrates, why does he go about questioning people to see whether they are wise? **(b) Deduce:** Why does his questioning make so many people his enemies?
3. **(a) Recall:** What does Socrates call "the pretense of wisdom"? **(b) Interpret:** In what respect does Socrates consider himself wiser than the people he questions? **(c) Define:** What kind of person does Socrates claim is wisest?
4. **(a) Recall:** Why does Socrates refuse to compromise and stop teaching? **(b) Evaluate:** Considering that Socrates' refusal to compromise will cost him his life, do you believe he has made the right choice? Explain.
5. **Speculate:** Do you agree with Socrates that "the unexamined life is not worth living"? Why or why not?

For: More about Plato
Visit: www.PHSchool.com
Web Code: ete-9405

Apply the Skills

from the *Apology*

Literary Analysis

Monologue

1. In the opening remarks of his monologue, Socrates portrays himself as a simple old man who is not very eloquent. Why might Socrates portray himself in this way?
2. Socrates frequently mentions the gods. Why might he do this?
3. In addressing the court, Socrates frequently asks questions and then answers them. How might this technique affect his audience?
4. Use a chart like the one shown to analyze the character of Socrates as revealed in his monologue. Choose three statements made by Socrates, and explain what each one reveals about his character.

Statement	What It Reveals
1.	1.
2.	2.
3.	3.

Connecting Literary Elements

5. At one point, Socrates compares himself to Achilles, the hero of the *Iliad.* How might this **analogy** affect Socrates' audience?
6. What point does Socrates make by describing himself as a gadfly?
7. What does Socrates mean when he compares Athenians to people "suddenly awakened from sleep"?

Reading Strategy

Challenging the Text

8. **(a) Challenge** Socrates' claim that "the men most in repute were all but the most foolish." How does he support this assertion? **(b)** Is his evidence convincing? Why or why not?
9. **(a)** Do you agree with Socrates' assertion that "he who will fight for the right . . . must have a private station and not a public one"? **(b)** What evidence from your experience or readings supports your opinion?

Extend Understanding

10. **Cultural Connection: (a)** What failures of the State and of politicians does Socrates seem to be criticizing in this text? **(b)** Would Socrates be critical of today's states and politicians? Explain.

QuickReview

A **monologue** is a long and revealing speech by one character.

An **analogy** is an extended comparison of relationships.

To **challenge the text,** critically evaluate the author's assertions and reasoning.

For: Self-test
Visit: www.PHSchool.com
Web Code: eta-6405

Answers

1. **Possible response:** He might do this to win the jurors' sympathy.
2. **Possible response:** Socrates might mention the gods to combat the charge of atheism.
3. **Possible response:** His audience may become more familiar with his technique, thus making them more informed.
4. **Possible response: Statement:** "A man who is good for anything . . . of living or dying"; "The fear of death . . . pretense of wisdom"; "The unexamined life is not worth living." **What It Reveals:** courage and commitment; rationality and analytical nature; commitment to ideals, ethical values, and responsibility. Another sample answer can be found on **Literary Analysis Graphic Organizer B,** p. 87 in ***Graphic Organizer Transparencies.***
5. **Possible response:** Listeners may find the comparison to be unfounded or arrogant.
6. He reinforces his role as the "conscience" of the Athenians, reproaching them and persuading them as needed.
7. He means that they have been oblivious to important moral values.
8. (a) **Possible response:** Socrates points out that poets are less capable of discussing their poems than are other people. (b) **Possible response:** Yes; poets or artisans should be able to explain their craft.
9. (a) **Possible response:** Yes; politicians become beholden to special interests. No; it is important to work to preserve the value of integrity in public life. (b) **Possible response:** Shakespeare's *Julius Caesar* supports this opinion.
10. (a) Socrates seems to criticize the ethics of the State and of politicians. (b) **Possible response:** Yes; modern politics is often marked by scandals.

Go Online Assessment — Students may use the **Self-test** to prepare for **Selection Test A** or **Selection Test B.**

EXTEND/ASSESS

Answers

1 Vocabulary Lesson

Word Analysis: Legal Terminology

1. Socrates' *prosecutors* wished to show that he was an atheist and a corrupter of youth.
2. The suspect was *arraigned* in court the day after he was arrested.
3. If thirty votes had changed sides, the result of Socrates' trial might have been *acquittal.*

Spelling Strategy

1. impudent; impudently
2. prudent; prudently
3. magnificent; magnificently
4. benevolent; benevolently

Vocabulary Builder

1. exhorting
2. piety
3. indictment
4. affidavit
5. eloquence
6. impudence
7. lamented
8. avenged

2 Grammar and Style Lesson

1. although; comparison and contrast
2. then; chronological
3. after; chronological
4. whereupon; cause and effect
5. still; compare and contrast

Writing Application

Possible response: First, Socrates was accused of atheism. Then, he defended himself in court. In order to show that he was humble, he described the process he undertook to learn what the oracle meant when she said no man was wiser than he.

WG Writing and Grammar Platinum Level

For support in teaching the Grammar and Style Lesson, use Chapter 10, Section 4.

Build Language Skills

1 Vocabulary Lesson

Word Analysis: Legal Terminology

Socrates uses the words *affidavit* and *indictment.* These are examples of legal terminology, or words that pertain to the law and to legal proceedings.

Socrates also uses the following legal terms. Use each word in a sentence.

1. prosecutors
2. arraigned
3. acquittal

Spelling Strategy

Nouns ending in *-ence* usually end in *-ent* in their adjective form and in *-ently* in their adverb form. For example, *eloquence* becomes *eloquent* and *eloquently.*

Write the adjective and adverb forms of each of the following words:

1. impudence
2. prudence
3. magnificence
4. benevolence

Vocabulary Builder: Sentence Completion

Review the vocabulary list on page 439. Then, select the vocabulary word that best completes each of the following sentences.

1. Socrates wandered the streets, questioning people and __?__ them to examine their lives.
2. He was charged with atheism, so he demonstrated his __?__ in court.
3. The charges were listed in the __?__.
4. The __?__ was signed by the witnesses.
5. Despite the __?__ of his speech, he failed to persuade the judges.
6. His __?__ angered the judges.
7. His tearful followers __?__ his death.
8. His death may be __?__ by angry gods.

2 Grammar and Style Lesson

Transitions and Transitional Phrases

Transitions are words that show chronological, spatial, comparison and contrast, cause and effect, and order of importance relationships among ideas. Groups of words that function in this way are called transitional phrases.

Chronological: *At last* I went to the artisans.
Spatial: *Outside the courtroom,* people speculated about the verdict.
Comparison and contrast: . . . *whereas* I, who am probably in danger. . .
Cause and effect: *Accordingly,* I went to one . . .
Order of importance: *Above all,* I shall . . .

Practice Identify the transitional word or phrase in each item below. Then, indicate the kind of relationship it reveals.

1. They have done me no harm, although they did not mean to do me any good.
2. Then I went to another who had still higher pretensions to wisdom.
3. After the politicians, I went to the poets.
4. Whereupon I made another enemy.
5. Still, I have a favor to ask them.

Writing Application Write a paragraph describing the occasion of Socrates' speech. Use at least three transitions in your writing.

WG *Prentice Hall Writing and Grammar Connection: Platinum Level, Chapter 10, Section 4*

Assessment Practice

Stated and Implied Main Ideas (For more practice, see *Test Preparation Workbook*, p. 21.)

In many tests, students will have to identify an implied main idea. Use the sample test item to demonstrate this skill.

"The hour of departure has arrived, and we go our ways—I to die, and you to live. Which is better God only knows."

Which of the following best describes Socrates' main idea in this passage?

A Socrates regrets that his life will end.
B God will punish Socrates' judges accordingly.
C Humans do not know whether death is worse than life.
D Some of those who will live on deserve to die.

Choice C is the correct answer. Socrates does not deplore the end of his life, so *A* is incorrect. He does not comment on God's justice, nor does he insist on retribution, so choices *B* and *D* are incorrect.

❸ Writing Lesson

Account of a Remarkable Person

Plato found Socrates to be a remarkable person. Review the excerpt from the *Apology,* and determine which character traits Plato admired most in Socrates. Use Plato's writing as a springboard for your own essay. Think about the character traits of a remarkable person whom you know, and write an essay describing that person.

Prewriting Use a chart like the one shown to record details about what makes Socrates remarkable. Then, complete the chart with details about what makes the person you know remarkable.

Socrates	A Remarkable Person I Know

Drafting Plato wrote the *Apology* as a dramatic re-creation of Socrates' trial, using Socrates' own words to reveal the philosopher's character and beliefs. As you draft your essay, include your own reactions and the actual words of your subject to reveal his or her character.

Revising Show your essay to classmates to see whether your subject's remarkable qualities are clear. Then, revise your writing, adding quotations and precise details to convey your subject's character.

WG Prentice Hall Writing and Grammar Connection: Platinum Level, Chapter 6, Section 2

❹ Extend Your Learning

Listening and Speaking With a partner, develop and role-play an **interview** with someone who witnessed or was involved in the trial of Socrates. Use the following strategies to capture the drama of the courtroom scene:

- Develop questions and answers that describe the crowd at the trial.
- Have the interviewee directly quote some of Socrates' statements.
- Have the interviewee describe the mood of the courtroom when the verdict is announced.

Present your interview for the class. Following the presentation, allow time for a question-and-answer period. **[Group Activity]**

Research and Technology Use library resources and the Internet to gather information on the justice system in ancient Athens. Write a research **report** describing the system, focusing on what behaviors were considered criminal, how a person was brought to trial, who were the judges, and what types of punishments were handed out. Share your research report with the class.

For: An additional research activity
Visit: www.PHSchool.com
Web Code: etd-7404

Assessment Resources

The following resources can be used to assess students' knowledge and skills.

Unit 4 Resources
- **Selection Test A,** pp. 94–96
- **Selection Test B,** pp. 97–99

General Resources
- **Rubrics for Descriptive Essay,** pp. 67–68
- **Rubrics for Research: Research Report,** pp. 51–52

Go Online Assessment Students may use the **Self-test** to prepare for **Selection Test A** or **Selection Test B.**

❸ Writing Lesson

You may use this Writing Lesson as timed-writing practice, or you may allow students to develop the essay as a writing assignment over several days.

- To give students guidance in writing this essay, give them the **Support for Writing Lesson,** p. 91 in ***Unit 4 Resources.***
- Read aloud the Writing Lesson instruction. Tell students that their accounts should touch on such character traits as commitment, courage, consistency, rational analysis, kindness, and perseverance.
- Remind students that the remarkable persons they describe should be fully rounded, credible characters. Plato, for example, includes traits such as stubbornness and boldness in his portrait of Socrates.
- Use the Descriptive Essay Rubrics in ***General Resources,*** pp. 67–68, to assess students' essays.

WG Writing and Grammar Platinum Level
For support in teaching the Writing Lesson, use Chapter 6, Section 2.

❹ Research and Technology

- Have students prepare to conduct research by writing lists of questions that they believe a report about the ancient Athenian justice system should answer.
- Use the Research Report rubrics in ***General Resources,*** pp. 51–52, to evaluate students' research reports.
- The **Support for Extend Your Learning** page (***Unit 4 Resources,*** p. 92) provides guided note-taking opportunities to help students complete the Extend Your Learning activities.

Go Online Research Have students type in the Web Code for another research activity.

Standard Course of Study

LT.5.01.2 Build knowledge of literary genres and explore how characteristics apply to literature of world cultures.

LT.5.01.3 Analyze literary devices and explain their effect on the work of world literature.

❶ Elements of Drama

- Tell students that they will study drama in Unit 4. **Ask** students: Describe what you think it would be like to read a play as if it were another type of literature, such as a short story.
  Possible response: Students may say that a play is meant to be performed. Therefore, reading the text of a play as one would read other literature makes for choppy reading because the dialogue is marked for each actor and interrupted by stage directions.
- Review the elements of drama. Clarify the information available on these pages, and suggest that students use these pages as a reference as they read drama in Unit 4 and in other units.

❷ Comedy and Tragedy

- Explain that comedies do not have to be extremely funny; they must, however, end happily. Point out to students that Shakespeare's *A Midsummer Night's Dream* is a comedy.
- Tell students that the tragic flaw often shows that the tragic hero is dealing with problems familiar to the audience and helps the audience identify with the hero. Note that a familiar example of tragedy is Shakespeare's *Romeo and Juliet.*
  Ask: What does a tragedy teach about the place of heroes or main characters in the world?
  Possible response: Tragedy teaches that despite how important heroes or main characters may be, they do not have total control over their lives.

Defining Drama

A **drama** is a story written to be performed by actors. Like a short story or novel, a drama focuses on characters in conflict. However, unlike fiction, a drama presents its action through **dialogue,** the conversation and speeches of the characters.

❶ Elements of Drama

A drama, or **play,** typically includes several key elements.

- The **plot** is the ordered sequence of events that make up the play. A play is often divided into large units called **acts,** which are then divided into smaller units called **scenes.** These divisions were unknown to the Greeks and Romans, but beginning in Elizabethan England, acts and scenes formed distinct units of action.
- The **characters** are the people who participate in the action of the play and are portrayed onstage by **actors.**

THEATRE OFFERS . . . ACTUAL PEOPLE DOING ACTUAL THINGS. —*Gary Blackwood*

- **Dialogue** is the conversation and speeches of the characters. The dialogue of a play may be written in either prose or poetry. All ancient Greek and Roman plays were written in verse, but the transition to prose began in England during the Middle Ages. Shakespeare and his contemporaries wrote their plays mainly in verse, but they also included prose passages, usually for the speech of comic and lower-class characters. Today, most plays are written in prose.
- **Stage directions** are notes included in the play to describe the sets, costumes, lighting, scenery, sound effects, and props (the objects used on stage). Stage directions indicate where a scene takes place, how it should look and sound, and how the actors should move and deliver their lines.

❷ Comedy and Tragedy

Ever since the development of Western drama in ancient Greece, plays have been divided into two broad categories.

- A **comedy** is a play that has a happy ending. Comedies often show ordinary characters in conflict with society—conflicts that arise from misunderstandings, deceptions, disapproving parents, or mistaken identities.
- A **tragedy** is a play that shows the downfall or death of the main character, or **tragic hero.** In ancient Greek tragedy, the hero is always a noble or outstanding person, such as the title character in Sophocles' *Oedipus the King,* page 468. The tragic hero's downfall is caused by a **tragic flaw:** a

mistake or unwise decision. Sometimes, this mistake is the result of an innate character weakness, such as excessive pride. However, the error may instead result from ignorance—for example, of some crucial piece of information. In modern tragedy, the main character is usually an ordinary person. The cause of the tragedy might be a character flaw, but it may instead be some weakness or evil in society itself.

3 Other Types of Drama

Not all drama fits neatly into one of these two broad categories. For example, in addition to writing comedies and tragedies, Shakespeare wrote **history plays** that chronicle the struggles of the English monarchy over several generations. Other types of drama include the following:

- A **melodrama** features stereotyped characters and exaggerated conflicts.
- A **tragicomedy** combines tragic and comic elements, as in the plays of the Russian writer Anton Chekhov (page 904).
- A **modern realistic drama** features ordinary language, realistic characters, and controversial issues, as in *A Doll House* by the Norwegian playwright Henrik Ibsen, page 942.

4 Dramatic Conventions

Dramatic conventions are literary devices that break the illusion of reality. In a practice called the **suspension of disbelief,** the audience agrees to accept these conventions while watching—or reading—a play.

- A **soliloquy** is a speech in which a character who is alone onstage reveals private thoughts and feelings to the audience. This character may appear to address the audience directly, but it is understood that the audience is overhearing the character talking or thinking out loud.
- An **aside** is a brief remark delivered by a character to express private thoughts while other characters are onstage. Like a soliloquy, it is directed to the audience and presumed to be unheard by the other characters.
- The transition from one scene or act to another might involve a considerable **passage of time** in the plot.

5 Strategies for Reading Drama

Use these strategies as you read drama.

Visualize the Action in Performance As you read, use your imagination to visualize the action onstage. If possible, watch a live performance or a film version of the play.

Analyze the Conflict As you read, analyze how the conflict develops and how it is eventually resolved. Look for the moment when the conflict reaches its greatest intensity or when the main character's fortunes change, for better or worse.

3 Other Types of Drama

- Review the other types of drama listed, and point out that these types have developed over time.
- Have students **brainstorm** for titles of plays, movies, or television shows that express the characteristics of these types of drama.
  Possible response: Soap operas have characteristics of a melodrama. Family sitcoms have characteristics of tragicomedy.

4 Dramatic Conventions

- Review the dramatic conventions. Lead students in a discussion of how dramatic conventions help the audience to understand the drama. Have students focus on the occasional need for the audience to know more background or information about the characters or the situation.
- Point out the need for the passage of time in a plot. **Ask** students: How can a playwright show the passage of time in a drama?
  Possible response: Students may say that the passage of time can be shown through changes in scenery, costume, use of older actors, or through dialogue.

5 Strategies for Reading Drama

- Tell students that they should not only visualize the action of a drama, but they should also visualize the characters and their voices.
- Point out that students may analyze the characters as well as the conflict. Analyzing the characters may help students visualize the characters and understand why they act as they do.

Differentiated Instruction Solutions for All Learners

Strategy for Less Proficient Readers

Instruct students to look at the term "suspension of disbelief." **Ask** students: What do the words *suspend* and *disbelief* mean? **Possible response:** *Suspend* means "to hold or withhold something"; *disbelief* means "to not believe something." Then, **ask** students what they think the term "suspension of disbelief" means. **Possible response:** Suspension of disbelief means "to purposefully and temporarily believe that the impossible is possible." Then, ask students when they have had to suspend disbelief. Have students brainstorm for a list of movies, television programs, or books that break the rules of reality. Finally, discuss what would happen to the audience and to the effectiveness of the work if the audience refused to "suspend disbelief." **Possible response:** The work would be ruined because the audience would find the work unbelievable.

Standard Course of Study

Goal 1: WRITTEN LANGUAGE

WL.1.03.2 Identify and analyze text components, and evaluate impact on personal reflection.

Goal 3: FOUNDATIONS OF ARGUMENT

FA.3.04.7 Identify and analyze influences, contexts, or biases in argument.

Goal 5: LITERATURE

LT.5.01.2 Build knowledge of literary genres, and explore how characteristics apply to literature of world cultures.

LT.5.03.9 Analyze and evaluate the effects of author's craft and style in world literature.

Goal 6: GRAMMAR AND USAGE

GU.6.01.4 Use vocabulary strategies to determine meaning.

GU.6.02.1 Edit for agreement, tense choice, pronouns, antecedents, case, and complete sentences.

Step-by-Step Teaching Guide	Pacing Guide
PRETEACH	
• Administer Vocabulary and Reading Warm-ups as necessary.	5 min.
• Engage students' interest with the motivation activity.	5 min.
• Read and discuss author and background features and From the Author's Desk features. **FT**	10 min.
• Introduce the Literary Analysis Skill: Tragedy. **FT**	5 min.
• Introduce the Reading Strategy: Reading Drama. **FT**	10 min.
• Prepare students to read by teaching the selection vocabulary. **FT**	
TEACH	
• Informally monitor comprehension while students read independently or in groups. **FT**	30 min.
• Monitor students' comprehension with the Reading Check notes.	as students read
• Reinforce vocabulary with Vocabulary Builder notes.	as students read
• Develop students' understanding of tragedy with the Literary Analysis annotations. **FT**	5 min.
• Develop students' ability to read drama with the Reading Strategy annotations. **FT**	5 min.
ASSESS/EXTEND	
• Assess students' comprehension and mastery of the Literary Analysis and Reading Strategy by having them answer the Apply the Skills questions. **FT**	15 min.
• Have students complete the Vocabulary Lesson and the Grammar and Style Lesson. **FT**	15 min.
• Apply students' understanding by using one or more of the Extend Your Learning activities.	20–90 min. or homework
• Administer Selection Test A or Selection Test B. **FT**	15 min.

Resources

Print

Unit 4 Resources

- Vocabulary Warm-up Word Lists **[L1, L2, EL]** .... p. 102
- Vocabulary Warm-up Practice **[L1, L2, EL]** .... p. 103
- Reading Warm-up A **[L1, L2, EL]** .... p. 104
- Reading Warm-up B **[L1, L2, L3]** .... p. 105

Transparency

Graphic Organizer Transparencies

- Literary Analysis Graphic Organizer A **[L3]** .... pp. 88, 90
- Literary Analysis Graphic Organizer B **[L1, L2, EL]** .... pp. 89, 91

Technology

From the Author's Desk DVD .... **Sophocles, Segment 2**

Print

Reader's Notebook [L2]

Reader's Notebook: Adapted Version [L1]

Reader's Notebook: English Learner's Version [EL]

Unit 4 Resources

- Literary Analysis **[L3]** .... p. 106
- Reading Strategy **[L3]** .... p. 107
- Vocabulary Builder **[L3]** .... p. 108

Technology

Listening to Literature Audio CDs [L2, EL]

Reader's Notebook: Adapted Version Audio CD [L1, L2]

Print

Unit 4 Resources

- Grammar and Style **[L3]** .... p. 109
- Support for Extend Your Learning **[L3]** .... p. 110
- Enrichment **[L4]** .... p. 111
- Selection Test A **[L1, L2, EL]** .... pp. 112–114
- Selection Test B **[L3, L4]** .... pp. 115–117

General Resources

- Rubrics for Response to Literature **[L3]** .... pp. 55–56

Technology

- **Go Online:** Research **[L3]**
- **Go Online:** Self-test **[L3]**
- ***ExamView®*, Test Bank [L3]**

Choosing Resources for Differentiated Instruction

[L1] Special Needs Students

[L2] Below-Level Students

[L3] All Students

[L4] Advanced Students

[EL] English Learners

For Vocabulary and Reading Warm-ups and for Selection Tests, **A** signifies "less challenging" and **B** "more challenging." For Graphic Organizer transparencies, **A** signifies "not filled in" and **B** "filled in."

FT Fast Track Instruction: To move the lesson more quickly, use the strategies and activities identified with **FT**.

Scaffolding for Less Proficient and Advanced Students

The leveled Critical Thinking questions after selections progress in the levels of thinking required to answer them. To address the needs of your different students, you may use the (a) level questions for your less proficient students and the (b) level questions with your on-level and advanced students. The occasional (c) level questions are appropriate for your advanced students.

Use this complete suite of powerful teaching tools to make lesson planning and testing quicker and easier.

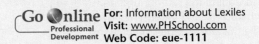

Use the interactive textbook (online and on CD-ROM) to make selections and activities come alive with audio and video support and interactive questions.

Go Online Professional Development **For:** Information about Lexiles
Visit: www.PHSchool.com
Web Code: eue-1111

Standard Course of Study

WL.1.02.3 Exhibit an awareness of cultural context of text in a personal reflection.

FA.3.04.10 Analyze connections between ideas, concepts, characters and experiences in argumentative work.

CT.4.05.6 Make inferences and draw conclusions based on critical text.

Background

Sphinxes in Ancient Cultures

The figure of the Sphinx originated in ancient Egypt, where the most famous depiction of the mythical monster can still be seen near the Great Pyramids. Sphinxes were known to Syrians, Phoenicians, and Mycenaean Greeks. In ancient Greece, sphinxes were often depicted on tombs and shields as a way of averting bad fortune.

Critical Viewing

Possible response: Each part of the Sphinx seems familiar (a woman's head, a lion's legs, a serpent's tail, and a bird's wings), but as a whole, the image, like the riddle, is mysterious and enigmatic. The Sphinx looks menacing, just as the unanswered riddle menaces the Thebans.

Activity

Organize students in groups. Suggest that each group first create a basic plot for a contemporary thriller. Then, have members of each group volunteer to update the setting, update the characters, and determine how to handle the oracle and its predictions about the main character. When members have completed their tasks, have them discuss their ideas and organize them for the presentation.

A Closer Look

Oedipus: The Myth

King Laius of Thebes learned from an oracle that he was destined to have a son who would kill his own father and marry his mother. When the king's wife, Jocasta, had a son, Laius pinned the baby's feet together and ordered a servant to leave him on a mountain to die. Instead, the servant gave the baby to a shepherd, who gave him to the king and queen of Corinth. They named the child Oedipus ("swollen foot") because of his wounded feet.

The Oracle As a young man, Oedipus learned from the oracle at Delphi that he was fated to kill his father and marry his mother. Horrified, he fled Corinth to avoid fulfilling the prophecy. During his travels, Oedipus encountered a chariot that tried to run him off the road. Enraged, he killed both the charioteer and the passenger and then continued on his way.

The Riddle of the Sphinx Oedipus arrived outside Thebes, where a monster called the Sphinx was terrorizing the city. The Sphinx had a woman's head, a lion's body, a serpent's tail, and an eagle's wings. She refused to let travelers enter the city unless they could answer her riddle: "What goes on four legs in the morning, two at midday, and three in the evening?" No one had solved her riddle, and she had eaten all who failed.

When the Thebans learned that King Laius had been killed on his way to Delphi, they had no time to find his murderer. Their priority was to save the city from the Sphinx. Queen Jocasta's brother offered her hand and the crown to any man who could solve the riddle. When Oedipus encountered the Sphinx, he gave the correct answer: "Man, who crawls in infancy, walks upright in his prime, and leans on a cane in old age." On hearing his answer, the Sphinx flung herself into the sea and died. In reward for saving the city, Oedipus married Jocasta and became the new king.

A New Prophecy Oedipus had ruled Thebes for almost twenty years when the city was struck with a devastating plague. Sophocles begins his tragedy *Oedipus the King* when Oedipus consults the oracle and learns that the plague will not end until Laius' murderer is exiled from Thebes.

Activity

Updating the Story

Though the setting of the Oedipus myth is ancient Greece, the basic plot is like a contemporary murder mystery—with Oedipus in the role of detective. With a group, discuss how the story of Oedipus could be turned into a contemporary thriller. Use these questions to guide your discussion:

- How would you update the setting and characters?
- How would you treat the idea of the oracle and its predictions?

Choose a point person to share your thoughts with the class.

▼ Critical Viewing In what way does this image of the Sphinx reinforce the frightening mystery of her riddle? **[Deduce]**

Enrichment

Freud and the Oedipus Complex

Sigmund Freud (1856–1939), the founder of modern psychoanalysis, coined the term "Oedipus complex" to refer to the unconscious desire of very young boys for the exclusive love of their mothers. Freud presented his theory in one of his landmark works, *The Interpretation of Dreams* (1899). The Oedipus complex is understood to be a short-lived phase of development that ends when boys repress their yearnings for their mothers and begin to accept the authority of their fathers.

The counterpart of the Oedipus complex in boys is the Electra complex in girls. Freud identified this as young girls' hostility toward their mothers, brought on by desire for their fathers. This complex is named for Electra, the avenging daughter of Clytemnestra and King Agamemnon, who killed Clytemnestra, the murderer of Agamemnon.

DAVID MAMET INTRODUCES

Oedipus the King *by Sophocles*

The Model of All Drama

Aristotle chooses *Oedipus the King* as the model of all drama. Understand this play, he says, and you understand how drama works.

Oedipus has a problem. In this case, there is a plague in Thebes, the city over which he rules.

He tries to find the cause of the plague.

In so doing, he accidentally uncovers facts about his own past.

His history is this: He is an orphan. He left the home of his adopted parents. On the road to Thebes he slew a man at a crossroads. He continued on, rose to power in Thebes, and married the widow of its ruler, Laius.

Now, Laius and and his widow, Jocasta, it seems, had an interesting history. They had a son. At his birth, it was prophesied that he would kill his father and marry his mother. So he was given to a shepherd, to be exposed and die upon a mountain.

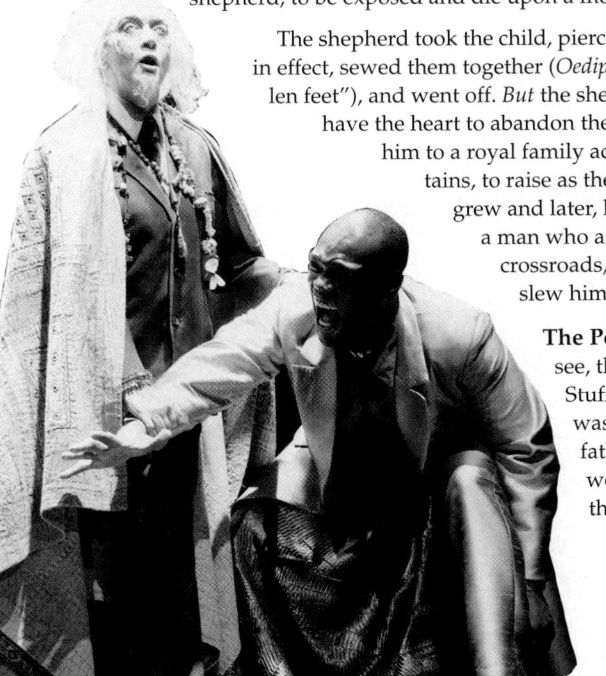

The shepherd took the child, pierced his feet–that is, in effect, sewed them together (*Oedipus* means "swollen feet"), and went off. *But* the shepherd did not have the heart to abandon the child, so he gave him to a royal family across the mountains, to raise as their own. The child grew and later, left home. He met a man who affronted him at a crossroads, and Oedipus slew him.

The Perfect Play As we see, this story is Hot Stuff. The man he slew was, of course, his father, Laius, and the woman he married, thus, his mother.

David Mamet

David Mamet is the author of the plays *American Buffalo, Glengarry Glen Ross, Speed the Plow,* and *Oleanna.* He wrote and directed the films *House of Games, The Spanish Prisoner, The Winslow Boy,* and *State and Main.*

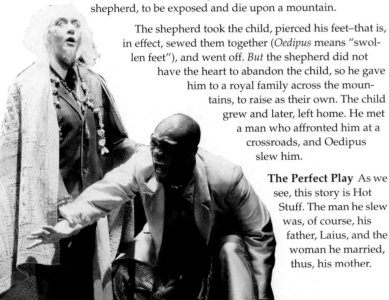

◀ **Critical Viewing** What emotions does each actor's facial expression, posture, and gesture convey? **[Interpret]**

From the Scholar's Desk

David Mamet

- You might wish to have students reread David Mamet's introduction to the unit on pages 348–349.
- Show segment 2 on David Mamet on ***From the Author's Desk DVD*** to provide insight into the history and elements of drama and the relevance of the elements of Greek drama today.
  Ask: What is the main question of drama?
  Answer: The main question of drama is "What does the protagonist want?"

The Model of All Drama

- After students have read Mamet's comments on these pages, **ask** students to summarize *Oedipus the King.*
  Possible response: Oedipus has a problem. Oedipus tries to solve the problem. Oedipus finds that he is the problem. Oedipus attempts to solve the problem.
- **Ask** students why Aristotle considers *Oedipus the King* to be the model of all drama.
  Answer: Aristotle considers it to be the model of all drama because if readers understand the drama in *Oedipus the King,* they will understand how drama works.

Critical Viewing

Possible response: The figure on the right conveys horror, shock, anger, or outrage. The standing figure conveys compassion; in addition, he seems to be blind.

Teaching Resources

The following resources can be used to enrich or extend the instruction for From the Scholar's Desk.

Unit 4 Resources
- **Support for Penguin Essay,** p. 100
- **Listening and Viewing,** p. 101

From the Author's Desk DVD
- **David Mamet,** Segment 2

Critical Viewing

Possible response: The contemporary costumes suggest that the drama of *Oedipus the King* could play out in the lives of people today.

Hiding in Plain Sight

- Ask students whether a solution to one of their problems was ever "hiding in plain sight." Point out that often people miss the cause of a problem because they are too close to the problem to see it for what it is.
- **Ask** students what Aristotle says happens when people find the cause of their troubles.
  Answer: Aristotle says that when people recognize the cause of their problems, they are transformed by self-knowledge.
- **Ask:** What does David Mamet mean when he emphasizes the importance of understanding the mechanism of *Oedipus the King?*
  Answer: Mamet means that the key to understanding *Oedipus the King* is to understand how Sophocles structured its drama. The solution to the problem is hidden in the beginning of the play, and the drama unfolds and progresses full circle until Oedipus discovers that he was the problem all along.

From the Scholar's Desk

These facts emerge, little by little, as Oedipus endeavors to discover the cause of the plague.

When the entire monstrous story comes out, Oedipus recognizes, of course, that *he himself*, that is, his monstrous actions, have angered the gods, and so have brought about the plague on Thebes.

He blinds himself in shame and leaves the throne to wander as a beggar.

Aristotle tells us this is the perfect play. Why?

Because the end is hidden in the beginning.

Oedipus, the King, is responsible for the welfare of his city, Thebes.

Thebes is cursed because someone angered the gods.

His efforts to uncover the corrupt cause of their sorrow lead back to himself. So, the play's close is both *surprising* ("How could we have foreseen that?") and *inevitable* ("Oh, yes, of course, we might have seen that all along").

Hiding in Plain Sight The progress of the *drama,* then, is like the progress of psychoanalysis, or any other attempt at self-knowledge: at the end of our journey we find the unknowable cause of our troubles in plain sight.

When we find it, Aristotle says, when we *recognize* it, our situation is immediately changed. We are transformed by self-knowledge: the all-powerful king becomes the blind beggar; the high is brought low, and (as Oedipus has committed patricide and murder), rightful order is restored.

▼ Critical Viewing
Why do you think the director and costume designer chose these costumes for their production of *Oedipus the King*? **[Speculate]**

We all understand this phenomenon naturally.

Consider that joke: What gets longer the more you cut it?

Answer: A *ditch.*

The difficulty is found to be not with the *problem* but with our *understanding.* It is revealed that there are two meanings to the verb *to cut,* and we laugh in recognition, as we are changed by the knowledge. We laugh because we *ourselves* are found to have been the problem we were laboring, to no avail, to solve. Just as with Oedipus.

The Mechanism of the Play One might discuss the *theme* of the play 'til the cows come home, as this is a matter of opinion; but the *mechanism* of the play is clear and definite: it is structural.

Just as with carpentry, chemistry, or physics, a simple understanding of the essential mechanism is the beginning of more generally useful *practical* knowledge.

Understand the internal combustion engine of a lawnmower and you may easily proceed to an understanding of a Formula One racing car. Understand Oedipus, and you may understand all drama.

Thinking About the Commentary

1. **(a) Recall:** According to Mamet, what does the Greek philosopher Aristotle say we will understand if we understand *Oedipus the King?* **(b) Make a Judgment:** Do you think that one play can provide such understanding, as Aristotle claims? Why or why not?
2. **(a) Recall:** Why is the play both surprising and inevitable? **(b) Interpret:** What does Mamet mean when he says that the progress of the drama is like any attempt at self-knowledge? **(c) Speculate:** In what ways might self-knowledge transform a person?

As You Read *Oedipus the King* . . .

3. Look for details throughout the play that seem to hint at the "inevitable" ending.
4. Think about the ways in which reading Mamet's commentary enriches your understanding of Sophocles' play.

ASSESS

Answers

1. (a) Aristotle says that if we understand *Oedipus the King,* we may understand all drama. (b) **Possible response:** Yes. Given the explanation in the text, readers should understand all drama because the structure of all drama is the same.
2. (a) The play is surprising because readers wonder how they could have foreseen the ending. The play is inevitable because readers might have seen the ending all along. (b) **Possible answer:** Mamet claims that the progress of drama is like any attempts at self-knowledge because in both cases, people come to realize that the problem is their understanding; the solution was there all along, but they did not recognize it. (c) Once people are aware that the source of a problem lies within them, they can make the choice to change and therefore solve the problem.
3. **Possible response:** Details include the prophecy about Oedipus when he was a baby and the fact that his life was spared in spite of the prophecy.
4. **Possible response:** Having an understanding of how the play is structured helps readers to make sense of the action of the play and how the play progresses. It may also help readers to see hints about the cause of the problem and the outcome.

PREETEACH

Motivation

Tell students they will be reading a play in which a good man who seems to be reaping the rewards of his superior intelligence, courage, and decency is in fact working out a tragic destiny. Have them think about what elements constitute tragedy: What kind of person makes us experience "pity and fear" if disaster afflicts him or her? Ask students to think of contemporary examples of tragic heroes who inspire pity and fear. Record students' suggestions on the board. Make sure that students explain their suggestions to the class.

❶ Background

More About the Author

Sophocles began his career not only as a playwright but as an actor. Throughout his life, he was well respected in Athens. In 442 B.C., for example, he served on a treasury board that supervised tribute payments to Athens from members of the Delian League, an association of city-states that Athens controlled. In his old age, his reputation for diplomacy and for exerting a moderating, sane influence assured his election to a governmental advisory board after the Athenian defeat in Sicily during the Peloponnesian War (413 B.C.).

Geography Note

Draw students' attention to the map above. Tell students that more than any other nation, Greece has influenced Western society in many spheres, from literature, philosophy, and science, to art, architecture, and language.

Build Skills | Drama

Oedipus the King ❶

Sophocles (496 B.C.–406 B.C.)

Sophocles' (säf´ ə klēz´) life corresponded with the splendid rise and tragic fall of fifth-century Athens. At 16, he was one of the young men chosen by the city to perform a choral ode, dancing and singing in a public celebration of the Athenian naval victory over the Persians at Salamis. In 442 B.C., he was one of the treasurers of the imperial league, which was organized to resist Persia. With Pericles, Sophocles served as one of the generals in the war against the island of Samos, which later tried to secede from the Athenian league. In 413 B.C., he was also appointed to a special government committee when the Athenian expedition to Sicily failed. He died in 406 B.C., two years before Athens surrendered to Sparta in the Peloponnesian War.

Winning Playwright Sophocles' life also coincided with the rise and fall of the Golden Age of Greek tragedy. His career as a dramatist began in 468 B.C. when he entered the Dionysia (dī´ ə nē´ sē ə), the annual theatrical competition dedicated to the god Dionysus (dī´ ə nī´ səs). Competing against the established and brilliant playwright Aeschylus (es´ ki ləs), Sophocles won first prize. Over the next 62 years, he wrote more than 120 plays, 24 of which won first prize; those that did not come in first placed second.

Enriching the Drama Greek plays had their origins in religious festivals honoring the god Dionysus. At first, a chorus narrated stories of the god's life in song. The choral leader would occasionally step forward to recite part of the story alone. Eventually, the recitation grew longer and involved a second speaker. Sophocles increased the number of singers in the chorus and introduced a third speaking part. The addition of a third actor allowed for more dramatically complex dialogue than that of the earlier Aeschylean plays.

Sophocles also introduced technical innovations to Greek tragedy. Originally, Greek drama was presented in an open-air theater with few sets or props. Sophocles expanded the use of stage machinery and sets. For instance, he was the first to use a crane that lowered actors "miraculously" onto the stage. These miraculous appearances were reserved for gods, who might appear at the end of a play to wrap up loose ends in the plot. The Romans called this device *deus ex machina* (dā´əs eks mak´ē nə)—literally "god from a machine." It came to signify a contrived ending, an unexpected last-minute reprieve, the intervention of a supernatural force in the nick of time.

Faithfulness to Human Experience In addition to his technical innovations, Sophocles is known for his fidelity to universal human experience. In his plays, the world order consists of human beings, nature, and the inscrutable forces of the gods and fate. Sophocles suggests that while gods can predetermine or influence human action, they do not necessarily define one's character. People are responsible for finding out who they are and where they belong; they must then take moral responsibility for their lives.

Only seven of Sophocles' plays have survived intact. These were carefully reconstructed in 303 B.C. by Athenians concerned with preserving this crucial part of their literary heritage. The extant plays are *Ajax, The Women of Trachis, Antigone, Oedipus the King, Electra, Philoctetes,* and finally, *Oedipus at Colonus. Oedipus the King* has often been considered not only the masterpiece among Sophocles' creations but the most important and influential drama ever written.

Preview

Connecting to the Literature

We often envision brave people as those who overcome a fear of death or injury to succeed in physical conflict. However, there are other ways of being brave. In this play, a bold king risks everything in his pursuit of a terrible truth. In doing so, he provides an unforgettable example of courage.

Standard Course of Study

- Build knowledge of literary genres, and explore how characteristics apply to literature of world cultures. (LT.5.01.2)
- Analyze and evaluate the effects of author's craft and style in world literature. (LT.5.03.9)

2 Literary Analysis

Tragedy

A **tragedy** is a work of dramatic literature that shows the downfall of a person, usually of high birth or noble status. Often, the *protagonist,* or main character, is a brilliant leader who has gained the love and respect of his or her subjects. In most tragedies, the protagonist initiates a series of events that lead to his or her own destruction.

Tragedies explore powerful emotions, such as love, hate, revenge, and loyalty. Aristotle wrote that tragedy triggers two main emotions in the audience—pity and fear. We pity the protagonist's suffering while we also fear for him or her and for ourselves.

Connecting Literary Elements

The **tragic hero** is the main character of a tragedy. Traditionally, the tragic hero possesses a fault or weakness in character that causes the hero's downfall. This weakness is called a **tragic flaw.** As you read, pay attention to details in Oedipus' actions and statements that suggest heroic qualities or a possible flaw. Use a chart like the one shown at right to organize your observations about his character.

Heroic Qualities	Actions
	Statements
"Flawed" Qualities	Actions
	Statements

3 Reading Strategy

Reading Drama

When you **read drama**, try to picture a live performance. Note stage directions, which are usually set in italics to provide information about characters' thoughts, attitudes, and behavior. As you read, try to picture how characters look, sound, move, and relate to one another.

Vocabulary Builder

blight (blīt) *n.* destructive disease (p. 470)

pestilence (pes′ tə lens) *n.* plague (p. 470)

induced (in do͞ost′) *v.* persuaded; caused (p. 474)

dispatch (di spach′) *v.* kill (p. 474)

invoke (in vōk′) *v.* summon; cause to appear (p. 477)

prophecy (präf′ ə sē) *n.* prediction of the future (p. 480)

countenance (koun′ tə nəns) *n.* the look on a person's face (p. 484)

malignant (mə lig′ nənt) *adj.* very harmful (p. 497)

2 Literary Analysis

Tragedy

- Tell students that they will focus on tragedy as they read Part I of *Oedipus the King.* Have students discuss some of the principal elements of tragedy: for example, the downfall of a noble, heroic person; strong emotions such as love and pride; and the evocation of pity and fear in the audience.
- Tell students to focus on the character of Oedipus as they read and to consider the following questions: What personality traits in Oedipus make him heroic? What traits might be considered flaws?
- Give students a copy of **Literary Analysis Graphic Organizer A,** p. 88 in ***Graphic Organizer Transparencies.*** Have them use it to organize their observations about Oedipus as they read.
- Remind students that the ancient Athenians were familiar with the plots of tragedies because these plots were drawn from well-known myths. However, playwrights were still able to include suspense in tragedy. The interest for the audience lay in seeing when and how the tragic hero would work out his or her destiny.

3 Reading Strategy

Reading Drama

- Remind students that dialogue in a play motivates the facial expressions, tone of voice, and gestures of each speaker.
- Tell students that dialogue may also contain clues to the reactions of nonspeaking characters.

Vocabulary Builder

- Pronounce each vocabulary word for students, and read the definitions as a class. Have students identify any words with which they are already familiar.

Differentiated Instruction Solutions for All Learners

Support for Special Needs Students
Have students complete the **Preview** and **Build Skills** pages for *Oedipus the King* Part I in the ***Reader's Notebook: Adapted Version.*** These pages provide a selection summary, an abbreviated presentation of the reading and literary skills, and the graphic organizer from the **Build Skills** page in the student book.

Support for Less Proficient Readers
Have students complete the **Preview** and **Build Skills** pages for *Oedipus the King* Part I in the ***Reader's Notebook.*** These pages provide a selection summary, an abbreviated presentation of the reading and literary skills, and the graphic organizer from the **Build Skills** page in the student book.

Support for English Learners
Have students complete the **Preview** and **Build Skills** pages for *Oedipus the King* Part I in the ***Reader's Notebook: English Learner's Version.*** These pages provide a selection summary, an abbreviated presentation of the reading and literary skills, additional contextual vocabulary, and the graphic organizer from the **Build Skills** page in the student book.

TEACH

Facilitate Understanding

Have students discuss their own experiences with literature or films whose plots revolve around good intentions leading to catastrophe or around actions resulting in an unexpected outcome. *The Lord of the Rings* trilogy is a good example. Lead students in a discussion about the extent to which characters act in avoidable ignorance or to what extent no human being can make a better decision, given the information available.

❶ About the Selection

Students may be familiar with the myth of Oedipus in a more modern, psychological context. Making the connection between what Sigmund Freud called the Oedipus complex and the ancient myth may furnish a good springboard for reading the play. Freud, in fact, quoted Jocasta's speech at lines 1071–1074 (in Part II) in his discussion of the Oedipus complex.

Sophocles

translated by David Grene

Background In the fifth century B.C., when Greek drama was at its height, plays were performed in Athens at annual festivals honoring Dionysus, the god of wine. The performances were staged in an outdoor theater, which held thousands of spectators. There were no curtains or lighting; scenery and props were minimal. Actors wore outsized masks appropriate to the characters they played. Although violent events were often central to plots, no violence occurred on stage. Such events took place offstage and were reported in dialogue.

Ancient Greek plays follow this consistent format:

- A prologue presents background and describes the conflict.
- Then, the chorus, or group of dancers, enters and sings a *parodos*, (par′ ə däs), or opening song.
- Choral songs, called odes, separate scenes. The odes are divided into alternating parts called strophe (strō′ fē) and antistrophe (an tis′ trə fē).

Greek tragedies took their plots from well-known myths and legends. For example, the audience in the fifth century B.C. would have known that the story of Oedipus involved a ruler who fulfilled a terrible destiny by killing his father and marrying his mother.

Differentiated Instruction Solutions for All Learners

Accessibility at a Glance

	Oedipus the King, Part I
Context	A drama presented in the fifth century B.C. in Athens
Language	Poetic and figurative language; challenging syntax; chorus's strophe and antistrophe with long compound-complex sentences
Concept Level	Accessible (Avoidable ignorance can lead to tragedy.)
Literary Merit	Classic tragic Greek drama
Lexile	NP
Overall Rating	Challenging

Characters

Oedipus, King of Thebes	**First Messenger**
Jocasta, His Wife	**Second Messenger**
Creon, His Brother-in-Law	**A Herdsman**
Teiresias, an Old Blind Prophet	**A Chorus of Old Men of Thebes**
A Priest	

Part I

Scene: *In front of the palace of Oedipus at Thebes. To the right of the stage near the altar stands the* PRIEST *with a crowd of children.* OEDIPUS *emerges from the central door.*

❷ **OEDIPUS:** Children, young sons and daughters of old Cadmus,[1]
why do you sit here with your suppliant crowns?[2]
The town is heavy with a mingled burden
of sounds and smells, of groans and hymns and incense;
I did not think it fit that I should hear
of this from messengers but came myself,—
I Oedipus whom all men call the Great.

[*He turns to the* PRIEST.]

❸ You're old and they are young; come, speak for them.
What do you fear or want, that you sit here
suppliant? Indeed I'm willing to give all
that you may need; I would be very hard
should I not pity suppliants like these.

PRIEST: O ruler of my country, Oedipus,
you see our company around the altar;
you see our ages; some of us, like these,
who cannot yet fly far, and some of us
heavy with age; these children are the chosen
among the young, and I the priest of Zeus.
Within the market place sit others crowned
with suppliant garlands,[3] at the double shrine
of Pallas[4] and the temple where Ismenus
gives oracles by fire.[5] King, you yourself
have seen our city reeling like a wreck

Reading Strategy
Reading Drama According to the stage directions and dialogue, whom does Oedipus address when he first appears?

Reading Strategy
Reading Drama As Oedipus turns to address the Priest, how might his tone of voice change?

❹ ***David Mamet* Scholar's Insight**
In an interview, David Mamet reflects on Sophocles: "Our job, as writers, is to do our jobs. I was thinking the other day, I have trouble sometimes finishing a lot of plays. But then I always try to remind myself it took Sophocles eighteen years to write *Oedipus Rex* [*Oedipus the King*]; that's also because he wasn't trying to write *Gigi* [a light musical comedy]."

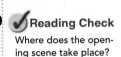

❺ 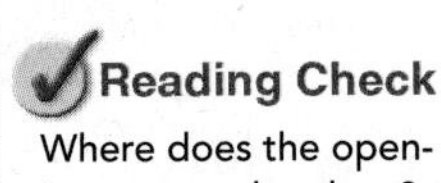
Reading Check
Where does the opening scene take place?

1. **Cadmus** (kad′ məs) *n.* mythical founder and first king of Thebes, a city in central Greece where the play takes place.
2. **suppliant** (sup′ lē ənt) **crowns** wreaths worn by people who ask favors of the gods.
3. **suppliant garlands** branches wound in wool, which were placed on the altar and left there until the suppliant's request was granted.
4. **double shrine of Pallas** the two temples of Athena.
5. **temple where Ismenus gives oracles by fire** Temple of Apollo, located by Ismenus, the Theban river, where the priests studied patterns in the ashes of sacrificial victims to foretell the future.

Differentiated Instruction
Solutions for All Learners

Strategy for Less Proficient Readers
Divide the class into groups of four, and have students discuss situations in which some decision or action of theirs created an undesired result. Ask students whether they think they should have known better. Invite students to write about one of the examples they share.

Vocabulary for English Learners
Point out the word *suppliant* in lines 2, 10, and 20. Then, urge students to determine the word's meaning from context clues, such as "What do you fear or want?" (line 9). Guide students to see that the context suggests the meaning of "beg" or "entreat."

Enrichment for Gifted/Talented Students
The priest refers to two ancient Greek gods: Zeus (line 18) and Athena (called "Pallas" in line 21). Have students compile a chart of ancient Greek divinities, with a list of characteristics or associations for each god or goddess. Then, encourage students to write a poem or short story about one or more of the gods.

❷ Reading Strategy
Reading Drama

- Have students read aloud the opening stage directions. Point out that the scene is set in public, outside the royal palace of Oedipus. A cross section of the city's inhabitants are onstage, suggesting that Thebes may be undergoing a crisis.
- Have students note that the stage directions call for an altar onstage. Elicit that this detail suggests prayers or sacrifices to the gods.
- Have students read lines 1–2 of the dialogue.
- **Ask** students the first Reading Strategy question: According to the stage directions and dialogue, whom does Oedipus address when he first appears?
Answer: Oedipus addresses the children of Thebes.

❸ Reading Strategy
Reading Drama

- Note the stage direction preceding line 8, and point out the contrast that Oedipus emphasizes in line 8 between the youth of the children and the age of the priest.
- **Ask** students the second Reading Strategy question: As Oedipus turns to address the Priest, how might his tone of voice change?
Possible response: Because Oedipus is now speaking to an adult who is an official, his tone might change to convey more urgency.

❹ Scholar's Insight

- Have students read the Scholar's Insight.
- Encourage students to explain what Mamet means by "our job . . . is to do our jobs." Then **ask** students what they think a writer's job is and why it might take eighteen years or even a lifetime to create a masterpiece.
Possible response: A writer's job is to express in words some poignant aspect of life or longing of the human spirit. Writing requires deep thought and many revisions, so it makes sense that a masterpiece may take many years to create.

❺ Reading Check

Answer: The opening scene takes place in front of the palace at Thebes.

❻ Literary Analysis

Tragedy

- Remind students that conflict is the mainspring of all dramatic plots. In tragedy, the conflict usually pits the tragic hero against overwhelming forces, which eventually combine to cause the hero's downfall.
- Have students summarize details from the priest's lengthy speech: for example, the description of suppliants in the marketplace, the account of the plague in the fields and the city, and the personal appeal to Oedipus, who has saved the city before in its hour of need.
- **Ask** students the Literary Analysis question: What major conflict or problem does the first scene introduce?
Answer: The major conflict involves the danger and destruction posed by the plague.

❼ Critical Thinking

Analyze

- Dramatic irony will be the Literary Analysis emphasis in Part II of the play. However, you may want to tell students at this point that dramatic irony is the contradiction between what characters think and what the audience knows to be true.
- **Ask** students: What irony would the ancient Athenian audience, familiar with the myth, immediately perceive in the statement that Oedipus came to the throne as the city's savior "with God's assistance" (line 45)?
Possible response: The audience would have realized that Oedipus' journey from Corinth to Thebes was closely linked to the fulfillment of the divine oracle that he would kill his father and marry his mother.

already; it can scarcely lift its prow
out of the depths, out of the bloody surf.
A blight is on the fruitful plants of the earth,
A blight is on the cattle in the fields,
a blight is on our women that no children
are born to them; a God that carries fire,
a deadly pestilence, is on our town,
strikes us and spares not, and the house of Cadmus
is emptied of its people while black Death
grows rich in groaning and in lamentation.[6]
We have not come as suppliants to this altar
because we thought of you as of a God,
but rather judging you the first of men
in all the chances of this life and when
we mortals have to do with more than man.
You came and by your coming saved our city,
freed us from tribute which we paid of old
to the Sphinx,[7] cruel singer. This you did
in virtue of no knowledge we could give you,
in virtue of no teaching; it was God
that aided you, men say, and you are held
with God's assistance to have saved our lives.
Now Oedipus, Greatest in all men's eyes,
here falling at your feet we all entreat you,
find us some strength for rescue.
Perhaps you'll hear a wise word from some God,
perhaps you will learn something from a man

Vocabulary Builder
blight (blīt) *n.* destructive disease
pestilence (pes´ tə ləns) *n.* plague

Literary Analysis
Tragedy What major conflict or problem does the first scene introduce?

6. **lamentation** (lam´ ən tā´ shən) *n.* expression of deep sorrow.
7. **Sphinx** (sfinks) winged female monster at Thebes that ate men who could not answer her riddle: "What is it that walks on four legs at dawn, two legs at midday, and three legs in the evening, and has only one voice; when it walks on most feet, it is weakest?" Creon, appointed ruler of Thebes, offered the kingdom and the hand of his sister Jocasta to anyone who could answer the riddle. Oedipus saved Thebes by answering correctly, "Man, who crawls in infancy, walks upright in his prime, and leans on a cane in old age." Outraged, the Sphinx destroyed herself, and Oedipus became King of Thebes.

Enrichment

Tyranny in Ancient Greece

The Greeks knew the play *Oedipus Rex (Oedipus the King)* as *Oedipus Tyrannos.* The word *tyrannos* is the source of the English word *tyrant.* Even in ancient Greece, the word eventually acquired the negative connotations associated with it today. Originally, however, it was simply the title given to a ruler who came to the throne through merit rather than inheritance. Consider the irony of the title: Oedipus thinks himself (and is thought to be) a *tyrannos,* someone who earned the throne through his ability to overcome the Sphinx. In fact, he is anything but an outsider; he is the legitimate heir of Laius, the true Theban king, and that is his tragedy.

(for I have seen that for the skilled of practice
the outcome of their counsels live the most).
Noblest of men, go, and raise up our city,
go,—and give heed. For now this land of ours
calls you its savior since you saved it once.
So, let us never speak about your reign
as of a time when first our feet were set
secure on high, but later fell to ruin.
Raise up our city, save it and raise it up.
Once you have brought us luck with happy omen;
be no less now in fortune.
If you will rule this land, as now you rule it,
better to rule it full of men than empty.
For neither tower nor ship is anything
when empty, and none live in it together.

8

OEDIPUS: I pity you, children. You have come full of longing,
but I have known the story before you told it
only too well. I know you are all sick,
yet there is not one of you, sick though you are,
that is as sick as I myself.
Your several sorrows each have single scope
and touch but one of you. My spirit groans
for city and myself and you at once.
You have not roused me like a man from sleep;
know that I have given many tears to this,
gone many ways wandering in thought,
but as I thought I found only one remedy
and that I took. I sent Menoeceus' son
Creon, Jocasta's brother, to Apollo,
to his Pythian temple,[8]
that he might learn there by what act or word
I could save this city. As I count the days,

8. **Pythian** (pith′ ē ən) **temple** shrine of Apollo at Delphi, below Mount Parnassus in central Greece.

9 ▲ Critical Viewing
What does this image of Oedipus and the Sphinx suggest about Oedipus' attitude toward the Sphinx and her riddle? **[Interpret]**

10 Reading Check
What great service did Oedipus provide the city when first arrived in Thebes?

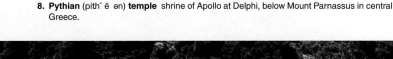

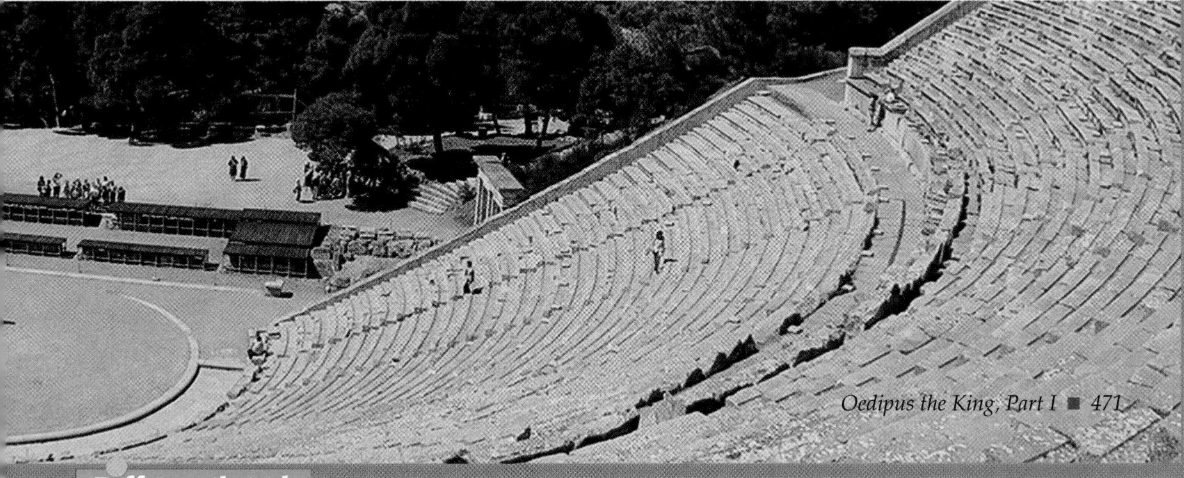

8 Reading Strategy
Reading Drama

- Remind students what they already know about Oedipus: they learned from the Sphinx story that he is intelligent and courageous. His initial speeches to the children and to the Priests show that he is sensitive to the needs of his subjects.
- **Ask** students: What new information do you learn about Oedipus in his speech in lines 66–77?
  Possible response: Oedipus reveals a deep sympathy for the suffering of his citizens: "My spirit groans for city and myself and you at once." Oedipus also shows himself a man of prompt action.

9 Critical Viewing

Possible response: The image suggests that Oedipus is relaxed and unafraid of the Sphinx. The artist is presenting Oedipus not as a man of action, but as a thinker—a man who will defeat the Sphinx with brains rather than brawn.

10 Reading Check

Answer: Oedipus solved the riddle of the Sphinx and saved Thebes from the terrifying monster.

Differentiated Instruction
Solutions for All Learners

Support for Less Proficient Readers
Make certain that students are aware of how poetic language works. For example, ask them to reread lines 31–33 carefully. Then, guide students in a discussion about the effect of the contrast between the house of Cadmus, emptied, and the rising death toll.

Support for English Learners
Tell students that Sophocles uses figurative language throughout the play. Model how to decode this figurative language, using the example of the city "reeling like a wreck" (line 23). Then, invite volunteers to take turns explaining other examples of figurative language.

Strategy for Advanced Readers
Invite students to consider the different types and layers of irony in the play. For example, how does Oedipus' claim to be more affected by the sickness than his subjects (lines 68–70) mean something different to the audience, who is aware that he is the cause of the plague?

⓫ Critical Thinking

Apply

- Tell students to notice the hopeful tone when Oedipus and the priest see that Creon has returned with news from Apollo.
- The repetition of the word *bright* (lines 89–90) in connection with the image of Creon's facial expression conveys Oedipus' hope.
- **Ask** students what other adjectives they would use to describe the tone established on these pages. Tell students to cite examples from the text to support their answers.
Possible response: Oedipus conveys a tone of anxiety when he says, "What you have said so far leaves me uncertain whether to trust or fear (lines 99–100)."

it vexes me what ails him; he is gone
far longer than he needed for the journey.
But when he comes, then, may I prove a villain,
if I shall not do all the God commands.

PRIEST: Thanks for your gracious words. Your servants here
signal that Creon is this moment coming.

⓫

OEDIPUS: His face is bright. O holy Lord Apollo,
grant that his news too may be bright for us
and bring us safety.

PRIEST: It is happy news,
I think, for else his head would not be crowned
with sprigs of fruitful laurel.[9]

OEDIPUS: We will know soon,
he's within hail. Lord Creon, my good brother,
what is the word you bring us from the God?

[CREON *enters.*]

⓬

CREON: A good word,—for things hard to bear themselves
if in the final issue all is well
I count complete good fortune.

OEDIPUS: What do you mean?
What you have said so far
leaves me uncertain whether to trust or fear.

9. **sprigs of fruitful laurel** Laurel symbolized triumph; a crown of laurel signified good news.

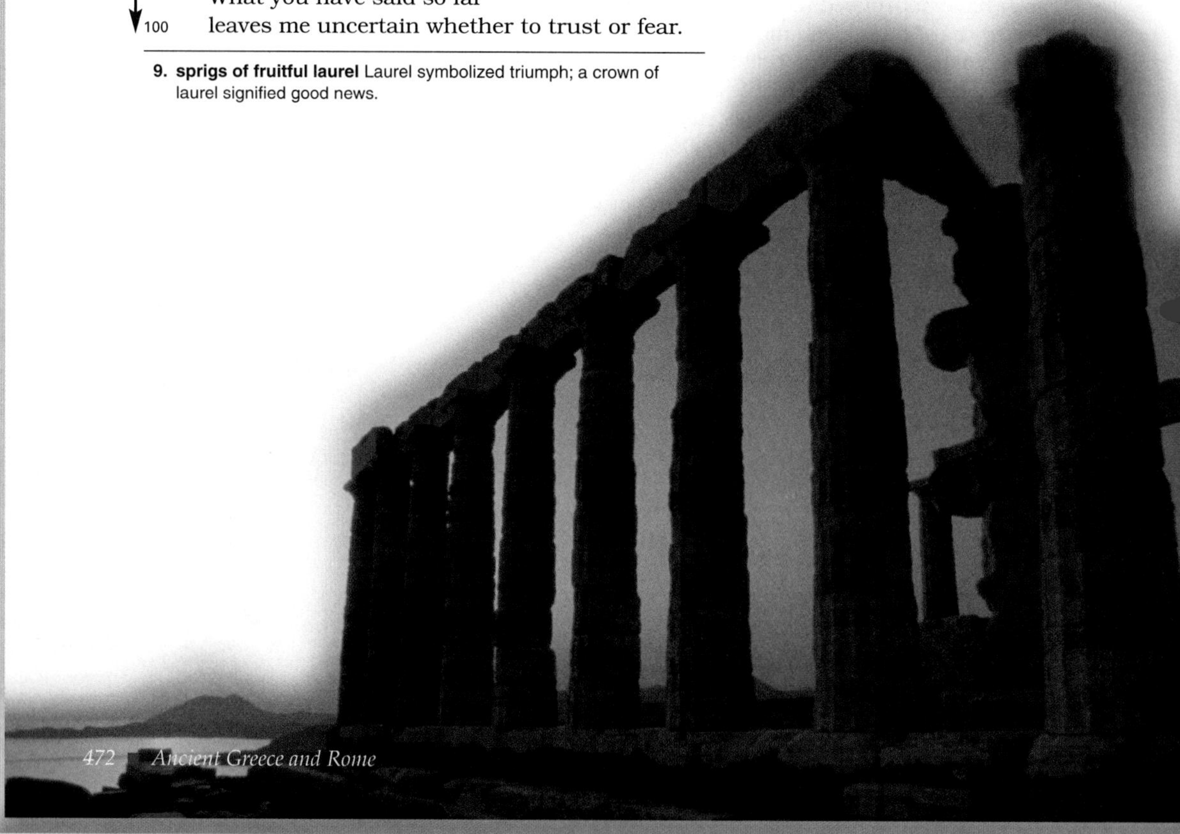

Enrichment

Tone

Tone refers to the author's attitude toward his or her subject. When a writer feels strongly about an issue, he or she may choose to write about it in a serious tone. Or, a writer may use an ironic tone to discuss an issue he or she considers ridiculous. Tone can be formal, informal, solemn, somber, playful, condescending, anxious, happy, or any other possible attitude. The effectiveness of a literary work—whether it communicates the author's intentions—can depend largely on the skill with which the author establishes tone. In *Oedipus the King,* Thebes is in crisis. The tone is serious because the Thebans are concerned about their city. They urgently need to discover the causes of the plague, and they are solemn while they wait for Creon to return with the answer from Apollo. The tone in the first scene sets the tone for the play.

CREON: If you will hear my news before these others
I am ready to speak, or else to go within.

OEDIPUS: Speak it to all;
the grief I bear, I bear it more for these
than for my own heart.

CREON: I will tell you, then,
what I heard from the God.
King Phoebus[10] in plain words commanded us
12 to drive out a pollution from our land,
pollution grown ingrained within the land;
drive it out, said the God, not cherish it,
till it's past cure.

OEDIPUS: What is the rite
of purification? How shall it be done?

CREON: By banishing a man, or expiation[11]
of blood by blood, since it is murder guilt
which holds our city in this destroying storm.

OEDIPUS: Who is this man whose fate the God pronounces?

CREON: My Lord, before you piloted the state
we had a king called Laius.

OEDIPUS: I know of him by hearsay. I have not seen him.

CREON: The God commanded clearly: let some one
punish with force this dead man's murderers.

OEDIPUS: Where are they in the world? Where would a trace
of this old crime be found? It would be hard
to guess where.

13 **CREON:** The clue is in this land;
that which is sought is found;
the unheeded thing escapes:
so said the God.

OEDIPUS: Was it at home,
or in the country that death came upon him,
or in another country travelling?

CREON: He went, he said himself, upon an embassy,[12]
but never returned when he set out from home.

OEDIPUS: Was there no messenger, no fellow traveller
who knew what happened? Such a one might tell
something of use.

10. **King Phoebus** (fē′ bəs) Apollo, god of the sun.
11. **expiation** (eks′ pē ā shən) *n.* the act of making amends for wrongdoing.
12. **embassy** (em′ be sē) *n.* important mission or errand.

Reading Strategy
Reading Drama What gestures and tones of voice do you imagine the actors playing Oedipus and Creon might use during this dialogue? Explain.

14 
Reading Check
Who was king of Thebes before Oedipus?

12 Reading Strategy

Reading Drama

- Have students review the characterization of Oedipus and Creon, as these figures have been portrayed so far in the drama. Make sure students recognize that Oedipus is urgent and intense, as shown by his repeated questions and prompt action. In contrast, Creon is cautious. Note, for example, his hesitation about speaking in public in lines 101–102.
- **Ask** students the Reading Strategy question: What gestures and tones of voice do you imagine the actors playing Oedipus and Creon might use during this dialogue? Explain.
Possible response: Because of Oedipus' repeated questions, the actor playing Oedipus may use an urgent tone of interrogation. He might stretch out his hands to encourage Creon's response. The actor playing Creon might use a more measured, cautious tone. At the mention of Oedipus as pilot of the state, Creon might incline his head in a respectful bow.

13 Background

Imagery

Sophocles introduces another dominant image: hunting. Oedipus as a tracker, hunting down prey, is also Oedipus the hunter whose arrow will hit his true mark but miss the target he thinks he sees.

14 Reading Check

Answer: Laius was the king of Thebes before Oedipus.

⑮ Scholar's Insight

- Read aloud the Scholar's Insight. Explain that it is common in plays for a hero to embark on a struggle, and the Scholar's Insight note gives an example of such a struggle.
- Have students read the bracketed section, and then **ask:** Which words in the bracketed section suggest that Oedipus will try to find the cause of the plague on Thebes? **Possible response:** "For when I drive pollution from the land," "so helping the dead king," and "let it meet upon the understanding that I'll do everything" suggest that Oedipus will act to find the cause of the plague.

⑯ Literary Analysis

Tragedy and Tragic Hero

- Have students note that Oedipus expresses two distinct reasons for his commitment to finding and punishing Laius' murderer: (1) This action will end the plague; (2) This action will protect Oedipus himself from the murderer.
- **Ask** students to explain the different ways in which Sophocles uses irony to make the audience feel both sympathetic and superior to Oedipus. **Answer:** The audience knows the truth about Oedipus' identity as the son and unwitting murderer of Laius. Consequently, Oedipus' speech both engages and distances the audience.
- **Ask** students the Literary Analysis question: According to the emotions Oedipus expresses toward both his subjects and himself, what kind of leader does he seem to be? Explain. **Possible response:** Toward his subjects, Oedipus expresses patriotism and concern, and toward himself he expresses confidence and courage. He seems to be a vigorous, committed leader, willing to take an active hand in the best interests of the state, and he asserts that these interests coincide with his own.

CREON: They were all killed save one. He fled in terror
and he could tell us nothing in clear terms
of what he knew, nothing, but one thing only.

OEDIPUS: What was it?
If we could even find a slim beginning
in which to hope, we might discover much.

CREON: This man said that the robbers they encountered
were many and the hands that did the murder
were many; it was no man's single power.

OEDIPUS: How could a robber dare a deed like this
were he not helped with money from the city,
money and treachery?

CREON: That indeed was thought.
But Laius was dead and in our trouble
there was none to help.

OEDIPUS: What trouble was so great to hinder you
inquiring out the murder of your king?

CREON: The riddling Sphinx <u>induced</u> us to neglect
mysterious crimes and rather seek solution
of troubles at our feet.

OEDIPUS: I will bring this to light again. King Phoebus
fittingly took this care about the dead,
and you too fittingly.
And justly you will see in me an ally,
a champion of my country and the God.
For when I drive pollution from the land
⑮ I will not serve a distant friend's advantage,
but act in my own interest. Whoever
he was that killed the king may readily
⑯ wish to <u>dispatch</u> me with his murderous hand;
so helping the dead king I help myself.

Come, children, take your suppliant boughs and go;
up from the altars now. Call the assembly
and let it meet upon the understanding
that I'll do everything. God will decide
whether we prosper or remain in sorrow.

PRIEST: Rise, children—it was this we came to seek,
which of himself the king now offers us.
May Phoebus who gave us the oracle
come to our rescue and stay the plague.

[*Exit all but the* CHORUS.]

Vocabulary Builder
induced (in do͞ost′) *v.* persuaded; caused

David Mamet
Scholar's Insight
In his book *Three Uses of the Knife*, Mamet says that at the beginning of a play, the hero "elects/consigns himself to a struggle," such as "to find the cause of the plague on Thebes. . . ."

Vocabulary Builder
dispatch (di spach′) *v.* kill

Literary Analysis
Tragedy and Tragic Hero
According to the emotions Oedipus expresses toward both his subjects and himself, what kind of leader does he seem to be? Explain.

Enrichment

The Plague in Athens

Sophocles wrote *Oedipus the King* when war-torn Athens had just been ravaged by a severe plague that devastated the city, killing its people and undermining faith in its laws and religious customs. The statesman Pericles died in the plague, depriving Athens of wise leadership at a critical time in the city's history. In his *History of the Peloponnesian War,* the historian Thucydides, himself a surviving plague victim, describes some of the social effects of the epidemic:

"There were other and worse forms of lawlessness which the plague introduced. . . . Men who had up to now concealed what they took pleasure in now grew bolder. Seeing sudden change and mutability—how the rich died in a moment and those who had nothing suddenly inherited property—they reflected that life and riches were transitory and resolved to enjoy themselves while they could, valuing only pleasure. . . ."

CHORUS:

Strophe

What is the sweet spoken word of God from the
shrine of Pytho[13] rich in gold
that has come to glorious Thebes?
I am stretched on the rack of doubt, and terror and
trembling hold
my heart, O Delian Healer,[14] and I worship full of fears
for what doom you will bring to pass, new or renewed
in the revolving years.
Speak to me, immortal voice,
child of golden Hope.

Antistrophe

18

First I call on you, Athene, deathless daughter of Zeus,
and Artemis, Earth Upholder,
who sits in the midst of the market place in the throne
which men call Fame,
and Phoebus, the Far Shooter, three averters of Fate,[15]
come to us now, if ever before, when ruin rushed upon
the state,
you drove destruction's flame away
out of our land.

Strophe

Our sorrows defy number;
all the ship's timbers are rotten;
taking of thought is no spear for the driving away of
the plague.
There are no growing children in this famous land;
there are no women bearing the pangs of childbirth.
You may see them one with another,
like birds swift on the wing,
quicker than fire unmastered,
speeding away to the coast of the
Western God.[16]

Antistrophe

In the unnumbered deaths
of its people the city dies;
those children that are born lie
dead on the naked earth

13. **Pytho** (pī´ thō) *n.* another name for Delphi, location of Apollo's oracular shrine. Delphi was the principal religious center for all ancient Greeks.
14. **Delian Healer** Born on the island of Delos, Apollo's title was "healer"; he caused and averted plagues.
15. **three averters of Fate** The chorus is praying to three gods—Athene, Artemis, and Apollo—as a triple shield against death.
16. **Western God** Since the sun sets in the west, this is the god of night, or Death.

Literature in Context

17 Humanities Connection

The Greek Chorus and Players

In Greek tragedies, the role of the chorus was central to the production and to the meaning of the play. The chorus consisted of 12 or 15 dancers called *choreuts,* who were young men about to enter the military. The chorus danced as it sang, moving from right to left during the strophe (strō´ fē), then left to right during the antistrophe (an tis´ trə fē).

Originally, plays included only one actor in addition to the chorus. Thespis, from whom we derive the English word *thespian,* or actor, is said to have been the first actor. The dramatist Aeschylus (es´ ki ləs) is said to have introduced the second actor, and Sophocles the third.

In most dramas, actors played several different parts each. Their costumes were long, flowing garments and expressive, wide-mouthed masks, which they changed as they changed characters. The actors' shoes also featured a high wooden sole called a *cothurnus* (kō thur´ nəs) to make the individual look taller and more impressive and to heighten visibility in the vast theater.

Connect to the Literature

How have you reacted to the words of the chorus as you read *Oedipus the King?*

19  **Reading Check**

What happened to King Laius?

17 Literature in Context

The Greek Chorus and Players

Dialogue, not physical action, is the principal form of dramatic expression in Greek drama. Constrained by large masks and balanced on towering shoes, actors (only men performed) are limited in their motions. Acts of violence happen offstage and are reported by messengers.

The chorus often represents a community and serves as a barometer of public opinion. The near-constant presence of the chorus reminds the audience of the societal impact of the protagonist's fate.

Connect to the Literature Have students form groups and do a choral reading of lines 174–230.

- **Ask:** What purpose does the chorus serve in this tragic drama?
  Possible response: The chorus provides a voice for the people of Thebes as they react to the Plague and to Oedipus' problems.
- **Ask:** How have you reacted to the words of the chorus as you read *Oedipus the King?*
  Possible response: The chorus can be annoying when it interrupts the flow of the narrative about Oedipus. However, it enriches the drama with details of the dreadful plague, the people's desperation, their belief in the gods, and their dependence on Oedipus. The chorus's advice to Oedipus also intensifies the drama.

18 Background

The Gods

As the chorus reminds the gods that they have helped Thebes before, the audience is also reminded that Apollo has in effect sent Oedipus both to save the city by killing the sphinx and to bring destruction on the city in working out his own destiny.

19 Reading Check

Answer: Laius was killed while on a journey, reportedly by robbers.

Differentiated Instruction Solutions for All Learners

Support for Special Needs Students
Students might mistake the terms *strophe* and *antistrophe* for the names of characters. Explain that these are titles for corresponding lyric stanzas. Details of meter are unimportant, but students should remember that each choral passage was accompanied by instrumental music.

Support for Less Proficient Readers
In the choral odes, lengthy sentences, dense allusions, and figurative language may challenge students. Remind students to read the footnotes for explanations of many allusions. Also, show students how to break down long sentences into shorter units of thought by using punctuation.

Strategy for Gifted/Talented Students
Invite students to form small groups and practice choral reading of the play's odes. Readings may effectively highlight the ritual element of ancient Greek drama, and they may also help bring out the meaning for Less Proficient Readers or for English learners.

20 Reading Strategy

Reading Drama

- Have students read the bracketed passage silently, noting vivid images such as the clash of shields, the cries of men, the racing course, the waves of the sea, and night and day.
- Review the Literature in Context feature on p. 475 about the chorus. Have students note the dancers' movements during an ode's strophe and antistrophe.
- **Ask** students the Reading Strategy question: What kinds of gestures might the chorus perform during this strophe? Why?
  Possible response: During the strophe, the chorus rotates from right to left. The dancers might gesture with special emphasis at the mention of the War God. For example, they might raise their hands over their heads in a gesture of invocation or placation.

21 Background

Mythological References

The chorus is saying that the plague is as devastating as war. For the Athenian audience engaged in war, the reference to Ares and to the devastation of war adds poignancy to the lament about the plague. The free association between Ares as the God "who burns us" and the heat of the sun lead the chorus to wish Ares would turn back in his course, seeing him as the Sun God Helios who races through the sky in his golden chariot. They want the War God to "set" in the sea, so night, and symbolically death, will give place to daylight.

unpitied, spreading contagion of death; and gray-haired mothers and wives
everywhere stand at the altar's edge, suppliant, moaning;
the hymn to the healing God[17] rings out but with it the wailing voices are blended.
From these our sufferings grant us, O golden Daughter of Zeus,[18] glad-faced deliverance.

Strophe

20

There is no clash of brazen[19] shields but our fight is with the War God,[20]
a War God ringed with the cries of men, a savage God who burns us;
grant that he turn in racing course backwards out of our country's bounds
to the great palace of Amphitrite[21] or where the waves of the Thracian sea
deny the stranger safe anchorage.
Whatsoever escapes the night
at last the light of day revisits;
so smite the War God, Father Zeus,
beneath your thunderbolt,
for you are the Lord of the lightning, the lightning that carries fire.

Antistrophe

And your unconquered arrow shafts, winged by the golden corded bow,
Lycean King,[22] I beg to be at our side for help;
and the gleaming torches of Artemis with which she scours the Lycean hills,
and I call on the God with the turban of gold,[23] who gave his name to this country of ours,
the Bacchic God with the wind flushed face,[24]
Evian One,[25] who travel
with the Maenad company,[26]
combat the God that burns us

Reading Strategy
Reading Drama What kinds of gestures might the chorus perform during this strophe? Why?

---

17. **healing God** Apollo.
18. **golden Daughter of Zeus** Athena.
19. **brazen** (brā′ zən) *adj.* of brass or like brass in color
20. **War God** Ares.
21. **Amphitrite** (am′ fi trīt′ ē) sea goddess who was the wife of Poseidon, god of the sea.
22. **Lycean** (lī sē′ ən) **King** Apollo, whose title *Lykios* means "god of light."
23. **God with the turban of gold** Dionysus, god of wine, who was born of Zeus and a woman of Thebes, the first Greek city to honor him. He wears an oriental turban because he has come from the East.
24. **Bacchic** (bak′ ik) **God with the wind flushed face** refers to Dionysus, who had a youthful, rosy complexion; Bacchus means "riotous god."
25. **Evian One** Dionysus,called Evios because his followers address him with the ritual cry "evoi."
26. **Maenad company** female followers of Dionysus.

Enrichment

Religious Context in the Play

The chorus (whose members are, of course, Athenian citizens although they are playing the parts of Thebans on stage) invokes Dionysus, who is a descendant of the house of Cadmus. *Oedipus the King* and other dramatic performances were part of a larger context of religious and civic ritual. The altar of Dionysus was at the center of the stage area, always visible to the audience. The priest of Dionysus was also one of the dignitaries sitting on a special seat in the center of the first row.

with your torch of pine;
for the God that is our enemy is a God unhonored among the
Gods.

[OEDIPUS *returns.*]

OEDIPUS: For what you ask me—if you will hear my words,
and hearing welcome them and fight the plague,
you will find strength and lightening of your load.

Hark to me; what I say to you, I say
as one that is a stranger to the story
as stranger to the deed. For I would not
be far upon the track if I alone
were tracing it without a clue. But now,
since after all was finished, I became
a citizen among you, citizens—
now I proclaim to all the men of Thebes:
who so among you knows the murderer
by whose hand Laius, son of Labdacus,
died—I command him to tell everything
to me,—yes, though he fears himself to take the blame
on his own head; for bitter punishment
he shall have none, but leave this land unharmed.
Or if he knows the murderer, another,
a foreigner, still let him speak the truth.
For I will pay him and be grateful, too.
But if you shall keep silence, if perhaps
some one of you, to shield a guilty friend,
or for his own sake shall reject my words—
hear what I shall do then:
I forbid that man, whoever he be, my land,
my land where I hold sovereignty[27] and throne;
and I forbid any to welcome him
or cry him greeting or make him a sharer
in sacrifice or offering to the Gods,
or give him water for his hands to wash.
I command all to drive him from their homes,
since he is our pollution, as the oracle
of Pytho's God[28] proclaimed him now to me.
So I stand forth a champion of the God
and of the man who died.
Upon the murderer I invoke this curse—
whether he is one man and all unknown,
or one of many—may he wear out his life
in misery to miserable doom!
If with my knowledge he lives at my hearth

27. **sovereignty** (säv′ rən tē) *n.* supreme authority.
28. **Pytho's God** Apollo.

Literary Analysis
Tragedy In lines 234–236, what aspects of his life story does Oedipus' description of himself emphasize?

Vocabulary Builder
invoke (in vōk′) *v.* summon; cause to appear

Reading Check 23
With which god is the chorus most distressed?

22 Literary Analysis
Tragedy

- Have students review the relevant details of the Oedipus myth that have occurred before the play begins: Oedipus believes himself the son of the king and queen of Corinth; he had left that city to avoid a terrible prophecy; arriving at Thebes, he solved the riddle of the Sphinx and married Queen Jocasta, the widow of King Laius.
- Elicit from students that Oedipus' description of himself in the bracketed lines is an example of dramatic irony because it presents a clash between what Oedipus believes to be true and what the audience knows to be true.
- **Ask** students the Literary Analysis question: In lines 234–236, what aspects of his life story does Oedipus' description of himself emphasize?
Answer: Oedipus thinks of himself as a "stranger" to the city and to the royal house. He is essentially saying, "I've never heard of this story, and I have nothing to do with the murder."

▶ **Monitor Progress** Lead students in a discussion about why Sophocles has chosen this particular way to have Oedipus phrase his claim.

▶ **Reteach** If students are having difficulty with the tragic elements of this myth, use **Literary Analysis** support, p. 106 in ***Unit 4 Resources.***

23 Reading Check

Answer: The chorus is most distressed with Ares.

㉔ Literary Analysis

Tragedy and Tragic Hero

- Point out that Oedipus' speech is a minefield of irony, containing promises that will explode on Oedipus later in the play. Make sure that students recognize the terrifying irony of Oedipus' curse: in cursing the murderer, Oedipus is damning himself to destruction.
- Also have students note that Oedipus' inclusion of the Theban genealogy in lines 286–288 is another ironic touch—the lines give a specific account of Oedipus' own ancestors.
- **Ask** students the Literary Analysis question: How does Oedipus' decision to seek out the murderer of Laius add to his stature as a hero? **Possible response:** Oedipus' decision derives from an active effort of will. In Greek tragedy, a hero meets his or her downfall as a result of his or her own actions and character traits.

㉕ Critical Viewing

Possible response: Both actors seem to be expressing strong emotions of anger or distress.

I pray that I myself may feel my curse.
On you I lay my charge to fulfill all this
for me, for the God, and for this land of ours
destroyed and blighted, by the God forsaken.

Even were this no matter of God's ordinance
it would not fit you so to leave it lie,
unpurified, since a good man is dead
and one that was a king. Search it out.
Since I am now the holder of his office,
and have his bed and wife that once was his,
and had his line not been unfortunate
we would have common children—(fortune leaped
upon his head)—because of all these things,
I fight in his defense as for my father,
and I shall try all means to take the murderer
of Laius the son of Labdacus
the son of Polydorus and before him
of Cadmus and before him of Agenor.
Those who do not obey me, may the Gods
grant no crops springing from the ground they plow
nor children to their women! May a fate
like this, or one still worse than this consume them!
For you whom these words please, the other Thebans,
may Justice as your ally and all the Gods
live with you, blessing you now and for ever!

CHORUS: As you have held me to my oath, I speak:
I neither killed the king nor can declare
the killer; but since Phoebus set the quest
it is his part to tell who the man is.

OEDIPUS: Right; but to put compulsion[29] on the Gods
against their will—no man can do that.

CHORUS: May I then say what I think second best?

OEDIPUS: If there's a third best, too, spare not to tell it.

CHORUS: I know that what the Lord Teiresias
sees, is most often what the Lord Apollo
sees. If you should inquire of this from him
you might find out most clearly.

OEDIPUS: Even in this my actions have not been sluggard.[30]
On Creon's word I have sent two messengers
and why the prophet is not here already
I have been wondering.

Literary Analysis
Tragedy and Tragic Hero How does Oedipus' decision to seek out the murderer of Laius add to his stature as a hero?

㉕ **Critical Viewing ▶** What emotions do these actors playing Oedipus (standing in foreground) and Teiresias (kneeling) convey? **[Interpret]**

---

29. **compulsion** (kəm pul′ shən) *n.* driving force; coercion.
30. **sluggard** (slug′ ərd) *adj.* lazy or idle.

Enrichment

Teiresias

According to one legend, during his youth, Teiresias came upon a male and a female snake on Mount Cithaeron, near Thebes. He struck them with his staff, killing the female. Immediately, Teiresias was transformed into a woman. Some time later, he came upon another pair of snakes. This time, he killed the male.

In another legend, Zeus and Hera were arguing whether men or women are more capable of enjoying physical pleasure. They called on Teiresias to resolve the dispute because he had been both male and female during his life. Teiresias answered that the pleasure is greater for women.

Infuriated, Hera blinded him on the spot, while Zeus rewarded him with the gift of prophecy.

In yet another legend, Teiresias accidentally caught sight of Athena bathing and was struck blind. But, because Teiresias' mother, Chariclo, was Athena's favorite nymph, the goddess gave him the gift of prophecy and long life in place of his sight.

CHORUS: His skill apart
there is besides only an old faint story.

OEDIPUS: What is it?
I look at every story.

CHORUS: It was said
that he was killed by certain wayfarers.

OEDIPUS: I heard that, too, but no one saw the killer.

CHORUS: Yet if he has a share of fear at all,
his courage will not stand firm, hearing your curse.

OEDIPUS: The man who in the doing did not shrink
will fear no word.

CHORUS: Here comes his prosecutor:
26 led by your men the godly prophet comes
in whom alone of mankind truth is native.

[*Enter* TEIRESIAS, *led by a little boy.*]

OEDIPUS: Teiresias, you are versed in everything,
things teachable and things not to be spoken,
things of the heaven and earth-creeping things.
You have no eyes but in your mind you know
with what a plague our city is afflicted.
My lord, in you alone we find a champion,

27 **Reading Check**

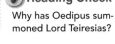

Why has Oedipus summoned Lord Teiresias?

26 Critical Thinking

Apply

- Draw students' attention to the fact that Oedipus' attempt to find out the truth—to find and convict Laius' murderer by calling witnesses to the stand and examining them—is modeled closely on legal procedures in fifth-century Athens.
- Lead students in a discussion about how this correspondence might affect Sophocles' audience.

27 Reading Check

Answer: Oedipus wants Teiresias to reveal the names of Laius' murderers.

28 Vocabulary Builder

Latin Prefix *pro-*

- Call students' attention to the word *prophecy* (line 336). Tell students that the Greek and Latin prefix *pro-* means "before in place or time" or "forward." A prophecy is a prediction of the future.
- **Ask** students to suggest other words containing this prefix, and write the words on the board. **Possible responses:** *Proceed, prologue, prognosis,* and *progeny* contain the prefix *pro-*.
- Ask volunteers to use the listed words in sentences that accurately reflect their meanings.

29 Reading Strategy

Reading Drama

- Suggest to students that in order to understand Oedipus' character fully, they should try to assume the king's point of view, or look at the world through his eyes. The audience knows that Teiresias has insight that Oedipus lacks. From Oedipus' point of view, however, does Teiresias sound reasonable? Is Oedipus' rage justified?
- Have volunteers read aloud the bracketed passage of dialogue. Urge students to note some emotionally charged phrases, such as "rob us," "kneel to you," and "betray us."
- Then, **ask** students the Reading Strategy question: How might the actor playing Oedipus vary his tone of voice in this dialogue with Teiresias? Explain. **Possible response:** In lines 349–352, Oedipus might sound reproachful. In lines 355–357, he might shift to a supplicating tone. In lines 360–362, he might express notes of anger and frustration.

in you alone one that can rescue us.
Perhaps you have not heard the messengers,
but Phoebus sent in answer to our sending
an oracle declaring that our freedom
from this disease would only come when we
should learn the names of those who killed King Laius,
and kill them or expel from our country.
Do not begrudge us oracles from birds,
or any other way of prophecy
within your skill; save yourself and the city,
save me; redeem the debt of our pollution
that lies on us because of this dead man.
We are in your hands; pains are most nobly taken
to help another when you have means and power.

TEIRESIAS: Alas, how terrible is wisdom when
it brings no profit to the man that's wise!
This I knew well, but had forgotten it,
else I would not have come here

OEDIPUS: What is this?
How sad you are now you have come!

TEIRESIAS: Let me
go home. It will be easiest for us both
to bear our several destinies to the end
if you will follow my advice.

OEDIPUS: You'd rob us
of this your gift of prophecy? You talk
as one who had no care for law nor love
for Thebes who reared you.

TEIRESIAS: Yes, but I see that even your own words
miss the mark; therefore I must fear for mine.

OEDIPUS: For God's sake if you know of anything,
do not turn from us; all of us kneel to you,
all of us here, your suppliants.

TEIRESIAS: All of you here know nothing. I will not
bring to the light of day my troubles, mine—
rather than call them yours.

OEDIPUS: What do you mean?
You know of something but refuse to speak.
Would you betray us and destroy the city?

TEIRESIAS: I will not bring this pain upon us both,
neither on you nor on myself. Why is it
you question me and waste your labor? I
will tell you nothing.

Vocabulary Builder
prophecy (präf´ ə sē) *n.* prediction of the future

Reading Strategy
Reading Drama How might the actor playing Oedipus vary his tone of voice in this dialogue with Teiresias? Explain.

Enrichment

Political Tricks

The Athenians were not wholly unfamiliar with collusion between politicians and the clergy. The historian Herodotus reports that in the early days of the democracy, the leader of one political faction got the Spartan Cleomenes to send a herald to Athens demanding the expulsion from Athens of Cleisthenes, a successful political rival, along with a large number of his associates.

The excuse was that Cleisthenes was under a curse and the city must "drive out the pollution." Before the beginning of the Peloponnesian War, the Spartans again used this device, demanding the expulsion of Pericles from Athens on the same grounds.

OEDIPUS: You would provoke a stone! Tell us, you villain,
tell us, and do not stand there quietly
unmoved and balking[31] at the issue.

TEIRESIAS: You blame my temper but you do not see
your own that lives within you; it is me
you chide.[32]

OEDIPUS: Who would not feel his temper rise
at words like these with which you shame our city?

TEIRESIAS: Of themselves things will come, although I hide them
and breathe no word of them.

OEDIPUS: Since they will come
tell them to me.

TEIRESIAS: I will say nothing further.
Against this answer let your temper rage
as wildly as you will.

31 **OEDIPUS:** Indeed I am
so angry I shall not hold back a jot
of what I think. For I would have you know
I think you were complotter[33] of the deed
and doer of the deed save in so far
as for the actual killing. Had you had eyes
I would have said alone you murdered him.

TEIRESIAS: Yes? Then I warn you faithfully to keep
the letter of your proclamation and
from this day forth to speak no word of greeting
to these nor me; you are the land's pollution.

OEDIPUS: How shamelessly you started up this taunt!
How do you think you will escape?

TEIRESIAS: I have.
I have escaped; the truth is what I cherish
and that's my strength.

OEDIPUS: And who has taught you truth?
Not your profession surely!

TEIRESIAS: You have taught me,
for you have made me speak against my will.

OEDIPUS: Speak what? Tell me again that I may learn it better.

TEIRESIAS: Did you not understand before or would you
provoke me into speaking?

31. **balking** (bôk′ iŋ) *v.* obstinately refusing to act.
32. **chide** (chīd) *v.* scold.
33. **complotter** (käm plät′ ər) *n.* person who plots against another person.

Literature in Context

30 History Connection

The Delphic Oracle

The Greeks called Delphi the "navel," or center, of the world. It was the place to which Greeks and foreigners alike traveled from all over the Mediterranean area to seek advice from the god Apollo.

The oracle at Delphi was a shrine to Apollo where the god, speaking through his priestess, would answer questions from mortals. No one would consider amending the constitution or establishing a new religious festival without advice from Delphi.

Sometimes Apollo gave straightforward answers. Often, however, the answers were ambiguous riddles that had to be solved with care and subtlety. Apollo knew all and always spoke the truth, but human beings could misinterpret his responses. For example, when King Croesus of Lydia, fabled for his wealth, asked whether he should invade Persia, the Oracle responded, "If you do, you will destroy a great kingdom." The king took this as a green light and invaded Persia as he had planned. Against everyone's expectations, he was defeated. Too late he realized that the "great kingdom" he had destroyed was his own.

Connect to the Literature

How has the ambiguity of the oracle's words trapped Oedipus?

32 **Reading Check**

Why is Oedipus angry with Teiresias?

Differentiated Instruction Solutions for All Learners

Strategy for Less Proficient Readers

Tell students Teiresias must only hint at Oedipus' guilt. Give one student a sheet of paper with a secret on it. Then, direct the student to talk to a class member, hinting at the secret but never stating it directly. Have the class members make guesses about the nature of the secret.

Vocabulary for English Learners

Remind students that using context clues can be a very effective strategy for decoding unfamiliar vocabulary items. For example, have students use the clues "truth" and "strength" to determine the meaning of the word *cherish* in line 394.

Enrichment for Advanced Readers

Have students discuss the notion of a tragic flaw with reference to other tragedies. Examples from Shakespearean tragedy might include ambition in *Macbeth,* indecision in *Hamlet,* and jealousy in *Othello.* Then, have them write essays about how a tragic flaw can lead to a hero's demise.

30 Literature in Context

The Delphic Oracle Greeks believed that Apollo established the oracle at Delphi after killing Python, the monstrous serpent that guarded the spot. The priestess of Apollo, called the Pythia or the Pythoness, was seated on a sacred tripod as questions were relayed to her via a male priest.

Delphic prophecies were notoriously puzzling; today, the adjective *Delphic* carries a connotation of obscurity or ambiguity. For the Greeks, even divine truth left ample room for human ingenuity and endeavor.

Connect to the Literature Point out to students that *ambiguous* means "capable of being understood in two or more ways."

- **Ask:** What is ambiguous about the oracle's words?
  Possible response: The oracle speaks of the dangers of "pollution" rather than identifying the killer.
- Ask: How does ambiguity trap Oedipus?
  Answer: Because Oedipus does not know that he killed his father, he promises to find the murderer and bring that person to justice. In this way, Oedipus traps himself into eventually being identified as the murderer and is punished accordingly.

31 Literary Analysis

Tragedy

- Remind students that in Greek tragedy the hero is traditionally of noble birth. Although the hero usually possesses outstanding character traits, he or she also exhibits one or more negative traits that constitute a "tragic flaw" which contributes directly to the hero's downfall.
- **Ask:** What flaw in Oedipus' character is suggested by his choosing to accuse Teiresias?
  Possible response: By accusing Teiresias of conspiring to kill Laius, Oedipus reveals that he is prone to fits of temper and irrational accusations against others. Perhaps he is nervous about the legitimacy of his rule.

32 Reading Check

Answer: Oedipus is angry because Teiresias refuses to reveal all that he knows about the murder.

33 Background

Terms of Endearment

The term rendered as "those you love best" (line 410) has a rich range of connotations in Greek; its primary sense is "those who are your closest kin," but it is also used by extension to refer to those who are like kin by virtue of being "most trusted allies," "dearest friends," or "most beloved."

34 Reading Strategy

Reading Drama

- Suggest to students that in order to determine Oedipus' tone of voice in this dialogue, they should first read through the passage silently and then consider how Oedipus' words fit into the context of the scene so far.
- **Ask** students the Reading Strategy question: How do you think the actor playing Oedipus should speak lines 428–436? Explain.
  Possible response: The actor may blend outrage with a note of self-pity.

OEDIPUS: I did not grasp it,
not so to call it known. Say it again.

TEIRESIAS: I say you are the murderer of the king
whose murderer you seek.

OEDIPUS: Not twice you shall
say calumnies[34] like this and stay unpunished.

TEIRESIAS: Shall I say more to tempt your anger more?

OEDIPUS: As much as you desire; it will be said
in vain.

TEIRESIAS: I say that with those you love best
you live in foulest shame unconsciously
and do not see where you are in calamity.[35]

OEDIPUS: Do you imagine you can always talk
like this, and live to laugh at it hereafter?

TEIRESIAS: Yes, if the truth has anything of strength.

OEDIPUS: It has, but not for you; it has no strength
for you because you are blind in mind and ears
as well as in your eyes.

TEIRESIAS: You are a poor wretch
to taunt me with the very insults which
every one soon will heap upon yourself.

OEDIPUS: Your life is one long night so that you cannot
hurt me or any other who sees the light.

TEIRESIAS: It is not fate that I should be your ruin,
Apollo is enough; it is his care
to work this out.

OEDIPUS: Was this your own design
or Creon's?

TEIRESIAS: Creon is no hurt to you,
but you are to yourself.

OEDIPUS: Wealth, sovereignty and skill outmatching skill
for the contrivance[36] of an envied life!
Great store of jealousy fill your treasury chests,
if my friend Creon, friend from the first and loyal,
thus secretly attacks me, secretly
desires to drive me out and secretly
suborns[37] this juggling, trick devising quack,
this wily beggar who has only eyes

Reading Strategy
Reading Drama How do you think the actor playing Oedipus should speak lines 428–436? Explain.

34. **calumnies** (kal´ əm nēz)) *n.* false and malicious statements; slander.
35. **calamity** (kə lam´ ə tē) *n.* extreme misfortune that leads to disaster.
36. **contrivance** (kən trī´ vəns) *n.* act of devising or scheming.
37. **suborns** (sə bôrnz´) *v.* instigates a person to commit perjury.

Enrichment

The Sophists

As Oedipus boasts that he is a better diviner than Teiresias, he echoes a position that was especially associated with the sophists of the late fifth century B.C. The sophists were the first paid professional teachers in Athens. Protagoras, one of the most distinguished of the sophists, became famous for his human-centered view of the universe: "Man is the measure of all things," he proclaimed. The sophist Antiphon defined prophecy as "the guess of an intelligent man." Less than twenty years after *Oedipus the King* was first performed, Euripides' character Helen asserted that "the best prophet is intelligence and good counsel." The validity or invalidity of the oracles was a crucial issue in Sophocles' time. The ancient audience would have recognized the applicability of this issue in their own lives.

for his own gains, but blindness in his skill.
For, tell me, where have you seen clear, Teiresias,
with your prophetic eyes? When the dark singer,
the sphinx, was in your country, did you speak
word of deliverance to its citizens?
And yet the riddle's answer was not the province
of a chance comer. It was a prophet's task
and plainly you had no such gift of prophecy
from birds nor otherwise from any God
to glean a word of knowledge. But I came,
Oedipus, who knew nothing, and I stopped her.
I solved the riddle by my wit alone.
Mine was no knowledge got from birds. And now
you would expel me,
because you think that you will find a place
by Creon's throne. I think you will be sorry,
both you and your accomplice, for your plot
to drive me out. And did I not regard you
as an old man, some suffering would have taught you
that what was in your heart was treason.

CHORUS: We look at this man's words and yours, my
king, and we find both have spoken them in anger.
We need no angry words but only thought
how we may best hit the God's meaning for us.

TEIRESIAS: If you are king, at least I have the right
no less to speak in my defense against you.
Of that much I am master. I am no slave
of yours, but Loxias', and so I shall not
enroll myself with Creon for my patron.
Since you have taunted me with being blind,
here is my word for you.
You have your eyes but see not where you are
in sin, nor where you live, nor whom you live with.
Do you know who your parents are? Unknowing
you are an enemy to kith and kin
in death, beneath the earth, and in this life.
A deadly footed, double striking curse,
from father and mother both, shall drive you forth
out of this land, with darkness on your eyes,
that now have such straight vision. Shall there be
a place will not be harbor to your cries,[38]
a corner of Cithaeron[39] will not ring
in echo to your cries, soon, soon,—
when you shall learn the secret of your marriage,

38. Shall . . . . cries Is there any place that won't be full of your cries?
39. Cithaeron (siˊ thər än) *n.* mountain near Thebes on which Oedipus was abandoned as an infant.

Reading Strategy
Reading Drama What change in the actor's posture or gestures should accompany lines 437–440?

36 ▼ Critical Viewing
Does this image of a sphinx suggest a creature that is a "cruel singer"? Why or why not? **[Evaluate]**

Literary Analysis
Tragedy What emotions might Teiresias' speech, which emphasizes a curse and Oedipus' "blindness," have evoked in the Athenian audience? Explain.

Reading Check
According to Teiresias, who is the murderer whom Oedipus seeks?

35 Reading Strategy
Reading Drama

- Review with the class the play's presentation of Oedipus' reputation at Thebes. For example, he is called "the Great" (line 7) and "Greatest in all men's eyes" (line 46).
- **Ask** students the Reading Strategy question: What change in the actor's posture or gestures should accompany lines 437–440?
Possible response: Oedipus should probably turn to face Teiresias in a confrontational pose.

36 Critical Viewing

Possible response: Because the sphinx seems to be smiling, it does not appear cruel.

37 Literary Analysis
Tragedy

- Remind students that the ancient Athenian audience—like many audiences and readers in modern times—was familiar with the main plots of Greek tragedies because these were drawn from well-known myths.
- **Ask** students the Literary Analysis question: What emotions might Teiresias' speech, which emphasizes a curse and Oedipus' "blindness," have evoked in the Athenian audience? Explain.
Possible response: By hinting at the guilt of Oedipus under his own curse, as well as at the agony of the king's self-blinding, the prophet may inspire the emotions of pity and fear.

38 Reading Check

Answer: Teiresias reveals that Oedipus himself is the murderer of the king.

Differentiated Instruction Solutions for All Learners

Strategy for Special Needs Students

To help students determine and analyze characters' motives, have students consider what makes each character behave the way he or she does. Suggest that students draw two-column charts to analyze characters' motives. Have them review the character list on p. 469 and list the main characters. Then, suggest that they review the play up to this point to analyze the motives for each character. Suggest that students ask themselves the following questions:

- Why does the character take certain actions?
- If I put myself in the character's place, what actions might I take and why?

Questioning the motives of the characters will enhance understanding of the plot and conflict found in the drama.

39 Critical Viewing

Possible response: The masks express emotions of shock, dread, and distress—appropriate responses to the play's unfolding events.

40 Literary Analysis

Tragedy

- Note to students that the dialogue on this page may be described as an unfair fight in which a blind man holds all the advantages and punches his opponent at will. Point out that in lines 482–494, Teiresias lands a left-right combination with dark references to Oedipus' children and his parents.
- **Ask:** How does Oedipus react to the mention of his parents? Why does he react in this way?
  Possible response: Oedipus stops the departure of Teiresias and urgently pursues a question. Significantly, he does not say, "My parents?" but rather, "What parents?" (line 495). This reaction suggests Oedipus' deep unease about his origin and identity.
- Read aloud the bracketed passage. Then, **ask** students: In what ways does line 512 echo Oedipus' description of himself in lines 234–236?
  Possible response: Line 512 echoes the notion of Oedipus as a "stranger" to the city of Thebes and the story of Laius. Whereas the tone of Oedipus' words is tinged with dramatic irony (because the audience is aware that Oedipus is truly a Theban), Teiresias' tone is far darker. His words ominously allude to the terrible truth about Oedipus' identity.

37

which steered you to a haven in this house,—
haven no haven, after lucky voyage?
And of the multitude of other evils
establishing a grim equality
between you and your children, you know nothing.
So, muddy with contempt my words and Creon's!
Misery shall grind no man as it will you.

OEDIPUS: Is it endurable that I should hear
such words from him? Go and a curse go with you!
Quick, home with you! Out of my house at once!

TEIRESIAS: I would not have come either had you not called me.

OEDIPUS: I did not know then you would talk like a fool—
or it would have been long before I called you.

TEIRESIAS: I am a fool then, as it seems to you—
but to the parents who have bred you, wise.

OEDIPUS: What parents? Stop! Who are they of all the world?

TEIRESIAS: This day will show your birth and will destroy you.

OEDIPUS: How needlessly your riddles darken everything.

TEIRESIAS: But it's in riddle answering you are strongest.

OEDIPUS: Yes. Taunt me where you will find me great.

TEIRESIAS: It is this very luck that has destroyed you.

OEDIPUS: I do not care, if it has saved this city.

TEIRESIAS: Well, I will go. Come, boy, lead me away.

OEDIPUS: Yes, lead him off. So long as you are here,
you'll be a stumbling block and a vexation;
once gone, you will not trouble me again.

TEIRESIAS: I have said
what I came here to say not fearing your
countenance; there is no way you can hurt me.
I tell you, king, this man, this murderer
(whom you have long declared you are in search of,
indicting him in threatening proclamation
as murderer of Laius)—he is here.
40
In name he is a stranger among citizens
but soon he will be shown to be a citizen
true native Theban, and he'll have no joy
of the discovery: blindness for sight
and beggary for riches his exchange,
he shall go journeying to a foreign country
tapping his way before him with a stick.
He shall be proved father and brother both
to his own children in his house; to her
that gave him birth, a son and husband both;
a fellow sower in his father's bed

Vocabulary Builder
countenance (koun′ tə nəns) *n.* the look on a person's face

39 **Critical Viewing** In what ways do the expressions of the masks in this image of the chorus reflect varied responses to the play's events? **[Analyze]**

Enrichment

Amphitheaters

Sophocles' tragedies were formally performed in *amphitheaters,* open-air structures built expressly for public performances. *Amphi-* means "on both sides," or "around," and an amphitheater is designed to place the audience on tiers of seats around the action of a play. The bowl-like structure of Greek amphitheaters resulted in remarkable acoustic properties; audiences could hear the actors' voices clearly, even when they spoke quietly.

A typical amphitheater might seat the audience in a semicircle facing the *proscenium,* or the front of the stage. At either side between audience and stage would be a corridor called a *parodos,* through which the chorus might enter.

with that same father that he murdered.
Go within, reckon that out, and if you find me
mistaken, say I have no skill in prophecy.

[*Exit separately* TEIRESIAS *and* OEDIPUS.]

CHORUS:

Strophe
Who is the man proclaimed
by Delphi's prophetic rock
as the bloody handed murderer,
the doer of deeds that none dare name?
Now is the time for him to run
with a stronger foot
than Pegasus[40]
for the child of Zeus leaps in arms upon him
with fire and the lightning bolt,
and terribly close on his heels
are the Fates that never miss.

Antistrophe
Lately from snowy Parnassus
clearly the voice flashed forth,
bidding each Theban track him down,
the unknown murderer.

40. **Pegasus** (peg´ ə səs) mythical winged horse.

41  **Reading Check**
How does Oedipus react to the information that Teiresias gives him?

42

41 Reading Check

Answer: Oedipus curses Teiresias and orders him to leave the city.

42 Humanities

During a two-week festival in the summer of 2000, the Greek National Theater presented a production of *Oedipus Rex* in an unlikely venue: the Colosseum in Rome. Celebrating completion of an eight-year restoration of the ancient amphitheater, the performance took place on a platform that partially replaced the long-missing wooden floor. For the first time in 1,500 years, the Colosseum rang with the sounds of a living spectacle: this time, not with the clangor of gladiators but with the emotions of a drama that is centuries older than the ancient Colosseum itself.

Photographs on this and other pages are from this unique production of *Oedipus Rex.*

Use the following question for discussion:

Why do some members of the chorus seem to react to the action on stage while others stand passive? **Possible response:** The chorus models the propensity of human beings not to hear what shocks or frightens them, not to understand when they are "in the thick of things," or not to acknowledge what with hindsight seems all too obvious.

Differentiated Instruction Solutions for All Learners

Strategy for Special Needs Students

Demonstrate the use of character webs to help students understand the personality traits of Oedipus and Teiresias. Encourage students to place what they think is each character's most important trait in each web's center cell and then to use the outer cells for subordinate character traits.

Strategy for Less Proficient Readers

Urge students to break down the long speeches of Oedipus and Teiresias into units of meaning and then to write a summary for each unit. Use lines 506–525 to model this strategy. **Sample summary:** "I said what I came here to say. I am not afraid of you. You cannot hurt me."

Enrichment for Gifted/Talented Students

Invite students to practice dramatic readings of Teiresias' final speech (lines 506–525). Have them experiment with such elements as tone, pitch, emphasis, volume, pacing, gestures, movements, and posture. Then, invite students to perform their readings for the class.

43 Reading Strategy

Reading Drama

- Call on a volunteer to read aloud Creon's speech. Point out that Creon is addressing the people of Thebes ("Citizens"). Oedipus is not on stage.
- Ask a volunteer to summarize briefly Creon's character as he has been portrayed so far. **Ask:** Is it likely that Creon would have conspired against Oedipus?
  Possible response: Creon has neither the temperament nor sufficient motive to conspire against Oedipus.
- **Ask** students the Reading Strategy question: Considering the content and tone of this passage, how should the actor playing Creon make his entrance?
  Possible response: The actor should enter urgently, in haste, with a self-righteous posture and tone.

In the savage forests he lurks and in
the caverns like
the mountain bull.
He is sad and lonely, and lonely his feet
that carry him far from the navel of earth;[41]
but its prophecies, ever living,
flutter around his head.

Strophe

The augur[42] has spread confusion,
terrible confusion;
I do not approve what was said
nor can I deny it.
I do not know what to say;
I am in a flutter of foreboding;
I never heard in the present
nor past of a quarrel between
the sons of Labdacus and Polybus,
that I might bring as proof
in attacking the popular fame
of Oedipus, seeking
to take vengeance for undiscovered
death in the line of Labdacus.

Antistrophe

Truly Zeus and Apollo are wise
and in human things all knowing;
but amongst men there is no
distinct judgment, between the prophet
and me—which of us is right.
One man may pass another in wisdom
but I would never agree
with those that find fault with the king
till I should see the word
proved right beyond doubt. For once
in visible form the Sphinx
came on him and all of us
saw his wisdom and in that test
he saved the city. So he will not be condemned by my mind.

[*Enter* CREON.]

CREON: Citizens, I have come because I heard
deadly words spread about me, that the king
accuses me. I cannot take that from him.
If he believes that in these present troubles
he has been wronged by me in word or deed

Reading Strategy
Reading Drama
Considering the content and tone of this passage, how should the actor playing Creon make his entrance?

41. navel of earth fissure, or crack, on Mount Parnassus from which mysterious vapors arose to inspire Pythia, priestess of the Oracle of Apollo at Delphi.
42. augur (ô´ gər) *n.* fortuneteller or prophet; refers here to Teiresias.

I do not want to live on with the burden
of such a scandal on me. The report
injures me doubly and most vitally—
for I'll be called a traitor to my city
and traitor also to my friends and you.

CHORUS: Perhaps it was a sudden gust of anger
that forced that insult from him, and no judgment.

CREON: But did he say that it was in compliance
with schemes of mine that the seer told him lies?

CHORUS: Yes, he said that, but why, I do not know.

CREON: Were his eyes straight in his head? Was his mind right
when he accused me in this fashion?

CHORUS: I do not know; I have no eyes to see
what princes do. Here comes the king himself.

[*Enter* OEDIPUS.]

44

OEDIPUS: You, sir, how is it you come here? Have you so much
brazen-faced daring that you venture in
my house although you are proved manifestly[43]
the murderer of that man, and though you tried,
openly, highway robbery of my crown?
For God's sake, tell me what you saw in me,
what cowardice or what stupidity,
that made you lay a plot like this against me?
Did you imagine I should not observe
the crafty scheme that stole upon me or
seeing it, take no means to counter it?
Was it not stupid of you to make the attempt,
to try to hunt down royal power without
the people at your back or friends? For only
with the people at your back or money can
the hunt end in the capture of a crown.

CREON: Do you know what you're doing? Will you listen
to words to answer yours, and then pass judgment?

OEDIPUS: You're quick to speak, but I am slow to grasp you,
for I have found you dangerous,—and my foe.

CREON: First of all hear what I shall say to that.

OEDIPUS: At least don't tell me that you are not guilty.

CREON: If you think obstinacy[44] without wisdom
a valuable possession, you are wrong.

OEDIPUS: And you are wrong if you believe that one,

43. **proved manifestly** (man′ ə fest lē) clearly proved with evidence.
44. **obstinacy** (äb′ stə nə sē) *n.* stubbornness; state of being unyielding to reason. Creon means that Oedipus cannot see—or refuses to see—the facts.

Literary Analysis
Tragedy, Tragic Hero, and Tragic Flaw Up to this point in the play, in what ways does Oedipus seem heroic and in what ways does he seem flawed? Explain.

45 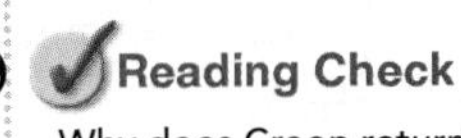

Why does Creon return?

44 Literary Analysis

Tragedy, Tragic Hero, and Tragic Flaw

- Remind students that the hero in a Greek tragedy is a round character who exhibits both positive and negative traits. Remind them also that the mix is usually biased toward the positive because the audience must be brought to sympathize with the hero and to experience pity and fear at his or her downfall.
- Have students review Oedipus' characterization in the major scenes so far: the king's first appearance, his first interview with Creon, his interrogation of Teiresias, and his second scene with Creon.
- Then, **ask** students the Literary Analysis question: Up to this point in the play, in what ways does Oedipus seem heroic and in what ways does he seem flawed? Explain. **Possible response:** Oedipus' heroic qualities include courage, intelligence, and patriotism. His flaws include a hot temper and irrational suspicion of others.

45 Reading Check

Answer: Creon has heard of Oedipus' accusations and has returned to defend himself.

Differentiated Instruction Solutions for All Learners

Enrichment for Less Proficient Readers

Explain that in a Readers Theatre presentation, dialogue is read rather than memorized, and the physical action is not staged. Have students brainstorm a list of qualities that make an oral presentation impressive, including expressive voices, clear diction, and dramatic facial expressions. Help groups select scenes and assign roles in preparation for a Readers Theatre presentation. Provide time for students to rehearse their scenes. You may choose to assign the chorus's lines to individual chorus members rather than have the chorus read in unison.

46 Background

Athenian Justice

One of the casualties of the Athenian empire was the legal system as it applied to allies and other noncitizens. As a "tyrant city," Athens meted out summary and often brutal retribution or "justice." Oedipus is not only an individual but the embodiment of imperial Athens, the *polis tyrannos.*

47 Literary Analysis

Tragedy and Tragic Flaw

- Encourage students to review Oedipus' flaws as well as his heroic qualities.
- **Ask** students the Literary Analysis question: What flaw in Oedipus' character is suggested by his choosing to accuse Creon? **Possible response:** By accusing Creon of conspiracy, Oedipus reveals that he is prone to fits of temper and irrational accusations against others.

a criminal, will not be punished only
because he is my kinsman.

CREON: This is but just—
but tell me, then, of what offense I'm guilty?

46 **OEDIPUS:** Did you or did you not urge me to send
to this prophetic mumbler?

CREON: I did indeed,
and I shall stand by what I told you.

OEDIPUS: How long ago is it since Laius. . . .

CREON: What about Laius? I don't understand.

OEDIPUS: Vanished—died—was murdered?

CREON: It is long,
a long, long time to reckon.

OEDIPUS: Was this prophet
in the profession then?

CREON: He was, and honored
as highly as he is today.

OEDIPUS: At that time did he say a word about me?

CREON: Never, at least when I was near him.

OEDIPUS: You never made a search for the dead man?

CREON: We searched, indeed, but never learned of anything.

OEDIPUS: Why did our wise old friend not say this then?

CREON: I don't know; and when I know nothing, I
usually hold my tongue.

OEDIPUS: You know this much,
and can declare this much if you are loyal.

CREON: What is it? If I know, I'll not deny it.

47 **OEDIPUS:** That he would not have said that I killed Laius
had he not met you first.

CREON: You know yourself
whether he said this, but I demand that I
should hear as much from you as you from me.

OEDIPUS: Then hear,—I'll not be proved a murderer.

CREON: Well, then. You're married to my sister.

OEDIPUS: Yes,
that I am not disposed to deny.

CREON: You rule
this country giving her an equal share
in the government?

Literary Analysis
Tragedy and Tragic Flaw
What flaw in Oedipus' character is suggested by his choosing to accuse Creon?

Enrichment

The City of Law Courts

The exchange between Oedipus and Creon in the scene on this page is very much like a modern courtroom cross-examination. To an Athenian audience, this method of finding out the facts and determining guilt, innocence, or mitigating circumstances was familiar. The Athenians themselves, as well as their detractors, spoke often of Athens as a "city of law courts" and of its citizens as devoted to litigation. Although they could poke fun at themselves, the Athenians prized their legal system because it afforded citizens a way to secure justice without violence.

OEDIPUS: Yes, everything she wants
she has from me.

CREON: And I, as thirdsman to you,
am rated as the equal of you two?

OEDIPUS: Yes, and it's there you've proved yourself false friend.

CREON: Not if you will reflect on it as I do.
Consider, first, if you think any one
would choose to rule and fear rather than rule
and sleep untroubled by a fear if power
were equal in both cases. I, at least,
I was not born with such a frantic yearning
to be a king—but to do what kings do.
And so it is with every one who has learned
wisdom and self-control. As it stands now,
the prizes are all mine—and without fear.
But if I were the king myself, I must
do much that went against the grain.
How should despotic[45] rule seem sweeter to me
than painless power and an assured authority?
I am not so besotted[46] yet that I
want other honors than those that come with profit.
Now every man's my pleasure; every man greets me;
now those who are your suitors fawn on me,—
success for them depends upon my favor.
Why should I let all this go to win that?
My mind would not be traitor if it's wise;
I am no treason lover, of my nature,
nor would I ever dare to join a plot.
Prove what I say. Go to the oracle
at Pytho and inquire about the answers,
if they are as I told you. For the rest,
if you discover I laid any plot
together with the seer, kill me, I say,
not only by your vote but by my own.
But do not charge me on obscure opinion
without some proof to back it. It's not just
lightly to count your knaves as honest men,
nor honest men as knaves. To throw away
an honest friend is, as it were, to throw
your life away, which a man loves the best.
In time you will know all with certainty;
time is the only test of honest men,
one day is space enough to know a rogue.

45. despotic (des pät′ ik) *adj.* absolute; unlimited; tyrannical.
46. besotted (bē sät′ əd) *v.* stupefied; foolish.

Reading Strategy
Reading Drama How do you think the actor playing Oedipus should react as Creon is making this speech?

Reading Check
What does Oedipus accuse Creon of doing?

48 Background

Political Philosophy

Creon here is expressing the political philosophy of those citizens who preferred not being involved in politics but still reaped the benefits of empire, such as those Pericles mentions in the *Funeral Oration:* security and a flourishing city with all its civic and religious festivals, its consumer goods, and its intellectual life.

49 Reading Strategy

Reading Drama

- Remind students that actors cannot simply stand on stage and wait to speak their next lines. They must react to the dialogue and action on stage at all times.
- **Ask** students the Reading Strategy question: How do you think the actor playing Oedipus should react as Creon is making this speech?
  Possible response: Oedipus must convey disbelief in reaction to Creon's speech, as the alternative is to turn the guilty eye on himself.

50 Reading Check

Answer: Oedipus accuses Creon of prompting Teiresias to suggest that he, Oedipus, is guilty of Laius' murder.

Differentiated Instruction Solutions for All Learners

Support for Less Proficient Readers
Some students may have difficulty recognizing Oedipus' tragic flaws in his exchange of words with Creon. To model a way of identifying tragic flaws, give students a copy of **Literary Analysis Graphic Organizer B**, p. 89 in ***Graphic Organizer Transparencies.*** The completed graphic organizer will give students insight into the process of identifying heroic qualities and tragic flaws. Students can use the process as a model for making their own observations about characters as they read. Finally, discuss with students the flaws that Oedipus manifests during this scene.

Enrichment for Gifted/Talented Students
Have students complete a *Lawyer/Witness* chart for the exchange between Creon and Oedipus beginning at line 622. Ask students to define the goal of each speaker and the tactics each speaker uses to accomplish his goal. Invite students to prepare a dramatic reading of this scene for the class using this chart as a guide. Students may enjoy staging this exchange within the setting of a courtroom they create within the classroom.

51 Reading Strategy
Reading Drama

- Review with the class the functions of the chorus in Greek drama. Have students recall that the chorus comments on the dramatic action and sets it in the overall context of Greek life and religion.
- Remind students that the chorus may also occasionally advise the characters or express sympathy with the tragic hero.
- Then, **ask** students the Reading Strategy question: From their words in lines 692–693, as well as in lines 709–711, what do you think the chorus wants Oedipus to do?
Answer: The chorus favors moderation and reconciliation.

52 Background
Pericles

Oedipus' viewpoint is very close to Pericles' rhetoric as reported by Thucydides. Seeing Oedipus as specifically one of them, a recognizable contemporary Athenian type, involves the audience on multiple levels.

CHORUS: His words are wise, king, if one fears to fall.
Those who are quick of temper are not safe.

OEDIPUS: When he that plots against me secretly
moves quickly, I must quickly counterplot.
If I wait taking no decisive measure
his business will be done, and mine be spoiled.

CREON: What do you want to do then? Banish me?

OEDIPUS: No, certainly; kill you, not banish you.

CREON: I do not think that you've your wits about you.

OEDIPUS: For my own interests, yes.

CREON: But for mine, too,
you should think equally.

OEDIPUS: You are a rogue.

CREON: Suppose you do not understand?

OEDIPUS: But yet
I must be ruler.

CREON: Not if you rule badly.

OEDIPUS: O, city, city!

CREON: I too have some share
in the city; it is not yours alone.

CHORUS: Stop, my lords! Here—and in the nick of time
I see Jocasta coming from the house;
with her help lay the quarrel that now stirs you.

[*Enter* JOCASTA.]

JOCASTA: For shame! Why have you raised this foolish squabbling
brawl? Are you not ashamed to air your private
griefs when the country's sick? Go in, you, Oedipus,
and you, too, Creon, into the house. Don't magnify
your nothing troubles.

CREON: Sister, Oedipus,
your husband, thinks he has the right to do
terrible wrongs—he has but to choose between
two terrors: banishing or killing me.

OEDIPUS: He's right, Jocasta; for I find him plotting
with knavish[47] tricks against my person.

CREON: That God may never bless me! May I die
accursed, if I have been guilty of
one tittle[48] of the charge you bring against me!

Reading Strategy
Reading Drama From their words in lines 692–693, as well as in lines 709–711, what do you think the chorus wants Oedipus to do?

47. **knavish** (nāv′ ish) *adj.* deceitful.
48. **tittle** (tit′ 'l) *n.* very small particle.

Enrichment
The Chorus

Even scholars familiar with the conventions of ancient tragedy have poked fun at the way tragic choruses always seem to miss the point—for example, by not noticing even a murder taking place within earshot or by participating in a lyric outburst that seems irrelevant. The role of the chorus is very important, however; in some ways the chorus is like us, both engaged and passive, both a participant and an observer. The members of the chorus were citizens; many members of the audience would have danced and sung in the chorus. For Sophocles' audience, a member of the chorus is in some way Everyman, an Athenian citizen.

JOCASTA: I beg you, Oedipus, trust him in this,
spare him for the sake of this his oath to God,
for my sake, and the sake of those who stand here.

CHORUS: Be gracious, be merciful,
we beg of you.

OEDIPUS: In what would you have me yield?

CHORUS: He has been no silly child in the past.
He is strong in his oath now.
Spare him.

OEDIPUS: Do you know what you ask?

CHORUS: Yes.

OEDIPUS: Tell me then.

CHORUS: He has been your friend before all men's eyes; do not cast
him away dishonored on an obscure conjecture.

53 **OEDIPUS:** I would have you know that this request of yours
really requests my death or banishment.

CHORUS: May the Sun God,[49] king of Gods, forbid! May I die
without God's blessing, without friends' help, if I had any such
thought. But my spirit is broken by my unhappiness for my
wasting country; and this would but add troubles
amongst ourselves to the other troubles.

OEDIPUS: Well, let him go then—if I must die ten times for it,
or be sent out dishonored into exile.
It is your lips that prayed for him I pitied,
not his; wherever he is, I shall hate him.

CREON: I see you sulk in yielding and you're dangerous
when you are out of temper; natures like yours
are justly heaviest for themselves to bear.

OEDIPUS: Leave me alone! Take yourself off, I tell you.

CREON: I'll go, you have not known me, but they have,
and they have known my innocence.

[*Exit.*]

CHORUS: Won't you take him inside, lady?

54 **JOCASTA:** Yes, when I've found out what was the matter.

CHORUS: There was some misconceived suspicion of a story, and
on the other side the sting of injustice.

JOCASTA: So, on both sides?

CHORUS: Yes.

JOCASTA: What was the story?

49. **Sun God** Apollo.

Literary Analysis
Tragedy Is Oedipus' interpretation of his own situation justified? Why or why not?

55 **Reading Check**
How does Oedipus want to punish Creon?

Differentiated Instruction
Solutions for All Learners

Enrichment for Gifted/Talented Students
Refer students to the exchange between Oedipus and Creon, lines 705–708. Point out that Oedipus and Creon are expressing differing views about government. Organize students into small groups. Have them research the fundamental differences between two political parties of their own choosing. After students have finished conducting research, have them brainstorm a list of possible campaign slogans for each party. Then, have students design campaign banners emblazoned with the slogans.

Enrichment for Advanced Students
Organize students into small groups. Have them research the fundamental differences between two political parties of their own choosing. After students have finished conducting research, have them brainstorm a list of possible campaign slogans for each party. The slogans should reflect the spirit and ideology of each party in a single concise statement. Students should present their slogans to the class, explaining the values or beliefs central to each party.

53 Literary Analysis
Tragedy
- Call on volunteers to identify previous points in the play at which Oedipus has expressed concern or anxiety about either violence or conspiracy against him. (Students may cite lines 159–164, 428–436, 449–455, and 595–610.)
- **Ask** students the Literary Analysis question: Is Oedipus' interpretation of his own situation justified? Why or why not?
Possible response: Oedipus' interpretation is unjustified because he has been unable to provide objective evidence that Creon is plotting against him.

54 Reading Strategy
Reading Drama
- Stress once again that when students read drama, they should try to form a mental picture of the action onstage.
- Tell students that a dramatic performance is seldom, if ever, static. The action in drama is driven by dialogue. In addition to the words they utter, speakers of dialogue use nonverbal means of communication—gestures and facial expressions—to convey meaning.
- Point out that Jocasta, in her first scene in the play, is responding to a crisis (a public quarrel between her brother and her husband) by seeking the truth of the situation.
- **Ask** students: In what ways do Jocasta's actions parallel those of her husband earlier in the play?
Possible response: Jocasta evinces the same urgency and determination to get to the bottom of the situation (line 758) as Oedipus did. Her questioning of Oedipus eerily recalls his earlier interrogation of Creon. Sophocles again speeds up the pace with rapid-fire questions and answers.

55 Reading Check
Answer: Oedipus wants to kill Creon.

56 Background

Ship-of-State

Draw students' attention to the implicit ship-of-state metaphor in lines 768–772. Have students think about why it is particularly appropriate for the Athenian maritime empire to think of rule in terms of navigation.

Speaking to the Athenians after the plague and working up enthusiasm for war, Pericles says: "I too have never mentioned it before, nor would I now, because the claim may seem too arrogant, if I did not see that you are unreasonably depressed. You think your empire is confined to your allies, but I say that of the two divisions of the world accessible to man, the land and the sea, there is one of which you are the absolute masters, and have, or may have the dominion to any extent which you please."

57 Critical Viewing

Possible response: This photograph emphasizes the individual, human qualities of the tragic hero while implying a static conformity on the part of the community.

CHORUS: I think it best, in the interests of the country, to leave it where it ended.

OEDIPUS: You see where you have ended, straight of judgment although you are, by softening my anger.

56 **CHORUS:** Sir, I have said before and I say again—be sure that I would have been proved a madman, bankrupt in sane council, if I should put you away, you who steered the country I love safely when she was crazed with troubles. God grant that now, too, you may prove a fortunate guide for us.

JOCASTA: Tell me, my lord, I beg of you, what was it that roused your anger so?

OEDIPUS: Yes, I will tell you.
I honor you more than I honor them.
It was Creon and the plots he laid against me.

JOCASTA: Tell me—if you can clearly tell the quarrel—

OEDIPUS: Creon says
that I'm the murderer of Laius.

JOCASTA: Of his own knowledge or on information?

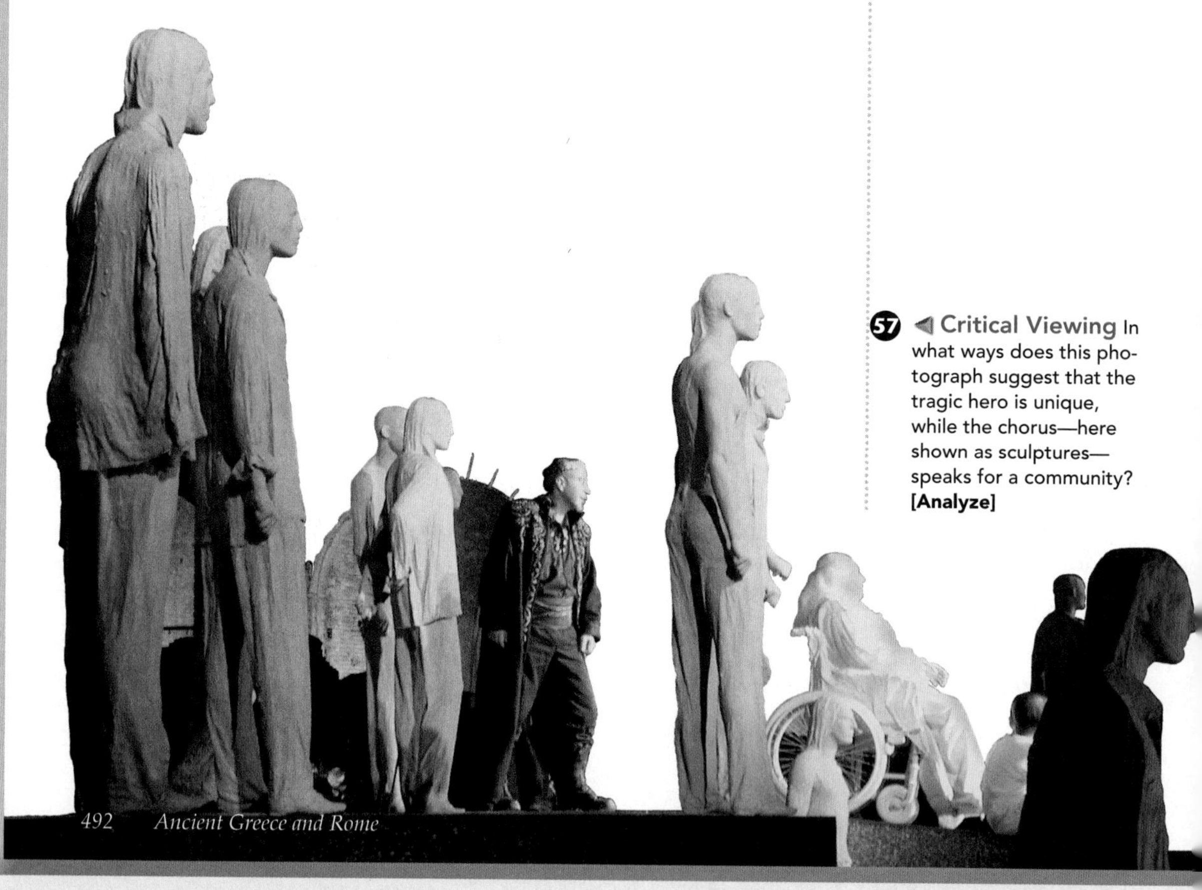

57 ◀ **Critical Viewing** In what ways does this photograph suggest that the tragic hero is unique, while the chorus—here shown as sculptures—speaks for a community? **[Analyze]**

Enrichment

Tragedy Then and Now

While Sophocles fulfilled the requirements for tragedy set forth by Aristotle in his *Poetics,* drama evolved and changed over history, so modern dramatists do not now feel that they must remain within the confines of Aristotle's famous definition. Hedda Gabler, in Henrik Ibsen's *Hedda Gabler,* and Blanche DuBois, in Tennessee Williams's *A Streetcar Named Desire,* for example, are not of noble birth or character. They are, on the other hand, very ordinary characters with whom the audience can identify.

Two other requirements for tragedy, however, do survive in modern drama: that the audience be made to feel pity and terror, and that at the end, a catharsis, a cleansing, purification, or purging of the emotions, takes place. In other words, the audience sympathizes with and fears for the protagonist, and then feels emotionally drained or exhausted at the end of the play.

OEDIPUS: He sent this rascal prophet to me, since
he keeps his own mouth clean of any guilt.

JOCASTA: Do not concern yourself about this matter;
listen to me and learn that human beings
have no part in the craft of prophecy.
Of that I'll show you a short proof.
There was an oracle once that came to Laius,—
I will not say that it was Phoebus' own,
but it was from his servants—and it told him
that it was fate that he should die a victim
at the hands of his own son, a son to be born
of Laius and me. But, see now, he,
the king, was killed by foreign highway robbers
58 at a place where three roads meet—so goes the story;
and for the son—before three days were out
after his birth King Laius pierced his ankles
and by the hands of others cast him forth
upon a pathless hillside. So Apollo
failed to fulfill his oracle to the son,
that he should kill his father, and to Laius
also proved false in that the thing he feared,
death at his son's hands, never came to pass.
So clear in this case were the oracles,
so clear and false. Give them no heed, I say;
what God discovers need of, easily
he shows to us himself.

OEDIPUS: O dear Jocasta,
as I hear this from you, there comes upon me
a wandering of the soul—I could run mad.

JOCASTA: What trouble is it, that you turn again
and speak like this?

59 **OEDIPUS:** I thought I heard you say
that Laius was killed at a crossroads.

JOCASTA: Yes, that was how the story went and still
that word goes round.

OEDIPUS: Where is this place, Jocasta,
where he was murdered?

JOCASTA: Phocis is the country
and the road splits there, one of two roads from Delphi,
another comes from Daulia.

OEDIPUS: How long ago is this?

JOCASTA: The news came to the city just before
you became king and all men's eyes looked to you.
What is it, Oedipus, that's in your mind?

Reading Strategy
Reading Drama From Oedipus' comment in lines 808–810, how do you think he should react during Jocasta's long speech in lines 784–807?

60 **Reading Check**
According to Jocasta, what did the oracle say would happen to Laius?

58 Critical Thinking

Analyze

- Read aloud the bracketed passage. Then, **ask** students to discuss how Jocasta's "proof" that oracles are meaningless and should not be heeded actually proves the opposite of what she intends.
  Possible response: Jocasta does not know that Oedipus actually killed Laius, nor does she know that Oedipus is a product of her union with Laius. Thus, she believes that Laius' death prevented the oracle's prophesy from coming true.
- **Ask:** What meaning is evident in Jocasta's concluding statement that Apollo shows what he wants to reveal by himself?
  Possible response: Jocasta seems to believe that humans will receive the information they need from Apollo himself, not from oracles or any other sources. She discredits the idea that Apollo speaks through others.

59 Reading Strategy

Reading Drama

- Have students read Jocasta and Oedipus' brief dialogue in lines 808–816. Make sure that students recognize the detail that snags Oedipus' attention (the crossroads).
- **Ask** students the Reading Strategy question: From Oedipus' comment in lines 808–810, how do you think he should react during Jocasta's long speech in lines 784–807?
  Possible response: At the mention of the crossroads (line 795), Oedipus should betray increasing anxiety and stress. The actor playing Oedipus might convey these emotions through facial expressions, movements, or posture. (On the Athenian stage, of course, the actor would not have the option of using facial expressions.)

60 Reading Check

Answer: The oracle said Laius would die a victim at the hands of his own son.

61 Background

Drama

According to tradition, the dramas that preceded true Greek tragedy featured only one character, who interacted with a chorus. The Greek tragedian Aeschylus (525–456 B.C.) is credited with introducing the second speaking character.

In the bracketed scene, Sophocles demonstrates the power of dialogue, the dramatic form that Aeschylus' innovation made possible. Because Oedipus is speaking to Jocasta, his exclamations to Zeus take on a heart-rending force they might not otherwise have. Jocasta does not yet see the implications of the information she reports to Oedipus. His exclamations make clear that he does. The dialogue between the two thus creates a charged, dramatic tension between Jocasta's ignorance and Oedipus' knowledge, between the happenstance facts of the past and what they mean for Oedipus' fate.

Here, it is not so much what dialogue allows characters to say that creates drama. Instead, it is what the form of dialogue allows to emerge as *unsaid,* as what will soon be said, that adds intense pathos and suspense to this scene.

62 Literary Analysis

Tragedy

- Point out that both Jocasta and Oedipus express fear to each other.
- **Ask** students: Why is Jocasta frightened? What is Oedipus' deadly fear? **Possible response:** At this point, Jocasta has no inkling of the fate that is gathering about them; she is frightened only by Oedipus' agitated behavior and desperate words. Oedipus' fears stem from his suspicion that his personal history—and his identity—are unraveling before his eyes. He may not have escaped the parricidal oracle; he may, in ignorance, have cursed and condemned himself.

OEDIPUS: What have you designed, O Zeus, to do with me?

JOCASTA: What is the thought that troubles your heart?

OEDIPUS: Don't ask me yet—tell me of Laius—
How did he look? How old or young was he?

(61)

JOCASTA: He was a tall man and his hair was grizzled
already—nearly white—and in his form
not unlike you.

OEDIPUS: O God, I think I have
called curses on myself in ignorance.

JOCASTA: What do you mean? I am terrified
when I look at you.

OEDIPUS: I have a deadly fear
that the old seer had eyes. You'll show me more
if you can tell me one more thing.

JOCASTA: I will.
I'm frightened,—but if I can understand,
I'll tell you all you ask.

OEDIPUS: How was his company?
Had he few with him when he went this journey,
or many servants, as would suit a prince?

JOCASTA: In all there were but five, and among them
a herald;[50] and one carriage for the king.

OEDIPUS: It's plain—it's plain—who was it told you this?

JOCASTA: The only servant that escaped safe home.

OEDIPUS: Is he at home now?

JOCASTA: No, when he came home again
and saw you king and Laius was dead,
he came to me and touched my hand and begged
that I should send him to the fields to be
my shepherd and so he might see the city
as far off as he might. So I
sent him away. He was an honest man,
as slaves go, and was worthy of far more
than what he asked of me.

OEDIPUS: O, how I wish that he could come back quickly!

JOCASTA: He can. Why is your heart so set on this?

(62)

OEDIPUS: O dear Jocasta, I am full of fears
that I have spoken far too much; and therefore
I wish to see this shepherd.

JOCASTA: He will come;

50. herald (her´ əld) *n.* person who makes proclamations and carries messages.

Enrichment

Dashes

Dashes are punctuation marks that indicate an abrupt break in thought. Like commas, semicolons, and parentheses, dashes signal pause, but dashes signal more striking, dramatic pauses. Dashes are frequently used in punctuating fast-paced dramatic scenes to capture the quick verbal exchange of speakers.

A single dash indicates an abrupt change of thought or emphasizes additional or explanatory information at the end of a sentence.

Sometimes dashes are used in pairs to emphasize interrupting information in the middle of a sentence; double dashes set off complete sentences within a construction.

Ask students to identify the ways in which dashes are used in the following lines: 779, 788–793, 793–799, 808–810, 823–825, 831–832, 838, and 865–868.

but, Oedipus, I think I'm worthy too
to know what it is that disquiets you.

OEDIPUS: It shall not be kept from you, since my mind
has gone so far with its forebodings. Whom
should I confide in rather than you, who is there
of more importance to me who have passed
through such a fortune?
Polybus was my father, king of Corinth,[51]
and Merope, the Dorian,[52] my mother.
I was held greatest of the citizens
in Corinth till a curious chance befell me
63 as I shall tell you—curious, indeed,
but hardly worth the store I set upon it.
There was a dinner and at it a man,
a drunken man, accused me in his drink
of being bastard. I was furious

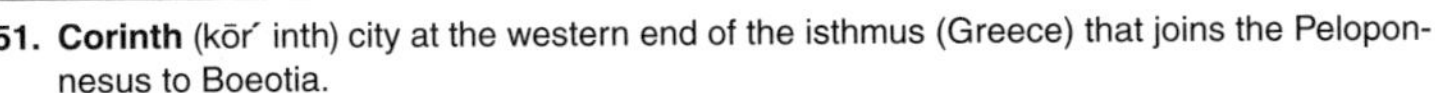

51. **Corinth** (kôr′ inth) city at the western end of the isthmus (Greece) that joins the Peloponnesus to Boeotia.
52. **Dorian** (dôr′ ē ən) *n.* one of the main branches of the Hellenes; the Dorians invaded the Peloponnesus.

Literary Analysis
Tragedy How does Oedipus' story about growing up in Corinth relate to Jocasta's description of Laius' murder?

64 **Reading Check**
What does the servant ask of Jocasta when he sees that Laius is dead and Oedipus is king?

Literature in Context

65 History Connection

The Theater of Dionysus at Athens

The great dramatic festivals of fifth-century Athens were staged in the Theater of Dionysus, an immense, semicircular, open-air theater set on the slope of the Acropolis (ə kräp′ ə lis). The theater held seventeen thousand spectators, who sat on long benches. The front row contained stone chairs with backs, which were reserved for priests and government officials. The performance area included a level circular area called the orchestra, or "dancing space." Beyond the orchestra stood the altar of the god Dionysus, and beyond that, the stage where the actors performed. Although scholars once believed that the masks the actors wore functioned like bullhorns, making their voices audible to the thousands of spectators, scholars now think that the theater was simply a perfect acoustical space in which even the smallest whisper could easily be heard.

Connect to the Literature

How do you think the performance space in the Theater of Dionysus would affect your experience of *Oedipus the King*?

Differentiated Instruction
Solutions for All Learners

For Special Needs Students
Have students reread Oedipus' long speech (lines 858–929) and then create timelines that list each event he describes. Tell students that the events must appear in chronological order. Students should find illustrations in magazines or draw images for each point on their timelines. In a subsequent discussion, ask students to explain how each event leads to the next.

For Less Proficient Readers
Have students reread Oedipus' long speech (lines 858–929) and then create timelines that list each event he describes. Tell students to make sure that their timelines are accurate. Students should find illustrations in magazines or draw images for each point on their timelines. Organize students into small groups in which they will present their timelines and explain how one event leads to another.

63 Literary Analysis
Tragedy
- Have a volunteer read aloud the bracketed passage. **Ask** students the Literary Analysis question: How does Oedipus' story about growing up in Corinth relate to Jocasta's description of Laius' murder?
  Possible response: Both stories involve a prophecy of parricide. Oedipus' tale complicates the plot by introducing the possibility that he was not truly the son of King Polybus of Corinth. Later, Oedipus also mentions his encounter at a crossroads, where he angrily killed an elderly traveler who had assaulted him. Oedipus begins to suspect that he may be guilty of the murder of Laius.

64 Reading Check
Answer: The servant asks Jocasta to send him to the countryside, far from the city, where he might work as a shepherd.

65 Literature in Context
The Theater of Dionysus at Athens Greek drama was not just entertainment; it was linked with sacred ritual and with Athenian social and political systems. The stage included an altar, and priests and public officials sat in the front row. The performance of plays might have originated as concerts—choral singing and dancing in ritual observance of a military victory or a seasonal festival. The singing and formal movements of the chorus in *Oedipus the King* reflect the ritual beginnings of Greek drama.

Connect to the Literature Have students discuss how public spaces such as theaters and sports facilities affect their enjoyment of a production or contest. Ask: What do you think it would be like to see *Oedipus the King* in the Theatre of Dionysus?
Possible response: Watching this play in an outdoor setting would be an extraordinary experience because of the large audience and the dignity of the surroundings. However, the scenery and noise might be distracting.

66 Critical Thinking

Make a Judgment

- Tell students that some critics have faulted Oedipus for fleeing and trying to escape his destiny.
- Lead students in a discussion about what they would have done under the circumstances and how they feel about Oedipus' attempt to take action rather than to submit passively.

67 Literary Analysis

Tragedy

- Point out to students that Oedipus uses a matter-of-fact tone as he recounts details of a mass killing: "And then I killed them all" (lines 907–908). **Ask** students how they are affected by Oedipus' description. What aspects of his character are reinforced by the way he tells this story?
  Possible response: Oedipus reveals the short temper that is contributing to his downfall.
- Discuss some of the inherent ironies in Oedipus' account; for example, he is on foot as he encounters the very man who lamed him as an infant. He kills Laius with his walking stick.

but held my temper under for that day.
Next day I went and taxed[53] my parents with it;
they took the insult very ill from him,
the drunken fellow who had uttered it.
So I was comforted for their part, but
still this thing rankled[54] always, for the story
crept about widely. And I went at last
to Pytho, though my parents did not know.
But Phoebus sent me home again unhonored
in what I came to learn, but he foretold
other and desperate horrors to befall me,
that I was fated to lie with my mother,
and show to daylight an accursed breed
which men would not endure, and I was doomed
to be murderer of the father that begot me.
When I heard this I fled, and in the days
that followed I would measure from the stars
the whereabouts of Corinth—yes, I fled
66 to somewhere where I should not see fulfilled
the infamies[55] told in that dreadful oracle.
And as I journeyed I came to the place
where, as you say, this king met with his death.
Jocasta, I will tell you the whole truth.
When I was near the branching of the crossroads,
going on foot, I was encountered by
a herald and a carriage with a man in it,
just as you tell me. He that led the way
and the old man himself wanted to thrust me
out of the road by force. I became angry
and struck the coachman who was pushing me.
When the old man saw this he watched his moment,
and as I passed he struck me from his carriage,
full on the head with his two pointed goad.[56]
But he was paid in full and presently
my stick had struck him backwards from the car
67 and he rolled out of it. And then I killed them
all. If it happened there was any tie
of kinship twixt this man and Laius,
who is then now more miserable than I,
what man on earth so hated by the Gods,
since neither citizen nor foreigner
may welcome me at home or even greet me,

---

53. **taxed** (takst) *v.* imposed a burden on; put a strain on.
54. **rankled** (raŋ′ keld) *v.* caused to have long-lasting anger and resentment.
55. **infamies** (in′ fə mēz) *n.* items of notorious disgrace and dishonor.
56. **goad** (gōd) *n.* sharp, pointed stick used to drive animals.

Enrichment

Fate

For the ancient Greeks, fate could be visualized like weaving: The parameters are fixed, as are some elements of the final cloth; some variation is possible, but it will not change the size of the cloth. What *Oedipus the King* reveals is that because they are human, all mortals have limited vision. For Aristotle, being who you are, in the culture or situation that constrains you, prevents you from understanding the information at hand.

but drive me out of doors? And it is I,
I and no other have so cursed myself.
And I pollute the bed of him I killed
by the hands that killed him. Was I not born evil?
Am I not utterly unclean? I had to fly
and in my banishment not even see
my kindred nor set foot in my own country,
or otherwise my fate was to be yoked
in marriage with my mother and kill my father,
Polybus who begot me and had reared me.
Would not one rightly judge and say that on me
these things were sent by some malignant God?
O no, no, no—O holy majesty
of God on high, may I not see that day!
May I be gone out of men's sight before
I see the deadly taint of this disaster
come upon me.

CHORUS: Sir, we too fear these things. But until you see this man face to face and hear his story, hope.

OEDIPUS: Yes, I have just this much of hope—to wait until the herdsman comes.

JOCASTA: And when he comes, what do you want with him?

OEDIPUS: I'll tell you; if I find that his story is the same as yours, I at least will be clear of this guilt.

JOCASTA: Why what so particularly did you learn from my story?

OEDIPUS: You said that he spoke of highway *robbers* who killed Laius. Now if he uses the same number, it was not I who killed him. One man cannot be the same as many. But if he speaks of a man travelling alone, then clearly the burden of the guilt inclines toward me.

JOCASTA: Be sure, at least, that this was how he told the story. He cannot unsay it now, for every one in the city heard it—not I alone. But, Oedipus, even if he diverges from what he said then, he shall never prove that the murder of Laius squares rightly with the prophecy—for Loxias declared that the king should be killed by his own son. And that poor creature did not kill him surely,—for he died himself first. So as far as prophecy goes, henceforward I shall not look to the right hand or the left.

OEDIPUS: Right. But yet, send some one for the peasant to bring him here; do not neglect it.

Vocabulary Builder
malignant (mə lig′ nənt) *adj.* very harmful

Literary Analysis
Tragedy On what details in the tale of Laius' murder does Oedipus base his hope that he is innocent?

Reading Check
What did Oedipus do to avoid fulfilling the horrors he was told awaited him?

68 Literary Analysis

Tragedy

- Ask students to review Jocasta's words in line 794. Point out that earlier in the play, Creon had referred to "robbers" in the plural when describing Laius' murder (line 141). Oedipus, surely unconsciously, changes the word to "robber" in the singular in line 144.
- Then, **ask** students the Literary Analysis question: On what details in the tale of Laius' murder does Oedipus base his hope that he is innocent?
  Answer: If the herdsman sticks to his story about "robbers," Oedipus believes that he can rest easy.

69 Reading Check

Answer: Oedipus fled Corinth, thinking that by doing so he would avoid his terrible fate.

Differentiated Instruction
Solutions for All Learners

Strategy for Advanced Readers

Lead students in a discussion about the way in which communication varies depending on the speaker's relationship to the listener. Ask students how people who are involved in romantic relationships communicate with each other. Record their responses on the board. Ask students how people who are involved in familial relationships communicate with one another. Record their responses on the board.

As Oedipus begins his speech at line 858, he speaks to Jocasta in a way appropriate to a loving husband confiding in his wife. However, his manner of speaking is also suggestive of the ways in which Jocasta is the closest kin he has. Ask students how awareness of the double relationship between Oedipus and Jocasta positions the audience to listen to the narrative. Have students write an essay analyzing the different ways in which Oedipus, Jocasta, and the audience can interpret the past events that Oedipus relates.

70 Literary Analysis

Tragedy

- Have students **paraphrase** the words of the chorus in the first strophe.
  Possible response: May I always obey the laws of the gods, which are unchanging and immortal.
- Have students explore how the chorus contrasts the pious person with the insolent tyrant in the antistrophe (lines 967–974).
- Call on volunteers to read aloud the second strophe and antistrophe.
- Then, **ask** students: In what ways do the second strophe and antistrophe present two different viewpoints about the relationship between the gods and humanity?
  Possible response: In the second strophe, the chorus seems confident that the gods will strike down the haughty and the lawless. In the second antistrophe, however, the chorus seems pessimistic about divine fulfillment of oracles and declares that its members may not participate in traditional worship if the gods fail them.
- Then, **ask** students the Literary Analysis question: How do you think this ode may have affected the audience? Explain.
  Possible response: At a moment of great tension in the drama, this passage enlists the audience's support of the play's fated outcome—whatever the audience's sympathy for Oedipus. The ode encourages this response by praising divine law, condemning those who reject that law, and then calling on the gods not to fail to enforce that law in the case of Oedipus.

JOCASTA: I will send quickly. Now let me go indoors. I will do nothing except what pleases you.

[*Exit.*]

CHORUS:

Strophe

May destiny ever find me
pious in word and deed
prescribed by the laws that live on high:
laws begotten in the clear air of heaven,
whose only father is Olympus;
no mortal nature brought them to birth,
no forgetfulness shall lull them to sleep;
for God is great in them and grows not old.

Antistrophe

Insolence[57] breeds the tyrant, insolence
if it is glutted with a surfeit,[58] unseasonable, unprofitable,
climbs to the roof-top and plunges
sheer down to the ruin that must be,
and there its feet are no service.
But I pray that the God may never
abolish the eager ambition that profits the state.
For I shall never cease to hold the God as our protector.

70

Strophe

If a man walks with haughtiness
of hand or word and gives no heed
to Justice and the shrines of Gods
despises—may an evil doom
smite him for his ill-starred pride of heart!—
if he reaps gains without justice
and will not hold from impiety
and his fingers itch for untouchable things.
When such things are done, what man shall contrive
to shield his soul from the shafts of the God?
When such deeds are held in honor,
why should I honor the Gods in the dance?

Antistrophe

No longer to the holy place,
to the navel of earth I'll go
to worship, nor to Abae
nor to Olympia,
unless the oracles are proved to fit,
for all men's hands to point at.

---

57. insolence (in´ sə ləns) *n.* arrogance; bold disrespectfulness.
58. surfeit (sur´ fit) *n.* excessive supply.

Literary Analysis
Tragedy How do you think this ode may have affected the audience? Explain.

Enrichment

Road Rage in Ancient Times

Travel in antiquity (and throughout most of human history, for that matter) was a risky proposition. No police force patrolled the open road; people usually journeyed in groups for mutual protection. Solitary travelers were responsible for their own safety and prepared accordingly. Chance meetings between armed and wary strangers easily escalated into violence; thus, salutes and handshakes evolved as signals of peaceful intent. However, no such gesture forestalled the quarrel of Oedipus and Laius, an event that was ironic, fatal, and tragic—but not rare.

O Zeus, if you are rightly called
the sovereign lord, all-mastering,
let this not escape you nor your ever-living power!
The oracles concerning Laius
are old and dim and men regard them not.
Apollo is nowhere clear in honor; God's service perishes.

Critical Reading

1. **Respond:** What do you think is Oedipus' most admirable character trait? What is his worst character trait?
2. **(a) Recall:** As the play opens, what disaster has struck Thebes? **(b) Infer:** In the opening scene, what does Oedipus' response to this disaster suggest about him as a ruler?
3. **(a) Recall:** What are Oedipus' two main reasons for seeking out Laius' murderer? **(b) Analyze Cause and Effect:** How does Oedipus' curse on the murderer foreshadow, or hint at, a tragic outcome for the drama?
4. **(a) Recall:** What physical ailment afflicts Teiresias? **(b) Classify:** Which details in Teiresias' speech in lines 460–486 refer to darkness, vision, and insight? **(c) Compare and Contrast:** Compare and contrast Oedipus and Teiresias in terms of blindness and insight at the end of Part I.
5. **(a) Recall:** Of what does Oedipus accuse Creon in the scene beginning at line 576? **(b) Assess:** How convincing is Creon's argument about his own motives in lines 654–691? Explain.
6. **(a) Recall:** In lines 784–807, what reasons does Jocasta give for not having faith in prophecy? **(b) Compare and Contrast:** At this point in the play, what do both Jocasta and Oedipus seem to believe about their abilities to control their own destinies? Explain.
7. **(a) Analyze:** What role does the chorus play in clarifying both the events and characters' emotions in the play? **(b) Analyze:** In what ways does the chorus heighten the dramatic tension?
8. **(a) Interpret:** In lines 705–708—the scene between Oedipus and Creon—what insights does Sophocles provide about the rights of the ruler and of the ruled? **(b) Evaluate:** In what ways are these ideas applicable to contemporary American life? Explain.

For: More about Sophocles
Visit: www.PHSchool.com
Web Code: ete-9410

ASSESS

Answers

1. **Possible response:** Oedipus' concern for his people is admirable; his frequent anger is his worst trait.
2. (a) The plague has struck Thebes. (b) Oedipus' concern and rapid action suggest that he is a fair and responsible ruler.
3. (a) Oedipus wants to end the plague and he wants to avoid Laius' fate. (b) The murderer will turn out to be none other than Oedipus himself.
4. (a) Teiresias is blind. (b) Lines 465, 467, and 474–475 refer to darkness, vision, and insight. (c) Although he is blind, Teiresias has unlimited insight. Although he has vision, Oedipus is blind metaphorically because he is ignorant of his real identity.
5. (a) Oedipus accuses Creon of treason. (b) Creon's argument, which depends on probability, is fairly convincing.
6. (a) Jocasta says that Laius was not killed by his own son, as the oracle had foretold. She adds that the son was abandoned in infancy to die. (b) They both believe that their actions have enabled them to avoid a predicted fate.
7. (a) The chorus clarifies such events as the plague and also comments on the characters' emotions, especially those of Oedipus. (b) The chorus comments intensely on the city's suffering and on the religious issues raised by the oracles.
8. (a) Rulers must govern justly and realize that the state is composed of many different people. (b) **Possible response:** Since students live in a democracy, they may point out that more than just one leader takes part in their government. Leaders may be removed if citizens do not think they are making just decisions.

Go Online Author Link For additional information about Sophocles, have students type in the Web Code, then select *S* from the alphabet, and then select Sophocles.

Assessment Practice

Stated and Implied Main Ideas **(For more practice, see *Test Preparation Workbook*, p. 22.)**

Students may encounter questions on standardized tests that require them to identify both stated and implied main ideas. For practice, give students the following sample test question.

> But I pray that the God may never abolish
> the eager ambition that profits the state.
> For I shall never cease to hold the God as
> our protector.
>
> — from *Oedipus the King*, Part I, lines 972–974

What is the implied main idea of these lines?

A Ambition is an undesirable quality.
B God favors the prosperity of the state.
C Eagerness makes people reckless.
D God is the protector of people.

A and *C* contain ideas neither stated nor implied in the passage. *D* contains information stated directly in the passage. *B* is the correct answer.

Answers

1. **Possible response:** Oedipus is outstanding for his intelligence and his concern for his people. He is also of high status because of his noble birth as a king's son.
2. **Possible response:** In choosing to run away from the prophecy, Oedipus condemns himself to living his life in dangerous ignorance. In choosing to kill or marry anyone, Oedipus risks fulfilling the prophecy.
3. **Possible response: Action or Event:** plague; search for murderer; **Issue/Question:** religious law; Oedipus' guilt or innocence; **Choral Commentary:** wish for piety (lines 175–230); defense of his reputation (lines 526–575)
4. **Possible response:** Oedipus persists in trying to find the plague's cause, the murderer of Laius, and the truth about Laius' death.
5. (a) The chorus asserts that human knowledge is limited and that divine knowledge is beyond humans' capacity for understanding. (b) Oedipus presses on relentlessly in his quest for knowledge. (c) **Possible response:** Oedipus can gain heroic status only by going beyond the chorus' passivity.
6. (a) **Possible response:** Oedipus' quick temper and his irrational assumptions about treason and conspiracy are negative traits. (b) Any negative trait becomes tragic if its practice brings about the downfall of a character.
7. **Possible response:** The play begins in front of the palace, which shows Oedipus' royal status; the altar and priest on the stage foreshadow the religious issues in the play; children on stage as the play begins emphasize the idea of legacies.
8. **Possible response:** Lines 261–274 should probably be delivered in a tone of solemn outrage, suggested by the opening words, "I command." Lines 808–819 should probably be delivered in hushed tones of dread, suggested by Oedipus' address of "O dear Jocasta."
9. (a) **Possible response:** Leaders need to be steady, intelligent, and courageous. (b) Oedipus has—these qualities, at least to some degree.

Apply the Skills

Oedipus the King, Part I

Literary Analysis

Tragedy

1. The leading figure in a **tragedy** is usually a person of high birth or noble status who also possesses outstanding personal traits. In what ways does Oedipus meet these requirements?
2. On the basis of what you have learned in Part I, which of Oedipus' choices have determined his destiny? Explain.
3. In Greek tragedies, the chorus often comments on universal issues raised by the action. Use a chart like the one shown to cite at least two specific examples of such choral commentary.

Connecting Literary Elements

4. Trace the motif, or idea, of the search for knowledge in Part I by noting three moments in which Oedipus persists in a quest for knowledge.
5. **(a)** How does the chorus try to modify Oedipus' insistence on acquiring knowledge? **(b)** How does Oedipus respond? **(c)** How does his response affect your view of him as a **tragic hero?**
6. **(a)** What negative traits do you see in Oedipus? **(b)** Might any of these be considered a **tragic flaw?** Explain.

Reading Strategy

Reading Drama

7. As you **read drama,** stage directions supply key information. List three details that appear in the stage directions in Part I. Then, write a brief comment on the significance of each detail.
8. Note two examples of dialogue in Part I that provide hints about a character's body language or tone of voice. Explain your choices.

Extend Understanding

9. **Social Studies Connection: (a)** Identify at least three qualities a leader needs in a time of crisis. **(b)** In your view, does Oedipus possess each of these qualities?

QuickReview

A **tragedy** is a work of literature—usually a play—that portrays the downfall of a noble or outstanding person.

The main character in a tragedy is the **tragic hero** who possesses a **tragic flaw** in his or her character that leads to his or her downfall.

To **read drama,** use the stage directions and other clues in the text to picture a live performance.

For: Self-test
Visit: www.PHSchool.com
Web Code: eta-6406

Go Online Assessment Students may use the **Self-test** to prepare for **Selection Test A** or **Selection Test B.**

Build Language Skills

❶ Vocabulary Lesson

Word Analysis: Prefix *pro-*

The prefix *pro-*, as in *prophecy*, means "before in place or time" or "forward." Add the prefix *pro-* to the word roots below. Then, write a definition of each word.

1. -ceed **2.** -gnosis **3.** -logue

Spelling Strategy

In words like *malignant*, the *g* and *n* have separate sounds. Sometimes, however, *gn* stands for only the *n* sound, as in *sign*. Finish spelling the words below; then, pronounce each word.

1. bring into line: al____
2. standing water: sta__ant

Vocabulary Builder: Synonyms

Select the letter of the word that is closest in meaning to each numbered vocabulary word.

1. blight: **(a)** glow, **(b)** disease, **(c)** harvest
2. pestilence: **(a)** plague, **(b)** heat, **(c)** omen
3. prophecy: **(a)** event, **(b)** death, **(c)** prediction
4. dispatch: **(a)** respond, **(b)** kill, **(c)** resent
5. invoke: **(a)** warn, **(b)** offer, **(c)** summon
6. induced: **(a)** caused, **(b)** stopped, **(c)** held
7. countenance: **(a)** joy, **(b)** expression, **(c)** exit
8. malignant: **(a)** harmful, **(b)** dull, **(c)** edgy

❷ Grammar and Style Lesson

Participial Phrases

A participle is a form of a verb that can act as an adjective. A **participial phrase** consists of a participle and its complements and modifiers.

Present Participle: King, you yourself have seen our city reeling like a wreck . . . (modifies *city*)

Past Participle: Within the marketplace sit others crowned with suppliant garlands . . . (modifies *others*)

Practice Identify each participial phrase, and explain the word it modifies.

1. Standing before the people, Oedipus curses.
2. They speak of waves crashing on the shore.
3. Teiresias, seeing deeply, refuses to answer.
4. Disturbed by his anger, the chorus urges calm.
5. Jocasta recalls a prophecy delivered by Apollo's servant.

Writing Application Write a paragraph describing an event that you recently witnessed. Include at least three participial phrases.

WG Prentice Hall Writing and Grammar Connection: Platinum Level, Chapter 20, Section 1

❸ Extend Your Learning

Writing Write a **news article** about the events in the play so far. Include details to address the 5 *w's*: *Who? What? When? Where? Why?*

Listening and Speaking Present a **dramatic reading** of a speech from Part I. Include music that complements the mood of the speech.

Assessment Resources

The following resources can be used to assess students' knowledge and skills.

Unit 4 Resources
- **Selection Test A**, pp. 112–114
- **Selection Test B**, pp. 115–117

General Resources
- **Rubrics for Response to Literature**, pp. 55–56

Go Online Assessment — Students may use the **Self-test** to prepare for **Selection Test A** or **Selection Test B.**

EXTEND/ASSESS

Answers

❶ Vocabulary Lesson

Word Analysis: Prefix *pro-*

1. proceed; move forward
2. prognosis; likely outlook
3. prologue; introduction

Spelling Strategy

1. align 2. stagnant

Vocabulary Builder: Synonyms

1. b 3. c 5. c 7. b
2. a 4. b 6. a 8. a

❷ Grammar and Style Lesson

1. "Standing—people"; modifies *Oedipus*
2. "Crashing—shore"; modifies *waves*
3. "Seeing deeply"; modifies *Teiresias*
4. "Disturbed—anger"; modifies *chorus*
5. "Delivered—servant"; modifies *prophecy*

Writing Application

Possible response: Fearing for its safety, the girl chased the dog from the road. The dog, **not knowing she was friendly,** growled. The police officer **assigned to that area** alerted animal control.

WG Writing and Grammar Platinum Level

For support in teaching the Grammar and Style Lesson, use Chapter 20, Section 1.

❸ Writing

- Remind students that their lead should contain the most compelling information in the story.
- The **Support for Extend Your Learning** page (*Unit 4 Resources*, p. 110) provides guided note-taking opportunities to help students complete the Extend Your Learning activities.
- Use the Response to Literature rubrics, pp. 55–56 in *General Resources* to evaluate students' work.

 Oedipus the King, **Part II**

Standard Course of Study

Goal 4: CRITICAL THINKING

CT.4.01.1	Interpret and make generalizations supported by specific references.
CT.4.02.3	Examine how elements such as irony and symbolism impact theme.

Goal 5: LITERATURE

LT.5.01.3	Analyze literary devices and explain their effect on the work of world literature.
LT.5.01.5	Analyze archetypal characters, themes, and settings in world literature.
LT.5.03.9	Analyze and evaluate the effects of author's craft and style in world literature.
LT.5.03.10	Analyze connections between ideas, concepts, characters and experiences in world literature.

Step-by-Step Teaching Guide	Pacing Guide
PRETEACH	
• Administer Vocabulary and Reading Warm-ups as necessary.	5 min.
• Engage students' interest with the motivation activity.	5 min.
• Read and discuss author and background features. **FT**	10 min.
• Introduce the Literary Analysis Skill: Irony. **FT**	5 min.
• Introduce the Reading Strategy: Questioning the Characters' Motives. **FT**	10 min.
• Prepare students to read by teaching the selection vocabulary. **FT**	
TEACH	
• Informally monitor comprehension while students read independently or in groups. **FT**	30 min.
• Monitor students' comprehension with the Reading Check notes.	as students read
• Reinforce vocabulary with Vocabulary Builder notes.	as students read
• Develop students' understanding of irony with the Literary Analysis annotations. **FT**	5 min.
• Develop students' ability to question the characters' motives with the Reading Strategy annotations. **FT**	5 min.
ASSESS/EXTEND	
• Assess students' comprehension and mastery of the Literary Analysis and Reading Strategy by having them answer the Apply the Skills questions. **FT**	15 min.
• Have students complete the Vocabulary Lesson and the Grammar and Style Lesson. **FT**	15 min.
• Apply students' ability to organize details into paragraphs by using the Writing Lesson. **FT**	45 min. or homework
• Apply students' understanding by using one or more of the Extend Your Learning activities.	20–90 min. or homework
• Administer Selection Test A or Selection Test B. **FT**	15 min.

Resources

Print

Unit 4 Resources

Transparency

Graphic Organizer Transparencies

Print

Reader's Notebook [L2]

Reader's Notebook: Adapted Version [L1]

Reader's Notebook: English Learner's Version [EL]

Unit 4 Resources

Technology

Listening to Literature Audio CDs [L2, EL]

Print

Unit 4 Resources

General Resources

Technology

Go Online: Research **[L3]**
Go Online: Self-test **[L3]**
***ExamView®*, Test Bank [L3]**

Choosing Resources for Differentiated Instruction

[L1] Special Needs Students
[L2] Below-Level Students
[L3] All Students
[L4] Advanced Students
[EL] English Learners

For Vocabulary and Reading Warm-ups and for Selection Tests, **A** signifies "less challenging" and **B** "more challenging." For Graphic Organizer transparencies, **A** signifies "not filled in" and **B** "filled in."

FT Fast Track Instruction: To move the lesson more quickly, use the strategies and activities identified with **FT**.

Scaffolding for Less Proficient and Advanced Students

The leveled Critical Thinking questions after selections progress in the levels of thinking required to answer them. To address the needs of your different students, you may use the (a) level questions for your less proficient students and the (b) level questions with your on-level and advanced students. The occasional (c) level questions are appropriate for your advanced students.

PRENTICE HALL **TeacherEXPRESS™** Plan · Teach · Assess Use this complete suite of powerful teaching tools to make lesson planning and testing quicker and easier.

PRENTICE HALL **StudentEXPRESS™** Learn · Study · Succeed Use the interactive textbook (online and on CD-ROM) to make selections and activities come alive with audio and video support and interactive questions.

Go Online Professional Development **For:** Information about Lexiles
Visit: www.PHSchool.com
Web Code: eue-1111

PRETEACH

❶ Literary Analysis

Irony

- Tell students that as they read Part II of the play, they will focus on irony. Review the three types of irony: verbal, situational, and dramatic. Call on volunteers to provide an example of each type, either from Part I of the play or from everyday life.
- Remind students that the notion of dramatic irony applies to the entire play. Because the ancient audience was already familiar with the broad outlines of the Oedipus myth, they knew of Oedipus' guilt from the beginning. Every key incident in the play is colored by dramatic irony.
- As they read, make sure students focus on linking Sophocles' use of dramatic irony to his manipulation of suspense. Ask students to consider how these two elements reinforce each other in Part II.

❷ Reading Strategy

Questioning the Characters' Motives

- Remind students that motive is the answer to the question *Why?*
- Point out that in a play, the audience usually relies on a character's words and actions to reveal the motives behind a given behavior. However, characters may be insincere about or unaware of the real reasons they act or speak as they do.
- Give students a copy of **Reading Strategy Graphic Organizer A,** p. 92 in ***Graphic Organizer Transparencies.*** Have them use it to monitor details in the play that reveal the actual motives of characters.

Vocabulary Builder

- Pronounce each vocabulary word for students, and read the definitions as a class. Have students identify any words with which they are already familiar.

Build Skills | *Drama*

❶ Literary Analysis

Irony

Irony is the result of a pointed contrast between appearances or expectations and reality. In literature, there are three main types of irony:

- **Verbal irony** is the use of words to suggest the opposite of their usual meaning.
- **Situational irony** occurs when the outcome of an action or situation directly contradicts expectations.
- **Dramatic irony** occurs when readers or audience members are aware of truths that the characters themselves do not perceive.

This play provides one of literature's best examples of dramatic irony. As you read Part II, notice the contrast between what Oedipus believes to be true and what the reader or viewing audience knows to be true.

Connecting Literary Elements

An outstanding example of **dramatic irony** occurs when the Corinthian Messenger tells Jocasta that Oedipus' father, believed to be Polybus, is dead. The audience knows that Oedipus' father is actually Laius, whom Oedipus killed on his way to Thebes. Sophocles reveals the painful truths to Oedipus only gradually. That gradual revelation builds **suspense**—a feeling of tension or uncertainty—as Oedipus relentlessly pursues the knowledge that will ultimately cause his downfall. As you read, notice the ways in which Oedipus' pursuit of the truth adds to the mounting suspense.

Standard Course of Study

- Analyze literary devices and explain their effect on the work. (LT.5.01.3)
- Analyze connections between ideas, concepts, characters and experiences. (LT.5.03.10)

❷ Reading Strategy

Questioning the Characters' Motives

Like people in real life, characters in literature are not always what they seem. To gain additional insight as you read, **question the characters' motives**—their reasons for behaving as they do. Ask whether characters are motivated by fear, greed, guilt, love, loyalty, revenge, or another emotion or desire. As you read, use a chart like the one shown at right to examine the motives of the characters in Part II of the play.

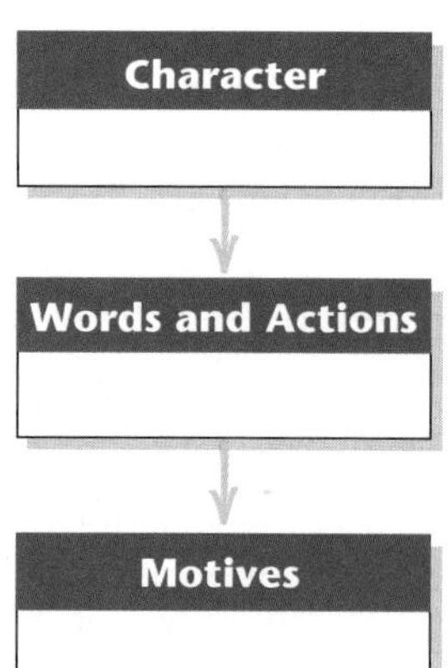

Vocabulary Builder

fettered (fet′ ərd) *adj.* shackled; chained (p. 507)

beneficent (bə nef′ ə sənt) *adj.* kind; helpful (p. 509)

consonant (kän′ sə nənt) *adj.* in harmony or agreement (p. 509)

gratify (grat′ i fī) *v.* please (p. 511)

infamous (in′ fə məs) *adj.* disgraceful (p. 516)

reverence (rev′ rəns) *v.* show great respect (p. 520)

Differentiated Instruction — Solutions for All Learners

Support for Special Needs Students
Have students complete the **Preview** and **Build Skills** pages for *Oedipus the King,* Part II in the ***Reader's Notebook: Adapted Version.*** These pages provide a selection summary, an abbreviated presentation of the reading and literary skills, and the graphic organizer on the **Build Skills** page in the student book.

Support for Less Proficient Readers
Have students complete the **Preview** and **Build Skills** pages for *Oedipus the King,* Part II in the **Reader's Notebook.** These pages provide a selection summary, an abbreviated presentation of the reading and literary skills, and the graphic organizer on the **Build Skills** page in the student book.

Support for English Learners
Have students complete the **Preview** and **Build Skills** pages for *Oedipus the King,* Part II in the ***Reader's Notebook: English Learner's Version.*** These pages provide a selection summary, an abbreviated presentation of the skills, additional contextual vocabulary, and the graphic organizer on the **Build Skills** page in the student book.

❶

Review and Anticipate In Part I of *Oedipus the King,* the people of Thebes beg Oedipus to save them from a disastrous plague. When Creon, the brother of Queen Jocasta, reports that the Delphic Oracle demands the punishment of King Laius' killer, Oedipus commits himself to solving the crime. He becomes enraged with the prophet, Teiresias, who tells Oedipus that he himself is the murderer. Teiresias adds that Oedipus will suffer a terrible destiny, blinded and outcast from society. Is Oedipus truly the murderer of King Laius? Will he suffer the terrible fate Teiresias has prophesied? Find the answers to these questions in Part II.

[*Enter* JOCASTA, *carrying garlands.*]

❷

JOCASTA: Princes of the land, I have had the thought to go
to the Gods' temples, bringing in my hand
garlands and gifts of incense, as you see.
For Oedipus excites himself too much
at every sort of trouble, not conjecturing,[1]
like a man of sense, what will be from what was,
but he is always at the speaker's mercy,
when he speaks terrors. I can do no good
by my advice, and so I came as suppliant
to you, Lycaean Apollo, who are nearest.
These are the symbols of my prayer and this
my prayer: grant us escape free of the curse.
Now when we look to him we are all afraid;
he's pilot of our ship and he is frightened.

[*Enter* MESSENGER.]

MESSENGER: Might I learn from you, sirs, where is
the house of Oedipus? Or best of all, if you
know, where is the king himself?

Reading Strategy
Questioning the Characters' Motives Which aspects of Oedipus' behavior have motivated Jocasta to visit the gods' temples?

❸ **Reading Check**
To which god does Jocasta direct her prayers?

1. **conjecturing** (kən jek′ chər iŋ) *v.* inferring or predicting from incomplete evidence.

TEACH

Facilitate Understanding

Tell students that Oedipus has made his way into popular culture. For example, filmmaker Woody Allen produced *New York Stories,* a series of short films, one of which is *Oedipus Wrecks*. In *Oedipus Wrecks,* a successful New York lawyer cannot escape his mother. She even looms over the Manhattan skyline after "disappearing" during a magic act.

❶ About the Selection

Jocasta enters, announcing that she has sacrificed to the god Apollo, entreating him to allow Oedipus to escape the curse. A messenger from Corinth arrives to announce the death of King Polybus. The relief of Oedipus and Jocasta is short-lived, however, for the Messenger reveals that Oedipus was not Polybus' true son. Jocasta, now realizing the truth, rushes offstage, but Oedipus pursues his quest, finally learning that he is the son of Laius.

❷ Reading Strategy

Questioning the Characters' Motives

- Remind students that in drama, characters reveal their motives through their speech.
- Read aloud the bracketed passage. Have students note that Jocasta refers explicitly to her inability to reassure Oedipus (lines 1002–1005).
- **Ask** students the Reading Strategy question: Which aspects of Oedipus' behavior have motivated Jocasta to visit the gods' temples?
  Answer: Jocasta notes that Oedipus is easily "excited," or disturbed, by everything he is hearing, no matter the source. He is troubled and afraid and unable to act "like a man of sense."

❸ Reading Check

Answer: Jocasta directs her prayers to Apollo.

Differentiated Instruction Solutions for All Learners

Accessibility at a Glance

	Oedipus the King, Part II
Context	Oedipus discovers his true identity and its consequences.
Language	Challenging syntax: long sentences embedded with clauses
Concept Level	Accessible (Always be aware of the motives for your actions.)
Literary Merit	Classic tragic Greek myth with dramatic irony
Lexile	NP
Overall Rating	Challenging

❹ Literary Analysis

Irony

- Remind students of the definition of irony as a literary element: a striking or pointed contrast between appearance or expectation and reality. Then, call on a volunteer to define situational irony: the direct contradiction of expectations by what occurs in fact.
- Point out that Jocasta has earlier exhibited skepticism about the validity of divine oracles (lines 804–807). Also remind students that the chorus has solemnly expressed concern about the oracles' apparent lack of fulfillment (lines 987–998).
- Remind students that the Delphic Oracle was frequently oblique, riddling, or ambiguous. (See Literature in Context, p. 480.)
- After students have read the bracketed passage, **ask** them the Literary Analysis question: In what ways is Jocasta's change of heart toward the oracles an example of situational irony?
  Possible response: Jocasta is now convinced that divine oracles are invalid. Ironically, a few moments earlier, she seemed reverent and respectful toward the gods.

CHORUS: This is his house and he is within doors. This lady is his wife and mother of his children.

MESSENGER: God bless you, lady, and God bless your household! God bless Oedipus' noble wife!

JOCASTA: God bless you, sir, for your kind greeting! What do you want of us that you have come here? What have you to tell us?

MESSENGER: Good news, lady. Good for your house and for your husband.

JOCASTA: What is your news? Who sent you to us?

MESSENGER: I come from Corinth and the news I bring will give you pleasure. Perhaps a little pain too.

JOCASTA: What is this news of double meaning?

MESSENGER: The people of the Isthmus will choose Oedipus to be their king. That is the rumor there.

JOCASTA: But isn't their king still old Polybus?

MESSENGER: No. He is in his grave. Death has got him.

JOCASTA: Is that the truth? Is Oedipus' father dead?

MESSENGER: May I die myself if it be otherwise!

❹ **JOCASTA** [*to a* SERVANT]**:** Be quick and run to the King with the news! O oracles of the Gods, where are you now? It was from this man Oedipus fled, lest he should be his murderer! And now he is dead, in the course of nature, and not killed by Oedipus.

[*Enter* OEDIPUS.]

Literary Analysis
Irony In what ways is Jocasta's change of heart toward the oracles an example of situational irony?

Enrichment

Freud on *Oedipus the King*

Sigmund Freud (1856–1939), the "father of psychoanalysis," made the Oedipus complex a well-known phenomenon. So famous is the Oedipus complex that many people have heard about it but have never read what Freud himself wrote. Here is an excerpt from *The Interpretation of Dreams,* written in 1899:

> The action of the play [Sophocles' *Oedipus the King*] consists in nothing other than the process of revealing, with cunning delays and ever-mounting excitement, a process that can be likened to the work of a psychoanalysis—that Oedipus himself is the murderer of Laius, but further that he is the son of the murdered man and of Jocasta.

Freud goes on to say that the play is known as a "tragedy of destiny" that moves the audience because the supreme will of the gods thwarts mankind's vain attempts to escape evil and suffering.

OEDIPUS: Dearest Jocasta, why have you sent for me?

JOCASTA: Listen to this man and when you hear reflect what is the
outcome of the holy oracles of the Gods.

OEDIPUS: Who is he? What is his message for me?

JOCASTA: He is from Corinth and he tells us that
your father Polybus is dead and gone.

OEDIPUS: What's this you say, sir? Tell me yourself.

MESSENGER: Since this is the first matter you want clearly told:
Polybus has gone down to death. You may be sure of it.

OEDIPUS: By treachery or sickness?

MESSENGER: A small thing will put old bodies asleep.

OEDIPUS: So he died of sickness, it seems,—poor old man!

MESSENGER: Yes, and of age—the long years he had measured.

OEDIPUS: Ha! Ha! O dear Jocasta, why should one
look to the Pythian hearth?[2] Why should one look
to the birds screaming overhead? They prophesied
that I should kill my father! But he's dead,
and hidden deep in earth, and I stand here
who never laid a hand on spear against him,—
5 unless perhaps he died of longing for me,
and thus I am his murderer. But they,
the oracles, as they stand—he's taken them
away with him, they're dead as he himself is,
and worthless.

JOCASTA: That I told you before now.

OEDIPUS: You did, but I was misled by my fear.

JOCASTA: Then lay no more of them to heart, not one.

OEDIPUS: But surely I must fear my mother's bed?

JOCASTA: Why should man fear since chance is all in all
6 for him, and he can clearly foreknow nothing?
Best to live lightly, as one can, unthinkingly.
As to your mother's marriage bed,—don't fear it.
Before this, in dreams too, as well as oracles,
many a man has lain with his own mother.
But he to whom such things are nothing bears
his life most easily.

OEDIPUS: All that you say would be said perfectly
if she were dead; but since she lives I must
still fear, although you talk so well, Jocasta:

JOCASTA: Still in your father's death there's light of comfort?

2. **Pythian hearth** (pī´ thē ən härth) *n.* the Delphic oracle that prophesied Oedipus' crime.

Literary Analysis
Irony In what ways is Jocasta and Oedipus' discussion about the Messenger's news an example of dramatic irony?

7 
Reading Check
What news does the Messenger bring from Corinth?

5 Literary Analysis

Irony

- Call on a volunteer to define dramatic irony: the clash between what a character believes to be true and what the audience or reader knows to be true.
- Read aloud the bracketed passage, and then **ask** students the Literary Analysis question: In what ways is Jocasta and Oedipus' discussion about the Messenger's news an example of dramatic irony?
  Possible response: Oedipus' lighthearted mockery of the oracles is dramatically ironic because readers know, in fact, that the prophecies have been fulfilled. Jocasta's reassurances concerning a son's incest with a mother are dramatically ironic for the same reason.

6 Critical Thinking

Apply

- Discuss Sigmund Freud's concept of the Oedipus complex: the attraction of a child to the parent of the opposite sex.
- Discuss with students whether Oedipus had the complex that bears his name. **Ask** students whether it is possible that Oedipus had no Oedipus complex.
  Possible response: Oedipus is completely unaware that Jocasta is his mother. He did not seek her out in marriage; rather, the marriage was a side effect of his rescue of Thebes.

7 Reading Check

Answer: The Messenger brings news that King Polybus, whom Oedipus believes to be his father, is dead.

Differentiated Instruction
Solutions for All Learners

Strategy for Less Proficient Readers
Ask students to read aloud lines 1020–1053. Tell them that the Messenger seems to imply more than Oedipus realizes during this exchange. Ask students to discuss what more the Messenger may hint at in lines 1048, 1051, and 1053.

Support for English Learners
Guide students in decoding some words or turns of phrase that may pose difficulties: for example, "the long years he had measured" (line 1053), "lay no more of them to heart" (line 1066), and "light of comfort" (line 1078).

Strategy for Advanced Readers
Have students discuss how skillfully Sophocles creates irony by having Oedipus wish his father dead because his father's (natural) death ensures that Oedipus will not kill him in the future. Have students consider ways in which the play opposes what one intends or what one must take responsiblity for.

8 Critical Viewing

Possible response: The actress playing Jocasta seems deeply disturbed or afraid; both her expression and posture suggest tension and fear. The expression and body language of the actor playing Oedipus suggest tension but also curiosity and confidence.

9 Reading Strategy

Questioning the Characters' Motives

- Suggest that students reread the Messenger's dialogue from his entrance at line 1013 up to this point in the scene. **Ask** students to describe this character's personality. **Possible response:** The Messenger is inquisitive, and though respectful to Oedipus, he is not reticent as one might be in the company of the king.
- Then, **ask** students the Reading Strategy question: Characterize the Messenger's demeanor since his first appearance. What might the Messenger seek from Oedipus in exchange for his "good news"? **Possible response:** The Messenger is talkative, ingratiating, and a trifle self-important or officious. The Messenger may expect Oedipus to reward him for his "good news."
- Note that Oedipus several times addresses the Messenger as "old man." Point out that the strenuous nature of messenger work makes it an unlikely role for an aged man. Tell students as they read to watch for other clues that the Messenger might be more than a simple news carrier.

OEDIPUS: Great light of comfort; but I fear the living.

MESSENGER: Who is the woman that makes you afraid?

OEDIPUS: Merope, old man, Polybus' wife.

MESSENGER: What about her frightens the queen and you?

OEDIPUS: A terrible oracle, stranger, from the Gods.

MESSENGER: Can it be told? Or does the sacred law
forbid another to have knowledge of it?

OEDIPUS: O no! Once on a time Loxias said
that I should lie with my own mother and
take on my hands the blood of my own father.
And so for these long years I've lived away
from Corinth; it has been to my great happiness;
but yet it's sweet to see the face of parents.

MESSENGER: This was the fear which drove you out of Corinth?

OEDIPUS: Old man, I did not wish to kill my father.

MESSENGER: Why should I not free you from this fear, sir,
since I have come to you in all goodwill?

9

OEDIPUS: You would not find me thankless if you did.

MESSENGER: Why, it was just for this I brought the news,—
to earn your thanks when you had come safe home.

OEDIPUS: No, I will never come near my parents.

MESSENGER: Son,
it's very plain you don't know what you're doing.

OEDIPUS: What do you mean, old man? For God's sake, tell me.

MESSENGER: If your homecoming is checked by fears like these.

OEDIPUS: Yes, I'm afraid that Phoebus may prove right.

MESSENGER: The murder and the incest?

OEDIPUS: Yes, old man;
that is my constant terror.

MESSENGER: Do you know
that all your fears are empty?

OEDIPUS: How is that,
if they are father and mother and I their son?

MESSENGER: Because Polybus was no kin to you in blood.

OEDIPUS: What, was not Polybus my father?

MESSENGER: No more than I but just so much.

OEDIPUS: How can
my father be my father as much as one
that's nothing to me?

8 ▼ Critical Viewing
Compare and contrast the emotions displayed by the actress playing Jocasta (below) and the actor playing Oedipus (facing page). **[Compare and Contrast]**

Reading Strategy
Questioning the Characters' Motives
Characterize the Messenger's demeanor since his first appearance. What might the Messenger seek from Oedipus in exchange for his "good news"?

Enrichment

Injury and Irony

It was Oedipus' fate to bear a name that proclaimed his injury to the world: "Here comes Big-foot." Oedipus' old injury poses interesting questions for actors playing the role: Should Oedipus limp? Use a cane? Wear orthopedic sandals? However a production may allude to Oedipus' childhood injury, there is no denying the stunning ironies it produces in the drama. According to the legend, it is a grazing injury to Oedipus' much-abused foot that precipitates the violent quarrel at the crossroads. With his walking staff, Oedipus kills the very man who maimed his feet. The poor Sphinx poses a riddle of human locomotion to a man exquisitely attuned by injury to the details of crawling, walking, and using a cane. In the end, blindness will put Oedipus on "three legs," using a staff—perhaps the same that murdered Laius—although he is in the prime of life.

MESSENGER: Neither he nor I
begat you.

OEDIPUS: Why then did he call me son?

MESSENGER: A gift he took you from these hands of mine.

OEDIPUS: Did he love so much what he took from another's hand?

MESSENGER: His childlessness before persuaded him.

OEDIPUS: Was I a child you bought or found when I
was given to him?

MESSENGER: On Cithaeron's slopes
in the twisting thickets you were found.

OEDIPUS: And why
were you a traveler in those parts?

MESSENGER: I was
in charge of mountain flocks.

(10) **OEDIPUS:** You were a shepherd?
A hireling vagrant?[3]

MESSENGER: Yes, but at least at that time
the man that saved your life, son.

OEDIPUS: What ailed me when you took me in your arms?

MESSENGER: In that your ankles should be witnesses.

OEDIPUS: Why do you speak of that old pain?

MESSENGER: I loosed you;
the tendons of your feet were pierced and fettered,—

OEDIPUS: My swaddling clothes[4] brought me a rare disgrace.

MESSENGER: So that from this you're called your present name.[5]

OEDIPUS: Was this my father's doing or my mother's?
For God's sake, tell me.

MESSENGER: I don't know, but he
who gave you to me has more knowledge than I.

OEDIPUS: You yourself did not find me then? You took me
from someone else?

MESSENGER: Yes, from another shepherd.

OEDIPUS: Who was he? Do you know him well enough
to tell?

MESSENGER: He was called Laius' man.

3. **hireling vagrant** (hīr′ liŋ vā grənt) person who wanders from place to place and works at odd jobs.
4. **swaddling** (swäd′ liŋ) **clothes** long, narrow bands of cloth wrapped around infants in ancient times.
5. **your present name** *Oedipus* means "swollen foot."

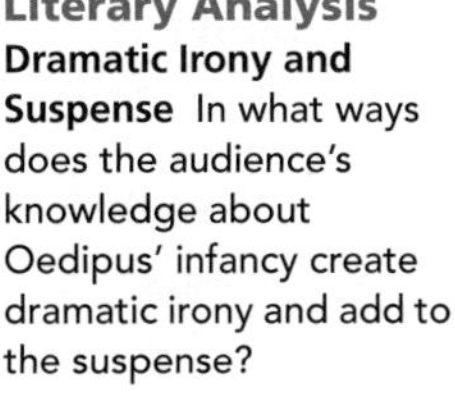

Literary Analysis
Dramatic Irony and Suspense In what ways does the audience's knowledge about Oedipus' infancy create dramatic irony and add to the suspense?

Vocabulary Builder
fettered (fet′ ərd) *adj.* shackled; chained

(11)

(12) 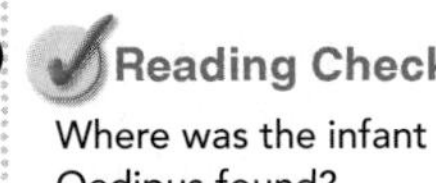

Reading Check
Where was the infant Oedipus found?

(10) Literary Analysis

Dramatic Irony and Suspense

- Have two students read the bracketed passage aloud. Point out that although Oedipus is well aware of the physical disfigurement he has had to bear ever since infancy, he does not know the identity of those who were responsible for treating him so cruelly.
- Then, **ask** the Literary Analysis question: In what ways does the audience's knowledge about Oedipus' infancy create dramatic irony and add to the suspense?
Possible response: The audience knows that Laius and Jocasta pinned Oedipus' ankles together and exposed him on the mountainside to die—because of the terrible prophecy that he would one day kill Laius and marry Jocasta. This knowledge increases suspense as the audience watches Oedipus come one step nearer to the truth about his own identity.

(11) Background

Costuming

You may wish to point out the large boot the actor is wearing. Use the material in the Enrichment note on the previous page to discuss how Oedipus' foot injury might be shown by the actor.

(12) Reading Check

Answer: The infant Oedipus was found on Mount Cithaeron.

Differentiated Instruction Solutions for All Learners

Vocabulary for English Learners

Remind students that Oedipus' name comes from the Greek words *oidus* and *pous,* which literally mean "swollen" and "foot." Give students the example *mnemonic,* and tell them that *-mnemon-* is a Greek root that means "to remember." Have students research other Greek root words in dictionaries or online. Ask each of them to put two or more Greek words together and then, in small groups, share the new "words" in sentences. Students should make educated guesses about what one another's "words" mean on the basis of previous knowledge and context clues. Start students with an example such as, "Those of us who do not have planomisia enjoyed our day at the nature preserve." Tell students that the new word is a combination of the Greek words *plano* ("wandering") and *misia* ("hate or hatred").

⓭ Reading Strategy

Questioning the Characters' Motives

- Remind students that actors onstage must remain "in character" even when they are not speaking; by observing their non-verbal cues such as gestures and body language, the audience can gain information to question the characters' motives.
- Have students recall some examples of actors' gestures in Part I of the play: for instance, Oedipus' reaction of anxiety when he hears Jocasta mention a crossroads as the scene of Laius' murder (line 795).
- Have students read the bracketed text, and then **ask** them to speculate about the dialogue in context. From the details provided by the Messenger and the comment of the chorus, what inferences is Jocasta likely to make?
  Possible response: Jocasta fears that the infant she gave away long ago is in fact Oedipus; if this is true, the prophesy is fulfilled.
- Then, **ask** students the Reading Strategy question: Why does Jocasta suddenly discourage Oedipus from pursuing information about his birth?
  Answer: The Messenger's revelation of being given a child by the Herdsman signals the truth to Jocasta; she now knows that her husband, Oedipus, is the child whom she abandoned long ago.

⓮ Critical Viewing

Possible response: In this scene, Jocasta's posture and tense facial expression suggest despair. Oedipus, though attempting to help Jocasta to her feet, wears an expression of worry.

OEDIPUS: You mean the king who reigned here in the old days?

MESSENGER: Yes, he was that man's shepherd.

OEDIPUS: Is he alive
still, so that I could see him?

MESSENGER: You who live here
would know that best.

OEDIPUS: Do any of you here
know of this shepherd whom he speaks about
in town or in the fields? Tell me. It's time
that this was found out once for all.

CHORUS: I think he is none other than the peasant
whom you have sought to see already; but
Jocasta here can tell us best of that.

OEDIPUS: Jocasta, do you know about this man
whom we have sent for? Is he the man he mentions?

⓭

JOCASTA: Why ask of whom he spoke? Don't give it heed;
nor try to keep in mind what has been said.
It will be wasted labor.

OEDIPUS: With such clues
I could not fail to bring my birth to light.

JOCASTA: I beg you—do not hunt this out—I beg you,
if you have any care for your own life.
What I am suffering is enough.

OEDIPUS: Keep up
your heart, Jocasta. Though I'm proved a slave,
thrice slave, and though my mother is thrice slave,
you'll not be shown to be of lowly lineage.

JOCASTA: O be persuaded by me, I entreat you;
do not do this.

OEDIPUS: I will not be persuaded to let be
the chance of finding out the whole thing clearly.

JOCASTA: It is because I wish you well that I
give you this counsel—and it's the best counsel.

OEDIPUS: Then the best counsel vexes me, and has
for some while since.

JOCASTA: O Oedipus, God help you!
God keep you from the knowledge of who you are!

OEDIPUS: Here, some one, go and fetch the shepherd for me;
and let her find her joy in her rich family!

JOCASTA: O Oedipus, unhappy Oedipus!
that is all I can call you, and the last thing
that I shall ever call you.

[*Exit.*]

⓮ ▲ **Critical Viewing**
What emotions does each actor's posture and facial expression convey? Explain. **[Interpret]**

Reading Strategy
Questioning the Characters' Motives Why does Jocasta suddenly discourage Oedipus from pursuing information about his birth?

CHORUS: Why has the queen gone, Oedipus, in wild
grief rushing from us? I am afraid that trouble
will break out of this silence.

OEDIPUS: Break out what will! I at least shall be
willing to see my ancestry, though humble.
Perhaps she is ashamed of my low birth,
for she has all a woman's high-flown pride.
But I account myself a child of Fortune,[6]
beneficent Fortune, and I shall not be
dishonored. She's the mother from whom I spring;
the months, my brothers, marked me, now as small,
and now again as mighty. Such is my breeding,
and I shall never prove so false to it,
as not to find the secret of my birth.

CHORUS:

Strophe
If I am a prophet and wise of heart
you shall not fail, Cithaeron,
by the limitless sky, you shall not!—
to know at tomorrow's full moon
that Oedipus honors you,
as native to him and mother and nurse at once;
and that you are honored in dancing by us, as finding favor in
sight of our king.
Apollo, to whom we cry, find these things pleasing!

Antistrophe
Who was it bore you, child? One of
the long-lived nymphs[7] who lay with Pan[8]—
the father who treads the hills?
Or was she a bride of Loxias, your mother? The grassy slopes
15 are all of them dear to him. Or perhaps Cyllene's king[9]
or the Bacchants' God that lives on the tops
of the hills received you a gift from some
one of the Helicon Nymphs, with whom he mostly plays?

[*Enter an* OLD MAN, *led by* OEDIPUS' SERVANTS.]

OEDIPUS: If some one like myself who never met him
may make a guess,—I think this is the herdsman,
16 whom we were seeking. His old age is consonant

Vocabulary Builder
beneficent (bə nef′ ə sənt) *adj.* kind, helpful

Literary Analysis
Dramatic Irony and Suspense How do the speculations of the chorus both create dramatic irony and increase suspense?

Vocabulary Builder
consonant (kän′ sə nənt) *adj.* in harmony or agreement

17 
Reading Check
What knowledge does Jocasta pray Oedipus will not learn?

6. **child of Fortune** Since Fortune, or good luck, saved him from death, Oedipus refuses to feel shame at being illegitimate or of humble origins.
7. **nymphs** (nimfs) *n.* minor female divinities with youthful, beautiful, and amorous qualities; "nymph" means young woman.
8. **Pan** Arcadian shepherd god who lived in the mountains, danced and sang with the nymphs, and played his pipes.
9. **Cyllene's king** Hermes, the messenger god.

15 Literary Analysis

Dramatic Irony and Suspense

- Remind students that dramatic irony results from the contrast between what the audience knows and what a character does not know.
- Read aloud the bracketed passage. Then, **ask** the Literary Analysis question: How do the speculations of the chorus both create dramatic irony and increase suspense?
Possible response: The words of the chorus are dramatically ironic because the audience or reader knows the truth: Oedipus will not turn out to be the glorious child of a divinity, but the mortal, and wretched, son of a father whom he unknowingly murdered. Suspense builds from uncertainty about how Oedipus will take the final step in his quest for self-knowledge and how he will react to the appalling truth of his own identity.

16 Vocabulary Builder

Latin Prefix: *con-*

- Call students' attention to the word *consonant,* and read its definition. Tell students that the Latin prefix *con-* means "with" or "together." Something consonant with something else "sounds with" it, or is harmonious or consistent.
- **Challenge** students to suggest other words containing this prefix.
Possible response: *Convert, conducive,* and *contest* are possible suggestions.
- After working with students to define the listed terms, ask volunteers to use each word appropriately in a sentence.

17 Reading Check

Answer: Jocasta prays that Oedipus will not learn who he truly is.

Differentiated Instruction
Solutions for All Learners

Strategy for Special Needs Students
Make sure students realize that Jocasta abruptly shifts course in line 1155. Ask students to determine Jocasta's level of understanding at this point in the scene. What does her discounting of the information reveal about how much she understands?

Strategy for Less Proficient Readers
Ask students to consider why Oedipus thinks Jocasta does not want the truth about his birth revealed. Encourage students to explain how his words in lines 1181–1191 reveal how much he understands.

Strategy for Advanced Readers
Ask students to evaluate Oedipus' treatment of Jocasta in lines 1181–1191. What do they think of his claim to be the son of "Lady Luck"? Remind students that Chance is an impartial divinity that "favors now one man, now another" and is intimately connected with reversal and mutability.

18 Reading Strategy

Questioning the Characters' Motives

- Have a volunteer read aloud the bracketed passage.
- Point out that the chorus describes the Herdsman as "honest." Encourage students to analyze carefully the story the Herdsman tells in order to establish what responsibility he has for the catastrophe that befalls Oedipus. Then, **ask** students to discuss whether the Herdsman is an honest man.
  Possible response: The Herdsman is honest because, in the end, he tells Oedipus the truth; on the other hand, the Herdsman's hesitation to answer Oedipus' questions directly indicates that he must be forced to tell the truth.
- **Ask** students the Reading Strategy question: What does Oedipus hope to learn from the Herdsman?
  Possible response: Oedipus wants the Herdsman to state that he received an infant from the Messenger to raise, thus confirming that the child was Oedipus, a presumed country orphan.

16 ↑

with the other. And besides, the men who bring him
I recognize as my own servants. You
perhaps may better me in knowledge since
you've seen the man before.

18

CHORUS: You can be sure
I recognize him. For if Laius
had ever an honest shepherd, this was he.

OEDIPUS: You, sir, from Corinth, I must ask you first,
is this the man you spoke of?

MESSENGER: This is he
before your eyes.

OEDIPUS: Old man, look here at me
and tell me what I ask you. Were you ever
a servant of King Laius?

HERDSMAN: I was,—
no slave he bought but reared in his own house.

OEDIPUS: What did you do as work? How did you live?

HERDSMAN: Most of my life was spent among the flocks.

OEDIPUS: In what part of the country did you live?

HERDSMAN: Cithaeron and the places near to it.

OEDIPUS: And somewhere there perhaps you knew this man?

HERDSMAN: What was his occupation? Who?

OEDIPUS: This man here,
have you had any dealings with him?

HERDSMAN: No—
not such that I can quickly call to mind.

Reading Strategy
Questioning the Characters' Motives
What does Oedipus hope to learn from the Herdsman?

Enrichment

Aristotle on Drama

Aristotle notes that Sophocles has kept all the irrational elements in the Oedipus story outside the play. Within the drama, Oedipus plays the hand that has been dealt him, and the audience must decide what kind of man he is. In the *Poetics,* Aristotle calls plot (literally, action) all-important because it is through action that essential character is revealed. (Indeed, the word *drama* itself comes from a Greek verb meaning "to do.") At different points in his treatise *Nicomachean Ethics,* Aristotle says, "We acquire the virtues by first exercising them. . . . We become just by doing just acts, temperate by doing temperate acts, brave by doing brave acts" and "The good state of mind may exist without producing any good result, as in a man who is asleep or in some other way quite inactive. . . ." Character, in some inner and abstract sense separate from action, is not of interest to Aristotle, insofar as it is at all detectable.

MESSENGER: That is no wonder, master. But I'll
make him remember what he does not know. For
I know, that he well knows the country of
Cithaeron, how he with two flocks, I with one
kept company for three years—each year half a
year—from spring till autumn time and then
when winter came I drove my flocks to our fold
home again and he to Laius' steadings. Well—am
I right or not in what I said we did?

HERDSMAN: You're right—although it's a long time ago.

MESSENGER: Do you remember giving me a child
to bring up as my foster child?

HERDSMAN: What's this?
Why do you ask this question?

MESSENGER: Look old man,
here he is—here's the man who was that child!

HERDSMAN: Death take you! Won't you hold your tongue?

OEDIPUS: No, no,
do not find fault with him, old man. Your words
are more at fault than his.

HERDSMAN: O best of masters,
how do I give offense?

OEDIPUS: When you refuse
to speak about the child of whom he asks you.

HERDSMAN: He speaks out of his ignorance, without meaning.

OEDIPUS: If you'll not talk to gratify me, you
will talk with pain to urge you.

HERDSMAN: O please, sir,
don't hurt an old man, sir.

19 **OEDIPUS** [*to the* SERVANTS]: Here, one of you,
twist his hands behind him.

HERDSMAN: Why, God help me, why?
What do you want to know?

OEDIPUS: You gave a child
to him,—the child he asked you of?

HERDSMAN: I did.
I wish I'd died the day I did.

OEDIPUS: You will
unless you tell me truly.

HERDSMAN: And I'll die
far worse if I should tell you.

Vocabulary Builder
gratify (grat′ i fī) *v.* please

Literary Analysis
Situational Irony Does Oedipus' sudden anger and threatening behavior surprise you? Explain.

20  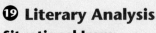 **Reading Check**
How does Oedipus try to make the Herdsman talk?

19 Literary Analysis

Situational Irony

- Remind students that situational irony often results when characters do not meet the expectations that the audience has for them.
- Ask students to read the bracketed text. Point out that Sophocles once again presents a rapid-fire interrogation, speeding up the action while increasing suspense. Despite a barrage of questions, the Herdsman stubbornly withholds the truth. This increases suspense for the audience, while provoking Oedipus to rage.
- **Ask** students the Literary Analysis question: Does Oedipus' sudden anger and threatening behavior surprise you? Explain.
  Possible responses: Yes; Oedipus acts disrespectfully toward the old man. No; Oedipus needs to know what the man tries to keep from him and Oedipus' quick temper is known.

▶ **Monitor Progress Ask** students to compare this scene with the story of Oedipus' long-ago crossroads encounter.
Possible response: Once again, Oedipus is at a (metaphorical) crossroads in his life. Once again, an old man provokes Oedipus' wrath. Once again, the intemperate Oedipus lashes out to inflict pain (and threaten death) on an old man.

▶ **Reteach** If students are having difficulty with situational irony, use **Literary Analysis** support, p. 122 in ***Unit 4 Resources.***

20 Reading Check

Answer: Oedipus tries to make the Herdsman talk by threatening him with pain.

Differentiated Instruction Solutions for All Learners

Support for Less Proficient Readers

Some students may have difficulty understanding the herdsman's motive for not telling Oedipus the story of his origins. To model a way to question characters' motives, give students a copy of **Reading Strategy Graphic Organizer B,** p. 93 in ***Graphic Organizer Transparencies.*** The completed graphic organizer will give students insight into the process of examining the motives of the characters. Students can use this process as a model for evaluating characters' motives as they continue to read.

Enrichment for Advanced Readers

Have students write a brief essay on the Greek dramatic convention of placing violent action offstage. Have students compare this practice with the explicit violence in many contemporary films. How do students evaluate the dramatic effects of onstage and offstage violence?

21 Reading Strategy

Questioning the Characters' Motives

- Remind students that reflecting on characters' behavior and reactions to earlier events can help them understand characters' motives in later passages.
- Have two volunteers read aloud the bracketed passage. Ask students to discuss parallels between this scene and Oedipus' earlier interrogation of Teiresias. For example, both the prophet and the Herdsman are reluctant to answer Oedipus' questions, and both of them possess knowledge that the king lacks. In both situations, Oedipus is unable to control his temper.
- Then, **ask** students the Reading Strategy question: Why does the Herdsman beg Oedipus to allow him to be silent?
  Possible response: The Herdsman is afraid to utter the terrible truth.

22 Scholar's Insight

- **Ask** students: What is "The Lie"?
  Answer: "The Lie" is what Oedipus has believed was true about his origins and the cause of the plague.
- Remind students that tension is a crucial element of drama. **Ask** students: Which part of the dialogue increases the scene's tension?
  Possible response: The unwillingness of the herdsman to tell the truth to Oedipus increases the tension.

23 Literary Analysis

Irony

- Review situational irony with the class. Call on volunteers to distinguish situational irony from verbal irony and dramatic irony. Read aloud the bracketed passage. Then, **ask** students why the Herdsman says Oedipus is "bred to misery."
  Answer: The Herdsman believes that Oedipus has no power to change the fate to which he was destined from birth.
- Then, **ask** the Literary Analysis question: In what way does the Herdsman's pity for the infant Oedipus present an example of situational irony?
  Possible response: The Herdsman's compassion and goodwill have the opposite effect of the result he intended. Instead of finding salvation, Oedipus encounters what he tried to avoid.

OEDIPUS: This fellow
is bent on more delays, as it would seem.

HERDSMAN: O no, no! I have told you that I gave it.

OEDIPUS: Where did you get this child from? Was
it your own or did you get it from another?

HERDSMAN: Not
my own at all; I had it from some one.

OEDIPUS: One of these citizens? or from what house?

HERDSMAN: O master, please—I beg you, master, please
don't ask me more.

OEDIPUS: You're a dead man if I
ask you again.

HERDSMAN: It was one of the children
of Laius.

OEDIPUS: A slave? Or born in wedlock?

HERDSMAN: O God, I am on the brink of frightful speech.

OEDIPUS: And I of frightful hearing. But I must hear.

HERDSMAN: The child was called his child; but she within,
your wife would tell you best how all this was.

OEDIPUS: *She* gave it to you?

HERDSMAN: Yes, she did, my lord.

OEDIPUS: To do what with it?

HERDSMAN: Make away with it.

OEDIPUS: She was so hard—its mother?

HERDSMAN: Aye, through fear
of evil oracles.

OEDIPUS: Which?

HERDSMAN: They said that he
should kill his parents.

OEDIPUS: How was it that you
gave it away to this old man?

HERDSMAN: O master,
I pitied it, and thought that I could send it
off to another country and this man
was from another country. But he saved it
for the most terrible troubles. If you are
the man he says you are, you're bred to misery.

OEDIPUS: O, O, O, they will all come,
all come out clearly! Light of the sun, let me
look upon you no more after today!
I who first saw the light bred of a match

Reading Strategy
Questioning the Characters' Motives Why does the Herdsman beg Oedipus to allow him to be silent?

David Mamet
Scholar's Insight
Oedipus is about to learn the truth. Mamet says, in *Three Uses of the Knife:* "And we have created the opportunity to face our nature, to face our deeds, to face our lies in The Drama. For the subject of the drama is The Lie."

Literary Analysis
Irony In what ways does the Herdsman's pity for the infant Oedipus present an example of situational irony?

accursed, and accursed in my living
with them I lived with, cursed in my killing.

[*Exit all but the* CHORUS.]

CHORUS:

Strophe
O generations of men, how I
count you as equal with those who live
not at all!
What man, what man on earth wins more
of happiness than a seeming
and after that turning away?
Oedipus, you are my pattern of this,
Oedipus, you and your fate!
Luckless Oedipus, whom of all men
I envy not at all.

24

Antistrophe
In as much as he shot his bolt
beyond the others and won the prize
of happiness complete—
O Zeus—and killed and reduced to nought
the hooked taloned maid of the riddling speech,[10]
standing a tower against death for my land:
hence he was called my king and hence
was honored the highest of all
honors; and hence he ruled
in the great city of Thebes.

Strophe
But now whose tale is more miserable?
Who is there lives with a savager fate?
Whose troubles so reverse his life as his?

O Oedipus, the famous prince
for whom a great haven
the same both as father and son
sufficed for generation,
how, O how, have the furrows plowed
by your father endured to bear you, poor wretch,
and hold their peace so long?

Antistrophe
Time who sees all has found you out
against your will; judges your marriage accursed,
begetter and begot at one in it.

O child of Laius,
would I had never seen you.

10. **hooked taloned maid of the riddling speech** the Sphinx; talons are claws.

Themes in World Masterpieces

25 ***Tragic Heroes***

In the *Poetics,* his analysis of tragedy, the Greek philosopher Aristotle wrote that the main character in a tragedy should be neither exceptionally good nor thoroughly evil. The hero's downfall should not be due to vice or crime, but rather to some error of judgment, or flaw. The Greek word Aristotle used for "flaw" is *hamartia,* which means "missing the mark"—as, for example, when an archer's arrow misses the target.

The myths from which ancient Greek tragic playwrights derived their plots usually revolved around royal or noble characters. Their destinies had widespread influence on the peoples they ruled. Thus, it became traditional for tragedies to present kings or other notable characters as heroes. In his tragic plays, for example, William Shakespeare portrays kings and princes such as Macbeth, Lear, and Hamlet.

In modern times, playwrights have written tragedies about ordinary people, highlighting the idea that daily life can contain the stuff of tragic emotion. Arthur Miller's *Death of a Salesman,* which centers on the failed life of Willy Loman, an ordinary person, is a famous example of such a modern tragedy.

Connect to the Literature

List two or three additional examples of tragic heroes, from literature or from film.

26  **Reading Check**

What fear drove Jocasta to give her child to the Herdsman?

Differentiated Instruction Solutions for All Learners

Vocabulary for English Learners

Post meanings for the following vocabulary words: *frightful* (line 1278), *accursed* (line 1301), *haven* (line 1326), *dirge* (line 1338), and *lamentation* (line 1338). Ask students to use each of these words in a sentence. Then, have students work in pairs to write a paragraph summarizing the action between lines 1272 and 1340.

Strategy for Advanced Readers

Have students prepare a Lincoln-Douglas style debate about the role that fate plays in Oedipus' decision making. Begin with this proposition: "There is no such thing as fate: Oedipus could have reversed his destiny by making better decisions." In addition to assigning students to two teams that will present the affirmative and negative position respectively, have students research the procedure for Lincoln-Douglas style debates. Instruct them to find specific passages in Parts I and II of the play to support their statements and counter the other team's claims.

24 Critical Thinking

Analyze

- Point out to students that in lines 1302–1322 the chorus refers to Oedipus as a "pattern." He exemplifies the fate of mankind, to be subject to mutability, to be "luckless" when seemingly most favored by "luck."
- **Ask** students: Do the words of the chorus suggest that Oedipus did anything to deserve his fate?
Possible response: The chorus links Oedipus' wretched destiny with the fact that he is human.

25 Themes in World Literature

Tragic Heroes In his *Poetics,* Aristotle illustrated many of his key principles with direct reference to Oedipus the King. For example, he believed that the plot of a tragedy must arouse pity and fear in the audience: "For the plot should be so constructed that even without seeing the play, anyone who merely hears the events unfold will shudder and feel pity as a result of what is happening—which is precisely what one would experience in listening to the plot of Oedipus."

In Aristotle's mind, pity and fear can be evoked through recognition and reversal. "Reversal is . . . a change from one state of affairs to its exact opposite, and this . . . should be in conformance with probability or necessity." For example, in *Oedipus,* the Messenger comes to cheer Oedipus by relieving him of his fear with regard to his mother; but by revealing Oedipus' true identity, he does just the opposite.

Connect to the Literature Review with students Oedipus' heroic qualities and tragic flaws. Ask: Who are your favorite tragic heroes from literature and film?
Possible response: Students may mention the following tragic heroes: from literature, Captain Ahab in Herman Melville's *Moby Dick* and Jay Gatsby in F. Scott Fitzgerald's *The Great Gatsby;* from drama, Tom Wingfield in *The Glass Menagerie;* and from films, Obi-Wan Kenobi in *Star Wars* and *The Return of the Jedi.*

26 Reading Check

Answer: The fear of what the oracles said drove Jocasta to give her child to the Herdsman.

27 Critical Viewing

Possible response: Oedipus' bowed head, fallen stance, and ragged clothing might evoke pity. The chorus members' clutching of one another might evoke pity, as well. The mournful and distressed expressions on the masks of the chorus members might evoke fear.

28 Reading Strategy

Questioning the Characters' Motives

- Have students read the bracketed passage, considering how the Second Messenger might feel as he enters, hearing the lamentation of the chorus.
- Then, **ask** students why the Second Messenger, before announcing his news, describes the effect that it will have.
  Possible response: The Messenger knows that the news he brings will result in further shock and horror and wishes to help his audience prepare for it; he wishes to add to the drama of his announcement.

I weep for you and cry
a dirge of lamentation.

To speak directly, I drew my breath
from you at the first and so now I lull
my mouth to sleep with your name.

[*Enter a* SECOND MESSENGER.]

SECOND MESSENGER: O Princes always honored by our country,
what deeds you'll hear of and what horrors see,
what grief you'll feel, if you as true born Thebans
care for the house of Labdacus's sons.

27 ▲ Critical Viewing
Which details in this image of Oedipus and the chorus might evoke both pity and fear in the audience? Explain. **[Analyze]**

Enrichment

Nietzsche on Tragedy

In 1872, the German philosopher Friedrich Nietzsche (1844–1900), who began his career as a professor of Greek, wrote about Sophocles' treatment of Oedipus in *The Birth of Tragedy:*

> The figure who suffers most on the Greek stage, the unfortunate Oedipus, was understood by Sophocles as the noble human being destined for error and misery despite his wisdom, but who nevertheless through his monstrous suffering exerts a magical healing power on all around him, a force that persists after his death.

Nietzsche here alludes to the last play Sophocles wrote, *Oedipus at Colonus*—performed more than twenty years after *Oedipus the King.* In this drama, Oedipus is purified by King Theseus of Athens and becomes in death a deified hero and protector of the city. The spot where he is buried becomes sacred ground.

Phasis nor Ister[11] cannot purge[12] this house,
I think, with all their streams, such things
it hides, such evils shortly will bring forth
into the light, whether they will or not;
and troubles hurt the most
when they prove self-inflicted.

CHORUS: What we had known before did not fall short
of bitter groaning's worth; what's more to tell?

29 ↓ **SECOND MESSENGER:** Shortest to hear and tell—our
glorious queen Jocasta's dead.

30  **Reading Check**

What news about Jocasta does the Second Messenger report?

---

11. **Phasis** (fā′ sis) . . . **Ister** (is′ tər) rivers that flow to the Black Sea.
12. **purge** (purj) *v.* cleanse of guilt or sin.

29 Background

Drama

Terrible events like murder and suicide take place off-stage, "in the house," rather than in public. Besides being a stage convention of the ancient theater, this convention keeps what is intensely personal out of public view, enclosed in the "haven," the house and the family.

30 Reading Check

Answer: The Second Messenger brings the news that Jocasta is dead.

Differentiated Instruction Solutions for All Learners

Enrichment for Advanced Readers

Ask students to reread the excerpt from Plato's *Apology* beginning on p. 440. Tell students to pay special attention to Plato's remarks about death. Ask students to compare Plato's remarks to Jocasta's suicide. Students should draw parallels between Plato's remarks about death, truth, and honor and Jocasta's action. Direct students to consider whether Plato would approve of Jocasta's suicide.

Students should state their opinions in the form of thesis statements and then support their thesis statements with evidence from Plato's *Apology* and Sophocles' *Oedipus the King.* Invite students to share insights from their papers orally with the class.

31 Reading Strategy

Questioning the Characters' Motives

- Read the bracketed passage aloud. Note that Sophocles screens Jocasta's death with a double veil: (1) it happens offstage, and (2) the eyewitness—the Second Messenger—is distracted by a raving Oedipus and does not witness Jocasta's demise.
- **Ask** students whether they think Oedipus intentionally distracted the Messenger to keep him from witnessing Jocasta's death. **Possible response:** Oedipus was likely too distraught to think about shielding the Messenger.
- **Ask** students the Reading Strategy question: What do you think motivates Oedipus to ask for a sword in line 1375? How might that motivation change in lines 1383–1385? **Possible response:** It may seem that Oedipus, in his horrified state, intends to kill Jocasta and perhaps himself. When he arrives in Jocasta's room, however, he uses the blade not to harm her but to release her body from the noose.

CHORUS: Unhappy woman! How?

SECOND MESSENGER: By her own hand. The worst of what was done
you cannot know. You did not see the sight.
Yet in so far as I remember it
you'll hear the end of our unlucky queen.
When she came raging into the house she went
straight to her marriage bed, tearing her hair
with both her hands, and crying upon Laius
long dead—Do you remember, Laius,
that night long past which bred a child for us
to send you to your death and leave
a mother making children with her son?
And then she groaned and cursed the bed in which
she brought forth husband by her husband, children
by her own child, an infamous double bond.
How after that she died I do not know,—
for Oedipus distracted us from seeing.
He burst upon us shouting and we looked
to him as he paced frantically around,
begging us always: Give me a sword, I say,
to find this wife no wife, this mother's womb,
this field of double sowing whence I sprang
and where I sowed my children! As he raved
some god showed him the way—none of us there.
Bellowing terribly and led by some
invisible guide he rushed on the two doors,—
wrenching the hollow bolts out of their sockets,
he charged inside. There, there, we saw his wife
hanging, the twisted rope around her neck.
When he saw her, he cried out fearfully
and cut the dangling noose. Then, as she lay,
poor woman, on the ground, what happened after,
was terrible to see. He tore the brooches—
the gold chased brooches fastening her robe—
away from her and lifting them up high
dashed them on his own eyeballs, shrieking out
such things as: they will never see the crime
I have committed or had done upon me!
Dark eyes, now in the days to come look on
forbidden faces, do not recognize
those whom you long for—with such imprecations[13]
he struck his eyes again and yet again
with the brooches. And the bleeding eyeballs gushed
and stained his beard—no sluggish oozing drops
but a black rain and bloody hail poured down.

Vocabulary Builder
infamous (in′ fə məs) *adj.* disgraceful

Reading Strategy
Questioning the Characters' Motives What do you think motivates Oedipus to ask for a sword in line 1375? How might that motivation change in lines 1383–1385?

13. **imprecations** (im′ pri kā′ shənz) *n.* acts of cursing and invoking evil.

Enrichment

Antigone

In 442 B.C., about twenty years before he wrote *Oedipus the King,* Sophocles wrote *Antigone,* naming the play after Oedipus' daughter. Even then he was attracted to the same theme: the great powers versus the ultimate limits of humanity. Sophocles shows distrust of the sophist Protagoras' view that "man is the measure of all things." In a famous ode in *Antigone,* the chorus explores human nature:

Many the wonders but nothing walks stranger than man. This thing crosses the sea in the winter's storm, making his path through the roaring waves. And she, the greatest of gods, the earth—ageless she is, and unwearied—he wears her away as the ploughs go up and down from year to year and his mules turn up the soil.

So it has broken—and not on one head
but troubles mixed for husband and for wife.
The fortune of the days gone by was true
good fortune—but today groans and destruction
and death and shame—of all ills can be named
not one is missing.

CHORUS: Is he now in any ease from pain?

SECOND MESSENGER: He shouts
for some one to unbar the doors and show him
to all the men of Thebes, his father's killer,
his mother's—no I cannot say the word,
it is unholy—for he'll cast himself,
out of the land, he says, and not remain
to bring a curse upon his house, the curse
he called upon it in his proclamation. But
he wants for strength, aye, and some one to guide him;
his sickness is too great to bear. You, too,
will be shown that. The bolts are opening.
Soon you will see a sight to waken pity
even in the horror of it.

[*Enter the blinded* OEDIPUS.]

CHORUS: This is a terrible sight for men to see!
I never found a worse!
Poor wretch, what madness came upon you!
What evil spirit leaped upon your life
to your ill-luck—a leap beyond man's strength!
Indeed I pity you, but I cannot
look at you, though there's much I want to ask
and much to learn and much to see.
I shudder at the sight of you.

OEDIPUS: O, O,
where am I going? Where is my voice
borne on the wind to and fro?
Spirit, how far have you sprung?

CHORUS: To a terrible place whereof men's ears
may not hear, nor their eyes behold it.

OEDIPUS: Darkness!
Horror of darkness enfolding, resistless, unspeakable
visitant sped by an ill wind in haste!
madness and stabbing pain and memory
of evil deeds I have done!

CHORUS: In such misfortunes it's no wonder
if double weighs the burden of your grief.

OEDIPUS: My friend,

Literary Analysis
Irony What is ironic about the chorus's finding the sight of Oedipus too painful to bear?

33  **Reading Check**
What injury does Oedipus inflict upon himself?

32 Literary Analysis

Irony

- Review with students some of the previous references to blindness and insight, especially in the scene between Oedipus and Teiresias (see, for example, lines 325, 417, 437, 465, 467, 474, and 518).
- Then, **ask** students the Literary Analysis question: What is ironic about the chorus's finding the sight of Oedipus too painful to bear?
Possible response: Members of the chorus, unlike Oedipus, have their eyes, but they cannot bear to look at the blinded king.

33 Reading Check

Answer: Oedipus blinds himself.

34 Critical Thinking

Interpret

- Read aloud the first bracketed passage. As students listen, encourage them to think about the degree of guilt or responsibility Oedipus should endure.
- Then, **ask** students for what actions does Oedipus take responsibility in these lines?
  Possible response: He takes responsibility for his self-blinding, but he attributes his evil destiny to the god Apollo.
- **Ask** students whether this was Oedipus' best course of action.
  Possible response: Oedipus' actions contradict his words. Oedipus' act of self-blinding suggests that he believes his choices have brought about his destiny and that he deserves punishment. Regardless, his blinding will not change the past, so it was probably not the best course of action.

35 Critical Thinking

Make a Judgment

- Point out that the chorus disapproves of Oedipus' form of self-punishment, stating that suicide would have been more fitting. Oedipus disagrees, noting that he has done things "deserving worse punishment than hanging."
- **Ask** students whether they believe that Oedipus has punished himself appropriately.
  Possible response: By choosing to endure inexpressible disgrace for the rest of his life as a blind outcast, Oedipus chooses a fate worse than death.

you are the only one steadfast, the only one that attends on me;
you still stay nursing the blind man.
Your care is not unnoticed. I can know
your voice, although this darkness is my world.

CHORUS: Doer of dreadful deeds, how did you dare
so far to do despite to your own eyes?
What spirit urged you to it?

OEDIPUS: It was Apollo, friends, Apollo,
that brought this bitter bitterness, my sorrows to completion.
But the hand that struck me
was none but my own.
Why should I see
whose vision showed me nothing sweet to see?

CHORUS: These things are as you say.

OEDIPUS: What can I see to love?
What greeting can touch my ears with joy?
Take me away, and haste—to a place out of the way!
Take me away, my friends, the greatly miserable,
the most accursed, whom God too hates
above all men on earth!

CHORUS: Unhappy in your mind and your misfortune,
would I had never known you!

OEDIPUS: Curse on the man who took
the cruel bonds from off my legs, as I lay in the field.
He stole me from death and saved me,
no kindly service.
Had I died then
I would not be so burdensome to friends.

CHORUS: I, too, could have wished it had been so.

OEDIPUS: Then I would not have come
to kill my father and marry my mother infamously.
Now I am godless and child of impurity,
begetter in the same seed that created my wretched self.
If there is any ill worse than ill,
that is the lot of Oedipus.

CHORUS: I cannot say your remedy was good;
you would be better dead than blind and living.

OEDIPUS: What I have done here was best
done—don't tell me
otherwise, do not give me further counsel.
I do not know with what eyes I could look
upon my father when I die and go
under the earth, nor yet my wretched mother—
those two to whom I have done things deserving

Enrichment

Causal Chains

Causality is a crucial element of Greek tragedy. The series of events that comprise the tragic plot must have a causal relationship so that the actions build on one another to create feelings of both mounting suspense and inevitability. By solving the riddle of the Sphinx, Oedipus relieves Thebes of the terrible monster, but eventually, as their king, he is the cause of a more destructive plague. Similarly, the character's relationship to the action is the causal, inevitable result of the character's personality. As the play unfolds, we see how each action Oedipus takes, how each choice he makes, shapes the next one. Ultimately, every choice he makes is the only one his character, or personality, will allow.

worse punishment than hanging. Would the sight
of children, bred as mine are, gladden me?
No, not these eyes, never. And my city,
its towers and sacred places of the Gods,
of these I robbed my miserable self
when I commanded all to drive *him* out,
the criminal since proved by God impure
and of the race of Laius.
To this guilt I bore witness against myself—
with what eyes shall I look upon my people?
No. If there were a means to choke the fountain
of hearing I would not have stayed my hand
from locking up my miserable carcass,[14]
seeing and hearing nothing; it is sweet
to keep our thoughts out of the range of hurt.

Cithaeron, why did you receive me? why
having received me did you not kill me straight?
And so I had not shown to men my birth.

O Polybus and Corinth and the house,
the old house that I used to call my father's—
what fairness you were nurse to, and what foulness
festered beneath! Now I am found to be
a sinner and a son of sinners. Crossroads,
and hidden glade, oak and the narrow way
at the crossroads, that drank my father's blood
offered you by my hands, do you remember
still what I did as you looked on, and what
I did when I came here? O marriage, marriage!
you bred me and again when you had bred
bred children of your child and showed to men
brides, wives and mothers and the foulest deeds
that can be in this world of ours.

Come—it's unfit to say what is unfit
to do.—I beg of you in God's name hide me
somewhere outside your country, yes, or kill me,
or throw me into the sea, to be forever
out of your sight. Approach and deign to touch me
for all my wretchedness, and do not fear.
No man but I can bear my evil doom.

CHORUS: Here Creon comes in fit time to perform
or give advice in what you ask of us.
Creon is left sole ruler in your stead.

OEDIPUS: Creon! Creon! What shall I say to him?
How can I justly hope that he will trust me?

14. **carcass** (kär′ kəs) *n.* dead body of an animal; here, scornful reference to Oedipus' own body.

Reading Strategy
Questioning the Characters' Motives What do you think motivates Oedipus to condemn his past actions—fear, shame, anger, or some other emotion? Explain.

Reading Check
Why does Oedipus curse the man who saved him when he was an infant?

36 Reading Strategy

Questioning the Characters' Motives

- Ask a volunteer to read the bracketed passage aloud.
- **Ask** students the Reading Strategy question: What do you think motivates Oedipus to condemn his past actions—fear, shame, anger, or some other emotion?
  Possible response: Oedipus probably acts out of the shock of experiencing all of these emotions simultaneously.
- **Ask** students to discuss what is surprising about what Oedipus says.
  Possible response: It is surprising that he talks about wanting to lose his senses because he has already "seen" and "heard" the truth about himself and his parents.

37 Reading Check

Answer: Oedipus curses the man who saved him because he believes that he would have been better off dead.

Differentiated Instruction Solutions for All Learners

Strategy for Less Proficient Readers

Students may have begun to notice a parallel between Oedipus at the end of the play and Teiresias, the blind prophet. Both men are blind, privy to insights that others do not possess, and nomadic, to name some of their similarities. Lead a discussion in which students compare and contrast these two characters. Students might benefit from using Venn diagrams or other comparison-and-contrast organizers.

Strategy for Advanced Readers

One of the predominant themes in *Oedipus the King* is the justice of the universe. In Greek, justice is *díkê*. Díkê in Homer's world meant getting one's fair portion. To Sophocles, díkê signified trial, judgment, and penalty. Tell students to write essays in which they show how Oedipus is on trial in the play. Tell students to define the charges against him and describe his defense. In their conclusions, students should determine whether justice has been achieved.

38 Literary Analysis

Irony

- Have students review the role Creon has played in the tragedy so far. Elicit that he has been a trusted advisor to the king, as well as a suspected adversary.
- **Ask** students to predict how Creon may behave now that Oedipus has been brought low.
  Possible response: Creon will show Oedipus mercy because they have a long history together; or Creon will treat Oedipus coldly because of the recent rift between them.
- Then, **ask** the Literary Analysis question: In what ways is Oedipus' changed position with respect to Creon an example of situational irony?
  Possible response: Earlier, Creon was subordinate and was accused by Oedipus of disloyalty. Now, Oedipus realizes that their roles have been reversed and that it is he who has wronged Creon. In a further irony, given Oedipus' unfounded suspicions, it now appears that Creon is the presumptive heir to the throne of Thebes. Oedipus is thus subordinate to him.

39 Critical Viewing

Possible response: The image suggests that Oedipus turns to the chorus for emotional and physical support and that the chorus loves and pities him.

In what is past I have been proved towards him
an utter liar.

[*Enter* CREON.]

38

CREON: Oedipus, I've come
not so that I might laugh at you nor taunt you
with evil of the past. But if you still
are without shame before the face of men
reverence at least the flame that gives all life,
our Lord the Sun, and do not show unveiled
to him pollution such that neither land
nor holy rain nor light of day can welcome.

[*To a* SERVANT.]

Be quick and take him in. It is most decent
that only kin should see and hear the troubles
of kin.

OEDIPUS: I beg you, since you've torn me from
my dreadful expectations and have come
in a most noble spirit to a man
that has used you vilely[15]—do a thing for me.
I shall speak for your own good, not for my own.

CREON: What do you need that you would ask of me?

OEDIPUS: Drive me from here with all the speed you can
to where I may not hear a human voice.

15. **vilely** (vīl′ lē) *adv.* wickedly.

Literary Analysis
Irony In what ways is Oedipus' changed position with respect to Creon an example of situational irony?

Vocabulary Builder
reverence (rev′ rəns) *v.* show great respect

39 ▼ **Critical Viewing**
What does this image of Oedipus and the chorus suggest about their relationship? Explain.
[Interpret]

Enrichment

Old Tales Retold

Like Sophocles in *Oedipus the King* and Shakespeare in *King Lear,* many poets bend old fairy tales to their own purposes. For instance, contemporary poets such as Randall Jarrell and Anne Sexton have retold familiar fairy tales like *Cinderella, Jack and the Beanstalk, Little Red Riding Hood, Snow White,* and others in such a way as to comment on tradition and suggest parables for their own time.

CREON: Be sure, I would have done this had not I
wished first of all to learn from the God the course
of action I should follow.

OEDIPUS: But his word
has been quite clear to let the parricide,[16]
the sinner, die.

CREON: Yes, that indeed was said.
But in the present need we had best discover
what we should do.

OEDIPUS: And will you ask about
a man so wretched?

CREON: Now even you will trust
the God.

40

OEDIPUS: So. I command you—and will beseech you—
to her that lies inside that house give burial
as you would have it; she is yours and rightly
you will perform the rites for her. For me—
never let this my father's city have me
living a dweller in it. Leave me live

16. **parricide** (par′ ə sīd) *n.* one who murders one's father.

41 

What information does Creon want to learn from the God?

40 Reading Strategy

Questioning the Characters' Motives

- Remind students that as events unfold, characters must react quickly; adapting to change can motivate them to alter the ways they think about themselves and others.
- Read the bracketed passage aloud. Tell students to listen for the requests Oedipus makes for Jocasta and himself.
- **Ask** students: In line 1558, how does Oedipus display awareness of his changed circumstances?
  Possible response: Oedipus catches himself in mid-sentence and switches his verb from *command* to *beseech*—a significant change from speaking from a position of power to asking for mercy.

41 Reading Check

Answer: Creon wants the God to reveal what should be done with Oedipus.

42 Background

Characterization

Oedipus is reeling from shock, and his words, up to this point, reveal the way in which his mind darts about in horror from one thought to another, always circling back to the horrible realization of his monstrous pollution. He now begins to sound more calm and rational.

43 Reading Strategy

Questioning the Characters' Motives

- Ask students to discuss the likely position of Oedipus' daughters now that their parentage and their father's situation are known to all.
- Have students speculate on what effect the appearance of the young daughters might have on the Athenian spectators.
- Then, **ask** students the Reading Strategy question: What is Creon's motivation for bringing Antigone and Ismene to their father? **Possible response:** Creon may have taken pity on Oedipus and decided to bring the king's daughters to him so that he could bid them farewell. Creon appears cautious but also sympathetic.

in the mountains where Cithaeron is, that's called
my mountain, which my mother and my father
while they were living would have made my tomb.
So I may die by their decree who sought
indeed to kill me. Yet I know this much:
42 no sickness and no other thing will kill me.
I would not have been saved from death if not
for some strange evil fate. Well, let my fate
go where it will.
Creon, you need not care
about my sons; they're men and so wherever
they are, they will not lack a livelihood.
But my two girls—so sad and pitiful—
whose table never stood apart from mine,
and everything I touched they always shared—
O Creon, have a thought for them! And most
I wish that you might suffer me to touch them
and sorrow with them.

[*Enter* ANTIGONE *and* ISMENE, OEDIPUS' *two daughters.*]

O my lord! O true noble Creon! Can I
really be touching them, as when I saw?
What shall I say?
Yes, I can hear them sobbing—my two darlings!
and Creon has had pity and has sent me
43 what I loved most?
Am I right?

CREON: You're right: it was I gave you this
because I knew from old days how you loved them
as I see now.

OEDIPUS: God bless you for it, Creon,
and may God guard you better on your road
than he did me!
O children,
where are you? Come here, come to my hands,
a brother's hands which turned your father's eyes,
those bright eyes you knew once, to what you see,
a father seeing nothing, knowing nothing,
begetting you from his own source of life.
I weep for you—I cannot see your faces—
I weep when I think of the bitterness
there will be in your lives, how you must live
before the world. At what assemblages
of citizens will you make one? to what
gay company will you go and not come home
in tears instead of sharing in the holiday?
And when you're ripe for marriage, who will he be,

Reading Strategy
Questioning the Characters' Motives What is Creon's motivation for bringing Antigone and Ismene to their father?

Enrichment

The *Iliad*

Oedipus' love for his children might be compared with what Andromache and Hector say when they look ahead to their son's life as an orphan in Homer's *Iliad.*

> [Andromache] joined [Hector] now, and following in her steps a servant holding the boy against her breast, in the first flush of life, only a baby, Hector's son, the darling of his eyes and radiant as a star. . . .
>
> [Andromache:] Reckless one, my Hector—your own fiery courage will destroy you! Have you no pity for *him,* our helpless son? . . . Pity me, please! Take your stand on the rampart here, before you orphan your son and make your wife a widow. . . .
>
> [Hector:] Zeus, all you immortals! Grant this boy, my son, may be like me, and rule all Troy in power and one day let them say, 'He is a better man than his father!'—when he comes home from battle bearing the bloody gear of the mortal enemy he has killed in war—a joy to his mother's heart.

the man who'll risk to take such infamy
as shall cling to my children, to bring hurt
on them and those that marry with them? What
curse is not there? "Your father killed his father
and sowed the seed where he had sprung himself
and begot you out of the womb that held him."
These insults you will hear. Then who will marry you?
No one, my children; clearly you are doomed
to waste away in barrenness unmarried.
Son of Menoeceus,[17] since you are all the father
left these two girls, and we, their parents, both
are dead to them—do not allow them wander
like beggars, poor and husbandless.
They are of your own blood.
And do not make them equal with myself
in wretchedness; for you can see them now
so young, so utterly alone, save for you only.
Touch my hand, noble Creon, and say yes.
If you were older, children, and were wiser,
there's much advice I'd give you. But as it is,
let this be what you pray: give me a life
wherever there is opportunity
to live, and better life than was my father's.

CREON: Your tears have had enough of scope; now go within the house.

OEDIPUS: I must obey, though bitter of heart.

CREON: In season, all is good.

OEDIPUS: Do you know on what conditions I obey?

CREON: You tell me them,
and I shall know them when I hear.

OEDIPUS: That you shall send me out
to live away from Thebes.

CREON: That gift you must ask of the God.

OEDIPUS: But I'm now hated by the Gods.

CREON: So quickly you'll obtain your prayer.

OEDIPUS: You consent then?

CREON: What I do not mean, I do not use to say.

OEDIPUS: Now lead me away from here.

CREON: Let go the children, then, and come.

OEDIPUS: Do not take them from me.

17. **Son of Menoeceus** (mə nē' sē əs) Creon.

Reading Strategy
Questioning the Characters' Motives What effect might Oedipus expect his statements to his daughters about their future to have on Creon?

45 Reading Check
What plea for his daughters does Oedipus make to Creon?

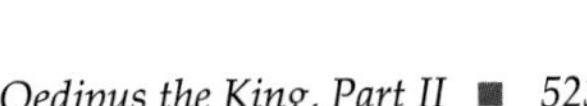

44 Reading Strategy

Questioning the Characters' Motives

- Read aloud the bracketed passage. Point out to students that after the almost unbearable emotion of Oedipus' meeting with his daughters, Oedipus turns to Creon for one last exchange.
- **Ask** students the Reading Strategy question: What effect might Oedipus expect his statements to his daughters about their future to have on Creon?
  Possible response: Oedipus likely expects his words to move Creon to pity, compelling him to help Antigone and Ismene.
- Have students **review** this last conversation as a sort of business negotiation. What does Oedipus want? How does Creon respond?
  Possible response: Oedipus wants Creon to protect his daughters and seeks a handshake ("Touch my hand") to seal the commitment. The text does not make clear whether Creon complies; his words are somewhat guarded and mysterious; he never explicitly agrees to any of Oedipus' requests.
- Creon has the "last word" before the chorus closes the play. **Ask** students whether they think his words are justified, well-meant, or unfriendly.
  Possible response: Creon may lack sympathy here, though his statement is accurate.

45 Reading Check

Answer: Oedipus begs Creon to protect his daughters and not allow them to "wander like beggars."

46 Scholar's Insight

- Have students read the Scholar's Insight.
- Explain that *catharsis* comes from a Greek word that means "to cleanse" or "to purge." Oedipus has been purged of the anxiety that results from having an opportunity to change his circumstances; he is resigned to his fate.
- After students have read the bracketed passage, **ask** them to contrast the results of Oedipus' willfulness throughout the play to the results of his resignation at the end of the play. **Possible response:** Oedipus' willfulness results in his discovering the terrible truth about himself and the cause of the plague on Thebes; it leads to his downfall and the suffering of his family. His resignation results in his acceptance of the truth of his life and affords him some measure of calm.

ASSESS

Answers

1. **Possible response:** Oedipus has suffered dreadfully for crimes he committed unknowingly; therefore, he inspires sympathy.
2. (a) Oedipus' name means "swollen-foot." (b) The name alludes to the painful fettering of his ankles when he was left on Mount Cithaeron to die as an infant.
3. (a) Oedipus wrongly infers that Jocasta may be ashamed at the possibility of his lowly birth. (b) **Possible response:** Oedipus is now so caught up in the search for his true identity that he must persist. (c) Sophocles may be suggesting that the quest for self-knowledge is irresistible, however much pain it may produce.
4. (a) The chorus addresses Cithaeron, the mountain near Thebes, where Oedipus had been exposed as an infant to die. (b) The chorus hopes that Oedipus will be shown to be the son of one of the gods.
5. (a) Oedipus establishes that the Herdsman gave a child to the Corinthian Messenger so that the infant could be reared in safety in Corinth. The infant had been given to the Herdsman by Jocasta; he was a son of Laius' royal line.

46

CREON: Do not seek to be master in everything,
for the things you mastered did not follow you throughout your life.

[*As* CREON *and* OEDIPUS *go out.*]

CHORUS: You that live in my ancestral Thebes, behold this Oedipus,—
him who knew the famous riddles and was a man most masterful;
not a citizen who did not look with envy on his lot—
see him now and see the breakers of misfortune swallow him!
Look upon that last day always. Count no mortal happy till
he has passed the final limit of his life secure from pain.

David Mamet Scholar's Insight
In *Three Uses of the Knife,* Mamet describes the strange sense of calm, sometimes called a *catharsis*, that comes at the end of tragedy: "Tragedy is a celebration not of our eventual triumph but of the truth—it is not a victory but a resignation. Much of its calmative power comes, again, from that operation described by Shakespeare: when remedy is exhausted, so is grief."

Critical Reading

1. **Respond:** At the end of the play, do you sympathize with Oedipus or blame him? Explain.
2. **(a) Recall:** What is the literal meaning of Oedipus' name? **(b) Assess:** What clue to Oedipus' identity does his name contain?
3. **(a) Recall:** What is Oedipus' reaction to Jocasta's abrupt exit at line 1177? **(b) Analyze:** Why do you think Oedipus continues his investigation despite Jocasta's strong objections? **(c) Extend:** What might the playwright be saying about the importance of "knowing thyself"?
4. **(a) Recall:** Whom or what does the chorus address in the strophe beginning at line 1192? **(b) Interpret:** What hope does the chorus express here?
5. **(a) Recall:** What facts does Oedipus establish by questioning the Herdsman? **(b) Draw Conclusions:** Why might this scene be considered the climax, or high point, of the tragedy?
6. **(a) Recall:** What events does the Second Messenger report? **(b) Relate:** Does this speech achieve the goal of dramatic tragedy? That is, does it evoke both pity and fear in you? Explain.
7. **(a) Recall:** What does Oedipus want Creon to do at the end of the play? **(b) Analyze:** Why does Oedipus insist that he is better off blind and living than dead? **(c) Make a Judgment:** At the play's end, do you think Oedipus is ennobled by suffering? Explain.

Go Online
Author Link
For: More about Sophocles
Visit: www.PHSchool.com
Web Code: ete-9410

Answers continued

(b) This scene may be considered the climax because it marks the point of highest tension, when Oedipus' downfall is conclusively established.

6. (a) The Second Messenger reports the suicide of Jocasta and the self-blinding of Oedipus. (b) **Possible response:** The vivid details and violent action succeed in evoking pity and fear.
7. (a) Oedipus wants Creon to send him into exile and to take care of his daughters. (b) **Possible response:** Oedipus believes that he has been marked for a special fate that he must not evade through an untimely death. (c) Yes; Oedipus has shouldered responsibility for his destiny. He does not blame others, nor does he try to end his life.

Go Online Author Link For additional information about Sophocles, have students type in the Web Code, then select *S* from the alphabet, and then select Sophocles.

Apply the Skills

Oedipus the King, Part II

Literary Analysis

Irony

1. At line 1042, Jocasta refers to "the holy oracles of the Gods." Given the context, what is **verbally ironic** about her words?
2. The Messenger attempts to cheer Oedipus when he reveals that Polybus and Merope were not the king's true parents. How do the Messenger's efforts result in a wrenching **situational irony?**
3. Oedipus misinterprets the reasons for Jocasta's departure at lines 1183–1184. **(a)** Use a chart like the one shown to examine elements of irony in his interpretation of her motives. **(b)** What does Oedipus' response to Jocasta's flight suggest about his character?

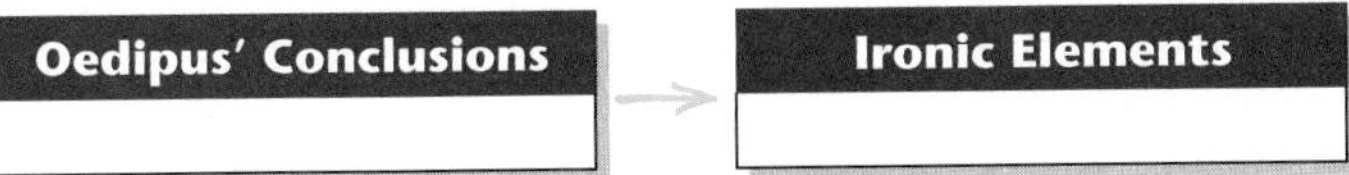

Connecting Literary Elements

4. What information about Oedipus' past underlies the **dramatic irony** in the scene involving Oedipus, Jocasta, and the Messenger from Corinth?
5. Why is Oedipus' description of himself as a "child of Fortune" (line 1185) dramatically ironic?
6. Sophocles reveals the truth of Oedipus' identity slowly, thus postponing the crisis, or climax, of the play. In what ways does this strategy add both to the play's dramatic irony and to its **suspense?**

Reading Strategy

Questioning the Characters' Motives

7. **(a)** Compare and contrast the attitudes of the Corinthian Messenger and the Herdsman toward the information they possess. **(b)** What contrasting **motives** are attributed to each?
8. Oedipus tries desperately to avoid his fate and at the same time learn his identity. How are both goals connected?

Extend Understanding

9. **Humanities Connection:** Chance plays a major role in the Oedipus story. In what other works of literature or film is chance important?

QuickReview

Irony is a contrast between appearance or expectation and reality.

Verbal irony is the use of words to suggest the opposite of their usual meaning.

Situational irony occurs when an outcome contradicts expectations.

Dramatic irony occurs when readers are aware of truths that the characters themselves do not perceive.

Suspense is a feeling of tension or uncertainty.

To gain insight as you read, **question the characters' motives,** or the reasons for their behavior.

For: Self-test
Visit: www.PHSchool.com
Web Code: eta-6407

Go Online Assessment Students may use the **Self-test** to prepare for **Selection Test A** or **Selection Test B.**

Answers

1. Jocasta means the opposite. She now believes that the oracles were mistaken.
2. The Messenger intends to assure Oedipus that he cannot possibly kill his father. Instead, the revelation triggers a catastrophic cascade of discovery.
3. (a) **Oedipus' Conclusions:** Jocasta is proud and may despise him for his lowly birth. **Ironic Elements:** Jocasta is horrified at her realization of the truth about Oedipus, who was not low-born, but rather her own son and the son of Laius. (b) Oedipus' response suggests he is self-conscious, insecure, and quick to take offense. Another sample answer can be found on **Literary Analysis Graphic Organizer B,** p. 95 in ***Graphic Organizer Transparencies.***
4. Information linked to dramatic irony includes the death of Polybus, the oracle about Oedipus and his mother, the revelation that Polybus and Merope were not Oedipus' true parents, and the facts about Oedipus' infancy on Mount Cithaeron.
5. Oedipus is indeed a "child of Fortune," but not in the way he means.
6. Dramatic irony derives from the audience's prior knowledge of the truth. The slow, incremental pace of revelations, however, increases the audience's uncertainty about how and when Oedipus will discover the truth.
7. (a) The Messenger is eager to tell what he knows, whereas the Herdsman is reluctant. (b) The Messenger expects a reward, but the Herdsman wants to shield Oedipus from the dreadful truth.
8. Oedipus' identity as Laius and Jocasta's son is his fate, as it was decreed that he would kill his father and marry his mother.
9. **Possible response:** Many of Shakespeare's works, such as *Romeo and Juliet* and *Othello,* explore the role of chance in the lives of human beings.

EXTEND/ASSESS

Answers

❶ Vocabulary Lesson

Word Analysis: Latin Prefix *con-*

1. concert: musical performance; At a concert, musicians play their instruments together.
2. conduct: lead; To conduct is to lead elements or people to work together.
3. conversation: dialogue; In a conversation, people speak together.
4. contemporary: modern, up-to-date; To be contemporary is to keep up with modern times.
5. consolation: sympathy; To offer consolation is to express sympathy to another person.
6. congratulate: offer good wishes; To congratulate is to express good wishes to another person.

Spelling Strategy

1. treasonous
2. gracious
3. bounteous

Vocabulary Builder

1. a
2. c
3. d
4. b
5. b
6. a

❷ Grammar and Style Lesson

1. Questioning; subject
2. respecting the oracles; object of a preposition
3. living and killing; objects of a preposition
4. blinding; direct object
5. counting any man happy; subject

Writing Application

Possible response: Running is my favorite hobby. Pacing myself gives me discipline to finish a race. I like accomplishing personal goals.

Build Language Skills

❶ Vocabulary Lesson

Word Analysis: Latin Prefix *con-*

The Latin prefix *con-* means "with" or "together." If something is *consonant* with something else, it "sounds with" it; the two are harmonious. Add the prefix *con-* to the word roots below. Then, define each word and explain how the prefix contributes to its meaning.

1. -cert **2.** -duct **3.** -versation **4.** -temporary **5.** -solation **6.** -gratulate

Spelling Strategy

You can form adjectives from some nouns by adding the suffix *-ous*. Sometimes, however, you will need to make a spelling change when adding this suffix. For example, *zeal* becomes *zealous; space* becomes *spacious; beauty* becomes *beauteous.* Use the suffix *-ous* to form an adjective from the following nouns.

1. treason **2.** grace **3.** bounty

Vocabulary Builder: Antonyms

Select the letter of the word most nearly opposite in meaning to each vocabulary word.

1. fettered: **(a)** loosened, **(b)** used, **(c)** hot, **(d)** angry
2. beneficent: **(a)** productive, **(b)** generous, **(c)** malignant, **(d)** polished
3. consonant: **(a)** loud, **(b)** joyful, **(c)** agreeing, **(d)** inconsistent
4. gratify: **(a)** please, **(b)** annoy, **(c)** resist, **(d)** steal
5. infamous: **(a)** notorious, **(b)** respectable, **(c)** glorious, **(d)** vivid
6. reverence: **(a)** insult, **(b)** respect, **(c)** grant, **(d)** report

❷ Grammar and Style Lesson

Gerunds and Gerund Phrases

A **gerund** is a verb form ending in *-ing* that can act as a noun. Like nouns, gerunds function in sentences as subjects, direct objects, predicate nominatives, and objects of prepositions. A **gerund phrase** consists of a gerund and its complements and modifiers.

Direct Object:
Do you remember giving me a child . . . ?

Object of Preposition:
—O God, I am on the brink of frightful speech.
—And I of frightful hearing. But I must hear.

Practice Identify each gerund or gerund phrase, and tell how it is used in the sentence.

1. Questioning is one of Oedipus' skills.
2. Jocasta doesn't believe in respecting the oracles.
3. Oedipus is cursed in living and killing.
4. The Messenger describes the blinding.
5. According to the chorus, counting any man happy until he is dead is a mistake.

Writing Application Write a paragraph in which you describe working at a hobby or playing a sport. Include at least three gerunds.

WG Prentice Hall Writing and Grammar Connection: Platinum Level, Chapter 20, Section 1

Assessment Practice

Cause and Effect, Predicting Outcomes

(For more practice, see *Test Preparation Workbook*, p. 23.)

Many tests require students to recognize cause and effect in order to predict an outcome. Use the following sample item to demonstrate.

Creon will likely—

A help Oedipus' daughters because he does not want more harm caused by Oedipus' past.
B help Oedipus' daughters because he wants to marry one of them.
C abandon Oedipus' daughters because Oedipus has wronged him in the past.
D abandon Oedipus' daughters because he does not believe that Oedipus loves them.

Answers *B, C,* and *D* are incorrect because Creon shows respect for Oedipus and concern for his daughters' welfare. Creon tells Oedipus, "Do not seek to be master in everything, for the things you mastered did not follow you throughout your life." This suggests that Creon will help the daughters because he thinks Oedipus has been treated unfairly by fate. The correct answer is *A*.

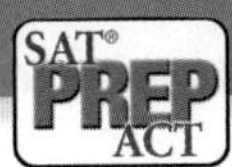

3 Writing Lesson

Timed Writing: Character Study

Some critics believe that Oedipus caused his own destruction through poor choices and character flaws. Others believe that his wrongdoing was involuntary and his suffering out of all proportion to the responsibility he truly bears. Write an essay in which you make your own judgment of Oedipus' character and guilt. ***(40 minutes)***

Prewriting *(10 minutes)* Reread the play, noting passages that describe or demonstrate Oedipus' reactions, statements, and decisions. Interpret these details, and write a statement, or working thesis, about his character.

Drafting *(20 minutes)* State your thesis in the introduction, and plan one main supporting idea for each paragraph. Organize the details from your notes into paragraphs.

Model: Organizing Details into Paragraphs

Main idea: One of Oedipus' worst flaws is his temper.

Supporting details:

- his anger at Laius
- his suspicion of Creon
- his anger at Teiresias
- his threats against the Herdsman

To be supported effectively, each main idea is defended by at least two specific examples from the text.

Revising *(10 minutes)* Review your essay, making sure that your opinion is well supported by the text. Underline main ideas and place marks next to supporting details. Identify opportunities to further elaborate with specific examples or accurate quotations from the play.

WG Prentice Hall Writing and Grammar Connection: Platinum Level, Chapter 13, Section 2

4 Extend Your Learning

Listening and Speaking Conduct a **debate** about Oedipus in the form of a mock trial, with one side acting as the defense team and the other side as the prosecution team. Use these tips to prepare:

- Look for evidence to support both positions, and then be prepared to debate on either side.
- Listen attentively while your opponents are speaking so that you can respond appropriately.

As you conduct the debate, use accurate quotations from the play as evidence. **[Group Activity]**

Research and Technology Write an **illustrated report** on ancient Greek theaters. Use Internet and library resources to locate information for your report. Explore topics such as location, size, acoustics, masks, and costumes. When you have finished, share your report with the class.

For: An additional research activity
Visit: www.PHSchool.com
Web Code: etd-7405

3 Writing Lesson

You may use this Writing Lesson as a timed-writing practice, or you may allow students to develop the character study essay as a writing assignment over several days.

- To give students guidance in writing this essay, give them the **Support for Writing Lesson,** p. 126 in ***Unit 4 Resources.***
- Remind students to take into account Oedipus' position as king of Thebes, as well as his choices and actions before the play begins.
- Use the Response to Literature rubrics in ***General Resources,*** pp. 55–56, to evaluate students' work.

WG Writing and Grammar Platinum Level

For support in teaching the Writing Lesson, use Chapter 13, Section 2.

4 Research and Technology

- Tell students that one of the best-preserved Greek theaters in Greece is located at Epidaurus. Also, remind them that the Greeks established many colonies in the Mediterranean. In some of these places, such as Syracuse in Sicily, there are still excellent examples of Greek theaters.
- The **Support for Extend Your Learning** page (***Unit 4 Resources,*** p. 127) provides guided note-taking opportunities to help students complete the Extend Your Learning activities.

Go Online Research Have students type in the Web Code for another research activity.

Assessment Resources

The following resources can be used to assess students' knowledge and skills.

Unit 4 Resources
- **Selection Test A,** pp. 129–131
- **Selection Test B,** pp. 132–134

General Resources
- **Rubrics for Response to Literature,** pp. 55–56

Go Online Assessment Students may use the **Self-test** to prepare for **Selection Test A** or **Selection Test B.**

Standard Course of Study

IR.2.03.1 Access cultural information from media sources.

FA.3.01.4 Compile response and research data to organize argument about controversial issues.

FA.3.03.1 Gather information to prove a point about issues in literature.

*See **Teacher Express™/Lesson View** for a detailed lesson for Reading Informational Material.*

About Web Research Sources

- Have students read the "About Web Research Sources" instruction. Then, **ask** them to offer appropriate examples of Web pages that they have visited.
  Possible response: Web sites related to hobbies, news, or games may be popular with students.
- Remind students that a Web research source differs from other Web pages in that its authors may represent an educational institution or a news organization.
- Discuss instances in which students might need to read and analyze Web research sources. Offer the example of using Web sites to conduct research for a term paper. Help students recognize the importance of ensuring that sites are credible.

Reading Skill

Analyzing the Usefulness and Credibility of Web Sources

- Point out that students must analyze Web sites for two factors: usefulness and credibility. **Ask** students to define these factors.
  Possible response: Usefulness refers to ease of navigation, ease in locating information, and organization of the site. Credibility refers to whether the site's information is reliable, current, and accurate.
- Explain that most Web sites share common elements such as hotlinks, icons, and search engines.
- Review the chart with students. Encourage them to refer to this chart as they examine the Perseus Digital Library Olympic Exhibit on the following pages.

Web Research Sources

About Web Research Sources

Web sites—sets of linked Web pages (screens) assembled by an individual or group and accessible via the Internet—offer a tremendous diversity of information, making the Web an attractive research tool. **Web research sources** include any Web site dedicated to providing information on a given topic for researchers. (See the Research and Technology Guide handbook on pages R25 and R26 for details about searching the Web.)

Unfortunately, not all "information" on the Web is of equal value. Furthermore, the information that you find on a Web site may be packaged in a confusing or misleading way. To make the best use of this great research tool, you need to read critically.

Reading Strategy

Analyzing the Usefulness and Credibility of Web Sources

Once you have located a Web site, you must **analyze the usefulness and credibility** of the source before using it for your research. A useful site is easy to understand and easy to navigate, and a credible site provides trustworthy, current information. Analyze and evaluate the site, basing your judgment on the factors listed in the chart shown.

A Useful Web Site . . .	A Credible Web Site . . .
• contains vocabulary and details appropriate to your research needs and that is suitable for your intended audience	• presents thorough coverage of a subject
• includes interesting and easy-to-follow graphics	• may be peer-reviewed: many sites are sponsored by academic institutions or endorsed by subject-matter specialists who have reviewed the content
• offers a clear site map or navigation bar	• includes a bibliography or identifies the source of its information
• features links to other pages within the site	• is updated periodically

As you review the Web pages from the Perseus Digital Library Olympics Exhibit on the following pages, note all the different factors that affect the usefulness and credibility of the site as a research tool.

Differentiated Instruction Solutions for All Learners

Reading Support

Give students reading support with the appropriate version of the **Reader's Notebooks:**

Reader's Notebook: [L2, L3]
Reader's Notebook: Adapted Version [L1, L2]
Reader's Notebook: English Learner's Version [EL]

Home Page

A home page such as this one is the "front door" of a Web site. A good home page identifies the sponsoring organization and provides an overview of the information on the site. Because the Perseus Web site features several different kinds of information, it offers this "secondary home page" for its Olympics Exhibit. From this page, you can access different categories of information by clicking on different links.

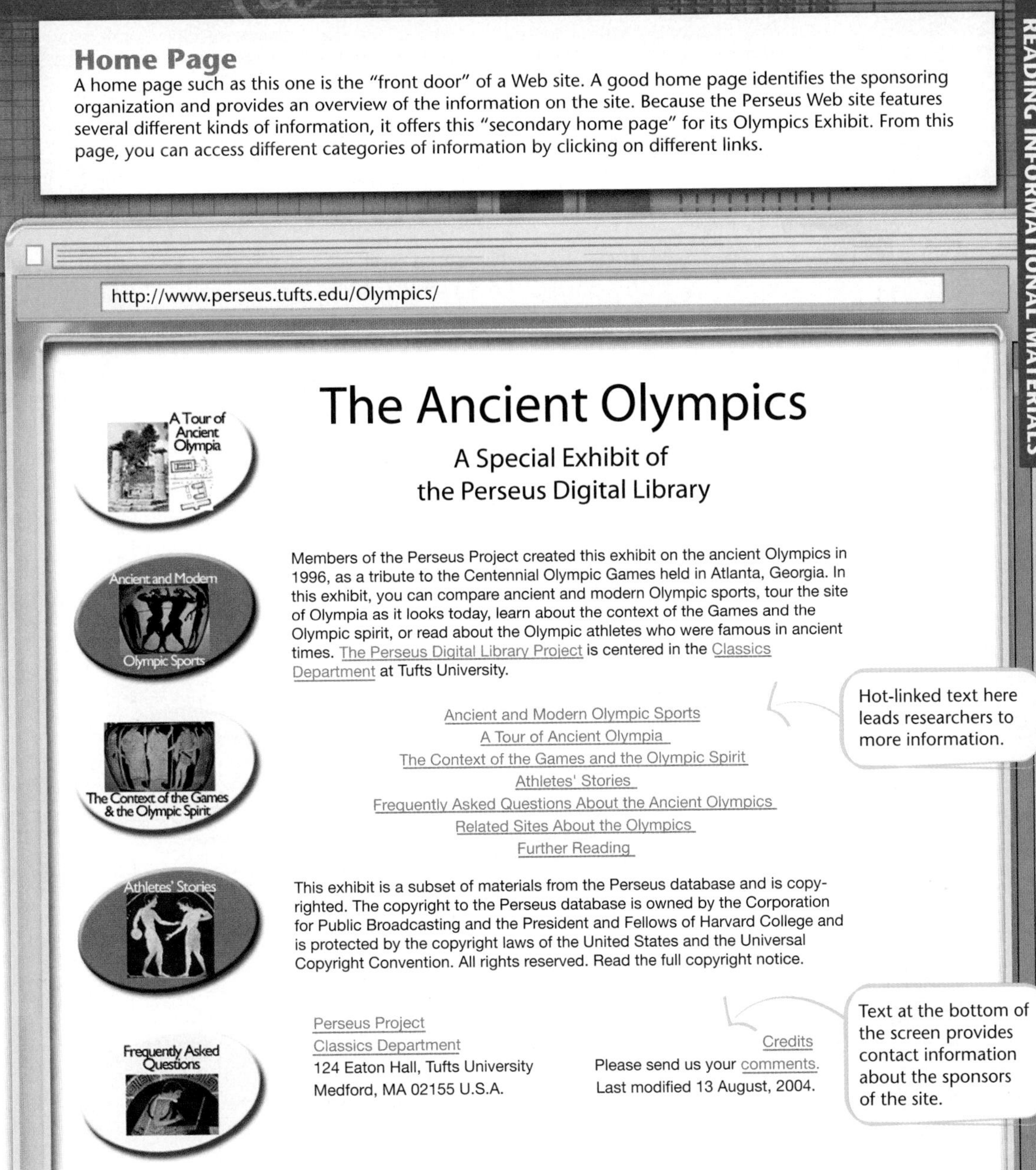
http://www.perseus.tufts.edu/Olympics/
A Tour of Ancient Olympia
Ancient and Modern Olympic Sports
The Context of the Games & the Olympic Spirit
Athletes' Stories
Frequently Asked Questions
The Ancient Olympics
A Special Exhibit of the Perseus Digital Library
Members of the Perseus Project created this exhibit on the ancient Olympics in 1996, as a tribute to the Centennial Olympic Games held in Atlanta, Georgia. In this exhibit, you can compare ancient and modern Olympic sports, tour the site of Olympia as it looks today, learn about the context of the Games and the Olympic spirit, or read about the Olympic athletes who were famous in ancient times. The Perseus Digital Library Project is centered in the Classics Department at Tufts University.
Ancient and Modern Olympic Sports
A Tour of Ancient Olympia
The Context of the Games and the Olympic Spirit
Athletes' Stories
Frequently Asked Questions About the Ancient Olympics
Related Sites About the Olympics
Further Reading
This exhibit is a subset of materials from the Perseus database and is copyrighted. The copyright to the Perseus database is owned by the Corporation for Public Broadcasting and the President and Fellows of Harvard College and is protected by the copyright laws of the United States and the Universal Copyright Convention. All rights reserved. Read the full copyright notice.
Perseus Project
Classics Department
124 Eaton Hall, Tufts University
Medford, MA 02155 U.S.A.
Credits
Please send us your comments.
Last modified 13 August, 2004.
Hot-linked text here leads researchers to more information.
Text at the bottom of the screen provides contact information about the sponsors of the site.

Differentiated Instruction Solutions for All Learners

Strategy for Special Needs Students
Have students examine Web sites that require little from the viewer in the way of navigation, such as "A Tour of Ancient Olympia." Provide a photocopy of the home page, and ask students to identify where they would click to begin the tour.

Strategy for Less Proficient Readers
Urge students to make full use of the picture icons on most Web sites. Point out on the example here, as well as on posted classroom examples, that picture icons may repeat text icons or may stand alone. Note on the "Credits" page that the sidebar icons allow users to navigate to additional links or to return to the home page.

Strategy for English Learners
Remind students that many Web sites can be accessed in a variety of languages. On some computers, students can set their Web browser for preferred languages by clicking on the "Preferences" option under "Tools." Then, have students search the Web for Olympic sites in their native languages.

Reading Web Research Sources

- If possible, post several home pages on classroom computers or provide students with photocopies. Ask students to discuss the function of home pages.
- Have students review the Perseus Digital Library pages and read the notes that identify its elements.
- After students read the opening text, have them **identify** on the Perseus Digital Library page the home page features it lists.
  Answer: The sponsoring organization, a summary of the site's information, and the search feature are present.
- Direct students' attention to the first call-out note and the picture icons. Point out that each of these icons bears a title that matches hot-linked text at mid-page. Explain that underlined text in an alternate color is usually a link to another page. Users can access the links from either the picture icon or the hot-linked text.
- **Elicit** from students the advantage that the hot-linked text offers.
  Answer: Hot-linked text offers two additional pages of information.
- Have a volunteer read aloud the paragraph at the bottom of the page that begins, "This exhibit is a subset . . ." **Ask** students what this information tells them and how they can use it to determine the Web site's credibility.
  Answer: The information tells users that the site is the property of the Corporation for Public Broadcasting and the President and Fellows of Harvard College. Because these are both recognized and respected institutions, users have some assurance of the site's credibility.
- Note that students can use an originating Web site's credibility to evaluate the credibility of the links it provides. In other words, if a user believes the originating Web site to be credible, then sites recommended on it are likely also to be credible.

continued on p. 530

Reading Web Research Sources *(cont.)*

- Point out the titles "Credits" and "The Context of the Games and the Olympic Spirit." Note that interior page titles help users navigate sites.
- **Ask** students what each interior page tells them.
  Answer: The upper page tells users who created and maintains the site. The lower page provides information about Olympic history.
- Point out the educational institutions associated with reviewing the site content. **Ask** students how this information helps them rate the site's credibility.
  Answer: This information helps users know that the site has been reviewed by respected academic institutions and should contain accurate information.
- Draw students' attention to the second call-out note. Point out that both interior pages feature the navigation bar at the left.
- **Ask** students why they think the navigation bar appears on both pages.
  Answer: The navigation bar allows users to move easily through the site.
- **Ask** students where on the lower page they would click to find what sports were played at the Olympics.
  Answer: Users would click on the "Sports" icon.

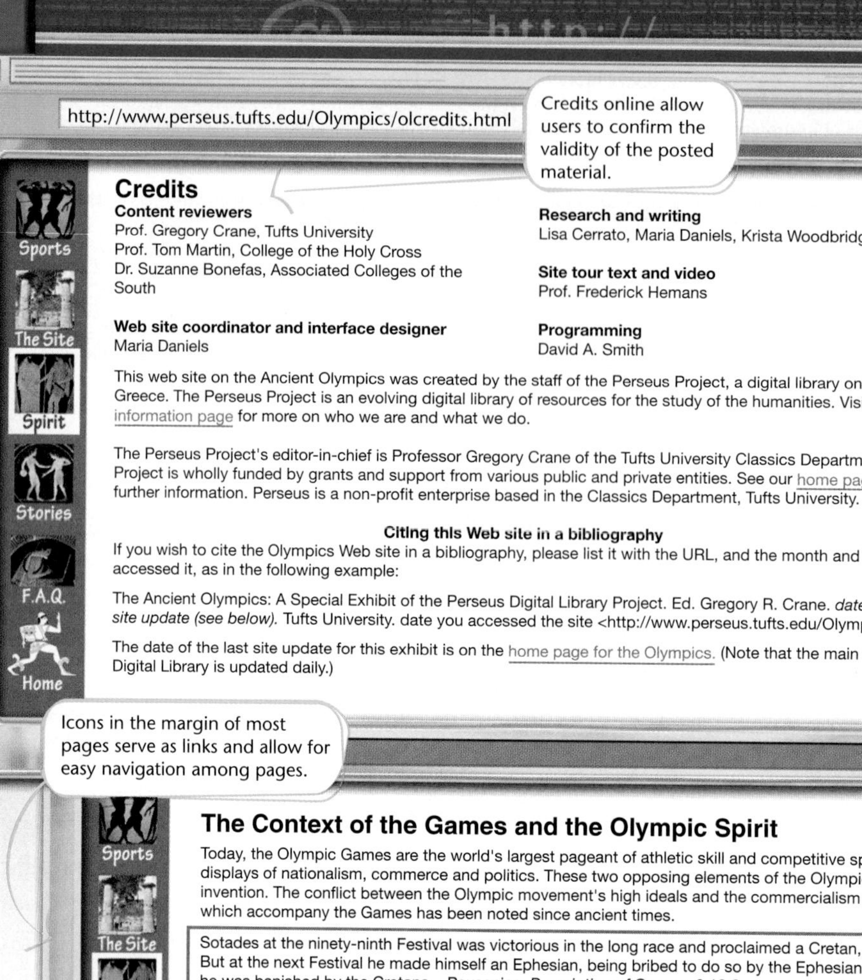

http://www.perseus.tufts.edu/Olympics/olcredits.html

Credits online allow users to confirm the validity of the posted material.

Sports
The Site
Spirit
Stories
F.A.Q.
Home

Credits

Content reviewers
Prof. Gregory Crane, Tufts University
Prof. Tom Martin, College of the Holy Cross
Dr. Suzanne Bonefas, Associated Colleges of the South

Web site coordinator and interface designer
Maria Daniels

Research and writing
Lisa Cerrato, Maria Daniels, Krista Woodbridge

Site tour text and video
Prof. Frederick Hemans

Programming
David A. Smith

This web site on the Ancient Olympics was created by the staff of the Perseus Project, a digital library on ancient Greece. The Perseus Project is an evolving digital library of resources for the study of the humanities. Visit our information page for more on who we are and what we do.

The Perseus Project's editor-in-chief is Professor Gregory Crane of the Tufts University Classics Department. The Project is wholly funded by grants and support from various public and private entities. See our home page for further information. Perseus is a non-profit enterprise based in the Classics Department, Tufts University.

Citing this Web site in a bibliography

If you wish to cite the Olympics Web site in a bibliography, please list it with the URL, and the month and year you accessed it, as in the following example:

The Ancient Olympics: A Special Exhibit of the Perseus Digital Library Project. Ed. Gregory R. Crane. *date of last site update (see below).* Tufts University. date you accessed the site <http://www.perseus.tufts.edu/Olympics/>.

The date of the last site update for this exhibit is on the home page for the Olympics. (Note that the main Perseus Digital Library is updated daily.)

Icons in the margin of most pages serve as links and allow for easy navigation among pages.

Sports
The Site
Spirit
Stories
F.A.Q.
Home

The Context of the Games and the Olympic Spirit

Today, the Olympic Games are the world's largest pageant of athletic skill and competitive spirit. They are also displays of nationalism, commerce and politics. These two opposing elements of the Olympics are not a modern invention. The conflict between the Olympic movement's high ideals and the commercialism or political acts which accompany the Games has been noted since ancient times.

> Sotades at the ninety-ninth Festival was victorious in the long race and proclaimed a Cretan, as in fact he was. But at the next Festival he made himself an Ephesian, being bribed to do so by the Ephesian people. For this act he was banished by the Cretans. Pausanias, *Description of Greece,* 6.18.6

The ancient Olympic Games, part of a major religious festival honoring Zeus, the chief Greek god, were the biggest event in their world. They were the scene of political rivalries and the site of controversies, boasts, public announcements and humiliations. In this section you can explore the context of the Olympics and read stories about the participants andspectators who came to Olympia from all over the Greek world.

To read more about these topics, see Further Resources.
- The Greek city-states and the religious festival
- Excellence and the competitive spirit
- The Olympic truce
- The ancient athlete: amateur or professional?
- Did politics ever affect the ancient Games?
- Spectators at the Games
- Cultural achievements and the Games

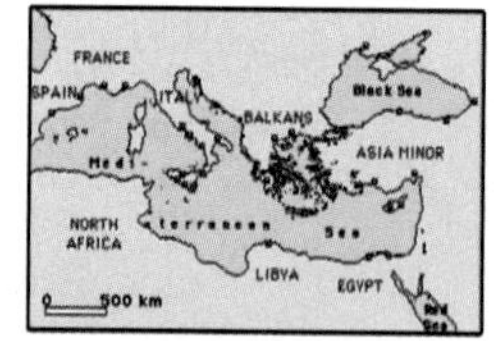

map of some cities which sent competitors to the Olympics in the 5th century B.C.

This exhibit is a subset of materials from the Perseus Project database and is copyrighted.
Please send us your comments

Monitor Your Progress

Assessment Practice

Reading: Analyzing the Usefulness and Credibility of Web Sources

Directions: *Choose the letter of the best answer to each question about the Web site.*

1. What element on the home page helps you evaluate the site's usefulness?
   A the modification date
   B the icons and hot-linked text
   C the copyright information
   D the link to Perseus Digital Library Project home page
2. What is one feature on the interior pages that helps you evaluate the site's credibility?
   A the list of content reviewers
   B the icons in the margins
   C the full-color map
   D the historical information about the athlete Sotades
3. How does the site's association with Tufts University help you judge its credibility?
   A It shows that only college students have access to the Web site.
   B It shows that the Web site is frequently updated.
   C It shows that scholars created the Web site.
   D It shows that the Web site is funded by grants.
4. What can you infer about the site from the information under the heading "Citing this Web site in a bibliography"?
   A The site cannot be cited as a source without permission.
   B The site is an acceptable source for a high school or college research paper.
   C The creators of the site believe that it is more credible than a print source.
   D The creators of the site intend it to be used as a source for research papers.

Reading: Comprehension and Interpretation

Directions: *Write your answers on a separate sheet of paper.*

5. From the Olympics Exhibit Web site, what is the best way to find out more about the Perseus Digital Library Project?
6. **(a)** Explain how the interior page "The Context of the Games and the Olympic Spirit" relates to the home page. **(b)** How can you move between these two pages?
7. **(a)** Rate the usefulness and credibility of this Web site on a scale of 1 to 5 for the following categories: subject, usefulness, and credibility. **(b)** Give at least two reasons to support each rating.

Timed Writing: Evaluation

Write a brief evaluation of this Web site, based on the three pages shown here and your ratings of the site's usefulness and credibility. As part of your evaluation, consider what information and features the site offers and whether its design makes it easy to navigate. Include your recommendations for any improvements that might make this site more useful or more credible as a source. ***(25 minutes)***

Extend the Lesson

Activity

To give students further exposure to Web research sources, have them search the Web for three sites for each of the following purposes:

- Writing a brief presentation of the Olympic Games for an audience of sixth graders.
- Writing a research paper on ancient Greek sports.

Then have students prepare a written analysis that evaluates each site's usefulness and credibility for each research purpose identified above.

Encourage students to look for Web sites that end in *.edu* or *.gov.* Students may wish to use the chart above to make notes on each Web site they review. Remind students to explain why each site would be useful to their purpose and to identify the criteria they used to determine credibility. Have students turn in a printout of each Web site's home page.

ASSESS

Answers

Reading: Analyzing the Usefulness and Credibility of Web Sources

1. B
2. A
3. C
4. D

Reading: Comprehension and Interpretation

5. **Answer:** From the Credits page, click on the "information page" link in the middle of the page.
6. **Possible response:** (a) The interior page provides information on one of the topics that you can link to from the home page. (b) You can reach this page from the home page by clicking on either the icon or the hot-linked text label "The Context of the Games and the Olympic Spirit." You can reach the home page from the interior page by clicking on the "Home" icon at the bottom left.
7. **Possible responses: subject 5:** The history of the Olympic games is thoroughly covered and is frequently updated, so it is also possible to follow modern Olympics. **usefulness 5:** The site is useful because it is easy to navigate and provides information both visually and verbally. **credibility 5:** The site is highly credible because it is associated with a respected educational institution and is responsibly maintained.

Timed Writing
Evaluation

- Advise students to include in their evaluations specific details about the most useful information found, as well as details about the site's design and any recommendations that they would like to make.
- Suggest that students plan their time to give 10 minutes to planning, 10 minutes to writing, and 5 minutes to revising and editing.

Standard Course of Study

Goal 1: WRITTEN LANGUAGE

- WL.1.02.2 Show awareness of culture in personal reflections.

Goal 3: FOUNDATIONS OF ARGUMENT

- FA.3.03.1 Gather information to prove a point about issues in literature.

Goal 5: LITERATURE

- LT.5.01.2 Build knowledge of literary genres, and explore how characteristics apply to literature of world cultures.
- LT.5.03.7 Analyze influences, contexts, or biases in world literature.
- LT.5.03.9 Analyze and evaluate the effects of author's craft and style in world literature.

Goal 6: GRAMMAR AND USAGE

- GU.6.01.4 Use vocabulary strategies to determine meaning.
- GU.6.02.1 Edit for agreement, tense choice, pronouns, antecedents, case, and complete sentences.

Step-by-Step Teaching Guide	Pacing Guide
PRETEACH	
• Administer Vocabulary and Reading Warm-ups as necessary.	5 min.
• Engage students' interest with the motivation activity.	5 min.
• Read and discuss author and background features. **FT**	10 min.
• Introduce the Literary Analysis Skill: National Epic. **FT**	5 min.
• Introduce the Reading Strategy: Applying Background Information. **FT**	10 min.
• Prepare students to read by teaching the selection vocabulary. **FT**	
TEACH	
• Informally monitor comprehension while students read independently or in groups. **FT**	30 min.
• Monitor students' comprehension with the Reading Check notes.	as students read
• Reinforce vocabulary with Vocabulary Builder notes.	as students read
• Develop students' understanding of national epic with the Literary Analysis annotations. **FT**	5 min.
• Develop students' ability to apply background information with the Reading Strategy annotations. **FT**	5 min.
ASSESS/EXTEND	
• Assess students' comprehension and mastery of the Literary Analysis and Reading Strategy by having them answer the Apply the Skills questions. **FT**	15 min.
• Have students complete the Vocabulary Lesson and the Grammar and Style Lesson. **FT**	15 min.
• Apply students' ability to clarify connections with transitions by using the Writing Lesson. **FT**	45 min. or homework
• Apply students' understanding by using one or more of the Extend Your Learning activities.	20–90 min. or homework
• Administer Selection Test A or Selection Test B. **FT**	15 min.

Resources

Print

Unit 4 Resources

- Vocabulary Warm-up Word Lists **[L1, L2, EL]** . . . . p. 135
- Vocabulary Warm-up Practice **[L1, L2, EL]** . . . . p. 136
- Reading Warm-up A **[L1, L2, EL]** . . . . p. 137
- Reading Warm-up B **[L1, L2, L3]** . . . . p. 138

Transparency

Graphic Organizer Transparencies

- Literary Analysis Graphic Organizer A **[L3]** . . . . p. 98
- Literary Analysis Graphic Organizer B **[L1, L2, EL]** . . . . p. 99
- Reading Strategy Graphic Organizer A **[L3]** . . . . p. 96
- Reading Strategy Graphic Organizer B **[L1, L2, EL]** . . . . p. 97

Print

Reader's Notebook [L2]

Reader's Notebook: Adapted Version [L1]

Reader's Notebook: English Learner's Version [EL]

Unit 4 Resources

- Literary Analysis **[L3]** . . . . p. 139
- Reading Strategy **[L3]** . . . . p. 140
- Vocabulary Builder **[L3]** . . . . p. 141

Technology

Listening to Literature Audio CDs [L2, EL]

Reader's Notebook: Adapted Version Audio CD [L1, L2]

Print

Unit 4 Resources

- Grammar and Style **[L3]** . . . . p. 142
- Support for Writing Lesson **[L3]** . . . . p. 143
- Support for Extend Your Learning **[L3]** . . . . p. 144
- Enrichment **[L4]** . . . . p. 145
- Selection Test A **[L1, L2, EL]** . . . . pp. 146–148
- Selection Test B **[L3, L4]** . . . . pp. 149–151

General Resources

- Rubrics for Response to Literature **[L3]** . . . . pp. 55–56
- Rubrics for Research: Research Report **[L3]** . . . . pp. 51–52

Technology

- **Go Online:** Research **[L3]**
- **Go Online:** Self-test **[L3]**
- ***ExamView®*, Test Bank [L3]**

Choosing Resources for Differentiated Instruction

[L1] Special Needs Students

[L2] Below-Level Students

[L3] All Students

[L4] Advanced Students

[EL] English Learners

For Vocabulary and Reading Warm-ups and for Selection Tests, **A** signifies "less challenging" and **B** "more challenging." For Graphic Organizer transparencies, **A** signifies "not filled in" and **B** "filled in."

FT Fast Track Instruction: To move the lesson more quickly, use the strategies and activities identified with **FT**.

Scaffolding for Less Proficient and Advanced Students

The leveled Critical Thinking questions after selections progress in the levels of thinking required to answer them. To address the needs of your different students, you may use the (a) level questions for your less proficient students and the (b) level questions with your on-level and advanced students. The occasional (c) level questions are appropriate for your advanced students.

PRENTICE HALL **TeacherEXPRESS™** Plan · Teach · Assess — Use this complete suite of powerful teaching tools to make lesson planning and testing quicker and easier.

PRENTICE HALL **StudentEXPRESS™** Learn · Study · Succeed — Use the interactive textbook (online and on CD-ROM) to make selections and activities come alive with audio and video support and interactive questions.

For: Information about Lexiles
Visit: www.PHSchool.com
Web Code: eue-1111

PRETEACH

Motivation

Invite students to discuss the concept of a national epic. Tell them that Virgil undertook the challenge of writing a national epic for the early Roman empire. By the time of the reign of Augustus, Rome had existed for more than seven centuries. It was Virgil's task to describe the founding of the city and to allude to the many landmarks on Rome's path to glory and domination of the Mediterranean. Ask students what a national epic for the United States might be like. What kind of story line would such an epic contain? Who would the major characters be? Perhaps most important, what distinctive and characteristic American values or talents would such an epic highlight?

❶ Background

More About the Author

Virgil was Augustus' poet laureate, the literary architect of the new Rome, whose national epic was part of a program that included monuments, works of art, and legislation. Although he was part of Augustus' inner circle, Virgil never became embroiled in political intrigue. He preferred to write in seclusion, away from the capital. He wrote slowly and spent much time on revision. We know, for example, that it took him seven years to finish his *Georgics,* a philosophic poem on the value of labor. At that rate he would have averaged less than a single line each day!

Geography Note

Draw students' attention to the map on this page. Remind them that Virgil was born on a farm in the northern frontier of the Roman Empire, in what is now northern Italy. He retained a lifelong love of rural life.

Build Skills | *Epic Poem*

from the Aeneid ❶

Virgil (70–19 B.C.)

Publius Vergilius Maro (pub′ lē əs vər jil′ ē əs ma′ rō), unquestionably the greatest Roman poet, was born near Mantua in what was then the province of Gaul. Virgil's childhood experiences on his family's farm marked his outlook in a profound and permanent way. Throughout his life, he would remain a person who was sensitive to nature and acutely aware of the beauty and wisdom of the natural world.

A Country Boy When Virgil was eleven years old, Julius Caesar came to govern Gaul. His arrival opened Virgil's eyes to a world different from his father's farm in a culturally isolated town. Virgil traveled to study in various cities, including Rome. It was there that he took courses in rhetoric, the construction and delivery of speeches. Rhetoric was an essential part of instruction for young Romans being trained for public affairs. Although Virgil was trained as a lawyer, he never pursued a legal career.

Virgil felt the effects of the ongoing Roman civil war directly. When Mark Antony, a factional leader, needed to reward his soldiers with land grants in 41 B.C., he confiscated many farms, including Virgil's. During this time, Virgil withdrew from the turmoil of the capital. He retreated to Naples and there began the study of Epicureanism, a Greek philosophy that emphasizes simple pleasures and serenity of mind.

Soon afterward, Octavian, who would eventually become the emperor Caesar Augustus, recognized the poet's genius and gave Virgil back his land. Understandably, Virgil felt deep and enduring gratitude to Octavian all his life. Virgil became the official poet of the empire. He was welcome at the emperor's court, but his heart remained in the countryside. Augustus had given Virgil an estate in the south of Italy, and the shy, delicate poet spent as much time there as he could.

Early Writing Virgil's early works were poetry collections called *Eclogues* and *Georgics.* Throughout these pastoral poems, Virgil idealizes the return to peace made possible by Caesar Augustus after a long civil war. One of the poems, the fourth *Eclogue,* had profound significance among later Christians. Written around 40 B.C., the poem speaks of a divine child whose birth would bring about peace and a return to the Golden Age. Many Christians believed Virgil had predicted the birth of Jesus, and so they considered the poet an honorary Christian and a prophet.

A National Epic When Caesar Augustus became the first emperor of Rome in 27 B.C., his new empire had no national epic. The Greeks had the *Iliad* and the *Odyssey,* venerated by Greeks and Romans alike, but Roman culture had produced nothing comparable. There were a number of impressive works of prose, theater, and even poetry by Roman writers. However, there was no national epic for Roman citizens, whose patriotism might be aroused by a mythic account of their origins.

Virgil undertook to remedy that deficiency. He spent the last eleven years of his life working on the *Aeneid* (ē nē′ id), Rome's national epic and the greatest single work of Latin literature. He wrote many drafts, revising and polishing his verse "like a she-bear licking her cubs into shape," as he put it. When he fell ill after a hard voyage and died, Virgil left instructions to destroy the manuscript he thought imperfect. Naturally, and luckily, Augustus intervened and saved the masterpiece.

Virgil's epic tells a story of adventure and bravery, with a beauty of language and style rarely equaled in world literature. During the Middle Ages and the Renaissance, Europeans considered the *Aeneid* to be the greatest literary work of all time—the ideal every writer dreamed of equaling, though none ever did.

Preview

Connecting to the Literature

Ancient Romans viewed Aeneas, the hero of the *Aeneid*, in much the same way that Americans view George Washington. Aeneas was considered the father of Rome and the embodiment of its ideals.

❷ Literary Analysis

National Epic

An epic is a long narrative—often a poem—about the adventures of gods or of a hero. A **national epic** tells a story about the founding or development of a nation or culture. Virgil's goal in writing the *Aeneid* was to give Rome a national epic that would equal Homer's *Iliad* and *Odyssey* in literary greatness and prove that Rome was as great a civilization as Greece. As you read, note details that would make Romans proud of their culture and their origins.

Connecting Literary Elements

An **epic hero** is the central figure of an epic. The hero of a national epic usually serves as a model for an entire culture. These characters are admired not just for their strength or skill in battle but for their integrity and beliefs. Ancient Roman values included the following:

- devotion to duty
- compassion and mercy for opponents in battle
- honesty and fairness

Note the ways in which Aeneas embodies and promotes these values in recounting the fall of Troy.

❸ Reading Strategy

Applying Background Information

When reading certain literary works, you must **apply background information** to fully understand them. Virgil makes frequent reference to characters and events in Homer's *Iliad*. Therefore, information about that work is useful when reading the *Aeneid*. Review the selections from the *Iliad* (p. 363). Then, use a chart like the one shown to apply that background information to Virgil's epic.

Vocabulary Builder

notions (nō′ shənz) *n.* ideas (p. 536)

perjured (pur′ jərd) *adj.* purposely false (p. 538)

guile (gīl) *n.* trickery (p. 539)

tumult (to͞o′ mult′) *n.* commotion; confusion (p. 540)

unfettered (un fet′ ərd) *adj.* unrestrained (p. 541)

blaspheming (blas fēm′ iŋ) *adj.* irreverent (p. 541)

desecrating (des′ i krāt′ iŋ) *v.* treating as not sacred (p. 542)

portents (pôr′ tents′) *n.* signs that suggest what is about to occur (p. 542)

NC Standard Course of Study

- Show awareness of culture in personal reflections. (WL.1.02.2)
- Analyze influences, contexts, or biases in world literature. (LT.5.03.7)

Reference

"cruel Achilles"

↓

Background Information

In the *Iliad*, Achilles shows no mercy to the Trojan hero Hector.

↓

Insight Gained

Virgil is presenting the Trojan side of the story told in the Greek *Iliad*.

❷ Literary Analysis

National Epic

- Read aloud the Literary Analysis instruction.
- Point out that a national epic has two purposes: to celebrate the deeds of a hero and to glorify the hero's nation and culture. The *Aeneid* may be said to have two heroes: Aeneas and Rome itself.
- Use the instruction for Connecting Literary Elements to help students understand the characteristics of an epic heo.
- Help students begin a character analysis chart for Aeneas. Have students list Aeneas' name in the left column and the three characteristics of an epic hero at the top of columns two, three, and four. As students read the *Aeneid,* tell them to list examples of Aeneas' behavior in the appropriate columns.

❸ Reading Strategy

Applying Background Information

- Encourage students to apply relevant background information as they read this excerpt from the *Aeneid*—including information from Homer's *Iliad.*
- Give students a copy of **Reading Strategy Graphic Organizer A,** p. 96 in ***Graphic Organizer Transparencies.*** Have them use it to record references and any backgound information they can use to gain greater insights into the selection.

Vocabulary Builder

- Pronounce each vocabulary word for students, and read the definitions as a class. Have students identify any words with which they are already familiar.

Differentiated Instruction Solutions for All Learners

Support for Special Needs Students

Have students read the adapted version of from the *Aeneid* Book II: How They Took the City in the ***Reader's Notebook: Adapted Version.*** This version provides basic-level instruction in an interactive format with questions and write-on lines. Completing these pages will prepare students to read the selection in the Student Edition.

Support for Less Proficient Readers

Have students read from the *Aeneid* Book II: How They Took the City in the ***Reader's Notebook.*** This version provides basic-level instruction in an interactive format with questions and write-on lines. After students finish the selection in the ***Reader's Notebook,*** have them complete the questions and activities in the Student Edition.

Support for English Learners

Have students read from the *Aeneid* Book II: How They Took the City in the ***Reader's Notebook: English Learner's Version.*** This version provides basic-level instruction in an interactive format with questions and write-on lines. Completing these pages will prepare students to read the selection in the Student Edition.

Facilitate Understanding

As students read, have them list the most important characters in the narrative and draw pictures of these characters. Display the drawings, and refer to them as students read.

❶ About the Selection

Romans as well as Greeks venerated the Homeric epics, the most ancient texts of Greek literature. To take his place beside Homer, Virgil uses the same meter, situates his story at the time of Troy's fall (1200 B.C.), and adopts epic conventions such as invoking the muse and involving Olympian gods.

❷ Humanities

Aeneas and Dido,
by Pierre Narcisse Guérin

This painting by Guérin (1774–1833) is representative of the work of the foremost follower of the neoclassical painter David. Guérin's classical and mythological pieces were a tremendous success in Paris. The artist was often seen sketching for his paintings in theaters around the city, a habit that strongly influenced his work.

Use the following questions for discussion:

- How would you describe the neoclassical style of painting?
  Possible response: The style is warm and balanced.
- What part of this painting draws the viewer's attention first?
  Possible response: The figure of Dido is most prominent.

❸ Critical Viewing

Answer: The listeners appear preoccupied or uninterested.

from the ❶ Aeneid

Book II: How They Took the City

Virgil *translated by* Robert Fitzgerald

❷

Aeneas and Dido, Pierre Narcisse Guérin, The Louvre, Paris, Reunion des Musees Nationaux

❸ ▲**Critical Viewing** As Aeneas speaks in this painting, what effect does he appear to have on his listeners? **[Infer]**

Differentiated Instruction Solutions for All Learners

Accessibility at a Glance

	from the Aeneid Book II: How They Took the City
Context	Aeneas recounts the fall of Troy in 1200 B.C.
Language	First-person point of view with some rhetorical questions
Concept Level	Accessible (Beware of trusting a fraudulent schemer.)
Literary Merit	Classic epic poem
Lexile	NP
Overall Rating	Challenging

Background Virgil opens the *Aeneid* with an invocation of the Muse, a goddess who presides over the arts. He calls on her to remind him why Aeneas, an exiled hero who survived the destruction of his native Troy by the Greeks, had to suffer so much before he could found Rome. The reason is that Juno (Hera, in Greek mythology), the queen of heaven, persecutes the Trojan hero. Juno is still angry that Aeneas' cousin Paris judged her to be less fair than Aeneas' mother, the goddess Venus (Aphrodite, in Greek mythology).

As the *Aeneid* begins, Aeneas is at sea, about to land safely in Italy, but Juno creates a storm that wrecks the hero's fleet. Aeneas is tossed about and lands on the African coast near Carthage, a city being built by Queen Dido. The Queen holds a banquet in the Trojans' honor. Disguised as Aeneas' son, the god Cupid attends the banquet and causes Dido to fall in love with Aeneas. To prolong his stay, Dido asks Aeneas to recount the fall of Troy and his subsequent wanderings, which he does as Book II begins.

4
The room fell silent, and all eyes were on him,
As Father Aeneas from his high couch began:

"Sorrow too deep to tell, your majesty,
You order me to feel and tell once more:
How the Danaans[1] leveled in the dust
The splendor of our mourned-forever kingdom—
Heartbreaking things I saw with my own eyes
And was myself a part of. Who could tell them,
Even a Myrmidon[2] or Dolopian[3]
Or ruffian of Ulysses,[4] without tears?
Now, too, the night is well along, with dewfall
Out of heaven, and setting stars weigh down
Our heads toward sleep. But if so great desire
Moves you to hear the tale of our disasters,
Briefly recalled, the final throes[5] of Troy,[6]
However I may shudder at the memory
And shrink again in grief, let me begin.

5
Knowing their strength broken in warfare, turned
Back by the fates, and years—so many years—
Already slipped away, the Danaan captains
By the divine handicraft of Pallas built
A horse of timber, tall as a hill,
And sheathed its ribs with planking of cut pine.
This they gave out to be an offering

1. **Danaans** (da´ nā ənz) tribal name for the Greeks.
2. **Myrmidon** (mʉr´ mə dän) Phthian warrior who fought under Achilles.
3. **Dolopian** (də lō´ pē ən) person from Thessaly, a Greek ally.
4. **Ulysses** (yoo lis´ ēz´) Roman name for Odysseus, a Greek warrior.
5. **throes** (thrōz) *n.* acts of struggling.
6. **Troy** (troi) city in Asia Minor, home of the Trojans.

Reading Strategy
Applying Background Information Use background information to explain why Aeneas is given the title "Father" here.

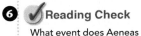

Reading Check
What event does Aeneas begin to recount?

4 Reading Strategy
Applying Background Information

- Remind students that the Romans traced the founding of their city to the Trojan leader Aeneas, who escaped from the burning city of Troy after the Greeks sacked it.
- Have students recall that Aeneas was considered the father of Rome and the embodiment of Roman ideals.
- Then, ask a volunteer to read aloud the bracketed passage. Call students' attention to the "high couch" from which Aeneas speaks. Explain that at banquets, the ancients reclined on couches placed around a low table. A "high couch" corresponds to the head table, where important guests were placed.
- **Direct** students to respond to the Reading Strategy note: Use background information to explain why Aeneas is given the title "Father" here.
  Answer: Aeneas is given the title "Father" to emphasize his preeminent position as the founder of Rome.

5 Background
Culture

Pallas Athene was notoriously pro-Greek and hostile to the Trojans. Many versions of the sack of Troy were told in epics and tragedies, and the trick of the Trojan horse was part of all of them. Virgil draws on the tradition while emphasizing the Trojan point of view.

6 Reading Check

Answer: Aeneas begins to recount the fall of Troy.

Differentiated Instruction Solutions for All Learners

Strategy for Special Needs Students

Tell students to reread carefully the Background note. Then, ask volunteers to name the major events in chronological order. Finally, have each student create a sequence chart that lists the events immediately preceding the action recounted in this excerpt. Help students begin a set of character cards that include the character's name, a description, and an illustration for a Muse, Aeneas, Juno, Paris, Venus, Dido, and Cupid.

Strategy for Less Proficient Readers

Discuss the importance of maps and charts to help sailors calculate time and distance. Ask students if they think Aeneas had maps to direct his adventures. Help students locate an ancient world map of the Mediterranean Sea and plot Aeneas' journey: Troy to Aenos to Delos to Crete to Strophades to Ithaca to Drepanum to Carthage to Drepanum to Cumae to Latium.

7 Critical Viewing

Possible response: Yes; the size of the horse and the ominous, somewhat violent mood in the depiction are consistent with Virgil's narrative.

8 Humanities

The Building of the Trojan Horse, by Giovanni Domenico Tiepolo

Tiepolo (1727–1804) was the most important Venetian artist and decorator of the eighteenth century. He was internationally famous for his draftsmanship and the clarity of his colors. Besides his work in Italy, Tiepolo also executed important commissions in Bavaria and Spain.

In this picture, the horse is being constructed outside the walls of Troy. The energetic, almost frantic stance of the figures emphasizes how much is at stake: nothing less than a winner-take-all effort to sack Troy after a siege of ten years. On the left, the posture of the onlookers may suggest the skepticism and resistance of Trojans such as Laocoön, who urged that the horse be rejected as a trick.

Use the following questions for discussion:

- Why do you think the artist shows the walls of the city prominently on the left?
  Possible response: The walls remind viewers of the Trojans' crucial decision to bring the horse inside the city's protected perimeter.
- Why do you think the builders of the horse are depicted as swarming over it in feverish poses?
  Possible response: This image prompts associations with violence and destruction.

For a safe return by sea, and the word went round.
But on the sly they shut inside a company
5 Chosen from their picked soldiery by lot,
Crowding the vaulted caverns in the dark—
The horse's belly—with men fully armed.

Offshore there's a long island, Tenedos,[7]
Famous and rich while Priam's kingdom[8] lasted,
A treacherous anchorage now, and nothing more.
They crossed to this and hid their ships behind it
On the bare shore beyond. We thought they'd gone,
Sailing home to Mycenae[9] before the wind,
So Teucer's[10] town is freed of her long anguish,
Gates thrown wide! And out we go in joy
To see the Dorian[11] campsites, all deserted,
The beach they left behind. Here the Dolopians
Pitched their tents, here cruel Achilles lodged,
There lay the ships, and there, formed up in ranks,
They came inland to fight us. Of our men
One group stood marveling, gaping up to see
The dire gift of the cold unbedded goddess,
The sheer mass of the horse.
Thymoetes[12] shouts
It should be hauled inside the walls and moored
High on the citadel[13]—whether by treason
Or just because Troy's fate went that way now.
Capys[14] opposed him; so did the wiser heads:
'Into the sea with it,' they said, 'or burn it,
Build up a bonfire under it,
This trick of the Greeks, a gift no one can trust,
Or cut it open, search the hollow belly!'

Contrary notions pulled the crowd apart.
Next thing we knew, in front of everyone,
Laocoön[15] with a great company
Came furiously running from the Height,[16]
9 And still far off cried out: 'O my poor people,
Men of Troy, what madness has come over you?

7. **Tenedos** (ten′ ə dōs) island off the coast of Troy.
8. **Priam's kingdom** Troy.
9. **Mycenae** (mi sē′ nē) Greek city ruled by Agamemnon, a principal character in the *Iliad*.
10. **Teucer's** (to͞o′ sər) **town** Troy; Teucer, from Crete, was the original king of Troy.
11. **Dorian** (dôr′ ē ən) Greek.
12. **Thymoetes** (thī mē′ tēz) a Trojan leader.
13. **citadel** (sit′ ə del) *n.* safe, fortified place of defense in a city.
14. **Capys** (kā′ pis) a Trojan leader.
15. **Laocoön** (lā äk′ə wän′) Trojan priest of the god Neptune.
16. **the Height** the Acropolis.

7 Critical Viewing ▶ Do you think this depiction of the wooden horse is consistent with the way Virgil describes it? Why or why not? **[Make a Judgment]**

Vocabulary Builder
notions (nō′ shənz) *n.* ideas

Enrichment

The National Epic

In his pioneering essay "Epic and Novel" (collected in *The Dialogic Imagination*), M. M. Bakhtin writes:

> The world of the epic is the national heroic past: it is a world of "beginnings" and "peak times" in the national history, a world of fathers and founders of families, a world of firsts and bests. The important point here is not that the past constitutes the content of the epic. The formally constitutive feature of the epic as a genre is rather the transferral of a represented world into the past. . . . The epic has been from the beginning a poem about the past, and the authorial position . . . is the environment of a man speaking about a past that is to him inaccessible, the reverent point of view of a descendent.

8 

Can you believe the enemy truly gone?
A gift from the Danaans, and no ruse?[17]
Is that Ulysses' way, as you have known him?
9 Achaeans[18] must be hiding in this timber,
Or it was built to butt against our walls,
Peer over them into our houses, pelt
The city from the sky. Some crookedness
Is in this thing. Have no faith in the horse!
Whatever it is, even when Greeks bring gifts
I fear them, gifts and all.'
He broke off then
And rifled his big spear with all his might
Against the horse's flank, the curve of belly.
It stuck there trembling, and the rounded hull
Reverberated[19] groaning at the blow.
If the gods' will had not been sinister,
If our own minds had not been crazed,
He would have made us foul that Argive[20] den
10 With bloody steel, and Troy would stand today—
O citadel of Priam,[21] towering still!

17. ruse (ro͞oz) *n.* trick.
18. Achaeans (ə kē′ ənz) Greeks.
19. reverberated (ri vur′ bə rāt′ id) *v.* echoed repeatedly.
20. Argive (är′ gīv) Greek.
21. Priam (prī ′ əm) King of Troy.

Literary Analysis
National Epic In this passage, how does Virgil contrast the Trojans, to whom the Romans traced their ancestry, with the Greeks?

Reading Check 11
What disagreement is taking place among the Trojans?

9 Literary Analysis
National Epic
- Tell students to reread Laocoön's impassioned speech in the bracketed passage, and ask them to summarize its main idea.
- Then, **ask** students the Literary Analysis question: In this passage, how does Virgil contrast the Trojans, to whom the Romans traced their ancestry, with the Greeks?
Answer: Laocoön contrasts Trojan credulousness or naiveté with Greek treachery.

Monitor Progress **Ask** students to explain the primary purpose of a national epic.
Answer: The purpose of a national epic is to tell about the founding or development of a nation or culture.

Reteach If students continue to have trouble with the idea of a national epic, use **Literary Analysis** support p. 139, in ***Unit 4 Resources.***

10 Background
Poetics
A device Virgil is fond of is the proleptic (from the Greek word meaning "anticipate") adjective. For example, in the phrase "bloody steel," the position of the adjective would indicate that the steel is bloody to begin with, before it is used to strike. However, logic leads us to see that the steel becomes bloody only after the act of violence. The effect is to compress time, to make the reader see the anticipation of the act, the act itself, and the result in a single frame.

11 Reading Check
Answer: Some Trojans want to bring the horse inside the walls; others fear that the horse is a Greek trick, and they urge that it be burned or thrown into the sea.

Differentiated Instruction Solutions for All Learners

Support for English Learners
The syntax of Laocoön's speech (lines 58–69) may pose some challenges for students. Remind them that the speech is meant to convey passionate excitement and foreboding. Thus, Laocoön begins with a series of rhetorical questions (lines 58–62). Point out the parallelism of the verbs *butt, peer,* and *pelt* in lines 64–65. To reinforce understanding, invite students to give choral readings of the speech, carefully observing the punctuation and the run-on lines.

Enrichment for Advanced Readers
Tell students that an archetype is a character who embodies certain readily identifiable character traits or who suggests familiar experiences. Ulysses is such a character. To his friends, he is a resourceful man and a persuasive speaker; to his foes, he is a rogue and a shameless liar. In modern television and film, Captain Kirk of *Star Trek* is a similar type. Encourage students to view the film *Star Trek.* Direct them to write a character analysis in which they compare and contrast Ulysses (Odysseus) and Captain Kirk.

⓬ Background

Literature

The "unknown fellow" is Sinon, who is wholly Virgil's creation, and his lying story is free invention. His "sinuous" name and the hissing words he uses in Latin mark him as the proverbial snake in the grass. He is as twisty and talented as Ulysses, his pretended enemy, and better suited for the job because no one knows him.

⓭ Literary Analysis

National Epic and Epic Hero

- Ask a volunteer to read aloud the bracketed passage.
- Remind students of the Roman values of compassion, mercy, and fairness. Stress that Virgil characterizes Aeneas as an embodiment of these values.
- Then, **ask** students the Literary Analysis question: What Roman value does Aeneas demonstrate in these lines?
  Answer: Aeneas demonstrates the value of fairness.

⓮ Vocabulary Builder

Latin Root *-jur-*

- Draw students' attention to the word *perjured* and its definition.
- Tell students that the Latin word *jurāre,* from which the root *-jur-* is derived, means "to swear an oath."
- Write the words *jury, jurisdiction,* and *abjure* on the board. Then, ask students to relate the root *-jur-* to the definitions of each of these words.
- Finally, challenge each student to use some of these vocabulary words in a short description of one of the epic heroes mentioned during the Motivation activity.

But now look: hillmen, shepherds of Dardania,[22]
Raising a shout, dragged in before the king
An unknown fellow with hands tied behind—
This all as he himself had planned,
Volunteering, letting them come across him,
So he could open Troy to the Achaeans.
Sure of himself this man was, braced for it
Either way, to work his trick or die.
From every quarter Trojans run to see him,
Ring the prisoner round, and make a game
Of jeering at him. Be instructed now
In Greek deceptive arts: one barefaced deed
Can tell you of them all.
As the man stood there, shaken and defenseless,
Looking around at ranks of Phrygians,[23]
'Oh god,' he said, 'what land on earth, what seas
Can take me in? What's left me in the end,
Outcast that I am from the Danaans,
Now the Dardanians will have my blood?'

The whimpering speech brought us up short; we felt
A twinge for him. Let him speak up, we said,
Tell us where he was born, what news he brought,
What he could hope for as a prisoner.
Taking his time, slow to discard his fright,
He said:
'I'll tell you the whole truth, my lord,
No matter what may come of it. Argive
I am by birth, and will not say I'm not.
That first of all: Fortune has made a derelict
Of Sinon,[24] but the witch
Won't make an empty liar of him, too.
Report of Palamedes[25] may have reached you,
Scion of Belus' line,[26] a famous man
Who gave commands against the war. For this,
On a trumped-up charge, on perjured testimony,
The Greeks put him to death—but now they mourn him,
Now he has lost the light. Being kin to him,
In my first years I joined him as companion,
Sent by my poor old father on this campaign,
And while he held high rank and influence

Literary Analysis
National Epic and Epic Hero What Roman value does Aeneas demonstrate in these lines?

Vocabulary Builder
perjured (pʉr′ jərd) *adj.* purposely false

---

22. **Dardania** (där dā′ nē ə) generalized name for Troy and its surrounding area.
23. **Phrygians** (fri′ jē ənz) Trojans.
24. **Sinon** (sī′ nän)
25. **Palamedes** (pal′ ə mē′ dēz) Greek warrior who advised Agamemnon to abandon the war against Troy; he was brought down by Ulysses, who forged proof that Palamedes cooperated with the enemy in the Trojan war.
26. **Scion of Belus**' (bel′ əs) **line** descendant of Belus, king of Egypt and father of Dido, queen of Carthage.

Enrichment

Roman Rhetoric

Like all educated Romans, Virgil was schooled in the art of rhetoric, or public speaking. Citizens were trained to plead cases in a court of law or to speak for or against legislation in the Senate. Many Roman authors (Cicero, Pliny, and Tacitus) enjoyed vigorous legal or political careers. Others (Catullus, Virgil, and Ovid) used their education in their writing and usually avoided law and politics. Everyone, however, knew the rules of the game, and the same techniques used to convince a jury appear in the speeches of Virgil's characters or in the fictitious letters of Ovid's heroes.

In Sinon, Virgil shows skill in building a many-layered character. Sinon, as a trickster or confidence man, creates his own plausible fictional character; simultaneously, Virgil reveals Sinon as a treacherous liar. In creating Sinon, Virgil displays his rhetorical skills as a speech-making poet.

In royal councils, we did well, with honor.
Then by the guile and envy of Ulysses—
Nothing unheard of there!—he left this world,
And I lived on, but under a cloud, in sorrow,
Raging for my blameless friend's downfall.
Demented, too, I could not hold my peace
But said if I had luck, if I won through
Again to Argos,[27] I'd avenge him there.
And I roused hatred with my talk; I fell
Afoul now of that man. From that time on,
Day in, day out, Ulysses
Found new ways to bait and terrify me,
Putting out shady rumors among the troops,
Looking for weapons he could use against me.
He could not rest till Calchas served his turn—
But why go on? The tale's unwelcome, useless,
If Achaeans are all one,
And it's enough I'm called Achaean, then
Exact the punishment, long overdue;
The Ithacan[28] desires it; the Atridae[29]
Would pay well for it.'
Burning with curiosity,
We questioned him, called on him to explain—
⑯ Unable to conceive such a performance,
The art of the Pelasgian.[30] He went on,
Atremble, as though he feared us:
'Many times
The Danaans wished to organize retreat,
To leave Troy and the long war, tired out.
If only they had done it! Heavy weather
At sea closed down on them, or a fresh gale
From the Southwest would keep them from embarking,
Most of all after this figure here,
This horse they put together with maple beams,
Reached its full height. Then wind and thunderstorms
Rumbled in heaven. So in our quandary[31]
We sent Eurypylus[32] to Phoebus' oracle,[33]
And he brought back this grim reply:

'Blood and a virgin slain
You gave to appease the winds, for your first voyage

---

27. Argos (är′ gōs) home city of Agamemnon and Menelaus; a generalized name for Greece.
28. Ithacan (ith′ ə kən) Ulysses, who comes from Ithaca in western Greece.
29. Atridae (ə trī′ dē) Agamemnon and Menelaus, the two sons of Atreus.
30. Pelasgian (pə laz′ jē ən) *n.* early inhabitant of Greece.
31. quandary (kwän′ də rē) *n.* state of uncertainty.
32. Eurypylus (yo͞o rip′ ə ləs) Greek.
33. Phoebus' oracle oracle of Apollo at Delphi.

Literature in Context

⑮ History Connection

The Reign of Augustus

In 27 B.C., Augustus, great-nephew of and heir to Julius Caesar, quashed all opposition and took power in Rome, putting an end to more than a hundred years of civil war. Many who had experienced the violence and terror of the late Republic welcomed the prospect of peace. Augustus marked the beginning of his reign by funding an ambitious building program and supporting poets and artists.

Augustus ruled as "first citizen" rather than as emperor, out of deference to the traditional Roman distrust of kings. Yet there was no doubt that his power was absolute. Peace, prosperity, and a long reign solidified his authority and legitimacy, and the Romans would never again return to a republican system of government.

Connect to the Literature

How might Virgil's epic be different if it had been written before the reign of Augustus?

Vocabulary Builder
guile (gīl) *n.* trickery

⑰ **Reading Check**

With which Greek soldier does Sinon say he is in conflict?

Differentiated Instruction Solutions for All Learners

Background for Special Needs Students
This page presents many names, which may challenge some students. Encourage students to use the footnotes. Explain the allusive or metaphorical uses of some of these names, for example, "Ithacan" for Ulysses. Finally, remind students that certain figures in literature and mythology are known by two names: one Greek and one Roman. Odysseus (Ulysses) is an example. Other examples include the Roman "Juno" for the Greek "Hera" and the Roman "Minerva" for the Greek "Athena."

Enrichment for Advanced Readers
A speaker trying to persuade his or her listeners to undertake a particular course of action may argue that the action is pleasant, just, or useful. Lead students to understand how Sinon uses the familiar structure of the persuasive argument to persuade the Trojans to do the opposite of what he advises them. Ask students to consider the persuasive tactics used in today's commercials and public service announcements. Suggest that students write analyses of a current anti-drug or anti-smoking advertisement.

⑮ Literature in Context

The Reign of Augustus

Perhaps Augustus' most notable shortcoming as a ruler was his difficulty in finding a suitable successor. Augustus had a daughter, Julia, but no male heir. One by one, the candidates whom Augustus identified as potential successors predeceased him: his nephew Marcellus, his son-in-law Agrippa, and his grandsons Gaius and Lucius. Finally, the emperor settled on his stepson Tiberius, whose mother was Livia, Augustus' second wife. Augustus adopted Tiberius and named him successor in his will. Tiberius, Rome's second emperor, began his rule in A.D. 14.

Connect to the Literature Remind students that the reign of Augustus brought peace to Rome after years of turmoil from the civil war in the Roman republic. Then ask students to suggest how this epic would be different if Virgil had written it before the reign of Augustus.
Possible response: Virgil might not have woven Roman values of compassion and mercy into his tale. If not, the Trojans would be too suspicious and watchful to have sympathy for Sinon, to listen to his tale, and to be tricked by his ploy to persuade them not to take the horse inside the walls of the city. Then the Greeks would not have destroyed Troy and won the war.

⑯ Critical Thinking

Analyze

- Ask a student to read aloud the bracketed passage.
- Point out to students that Aeneas calls attention to the Trojans' innocence resulting from their own decency and lack of duplicity.
- **Ask** students why he is doing this.
Possible response: A Roman belief about Greeks is that they were cunning speakers and devious actors as opposed to the strong and silent Romans.

⑰ Reading Check

Answer: Sinon is in conflict with Ulysses (Odysseus).

⓲ Humanities

The Wooden Horse of Troy

This complex rendering of the Trojan horse (c. 1525–1540) is an extraordinary example of the art of enamel painting. This technique employs colored-glass powders fused to a copper or silver base, using a frame.

This extremely difficult process was brought to the status of high art by the fifteenth- and sixteenth-century French artists of the city of Limoges. By applying the powdered glass with a brush, artists could capture the finest details.

The name of the artist who created this series of plaques on the themes of the *Aeneid* has been lost. It is thought, however, that they may be the work of Jean I. Penicaud, known as "The Master of the *Aeneid*."

Use the following questions for discussion:

- How does this artist's conception of the Trojan horse compare with your own notion of it?
  Possible response: The horse seems smaller in the painting than it might have been in real life.
- Choose one element of the illustration that you would remove and another that you would add if you were going to depict this scene differently. Explain your choices.
  Possible response: If the horse were made larger, it would be more realistic. Removing the blacks and browns from the painting and using more color would make the action easier for the viewer to see.

⓳ Critical Viewing

Possible response: Such details include the small size of the horse and the architectural style of the buildings of Troy.

⓲

The Wooden Horse of Troy, Limoges Master of the Aeneid, Louvre, Paris

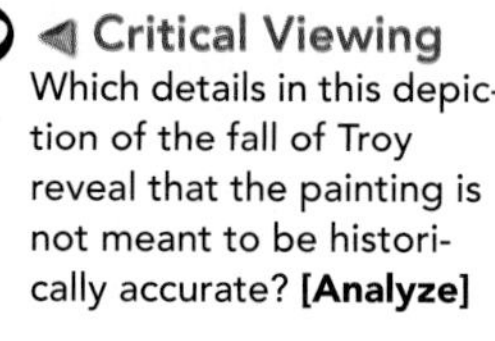

⓳ ◀ Critical Viewing
Which details in this depiction of the fall of Troy reveal that the painting is not meant to be historically accurate? **[Analyze]**

Troyward, O Danaans. Blood again
And Argive blood, one life, wins your return.'

When this got round among the soldiers, gloom
Came over them, and a cold chill that ran
To the very marrow. Who had death in store?
Whom did Apollo call for? Now the man
Of Ithaca haled Calchas out among us
In tumult, calling on the seer to tell
The true will of the gods. Ah, there were many
Able to divine the crookedness
And cruelty afoot for me, but they
Looked on in silence. For ten days the seer
Kept still, kept under cover, would not speak
Of anyone, or name a man for death,
Till driven to it at last by Ulysses' cries—
By prearrangement—he broke silence, barely
Enough to designate me for the altar.
Every last man agreed. The torments each
Had feared for himself, now shifted to another,
All could endure. And the infamous day came,
The ritual, the salted meal, the fillets[34] . . .

⓴

Vocabulary Builder
tumult (to͞o′ mult′) *n.* commotion; confusion

34. fillets (fil′ its) *n.* woolen bands worn by sacrificial victims.

Enrichment

The Sacrifice at Aulis

In lines 154–157, the oracular utterance refers to Agamemnon's sacrifice of his daughter Iphigeneia. The sacrifice was performed at Aulis so that the winds would blow and the Greek fleet could sail from Aulis to Troy. In the tragedian Euripides' dramatic version of the myth, staged at Athens in the late fifth century B.C., Odysseus (Ulysses), with the deceitful cooperation of the seer Calchas, engineers the human sacrifice for his own ambitious ends. Virgil would expect his audience to remember not only the myth but the popular Euripidean play.

I broke free, I confess it, broke my chains,
Hid myself all night in a muddy marsh,
Concealed by reeds, waiting for them to sail
If they were going to.
Now no hope is left me
Of seeing my home country ever again,
My sweet children, my father, missed for years.
Perhaps the army will demand they pay
For my escape, my crime here, and their death,
Poor things, will be my punishment. Ah, sir,
I beg you by the gods above, the powers
In whom truth lives, and by what faith remains
Uncontaminated to men, take pity
On pain so great and so unmerited!'

For tears we gave him life, and pity, too.
Priam himself ordered the gyves[35] removed
And the tight chain between. In kindness then
He said to him:
'Whoever you may be,
The Greeks are gone; forget them from now on;
You shall be ours. And answer me these questions:
Who put this huge thing up, this horse?
Who designed it? What do they want with it?
Is it religious or a means of war?'

These were his questions. Then the captive, trained
In trickery, in the stagecraft of Achaea,
Lifted his hands unfettered to the stars.
'Eternal fires of heaven,' he began,
'Powers inviolable, I swear by thee,
As by the altars and blaspheming swords
I got away from, and the gods' white bands[36]
I wore as one chosen for sacrifice,
This is justice, I am justified
In dropping all allegiance to the Greeks—
As I had cause to hate them; I may bring
Into the open what they would keep dark.
No laws of my own country bind me now.
Only be sure you keep your promises
And keep faith, Troy, as you are kept from harm
If what I say proves true, if what I give
Is great and valuable.

35. gyves (gīvz) *n.* fetters or shackles used to restrain.
36. gods' white bands fillets.

Vocabulary Builder

unfettered (un fet′ ərd) *adj.* unrestrained

blaspheming (blas fēm′ iŋ) *adj.* irreverent

Reading Check

Why does Sinon say he deserted the Greeks?

20 Critical Thinking

Analyze Cause and Effect

- Have students read the bracketed passage. Then, ask them to think about how Sinon is working to arouse sympathy and increase his credibility.
- **Ask:** What is the purpose of "confessing" a weakness?
  Possible response: When a speaker confesses a weakness, it allows the listener to feel both sympathy for and superiority over the speaker.

21 Critical Thinking

Infer

- Have students reread lines 180–185 carefully.
- Then, **ask** why Sinon mentions his home country, his children, and his father.
  Possible response: The references are calculated to stimulate pity and compassion in Sinon's audience—an objective he accomplishes successfully.

22 Background

Culture

Falsely swearing a solemn oath was a serious offense. During the long years of the civil wars in Rome, however, Virgil's audience would have seen more than one solemn oath of state made only to be broken. Aeneas may be thinking that only Greeks are treacherous, but Virgil wants his audience to think about treachery as a human problem.

23 Reading Check

Answer: Sinon says that he deserted the Greeks to avoid being sacrificed. He also wishes to convince the Trojans of his hatred for the Greeks.

Differentiated Instruction — Solutions for All Learners

Support for English Learners

Review with students that phrases made up of prepositions and their objects are modifiers, used as either adjectives or adverbs. As adjectives, they usually modify nouns; while as adverbs, they modify verbs, adjectives, or other adverbs. Note that a gerund, a verbal noun, can be the object of a preposition (*of seeing* in line 181); a participle, a verbal adjective, can be modified by a prepositional phrase (*trained in trickery* in lines 199–200).

Tell students to continue reading and then write paragraphs in which they tell in their own words Sinon's explanation for the construction of the wooden horse and the penalty involved in transporting it into Troy. Suggest that students include two prepositional phrases used as adjectives and two prepositional phrases used as adverbs.

24 Reading Strategy

Applying Background Information

- Have students recall which side—Greek or Trojan—was favored by the leading Greek divinities.
- Remind students that Athena and Hera favored the Greeks as a result of the Judgment of Paris.
- Guide students to understand how Athena's well-known preference for the Greek cause makes Sinon's narrative—in which the goddess is momentarily offended—seem more plausible.
- Have a student read aloud the bracketed passage. Then, **ask** students to respond to the Reading Strategy item: Explain how knowing Athena's role in the *Iliad* adds to your understanding of this passage.
Possible response: Knowing Athena's role in the *Iliad* as a protector and helper of the Greeks adds an ironic level of understanding to the passage. Sinon's pretenses to the contrary, Athena is actually helping the Greeks with the stratagem of the horse.

The whole hope
Of the Danaans, and their confidence
In the war they started, rested all along
In help from Pallas. Then the night came
24 When Diomedes and that criminal,
Ulysses, dared to raid her holy shrine.
They killed the guards on the high citadel
And ripped away the statue, the Palladium,[37]
Desecrating with bloody hands the virginal
Chaplets[38] of the goddess. After that,
Danaan hopes waned and were undermined,
Ebbing away, their strength in battle broken,
The goddess now against them. This she made
Evident to them all with signs and portents.
Just as they set her statue up in camp,
The eyes, cast upward, glowed with crackling flames,

Reading Strategy
Applying Background Information Explain how knowing Athena's role in the *Iliad* adds to your understanding of this passage.

Vocabulary Builder
desecrating (des′ i krāt′ iŋ) *v.* treating as not sacred

portents (pôr′ tents′) *n.* signs that suggest what is about to occur

37. Palladium (pə lā′ dē əm) statue of Pallas Athena at her shrine in Troy. According to the oracle, Troy could not be captured as long as the Palladium remained in place.
38. Chaplets (chap′ lits) *n.* fillets; garlands.

25 

Enrichment

Imagery in the *Aeneid*

Virgil uses imagery to influence his readers' reactions to characters and events. Without needing to make editorial comments or to interpret, Virgil suggests possible interpretations by his use of figurative language. Serpents and flames play a large part in the story of the fall of Troy. The wisdom of the serpent is sacred to Athena (Minerva), who favors the Greeks. Three celestial serpents grace the breastplate of Agamemnon, the Greek father of Helen, whose kidnapping began the Trojan War. An angry Apollo sends monstrous sea snakes to kill Laocoön and his two sons when Laocoön seeks to warn the Trojans against the wooden horse. Sinon's name hisses and is sinuous like a snake. Recurrent use of the serpent and the flame in metaphors and similes dominate the story of Dido, as well.

And salty sweat ran down the body. Then—
I say it in awe—three times, up from the ground,
The apparition of the goddess rose
In a lightning flash, with shield and spear atremble.
Calchas divined at once that the sea crossing
Must be attempted in retreat—that Pergamum[39]
Cannot be torn apart by Argive swords
Unless at Argos first they get new omens,
Carrying homeward the divine power
Brought overseas in ships. Now they are gone
Before the wind to the fatherland, Mycenae,
Gone to enlist new troops and gods. They'll cross
The water again and be here, unforeseen.
So Calchas read the portents. Warned by him,
They set this figure up in reparation
For the Palladium stolen, to appease
The offended power and expiate[40] the crime.
Enormous, though, he made them build the thing
With timber braces, towering to the sky,

27 **Reading Check**
According to Sinon, why did the Greeks build the wooden horse?

39. **Pergamum** (pur´ gə məm) *n.* the citadel of Troy.
40. **expiate** (eks´ pē āt´) *v.* atone for; make amends for.

26 **Critical Viewing**
How do you think Trojan citizens would have reacted to a horse like this one being brought inside their city's walls? **[Speculate]**

Differentiated Instruction Solutions for All Learners

Enrichment for Gifted/Talented Students

Tell students to imagine that they are Greek warriors inside the wooden horse. Tell them to freewrite about their thoughts and feelings. Suggest that students use these questions as writing prompts: What are you experiencing? It is too dark to see, but what are you feeling, smelling, and hearing? What are your reactions to events like Laocoön's striking the horse's belly? Tell students to create first-person narratives of this experience. Recommend that students prepare dramatic readings for the class.

Enrichment for Advanced Readers

Encourage students to think about how often classical rhetoric is used in today's political speeches and advertising. Examples abound in literature as well. Students might think of the king and the duke in Mark Twain's *The Adventures of Huckleberry Finn,* or of the main character in Sinclair Lewis's *Elmer Gantry,* or of Manley Pointer in Flannery O'Connor's "Good Country People." Suggest that students write essays in which they analyze the use of classical rhetoric in one of the examples noted above.

25 Humanities

The Wooden Horse of Troy,
by the Circle of Paul Bril

Bril (1554–1626) was a Flemish landscape painter who settled in Rome in about 1575. He was known for landscapes and for small easel paintings, in which he blended the sixteenth-century Mannerist style with the more balanced, idealized style of seventeenth-century Italian painting. Bril had considerable influence on Claude Lorrain, who would become one of the most famous seventeenth-century painters of classical Greek and Roman scenes.

In *The Wooden Horse of Troy,* the composition is dominated by the city walls and the gigantic horse, which dwarfs the many Trojans who are about to bring it into the city. The urban buildings, of course, are anachronistic. The picture's emotional effect is unmistakable: the monstrous horse symbolizes the death and destruction that will shortly be the Trojans' fate.

Use the following questions for discussion:

- What do the size of the walls and high turrets suggest about Troy's defenses?
  Possible response: Troy is well-defended. Only a trick such as the horse could lead to its defeat.
- What emotions are suggested by the depiction of the Trojans struggling to bring the horse into the city?
  Possible response: The size of the Trojans suggests elements of foreboding and perhaps even compassion.

26 Critical Viewing

Possible response: Trojans might have reacted with fear for the following reasons: the horse is a gift from the Greeks; it is unusual; and it is enormous.

27 Reading Check

Answer: The Greeks built the horse in reparation for the insult to Athena occasioned by the offensive theft of the Palladium.

ASSESS

Answers

1. **Possible response:** No; Sinon's story sounds too pat, and the consequences of trusting him are too deadly.
2. (a) Aeneas recounts the story at the court of Dido in Carthage. (b) **Possible response:** The first-person point of view adds vividness and immediacy to the tale. Aeneas may be trying to impress Dido, the Queen of Carthage, with his story.
3. (a) The Danaans left Sinon behind because he fled from them to avoid being sacrificed. (b) **Possible response:** Sinon's denunciation of Ulysses' treachery and deceit may ring true in Trojan ears.
4. (a) The Danaans built the horse as an offering in reparation for the theft of Athena's sacred statue, the Palladium. (b) **Possible response:** Sinon may be appealing to the Trojans' feelings of piety or their respect for the gods.
5. **Possible response:** The poem shows that the Greeks won only through unscrupulous cunning, not superior courage and strength, while the Trojans defeated themselves through their own generosity, honesty, and mercy.

Go Online **Author Link** For additional information about Virgil, have students type in the Web Code, then select *V* from the alphabet, and then select Virgil.

Too big for the gates, not to be hauled inside
And give the people back their ancient guardian.
If any hand here violates this gift
To great Minerva, then extinction waits,
Not for one only—would god it were so—
But for the realm of Priam and all Phrygians.
If this proud offering, drawn by your hands,
Should mount into your city, then so far
As the walls of Pelops' town[41] the tide of Asia
Surges in war: that doom awaits our children.'

This fraud of Sinon, his accomplished lying,
Won us over; a tall tale and fake tears
Had captured us, whom neither Diomedes
Nor Larisaean Achilles[42] overpowered,
Nor ten long years, nor all their thousand ships."

Despite warnings that Greeks are hiding in the horse, the Trojans bring it inside the walls of Troy. During the night, the Greeks emerge from the horse, ready for combat. Aeneas is also ready. In fierce spirit, he and his men fight against desperate odds. Toward daybreak, Aeneas finds a crowd of refugees gathered for exile, waiting for him to lead them to safety. He does so, with characteristic courage.

---

41. **Pelops'** (pel′ əps) **town** Argos. Pelops was an early king of Mycenae and an ancestor of Menelaus and Agamemnon.
42. **Larisaean Achilles** (lə ris′ ē ən ə kil′ ēz) Achilles, the foremost Greek warrior, was so called after Larissa, a town in his homeland of Thessaly.

Critical Reading

1. **Respond:** If you were a Trojan listening to Sinon's lying tale, do you think you would have sympathized with him? Why or why not?
2. **(a) Recall:** Who recounts the story of Troy's fall, and where? **(b) Interpret:** In what way do this perspective and setting color the narrative?
3. **(a) Recall:** According to Sinon, why did the Danaans leave him behind? **(b) Infer:** In what way does his explanation help him gain the Trojans' trust?
4. **(a) Recall:** Why did the Danaans build the wooden horse, according to Sinon's story? **(b) Analyze:** To what Trojan feelings might Sinon be trying to appeal with this story?
5. **Make a Judgment:** Do you think the Trojans' compassion is what allows Sinon to trick them, or do you think the Trojans were really blinded by pride? Explain.

For: More about Virgil
Visit: www.PHSchool.com
Web Code: ete-9407

Apply the Skills

from the *Aeneid*

Literary Analysis

National Epic

1. **(a)** Who is Aeneas' mother? **(b)** Why might this fact have been a source of pride for ancient Romans reading their **national epic**?
2. Why do you think Virgil repeatedly portrays the Greeks in the *Aeneid* as ruthless liars?
3. In what way do the last five lines of this selection allow Romans to remain proud of their origins despite the Trojans' defeat?

Connecting Literary Elements

4. The **epic hero** Aeneas recounts the fall of Troy even though it grieves him to do so. What Roman value does he demonstrate by agreeing to tell the story?
5. Which qualities of Aeneas and the Trojans might Romans have admired even though those qualities bring about Troy's downfall?
6. **(a)** Based on what the *Aeneid* reveals or suggests about each character, compare and contrast Aeneas with Ulysses (Odysseus), the epic hero of Homer's *Odyssey*. Use a Venn diagram like the one shown.

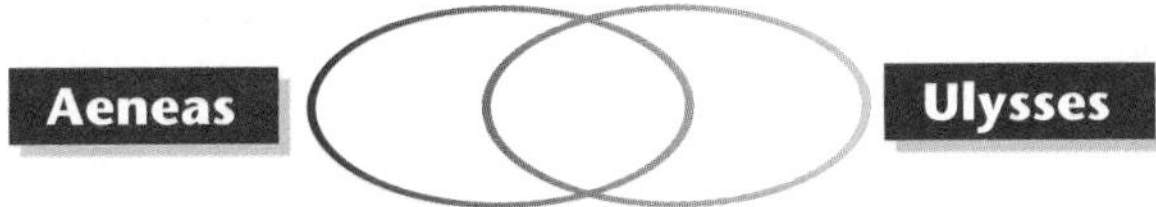

(b) By contrasting the two heroes in the way that he does, what do you think Virgil suggests about the difference between Roman and Greek culture?

Reading Strategy

Applying Background Information

7. Knowing that Ulysses' (Odysseus') reputation in Homer's epics is that of a cunning and resourceful warrior, what do you think Laocoön means in the following lines?

   A gift from the Danaans, and no ruse?
   Is that Ulysses' way, as you have known him?

Extend Understanding

8. **Psychology Connection:** Sometimes a talent or strength can also be a weakness. In what way does the story of Troy's fall support this paradox, or seeming contradiction?

QuickReview

A **national epic** is a long narrative that tells a story about the founding or development of a nation or culture.

An **epic hero** is the central figure of an epic.

When you **apply background information** about a literary work, you consider its author or its context in order to understand it.

For: Self-test
Visit: www.PHSchool.com
Web Code: eta-6408

Answers

1. (a) Aeneas' mother is the goddess Aphrodite. (b) **Possible response:** The fact that the founder of their city had one divine parent might have been a source of pride to the Romans.
2. **Possible response:** Virgil may want to stress a contrast between the Greeks (creative but deceitful) and the Romans (straightforward, practical, compassionate, and just).
3. **Possible response:** The final lines stress the effectiveness and courage with which the Trojans resisted the ten-year Greek siege.
4. **Possible response:** Aeneas demonstrates the value of endurance.
5. **Possible response:** The Romans might have admired the values of compassion and fairness.
6. (a) **Possible response: Aeneas:** compassionate, honest, fair; **Overlap:** national heroes, warriors, leaders, intelligent; **Odysseus:** deceitful, ruthless (b) **Possible response:** Virgil implies that Roman culture is morally superior to Greek culture.
   Another sample answer can be found on **Literary Analysis Graphic Organizer B**, p. 99 in ***Graphic Organizer Transparencies.***
7. **Possible response:** Laocoön means that any gift presented by Ulysses should automatically be suspected as a trick or delusion.
8. **Possible response:** The story of Troy's fall paradoxically presents some of the Trojans' moral strengths—their compassion and sense of justice, for example—as factors that contributed to their destruction.

Go Online Assessment Students may use the **Self-test** to prepare for **Selection Test A** or **Selection Test B.**

EXTEND/ASSESS

Answers

1 Vocabulary Lesson

Word Analysis: Latin Root *-jur-*

1. panel at a trial or legal proceeding
2. sphere of authority
3. to renounce

Spelling Strategy

1. *oo*
2. *wi*
3. *ī*

Vocabulary Builder

1. perjured
2. tumult
3. portents
4. guile
5. notions
6. blaspheming
7. unfettered
8. desecrating

2 Grammar and Style Lesson

1. At Dido's request, Aeneas told his story.
2. For ten long years, the Greeks laid siege to Troy.
3. With expert skill, Sinon wove his deceptive tale.
4. In the dead of night, the Greeks emerged.
5. In the eyes of the Greeks, Sinon could be considered a hero.

Writing Application

Possible response:

Trojan 1: "At Sinon's suggestion, we bring the horse inside the city."

Trojan 2: "For ten long years, we have known the Greeks to be our enemy."

Trojan 1: "In the dead of night, the Greeks ran from our superior skill."

Trojan 2: "In the eyes of Romans to come, we will be seen as fools."

WG Writing and Grammar Platinum Level

For support in teaching the Grammar and Style Lesson, use Chapter 21, Section 3.

Build Language Skills

1 Vocabulary Lesson

Word Analysis: Latin Root *-jur-*

The word root *-jur-* comes from the Latin word *jurare*, meaning "to swear an oath." For example, the word *perjury* (lying while under oath) literally means a statement that runs "through" or "against" an oath. The root *-jur-* is also related to the Latin words *jus* and *juris*, which mean "law."

Using the meaning of *-jur-*, write a brief definition of each of the following words.

1. jury **2.** jurisdiction **3.** abjure

Spelling Strategy

The letters *ui* in English can represent several different sounds, including *ī (guile)*, *i (biscuit)*, *o͞o (fruit)*, and *wi (languish)*. Indicate the sound that the letters *ui* make in each of these words.

1. suitable **2.** liquid **3.** disguise

Vocabulary Builder: Analogies

For each of the following items, study the relationship presented in the first word pair. Then, complete the analogies by using the vocabulary words on p. 533 to build word pairs expressing the same relationship.

1. forged : signature :: __?__ : testimony
2. riot : order :: __?__ : calm
3. memories : past :: __?__ : future
4. honesty : integrity :: __?__ : treachery
5. actions : concrete :: __?__ : abstract
6. fleeting : temporary :: __?__ : disrespectful
7. confined : released :: restrained : __?__
8. polishing : lustrous :: __?__ : unholy

2 Grammar and Style Lesson

Sentence Beginnings: Adverb Phrases

One way in which writers create sentence variety and interest is by beginning a sentence with an **adverb phrase.** An adverb phrase is a group of words acting together to modify a verb, an adjective, or an adverb by pointing out *where, when, in what way,* or *to what extent.*

Examples: From that time on, / Day in, day out, Ulysses / Found new ways . . . (modifies *Found,* tells when)

Inside the wooden horse, the Greeks stood poised to attack. (modifies *stood,* tells where)

Practice Rewrite each of these sentences so that it begins with an adverb phrase.

1. Aeneas told his story at Dido's request.
2. The Greeks laid siege to Troy for ten long years.
3. Sinon wove his deceptive tale with expert skill.
4. The Greeks emerged in the dead of night.
5. Sinon could be considered a hero in the eyes of the Greeks.

Writing Application Write a dialogue in which the Trojans debate what to do with the wooden horse. Begin at least two sentences with adverb phrases.

WG Prentice Hall Writing and Grammar Connection: Platinum Level, Chapter 21, Section 3

Assessment Practice

Cause and Effect; Predicting Outcomes

(For more practice, see *Test Preparation Workbook*, p. 24.)

In many tests, students will need to analyze causes and effects to predict outcomes. Use the following sample test item to demonstrate.

This fraud of Sinon, his accomplished lying,
Won us over; a tall tale and fake tears
Had captured us, whom neither Diomedes
Nor Larisaean Achilles overpowered,
Nor ten long years, nor all their thousand ships.

—from the *Aeneid*, Book II, lines 260–264

Sinon will be remembered by the Greeks—

A as a manipulative liar.
B as a superior orator.
C as a cunning deceiver.
D as a dangerous traitor.

A, C, and *D* represent how Sinon is likely to be remembered by the Romans, not by the Greeks. The Greeks are likely to remember Sinon as a superior orator because he convinces the Trojans to bring the horse into Troy. *B* is the correct answer.

❸ Writing Lesson

Timed Writing: Analysis of Storytelling Technique

In the *Aeneid,* Virgil interweaves Aeneas' account of the fall of Troy with long speeches by Sinon. Thus, Virgil, Aeneas, and Sinon can all be considered tellers of this story. Write an analysis of Virgil's storytelling technique, explaining how it supports the overall purpose of his epic: to glorify the origins of Rome and Roman culture. ***(40 minutes)***

Prewriting ***(10 minutes)*** Review the selection, noting passages in which your perceptions of characters and events are influenced by the way in which they are presented. For example, consider how your impressions of Sinon are colored by the comments Aeneas interjects about him.

Drafting ***(20 minutes)*** Organize and draft your essay, citing passages that demonstrate how Virgil's narrative technique helps portray the Trojans positively.

Revising ***(10 minutes)*** As you review your work, make sure that you have clearly linked your ideas. Add transitions such as *therefore, furthermore,* and *in contrast* to clarify connections between ideas.

Model: Clarifying Connections With Transitions

Sinon tells a convincing story that appeals to his listeners' emotions. Therefore, Readers can understand how he was able to deceive the Trojans.

Words like *therefore* strengthen the connections between ideas.

Prentice Hall Writing and Grammar Connection: Platinum Level, Chapter 13, Section 4

❹ Extend Your Learning

Listening and Speaking Write a **persuasive speech** in which you argue that the Trojans should not let the horse inside the city gates. Consider using the following to strengthen your speech:

- arguments from the speech of Laocoön (lines 58–69)
- references to some of the less credible assertions of Sinon

Rehearse and deliver your speech before an audience of classmates.

Research and Technology With a group of classmates, research the complete story of the *Aeneid.* Then, create an illustrated **travelogue** showing the wanderings of Aeneas on his journey from Troy to Italy. Include pictures of the places he visited. **[Group Activity]**

For: An additional research activity
Visit: www.PHSchool.com
Web Code: etd-7406

Assessment Resources

The following resources can be used to assess students' knowledge and skills.

Unit 4 Resources
Selection Test A, pp. 146–148
Selection Test B, pp. 149–151

General Resources
Rubrics for Response to Literature, pp. 55–56
Rubrics for Research: Research Report, pp. 51–52

Go Online Assessment Students may use the **Self-test** to prepare for **Selection Test A** or **Selection Test B.**

❸ Writing Lesson

You may use this Writing Lesson as a timed-writing practice, or you may allow students to develop the analytical essay as a writing assignment over several days.

- To give students guidance in writing this analytical essay, give them the **Support for Writing Lesson,** p. 143, in ***Unit 4 Resources.***
- Have the class discuss the main purpose of each storyteller in this passage: Virgil, Aeneas, and Sinon.
- Tell students to consider the *audience* for each of the three storytellers. If Virgil's audience consists of educated Roman listeners and readers in the age of Augustus, who constitutes Aeneas' audience? Who is Sinon's audience? How does the audience influence the content and manner of the storytelling?
- Use the Response to Literature rubrics on pp. 55–56 in ***General Resources*** to assess students' work.

WG Writing and Grammar Platinum Level
For support in teaching the Writing Lesson, use Chapter 13, Section 4.

❹ Research and Technology

- Direct students to a handbook of Greek and Roman literature to find a plot summary of Books I–VI of Virgil's epic.
- Before students begin their travelogues, encourage them to obtain maps of the Mediterranean region.
- Use the Research Report rubrics in ***General Resources,*** pp. 51–52, to evaluate students' work.
- The **Support for Extend Your Learning** page (***Unit 4 Resources,*** p. 144) provides guided note-taking opportunities to help students complete the Extend Your Learning activities.

Go Online Research Have students type in the Web Code for another research activity.

The Story of Daedalus and Icarus

Standard Course of Study

Goal 1: WRITTEN LANGUAGE

WL.1.03.10	Analyze connections between ideas, concepts, characters and experiences in reflection.

Goal 2: INFORMATIONAL READING

IR.2.02.4	Develop appropriate strategies to illustrate points about cause/effect relationships.

Goal 5: LITERATURE

LT.5.01.2	Build knowledge of literary genres, and explore how characteristics apply to literature of world cultures.
LT.5.01.2	Build knowledge of literary genres, and explore how characteristics apply to literature of world cultures.

Goal 6: GRAMMAR AND USAGE

GU.6.01.3	Use recognition strategies to understand vocabulary and exact word choice.

Step-by-Step Teaching Guide	Pacing Guide
PRETEACH	
• Administer Vocabulary and Reading Warm-ups as necessary.	5 min.
• Engage students' interest with the motivation activity.	5 min.
• Read and discuss author and background features. **FT**	10 min.
• Introduce the Literary Analysis Skill: Narrative Poetry. **FT**	5 min.
• Introduce the Reading Strategy: Anticipating Events. **FT**	10 min.
• Prepare students to read by teaching the selection vocabulary. **FT**	
TEACH	
• Informally monitor comprehension while students read independently or in groups. **FT**	30 min.
• Monitor students' comprehension with the Reading Check notes.	as students read
• Reinforce vocabulary with Vocabulary Builder notes.	as students read
• Develop students' understanding of narrative poetry with the Literary Analysis annotations. **FT**	5 min.
• Develop students' ability to anticipate events with the Reading Strategy annotations. **FT**	5 min.
ASSESS/EXTEND	
• Assess students' comprehension and mastery of the Literary Analysis and Reading Strategy by having them answer the Apply the Skills questions. **FT**	15 min.
• Have students complete the Vocabulary Lesson and the Grammar and Style Lesson. **FT**	15 min.
• Apply students' ability to follow script formats by using the Writing Lesson. **FT**	45 min. or homework
• Apply students' understanding by using one or more of the Extend Your Learning activities.	20–90 min. or homework
• Administer Selection Test A or Selection Test B. **FT**	15 min.

Resources

Print

Unit 4 Resources

Vocabulary Warm-up Word Lists [**L1, L2, EL**] . . . . . . p. 152
Vocabulary Warm-up Practice [**L1, L2, EL**] . . . . . . p. 153
Reading Warm-up A [**L1, L2, EL**] . . . . . . p. 154
Reading Warm-up B [**L1, L2, L3**] . . . . . . p. 155

Transparency

Graphic Organizer Transparencies

Literary Analysis Graphic Organizer A [**L3**] . . . . . . p. 102
Literary Analysis Graphic Organizer B [**L1, L2, EL**] . . . . . . p. 103
Reading Strategy Graphic Organizer A [**L3**] . . . . . . p. 100
Reading Strategy Graphic Organizer B [**L1, L2, EL**] . . . . . . p. 101

Print

Reader's Notebook [L2]
Reader's Notebook: Adapted Version [L1]
Reader's Notebook: English Learner's Version [EL]
Unit 4 Resources

Literary Analysis [**L3**] . . . . . . p. 156
Reading Strategy [**L3**] . . . . . . p. 157
Vocabulary Builder [**L3**] . . . . . . p. 158

Technology

Listening to Literature Audio CDs [L2, EL]

Print

Unit 4 Resources

Grammar and Style [**L3**] . . . . . . p. 159
Support for Writing Lesson [**L3**] . . . . . . p. 160
Support for Extend Your Learning [**L3**] . . . . . . p. 161
Enrichment [**L4**] . . . . . . p. 162
Selection Test A [**L1, L2, EL**] . . . . . . pp. 163–165
Selection Test B [**L3, L4**] . . . . . . pp. 166–168

General Resources

Rubrics for Multimedia Report [**L3**] . . . . . . pp. 57–58

Technology

Go Online: Research [**L3**]
Go Online: Self-test [**L3**]
***ExamView®,* Test Bank [L3]**

Choosing Resources for Differentiated Instruction

[**L1**] Special Needs Students
[**L2**] Below-Level Students
[**L3**] All Students
[**L4**] Advanced Students
[**EL**] English Learners

For Vocabulary and Reading Warm-ups and for Selection Tests, **A** signifies "less challenging" and **B** "more challenging." For Graphic Organizer transparencies, **A** signifies "not filled in" and **B** "filled in."

FT Fast Track Instruction: To move the lesson more quickly, use the strategies and activities identified with **FT**.

Scaffolding for Less Proficient and Advanced Students

The leveled Critical Thinking questions after selections progress in the levels of thinking required to answer them. To address the needs of your different students, you may use the (a) level questions for your less proficient students and the (b) level questions with your on-level and advanced students. The occasional (c) level questions are appropriate for your advanced students.

PRENTICE HALL **TeacherEXPRESS™** Plan · Teach · Assess Use this complete suite of powerful teaching tools to make lesson planning and testing quicker and easier.

PRENTICE HALL **StudentEXPRESS™** Learn · Study · Succeed Use the interactive textbook (online and on CD-ROM) to make selections and activities come alive with audio and video support and interactive questions.

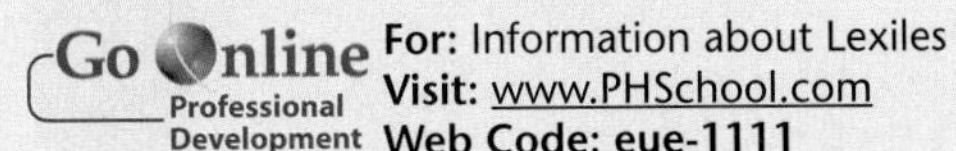

For: Information about Lexiles
Visit: www.PHSchool.com
Web Code: eue-1111

PREETEACH

Motivation

Write the phrase "urban legend" on the board. Rather than asking students to offer examples, ask them to discuss why these stories, often neither credible nor attributable to any definite source, continue to circulate. Tell students that myths, like their contemporary counterparts, were passed down for entertainment. Myths also attempted to explain things that at the time were mysteries, such as the change in seasons. From a historical perspective, myths often revealed cultural beliefs, attitudes, or preoccupations of the day. Ask students to discuss connections between urban legends and their reflections of contemporary culture.

❶ Background

More About the Author

During the miserable decade he spent in exile, Ovid wrote autobiographical poetry. He kept a sort of verse journal in the form of letters to friends in Rome. He complained that no one spoke Latin, so he had to talk to himself. His fear of forgetting his Latin is hyperbolic because his style and sly wit come across undiminished in his descriptions of life on the frontier.

Geography Note

Draw students' attention to the map on this page, point out Italy, and tell students that Ovid was born in Sulmo, a village in central Italy. Sulmo, now known as Sulmona, is an important agricultural and commercial center.

Build Skills | Narrative Poem

The Story of Daedalus and Icarus ❶

Ovid (43 B.C.–A.D. 17)

Publius Ovidius Naso (pub′ lē əs ä vid′ ē əs nā′ sō), known as Ovid (äv′ id), was born in Sulmo, a small village about ninety miles east of Rome, in the year after Julius Caesar's assassination. Ovid's father wanted him to go into public life, so he sent Ovid to Rome to be educated. After completing his studies in Rome, Ovid went on a long tour of the major cities of the ancient world in Greece, Asia Minor, and Sicily. On his return, Ovid dutifully joined the legal profession and became a judge. However, Ovid preferred to be a poet. His father discouraged him from writing poetry, reminding him that Homer died poor, but Ovid pursued his goal.

Poetry and Politics Ovid was only twelve when Octavian defeated Antony and effectively established himself as the absolute ruler of Rome. Therefore, the Rome that Ovid knew was untroubled by the civil wars that had haunted the work of earlier writers. Perhaps as a reaction to this more secure, carefree society, Ovid's poetry usually speaks of pleasure, and especially love. His first work was the *Amores* (c. 20 B.C.), a series of love lyrics addressed to an imaginary woman named Corinna. He followed this work with the *Heroides*, a collection of fifteen fictional verse letters from famous women of the past to the men they loved. He then went on to a more theoretical study in three books called *Ars amatoria* (The Art of Love), which appeared around 9 B.C.

Unfortunately for Ovid, he was producing provocative literature at a time when Octavian, now the emperor Caesar Augustus, was seeking to improve Roman life through a series of laws that punished adultery and other kinds of immoral conduct. The poet soon turned to less controversial subjects that would not be seen as disrespectful to the new emperor and his vision of an ideal Roman state.

Ovid's Masterpiece The *Metamorphoses* (Transformations) stands as Ovid's greatest literary achievement. A poem of nearly 12,000 lines, it tells a series of stories beginning with the creation of the world and ending with the death of Julius Caesar. Among these stories is "The Story of Daedalus and Icarus," a famous myth about a boy who flies too close to the sun. Others include the well-known myths of King Midas, Echo and Narcissus, Hercules, and Orpheus. In each story, someone or something undergoes a change. The stories are linked by clever transitions, so that the entire work reads as one long, uninterrupted tale. In addition to its literary value, the *Metamorphoses* also has historical value because it documents some of the most famous myths of ancient Mediterranean culture.

The *Metamorphoses* is divided into fifteen books and is written in the same meter as Virgil's *Aeneid*. Ovid knew that he was writing in the shadow of Virgil's great epic, and he met this challenge by producing a lighthearted and entertaining poem that seems to mock the very serious *Aeneid*.

Banishment Shortly after Ovid completed the *Metamorphoses* in A.D. 8, Caesar Augustus banished him to Tomis, a remote village on the Black Sea. The reasons for the poet's exile are not entirely clear, but the emperor might have felt that Ovid endangered public morals.

Banishment to a half-civilized place at the far edge of the empire was a severe punishment for this worldly poet. Although he kept his property and continued to write, he was never allowed to return to Rome.

Preview

Connecting to the Literature

World literature is filled with tales that teach the dangers of excessive ambition. In this famous story, a boy ignores his father's warnings and meets a tragic end.

2 Literary Analysis

Narrative Poetry

A **narrative poem** is a poem that tells a story. Narrative poems are distinct from lyric poems, in which the main purpose is to express the thoughts or feelings of the speaker. Ballads are one type of narrative poetry; epic poems like Virgil's *Aeneid* are another.

In the *Metamorphoses*, Ovid uses the epic form. Unlike Virgil, however, Ovid does not tell the story of an important historical event or a famous hero. Instead, he weaves together entertaining tales about gods, demigods, and mortals. As you read "The Story of Daedalus and Icarus" from the *Metamorphoses*, notice how Ovid makes use of both narrative and poetic techniques.

Connecting Literary Elements

A **myth** is a fictional tale that arises out of a culture's oral tradition and usually involves supernatural characters or events. In addition to providing entertainment, myths often teach the values and ideals of a culture or attempt to explain such unknowns as the following:

- causes of natural phenomena, such as the origins of earthly life
- origins of place names
- reasons for certain customs

Consider what lesson "The Story of Daedalus and Icarus" might be meant to teach and what questions it might answer.

3 Reading Strategy

Anticipating Events

As you read this story, you will probably find yourself **anticipating events**—looking forward to what happens next. More emotional than the logical process of predicting, anticipating events leads you to connect with characters as you watch their lives unfold. As you read "The Story of Daedalus and Icarus," use a chart like the one shown to note clues that cause you to anticipate later events in the story.

Vocabulary Builder

dominion (də min′ yən) *n.* kingdom; area of rule (p. 551)

sequence (sē′ kwəns) *n.* order; succession (p. 551)

poised (poizd) *adj.* balanced and steady, as though suspended (p. 551)

NC Standard Course of Study

- Analyze connections between ideas, concepts, characters and experiences in reflection. (WL.1.03.10)
- Build knowledge of literary genres, and explore how characteristics apply to literature of world cultures. (LT.5.01.2)

2 Literary Analysis

Narrative Poetry

- Read aloud the Literary Analysis instruction. Make sure students understand that in addition to characters, actions, and conflict, the narrative poem contains atmosphere, tone, and theme.
- Then, ask students to give examples of songs that tell a story.
- Remind students that song lyrics or poems that tell a story have rhythmic qualities.
- Tell students that "The Story of Daedalus and Icarus" is part of an epic poem; ask them to listen to the rhythm of the lines as they read.

3 Reading Strategy

Anticipating Events

- Read aloud the Reading Strategy instruction.
- Write the words *anticipate* and *predict* on the board. **Ask** students to use each word in a sentence to demonstrate the difference between them.
  Possible response: Anna *anticipated* her friend's usual forgetfulness, so she packed an extra sandwich. The mayor *predicts* record attendance at the town festival.
- Explain that anticipation suggests a personal involvement and a need to respond to the situation, whereas prediction may rely on logic and require nothing more than reporting what will likely happen.
- Tell students that as readers become involved with the lives of characters, they anticipate what will happen next.
- Give students a copy of **Reading Strategy Graphic Organizer A,** p. 100 in ***Graphic Organizer Transparencies.*** Have them use it to note clues that cause anticipation of later events in the story.

Vocabulary Builder

- Pronounce each vocabulary word for students, and read the definitions as a class. Have students identify any words with which they are already familiar.

Differentiated Instruction — Solutions for All Learners

Support for Special Needs Students

Have students complete the **Preview** and **Build Skills** pages for "The Story of Daedalus and Icarus" in the ***Reader's Notebook: Adapted Version.*** These pages provide a selection summary, an abbreviated presentation of the reading and literary skills, and the graphic organizer on the **Build Skills** page in the student book.

Support for Less Proficient Readers

Have students complete the **Preview** and **Build Skills** pages for "The Story of Daedalus and Icarus" in the ***Reader's Notebook.*** These pages provide a selection summary, an abbreviated presentation of the reading and literary skills, and the graphic organizer on the **Build Skills** page in the student book.

Support for English Learners

Have students complete the **Preview** and **Build Skills** pages for "The Story of Daedalus and Icarus" in the ***Reader's Notebook: English Learner's Version.*** These pages provide a selection summary, an abbreviated presentation of the skills, additional contextual vocabulary, and the graphic organizer on the **Build Skills** page in the student book.

Facilitate Understanding

Tell students that they will be reading an etiological myth, and explain that etiology means "the study of causes, origins, or reasons." Ask for examples of other myths that explain how something came to be. Start a discussion about familiar tales such as Kipling's "How the Elephant Got His Trunk" from *Just So Stories.*

❶ About the Selection

Daedalus and his son Icarus are imprisoned in the Labyrinth by King Minos. Daedalus designs wings out of wax and feathers to facilitate an escape. Icarus, despite his father's warnings, flies too close to the sun. The wings melt, and Icarus falls into the sea and drowns.

❷ Humanities

The Fall of Icarus,
by Paul-Ambroise Slodtz

Paris-born Slodtz (1702–1758) came from a family of sculptors who had emigrated from Flanders to France. Slodtz and his brothers worked in the rococo style, a highly ornate variation of the baroque style that was popular in eighteenth-century Europe. Slodtz created *The Fall of Icarus* in 1743.

Use this question for discussion:

What details in this sculpture create a sense of tragedy?
Possible response: Icarus is sprawled helplessly upon a stone. This depiction creates a feeling of wasted youth and potential. In addition, the wings—created with such care by Daedalus—are crushed beneath Icarus' body.

❸ Critical Viewing

Possible response: The sculpture evokes emotions such as shock, dismay, and compassion.

from the *Metamorphoses*

The Story of 1 *Daedalus and Icarus*

Ovid *translated by* Rolphe Humphries

Background "The Story of Daedalus and Icarus" is just one of a series of myths in the *Metamorphoses* involving artists or craftspeople. In most of these myths, Ovid associates skill and ingenuity with pride, danger, and risk. Daedalus' very name means "cunning craftsman." As you read "The Story of Daedalus and Icarus," you will recognize the theme of danger, loss, or grief associated with artistic or technological achievement.

The myth begins with Daedalus and his son Icarus in exile on the island of Crete, where King Minos rules. Daedalus has been exiled from Athens for the murder of his nephew Perdix, who had shown signs of surpassing his uncle in artistic ability.

2

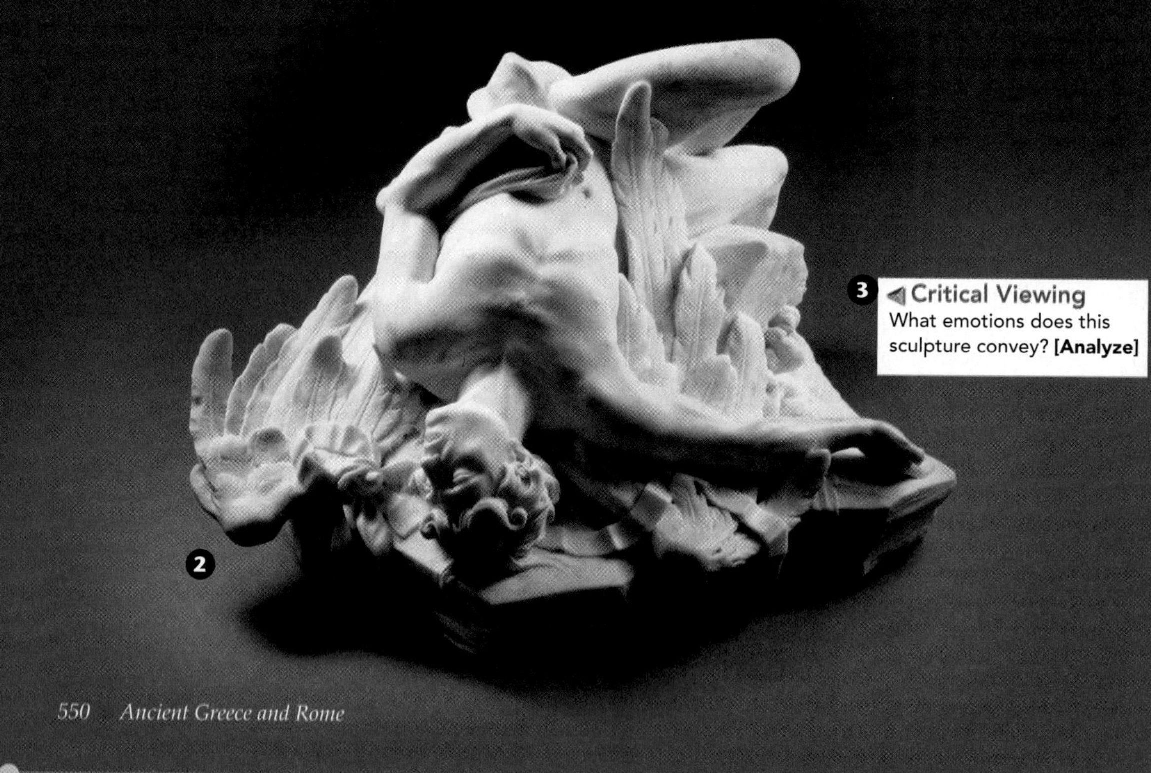

3 ◀ **Critical Viewing** What emotions does this sculpture convey? **[Analyze]**

Differentiated Instruction Solutions for All Learners

Accessibility at a Glance

	From the Metamorphoses: The Story of Daedalus and Icarus
Context	King Minos' imprisonment of Daedalus and son Icarus on the island of Crete
Language	Accessible: poetic with some similes
Concept Level	Accessible (Avoid taking extreme measures to solve a problem.)
Literary Merit	Classic narrative poem
Lexile	1330L
Overall Rating	Average

Homesick for homeland, Daedalus hated Crete
And his long exile there, but the sea held him.
"Though Minos blocks escape by land or water,"
Daedalus said, "surely the sky is open,
4 And that's the way we'll go. Minos' dominion
Does not include the air." He turned his thinking
Toward unknown arts, changing the laws of nature.
He laid out feathers in order, first the smallest,
A little larger next it, and so continued,
The way that pan-pipes[1] rise in gradual sequence.
He fastened them with twine and wax, at middle,
At bottom, so, and bent them, gently curving,
So that they looked like wings of birds, most surely.
And Icarus, his son, stood by and watched him,
Not knowing he was dealing with his downfall,
Stood by and watched, and raised his shiny face
To let a feather, light as down,[2] fall on it,
Or stuck his thumb into the yellow wax,
Fooling around, the way a boy will, always,
Whenever a father tries to get some work done.
Still, it was done at last, and the father hovered,
Poised, in the moving air, and taught his son:
"I warn you, Icarus, fly a middle course:
Don't go too low, or water will weigh the wings down;
Don't go too high, or the sun's fire will burn them.
Keep to the middle way. And one more thing,
No fancy steering by star or constellation,
Follow my lead!" That was the flying lesson,
And now to fit the wings to the boy's shoulders.
Between the work and warning the father found
His cheeks were wet with tears, and his hands trembled.
He kissed his son (*Good-bye*, if he had known it),
5 Rose on his wings, flew on ahead, as fearful
As any bird launching the little nestlings[3]
Out of high nest into thin air. *Keep on,*
Keep on, he signals, *follow me!* He guides him
In flight—O fatal art!—and the wings move
And the father looks back to see the son's wings moving.
Far off, far down, some fisherman is watching
As the rod dips and trembles over the water,
Some shepherd rests his weight upon his crook,[4]

1. **pan-pipes** musical instrument consisting of a series of tubes of varying lengths bound together and played by blowing across the open upper ends.
2. **down** soft, fluffy feathers, like those of a young bird.
3. **nestlings** young birds that have not yet left the nest.
4. **crook** shepherd's staff, with a hook at one end.

Vocabulary Builder
dominion (də min′ yən) *n.* kingdom; area of rule
sequence (sē′ kwəns) *n.* order; succession

Vocabulary Builder
poised (pɔizd) *adj.* balanced and steady, as though suspended

Reading Strategy
Anticipating Events Based on the clues in these lines, what do you anticipate will happen later in the poem?

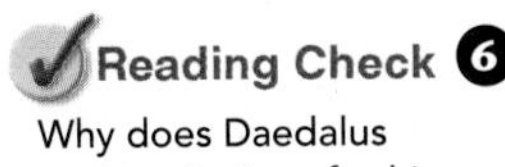
Reading Check 6
Why does Daedalus construct wings for himself and Icarus?

4 Vocabulary Builder

The Latin Root *-domin-*

- Draw students' attention to the word *dominion* and its definition.
- Tell students that the Latin root *-domin-* means "rule" or "master."
- **Ask** students to explain the connection between the root *-domin-* and the word *dominion.*
  Possible response: *Dominion* refers to an area under rule or mastery.

5 Reading Strategy

Anticipate Events

- Tell students that clues that suggest, or foreshadow, future events help readers understand what may befall a character and may reveal irony.
- Have a volunteer read aloud lines 28–38. Then, **ask** students the Reading Strategy question: Based on the clues in these lines, what do you anticipate will happen later in the poem?
  Answer: Daedalus' warning, his tears, his trembling hands, the parenthetical mention of "Goodbye," and the reference to flight as a "fatal art" all suggest that the flight will end in disaster.

➤ **Monitor Progress** **Ask** students what the clues in lines 28–38 reveal about Daedalus.
Possible response: Daedalus' warning, tears, and trembling hands suggest that he senses impending disaster. He chooses to ignore these clues, however, and urges Icarus to "keep on."

➤ **Reteach** If students have difficulty answering the Monitor Progress question, review the Reading Strategy instruction on p. 549.

6 Reading Check

Answer: Daedalus constructs wings to escape from Crete.

Enrichment

Roman History

The period in which Ovid lived coincided with the reign of the Emperor Augustus (27 B.C.–A.D. 14). This period was viewed by Ovid and his contemporary, the Roman historian Livy, as a period of decadence and decline. Livy's pessimistic tone profoundly influenced future Roman historians. Livy looked back on the final years of the Roman Republic, which ended when Augustus became emperor, as a golden age of intellectual and artistic achievement. Rome's greatest poets, Virgil (70–19 B.C.) and Horace (65–8 B.C.), were born during the Republic. Livy regretted most what he thought was a loss of Roman virtue—love of family and country, intellectual honesty, and self-reliance. He downplayed strife and civil war, as well as political corruption, that characterized much of the Republican period. He also chose not to see that more Romans were better off under Augustus. The view of the present as inferior to the past characterized the writings of future Roman historians.

7 Literary Analysis

- Invite a volunteer to read the bracketed passage aloud.
- **Ask:** How does Ovid combine both narrative and poetic techniques in this passage?
  Possible response: Ovid compresses Icarus' death scene by using imagery such as "the blue sea hushed him" and "the wings on the waves."

ASSESS

Answers

1. **Possible responses:** Yes; Icarus willfully ignores his father's warning. No; Icarus' mistake does not warrant death.
2. (a) As he watches his father work, Icarus plays with the materials Daedalus is using. (b) These details underscore Icarus' youth, innocence, and curiosity and help the reader anticipate what may go wrong during the escape.
3. (a) Daedalus tells Icarus to follow his lead, keeping a steady, middle course to avoid danger.
   (b) **Possible response:** The "middle path" can be interpreted as using moderation in decision-making in order to avoid danger.
4. (a) Icarus, ignoring his father's warning, soars too high; the sun's heat melts the wax that holds his wings together and he plummets to the sea. (b) **Possible responses:** Yes; Icarus feels invincible and disobeys on the basis of this emotion. No; The risk of flying across the sea would have made Icarus afraid to disobey his father.
5. **Possible response:** Yes; Daedalus curses his artistic talent and takes responsibility for his son's death. No; Daedalus needs to take more responsibility for his desire to manipulate nature.

Go Online Author Link For additional information about Ovid, have students type in the Web Code, then select *O* from the alphabet, and then select Ovid.

Some ploughman on the handles of the ploughshare,[5]
And all look up, in absolute amazement,
At those air-borne above. They must be gods!
They were over Samos, Juno's sacred island,
Delos and Paros toward the left, Lebinthus
Visible to the right, and another island,
Calymne,[6] rich in honey. And the boy
Thought *This is wonderful!* and left his father,
Soared higher, higher, drawn to the vast heaven,
Nearer the sun, and the wax that held the wings
Melted in that fierce heat, and the bare arms
Beat up and down in air, and lacking oarage[7]
Took hold of nothing. *Father!* he cried, and *Father!*
Until the blue sea hushed him, the dark water
Men call the Icarian now. And Daedalus,
Father no more, called "Icarus, where are you!
7 Where are you, Icarus? Tell me where to find you!"
And saw the wings on the waves, and cursed his talents,
Buried the body in a tomb, and the land
Was named for Icarus.[8]

---

5. **ploughshare** cutting blade of a plow.
6. **Samos** (sā′ mäs) . . . **Delos** (dē′ läs) . . . **Paros** (per′ äs′) . . . **Lebinthus** (lə bin′ thəs) . . . **Calymne** (kə lim′ nē) islands in the Aegean Sea, between mainland Greece and Asia Minor.
7. **oarage** something functioning as oars with which to row.
8. **the land was named for Icarus** a reference to the island now called Icaria.

Critical Reading

1. **Respond:** Do you think Icarus deserved his fate? Explain.
2. **(a) Recall:** In lines 14–20, what does Icarus do as he watches his father prepare the wings? **(b) Infer:** Why do you think Ovid includes these details?
3. **(a) Recall:** What warning does Daedalus give his son as the two prepare to take off? **(b) Apply:** In what way might this advice apply to life in general?
4. **(a) Recall:** What does Icarus do to cause his demise?
   (b) Evaluate: In your opinion, is his motivation for taking this action believable?
5. **Make a Judgment:** Do you think Daedalus takes proper responsibility for what happened to Icarus? Explain your answer.

Author Link

For: More about Ovid
Visit: www.PHSchool.com
Web Code: ete-9408

Apply the Skills

The Story of Daedalus and Icarus

Literary Analysis

Narrative Poetry

1. **(a)** What conflict sets the plot of this **narrative poem** in motion? **(b)** How does Daedalus plan to resolve this conflict?
2. **(a)** To what does Ovid compare Daedalus and Icarus when they first take flight? **(b)** How does this comparison enrich the story?
3. What does Ovid do to make his narrative interesting and suspenseful even for readers who are familiar with the story? Explain.

Connecting Literary Elements

4. **(a)** Which details in this **myth** would you point to as supernatural? **(b)** Which details are realistic? **(c)** Why do you think Ovid includes both supernatural and realistic elements? Explain.
5. **(a)** Using a chart like the one shown, show how certain details in "The Story of Daedalus and Icarus" teach lessons or convey values.

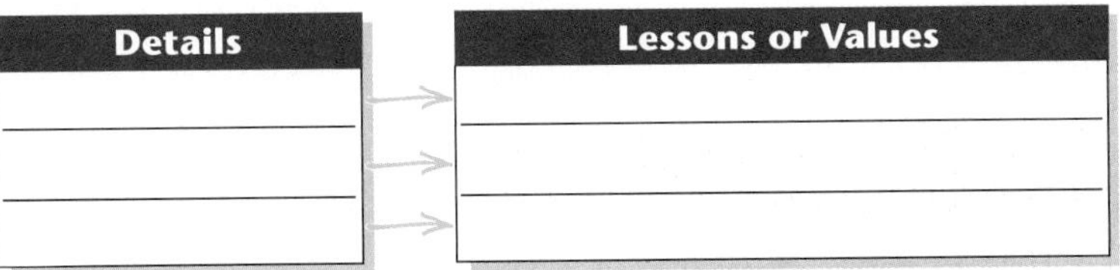

(b) What would you say is the main lesson of the story?

6. What do you think "The Story of Daedalus and Icarus" suggests about the uses of art and technology? Explain your answer with examples from the story.

Reading Strategy

Anticipating Events

7. At what point in the story can readers first **anticipate** that Daedalus' plan might lead to disaster? Cite specific lines.
8. What do you think Daedalus' life will be like after the point at which the narrative ends? Explain.

Extend Understanding

9. **Psychology Connection:** Psychologists sometimes refer to an "Icarus complex." Based on "The Story of Daedalus and Icarus," what do you think this term means?

QuickReview

Narrative poetry is poetry that tells a story.

A **myth** is a fictional tale that arises out of a culture's oral tradition. It usually involves supernatural characters or events.

When you **anticipate events,** you connect to characters' lives and look forward to what might happen next.

Go Online Assessment

For: Self-test
Visit: www.PHSchool.com
Web Code: eta-6409

Answers

1. (a) Daedalus wishes to escape from Crete, where he is held by King Minos. (b) Daedalus plans to construct wings for himself and his son so that they can fly away.
2. (a) Ovid compares Daedalus and Icarus to gods. (b) The comparison implies that the father and son have overstepped the boundaries for human potential.
3. Ovid includes vivid, realistic details; he develops similes; he includes the perspectives of the fisherman, the shepherd, and the ploughman; and he includes foreshadowing.
4. (a) The wings' functioning is supernatural. (b) The characters' motivation to be free and the geographical place names are realistic. (c) **Possible response:** Ovid wishes to entertain, but he also wants the story to seem believable so that readers sympathize with the characters.
5. (a) **Detail:** Daedalus warns Icarus of flying too low and too high. **Lesson:** Moderation is a virtue. **Detail:** Icarus strays from his father and suffers the consequences. **Lesson:** It is important to obey one's elders. **Detail:** Daedalus curses his artistic talents. **Lesson:** When used to imitate nature or the divine, art is a dangerous endeavor. Another sample answer can be found on **Literary Analysis Graphic Organizer B**, p. 103 in ***Graphic Organizer Transparencies.*** (b) **Possible response:** The main lesson of the myth is to avoid extremes.
6. **Possible response:** Daedalus' construction of the wings and his son's subsequent fate show that art and technology should not be counted on to exceed their capacity.
7. In line 7, the narrator says that Daedalus is tinkering with "unknown arts, changing the laws of nature." This is the first example of foreshadowing.
8. **Possible response:** Daedalus' life will be lonely and guilt-ridden.
9. **Possible response:** The term may refer to an obsession with aspiration or striving, or it may refer to a feeling of invincibility.

Students may use the **Self-test** to prepare for **Selection Test A** or **Selection Test B.**

Answers

❶ Vocabulary Lesson

Word Analysis: Latin Root *-domin-*

1. For decades, no one disputed the *dominance* of Augustus.
2. Men from wealthy, long-established families would *dominate* the Roman Senate.
3. Classmates, finding Tim's behavior *domineering,* avoided him.
4. That particular group is *predominantly* made up of musicians.

Spelling Strategy

1. grievance
2. aspiring
3. synthesized
4. intensity

Vocabulary Builder

1. True; a king holds power.
2. False; a book's pages are usually numbered consecutively.
3. False; fish out of water look awkward, the opposite of poised.

❷ Grammar and Style Lesson

1. Daedalus, a clever artisan, devised an escape plan.
2. He fitted his son Icarus with wings.
3. The boy, a novice at flying, ignored his father's advice.
4. Daedalus and Icarus flew over Samos, Juno's sacred island.
5. Daedalus, a father no more, lamented his son's death.

Writing Application

Possible response: I visited Mt. Vernon, *Washington's home,* in July. I went with my cousin *Ann* and my brother *Ted.* Visitors, *people from all over the world,* crowded the porch.

WG Writing and Grammar Platinum Level

For support in teaching the Grammar and Style Lesson, use Chapter 20, Section 1.

Build Language Skills

❶ Vocabulary Lesson

Word Analysis: Latin Root *-domin-*

The word *dominion* contains the Latin root *-domin-*, which means "rule" or "master." Thus, *dominion* means "region or area of rule." Applying the meaning of the root *-domin-*, use each of the following words in a sentence.

1. dominance
2. dominate
3. domineering
4. predominantly

Spelling Strategy

Words ending in a silent *e* usually drop the *e* before adding suffixes that start with vowels. For example, *poise* + *-ed* = *poised.* Combine each of the following words with its suffix.

1. grieve + *-ance*
2. aspire + *-ing*
3. synthesize + *-ed*
4. intense + *-ity*

Vocabulary Builder: True or False

Review the vocabulary words on page 549. Then, indicate whether each of the following statements is true or false. Explain the reason for each of your answers.

1. An emperor or a king is someone who might hold *dominion* over an entire nation or region.
2. The pages of a book are usually numbered in no particular *sequence.*
3. Fish generally appear more *poised* when they are out of water than when they are swimming.

❷ Grammar and Style Lesson

Appositives and Appositive Phrases

An **appositive** is a noun or pronoun placed next to another noun or pronoun to provide more information about it. When an appositive is accompanied by its own modifiers, it forms an **appositive phrase.**

If an appositive can be omitted from a sentence without altering its basic meaning, it must be set off by commas. If the appositive is essential to the meaning of a sentence, commas are not used. Appositive phrases are always set off by commas or dashes.

Nonessential: Ovid, a Roman poet, wrote the *Metamorphoses.*

Essential: The Roman poet Ovid wrote the *Metamorphoses.*

Practice Rewrite each sentence below, incorporating the information given as an appositive. Add words as necessary.

1. Daedalus devised an escape plan. *(clever artisan)*
2. He fitted Icarus with wings. *(his son)*
3. The boy ignored his father's advice. *(novice at flying)*
4. Daedalus and Icarus flew over Samos. *(Juno's sacred island)*
5. Daedalus lamented his son's death. *(father no more)*

Writing Application Write a paragraph about a journey that you or someone you know has taken recently. Use at least three appositives or appositive phrases in your writing.

WG Prentice Hall Writing and Grammar Connection: Platinum Level, Chapter 20, Section 1

Assessment Practice

Cause and Effect; Predicting Outcomes

(For more practice, see *Test Preparation Workbook*, p. 26.)

Use the following sample test item to demonstrate cause and effect.

> They were over Samos, Juno's sacred island, / Delos and Paros toward the left, Lebinthus / Visible to the right, and another island, Calymne, rich in honey. And the boy / Thought *This is wonderful!* and left his father, / Soared higher, higher, drawn to the vast heaven . . .
>
> —from "The Story of Daedalus and Icarus," lines 45–50

What causes Icarus to leave his father?

A He is angry with Daedalus.
B He is awed by the experience of flying.
C He wants to show his father a trick.
D He cannot control his wings.

Choices *A, C,* and *D* cannot be supported with details from the passage. Choice *B* is correct: Icarus is in awe, as evidenced by his thought *"This is wonderful!"* and the description of him "drawn to the vast heaven."

❸ Writing Lesson

Script for the Multimedia Presentation of a Story

In his story, Ovid conjures up vivid scenes and dialogue. Plan a multimedia presentation of "The Story of Daedalus and Icarus." Prepare a script describing the audio-visual aids that will bring out the imagery and emotion of the work.

Prewriting Reread the selection, making a list of photographs, artwork, music, video clips, and sound effects that could highlight the poem's images and emotional dynamics.

Drafting Draft your script, clearly showing the line-by-line relationship between the text and the sounds and images you will use.

Revising Make sure that the format of your script is clear and easy to follow. Adjust the script to achieve the clearest, strongest arrangement of multimedia elements.

Model: Following Script Format

SPEAKER: . . . surely the sky is open,
[VISUAL: video slide of sky with sea gulls soaring]
And that's the way we'll go. Minos' dominion
Does not include the air.
[VISUAL: slide dissolves into picture of Daedalus]
[AUDIO: fade in music with brass instrument
playing a melody that conveys a sense of hope]

Bracketed directions convey the timing of audiovisual effects with the reading of the poem.

WG Prentice Hall Writing and Grammar Connection: Platinum Level, Chapter 29, Section 3

❹ Extend Your Learning

Listening and Speaking As a news anchor, present a **videotaped news report** on the fall of Icarus. Interview Daedalus, as well as the other witnesses to the tragedy: the fisherman, the shepherd, and the ploughman.

- In a group, assign roles and rehearse.
- Create pacing by timing segments.
- Use lighting or staging to direct audience attention from one speaker to the next.

Videotape your broadcast, and then play it for the class. **[Group Activity]**

Research and Technology Using a historical atlas, draw a **map of the Roman Empire** in Ovid's time. On your map, trace the route that Ovid might have taken from Rome to his place of exile—on the site of present-day Constanta in Romania.

For: An additional research activity
Visit: www.PHSchool.com
Web Code: etd-7407

❸ Writing Lesson

You may use this Writing Lesson as timed-writing practice, or you may allow students to develop the script as a writing assignment over several days.

- To give students guidance in writing this script, give them the **Support for Writing Lesson,** p. 160, in ***Unit 4 Resources.***
- Before students begin their multimedia presentations, suggest that they research depictions of this myth, such as Pieter Brueghel's painting *The Fall of Icarus* and W. H. Auden's poem "Musée des Beaux Arts." Students may choose to incorporate other depictions into their presentations.
- Use the Writing Lesson to guide students as they create their presentations. Remind students that their presentations should engage the audience's interest with details and appropriate narration.
- Use the Multimedia Report rubrics in ***General Resources,*** pp. 57–58, to assess students' presentations.

WG Writing and Grammar Platinum Level

For support in teaching the Writing Lesson, use Chapter 29, Section 3.

❹ Research and Technology

- Students may be able to locate an appropriate map on the Internet and print it.
- Suggest that interested students plot two alternate routes: one a journey taken wholly by land and a second route that incorporates some travel by sea.
- The **Support for Extend Your Learning** page (***Unit 4 Resources,*** p. 161) provides guided note-taking opportunities to help students complete the Extend Your Learning activities.

Go Online Research Have students type in the Web Code for another research activity.

Assessment Resources

The following resources can be used to assess students' knowledge and skills.

Unit 4 Resources
- **Selection Test A,** pp. 163–165
- **Selection Test B,** pp. 166–168

General Resources
- **Rubrics for Multimedia Report,** pp. 57–58

Go Online Assessment Students may use the **Self-test** to prepare for **Selection Test A** or **Selection Test B.**

Standard Course of Study

Goal 1: WRITTEN LANGUAGE

WL.1.03.9 Analyze effects of author's craft and style in reflection.

Goal 2: INFORMATIONAL READING

IR.2.01.3 Provide evidence to support understanding of and response to research text.

IR.2.01.11 Identify and analyze information in light of purpose, audience, and context.

Goal 4: CRITICAL THINKING

CT.4.01.3 Distinguish fact from fiction and recognize personal bias in interpretation.

Goal 5: LITERATURE

LT.5.03.7 Analyze influences, contexts, or biases in world literature.

Goal 6: GRAMMAR AND USAGE

GU.6.01.2 Analyze author's use of language to demonstrate understanding of expression.

Step-by-Step Teaching Guide	Pacing Guide
PRETEACH	
• Administer Vocabulary and Reading Warm-ups as necessary.	5 min.
• Engage students' interest with the motivation activity.	5 min.
• Read and discuss author and background features. **FT**	10 min.
• Introduce the Literary Analysis Skill: Annals. **FT**	5 min.
• Introduce the Reading Strategy: Recognize Author's Bias. **FT**	10 min.
• Prepare students to read by teaching the selection vocabulary. **FT**	
TEACH	
• Informally monitor comprehension while students read independently or in groups. **FT**	30 min.
• Monitor students' comprehension with the Reading Check notes.	as students read
• Reinforce vocabulary with Vocabulary Builder notes.	as students read
• Develop students' understanding of the Annals with the Literary Analysis annotations. **FT**	5 min.
• Develop students' ability to recognize author's bias with the Reading Strategy annotations. **FT**	5 min.
ASSESS/EXTEND	
• Assess students' comprehension and mastery of the Literary Analysis and Reading Strategy by having them answer the Apply the Skills questions. **FT**	15 min.
• Have students complete the Vocabulary Lesson and the Grammar and Style Lesson. **FT**	15 min.
• Apply students' ability to add transitions to clarify sequence of events by using the Writing Lesson. **FT**	45 min. or homework
• Apply students' understanding by using one or more of the Extend Your Learning activities.	20–90 min. or homework
• Administer Selection Test A or Selection Test B. **FT**	15 min.

Resources

Print

Unit 4 Resources

- Vocabulary Warm-up Word Lists **[L1, L2, EL]** .... p. 169
- Vocabulary Warm-up Practice **[L1, L2, EL]** .... p. 170
- Reading Warm-up A **[L1, L2, EL]** .... p. 171
- Reading Warm-up B **[L1, L2, L3]** .... p. 172

Transparency

Graphic Organizer Transparencies

- Literary Analysis Graphic Organizer A **[L3]** .... p. 106
- Literary Analysis Graphic Organizer B **[L1, L2, EL]** .... p. 107
- Reading Strategy Graphic Organizer A **[L3]** .... p. 104
- Reading Strategy Graphic Organizer B **[L1, L2, EL]** .... p. 105

Print

Reader's Notebook [L2]

Reader's Notebook: Adapted Version [L1]

Reader's Notebook: English Learner's Version [EL]

Unit 4 Resources

- Literary Analysis **[L3]** .... p. 173
- Reading Strategy **[L3]** .... p. 174
- Vocabulary Builder **[L3]** .... p. 175

Technology

Listening to Literature Audio CDs [L2, EL]

Print

Unit 4 Resources

- Grammar and Style **[L3]** .... p. 176
- Support for Writing Lesson **[L3]** .... p. 177
- Support for Extend Your Learning **[L3]** .... p. 178
- Enrichment **[L4]** .... p. 179
- Selection Test A **[L1, L2, EL]** .... pp. 180–182
- Selection Test B **[L3, L4]** .... pp. 183–185

General Resources

- Rubrics for Narration: Autobiographical Narrative **[L3]** .... pp. 43–44

Technology

- **Go Online:** Research **[L3]**
- **Go Online:** Self-test **[L3]**
- ***ExamView®*, Test Bank [L3]**

Choosing Resources for Differentiated Instruction

[L1] Special Needs Students

[L2] Below-Level Students

[L3] All Students

[L4] Advanced Students

[EL] English Learners

For Vocabulary and Reading Warm-ups and for Selection Tests, **A** signifies "less challenging" and **B** "more challenging." For Graphic Organizer transparencies, **A** signifies "not filled in" and **B** "filled in."

FT Fast Track Instruction: To move the lesson more quickly, use the strategies and activities identified with **FT**.

Scaffolding for Less Proficient and Advanced Students

The leveled Critical Thinking questions after selections progress in the levels of thinking required to answer them. To address the needs of your different students, you may use the (a) level questions for your less proficient students and the (b) level questions with your on-level and advanced students. The occasional (c) level questions are appropriate for your advanced students.

PRENTICE HALL **TeacherEXPRESS™** Plan · Teach · Assess Use this complete suite of powerful teaching tools to make lesson planning and testing quicker and easier.

PRENTICE HALL **StudentEXPRESS™** Learn · Study · Succeed Use the interactive textbook (online and on CD-ROM) to make selections and activities come alive with audio and video support and interactive questions.

Benchmark

After students have completed reading the excerpts from the *Annals,* administer **Benchmark Test 5 *(Unit 4 Resources,* pp. 193–198).** If the Benchmark Test reveals that some of the students need further work, use the **Interpretation Guide** to determine the appropriate reteaching page in the **Reading Kit** and on **Success Tracker.**

For: Information about Lexiles
Visit: www.PHSchool.com
Web Code: eue-1111

PREACH

Motivation

Ask students to imagine that a nearby city or town has been struck by a great catastrophe, such as a flood or fire that destroyed most of the city. Ask them to imagine that they are newspaper reporters covering the event. What would they be likely to see? What details might they include in the story? What details might they leave out? What might they say about the role that local government played in the catastrophe? Tell students that in the following excerpt, the ancient historian Tacitus describes the great fire of Rome. Encourage them to notice what details he describes, especially the information he relates about Nero, the Roman emperor at the time.

❶ Background

More About the Author

Tacitus survived the bloody reign of Domitian by keeping his own counsel. Unlike his garrulous friend Pliny the Younger, many of whose letters survive, Tacitus says very little about himself, mentioning only that his official honors were "begun by Vespasian, increased by Titus, and further advanced by Domitian." He also says that he spent four years in an official capacity in one of the provinces.

Geography Note

Draw students' attention to the map on this page. Tell them that Tacitus' birthplace is unknown, although he probably came from either southern France or northern Italy. He served as a government official in Asia (modern Turkey).

Build Skills *Primary Source*

from the Annals ❶

Tacitus (A.D. 56–c. 120)

The worldview and the works of the Roman historian Publius Cornelius Tacitus (pub′ lē əs kôr nēl′ yəs tas′ ət əs) were shaped by the tumultuous era in which he lived. Nearly one hundred years before his birth, a long period of civil strife had brought an end to the Roman republic. In 27 B.C., Octavian, the grand-nephew and adopted son of Julius Caesar, had seized power as emperor, given himself the name "Augustus"—from a Latin word meaning "to increase"—and launched the Roman Empire.

Rubber-Stamp Senators The rule of Augustus was marked by a loss of liberty for his subjects. Senators merely rubber-stamped his decisions, and his displeasure could mean—as it did for the poet Ovid—perpetual exile, with no legal right of appeal. Nonetheless, Augustus was an able and sane leader, and under him the empire enjoyed relative peace and prosperity.

His immediate successors, however, form a parade of irresponsible, capricious individuals who managed the state poorly. Understandably, many Romans longed for the days when a dutiful citizen could play a role in governing the state.

A Survivor Tacitus not only survived the sometimes brief and always repressive reigns of more than half a dozen emperors but even managed to enjoy a successful public career as a brilliant trial lawyer and judge. He seems to have been able to do that by keeping his political views to himself and spending some of the most tumultuous years away from Rome, in a government office overseas.

When the vicious emperor Domitian died in A.D. 96 and was succeeded by more reasonable rulers, Tacitus returned to Rome. He then enjoyed a distinguished public career, first in Rome and later in Asia. He was also finally able to turn his pen against the depraved rule of the emperors who immediately followed Augustus.

Influencing Future Opinion Through his incisive *Annals*, Tacitus has helped shape the world's opinion of Augustus' first four successors, particularly Nero, who is rumored to have sung while Rome burned. To be Nero's relative or close friend often marked one for an untimely death. It was his persecution of vulnerable groups like the early Christians, however, that earned him a lasting reputation for savagery.

The Dangers of Dynasty Tacitus' purpose in writing the *Annals* was to show how the four emperors who followed Augustus reduced Romans' freedoms. Rome's greatest historian did not object to strong leadership. He was distressed, however, by the way in which domination of the government by a single family, or dynasty, could deny power to men of ability.

Tacitus had planned to write about good emperors like Nerva and Trajan, and perhaps about Augustus as well, but the historian died before he could fulfill this goal. Perhaps he could not bring himself to turn his keen analytical gaze on good government for fear of having to recognize its imperfections.

Tacitus Today It is a tribute to Tacitus that after almost 2,000 years, historians still read his works to understand the beginnings of the Roman Empire. Yet they study his writings with a critical eye, knowing that he is not a completely objective observer. All readers, however, can appreciate the style of this ancient historian and his ability to portray vivid personalities and stirring events. You will see evidence of these talents in "The Burning of Rome."

Preview

Connecting to the Literature

You have probably seen news stories about disasters like fires, earthquakes, and floods. This selection tells about one of the greatest disasters of the ancient world: the fire that devastated Rome in A.D. 64.

❷ Literary Analysis

Annals

Annals are histories that present a year-by-year account of events—the word *annus* is Latin for "year." In the *Annals*, for example, Tacitus records important events of the first century of the Roman Empire. Yet he also includes these elements:

- narratives of events or incidents
- vivid descriptions
- explanations of causes and effects

As you read, look for ways in which Tacitus uses narratives, descriptions, and explanations of causes and effects to go beyond a mere listing of events.

Connecting Literary Elements

Tacitus uses several types of **descriptive detail** to enhance his account—details that appeal to the senses, give a precise fact, or name something specific. One precise fact, for example, is the selling price of corn. This detail and others make the *Annals* more vivid and believable. Look for descriptive details as you read.

❸ Reading Strategy

Recognize Author's Bias

If you **recognize the author's bias,** or point of view on details and events, you will be able to understand why he or she stresses certain facts or makes certain statements. Clues to bias include phrases or assertions with negative or positive associations. For example, in Tacitus' descriptions of Nero, words like *brutality* and suggestions of ambition and cruelty reflect the historian's negative opinion of the emperor. To uncover this bias, use a chart like the one shown.

Vocabulary Builder

conflagration (kän′ flə grā′ shən) *n.* large, destructive fire (p. 558)

unhampered (un ham′ pərd) *adv.* freely; without interference (p. 559)

destitute (des′ tə to͞ot′) *adj.* extremely poor (p. 560)

antiquity (an tik′ wə tē) *n.* early period of history (p. 560)

precipitous (prē sip′ ə təs) *adj.* steep like a precipice; sheer (p. 561)

demarcation (dē′ mär kā′ shən) *n.* boundary (p. 561)

munificence (myo͞o nif′ ə səns) *n.* great generosity (p. 562)

Standard Course of Study

- Identify and analyze information in light of purpose, audience, and context. (IR.2.01.11)
- Analyze influences, contexts, or biases in world literature. (LT.5.03.7)

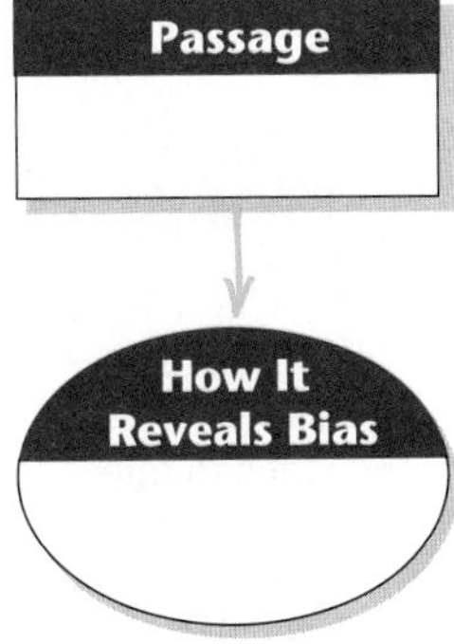

❷ Literary Analysis

Annals

- Tell students that as they read this selection, they will focus on annals, or histories that present a year-by-year account of events.
- Have students read the instruction carefully. Point out that Tacitus' inclusion of narratives, descriptions, and explanations shows that he worked to analyze what he witnessed, rather than recite dry facts.
- After students read the Connecting Literary Elements instruction, ask them to suggest ways in which descriptive details can make a historical account more vivid and interesting.

❸ Reading Strategy

Recognize Author's Bias

- Point out that identifying how a writer's attitude or bias determines the details of nonfiction narrative is similar to analyzing point of view in fiction.
- Explain to students that they can uncover an author's bias by analyzing how the writer uses language and by questioning details, reports, and rumors included in the narrative. Remind students that sometimes they may need to read critically to recognize attitudes that are implied rather than stated directly.
- Give students a copy of **Reading Strategy Graphic Organizer A,** p. 104 in ***Graphic Organizer Transparencies.*** Have them use it to evaluate the author's bias.

Vocabulary Builder

- Pronounce each vocabulary word for students, and read the definitions as a class. Have students identify any words with which they are already familiar.

Differentiated Instruction Solutions for All Learners

Support for Special Needs Students

Have students complete the **Preview** and **Build Skills** pages for *from the* Annals, from *The Burning of Rome* in the ***Reader's Notebook: Adapted Version.*** These pages provide a selection summary, an abbreviated presentation of the reading and literary skills, and the graphic organizer on the **Build Skills** page in the student book.

Support for Less Proficient Readers

Have students complete the **Preview** and **Build Skills** pages for *from the* Annals, from *The Burning of Rome* in the ***Reader's Notebook.*** These pages provide a selection summary, an abbreviated presentation of the reading and literary skills, and the graphic organizer on the **Build Skills** page in the student book.

Support for English Learners

Have students complete the **Preview** and **Build Skills** pages for *from the* Annals, from *The Burning of Rome* in the ***Reader's Notebook: English Learner's Version.*** These pages provide a selection summary, an abbreviated presentation of the skills, additional contextual vocabulary, and the graphic organizer on the **Build Skills** page in the student book.

TEACH

Facilitate Understanding

Students will probably have learned that Nero was a villain who "fiddled while Rome burned." Direct their attention to Tacitus' account of Nero's personal involvement in the disaster; have them note both his positive and his negative contributions. From a newly informed perspective, ask them to reconsider any previous estimations they had about his reputation.

❶ About the Selection

The ancient historian Tacitus makes this account of the great fire at Rome come alive with his vivid description of burning buildings and terrified people. Tacitus also uses the *Annals* not only to portray how human lives are disrupted by this frightening force of nature but also to expose the depravity of Nero.

❷ Vocabulary Builder

The Latin Suffix *-tion*

- Draw students' attention to the word *conflagration* and its definition.
- Tell students that the Latin suffix *-tion* forms nouns that indicate the action, state, or quality of something.
- Write the words *demarcation, definition,* and *medication* on the board. Then, ask students to relate the suffix *-tion* to the definitions of each of these words.
- Have students **list** other words formed by *-tion*.
  Possible response: Some words are *rotation, realization, location, ignition, assumption,* and *creation.*

❸ Critical Viewing

Possible response: The image of red-hot surfaces engages the sense of touch; the frantic gestures of the fleeing people make the viewer wonder what the citizens may be yelling to one another and how loudly the flames roar, engaging the sense of hearing.

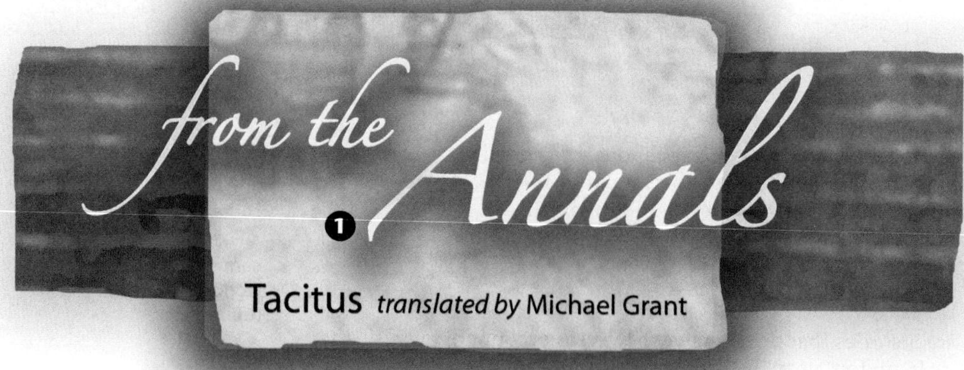

Background Nero became emperor of Rome—and potentially the most powerful person in the world—when he was just sixteen years old. The scheming of his mother, Agrippina, had cleared the way to the throne for him. As emperor, Nero at first enacted wise measures. Soon, however, he had both his mother and his wife put to death. He combined cruelty with artistic pretensions, shocking Romans by acting the parts of low-ranking characters on stage. By the time the great fire broke out ten years into his reign, Nero was so hated that many thought he had started the fire just to rebuild Rome as a monument to himself. Tacitus reports this popular belief in the *Annals*, but modern historians doubt the truth of this rumor.

The fire, which broke out in July, spread rapidly because summer winds fanned it and many Roman buildings were made of wood. A new, more splendid Rome of marble and stone was born from the ruins of this disaster.

from *The Burning of Rome*

Now started the most terrible and destructive fire which Rome had ever experienced. It began in the Circus,[1] where it adjoins the Palatine and Caelian hills.[2]

❷ Breaking out in shops selling inflammable goods, and fanned by the wind, the conflagration instantly grew and swept the whole length of the Circus. There were no walled mansions or temples, or any other

Vocabulary Builder
conflagration (kän′ flə grā′ shən) *n.* large, destructive fire

Critical Viewing ▶ ❸ Which senses does this depiction of the burning of Rome engage, other than the sense of sight? Explain. **[Analyze]**

1. **Circus** (sʉr′ kəs) In ancient Rome, games and chariot races were held in the Circus, an oval arena surrounded by tiers of seats.
2. **Palatine** (pal′ ə tīn) **and Caelian** (kē′ lē ən) **hills** locations of Nero's imperial palaces.

Differentiated Instruction Solutions for All Learners

Accessibility at a Glance

	from the Annals from *The Burning of Rome*
Context	The great fire of Rome in A.D. 64 when Nero was emperor
Language	Challenging vocabulary and syntax: long sentences with embedded clauses
Concept Level	Accessible (Bias distorts the recounting of an event.)
Literary Merit	Classic historical primary source
Lexile	1120L
Overall Rating	Challenging

obstructions, which could arrest it. First, the fire swept violently over the level spaces. Then it climbed the hills—but returned to ravage the lower ground again. It outstripped every counter-measure. The ancient city's narrow winding streets and irregular blocks encouraged its progress.

Terrified, shrieking women, helpless old and young, people intent on their own safety, people unselfishly supporting invalids or waiting for them, fugitives and lingerers alike—all heightened the confusion. When people looked back, menacing flames sprang up before them or outflanked them. When they escaped to a neighboring quarter, the fire followed—even districts believed remote proved to be involved. Finally, with no idea where or what to flee, they crowded on to the country roads, or lay in the fields. Some who had lost everything—even their food for the day—could have escaped, but preferred to die. So did others, who had failed to rescue their loved ones. Nobody dared fight the flames. Attempts to do so were prevented by menacing gangs. Torches, too, were openly thrown in, by men crying that they acted under orders. Perhaps they had received orders. Or they may just have wanted to plunder unhampered. ❹

Vocabulary Builder
unhampered (un ham′ pərd) *adv.* freely; without interference

Reading Check ❺
According to Tacitus, where did the fire begin?

The Burning of Rome, Hubert Robert, Giraudon

❹ Humanities

The Burning of Rome,
by Hubert Robert

The French painter Hubert Robert (1733–1808) specialized in depicting Italian ruins and classical scenes that combined architectural views with imaginary events.

The Burning of Rome is an example of such a scene. This highly evocative landscape is based on actual ruins that Robert studied and drew in Italy. He combined them with the story of the burning of Rome to create this dramatic painting. The ancient buildings stand stately and immobile amid leaping flames and fleeing people.

The paintings of Hubert Robert were highly regarded in their day and earned him the nickname of "Robert of the Ruins."

Use the following questions for discussion:

- Does this painting capture the burning of Rome as Tacitus describes it? Explain.
  Possible responses: Yes; The architectural elements suggest ancient Rome. No; There probably would have been more panic and crowds in the burning city.
- What does the statue at the top of the archway suggest about this event?
  Possible response: Rome's history of greatness cannot stop the destruction; the fire may bring about the end of Rome's greatness.

❺ Reading Check

Answer: The fire began in the Circus, an arena.

Differentiated Instruction
Solutions for All Learners

Support for English Learners

To assist with syntax, point out the inverted order in the first sentence of this excerpt and its subject *(fire)*. Then discuss the participial phrases. Explain that both *Breaking out in shops* and *fanned by the wind* work as adjectives modifying the subject *conflagration*. Ask students what *selling inflammable goods* modifies *(shops)*. Note the following participles in the rest of the paragraph: *walled* modifying *mansions or temples*, and *winding* modifying *streets*. Then, ask students to make a list of participles and participial phrases in the next paragraph and the words that they modify.

Enrichment for Advanced Readers

Ask students to write reports about a community or national event that happened when they were about seven years old. Tell them to supplement their own memories by interviewing older people, but ask them to refrain from conducting additional print or Internet research until they have finished writing. Ask students to present their reports, reveal any inaccuracies that resulted from relying on memory alone, and share news articles published at the time of the event.

❻ Critical Viewing

Possible response: The sculpture seems to convey foolishness, laziness, self-indulgence, and superficiality.

❼ Critical Thinking

Analyze

- Have students reread the bracketed passage.
- Then, **ask** students to explain some of the specific techniques Tacitus uses to convey the magnitude of the disaster.
  Possible response: Tacitus uses specific, quantitative measures; he refers to specific temples of great antiquity; he also mentions losses such as Greek artistic masterpieces. The magnitude of the disaster is underlined by the phrase "irreplaceable objects."

❽ Reading Strategy

Recognize Author's Bias

- Remind students that bias is often revealed in an author's word choice.
- **Ask** students to identify details in the bracketed passage that reveal Tacitus' feelings about Rome.
  Possible response: "Precious spoils of countless victories," "artistic masterpieces," and "Roman genius" all reveal the author's feelings.
- **Ask** students how the author feels about Rome, on the basis of these word choices.
  Possible response: He shows a deep admiration for the city.
- **Ask** students how the author's bias may affect his account of the fire.
  Possible response: The author may write about the fire in more emotional terms than another writer might; he also may be more likely than a less involved writer to find someone or something to blame for the fire.

Nero was at Antium.[3] He only returned to the city when the fire was approaching the mansion he had built to link the Gardens of Maecenas to the Palatine. The flames could not be prevented from overwhelming the whole of the Palatine, including his palace. Nevertheless, for the relief of the homeless, fugitive masses he threw open the Field of Mars, including Agrippa's public buildings, and even his own Gardens. Nero also constructed emergency accommodation for the destitute multitude. Food was brought from Ostia[4] and neighboring towns, and the price of corn was cut to less than one quarter sesterce[5] a pound. Yet these measures, for all their popular character, earned no gratitude. For a rumor had spread that, while the city was burning, Nero had gone on his private stage and, comparing modern calamities with ancient, had sung of the destruction of Troy.

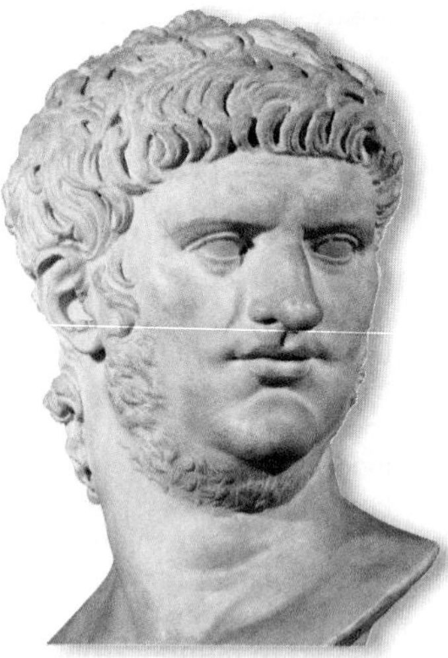

▲ **Critical Viewing** ❻ What impression of Nero do you think this sculpture is meant to convey? **[Infer]**

By the sixth day enormous demolitions had confronted the raging flames with bare ground and open sky, and the fire was finally stamped out at the foot of the Esquiline Hill. But before panic had subsided, or hope revived, flames broke out again in the more open regions of the city. Here there were fewer casualties; but the destruction of temples and pleasure arcades was even worse. This new conflagration caused additional ill-feeling because it started on Tigellinus' estate[6] in the Aemilian district. For people believed that Nero was ambitious to found a new city to be called after himself.

Vocabulary Builder

destitute (des′ tə to͞ot′) *adj.* extremely poor

antiquity (an tik′ wə tə) *n.* early period of history

❼ Of Rome's fourteen districts only four remained intact. Three were leveled to the ground. The other seven were reduced to a few scorched and mangled ruins. To count the mansions, blocks, and temples destroyed would be difficult. They included shrines of remote antiquity, such as Servius Tullius' temple of the Moon, the Great Altar and holy place dedicated by Evander to Hercules, the temple vowed by Romulus to Jupiter the Stayer, Numa's sacred residence, and Vesta's shrine containing Rome's household gods. ❽ Among the losses, too, were the precious spoils of countless victories, Greek artistic masterpieces, and authentic records of old Roman genius. All the splendor of the rebuilt city did not prevent the older generation from remembering these irreplaceable objects. It was noted that the fire had started on July 19th, the day on which the Senonian Gauls[7] had captured and burnt the city. Others elaborately calculated that the two fires were separated by the same number of years, months, and days.[8]

But Nero profited by his country's ruin to build a new palace. Its wonders were not so much customary and commonplace luxuries like gold and jewels, but lawns and lakes and faked rusticity—woods here,

3. **Antium** (an′ tē əm) town in central Italy where Nero was born.
4. **Ostia** (äs′ tē ə) Roman port at the mouth of the Tiber River.
5. **sesterce** (ses′ tərs) Roman coin, equal in value to two and a half cents.
6. **Tigellinus' estate** (tī′ jə lī′ nəs) land belonging to Tigellinus, second to Nero in power.
7. **Senonian Gauls** (sə nō′ nē ən gôlz) barbarians from Gaul, an ancient region in western Europe; they burned Rome in 390 B.C.
8. **the same number of years, months, and days** 418 years, 418 months, and 418 days.

Enrichment

History and Moral Judgments

Tacitus believed that his writing had a moral purpose. For him, writing history was not merely recording facts but making clear the distinctions between good and evil. Writing about the moral and political climate under the emperor Tiberius, Tacitus states, "My purpose is not to relate at length every motion of the senate, but only such as were conspicuous for excellence or notorious for infamy. This I regard as history's highest function, to let no worthy action be uncommemorated, and to hold out the reprobation of posterity as a terror to evil words and deeds."

Organize students into small discussion groups, and have them address this question: Is it a historian's responsibility to make moral judgments about the "words and deeds" of historical figures to pass on to later generations? Have groups present the results of their discussion to the class.

open spaces and views there. With their cunning, impudent[9] artificialities, Nero's architects and engineers, Severus and Celer, did not balk at effects which Nature herself had ruled out as impossible.

They also fooled away an emperor's riches. For they promised to dig a navigable canal from Lake Avernus to the Tiber estuary,[10] over the stony shore and mountain barriers. The only water to feed the canal was in the Pontine marshes. Elsewhere, all was precipitous or waterless. Moreover, even if a passage could have been forced, the labor would have been unendurable and unjustified. But Nero was eager to perform the incredible; so he attempted to excavate the hills adjoining Lake Avernus. Traces of his frustrated hopes are visible today.

10 In parts of Rome unfilled by Nero's palace, construction was not—as after the burning by the Gauls—without plan or demarcation. Street-fronts were of regulated alignment, streets were broad, and houses built round courtyards. Their height was restricted, and their frontages protected by colonnades. Nero undertook to erect these at his own expense, and also to clear debris from building-sites before transferring them to their owners. He announced bonuses, in proportion to rank and resources, for the completion of houses and blocks before a given date. Rubbish was to be dumped in

11 the Ostian marshes by corn-ships returning down the Tiber.

A fixed proportion of every building had to be massive, untimbered stone from Gabii[11] or Alba[12] (these stones being fireproof). Furthermore, guards were to ensure a more abundant and extensive public water-supply, hitherto diminished by irregular private enterprise. Householders were obliged to keep fire-fighting appartus in an accessible place; and semi-detached houses were forbidden—they must have their own walls. These measures were welcomed for their practicality, and they beautified the new city. Some, however, believed

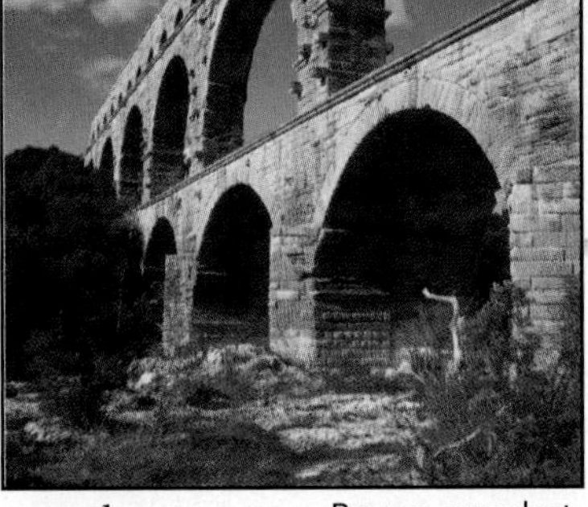

Roman aqueduct

9. **impudent** (im´ pyo͞o dənt) *adj.* shamelessly bold and disrespectful.
10. **Tiber estuary** (tī´ bər es´ tyo͞o er ē) the wide mouth of the Tiber, a river in central Italy that flows south through Rome.
11. **Gabii** (gā´ bē ī) ancient Roman town where Romulus, legendary founder of Rome, was reared. Gabii supposedly resisted a siege and was an important city until it was overshadowed by Rome.
12. **Alba** (äl´ bə) Alba Longa, a powerful ancient Roman city; legendary birthplace of Romulus and Remus.

Literature in Context

9 Science Connection

Roman Engineering

Tacitus refers to an expensive scheme "to dig a navigable canal." In this case, Tacitus is sarcastic, but Roman architects and engineers accomplished amazing feats, including the rebuilding of Rome after the fire. For example, they built about 50,000 miles of roads, some of which are still in use today. These carefully layered roads had a slight downward curve at the edges to facilitate drainage. Engineers also built many miles of aqueducts,"conduits for carrying water," to supply Rome and other cities. These aqueducts brought water from miles away and sometimes crossed over valleys on great stone arches.

Connect to the Literature

Why do you think Tacitus' reference to a "navigable canal" is sarcastic?

Vocabulary Builder

precipitous (prē sip´ ə təs) *adj.* steep like a precipice; sheer

demarcation (dē´ mär kā´ shən) *n.* boundary

12  

In what way did Nero profit from the fire, according to Tacitus?

9 Literature in Context

Roman Engineering The first recorded Roman aqueduct was the Aqua Appia, constructed in 312 B.C., just as the Romans were beginning to build the Via Appia, the first Roman road. The Aqua Appia brought water to the city from natural springs located about ten miles away. Over the next 500 years, the growing city added ten more aqueducts to provide water for its residents. In 125 B.C., with the Aqua Tepula, the Romans started to use poured concrete in their aqueducts. Water pipes were made of clay, lead, and bronze.

Connect to the Literature Point out to students that Tacitus' bias shows in his discussion of Nero's plan to build a navigable canal when he writes, "They also fooled away an emperor's riches." Ask why Tacitus is sarcastic.

Possible response: Tacitus knows that this is a foolish idea because the water is that from a marsh, and it is not deep and wide enough to provide passage for vessels.

10 Vocabulary Builder

The Latin Suffix *-tion*

- Draw students' attention to the word *demarcation* and its definition.
- Tell students that the Latin suffix *-tion* forms nouns that indicate the action, state, or quality of something.
- **Ask** students what word is imbedded within the word *demarcation.*
  Answer: The word *mark* is embedded within *demarcation.*
- Tell students that *demarcation* is the quality or state of "being marked," as a boundary. Then, ask them to use the word in a paragraph that contains three other words that end with the suffix *-tion.*

11 Background

Shipping

Corn refers to grain in general. Rome was a great importer of grains from other parts of the Mediterranean world. Ships from other regions that carried grain sailed up the Tiber to be delivered to Roman ports.

12 Reading Check

Answer: Nero was able to build a new palace.

Differentiated Instruction Solutions for All Learners

Strategy for Special Needs Students

Have students compile a chart of the specific requirements Nero makes for houses built after the fire. Ask students to offer reasons why Nero might have made these rules. Ask students to conclude whether each rule had to do with fire prevention, beautification of the city, or both.

Strategy for Less Proficient Readers

Have students compile a chart of the specific requirements Nero makes for houses built after the fire. Then, organize students into two groups. Have one group create a list of positive reactions people might have had to these requirements, and have the other group compile a list of possible objections to these requirements. Have both sides present their arguments, and give them a chance to respond to the opposition's position on each matter.

13 Critical Thinking

Analyze

- Read the bracketed passage aloud. **Ask** students to evaluate the measures taken by Nero to safeguard against future fires.
  Possible response: The measures seem reasonable and would probably protect against fire.
- **Ask** students what drawback some of the citizens saw in these measures.
  Possible response: Some people believed that the old houses cast shadows that provided protection from the sun's intensity. The new requirement of open spaces instead of narrow streets also made the people more aware of the sun's intensity.
- **Ask** students what some people might have concluded about Nero's requirements.
  Possible response: Even though Nero had fire safety in mind when he created the regulations, his decisions brought discomfort to the Romans' daily lives. Therefore, some people might have concluded that Nero did not care about the comfort or concerns of his citizens.

14 Humanities

A View of Rome, by Antonio Basoli

Basoli (1774–1848) painted *A View of Rome* in 1838, a time when landscape painting flourished. Unlike many landscape painters who take their canvases to the site they wish to paint, Basoli conjured a vision of ancient Rome in his imagination.

Use the following question for discussion:

What does this painting tell the viewer about ancient Rome?
Possible response: The city was vast, filled with remarkable architecture and majestic vistas; the people assembled there seem to be moving in an orderly and efficient way.

15 Critical Viewing

Possible response: This painting shows the open spaces of Rome, perhaps following its reconstruction during Nero's reign. The rich tones of the painting capture the beauty of the city that Tacitus articulates in his writing. The recurring images of monuments in the foreground seem both impressive and ominous, reminding the viewer of the mixed feelings people had about Nero.

13 that the old town's configuration had been healthier, since its narrow streets and high houses had provided protection against the burning sun, whereas now the shadowless open spaces radiated a fiercer heat.

So much for human precautions. Next came attempts to appease heaven. After consultation of the Sibylline books,[13] prayers were addressed to Vulcan, Ceres, and Proserpina. Juno, too, was propitiated.[14] Women who had been married were responsible for the rites—first on the Capitol, then at the nearest sea-board, where water was taken to sprinkle her temple and statue. Women with husbands living also celebrated ritual banquets and vigils.

16 But neither human resources, nor imperial munificence, nor appeasement of the gods, eliminated sinister suspicions that the fire

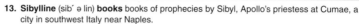

Vocabulary Builder
munificence (myo͞o nif′ ə səns) *n.* great generosity

15 ▼ **Critical Viewing**
Compare and contrast this artist's rendering of Rome with Tacitus' description of the city. **[Compare and Contrast]**

13. **Sibylline** (sib′ ə lin) **books** books of prophecies by Sibyl, Apollo's priestess at Cumae, a city in southwest Italy near Naples.
14. **propitiated** (prō pish′ ē āt′ id) *v.* appeased.

14

Enrichment

Christians in the Early Roman Empire

Written nearly fifty years after Nero's persecution of Christians, two letters document the growth of Christianity in the Roman Empire. The first letter was written by Tacitus' friend Pliny the Younger, who served as the governor of the province of Pontus/Bithynia (modern-day northern Turkey) in A.D. 111–113. Addressing the emperor Trajan (who ruled A.D. 98–117), Pliny seeks advice about handling alleged Christians. In his reply to Pliny, Trajan states that Christians are not to be sought out but that they should be punished if they refuse to worship the Roman gods. Trajan also warns Pliny of the dangers of allowing people to anonymously accuse one another of practicing Christianity. He believed that this was not in "the spirit of our age."

had been instigated. To suppress this rumor, Nero fabricated scapegoats—and punished with every refinement the notoriously depraved Christians (as they were popularly called). Their originator, Christ, had been executed in Tiberius' reign[15] by the governor of Judaea,[16] Pontius Pilatus. But in spite of this temporary setback the deadly superstition had broken out afresh, not only in Judaea (where the mischief had started) but even in Rome. All degraded and shameful practices collect and flourish in the capital.

First, Nero had self-acknowledged Christians arrested. Then, on their information, large numbers of others were condemned—not so much for incendiarism[17] as for their anti-social tendencies. Their deaths were made farcical. Dressed in wild animals' skins, they were torn to pieces by dogs, or crucified, or made into torches to be ignited after dark as substitutes for daylight. Nero provided his Gardens for the spectacle, and exhibited displays in the Circus, at which he mingled with the crowd—or stood in a chariot, dressed as a charioteer. Despite their guilt as Christians, and the ruthless punishment it deserved, the victims were pitied. For it was felt that they were being sacrificed to one man's brutality rather than to the national interest.

Meanwhile Italy was ransacked for funds, and the provinces were ruined—unprivileged and privileged communities alike. Even the gods were included in the looting. Temples at Rome were robbed, and emptied of the gold dedicated for the triumphs and vows, the ambitions and fears, of generations of Romans. Plunder from Asia and Greece included not only offerings but actual statues of the gods. Two agents were sent to these provinces. One, Acratus, was an ex-slave, capable of any depravity. The other, Secundus Carrinas, professed Greek culture, but no virtue from it percolated to his heart.

17 Seneca,[18] rumor went, sought to avoid the odium of this sacrilege by asking leave to retire to a distant country retreat, and then—permission being refused—feigning a muscular complaint and keeping to his bedroom. According to some accounts one of his former slaves, Cleonicus by name, acting on Nero's orders intended to poison Seneca but he escaped—either because the man confessed or because Seneca's own fears caused him to live very simply on plain fruit, quenching his thirst with running water.

At this juncture there was an attempted break-out by gladiators at Praeneste.[19] Their army guards overpowered them. But the Roman public, as always terrified (or fascinated) by revolution, were already talking of ancient calamities such as the rising of Spartacus.[20] Soon afterwards a naval disaster occurred. This was not on active service; never had there been such profound peace. But Nero had ordered the

15. **Tiberius'** (tī bir´ ē əs) **reign** Tiberius was emperor of Rome A.D. 14–37.
16. **Judaea** (jo͞o dē´ ə) ancient region of South Palestine.
17. **incendiarism** (in sen´ dē ə riz´ əm) *n.* willful destruction of property by fire.
18. **Seneca** (sen´ ə kə) philosopher and minister of Nero.
19. **Praeneste** (prī nest) town in central Italy.
20. **Spartacus** (spärt´ ə kəs) ancient Thracian slave and gladiator who led a slave revolt.

Literary Analysis
Annals According to Tacitus, what chain of causes and effects links the fire to the persecution of Christians?

Reading Strategy
Recognize Author's Bias How does the implied contrast of Seneca's actions with Nero's reveal Tacitus' bias against Nero?

Reading Check 18
According to Tacitus, what group of people were Nero's "fabricated scapegoats"?

16 Literary Analysis
Annals
- Have students read the bracketed passage.
- Point out that Tacitus introduces the topic of the persecution of the Christians with a cause-and-effect chain.

Monitor Progress Ask students to explain the concept of a cause-and-effect chain.

- **Ask** students the Literary Analysis question: According to Tacitus, what chain of causes and effects links the fire to the persecution of Christians?
Answer: Persistent rumors that the fire had been instigated led Nero to deflect attention from himself by making a public spectacle of persecuting Christians.

Reteach Discuss how one event often leads to another, and ask students to give examples of cause-and-effect chains in their daily lives.

17 Reading Strategy
Recognize Author's Bias
- Have students reread the bracketed passage.
- Ask students to characterize Seneca and Nero based on how they are described in this paragraph.
- **Ask** students to respond to the Reading Strategy question: How does the implied contrast of Seneca's actions with Nero's reveal Tacitus' bias against Nero?
Answer: Tacitus relates two rumors—Seneca's disgust at the plundering and Nero's plan to have him poisoned—in his account of the events. The inclusion of the rumors shows that he believes them and in turn reveals his own bias.

18 Reading Check
Answer: Christians were Nero's "fabricated scapegoats" for the fire.

Differentiated Instruction Solutions for All Learners
Enrichment for Gifted/Talented Students
Have students visit the library to find works of art that depict the events described in the Tacitus excerpt they have just read. Students will create a mural that depicts the fire and reconstruction of Rome and the persecution of Christians. Tell students to begin drawing or painting the fire on the left edge of the mural and then move to the reconstruction of Rome and the persecution of Christians as they move to the right edge of the mural. Tell students that their mural will serve as a visual timeline for the events Tacitus describes. Students will need to conduct additional research about Roman life so that they can render architectural and other details accurately. When the mural is finished, students will present it to the class with a brief, informal talk. Allow students to use a wooden or laser pointer to draw the audience's attention to details in the mural as the artists explain them.

ASSESS

Answers

1. Tacitus' account of Nero's selfishness, ambition, deceitfulness, and cruelty is shocking. It is surprising that the historian included any positive remarks about Nero.
2. (a) The fire first broke out in shops selling inflammable goods. (b) Narrow, winding streets and irregular blocks encouraged the fire's progress.
3. (a) **Possible response:** He opened the Field of Mars, as well as his own gardens, to the city dwellers. He provided for emergency accommodation, arranged for food deliveries, and cut the price of corn. (b) The rumor of Nero's stage performance seems to have eclipsed any gratitude the people felt toward the emperor; their cynicism suggests that Nero had a poor reputation for leadership.
4. (a) Regulations included aligned street fronts, restrictions on building heights, and clearing of debris from building sites. (b) The regulations seem sensible because they contributed to greater order and safety.
5. (a) Nero wanted to make Christians the scapegoats for the fire because rumors persisted that the conflagration had been instigated. (b) The treatment of the Christians was so cruel that people were disinclined to believe that they deserved such suffering.
6. (a) Omens include the appearance of a comet and the birth of a calf with its head fastened to one of its legs. (b) The omens seem to reinforce the atmosphere of destruction and deceit that characterizes the account of the fire.
7. **Possible response:** A modern historian might praise Tacitus' factual precision about the location of the fire and his cause-and-effect analysis of Nero's persecution of the Christians; he or she might criticize Tacitus' inclusion of the rumor of Nero's stage performance and the final paragraph on the omens.

fleet to return to Campania by a fixed date regardless of weather. So, despite heavy seas the steersmen started from Formiae. But when they tried to round Cape Misenum a south-westerly gale drove them ashore near Cumae and destroyed numerous warships and smaller craft.

As the year ended omens of impending misfortune were widely rumored—unprecedentedly frequent lightning; a comet (atoned for by Nero, as usual, by aristocratic blood); two-headed offspring of men and beasts, thrown into the streets or discovered among the offerings to those deities to whom pregnant victims are sacrificed. Near Placentia a calf was born beside the road with its head fastened to one of its legs. Soothsayers deduced that a new head was being prepared for the world—but that it would be neither powerful nor secret since it had been deformed in the womb and given birth by the roadside.

Critical Reading

1. **Respond:** Based on this account, what is your reaction to the emperor Nero? Why?
2. **(a) Recall:** In what part of Rome did the fire first break out? **(b) Analyze:** In what way did the city's layout encourage the fire's progress?
3. **(a) Recall:** What are two ways in which Nero tried to help people during the fire? **(b) Interpret:** What does the people's reaction to Nero's help suggest about his reputation as their leader? Explain.
4. **(a) Recall:** What are three regulations that were part of Nero's plan to rebuild the city? **(b) Evaluate:** Do these regulations make sense? Why or why not?
5. **(a) Recall:** Why did Nero turn against the Christians? **(b) Interpret:** Why do you think people felt the Christians "were being sacrificed to one man's brutality rather than to the national interest"?
6. **(a) Recall:** What are two "omens" that Tacitus mentions in the final paragraph? **(b) Connect:** What is the relationship between these omens and the account of the fire?
7. **Evaluate:** What are two details in this account that a modern historian might praise and two details that he or she might criticize? Explain.

Go Online
Author Link
For: More about Tacitus
Visit: www.PHSchool.com
Web Code: ete-9409

Go Online Author Link For additional information about Tacitus, have students type in the Web Code, then select *T* from the alphabet, and then select Tacitus.

Apply the Skills

from the *Annals*

Literary Analysis

Annals

1. On the right side of a chart like the one shown, give an example from the selection for each element of an **annal** listed on the left.

Elements of an Annal	Examples From the *Annals* of Tacitus
review of a year's important events	
explanation of cause-effect relationships	
vivid descriptions	

2. Do the *Annals* follow a chronological sequence? Why or why not?
3. To what extent does Tacitus report verified facts and to what extent does he report rumors? Explain.
4. **(a)** What are three sources that a modern annals writer could use? **(b)** Explain the type of information available from each.

Connecting Literary Elements

5. Give an example of each type of **descriptive detail** in the *Annals:* precise fact, specific name, and detail that appeals to the senses.
6. What does each type of detail add to the account of the year's events?

Reading Strategy

Recognizing Author's Bias

7. You can **recognize the author's bias** by analyzing both positive and negative statements about Nero. **(a)** Which type of statement tends to come at the end of a paragraph? **(b)** What is the effect of this pattern of placement?
8. What are two examples in which Tacitus, rather than criticizing Nero directly, allows the voice of public opinion to criticize him?
9. What are two phrases that reveal Tacitus' attitude toward Christianity? Explain.

Extend Understanding

10. **Media Connection:** Do you think that today's newspaper or television reporters ever reveal a bias as Tacitus does? Why or why not?

QuickReview

Annals are histories that present a year-by-year account of events.

A **descriptive detail** is one that appeals to the senses, gives a precise fact, or names something specific.

When reading, use clues to **recognize the author's bias**—his or her point of view on people or events.

For: Self-test
Visit: www.PHSchool.com
Web Code: eta-6410

Answers

1. **Possible response: Review of a year's important events:** the account of the fire and Nero's persecution of the Christians; **Explanation of cause-effect relationships:** "But neither human resources, nor imperial munificence nor appeasement of the gods, eliminated sinister suspicions that the fire had been instigated."; **Vivid descriptions:** "Dressed in wild animals' skins, they were torn to pieces by dogs, or crucified, or made into torches to be ignited after dark as substitutes for daylight."
2. **Possible response:** The *Annals* report events year by year, but the events within a year may be grouped thematically.
3. He reports verified facts about the fire and the regulations for rebuilding houses; he reports rumors regarding Nero's dramatic performance while the city burned and the alleged plot against Seneca's life.
4. (a) A modern annals writer might use newspaper articles, autobiographies, and the Internet.
(b) Newspapers supply objective reports about events; autobiographies supply the writer's description of events; the Internet supplies a wide range of fact and opinion.
5. **Possible response: Precise fact:** the price of corn as less than one quarter sesterce per pound; **Specific name:** Nero, Cleonicus, or Seneca; **Details appealing to the senses:** The shadowless open spaces of the rebuilt city radiated fierce heat.
6. Each type of detail contributes vividness and believability.
7. **Possible response:** (a) Tacitus often concludes with a negative statement. (b) These statements linger in the reader's mind.
8. Tacitus mentions that "some people" thought Rome's old configuration was better, and he lists the "omens of impending misfortune" that people connected to Nero's leadership.
9. Phrases include "the deadly superstition" and "the ruthless punishment it [Christianity] deserved."

Answers continued

10. **Possible response:** The journalistic ideal today is to remain objective, although absolute neutrality may be impossible.

Go Online Assessment Students may use the **Self-test** to prepare for **Selection Test A** or **Selection Test B.**

Answers

❶ Vocabulary Lesson

Word Analysis: Latin Suffix *-tion*

1. Large fire; The *conflagration* in Rome in the year A.D. 64 destroyed or damaged much of the city.
2. Boundary; The *demarcation* between districts was hard to discern.
3. Substance for curing or healing; After she injured her knee, she took pain *medication.*
4. Meaning; Use a dictionary to find the *definition* of new words.
5. Change; After the fire, there was *alteration* in Rome's appearance.
6. Gradual wearing away or weakening; The staff became leaner through *attrition,* in which retiring employees were not replaced.

Vocabulary Builder

1. d 4. c 7. b
2. g 5. a
3. f 6. e

Spelling Strategy

1. calamity 3. variety
2. levity

❷ Grammar and Style Lesson

1. fewer 3. fewer 5. less
2. less 4. less

Writing Application

Possible response: New streets could not be *less* than a certain width. There would be *fewer* narrow streets. *Less* rubbish was permitted to remain.

Writing and Grammar Platinum Level

For support in teaching the Grammar and Style Lesson, use Chapter 26, Section 2.

Build Language Skills

❶ Vocabulary Lesson

Word Analysis: Latin Suffix *-tion*

The Latin suffix *-tion* forms nouns that indicate the action, state, or quality of something. The word *conflagration,* for example, means "the act of burning"—the Latin *conflagare* means "to burn."

Use your understanding of the suffix *-tion* to define each of the following words. If necessary, check the definition of the root in a dictionary. Then, use each word in an original sentence.

1. conflagration
2. demarcation
3. medication
4. definition
5. alteration
6. attrition

Vocabulary Builder: Synonyms

Identify the letter of the word or phrase that is closest in meaning to each numbered word below.

1. conflagration — a. steep
2. unhampered — b. generosity
3. destitute — c. early era
4. antiquity — d. large fire
5. precipitous — e. boundary
6. demarcation — f. very poor
7. munificence — g. not impeded

Spelling Strategy

The suffix *-ity* is more common than *-ety,* which often follows the letter *i.* Complete each word below with the correct suffix.

1. calam___ 2. lev___ 3. vari___

❷ Grammar and Style Lesson

Commonly Confused Words: *less* and *fewer*

Use the word *less* with qualities or amounts that cannot be counted. It modifies a singular noun and answers the question "How much?"

> It takes *less* time to start a conflagration than it does to extinguish it.

Use the word *fewer* with objects that can be counted. It modifies a plural noun and answers the question "How many?"

> Here there were *fewer* casualties; but the destruction of temples and pleasure arcades was even worse.

Practice In your notebook, complete each sentence below by inserting *fewer* or *less.*

1. Does this selection contain __?__ details than you expected?
2. Tacitus had __?__ admiration for the empire than for the republic.
3. No __?__ than ten of Rome's fourteen districts were destroyed by the fire.
4. The fire caused __?__ damage on the seventh day than on the fifth.
5. There was __?__ wealth in the provinces after Nero's agents visited them.

Writing Application Write a paragraph to describe Rome's building laws after the fire. Use the words *less* and *fewer* at least once each.

Prentice Hall Writing and Grammar Connection: Platinum Level, Chapter 26, Section 2

Assessment Practice

Cause and Effect; Predicting Outcomes

(For more practice, see *Test Preparation Workbook*, p. 27.)

In many tests, students will have to identify causes and effects to predict outcomes. Use the following sample test item to demonstrate.

"Nero was at Antium. He only returned to the city when the fire was approaching the mansion he had built to link the Gardens of Maecenas to the Palatine."

Which of the following is a likely outcome of Nero's popularity with the Romans?

A The people will appreciate Nero's help, and his popularity will rise.
B The people will understand Nero's delay, and his popularity will rise.
C The people will view Nero as selfish, and his popularity will decline.
D The people will be forced to rebuild Nero's mansion, and his popularity will decline.

It is likely that the people will make the inference that Nero selfishly returned to Rome only when his personal possessions were threatened, causing his popularity to suffer. C is the correct answer.

❸ Writing Lesson

Eyewitness Narrative Essay

People enjoy reading reports of events by those who witnessed them. Such eyewitness accounts often contain vivid details and convey the excitement of firsthand impressions. Using the *Annals* as a model, write an eyewitness narrative essay about an event that you have witnessed.

Prewriting After choosing an exciting event that you have witnessed, freewrite to gather details about it. Review what you have written. Next, arrange your details in chronological order.

Drafting Begin with an introduction that creates the proper mood and provides necessary background information. Then, tell what happened in chronological order, including descriptive details that appeal to the senses.

Revising Reread your draft. Add transitions where necessary—words like *then, next, first, before, during, while,* and *after*—to clarify the sequence of events.

Model: Adding Transitions to Clarify the Sequence of Events

First, ^Coach Donaldson welcomed everyone to the pep rally. Then, ^As each player's name was called, the player stood up to the accompaniment of the band.

Time transitions clarify the sequence of events.

WG Prentice Hall Writing and Grammar Connection: Platinum Level, Chapter 9, Section 4

❹ Extend Your Learning

Listening and Speaking With a small group, develop a **skit,** or brief dramatic scene, in which a group of Romans gossip about the fire. Consider these tips:

- Include historical details from the *Annals*.
- Have characters express the concerns of their social class and occupation.
- In rehearsals, allow actors to improvise, and include improvised dialogue in the script.

Present your skit to the class. **[Group Activity]**

Research and Technology Use library and Internet resources to create an **illustrated timeline of Roman history** during the first century A.D. Include a portrait of each emperor and illustrations for each major event, like the fire of A.D. 64.

For: An additional research activity
Visit: www.PHSchool.com
Web Code: etd-7408

❸ Writing Lesson

You may use this Writing Lesson as timed-writing practice, or you may allow students to develop the narrative essay as a writing assignment over several days.

- To give students guidance in writing this narrative essay, give them the **Support for Writing Lesson,** p. 177 in ***Unit 4 Resources.***
- As students consider possible topics, remind them to choose events that they have closely observed firsthand.
- Remind students to use chronological order to organize their accounts. Writers may need to use flashback, however, in order to provide essential background information.
- Use the rubrics for Narration: Autobiographical Narrative in ***General Resources,*** pp. 43–44, to evaluate students' work.

WG Writing and Grammar Platinum Level

For support in teaching the Writing Lesson, use Chapter 9, Section 4.

❹ Listening and Speaking

- Encourage students to reread the selection thoroughly before they plan their skits. Suggest students make a list of details that they consider suitable springboards for dialogue.
- Have students make a list of occupations that might be represented by the speakers.
- The **Support for Extend Your Learning** page (***Unit 4 Resources,*** p. 178) provides guided note-taking opportunities to help students complete the Extend Your Learning activities.

Go Online Research Have students type in the Web Code for another research activity.

Assessment Resources

The following resources can be used to assess students' knowledge and skills.

Unit 4 Resources

- **Selection Test A,** pp. 180–182
- **Selection Test B,** pp. 183–185
- **Benchmark Test 5,** pp. 193–198

General Resources

- **Rubrics for Narration: Autobiographical Narrative,** pp. 43–44

Go Online Assessment Students may use the **Self-test** to prepare for **Selection Test A** or **Selection Test B.**

Benchmark

Administer **Benchmark Test 5.** If some students need further work, use the **Interpretation Guide** to determine the appropriate reteaching page in the **Reading Kit** and on **Success Tracker.**

Standard Course of Study

FA.3.04.7 Identify and analyze influences, contexts, or biases in argument.

LT.5.03.9 Analyze and evaluate the effects of author's craft and style in world literature.

LT.5.03.11 Analyze elements of literary environment in world literature.

Prewriting

- Ask students to brainstorm words and concepts related to citizenship. Then, ask students to review the works in this unit, looking for passages that deal with key concepts from the brainstorming session.
- Ask students to begin with three works that are especially relevant for review: *Pericles' Funeral Oration, Apology,* and *Oedipus the King.*
- As students review the works, ask them to begin to frame a thesis statement that expresses their findings. Remind students that a thesis statement is a fairly general statement that every paragraph of the essay will support.
- Tell students to gather evidence from each work in the unit. They should look for information that supports their thesis about citizenship. As they write about each work, they will need to provide enough context to explain the evidence sufficiently; however, they need not summarize the entire work.

Tips for Test Taking

A writing prompt on the SAT or ACT test may assess students' ability to analyze a topic such as literary themes, state a point of view regarding that topic, and support the point of view with evidence. When writing under timed circumstances, students will need to quickly clarify a point of view (their thesis statement) and the evidence that supports it. Because students will not be referring to a text, their evidence must be based on their own experiences, readings, or observations.

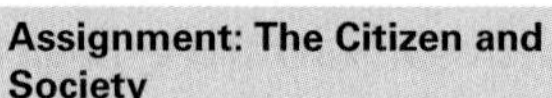

Analyze Literary Themes

The ancient Greek writers whose works appear in this unit speak to the modern era across great expanses of time, revealing not only their individual points of view but also the values that drove their culture. One such value was the importance of citizenship—the idea that the individual owes certain obligations to the community. Use the assignment outlined in the yellow box to analyze the concept of citizenship as the ancient Greeks saw it.

Assignment: The Citizen and Society

Write an analytical essay that explores the ancient Greek perspective on citizenship as it is expressed in the works in this unit.

Criteria:
- Include an explanation of each writer's position on the theme of citizenship.
- Include a thesis statement that states your main idea.
- Support your ideas with examples from the selections.
- Approximate length: 700 words

Prewriting

Review the material. Review each selection in the unit, gathering details relevant to the theme of citizenship. These questions can help you identify useful information:

- Which qualities does the author praise in his fellow citizens?
- How does the author see his fellow citizens in comparison with people in the rest of the world?
- How does the author describe what he or another citizen has done for the good of society?
- How does the author criticize citizens who do not live up to their obligations?

As you review the material, note any especially clear or compelling passages that you may want to use as quotations in your essay.

Read to Write

As you reread the selections, note direct statements, but also draw inferences—make informed guesses—about each author's position on the topic.

Find a focus. Use a chart like the one below to organize the details you have gathered. As you work, note both similarities and differences in the authors' positions.

Model: Charting to Find a Focus

Title	Point # 1	Point # 2	Point #3
Pericles' Funeral Oration	Obey the laws and those in authority.	Show courage and loyalty in times of war.	Get involved in affairs of the state.

Identify the beliefs about citizenship that these writers share and that may express a typical Greek point of view. Write a sentence expressing this main idea. This sentence will be the focus of your essay—your working thesis statement. Remember that you can modify your thesis as you draft and revise.

Teaching Resources

The following resources can be used to extend or enrich the instruction for Writing About Literature.

Unit Resources
Writing About Literature, pp. 186–187

General Resources
Response to Literature rubrics, pp. 55–56

Graphic Organizer Transparencies
Author's Purpose Chart, p. 274
Outline Organizer, p. 279

Drafting

Write an outline. Prepare an outline like the one shown below to plan the logical progression of your ideas and to identify the best placement of supporting details.

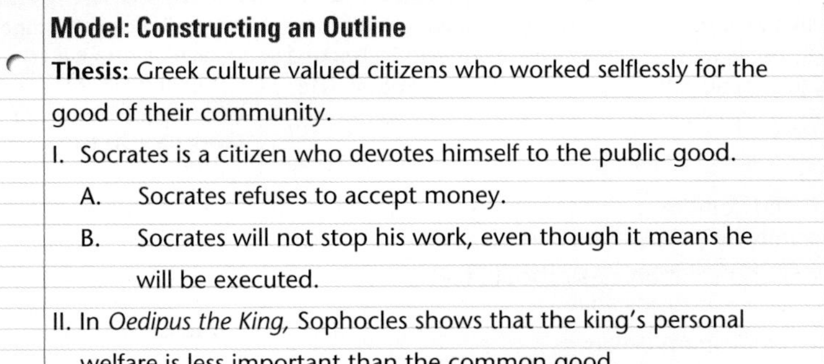

Model: Constructing an Outline

Thesis: Greek culture valued citizens who worked selflessly for the good of their community.

I. Socrates is a citizen who devotes himself to the public good.

A. Socrates refuses to accept money.

B. Socrates will not stop his work, even though it means he will be executed.

II. In *Oedipus the King,* Sophocles shows that the king's personal welfare is less important than the common good.

Write a memorable conclusion. The most effective essays end with a strong, memorable paragraph. For this assignment, end by presenting a final thought that ties your analysis together. For example, you might make a statement that emphasizes the relevance of ancient Greek values and ideas to the modern world.

Write to Learn

As you write, you may change your mind or discover a surprising idea. Allow for such changes in opinion; recognize that the writing process can give you a new perspective on a topic.

Revising and Editing

Review content: Revise to support ideas with details. Ensure that each point you make about the theme of citizenship is supported with details from at least one of the selections. Underline main ideas in your essay, and make sure that each one is supported. Add more proof as needed.

Review style: Revise to improve word choice. Be sure that you know the meanings of all the words you have used and that you have used the words accurately. Note whether you have repeated certain words, such as *citizenship* or *theme*, too often. Your essay will be more effective if you carefully edit to avoid such word-choice problems.

Write to Explain

You need clear, specific details from the selections—including quotations, where appropriate—to support your points. Vague references will not get the job done.

Publishing and Presenting

Hold a panel discussion. Begin by having each participant present a summary version of his or her essay on the Greek concept of citizenship. After each student has spoken, hold a panel discussion on the relevance of Greek ideas about citizenship to today's world. One student should act as the moderator and call for questions from the audience.

WG Prentice Hall Writing and Grammar Connection: Platinum Level, Chapter 13

Differentiated Instruction — Solutions for All Learners

Strategy for Less Proficient Writers

Offer students a strategy to organize information visually. Encourage them to re-create the chart on p. 568 so that it also includes the selections by Thucydides, Plato, and Sophocles. Then, have students find connections between the entries on their completed charts in order to help them generate concise thesis statements.

Vocabulary for English Learners

If students have trouble finding appropriate words to state a thesis and supporting arguments, have them use **Vocabulary Warm-up Word Lists** and **Vocabulary Warm-up Practice,** pp. 169–170 in ***Unit 4 Resources.*** Also encourage students to develop the habit of using a dictionary to look up any unfamiliar words.

Strategy for Advanced Writers

Invite students to construct more complex thesis statements. For example, suggest that students compare and contrast fourth- and fifth-century Athenian writers' outlooks on citizenship with the heroic code of Homeric society found in the *Iliad* excerpts.

Drafting

- Instruct students to begin their outlines with the thesis statement. Tell them this technique will help them find the most relevant evidence from each work.
- Remind students that an effective conclusion clearly restates the essay's main idea and presents a thought-provoking final comment.

Revising and Editing

- As students underline or highlight their drafts, ask them to check that the main idea in each body paragraph supports the thesis statement. If the connection between a detail and a main idea is unclear, ask students to revise the detail so that the connection is clear.
- Explain that varied word choice and sentence structure make an essay more interesting and enjoyable to read.

Publishing and Presenting

- Have students write the thesis statement and all of the main ideas on note cards so that they can "talk" their way through the points, rather than reading them aloud.
- Encourage students to ask questions after each presentation.

WG Writing and Grammar Platinum Level

Students will find additional instruction on writing an analytical essay in Chapter 9.

Writing and Grammar Interactive Textbook CD-ROM

Students can use the following tools as they complete their analytical essays:

- Customizable Outliner
- Descriptive Word Bin

Six Traits Focus

✓	Ideas	✓	Word Choice
✓	Organization	✓	Sentence Fluency
	Voice	✓	Conventions

Assessing the Essay

To evaluate students' analytical essays, use the Response to Literature rubrics in ***General Resources,*** pp. 55–56.

Standard Course of Study

IR.2.02.3 Use transitions to make logical connections.

FA.3.02.1 State position or proposed solution in an editorial or response.

GU.6.01.1 Employ varying sentence structures and sentence types.

GU.6.01.6 Use correct format for writing.

From the Scholar's Desk

David Mamet

Show students Segment 3 on David Mamet on ***From the Author's Desk DVD.*** Discuss his techniques for drafting, including the ways that he develops characters, action, and dialogue. Discuss also the extent of his revisions and his views about the performance of his plays.

Writing Genres

Using the Form Remind students that problem-and-solution essays are often used in the real world. Point out these examples:

- A person involved in government or local school governance may have to write a problem-and-solution essay to explain how to resolve an economic, political, or social problem.
- A letter to a government official may include part of a problem-and-solution essay.
- An employee may have to write a problem-and-solution essay to address an issue in the workplace.

Online Essay Scorer

A writing prompt for this mode of writing can be found on the ***PH Online Essay Scorer*** at PHSuccessNet.com.

Writing Workshop

Exposition:
Problem-and-Solution Essay

In real life, you solve problems all the time—at home, at work, at school, and in your community. Writing a **problem-and-solution essay** allows you to share your ideas about one way to make the world a better place—or at least to improve a small corner of it. Such writing could even spur you to make a real change, enlisting others to join you in constructive action. Follow the steps outlined in this workshop to write your own problem-and-solution essay.

Assignment Write a problem-and-solution essay analyzing a particular issue in your school or community and evaluating various solutions for it.

What to Include Your problem-and-solution essay should feature the following elements:

- a statement describing a significant problem
- details and examples that develop the problem and show its significance
- description and evaluation of one or more solutions to the problem

To preview the criteria on which your problem-and-solution essay may be assessed, see the rubric on page 577.

Standard Course of Study

- Use transitions to make logical connections. (IR.2.02.3)
- State position or proposed solution in an editorial or response. (FA.3.02.1)
- Use correct format for writing. (GU.6.01.6)

Using the Form

You may use elements of problem-and-solution writing in these situations:

- persuasive essays
- newspaper editorials
- speeches

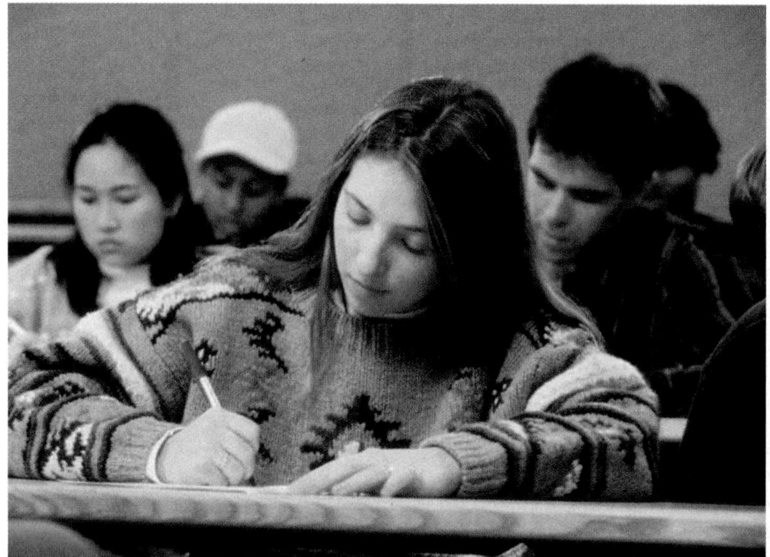

Teaching Resources

The following resources can be used to enrich or extend the instruction for the Writing Workshop.

Unit 4 Resources
- **Writing Workshop: Problem-and-Solution Essay,** p. 188

General Resources
- **Rubrics for Exposition: Problem-Solution Essay** pp. 49–50

Graphic Organizer Transparencies
- **Rubric for Self-Assessment,** p. 108
- **Two-column Chart,** p. 285

From the Author's Desk, DVD
- **David Mamet,** Segments 3 and 4

Prewriting

Choosing Your Topic

Write your problem-and-solution essay about a consumer, community, school, or social issue that is significant to you. To find a topic, use any of the following strategies:

- **Freewriting** Write for five minutes using one or more of the following **sentence starters:**

  The problem with many products on the market today is that _________.

  I bet most people would vote for a politician who could _________.

  Sometimes the best way to solve a big problem is to break it up into small parts. For example, _________.

- **Scan a newspaper.** Highlight intriguing news stories, and think about the problems they suggest. Then, list the problems and possible solutions, as shown here.

Problem	Ideas for Solutions
car accidents at dangerous intersections	speed bumps, traffic-calming devices, more traffic lights
false advertising for a cell phone	better monitoring of ads, networks of consumer information
students' struggles with college applications	break down task into smaller bits, budget time, make schedules

- **Talk with a classmate.** Talking with someone else can open up new issues for you to focus on. Begin by brainstorming together about consumer, community, or social problems. As you brainstorm, jot down the most promising possibilities.

Narrowing Your Topic

Target your topic. Use a target diagram like the one shown to narrow a broad topic. In the outer circle, write your general topic. Then, to narrow your topic, consider what part of your topic affects you. In the second circle, identify a single aspect of the broad topic. To complete the diagram, challenge yourself to write an even narrower topic in the center of the target.

NARROWING A TOPIC WITH A TARGET DIAGRAM

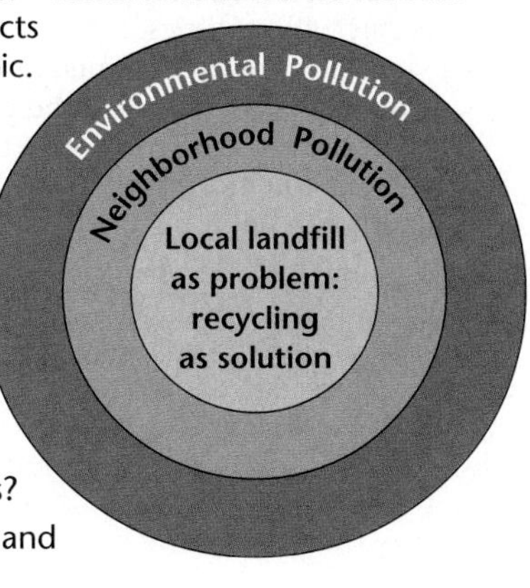

Gathering Details

Analyze your audience. Always keep your audience in mind: readers who can recognize the problem and put your solutions into practice. Ask yourself these questions:

- Who is my audience?
- What does my audience already know about my topic? What information do they need?
- How can I show this audience how important this problem is?

Let your answers to these questions guide the level of evidence and information you gather before you write.

TEACH

Prewriting

- Point out that the problem of the plague in *Oedipus the King* is relevant to both Oedipus' life and the lives of others. As students consider topics, suggest that they freewrite about something that they care about and that affects others.
- Suggest that students search Internet news sites as they choose their topics. When students have listed several possible topics, organize students in small groups to discuss their findings and to narrow their topics, following the instruction on the student page.
- Tell students that although the audience may have some knowledge of or interest in the topic, students' essays should show or explain the importance of the problem.
- When students focus on possible solutions to the problem, ask them to consider which option makes the most sense and why. Remind them to inform the audience about the urgency and the appropriateness of the solution.
- Use the Writing Workshop support, pp. 188–189 from ***Unit 4 Resources,*** as students write their problem-and-solution essays.

Six Traits Focus

✓	Ideas		Word Choice
	Organization		Sentence Fluency
	Voice		Conventions

Writing and Grammar Platinum Level

Students will find additional instruction on prewriting for a problem-and-solution essay in Chapter 11, Section 2.

Writing and Grammar Interactive Textbook CD-ROM

Students can use the following tools as they complete their reflective essays:

- List Organizer
- Topic Bin
- Sentence Length Revising Tool

Tips for Using Rubrics

- Before students begin work on this assignment, have them preview the Rubric for Self-Assessment, p. 577, to know what is expected.
- Review the Assessment criteria in class. Before students use the Rubric for Self-Assessment, work with them to rate the student model by applying one or two criteria to it.
- If you wish to assess students' problem-and-solution essays with a 4-point, 5-point, or 6-point scoring rubric, see ***General Resources,*** pp. 49 and 50.

Drafting

- Explain that solutions with multiple parts or steps benefit from the point-by-point strategy because this strategy allows writers to present each part of the solution in the most logical and orderly way.
- Remind students that the types of supporting details they use will vary, depending on their topics. In the Student Model, for example, Andrew cited professional studies to support both his diagnosis of the problem and his proposed solution. In problem-and-solution essays that deal with topics relevant to students' school or local community, students may need to conduct interviews or take polls to find the information they need.
- Warn students to be sure that their statistics come from a reliable source. The misuse of statistics can seriously damage the credibility of their problem-and-solution essays, and they should always cite the source for any statistics included in their paper.
- Point out that expert testimony should also be cited. Tell students that "nine out of ten doctors" is not expert testimony. Students must provide specific names of experts or reliable studies that yielded the testimony they cite.

Six Traits Focus

✓	Ideas		Word Choice
✓	Organization		Sentence Fluency
	Voice		Conventions

WG Writing and Grammar Platinum Level

Students will find additional instruction on drafting a problem-and-solution essay in Chapter 11, Section 3.

Drafting

Shaping Your Writing

Choose an organization. You need to decide on a method of organization that will present your problem and solution in a clear, coherent matter. Here are two basic methods for organizing your thoughts:

- **Point by Point** If you use this approach, break the main problem down into a group of smaller problems, and then address each one, point by point, offering small-scale solutions.
- **Block** In this approach, present the problem as a whole and then propose a comprehensive solution.

Review your notes, and pick an organization that suits the problem and solution that you will present.

Providing Elaboration

Include a variety of support. Support all statements with concrete and precise evidence. Such support will make your ideas more credible and compelling.

- **Details** Specific and concrete details can make your essay more interesting and believable, grounding it in everyday reality.
- **Examples and anecdotes** You can use anecdotes—real-life examples—to show how the problem affects actual people, including you.
- **Facts and statistics** A few hard facts and well-chosen statistics can help emphasize the extent of the problem or indicate how workable a solution might be. Be careful, however, not to overwhelm your readers with statistics.
- **Expert testimony** Informed opinions by experts who have studied the problem can bolster your own views of the problem and its best solution. Your experts can hold strong views, but look for credible sources and opinions that are supported by facts.

Use a chart like the one shown here to generate, organize, and choose the best evidence to support your ideas.

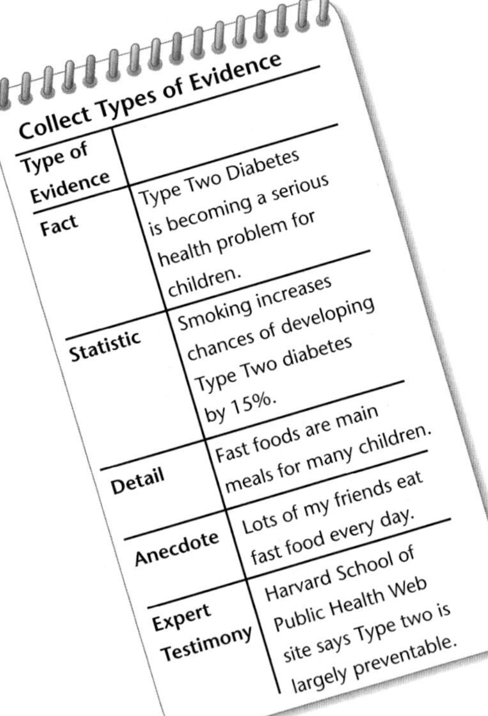
Collect Types of Evidence
Type of Evidence
Fact
Type Two Diabetes is becoming a serious health problem for children.
Statistic
Smoking increases chances of developing Type Two diabetes by 15%.
Detail
Fast foods are main meals for many children.
Anecdote
Lots of my friends eat fast food every day.
Expert Testimony
Harvard School of Public Health Web site says Type two is largely preventable.

From the Scholar's Desk
David Mamet on Writing Dialogue

David Mamet

David Mamet is known for his distinctive dialogue, whose abrupt rhythm gives even apparently trivial conversations a tense, mysterious poetry. This "poetry" can be both nasty and humorous. Asked by theater critic John Lahr where he learned to write such dialogue, Mamet responded, "In my family, in the days prior to television, we liked to wile away the evenings by making ourselves miserable, solely based on our ability to speak the language viciously." In the following example, as two salesman consider whether to steal lists of sales prospects and sell them to a competitor, the pauses, the one-word answer, and stressed words all contribute to the effect.

> *"There's no such thing as talent; you just have to work hard enough."*
> —David Mamet

Professional Model:
from *Glengarry Glen Ross*

Aaronow: And you're saying a fella could take and sell these leads to Jerry Graff.

Moss: Yes.

Aaronow: How do you know he'd buy them?

Moss: Graff? Because I worked for him.

Aaronow: You've haven't talked to him.

Moss: No. What do you mean? Have I talked to him about *this*? (*Pause.*)

Aaronow: Yes. I mean are you actually *talking* about this, or are we just . . .

Moss: No, we're just . . .

Aaronow: We're just *"talking"* about it.

Moss: We're just *speaking* about it. (*Pause.*) As an *idea.*

Aaronow: As an idea.

Moss: Yes.

Aaronow: We're not actually *talking* about it.

Moss: No.

Mamet's general answers to interviewers' questions reveal his writing process and help explain his techniques in this particualr excerpt:

"I write [dialogue] to be spoken, and I think that almost all actors appreciate that."

"I [compose dialogue] fairly spontaneously, and then sometimes, for various reasons, it has to be re-crafted."

"I'm always trying to keep [my dialogue] spare. For me the real division between a serious writer and an unserious one is whether they're willing to cut."

From the Scholar's Desk
David Mamet

- Show students Segment 4 on David Mamet on **From the Author's Desk DVD.** Discuss his comments on hard work and the success he has enjoyed from his career in film. Call students' attention to his statement about the importance of writing in all types of work.
- Point out that David Mamet believes hard work is the key to good writing. Tell students that all serious writers must work diligently at their craft. Often writers receive dozens of rejection letters when they first try to publish their work, so they revise the work and submit it to other publishers. This process can be discouraging and time consuming, but determined writers continue to try.
- Review Mamet's comments about writing dialogue. **Ask** students why they think his dialogue might need to be re-crafted and why he says, "the real division between a serious writer and an unserious one is whether they're willing to cut."
  Possible response: Because Mamet writes dialogue "fairly spontaneously," he may need to re-craft it so that one dialogue sequence or scene can smoothly transition to the next scene.

Tips for Improving Word Choice

Give students these suggestions for revising for word choice.

1. The verb should be precise. Replace verbs like *run* with *dash, gallop, dart,* or *trot.* By using strong and precise verbs, you may be able to eliminate adverbs.
2. Use the passive voice for special situations, such as times that you wish to be vague about who did something. Otherwise, avoid the passive voice because it is less direct and leads to heavy and boring writing.
3. In writing dialogue, use words that the characters or people would use when speaking. Dialogue is often composed of short sentences or fragments. It is speech and should sound natural.

Revising

- Have students highlight or underline the thesis statement and main ideas in the first draft of their essays. This strategy will help them identify ideas that need more support and eliminate sections that do not fit.
- Tell students to address at least one opposing argument or potential objection to their solution. Point out that they must address a significant objection or argument, or their position will appear too weak to withstand significant disagreements.
- Remind students to consider their audience when they make word choices and to consider the needs of their audience when they address how much evidence to present. For example, if a student is writing an essay on solutions to misbehaving toddlers, an audience of parents may need fewer terms defined than if the audience were composed of high school students.
- Have each student ask a peer to read his or her essay and help identify difficult or obscure terms. Tell students to revise by using synonyms or providing context clues for definitions.

Six Traits Focus

✓	Ideas	✓	Word Choice
✓	Organization		Sentence Fluency
✓	Voice	✓	Conventions

Writing and Grammar Platinum Level
Students will find additional guidance for revising a problem-and-solution essay in Chapter 11, Section 4.

Writing Workshop

Revising

Revising Your Paragraphs

Strengthen your support. Look for weaknesses in your essay by identifying ideas that are not supported or with which critics might disagree. Strengthen these ideas by adding support and answering any objections. A few common objections are listed here, along with strategies you could use to address them as you revise.

"It is not true." Add facts, statistics, and other information to eliminate doubts about your credibility. Credit your sources to show readers that you have used reliable information and evidence.

"It is too hard." Persuade readers that the solution is feasible. Consider breaking the solution into small steps or showing how it could work over time.

"Why should I care?" Add support that shows how the problem directly affects your audience. Look for examples that bring the issue into your readers' lives.

Model: Strengthen Your Support

Another controllable risk factor for diabetes is the choice to smoke. Smoking has numerous associated health risks, including a direct link with diabetes.

Evidence shows that smoking increases a person's chance of developing Type Two diabetes by fifteen percent.

Kellsi added a statistic to support her point.

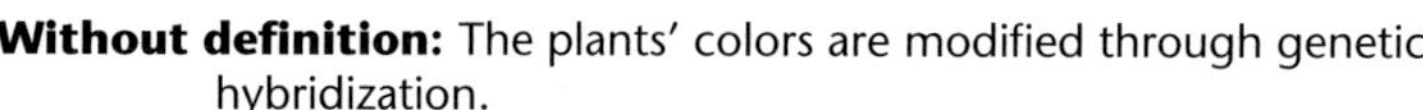

Revising for Word Choice

Remember your audience. Review your draft with your readers in mind. Circle any specialized terms that need to be defined for your audience, as well as language that seems inappropriate for your readers. For example, in the following passage, the technical word *hybridization* is defined for a non-expert audience:

Without definition: The plants' colors are modified through genetic hybridization.

With definition: The plants' colors are modified through genetic hybridization, or blending.

Peer Review: Ask a classmate to review your draft, marking any words that may need clarification or definition. Consider these suggestions for further revision. After you have made your revisions, ask your partner to review your definitions to see if they are clear or require further explanation.

To read the complete Student Model, see p. 577.

Tips for Using Technology in Writing

After students have composed their essays, ask them to print hard copies to review before revising their work on the screen. As they work on paper, students should concentrate on finding the best order for their paragraphs and then renumber them in the margin. Because word processing programs allow students to move large blocks of text within a document, making changes (or undoing them) is easy.

Students can also use the Unity and Coherence or Editing features of the **Writing and Grammar Interactive Textbook CD-ROM** to revise their essays.

Developing Your Style

Smooth Writing

Combining Sentences Although short sentences can add impact when used sparingly, clusters of short sentences usually make your writing choppy. One way to improve sentence flow is to combine short sentences that express related ideas. Sentences can be combined in a variety of ways.

- Join two independent clauses with a comma and a coordinating conjunction such as *and, but, or, nor,* or *for* to create a compound sentence.

Choppy: The painting's colors were beautiful. The texture was lovely.
Compound sentence: The painting's colors were beautiful, *and* the texture was lovely.

- When ideas are closely related, join two independent clauses with a semicolon to create a compound sentence.

Choppy: The artwork was impressive. We stood in awe.
Compound sentence: The artwork was impressive; we stood in awe.

- Take key information from one sentence and insert it into the other. Using a subordinating conjunction like those shown in the chart, rewrite one sentence to link it to the other.

Choppy: I like the watercolors. I like the sculpture even more.
Compound sentence: *Although* I like the watercolors, I like the sculpture even more.

Common Subordinating Conjunctions

after	because	that
although	before	when
as if	even if	whenever
as soon as	in order that	while
until	since	unless
wherever	while	if

Find It in Your Reading Read or review "The Cat Who Lived in the Palace" from *The Pillow Book* on page 309. Find three consecutive sentences that flow particularly well. Identify the connecting words or punctuation that allow the writer to present the passage smoothly.

Apply It to Your Writing Review the draft of your essay with the goal of improving the flow and variety of your sentences. For each paragraph, use the methods presented here to eliminate choppy writing.

WG *Prentice Hall Writing and Grammar Connection: Platinum Level, Chapter 3, Section 1*

Developing Your Style

- Point out to students that using too many short, choppy sentences may make their writing sound juvenile and boring.
- Tell students to join two equally important sentences to create a compound sentence.
- Point out to students that they can easily remember the coordinating conjunctions because the first letter of each conjunction combines to spell the phrase *boy fans (but, or, yet, for, and, nor, so).*
- Tell students to create a complex sentence when they have two closely related sentences but the information in one is more important than the information in the other.
- You may wish to allow students to work in small groups or with partners to find the passages in **Find It in Your Reading.**
  Possible response: "The Imperial guards quickly succeeded in catching Okinamaro and drove him out of the palace grounds. Poor dog! He used to swagger about so happily"; the guards caught the dog and banished him. Placing a short sentence between two longer sentences makes for smooth reading. The second and third sentences, respectively, act as commentaries on the sentences that precede them.
- Have students read their essays aloud, listening for short, choppy sentences. Provide students with highlighters, and have them mark the choppy sentences so that they can combine them later.

WG **Writing and Grammar Platinum Level**
Students will find additional instruction on smooth writing in Chapter 3, Section 1.

Tips for Using Technology in Writing

If students are using word processors to write their essays, have them read the essays and use the highlight feature to mark choppy sentences. Then they can make revisions on the computer. If the program has a grammar check, they can then review their revisions to make sure that the sentences are correct.

Student Model

- Explain that the Student Model is a sample and that students' own essays may be longer.
- Have students read the model silently. Point out that Kellsi has chosen to discuss an issue with which many people are familiar and that students this age can address. This topic may give students ideas for their own essays.
- Call students' attention to the statistic in the second paragraph. Tell students that when they support their claims with reliable information, they add credibility to their essays.
- Point out that in the third paragraph, Kellsi discusses a second cause of the problem: lack of exercise. This second cause shows that she has explored the problem, and she provides ways to address this problem as well.
- **Ask** students why Kellsi might have included a statistic about smoking in the fourth paragraph.
  Possible response: Because many people may not link smoking and Type Two diabetes, using a statistic helps provide credibility and emphasize the point.
- Point out that Kellsi concludes her essay by restating the solutions she presented earlier.

Writing Genres

Problem-and-Solution Essays in the Workplace Many jobs require the ability to propose solutions to problems. For example, politicians and community leaders routinely have to make speeches that outline problems and propose solutions. Mathematics, law, medicine, teaching, and archaeology are other fields in which people consider problems carefully in order to find the best solutions.

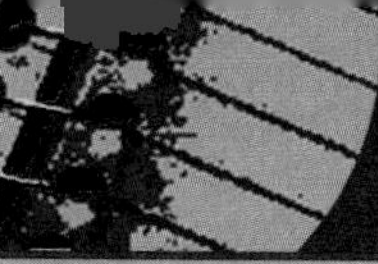

Student Model: Kellsi Wallace, Black Mountain, North Carolina

Childhood Diabetes

Diabetes has recently become one of the most serious health problems facing the youngest members of our society. In the United States alone, each year more than 13,000 children are diagnosed with Type One diabetes. The more serious problem, however, is that one third to one half of all new cases of childhood diabetes are now Type Two. Type Two diabetes develops when muscle, liver, and fat cells do not use or process insulin effectively to meet the body's needs. As a result, glucose builds up in the blood, and body tissues become starved for energy. This disorder used to be found mainly in adults over the age of 40 who do not follow a healthy lifestyle. You see, Type Two diabetes is mostly preventable—so the fact that children are now being diagnosed with it is devastating. Why aren't preventive measures in place to stop children from getting this terrible disease?

> Kellsi states the problem and then asks why we are not doing what is necessary to solve the problem.

A well-rounded, nutritious diet is one of the main components of a healthy lifestyle. The growing popularity of fast food restaurants is one of the major reasons children are developing Type Two diabetes. Fruits and vegetables should be part of nearly every meal, yet with fast foods serving as many children's main meals, this goal is not being met. School lunches also frequently fail to meet the nutritional needs of children. Poor nutrition is associated with weight gain. Childhood obesity is growing at an alarming rate, and childhood diabetes is rising as a result. Studies show that if a person is already at risk for developing Type Two diabetes, a five to seven percent weight loss can delay and even prevent the onset of the disease.

> After explaining one of the causes of the problem, Kellsi presents a statistic that offers a workable solution.

Weight loss is achieved not only through a healthy diet, however. Exercise is also a large factor in overall well-being. Exercising for a mere 30 minutes every other day dramatically improves a person's physical condition. The physical education programs in schools help accomplish this goal, but the restraints on some school districts have led to reduced time spent on the physical education curriculum, as well as less time available for recess. Leading a sedentary lifestyle as a child is highly dangerous, even if it doesn't seem like a health risk at the time. Adults need to model an active lifestyle. Children need to be up and moving—choosing to walk instead of ride, to take the stairs instead of the elevator, or to play outside instead of watching television.

> Kellsi discusses another cause of the problem and lays out some solutions.

Another controllable risk factor for diabetes is smoking. Studies show that smoking increases a person's chance of developing Type Two diabetes by fifteen percent. Being around smokers also places children at risk.

> Kellsi presents a statistic to support her statement that smoking is also part of the problem.

Type Two diabetes is a lifestyle disease that can be prevented. Especially among children, the growing number of people with this disease is a problem that we must work to solve. Making sure that children eat well-balanced meals is a step in the right direction. Getting kids to be physically active will also help solve the problem. The dilemma of childhood diabetes does have answers, if people will just reflect on the choices they make regarding their own health as well as the health of the people around them.

> Kellsi concludes by pointing out that people can solve the problem by making the right choices, both for themselves and others.

Differentiated Instruction
Solutions for All Learners

Strategy for Less Proficient Writers
Have students use outlines to organize their ideas from the prewriting stage. First, have them state their main argument. Then, guide them to organize their main ideas by identifying each main idea. Next, have them select a type of order for their main ideas, such as least important to most important, or chronological if the problem has developed over time. Guide students to identify the opposing arguments and their refutations and to include these in their outlines.

Strategy for English Learners
During the prewriting stage, meet with students individually to discuss their topics. Students may find it helpful to select a problem they have experienced and solved or a problem with which they are otherwise familiar. Guide students away from extensive research if they lack the vocabulary to support what they read.

Editing and Proofreading

Review your draft to correct errors in grammar, usage, punctuation, and spelling.

Focus on Word Meanings: Confirm that you know the meaning of every word in your draft and that you have used each word correctly. Use a dictionary or thesaurus for help, and replace words that confuse you.

Publishing and Presenting

Consider the following ways to share your writing with a wider audience.

Write a letter to the editor. If your problem-and-solution essay is based on a newspaper article, turn the essay into a letter addressed to the editor of the paper. If your essay addresses a problem at school, consider sending it to the editors of your school newspaper.

Deliver an oral presentation. Read your problem-and-solution essay aloud to your class. When you have finished, invite comments and questions. Survey your classmates to determine whether they agree with you about the problem and the solution.

Reflecting on Your Writing

Writer's Journal Jot down your thoughts on the experience of writing a problem-and-solution essay. Begin by answering these questions:

- What strategies might you use again? Why?
- What insights did you gain into the problem and its solution?

WG *Prentice Hall Writing and Grammar Connection: Platinum Level, Chapter 11*

Rubric for Self-Assessment

Evaluate your problem-and-solution essay *using the following criteria and rating scale, or, with your classmates, determine your own reasonable evaluation criteria.*

NC Criteria	Rating Scale				
	not very				very
Focus: How clearly do you state a significant problem?	1	2	3	4	5
Organization: How well organized is your description of the problem and its solution?	1	2	3	4	5
Support/Elaboration: How well do you provide details and examples to describe and evaluate the problem?	1	2	3	4	5
Style: How well do you use a variety of sentences to express your solution?	1	2	3	4	5
Conventions: How correct is your usage, especially your use of appropriate word meanings?	1	2	3	4	5

Tips for Test Taking

When students encounter a prompt on a standardized test that asks them to write a problem-and-solution essay, they should think carefully about a problem and then brainstorm for a list of possible solutions. Given the time pressure, if students cannot think of two or three feasible solutions in just a minute or two, students should consider writing about a different problem. Tell students that they will be scored for the strength of their writing and the way in which they support the thesis. A problem-and-solution essay that does not explain solutions to the problem will not score high.

Editing and Proofreading

- Remind students that editing and proofreading skills are different from revising skills. When students revise, they check their organizations and clarify their ideas; in editing and proofreading, students read for errors in spelling, usage, and grammar.
- Review class or school conventions for citing sources, and remind students to check that they cited their sources and copied quotations accurately. Failure to do so will destroy the credibility of their papers.

Six Traits Focus

	Ideas		Word Choice
	Organization		Sentence Fluency
	Voice	✓	Conventions

ASSESS

Publishing and Presenting

- Organize students in small groups to discuss the problems that they have analyzed in their essays. Direct each student to read his or her essay aloud to group members and then receive questions or suggestions about the problems and solutions that were addressed. Tell students to be prepared to answer questions and entertain their classmates' ideas about alternative solutions.
- If students choose to submit their essays to their school or community newspapers, suggest that they write cover letters to accompany them.

Reflecting on Your Writing

- Have each student identify another problem that would lend itself to analysis in a problem-and-solution essay. Encourage students to identify a problem on something that is related to the problem in their previous essay. Tell students to list ideas about how they would approach writing about the problem, now that they have experience writing a problem-and-solution essay.

WG Writing and Grammar Platinum Level

Students will find additional guidelines for editing and proofreading and publishing and presenting a problem-and-solution essay in Chapter 11, Sections 5 and 6.

Standard Course of Study

CT.4.03.4 Analyze how writers use effective word choice as a basis for coherence.

LT.5.03.5 Summarize key events and points from world literature.

LT.5.03.6 Make inferences, predictions, and draw conclusions based on world literature.

Know Your Terms: Understanding Meaning

Explain that the terms listed under Terms to Learn will be used in standardized-test situations when students are asked to describe or infer what is happening in a reading passage.

Terms to Learn

- Review *describe.* Tell students that to describe is to offer detailed observation. When describing, have students ask themselves, "What details do I need to answer this question thoroughly?"
- Review *infer.* When students are asked to infer, they must pay close attention to text details. Remind them that their inferences must not contradict the details. Tell students that inferring means they are making logical assumptions on the basis of the text and on what they know.

ASSESS

Answers

1. The Spartan attitude toward military security included deportations of people to prevent them from learning military secrets.
2. The Spartans have "state-induced courage" because they are forcibly trained from their youth.
3. Athenians serve in the military because they believe their cause is right.
4. Pericles believes that Sparta is weak and cowardly. Even when Spartans defend their homeland, they exaggerate their enemy's strength and rarely fight without the help of allies.

Vocabulary Workshop

High-Frequency Academic Words

High-frequency academic words are words that appear often in textbooks and on standardized tests. Though you may already know the meaning of many of these words, they usually have a more specific meaning when they are used in textbooks and on tests.

Know Your Terms: Understanding Meaning

Each of the words listed is a verb that tells you to show that you understand the meaning of details in the text and the relationships among them. The words indicate the kind of information you should provide in your answer.

Terms to Learn

Describe Show that you understand something by explaining it in detail.

Sample test item: ***Describe*** the relationship between Agamemnon and the other Greek leaders.

Infer Use text details to figure out what is not stated.

Sample test item: What can you ***infer*** about Apollo's relationship with his priests?

Standard Course of Study

- Analyze how writers use effective word choice as a basis for coherence. (CT.4.03.4)
- Summarize key events and points from world literature. (LT.5.03.5)
- Make inferences, predictions, and draw conclusions based on world literature. (LT.5.03.6)

Practice

Directions: *Read this passage from a speech by the Athenian statesman Pericles. Then, on a separate sheet of paper, answer items 1–4.*

Then there is a great difference between us and our opponents in our attitude toward military security. Here are some examples: Our city is open to the world, and we have no periodical deportations in order to prevent people observing or finding out secrets which might be of military advantage to the enemy. This is because we rely, not on secret weapons, but on our own real courage and loyalty. There is a difference, too, in our educational systems. The Spartans, from their earliest boyhood, are submitted to the most laborious training in courage; we pass our lives without all these restrictions, and yet are just as ready to face the same dangers as they are. Here is a proof of this: When the Spartans invade our land, they do not come by themselves, but bring all their allies with them; whereas we, when we launch an attack abroad, do the job by ourselves, and, though fighting on foreign soil, do not often fail to defeat opponents who are fighting for their own hearths and homes. There are certain advantages, I think, in our way of meeting danger voluntarily, . . . instead of with a laborious training, with natural rather than with state-induced courage. . . .

1. *Describe* the Spartan attitude toward military security.
2. *Describe* what Pericles means by "state-induced courage."
3. What can you *infer* about why an Athenian serves in the military?
4. *Infer* Pericles' opinion about Sparta, using details from the text.

Tips for Test Taking

- When students are asked to select the best description on a multiple-choice test, they should look carefully at all the details included in each answer choice. The addition of one extraneous detail may invalidate an answer.
- If students are asked to infer an answer, they must ask themselves the question, "How can I show that this is a logical inference based on the details given in the text?"

Go Online Vocabulary **For:** An Interactive Crossword Puzzle **Visit:** www.PHSchool.com **Web Code:** etj-5401

This crossword puzzle contains vocabulary that reflects the concepts in Unit 4. After students have completed Unit 4, give students the Web Code and have them complete the crossword puzzle.

Critical Reading: Inferences and Generalizations

Standard Course of Study

- CT.4.01.1
- IR.2.01.6
- WL.1.02.1

In the reading sections of some tests, you are often required to read a passage of fiction and draw inferences and make generalizations about the plot, setting, characters, and mood. The following strategies will help you answer such test questions:

- Remember that to clarify a passage, you may have to read between the lines, inferring the implied message of a selection.
- Look in the passage for clues about the characters, setting, plot, and mood.
- Identify significant word choices, patterns of events, and other clues that can help you understand the writer's implied message.

Practice

Directions: *Read the passages below, and then answer the questions that follow.*

Passage A. Penelope tried to scoot out the front door, but it closed too quickly. It was spring, and that meant it was time to chase squirrels and roll in puddles of sunshine. She had spent most of the winter in the house, where she was warm and coddled, but fresh air and the thrill of the hunt beckoned now. She wound herself around Jenna's ankles and glanced at the door, but her efforts prompted no response.

Passage B. If his parents had their way, David would buy the most sensible car on the lot. But he had other ideas in mind. After two years of driving the family car, he wanted something new, something splashy that would make heads turn. He was a working man now, and it was high time he owned his own car. When David saw the metallic blue sports model in the corner of the lot, he knew he had found the perfect set of wheels.

1. In Passage A, Penelope can best be described as

- **A** a stubborn child.
- **B** a frightened squirrel.
- **C** an impatient cat.
- **D** an eager student.

2. In Passage B, which of the following inferences about the family car does the passage support?

- **A** It is sporty and fast.
- **B** It is conservative and slow.
- **C** It was very expensive.
- **D** It is a metallic blue.

3. In Passage B, which of the following most accurately describes David?

- **A** headstrong
- **B** cautious
- **C** lucky
- **D** hesitant

Test-Taking Strategies

- Before answering questions, review the passage to clarify the main points.
- Look for descriptive details to help you make inferences about characters, setting, plot, and mood. Categorize these details according to their importance.

Standard Course of Study

WL.1.02.1 Relate personal knowledge to textual information in a written reflection.

IR.2.01.6 Make inferences, predict, and draw conclusions based on research questions.

CT.4.01.1 Interpret and make generalizations about events supported by specific references.

Critical Reading

- Remind students of the meaning of the word *infer* that they learned in the Vocabulary Workshop in Unit 4. Point out that "reading between the lines" requires thinking deeply about a passage and going beyond its literal meaning.
- Remind students that in fiction, things are not always as they seem. For example, a character's actions and other characters' attitudes toward that character may show more about the character than the character's self-description does.
- Tell students that an implied message is inferred or hinted in a passage. Students must be alert in order to find the clues that reveal the implied message.
- After students have read the Practice passages and have answered the questions, point out that Penelope wanted to chase squirrels, and she wound herself around Jenna's ankles to get attention. These details indicate that the correct answer to question 1 is C.
- Point out that David wanted something splashy that would make heads turn, and he liked the sporty model. These facts indicate that B is the correct answer to question 2.
- Point out that David disagrees with his parents' idea. Therefore, A is the only correct choice to question 3.

Tips for Test Taking

When students are asked to make inferences on standardized-test questions, they must remember that sometimes authors do not state everything directly; often the author implies or suggests ideas. Students must use the information or details that the passage provides and make inferences from these suggested ideas.

Remind students to review the answer choices and select the inference that the passage suggests or implies. Students should be able to support their choice with information from the passage.

ASSESS

Answers

1. C
2. B
3. A

Standard Course of Study

FA.3.04.8 Make connections between works, self and related topics in argument.

CT.4.05.4 Comprehend main idea and supporting details in critical text.

GU.6.01.5 Examine language for elements to apply effectively in own writing/speaking.

Prepare to Listen

- Have students discuss the concept of "cultural context." Encourage them to give a specific account of the context for Pericles' funeral oration in Thucydides or for Socrates' speech at his trial in Plato's *Apology*. **Possible response:** Pericles speaks as a respected democratic leader in a time of crisis; Socrates speaks as a philosopher whose ideals and methods have been misinterpreted.
- Invite students to link what they may know about funeral eulogies and courtroom speeches to the orations reported by Thucydides and Plato. What prior knowledge influenced students' expectations for these speeches?

Analyze What You Have Heard

- Review with students the bulleted list of steps for analyzing a speech, as well as the three sections of the Feedback Form. Make sure that students understand each bulleted item on the list and each line item on the form.
- Tell students that taking notes while listening to a speech can help them remember the speaker's important points; these notes will help students thoroughly evaluate the speaker's evidence after the speech has ended.

Assess the Activity

To evaluate students' analyses, use the Effective Listening rubric, p. 83 in ***General Resources.***

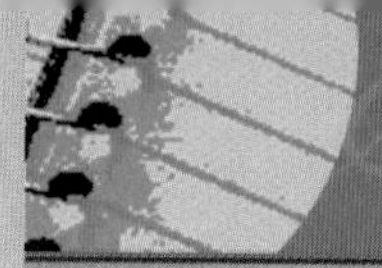

Communications Workshop

Listening to Speeches

Standard Course of Study

- Make connections between works, self and related topics in argument. (FA.3.04.8)

Imagine being in the audience when the orations you read in this unit were delivered. To fully appreciate them, you would need to do more than just sit there; you would need to listen effectively. Effective listening involves two parts—preparation and analysis.

Prepare to Listen

To prepare to listen to a speech, use the following guidelines:

- **Identify cultural context.** In addition to expressing an individual's point of view, speeches also express a cultural context—the values, traditions, beliefs, and assumptions of the culture that produced them. To get the most out of a presentation from another culture, determine its cultural context. If you understand the underlying values and beliefs, you will be able to listen more effectively.
- **Connect to personal knowledge and experience.** Your own life experience and knowledge are great resources for effective listening. To prepare to listen to a speech, learn what topics it will cover and think about your own familiarity with those subjects.

Feedback Form for Listening to Speeches

Preparation:
What is the cultural context of the speech?____
What is the subject of the speech? __________
What personal knowledge do you have of the subject?__________

Analysis:
Note the main idea: __________
Note three supporting details or points:
1. Persuasive facts: __________
2. Speaker's values: __________
3. Effective words: __________

What visual aids, if any, are being used?______

Response:
1. What were the most persuasive elements of the speech?__________
2. If visual aids were used, were they effective?__________
3. Do you agree or disagree with the speaker?________ Why?________

Analyze What You Have Heard

After you listen to a speech, follow these steps to analyze the information and attitudes it conveys:

- Summarize the main ideas and identify supporting details.
- Note key facts and arguments that you found persuasive.
- Note statements that reveal the speaker's values and perspective.
- Note any words or statements that were especially effective.
- Note visual aids that were used and whether or not they were effective.
- Identify the purpose of the speaker.
- Decide whether you agree with the speech as a whole, in part, or not at all, and be prepared to explain why.
- Ask additional questions to gain further understanding.

Activity *Analyzing an Oration* In small groups, deliver and analyze orations from the unit. One member of the group should rehearse and present one of the orations. The others should prepare to listen and then analyze the presentation. Use the Feedback Form shown above to focus your preparation and analysis.

Differentiated Instruction — Solutions for All Learners

Strategy for Less Proficient Readers
Have students listen to a recorded speech, taking notes on the bulleted items in the Analyze What You Have Heard section. Give students time to finish their notes, and then organize them into small groups in which they will share their responses.

Strategy for English Learners
Listen to a recorded speech with students, pausing the tape to model note-taking techniques. Use the board to record responses to each bulleted item in the Analyze What You Have Heard section. Then, play a second speech to give students additional practice with taking notes.

Strategy for Advanced Readers
Have students research issues addressed in a recorded speech. As they listen to the speech a second time, ask students to take notes and then review their research findings. Have students write short reports in which they identify the cultural context of the speech as well as the cultural values, attitudes, and beliefs expressed by the speaker.

Suggestions for Further Reading

Featured Titles:

The Three Theban Plays

Sophocles, *translated by Robert Fagles, Penguin Classic, 1984*

Drama This collection contains Sophocles' three tragedies about the royal house of Thebes. In addition to *Oedipus the King,* which appears in Unit 4 of *Prentice Hall World Masterpieces,* the collection includes the plays *Oedipus at Colonus* and *Antigone. Oedipus at Colonus* focuses on the end of Oedipus' life, following his downfall in *Oedipus the King.* In *Antigone,* Oedipus is gone, but his legacy remains. His daughter Antigone refuses to compromise her ideals and submit to the orders of Creon, the new king of Thebes. Like her father, Antigone is strong-willed, and like him, she meets a tragic fate. These three plays are considered to be not only the greatest works by Sophocles but also the finest examples of Greek tragedy. They are ably translated by Robert Fagles, who also translated Homer's *Iliad* and *Odyssey.*

The Fall of the Roman Republic (Six Lives)

Plutarch, *translated by Rex Warner, Penguin Classic, 1954*

Historical Nonfiction The Roman historian Plutarch was especially interested in the biographies of great men and the lessons that could be drawn from them. In this volume, he narrates the lives of six prominent Romans involved in the violence leading to the fall of the Roman republic: Marius, Sulla, Crassus, Pompey, Caesar, and Cicero. Plutarch had a flair for capturing vivid details. That is why Shakespeare relied so heavily on *Plutarch's Lives* while writing plays like *Julius Caesar.* Opening this book is like pulling aside the curtains of a stage and viewing the most dramatic events of Roman history.

Works Presented in Unit Four:

If sampling a portion of the following texts has built your interest, treat yourself to the full works.

The Iliad

Homer, *translated by Robert Fagles, Penguin Classic, 1991*

The Aeneid

Virgil, *translated by Patric Dickinson, Signet Classic, 2002*

Related British Literature:

The Extraordinary Voyage of Pytheas the Greek

Barry Cunliffe, *Penguin, 2002*

A British archaeologist tells the true story of a Greek who, more than 2,000 years ago, made a dangerous sea voyage all the way to Iceland.

Related American Literature:

The Federalist Papers

Alexander Hamilton et al., *Penguin Classic, 1987*

Looking to the classical world as their model, three of America's greatest founding fathers set forth the principles of government that still guide us today.

Many of these titles are available in the* Prentice Hall/Penguin Literature Library. *Consult your teacher before choosing one.

Planning Students' Further Reading

Discussions of literature can raise sensitive and often controversial issues. Before you recommend further reading to your students, consider the values and sensitivities of your community as well as the age, ability, and sophistication of your students. It is also good policy to preview literature before you recommend it to students. The notes below offer some guidance on specific titles.

The Three Theban Plays by Sophocles

Sophocles' great tragedies tell of incest and suicide. They include references to torture as well as expressions of sexist attitudes. The introduction to *Oedipus the King* quotes Sigmund Freud on the Oedipus Complex. To prepare students to read the plays, discuss the way tragedy traces the boundaries of our common experience through extreme events and actions.
Lexile: NP

***The Fall of the Roman Republic* (Six Lives)** by Plutarch

Throughout these classic biographies, a source for Shakespeare and later writers, Plutarch describes battle and death. The text also refers to sexual relationships, including incest and homosexuality, and to suicide. There are suggestions of anti-Semitic attitudes. To prepare students to read this work, discuss Roman attitudes toward war and the state.

Lexile: Appropriate for high school students

The *Iliad* by Homer

The *Iliad* contains graphic and bloody descriptions of war and death that may be difficult for students. There is some bad language, especially directed toward women. The status of women in the era will be considered degrading by most students, but it is a true picture of classical times.
Lexile: 1330L

The *Aeneid* by Virgil

Violence, occasionally graphic, is depicted throughout Virgil's *Aeneid.* There are also occasional references to suicide, rape, and drinking, as well as a reference to Romans as "the master-race." To prepare students to read this work, discuss Virgil's use of Homeric models and the relationship of the work to Roman ideology.

Lexile: NP

The Extraordinary Voyage of Pytheas the Greek by Barry Cunliffe

Most issues arise in the context of anthropological discussions of the people whom Pytheas probably encountered on his journey. These issues include a reference to wife-sharing among male family members, cannibalism, and the consumption of beer and wine.

Lexile: Appropriate for high school students

The Federalist Papers by Alexander Hamilton et al.

The framers of the Constitution did not include African Americans, Native Americans, or women in their concept of self-government. This historical and cultural limitation of the Constitution can serve as a fruitful point of departure for a discussion of the subsequent evolution of American democracy.
Lexile: 1450L

Standard Course of Study

CT.4.02.3	Examine how elements such as irony and symbolism impact theme.
CT.4.05.10	Analyze connections between ideas, concepts, characters and experiences in critical text.
LT.5.01.5	Analyze archetypal characters, themes, and settings in world literature.
LT.5.01.7	Understand the cultural and historical impact on world literature texts.

Unit Instructional Resources

In *Unit 5 Resources,* you will find materials to support students in developing and mastering the unit skills and to help you assess their progress.

Vocabulary and Reading Additional vocabulary and reading support, based on Lexile scores of vocabulary words, is provided for each selection or grouping.

- **Word Lists A and B** and **Practices A and B** provide vocabulary-building activities for students reading two grades or one grade below level, respectively.
- **Reading Warm-ups A and B,** for students reading two grades or one grade below level, respectively, consist of short readings and activities that provide a context and practice for newly learned vocabulary.

Selection Support Practice and reinforcement pages support each selection:

- Reading Strategy
- Literary Analysis
- Vocabulary Builder
- Grammar and Style
- Support for Writing
- Support for Extend Your Learning
- Enrichment

PRENTICE HALL TeacherEXPRESS™ Plan · Teach · Assess You may also access these resources at TeacherExpress.

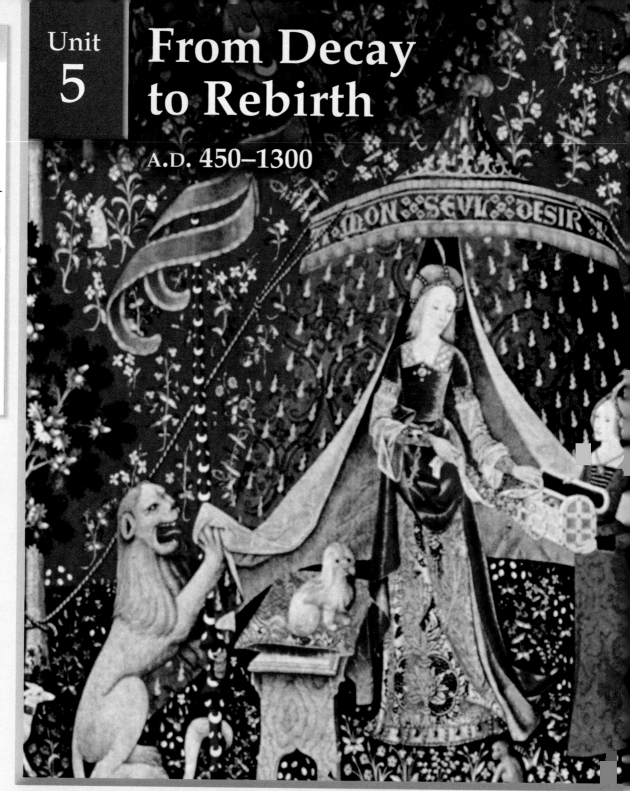

Unit 5 From Decay to Rebirth

A.D. 450–1300

MON SEVL DESIR

Assessment Resources

Listed below are the resources available to assess and measure students' progress in meeting the unit objectives and your state standards.

Skills Assessment

Unit 5 Resources
- Selection Tests A and B

TeacherExpress™
- *ExamView®* Test Bank Software

Adequate Yearly Progress Assessment

Unit 5 Resources
- Diagnostic Tests 6 and 7
- Benchmark Test 6

Standardized Assessment

Standardized Test Preparation Workbook

The Middle Ages

Standard Course of Study
In This Unit You Will

- Demonstrate an understanding of media's impact on analyses and personal reflection. (WL.1.02.5)
- Access cultural information from media sources. (IR.2.03.1)
- Examine how elements such as irony and symbolism impact theme. (CT.4.02.3)
- Apply criteria to evaluate others using reasoning and substantiation. (CT.4.04.2)
- Analyze archetypal characters, themes, and settings in world literature. (LT.5.01.5)
- Understand the cultural and historical impact on world literature texts. (LT.5.01.7)
- Edit for appropriate and correct mechanics. (GU.6.02.2)

◀ Many medieval tapestries, like this one, have a background of *millefleurs*, a French word meaning "a thousand flowers."

Introduce Unit 5

- Direct students' attention to the title and time period of this unit. Have a student read the quotation. **Ask** them: What is the connection between the quotation and the scene taking place in the tapestry?
  Possible response: The woman exemplifies the meaning of the quotation. She appears peaceful and serene. She is surrounded by animals, who either attend to her needs or seem comfortable in her presence.
- Have students look at the art. Read the Humanities note to them, and ask the discussion question.
- Then **ask:** What kinds of literature or themes in literature do you think might come out of this period in literary history?
  Possible response: The medieval outlook on life was highly religious. Themes in literature might include aspects of human existence as seen through the narrative of faith.

Humanities

The Lady and the Unicorn

Tapestries flourished in Europe in the Middle Ages. Many medieval tapestries, like this one, have a background of *millefleurs,* a French word meaning "a thousand flowers." Tapestries were made of wool and served as both decoration and insulation against the cold.

Use the item for discussion:

Describe what is taking place in the scene.
Answer: A woman of the noble class is standing under a protective canopy, receiving something from a maidservant. The animals witnessing the scene seem to be attendants for the noblewoman. A creature resembling a lion holds up one side of the canopy. A unicorn is prominent in the lower right side of the tapestry.

Unit Features

Marilyn Stokstad
Each unit features commentary by a contemporary writer or scholar under the heading "From the Author's Desk." Scholar Marilyn Stokstad introduces Unit 5 in Setting the Scene, in which she discusses the contributions of Eleanor of Aquitaine and other medieval women during the Middle Ages. Later in the unit, she introduces the medieval poem, Perceval. She also contributes her insights on revising texts for clarity by eliminating unnecessary words in the Writing Workshop.

Connections
Every unit contains a feature that connects literature to a related topic, such as art, science, or history. In this unit, students will read Alfred, Lord Tennyson's **Sir Galahad** on pp. 652–655.

Use the information and questions on the Connections pages to help students enrich their understanding of the selections presented within the unit.

Reading Informational Materials
These selections will help students learn to analyze and evaluate informational texts, such as workplace documents, technical directions, and consumer materials. They will expose students to the organization and features unique to nonnarrative texts.

In this unit, the focus is on Interviews. The ***ComicFan*** interview is on pp. 622–625.

From the Scholar's Desk

Introduce Marilyn Stokstad

- Marilyn Stokstad, an art historian and professor, introduces the unit and provides insights into life in the Middle Ages. Her commentary about medieval life appears later in the unit on pages 626–627.
- Have students read the introductory paragraph about Marilyn Stokstad. Tell them that she is an expert in medieval and Spanish art and is a distinguished professor of art history at Kansas University.
- Use *From the Author's Desk DVD* to introduce Marilyn Stokstad. Show Segment 1 to provide insight into her career as a scholar. After students have watched the segment, **ask:** Why did Marilyn Stokstad write a series of books on art history?
Answer: She wanted to make famous works of art understandable and accessible to the average viewer.

Eleanor of Aquitaine

- After students have read Stokstad's commentary on Eleanor of Aquitaine and women in medieval studies, **ask:** Why is Eleanor of Aquitaine so important in medieval studies?
Answer: She was one of the most brilliant women in medieval history, and she ruled both France and England. She is one of the few women predominantly mentioned in the history of this period.
- Tell students that they will also read Marilyn Stokstad's introduction to the selection from *Perceval,* "The Grail" by Chrétien de Troyes later in this unit. Stokstad will explain the medieval history that accompanies *Perceval.*

Critical Viewing

Possible response: The book may be meant to represent Eleanor's brilliance or her encouragement of writers and artists.

Setting the Scene

Unit 5 contains European works of literature written during the Middle Ages. The following essay by art historian Marilyn Stokstad discusses Eleanor of Aquitaine and other women during this period. As you read Stokstad's essay, the unit introduction that follows, and the literature in Unit 5, consider how historical and cultural developments during this era still influence us today.

From the Scholar's Desk
Marilyn Stokstad Talks About the Time Period

Marilyn Stokstad

Introducing Marilyn Stokstad (b. 1929) Art historian Marilyn Stokstad is the author of *Art History.* Widely used across the country in colleges and universities, this book brings fresh perspectives to art studies and gives new emphasis to the achievements of women.

Eleanor of Aquitaine and Women in Medieval Studies

When I was an art student in college, history seemed to be just one battle after another. Kings, nobles, and popes plotted against each other, and peasant lads escaped to towns where they became wealthy and ended up as the mayor. I assumed that women had to be around somewhere because kings were always producing sons to inherit the kingdom, and they certainly couldn't do that by themselves. Once in a while an empress or a queen might be mentioned. "Thank heavens," some of us said, "for Eleanor of Aquitaine." These days, we study not only Eleanor of Aquitaine, one of the most brilliant women in medieval history, but many other prominent women of this era as well.

Queen of Courtly Love Eleanor still stands out from the rest. She inherited the rich and cultivated lands of southwestern France from her grandfather, William IX (1071–1127). William had sponsored music, poetry, and the visual arts and was a poet himself. Similarly, in the courts presided over by Eleanor and her daughters, music and literature flourished, and courtly love became a game with elaborate rules that forced rude warriors to learn courtesy and etiquette.

Queen of France *and* England When both her father and brother died, Eleanor became Duchess of Aquitaine and Countess of Poitou. In 1137 Eleanor married Louis VII, the king of France. Eleanor and Louis had two daughters but no son to inherit the kingdom.

▼ **Critical Viewing** Why might the sculptor have chosen to portray Eleanor of Aquitaine holding a book? **[Speculate]**

Teaching Resources

The following resources can be used to enrich or extend the instruction for Unit 5 Introduction.

From the Author's Desk DVD
- **Marilyn Stokstad,** Segment 1

Unit 5 Resources
- **Support for Penguin Essay,** p. 24
- **Unit Introduction: Names and Terms to Know,** p. 5
- **Unit Introduction: Focus Questions,** p. 6
- **Listening and Viewing,** p. 25

Eleanor separated from Louis, and their marriage was annulled in 1152. Only two months later she married Henry Plantagenet. Between them, Eleanor and Henry ruled all of western France from the English Channel to the Pyrenees Mountains. Then, in 1154, Henry inherited the English throne. For the second time in her life, Eleanor was a queen, this time queen of England. The couple had five sons and three daughters—two sons became kings of England, and the daughters married powerful rulers.

Eleanor ruled her French lands with great political skill and often acted for her husband and sons when they were off at war, although the royal couple quarreled bitterly. Her sons—Richard the Lion Hearted and John Lackland—ruled after their father, while Eleanor remained a powerful political figure until her death at age eighty-one.

Women and Medieval Studies Today—in addition to Eleanor—we study women writers like Marie de France and women painters like Ende of Spain and Guda of Germany. We know that, also in Germany, Hroswitha wrote plays and music, that Hildegard recorded her visions and wrote practical letters of advice to noblemen and even the Pope, and that Herrad wrote an encyclopedia. We know that the king of England paid Mabel of Bury St. Edmonds very well for her embroidery. We know, too, that Christine de Pizan, living in France, supported her family with her writing and hired a woman painter, Anastasia, to decorate her books.

As a woman who studies medieval history, I share a love of the time period with other women who teach medieval studies, run archaeological excavations, write books on the Middle Ages, organize exhibitions of medieval art, play medieval music, and stage medieval drama. I celebrate the new focus on women in medieval history, and I think, perhaps, that Eleanor of Aquitaine would have approved.

Go Online
Author Link

For: An online video
Visit: www.PHSchool.com
Web Code: ete-8501

For: More about Marilyn Stokstad
Visit: www.PHSchool.com
Web Code: ete-9504

Reading the Unit Introduction

Reading for Information and Insight Use the following terms and questions to guide your reading of the unit introduction on pages 588–595.

Names and Terms to Know
Middle Ages
Renaissance
Roman Empire
Feudalism
Charlemagne
Crusades
Gothic
Vernacular

Focus Questions As you read this introduction, use what you learn to answer these questions:

- In what ways did the structure of Europe change during this period?
- What were the important elements of the code of chivalry?
- During this period, how did poetry influence attitudes toward women?

Reading the Unit Introduction

Tell students that the terms and questions listed here are the key points in this introductory material. This information provides a context for the selections in this unit. Students should use the terms and questions as a guide to focus their reading of the unit introduction. When students have completed the unit introduction, they should be able to identify or explain each of these terms and answer or discuss the Focus Questions.

Concept Connector

After students have read the unit introduction, return to the Focus Questions to review the main points. For key points, see p. 595.

Go Online Author Link Typing in the Web Codes when prompted will bring students to a video clip and more information on Marilyn Stokstad.

Using the Timeline

The Timeline can serve a number of instructional purposes, as follows:

Getting an Overview

Use the Timeline to help students get a quick overview of themes and events of the period. This approach will benefit all students but may be especially helpful for Visual/Spatial Learners, English Learners, and Less Proficient Readers. (For strategies in using the Timeline as an overview, see the bottom of this page.)

Thinking Critically

Questions are provided on the facing page. Use these questions to have students review the events, discuss their significance, and examine the *so what* behind the *what happened.*

Connecting to Selections

Have students refer to the Timeline when they begin to read individual selections. By consulting the Timeline regularly, students will gain a better sense of the period's chronology. In addition, they will appreciate world events that gave rise to these works of literature.

Projects

Students can use the Timeline as a launching pad for projects like these:

- **Customized Timeline** Have students create period timelines in their notebooks, adding key details as they read new selections. They can use dates from this Timeline as a starting framework. If they wish, students can create a specialized timeline for political, scientific, or artistic developments.
- **Headline History** Have students scan the Timeline for ten especially newsworthy items. Then, ask students to write news headlines for each of these items. Have students research one of the items and write a news story about it.

European and World Events

450

EUROPEAN EVENTS

- **476** The Western Roman Empire ceases to exist.
- **476–750** Merovingian kings rule the Franks.
- **511** Merovingian King Clovis dies; he was the first important Catholic king.
- **597** Roman cleric Saint Augustine converts English King Ethelbert to Christianity.

- **700** This is the earliest possible date for the composition of the English epic *Beowulf.* ◄

WORLD EVENTS

- **400s and 500s (India)** Using the concept of zero, mathematicians develop decimals.
- **c. 400 (Middle East)** Jews compile religious teachings called the Palestinian Talmud.
- **500s (India)** The game of chess is invented.
- **618–907 (China)** The T'ang dynasty rules.
- **622 (Middle East)** Muhammad journeys from Mecca to Yathrib, an event that marks the rise of Islam.
- **600s (Africa)** Islam spreads to North Africa.
- **c. 600s (Tibet)** Buddhism begins to take hold.

700

EUROPEAN EVENTS

- **711** The Moors invade Spain.
- **732** Charles Martel defeats the Moors at the Battle of Tours.
- **778** Charlemagne crosses the Pyrenees to fight the Moors in Spain.
- **800** Charlemagne is crowned Holy Roman Emperor by Pope Leo III.

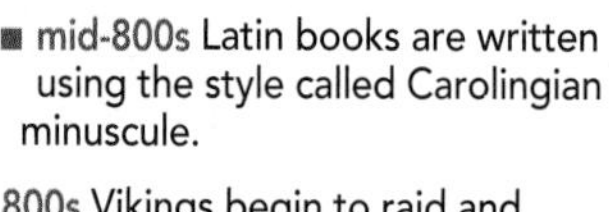

- **mid-800s** Latin books are written using the style called Carolingian minuscule.
- **800s** Vikings begin to raid and settle in Europe. ▼

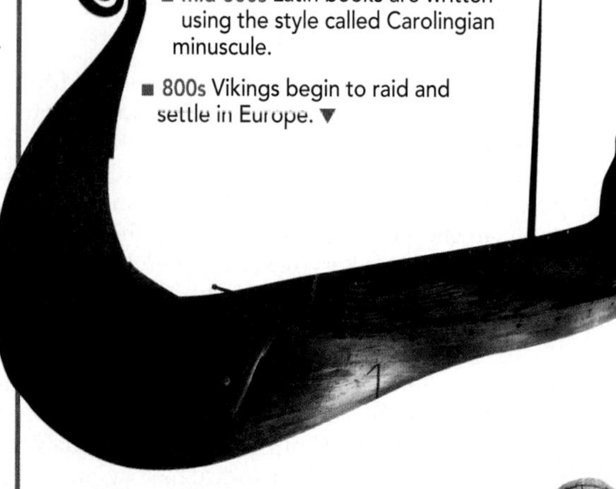

WORLD EVENTS

- **early 700s (Japan)** The first works of Japanese prose appear.
- **700s (Japan)** "Collection of Ten Thousand Leaves," an early poetry anthology, appears.
- **762–763 (Middle East)** Baghdad is founded as the new capital of the Abassid dynasty.
- **794 (Japan)** A new imperial capital is built at Heian (Kyoto).
- **800 (New Zealand)** This is the earliest known date for habitations of the Polynesian people known as the Maori. ►
- **813–833 (Middle East)** Science and scholarship thrive during Ma'mun's reign (Abassid dynasty).
- **c. 850 (Africa)** The trading empire of Kanem-Bornu is founded.

Getting an Overview of the Period

Introduction To give students an overview of the period, have them indicate the span of dates in the title of the Timeline. Next, point out that the Timeline is divided into European Events (on the top) and World Events (on the bottom). Have students scan the Timeline, looking at both the European Events and the World Events. Finally, point out that the events in the Timeline often represent beginnings, turning points, and endings (for example, the Moors' invasion of Spain in 711).

Key Events Have students **identify** key events related to the rise of Islam and its struggle with Christianity.
Answer: In 622, Muhammad journeys from Mecca to Yathrib; In the 600s, Islam spreads to North Africa; In 1095, Pope Urban II urges a crusade to retake the Holy Land; In 1099, Crusaders retake Jerusalem; In 1187, Jerusalem is again under Islamic control.

Ask students to **describe** the A.D. 700s in Europe.
Possible response: It was a turbulent century, with much warfare.

900 1100 1300

- 900s The game of chess is introduced into Europe. ▼
- 1000s Serious efforts begin to drive the Moors from Spain.
- 1043–1099 Rodrigo Díaz de Vivar, Spain's national hero, lives and battles the Moors.
- 1066 William the Conqueror successfully invades England.
- 1095 Pope Urban II urges a crusade to retake the Holy Land from Muslims.
- 1099 Crusaders retake Jerusalem from Muslims.

- 1100s Use of windmills starts to spread.
- 1100s Society experiences a rebirth; the Gothic style develops.
- 1122–1204 Eleanor of Aquitane, the most influential woman of her time, lives.

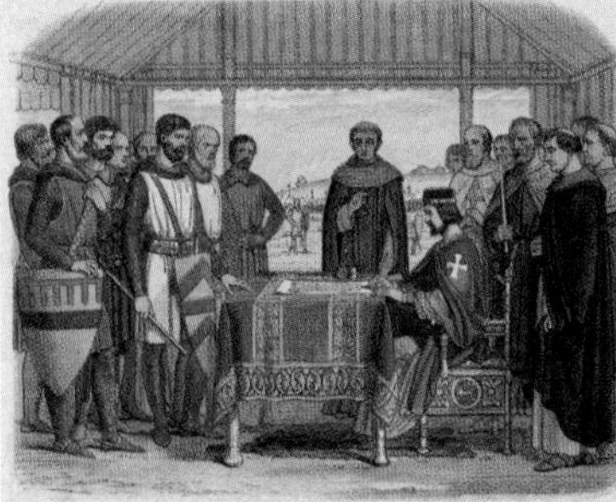

- 1215 King John of England signs the Magna Carta, limiting royal power. ▲
- mid-1200s Eyeglasses are in use.
- 1300 Universities exist in a number of European cities.
- early 1300s Dante, exiled from Florence, writes the *Divine Comedy*.
- 1300s Paper mills exist in Europe.

- c. 900 **(Mexico/Central America)** Classic period of Mayan culture ends.
- c. 1000 **(Japan)** Lady Murasaki Shikibu writes *The Tale of Genji*.
- c. 1020 **(Persia)** The poet Firdawsi, author of the *Book of Kings*, dies.
- 1048–1131 **(Persia)** Omar Khayyam—poet, mathematician, and astronomer—lives.

- 1100 **(Africa)** The city of Timbuktu is founded in West Africa.
- c. 1100s **(Mexico/Central America)** The Aztecs first appear.
- 1187 **(Middle East)** Jerusalem is again under Islamic control.▼

Analyzing the Timeline

1. (a) In which entry on this timeline are the Moors first mentioned? In which entry are they last mentioned? (b) What do these entries suggest about Spanish culture during the dates concerned? **[Infer]**
   Answer: (a) The first time the Moors are mentioned is in the entry for 711; the last time is in the entry for 1043–1099. (b) Spanish culture must have had a heavy Moorish influence during this time.
2. (a) What happened in England in 597? (b) How might this event have impacted the future of the political climate in England? **[Speculate]**
   Answer: (a) In 597, the Roman cleric Saint Augustine converted English King Ethelbert to Christianity. (b) Christianity would have influenced the kings' decisions.
3. (a) Which entries mention the Holy Land or Jerusalem? (b) What do these entries suggest about the relationship between Christianity and Islam? **[Infer]**
   Answer: (a) The entries for 1095, 1099, and 1187 mention the Holy Land or Jerusalem. (b) These entries suggest a long-standing conflict between Christianity and Islam over possession of the Holy Land.
4. (a) By what date did universities and paper mills exist in Europe? (b) What does this fact indicate about the spread of knowledge? **[Analyze]**
   Answer: (a) Universities and paper mills existed in Europe by the 1300s. (b) This fact indicates that literacy was becoming more widespread and that education was more widely available.
5. (a) What happened in India in the 500s? (b) Why was this surprising, and what does it tell you about the world at that time? **[Analyze]**
   Answer: (a) The game of chess was invented. (b) The game of chess features social ranks that were common in Europe but not in India. This suggests that international trade and travel were common among the commercial and educated classes.

Critical Viewing

1. What does the illustration for the English epic *Beowulf* (700) suggest about one of the characters in that poem? Explain. **[Interpret]**
   Possible response: The illustration suggests that one of the characters is a monster. His claws, large teeth, horns, and angry expression convey an air of danger and malice.
2. What can you infer about the Maori (800) from the sculpture? **[Distinguish]**
   Possible response: Maori artists were skilled craftspeople.
3. What mood does the picture of King John of England signing the Magna Carta (1215) convey? **[Analyze]**
   Possible response: The mood is one of solemnity and significance. It appears that the moment is one of great ceremony, requiring many witnesses, who seem to be observing with approval.

Literature of the Period

- Central to the medieval epic are the deeds—often exaggerated—of heroic figures. Students will find examples of this theme in the excerpts from the *Song of Roland,* p. 600, and *The Nibelungenlied,* p. 610.
- Another theme in medieval literature is the quest, or the journey toward a spiritual goal. Students will read about two different types of quests in the excerpts from de Troyes's *Perceval,* p. 630, and Dante's *Divine Comedy,* p. 658.

Critical Viewing

Possible response: The statue of the Roman soldier suggests that people in the Roman Empire valued youth, strength, military power, courage, and artistic skill.

Historical Background

From the Fall of Rome to the Renaissance Scholars usually refer to the historical period between approximately A.D. 450 and 1300 as the Middle Ages—but why is this considered a "middle" period? The Middle Ages may be seen as a historical filling, sandwiched between the Latin civilization of the Roman Empire and the later rediscovery of the classical civilizations of Greece and Rome in the Renaissance.

The dates of the Middle Ages are somewhat arbitrary. The fifth century, a period marked by the rapid decay of those institutions that held the Roman Empire together, is the beginning of this period: Rome was sacked by the Visigoths, a Germanic tribe, in 410 and the western part of the empire ceased to exist in 476. The end of the Middle Ages, however, is more complex an issue. The Renaissance began in the south of Europe. In Italy, the early fourteenth century brought the rediscovery of classical forms in art and architecture, together with the production of new editions of classical literature. In northern Europe, however, such innovations did not occur until the end of the fifteenth century.

A New European Structure In the third century A.D., Rome was master of most of Europe. The empire extended from England in the north to Africa in the south and from Portugal in the west to Syria in the east. Ultimately, this territory was far too large to administer, both politically and militarily. The Roman Empire was then divided into two distinct empires, with the emperor of the West ruling from Rome and the emperor of the East ruling from Constantinople (now Istanbul, Turkey).

For some time, the northern frontiers of the empire had been experiencing pressure from several Germanic tribes. The northern border, however, had generally remained secure. Then, a population explosion among these tribes triggered a need for expansion. This need for more territory, coupled with the tribes' warlike disposition, provoked what is sometimes called the "barbarian invasions." In reality, the incursion of the Germanic tribes into Roman territory more accurately resembled a mass migration sometimes marked by hostilities. Germanic historians, sensitive about using the word "invasion," called this period in history the *Volkerwanderung*—the wandering of the peoples.

The Germanic Contribution Hardly a portion of the old Western Roman Empire was left untouched by the various Germanic tribes: Lombards, Visigoths, and Ostrogoths settled in Italy; Visigoths, in southern France and Spain; Franks, in northern France; Angles and Saxons, in England. The presence of these peoples radically changed the political structure of what had been, until then, a unified empire. As these tribes began to dominate the land in which they settled, they established individual kingdoms, ending Roman rule once and for all.

▼ **Critical Viewing** What does this statue of a Roman soldier suggest about the values of the Roman Empire? Explain. **[Infer]**

Enrichment

Western Europe

One quarter of Western Europe consists of lowland plains located along seacoasts and in river valleys. The largest and most important is the North European Plain, which stretches more than 1,000 miles from Britain through France and Germany and into Eastern Europe. From about 500 to 1000, this region was a frontier land, sparsely populated and relatively undeveloped. Much of the region was covered with dense forests or mosquito-ridden marshes. By the late Middle Ages, Europeans began to develop the technology to drain the marshlands and open up rich new land for farming.

Today, the North European Plain still contains some of the world's most productive farmland and a number of major cities. Many navigable rivers flow through Europe's plains. In addition, the plains have few natural barriers. For centuries, the lowlands served as routes for migration and trade. Yet, the absence of natural barriers has also contributed to warfare, enabling rival groups and nations to invade neighboring lands with relative ease.

Themes in World Masterpieces — Close-up on Culture

The Code of Chivalry

Superheroes who defend the weak are today's knights, following the code of chivalry first developed in the Middle Ages.

The chivalric code evolved slowly out of the feudal system. Under this system, the king granted land to his lords, or vassals, so that they could afford to maintain mounted troops. Each lord, therefore, had a group of loyal knights ready to serve him in battle at a moment's notice.

Knights were experienced horsemen. They were also experienced in the use and repair of elaborate metal armor and of weapons such as lances, long wooden shafts tipped with iron or steel; maces, heavy clublike weapons with metal spikes at the end; and double-edged broadswords, about three feet long but weighing only a few pounds.

Equally important as these weapons, however, was the code of chivalry that dictated their use. A knight's loyalty to his lord was crucial, as was the obligation to defend those weaker than himself, especially women. Knights also offered their services to the greater glory of God. The Crusades, campaigns to retake Jerusalem and the Holy Land from Muslims, were opportunities for knights to fight for their most powerful lord, God himself.

The code of chivalry was impossibly idealistic. Yet the view of the perfect knight offered by medieval literature softened a brutal feudal system based on warlike qualities. Eventually, however, knights became less effective in warfare. In various fourteenth-century battles, French knights were like tin cans on horseback, easy targets for English archers with longbows.

Nevertheless, the code of chivalry has survived its armored adherents. It is still practiced by Batman and Spiderman, and it lives every time a man treats a woman with courtesy and respect.

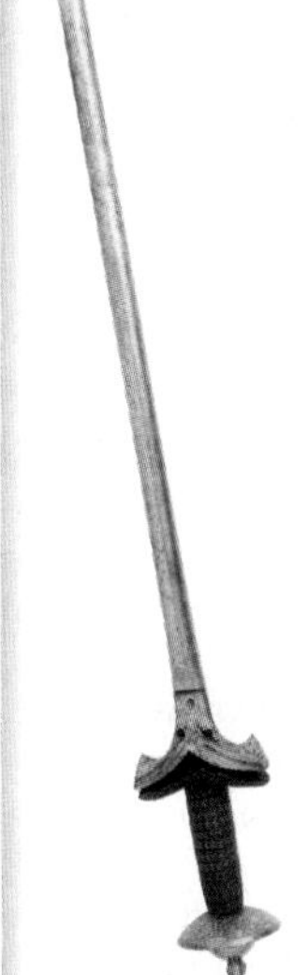

▲ **Critical Viewing** This weapon is a spiked mace. What does it indicate about the importance of armor to a knight? Why? **[Infer]**

The Birth of Feudalism These tribes also helped shape the feudal system that spread through medieval Europe. The act of vassalage, in which one lord swears allegiance to another in exchange for privileges or "feuds," originated in tribal organization. The concepts of kingship, knighthood, and chivalry all emerged from these Germanic peoples. (See Close-up on Culture, above.) After settling in the empire, Germanic tribes were quickly converted to Christianity, which had become the empire's official religion during the fourth century A.D. Because of this religious conversion, their political institutions were also Christianized. With their adoption of Roman religion, they also adopted Latin, the official language of the Western Church, as their language. Many linguists believe that the Romance languages descended from Latin—such as French, Spanish, Portuguese, Italian, and Romanian—owe their modern differences to the various Germanic tribes that learned Latin in an imperfect manner. Many words of Germanic origin, especially those relating to warfare and feudalism, still exist in these languages.

Critical Viewing

Possible response: The spiked mace appears to be a formidable weapon that could do a great deal of damage to anything it struck. Armor was, therefore, a necessary means of protection for a knight.

Background

The Knight

The word *knight* comes from the Old English word *cniht,* which means "household retainer."

Themes in World Literature

Close-up on Culture

Note the irony of the code of chivalry's having been introduced under a brutal feudal system that kept knights defending their Lord with fierce loyalty and fighting in wars, and peasants working the land without any hope of fulfilling their own needs. Tell students that before the code of chivalry, women in Europe had no rights, and were often mistreated and brutalized. Christianity raised women to a level requiring protection, and knights were expected to keep women from harm's way.

Ask: How does the code of chivalry manifest itself in modern life?

Possible response: Courteous behavior of any kind is a sign of chivalry, whether it be at home, at school, in the workplace, or elsewhere. When a male displays good manners toward a female, such as listening respectfully, offering to assist with heavy physical tasks, or honoring her achievements, he displays chivalry. However, some feminists are offended by any male behavior that suggests a woman's weakness.

Differentiated Instruction — Solutions for All Learners

Strategy for Less Proficient Readers

Have students preview the art and illustrations for this period before they read the "Historical Background" portion of the text. Then, have them write one or two questions about the illustrations and then read the text to find the answers.

Strategy for English Learners

Have students preview the subheadings for the Historical Background and Literature sections of the unit opener material. Then, guide students to use these headings to create an outline. As students read, they can take notes in the outline, organizing the main points and supporting details of the text.

Enrichment for Advanced Readers

Challenge students to find links between this historical period and their own times. Students can look for parallels or cause-and-effect relationships. Ask students to discuss whether they see any parallels between the global conflicts of the medieval period and those of our own era.

Background

The Latin Mass

Latin was used for celebrating Mass by the Roman Catholic Church until the 1960s, when Vatican Council II permitted the vernacular to be used.

Critical Viewing

Possible response: Details in the scene that suggest a close association between religious and political power include the Pope placing the crown on Charlemagne's head and the clerics standing nearby as witnesses.

Humanities

***Scenes from the life of Charlemagne,* 15th century**

The emperor Charlemagne was a favorite subject for illumination and study in the Middle Ages. King Charles V of France revived historic interest in the great leader. That interest led to the establishment of Charlemagne as a cult figure.

In his day, Charlemagne was a firm champion of books, libraries, and illumination. He sponsored many projects to promote the literary arts. His appearance in this manuscript is suitable tribute to this legendary hero.

Background

The Effects of the Crusades

The demand for the new and exotic goods that returning crusaders introduced to Europe helped fuel an increase in commerce. The increase in trade led to the development of a new merchant class centered first in such Italian city-states as Genoa and Venice. Soon, other small towns throughout Europe experienced a commercial growth that led to their transformation into large trading centers.

Feudalism and Peasants The feudal system did not involve only lords and knights. It also spelled out the duties of poor farmers known as peasants. They lived on a lord's manor—a village and its surrounding fields—and owed service to the lord in exchange for protection. Usually, they were not free to leave the land. They contributed to the manor by raising sheep and cattle and growing grain and vegetables. Their self-sufficient community often included a mill, a blacksmith shop, and a church.

The Moors Threaten Europe In A.D. 711, the Muslims, or Moors, inspired by their successful subjugation of the Middle East and North Africa, swept into Spain and quickly conquered all but a few mountain strongholds. The Muslim advance into Europe's heartland was not stopped until A.D. 732, when Charles Martel (mär tel′), "the Hammer," defeated the Moors at the Battle of Tours, in central France. The struggle between Christianity and Islam became one of the most important conflicts in medieval Europe.

A New Stability: The Reemergence of Learning On December 25, A.D. 800, Charles I, King of the Franks, also known as Charles the Great or Charlemagne (shär′ lə mān′), was crowned Holy Roman Emperor by Pope Leo III. (For the size of this empire four hundred years later, see the map on page 591.) This event represents the complete integration of the Germanic peoples into the mainstream of European society. In addition, the use of a title and an office linked to the traditions of the ancient Roman Empire was an attempt at creating a new unified political order. This action revealed a need and willingness to revive some kind of historical continuity, and there is little doubt that at this time Europe needed all the unity it could muster.

A Crusade Having contained the Islamic threat in Europe, the Christian rulers of Europe turned their eyes to the Holy Land. This Middle Eastern region, located in what is now Jordan and Israel, was at that time a Muslim stronghold. Its sacred associations, however, made it "holy" for Jews and Christians as well. In 1095, Pope Urban II preached a sermon in Clermont, France, urging European knights to participate in a crusade that would win back the Holy Land.

A Powerful Sermon Urban's sermon was perhaps one of the most effective orations in history. The pope even claimed that he was not ready for the intense fervor generated by his discourse. Nevertheless, one year later, the first crusade was launched. This army, under the leadership of several powerful lords, initially met with great success. They regained Jerusalem in 1099, but the Arabs reorganized and began to exploit the internal discord of the crusaders. Several crusades were subsequently undertaken. Their success was minimal because

▼ Critical Viewing These images from an illuminated manuscript show scenes from the life of Charlemagne. The upper picture, for example, shows him being crowned. Which details in this scene suggest a close association between religious and political power? Explain. **[Interpret]**

Enrichment

Charlemagne (742–814)

Charlemagne's influence was felt well beyond the geographic confines of his kingdom. At various points during his rule, Charlemagne, or Charles the Great, influenced events in England and Spain and carried on diplomatic relations with rulers in the Middle East. Charlemagne's enormous influence over many aspects of life—protector of the Church, patron of the arts, initiator of governmental reforms and organization, and guarantor of military stability—inspired numerous artistic and literary tributes.

Among Charlemagne's reforms was the establishment of the feudal system of government, which lasted for the next 400 years. In addition, Charlemagne protected and extended the power of the Christian church. To strengthen his alliance further, on Christmas Day, A.D. 800, Pope Leo III crowned Charlemagne emperor of the Romans. When Charlemagne died in 814, his empire passed to his son, Louis I. In 843, Louis's sons drew up the Treaty of Verdun, which split the empire into three regions.

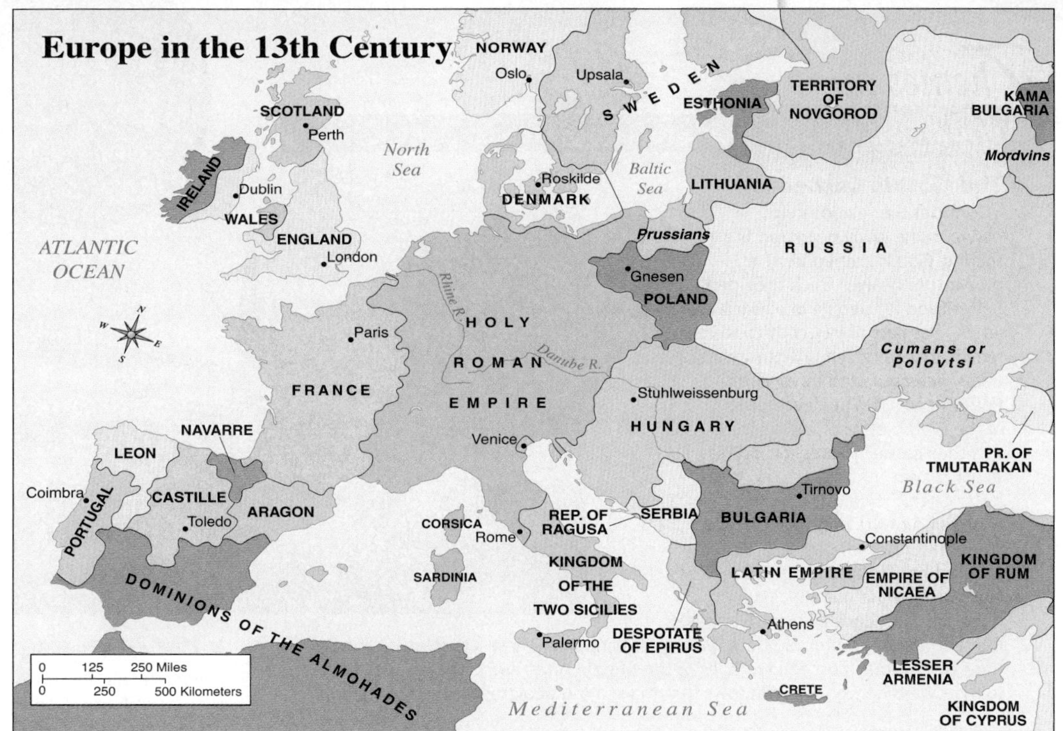

the European lords were more interested in protecting and expanding their own domains than in pursuing any international cooperative venture. By 1187, Jerusalem was once again under Islamic control.

Stirrings of Nationalism With nationalism beginning to take hold in Europe, there arose a natural antagonism between the single most important international office, the Catholic Church, and the various kingdoms. This conflict of interest between the papacy and the secular order reshaped the political landscape of Europe. One of the most famous victims of this controversy was the great Italian poet Dante (dän′ tā). Exiled from his native Florence in 1302 for opposing papal meddling in Florentine politics, he expressed his aversion to the worldly pursuits of the papacy as a recurring theme in the *Inferno,* the first part of his epic poem, the *Divine Comedy*.

The Impact of the Crusades Despite their limited military success, the crusades had a tremendous impact on medieval civilization. As crusaders returned from the Middle East, they brought back with them new spices, textiles, and other products. A demand for these new and exotic items inspired commerce. This trading created a new merchant class in the Italian city-states of Genoa, Florence, and Venice, and new markets

▲ Critical Viewing
In thirteenth-century Europe, what was the status of present-day Spain, Germany, and Italy? Explain. **[Read a Map]**

Critical Viewing

Answer: In thirteenth-century Europe, present-day Spain was divided into five different regions: Leon, Castille, Navarre, Aragon, and the Dominions of the Almohades. Germany was part of the Holy Roman Empire. Northern Italy was part of the Holy Roman Empire, and southern Italy was the Kingdom of the Two Sicilies.

Background

Richard the Lionheart and Saladin

England's King Richard I (or Richard the Lionheart) and Saladin, a Muslim warrior, were determined but honorable foes during the Crusades. In 1189, following Saladin's capture of Jerusalem, Richard set out on the Third Crusade to try to recapture and reclaim the Holy City. In 1192, Richard and Saladin concluded a treaty that allowed Christians access to the holy places of Jerusalem. Both Richard and Saladin were known for their chivalry, and their conflict has been celebrated in chivalric romance literature.

Humanities

To give students insight into medieval life, display **Art Transparency 5: The Meeting of St. Nicholas With the Emperor's Messenger and the Miraculous Rescue of a Ship,** by Fra Angelico, in the **Fine Art Transparencies** booklet.

Themes in World Literature

Art in the Historical Context

Note that throughout Europe, grand Gothic cathedrals are among the most popular tourist attractions. Point out that these astonishing buildings were constructed before machinery such as cranes and ladders were available.

Ask: How do you think the Gothic style represented spiritual expression?

Possible response: When one stands near or in a Gothic cathedral, one tends to look up at the huge spires, towers and ceilings enhanced with beautiful paintings and stained-glass windows. This architecture stimulates looking up toward heaven and thinking of God.

Critical Viewing

Answer: The flying buttresses and the tall stone towers are two major elements of the Gothic style.

Historical Background

Comprehension Check

1. Between which two major historical periods did the Middle Ages take place?
   Answer: The Middle Ages took place between the Latin civilization of the Roman Empire and the Renaissance.
2. How did the feudal system work?
   Answer: The king granted land to his lords, or vassals, so that they could afford to maintain mounted troops. Each lord, therefore, had a group of loyal knights ready to serve him. Poor farmers known as peasants lived on a lord's manor and owed service to the lord in exchange for protection. These peasants contributed to the manor by raising livestock and by growing crops.
3. Which two religions carried on one of the most important conflicts in medieval Europe?
   Answer: Islam and Christianity carried on this conflict.

Themes in World Masterpieces

Art in the Historical Context

The Gothic Cathedral

Consider the relationship between the lowly bean and the soaring Gothic cathedral. The growing of beans, which provided better food for people of all social levels, was part of a twelfth-century renaissance in which towns thrived, trade increased, and travel conditions improved. The development of the Gothic style of architecture was the spiritual expression of this social rebirth.

The Gothic style was also an expression of the brilliance of stonemasons. These artisans discovered how to use flying buttresses (supports on the outer walls) to build tall cathedrals whose walls were thin enough to accommodate stained-glass windows. These architectural innovations give us our most vivid images of the Middle Ages: stone towers that seem to fly toward heaven and windows that make a multicolored heaven of sunlight.

▲ Critical Viewing Which details in these pictures of Notre Dame Cathedral, Paris, reveal two major elements of the Gothic style? Explain. **[Connect]**

sprang up elsewhere as well. Small towns in Europe were quickly transformed into large trading centers. By the effective end of the crusades in the late thirteenth century, the merchant class was becoming increasingly important in many parts of Europe.

As the medieval city grew, so did the new centers of learning. By 1300, universities existed in a number of important European cities. The University of Paris was the most eminent center of theology and philosophy in the Western world, and the University of Bologna in Italy was the most important center for the study of law.

Transformation of Medieval Life Despite disease and poverty during this time, new capital generated by commerce stimulated the quest for learning and the rediscovery of classical literature. In addition, explorers searching for better trade routes would soon expand European knowledge of the world. Europe was entering the period of rebirth that we now call the Renaissance.

Critical Thinking

1. Why might the rediscovery of classical forms of art, architecture, and literature have occurred later in northern Europe than in southern Europe? **[Infer]**
   Possible response: Southern Europe is closer to the seat of these classical civilizations, therefore, the occupants of southern Europe had easier access to the classical forms than occupants of northern Europe.
2. What might the period of "barbarian invasion" have been like? **[Speculate]**
   Possible response: This period probably was marked by violence and destruction as the fearsome Germanic tribes attempted to claim land in Roman territory.
3. Do you think the peasants in the feudal system were fortunate? Explain your answer. **[Make a Judgment]**
   Possible response: No; although the peasants had a place to live, they could never own their own land and they were not free to leave the place where they lived.

Literature

Literature in Native Languages As previously mentioned, Latin became the language of religion, scholarship, and government. It was no longer understood by common people, who spoke German or one of the Romance languages that were evolving from Latin, such as Italian, French, and Spanish. These languages were known as the vernacular, or "the native language of a place."

This new linguistic situation affected the way culture was passed on. Two cultures existed side by side: a high culture based on Latin and a popular culture based on vernacular languages. The history of medieval literature is the story of how the various national literatures emerged in native languages while Latin became increasingly specialized.

▲ **Critical Viewing** This fifteenth-century Holy Book provides some idea of what a medieval illuminated manuscript looked like. Compare and contrast the relationship between words and pictures in such a manuscript and in a modern illustrated book. **[Compare and Contrast]**

Reforms in Latin As vernacular literatures were emerging, however, Latin underwent important reforms that ensured the more accurate transmission of texts. Under Charlemagne's patronage, monks created a new writing style called the Carolingian minuscule. This style, featuring a neater script penmanship and distinct breaks between words, made documents much easier to read. In addition, new Latin grammars helped to standardize the language by eliminating elements introduced from the vernacular.

A New Kind of Vernacular Epic While monks in monasteries were refining Latin and copying out libraries of books, the oral tradition was thriving in the rough-and-tumble world. Germanic storytellers, for example, developed a new kind of epic, or long narrative heroic poem. Epic poetry existed in classical Latin, but these Latin poems, such as Virgil's *Aeneid*, were extremely refined and literary. The Germanic epics existed in oral form centuries before they were written down. Their verse form is irregular, and they were meant to be performed to stimulate a warrior's courage before battle. The most famous Germanic epic is the *Nibelungenlied* ("Song of the Nibelungs"), which an unknown author composed from earlier tales sometime around 1200.

Epic Heroes for Different Nationalities The Spanish *Song of My Cid* and the French *Song of Roland*, although written in medieval Spanish and medieval French, respectively, are also descendants of this ancient Germanic tradition. These two epics describe conflicts between Christians and Moors.

Background

Medieval Manuscripts

The illuminated manuscripts of the Middle Ages are probably the most important pictorial sources for our understanding of medieval culture and society. Because most illuminated manuscripts were produced in monasteries, they address mostly religious topics. However, many illuminated manuscripts feature scenes from daily life, providing both a rewarding aesthetic experience and an invaluable picture into medieval culture.

Critical Viewing

Possible response: The art is meant to enhance and clarify the words, as it does in modern illustrated books. However, in a medieval illuminated manuscript, much more space is devoted to art than in a modern illustrated book (except, of course, in children's picture books).

Literature Connection

For more insight into medieval attitudes, fears, and superstitions, students can read "The Lay of the Werewolf" on p. 642.

Critical Viewing

Possible response: The picture reveals that the instruments the troubadours played were light enough to be carried easily. This portability made it easy for the troubadours to travel from place to place.

The Moors had invaded Spain and Portugal in the early 700s. Charlemagne took part in early efforts to expel the Moors. In 778, he crossed the Pyrenees into Spain to accomplish this goal. The *Song of Roland*, dating from around 1100, relates the tragedy that befell Charlemagne's nephew, Roland, during this campaign.

In the eleventh century, Christians in Spain launched a new campaign against the Moors. Eventually, several independent Christian kingdoms emerged. *Song of My Cid*, written in the mid-1100s, tells the story of Spain's national hero, Rodrigo Díaz de Vivar (1043–1099), who helped spearhead the expansion of these Christian kingdoms.

Icelandic Sagas Meanwhile, from the ninth through the eleventh centuries, conflicts also occurred between Europeans and Viking raiders from Scandinavia. These Vikings, or Norsemen, settled in England and in northern France, where they became known as Normans. Under William the Conqueror, a Norman army conquered England in 1066.

Vikings also settled in Iceland. There, in the late 1100s, they carried their restless, adventurous spirit into literature, producing works like *Njáls saga* and *Egils saga*. These tales draw upon oral traditions and fictionalize historical events.

Troubadour Poetry In the second half of the eleventh century, a group of poets began writing verse in Provençal (prō′ vän säl′), a Romance language spoken in the south of France. These troubadours—from *trobar*, meaning "to find or invent"—were associated with the courts of certain powerful lords and invented new ways to sing about love. As a result, the theme of their poetry became known as courtly love. The rules of courtly love required a troubadour to praise in poetry a distant, unattainable lady, usually someone else's wife.

Courtly Love and the Status of Women This type of poetry, which helped foster enlightened attitudes toward women, took Europe by storm. Poets followed courtly love traditions, writing in their own native languages rather than in Latin. Among those who helped popularize the new poetry was Eleanor of Aquitane (c. 1122–1204). As queen of France and England, successively, she was the most influential woman of her time.

Chrétien de Troyes (krā tyän də trwä′), writing at the court of France's Marie de Champagne in the twelfth century, created a new poetic form, the courtly romance. This form combined the elements of courtly love with the longer narrative form of the romance. Many of his works, like *Perceval*, recount adventures associated with the legendary King Arthur of Britain.

▼ **Critical Viewing** Troubadours played music and composed poetry. What does this picture of medieval troubadours reveal about the kinds of instruments they played? Explain. **[Infer]**

Enrichment

Books in the Middle Ages

In the Middle Ages, books achieved a previously unknown prominence. Although books were still produced by laborious hand processes, groups of scribes and artists banded together to form workshops that turned out remarkable quantities of books. The subjects varied widely, ranging from personal prayer books to ambitious histories. Book formats were both the rolled manuscripts and the leaved, bound codex. Some of these books used elaborate decorative works of art; others were quite simple. All contained important clues to everyday life in the Middle Ages.

Themes in World Masterpieces — A Writer's Voice

François Villon, Outlaw Poet

Today, gangsta rappers stir up controversy with lyrics about their outlaw lives. Yet medieval French poet François Villon (frän swä´ vē yōn´) (1431–c. 1463) beat rappers like Dr. Dre to the punch. Villon, who came from a poor family, ran with the roughest crowds in Paris. Although he studied at the Sorbonne, a college that taught religion, he was involved in brawling and thievery. He even killed a priest but was pardoned due to extenuating circumstances.

Villon wrote his poem "Ballade" at a time when he thought he would be hanged. In the poem, he speaks as a dead man and asks forgiveness of those who view his body. Villon's actual death, however, remains mysterious. Instead of being executed, he was exiled from Paris. At this point, he vanishes from history and enters legend as an outlaw poet.

from "Ballade" by François Villon, translated by Galway Kinnell

Brother humans who live on after us
Don't let your hearts harden against us
For if you have pity on wretches like us
More likely God will show mercy to you
You see us five, six, hanging here
As for the flesh we loved too well
A while ago it was eaten and has rotted away
And we the bones turn to ashes and dust
Let no one make us the butt of jokes
But pray God that he absolve us all. . . .

▲ Critical Viewing
Do any details in this picture of François Villon suggest that he was an outlaw poet? Why or why not? **[Interpret]**

Dante Makes a Fateful Choice As medieval society evolved and education became more available with the growth of the universities, popular and Latin culture at times intersected. These traditions combined in the greatest poem of medieval times, Dante's *Divine Comedy*, written in the early 1300s. This epic, which expresses a Christian vision of the world, is based in part on Latin culture. Dante's guide for his imaginary trip through Hell, for example, is the great Roman poet Virgil. At the same time, Dante chose to write his poem in Italian rather than in Latin. His choice gave added prestige to the vernacular and caused other writers to use it as well.

The Dark Side Starting in the 1100s, European towns began to increase rapidly in size. Although this urbanization was part of a social rebirth, it had its dark side as well. Impoverished city-dwellers, menaced by crime and disease, had a hard time surviving. Especially threatening was the plague, a highly contagious disease carried from rats to humans by fleas. The dark side of medieval life found expression in the work of Parisian poet François Villon (see above).

Themes in World Literature

A Writer's Voice

Point out to students that rap is defined as "a form of popular music characterized by spoken rhyming lyrics with a syncopated, repetitive rhythmic accompaniment."
Ask: What is it about the style of gangsta rappers that would legitimize their being called "outlaw poets"?
Possible response: The lively rhythm and beat of the music do give the rappers' words, as vulgar as they may be, a poetic punch that evokes emotions of both joy and anger, as well as disgust, in listeners.

Critical Viewing

Possible response: His posture, clothing, and knife indicate an attitude consistent with that of an outlaw.

Literature of the Period

Comprehension Check

1. What language was used in matters of religion, scholarship, and government during the Middle Ages?
   Answer: Latin was used.
2. In what way did Dante increase the prestige of the vernacular?
   Answer: Dante chose to write his *Divine Comedy* in Italian rather than in Latin.

Critical Thinking

1. Why do you think Latin, rather than one of the vernacular languages, became the language of religion, scholarship, and government? **[Analyze]**
   Possible response: Only the well educated—those involved in matters of religion, scholarship, and government—understood Latin. Because documents dealing with these matters were written in Latin, the educated classes of all European countries were obliged to maintain their understanding and use of Latin.
2. What qualities might a successful medieval storyteller have had? **[Infer]**
   Possible response: A successful storyteller would have had a good memory, an exciting performance style, and the ability to play a musical instrument.

Concept Connector

Have students return to the Focus Questions on p. 585. Ask them to summarize the main points in the Unit Introduction. Students' summaries should include the following:

Ways Europe's structure changed:
- The Roman Empire was too large to administer effectively and was split into Eastern and Western Empires.
- Germanic tribes established individual kingdoms and developed feudalism.

The code of chivalry:
- Chivalry dictated the conduct of knights in war and in personal relationships.
- A knight was loyal to his lord and defended those weaker than him, especially women.
- Knights fought to preserve Christian lands.

Ways the Crusades changed Europe:
- Crusaders returned with spices, textiles, and other products from foreign lands.
- Demand for these items increased commerce and small villages grew into trading centers.
- Centers of learning developed.

Poetry's influence on attitudes toward women:
- The development of courtly love helped foster enlightened attitudes toward women.

PRETEACH/TEACH

Standard Course of Study

LT.5.01.2	Build knowledge of literary genres and explore how characteristics apply to literature of world cultures.
LT.5.01.3	Analyze literary devices and explain their effect on the work of world literature.

❶ Origin and Development of the Term

- Tell students that they will study medieval romance sagas in Unit 5. **Ask** students what comes to mind when they think of the word *romance.*
  Possible responses: Students may say that the word *romance* triggers thoughts about falling in love, having feelings of attraction for another person, or being in a dating relationship with someone.
- Then review the material that explains the origin of the term. **Ask** students to indicate what aspects of the literary meaning of *romance* apply to the contemporary everyday use of the term.
  Answer: Central to the literary meaning of *romance* was chivalry, which had much to do with courtly love. Courtly love and the contemporary meaning of romantic love are similar.
- Point out that the word *chivalry* referred to an ethical code that fused together Christian ethics and military codes of conduct. Chivalric virtues included piety, honor, valor, courtesy, chastity, and loyalty. A knight was loyal to God, an earthly master, and a woman to whom the knight pledged his devotion.

❷ Romance and Legend

- Review the material about romance and legend. Have students **compare** the qualities of legends with the qualities of epics.
  Answer: Legends, like epics, reflect a people's cultural identity and values and often tell about a hero or a person who performed extraordinary deeds.

Focus on Literary Forms

Defining Romance

A **romance** is a narrative that tells of strange, sometimes supernatural, events in exotic settings. In the Middle Ages, the term referred to tales that depicted the heroic deeds and courtly loves of noble knights and ladies. The genre has expanded to include any work that features idealized characters in an exotic setting, particularly one that focuses on a struggle between good and evil. The term **saga**, derived from an Old Norse word meaning "say," refers to a long story of adventure or heroic deeds.

❶ Origin and Development of the Term

The word *romance* comes from the French word *roman*, which is similar in meaning to the English word *novel*. Originally, romances did not have any connection to love, except in an indirect way. However, courtly love is an important element of chivalry, and chivalry is the real core of the medieval romance. For this reason, romance sagas are sometimes known as **chivalric romances** or **courtly romances.**

Over the centuries, the link between the romance as a literary form and romantic love became stronger. Since the eighteenth century, the term *romance* has been used to describe sentimental popular novels about love.

> ROMANCE MEANS NOTHING IF IT DOES NOT CONVEY SOME NOTION OF MYSTERY AND FANTASY. —*W. P. Ker*

❷ Romance and Legend

Medieval romance sagas are often closely related to **legends,** traditional stories about the past that are usually based on historical fact. Legends often tell about a hero who is human yet larger than life—a king, a saint, or a person who performed extraordinary deeds. Medieval romances were often based on legends. For example, legends about the adventures of King Arthur and his Knights of the Round Table were adapted to form the plots of numerous romance sagas, such as Chrétien de Troyes's twelfth-century French narrative poem *Perceval*, page 630.

❸ Features of the Medieval Romance Saga

The medieval romance saga is characterized by these key features:

- **Romance Hero** A romance focuses on the exciting adventures and courageous deeds of a heroic main character. This **romance hero** is usually a king, a knight, or a brave warrior who follows the chivalric code of

Extend the Lesson

Quests in Literature and Film

- Review the idea of a quest with students.
- Have students brainstorm for a list of quests found in literature and film.
  Possible responses: Luke Skywalker from *Star Wars,* Bilbo Baggins from *Lord of the Rings,* and Nathaniel in *Last of the Mohicans.*
- Group students into pairs. Then have each pair select a quest from the brainstorming list. Have students research and compare the qualities seen in medieval romance sagas with those seen in the film or piece of literature they have selected. Have them include the following.

1. hero
2. heroic quest
3. supernatural elements
4. cultural values
5. the role of the fantastic
6. symbols and archetypes

- Have students compare the change in the hero with the changes listed for a medieval romance hero. Then have students share their results either in a report to the class or on a chart posted in the room.

Medieval Romance Saga

▲ Critical Viewing
What features of a medieval romance does this painting reflect? **[Connect]**

behavior, which values courage, virtue, piety, loyalty to a ruler, and the idealized love of a noble lady. The romance hero is often raised in humble surroundings and does not discover his true identity until he approaches manhood. For example, King Arthur is does not learn that he is the rightful king of England until he pulls a magical sword from a stone.

- **A Heroic Quest** The plot of a romance usually focuses on a **quest**, a hero's dangerous journey in search of something of value. For example, in *Perceval*, the hero's quest is to find the Holy Grail, which will enable King Arthur to save his kingdom.
- **Supernatural Elements** A romance blends realistic and fantastic elements, including supernatural characters, fantastic plot elements, and exotic or even magical settings. For example, Marie de France's *Lay of the Werewolf*, page 642, includes a character who is a werewolf.
- **Symbols and Archetypes** A romance features characters, plot elements, settings, images, and themes that take on greater importance. A **symbol** is a person, a place, an animal, or an object that suggests a meaning larger than itself. For example, in *Perceval*, the Holy Grail is a symbol that represents more than simply a golden cup. An **archetype** is a symbolic narrative element that appears in the literature, mythology, or folklore of many different cultures. For example, *The Lay of the Werewolf* includes the archetype of disguised identity, which is found in folk tales, myths, and legends throughout the world.

4 Strategies for Reading Medieval Romance Sagas

Use these strategies as you read medieval romance sagas.

Identify Cultural Values Pay close attention to plot elements, characterizations, and settings that reflect cultural values, particularly those relating to medieval chivalry and religious ideals.

Analyze the Hero's Quest Make sure you understand what the hero seeks on his quest and how that object will help him or his people. If the hero's quest is not successful, think about what may have prevented its success.

Interpret Symbols and Archetypes Decide whether there are characters, images, objects, or settings that suggest a symbolic meaning. Also look for archetypal elements that appear in the literature of many different cultures. Then, work to interpret the larger meaning that these symbols and archetypes suggest.

3 Features of the Medieval Romance Saga

- Review the features of medieval romance sagas. Suggest that students use these pages as a reference as they read the medieval romance sagas in Unit 5.
- Clarify the idea of symbols.
  Ask students: What is one symbol in modern life?
  Answer: The flag of a country is a symbol.
- Reinforce the idea that a symbol is a real object, place, or person that represents more than what it actually is. Ask students what the flag means to them, and make sure they understand that it is more than a piece of colored cloth.
- Point out that much literature focuses on the struggle between good and evil, just as the medieval romance saga does.

4 Strategies for Reading Medieval Romance Sagas

- Before reading a medieval romance saga, tell students to read its background to determine what the culture of the saga is. This will help students to identify the cultural values present in the saga.
- Tell students to identify who the hero is and what qualities the hero brings to his or her quest. Suggest that students look at the character and evaluate those qualities that will serve him or her well, as well as those qualities that may interfere with the quest.
- Suggest that students analyze how the fantastic is used in the literature and whether it strains credibility or works well with the reality of the piece.
- Point out that symbols in a medieval romance saga are often recurring. If students see a symbol repeated throughout a saga, the symbol probably has a great deal of significance in the story.

Critical Viewing

Possible response: The painting depicts a knight who appears ready for battle. The features of a medieval romance, then, are the romance hero and the heroic quest.

Standard Course of Study

Goal 3: FOUNDATIONS OF ARGUMENT

- **FA.3.03.1** Gather information to prove a point about issues in literature.

Goal 4: CRITICAL THINKING

- **CT.4.02.1** Show an understanding of cultural context in analyzing thematic connections.
- **CT.4.05.7** Identify and analyze influences, contexts, or biases in critical text.

Goal 5: LITERATURE

- **LT.5.01.2** Build knowledge of literary genres, and explore how characteristics apply to literature of world cultures.
- **LT.5.01.7** Understand the cultural and historical impact on world literature texts.
- **LT.5.03.5** Summarize key events and points from the text.

Step-by-Step Teaching Guide	Pacing Guide
PRETEACH	
• Administer Vocabulary and Reading Warm-ups as necessary.	5 min.
• Engage students' interest with the motivation activity.	5 min.
• Read and discuss author and background features. **FT**	10 min.
• Introduce the Literary Analysis Skill: Medieval Epic. **FT**	5 min.
• Introduce the Reading Strategy: Recognizing Feudal Values. **FT**	10 min.
• Prepare students to read by teaching the selection vocabulary. **FT**	
TEACH	
• Informally monitor comprehension while students read independently or in groups. **FT**	30 min.
• Monitor students' comprehension with the Reading Check notes.	as students read
• Reinforce vocabulary with Vocabulary Builder notes.	as students read
• Develop students' understanding of medieval epics with the Literary Analysis annotations. **FT**	5 min.
• Develop students' ability to recognize feudal values with the Reading Strategy annotations. **FT**	5 min.
ASSESS/EXTEND	
• Assess students' comprehension and mastery of the Literary Analysis and Reading Strategy by having them answer the Apply the Skills questions. **FT**	15 min.
• Have students complete the Vocabulary Lesson and the Grammar and Style Lesson. **FT**	15 min.
• Apply students' ability to analyze details by using the Writing Lesson. **FT**	45 min. or homework
• Apply students' understanding by using one or more of the Extend Your Learning activities.	20–90 min. or homework
• Administer Selection Test A or Selection Test B. **FT**	15 min.

Resources

Print

Unit 5 Resources

Transparency

Graphic Organizer Transparencies

Print

Reader's Notebook [L2]

Reader's Notebook: Adapted Version [L1]

Reader's Notebook: English Learner's Version [EL]

Unit 5 Resources

Technology

Listening to Literature Audio CDs [L2, EL]

Print

Unit 5 Resources

General Resources

Technology

Go Online: Research **[L3]**
Go Online: Self-test **[L3]**
***ExamView®*, Test Bank [L3]**

Choosing Resources for Differentiated Instruction

[L1] Special Needs Students
[L2] Below-Level Students
[L3] All Students
[L4] Advanced Students
[EL] English Learners

For Vocabulary and Reading Warm-ups and for Selection Tests, **A** signifies "less challenging" and **B** "more challenging." For Graphic Organizer transparencies, **A** signifies "not filled in" and **B** "filled in."

FT Fast Track Instruction: To move the lesson more quickly, use the strategies and activities identified with **FT**.

Scaffolding for Less Proficient and Advanced Students

The leveled Critical Thinking questions after selections progress in the levels of thinking required to answer them. To address the needs of your different students, you may use the (a) level questions for your less proficient students and the (b) level questions with your on-level and advanced students. The occasional (c) level questions are appropriate for your advanced students.

Use this complete suite of powerful teaching tools to make lesson planning and testing quicker and easier.

Use the interactive textbook (online and on CD-ROM) to make selections and activities come alive with audio and video support and interactive questions.

Monitoring Progress

Before students read these selections, administer **Diagnostic Test 6 (*Unit 5 Resources*, pp. 2–4).** This test will determine students' level of readiness for the reading and vocabulary skills.

Go Online Professional Development
For: Information about Lexiles
Visit: www.PHSchool.com
Web Code: eue-1111

PRETEACH

Motivation

Tell students that they will be reading the stories of two great heroes of the Middle Ages. Both are powerful warriors and leaders. One dies while fighting against overwhelming odds; the other dies at the hands of traitors. The two heroes epitomize the qualities and values of the medieval knight. Ask students to recall stories they have heard and read that tell of contemporary heroes. Have them discuss their ideas of heroism. Then, tell them to compare these qualities with those of the knights they will read about in the following epics.

❶ Background

More About the Authors

Authorship in the Middle Ages was either undetermined or unimportant. Because of the nature of the *Song of Roland* as an oral composition, the tale was sung as a collective performance. Each singer contributed to the composition of the *Song of Roland* as it was passed from one singer to another and from one generation to the next. Although some attributions have been suggested for *The Nibelungenlied,* the idea of anonymous authorship is important to this poetic form and reinforces the collective experience and primacy of the performance.

Geography Note

Call students' attention to the map on this page, and explain that the *Song of Roland* and *The Nibelungenlied* come from the heart of Europe: France and Germany. France and part of Western Germany—along with Belgium, Luxembourg, and the Netherlands—were once part of the Frankish kingdom. This area was ruled by Charlemagne, or Charles the Great.

Build Skills | Epics

from the Song of Roland • *from* The Nibelungenlied

❶

About the *Song of Roland*

Some scholars believe that French literature begins with the *Chanson de Roland* (shän sōn′ də rō län′), or *Song of Roland*. This poem about a great warrior is by far the best known of all medieval epics. Despite its popularity, scholars cannot determine exactly when it was written or who wrote it. The manuscript at Oxford University, England, dates from the decades after A.D. 1100 and is written in the Norman dialect of Old French. The original poem, however, is much older.

Death of Roland, Vincent de Beauvais, Giraudon

Tales of a Great King The *Song of Roland* treats one of the great themes of medieval heroic literature: the deeds surrounding Charlemagne (shär′ lə mān′) and his court. Charlemagne, or Charles the Great, was king of the Franks from 768 to 814 and emperor of the Holy Roman Empire from 800 to 814. Because Charlemagne ruled France about 300 years before the *Song of Roland* was composed, there is a great distance between the poem and the events it narrates.

The poem transforms a rather minor historical event. In 778, Charlemagne intervened in a dispute in Spain between two rival Moorish rulers. The Moors were Muslims from northwest Africa who invaded Spain in the eighth century. While returning to France through the Pyrenees (pir′ ə nēz), Charlemagne's rear guard, led by his nephew Roland, was attacked in the valley of Roncesvalles (rän′ sə valz′) by a band of Basques (bäsks). To a man, the rear guard perished.

Fiction Not Fact The author of the *Song of Roland* takes considerable poetic license with the historical facts. Most significantly, the Basques become Moors, a more contemporary and meaningful foe for a twelfth-century audience. Charlemagne, thirty-six years old at the time of the massacre at Roncesvalles, is transformed into a miraculous two-hundred-year-old figure.

Because Roland is the victim of a treacherous betrayal, his demise is narrated far more dramatically than history could ever have witnessed.

About *The Nibelungenlied*

Composed more than 800 years ago by a now-unknown author, *The Nibelungenlied* (nē′ bə lo͝oŋ′ ən lēt′) is one of the great works of German literature. The name means "song of the Nibelungs," a term that is sometimes used in the poem as another name for Burgundians.

Love and Deception *The Nibelungenlied* is a tragedy in two parts. The first part describes the life and death of Siegfried, who falls in love with the lovely Burgundian princess Kriemhild. The second part of the tragedy features the vengeance of Kriemhild after Siegfried's murder.

A Window Into History Scholars believe that elements of the story reflect historical facts. For example, the destruction of the Burgundians was inspired by the overthrow of the Burgundian kingdom by the Huns in A.D. 437. Likewise, the story of Brunhild and Siegfried may have been inspired by actual events that took place among the Franks around A.D. 600.

With its potent combination of romance, power, betrayal, and violence, *The Nibelungenlied* has survived the ages and inspired numerous adaptations and dramatizations, including Richard Wagner's famous four-part opera, *The Ring of the Nibelung* (1874).

Preview

Connecting to the Literature

Hollywood movies portray action heroes as infallible. While Roland and Siegfried, the champions in these stories, are prototypes of the modern action hero, they show that being heroic does not mean being perfect.

Standard Course of Study

- Build knowledge of literary genres, and explore how characteristics apply to literature of world cultures. (LT.5.01.2)
- Understand the cultural and historical impact on world literature texts. (LT.5.01.7)

2 Literary Analysis

Medieval Epic

Medieval epics originated in the great halls of the Germanic tribes and focused on ideas, such as loyalty and valor, that bound societies together. In addition, medieval epics

- defined and expressed the character of a people.
- were based on historical events but prized adventure more than accuracy.
- were performed long before they were written down.

The early Germanic epics dealt with conflicts between traditional beliefs and the tribes' newfound Christianity. However, as the tribes migrated southward, epics were altered to address a different threat—the religion of Islam. With Muslims settled in Spain and southern France, Christendom felt menaced. As you read, identify the values these stories express.

Comparing Literary Works

The **epic hero** is a person of extraordinary abilities who represents a culture's highest values. In most epics, the hero also possesses a **heroic flaw**—a defect of character that may lead to suffering or even death. As you read, compare the ways in which both Roland and Siegfried exemplify the highest values of their cultures, and identify the flaw in each that leads to his demise.

3 Reading Strategy

Recognizing Feudal Values

Feudalism was the economic, political, and social system of medieval Europe. Under the feudal system, serfs worked the land, which was held by vassals, who took oaths of loyalty to their lords. The society emphasized the warrior virtues of military prowess, loyalty, and honor. As you read, use a chart like the one shown to identify **feudal values.**

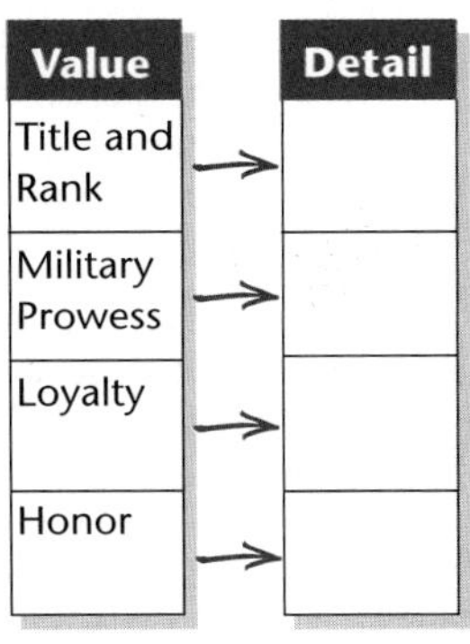

Vocabulary Builder

vassal (vas′ əl) *n.* person who holds land under the feudal system, pledging loyalty to an overlord (p. 602)

prowess (prou′ is) *n.* ability (p. 602)

exulting (eg zult′ iŋ) *v.* rejoicing (p. 602)

unrestrained (un ri strānd′) *v.* not checked or controlled (p. 611)

malice (mal′ is) *n.* ill will; spite (p. 611)

sinister (sin′ is tər) *adj.* wicked; threatening harm (p. 611)

intrepid (in trep′ id) *adj.* brave; fearless (p. 612)

thwarted (thwôrt′ əd) *v.* hindered; frustrated (p. 613)

Differentiated Instruction — Solutions for All Learners

Support for Special Needs Students
Have students complete the **Preview** and **Build Skills** pages for these selections in the ***Reader's Notebook: Adapted Version.*** These pages provide a selection summary, an abbreviated presentation of the reading and literary skills, and the graphic organizer on the **Build Skills** page in the student book.

Support for Less Proficient Readers
Have students complete the **Preview** and **Build Skills** pages for these selections in the ***Reader's Notebook.*** These pages provide a selection summary, an abbreviated presentation of the reading and literary skills, and the graphic organizer on the **Build Skills** page in the student book.

Support for English Learners
Have students complete the **Preview** and **Build Skills** pages for these selections in the ***Reader's Notebook: English Learner's Version.*** These pages provide a selection summary, an abbreviated presentation of the skills, additional contextual vocabulary, and the graphic organizer on the **Build Skills** page in the student book.

2 Literary Analysis

Medieval Epic

- Read aloud and discuss with students the characteristics of the medieval epic. Remind students that an epic is a long, narrative poem in which characters of high birth or national status are engaged in a quest, a series of adventures important to the history of a nation or race.
- Read aloud the Comparing Literary Works instruction. Have students **recall** other epic heroes about whom they have read.
- **Possible response:** Achilles, Hector, and Aeneas are possible heroes.
- Explain to students that in the medieval epic, the heroic image serves something larger than the individual. Unlike the heroes of earlier epics, the heroes of medieval epics do not fight for the glory of their own names.
- Emphasize that the epic hero is an incomplete person, usually dominated by one emotion and incapable of a reasonable consideration of the problems at hand. The epic hero leaps into action without careful thought.

3 Reading Strategy

Recognizing Feudal Values

- After reading aloud the Reading Strategy instruction, explain to students that feudalism was the mortar that held medieval European society together.
- Explain the use of the graphic organizer. Then, give students a copy of **Reading Strategy Graphic Organizer A,** p. 109 in ***Graphic Organizer Transparencies.*** As students read, have them use the organizer to record details that illustrate the value of title and rank, military prowess, loyalty, and honor to people of the Middle Ages.

Vocabulary Builder

- Pronounce each vocabulary word for students, and read the definitions as a class. Have students identify any words with which they are already familiar.

TEACH

Facilitate Understanding

Ask students to think of modern heroes who are flawed. Encourage them to name champions or winners of various contests. Then, ask them how some of these outstanding individuals also suffer from the pride or impatience that tainted the personalities of classical heroes.

❶ About the Selection

This excerpt from the *Song of Roland* beautifully illustrates many of the values of the Middle Ages: the importance of valor and bravery in fighting; the need for loyalty and devotion to one's lord and one's land; the difficulty of finding trustworthy followers. Roland's faults, as well as his virtues, go a long way toward making him an ideal knight: fiercely loyal to his king and brave in any combat with the enemy. He also shows his weakness through pride. *The Song of Roland,* ending as it does with the hero's death, explores the contradictions of the hero's role.

❷ Critical Viewing

Possible response: The illustration does not glorify war because it depicts chaos and death, however cartoonishly.

from the Song of Roland ❶

translated by **Frederick Goldin**

Background After seven years of war between the French Christians and the Spanish Muslims, or Saracens, a single Muslim stronghold remains—the city of Saragossa, which is ruled by King Marsile. Certain of his own defeat, Marsile sends a message to King Charlemagne saying that he will convert to Christianity and become Charlemagne's vassal if the French will leave Spain. (Once Charlemagne is gone, however, Marsile intends to break his promises.) Roland, Charlemagne's greatest knight, suggests that his stepfather, Ganelon, serve as the emissary to Marsile to discuss the offer. Ganelon perceives this nomination for the perilous mission as a thinly veiled attempt at his murder. He accepts the mission but then plots with Marsile to defeat the French by ambushing Charlemagne's rear guard, which Ganelon knows will be led by Roland.

Ganelon returns to Charlemagne with assurances of Marsile's good faith, and they organize the departure from Spain. As Ganelon promised, Roland is chosen to lead the rear guard, which also includes the Twelve Peers—Charlemagne's most beloved vassals—the Archbishop Turpin, and Oliver, Roland's best friend. All told, the French rear guard constitutes a force of 20,000 men, but at the pass of Roncevalles, the rear guard meets a Saracen force numbering in the hundreds of thousands. Oliver begs Roland to blow his horn, the Olifant, to call back Charlemagne's main army, but Roland refuses, saying,

"I'd be a fool to do it.
I would lose my good name all through sweet France.
I will strike now, I'll strike with Durendal,
the blade will be bloody to the gold from striking!
These pagan traitors came to these passes doomed!
I promise you, they are marked men, they'll die."

This excerpt begins as Roland, Oliver, and the rest of the French rear guard face the massive Saracen army.

❷ **Critical Viewing ▶** Do you think this medieval illustration of Roland's battle glorifies war? Why or why not? **[Make a Judgment]**

Differentiated Instruction — Solutions for All Learners

Accessibility at a Glance

	from the Song of Roland	*from* The Niebelungenlied How Seigfried Was Slain
Context	The eighth-century war between French Christians and Saracens	Rituals of hunting and its reflection of feudal values
Language	Lyrical poetic elements: alliteration, assonance, consonance	Narrative prose with many action verbs and vivid adjectives
Concept Level	Accessible (Disaster of pride)	Accessible (Power of treachery)
Literary Merit	Medieval epic poem	Medieval epic poem
Lexile	NP	1110L
Overall Rating	Challenging	Challenging

110

The battle is fearful and full of grief.
Oliver and Roland strike like good men,
the Archbishop, more than a thousand blows,
and the Twelve Peers do not hang back, they strike!
the French fight side by side, all as one man.
The pagans die by hundreds, by thousands:
whoever does not flee finds no refuge from death,
like it or not, there he ends all his days.
And there the men of France lose their greatest arms;
they will not see their fathers, their kin again,
or Charlemagne, who looks for them in the passes.
Tremendous torment now comes forth in France,
a mighty whirlwind, tempests of wind and thunder,
rains and hailstones, great and immeasurable,
bolts of lightning hurtling and hurtling down:
it is, in truth, a trembling of the earth.
From Saint Michael-in-Peril to the Saints,
from Besançon to the port of Wissant,[1]
there is no house whose veil of walls does not crumble.
A great darkness at noon falls on the land,
there is no light but when the heavens crack.
No man sees this who is not terrified,
and many say: "The Last Day! Judgment Day!

Literary Analysis

Medieval Epic In what ways does this description of the battle suggest both the tribal origins of this epic and the values of military prowess?

Reading Check

What is the nature of the battle at Roncesvalles?

1. **Saint Michael-in-Peril . . . Saints . . . Besançon** (bə zän sōn′) **. . . Wissant** (wə sän′) four points marking out tenth-century France.

Battle of Ronceveaux and the Death of Roland, Giraudon

Differentiated Instruction Solutions for All Learners

Support for Special Needs Students

Because this selection is an excerpt, some of the characters are not introduced or well developed. Help students understand the epic better by having them identify each of the characters mentioned. List the names and discuss each character, guiding students as they suggest a brief sentence or two that reminds them of who these characters are and why they are important. Leave the descriptions on the board so that students can refer back to them as they read.

Support for Advanced Readers

Point out to students that the *Song of Roland* was meant to be read aloud. Even in translation, it has rich musical elements. On the board, write the terms *alliteration, consonance,* and *assonance,* and explain them to students. Then, read stanza 110 aloud, pausing to point out examples of these devices. (Possible examples: alliteration: "*f*earful and *f*ull"; consonance: "stri*k*e li*k*e"; assonance: "f*ea*rful and full of gr*ie*f.") Discuss how these devices add a lyrical effect to the poem.

3 Literary Analysis

Medieval Epic

- Remind students that the medieval epic focuses on ideals such as loyalty, valor, and military prowess. Then, read aloud the bracketed passage. Have students **characterize** the French forces on the basis of this description.
  Answer: The French are powerful, unified, and fearsome.
- Then, **ask** students the Literary Analysis question: In what ways does this description of the battle suggest both the tribal origins of this epic and the values of military prowess?
  Answer: The passage describes the French forces as fighting "side by side," which indicates their close, tribelike relationship. In addition, the French knights are described as relentless, which earns them the title of "good men."

4 Reading Check

Answer: The battle is violent and deadly. The French fight bravely and kill many thousands of the enemy.

5 Humanities

The Battle of Roncevaux and the Death of Roland, from the French illuminated manuscript, *The History of the Emperors*

An *illumination* is an illustration that forms part of a medieval manuscript. Before the days of the printing press, all texts were manuscripts—that is, handwritten—and illuminations were one-of-a-kind handpainted decorations. In this illustration, the feverish battle scene contrasts with the delicately painted rock formations and lacy trees of the landscape. The lively rhythm of the figures in motion is a trademark of the Gothic style of painting.

Use the following question for discussion:

Do you think this is a realistic portrayal of medieval warfare?
Possible response: The portrayal is not realistic because the characters are stiff and pale.

6 Literary Analysis

Medieval Epic and Epic Heroes

- Remind students that an epic focuses on one heroic man and his impact on a great cause or event in history. The battle depicted in this selection is important partly because it is part of a larger war and also because it causes the death of the hero. **Ask** students to identify the cause of this larger war.
  Answer: The cause of the larger war was the conflict between Christianity and Islam for control of Europe.
- Have students read independently the bracketed passage that begins on p. 601. Then, **ask** students to respond to the Literary Analysis item: The poet associates the death of Roland with the chaos of the end of the world. What does this suggest about the importance of Roland, the epic hero?
  Answer: The association suggests that Roland was an extremely important Christian warrior. It further suggests that Roland acts as a symbol for Christianity and feudal values and that these institutions—as well as the fate of the world—are in jeopardy as a result of Roland's death.

7 Reading Strategy

Recognizing Feudal Values

- Review with students the Reading Strategy instruction on p. 599.
- Have volunteers take turns reading aloud the bracketed passage. Then, **ask** students the Reading Strategy question: What lesson about being a good vassal does Oliver point out to Roland?
  Answer: Oliver wants Roland to understand that being a good vassal means protecting those in his charge, not sacrificing them in a show of his own courage.

▶ **Reteach** If students have difficulty answering the Reading Strategy question, use the **Reading Strategy** support, p. 12 in ***Unit 5 Resources,*** to help them identify feudal values.

6
The end! The end of the world is upon us!"
They do not know, they do not speak the truth:
it is the worldwide grief for the death of Roland.

130

And Roland says: "We are in a rough battle.
I'll sound the olifant,[2] Charles will hear it."
Said Oliver: "No good vassal would do it.
When I urged it, friend, you did not think it right.
If Charles were here, we'd come out with no losses.
Those men down there—no blame can fall on them."
Oliver said: "Now by this beard of mine,
If I can see my noble sister, Aude,[3]
once more, you will never lie in her arms!" AOI.[4]

131

And Roland said: "Why are you angry at me?"
7
Oliver answers: "Companion, it is your doing.
I will tell you what makes a vassal good:
it is judgment, it is never madness;
restraint is worth more than the raw nerve of a fool.
Frenchmen are dead because of your wildness.
And what service will Charles ever have from us?
If you had trusted me, my lord would be here,
we would have fought this battle through to the end,
Marsilion would be dead, or our prisoner.
Roland, your prowess—had we never seen it!
And now, dear friend, we've seen the last of it.
No more aid from us now for Charlemagne,
a man without equal till Judgment Day,
you will die here, and your death will shame France.
We kept faith, you and I, we were companions;
and everything we were will end today.
We part before evening, and it will be hard." AOI.

132

Turpin the Archbishop hears their bitter words,
digs hard into his horse with golden spurs
and rides to them; begins to set them right:
"You, Lord Roland, and you, Lord Oliver,
I beg you in God's name do not quarrel.
To sound the horn could not help us now, true,
but still it is far better that you do it:
let the King come, he can avenge us then—
these men of Spain must not go home exulting!

Literary Analysis
Medieval Epic and Epic Heroes The poet associates the death of Roland with the chaos of the end of the world. What does this suggest about the importance of Roland, the epic hero?

Vocabulary Builder
vassal (vas′ əl) *n.* person who holds land under the feudal system, pledging loyalty to an overlord

prowess (prou′ is) *n.* ability

Reading Strategy
Recognizing Feudal Values What lesson about being a good vassal does Oliver point out to Roland?

Vocabulary Builder
exulting (eg zult′ iŋ) *v.* rejoicing

2. **olifant** Roland's horn, the name of which derives from the word *elephant* because it was carved from a tusk.
3. **Aude** (ōd) Roland's intended bride.
4. **AOI:** These three mysterious letters appear at certain points throughout the text, 180 times in all. No one has ever adequately explained them.

Enrichment

Paradox in the *Song of Roland*

Throughout the *Song of Roland,* and in epic poetry in general, hyperbole and exaggerations are used. Frequently, Charlemagne's age is overdrawn. The reasons for such figures of speech are part of the preservation of the epic form in an almost self-conscious gesture. In the case of Charlemagne's age, it was a popular myth to believe that the king lived for hundreds of years. It is also a comment on the epic form itself. The *Song of Roland,* like many epics, serves two paradoxical functions: The work is both "timely"—describing a specific historical moment—and "timeless"—enduring forever as the story is told and retold, holding lasting interest and value. The singers or composers of the tale were aware that they were singing an old song.

Our French will come, they'll get down on their feet,
and find us here—we'll be dead, cut to pieces.
They will lift us into coffins on the backs of mules,
and weep for us, in rage and pain and grief,
and bury us in the courts of churches;
and we will not be eaten by wolves or pigs or dogs."
Roland replies, "Lord, you have spoken well." AOI.

133

Roland has put the olifant to his mouth,
he sets it well, sounds it with all his strength.
The hills are high, and that voice ranges far,
they heard it echo thirty great leagues away.
King Charles heard it, and all his faithful men.
And the King says: "Our men are in a battle."
And Ganelon disputed him and said:
"Had someone else said that, I'd call him liar!" AOI.

134

And now the mighty effort of Roland the Count:
he sounds his olifant; his pain is great,
and from his mouth the bright blood comes leaping out,
and the temple bursts in his forehead.
That horn, in Roland's hands, has a mighty voice:
King Charles hears it drawing through the passes.
Naimon heard it, the Franks listen to it.
And the King said: "I hear Count Roland's horn;
he'd never sound it unless he had a battle."
8 Says Ganelon: "Now no more talk of battles!
You are old now, your hair is white as snow,
the things you say make you sound like a child.
You know Roland and that wild pride of his—
what a wonder God has suffered it so long!
Remember? he took Noples without your command:
the Saracens rode out, to break the siege;
they fought with him, the great vassal Roland.
Afterward he used the streams to wash the blood
from the meadows: so that nothing would show.
He blasts his horn all day to catch a rabbit,
he's strutting now before his peers and bragging—
who under heaven would dare meet him on the field?
So now: ride on! Why do you keep on stopping?
The Land of Fathers lies far ahead of us." AOI.

135

The blood leaping from Count Roland's mouth,
the temple broken with effort in his forehead,
he sounds his horn in great travail and pain.
King Charles heard it, and his French listen hard.
10 And the King said: "That horn has a long breath!"

9 
Reading Check
Why is Oliver mad at Roland?

8 Critical Thinking

Draw Conclusions

- Remind students that a reader must use information from the text and what he or she knows to draw a conclusion.
- Read aloud the bracketed passage. Then, **ask** students how they would characterize Ganelon's attitude toward King Charles.
  Answer: Ganelon's attitude toward King Charles is one of disrespect.
- **Ask:** On the basis of the passage, what can you conclude about the characters of King Charles and Ganelon?
  Possible response: King Charles is a good and loyal king who recognizes his duty to protect his vassal, Roland. Ganelon is an evil and scheming individual who does not value loyalty or honor.

9 Reading Check

Answer: Roland, out of pride, has gotten Oliver into a battle he and the other French knights will not survive.

Differentiated Instruction Solutions for All Learners

Enrichment for Gifted/Talented Students

Have students create illustrations that depict the action on these two pages. Encourage students to reread these pages and take notes on the visual details they will include in their illustrations. Students can even create a multiple-framed comic strip with captions to show the progression of events. When students have finished their illustrations, ask them to share their work with the class and explain their artistic intent.

Enrichment for Advanced Readers

Remind students that the *Song of Roland* is fiction but that it is based on historic fact. Tell students to review the selection and identify details that they believe to be fact and those that they believe to be fiction. Have them discuss the reasons for their choices. Then, ask them to do research using library resources or the Internet to learn more about the history of this conflict between the French and the Moors. Initiate a panel discussion in which students share their findings with the class.

10 Reading Strategy

Recognizing Feudal Values

- Ask a volunteer to read aloud the bracketed passage. Then, have students **explain** the feudal values that Naimon is exhibiting in the passage.
  Answer: Naimon is exhibiting loyalty to Roland by urging King Charles to return and help Roland. Naimon is exhibiting loyalty to King Charles because he is counseling him wisely. He is exhibiting a willingness to go into battle to fight for his king and for honor.
- **Ask** students the Reading Strategy question: What is the fundamental feudal value that Ganelon has violated?
  Answer: Ganelon has shown loyalty neither to Roland nor to King Charles.

11 Humanities

Roland

This illustration provides a romantic interpretation of the later moments of the confrontation at Roncesvalles. In contrast to the manuscript illumination on p. 601, this depiction is highly detailed and realistic.

Use the following questions for discussion:

- Does this depiction of Roland blowing his olifant correspond with what you visualized while reading the poem? Explain.
  Possible response: No; Oliver and the Archbishop do not appear to be present.
- Does the setting of the painting match the setting of the poem?
  Answer: Yes; the action takes place high in the Pyrenees, which are shown in the illustration.

12 Critical Viewing

Possible response: Roland is powerfully built, and his head is lifted high as he blows on the olifant. He rides proudly on a powerful horse and seems to be fighting alone against the pressing army of Saracens.

10
Naimon answers: "It is a baron's breath.
There is a battle there, I know there is.
He betrayed him! and now asks you to fail him!
Put on your armor! Lord, shout your battle cry,
and save the noble barons of your house!
You hear Roland's call. He is in trouble."

136

The Emperor commanded the horns to sound,
the French dismount, and they put on their armor:
their hauberks, their helmets, their gold-dressed swords,
their handsome shields; and take up their great lances,
the gonfalons of white and red and blue.
The barons of that host mount their war horses
and spur them hard the whole length of the pass;

Reading Strategy
Recognizing Feudal Values What is the fundamental feudal value that Ganelon has violated?

11

12 ◀ **Critical Viewing** Which details in this image help portray Roland as a heroic figure? **[Analyze]**

Enrichment

Oral Traditions

In A.D. 1066, a fleet of Norman knights set sail for England under the leadership of their duke, William, in order to settle a dispute with Harold, king of England. William met and defeated Harold in battle on the field at Hastings. In a twelfth-century history of the Norman conquest of England, the historian Wace writes of a *jongleur,* or minstrel, named Taillefer who, while riding at the head of William's army, led the Norman knights into battle singing "of Charlemagne and of Roland and of Olivier and of the vassals who died at Roncesvalles." Taillefer was, of course, referring to Charles the Great of France and to events that had occurred almost three hundred years earlier. He was singing a version of the *Song of Roland*—perhaps not the same version as the poem we read today, but very likely something similar.

and every man of them says to the other:
"If only we find Roland before he's killed,
we'll stand with him, and then we'll do some fighting!"
What does it matter what they say? They are too late.

138

High are the hills, and tenebrous,[5] and vast, AOI.
the valleys deep, the raging waters swift;
to the rear, to the front, the trumpets sound:
13 they answer the lone voice of the olifant.
The Emperor rides on, rides on in fury,
the men of France in grief and indignation.
There is no man who does not weep and wail,
and they pray God: protect the life of Roland
till they come, one great host, into the field
and fight at Roland's side like true men all.
What does it matter what they pray? It does no good.
They are too late, they cannot come in time. AOI.

Literary Analysis
Medieval Epic Which details in stanzas 136 and 138 suggest that this poem was originally performed before live audiences?

156

Roland the Count fights well and with great skill,
but he is hot, his body soaked with sweat;
has a great wound in his head, and much pain,
his temple broken because he blew the horn.
But he must know whether King Charles will come;
draws out the olifant, sounds it, so feebly.
The Emperor drew to a halt, listened.
"Seigneurs," he said, "it goes badly for us—
My nephew Roland falls from our ranks today.
I hear it in the horn's voice: he hasn't long.
Let every man who wants to be with Roland
ride fast! Sound trumpets! Every trumpet in this host!"
Sixty thousand, on these words, sound, so high
the mountains sound, and the valleys resound.
The pagans hear: it is no joke to them;
cry to each other: "We're getting Charles on us!"

160

Say the pagans: "We were all born unlucky!
The evil day that dawned for us today!
We have lost our lords and peers, and now comes Charles—
that Charlemagne!—with his great host. Those trumpets!
that shrill sound on us—the trumpets of the French!
And the loud roar of that Munjoie! This Roland
14 is a wild man, he is too great a fighter—
What man of flesh and blood can ever hope
to bring him down? Let us cast at him, and leave him there."

Literary Analysis
Medieval Epic and Heroic Flaw In what ways does the description of Roland as a "wild man" have elements of truth? Explain.

15  **Reading Check**
What truth about Roland's situation does Charlemagne hear in the "horn's voice"?

5. **tenebrous** (ten′ ə brəs) *adj.* dark; gloomy.

13 Literary Analysis
Medieval Epic

- Remind students that the medieval epic focuses on ideas that bound medieval societies together, such as loyalty and valor.
- Have students read the bracketed passage that begins on the previous page. **Ask:** What do you learn about the character of the soldiers in the French army from the description in this passage?
Answer: They are loyal to Roland, courageous going into battle, and sensitive in the face of the tragic loss of a leader.
- **Ask** students the first Literary Analysis question: Which details in stanzas 136 and 138 suggest that this poem was originally performed before live audiences?
Answer: The many descriptive details would help an audience visualize the scene, and these details are presented very clearly, almost methodically. The sensory detail of the horns sounding would also provide an opportunity for a dramatic performance.

14 Literary Analysis
Medieval Epic and Heroic Flaw

- Review with students the Comparing Literary Works instruction on p. 599. Remind them that a character's flaw can be his or her pride, vanity, selfishness, or any other trait that brings about the hero's downfall.
- Then, **ask** students the second Literary Analysis question: In what ways does the description of Roland as a "wild man" have elements of truth? Explain.
Answer: Roland acts without thinking, as he did when he charged into battle with the Saracens without calling for King Charles's aid.

15 Reading Check

Answer: When Charlemagne hears the feebleness of Roland's olifant, he knows that Roland is injured and near death.

Differentiated Instruction — Solutions for All Learners

Support for Less Proficient Readers
Tell students that many phrases in the *Song of Roland* are brought together in juxtaposition through the use of colons and semicolons. Then, explain that the colon can introduce a list after an independent clause, introduce quotations, introduce summative remarks, and introduce an appositive following an independent clause. The semicolon joins independent clauses that express similar or contrasting ideas. Guide students to identify in the selection uses of the colon and the semicolon and discuss the purpose and effect of each use.

Enrichment for Gifted/Talented Students
Remind students that the *Song of Roland* was intended for recital and was influenced by an oral tradition. Invite students to revive this tradition by giving an oral presentation of a passage from the *Song of Roland.* Tell them to memorize their passage and practice its recitation. Remind students to use appropriate gestures and tone of voice to convey the emotion of the action taking place. Then, have students present their passages to the class.

16 Critical Thinking

Analyze

- Read aloud the bracketed passage. **Ask:** Why do the pagans flee in "bitterness and rage"?
  Answer: The pagans are bitter and enraged because they have not killed Roland in spite of their great efforts and overwhelming numbers. They realize that they must now contend with King Charles.
- **Ask** students: How do the details in this stanza reinforce Roland's heroic status?
  Answer: Despite his injuries, Roland rushes to the aid of Archbishop Turpin. With this action, Roland demonstrates the qualities of loyalty and honor, which are so often attributed to heroes.

17 Background

Weaponry

It was customary for Medieval European heroes to name their swords (such as King Arthur's sword, Excalibur). The custom was a sign of how much the hero relied upon his sword and what a great loss it was if a sword were destroyed or taken in battle. Medieval swords were forged with great skill, and fighters no doubt preferred swords whose weight and balance they were accustomed to.

And so they did: arrows, wigars, darts,
lances and spears, javelots dressed with feathers;
struck Roland's shield, pierced it, broke it to pieces,
ripped his hauberk, shattered its rings of mail,
but never touched his body, never his flesh.
They wounded Veillantif in thirty places,
struck him dead, from afar, under the Count.
The pagans flee, they leave the field to him.
Roland the Count stood alone, on his feet.[6] AOI.

161

The pagans flee, in bitterness and rage,
strain every nerve running headlong toward Spain,
and Count Roland has no way to chase them,
he has lost Veillantif, his battle horse;
he has no choice, left alone there on foot.
He went to the aid of Archbishop Turpin,
unlaced the gold-dressed helmet, raised it from his head,
lifted away his bright, light coat of mail,
cut his under tunic into some lengths,
16 stilled his great wounds with thrusting on the strips;
then held him in his arms, against his chest,
and laid him down, gently, on the green grass;
and softly now Roland entreated him:
"My noble lord, I beg you, give me leave:
our companions, whom we have loved so dearly,
are all dead now, we must not abandon them.
I want to look for them, know them once more,
and set them in ranks, side by side, before you."
Said the Archbishop: "Go then, go and come back.
The field is ours, thanks be to God, yours and mine."

168

Now Roland feels that death is very near.
His brain comes spilling out through his two ears;
prays to God for his peers: let them be called;
and for himself, to the angel Gabriel;
took the olifant: there must be no reproach!
17 took Durendal his sword in his other hand,
and farther than a crossbow's farthest shot
he walks toward Spain, into a fallow land,[7]
and climbs a hill: there beneath two fine trees
stand four great blocks of stone, all are of marble;
and he fell back, to earth, on the green grass,
has fainted there, for death is very near.

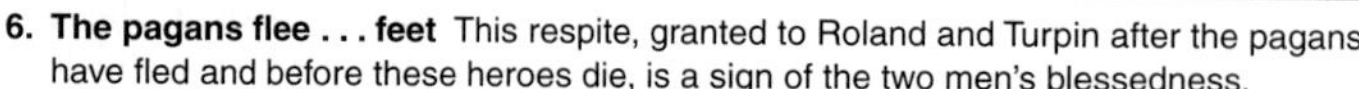

6. **The pagans flee . . . feet** This respite, granted to Roland and Turpin after the pagans have fled and before these heroes die, is a sign of the two men's blessedness.
7. **fallow land** land plowed but not seeded for one or more growing seasons.

Enrichment

Medieval Instruments

Epics such as the *Song of Roland* flourished at a time when oral transmission was the only way in which a poet could guarantee that he or she would be heard. The *jongleur,* or minstrel, would stand in a public square and sing or chant the poem, perhaps accompanying himself or herself on a type of fiddle or harp.

Other instruments played in the Middle Ages include those of the viol family—a family of stringed instruments played with bows. Viols have soft, sweet tones and a far gentler sound than their descendant, the violin. A viol is usually played upright, with the instrument resting on the musician's knees and the bow held with the palm upward.

Other medieval instruments included the lute and the psaltery, ancestors of the banjo and guitar, whose strings were plucked. Various wind instruments and horns were also played during the Middle Ages.

169

High are the hills, and high,
 high are the trees;
there stand four blocks of
 stone, gleaming of marble.
Count Roland falls fainting on
 the green grass,
and is watched, all this time, by
 a Saracen:
who has feigned death and lies
 now with the others,
has smeared blood on his face
 and on his body;
and quickly now gets to his feet
 and runs—
a handsome man, strong,
 brave, and so crazed with
 pride
that he does something mad
 and dies for it:
laid hands on Roland, and on
 the arms of Roland,
and cried: "Conquered!
 Charles's nephew conquered!
I'll carry this sword home to Arabia!"
As he draws it, the Count begins to come round.

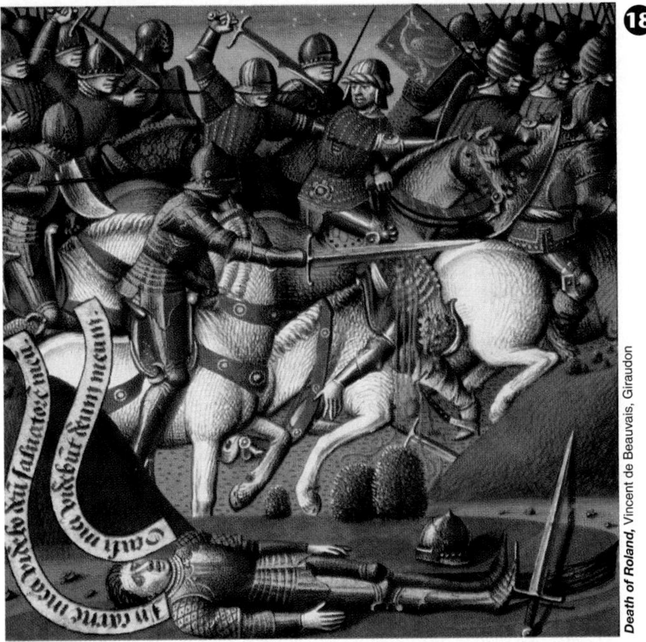
18

Death of Roland, Vincent de Beauvais, Giraudon

170

20
Now Roland feels: *someone taking his sword!*
opened his eyes, and had one word for him:
"I don't know you, you aren't one of ours";
grasps that olifant that he will never lose,
strikes on the helm beset with gems in gold,
shatters the steel, and the head, and the bones,
sent his two eyes flying out of his head,
dumped him over stretched out at his feet dead;
and said: "You nobody! how could you dare
lay hands on me—rightly or wrongly: how?
Who'll hear of this and not call you a fool?
Ah! the bell-mouth of the olifant is smashed,
the crystal and the gold fallen away."

171

Now Roland the Count feels: his sight is gone;
gets on his feet, draws on his final strength,
the color on his face lost now for good.
Before him stands a rock; and on that dark rock
in rage and bitterness he strikes ten blows:
the steel blade grates, it will not break, it stands unmarked.

19 ▲ **Critical Viewing**
Which details from the epic appear in this medieval illustration of the death of Roland? **[Connect]**

Literary Analysis
Medieval Epic What quality of the medieval epic is suggested by Roland's words, "you aren't one of ours"?

21 ✓ **Reading Check**
What object does a Saracen try to take from Roland?

18 Humanities

Death of Roland

This is another illumination that depicts the battle in which Roland dies. It was found in a fifteenth-century French manuscript. The full fury of the conflict is fashioned in such a way that the viewer cannot help but become engaged in the turmoil.

Use the following question for discussion:

On the basis of this picture, how do you think the artist feels about death in battle? Explain.
Possible response: Death is graphically but not painfully portrayed, so the artist must feel that death in battle is honorable.

19 Critical Viewing

Answer: The illustration conveys the brutality of the battle and shows Roland lying on the grass with his sword, Durendal.

20 Literary Analysis

Medieval Epic

- **Ask** students to read the bracketed passage independently and then paraphrase what is happening.
  Possible response: As Roland is lying on the ground, he feels someone trying to steal Durendal. Roland rouses and dispatches the offending Saracen by striking him with the olifant. Roland then admonishes the dead man for his gall and foolishness.
- **Ask** students the Literary Analysis question: What quality of the medieval epic is suggested by Roland's words, "you aren't one of ours"?
  Answer: These words indicate a solidarity or loyalty among forces. Roland recognizes that the Moor does not share his beliefs and thus is disloyal.

21 Reading Check

Answer: A Saracen tries to take Roland's sword.

Differentiated Instruction Solutions for All Learners

Support for English Learners

Point out the word *mail* on p. 606. Explain to students that as a noun, this word has several meanings. It can mean "something sent or carried in the postal system" or "armor made of metal links." Make sure that students understand that the word *mail* is a homograph, or one of two or more words that are spelled alike but have different meanings, derivations, or pronunciations. Encourage students to suggest other homographs, and record their suggestions on the board.

Enrichment for Gifted/Talented Students

Have students find music to accompany this poem. Encourage them first to review the text they have read thus far to identify key events or turning points. Also, have students brainstorm a list of moods evoked by the poem. Remind students that their musical selections should reflect both the action of the poem and the appropriate moods. Then, make available to students a cassette or CD player, and ask volunteers to present their musical selections to the class.

㉒ Reading Strategy

Recognizing Feudal Values

- Remind students that under the feudal system, military prowess, loyalty, and honor were valued.
- Read aloud the bracketed passage. Point out to students that Roland's sword contains sacred relics. Discuss the great value that people of the Middle Ages placed on such relics and the faith they had in them.
  Ask: What do these holy relics symbolize?
  Answer: These relics symbolize faith and Christianity as a whole.
- Then, **ask** students the Reading Strategy question: In what ways does Roland's concern for his sword demonstrate the feudal value of military prowess?
  Answer: By imbuing Durendal with spiritual significance, this epic shows that military prowess is next to godliness. Roland's concern for his sword demonstrates not only his interest in preserving his own reputation as a warrior but also his concern for preserving Christianity and the Christian cause. Military prowess is also an extension of Christian loyalty. This is evidenced when Roland says, "your power must not fall to the pagans."

➤ **Monitor Progress Ask** students: Does Roland exhibit feudal values? Explain.
Answer: Roland does exhibit feudal values through his loyalty to Charlemagne and his honorable character. He also demonstrates the feudal value of military prowess through his skill as a warrior and his concern for his sword.

"Ah!" said the Count, "Blessed Mary, your help!
Ah Durendal, good sword, your unlucky day,
for I am lost and cannot keep you in my care.
The battles I have won, fighting with you,
the mighty lands that holding you I conquered,
that Charles rules now, our King, whose beard is white!
Now you fall to another: it must not be
 a man who'd run before another man!
For a long while a good vassal held you:
there'll never be the like in France's holy land."

173

Roland the Count strikes down on a dark rock,
and the rock breaks, breaks more than I can tell,
and the blade grates, but Durendal will not break,
the sword leaped up, rebounded toward the sky.
The Count, when he sees that sword will not be broken,
softly, in his own presence, speaks the lament:
"Ah Durendal, beautiful, and most sacred,
the holy relics in this golden pommel!
㉒ Saint Peter's tooth and blood of Saint Basile,
a lock of hair of my lord Saint Denis,
and a fragment of blessed Mary's robe:[8]
your power must not fall to the pagans,
you must be served by Christian warriors.
May no coward ever come to hold you!
It was with you I conquered those great lands
that Charles has in his keeping, whose beard is white,
the Emperor's lands, that make him rich and strong."

174

Now Roland feels: death coming over him,
death descending from his temples to his heart.
He came running underneath a pine tree
and there stretched out, face down, on the green grass,
lays beneath him his sword and the olifant.
He turned his head toward the Saracen hosts,
and this is why: with all his heart he wants
King Charles the Great and all his men to say,
he died, that noble Count, a conqueror;
makes confession, beats his breast often, so feebly,
offers his glove, for all his sins, to God. AOI.

176

Count Roland lay stretched out beneath a pine;
he turned his face toward the land of Spain,
began to remember many things now:

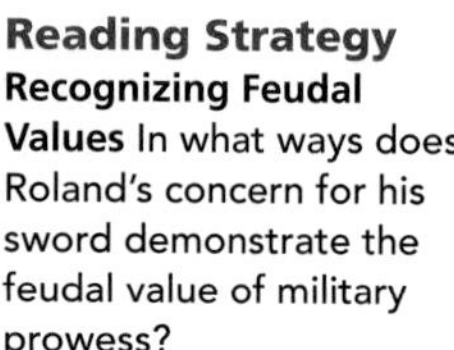

Reading Strategy
Recognizing Feudal Values In what ways does Roland's concern for his sword demonstrate the feudal value of military prowess?

8. **Saint Peter's tooth . . . Mary's robe** Such relics—remains of holy men and women—were thought to have miraculous power.

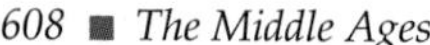

how many lands, brave man, he had conquered;
and he remembered: sweet France, the men of his line,
remembered Charles, his lord, who fostered him:
cannot keep, remembering, from weeping, sighing;
but would not be unmindful of himself:
23 he confesses his sins, prays God for mercy:
"Loyal Father, you who never failed us,
who resurrected Saint Lazarus from the dead,
and saved your servant Daniel from the lions:[9]
now save the soul of me from every peril
for the sins I committed while I still lived."
Then he held out his right glove to his Lord:[10]
Saint Gabriel took the glove from his hand.
He held his head bowed down upon his arm,
he is gone, his two hands joined, to his end.
Then God sent him his angel Cherubin
and Saint Michael, angel of the sea's Peril;
and with these two there came Saint Gabriel:
they bear Count Roland's soul to Paradise.

Reading Strategy
Recognizing Feudal Values Which feudal values does Roland express in his final thoughts? Explain.

9. **Saint Lazarus . . . Daniel from the lions** reference to two famous miracles described in the Bible (John 11:1–44 and Daniel 6:16–23, respectively).
10. **he held out . . . to his Lord** ritual act of resignation to a feudal lord.

Critical Reading

1. **Respond:** If you could speak to Roland as he heads into battle, what advice would you give him?
2. **(a) Recall:** In the second line of stanza 130, what does Roland say he will now do? **(b) Analyze Cause and Effect:** Why does he decide to take this action?
3. **(a) Recall:** According to Oliver, what makes one a good vassal? **(b) Interpret:** According to Oliver, why would Roland not be considered a good vassal?
4. **(a) Recall:** In stanza 171, as he tries to destroy his sword, how does Roland describe himself? **(b) Interpret:** How does Roland seem to feel about the service he has rendered to Charlemagne? **(c) Analyze:** In what ways does this stanza suggest that Roland is undergoing an internal struggle about his own life and identity?
5. **Analyze:** What truth about himself, if any, do you think Roland faces as he lies dying? Explain your answer.
6. **Evaluate:** Would Roland be considered a hero in today's world? Explain your answer.

Differentiated Instruction Solutions for All Learners

Strategy for Special Needs Students

Students may have difficulty with words such as *fostered, unmindful, resurrected,* and *peril.* Have students work in pairs, using dictionaries to find the definitions of these words. Then, guide students to use each word in a sentence, and record these sentences on the board. Encourage students to preview the next selection, *The Nibelungenlied,* to list and define difficult or unfamiliar words. Students can refer to their lists as they read the selection.

Support for Less Proficient Readers

Tell students that in the *Song of Roland,* inanimate objects are sometimes given animate qualities. This technique is called *personification.* For example, in the lines "Now Roland feels: death coming over him, / death descending from his temples to his heart," death is described almost as if it were a person walking down a stairway through the home of Roland's body. Have students identify other examples of personification in the poem.

23 Reading Strategy

Recognizing Feudal Values

- Have volunteers take turns reading aloud the bracketed passage.
- Then, **ask** students the Reading Strategy question: Which feudal values does Roland express in his final thoughts? Explain.
  Answer: Roland remembers his country, his men, and his king. He then remembers God and the saints. To all of these, he owed his loyalty.

ASSESS

Answers

1. **Possible response:** Roland should think before rushing into action. Roland should blow the olifant to call King Charles before the battle begins.
2. (a) Roland says that he will sound the olifant to call King Charles. (b) Roland sees that the battle is hopeless and that he and his men will die if King Charles does not come to their aid.
3. (a) Oliver says that a good vassal uses good judgment and shows restraint. (b) Roland entered the battle out of pride in his military prowess; he did not use good judgment or consider the lives of his men.
4. (a) Roland describes himself as a good vassal who has served his king and country well. (b) He believes that he has served Charlemagne well by fighting for him and gaining new lands for his realm. (c) Roland seems to be coming to grips with his heroic flaw. He probably realizes that he has been too proud and, consequently, has not been the best vassal, but he stifles this realization by boasting.
5. **Possible response:** Roland asks the Lord to forgive his sins, so Roland realizes that he has not lived a perfect life.
6. **Possible response:** Yes; the same reasons that Roland was considered a hero then would apply now. He was a strong, determined, and successful warrior who never turned from or lost a fight.

24 About the Translation

Translators sometimes decide to render poems in prose. This choice can be prompted by linguistic or literary incompatibilities between two languages that make it difficult or impossible to re-create in translation the verse form of the original. Such is the motivation behind A. T. Hatto's prose translation of *The Nibelungenlied.*

In its original medieval German, the epic is a poem composed in stanzas. The system of versification is based on both quantity (relative length of sound) and stress (relative emphasis of sound) in a way that is foreign to English versification, with its reliance on stress. Hatto therefore decided to render the poem in prose rather than try to imitate medieval German prosody. In fact, Hatto doubts that modern German itself could reproduce the versification of medieval German.

In his discussion of previous translations of *The Nibelungenlied* into English prose, Hatto raises another important point: Even the best translation often has a limited life. Because the language of a particular era begins to seem old-fashioned as time passes, each generation must retranslate important works. As Hatto says of a respected earlier prose translation of *The Nibelungenlied:* "The rendering of Margery Armour is the prose that was considered appropriate in her own generation."

25 Humanities

The Hunt,
by Paolo Uccello

Paolo Uccello (1397–1475) was a Florentine painter who was concerned with creating three-dimensional perspective in two dimensions. In *The Hunt,* all the people and animals that are near to the viewer are about the same size, but they gradually get smaller as they recede from the viewer. This technique of depicting space and depth was just appearing during this period.

Use the following question for discussion:

The hunt depicted takes place at night. What is the location of the source of light? Explain.
Answer: The light comes from the left side of the picture, as evidenced by the illuminated left sides of the people and the shadowed right sides.

from *The Nibelungenlied*

24 How Siegfried Was Slain

translated by A. T. Hatto

Background Brave prince Siegfried has proven gifts as a warrior and hero. He has captured a treasure, a fabled sword, and a cloak of invisibility. He has slain a dragon and bathed in its blood, thus becoming almost invincible—just one small spot between his shoulder blades remains vulnerable to attack.

Siegfried has heard of Princess Kriemhild's great beauty and has journeyed to the city of Worms, the capital of Burgundy, to woo her. He enters into the service of her brother, King Gunther. After leading the Burgundian forces in battle, he becomes Gunther's trusted vassal and friend. Using his cloak of invisibility, he also helps Gunther win the hand of Brunhild, a powerful warrior queen. However, Kriemhild reveals the deception, and Brunhild vows revenge. With Hagen, her loyal servant, and Gunther, who appears to have forgotten both his friendship and his debt to Siegfried, Brunhild plots to kill the hero. Kriemhild then makes a terrible mistake by revealing the location of Siegfried's vulnerable spot.

This excerpt describes Siegfried's death, the pivotal point of the epic.

25

The Hunt, Paolo Uccello

Enrichment

Hunting Rituals

Although hunting was necessary for survival in the Middle Ages, it was also a type of ritual with almost religious significance. Noblemen proved their courage and strength by hunting large game. The larger the animal, the greater the prestige of the hunter. In this epic, Siegfried's pursuit of beasts proves he is the greatest hero in the story, in which hunting is a sort of contest, but one in which competing hunters are supposed to cooperate. Thus, hunting reinforces bonds of kinship and friendship.

In medieval literature, hunting often symbolizes the quest for truth. In the hunt, the hero confronts certain aspects of himself and reevaluates his place in society. The heroic hunter prefers to meet his prey in what almost becomes hand-to-hand combat. As he confronts the beast, he confronts his own natural instinct for survival.

The fearless warriors Gunther and Hagen treacherously proclaimed a hunt in the forest where they wished to chase the boar, the bear, and the bison—and what could be more daring? Siegfried rode with their 26 party in magnificent style. They took all manner of food with them; and it was while drinking from a cool stream that the hero was to lose his life at the instigation of Brunhild, King Gunther's queen.

Bold Siegfried went to Kriemhild while his and his companions' hunting-gear was being loaded on to the sumpters in readiness to cross the Rhine,[1] and she could not have been more afflicted. "God grant that I may see you well again, my lady," he said, kissing his dear wife, "and that your eyes may see me too. Pass the time pleasantly with your relations who are so kind to you, since I cannot stay with you at home."

Kriemhild thought of what she had told Hagen, but she dared not mention it and began to lament that she had ever been born. "I dreamt last night—and an ill-omened dream it was—" said lord Siegfried's noble queen, weeping with unrestrained passion, "that two boars chased you over the heath and the flowers were dyed with blood! How can I help weeping so? I stand in great dread of some attempt against 27 your life.—What if we have offended any men who have the power to vent their malice on us? Stay away, my lord, I urge you."

"I shall return in a few days time, my darling. I know of no people here who bear me any hatred. Your kinsmen without exception wish me well, nor have I deserved otherwise of them."

"It is not so, lord Siegfried. I fear you will come to grief. Last night I had a sinister dream of how two mountains fell upon you and hid you

1. **sumpters . . . Rhine** Sumpters are pack horses; the Rhine River flows from eastern Switzerland north through Germany, then west through the Netherlands into the North Sea.

Reading Strategy
Recognizing Feudal Values Which details in this description of the planned hunt reflect the feudal values of bravery, skill with weaponry, and pageantry, or theatrical display? Explain.

Vocabulary Builder

unrestrained (un ri strānd′) *adj.* not checked or controlled

malice (mal′ is) *n.* ill will; spite

sinister (sin′ is tər) *adj.* wicked; threatening harm

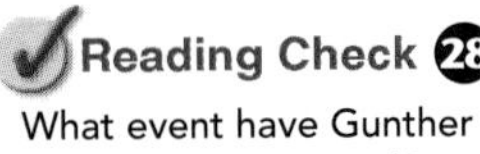

Reading Check 28
What event have Gunther and Hagen organized?

◄ Critical Viewing 29
Based on this image of a medieval hunt, why might such an event spark rivalry or jealousy among the participants? **[Deduce]**

26 Reading Strategy
Recognizing Feudal Values

- Read aloud the bracketed passage. Then, **ask** students why the hunt is described as "daring."
  Answer: The hunt is described as daring both because of the danger associated with hunting wild game and because Gunther and Hagen are using it as a ruse to lure Siegfried to his death.
- Then, **ask** students the Reading Strategy question: Which details in this description of the planned hunt reflect the feudal values of bravery, skill with weaponry, and pageantry, or theatrical display? Explain.
  Answer: The listing of the large game suggests that only the bravest and most skilled hunters can hunt such powerful animals. The scale of the hunt implies that this is a magnificent party worthy of royalty. The hunt itself is theatrical in that Gunther and Hagen have staged it in order to murder Siegfried.

27 Vocabulary Builder
Latin Prefix *mal-*

- Draw students' attention to the word *malice* on this page, and read its definition. Tell students that *malice* contains the prefix *mal-*, meaning "bad." This prefix derives from the Latin word *malus,* which means "evil."
- Have students **discuss** how the prefix *mal-* relates to the meaning of *malice.*
  Answer: *Malice* means "ill will," which is consistent with the word's derivation from *malus,* or "evil."
- **Ask** students to suggest and define other words that contain the prefix *mal-*.
  Possible response: *Malignant, malicious,* or *malevolent* all contain the Latin prefix *mal-*.

28 Reading Check

Answer: Gunther and Hagen have organized a hunt.

29 Critical Viewing

Possible response: The hunt takes place within close quarters, and there is certain to be friction as one hunter impedes another hunter or infringes on another's kill.

Differentiated Instruction
Solutions for All Learners

Support for Special Needs Students
Make sure that students understand that *The Nibelungenlied* is a story about love and treachery. Students may be surprised to find how familiar they already are with this genre. This epic is a bit like the television epics of soap opera fame. Like a medieval *All My Children* or *Days of Our Lives,* this German narrative weaves a tale of abundance and greed. Ask students to discuss why these types of stories are so popular.

Enrichment for Advanced Readers
Explain to students that this translation is a prose version of the original composition, which was a long, narrative poem. There is a long tradition of translating works of poetry into prose. Both the *Song of Roland* and the *Divine Comedy* have been treated in prose. Ask students to find a prose version of the *Song of Roland* or a poetry version of *The Nibelungenlied.* Ask them to compare the prose and poetry.

30 Literary Analysis

Medieval Epic and Epic Heroes

- After reading aloud the bracketed passage, **ask:** Why does Hagen want the hunting group to split up? What does his reason say about the attitude he and the other knights have toward their hunt?
  Answer: Hagen wants the group to split up so that he can accurately gauge their skill as hunters. This reveals that the hunters regard the hunt not as a chance to enjoy the outdoors or to put meat on the table but as a chance to show off their skills.
- **Ask** students the Literary Analysis question: What does Siegfried's comment reveal about his character?
  Answer: Siegfried's claim that he needs only one hound reveals his confidence and arrogance.

31 Background

Language

The word *hart* is a somewhat archaic term for stag, or male deer. *Hind* refers to the doe, or female deer.

from my sight! I shall suffer cruelly if you go away and leave me." But he clasped the noble woman in his arms and after kissing and caressing her fair person very tenderly, took his leave and went forthwith. Alas, she was never to see him alive again.

They rode away deep into the forest in pursuit of their sport. Gunther and his men were accompanied by numbers of brave knights, but Gernot and Giselher stayed at home. Ahead of the hunt many horses had crossed the Rhine laden with their bread, wine, meat, fish, and various other provisions such as a King of Gunther's wealth is bound to have with him.

The proud and intrepid hunters were told to set up their lodges on a spacious isle in the river on which they were to hunt, at the skirt of the greenwood over towards the spot where the game would have to break cover. Siegfried, too, had arrived there, and this was reported to the King. Thereupon the sportsmen everywhere manned their relays.[2]

Vocabulary Builder
intrepid (in trep′ id) *adj.* brave; fearless

"Who is going to guide us through the forest to our quarry, brave warriors?" asked mighty Siegfried.

30 "Shall we split up before we start hunting here?" asked Hagen. "Then my lords and I could tell who are the best hunters on this foray into the woods. Let us share the huntsmen and hounds between us and each take the direction he likes—and then all honor to him that hunts best!" At this, the hunters quickly dispersed.

"I do not need any hounds," said lord Siegfried, "except for one tracker so well fleshed that he recognizes the tracks which the game leave through the wood: then we shall not fail to find our quarry."

Literary Analysis
Medieval Epic and Epic Heroes What does Siegfried's comment reveal about his character?

An old huntsman took a good sleuth-hound and quickly led the lord to where there was game in abundance. The party chased everything that was roused from its lair, as good hunting-men still do today. Bold Siegfried of the Netherlands killed every beast that his hound started, for his hunter was so swift that nothing could elude him. Thus, versatile as he was, Siegfried outshone all the others in that hunt.

The very first kill was when he brought down a strong young tusker,[3] after which he soon chanced on an enormous lion. When his hound had roused it he laid a keen arrow to his bow and shot it so that it dropped in its tracks at the third bound. Siegfried's fellow-huntsmen acclaimed him for this shot. Next, in swift succession, he killed a wisent, an elk, four mighty aurochs,[4] and a fierce and monstrous

buck—so well mounted was he that nothing, be it hart or hind, could evade him. His hound then came upon a great boar, and, as this turned to flee, the champion hunter at once blocked his path, bringing him to bay; and when in a trice the beast sprang at the hero in a fury,

2. **relays** fresh horses brought in to relieve tired ones.
3. **tusker** (tusk′ ər) wild boar.
4. **wisent** (vē′ zənt) . . . **aurochs** (ô′ räks′) European bison and wild oxen.

Enrichment

Star Wars

The movie trilogy known as *Star Wars* is a modern epic. It is a futuristic tale of a young hero and his battle to overcome obstacles and to fight evil. Like other epic heroes, Luke Skywalker has his weaknesses as well as his strengths. He has to overcome the fears and disadvantages that come with being an ordinary human, as well as a hero. In the tradition of other heroes, Skywalker has trustworthy companions and a spiritual guide, from whom he receives the gifts of the force.

As often happens in epics, Skywalker is separated from his companions. Alone, he must seek out a spiritual teacher on a long journey or quest. When he returns, he is prepared to confront the forces and temptations that would defeat an ordinary man. Therefore, when he confronts his nemesis, Darth Vader, Skywalker is strong enough to suffer serious injury rather than give up the struggle for his cause.

Siegfried slew him with his sword, a feat no other hunter could have performed with such ease. After the felling of this boar, the tracker was returned to his leash and Siegfried's splendid bag was made known to the Burgundians.

32 "If it is not asking too much, lord Siegfried," said his companions of the chase, "do leave some of the game alive for us. You are emptying the hills and woods for us today." At this the brave knight had to smile.

There now arose a great shouting of men and clamor of hounds on all sides, and the tumult grew so great that the hills and the forest re-echoed with it—the huntsmen had unleashed no fewer than four and twenty packs! Thus, many beasts had to lose their lives there, since each of these hunters was hoping to bring it about that *he* should be given the high honors of the chase. But when mighty Siegfried appeared beside the camp fire there was no chance of that.

The hunt was over, yet not entirely so. Those who wished to go to the fire brought the hides of innumerable beasts, and game in plenty—what loads of it they carried back to the kitchen to the royal retainers! And now the noble King had it announced to those fine hunters that he wished to take his repast, and there was one great blast of the horn to tell them that he was back in camp.

At this, one of Siegfried's huntsmen said: "Sir, I have heard a horn-blast telling us to return to our lodges.—I shall answer it." There was much blowing to summon the companions.

"Let us quit the forest, too," said lord Siegfried. His mount carried him at an even pace, and the others hastened away with him but with the noise of their going they started a savage bear, a very fierce beast.

"I shall give our party some good entertainment," he said over his shoulder. "Loose the hound, for I can see a bear which will have to come back to our lodges with us. It will not be able to save itself unless it runs very fast." The hound was unleashed, and the bear made off at speed. Siegfried meant to ride it down but soon found that his way was blocked and his intention thwarted, while the mighty beast fancied it would escape from its pursuer. But the proud knight leapt from his horse and started to chase it on foot, and the animal, quite off its guard, failed to elude him. And so he quickly caught and bound it, without having wounded it at all—nor could the beast use either claws or teeth on the man. Siegfried tied it to his saddle, mounted his horse, and in his high-spirited fashion led it to the camp fire in order to amuse the good knights.

34 And in what magnificent style Siegfried rode! He bore a great spear, stout of shaft and broad of head; his handsome sword reached down to his spurs; and the fine horn which this lord carried was of the reddest gold. Nor have I ever heard tell of a better hunting outfit: he wore a surcoat of costly black silk and a splendid hat of sable,[5] and you should

5. **surcoat . . . sable** (sā´ bəl) A surcoat is a loose, short cloak worn over armor, and sable is the costly fur of the marten.

Reading Strategy
Recognizing Feudal Values Which feudal ideals are reflected in each huntsman's desire to win "the high honors of the chase"?

Vocabulary Builder
thwarted (thwôrt´ əd) *v.* hindered; frustrated

33 **Reading Check**
Which hunter kills the most game?

32 Reading Strategy
Recognizing Feudal Values

- Read aloud the bracketed passage, and invite students to discuss what a huge gathering of knights—such as the one described—might be like.
- Then, **ask:** How might such a gathering help reinforce feudal ideals? **Answer:** A gathering such as the one described would be rife with competitive tension. This competition would reinforce a knight's need for bravery and skill with weaponry in order to claim the title of best huntsman. Despite this competition, the knights would experience a degree of camaraderie and loyalty brought about by their common participation in such a dangerous event.
- **Ask** students the Reading Strategy question: Which feudal ideals are reflected in each huntsman's desire to win "the high honors of the chase"? **Answer:** The feudal ideals of bravery, skill with weaponry, and honor are reflected in this desire.

33 Reading Check
Answer: Siegfried kills the most game.

Differentiated Instruction
Solutions for All Learners

Strategy for Less Proficient Readers
To help students visualize the hunt scene, have them use the Internet to find images of the animals mentioned on these pages, such as the boar, the wisent, the auroch, and the buck. Students can print out images and write short captions that describe the characteristics of each animal. Then, have students discuss why the hunt for these animals might be extremely dangerous.

Enrichment for Advanced Readers
Challenge students to read the full text of *The Nibelungenlied* to learn more about the plot and characters of this complex epic. Organize students into groups, and assign each group a portion of the text. After students have finished reading, have each group present to the class a summary of their assigned portion. Ask them to address the following questions in their presentations: Who are the key characters? What are the key events? What is the theme of this portion of the text?

34 Literary Analysis

Medieval Epic

- Ask volunteers to take turns reading the bracketed passage. Then, have students describe Siegfried.
- **Ask:** What does this description of Siegfried tell you about the culture and society of the people at this time?
  Answer: The people of the upper classes lived in extreme luxury and wealth and proudly displayed their wealth in their clothing, equipment, and other possessions.
- **Ask** students the Literary Analysis question: In what ways does the long description of Siegfried's appearance reflect the origins of the medieval epic in the oral tradition?
  Answer: The storytellers would give long, detailed descriptions of their heroes in order to create vivid images for the audience.

35 Humanities

Siegfried's Death

By the fourteenth century, the art of manuscript illumination in Germany was reduced to a role of secondary importance. The miniatures that were produced drew their influence from the French style. Secular manuscripts were produced in greater numbers than the sacred ones at this time. *Siegfried's Death* is from a German manuscript of this era. Although the dynamic curves and colors of the composition are pleasing, they are overly stylized and lack the refinement of earlier work.

Use the following question for discussion:

Does anything in this miniature resemble modern art?
Possible response: The primitive quality of the art and the lack of realistic proportion of some figures resembles modern art.

36 Critical Viewing

Possible response: The illustration shows the types of animals being hunted.

have seen the gorgeous silken tassels on his quiver, which was covered in panther-skin for the sake of its fragrant odor![6] He also bore a bow so strong that apart from Siegfried any who wished to span it would have had to use a rack. His hunting suit was all of otter-skin, varied throughout its length with furs of other kinds from whose shining hair clasps of gold gleamed out on either side of this daring lord of the hunt. The handsome sword that he wore was Balmung, a weapon so keen and with such excellent edges that it never failed to bite when swung against a helmet. No wonder this splendid hunter was proud and gay.  And (since I am bound to tell you all) know that his quiver was full of good arrows with gold mountings and heads a span[7] in width, so that any beast they pierced must inevitably soon die.

Thus the noble knight rode along, the very image of a hunting man. Gunther's attendants saw him coming and ran to meet him to take his horse—tied to whose saddle he led a mighty bear! On dismounting, he loosed the bonds from its muzzle and paws, whereupon all the hounds that saw it instantly gave tongue. The beast made for the forest and the people were seized with panic. Affrighted by the tumult, the bear strayed into the kitchen—and how the cooks scuttled from their fire at its approach! Many cauldrons were sent flying and many fires were

Literary Analysis
Medieval Epic In what ways does the long description of Siegfried's appearance reflect the origins of the medieval epic in the oral tradition?

6. **panther-skin . . . odor** The odor of panther skin was supposed to lure other animals and therefore help with the hunt.
7. **span** nine inches.

35

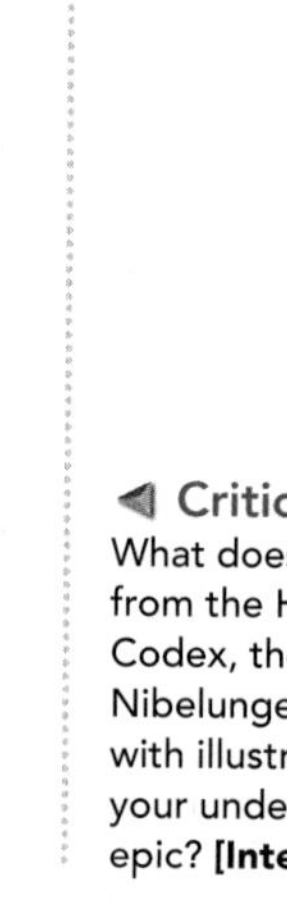
Siegfried's Death, Staatsbibliothek Preussischer Kulturbesitz, Berlin

◀ **Critical Viewing** 36 What does this illustration from the Hundeshagen Codex, the only surviving Nibelungen manuscript with illustrations, add to your understanding of the epic? **[Interpret]**

Enrichment

The Operas of Richard Wagner

The great German composer Richard Wagner (1813–1883) drew on the traditional literature of his people for inspiration for his operas. Perhaps his finest work, *Der Ring des Nibelungen (The Ring of the Nibelung)* is based on the tales and stories in the medieval classic *The Nibelungenlied.* Comprising four interwoven operas, the Ring cycle changes the focus of the original from human beings to the gods. The war saga is overshadowed by a divine conflict—Wotan, king of the gods, battles for control of the world.

Wagner transforms *The Nibelungenlied,* an epic about petty characters, into a story of superheroes who can be destroyed only by fate. In *The Nibelungenlied,* Brunhild's jealousy destroys Siegfried, and Kriemhild vengefully eliminates the Burgundians. In *The Ring,* Brunnhilde and Siegfried are controlled by evil forces, yet their love is undying and pure. It is the gods themselves who are tainted by greed.

37 scattered, while heaps of good food lay among the ashes. Lord and retainers leapt from their seats, the bear became infuriated, and the King ordered all the hounds on their leashes to be loosed—and if all had ended well they would have had a jolly day! Bows and spears were no longer left idle, for the brave ones ran towards the bear, yet there were so many hounds in the way that none dared shoot. With the whole mountain thundering with people's cries the bear took to flight before the hounds and none could keep up with it but Siegfried, who ran it down and then dispatched it with his sword. The bear was later carried to the camp fire, and all who had witnessed this feat declared that Siegfried was a very powerful man.

The proud companions were then summoned to table. There were a great many seated in that meadow. Piles of sumptuous dishes were set before the noble huntsmen, but the butlers who were to pour their wine were very slow to appear. Yet knights could not be better cared for than they and if only no treachery had been lurking in their minds those warriors would have been above reproach.

"Seeing that we are being treated to such a variety of dishes from the kitchen," said lord Siegfried, "I fail to understand why the butlers bring us no wine. Unless we hunters are better looked after, I'll not be a companion of the hunt. I thought I had deserved better attention."

"We shall be very glad to make amends to you for our present lack," answered the perfidious[8] King from his table. "This is Hagen's fault—he wants us to die of thirst."

"My very dear lord," replied Hagen of Troneck, "I thought the day's hunting would be away in the Spessart and so I sent the wine there. If we go without drink today I shall take good care that it does not happen again."

"Damn those fellows!" said lord Siegfried. "It was arranged that they were to bring along seven panniers of spiced wine and mead[9] for me. Since that proved impossible, we should have been placed nearer the Rhine."

"You brave and noble knights," said Hagen of Troneck, "I know a cool spring nearby—do not be offended!—let us go there."—A proposal which (as it turned out) was to bring many knights into jeopardy.

Siegfried was tormented by thirst and ordered the board to be removed all the sooner in his eagerness to go to that spring at the foot of the hills. And now the knights put their treacherous plot into execution.

Word was given for the game which Siegfried had killed to be conveyed back to Worms on wagons, and all who saw it gave him great credit for it.

Hagan of Troneck broke his faith with Siegfried most grievously, for as they were leaving to go to the spreading lime-tree he said: "I have often been told that no one can keep up with Lady Kriemhild's lord when he cares to show his speed. I wish he would show it us now."

8. **perfidious** (pər fid´ ē əs) *adj.* treacherous.
9. **panniers** (pan´ yərz) . . . **mead** (mēd) Panniers are pairs of large baskets that straddle the backs of pack animals; mead is an alcoholic liquor made of fermented honey and water.

Literary Analysis
Medieval Epic and Epic Heroes In what ways does this episode with the bear add to Siegfried's mystique?

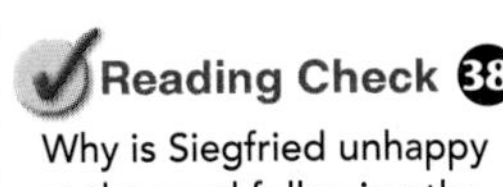
Reading Check 38
Why is Siegfried unhappy at the meal following the hunt?

37 Literary Analysis
Medieval Epic and Epic Heroes

- Remind students that an epic hero has extraordinary abilities and exemplifies the highest values in his or her culture.
- Then, have students read the bracketed passage that begins on the previous page.
  Ask: What purpose does the episode with the bear serve in the epic?
  Possible response: The episode is intended to entertain the reader, to provide a characterization of Siegfried, and to reinforce his heroic qualities.
- Then, **ask** students the Literary Analysis question: In what ways does this episode with the bear add to Siegfried's mystique?
  Answer: The episode with the bear describes such a fantastic feat that it adds to Siegfried's image as a larger-than-life hero.

➤ **Monitor Progress** Point out to students that the episode with the bear is brief, colorful, and entertaining. **Ask** students how episodes like this would be especially suitable to a narrative drawn from an oral tradition.
Answer: These episodes are brief, so they do not demand extended attention from the storyteller's audience; they are exciting, so they hold an audience's attention.

38 Reading Check

Answer: Siegfried is unhappy because there is no wine or mead.

Differentiated Instruction
Solutions for All Learners

Support for English Learners
Draw students' attention to the word *quiver* at the top of p. 614. Explain that in this selection, *quiver* means "a case for carrying arrows," not "to shake or tremble" (the definition with which students are probably more familiar). Then, explain that *quiver* is a homograph, one of two or more words that have the same spelling but different meanings, derivations, or pronunciations. Encourage students to suggest other homographs, and record their suggestions on the board.

Enrichment for Gifted/Talented Students
Tell students that translating a text from one literary form to another may be a challenging exercise. Organize the class into small groups, and have each group select a different passage. Then, have each group write the passage in verse form. A further challenge would be to have students use the original form, which had a rhyme pattern of *aabb* with each line consisting of six syllables, then seven, then six, and so on. After students have finished their translations, have each group present its work to the class.

39 Literary Analysis

Medieval Epic and Epic Heroes

- Ask a volunteer to read aloud the bracketed passage. Then, discuss how the simile "like a pair of wild panthers" creates a picture of Siegfried and Hagen as fierce and formidable hunters. Point out that this characterization is consistent with that of an epic hero.
- Then, **ask** students the Literary Analysis question: What does Siegfried fail to realize about the effects his unrivaled abilities are having on the other knights? **Answer:** Siegfried fails to realize that many of the other knights resent his superiority and his arrogance.

40 Reading Strategy

Recognizing Feudal Values

- Read aloud the bracketed passage. Then, **ask** students the Reading Strategy question: How does Siegfried's treatment of Gunther exemplify the ideal relationship between a vassal and his king? **Answer:** A vassal's duty is to his king. Here, Siegfried shows high respect for Gunther by waiting for him to drink first.

Monitor Progress **Ask** students: Why are Hagen's actions (killing Siegfried and running away) contrary to feudal values? **Answer:** According to feudal values, Hagen should have been loyal to Siegfried because he was a member of the same court. In a society that valued valor and military prowess, he should never have fled the wounded Siegfried.

Reteach If students have difficulty answering the Monitor Progress question, review the Reading Strategy instruction on Recognizing Feudal Values on p. 599.

41 Critical Viewing

Possible answer: The characters in the painting seem more primitive. They are not dressed in fine skins such as Siegfried is described as wearing for the hunt.

"You can easily put it to the test by racing me to the brook," replied gallant Siegfried of the Netherlands. "Then those who see it shall declare the winner."

"I accept your challenge," said Hagen.

39 "Then I will lie down in the grass at your feet, as a handicap," replied brave Siegfried, much to Gunther's satisfaction. "And I will tell you what more I shall do. I will carry all my equipment with me, my spear and my shield and all my hunting clothes." And he quickly strapped on his quiver and sword. The two men took off their outer clothing and stood there in their white vests. Then they ran through the clover like a pair of wild panthers. Siegfried appeared first at the brook.

40 Gunther's magnificent guest who excelled so many men in all things quickly unstrapped his sword, took off his quiver, and after leaning his great spear against a branch of the lime, stood beside the rushing brook. Then he laid down his shield near the flowing water, and although he was very thirsty he most courteously refrained from drinking until the King had drunk. Gunther thanked him very ill for this.

The stream was cool, sweet, and clear. Gunther stooped to its running waters and after drinking stood up and stepped aside. Siegfried in turn would have liked to do the same, but he paid for his good manners. For now Hagen carried Siegfried's sword and bow beyond his reach, ran back for the spear, and searched for the sign on the brave man's tunic.[10] Then, as Siegfried bent over the brook and drank, Hagen hurled the spear at the cross, so that the hero's heart's blood leapt from the wound and splashed against Hagen's clothes. No warrior will ever do a darker deed. Leaving the spear fixed in Siegfried's heart, he fled in wild desperation, as he had never fled before from any man.

When lord Siegfried felt the great wound, maddened with rage he bounded back from the stream with the long shaft jutting from his heart. He was hoping to find either his bow or his sword, and, had he succeeded in doing so, Hagen would have had his pay. But finding no sword, the gravely wounded man had nothing but his shield. Snatching this from the bank he ran at Hagen, and King Gunther's vassal was unable to elude him. Siegfried was wounded to death, yet he struck so powerfully that he sent many precious stones whirling from the shield as it smashed to pieces. Gunther's noble guest would dearly have loved to avenge himself. Hagen fell reeling under the weight of the blow and the riverside echoed loudly. Had Siegfried had his sword in his hand it would have been the end of Hagen, so enraged was the wounded man, as indeed he had good cause to be.

The hero's face had lost its color and he was no longer able to stand. His strength had ebbed away, for in the field of his bright countenance he now displayed Death's token. Soon many fair ladies would be weeping for him.

Literary Analysis
Medieval Epic and Epic Heroes What does Siegfried fail to realize about the effects his unrivaled abilities are having on the other knights?

Reading Strategy
Recognizing Feudal Values How does Siegfried's treatment of Gunther exemplify the ideal relationship between a vassal and his king?

Critical Viewing 41
In this painting depicting Siegfried's funeral, how does the artist's portrayal of the characters compare to the images you had formed in your mind? **[Compare and Contrast]**

10. **sign . . . tunic** Siegfried is invulnerable except for a spot beween his shoulder blades. Earlier, Hagen had tricked Kriemhild into sewing a cross-shaped patch on Siegfried's tunic to indicate the exact location of the spot.

The lady Kriemhild's lord fell among the flowers, where you could see the blood surging from his wound. Then—and he had cause—he rebuked those who had plotted his foul murder. "You vile cowards," he
42 said as he lay dying. "What good has my service done me now that you have slain me? I was always loyal to you, but now I have paid for it. Alas, you have wronged your kinsmen so that all who are born in days to come will be dishonored by your deed. You have cooled your anger on me beyond all measure. You will be held in contempt and stand apart from all good warriors."

The knights all ran to where he lay wounded to death. It was a sad day for many of them. Those who were at all loyal-hearted mourned for him, and this, as a gay and valiant knight, he had well deserved.

The King of Burgundy too lamented Siegfried's death.

"There is no need for the doer of the deed to weep when the damage is done," said the dying man. "He should be held up to scorn. It would have been better left undone."

"I do not know what you are grieving for," said Hagen fiercely. "All our cares and sorrows are over and done with. We shall not find many who will dare oppose us now. I am glad I have put an end to his supremacy."

"You may well exult," said Siegfried. "But had I known your murderous bent I should easily have guarded my life from you. I am sorry for
45 none so much as my wife, the lady Kriemhild. May God have mercy on me for ever having got a son who in years to come will suffer the

Reading Strategy
Recognizing Feudal Values What feudal values does Siegfried's condemnation of his murderers express?

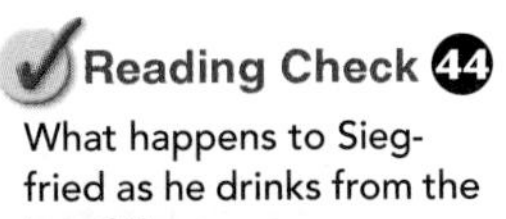

Reading Check 44
What happens to Siegfried as he drinks from the brook?

43

The Burial of Siegfried, Richard Jack, City of New York Art Gallery

42 Reading Strategy

Recognizing Feudal Values

- Ask students to list feudal values, and record their suggestions on the board. Then, have a volunteer read aloud the bracketed passage.
- **Ask** students the Reading Strategy question: What feudal values does Siegfried's condemnation of his murderers express?
  Answer: Siegfried condemns his murderers for not showing loyalty to him, a member of the same court and one who fought the same enemies.
- Then, **ask:** Has King Gunther treated Siegfried according to feudal values? Explain.
  Answer: Gunther has not treated Siegfried according to feudal values. As a king, he must remain loyal to his vassals just as they must remain loyal to him.

43 Humanities

The Burial of Siegfried,
by Richard Jack

Painter Richard Jack was born in Sunderland, England, in 1866. He emigrated to Canada. In 1916, he was appointed Canada's first official war artist. Jack was lauded for his realistic depictions of Canadian soldiers fighting in World War I battles. He was also a noted portrait artist.

Use the following questions for discussion:

- What is the mood of this painting? What elements help create this mood?
  Possible response: The mood of this painting is one of solemnity. The roiling dark clouds, the profusions of blues and violets, and the postures of the men create this mood.
- How is Siegfried set apart from the men carrying him?
  Answer: Siegfried is draped in a magenta shroud. Unlike the other men, Siegfried has golden, flowing hair.

44 Reading Check

Answer: Hagen throws a spear into Siegfried's back, striking the hero's one vulnerable spot.

Differentiated Instruction Solutions for All Learners

Enrichment for Gifted/Talented Students

Tell students to imagine that one of the knights loyal to Siegfried returns to tell Kriemhild what has happened. Have them write their own versions of the conversation between the knight and Kriemhild. Students should consider the following questions: Which details of the hunt and the death of Siegfried would the knight give Kriemhild? How would Kriemhild react? What words would she use to explain her response? Remind students to make sure that the language and sentiments are consistent with the characters.

Enrichment for Advanced Readers

Tell students that the writer Robert Service writes, "Fate has written a tragedy; its name is the Human Heart." Have students write brief essays in which they address the following questions: How do Service's words relate to Siegfried? How do his words relate to life in general? Before beginning their essays, students can conduct a class discussion in which they consider Siegfried's tragic flaws and their role in his downfall.

45 Critical Thinking

Apply

- Remind students that dramatic irony is contradiction between what a character thinks and what the reader or audience knows to be true.
- Read aloud the bracketed passage. Then, **ask** students: How is this passage ironic?
  Answer: The passage is ironic because Siegfried pleads for Gunther's loyalty to Kriemhild, yet Kriemhild has not remained loyal to Siegfried.

ASSESS

Answers

1. **Possible response:** The death of Siegfried is tragic and depressing because he does not die nobly. His death is a result of a great betrayal, not only by Hagen and Gunther but also by Kriemhild.
2. (a) Kriemhild dreams that two boars kill Siegfried and that two mountains fall on him. (b) Kriemhild fears that Siegfried will die during the hunt. (c) Siegfried dismisses the dreams, believing that he is invincible. Kriemhild, knowing that she had divulged too much to Hagen, recognizes Siegfried's vulnerability.
3. (a) Siegfried takes a sword, a bow and arrows, and his spear. (b) Siegfried wears a sable hat, his quiver is covered with panther skin, and his hunting suit is made of otter-skin and other furs.
4. (a) Siegfried kills more game than the other knights, catches and kills the bear when no other knight can, and outraces Hagen to the brook. (b) Siegfried feels superior to the other knights. (c) **Possible response:** Siegfried's arrogance may have dissuaded other knights from coming to his aid.
5. **Possible response:** Those who think disaster has befallen them are correct. Murdering such a strong warrior and leader will weaken the kingdom, making it more vulnerable to attack from within and without.

45 reproach that his kinsmen were murderers. If I had the strength I would have good reason to complain. But if you feel at all inclined to do a loyal deed for anyone, noble King," continued the mortally wounded man, "let me commend my dear sweetheart to your mercy. Let her profit from being your sister. By the virtue of all princes, stand by her loyally! No lady was ever more greatly wronged through her dear friend. As to my father and his vassals, they will have long to wait for me."

The flowers everywhere were drenched with blood. Siegfried was at grips with Death, yet not for long, since Death's sword ever was too sharp. And now the warrior who had been so brave and gay could speak no more.

When those lords saw that the hero was dead they laid him on a shield that shone red with gold, and they plotted ways and means of concealing the fact that Hagen had done the deed. "A disaster has befallen us," many of them said. "You must all hush it up and declare with one voice that Siegfried rode off hunting alone and was killed by robbers as he was passing through the forest."

"I shall take him home," said Hagen of Troneck. "It is all one to me if the woman who made Brunhild so unhappy should come to know of it. It will trouble me very little, however much she weeps."

Critical Reading

1. **Respond:** Did you find the death of Siegfried noble and uplifting or tragic and depressing? Explain your answer.
2. **(a) Recall:** Before the hunt, what does Kriemhild dream?
   (b) Interpret: What does Kriemhild fear her dream may represent?
   (c) Analyze: In what ways do Siegfried's and Kriemhild's responses to her dream reveal differences in their characters?
3. **(a) Recall:** What three weapons does Siegfried take to the hunt?
   (b) Analyze: What other details convey the sense that Siegfried is "the very image of a hunting man"?
4. **(a) Classify:** Identify three moments in which Siegfried bests the other knights in a physical challenge. **(b) Interpret:** What is Siegfried's attitude toward the other knights? **(c) Make a Judgment:** Do you think Siegfried's character contributes to his death? Explain your answer.
5. **Take a Position:** At the end of the excerpt, Hagen says, "All our cares are over and done with," while others say, "A disaster has befallen us." Which opinion do you think is accurate? Explain your answer.

Apply the Skills

from the *Song of Roland* • from *The Nibelungenlied*

Literary Analysis

Medieval Epic

1. **Medieval epics** favored adventure over factual accuracy. **(a)** How might this emphasis have aided a storyteller? **(b)** How might this emphasis have affected a people's sense of its own history?
2. Which elements in the following passage suggest that the *Song of Roland* was first performed as an entertainment for live audiences?

   The French dismount, and they put on their armor: / their hauberks, their helmets, their gold-dressed swords, / their handsome shields; and take up their great lances, / the gonfalons of white and red and blue . . .
3. **(a)** In what ways do you think these stories might have inspired their audiences? **(b)** In what ways might these stories have been viewed as cautionary tales? Explain.

Comparing Literary Works

4. Use a chart like the one shown to identify details that reveal specific elements of each **epic hero's** character.

Hero	Appearance	Abilities and Skills	Others' Opinions of Him	Opinion of Himself
Roland				
Siegfried				

5. **(a)** Identify three examples of Siegfried's thoughtlessness about other people. **(b)** What is Siegfried's **heroic flaw?**
6. **(a)** Why does Roland not call for help? **(b)** What is his heroic flaw?

Reading Strategy

Recognizing Feudal Values

7. Loyalty was one of the most esteemed **feudal values,** and betrayal was one of the most serious violations. Does Roland betray Charlemagne by his actions? Explain.
8. **(a)** In what ways does Siegfried express respect for Gunther? **(b)** In what ways does Roland express respect for Charlemagne?

Extend Understanding

9. **Social Studies Connection:** Which elements of these epic works provide insight into the conditions of life during the Middle Ages?

QuickReview

Medieval epics are long works that were originally performed in dramatic theatricals to present the exploits of larger-than-life heroes.

The **epic hero** is a person of extraordinary abilities who embodies a people's core beliefs and values.

A **heroic flaw** is a character defect that may lead to the failure, suffering, or death of the hero.

To **recognize feudal values** as you read, identify those details of a literary work that reveal the values underlying the economic, political, and social system of medieval Europe.

For: Self-test
Visit: www.PHSchool.com
Web Code: eta-6501

Go Online Assessment — Students may use the **Self-test** to prepare for **Selection Test A** or **Selection Test B.**

Answers

1. (a) The storyteller could fabricate details and embellish episodes to add more interest to an historic event. (b) The emphasis might have skewed a people's understanding of its own history by making that history grander than it actually was.
2. The lines are musical with a regular cadence, parallel structure, and repetition. The mention of all the "props" enables listeners to envision the action.
3. (a) **Possible response:** The stories depicting heroes who are courageous and loyal to king and country might have inspired listeners to emulate such legendary figures. (b) Both tales tell of flaws or imbalances that lead to tragedy. Listeners might have viewed them as warnings to deal with their own flaws.
4. **Possible response: Roland—Appearance:** strong; **Abilities and Skills:** skilled and powerful warrior; **Others' Opinions of Him:** arrogant, lacks judgment; **Opinion of Himself:** great warrior, good vassal. **Siegfried—Appearance:** handsome, strong; **Abilities and Skills:** great warrior and hunter; **Others' Opinions of Him:** arrogant, thought skillful as a warrior and hunter; **Opinion of Himself:** skilled warrior, hunter, and leader.
5. (a) Siegfried shows up the other knights with his hunting skills; he releases the bear among the lodges; and he defeats Hagen in a race to the brook. (b) Siegfried's heroic flaw is his pride.
6. (a) Roland arrogantly believes that he can win the battle without Charlemagne's help. (b) Roland's heroic flaw is his pride.
7. **Possible response:** Roland betrays Charlemagne by allowing his army to be destroyed and by losing his life, both of which weaken the king.
8. (a) Siegfried serves Gunther faithfully. He waits for Gunther to drink first at the brook. (b) Roland fights faithfully for Charlemagne and serves him as a good vassal.
9. **Possible response:** The social attitudes reflected in the leaders' respect for feudal values, as well as their wealth and luxury, provide insight into the conditions of medieval life.

EXTEND/ASSESS

Answers

1 Vocabulary Lesson

Word Analysis: Latin Prefix *mal-*

1. malpractice
2. malady
3. malfunction

Spelling Strategy

1. chalice
2. edifice
3. apprentice

Vocabulary Builder: Context

vassal; prowess; exulting; intrepid; unrestrained; sinister; thwarted; malice

2 Grammar and Style Lesson

1. I read the *Song of Roland*—what a great work!
2. *The Nibelungenlied*—the medieval epic—reminds me of *The Lord of the Rings.*
3. The death of Roland—someday you must read it—is a powerful scene.
4. Roland's friend Oliver—I just recalled his name—tries to give him advice.
5. Monday—what an amazing day it was!—I felt like Roland at Roncesvalles.

Writing Application

Possible response: The *Song of Roland* is a great epic. Roland—what a sensational warrior!—almost won the battle singlehandedly. Sure, he made a mistake in failing to call for support—Charlemagne would have come immediately—but he made the best of the situation.

WG Writing and Grammar Platinum Level

For support in teaching the Grammar and Style Lesson, use Chapter 28, Section 5.

Build Language Skills

1 Vocabulary Lesson

Word Analysis: Latin Prefix *mal-*

The prefix *mal-*, which means "bad," derives from the Latin word *malus*, which means "evil." Thus, *malice* means "ill will." Fill in each blank below with the word that best completes each sentence.

a. malady **b.** malfunction **c.** malpractice

1. The doctor was sued for ___________.
2. The patient recovered from her _______.
3. The engine started to _________.

Spelling Strategy

When words that derive from French end in the *is* sound, they are often spelled with the letter combination *ice*, as in *malice*. Use the clues below to finish the spelling of each word.

1. a cuplike vessel chal______________
2. building edif______________
3. trainee apprent___________

Vocabulary Builder: Context

Review the vocabulary list on page 599, and notice the way the words are used in the context of the selection. Then, fill in the blanks in the paragraph below with the best word from the vocabulary list.

vassal	malice
prowess	sinister
exulting	intrepid
unrestrained	thwarted

When the knights gathered at the tournament, the young __?__ displayed his strength and __?__. He left the field __?__ in his victory. He had proved he was fearless and __?__, and his celebration was __?__. However, his __?__ enemy, who wanted attention for himself, saw his own plans __?__. He looked at the young knight with __?__.

2 Grammar and Style Lesson

Interrupting Phrases and Clauses

Writers sometimes interrupt sentences with phrases and clauses that express strong feeling. When such interrupters break into the middle of a sentence, they are often set off with dashes. When they end a sentence, they are often preceded by a dash. **Interrupting phrases and clauses** may imitate speech, provide explanations, or suggest an intense, irrepressible feeling.

> Roland, your prowess—had we never seen it!
>
> Charles—that Charlemagne!—with his great host.

Practice Correctly punctuate the following items.

1. I read the *Song of Roland* what a great work
2. *The Nibelungenlied* the medieval epic reminds me of *The Lord of the Rings*
3. The death of Roland someday you must read it is a powerful scene
4. Roland's friend Oliver I just recalled his name tries to give him advice
5. Monday what an amazing day it was I felt like Roland at Roncesvalles

Writing Application Write a paragraph about heroes. Use at least two interrupting phrases or clauses.

WG Prentice Hall Writing and Grammar Connection: Platinum Level, Chapter 28, Section 5

Assessment Practice

Evaluate and Make Judgments **(For more practice, see *Test Preparation Workbook*, p. 28.)**

Many tests require students to evaluate and make judgments about text in a reading passage. Use the following sample test item to give students practice using this skill.

"I do not need any hounds," said lord Siegfried, "except for one tracker so well fleshed that he recognizes the tracks which the game leave through the wood: then we shall not fail to find our quarry."

This passage provides evidence that Siegfried is—

A frightened.
B confident.
C pessimistic.
D frustrated.

Answers *A, C,* and *D* are not supported by the text and are inconsistent with Siegfried's character. Siegfried's refusal to use a group of hunting hounds reveals his self-assuredness. The correct answer is *B*.

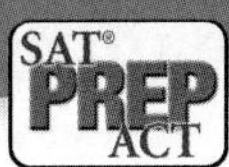

❸ Writing Lesson

Timed Writing: Persuasive Essay on Values

Roland and Siegfried demonstrate many virtues, including courage and strength. However, when it comes to prudence, they are less gifted. Using the stories of Roland and Siegfried as evidence, write an essay defining the virtues of courage and prudence and determining whether one is more important than the other. ***(40 minutes)***

Prewriting ***(10 minutes)*** Use a chart to examine details from the stories that demonstrate either courage or prudence. Under "Conclusions Drawn," describe what each detail reveals about the value of that virtue.

Model: Charting to Analyze Details

Selection	Detail	Virtue Shown	Conclusions Drawn
Song of Roland	Roland refuses to blow his horn.	courage	Courage can erase prudence; a virtue can be destructive.
Nibelungenlied			

Drafting ***(20 minutes)*** Decide on a structure for your essay. For example, you might discuss all your observations about courage and then all your observations about prudence, or you might list all your ideas about Roland and then all your ideas about Siegfried.

Revising ***(10 minutes)*** Reread your essay, making sure you have presented your ideas persuasively by organizing them clearly and including strong support from the text. Add quotations or other details as needed.

WG Prentice Hall Writing and Grammar Connection: Platinum Level, Chapter 7, Section 2

❹ Extend Your Learning

Listening and Speaking In a small group, conduct a **press conference** in which Charlemagne describes the events at Roncevalles. Have one student play Charlemagne, while the others act as reporters. Use these tips to prepare:

- Reporters should prepare at least two questions in advance.
- Follow-up questions should be allowed after Charlemagne's responses.

You may also create a map as a visual aid for use during the press conference. **[Group Activity]**

Research and Technology Use electronic and print resources to create an **informative poster** about medieval dress. Consider organizing the material according to occupation or social status. Alternatively, present outfits worn for various occasions or times of day. Clearly identify the different styles and purposes of dress in your poster.

For: An additional research activity
Visit: www.PHSchool.com
Web Code: etd-7501

❸ Writing Lesson

You may use this Writing Lesson as a timed-writing practice, or you may allow students to develop the persuasive essay as a writing assignment over several days.

- To give students guidance in writing this persuasive essay, give them **Support for Writing,** p. 15 in ***Unit 5 Resources.***
- Use the Writing Lesson to guide students as they create their essays. Tell students to determine why a reader might disagree with their position and to address those reasons in their essays.
- When students have finished their essays, use the Persuasion: Persuasive Essay rubrics in ***General Resources,*** pp. 47–48, to evaluate their work.

WG Writing and Grammar Platinum Level

For support in teaching the Writing Lesson, use Chapter 7, Section 2.

❹ Listening and Speaking

- After reading aloud the Listening and Speaking instruction, organize students to choose the time frame in which their press conferences will take place. Encourage students to use costumes or props as part of their presentations.
- The **Support for Extend Your Learning** page ***(Unit 5 Resources,*** p. 16) provides guided note-taking opportunities to help students complete the Extend Your Learning activities.

Go Online Research Have students type in the Web Code for another research activity.

Assessment Resources

The following resources can be used to assess students' knowledge and skills.

Unit 5 Resources

Selection Test A, pp. 18–20
Selection Test B, pp. 21–23

General Resources

Rubrics for Persuasion: Persuasive Essay, pp. 47–48

Go Online Assessment Students may use the **Self-Test** to prepare for **Selection Test A** or **Selection Test B.**

Standard Course of Study

WL.1.02.4	Explain how culture affects personal responses.
IR.2.03.1	Access cultural information from media sources.
CT.4.05.1	Select, monitor, and modify reading strategies appropriate to critical interpretation.

*See **Teacher Express™/Lesson View** for a detailed lesson for Reading Informational Material.*

About Interviews

- Have students read the "About Interviews" instruction. Then, ask them to share interviews they have seen or read.
- Explain the types of information students may learn from an interview and how the interviewer's relationship to the interviewee may influence what is said.
- **Ask** students why it is important to know whether written text is an interview or an article.
  Possible response: An interview contains the speaker's own words, whereas the author of an article may interpret what was said.
- Remind students that interviews often include both facts and opinions. **Ask** students to list words and phrases that might signal that an opinion is being provided.
  Possible response: Phrases such as *I think* and *I believe* and comparative and superlative adjectives such as *better, best, worse,* and *worst* might signal opinions.

Reading Strategy

Analyzing Purpose

- Have students read aloud the Reading Strategy instruction.
- **Ask** students why it is important to understand the purpose of an interview.
  Possible response: Understanding why an interview takes place helps the reader evaluate the information in the interview.
- Draw students' attention to the graphic organizer. As they read, have students record the details that point to the interview's purpose.

Reading Informational Materials

Interviews

About Interviews

An **interview** is a record of an exchange between two or more people for the purpose of obtaining specific information about a person, a topic, or an event. Interviews may be formal, with the interview and the questions planned in advance, or informal and occurring spontaneously, as in a news report. An interview can provide an expert opinion or a firsthand account—an eyewitness recollection or a description of an event. Sometimes, an interview previews the release of a movie, a book, or even a comic book, as does the interview you are about to read.

Interviews are published in print and online newspapers and magazines or broadcast on television and radio shows. Most written interviews include these elements:

- Initials, formatting, or other design elements to distinguish between the words of the interviewer and those of the interviewee
- A limited scope with questions that focus on a particular subject or time period
- Introductory and closing material providing background information about the topic of the interview or the person being interviewed

Reading Strategy

Analyzing Purpose

Interviews are held for many reasons, such as to entertain, inform, inspire, or persuade readers, listeners, or viewers. **Analyzing the purpose** of an interview will help you to understand why it took place.

Start by examining the writer's language, including words, details, and events. Look for specific information that points to a particular purpose. Keep in mind that an interview may have more than one purpose.

As you read the *ComicFan* interview, use a chart like the one shown to list the details that help you determine the interview's main purpose and decide if it has more than one purpose.

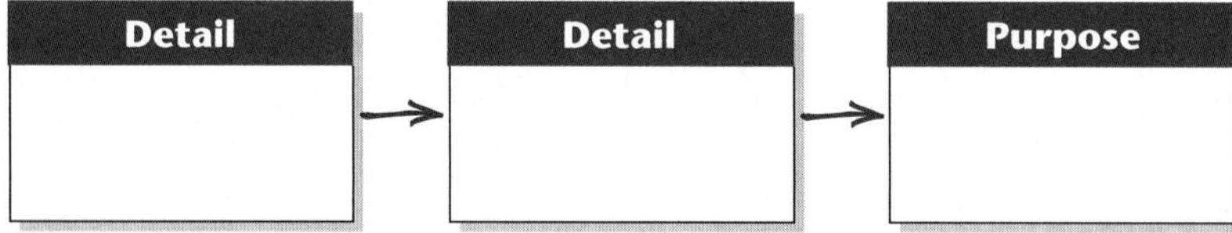

Differentiated Instruction Solutions for All Learners

Reading Support

Give students reading support with the appropriate version of the **Reader's Notebooks:**

Reader's Notebook: [L2, L3]
Reader's Notebook: Adapted Version [L1, L2]
Reader's Notebook: English Learner's Version [EL]

from ComicFan

INTERVIEW WITH SHANE L. AMAYA, Writer of the comic *Roland: Days of Wrath*

The boldface titles identify the publication and the person who is being interviewed.

Slated for release in July [1999], Shane L. Amaya's *Roland: Days of Wrath* has all the ingredients to be a hit. Recently chosen worthy of the Small Press Snapshot and Certified Cool mentions in May's Previews catalogue, *Roland: Days of Wrath* promises beautiful art and an epic storyline. We recently caught up with the busy writer for a little one-on-one.

Names in boldface type followed by a colon identify each speaker.

ComicFan: I understand that *Roland: Days of Wrath* is your first published work. Do you see this series as a springboard to other projects or have you committed yourself to this project for the long run?

Shane: The Roland comic is my first self-published work. My artists and I see this comic as our debut—as a way of getting our foot in the industry door. I hope to continue to self-publish and write comics after Roland: I am already thinking about two new projects for next year; I know my artists, Gabriel Ba and Fabio Moon, have stories to tell as well. Since our collaboration on the Roland comic has gone so well, we will definitely work together again, and sooner rather than later.

ComicFan: Now, for those not familiar with your upcoming comic *Roland: Days of Wrath.* How would you describe the story and characters?

Shane: The Roland comic is based on the early medieval French war epic the *Song of Roland.* It was probably written late in the 11th century but the action is set in a glorified past—Charlemagne's 8th century Holy Roman Empire. It is the story of Roland's sacrifice, his stepfather's betrayal, and Charlemagne's eternal embattlement. The story is incredibly powerful and the language—having been refined orally for over three hundred years—is strong and beautiful. The characters are all warriors, feudal lords, kings, and vassals. They are cut sharply: Roland is brave and Oliver is wise; they boast and betray; they weep and roar with anger—and these men fight, with all the strength in their hearts, and kill and die on the battlefield.

This page from the comic book helps readers visualize the characters Amaya is describing.

ComicFan: So what do you think fuels your passion for comic books, is there a particular aspect?

Shane: Comic books tell more powerful, more emotionally evocative and more stimulating stories than any other medium. Comics are capable of the best storytelling Art and Literature can offer: they feature the best of two infinitely productive universes—the imagination Literature excites coupled with the emotion Art evokes. There is no medium more potential than comics, more intelligent, or more

Reading Interviews *(cont.)*

- Have students read the selection and the notes that identify the elements of the interview. Draw students' attention to the first call-out note. **Ask** why it is important to identify at the beginning of the interview the publication and the person being interviewed.
  Possible response: This information sets the context for the interview and helps the reader understand the circumstances under which the interview was conducted.
- Have students read the second call-out note. **Ask** students why the names in boldface type are important.
  Answer: The names tell the reader who is speaking.
- Point out the illustration and its accompanying note. **Ask** students why the picture of the character is important.
  Possible response: In addition to helping readers visualize the character, the illustration may attract the interest of readers who otherwise might not read the story.

continued on page 624

Differentiated Instruction Solutions for All Learners

Support for Less Proficient Readers
Draw students' attention to the first call-out note. Discuss with students the possible purpose of the magazine *ComicFan* and how this purpose and the magazine's audience might impact the interview. Remind students that interviews can serve several purposes, including to entertain, to inform, and to persuade.

Support for English Learners
Students may be unfamiliar with the term *comic book.* Explain the term *comic book* and, if possible, show students an example. Then, discuss with students their experiences with similar types of literature.

Reading Interviews *(cont.)*

- Have students read the first call-out note. Then, **ask** students why it is important for an interviewer to ask highly focused questions.
  Answer: In order to provide the information the interviewer wants, the interviewee needs a specific question. Focused questions prevent the interviewee from digressing and from speaking in abstractions.
- Direct students' attention to the second call-out note. **Ask** students why they think art was added to the report of the interview.
  Possible response: The note illustrates that clever art and writing bring characters to life, which further motivates readers to buy the magazine.
- Point out the last call-out note. **Ask** students why this information is important for this particular interview.
  Possible response: Part of the reason for this interview is to interest people in this new comic book, which had just come out, and to encourage them to purchase it. Therefore, including information about the availability of the comic book would help sell it.

Reading Informational Materials

interactive. Reading a comic is not a passive experience: it requires work, it demands your imagination at the same time it feeds your eyes and heart with visual inspirations. This is the aspect of comics that I love the most: its ability to express, relate, share and encourage the creativity of two art forms in one unique—and amazing—medium.

ComicFan: I know you've done a lot of research into the historical aspects of the *Song of Roland,* which your comic is based on. What do you find so captivating about the *Song of Roland*?

The interviewer's questions focus carefully on the particular subject of the interview.

Shane: The Middle Ages are an incredibly fascinating, important and—despite popular belief—creatively astounding period. I love the medieval imagination; medieval imagination has, I think, influenced the modern world in profound, unshakable ways. *The Song of Roland* captivates me in more ways than I can say here: but for one, it is an amazing example of medieval ingenuity. How does Charlemagne's actual, historical and shameful defeat become a poem that, throughout time, transforms this skirmish into a story of apocalyptic struggle and Christ-like sacrifice; of battlefields packed with hundreds of thousands of warriors; of Anti-Gods and Judas figures; and where the stakes are no higher than the fate of the entire universe?!

ComicFan: Which writers do you think have had the most influence on you?

Shane: The works I enjoy reading most of all are those created by countless, anonymous authors. This includes ancient epics and sagas, much of medieval literature, folk tales and other oral narratives. I enjoy medieval literature especially for the way it is created: through the hands and voices of many, . . . through marginalia and glosses upon glosses, and because of the way it is constantly interpreted, translated—and forever changing. To a medieval mind, authorship is wholly unimportant: it is only the story the matters, and still more important than the story is the way that it is well told. . . .

This panel from the comic gives readers an idea of both the art and the writing.

ComicFan: What do you think you enjoy more, the creating of Roland or the reading of it?

Shane: I never get tired of reading either the *Song of Roland* or my comic! Though the process of creation is a lot of fun, there's nothing like seeing the finished product.

ComicFan: Finally, what can readers expect to see in the coming issues of *Roland: Days of Wrath*?

Shane: The Roland comic is a moving and poignant story of war and vengeance, fraternity and betrayal, faith and wisdom. Readers can expect a beautifully drawn and colored mini-series that will take them into a vivid medieval world of tenuous politics and treacherous pagan citadels; they will witness justice, bloody vengeance, epic battle-storm and battlefields choked with dying warriors; readers will know the depths Charlemagne's terrible grief, and the heart of one of the world's greatest heroes!

ComicFan: Thanks again for your time, Shane, and good luck with your great comic! You've got what looks like a hit on your hands. Keep it up.

Roland: Days of Wrath from Terra Major debuts in July [1999] at comic book shops everywhere.

The closing paragraph provides information about the availability of the comic book discussed in the interview.

Monitor Your Progress

Assessment Practice

Reading: Analyzing Purpose

Directions: *Choose the letter of the best answer to each question about the article.*

1. Which detail **best** supports the interview's purpose of entertaining?
   - **A** information about upcoming issues
   - **B** information about awards the comic book has won
   - **C** details about the comic's release date
   - **D** images from the comic book
2. Which detail **best** supports the interview's purpose of informing?
   - **A** Amaya's answer to the question about what fuels his passion for comic books
   - **B** Amaya's description of the historical basis of the comic's story
   - **C** Amaya's use of vivid language to describe his characters
   - **D** the interviewer's prediction that Amaya's comic will be a hit
3. What is the **overall** purpose of this interview?
   - **A** to increase sales of *ComicFan*
   - **B** to inform *ComicFan* readers about the historical background of the comic
   - **C** to introduce Amaya and his work to the magazine's readers
   - **D** to inspire *ComicFan* readers to create their own historical comic books
4. Which of the following is probably **not** another purpose of the interview?
   - **A** to persuade readers to subscribe to *ComicFan*
   - **B** to persuade readers of *ComicFan* to read *Roland: Song of Wrath*
   - **C** to increase sales of Amaya's comic book
   - **D** to advance Amaya's career

Reading: Comprehension and Interpretation

Directions: *Write your answers on a separate sheet of paper.*

5. **(a)** On which work of literature did Amaya base his comic book? **(b)** Summarize Amaya's analysis of this work's story and characters.
6. **(a)** What is Amaya's attitude toward the Middle Ages and medieval literature? **(b)** According to Amaya, why is the *Song of Roland* an example of "medieval ingenuity"?
7. **(a)** According to Amaya, in what way do comic books contrast with other forms of artistic expression? **(b)** What aspect of comics does Amaya love the most?

Timed Writing: Exposition

Write a proposal explaining how you would turn a specific work of literature into a comic book or an animated cartoon. Summarize the plot, describe the main characters, and provide an overview of the theme your comic or cartoon would address. Then, describe the style of art you would use. In writing your proposal, discuss why the work you have chosen is well suited to a comic form. ***(25 minutes)***

Extend the Lesson

Conducting an Interview

Have students interview a classmate about one of his or her accomplishments. Point out these five tips for conducting an interview:

1. Contact the person to set up a day and time for the interview.
2. Write your questions in advance.
3. Gather the materials you need, such as a note pad, pens or pencils, and a tape recorder.
4. While interviewing, listen carefully to the interviewee's responses. A response to one question might give you ideas for another question.
5. Take thorough notes during your interview.

Emphasize that the students' interview questions should relate only to the interviewee's accomplishments. Students should ask permission to tape the interview. Also point out that the interviewers must write the interviewee's words exactly so that comments do not get distorted. After students have finished their rough drafts, have them compare the drafts with their tapes and replace any incorrect information. Then, have them write and submit their final drafts.

ASSESS

Answers

Reading: Analyzing Purpose

1. D
2. B
3. C
4. A

Reading: Comprehension and Interpretation

5. (a) Amaya's comic is based on the *Song of Roland,* a medieval French war epic. (b) The story takes place in the eighth century in Charlemagne's Holy Roman Empire and includes Roland's sacrifice, his stepfather's betrayal, and Charlemagne's embattlement. The characters are warriors, feudal lords, kings, and vassals who are fighting, killing, and dying on the battlefields.
6. (a) Amaya thinks that the Middle Ages are not only a fascinating period but also "a creatively astounding period." He believes that medieval imagination has had a profound effect on the modern world. (b) He is astonished by the ingenuity of the *Song of Roland* because even though Chalemagne's actual defeat was a shameful mark on history, the story presents a battle of extraordinary struggle and sacrifice with good and evil characters of immense status and thousands of warriors. This story still resonates with readers today.
7. (a) Amaya believes that comic books offer the best storytelling and evoke a more emotional response than other types of literature. He says that reading a comic book is interactive and requires that the reader use his or her imagination. (b) Amaya loves the ability of comic books to express, relate, and share. Comic books also encourage the creativity of the two art forms of writing and illustrating in one medium.

Timed Writing

- Tell students that their proposals should clearly persuade readers that this project will be well worth reading.
- Suggest that students plan their time to give 10 minutes to planning, 10 minutes to writing, and 5 minutes to revising and editing.

Standard Course of Study

Goal 2: INFORMATIONAL READING

IR.2.01.2 Analyze text components and evaluate their impact on research questions.

Goal 4: CRITICAL THINKING

CT.4.02.3 Examine how elements such as irony and symbolism impact theme.

Goal 5: LITERATURE

LT.5.01.3 Analyze literary devices and explain their effect on the work of world literature.

LT.5.01.5 Analyze archetypal characters, themes, and settings in world literature.

LT.5.03.10 Analyze connections between ideas, concepts, characters and experiences in world literature.

Goal 6: GRAMMAR AND USAGE

GU.6.01.1 Employ varying sentence structures and sentence types.

Step-by-Step Teaching Guide	Pacing Guide
PRETEACH	
• Administer Vocabulary and Reading Warm-ups as necessary.	5 min.
• Engage students' interest with the motivation activity.	5 min.
• Read and discuss author, background, and From the Scholar's Desk features. **FT**	10 min.
• Introduce the Literary Analysis Skill: Archetypes. **FT**	5 min.
• Introduce the Reading Strategy: Interpreting Symbols. **FT**	10 min.
• Prepare students to read by teaching the selection vocabulary. **FT**	
TEACH	
• Informally monitor comprehension while students read independently or in groups. **FT**	30 min.
• Monitor students' comprehension with the Reading Check notes.	as students read
• Reinforce vocabulary with Vocabulary Builder notes.	as students read
• Develop students' understanding of archetypes with the Literary Analysis annotations. **FT**	5 min.
• Develop students' ability to interpret symbols with the Reading Strategy annotations. **FT**	5 min.
ASSESS/EXTEND	
• Assess students' comprehension and mastery of the Literary Analysis and Reading Strategy by having them answer the Apply the Skills questions. **FT**	15 min.
• Have students complete the Vocabulary Lesson and the Grammar and Style Lesson. **FT**	15 min.
• Apply students' ability to revise to enrich symbolic meaning by using the Writing Lesson. **FT**	45 min. or homework
• Apply students' understanding by using one or more of the Extend Your Learning activities.	20–90 min. or homework
• Administer Selection Test A or Selection Test B. **FT**	15 min.

Resources

Print

Unit 5 Resources

Transparency

Graphic Organizer Transparencies

Technology

From the Author's Desk DVD . . . . Marilyn Stokstad, Segment 2

Print

Reader's Notebook [L2]

Reader's Notebook: Adapted Version [L1]

Reader's Notebook: English Learner's Version [EL]

Unit 5 Resources

Technology

Listening to Literature Audio CDs [L2, EL]

Reader's Notebook: Adapted Version Audio CD [L1, L2]

Print

Unit 5 Resources

General Resources

Technology

Go Online: Research **[L3]**
Go Online: Self-test **[L3]**
ExamView®, **Test Bank [L3]**

Choosing Resources for Differentiated Instruction

[L1] Special Needs Students
[L2] Below-Level Students
[L3] All Students
[L4] Advanced Students
[EL] English Learners

For Vocabulary and Reading Warm-ups and for Selection Tests, **A** signifies "less challenging" and **B** "more challenging." For Graphic Organizer transparencies, **A** signifies "not filled in" and **B** "filled in."

FT Fast Track Instruction: To move the lesson more quickly, use the strategies and activities identified with **FT**.

Scaffolding for Less Proficient and Advanced Students

The leveled Critical Thinking questions after selections progress in the levels of thinking required to answer them. To address the needs of your different students, you may use the (a) level questions for your less proficient students and the (b) level questions with your on-level and advanced students. The occasional (c) level questions are appropriate for your advanced students.

Use this complete suite of powerful teaching tools to make lesson planning and testing quicker and easier.

Use the interactive textbook (online and on CD-ROM) to make selections and activities come alive with audio and video support and interactive questions.

Go Online Professional Development **For:** Information about Lexiles
Visit: www.PHSchool.com
Web Code: eue-1111

 From the Scholar's Desk

Marilyn Stokstad

- You might wish to have students read Marilyn Stokstad's introduction to the unit on pages 584–585.
- Show Segment 2 on Marilyn Stokstad on ***From the Author's Desk DVD*** to provide insight into her interest in medieval art and the Grail legend. After students have watched the segment, **ask:** What is the Grail legend?
  Answer: The Grail legend describes the quest for the Holy Grail, or the cup that was supposedly used by Jesus at the Last Supper.

The Medieval Castle

- After students have read Stokstad's comments on these pages, **ask:** How does Stokstad explain the slow appearance of the castle?
  Answer: When she last visited Windsor Castle in England, she could only see "ghostly towers" through the thick fog; the rest of the castle slowly became visible through the fog. This type of sight is not uncommon in England.
- **Ask:** What features of castles provided protection?
  Answer: Castles were built with two towers that flanked the entrance; a moat or river protected the castle and required a drawbridge to enter it; and the door of heavy wood, fortified by metal, was protected by a sliding wood and metal grill.

Critical Viewing

Answer: The following details in the picture reflect Stokstad's description of medieval castles: The tops of the towers are notched; the castle is surrounded by water; high walls offer protection; and the door is flanked by two high towers and appears to be heavily fortified.

From the Scholar's Desk

MARILYN STOKSTAD INTRODUCES
from Perceval, *"The Grail" by Chrétien de Troyes*

The Medieval Castle: Picturing the Encounter

In Chrétien de Troyes's poem *Perceval,* the hero, Perceval, encounters the Holy Grail in a mysterious castle. To picture this episode in his quest, it helps to know something about medieval castles. The information that follows each of these four quotations from the poem will help you picture what Perceval sees.

"He caught sight / of a tower starting to appear . . ." That Perceval should find a castle slowly becoming visible, as if it were emerging out of the mist, is not surprising. The last time I visited Windsor Castle in England, I felt like Perceval. The fog was thick, and I could see only ghostly towers. Perceval sees a tower across the river, then more towers, and finally the Great Hall.

Medieval castles usually stood on hills or beside rivers. Where there was no river, deep ditches (moats) and high walls reinforced with towers surrounded courtyards and buildings. The walls and towers were crenellated, or notched, to form protective shields for men standing on top. A Great Tower served as the final refuge for the residents in wartime. The lord's hall and residence was a separate building.

"The youth went toward the gate and found / the drawbridge lowered . . ." Perceval enters the Grail Castle by crossing a drawbridge and passing through a gate into the castle yard. Castle gates

Marilyn Stokstad

Marilyn Stokstad, a distinguished professor of art history at Kansas University, is an expert in medieval and Spanish art. She enjoys writing about art for students and for the general public.

▼ **Critical Viewing**
What details in this photograph reflect Stokstad's description of a medieval castle? **[Connect]**

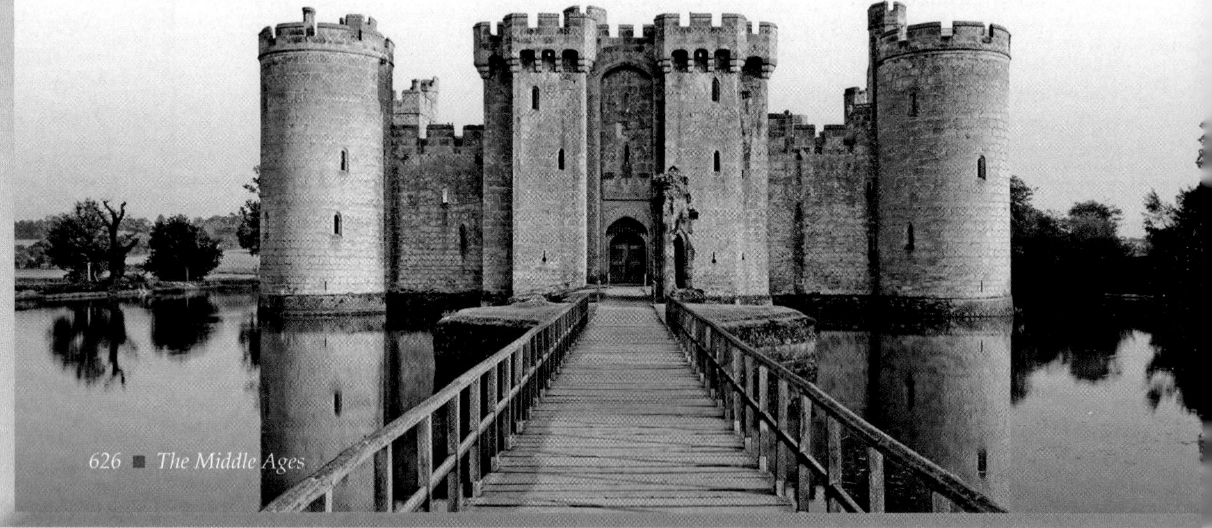

Teaching Resources

The following resources can be used to enrich or extend the instruction for From the Scholar's Desk.

Unit 5 Resources
- **Support for Penguin Essay,** p. 24
- **Listening and Viewing,** p. 25

From the Author's Desk DVD
- **Marilyn Stokstad,** Segment 2

were always heavily fortified. A pair of towers flanked the entrance, which consisted of a massive wooden door reinforced with metal. A sliding wood and metal grill (the portcullis) could be dropped in front of the door. When the drawbridge was raised, it also added to the strength of the door as well as the water defense. By the time a visitor, like Perceval, had passed these outer defenses, he would have been impressed, if not intimidated. Of course, that was the point. The castle symbolized the authority and military power of its lord.

"two squires escort him to the hall . . ." A medieval castle was not a single building. It was like a village with the lord's residence and hall, chapel, guardrooms, kitchen, dormitories, barns, craft shops, storehouses, and gardens. The most important building was the Great Hall.

In the Middle Ages, life revolved around the hall. The room served as a banquet hall, audience chamber, and courtroom, and at night servants, travelers, and even guests might sleep there. Furniture was simple: chests served as both seats and storage places, and trestle tables were stacked by the walls and assembled at meal times. In a wealthy household, gold and silver vessels and platters might be displayed on special ornate cupboards. Textiles provided color and luxury.

"a squire came, clasping / a lance of purest white . . ." As Perceval and the lord sit talking, a mysterious procession enters the hall. Young men carry a bleeding lance and two candelabra. Maidens bear a glowing, golden chalice and a silver platter. The procession itself is not surprising, since servants normally carried in the food in a procession. Food had to be brought into the hall from the kitchen beyond the screened passage at the far end of the hall.

But the lance and grail procession, which passes by the table and enters an inner room at the beginning and before every course in the banquet, is a strange form of this familiar ritual. To see what it might mean, join Perceval on his quest.

Thinking About the Commentary

1. **(a) Recall:** What did a castle look like from the outside? **(b) Connect:** In what ways did its position in the landscape and the details of its appearance relate to its main purpose of protection?
2. **(a) Recall:** How did a medieval castle resemble a village? **(b) Infer:** Why is it logical that Perceval's encounter with the grail occurs in the hall?

As You Read from *Perceval*, "The Grail" . . .

3. Use what you have learned about medieval castles to picture the action and descriptions in as much detail as possible.
4. Consider how the setting relates to the poem's theme.

- Point out that the Great Hall was a very practical room in the castle.
  Ask: What purposes did it serve?
  Answer: The Great Hall functioned as a banquet hall, audience chamber, courtroom, and sleeping quarters for servants, travelers, and guests.
- Then **ask:** How could a visitor in the Great Hall tell that a household was wealthy?
  Answer: Visitors might see gold and silver platters displayed on fancy cupboards or elegant tapestries.
- Point out that the kitchen was separate from the Great Hall, and servants walked the food from the kitchen to the hall in a procession.
  Ask: What kind of inconveniences might this process have caused?
  Possible response: The food could get cold sooner; if a servant forgot something or if a guest requested something, the requested item might not be ready at hand.

ASSESS

Answers

1. (a) A castle towered over the landscape with towers near its entrance and a moat or river that provided protection. Visitors and residents alike used the drawbridge to gain entrance to the heavy, fortified door. Often lords built castles on a hill. (b) The placement on a hill gave defenders a view of the countryside and of anyone trying to attack. The location near water made attack more difficult, and the towers and crenellated walls provided protection from attackers.
2. (a) A medieval castle contained the residence of the lord and lady, a chapel, guardrooms, a kitchen, dormitories, barns, craft shops, storehouses, and gardens, with the Great Hall at the center of castle life. (b) Perceval's encounter with the grail occurs in the hall because this is where the lord of the castle receives visitors and serves meals.
3. **Possible response:** Students may describe a battle scene that involves men shooting arrows from between a castle's crenellated towers, or students may describe an elaborate procession of servants who are carrying food into the Great Hall.
4. **Possible response:** The castle may seem like heaven and the poem's theme is about faith.

PRETEACH

Motivation

Have students work in pairs to brainstorm a list of words and phrases they think describe King Arthur and his Knights of the Round Table. Suggest that they consider what they have heard and read in sources such as books and television shows. After compiling a representative class list, encourage students to keep these ideas in mind as they read and to compare them with their impressions of Perceval in this selection.

❶ Background

More About the Authors

Very little is known about the author Chrétien de Troyes. He was from Brittany, a region populated by Celts who fled from Britain and who still speak a Celtic language today. Breton mythology is Celtic, and the story of Perceval fits well into the traditions of dragons, enchanted forests, and mysterious elements that abound in these Celtic legends.

Little is also known of Marie de France's life. Even her name is subject to conjecture; it is based on a line in a manuscript found in 1581 that said, "At the end of this text, which I have composed in romance [the vernacular], I shall name myself for the sake of posterity: Marie is my name and I am from France."

Geography Note

Call students' attention to the map on this page. Explain that both Chrétien de Troyes and Marie de France probably lived in northern France, possibly in Brittany and Normandy. Marie de France spoke an Anglo-Norman dialect that was popular at the time with the aristocracy. Dialects around the country were gradually replaced with a standard French by the nineteenth century.

Build Skills | *Poem • Short Story*

❶ *from* Perceval • The Lay of the Werewolf

Chrétien de Troyes (1135–1180)

Chrétien de Troyes (krā tyan də trwá) was one of the first and most gifted authors of Arthurian romances. Details about his life are lost to time, but his name provides the clue that he probably came from the town of Troyes, located in the heart of the Champagne region of France. The name *Chrétien,* which means Christian, may simply be an indication of his religion.

An Educated Courtier Most of what scholars know about Chrétien's life is based on an analysis of his work. Clearly, he was well educated. His work reflects knowledge of Latin as well as the cultures of Provence, a region in southern France, and Bretagne (Brittany), a region in northwest France. He wrote in the vernacular—the language of common people—and was inspired by a French translation of Geoffrey of Monmouth's *Historia Regum Britanniae,* which introduced the British legends of King Arthur to continental Europe.

The Grail Tale Chrétien's *Perceval* is the earliest known version of the Grail legend, which describes the quest for the Holy Grail, the cup from which Jesus drank at the Last Supper. According to medieval legend, both this cup and the lance that pierced Jesus' side during the Crucifixion were hidden in a magical castle. Sometime in the late Middle Ages, the Grail legend was woven into the tales of King Arthur and his knights. The knights sought to find this mystical object, which would then enable Arthur to found a new holy kingdom. Only a knight of absolute purity would be able to find the Grail. In *Perceval,* Chrétien created a knight virtuous enough to see the Grail but not quite pure enough to obtain it. Chrétien died before completing this story; nevertheless, it remains one of the most enduring tales to emerge from the Middle Ages.

Marie de France (c. 1155–1190)

Little is known about the life of Marie de France, one of the finest storytellers of the Middle Ages. Yet her works, which were read by Boccaccio and Chaucer, were crucial to the development of the short story. Scholars know that she lived in the French-speaking English court of the late twelfth century, about one hundred years after the Norman Conquest. She was well educated, a member of the nobility, and possibly an abbess. Her name suggests that she came from France.

Magical Worlds Marie's work combines elements of the classical, Christian, and Celtic traditions. For example, in *Saint Patrick's Purgatory,* which she translated from the Latin, the hero travels to another land, where he learns the secrets of the Christian faith. The theme of a voyage to another world, usually the magical world of the dead, is typical of Celtic mythology. In Marie's work, however, the magical journey reinforces Christian morality.

Radical Ideas Marie's most original works, the *lais* (lā), explore the conflict between passionate love and marital duty. The *lais* are short stories, written in verse, that combine folkloric elements of magic with the newly popular concept of courtly love. Initially, the idea of courtly love involved the hopeless adoration of an unobtainable woman by a young man of inferior social standing. Marie revised this perception to achieve a more realistic view of human relationships. For Marie, a man and a woman should choose each other because of a genuine affinity. In an era when most marriages were based on political or economic interests, this idea was a radical departure from the norm. Through her work, Marie helped lay the foundations for modern ideas about love and marriage.

Preview

Connecting to the Literature

You have probably had dreams in which odd things happen. You may fly over rooftops or find yourself in a strange situation that nevertheless seems familiar. The adventures in these selections echo such dreamlike images.

NC Standard Course of Study

- Examine how elements such as irony and symbolism impact theme. (CT.4.02.3)
- Analyze archetypal characters, themes, and settings in world literature. (LT.5.01.5)

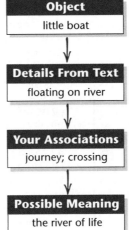

❷ Literary Analysis

Archetypes

Archetypes are details, plot patterns, character types, or themes that appear in the literature of many different cultures. Chrétien de Troyes's tale contains the archetype of the quest, while Marie de France's story contains the archetype of disguised identity.

- *The quest:* A quest is the pursuit of someone or something of great importance. While on a quest, a hero journeys great distances, defeats evil, demonstrates valor, and grows in wisdom and maturity.
- *Disguised identity:* Characters use disguises, transformations, and tricks to hide their true identities.

As you read these selections, notice the ways in which they follow archetypal patterns.

Comparing Literary Works

Archetypes almost always have a deeper, symbolic significance. A **symbol** is a person, a place, an animal, or an object that has its own meaning but also suggests a larger meaning. For example, a rose might symbolize love. In many medieval tales, the entire story centers on a symbol. In *Perceval,* the grail is not merely a golden cup but an object symbolizing the story's most important ideas. As you read these selections, compare the ways in which symbols express each tale's central meaning.

❸ Reading Strategy

Interpreting Symbols

To **interpret a symbol** and better appreciate archetypal narratives, examine the details associated with characters, places, objects, or events, and consider them in the context of the story. For example, when Perceval nears the edge of a cliff, the cliff might symbolize the danger of his quest. As you read these selections, use a chart like the one shown to interpret symbols.

Object
little boat
↓
Details From Text
floating on river
↓
Your Associations
journey; crossing
↓
Possible Meaning
the river of life

Vocabulary Builder

sovereign (säv´ rən) *adj.* chief; superior; highest (p. 630)

navigated (nav´ i gāt´ əd) *v.* piloted; steered (a boat) (p. 631)

elated (ē lāt´ əd) *adj.* extremely happy; joyful (p. 633)

serene (sə rēn´) *adj.* clear; calm; peaceful (p. 637)

nimble (nim´ bəl) *adj.* able to move quickly and lightly; agile (p. 639)

esteemed (e stēmd´) *v.* valued; respected (p. 642)

importunity (im´ pôr to͞on´ i tē) *n.* persistence (p. 644)

abases (ə bās´ əz) *v.* lowers; brings down (p. 645)

Differentiated Instruction
Solutions for All Learners

Support for Special Needs Students

Have students use the support pages for these selections in the ***Reader's Notebook: Adapted Version.*** Completing these pages will prepare students to read the selections in the Student Edition.

Support for Less Proficient Readers

Have students use the support pages for these selections in the ***Reader's Notebook.*** Completing these pages will prepare students to read the selections in the Student Edition.

Support for English Learners

Have students use the support pages for these selections in the ***Reader's Notebook: English Learner's Version.*** Completing these pages will prepare students to read the selections in the Student Edition.

❷ Literary Analysis

Archetypes

- Have a student read aloud the Literary Analysis instruction.
- Point out that the quest is a theme found in many cultures. Tell students that in addition to "The Grail," other examples of quests include the Ashanti legend *Journey to Asamando, Land of the Dead; The Odyssey;* and such contemporary entertainment as *The Wizard of Oz.* **Invite** students to give more examples of quests.
  Possible response: The Spanish story *The Poem of the Cid* and *The Lord of the Rings* are possible suggestions.
- Tell students to look for ways in which "The Grail" resembles other quests they have read about or seen in movies or on television.

❸ Reading Strategy

Interpreting Symbols

- Remind students that a symbol is something that has two or more meanings. An apple, for example, is a fruit that one eats. Its symbolic meanings can include knowledge or sin.
- Explain that in "The Grail," the central symbol is the Grail, or cup of Jesus. Elicit from students that the Grail can have many meanings, such as forgiveness, love, or eternal life.
- Give students a copy of **Reading Strategy Graphic Organizer A,** p. 113 in ***Graphic Organizer Transparencies.*** Have them use it to examine elements in "The Grail" and "The Lay of the Werewolf" that may have symbolic importance.

Vocabulary Builder

- Pronounce each vocabulary word for students, and read the definitions as a class. Have students identify any words with which they are already familiar.

Facilitate Understanding

Tell students to keep in mind that Perceval is a youth. Have them picture someone their own age as they read about Perceval's quest.

❶ About the Selection

Perceval tells the story of an innocent young knight of King Arthur's Round Table who is on a personal and spiritual quest to become a worthy knight. In "The Grail," Perceval attends a lavish dinner at a magnificent castle. During the dinner, he observes two remarkable items that puzzle him—a Grail and a lance. The selection raises questions about the meaning of a personal quest and the personal qualities needed to overcome challenges.

❷ Scholar's Insight

- Point out Stokstad's comments about the value of the King Arthur stories during the twelfth century.
- **Ask** students what lessons the King Arthur stories still hold today.
  Answer: The stories teach about bravery and loyalty. Reading the stories is both educational and entertaining.

❸ Reading Strategy

Interpreting Symbols

- Have a student read aloud the second bracketed passage.
- **Ask** students the Reading Strategy question: Which details in the description of the river suggest its possible symbolic meaning? Explain.
  Possible response: The rapid current, deep water, and high cliff suggest the river's symbolic meaning. Each is a challenge that Perceval must face on his quest.

from *Perceval*

❶ The Grail

Chrétien de Troyes *translated by* Ruth Harwood Cline

Background Perceval is a young man whose mother raised him in isolation after losing her husband and two other sons to chivalric combat. One day, Perceval meets a group of knights, who so impress him that he decides to become a knight himself. He journeys to King Arthur's court, proves his valor, and is accepted. As part of his training for knighthood, Perceval learns never to ask questions and never to speak until spoken to first. Once his training is complete, Perceval sets out on a quest for the Grail, or holy cup. This excerpt begins just before Perceval stumbles upon a mysterious castle, that of the ailing Fisher King.

The youth began his journey from
the castle, and the daytime whole
he did not meet one living soul:
no creature from the wide earth's span,
no Christian woman, Christian man
who could direct him on his way.
The young man did not cease to pray
the sovereign father, God, Our Lord,
if He were willing, to accord
that he would find his mother still
alive and well. He reached a hill
and saw a river at its base.
❸ So rapid was the current's pace,
so deep the water, that he dared
not enter it, and he declared,
"Oh God Almighty! It would seem,
if I could get across this stream,
I'd find my mother, if she's living."
He rode the bank with some misgiving
and reached a cliff, but at that place
the water met the cliff's sheer face
and kept the youth from going through.

Marilyn Stokstad
❷ Scholar's Insight
In the late twelfth century, men and women read for pleasure as well as enlightenment. The stories of King Arthur and his knights provided entertainment and moral lessons.

Vocabulary Builder
sovereign (säv′ rən) *adj.* chief; superior; highest

Reading Strategy
Interpreting Symbols
Which details in the description of the river suggest its possible symbolic meaning? Explain.

Differentiated Instruction Solutions for All Learners

Accessibility at a Glance

	from *Perceval* The Grail	The Lay of the Werewolf
Context	A knight's quest for the Holy Grail	The concealment of one's personal identity by outward appearance
Language	Old-fashioned vocabulary to reflect the legend's antiquity	Narrative prose with some dialogue and words with symbolic meaning
Concept Level	Accessible (The price of too much passivity)	Challenging (The paradox of man's duality)
Literary Merit	Earliest known version of the Grail legend	Classic story containing the archetype of disguised identity
Lexile	NP	1010L
Overall Rating	Average	Challenging

A little boat came into view;
it headed down the river, floating
and carrying two men out boating.
The young knight halted there and waited.
(4) He watched the way they navigated
and thought that they would pass the place
he waited by the cliff's sheer face.
They stayed in mid-stream, where they stopped
and took the anchor, which they dropped.
The man afore,[1] a fisher, took
a fish to bait his line and hook;
in size the little fish he chose
was larger than a minnow grows.
The knight, completely at a loss,
not knowing how to get across,
first greeted them, then asked the pair,
(5) "Please, gentlemen, nearby is there
a bridge to reach the other side?"
To which the fisherman replied,
"No, brother, for besides this boat,
the one in which we are afloat,
which can't bear five men's weight as charge,
there is no other boat as large
for twenty miles each way and more,
and you can't cross on horseback, for
there is no ferry, bridge, nor ford."
(6) "Tell me," he answered, "by Our Lord,
where I may find a place to stay."
The fisherman said, "I should say
you'll need a roof tonight and more,
so I will lodge you at my door.
First find the place this rock is breached
and ride uphill, until you've reached
the summit of the cliff," he said.
"Between the wood and river bed
you'll see, down in the valley wide,
the manor house where I reside."
The knight rode up the cliff until
he reached the summit of the hill.
He looked around him from that stand
but saw no more than sky and land.
(10) He cried, "What have I come to see?
Stupidity and trickery!
May God dishonor and disgrace
the man who sent me to this place!
He had the long way round in mind,

Vocabulary Builder
navigated (nav′ i gāt′ əd) *v.* piloted; steered (a boat)

Literary Analysis
Archetypes At this stage of the quest, is the challenge the knight faces physical, emotional, or intellectual? Explain.

Reading Strategy
Interpreting Symbols Which details in this exchange suggest that the fisherman might be more than he seems to be?

(7) 
Reading Check
Whom does Perceval meet at the river?

1. **afore** (ə fôr′) before.

(4) Vocabulary Builder

Latin Root *-naviga-*

- Call students' attention to the word *navigated* and its use in line 27.
- Explain that *-naviga-* is a Latin root that means "to steer a ship." Have students **brainstorm** words that contain *-naviga-* and then use those words in sentences.
  Possible response: *Navigation* and *navigator* contain the Latin root *-naviga-*.

(5) Literary Analysis

Archetypes

- **Ask** students how meeting the fisherman might contribute to Perceval's quest.
  Possible response: The fisherman may help Perceval on his journey or give him knowledge that might assist him later.
- Allow students time to independently read the bracketed passage. Then, **ask** the Literary Analysis question: At this stage of the quest, is the challenge the knight faces physical, emotional, or intellectual? Explain.
  Answer: The challenge that Perceval faces is physical. He must find a way to cross the river.

(6) Reading Strategy

Interpreting Symbols

- Review with students the information on p. 629 about interpreting symbols. **Ask** students: Do you think the fisherman is a symbol? Explain.
  Possible response: The fisherman is a symbol because he is someone who knows the water and the things beneath the surface.
- Then, have students **respond** to the Reading Strategy question: Which details in this exchange suggest that the fisherman might be more than he seems to be?
  Possible response: The fisherman says that he lives in a manor, which means that he may be more than he appears.

(7) Reading Check

Answer: Perceval meets a fisherman at the river.

Differentiated Instruction — Solutions for All Learners

Support for English Learners

Students may have difficulty with some of the vocabulary words in "The Grail." Explain that the language used is deliberately old-fashioned; it suggests the antiquity of the legend. Have students work in pairs on the **Vocabulary Warm-up List** and **Vocabulary Warm-up Practice**, pp. 26–27 in *Unit 5 Resources.* Then post the meanings of the following words on these pages: *span* (line 4), *pace* (line 13), *sheer* (line 21), and *breached* (line 54). Work with students to make up additional sentences using the words in another context (for example, "He read at a rapid pace.").

Enrichment for Advanced Readers

All students may find the selection from *Perceval* more enjoyable and rewarding if they know more about King Arthur and the Round Table. Have students learn about the legend through research and additional readings. Organize students into small groups, and have them divide the tasks. For example, some students might research the history of the legend, others its links to historical fact, and others the tales and poems that have been inspired by it. Have each group share its findings in a class discussion.

8 Humanities

Parsifal Sees the Grail's Castle, by Martin Weigand

This painting, which dates from the early twentieth century, gives a romantic rather than a realistic interpretation of Perceval's arrival at the castle. Note that he is fully armed and carrying his lance as though ready for battle—an unlikely way to carry a weapon during an all-day ride. Likewise, he is not carrying a satchel or saddlebags, which he would need to hold a change of clothing, food, or other supplies for a long journey.

Use the following questions for discussion:

- What is the mood of the painting? Explain your answer.
  Possible response: The mood is romantic and adventurous. The details of the castle suggest endless possibilities: Anything might happen. Perceval is armed and ready for any adventure that might come his way.
- Why might the artist have decided not to give Perceval a bundle of supplies such as a traveler might carry?
  Possible response: It is more romantic to have Perceval appear unencumbered by a bundle of supplies. This lack of supplies also elevates Perceval above normal human needs; he is somehow greater than the viewer.

9 Critical Viewing

Possible response: The castle is wrapped in clouds and appears almost to be floating in the air. The castle itself seems insubstantial, as though it is not entirely real.

8

Parsifal Sees the Grail's Castle, Martin Wiegand

9 ▲ **Critical Viewing** Which details in this painting of Perceval suggest that the castle has magical or supernatural qualities? **[Analyze]**

Enrichment

Perceval and His Mother

Perceval's naïveté throughout "The Grail" can be better understood by learning about his life before the Grail quest. Perceval's father and brothers are killed in battle, leaving Perceval's mother to raise him on her own. His mother fears that Perceval will meet a similar fate, so she shelters her son from the outside world. Perceval knows nothing about knights, chivalry, or courtly love; in fact, he does not even know his own name. When Perceval encounters King Arthur's knights in the forest, he decides that he wants to become a knight, too.

Perceval's mother is devastated to learn of her son's desire to become a knight. Despite her pleas, Perceval remains committed to his decision. His mother falls to the ground in grief at his departure, but Perceval continues on to King Arthur's court. Later, Perceval encounters a maiden who tells him the story behind the Fisher King—and informs him of his mother's death.

when he told me that I would find
a manor when I reached the peak.
Oh, fisherman, why did you speak?
For if you said it out of spite,
you tricked me badly!" He caught sight
of a tower starting to appear
down in a valley he was near,
and as the tower came into view,
if people were to search, he knew,
as far as Beirut,[2] they would not
10 find any finer tower or spot.
The tower was dark gray stone, and square,
11 and flanked by lesser towers, a pair.
Before the tower the hall was laid;
before the hall was the arcade.[3]
On toward the tower the young man rode
in haste and called the man who showed
the way to him a worthy guide.
No longer saying he had lied,
he praised the fisherman, elated
to find his lodgings as he stated.
The youth went toward the gate and found
the drawbridge lowered to the ground.
He rode across the drawbridge span.
Four squires awaited the young man.
Two squires came up to help him doff
his arms and took his armor off.
The third squire led his horse away
to give him fodder, oats, and hay.
The fourth brought a silk cloak, new-made,
and led him to the hall's arcade,
which was so fine, you may be sure
you'd not find, even if you were
to search as far as Limoges,[4] one
as splendid in comparison.
The young man paused in the arcade,
until the castle's master made
two squires escort him to the hall.
The young man entered with them all
and found the hall was square inside:
it was as long as it was wide;
and in the center of its span
12 he saw a handsome nobleman
with grayed hair, sitting on a bed.

Literary Analysis
Archetypes What lesson should Perceval learn from accusing, and then praising, the fisherman?

Vocabulary Builder
elated (ē lāt′ əd) *adj.* extremely happy; joyful

Marilyn Stokstad
Scholar's Insight
Since the bed was often the largest and most important piece of furniture in a house, it was not unusual to find it in one of the principal rooms.

13 

Reading Check
What appears "down in a valley" as Perceval watches?

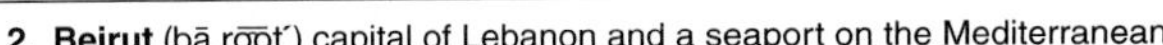

2. **Beirut** (bā ro͞ot′) capital of Lebanon and a seaport on the Mediterranean.
3. **arcade** (är kād′) passage with an arched roof, or any covered passageway.
4. **Limoges** (lē mōzh′) city in west central France.

10 Literary Analysis
Archetypes

- Read aloud the bracketed passage. **Ask** students how Perceval's feelings toward the man in the boat change in lines 64–89 and why.
  Answer: Initially, when Perceval does not see the castle, he thinks the man has tricked him; by the end of this passage, he praises the man because the castle looks so grand.
- **Ask** students the Literary Analysis question: What lesson should Perceval learn from accusing, and then praising, the fisherman?
  Answer: Perceval should learn not to be so hasty in condemning others.

11 Critical Thinking
Draw Conclusions

- Explain to students that Perceval is one of the few knights who will be allowed to see the Fisher King's castle and the mysteries within. Guide students to recognize that this is a tribute to Perceval's innocent, virtuous character.
- **Ask** students what conclusions they can draw about Perceval's character from the change in his feelings in the bracketed passage.
  Possible response: Perceval has a temper and jumps to incorrect conclusions, but he also has the ability to admit his mistakes and correct himself.

12 Scholar's Insight

- Direct students' attention to Stokstad's comment about medieval furniture. Point out that today people consider beds and sleeping areas very personal and private. Although it may seem odd to us to receive guests on a bed in the main room, Perceval would not consider this unusual.
- **Ask:** How might you feel if your bed was moved to such a public space as a living room or open hall?
  Answer: Students might answer that they would feel uncomfortable because they would have very little privacy, or feel that their sleep would be disturbed if their bedroom were out in the open.

13 Reading Check

Answer: The castle appears "down in the valley."

Differentiated Instruction
Solutions for All Learners

Strategy for Special Needs Students
Explain that Perceval will grow and change as the story progresses. Have each student begin a character analysis map and develop it as he or she continues reading. First, tell students to create cluster maps by writing "Perceval" in a center circle on a sheet of paper. Then, have them add details of Perceval's physical, psychological, and intellectual qualities in surrounding circles.

Support for Less Proficient Readers
Have students listen to the **Listening to Literature Audio CDs** for Perceval. Encourage them to visualize the descriptions of Perceval, his meeting with the fisherman, and his stay at the castle. When the recording is finished, lead a discussion of the story. Which scenes did students find most appealing? Which scenes did they find confusing or unclear? Discuss these scenes in more detail.

14 Themes in World Literature

Quest Narratives

Joseph Campbell, author of *Hero With a Thousand Faces,* observes that the quest is essentially the same in every culture and every myth. He describes the journey as a series of steps. The quest begins with the call to adventure. The hero soon finds allies, people who in some manner aid the hero on his or her way. (The nobleman is such a figure.) The hero then steps into the unknown and passes through a series of trials that will ultimately allow the hero to progress and change into someone better. The hero may meet more helpers along the way, and he or she eventually achieves the goal of the quest. Then, the hero must return home—a journey that he or she may resist. Finally, the hero shares the gift—usually of wisdom or faith—that he or she earned on the quest.

Connect to the Literature Point out that the Grail is the main symbol of this tale, but Perceval doesn't understand its significance. Note that a mystery surrounds the appearance of the Grail in the Fisher King's domain. Ask students what they think is Perceval's motive for traveling about. **Possible response:** After his training to become a knight, Perceval, who yearns to be a worthy knight, sets out on a quest to find the Holy Grail for King Arthur. He also hopes to visit his mother along the way.

15 Scholar's Insight

- Have students note Stokstad's comment about the watchman's horn and the church bell.
- Point out that in medieval times these were ways to notify people of time and important events since there were no clocks.
- **Ask:** Why would it have been important to communicate time by horns or bells?
  Answer: The closing and opening of city gates would have been important for safety reasons. Also, religion played a large role in medieval life so calling people to church was important as well.

The nobleman wore on his head
a mulberry-black sable cap
and wore a dark silk robe and wrap.
He leaned back in his weakened state
and let his elbow take his weight.
Between four columns, burning bright,
a fire of dry logs cast its light.
In order to enjoy its heat,
four hundred men could find a seat
around the outsized fire, and not
one man would take a chilly spot.
The solid fireplace columns could
support the massive chimney hood,
which was of bronze, built high and wide.
The squires, one squire on either side,
appeared before their lord foremost
and brought the youth before his host.
He saw the young man, whom he greeted.
"My friend," the nobleman entreated,
"don't think me rude not to arise;
I hope that you will realize
that I cannot do so with ease."
"Don't even mention it, sir, please,
I do not mind," replied the boy,
"may Heaven give me health and joy."
The lord rose higher on the bed,
as best he could, with pain, and said,
"My friend, come nearer, do not be
embarrassed or disturbed by me,
for I command you to come near.
Come to my side and sit down here."
The nobleman began to say,
"From where, sir, did you come today?"
He said, "This morning, sir, I came
from Belrepeire, for that's its name."
"So help me God," the lord replied,
"you must have had a long day's ride:
to start before the light of morn
before the watchman blew his horn."
"Sir, I assure you, by that time
the morning bells had rung for prime,"[5]
the young man made the observation.
While they were still in conversation,
a squire entered through the door
and carried in a sword he wore
hung from his neck and which thereto

5. **prime** first hour of daylight, usually 6 A.M.

14 Quest Narratives

The quest archetype is central to literature because it is central to the imagination. The journey, which is motivated by the pursuit of love or glory, filled with peril, stalled by monsters, aided by friends, and completed in a joyous homecoming, mirrors the path of life. Many of literature's most compelling narratives—including Jason's search for the Golden Fleece, Don Quixote's struggle against imaginary monsters, Frodo's passage into the heart of evil, and even Indiana Jones's pursuit of ancient treasures—are quest tales. The quest is the archetypal pattern that people follow in order to become the heroes of their own lives.

Connect to the Literature

What do you think motivates Perceval's quest?

***Marilyn Stokstad* Scholar's Insight**

Watchmen blew horns to signal the closing of castle or city gates at sunset and the opening at sunrise. Church bells called the community together for services at appointed hours.

he gave the rich man, who withdrew
the sword halfway and checked the blade
to see where it was forged and made,
which had been written on the sword.
The blade was wrought, observed the lord,
of such fine steel, it would not break
save with its bearer's life at stake
on one occasion, one alone,
a peril that was only known
to him who forged and tempered it.
The squire said, "Sir, if you permit,
your lovely blonde niece sent this gift,
and you will never see or lift
a sword that's lighter for its strength,
considering its breadth and length.
Please give the sword to whom you choose,
but if it goes to one who'll use
the sword that he is given well,
you'll greatly please the demoiselle.
The forger of the sword you see
has never made more swords than three,
and he is going to die before
he ever forges any more.
No sword will be quite like this sword."
Immediately the noble lord
bestowed it on the newcomer,
who realized that its hangings were
a treasure and of worth untold.
The pommel[6] of the sword was gold,
the best Arabian or Grecian;
the sheath's embroidery gold Venetian.
Upon the youth the castle's lord
bestowed the richly mounted sword
and said to him, "This sword, dear brother,
was destined for you and none other.
I wish it to be yours henceforth.
Gird on the sword and draw it forth."
He thanked the lord, and then the knight
made sure the belt was not too tight,
and girded on the sword, and took
the bare blade out for a brief look.
Then in the sheath it was replaced:
it looked well hanging at his waist
and even better in his fist.
It seemed as if it would assist

18 ▲ Critical Viewing
The bottom band of this illustrated manuscript shows Perceval and others nearing the Castle of the Grail. Is the mood of this scene similar to or different from the mood created by the poem? **[Compare and Contrast]**

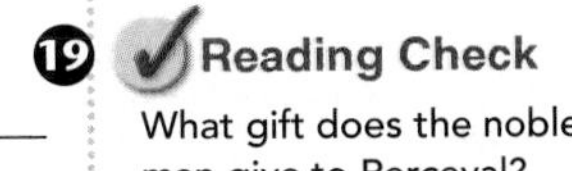

19 Reading Check
What gift does the nobleman give to Perceval?

6. **pommel** (pum′ el) *n.* knob on the end of the hilt of a sword or dagger.

16 Critical Thinking

Speculate

- Read the bracketed passage beginning on the previous page.
  Ask students why they think the nobleman would give a sword with such a secret to Perceval.
  Possible response: The nobleman foresees the future and knows that Perceval will need the weapon in a moment of particular danger.
- **Ask:** Was this entire scene prepared in advance for Perceval? Explain.
  Possible response: The nobleman tells Perceval that the "sword . . . was destined for you," which implies that it was made, with its special secret, to be presented to Perceval at just this time.

17 Humanities

Kundry and Feirefiz Ride to the Grail Castle Where a Feast Is Held

This section of the German illuminated manuscript of *Perceval* dates from the mid-thirteenth century. The artist, who is unknown, chose to show three different scenes from the text displayed in horizontal bands on a single page. The first band shows King Arthur and King Gramoflanz in their separate tents; the second band illustrates their meeting at an elaborate banquet; and the third band shows Perceval, Kundry, and Feirefiz approaching the Grail Castle. Each scene is crowded with figures and details, resulting in a lively presentation of the story.

Use the following question for discussion:

What impression does the viewer receive about life in the Middle Ages when viewing this painting?
Possible response: Life in the Middle Ages seems romantic and adventurous, an era of horses, armor, swords, rich banquets, and castles. However, it may be a difficult life, if one were not a knight.

18 Critical Viewing

Possible response: The celebratory mood of the characters in the scene is more uplifting than the darker, mysterious mood evoked by the poem.

19 Reading Check

Answer: The nobleman gives Perceval a sword.

Differentiated Instruction Solutions for All Learners

Support for English Learners

Tell students that *demoiselle* is a French word for "young lady." Some students will be more familiar with the term *mademoiselle.* Invite student groups to discuss the denotations and connotations of English words for young lady such as *woman, girl, lady, chick,* and *gal.* Students may benefit from using dictionaries as they discuss each of these words. Tell students to construct language charts, noting words, definitions, and connotations.

Enrichment for Gifted/Talented Students

Remind students that Perceval is looking for a place to spend the night; and instead, he walks into a castle where he is entertained by a wealthy nobleman who generously gives him a very fine sword. Throughout the encounter, Perceval says little and expresses no surprise. Ask students to imagine what is going on in Perceval's mind. How does this treatment make him feel? Is he suspicious of the nobleman's motives? Have students rewrite the scene to include what they imagine to be Perceval's thoughts and feelings.

20 Reading Strategy

Interpreting Symbols

- Read the bracketed passage to students.
- Explain that this lance was thought by medieval Christians to be the one used by a Roman soldier to pierce Jesus' side after his death. **Ask** students why it might be fitting that this special lance drips blood.
  Answer: The lance symbolizes the crucifixion of Jesus.

21 Humanities

The Damsel of Sanct Grael,
by Dante Gabriel Rossetti

British artist Dante Gabriel Rossetti (1828–1882) was a poet as well as a painter. Rossetti painted this watercolor in 1857. The single figure that fills the picture is fashioned with a spare and angular grace. Her hair and expression provide an almost mystical appearance. The symbolism of the dove and the covered basket of bread enhance this effect.

Rossetti's model for this and many other paintings was Elizabeth Siddal, a fellow poet and painter who became his wife.

Use the following questions for discussion:

- What is the effect in this painting of the radiant hair and the expression on the damsel's face?
  Possible response: The damsel's radiant hair and facial expression produce a peaceful, mystical effect. They create the feeling that the damsel is floating or stepping lightly.
- Why do you think the artist chose to fill the entire picture with the damsel?
  Possible response: The artist wanted to emphasize the importance of the damsel carrying the Grail.

22 Critical Viewing

Possible response: The woman carrying the Grail in the painting looks "noble," "well dressed," and "serene," just as the poet describes her. However, the Grail is not casting a light in the picture, although the poet describes it as doing so.

the youth in any time of need
to do a brave and knightly deed.
Beside the brightly burning fire
the youth turned round and saw a squire,
who had his armor in his care,
among the squires standing there.
He told this squire to hold the sword
and took his seat beside the lord,
who honored him as best he might.
The candles cast as bright a light
as could be found in any manor.
They chatted in a casual manner.
Out of a room a squire came, clasping
a lance of purest white: while grasping
the center of the lance, the squire
walked through the hall between the fire
and two men sitting on the bed.
All saw him bear, with measured tread,
the pure white lance. From its white tip
a drop of crimson blood would drip
and run along the white shaft and
drip down upon the squire's hand,
and then another drop would flow.
The knight who came not long ago
beheld this marvel, but preferred
not to inquire why it occurred,
for he recalled the admonition
the lord made part of his tuition,[7]
since he had taken pains to stress
the dangers of loquaciousness.[8]
The young man thought his questions might
make people think him impolite,
and that's why he did not inquire.
Two more squires entered, and each squire
held candelabra, wrought of fine
pure gold with niello work design.[9]
The squires with candelabra fair
were an extremely handsome pair.
At least ten lighted candles blazed
in every holder that they raised.
The squires were followed by a maiden
who bore a grail, with both hands laden.

The Damsel of Sanct Grael, 1857, Dante Gabriel Rossetti, Tate Gallery, London

22 ▲ Critical Viewing
Which details in the poet's description of the grail and the maiden have been included in this painting, and which have been changed or omitted? Explain. **[Distinguish]**

7. **the admonition . . . tuition** the warning that the lord made part of his teaching.
8. **loquaciousness** (lō kwā′ shəs nis) *n.* talkativeness.
9. **niello** (nē el′ ō) **work design** deep black inlaid work used to decorate metal.

Enrichment

Joseph of Arimathea

A key figure in the legends that grew up around the Holy Grail was Joseph of Arimathea. He was a wealthy Jewish man who was said to have asked for Jesus' body after his death and whose tomb was used to bury Jesus. According to legend, he was also given the Holy Grail for safekeeping. Joseph is said to have caught the blood of Jesus in the cup. Romances from the 1200s claim that Joseph went to Glastonbury, a city in western England, as a missionary.

He carried the cup with him, and it was passed down from generation to generation. The Grail is reputed to have many miraculous qualities, including the power to provide food for those without sin, the power to blind the sinner, and the power to strike dumb the unfaithful who come near it. Glastonbury is also associated with King Arthur, linking the two legends highlighted in *Perceval.*

The bearer was of noble mien,[10]
well dressed, and lovely, and serene,
and when she entered with the grail,
23 the candles suddenly grew pale,
the grail cast such a brilliant light,
as stars grow dimmer in the night
when sun or moonrise makes them fade.
A maiden after her conveyed
a silver platter past the bed.
The grail, which had been borne ahead,
was made of purest, finest gold
and set with gems; a manifold
display of jewels of every kind,
24 the costliest that one could find
in any place on land or sea,
the rarest jewels there could be,
let not the slightest doubt be cast.
The jewels in the grail surpassed
all other gems in radiance.
They went the same way as the lance:
they passed before the lord's bedside
to another room and went inside.
The young man saw the maids' procession
and did not dare to ask a question
about the grail or whom they served;
the wise lord's warning he observed,
25 for he had taken it to heart.
I fear he was not very smart;
26 I have heard warnings people give:
that one can be too talkative,
but also one can be too still.
But whether it was good or ill,
I do not know, he did not ask.
The squires who were assigned the task
of bringing in the water and
the cloths obeyed the lord's command.
The men who usually were assigned
performed these tasks before they dined.
They washed their hands in water, warmed,
and then two squires, so I'm informed,
brought in the ivory tabletop,
made of one piece: they had to stop
and hold it for a while before

Vocabulary Builder
serene (sə rēn′) *adj.* clear; calm; peaceful

Marilyn Stokstad
Scholar's Insight
A grail was a large, deep serving dish. This grail is unusual in that it is made of gold studded with jewels, is carried in a procession but not used for dinner, and glows.

Literary Analysis
Archetypes and Symbols
What might the radiant light of the grail symbolize?

Marilyn Stokstad
Scholar's Insight
Perceval, who learned knightly virtues and won a place in Arthur's court as well as a kingdom for himself, could be portrayed as morally flawed in spite of personal heroism.

Literary Analysis
Archetypes Quests often include tests—some difficult, some easy. How would you characterize Perceval's test? Explain.

27 
Reading Check
What two extraordinary objects does Perceval observe as they are paraded around the hall?

10. **grail** (grāl) . . . **mien** (mēn) The Grail is the legendary cup or platter used by Jesus at the Last Supper and by Joseph of Arimathea to collect drops of Jesus' blood at the Crucifixion. *Mien* signifies "appearance."

Differentiated Instruction Solutions for All Learners

Strategy for Less Proficient Readers
Emphasize to students that the Grail is one of the most important symbols in *Perceval.* Organize students in groups, and have each group create a word web to record details about the Grail. Students should write "Grail" in the center circle and add in the surrounding circles details that summarize the appearance and characteristics of the Grail. Direct them to begin by reading lines 247–263 on p. 637. Have groups compare their finished word webs.

Enrichment for Advanced Readers
Tell students that the Holy Grail, referred to in this selection as the Grail, was a sacred object. The word *holy* comes from an Old English word, *halig,* meaning "holy" or "sacred." Etymologists have identified an even older Indo-European root that is the basis of the words *whole, wholesome, health, healthy, heal, holy,* and *hallow.* Tell students to use an etymological dictionary to look up the derivation of these words. Then, ask students to speculate on why the ideas of holiness, wholeness, and health are linked.

23 Scholar's Insight

- Have students read Stokstad's comment about the Grail's great significance.
- **Ask:** Of what importance is the Grail in the story?
  Answer: Medieval people believed in the magical power of religious objects such as the Grail.

24 Literary Analysis

Archetypes and Symbols

- Point out that Chrétien de Troyes describes the Grail as being set with incredible gems. **Ask** students why he makes a point of embellishing the value of the Grail.
  Possible response: The gems enhance the symbolic value of the Grail as an item of inestimable worth.
- **Ask** students the first Literary Analysis question.
  Possible response: The radiant light might symbolize the light of Jesus, whom Christians call the Light of the World.

25 Scholar's Insight

- Direct students' attention to Stokstad's comment about Perceval's virtues. Note that in the medieval court, one could gain or lose respect based on a certain set of traits, or virtues.
- **Ask:** What virtues do you find in Perceval that would win him the friendship and respect of the men and women at court?
  Answer: Perceval is determined, loyal, and polite.

26 Literary Analysis

Archetypes

- **Ask** students to respond to the second Literary Analysis question.
  Possible response: Perceval's test is mentally difficult because he is torn between following the directions of the wise lord not to ask questions and satisfying his curiosity by asking questions.

27 Reading Check

Answer: Perceval observes a white lance that bleeds from its tip and a golden Grail studded with gems.

28 Literary Analysis

Archetypes and Symbols

- Allow time for students to read silently the bracketed passage. Then, **ask** the Literary Analysis question: In what ways does the long description of the meal add to the air of mystery surrounding the nobleman?
  Possible response: The meal is so large and spectacular for just two people that it suggests something fantastic and special about the man who dines in this way.
- Call students' attention to the repeated passage of the Grail through the hall. Then, **ask** what the meal might symbolize.
  Possible response: The meal might symbolize The Last Supper.
- Remind students that during The Last Supper, Jesus began the institution of the Eucharist by serving bread and wine to his twelve disciples.

➤ **Monitor Progress Ask** students how the symbolism of the Grail and the feast adds to students' understanding of events in the story.
Possible response: The symbolism broadens the meaning of the adventure. The story is no longer just about a wayfaring knight who is having dinner with a rich nobleman. It is now apparent that the quest involves the mystery of faith, the Holy Grail, and possession of the Grail and the lance.

➤ **Reteach** Use **Literary Analysis** support, p. 30 in ***Unit 5 Resources,*** to review the characteristics of archetypes with students.

the lord and youth, until two more
squires entered, each one with a trestle.[11]
The trestles had two very special,
rare properties, which they contained
since they were built, and which remained
in them forever: they were wrought
of ebony, a wood that's thought
to have two virtues: it will not
ignite and burn and will not rot;
these dangers cause no harm nor loss.
They laid the tabletop across
the trestles, and the cloth above.
What shall I say? To tell you of
the cloth is far beyond my scope.
No legate, cardinal, or pope
has eaten from a whiter one.
The first course was of venison,
a peppered haunch, cooked in its fat,
accompanied by a clear wine that
was served in golden cups, a pleasant,
delicious drink. While they were present
a squire carved up the venison.
He set the peppered haunch upon
a silver platter, carved the meat,
and served the slices they would eat
by placing them on hunks of bread.
Again the grail passed by the bed,
and still the youth remained reserved
about the grail and whom they served.
he did not ask, because he had
been told so kindly it was bad
to talk too much, and he had taken
these words to heart. He was mistaken;
though he remembered, he was still
much longer than was suitable.
At every course, and in plain sight,
the grail was carried past the knight,
who did not ask whom they were serving,
although he wished to know, observing
in silence that he ought to learn
about it prior to his return.
So he would ask: before he spoke
he'd wait until the morning broke,
and he would ask a squire to tell,
once he had told the lord farewell

Literary Analysis
Archetypes and Symbols
In what ways does the long description of the meal add to the air of mystery surrounding the nobleman?

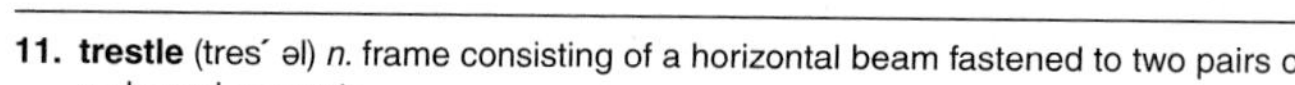

11. **trestle** (tres´ əl) *n.* frame consisting of a horizontal beam fastened to two pairs of v-shaped supports.

Enrichment

An Opera About Perceval

Perceval's quest for the Holy Grail is the subject of the last opera by the German composer Richard Wagner. Wagner (1813–1883) was fascinated with northern European legends, including the King Arthur stories. *Parsifal,* which Wagner called a "sacred festival drama" rather than an opera, addresses themes such as love, faith, redemption, and suffering. Both the Grail and the lance play important parts in the action. Wagner's Parsifal is often described as a "holy fool," the only man pure enough to become the guardian of the Grail.

Unlike almost all other opera composers, Wagner wrote the story and the libretto himself. He based his opera in part on Chrétien de Troyes's poem. His musical style was considered revolutionary for its unusual harmonies and melodies and daring use of different instrumental textures. Consider obtaining a recording of *Parsifal.* The beautiful prelude that begins the opera includes its most important musical phrase, which represents the Grail.

and all the others in his train.
He put the matter off again
and turned his thoughts toward drink
and food.
They brought, and in no stingy mood,
the foods and different types of wine,
which were delicious, rich and fine.
The squires were able to provide
the lord and young knight at his side
with every course a count, king, queen,
and emperor eat by routine.
At dinner's end, the two men stayed
awake and talked, while squires made
28 the beds and brought them fruit: they ate
the rarest fruits: the nutmeg, date,
fig, clove, and pomegranate red.
With Alexandrian gingerbread,
electuaries[12] at the end,
restoratives, a tonic blend,
and pliris archonticum
for settling his stomachum.
Then various liqueurs were poured
for them to sample afterward:
straight piment, which did not contain
sweet honey or a single grain
of pepper, wine of mulberries,
clear syrups, other delicacies.
The youth's astonishment persisted;
he did not know such things existed.
"Now, my dear friend," the great lord said,
"the time has come to go to bed.
I'll seek my room—don't think it queer—
and you will have your bed out here
and may lie down at any hour.
I do not have the slightest power
over my body anymore
and must be carried to my door."
Four nimble servants, strongly set,
came in and seized the coverlet
by its four corners (it was spread
beneath the lord, who lay in bed)
and carried him away to rest.
The others helped the youthful guest.
As he required, and when he chose,
they took his clothing off, and hose,

12. **electuaries** (ē lek´ cho͞o er´ ēz) medicines made by mixing drugs with honey or syrup to form a paste. Pliris archonticum, mentioned two lines later, is such a medicine.

29

Perceval at Amfortas, wall painting from the "Parsifal saga," Ferdinand Piloty, the Younger

30 ▲ Critical Viewing

Is this painting a faithful rendering of the grail scene as described by the poet? Explain. **[Evaluate]**

Vocabulary Builder

nimble (nim´ bəl) *adj.* able to move quickly and lightly; agile

31  Reading Check

What question about the lord of the castle does Perceval fail to ask?

29 Humanities

Perceval at Amfortas,
by Ferdinand Piloty, the Younger

In this selection, Chrétien de Troyes never names the nobleman in the castle. Wolfram von Eschenbach, however, gives the Fisher King the name of Amfortas. Eschenbach was inspired by the Chrétien de Troyes's story and wrote the German poem *Parzival* around 1200–1210. Richard Wagner also adopts Amfortas as the name of The Fisher King in his opera, *Parsifal.*

Use the following questions for discussion:

- How can you identify Amfortas, the old nobleman, in this painting?
  Answer: Amfortas is the one sitting on the bed because he is unable to stand.
- What symbols in the painting reinforce the interpretation of *Perceval* as a Christian allegory?
  Possible response: The structure behind the bed looks like an altar and is carved with figures that may be saints.

30 Critical Viewing

Answer: The painting is a faithful rendering with the exception that the poet describes another maiden bearing a silver platter who follows the maiden holding the Grail.

31 Reading Check

Answer: Perceval fails to ask the lord who is being served from the Grail.

Differentiated Instruction Solutions for All Learners

Enrichment for Gifted/Talented Students

Draw students' attention to the magnificence of the table and the feast that Perceval enjoys. Have students reread these pages and identify some of the details that Chrétien de Troyes includes. Then, have each student create a painting, drawing, print, sculpture, collage, or other artwork that represents some aspect of the scene. Remind students to examine the text closely for details that will help them visualize the banquet. Display their finished work in the classroom.

Enrichment for Advanced Readers

Tell students that the excerpt they are reading is only a small part of the legend of Perceval. The story begins when Perceval is a young man still living with his mother. It then traces his wanderings as he visits King Arthur and becomes a knight. This selection occurs next. The story then continues as Perceval matures and continues his search for knowledge of the Grail. Ask interested students to research the plot of *Perceval* or to read other parts of the poem. Have students summarize their readings for the class.

㉜ Scholar's Insight

- Have students read Stokstad's comment about Perceval's bed. **Ask** students: What other special treatment, besides the white linen sheets, is Perceval given?
  Answer: The servants help Perceval change his clothes and get ready for bed.
- **Ask:** Why would the lord of the castle give such special treatment to Perceval?
  Answer: The lord is a gracious host, but he also sees something in Perceval that he admires.

㉝ Reading Strategy

Interpreting Symbols

- Read aloud the bracketed passage. Then, **ask** students the Reading Strategy question: What does the complete absence of people suggest about Perceval's experience of the night before?
  Possible response: The absence of people suggests that Perceval's experience was a dream or an illusion.

Monitor Progress Call students' attention to lines 392–397. **Ask:** What might the locked doors symbolize?
Possible response: The locked doors might symbolize the difficulty of learning the truth about the Grail, the lance, and the person who was served from the Grail.

Reteach Use **Reading Strategy** support, p. 31 in *Unit 5 Resources,* to help students interpret the symbol of the locked doors.

㉜ and put him in a bed with white,
smooth linen sheets; he slept all night
at peace until the morning broke.
But when the youthful knight awoke,
he was the last to rise and found
that there was no one else around.
Exasperated and alone,
he had to get up on his own.
He made the best of it, arose,
and awkwardly drew on his hose
without a bit of help or aid.
He saw his armor had been laid
㉝ at night against the dais' head
a little distance from his bed.
When he had armed himself at last,
he walked around the great hall past
the rooms and knocked at every door
which opened wide the night before,
but it was useless: juxtaposed,[13]
the doors were tightly locked and closed.
He shouted, called, and knocked outside,
but no one opened or replied.
At last the young man ceased to call,
walked to the doorway of the hall,
which opened up, and passed through there,
and went on down the castle stair.
His horse was saddled in advance.
The young man saw his shield and lance
were leaned against the castle wall
upon the side that faced the hall.
He mounted, searched the castle whole,
but did not find one living soul,
one servant, or one squire around.
He hurried toward the gate and found
the men had let the drawbridge down,
so that the knight could leave the town
at any hour he wished to go.
His hosts had dropped the drawbridge so
the youth could cross it undeterred.
The squires were sent, the youth inferred,
out to the wood, where they were set
to checking every trap and net.
The drawbridge lay across the stream.
He would not wait and formed a scheme
of searching through the woods as well
to see if anyone could tell

13. juxtaposed (juks′ tə pōzd′) *adj.* placed side by side or close together.

Marilyn Stokstad
Scholar's Insight
The hall became a dormitory at night where travelers, guests, and servants could sleep. Perceval gets special treatment—white linen sheets would be saved for important guests.

Reading Strategy
Interpreting Symbols
What does the complete absence of people suggest about Perceval's experience of the night before?

Enrichment

Castles in the Middle Ages

When Perceval first glimpses the mysterious castle of the Fisher King rising from the valley, he observes that one could search the world over and never find "any finer tower." However, most castles in the Middle Ages were built for the sole purpose of providing protection; living quarters were of secondary concern. In addition, castles were built in places that afforded clear views of the surrounding area—on the edges of cliffs, for example, or at river bends. A typical castle was surrounded by a deep moat, which was often dry. A drawbridge controlled from inside the castle crossed the moat; and a walled area, known as a *bailey,* separated the moat from the castle.

Encourage interested students to further research castles in the Middle Ages. They might wish to learn how castles were designed and constructed, what it was like to live in a castle, or why castles declined in popularity. Have students prepare multimedia presentations for the class.

about the lance, why it was bleeding,
about the grail, whom they were feeding,
and where they carried it in state.
The youth rode through the castle gate
and out upon the drawbridge plank.
Before he reached the other bank,
the young man started realizing
the forefeet of his horse were rising.
His horse made one great leap indeed.
Had he not jumped well, man and steed
would have been hurt. His rider swerved
to see what happened and observed
the drawbridge had been lifted high.
He shouted, hearing no reply,
"Whoever raised the bridge," said he,
"where are you? Come and talk to me!
Say something to me; come in view.
There's something I would ask of you,
some things I wanted to inquire,
some information I desire."
His words were wasted, vain and fond;
no one was willing to respond.

34

Critical Reading

1. **Respond:** Which aspect of Perceval's adventure do you find most interesting? Explain.
2. **(a) Recall:** What invitation does the fisherman extend to Perceval? **(b) Analyze:** Do you think the fisherman and the Fisher King are the same person? Explain.
3. **(a) Recall:** What is the Fisher King's physical condition? **(b) Analyze:** What do you think might be causing his condition? Support your answer.
4. **(a) Interpret:** When Perceval sees the lance and the Grail, what fateful decision does he make? **(b) Analyze Causes and Effects:** Why do you think he makes this decision?
5. **(a) Speculate:** In what ways, if any, do you think Perceval will grow as a result of this adventure? **(b) Support:** Which details in the excerpt support your position? Explain.
6. **Evaluate:** What do you think the story of Perceval suggests about the pros and cons of innocence? Explain.

For: More about Chrétien de Troyes
Visit: www.PHSchool.com
Web Code: ete-9501

Differentiated Instruction Solutions for All Learners

Strategy for Special Needs Students

Ask students to work in pairs. Then, divide the selection into passages and assign one of the passages to each pair. Have pairs write summaries of their passage, using the following questions to guide their writing:

- What is the situation when the passage begins?
- Who is involved in the passage?
- What happens or changes in the passage?
- What is the situation when the passage ends?

Strategy for Less Proficient Readers

Ask students to evaluate Perceval's actions and behavior while at the castle. Have them determine whether the decisions he makes, such as not asking about the lance and Grail and remaining passive at the banquet, are good ones. Have students list each decision and then their opinions of it. Students should support their opinions with evidence from the text. Ask students to share their thoughts in a class discussion.

34 Humanities

The Tassilo Chalice

This chalice from the Kremsmünster Abbey in Austria (c. 770) is one of the few surviving chalices from this period. Made of copper-gilt, the chalice shows clear influences of Irish craftsmanship of the period. It was almost certainly crafted by a monk.

Use this question for discussion:

Why do you think cups such as this one were made with such beautiful craftsmanship?
Possible response: The cup had to be worthy of being used in special religious ceremonies.

ASSESS

Answers

1. **Possible response:** The most interesting aspect is the mystery surrounding the identity of the person being served from the Grail.
2. (a) The fisherman invites Perceval to stay with him at his manor. (b) **Possible response:** The fisherman said that Perceval could stay with him, and he told him how to get to his home, so he is probably the same man as the Fisher King.
3. (a) The Fisher King is ill and unable to stand up. (b) **Possible response:** The Fisher King was probably wounded in a battle. He seems familiar with weapons, and noblemen of that time would have reason to use them.
4. (a) Perceval fails to ask questions about the lance and the Grail. (b) **Possible response:** Perceval has been taught not to ask questions or talk too much.
5. (a) **Possible response:** Perceval will learn to ask questions and speak more quickly. (b) **Possible response:** Perceval is insistent on finding the answers when it is too late. He has already learned that he should have asked questions when he had the opportunity.
6. **Possible response:** The story suggests that people must eventually outgrow their innocence.

Go Online Author Link For additional information about Chrétien de Troyes, have students type in the Web Code, then select *T* from the alphabet, and then select Chrétien de Troyes.

35 About the Selection

"The Lay of the Werewolf" is not just another story about a man who turns into a werewolf. This wolf behaves like the perfect courtier, saluting his king with the proper feudal gesture. It is his wife who seems less than human in her actions, which condemn her husband to the life of a beast. In this reversal of expected behavior, Marie de France contradicts the popular medieval notion that a person's appearance announces his or her character. She affirms the sad reality that appearances deceive and that good people often suffer for no reason other than bad fortune. Through her use of the werewolf, Marie de France combats the effects of the very superstition that created such a monster.

36 Literary Analysis

Archetypes and Symbols

- Read aloud the bracketed passage with students. **Ask** them why people have chosen the wolf as the form that evil humans often take when they turn into beasts.
  Possible response: The wolf is a smart, fearsome animal that ranks just below humans as the top predator in many places around the world.
- Then, have students **respond** to the Literary Analysis question: Based on this description, which human emotions do werewolves seem to embody?
  Answer: Werewolves seem to embody the human emotions of anger and hate.

35 The Lay of the Werewolf

Marie de France
***translated by* Eugene Mason**

Background The ancient Greeks wrote that people could be transformed into wolves, remain in that form for years, and then return to their human form. Medieval intellectuals were ready to dismiss werewolves as mere hallucinations, but the common people believed these creatures truly existed. For medieval villagers, such creatures were either demons or men being punished for horrible sins. However, in this story, Marie de France questions the assumption that the beast is evil or sinful. Instead, the werewolf displays a deep, sensitive humanity, while human beings show themselves to be the real beasts.

Amongst the tales I tell you once again, I would not forget the Lay of the Werewolf. Such beasts as he are known in every land. Bisclavaret he is named in Brittany; whilst the Norman[1] calls him Garwal.

36 It is a certain thing, and within the knowledge of all, that many a christened man has suffered this change, and ran wild in woods, as a Werewolf. The Werewolf is a fearsome beast. He lurks within the thick forest, mad and horrible to see. All the evil that he may, he does. He goeth to and fro, about the solitary place, seeking man, in order to devour him. Hearken, now, to the adventure of the Werewolf, that I have to tell.

In Brittany there dwelt a baron who was marvelously esteemed of all his fellows. He was a stout knight, and a comely, and a man of office and repute. Right private was he to the mind of his lord, and dear to the counsel of his neighbors. This baron was wedded to a very worthy dame, right fair to see, and sweet of semblance. All his love was set on her, and all her love was given again to him. One only grief had this

Literary Analysis
Archetypes and Symbols
Based on this description, which human emotions do werewolves seem to embody?

Vocabulary Builder
esteemed (e stēmd′) v. valued; respected

1. **Brittany** (brit′ ′n ē) . . . **Norman** Brittany is a region of northwestern France, adjacent to Normandy.

Enrichment

Werewolves

A belief in the existence of werewolves was a fact of life in medieval Europe, and rumors about the beasts abounded. Some people had heard of men who boasted of the power to turn into wolves. Others claimed that people who were in league with the devil were granted the power to transform themselves into werewolves at will. Medieval people sometimes explained epileptics as werewolves whose seizures revealed them in midtransformation, and they viewed people with autism or schizophrenia as werewolves as well.

These and other rumors and beliefs spread around Europe throughout the Middle Ages. Like the suspected witches at the trials of Salem, suspected werewolves were tortured until they confessed their guilt.

lady. For three whole days in every week her lord was absent from her side. She knew not where he went, nor on what errand. Neither did any of his house know the business which called him forth.

On a day when this lord was come again to his house, altogether joyous and content, the lady took him to task, right sweetly, in this fashion,

"Husband," said she, "and fair, sweet friend, I have a certain thing to pray of you. Right willing would I receive this gift, but I fear to anger you in the asking. It is better for me to have an empty hand, than to gain hard words."

When the lord heard this matter, he took the lady in his arms, very tenderly, and kissed her.

"Wife," he answered, "ask what you will. What would you have, for it is yours already?"

"By my faith," said the lady, "soon shall I be whole. Husband, right long and wearisome are the days that you spend away from your home. I rise from my bed in the morning, sick at heart, I know not why. So fearful am I, lest you do aught to your loss, that I may not find any comfort. Very quickly shall I die for reason of my dread. Tell me now, where you go, and on what business! How may the knowledge of one who loves so closely, bring you to harm?"

"Wife," made answer the lord, "nothing but evil can come if I tell you this secret. For the mercy of God do
42 not require it of me. If you but knew, you would withdraw yourself from my love, and I should be lost indeed."

37

Werewolf Attacking a Man, German woodcut, 15th century

When the lady heard this, she was persuaded that her baron sought to put her by with jesting words. Therefore she prayed and required him the more urgently, with tender looks and speech, till he was overborne, and told her all the story, hiding naught.

"Wife, I become Bisclavaret. I enter in the forest, and live on prey and roots, within the thickest of the wood."

After she had learned his secret, she prayed and entreated the more as to whether he ran in his raiment, or went spoiled of vesture.

"Wife," said he, "I go naked as a beast."

"Tell me, for hope of grace, what you do with your clothing?"

"Fair wife, that will I never. If I should lose my raiment, or even be marked as I quit my vesture, then a Werewolf I must go for all the days of my life. Never again should I become man, save in that hour my clothing were given back to me. For this reason never will I show my lair."

"Husband," replied the lady to him, "I love you better than all the world. The less cause have you for doubting my faith, or hiding any

▼ Critical Viewing 38

Compare and contrast the portrayal of the werewolf in this fifteenth-century woodcut with the description of werewolves in the story. **[Compare and Contrast]**

Reading Check 39

What happens to the baron for three days of every week?

37 Humanities

Werewolf Attacking a Man

The earliest form of printing in Europe was the wood block of the fifteenth century. The wood block was used not only for printing letters but also for illustrations. Images were deeply cut in reverse into soft wood. The block was then inked and pressed onto paper, leaving an image in black and white. The image was then sometimes handpainted. *Werewolf Attacking a Man,* by an unknown artist, is a woodcut illustration from this era.

Use the following questions for discussion:

- What does the illustration tell you about the nature of life in fifteenth-century Germany?
  Possible response: People lived very close to nature, as evidenced by this werewolf that comes right to the man's door.
- What words would you use to describe this illustration?
  Possible response: The illustration is primitive, colorful, frightening, and lacking in fine detail.

38 Critical Viewing

Possible response: Both werewolves look like ordinary wolves, but the werewolf in the story does not attack humans unless he has reason to do so. The werewolf in the woodcut seems eager to attack people.

39 Reading Check

Answer: The baron disappears into the woods as a werewolf.

Differentiated Instruction Solutions for All Learners

Strategy for English Learners

Tell students that transformation, or shapeshifting, in which humans turn into something else, is an archetypal theme that runs through the literature of many cultures. The Lakota tell of Iktomi, the shapeshifting spiderman. In Asia, legends tell of a were-tiger. The Navaho never talk to outsiders about the Skinwalker; and in the Amazon, people fear the jaguarmen. Encourage students to provide examples of stories of shapeshifting from their native cultures. Ask them to tell the stories orally, as a storyteller might.

Strategy for Advanced Readers

The theme of transformation, or shapeshifting, is common in literature. Ask students to name other stories, novels, and movies that describe transformations. (Examples include *The Strange Case of Dr. Jekyll and Mr. Hyde* by Robert Louis Stevenson and *The Metamorphosis* by Franz Kafka.) Have students describe the transformation and how the victim responds to the event. Ask students to answer this question: Are these changed persons evil or good?

40 Humanities

Tree Umbrellas,
by Diantha York-Ripley

York-Ripley is a contemporary artist who often paints outdoor scenes. She creates texture by adding thick strokes of paint that give this painting an almost three-dimensional appearance. York-Ripley gives the impression of details through the effect of her brush strokes.

Use the following question for discussion:

Does this forest look realistic? Explain.
Possible response: The forest does not look realistic because the trees are bent and twisted more than is typical of real trees.

41 Critical Viewing

Possible response: The forest is dense and dark, and few people would want to venture into it; thus, it would offer Bisclavaret the kind of secrecy he seeks.

42 Literary Analysis

Archetypes

- Have students read the bracketed passage.
- Then, **ask** the Literary Analysis question: How does the wife manipulate her husband into revealing the entirety of his secret?
Answer: The wife wears her husband down with her persistent questions and pledges of love. She says that if he really loves her, he will reveal his secret.

43 Critical Thinking

Predict

- Emphasize that people's actions in certain circumstances tend to be predictable from culture to culture and time period to time period.
- Have students **predict** the wife's reaction to her husband's secret.
Possible response: The wife will be repelled by her husband and seek to escape him.

40

◀ **Critical Viewing** 41 Would the forest portrayed in this painting offer Bisclavaret the kind of secrecy he seeks? Why or why not? **[Interpret]**

42 tittle from me. What savor is here of friendship? How have I made forfeit of your love; for what sin do you mistrust my honor? Open now your heart, and tell what is good to be known."

So at the end, outwearied and overborne by her <u>importunity</u>, he could no longer refrain, but told her all.

43 "Wife," said he, "within this wood, a little from the path, there is a hidden way, and at the end thereof an ancient chapel, where oftentimes I have bewailed my lot. Near by is a great hollow stone, concealed by a bush, and there is the secret place where I hide my raiment, till I would return to my own home."

On hearing this marvel the lady became sanguine[2] of visage, because of her exceeding fear. She dared no longer to lie at his side, and turned over in her mind, this way and that, how best she could get her from him. Now there was a certain knight of those parts, who, for a great while, had sought and required this lady for her love. This knight had spent long years in her service, but little enough had he got thereby, not even fair words, or a promise. To him the dame wrote a letter, and meeting, made her purpose plain.

"Fair friend," said she, "be happy. That which you have coveted so long a time, I will grant without delay. Never again will I deny your suit. My heart, and all I have to give, are yours, so take me now as love and dame."

Literary Analysis
Archetypes How does the wife manipulate her husband into revealing the entirety of his secret?

Vocabulary Builder
importunity (im´ pôr to͞on´ i tē) *n.* persistence

2. **sanguine** (saŋ´ gwin) *adj.* reddish; ruddy.

Enrichment

The Jongleurs and the Celts

Marie de France's *lais,* such as "The Lay of the Werewolf," are based on similar verse stories told by Breton minstrels who traveled from village to village, accompanying their singing on the harp or other instruments. Often these *jongleurs,* as they were called, performed acrobatics and juggling in the village square in order to attract an audience. They lived on whatever this audience gave them, so they entertained well.

These minstrels were the guardians of Celtic culture, which was largely oral in the Middle Ages, so they memorized many stories. The Celts believed that the dead lived on Earth, that the springs, rivers, mountains, and forests were guarded by gods or spirits, and that animals had human consciousness and supernatural powers.

Right sweetly the knight thanked her for her grace, and pledged her faith and fealty. When she had confirmed him by an oath, then she told him all this business of her lord—why he went, and what he became, and of his ravening[3] within the wood. So she showed him of the chapel, and of the hollow stone, and of how to spoil the Werewolf of his vesture. Thus, by the kiss of his wife, was Bisclavaret betrayed. Often enough had he ravished his prey in desolate places, but from this journey he never returned. His kinsfolk and acquaintance came together to ask of his tidings, when this absence was noised abroad. Many a man, on many a day, searched the woodland, but none might find him, nor learn where Bisclavaret was gone.

The lady was wedded to the knight who had cherished her for so long a space. More than a year had passed since Bisclavaret disappeared. Then it chanced that the King would hunt in that self-same wood where the Werewolf lurked. When the hounds were unleashed they ran this way and that, and swiftly came upon his scent. At the view the huntsman winded on his horn, and the whole pack were at his heels. They followed him from morn to eve, till he was torn and bleeding, and was all adread lest they should pull him down. Now the King was very close to the quarry, and when Bisclavaret looked upon his master, he ran to him for pity and for grace. He took the stirrup within his paws, and fawned upon the prince's foot. The King was very fearful at this sight, but presently he called his courtiers to his aid.

45 "Lords," cried he, "hasten hither, and see this marvelous thing. Here is a beast who has the sense of man. He abases himself before his foe, and cries for mercy, although he cannot speak. Beat off the hounds, and let no man do him harm. We will hunt no more today, but return to our own place, with the wonderful quarry we have taken."

The King turned him about, and rode to his hall, Bisclavaret following at his side. Very near to his master the Werewolf went, like any dog, and had no care to seek again the wood. When the King had brought him safely to his own castle, he rejoiced greatly,
47 for the beast was fair and strong, no mightier had any man seen. Much pride had the King in his marvelous beast. He held him so dear, that he bade all those who wished for his love, to cross the Wolf in naught, neither to strike him with a rod, but ever to see that he was richly fed and kenneled warm. This commandment the Court observed willingly. So all the day the Wolf sported with the lords, and at night he lay within

Literature in Context

44 History Connection

Wolves in the Middle Ages

During the Middle Ages, the natural world was far more threatening than it is today. Dense forest covered most of Europe. Residents of villages only a few miles apart often spoke different languages and never encountered each other.

Wolves embodied the threat posed by the natural world. Wolves wandered the forest, sometimes venturing into villages to snatch up small livestock. The terror people felt for wolves is captured in familiar fairy tales, such as the story of Little Red Riding Hood.

As frightening as wolves were, human beings could be worse. Only vagabonds and thieves ventured into the forest, and they were more terrifying than the wolves. The brutality of life in the Middle Ages sometimes diminished the distance between human and animal behavior—a harsh fact of life reflected in literature like Marie de France's tale.

Connect to the Literature

How does this information about wolves make the King's behavior particularly remarkable?

Vocabulary Builder

abases (ə bās′ əz) *v.* lowers; brings down

Reading Check 46

Who betrayed Bisclavaret?

3. **ravening** (rav′ ən iŋ) *n.* greedy searching for prey.

44 Literature in Context

Wolves in the Middle Ages

Stories of wolves killing humans puzzle scientists; wolf attacks on humans in North America are almost nonexistent. In fact, there is no documentation that a wolf has ever killed anyone in North America. Nonetheless, the stories of wolves attacking humans during the Middle Ages in Europe are common enough that researchers believe there must be some basis for it. They conjecture that rabies might have been the cause of some of the attacks because wolves would have had frequent contact with rabid dogs. Other attacks may have occurred when starving wolves happened upon unarmed people.

Connect to the Literature Point out to students that two people in this tale respond differently to the threat of the werewolf. The baron's frightened yet crafty wife uses treachery to get rid of the werewolf by showing the knight where the baron's clothes are hidden, and thus robs her husband of his humanity. Ask students to discuss how the King reacts to the werewolf.

Possible response: Given the fears people have of this animal, the king's reaction to the werewolf is remarkable, because he correctly interprets the wolf's behavior as harmless and then treats it like a beloved pet.

45 Critical Thinking

Interpret

- Call students' attention to the bracketed passage. **Ask** students: Can the observation of Bisclavaret's "cries for mercy" be taken literally?
  Answer: The observation can be taken literally. Even though Bisclavaret cannot speak, he can bark, growl, whine, and use body language to communicate.
- Ask students what humor is suggested in the King's comment that Bisclavaret "cannot speak."
  Possible response: The comment may be the writer's play on the fact that Bisclavaret is in fact part human.

46 Reading Check

Answer: Bisclavaret's wife betrayed him.

Differentiated Instruction Solutions for All Learners

Support for English Learners

Encourage students to follow the written text as they listen to a recording of "The Lay of the Werewolf" on the **Listening to Literature Audio CDs.** Stop the recording after portions of text, and discuss with students any unfamiliar words. Then, reread the text aloud with students, and ask them to identify the main idea.

Enrichment for Gifted/Talented Students

Explain to students that the typical hunt has certain rituals such as colorful dress, a musical instrument announcing the start of the hunt, a feast after the hunt, and the like. Have students use the Internet to research the sport of hunting in medieval days. Then have them work in pairs to draw a mural of the King's hunt, the appearance of the werewolf, and the aftermath. Have them exhibit their murals for the class.

47 Reading Strategy

Interpreting Symbols

- Have students read the bracketed passage that begins on the previous page. Guide students in concluding that the wolf behaves and is treated like a pet dog.
- Then, **ask:** How are his behavior and treatment different from the way werewolves would typically act and be treated in literature or film?
  Answer: Typically, werewolves would be vicious and would be destroyed as quickly as possible.
- Have students **respond** to the Reading Strategy question: Why do you think the author emphasizes the marvel of the beast's good conduct?
  Possible response: The author wants to emphasize that although the baron is in the form of a wolf, he retains the intellect and values of a human.

➤ **Monitor Progress Ask** students what they think the werewolf symbolizes.
Possible response: The werewolf symbolizes the duality of the human spirit—its wild side (the beast) and its civilized side (the human).

48 Humanities

Marriage of Philip the Good and Isabella de Portugal in 1430,
detail of a group around a table

This anonymous painting depicts the marriage of two fifteenth-century nobles. Philip the Good was the duke of Burgundy from 1419 to 1467. The fiefdom of Burgundy included parts of present-day France, Holland, and Belgium and was one of the largest and most magnificent courts of its time.

Use the following question for discussion:

What does this painting indicate about an early fifteenth-century celebration?
Possible response: There was probably a good deal of fanfare at the celebration, as seen by the figures holding instruments and banners, yet the outdoor setting and the presence of dogs make the scene seem more informal.

49 Critical Viewing

Answer: Everyone is richly dressed and in a festive mood, much like the king and his court in the story.

47 the chamber of the King. There was not a man who did not make much of the beast, so frank was he and debonair.[4] None had reason to do him wrong, for ever was he about his master, and for his part did evil to none. Every day were these two companions together, and all perceived that the King loved him as his friend.

Hearken now to that which chanced.

The King held a high Court, and bade his great vassals and barons, and all the lords of his venery[5] to the feast. Never was there a goodlier feast, nor one set forth with sweeter show and pomp. Amongst those who were bidden, came that same knight who had the wife of Bisclavaret for dame. He came to the castle, richly gowned, with a fair company, but little he deemed whom he would find so near. Bisclavaret marked his foe the moment he stood within the hall. He ran towards him, and seized him with his fangs, in the King's very presence, and to the view of all. Doubtless he would have done him much mischief, had not the King called and chidden him, and threatened him with a rod. Once, and twice, again, the Wolf set upon the knight in the very light of day. All men marveled at his malice, for sweet and serviceable was the beast, and to that hour had shown hatred of none. With one consent the household deemed that this deed was done with full reason, and that the Wolf had suffered at the knight's hand some bitter wrong. Right wary of his foe was the knight until the feast had ended, and all the barons had taken farewell of their lord, and departed, each to his own house. With these, amongst the very first, went that lord whom Bisclavaret so fiercely had assailed. Small was the wonder that he was glad to go.

No long while after this adventure it came to pass that the courteous King would hunt in that forest where Bisclavaret was found. With the prince came his wolf, and a fair company. Now at nightfall the King abode

4. **debonair** (deb´ ə ner´) *adj.* pleasant, charming, and friendly.
5. **venery** (ven´ ər ē) the act or practice of hunting game.

Reading Strategy
Interpreting Symbols
Why do you think the author emphasizes the marvel of the beast's good conduct?

▼ **Critical Viewing** 49
In what ways does this painting of a festive gathering of medieval nobility emphasize the qualities shown by the king and his court in this story?
[Analyze]

Enrichment

The Lay of Marie de France

Critic Emanuel J. Mickel observes that the *lais,* or *lay,* is different from the quests in other narrative poems.

> In the *lais* it is the adventure which comes to the hero. Far from setting forth on an adventurous quest, the hero of the *Lais* is essentially passive. . . . In a sense, it is the adventure which seems to seek out the hero. It is an encounter which seems deliberately directed toward him, an experience which he seems destined to have and which totally transforms his existence, and at times introduces him to another order of reality. . . . There is no special relationship between the destiny of society and that of the hero. Society remains unchanged by the hero's adventure. The experience is a personal one which leads to a private fulfillment and happiness. . . .

within a certain lodge of that country, and this was known of that dame who before was the wife of Bisclavaret. In the morning the lady clothed her in her most dainty apparel, and hastened to the lodge, since she desired to speak with the King, and to offer him a rich present. When the lady entered in the chamber, neither man nor leash might restrain the fury of the Wolf. He became as a mad dog in his hatred and malice. Breaking from his bonds he sprang at the lady's face, and bit the nose from her visage. From every side men ran to the succor of the dame. They beat off the wolf from his prey, and for a little would have cut him in pieces with their swords. But a certain wise counselor said to the King,

Werewolf of Eschenbach, 1685, German colored engraving 50

52 "Sire, hearken now to me. This beast is always with you, and there is not one of us all who has not known him for long. He goes in and out amongst us, nor has molested any man, neither done wrong or felony to any, save only to this dame, one only time as we have seen. He has done evil to this lady, and to that knight, who is now the husband of the dame. Sire, she was once the wife of that lord who was so close and private to your heart, but who went, and none might find where he had gone. Now, therefore, put the dame in a sure place, and question her straitly, so that she may tell—if perchance she knows thereof—for what reason this Beast holds her in such mortal hate. For many a strange deed has chanced, as well we know, in this marvelous land of Brittany."

The King listened to these words, and deemed the counsel good. He laid hands upon the knight, and put the dame in surety in another place. He caused them to be questioned right straitly, so that their torment was very grievous. At the end, partly because of her distress, and partly by reason of her exceeding fear, the lady's lips were loosed, and she told her tale. She showed them of the betrayal of her lord, and how his raiment was stolen from the hollow stone. Since then she knew not where he went, nor what had befallen him, for he had never come again to his own land. Only, in her heart, well she deemed and was persuaded, that Bisclavaret was he.

Straightway the King demanded the vesture of his baron, whether this were to the wish of the lady, or whether it were against her wish. When the raiment was brought him, he caused it to be spread before Bisclavaret, but the Wolf made as though he had not seen. Then that cunning and crafty counselor took the King apart, that he might give him a fresh rede.[6]

▲ Critical Viewing 51
Do you think contemporary viewers would have found this seventeenth-century engraving of a werewolf frightening? Explain. **[Speculate]**

Reading Check 53
How does Bisclavaret react to his ex-wife and her new husband?

6. **rede** (rēd) counsel; advice.

50 Humanities

Werewolf of Eschenbach

This colored wood engraving was produced in Germany in 1685 by an unknown artist. The artist shows the werewolf walking upright and wearing a man's garment. The man looks back at this fearsome monster as he tries to escape.

Use the following question for discussion:

How does the artist's depiction of the werewolf compare to others you have seen?
Possible response: This werewolf seems less threatening than in other depictions.

51 Critical Viewing

Possible response: Contemporary viewers will probably find this engraving more comical than frightening because of the werewolf's body language and the man's bland expression.

52 Literary Analysis

Archetypes

- Ask a student to read aloud the bracketed passage. Then, **ask** students whether Bisclavaret behaves differently in his attack than he would have had he been in human form. Have students explain their answers.
  Possible response: Bisclavaret probably responds with more violence and anger than he would have had he been in human form. As an animal, he can react to events only physically, not verbally.
- **Ask** students: The husband's condition is a form of disguised identity. What deeper truth do the people of the household suspect?
  Answer: The people suspect that Bisclavaret's former wife and her new husband have done something terribly wrong to Bisclavaret.

➤ **Monitor Progress** How does the baron's disguise help him find justice?
Answer: Disguised as a wolf, the baron is able to live in the king's company and to act decisively at the right moment. In doing so, he draws attention to his former wife and her new husband and raises the question of what they did to wrong him.

53 Reading Check

Answer: Bisclavaret viciously attacks his ex-wife and her new husband.

Differentiated Instruction Solutions for All Learners

Strategy for Special Needs Students

Aid students' comprehension by asking them to create a sequence-of-events chart. Assign each student one passage from the selection, and ask him or her to record on a sheet of paper the most important event in the passage. Collect the papers, and read the events in random order. Work with students to order the events in sequence. Have students record the events in individual sequence-of-events charts.

Enrichment for Advanced Readers

Ask students whether they think "The Lay of the Werewolf" would be different if it were centered around a female character instead of a male. Discuss what would happen if the transformation happened to the wife. Challenge interested students to rewrite the story with this twist in the characters' roles. Have the class predict how this change would alter the plot, and then have volunteers read their stories.

ASSESS

Answers

1. **Possible response:** The secret would be an astonishing piece of news to accept. Given the attitude prevalent during the Middle Ages, it would be hard to continue living with a man who had been so cursed.
2. (a) The wife's one grief is that her husband goes away for three days each week, leaving her alone. (b) The wife repeatedly asks her husband to tell her where he goes. (c) **Possible response:** The wife's pursuit of the secret suggests that she wants to be in control and know everything about her husband.
3. (a) The wife turns to a knight who has long been interested in her. (b) The narrator describes the wife's betrayal by saying, "thus, by the kiss of his wife, was Bisclavaret betrayed." (c) The wife not only leaves her husband and lies to him, but she also takes away his humanity.
4. (a) The wife is described as having a fair, sweet appearance. (b) Bisclavaret bites off his ex-wife's nose, thereby making her ugly. Her external appearance now matches the ugliness of her inner self.
5. (a) The wife and her new husband are chased from the land and go to a foreign country to live. (b) The couple's fate is similar because they lose everything they once took for granted. Their fate is different because they retain their human form.
6. **Possible responses:** The tale has a happy ending because the baron regains his human form and all his possessions; the tale does not have a happy ending because the baron will forever be associated with his experience of being a werewolf.

Go Online Author Link For additional information about Marie de France, have students type in the Web Code, then select *F* from the alphabet, and then select Marie de France.

"Sire," said he, "you do not wisely, nor well, to set this raiment before Bisclavaret, in the sight of all. In shame and much tribulation must he lay aside the beast, and again become man. Carry your wolf within your most secret chamber, and put his vestment therein. Then close the door upon him, and leave him alone for a space. So we shall see presently whether the ravening beast may indeed return to human shape."

The King carried the Wolf to his chamber, and shut the doors upon him fast. He delayed for a brief while, and taking two lords of his fellowship with him, came again to the room. Entering therein, all three, softly together, they found the knight sleeping in the King's bed, like a little child. The King ran swiftly to the bed and taking his friend in his arms, embraced and kissed him fondly, above a hundred times. When man's speech returned once more, he told him of his adventure. Then the King restored to his friend the fief that was stolen from him, and gave such rich gifts, moreover, as I cannot tell. As for the wife who had betrayed Bisclavaret, he bade her avoid his country, and chased her from the realm. So she went forth, she and her second lord together, to seek a more abiding city, and were no more seen.

The adventure that you have heard is no vain fable. Verily and indeed it chanced as I have said. The Lay of the Werewolf, truly, was written that it should ever be borne in mind.

Critical Reading

1. **Respond:** If you were the wife in this story, how would you feel about your husband's secret? Explain.
2. **(a) Recall:** What is the wife's "one grief"? **(b) Infer:** What does she do to address this grief? **(c) Interpret:** What does her pursuit of her husband's secret suggest about her character?
3. **(a) Recall:** To whom does the wife turn for help? **(b) Distinguish:** With what telling words does the narrator describe the nature of the wife's betrayal? **(c) Analyze:** Why do the wife's actions constitute a particularly terrible form of treachery?
4. **(a) Interpret:** At the beginning of the story, how does the narrator describe the wife's appearance? **(b) Analyze:** In what ways does the injury inflicted by Bisclavaret upon his ex-wife reveal her true nature?
5. **(a) Infer:** What happens to the wife and her new husband at the end of the tale? **(b) Compare and Contrast:** In what ways is their fate both similar to and different from the harm they inflicted on Bisclavaret?
6. **Evaluate:** On the surface, this tale seems to have a happy ending. Does it? Explain.

For: More information about Marie de France
Visit: www.PHSchool.com
Web Code: ete-9502

Apply the Skills

from *Perceval* • *The Lay of the Werewolf*

Literary Analysis

Archetypes

1. Use a chart like the one shown to examine the ways in which the story of Perceval exemplifies the **archetype** of the **quest.**

Elements of the Quest Archetype		
Characters	**Young hero:** Perceval	**Wise teacher:**
Goals	**Valuable object:**	**Restoration of kingdom/rescue:**
Obstacles	**Natural:**	**Supernatural:**
Magical Objects	**Devices:**	**Weapons:**

2. **(a)** In "The Lay of the Werewolf," in what ways is the archetype of **disguised identity** present in a physical sense? **(b)** How is it present in an emotional sense?

Comparing Literary Works

3. **(a)** In *Perceval,* which object serves as the story's main **symbol**? Explain. **(b)** In "The Lay of the Werewolf," which character serves as the central symbol? Explain.
4. **(a)** Which characters in each story fail to understand the meaning of the main symbol? Explain. **(b)** How does this lack of understanding affect their actions?

Reading Strategy

Interpreting Symbols

5. Jesus has been referred to as a fisher of men. Does this information affect your **interpretation** of the Fisher King as a symbol in *Perceval?*
6. **(a)** Near the end of "The Lay of the Werewolf," what advice does the counselor give the king regarding Bisclavaret's clothing? **(b)** In what ways does his advice add to your understanding of the werewolf as a symbol?

Extend Understanding

7. **Cultural Connection:** What object or idea might be called the "holy grail" of contemporary American culture? Explain.

QuickReview

An **archetype** is a detail, plot pattern, character type, or theme that recurs in the literature of many different cultures. The **quest,** a common archetype, is the danger-filled pursuit of someone or something of great importance. **Disguised identity** is an archetypal plot pattern in which a character's true identity is concealed by outward appearances.

A **symbol** is a person, place, animal, or object that has its own meaning but also suggests a larger meaning.

To **interpret symbols** as you read, examine the details surrounding important characters, places, objects, or events, and consider their deeper meaning.

For: Self-test
Visit: www.PHSchool.com
Web Code: eta-6502

Answers

1. **Possible response:** **Characters**—Young hero: Perceval; Wise teacher: the lord who trained Perceval; **Goals**—Valuable object: Grail; Restoration of kingdom/ rescue: acquisition of the Grail, allowing the creation of a new holy kingdom; **Obstacles**—Natural: the raging river; Supernatural: the mysterious Fisher King; **Magical Objects**—Devices: Grail; Weapons: sword
   Another sample answer can be found on **Literary Analysis Graphic Organizer B,** p. 116 in ***Graphic Organizer Transparencies.***
2. (a) The baron turns into a werewolf. (b) The baron's human qualities remain intact although he appears to be a werewolf.
3. (a) The Grail is the story's main symbol. Acquiring it, which is the purpose of Perceval's quest, would allow the creation of a new holy kingdom. (b) The baron, Bisclavaret, serves as the central symbol. He represents the paradox of the beast versus the humanity in each of us.
4. (a) Perceval fails to understand the meaning of the Grail; he does not ask the necessary questions about it. The wife fails to understand the meaning of Bisclavaret; she cannot see past his appearance. (b) Perceval remains quiet and loses the opportunity to learn about the Grail. The wife tries to destroy Bisclavaret instead of recognizing the human qualities that prevail even inside his bestial form.
5. **Possible response:** The Fisher King offers Perceval the chance to grow and be saved, but Perceval does not recognize the opportunity, fails to ask the necessary questions, and so misses his chance at salvation.
6. (a) The counselor tells the king to place the clothing in another room so that Bisclavaret can change back into a human in private. (b) The advice suggests that no one wants his or her bestial, or lower, self to be seen by others.

Answers continued

7. **Possible response:** Money might be seen as the "holy grail" of contemporary culture. People believe that acquiring it will transform their lives.

Go Online Assessment Students may use the **Self-test** to prepare for **Selection Test A** or **Selection Test B.**

EXTEND/ASSESS

Answers

1 Vocabulary Lesson

Word Analysis: Latin Root *-naviga-*

1. navigator
2. navigable
3. navigate

Spelling Strategy

1. weigh
2. transient
3. brief

Vocabulary Builder: Synonyms

1. c 2. a 3. c 4. c
5. c 6. a 7. b 8. c

2 Grammar and Style Lesson

1. Independent: Nearby is a hollow stone; there is the place; Dependent: where I hide my clothes
2. Independent: This beast is always with you; there is not one of us; Dependent: who has not known him for long
3. Independent: The King was close to the quarry; he ran to him; Dependent: when Bisclavaret looked upon his master
4. Independent: The young man saw the maid's procession; he did not ask a question about the grail; Dependent: whom they served
5. Independent: he walked around the great hall; he knocked at every door; Dependent: When he was ready

Writing Application

Possible response: I like to read biographies, but I also like science fiction books, especially those that are set in outer space. When I read, I forget about the outside world, and I sometimes lose track of time.

Build Language Skills

1 Vocabulary Lesson

Word Analysis: Latin Root *-naviga-*

The root *-naviga-* means "to steer a ship." Words from sailing are also used when speaking of air travel or driving. Fill in each blank below with a word that contains the root *-naviga-*.

1. The __?__ changed the route.
2. The river was __?__ by the barges.
3. If you give me the map, I'll __?__.

Spelling Strategy

The *ay* sound can be spelled *ei*, as in *neighbor*, but never *ie*. Use the clues on the left to finish the spelling of each word below.

1. measure: w___gh
2. temporary: trans___nt
3. short-lived: br___f

Vocabulary Builder: Synonyms

Select the letter of each word or phrase below that is closest in meaning to the first word.

1. navigated: (a) reached an agreement, (b) became sick, (c) steered a boat
2. sovereign: (a) highest, (b) lowest, (c) wealthiest
3. elated: (a) late, (b) raised, (c) joyful
4. serene: (a) proud, (b) pretty, (c) calm
5. nimble: (a) cloudy, (b) careless, (c) agile
6. abases: (a) lowers, (b) raises, (c) establishes
7. esteemed: (a) heated, (b) valued, (c) ignored
8. importunity: (a) chance, (b) laziness, (c) persistence

2 Grammar and Style Lesson

Compound-Complex Sentences

A clause is a group of words with a subject and a verb. An independent clause can stand alone as a sentence; a subordinate clause cannot. A **compound-complex sentence** contains two independent clauses and one subordinate clause.

Example: [SUBORDINATE CLAUSE: If you but knew,] [INDEPENDENT CLAUSE: you would withdraw yourself from my love,] and [INDEPENDENT CLAUSE: I should be lost indeed.]

Practice Identify the independent and dependent clauses in each item below.

1. Nearby is a hollow stone, concealed by a bush, and there is the place where I hide my clothes.
2. This beast is always with you, and there is not one of us who has not known him for long.
3. The King was close to the quarry, and when Bisclavaret looked upon his master, he ran to him.
4. The young man saw the maid's procession, but he did not ask a question about the grail or whom they served.
5. When he was ready, he walked around the great hall and he knocked at every door.

Writing Application Write a paragraph about the kinds of stories that you like. Use at least two compound-complex sentences.

WG *Prentice Hall Writing and Grammar Connection: Platinum Level, Chapter 20, Section 2*

Assessment Practice

Evaluate and Make Judgments **(For more practice, see *Test Preparation Workbook*, p. 29.)**

Standardized tests often require students to evaluate and make judgments about written information. Write on the board lines 227–233 from "The Grail." Have students read the passage and then respond to the following question to help them practice evaluating and making judgments.

This passage provides evidence that the knight (Perceval) is—

A obedient.
B talkative.
C rebellious.
D brave.

A is the correct answer. Perceval does not ask questions about the marvel, so *B* is incorrect; *C* is incorrect because Perceval obeys what his lord teaches him; *D* is incorrect because the situation in the passage does not concern bravery.

❸ Writing Lesson

Modern Symbolic Tale

Write either a tale of a quest or a tale of disguised identity set in the modern world. For a quest story, select an object or a person to serve as both the goal of the quest and the story's main symbol. For a story of disguised identity, feature a disguise that also has symbolic value.

Prewriting Write an outline of the plot. If your story is a quest, specify the hero's skills, weapons, obstacles, and goal. If your story involves a transformation of identity, specify the physical, emotional, and moral traits of both identities.

Drafting Using your plot outline, write a rough draft. Include sensory details, descriptions, and dialogue to make each scene vivid and believable.

Revising As you review your draft, pay attention to the descriptions of the symbolic object or person. Consider adding details to enrich the meaning.

Model: Revising to Enrich Symbolic Meaning

Mark had turned into a human DVD player, ^a walking cinema. He spoke only in movie dialogue, and he found himself sounding like all the characters of every movie he had ever seen. ^He even made sound effects. Worst of all, he kept "playing back" the same movies, over and over.

Vivid and precise details enrich the meaning of a symbol.

Prentice Hall Writing and Grammar Connection: Platinum Level, Chapter 5, Section 4

❹ Extend Your Learning

Listening and Speaking With a group of classmates, present a **panel discussion** on the topic of symbolism in *Perceval* and "The Lay of the Werewolf." Use these tips to prepare:

- Include four to six panelists and a moderator.
- Ask each panelist to prepare an opening statement.
- Ask the moderator to develop questions to encourage discussion.

End the discussion with several critical comments on which all panelists agree. **[Group Activity]**

Research and Technology Using both print and electronic sources, create a **research presentation** on the historical foundations of the Arthurian legends. Illustrate the information with maps, artworks, and photographs.

For: An additional research activity
Visit: www.PHSchool.com
Web Code: etd-7502

❸ Writing Lesson

- To give students guidance in writing this story, give them **Support for Writing**, p. 34 in ***Unit 5 Resources.***
- Have students read the Writing Lesson instruction. Explain that a symbolic tale should have one principal symbol that serves as a focal point and helps develop and explain the main idea of the story.
- Tell students to begin by developing a story line, or plot. They should then create a symbol that represents the lesson or experience that challenges the main character.
- Use the Narration: Short Story rubrics in General Resources, pp. 63–64, to evaluate students' work.

Writing and Grammar Platinum Level
For support in teaching the Writing Lesson, use Chapter 5, Section 4.

❹ Research and Technology

- Tell students to brainstorm for topics for their presentations.
- Suggest that they consider several subjects to help narrow their research. For example, they might read about Arthurian legends in encyclopedias. They can then select more specific topics on which to focus.
- The **Support for Extend Your Learning** page (***Unit 5 Resources,*** p. 35) provides guided note-taking opportunities to help students complete the Extend Your Learning activities.

Go Online Research Have students type in the Web Code for another research activity.

Assessment Resources

The following resources can be used to assess students' knowledge and skills.

Unit 5 Resources
Selection Test A, pp. 37–39
Selection Test B, pp. 40–42

General Resources
Rubrics for Narration: Short Story, pp. 63–64

Go Online Assessment Students may use the **Self-test** to prepare for **Selection Test A** or **Selection Test B.**

Standard Course of Study

CT.4.05.8 Make connections between works, self and related topics in critical texts.

LT.5.01.2 Build knowledge of literary genres, and explore how characteristics apply to literature of world cultures.

LT.5.03.9 Analyze and evaluate the effects of author's craft and style.

Connections

British Literature

Both *Perceval* and "Sir Galahad" tell the story of a knight's quest for the Holy Grail. Faith is the central theme in both poems. After students have read "Sir Galahad," have them reread *Perceval.* Challenge students to compare and contrast the central figures' approaches to problems.

Searching for the Holy Grail

- Read excerpts from both poems, and encourage students to listen for ways that each poet describes the central character. For example, students might listen for details that suggest each knight's level of sophistication and intelligence. Perceval is an innocent and humorous character who gains knowledge and faith. Galahad avoids human love because of his faith in God and his determination to find the Grail.
- Clarify that Chrétien de Troyes (1135–1180) lived in France during the Middle Ages. He used humor to depict Perceval's naiveté, which fades as Perceval adopts the ideals of knighthood. Tennyson, on the other hand, wrote Sir Galahad and many other Arthurian poems (see *Idylls of the King*) in Victorian England, a culture that prized the moral, spiritual, and intellectual aspects of life.

British Literature

Searching for the Holy Grail

At some time during their lives, most people take a long journey, work hard to reach a goal, make a series of difficult decisions, or even face personal danger. In the literature of the Middle Ages, such a quest fires the imagination in long poems like *Perceval,* in which a young knight sets out to find the Holy Grail, the legendary cup from which Christ drank at the Last Supper.

A Failed Search The section of Chrétien de Troyes's poem *Perceval* in this unit (page 630) recounts Perceval's failure to find the Grail. In spite of the purity of his heart and his stature as one of the bravest knights in the court of King Arthur, Perceval has much to learn about his own weaknesses and the need to ask for help from others. Until he learns those lessons, the Grail remains elusive.

The Grail legend and the other tales of the famous knights of King Arthur's Round Table had such a hold on the imagination of poets and readers that one of nineteenth-century England's most renowned poets, Alfred, Lord Tennyson, used them in several of his poems, including "Sir Galahad." Like Perceval, Galahad sets out with a pure heart on a mystical quest—but neither knight ever finds the Holy Grail. The magical cup has, over centuries and across cultures, become a symbol for all unfulfilled desires and unattainable goals.

Alfred, Lord Tennyson

Enrichment

The Holy Grail

The Holy Grail was the object of many legendary quests in Arthurian romances (and in stories since then—for example, the film *Indiana Jones and the Last Crusade*).

In Arthurian legend, the Grail was the cup Jesus used at the Last Supper. However, at least some of the mystical properties attributed to the cup were probably inspired by classical or Celtic mythologies, in which one finds many magic drinking horns or life-restoring caldrons.

Stories of the search for the Grail first appeared in the 1100s and introduced such heroes as Sir Galahad and Sir Lancelot. Robert de Borron's thirteenth-century poem, *Roman de l'estoire dou Graal,* had a particularly large impact on the image of the Grail in Arthurian legend; it was one of the texts used by Sir Thomas Malory to create *Le Morte d'Arthur.*

In the thirteenth-century *Queste del Sainte Graal,* the final disasters that befall Camelot are linked with the withdrawal of the Grail, which was lost.

My good blade carves the casques[1] of men,
  My tough lance thrusteth sure,
My strength is as the strength of ten,
  Because my heart is pure.
The shattering trumpet shrilleth high,
  The hard brands shiver on the steel,
The splinter'd spear-shafts crack and fly,
  The horse and rider reel:
They reel, they roll in clanging lists,
  And when the tide of combat stands,
Perfume and flowers fall in showers,
  That lightly rain from ladies' hands.

How sweet are looks that ladies bend
  On whom their favours fall!
From them I battle till the end,
  To save from shame and thrall:[2]
But all my heart is drawn above,
  My knees are bow'd in crypt and shrine:
I never felt the kiss of love,
  Nor maiden's hand in mine.
More bounteous aspects on me beam,
  Me mightier transports move and thrill;
So keep I fair thro' faith and prayer
  A virgin heart in work and will.

When down the stormy crescent goes,
  A light before me swims,
Between dark stems the forest glows,
  I hear a noise of hymns:
Then by some secret shrine I ride;
  I hear a voice but none are there;
The stalls are void, the doors are wide,
  The tapers burning fair.
Fair gleams the snowy altar-cloth,
  The silver vessels sparkle clean,
The shrill bell rings, the censer[3] swings,
  And solemn chaunts[4] resound between.

Sometime on lonely mountain-meres
  I find a magic bark;
I leap on board: no helmsman steers:
  I float till all is dark.

---

1. **casques** (kasks) *n.* helmets.
2. **thrall** (thrôl) *n.* slavery.
3. **censer** (sen′ sər) *n.* a container in which incense is burned during religious rites.
4. **chaunts** (chänts) *n.* chants.

CONNECTIONS

Sir Galahad, George Frederick Watts, Trustees of the National Museum & Galleries on Merseyside, England

▲ Critical Viewing
Does this painting of Sir Galahad match your mental picture of the knight? Why or why not? **[Analyze]**

Humanities

Sir Galahad,
by George Frederick Watts

Watts (1817–1904), a British Victorian-era painter and sculptor, began his artistic education at age ten by apprenticing to Neoclassical sculptor William Behnes. (Neoclassicism often dealt with heroic and idealistic universal themes, as do the Arthurian legends.) After a brief time at the Royal Academy, Watts continued his artistic education on his own, focusing on painting universal ideals and symbols, rejecting the emotionalism and sensuality of Romanticism. Ironically, although he despised portraiture, he is admired today for his many effective and revealing portraits of his contemporaries, including the author of "Sir Galahad," Alfred, Lord Tennyson.

Use the following questions for discussion:

- What effect does Watts create by painting both horse and knight in profile?
  Possible response: Watts creates a sense of camaraderie between the two figures. They are depicted as almost supporting each other.
- Examine Galahad's posture. What does he appear to be doing?
  Possible response: Galahad's hands are clasped, his head is slightly tilted, and his eyes appear to be closed—these details make it appear as if he is thinking deeply or engaging in a moment of prayer.

Critical Viewing

Possible responses: Yes; Sir Galahad looks like a journeying knight in full and shining armor. The figure's calm, contemplative demeanor is consistent with Tennyson's depiction of a deeply spiritual Galahad. No; The fierce and skilled warrior described in the first few lines of the poem is altogether absent in Watts' painting.

Differentiated Instruction Solutions for All Learners

Support for Less Proficient Readers

Students may be confused by words in the selection that use the archaic suffix *-eth,* such as *thrusteth* (line 2) and *shrilleth* (line 5). Explain that this suffix is used to form the third person singular present tense of verbs. *Thrusteth* is really just *thrust,* and *shrilleth* is really just *shrill.* Encourage students to read the words without the suffix.

Support for English Learners

Students will probably find Tennyson's verse difficult to understand. Work through several stanzas of the poem with them, line by line, offering definitions and synonyms. Then, organize students into small groups, assigning one unread stanza to each group. Then, have each group interpret their stanza for the class.

Strategy for Advanced Readers

Point out to students that the speaker of "Sir Galahad" is the knight himself. Ask them to discuss how the use of first person contributes to the meaning of the poem. Then, ask students how the meaning of the poem would change if the speaker were someone other than Sir Galahad.

A gentle sound, an awful light!
  Three angels bear the holy Grail:
With folded feet, in stoles of white,
  On sleeping wings they sail.
Ah, blessed vision! blood of God!
  My spirit beats her mortal bars,
As down dark tides the glory slides,
  And star-like mingles with the stars.

When on my goodly charger borne
  Thro' dreaming towns I go,
The cock crows ere the Christmas morn,
  The streets are dumb with snow.

◀ **Critical Viewing**
In what ways is the mood created by the colors and light of this painting similar to the mood of this poem? **[Compare]**

Humanities

The Last Appearance of the Sangreal: Sir Galahad Kneels at the Sight of the Holy Grail, by Donn P. Crane

This intricate engraving depicts a religious figure presenting the Holy Grail to Sir Galahad as three angels observe. The combination of cross-hatching, negative space, and color makes the engraving appear as if it is radiating light. This permeation of "divine light" emphasizes the work's spiritual content.

Use the following questions for discussion:

- Which lines in the poem apply to the events in this engraving?
  Possible response: Lines 42–43 describe the three angels in "stoles of white" who bear the Holy Grail. Although this engraving shows another holy figure bearing the grail, the angels shown match those that Sir Galahad encounters in the poem. In lines 45–48, Sir Galahad is described as being in awe, his spirit filled with wonder. The Galahad in the engraving appears to share these emotions. Both the engraving and poem share images of radiant light, a traditional symbol of divine presence.
- Which details in the engraving reveal Sir Galahad's religious devotion?
  Possible response: Galahad looks upon the holy figure and the Grail with reverence. His hands are joined as if to honor the relic and all it symbolizes.

Critical Viewing

Possible response: The engraving's lucid colors—especially blue and gold—and halo of radiating light create a mood of spiritual enlightenment. Words and phrases in the poem—such as "beam" (line 21), "A light before me swims" (line 26), "the forest glows" (line 27), "The tapers burning fair" (line 32), "Fair gleams" (line 33), "an awful light" (line 41), and "But o'er the dark a glory spreads" (line 55)—create a similar mood of enlightenment.

Enrichment

Fens

Fens are peat-producing wetland areas fed by groundwater sources or drainage water. On the surface, these large tracts of land may appear to be the desolate wastelands Tennyson describes in "Sir Galahad," but in fact, fens are diverse ecosystems that support a wide variety of plant and animal life. Grasses, sedges, and some varieties of orchids thrive in the nutrient-rich soil. Insects such as aquatic beetles, dragonflies, and spiders; mammals such as otters and bats; amphibians such as frogs and newts; and birds such as warblers and buntings all make their homes in fens.

Most fens exist in the northern hemisphere. The United Kingdom features several fens, the largest of which is the Insh Marshes, which lie in the floodplain of Scotland's River Spey. The fens Tennyson mentions in "Sir Galahad" may be those of Eastern England. For hundreds of years, "fenmen" have lived on these flat marshy areas, hunting wildfowl, fishing, and grazing their cattle on the abundant vegetation.

The tempest crackles on the leads,
And, ringing, springs from brand and mail;[5]
But o'er the dark a glory spreads,
And gilds the driving hail.
I leave the plain, I climb the height;
No branchy thicket shelter yields;
But blessed forms in whistling storms
Fly o'er waste fens[6] and windy fields.

A maiden knight—to me is given
Such hope, I know not fear;
I yearn to breathe the airs of heaven
That often meet me here.
I muse on joy that will not cease,
Pure spaces clothed in living beams,
Pure lilies of eternal peace,
Whose odours haunt my dreams;
And, stricken by an angel's hand,
This mortal armour that I wear,
This weight and size, this heart and eyes,
Are touch'd, are turn'd to finest air.

The clouds are broken in the sky,
And thro' the mountain-walls
A rolling organ-harmony
Swells up, and shakes and falls.
Then move the trees, the copses nod,
Wings flutter, voices hover clear:
"O just and faithful knight of God!
Ride on! the prize is near!"
So pass I hostel, hall, and grange;
By bridge and ford, by park and pale,
All-arm'd I ride, whate'er betide,
Until I find the holy Grail.

5. **brand and mail** sword and armor.
6. **fens** swamp or bogs.

Alfred, Lord Tennyson (1809–1892)

Tennyson was born in the rural town of Somersby in Lincolnshire, England, the fourth of twelve children. His father, a clergyman, had a large library and supervised Tennyson's early education. At Cambridge University, Tennyson met Arthur Henry Hallam, who became his closest friend and encouraged him to publish his poems. When Hallam died suddenly in 1833, Tennyson was devastated, but his grief inspired one of his greatest works, *In Memoriam, A.H.H.* The royalties from this poem enabled Tennyson and his wife to buy a farm on the Isle of Wight, where they raised two children and Tennyson continued to write poetry into his eighties.

Connecting British Literature

1. **(a)** In what way are Perceval and Sir Galahad similar? **(b)** How are the two characters different?
2. Which of the two characters do you find more interesting or sympathetic? Explain.
3. What details in each poem express a universal human desire for adventure?

ASSESS

Answers

1. (a) Both Perceval and Sir Galahad are devout Christians and knights searching for the Holy Grail.
(b) Perceval, apparently quite young or very naïve, throws himself into his quest unquestioningly, responding to all advice, good and bad, with blind obedience. He struggles to find his way, gets lost, and refuses to ask for help because once, in an entirely different situation, he was told not to do so. By the end of *Perceval,* he has learned his lesson about asking for help. Sir Galahad, a model of devout knighthood, single-mindedly searches for the Grail, never tempted by physical desires to delay his quest.
2. **Possible response:** Perceval is more interesting, sympathetic, and even humorous because he shows more human flaws and grows over the course of the poem.
3. **Possible response:** The desire for adventure is reflected in Perceval's willingness to wander in search of the castle and to enter a strange place where he seems to know no one and understand nothing. In "Sir Galahad," the last five lines reflect the human compulsion to reject the comforts at home to seek rewards—both literal and figurative—elsewhere.

Differentiated Instruction Solutions for All Learners

Strategy for Special Needs Students

Point out the words "thro'" (lines 50, 74), "o'er" (lines 55, 60), "touch'd" (line 72), and "all-arm'd" (line 83). Remind students that an apostrophe replaces letters that are omitted from a word. Ask students to write the spellings on the board. (thro'/through; o'er/over; touch'd/touched; all-arm'd/all-armed)

Enrichment for Gifted/Talented Students

Invite students to write their own poems or stories about the quest for the Holy Grail. Students can use Perceval or Sir Galahad or create a protagonist of their own. Have them create drawings to illustrate their works. Then, ask volunteers to share their versions with the class, displaying the accompanying illustrations.

Strategy for Advanced Readers

Challenge students to find examples of alliteration within Tennyson's first stanza: "carves/casques" (line 1); "shattering/shrilleth" (line 5); "shiver/steel" (line 6); "splinter'd/spear-shafts" (line 7); "rider/reel" (line 8); "reel/roll" (line 9); "flowers/fall" (line 11). Ask students to consider the purpose and effect of this technique.

Standard Course of Study

Goal 1: WRITTEN LANGUAGE

WL.1.03.11 Identify and analyze elements of expressive environment in personal reflections.

Goal 5: LITERATURE

LT.5.01.3 Analyze literary devices and explain their effect on the work of world literature.

LT.5.03.9 Analyze and evaluate the effects of author's craft and style in world literature.

Goal 6: GRAMMAR AND USAGE

GU.6.01.3 Use recognition strategies to understand vocabulary and exact word choice.

GU.6.01.4 Use vocabulary strategies to determine meaning.

GU.6.01.7 Use language effectively to create mood and tone.

Step-by-Step Teaching Guide	Pacing Guide
PRETEACH	
• Administer Vocabulary and Reading Warm-ups as necessary.	5 min.
• Engage students' interest with the motivation activity.	5 min.
• Read and discuss author and background features. **FT**	10 min.
• Introduce the Literary Analysis Skill: Allegory. **FT**	5 min.
• Introduce the Reading Strategy: Interpreting Imagery. **FT**	10 min.
• Prepare students to read by teaching the selection vocabulary. **FT**	
TEACH	
• Informally monitor comprehension while students read independently or in groups. **FT**	30 min.
• Monitor students' comprehension with the Reading Check notes.	as students read
• Reinforce vocabulary with Vocabulary Builder notes.	as students read
• Develop students' understanding of allegory with the Literary Analysis annotations. **FT**	5 min.
• Develop students' ability to interpret imagery with the Reading Strategy annotations. **FT**	5 min.
ASSESS/EXTEND	
• Assess students' comprehension and mastery of the Literary Analysis and Reading Strategy by having them answer the Apply the Skills questions. **FT**	15 min.
• Have students complete the Vocabulary Lesson and the Grammar and Style Lesson. **FT**	15 min.
• Apply students' understanding by using one or more of the Extend Your Learning activities.	20–90 min. or homework
• Administer Selection Test A or Selection Test B. **FT**	15 min.

Resources

Print

Unit 5 Resources

- Vocabulary Warm-up Word Lists **[L1, L2, EL]** .... p. 43
- Vocabulary Warm-up Practice **[L1, L2, EL]** .... p. 44
- Reading Warm-up A **[L1, L2, EL]** .... p. 45
- Reading Warm-up B **[L1, L2, L3]** .... p. 46

Transparency

Graphic Organizer Transparencies

- Literary Analysis Graphic Organizer A **[L3]** .... p. 119
- Literary Analysis Graphic Organizer B **[L1, L2, EL]** .... p. 120
- Reading Strategy Graphic Organizer A **[L3]** .... p. 117
- Reading Strategy Graphic Organizer B **[L1, L2, EL]** .... p. 118

Print

Reader's Notebook [L2]

Reader's Notebook: Adapted Version [L1]

Reader's Notebook: English Learner's Version [EL]

Unit 5 Resources

- Literary Analysis **[L3]** .... p. 47
- Reading Strategy **[L3]** .... p. 48
- Vocabulary Builder **[L3]** .... p. 49

Technology

Listening to Literature Audio CDs [L2, EL]

Reader's Notebook: Adapted Version Audio CD [L1, L2]

Print

Unit 5 Resources

- Grammar and Style **[L3]** .... p. 50
- Support for Extend Your Learning **[L3]** .... p. 51
- Enrichment **[L4]** .... p. 52
- Selection Test A **[L1, L2, EL]** .... pp. 53–55
- Selection Test B **[L3, L4]** .... pp. 56–58

Technology

- **Go Online:** Research **[L3]**
- **Go Online:** Self-test **[L3]**
- ***ExamView®,* Test Bank [L3]**

Choosing Resources for Differentiated Instruction

[L1] Special Needs Students

[L2] Below-Level Students

[L3] All Students

[L4] Advanced Students

[EL] English Learners

For Vocabulary and Reading Warm-ups and for Selection Tests, **A** signifies "less challenging" and **B** "more challenging." For Graphic Organizer transparencies, **A** signifies "not filled in" and **B** "filled in."

FT Fast Track Instruction: To move the lesson more quickly, use the strategies and activities identified with **FT**.

Scaffolding for Less Proficient and Advanced Students

The leveled Critical Thinking questions after selections progress in the levels of thinking required to answer them. To address the needs of your different students, you may use the (a) level questions for your less proficient students and the (b) level questions with your on-level and advanced students. The occasional (c) level questions are appropriate for your advanced students.

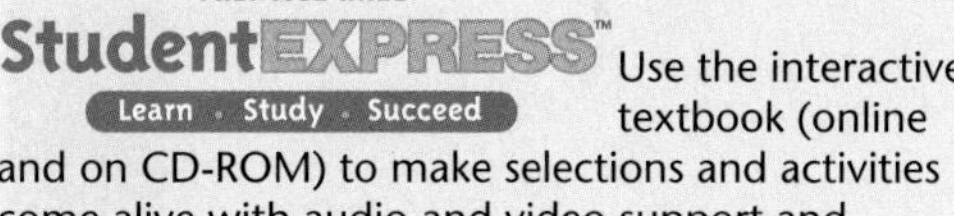

Use this complete suite of powerful teaching tools to make lesson planning and testing quicker and easier.

PRENTICE HALL
StudentEXPRESS™
Learn · Study · Succeed

Use the interactive textbook (online and on CD-ROM) to make selections and activities come alive with audio and video support and interactive questions.

Benchmark

After students have completed reading these excerpts from the *Inferno,* administer **Benchmark Test 6 *(Unit 6 Resources,* pp. 59–64).** If the Benchmark Test reveals that some of the students need further work, use the **Interpretation Guide** to determine the appropriate reteaching page in the **Reading Kit** and on **Success Tracker.**

For: Information about Lexiles
Visit: www.PHSchool.com
Web Code: eue-1111

PRETEACH

Motivation

Capture students' attention by explaining that the selection describes a symbolic journey. Ask students to work in pairs to brainstorm for other stories, poems, films, songs, or works of art that use the theme of a journey. Have volunteers explain the journey in each of the works cited, its symbolic importance to the narrator or main character, and why the creator might have used a journey as the theme in each of the works cited. Then, have students list features of journeys that make them appropriate symbolic structures.

❶ Background

More About the Author

Two men in particular influenced Dante. Brunetto Latini taught Dante to think and speak effectively and to participate in public life. Guido Cavalcanti, a poet, encouraged Dante to make the important switch to writing in Italian.

Geography Note

Draw students' attention to the map on this page. Explain that after his exile from Florence, Dante spent great effort pleading his case for being allowed to return. He failed and remained on his own journey until he died in Ravenna.

Build Skills *Epic Poem*

❶ *from the* Divine Comedy: Inferno

Dante Alighieri (1265–1321)

Dante Alighieri (dän′ tā al əg yer′ ē), whose visions of Hell have haunted readers for centuries, is widely considered one of the greatest poets of Western civilization. T. S. Eliot wrote, "Dante and Shakespeare divide the modern world between them. There is no third."

Political Chaos Dante was born into a poor but noble family in Florence, Italy. At the time, Italy was not a unified country but a collection of independent city-states. These city-states were marked by fierce political turbulence and power struggles between ruling families. The states were constantly at war with each other while they simultaneously battled civil unrest within their own borders.

Painful Exile As a member of the nobility, Dante became an elected official. Along with six other officials, he ran Florence's government. However, in 1300, a street accident led to a skirmish, which escalated into a full-blown civil war. Dante's political party and all its representatives were overthrown. In 1302, Dante was officially exiled from his beloved city, never to return. His experience of exile would later play an important role in his writing.

Writing in Italian Scholars believe that Dante studied law and rhetoric at the University of Bologna, one of Europe's most prestigious institutions of higher learning. Bologna also boasted a great poetic tradition, and it was there that Dante discovered a school of writers who sought to free poetry from the limitations imposed by the church and government. At the time, most writers wrote in Latin, the language of scholars. Dante believed that poets should write in the language of the people—in his case, Italian. In 1304, he published *De Vulgari Eloquentia,* in which he argued for the use of the common tongue in works of literature. He wrote many lyric poems in Italian; however, it was with his *Divine Comedy* that he created the crowning achievement of medieval literature.

Principle of the Trinity Completed shortly before his death, the *Commedia,* which later gained the honorific title *Divina,* documents the physical and spiritual journey of a man who is also named Dante. Dante used the number three, which represents the Christian concept of the trinity, as an organizing principle for the *Divine Comedy.* Consisting of 100 cantos, the poem is divided into three parts—the *Inferno,* the *Purgatorio,* and the *Paradiso.* Each part contains thirty-three cantos; there is also an introductory first canto for the *Inferno,* the only one that takes place on Earth. Within each canto, the verse form is *terza rima,* a stanza of three lines. In addition, Dante's journey takes three days, beginning on Good Friday and ending on Easter Sunday.

The Love of His Life Guiding Dante on his pilgrimage is his beloved Beatrice, whose name means "she who blesses." It is believed that Dante modeled his literary Beatrice on the real-life Bea-trice Portinari. Although evidence suggests that Dante saw the real Beatrice only twice in his life—first when he was nine years old and then again nine years later—she became for Dante the force that led him out of his despair. She was first the subject of his love poetry; later, she became both the object of his religious quest and a symbol of spiritual purity. Beatrice, the guiding presence in Dante's life and in his poem, is literally and symbolically his link between heaven and Earth.

In 1321, shortly after completing the *Paradiso,* Dante died in the city of Ravenna in northern Italy.

Preview

Connecting to the Literature

Imagine a movie that begins with a lone man lost in a dark forest. Suddenly, a leopard and a lion leap from the shadows, baring their fangs. The man runs, only to come face to face with a vicious wolf. This selection opens with just such a scene and contains all the drama of a Hollywood film.

NC Standard Course of Study

- Analyze literary devices and explain their effect on the work of world literature. (LT.5.01.3)
- Use language effectively to create mood and tone. (GU.6.01.7)

❷ Literary Analysis

Allegory

An **allegory** is a literary work with two levels of meaning—the literal and the symbolic. In an allegory, every detail, character, and plot point has an equivalent symbolic meaning. For example, an allegory in which a rowboat floating down a river symbolizes the journey of life might have these symbolic equivalents:

- rowboat = person
- water = flow of time
- two oars = hard work and persistence
- rudder = love or guidance

The *Divine Comedy* is a complex allegory in which a literal journey symbolizes a man's struggle for redemption. As you read, try to identify the allegorical meanings of the places and characters Dante encounters.

Connecting Literary Elements

Imagery is the use of language that appeals to one or more of the five senses and creates mental pictures for the reader. Dante uses imagery to make the allegorical world of his poem seem tangible and real, helping the reader *feel* the ideas. As you read, notice language that appeals to the senses and creates powerful word pictures in your mind.

❸ Reading Strategy

Interpreting Imagery

To **interpret an image,** identify which of the five senses it involves. Then, classify the physical experience the image creates by the sight, sound, taste, smell, or sense of touch it evokes. Finally, define the emotion or idea the image conveys. As you read, use a chart like the one shown to interpret imagery.

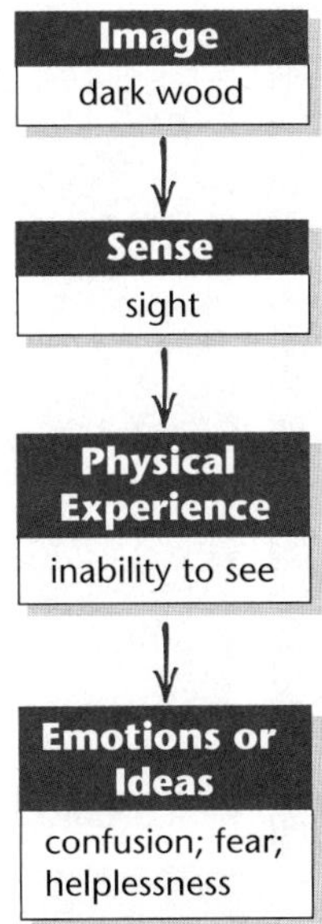

Vocabulary Builder

flounders (floun′ dərz) *v.* struggles to move (p. 660)

tremulous (trem′ yo͞o ləs) *adj.* quivering; shaking (p. 662)

zeal (zēl) *n.* ardor; fervor (p. 662)

putrid (pyo͞o′ trid) *adj.* rotten; stinking (p. 665)

despicable (dəs′ pi kə bəl) *adj.* deserving to be despised; contemptible (p. 667)

lamentation (lam′ ən tā′ shən) *n.* weeping; wailing (p. 667)

scorn (skôrn) *v.* reject (p. 667)

reprimand (rep′ rə mand′) *n.* a severe or formal rebuke (p. 668)

❷ Literary Analysis

Allegory

- Tell students that they will focus on allegory—the discussion of one subject disguised as another—as they read the excerpts from the *Inferno.*
- Explain that allegories often tell moral or religious lessons, and urge students to watch for these as they read.

❸ Reading Strategy

Interpreting Imagery

- Remind students that visualizing and analyzing Dante's imagery will help them follow and relate to the story.
- As they read Dante's poem, have students watch for language that creates vivid mental pictures.
- Give students a copy of **Reading Strategy Graphic Organizer A,** p. 117 in ***Graphic Organizer Transparencies.*** Have them use it to track and interpret the images from the poem.

Vocabulary Builder

- Pronounce each vocabulary word for students, and read the definitions as a class. Have students identify any words with which they are already familiar.

Differentiated Instruction Solutions for All Learners

Support for Special Needs Students
Have students use the support pages for these selections in the ***Reader's Notebook: Adapted Version.*** Completing these pages will prepare students to read the selections in the Student Edition.

Support for Less Proficient Readers
Have students use the support pages for these selections in the ***Reader's Notebook.*** Completing these pages will prepare students to read the selections in the Student Edition.

Support for English Learners
Have students use the support pages for these selections in the ***Reader's Notebook: English Learner's Version.*** Completing these pages will prepare students to read the selections in the Student Edition.

Facilitate Understanding

Ask students whether they have ever visited a haunted house or house of horrors. Inform them that Dante is about to take them on a journey that is in some way comparable to such an adventure. Then, ask them to describe briefly the feelings they experienced when they first approached such attractions.

1 About the Selection

In this vivid and gripping canto, the first of the *Inferno,* Dante describes the horrors of Hell. The poet is beginning a journey from despair to hope, as he confronts the nature and consequences of sin.

Canto I relates how the middle-aged poet, having lost faith, finds himself lost and alone in a dark wood. There he finds a guide, the Roman poet Virgil, who will lead him out of his errors and back onto the path toward hope.

2 Humanities

The Forest, Inferno I,
by Gustave Doré

The French artist Doré (1832–1883) published several large-scale illustrated books at the height of his career. He lavishly illustrated these deluxe editions with engravings of his drawings. Dante's *Inferno,* one of the works selected, enjoyed tremendous success.

In this engraving, the poet is shown standing "alone in a dark wood."

Use the following questions for discussion:

- Why do you suppose the figure is looking around?
  Answer: He is worried and wants to make sure that nothing dangerous is nearby.
- What lines in the poem might the artist have been referring to when creating his illustration?
  Answer: The artist might have been referring to lines 1–7.

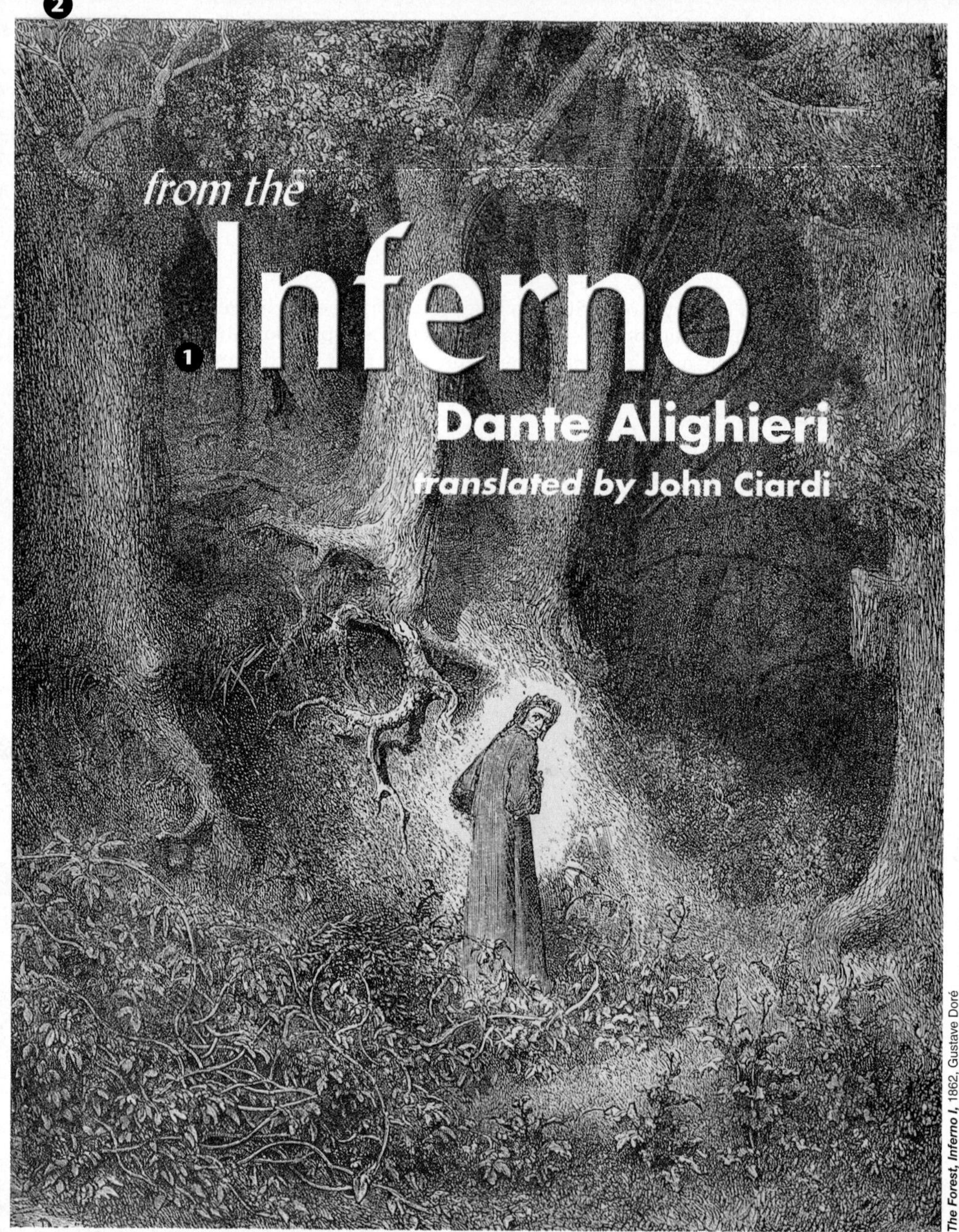

from the Inferno

Dante Alighieri

translated by John Ciardi

The Forest, Inferno I, 1862, Gustave Doré

Differentiated Instruction
Solutions for All Learners

Accessibility at a Glance

	Canto I	Canto III
Context	Dante realizes his problem and meets his guide, Virgil.	Virgil leads Dante through the Gate and into Hell.
Language	Long sentences with symbolic words	Some dialogue within poetic narration
Concept Level	Accessible (Sin is dangerous.)	Accessible (Sinners will be punished.)
Literary Merit	Classic allegorical epic poem	Classic allegorical epic poem
Lexile	NP	NP
Overall Rating	Challenging	Challenging

Background The *Divine Comedy* is composed of three sections—the *Inferno*, the *Purgatorio*, and the *Paradiso*. In the *Inferno*, the poet Virgil has been sent by Beatrice to lead Dante through Hell. Hell, a series of downward spiraling circles, is organized according to the gravity of the sin being punished. The lowest circle is reserved for traitors and Lucifer himself, the ultimate betrayer.

In Canto I of the *Inferno*, Dante first awakens to his plight and meets his guide. In Canto III, Virgil leads Dante through the Gate and into Hell itself.

Canto I

THE DARK WOOD OF ERROR

Midway in his allotted threescore years and ten, Dante comes to himself with a start and realizes that he has strayed from the True Way into the Dark Wood of Error (Worldliness). As soon as he has realized his loss, Dante lifts his eyes and sees the first light of the sunrise (the Sun is the Symbol of Divine Illumination) lighting the shoulders of a little hill (The Mount of Joy). It is the Easter Season, the time of resurrection, and the sun is in its equinoctial rebirth.[1] This juxtaposition of joyous symbols fills Dante with hope and he sets out at once to climb directly up the Mount of Joy, but almost immediately his way is blocked by the Three Beasts of Worldliness: *The Leopard of Malice and Fraud, The Lion of Violence and Ambition,* and *The She-Wolf of Incontinence.*[2] These beasts, and especially the She-Wolf, drive him back despairing into the darkness of error. But just as all seems lost, a figure appears to him. It is the shade of *Virgil,*[3] Dante's symbol of *Human Reason.*

Virgil explains that he has been sent to lead Dante from error. There can, however, be no direct ascent past the beasts: the man who would escape them must go a longer and harder way. First he must descend through Hell (The Recognition of Sin), then he must ascend through Purgatory (The Renunciation of Sin), and only then may he reach the pinnacle of joy and come to the Light of God. Virgil offers to guide Dante, but only as far as Human Reason can go. Another guide (*Beatrice,* symbol of *Divine Love*) must take over for the final ascent, for Human Reason is self-limited. Dante submits himself joyously to Virgil's guidance and they move off.

3 Midway in our life's journey,[4] I went astray
from the straight road and woke to find myself
alone in a dark wood. How shall I say

1. **equinoctial** (ē′ kwi näk′ shəl) **rebirth** After the vernal equinox, which occurs about March 21, days become longer than nights.
2. **incontinence** (in kän′ tə nəns) *n.* lack of self-restraint.
3. **Virgil** (vʉr′ jəl) great Roman poet (70–19 B.C.).
4. **Midway in our life's journey** The biblical life span is threescore years and ten—seventy years. The action opens in Dante's thirty-fifth year, i.e., A.D. 1300.

4 ◀ **Critical Viewing** Which elements in this engraving portray Dante's "dark wood of error" as an ominous, threatening place? **[Analyze]**

Literary Analysis
Allegory Which details in the opening lines immediately suggest the allegorical nature of the poem? Explain.

5 

Reading Check
At what time of year does Dante's tale take place?

3 Literary Analysis

Allegory

- Review with students the defining characteristics of an allegory on p. 657.
- Have students review lines 1–3 and consider details that indicate allegory. For example, point out the use of both the plural and singular first-person pronoun ("our" and "I"). Explain that this usage suggests the poem will be about both a single man, the poet, and, allegorically, about the entire human race.
- Then, **ask** students the Literary Analysis question: Which details in the opening lines immediately suggest the allegorical nature of the poem? Explain.
Answer: The reference to a life's journey, to veering from the straight road, and to being alone in a dark wood all suggest an allegorical, not literal, journey.

4 Critical Viewing

Answer: Students might note the shadows; the tiny figure amidst a large, dark wood; and the tangled undergrowth as elements that suggest an ominous, threatening place.

5 Reading Check

Answer: It takes place in the spring, near the Christian holiday of Easter.

Differentiated Instruction
Solutions for All Learners

Strategy for Less Proficient Readers
Have students write out difficult passages and work to identify sentence parts. If necessary, help students paraphrase sentences or rearrange the syntax to clarify meaning. Also, urge students to use the dictionary to find the meanings of unfamiliar words not treated in the accompanying notes.

Support for English Learners
Before students read, choose some longer sentences and model the process of breaking a sentence into its main subject and verb to determine its basic meaning. Ask: "Who is this sentence about? What is happening to this subject? What symbolic meaning might the text have?"

Enrichment for Advanced Readers
Challenge students to discuss their experiences with films and stories that contain elements of allegory. Remind them of how allegory works in Orwell's *Animal Farm,* a novel many will know. Ask them to explain how the characters in this novel represent concepts.

6 Reading Strategy

Interpreting Imagery

- Read aloud the bracketed passage. Point out that the speaker describes his state as "drugged and loose with sleep."
- Ask students to describe the image that these words bring to mind.
- **Ask** students what sense this narcotic state gives to Dante's tale.
Possible response: It gives the story a surreal quality, as if it were a dream.

7 Literary Analysis

Allegory

- Ask a volunteer to read aloud lines 31–36. Have students identify the character of the leopard introduced here.
- Explain that the animal is a real threat but that it also represents an abstract idea. Recall with students the old story about the leopard that changed his spots to fool the other animals.
- **Ask** students to predict what abstract ideas Dante might represent through the leopard.
Possible response: Predictions should include ideas of danger, deceit, or fraud.

8 Critical Viewing

Possible response: The illustrations emphasize the fierce and frightening qualities associated with each animal. The illustrations are not intended to be realistic; rather, they portray the animals in a way that taps into the viewer's primal fear of what is "wild."

what wood that was! I never saw so drear,
so rank, so arduous[5] a wilderness!
Its very memory gives a shape to fear.

Death could scarce be more bitter than that place!
But since it came to good, I will recount
all that I found revealed there by God's grace.

How I came to it I cannot rightly say,
so drugged and loose with sleep had I become
when I first wandered there from the True Way.

But at the far end of that valley of evil
whose maze had sapped my very heart with fear
I found myself before a little hill

and lifted up my eyes. Its shoulders glowed
already with the sweet rays of that planet[6]
whose virtue leads men straight on every road,

and the shining strengthened me against the fright
whose agony had wracked the lake of my heart
through all the terrors of that piteous night.

Just as a swimmer, who with his last breath
flounders ashore from perilous seas, might turn
to memorize the wide water of his death—

so did I turn, my soul still fugitive
from death's surviving image, to stare down
that pass that none had ever left alive.

And there I lay to rest from my heart's race
till calm and breath returned to me. Then rose
and pushed up that dead slope at such a pace

each footfall rose above the last. And lo!
almost at the beginning of the rise
I faced a spotted Leopard,[7] all tremor and flow

Vocabulary Builder
flounders (floun′ dərz) v. struggles to move

8 ▲ Critical Viewing Do you think these illustrations of the leopard (this page), the lion, and the wolf (facing page) emphasize each animal's realistic appearance or its symbolic meaning? Explain. **[Make a Judgment]**

5. **so rank, so arduous** (är′ jo͞o əs) so overgrown, so difficult to cross.
6. **that planet** the sun. Medieval astronomers considered the sun a planet. In the *Divine Comedy,* the sun is also symbolic of God.
7. **a spotted Leopard** The three beasts that Dante encounters are taken from the Bible, Jeremiah 5:6. While numerous interpretations have been advanced for them, many scholars agree that they foreshadow the three divisions of Hell (incontinence, violence, and fraud), which Virgil explains at length in Canto XI, 16–111.

Enrichment

Language of the Common People

Dante was one of the first great authors in history to write in the language spoken by ordinary people in his time and country. By choosing Italian instead of Latin, Dante knew that his writing and message would reach more people.

At the time, learned people from many countries would have known Latin and would have communicated with one another in that language. Even today, some Roman Catholic religious orders communicate to members across the world in Latin, and the supporters of Esperanto seek to encourage the development of a common language to be used throughout the world. Ask students to brainstorm for challenges that Dante would have faced, as well as advantages he would have gained, by his decision. Then, have students speculate on the advantages of having a more universal language, like the Latin that Dante put aside when writing *The Divine Comedy.*

and gaudy pelt. And it would not pass, but stood
so blocking my every turn that time and again
I was on the verge of turning back to the wood.

This fell at the first widening of the dawn
as the sun climbing Aries with those stars
that rode with him to light the new creation.[8]

Thus the holy hour and the sweet season
of commemoration did much to arm my fear
of that bright murderous beast with their good omen.

Yet not so much but what I shook with dread
at sight of a great Lion that broke upon me
raging with hunger, its enormous head

held high as if to strike a mortal terror
into the very air. And down his track,
a She-Wolf drove upon me, a starved horror

ravening and wasted beyond all belief.
She seemed a rack for avarice,[9] gaunt and craving.
9 Oh many the souls she has brought to endless grief!

10 She brought such heaviness upon my spirit
at sight of her savagery and desperation,
I died from every hope of that high summit.

And like a miser—eager in acquisition
but desperate in self-reproach when Fortune's wheel
turns to the hour of his loss—all tears and attrition[10]

I wavered back; and still the beast pursued,
forcing herself against me bit by bit
till I slid back into the sunless wood.

Literary Analysis
Allegory In what ways is Dante's reaction to the beasts more realistic than heroic? Explain.

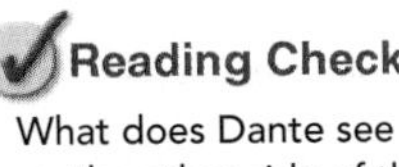

Reading Check 11
What does Dante see on the other side of the "valley of evil"?

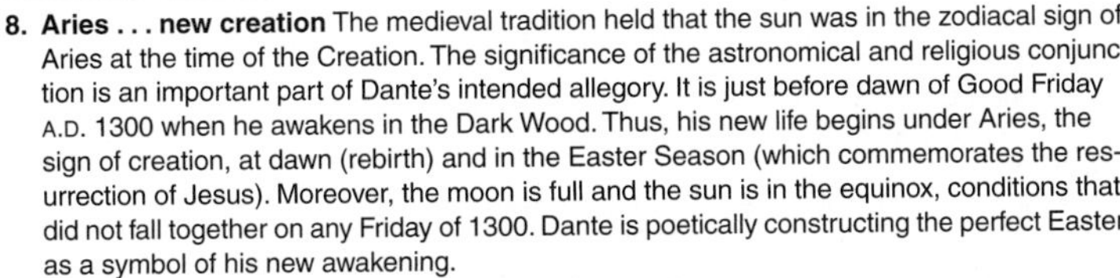

8. **Aries . . . new creation** The medieval tradition held that the sun was in the zodiacal sign of Aries at the time of the Creation. The significance of the astronomical and religious conjunction is an important part of Dante's intended allegory. It is just before dawn of Good Friday A.D. 1300 when he awakens in the Dark Wood. Thus, his new life begins under Aries, the sign of creation, at dawn (rebirth) and in the Easter Season (which commemorates the resurrection of Jesus). Moreover, the moon is full and the sun is in the equinox, conditions that did not fall together on any Friday of 1300. Dante is poetically constructing the perfect Easter as a symbol of his new awakening.
9. **a rack for avarice** an instrument of torture for greed.
10. **attrition** (ə trish´ ən) *n.* weakening; wearing away.

9 Literary Analysis

Allegory

- Point out that Dante faces a leopard, a lion, and a wolf. Then, discuss the qualities of a hero: larger than life, extraordinarily brave.
- Invite a volunteer to read aloud lines 43–60, conveying the emotions reflected by the situation and language.
- Then, **ask** students the Literary Analysis question: In what ways is Dante's reaction to the beasts more realistic than heroic? Explain.
  Answer: Dante's reaction is more realistic than heroic because Dante shakes with dread, feels despair, and runs from the beasts, whereas a heroic character would likely face down the beasts and fight.

Monitor Progress As students consider the questions, urge them to think about how Dante's ordinary reactions function allegorically.

10 Critical Thinking

Infer

- Discuss Dante's reaction to the She-Wolf.
- **Ask** students why Dante seems so frightened of the She-Wolf and convinced that the animal will destroy his hopes for reaching the "high summit."
  Answer: Representing the temptation to sin, the She-Wolf, as Dante knows, has "devoured" many—that is, many have been destroyed by their greed.

11 Reading Check

Answer: Dante sees a spotted leopard.

Differentiated Instruction Solutions for All Learners

Support for Special Needs Students
Some students will have difficulty with imagery. Give them a copy of **Reading Strategy Graphic Organizer B,** p. 118 in ***Graphic Organizer Transparencies.*** They can use the completed graphic organizer as a model for identifying an image, determining what senses are involved in the image, and interpreting imagery as they read.

Strategy for Less Proficient Readers
Encourage students to read each canto all the way through in one sitting. Suggest that they make notes about passages they find confusing, such as Dante's encounter with the three beasts. Reading further may clarify points. If this strategy does not prove helpful, students can return to the passages and ask questions.

Support for English Learners
Students may have difficulty interpreting Dante's verses and imagery. Review the Reading Strategy instruction on p. 657. Then give them **Reading Warm-up A,** page 45 in ***Unit 5 Resources.*** Have students keep a list of images they encounter as they read. Encourage them to ask questions about the meaning of those images they do not understand.

⓬ Humanities

15th-century Italian manuscript illumination from Dante's *Inferno*

This illustration appeared as the frontispiece for Dante's *Inferno.* Created as an illumination, it would have featured strong colors, such as this red.

Use the following question to stimulate discussion:

How does the artist use color to focus viewers' attention on important elements?
Answer: Virgil and Dante, both crucial elements of the image, appear in vibrant red and blue (respectively), colors that attract viewers' attention.

⓭ Critical Viewing

Possible response: Virgil may be reassuring the poet. He also may be telling Dante to trust and rely on him for help.

⓮ Critical Thinking

Interpret

- Read aloud the bracketed passage. Ask students to discuss what Virgil means by "false and lying gods."
- Then, **ask** why this statement points to a significant difference between Virgil and Dante.
  Answer: Virgil implies that he was not a Christian in life but rather a follower of the ancient Roman religion; therefore, although he represents the highest insights open to unaided reason, he is lacking the insights Dante believed Christianity offers as well as the accompanying sense of hope.

⓯ Vocabulary Builder

Latin Root *-trem-*

- Call students' attention to the word *tremulous* and its definition. Explain that the Latin word root *-trem-* means "tremble."
- Discuss how and why a voice might tremble.
- Invite volunteers to demonstrate a tremulous voice.

And as I fell to my soul's ruin, a presence
gathered before me on the discolored air,
the figure of one who seemed hoarse from long silence.

At sight of him in that friendless waste I cried: ⓬
"Have pity on me, whatever thing you are,
whether shade or living man." And it replied:

"Not man, though man I once was, and my blood
was Lombard, both my parents Mantuan.[11]
I was born, though late, *sub Julio,*[12] and bred

⓮ in Rome under Augustus in the noon
of the false and lying gods.[13] I was a poet
and sang of old Anchises' noble son

who came to Rome after the burning of Troy.[14]
But you—why do *you* return to these distresses
instead of climbing that shining Mount of Joy

which is the seat and first cause of man's bliss?"
⓯ "And are you then that Virgil and that fountain
of purest speech?" My voice grew tremulous:

"Glory and light of poets! now may that zeal
and love's apprenticeship that I poured out
on your heroic verses serve me well!

For you are my true master and first author,
the sole maker from whom I drew the breath
of that sweet style whose measures have
brought me honor.

See there, immortal sage, the beast I flee.
For my soul's salvation, I beg you, guard me from her,
for she has struck a mortal tremor through me."

⓭ ▼ **Critical Viewing** In this fifteenth-century illustration of Canto I, what do you think Virgil, in red, is telling Dante? **[Connect]**

Vocabulary Builder

tremulous (trem′ yo͞o ləs) *adj.* quivering; shaking

zeal (zēl) *n.* ardor; fervor

11. **Lombard . . . Mantuan** Lombardy is a region of northern Italy; Mantua, the birthplace of Virgil, is a city in that region.
12. ***sub Julio*** in the reign of Julius Caesar. It would be more accurate to say that he was born during the lifetime of Caesar (102?–44 B.C.). Augustus did not begin his rule as dictator until long after Virgil's birth, which occurred in 70 B.C.
13. **under Augustus . . . gods** Augustus, the grandnephew of Julius Caesar, was the emperor of Rome from 27 B.C. to A.D.14. The "lying gods" are the gods of classical mythology.
14. **and sang . . . Troy** Virgil's epic poem, the *Aeneid*, describes the destruction of Troy by the Greeks and the founding of Roman civilization by the Trojan Aeneas, son of Anchises (an kī′ sēz).

Enrichment

Mentoring Programs

Dante calls Virgil his "true master" and means it in two senses: Virgil was his poetic model and has now become his guide and teacher on his journey through Hell and Purgatory. The word *mentor,* meaning a wise and trusted advisor, also comes from a classical epic. Mentor was the teacher of Telemachus, the son of Odysseus, hero of Homer's great epic poem the *Odyssey.* Today, many communities have instituted mentoring programs, in which older people become mentors to younger people. These programs have been especially successful in helping young people learn about careers, take personal responsibility in their lives, and improve their communities.

Ask students to work together in small groups to research the availability and activities of mentoring programs in your community. After student groups report to the class on their findings, have them compare activities of community mentors with the help Virgil provides to Dante.

And he replied, seeing my soul in tears:
"He must go by another way who would escape
this wilderness, for that mad beast that fleers[15]

before you there, suffers no man to pass.
She tracks down all, kills all, and knows no glut,
but, feeding, she grows hungrier than she was.

She mates with any beast, and will mate with more
before the Greyhound comes to hunt her down.
He will not feed on lands nor loot, but honor

16

and love and wisdom will make straight his way.
He will rise between Feltro and Feltro,[16] and in him
shall be the resurrection and new day

of that sad Italy for which Nisus died,
and Turnus, and Euryalus, and the maid Camilla.[17]
He shall hunt her through every nation of sick pride

till she is driven back forever to Hell
whence Envy first released her on the world.
Therefore, for your own good, I think it well

you follow me and I will be your guide
and lead you forth through an eternal place.
There you shall see the ancient spirits tried

in endless pain, and hear their lamentation
as each bemoans the second death[18] of souls.
Next you shall see upon a burning mountain[19]

17

souls in fire and yet content in fire,
knowing that whensoever it may be
they yet will mount into the blessed choir.

Literary Analysis
Allegory Based on Virgil's comments, do you think the She-Wolf symbolizes Dante's social, political, religious, or moral concerns? Explain.

Reading Check 18
What assistance does Virgil offer Dante?

15. **fleers** (flirz) laughs scornfully.
16. **the Greyhound . . . Feltro and Feltro** The Greyhound almost certainly refers to Can Grande della Scala (1290–1329), a great Italian leader born in Verona, which lies between the towns of Feltre and Montefeltro.
17. **Nisus . . . Camilla** All were killed in the war between the Trojans and the Latians when, according to legend, Aeneas led the survivors of Troy into Italy. Nisus and Euryalus (*Aeneid* IX) were Trojan comrades-in-arms who died together. Camilla (*Aeneid* XI) was the daughter of the Latian king and one of the warrior women. She was killed in a horse charge against the Trojans after displaying great gallantry. Turnus (*Aeneid* XII) was killed by Aeneas in a duel.
18. **the second death** damnation.
19. **a burning mountain** Mountain of Purgatory.

16 Literary Analysis

Allegory

- Explain that gluttony is one of the seven deadly sins in Christianity, so Dante's depiction of the She-Wolf suggests concern about excessive appetite in some area.
- Draw students' attention to footnote 16, and point out the political context that it suggests. Discuss how appetite could pose problems in the political context.
- Then, read aloud the bracketed passage. **Ask** students the Literary Analysis question: Based on Virgil's comments, do you think the She-Wolf symbolizes Dante's social, political, religious, or moral concerns? Explain.
  Possible response: The wolf symbolizes Dante's political concerns—perhaps his political ambition, which can consume all judgment.

17 Critical Thinking

Interpret

- Have a volunteer read aloud lines 111–112. **Ask** students what Dante might mean by "souls in fire and yet content in fire."
  Possible response: The souls are in pain but willing to submit to the pain for some reason.
- **Ask** why someone might be content to be in great physical or psychological pain.
  Possible response: As the footnote says, the burning mountain refers to Purgatory, where Dante will travel after passing through Hell. In Purgatory, the suffering is borne in hope because it is a part of purification that will result in the ascension to Paradise.

18 Reading Check

Answer: Virgil offers to be Dante's guide, to lead him through the dangers of Hell and Purgatory to the far reaches of Heaven.

Differentiated Instruction Solutions for All Learners

Strategy for Special Needs Students
Focus attention on the introduction of Virgil as Dante's guide. Explain that on p. 664, Dante asks Virgil to be his guide on his journey through the "sad halls of Hell." Ask what person, either real or fictional, students might choose to guide them on a difficult but important journey. Have them explain their choices.

Enrichment for Gifted/Talented Students
Challenge students to explain why Dante's view of Virgil led him to include the ancient poet as his guide through the *Inferno.* Ask them to research and prepare a short presentation on Virgil and his epic, the *Aeneid.* Urge them to demonstrate why Dante held Virgil in high esteem.

Strategy for Advanced Readers
Tell students that at this point in the epic, Dante gains his remarkable guide for his journey through Hell: Virgil. As students read, have them analyze Virgil's role and what he symbolizes. Ask students whether Virgil is lacking any quality or characteristic that might prevent him from being the perfect guide.

19 Literary Analysis

Allegory

- Remind students that the central allegory in the poem is the journey as a symbol for life. Remind them that Dante divides the poem, and his journey, in three: He travels from Hell (sin) to Purgatory (penitence) to Paradise (beatitude).
- Then, **ask** students the Literary Analysis question.
  Possible response: Readers who are aware of Dante's route and ultimate destination will grasp that his journey corresponds allegorically to the education of the soul, passing from sin to redemption.

ASSESS

Answers

1. **Possible response:** Students might find the experience of facing the angry She-Wolf most terrifying.
2. (a) The Leopard, the Lion, and the She-Wolf block Dante's path. (b) The leopard represents deceit; the lion, pride or cruelty; and the She-Wolf, greed. (c) The leopard's looks vary and can fool viewers, depending on how many spots it has; people often think of the lion not only as the proud king of the animals but also as a cruel hunter; the wolf is viewed as ravenous.
3. (a) The Roman poet Virgil rescues Dante. (b) It suggests that Dante values the literature and ideas of ancient (or classical) times.
4. (a) **Possible response:** In lines 40–54, Dante speaks of his dread of the Lion and the She-Wolf; in lines 79–88, Dante speaks of his admiration for Virgil. (b) Dante is learned and educated. He values antiquity and lacks arrogance. He is emotional and perhaps feels repentant. (c) He will be strongly affected by them because he feels emotion intensely.
5. **Possible response:** The situation seems like a fantasy—the characters appear much larger than life, the setting is reminiscent of scary stories, and a character (Virgil) appears from the afterlife.

Go Online Author Link For additional information about Dante Alighieri, have students type in the Web Code, then select A from the alphabet, and then select Dante Alighieri.

To which, if it is still your wish to climb,
  a worthier spirit[20] shall be sent to guide you.
  With her shall I leave you, for the King of Time,

who reigns on high, forbids me to come there[21]
  since, living, I rebelled against his law.
  He rules the waters and the land and air

and there holds court, his city and his throne.
  Oh blessed are they he chooses!" And I to him:
  "Poet, by that God to you unknown,

lead me this way. Beyond this present ill
  and worse to dread, lead me to Peter's gate[22] (19)
  and be my guide through the sad halls of Hell."

And he then: "Follow." And he moved ahead
in silence, and I followed where he led.

Literary Analysis
Allegory At the end of Canto I, Dante lays out the structure of his entire poem. In what ways does this help the reader grasp the allegory?

20. **a worthier spirit** Beatrice.
21. **forbids me to come there** In Dante's theology, salvation is achieved only through Christ. Virgil lived and died before the establishment of Christ's teachings in Rome and therefore cannot enter Heaven.
22. **Peter's gate** the gate of Purgatory. The gate is guarded by an angel with a gleaming sword. The angel is Peter's vicar and is entrusted with the two great keys.

Critical Reading

1. **Respond:** Which part of Dante's experience in the Dark Wood did you find most frightening? Explain.
2. **(a) Recall:** Which three beasts block Dante's path?
   (b) Interpret: What emotion or idea does each beast represent?
   (c) Analyze: Why is each beast an appropriate choice for the emotion or idea it represents?
3. **(a) Recall:** Who rescues Dante? **(b) Infer:** What does the author's choice of rescuer and guide reveal about Dante's values?
4. **(a) Interpret:** Identify at least two lines in Canto I that reveal strong emotion in Dante. **(b) Analyze:** Based on his thoughts, emotions, and actions thus far, how would you describe Dante's character?
   (c) Speculate: Based on your understanding of his character, how do you think Dante will respond to the sights and sounds of Hell? Explain.
5. **Evaluate:** Does Dante the character seem like a real man on a real journey, or does the whole situation presented in Canto I seem like a fantasy? Explain.

Author Link
For: More about Dante Alighieri
Visit: www.PHSchool.com
Web Code: ete-9503

Enrichment

A Dante Symphony

Dante's poem *The Divine Comedy* has inspired other artists, writers, and even composers. The great Hungarian composer, pianist, and conductor Franz Liszt (1811–1886) was one of the best-known figures of his day. His fame and charisma matched that of today's rock stars or professional athletes. In 1856, he composed his *Dante Symphony,* the first movement of which is entitled "Inferno." In this work, Liszt used music to re-create the emotions and ideas of Dante's poem.

Obtain a recording of the *Dante Symphony,* and play the first movement for students. Ask them to discuss how well Liszt succeeds in portraying Dante's thoughts and images, as well as differences in the way music and language portray emotional states. Have students point out passages in the music that they believe reflect the moods in Canto I and later in Canto III. Conclude by asking students whether they can name other musical works that are based on works of literature.

20 Canto III

THE VESTIBULE OF HELL *The Opportunists*

The Poets pass the Gate of Hell and are immediately assailed by cries of anguish. Dante sees the first of the souls in torment. They are *The Opportunists*, those souls who in life were neither for good nor evil but only for themselves. Mixed with them are those outcasts who took no sides in the Rebellion of the Angels.[1] They are neither in Hell nor out of it. Eternally unclassified, they race round and round pursuing a wavering banner that runs forever before them through the dirty air; and as they run they are pursued by swarms of wasps and hornets, who sting them and produce a constant flow of blood and putrid matter which trickles down the bodies of the sinners and is feasted upon by loathsome worms and maggots who coat the ground.

The law of Dante's Hell is the law of symbolic retribution. As they sinned so are they punished. They took no sides, therefore they are given no place. As they pursued the ever-shifting illusion of their own advantage, changing their courses with every changing wind, so they pursue eternally an elusive, ever-shifting banner. As their sin was a darkness, so they move in darkness. As their own guilty conscience pursued them, so they are pursued by swarms of wasps and hornets. And as their actions were a moral filth, so they run eternally through the filth of worms and maggots which they themselves feed.

21

Dante recognizes several, among them *Pope Celestine V*,[2] but without delaying to speak to any of these souls, the Poets move on to *Acheron*,[3] the first of the rivers of Hell. Here the newly arrived souls of the damned gather and wait for monstrous *Charon*[4] to ferry them over to punishment. Charon recognizes Dante as a living man and angrily refuses him passage. Virgil forces Charon to serve them, but Dante swoons with terror, and does not reawaken until he is on the other side.

I AM THE WAY INTO THE CITY OF WOE.
I AM THE WAY TO A FORSAKEN PEOPLE.
I AM THE WAY INTO ETERNAL SORROW.

Vocabulary Builder
putrid (pyo͞o′ trid) *adj.* rotten; stinking

22 **▼ Critical Viewing**
Which details in this illustration of Dante help convey the fear and horror he is experiencing? Explain. **[Interpret]**

23  
Reading Check
What is the law of Dante's Hell?

1. **Rebellion of the Angels** In Christian tradition, Satan and other angels who rebelled against God were cast out of heaven; see the Bible, Revelation 12:7–9.
2. **Pope Celestine V** He lived from 1215 to 1296.
3. **Acheron** (ak′ ər än′)
4. **Charon** (ker′ ən)

20 About the Selection

In Canto III, Dante and Virgil meet the boatman Charon and see the multitudes of damned. As might be expected, the journey is filled with macabre images.

21 Humanities

Dante in the Dark Woods, by Suloni Robertson

This image—as well as those of the leopard, lion, and wolf on pp. 660–661—was created by the graphic artist Suloni Robertson. Robertson's illustrations are featured in *Dante-worlds* (http://danteworlds.laits.utexas.edu), an online multimedia presentation that guides viewers through Dante's *Inferno.*

Use the following question to stimulate discussion:

What emotions does this illustration evoke? Explain.
Possible response: The dark tones of red and orange, Dante's pained expression, and his gesture evoke feelings of fear.

22 Critical Viewing

Possible response: Dante averts his eyes and uses his hands as if to protect himself from the horrors he sees. A heavy cloak and hood protect his figure.

23 Reading Check

Answer: The law of Dante's Hell is the law of symbolic retribution.

Differentiated Instruction Solutions for All Learners

Support for Special Needs Students

Ask students to consider the effect of first impressions when they enter a house or building. What purposes do entrances serve? How do they make people feel? Have students imagine different types of entrances: the front doors of a school, the mechanical doors of a supermarket, the pillars guarding the entrance to a public building. How does each make someone entering the building feel? Link answers to Dante's vestibule of Hell and the fear such an image suggests.

Support for English Learners

Help students clarify the central images that Dante uses to open Canto III, beginning with the title. Explain that a vestibule is a hallway or antechamber located at the entrance of a house or building. If possible, show pictures or take students to a vestibule on school property. Discuss how a vestibule could symbolize the beginning in the context of a journey, and help students see how this image fits with the overall journey structure of Dante's work.

24 Literary Analysis

Allegory

- Discuss the many everyday journeys on which medieval people might pass through a gate. Remind students that cities had walls and that people had to pass through gates to enter the cities. Then, explain that gates, like doorways, often symbolize transitions or beginnings in literature.
- Have students read the bracketed text carefully and consider the situation it describes.
- Then, **ask** students the first Literary Analysis question: In what ways does Dante's use of a gate, an object familiar to all medieval people, make his allegory seem all the more real?
  Possible response: Medieval people used gates to pass from field to field or from town to town. The image of passing through a gate to reach Hell makes the allegory seem very ordinary and possible.

25 Literary Analysis

Allegory and Imagery

- Invite a volunteer to read aloud the bracketed passage. Call on another student to **review** the definitions of allegory and imagery.
  Answer: Allegory is a literary work with both literal and symbolic meanings. Imagery is the use of language that creates mental pictures for readers by appealing to the five senses.
- **Ask** students the second Literary Analysis question: Why do you think the imagery at this point in the poem appeals almost solely to the sense of hearing?
  Possible response: Perhaps because it is dark in Hell, Dante's imagery appeals to the sense of hearing. It might be the strongest sense in such a situation.

Monitor Progress Ask students to discuss different types of images that would appeal to each of the five senses.

Reteach Have students focus on two or three images. Explain that the sense of touch involves not only the fingers touching a surface or an object but also the sensations of heat, cold, wind, dampness, and so on.

SACRED JUSTICE MOVED MY ARCHITECT.
I WAS RAISED HERE BY DIVINE OMNIPOTENCE,
PRIMORDIAL[5] LOVE AND ULTIMATE INTELLECT.

ONLY THOSE ELEMENTS TIME CANNOT WEAR[6]
WERE MADE BEFORE ME, AND BEYOND TIME I STAND.[7]
ABANDON ALL HOPE YE WHO ENTER HERE.

These mysteries I read cut into stone
above a gate. And turning I said: "Master,
what is the meaning of this harsh inscription?"

And he then as initiate to novice:[8]
"Here must you put by all division of spirit
and gather your soul against all cowardice.

This is the place I told you to expect.
Here you shall pass among the fallen people,
souls who have lost the good of intellect."

So saying, he put forth his hand to me,
and with a gentle and encouraging smile
he led me through the gate of mystery.

Here sighs and cries and wails coiled and recoiled
on the starless air, spilling my soul to tears.
A confusion of tongues and monstrous accents toiled

in pain and anger. Voices hoarse and shrill
and sounds of blows, all intermingled, raised
tumult and pandemonium[9] that still

whirls on the air forever dirty with it
as if a whirlwind sucked at sand. And I,
holding my head in horror, cried: "Sweet Spirit,

what souls are these who run through this black haze?"
And he to me: "These are the nearly soulless
whose lives concluded neither blame nor praise.

Literary Analysis
Allegory In what ways does Dante's use of a gate, an object familiar to all medieval people, make his allegory seem all the more real?

Literary Analysis
Allegory and Imagery Why do you think the imagery at this point in the poem appeals almost solely to the sense of hearing?

---

5. **primordial** (prī môr′ dē əl) *adj.* existing from the beginning.
6. **only . . . wear** The Angels, the Empyrean (the highest heaven), and the First Matter are the elements time cannot wear, for they will last forever. Human beings, being mortal, are not eternal. The Gate of Hell, therefore, was created before people.
7. **and . . . stand** So odious is sin to God that there can be no end to its just punishment.
8. **as initiate to novice as one who knows to one who does not.**
9. **pandemonium** (pan′ də mō′ nē əm) word coined by English poet John Milton (1608–1674) to identify the demons' capital in hell; now describes any place or scene of noise, wild disorder, and confusion.

(26) They are mixed here with that despicable corps
of angels who were neither God nor Satan,
but only for themselves. The High Creator

scourged[10] them from Heaven for its perfect beauty,
and Hell will not receive them since the wicked
might feel some glory over them." And I:

(27) "Master, what gnaws at them so hideously
their lamentation stuns the very air?"
"They have no hope of death," he answered me,

"and in their blind and unattaining state
their miserable lives have sunk so low
that they must envy every other fate.

No word of them survives their living season.
Mercy and Justice deny them even a name.
Let us not speak of them: look, and pass on."

(28) I saw a banner there upon the mist.
Circling and circling, it seemed to scorn all pause.
So it ran on, and still behind it pressed

a never-ending rout of souls in pain.
I had not thought death had undone so many
as passed before me in that mournful train.

And some I knew among them; last of all
I recognized the shadow of that soul
who, in his cowardice, made the Great Denial.[11]

At once I understood for certain: these
were of that retrograde[12] and faithless crew
hateful to God and to His enemies.

These wretches never born and never dead
ran naked in a swarm of wasps and hornets
that goaded them the more the more they fled,

Vocabulary Builder
despicable (des′ pi kə bel) *adj.* deserving to be despised; contemptible

Vocabulary Builder
lamentation (lam′ ən tā′ shen) *n.* weeping; wailing

Vocabulary Builder
scorn (skôrn) *v.* reject

10. **scourged** (skurj′d) *v.* whipped.
11. **who, in . . . Denial** This is almost certainly intended to be Celestine V, who became pope in 1294. He was a man of saintly virtue, but he allowed himself to be convinced by a priest named Benedetto that his soul was in danger since no man could live in the world without being damned. In fear for his soul, he withdrew from all worldly affairs and renounced the papacy. Benedetto promptly assumed the mantle himself and became Boniface VIII, a pope who became for Dante a symbol of all the worst corruptions of the church.
12. **retrograde** (re′ trə grād′) *adj.* moving backward.

Reading Check (29)
In the vestibule of Hell, with whom are the "nearly soulless" souls mixed?

Differentiated Instruction
Solutions for All Learners

Support for Special Needs Students
Highlight dialogue and quotation marks in lines 11–18 and 29–39. Explain that dialogue is conversation between characters and that quotation marks indicate its beginning and end. Write lines 11–18 on the board; then, read aloud the lines in character. Stress the difference between the dialogue and narration in lines 11 and 13.

Support for Less Proficient Readers
Point out the dialogue in lines 11–18 and the quotation marks signaling the beginning and end of dialogue. Explain that Dante uses dialogue, or conversation, to give direction and purpose to the journey. Help students paraphrase lines 32–33: "these are the nearly soulless / whose lives concluded neither blame nor praise.

Strategy for English Learners
Review the dialogue in Canto III with students. Remind them that quotation marks signal the beginning and end of dialogue. Have students work in pairs to practice reading the dialogue in lines 11–18 and 29–39. If appropriate, have students read the passages aloud to gain experience in recognizing and reading English dialogue.

(26) Background
Comedy
Point out how the inhabitants here have been rejected by both Heaven and Hell. There is a bit of comedy, even if unintended, in Dante's description, which is similar to this old joke: "They said you weren't fit to live with pigs, but I defended you; I said you were."

(27) Critical Thinking
Connect
- Read the bracketed lines aloud for students. Have students **restate** the lines in their own words.
  Possible response: What makes these people so terribly unhappy? They have no hope of ending their misery through death.
- **Ask** students to imagine situations in which death might seem welcome because of some circumstance. Invite them to suggest alternatives to despair.
  Answer: Students may mention terminal illness or terrible grief. Alternatives could include counseling, support of clergy, or medication.

(28) Reading Strategy
Interpreting Imagery
- Remind students that imagery is the use of language that appeals to the senses and that creates mental pictures.
- After students read the bracketed passage, **ask** them what central image it contains.
  Answer: It contains the central image of circles.
- Note that circles are endless. Then, **ask** students how this endlessness might contribute to the larger themes of Dante's work.
  Possible response: It contributes to the theme of life as a journey that leads back to its beginnings.

(29) Reading Check
Answer: These souls are mixed with the angels who would not commit to either God or Satan, choosing instead to serve their own interests.

30 Literary Analysis

Allegory

- Review with students footnote 13, which identifies the old man as Charon, a figure from classical mythology.
- Have students read the bracketed passage carefully, and draw their attention to the clue "ancient."
- Then, **ask** students the Literary Analysis question: Judging from this character, in what ways has the mythology of ancient Greece and Rome provided Dante with source materials for his allegory?
Possible response: Mythology has given Dante characters, places, and concepts, which readers will recognize. He takes a figure from mythology and uses it for a Christian allegory.

Monitor Progress Have students **explain** the allegory presented in the bracketed text. What do the shores and the river represent?
Answer: The shores are Life and Hell, or eternal punishment. The river is the boundary between these places.

Reteach Use **Literary Analysis** support, page 47 in ***Unit 5 Resources,*** to reinforce students' understanding of allegory.

and made their faces stream with bloody gouts
of pus and tears that dribbled to their feet
to be swallowed there by loathsome worms and maggots.

Then looking onward I made out a throng
assembled on the beach of a wide river,
whereupon I turned to him: "Master, I long

to know what souls these are, and what strange usage
makes them as eager to cross as they seem to be
in this infected light." At which the Sage:

"All this shall be made known to you when we stand
on the joyless beach of Acheron." And I
cast down my eyes, sensing a reprimand

in what he said, and so walked at his side
in silence and ashamed until we came
through the dead cavern to that sunless tide.

There, steering toward us in an ancient ferry
came an old man[13] with a white bush of hair,
bellowing: "Woe to you depraved souls! Bury

here and forever all hope of Paradise:
I come to lead you to the other shore,
into eternal dark, into fire and ice.

And you who are living yet, I say begone
from these who are dead." But when he saw me stand
against his violence he began again:

"By other windings[14] and by other steerage
shall you cross to that other shore. Not here! Not here!
A lighter craft than mine must give you passage."

And my Guide to him: "Charon, bite back your spleen:
this has been willed where what is willed must be,
and is not yours to ask what it may mean."[15]

Vocabulary Builder
reprimand (rep′ rə mand′) *v.* chastise; blame

Literary Analysis
Allegory Judging from this character, in what ways has the mythology of ancient Greece and Rome provided Dante with source material for his allegory?

---

13. **an old man** Charon, the ferryman who transports dead souls across the Acheron in all classical mythology.
14. **By other windings** Charon recognizes Dante not only as a living man but as a soul in grace and knows, therefore, that the Infernal Ferry was not intended for him. He is probably referring to the fact that souls destined for Purgatory and Heaven assemble not at his ferry point but on the banks of the Tiber (a river that runs through Rome), from which they are transported by an Angel.
15. **Charon . . . mean** Virgil tells Charon to suppress his bad temper because God has ordained that Dante shall make this journey. Charon has no right to question God's orders.

Enrichment

Classical Influences

Dante is basing his *Divine Comedy* in part on classical epics, particularly Virgil's *Aeneid,* which tells the story of the founding of Rome. Aeneas, the epic hero, flees Troy and wanders throughout the Mediterranean region in his quest for a new land. In Book VI of the *Aeneid,* Virgil describes Aeneas' descent into Hades, divided into the Elysian Fields where souls of good men and women wander, and the realm of punishment, where souls of the wicked suffer. Aeneas is guided by the Cumaean Sybil and protected by a golden bough as he journeys toward self-discovery. The importance of this episode for Dante is hinted at by the numerous details the later poet transposes from the classical epic. Charon is found in Dante's Hell. Dante finds himself in places, like Cocytus, that originated in the classical Hades. But Dante replaces pagan ceremonies and creeds with his own religious beliefs.

The steersman of that marsh of ruined souls,
who wore a wheel of flame around each eye,
stifled the rage that shook his woolly jowls.

But those unmanned and naked spirits there
turned pale with fear and their teeth began to chatter
at sound of his crude bellow. In despair

they blasphemed God, their parents, their time on earth,
the race of Adam, and the day and the hour
and the place and the seed and the womb that gave
them birth.

But all together they drew to that grim shore
where all must come who lose the fear of God.
Weeping and cursing they come for evermore,

and demon Charon with eyes like burning coals
herds them in, and with a whistling oar
flails on the stragglers to his wake[16] of souls.

As leaves in autumn loosen and stream down
until the branch stands bare above its tatters
spread on the rustling ground, so one by one

the evil seed of Adam in its Fall[17]
cast themselves, at his signal, from the shore
and streamed away like birds who hear their call.

So they are gone over that shadowy water,
and always before they reach the other shore
a new noise stirs on this, and new throngs gather.

"My son," the courteous Master said to me,
"all who die in the shadow of God's wrath
converge to this from every clime and country.

And all pass over eagerly, for here
Divine Justice transforms and spurs them so
their dread turns wish: they yearn for what they fear.[18]

The Vulgar Tongue 

By composing the *Divine Comedy* in Italian, Dante implicitly rejected the use of Latin, the literary language of his day, in favor of the "vulgar" tongue. A vulgar tongue is the language spoken by the *vulgus*, the common people. In many cultures, centuries passed before the language spoken by ordinary people was accepted as a medium for the composition of literature. For example, in Japan, works written in Japanese were considered less significant than works written in Chinese until well into the twentieth century.

Works composed in "vulgar" tongues are more accessible to more people. As the common tongue becomes the dominant literary language, literature takes an increasingly important place in the life of a society. Literary works better express the real lives of the people; in turn, literature exerts a greater influence on the culture itself.

Connect to the Literature

Choose three or four words from this page and the facing page that seem to you to reflect the language of ordinary people.

16. **wake** *n.* a watch over a corpse before burial, with a pun on waking up.
17. **Fall** This word has at least three different meanings: the season of fall, the fall of all humans with the sin of Adam and Eve, and the fall of individual sinners.
18. **they yearn . . . fear** Hell (allegorically, Sin) is what the souls of the damned really wish for. Hell is their actual and deliberate choice, for divine grace is denied to none who wish for it in their hearts.

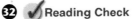

Reading Check

What hope does Charon tell the dead souls they must abandon?

31 Themes in World Literature

The Vulgar Tongue

In many cultures, the authors of important literature become prominent people in society with influence of their own. Dante, for example, is often seen as the father of Italian letters. Nearly all Italians, and many Italian Americans too, feel a great sense of pride in Dante's work. Like William Shakespeare to the British and James Joyce to the Irish, Dante represents the writer as national hero. In this sense the writer shares the celebrated status of military leaders, diplomats, and athletes. Streets and schools in Italy are named for Dante as well as for other writers.

Connect to the Literature Point out to students that this translation uses many words that are immediately recognized by most ordinary speakers of English. This word choice reflects Dante's use of the "vulgar" tongue—the Italian language—rather than Latin, so that ordinary people of Italy would be comfortable reading his epic poem. Ask students to list three or four words from these two pages that reflect such word choice. **Possible response:** Students may select *bloody, pus, tears, beach, silence, bite, rage, naked, pale, fear, teeth, despair, God, parents, earth, weeping,* or *cursing.*

32 Reading Check

Answer: The dead souls must give up all hope of Paradise.

Differentiated Instruction

Solutions for All Learners

Support for Special Needs Students

Point out that a particular image or group of images seems to guide each canto. In Canto III, the ideas of decay and general unpleasantness are echoed throughout. For example, the image is repeated through words such as "despicable corps," "gnaws," "miserable," "wretches, "bloody gouts," "pus and tears," and "loathsome worms and maggots." Have student pairs reread the canto, listing words that repeat images. Students might look for words linked to movement, light, or carnality.

Enrichment for Advanced Readers

Highlight images such as "bloody gouts of pus," "wheel of flame around each eye," "eyes like burning coals," and recall that imagery is the use of terms that repeat or echo a particular quality. Discuss the quality or theme Dante seeks to echo (horror). Then, have students write a descriptive paragraph employing a variety of images, each of which conveys the same quality. The subject should be something or someone familiar to students.

33 Humanities

Fifteenth-century Italian manuscript illumination from Dante's *Inferno*

Like others of Dante's time, this fifteenth-century illumination features bright colors and gold or silver detailing. Illuminations were hand-painted in the days before printing, when books were hand-scribed as well.

Use the following questions for discussion:

- On which bank of the river do lighter colors predominate? On which do darker colors predominate?
  Answer: The colors are lighter on the bank to the right, darker on the bank to the left.
- On the basis of the use of light and shadow, toward which shore do you think the boat is traveling? Why?
  Answer: It is traveling toward the left side; this is the darkness of Hell.

34 Critical Viewing

Answer: The ferryman stands erect and seems unafraid of and unmoved by his surroundings. Virgil is calm and protective of Dante. Dante, seated with Virgil in the boat, is visibly shocked.

35 Reading Strategy

Interpreting Imagery

- Review the definition of imagery on p. 657, and have students name the five senses to which imagery can appeal.
- Then, have a volunteer read aloud the bracketed passage, as other students listen carefully for words that signal particular sensory images.
- **Ask** students the Reading Strategy question: To which senses do the images in this passage appeal?
  Answer: The images appeal to the senses of hearing, sight, and touch.

33

◀ **Critical Viewing** 34
In this fifteenth-century illumination of Dante and Virgil crossing the river into Hell, how do Dante's posture and attitude compare and contrast with those of both Virgil and the ferryman? **[Compare and Contrast]**

35

No soul in Grace comes ever to this crossing;
therefore if Charon rages at your presence
you will understand the reason for his cursing."

When he had spoken, all the twilight country
shook so violently, the terror of it
bathes me with sweat even in memory:

Reading Strategy
Interpreting Imagery
To which senses do the images in this passage appeal?

Enrichment

Translation as an Act of Composition

The translation used in this book is that of the American poet John Ciardi. This translation is popular and critically acclaimed. Without maintaining accuracy on a lexical level, it conveys the spirit of the original.

Translation is an act of composition and betrayal; each translation represents a decomposition and rewriting. The word *translation* often means "to move or change into 'one's own language'." Literature, like language, is a kind of social property, and the act of translating is like buying a new house. The structure remains the same but the change of ownership gives the house a different quality.

Have students examine other translations of the *Inferno* to compare and contrast approaches to the text. Henry Wadsworth Longfellow, Charles S. Singleton, Dorothy Sayers, Allen Mandelbaum, and Robert Pinsky have translated Dante into English.

the tear-soaked ground gave out a sigh of wind
  that spewed itself in flame on a red sky,
  and all my shattered senses left me. Blind,

like one whom sleep comes over in a swoon,[19]
I stumbled into darkness and went down.

---

19. **swoon** the act of fainting. This device (repeated at the end of Canto V) serves a double purpose. The first is technical: Dante uses it to cover a transition. We are never told how he crossed Acheron, for that would involve certain narrative matters he can better deal with when he crosses Styx (stiks), another river of the underworld, in Canto VII. The second purpose is to provide a point of departure for a theme that is carried through the entire descent: Dante's emotional reaction to Hell. These two swoons early in the descent show him most susceptible to the grief about him. As he descends, pity leaves him, and he even goes so far as to add to the torments of one sinner.

Critical Reading

1. **Respond:** Do you think that the Opportunists deserve the punishment Dante envisioned for them? Why or why not?
2. **(a) Recall:** According to the inscription on the Gate of Hell, which feeling must be abandoned by all who enter?
   (b) Analyze Causes and Effects: What effect do you think Dante intends this passage to have on the reader? Explain.
3. **(a) Recall:** Which creatures torment the Opportunists?
   (b) Analyze: In what ways do these small but fierce creatures suggest Dante's attitude toward the sins of the Opportunists? Explain.
4. **(a) Recall:** As they prepare to cross the river Acheron into Hell itself, what physical reactions do the spirits have?
   (b) Interpret: Judging from their outbursts, what emotional reactions do they experience? **(c) Infer:** Based on the details presented, what is the greatest spiritual torment of Hell? Explain.
5. **Analyze:** Why do you think Dante dwells on the physical torments of Hell?
6. **(a) Draw Conclusions:** What message does this Canto provide to readers about those who will not or cannot make a commitment to God? Explain. **(b) Synthesize:** What image might be appropriate to appear on the banner pursued by the Opportunists? Explain your answer.

For: More about Dante Alighieri
Visit: www.PHSchool.com
Web Code: ete-9503

Assessment Practice

Evaluate and Make Judgments **(For more practice, see *Test Preparation Workbook*, p. 30.)**

Many tests require students to evaluate and make judgments about characters or situations. Use the following sample test item, from Canto III of the Inferno (lines 19–21), to help students practice this skill:

So saying, he put forth his hand to me, and with a gentle and encouraging smile he led me through the gate of mystery.

According to the passage, what kind of guide do you think Virgil is?

A kind
B incompetent
C deceitful
D pushy

Lead students to recognize that the correct answer is *A*. Readers would not likely make the evaluations or judgments in choices *B, C,* and *D* based on the clues in the passage.

36 Reading Strategy

Interpreting Imagery

- Read the bracketed text aloud, emphasizing the word "down."
- Point out the repeated images of a downward, spiraling motion.
- Then, **ask** students how they imagine this motion would "feel."
  Possible response: It would feel frightening, as if the ground were falling away, as on a roller coaster.

ASSESS

Answers

1. **Possible responses:** Yes; the punishment is just, for serving oneself above all represents selfishness. No; we have the right to put ourselves first, so the punishment is unfair.
2. (a) Hope must be abandoned.
   (b) **Possible response:** Dante wants readers to experience the horror of going to Hell and wants them to know that Hell's punishments are eternal.
3. (a) The Opportunists are tormented by a swarm of wasps and hornets and by worms and maggots at their feet. (b) **Possible response:** Just as they pursued their interests in life, the Opportunists are pursued by insects that try to sting the Opportunists' consciences. As the Opportunists' actions suggest moral filth, the sinners run eternally through worms and maggots.
4. (a) The spirits turn pale with fear, and their teeth chatter at the thought of crossing the river.
   (b) The spirits experience terror but also regret. (c) **Possible response:** The greatest torment may be the realization that one's own actions and attitudes have brought one to Hell and that the torment is endless.
5. **Possible response:** Dante dwells on the torments to make them concrete and more memorable.
6. (a) The canto warns the uncommitted by describing the torments of those damned for lack of commitment. (b) **Possible responses:** Images of mercy, heaven, or even of death as a release might be appropriate.

Answers

1. **Possible response:** Dante represents the good Christian who, in midlife, realizes that he has strayed from the True Way.
2. **Literal Meanings:** road that doesn't wind; forest with little light; large, spotted cat; stinging insects **Allegorical Meanings:** moral behavior; despair and confusion; deceit and trickery; stings of conscience
   Another sample answer can be found on **Literary Analysis Graphic Organizer B,** p. 120 in ***Graphic Organizer Transparencies.***
3. **Possible response:** Dante admires the qualities of poetic vision and creativity.
4. (a) The Greyhound will hunt the She-Wolf down and drive her back to Hell. (b) **Possible response:** The prediction refers to the She-Wolf both as a symbol for temptation and greed and as a real animal that mates without judgment.
5. Dante's imagery includes subject matter with which readers are familiar. He translates abstract ideas into comprehensible, concrete situations.
6. The image of souls as falling leaves contributes to a sense of lifelessness and despair. Readers feel the eternal helplessness and fragility of these souls.
7. (a) **Possible response:** Images of light include "shoulders glowed," "sweet rays of that planet," "shining," "widening of the dawn," "light the new creation," "shining Mount of Joy," "light of poets," "burning mountain," "souls in fire." (b) **Possible response:** Light represents purity and salvation to Dante.
8. (a) These stanzas appeal to the senses of touch, hearing, and sight. (b) Dante is overcome by what he feels.
9. Students should give reasons for their choices. They might mention Benjamin Franklin or Mark Twain. However, it would be difficult to name an American writer who has been as revered by Americans as Dante is by Italians.

Apply the Skills

from the *Divine Comedy: Inferno*

Literary Analysis

Allegory

1. Who or what do you think Dante the character represents in this **allegory**?
2. Use a chart like the one shown to explore the allegorical meanings of other elements in Cantos I and III.

Detail	Literal Meaning	Allegorical Meaning
straight road		
dark wood		
leopard		
wasps and hornets		

3. Dante chose the poet Virgil rather than a philosopher, such as Socrates or Aristotle, to be his symbol of human reason. What does this choice suggest about the intellectual qualities he admires most?
4. **(a)** In Canto I, what prediction does Virgil make about the She-Wolf and the Greyhound? **(b)** How does this prediction reveal Dante's intention to explore both spiritual matters and earthly concerns in this allegory?

Connecting Literary Elements

5. How does Dante's **imagery** in Canto I contribute to the poem's verisimilitude—its sense of reality or truth?
6. Does the image of souls as falling leaves merely convey a sense of great numbers, or does it contribute to the sense of despair in Canto III? Explain.

Reading Strategy

Interpreting Imagery

7. **(a)** Begin to **interpret imagery** by listing images of light in Canto I. **(b)** What do you think light represents to Dante? Explain.
8. **(a)** Identify the senses to which the images in the last three stanzas of Canto III appeal. **(b)** Why do you think Dante swoons at this point?

Extend Understanding

9. **Cultural Connection:** Dante is a national hero for the Italians. Which writers, if any, play a similar role for Americans? Explain.

QuickReview

An **allegory** is a literary work with two or more levels of meaning—the literal and the symbolic.

Imagery is the use of language that appeals to one or more of the five senses and creates word pictures for the reader.

To **interpret imagery** as you read, identify the senses to which each image appeals, note the physical experience it suggests, and identify the emotion or idea it conveys.

For: Self-test
Visit: www.PHSchool.com
Web Code: eta-6503

Go Online Assessment Students may use the **Self-test** to prepare for **Selection Test A** or **Selection Test B.**

Build Language Skills

❶ Vocabulary Lesson

Word Analysis: Latin Root *-trem-*

The word *tremulous,* which means "trembling, as with fear," is based on the Latin root *-trem-*, meaning "tremble." Match each of the following words with its definition.

1. tremble
2. tremor
3. tremolo

a. musical vibration
b. vibration
c. shiver; vibrate

Spelling Strategy

The *us* sound at the end of a word is often spelled *ous* when it represents the suffix *-ous,* meaning "full of " (*tremulous* = "full of trembling"). Write a word ending in the *us* sound that meets each definition below.

1. full of fame
2. full of caution

Vocabulary Builder: Sentence Completion

Review the vocabulary list on page 657, and notice the way the words are used in the context of the selection. Then, complete each sentence below with the appropriate words.

1. They looked down with __?__ on the __?__ criminals.
2. "Please do not give me a __?__," the driver says to the policeman in a __?__ voice.
3. The __?__ smell of rotting food dampened the __?__ of the diners.
4. She hears the cries and __?__ and sees the poor soul who __?__ in the waves.

❷ Grammar and Style Lesson

Present Perfect Verb Tense

The **present perfect tense** shows either a single action or repeated actions that were completed at an indefinite time before the present.

Single action . . . this has been willed
Repeated action . . . that sweet style whose measures have brought me honor . . .

Practice Identify the example of the present perfect tense in each item, and state whether it describes a single or a repeated action.

1. For centuries, Dante has been considered the greatest Italian writer.
2. Have you read his *Divine Comedy*?
3. Do you know someone who has read it?
4. The *Inferno* has become my favorite.
5. The *Divine Comedy* is the most complex allegory we have studied.

Writing Application Write a paragraph about an amazing sight that you have seen. Include at least three examples of the present perfect tense.

WG Prentice Hall Writing and Grammar Connection: Platinum Level, Chapter 22, Section 1

❸ Extend Your Learning

Listening and Speaking Dante's crisis occurred "midway" through his life. With a small group, create a **presentation** on changing images of middle age. **[Group Activity]**

Writing Write a **new version** of this part of the journey from Virgil's point of view.

Assessment Resources

The following resources can be used to assess students' knowledge and skills.

Unit 5 Resources
Selection Test A, pp. 53–55
Selection Test B, pp. 56–58
Benchmark Test 6, pp. 59–64

Go Online **Assessment** Students may use the **Self-test** to prepare for **Selection Test A** or **Selection Test B.**

Benchmark
Administer **Benchmark Test 6.** If some students need further work, use the **Interpretation Guide** to determine the appropriate reteaching page in the **Reading Kit** and on **Success Tracker.**

EXTEND/ASSESS

Answers

❶ Vocabulary Lesson

Word Analysis: Latin Root *-trem-*
1. c 2. b 3. a

Spelling Strategy
1. famous 2. cautious

Vocabulary Builder: Sentence Completion
1. scorn, despicable
2. reprimand, tremulous
3. putrid, zeal
4. lamentations, flounders

❷ Grammar and Style Lesson

1. *has been,* repeated action
2. *have read,* single action
3. *has read,* single action
4. *has become,* repeated action
5. *have studied,* repeated action

Writing Application
Sample sentence: This vision has brought me hope.

WG Writing and Grammar Platinum Level
For support in teaching the Grammar and Style Lesson, use Chapter 22, Section 1.

❸ Listening and Speaking

- Have students narrow their topics and choose a presentation medium, such as slides or skits.
- The **Support for Extend Your Learning** page (*Unit 5 Resources,* p. 51) provides guided note-taking opportunities to help students complete the Extend Your Learning activities.

Go Online **Research** Have students type in the Web Code for another research activity.

Standard Course of Study

Goal 1: WRITTEN LANGUAGE

WL.1.03.3 Provide textual evidence to support understanding and response to personal reflection.

Goal 3: FOUNDATIONS OF ARGUMENT

FA.3.04.4 Demonstrate comprehension of main idea and supporting details in argument.

Goal 4: CRITICAL THINKING

CT.4.04.2 Apply criteria to evaluate others using reasoning and substantiation.

Goal 5: LITERATURE

LT.5.01.2 Build knowledge of literary genres, and explore how characteristics apply to literature of world cultures.

LT.5.03.10 Analyze connections between ideas, concepts, characters and experiences in world literature.

Goal 6: GRAMMAR AND USAGE

GU.6.02.1 Edit for agreement, tense choice, pronouns, antecedents, case, and complete sentences.

Step-by-Step Teaching Guide	Pacing Guide
PRETEACH	
• Administer Vocabulary and Reading Warm-ups as necessary.	5 min.
• Engage students' interest with the motivation activity.	5 min.
• Read and discuss author and background features. **FT**	10 min.
• Introduce the Literary Analysis Skill: Characterization. **FT**	5 min.
• Introduce the Reading Strategy: Distinguishing Between the Speaker and the Poet. **FT**	10 min.
• Prepare students to read by teaching the selection vocabulary. **FT**	
TEACH	
• Informally monitor comprehension while students read independently or in groups. **FT**	30 min.
• Monitor students' comprehension with the Reading Check notes.	as students read
• Reinforce vocabulary with Vocabulary Builder notes.	as students read
• Develop students' understanding of characterization with the Literary Analysis annotations. **FT**	5 min.
• Develop students' ability to distinguish between the speaker and the poet with the Reading Strategy annotations. **FT**	5 min.
ASSESS/EXTEND	
• Assess students' comprehension and mastery of the Literary Analysis and Reading Strategy by having them answer the Apply the Skills questions. **FT**	15 min.
• Have students complete the Vocabulary Lesson and the Grammar and Style Lesson. **FT**	15 min.
• Apply students' ability to elaborate with supporting quotations by using the Writing Lesson. **FT**	45 min. or homework
• Apply students' understanding by using one or more of the Extend Your Learning activities.	20–90 min. or homework
• Administer Selection Test A or Selection Test B. **FT**	15 min.

Resources

Print

Unit 5 Resources

Transparency

Graphic Organizer Transparencies

Print

Reader's Notebook [L2]

Reader's Notebook: Adapted Version [L1]

Reader's Notebook: English Learner's Version [EL]

Unit 5 Resources

Technology

Listening to Literature Audio CDs [L2, EL]

Print

Unit 5 Resources

General Resources

Technology

Go Online: Research **[L3]**
Go Online: Self-test **[L3]**
***ExamView®*, Test Bank [L3]**

Choosing Resources for Differentiated Instruction

[L1] Special Needs Students
[L2] Below-Level Students
[L3] All Students
[L4] Advanced Students
[EL] English Learners

For Vocabulary and Reading Warm-ups and for Selection Tests, **A** signifies "less challenging" and **B** "more challenging." For Graphic Organizer transparencies, **A** signifies "not filled in" and **B** "filled in."

FT Fast Track Instruction: To move the lesson more quickly, use the strategies and activities identified with **FT**.

Scaffolding for Less Proficient and Advanced Students

The leveled Critical Thinking questions after selections progress in the levels of thinking required to answer them. To address the needs of your different students, you may use the (a) level questions for your less proficient students and the (b) level questions with your on-level and advanced students. The occasional (c) level questions are appropriate for your advanced students.

Use this complete suite of powerful teaching tools to make lesson planning and testing quicker and easier.

Use the interactive textbook (online and on CD-ROM) to make selections and activities come alive with audio and video support and interactive questions.

Monitoring Progress

Before students read the excerpts from the *Inferno*, administer **Diagnostic Test 7** (***Unit 5 Resources*, pp. 65–67**). This test will determine students' level of readiness for the reading and vocabulary skills.

Go Online Professional Development **For:** Information about Lexiles
Visit: www.PHSchool.com
Web Code: eue-1111

PREFEACH

❶ Literary Analysis

Characterization

- Invite volunteers to read aloud the definitions of direct and indirect characterization.
- Confirm students' understanding by eliciting or providing examples of each.
- Highlight the point-of-view discussion under Reading Strategy, and discuss the limitations that a first-person speaker has for characterization. For example, such a speaker can describe characters only through his or her own view.

❷ Reading Strategy

Distinguishing Between the Speaker and the Poet

- Remind students that the speaker is the voice that tells a story. Stress that good readers analyze the speaker's views to determine whether they match those of the poet.
- Read aloud to students the text in the graphic organizer. Model its use by explaining that the first two boxes identify a text example, and the second two boxes features inferences made (on the basis of the examples) about the poet's views and purpose.
- Give students a copy of **Reading Strategy Graphic Organizer A,** p. 121 in ***Graphic Organizer Transparencies.*** Have them use it to distinguish between the speaker and the poet as they read.

Vocabulary Builder

- Pronounce each vocabulary word for students, and read the definitions as a class. Have students identify any words with which they are already familiar.

Build Skills *Epic Poem*

Inferno, Cantos V and XXXIV

NC Standard Course of Study

- Apply criteria to evaluate others using reasoning and substantiation. (CT.4.04.2)
- Analyze connections between ideas, concepts, characters and experiences in world literature. (LT.5.03.10)

❶ Literary Analysis

Characterization

Characterization is the art of revealing character. There are two main types of characterization:

- In *direct characterization*, a writer simply tells the reader what a character is like.
- In *indirect characterization*, a writer suggests what a character is like by showing what the character says and does, what other characters say about him or her, or how other characters behave toward him or her.

As you read, notice the techniques Dante uses to paint vivid portraits of his characters.

Connecting Literary Elements

An **allusion** is a reference within a literary work to something outside the work. Allusions are a kind of literary shorthand because they quickly add layers of meaning. For example, when Francesca alludes to the story of Lancelot, she associates her misadventure with the well-known romance of the tragic knight. Pay attention to Dante's use of allusions, and identify the layers of meaning they add to his tale.

❷ Reading Strategy

Distinguishing Between the Speaker and the Poet

The *Inferno* uses the first-person point of view—the reader sees events through the speaker's eyes. Yet, the Dante who relates this tale is simply a literary character created by the poet. Along with Virgil, Francesca, and other characters, Dante the poet uses Dante the character to express his ideas. As you read, use a chart like the one shown to **distinguish between the speaker and the poet.**

Speaker
Dante the character

↓

Statement
Francesca's suffering "melts me to tears."

↓

Poet's Judgment
He has written Francesca into Hell, suggesting a lack of sympathy.

↓

Poet's Purpose
to show that Dante the character needs to outgrow his sympathy for sinners

Vocabulary Builder

grotesque (grō tesk′) *adj.* strangely distorted (p. 676)

degree (di grē′) *n.* step; stage; level (p. 676)

anguish (aŋ′ gwish) *n.* great suffering; agony (p. 677)

tempest (tem′ pist) *n.* storm (p. 679)

perilous (per′ ə ləs) *adj.* dangerous (p. 681)

awe (ô) *n.* feelings of reverence, fear, and wonder (p. 685)

writhes (rīthz) *v.* twists and turns the body, as in agony (p. 686)

nimble (nim′ bəl) *adj.* able to move quickly and lightly; agile (p. 687)

Review and Anticipate In Canto III, Dante and Virgil paused at Hell's outer edge, where they witnessed the torments suffered by the Opportunists. As they prepared to cross the river Acheron into the first circle of Hell, Dante was so overcome by terror he fell into a swoon.

In Canto V, Dante and Virgil will enter the second circle of Hell, where they will observe the carnal sinners.

Then, in Canto XXXIV, Dante and his guide will enter the ninth and lowest circle of Hell, the lair of Satan himself. How do you think Dante will react when he witnesses the horrors ahead? Read to find out.

❶ Canto V

CIRCLE TWO — *The Carnal*

The Poets leave Limbo and enter the *Second Circle*. Here begin the torments of Hell proper, and here, blocking the way, sits *Minos*,[1] the dread and semi-bestial judge of the damned who assigns to each soul its eternal torment. He orders the Poets back; but Virgil silences him as he earlier silenced Charon, and the Poets move on.

They find themselves on a dark ledge swept by a great whirlwind, which spins within it the souls of the *Carnal*, those who betrayed reason to their appetites. Their sin was to abandon themselves to the tempest of their passions: so they are swept forever in the tempest of Hell, forever denied the light of reason and of God. Virgil identifies many among them.[2] *Semiramis* is there, and *Dido, Cleopatra, Helen, Achilles, Paris*, and *Tristan*. Dante sees *Paolo* and *Francesca* swept together, and in the name of love he calls to them to tell their sad story. They pause from their eternal flight to come to him, and Francesca tells their history while Paolo weeps at her side. Dante is so stricken by compassion at their tragic tale that he swoons once again.

So we went down to the second ledge alone;
  a smaller circle[3] of so much greater pain
  the voice of the damned rose in a bestial moan.

1. **Minos** (mī´ näs´) Like all the monsters Dante assigns to the various offices of Hell, Minos is drawn from classical mythology. He was the son of Europa and of Zeus, who descended to her in the form of a bull. Minos became a mythological king of Crete, so famous for his wisdom and justice that after death his soul was made judge of the dead. In the *Aeneid*, Virgil presents him fulfilling the same office at Aeneas' descent to the underworld. Dante, however, transforms him into an irate and hideous monster with a tail.
2. **many among them** The names that follow are those of famous lovers from legend and history: Semiramis (si mir´ ə mis); Dido (dī´ dō); Cleopatra (klē´ ō pa´ trə); Achilles (ə kil´ ēz´); Tristan (tris´ tən); Paolo (pä´ ô lô); Francesca (frän ches´ kä).
3. **a smaller circle** The pit of Hell tapers like a funnel. The circles of ledges accordingly grow smaller as they descend.

❷ 

What function does Minos perform?

TEACH

Facilitate Understanding

Ask students this question: How do you feel when friends talk about a movie that you have not seen? Explain that modern readers may feel "left out" by Dante's many allusions. Review the definition of allusion; then, direct students to the many footnotes in the selection. Explain that these notes will help readers understand Dante's allusions and add layers of meaning to the reading.

❶ About the Selection

Canto V offers a poignant exploration of the battle between body and mind as Dante and Virgil travel into Hell proper. They meet the lovers Francesca and Paolo, and Dante learns of the danger facing those who succumb to uncontrolled emotion. He struggles with his own compassion for these damned souls.

❷ Reading Check

Answer: Minos assigns each damned soul its specific torment.

Differentiated Instruction — Solutions for All Learners

Accessibility at a Glance

	Canto V	Canto XXXIV
Context	Virgil and Dante enter the second circle of Hell.	Virgil and Dante enter the last circle of Hell, where they find Satan.
Language	Footnotes identify Dante's many allusions.	Words describing physical sensations and many sensory images
Concept Level	Accessible (Dangers of uncontrolled emotions)	Accessible (Dangers of betrayal and the consequent punishments)
Literary Merit	Classic allegorical epic poem	Classic allegorical epic poem
Lexile	NP	NP
Overall Rating	Challenging	Challenging

3 Humanities

Minos, the infernal judge, sitting at the entrance to the second circle of hell, waiting to pass sentence on the souls brought before him, by Gustave Doré

Although he was self-taught, Gustave Doré (1832–1883) became the most accomplished and admired illustrator of his time. His editions of such authors as Milton, Coleridge, and Dante showcase his elegant and detailed drawings.

Use the following questions to stimulate discussion:

- On which lines in the poem is the engraving based?
  Answer: The engraving is based on lines 4–12.
- What details in the artwork echo information from the poem?
  Answer: Details such as Minos' tail and the cowering souls on the ledge echo information from the poem.

4 Critical Viewing

Answer: Minos is many times the size of those who stand before him. His size adds drama to the scene by emphasizing his power over these individuals.

5 Literary Analysis

Characterization

- Explain that the use of descriptive adjectives is one way a writer constructs a characterization.
- Have a volunteer read aloud the bracketed line as students **identify** the three adjectives Dante uses to describe Minos.
  Answer: Dante describes Minos as "grinning, grotesque, and hale."
- Discuss what each adjective means, referring students to footnote 4 for a definition of "hale."
- Then, **ask** students the Literary Analysis question: Dante uses three adjectives to directly characterize Minos. Which adjective do you find surprising? Explain.
  Possible answer: The adjective "hale" may be most surprising because it contrasts dramatically with "grotesque." One might expect grotesqueness more than health in Hell.

3

Minos, the infernal judge, sitting at the entrance to the second circle of hell, waiting to pass sentence on the souls brought before him, Gustave Doré

4 ◀ **Critical Viewing** In this illustration of Minos sitting in judgment, how do the relative sizes of the figures emphasize the drama of the scene? **[Interpret]**

5

There Minos sits, grinning, grotesque, and hale.[4]
He examines each lost soul as it arrives
and delivers his verdict with his coiling tail.

That is to say, when the ill-fated soul
appears before him it confesses all,[5]
and that grim sorter of the dark and foul

decides which place in Hell shall be its end,
then wraps his twitching tail about himself
one coil for each degree it must descend.

The soul descends and others take its place:
each crowds in its turn to judgment, each confesses,
each hears its doom and falls away through space.

"O you who come into this camp of woe,"
cried Minos when he saw me turn away
without awaiting his judgment, "watch where you go

once you have entered here, and to whom you turn!
Do not be misled by that wide and easy passage!"
And my Guide to him: "That is not your concern;

Literary Analysis
Characterization Dante uses three adjectives to directly characterize Minos. Which adjective do you find surprising? Explain.

Vocabulary Builder
grotesque (grō tesk′) *adj.* strangely distorted

degree (di grē′) *n.* step; stage; level

4. **hale** (hāl) *adj.* healthy.
5. **it confesses all** Just as the souls appeared eager to cross Acheron, so they are eager to confess even while they are filled with dread. Dante is once again making the point that sinners elect their Hell by an act of their own will.

Enrichment

Carnival Celebrations

Recall the subtitle *The Carnal* for students. The theme of carnality—of the struggle between body and mind—runs throughout Canto V. Explain that the word *carnal* is based on the Latin word *carnalis,* meaning "fleshly" as opposed to "spiritual." Canto V deals with the punishment of the souls of people who have committed sins of the flesh.

Other English words share a common idea with *carnal. Carnival* is derived from the medieval Italian phrase *carne vale,* meaning "O flesh farewell!" In the Middle Ages, *carnival* referred to Mardi Gras (Fat Tuesday). Mardi Gras festivities were a last, boisterous round of amusement and pleasure on the eve of the Lenten season, during which Christians were required to abstain from meat. Lent is still observed by Christians; it falls during the forty days before Easter. Even though abstinence from meat during Lent is now optional in many denominations, Mardi Gras continues to be celebrated with exuberant carnival festivities in New Orleans and other cities around the world.

it is his fate to enter every door.
This has been willed where what is willed must be,
and is not yours to question. Say no more."

Now the choir of anguish, like a wound,
strikes through the tortured air. Now I have come
to Hell's full lamentation, sound beyond sound.

I came to a place stripped bare of every light
and roaring on the naked dark like seas
6 wracked by a war of winds. Their hellish flight

of storm and counterstorm through time foregone,
sweeps the souls of the damned before its charge.
Whirling and battering it drives them on,

and when they pass the ruined gap of Hell[6]
through which we had come, their shrieks begin anew.
There they blaspheme the power of God eternal.

And this, I learned, was the never ending flight
7 of those who sinned in the flesh, the carnal and lusty
who betrayed reason to their appetite.

As the wings of wintering starlings bear them on
in their great wheeling flights, just so the blast
wherries[7] these evil souls through time foregone.

Here, there, up, down, they whirl and, whirling, strain
with never a hope of hope to comfort them,
not of release, but even of less pain.

As cranes go over sounding their harsh cry,
leaving the long streak of their flight in air,
so come these spirits, wailing as they fly.

And watching their shadows lashed by wind, I cried:
"Master, what souls are these the very air
lashes with its black whips from side to side?"

"The first of these whose history you would know,"
he answered me, "was Empress of many tongues.[8]
Mad sensuality corrupted her so

6. **the ruined gap of Hell** At the time of the Harrowing of Hell—the supposed descent of Christ into Limbo to rescue and bring to Heaven his "ancestors" from the Hebrew Bible—a great earthquake shook the underworld, shattering rocks and cliffs.
7. **wherries** (hwer´ ēz) *v.* transports.
8. **Empress of many tongues** Semiramis, a legendary queen of Assyria.

Vocabulary Builder
anguish (aŋ´ gwish) *n.* great suffering; agony

Reading Strategy
Distinguishing Between the Speaker and the Poet Which images does Dante the poet use to convey the physical experience of Dante the character?

Literary Analysis
Characterization In lines 38–39, what does Dante's definition of carnal sin reveal about his values?

8 
Reading Check
What force whirls and batters the souls of the damned?

6 Reading Strategy
Distinguishing Between the Speaker and the Poet

- Review the definition of imagery from p. 657, and list the senses to which it can appeal: touch, sight, smell, taste, and hearing.
- Read the bracketed text aloud, as students work in pairs to list sensory details.
- Then, **ask** students the Reading Strategy question: Which images does Dante the poet use to convey the physical experience of Dante the character?
  Answer: Images such as "choir of anguish," "sound beyond sound," "a place stripped bare of every light," "naked dark like seas wracked by a war of winds," "whirling and battering it drives them on" all paint a picture of what Dante the character is seeing and hearing.

7 Literary Analysis
Characterization

- Share the discussion of *carnal* and its meaning from Enrichment.
- Have students keep the definition in mind as they reread the bracketed text. Then, **ask** them to paraphrase Dante's definition of carnal sin.
  Answer: Dante defines carnal sins as those that put the appetites of the flesh beyond the control of reason.
- Then, **ask** the Literary Analysis question: In lines 38–39, what does Dante's definition of carnal sin reveal about his values?
  Possible response: Dante's use of the word "betrayed" suggests that he believes reason is a better guide to life, a more important value, than carnal appetite.

8 Reading Check
Answer: Uncontrolled desire whirls and batters the souls of the damned.

Differentiated Instruction
Solutions for All Learners

Support for Special Needs Students
Sometimes, it is hard for readers to find the sentence structure beneath the many descriptive images. Read lines 28–30 aloud for students, pausing after the word *dark.* Explain that in this context, *dark* is used as a noun rather than an adjective. The *dark* is "naked" and sounds like "seas wracked by a war of winds."

Strategy for Advanced Readers
Tell students that Dante frequently employs adjectives to create moods and to emphasize the point of his writing. For example, Dante's starlings (line 40) are "wintering starlings." Their flights are "great wheeling flights." Have students list other strings of adjectives employed by Dante in this canto. Then, have them follow Dante's example by writing a brief description of a familiar place, using adjectives to paint a vivid picture.

9 Critical Viewing

Answer: The map shows the different layers of Hell that Dante and Virgil visit and thus helps readers follow the journey. It also shows which sins the poet considers least and most heinous.

10 Humanities

Dante's Inferno,
sixteenth-century woodcut

This illustration was created for a sixteenth-century Venetian edition of the *Divine Comedy.* Like a map, it provides a graphic reference to Dante's journey.

Use the following questions for discussion.

- Where on the map does Dante's encounter with Minos appear?
  Answer: Minos appears in the third layer from the top of the map (the layer just below Limbo).
- What does this placement suggest about the journey ahead?
  Answer: It suggests that Dante has a long way to go to reach the bottom of Hell.

that to hide the guilt of her debauchery
she licensed all depravity alike,
and lust and law were one in her decree.

She is Semiramis of whom the tale is told
how she married Ninus and succeeded him
to the throne of that wide land the Sultans hold.

9 ▼ **Critical Viewing** In what ways does this map of Dante's Hell help you better understand the poem? **[Connect]**

10

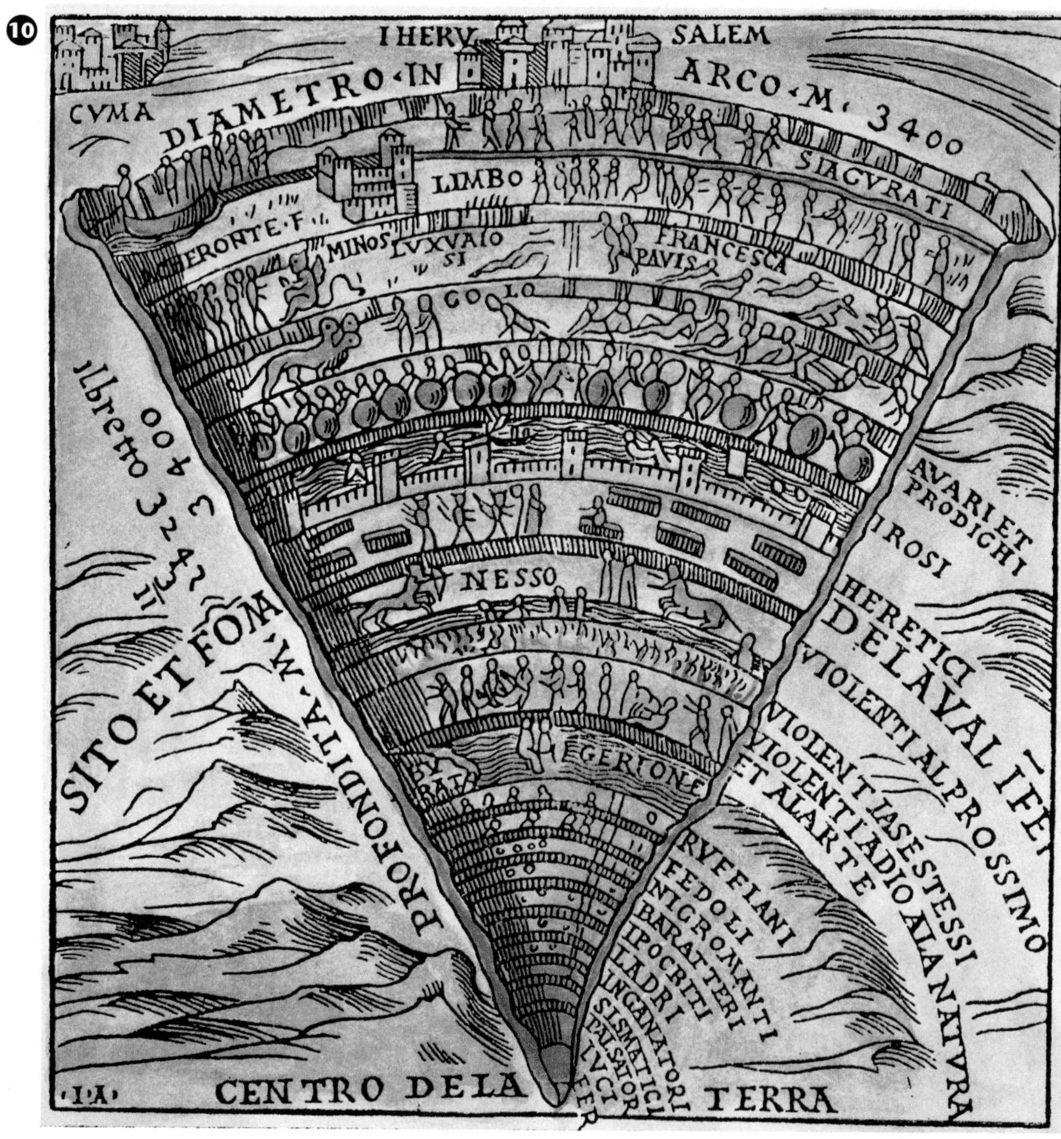

Enrichment

High and Low Art

Much respected art combines high and low forms of culture. Just as dandies and groundlings made up the audience of Shakespeare's plays, so do works themselves often combine the varied aspects of culture.

Dante's writing also attempts to combine diverse aspects of culture. Through his choice of language, he bridges these opposite ends of culture and raises the low form to a high level of art. He does this by writing in the vernacular, Italian, and rejecting Latin.

Dante's goals were many. In one sense, he was trying to address his audience directly.

Every day we employ many different modes of speaking depending on purpose and audience. For example, students may use slang among themselves but more formal language in the classroom.

11 The other is Dido;[9] faithless to the ashes
of Sichaeus, she killed herself for love.
The next whom the eternal tempest lashes

is sense-drugged Cleopatra. See Helen[10] there,
from whom such ill arose. And great Achilles,[11]
who fought at last with love in the house of prayer.

And Paris. And Tristan."[12] As they whirled above
he pointed out more than a thousand shades
of those torn from the mortal life by love.

I stood there while my Teacher one by one
named the great knights and ladies of dim time;
and I was swept by pity and confusion.

12 At last I spoke: "Poet, I should be glad
to speak a word with those two swept together[13]
so lightly on the wind and still so sad."

And he to me: "Watch them. When next they pass,
call to them in the name of love that drives
and damns them here. In that name they will pause."

Thus, as soon as the wind in its wild course
brought them around, I called: "O wearied souls!
if none forbid it, pause and speak to us."

As mating doves that love calls to their nest
glide through the air with motionless raised wings,
borne by the sweet desire that fills each breast—

Literary Analysis
Characterization and Allusion In what ways do these allusions to both historical and legendary figures add to the sense of reality in Dante's tale? Explain.

Vocabulary Builder
tempest (tem′ pist) *n.* storm

Literary Analysis
Characterization How does the poet's use of the word "swept" enrich his characterization of Dante's character?

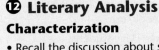

9. **Dido** Queen and founder of Carthage, an ancient kingdom in northern Africa. She had vowed to remain faithful to her husband, Sichaeus (sə kē′ əs), but she fell in love with Aeneas.
10. **Cleopatra . . . Helen** Cleopatra was a queen of Egypt (51–49; 48–30 B.C.) and the mistress of the powerful Romans Julius Caesar and Mark Antony. Helen was the beautiful wife of the King of Sparta. According to legend, the Trojan War was started when she was forcibly taken away to Troy by Paris, a son of the Trojan king Priam.
11. **Achilles** greatest warrior on the Greek side during the Trojan War; placed in this company because of his passion for Polyxena (pō lik′ sə nə), the daughter of Priam. For love of her, he agreed to desert the Greeks and to join the Trojans, but when he went to the temple for the wedding (according to the legend Dante has followed), he was killed by Paris.
12. **Tristan** knight sent to Ireland by King Mark of Cornwall to bring back the princess Isolde (i sōl′ də) to be the king's bride. Isolde and Tristan fell in love and tragically died together.
13. **those two swept together** Paolo and Francesca. In 1275, Giovanni Malatesta (jō vä′ nē mä′ lä tes′ tä) of Rimini made a political marriage with Francesca, daughter of Guido da Polenta (gwē′ dō dä pō len′ tä) of Ravenna. Francesca came to Rimini and fell in love with Giovanni's younger brother Paolo. Paolo had married in 1269 and had had two daughters by 1275, but his affair with Francesca continued for many years. Sometime between 1283 and 1286, Giovanni surprised and killed them in Francesca's bedroom.

13  **Reading Check**
According to Virgil, what tore the souls in this circle of Hell from their mortal lives?

11 Literary Analysis
Characterization and Allusion

- Read aloud footnotes 9–12 for students, and then read aloud the bracketed text.
- Discuss how meeting named people, of whom readers have a familiar image, might differ from meeting unfamiliar or unnamed characters.
- **Ask** students the first Literary Analysis question: In what ways do these allusions to both historical and legendary figures add to the sense of reality in Dante's tale? Explain.
Possible response: Because historical and legendary figures are more familiar to readers, they seem more individualized and more real than unfamiliar fictional characters.

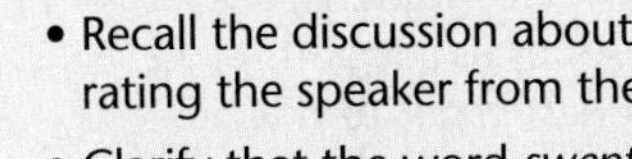

12 Literary Analysis
Characterization

- Recall the discussion about separating the speaker from the poet.
- Clarify that the word *swept* is used by Dante the character. **Ask** students what images and characteristics they associate with this word.
Possible response: Students may mention leaves swept on the wind or other images that suggest a lack of control.
- Have students read the bracketed text carefully and then **respond** to the second Literary Analysis question: How does the poet's use of the word *swept* enrich his characterization of Dante's character?
Answer: The character's use of the word *swept* suggests his acknowledgement of the uncontrollability of emotion. It sweeps one along. The poet's use of this word helps him suggest Dante's sympathy for those damned by uncontrolled emotion.

13 Reading Check

Answer: Virgil says that the souls in this circle were torn from their mortal lives by love.

Differentiated Instruction
Solutions for All Learners

Support for Less Proficient Readers
Help students identify the figures named in lines 61–67. Point out the text numbers, and refer students for explanation to footnotes 9–12. Read each footnote aloud, and have students **explain** why each character ended up in the *Carnal.*
Answer: Dido fell in love outside marriage; Cleopatra caused war by her passion; Achilles broke a promise in the pursuit of love; Tristan fell in love with Isolde, who was promised to his king.

Enrichment for Gifted/Talented Students
Review the historical and legendary characters to whom Dante refers in lines 61–67. Then, invite students to research each character. Encourage students to begin their research with the information in footnotes 9–12 and then to continue it with an Internet search that uses each character name as a key word. Students can share their findings with the class.

14 Literary Analysis

Characterization

- Direct students to read the bracketed passage. Explain that the repetition that appears in the bracketed stanzas is called anaphora.
- **Ask** students the Literary Analysis question: What does the repetition of the word "Love" at the beginning of these three stanzas add to Francesca's characterization?
  Answer: The repetition suggests how important this concept is to her.

Monitor Progress Have students review the definition of indirect characterization on p. 674. Clarify with them that Dante paints a picture of Francesca by his choice of the words she uses. Discuss with students how they draw conclusions about the characters of people they know on the basis of the words these people use.

Reteach Have students use **Literary Analysis** support, p. 72 in ***Unit 5 Resources,*** to practice identifying examples of indirect characterization.

Just so those spirits turned on the torn sky
    from the band where Dido whirls across the air;
    such was the power of pity in my cry.

"O living creature, gracious, kind, and good,
    going this pilgrimage through the sick night,
    visiting us who stained the earth with blood,

were the King of Time our friend, we would pray His peace
    on you who have pitied us. As long as the wind
    will let us pause, ask of us what you please.

The town where I was born lies by the shore
    where the Po[14] descends into its ocean rest
    with its attendant streams in one long murmur.

Love, which in gentlest hearts will soonest bloom
    seized my lover with passion for that sweet body
    from which I was torn unshriven[15] to my doom.

Love, which permits no loved one not to love,
    took me so strongly with delight in him
    that we are one in Hell, as we were above.[16]

Love led us to one death. In the depths of Hell
    Caïna waits for him[17] who took our lives."
    This was the piteous tale they stopped to tell.

And when I had heard those world-offended lovers
    I bowed my head. At last the Poet spoke:
    "What painful thoughts are these your lowered brow covers?"

When at length I answered, I began: "Alas!
    What sweetest thoughts, what green and young desire
    led these two lovers to this sorry pass."

Then turning to those spirits once again,
    I said: "Francesca, what you suffer here
    melts me to tears of pity and of pain.

Literary Analysis
Characterization What does the repetition of the word "Love" at the beginning of these three stanzas add to Francesca's characterization?

14. **Po** (pō) river in northern Italy.
15. **unshriven** unconfessed and so with her sin unforgiven.
16. **that we . . . above** Dante frequently expresses the principle that the souls of the damned are locked so blindly into their own guilt that none can feel sympathy for another. The temptation of many readers is to interpret this line romantically. The more Dantean interpretation, however, is that Paolo and Francesca add to each other's anguish as mutual reminders of their sin.
17. **Caïna . . . him** Giovanni Malatesta was still alive at the time this was written. According to Dante, his fate is already decided, however, and upon his death, his soul will fall to Caïna, the first ring of the last circle (Canto XXXII), where lie those who performed acts of treachery against their kin.

Enrichment

Tale Within a Tale

Canto V includes Francesca's first-person tale, as recounted by Dante. As Francesca tells her story, she draws the pilgrim Dante into her tragedy. She captures his sympathy immediately by addressing him as "gracious, kind, and good" and invokes God to show her gratitude to him. Her repetition of "love" and her description of it as a noble sentiment render her argument all the more convincing. The pilgrim is immediately touched and anguished.

Francesca never speaks directly of her transgression and leaves the listener and reader to think that she is unjustly punished. Thus, the poet shows us the danger of the same language he himself uses. Anyone may mislead others by omitting certain details and emphasizing others. Here the reader learns to distrust the first-person narrative that has previously engaged his or her sympathy.

Paolo and Francesca, 1855, Dante Gabriel Rossetti, Tate Gallery, London

But tell me: in the time of your sweet sighs
  by what appearances found love the way
  to lure you to his perilous paradise?"

And she: "The double grief of a lost bliss
  is to recall its happy hour in pain.
  Your Guide and Teacher knows the truth of this.

But if there is indeed a soul in Hell
  to ask of the beginning of our love
  out of his pity, I will weep and tell:

On a day for dalliance we read the rhyme
  of Lancelot,[18] how love had mastered him.
  We were alone with innocence and dim time.[19]

Pause after pause that high old story drew
  our eyes together while we blushed and paled;
  but it was one soft passage overthrew

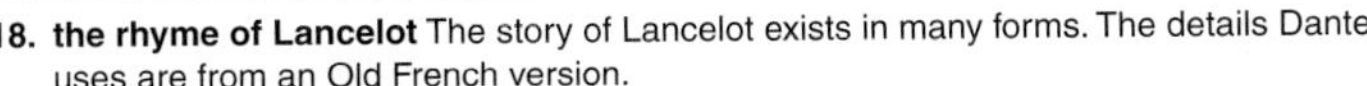

18. the rhyme of Lancelot The story of Lancelot exists in many forms. The details Dante uses are from an Old French version.

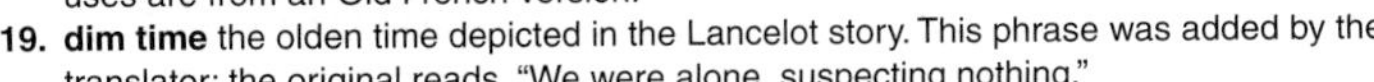

19. dim time the olden time depicted in the Lancelot story. This phrase was added by the translator; the original reads, "We were alone, suspecting nothing."

16 ▲ Critical Viewing This three-part illustration shows Paolo and Francesca in life, Virgil and Dante, and Paolo and Francesca in Hell. Do you think the artist shares Dante's sympathy for the doomed pair? Explain. **[Take a Position]**

Vocabulary Builder
perilous (per′ ə ləs) *adj.* dangerous

Reading Check
With which condemned soul does Dante speak?

15 Humanities

Paolo and Francesca,
by Dante Gabriel Rossetti

Rossetti (1828–1882) was an English painter and poet. Well-read and educated, Rossetti worked extensively with literary subjects, such as Dante's lovers. As part of the Pre-Raphaelite movement, Rossetti and other artists looked for inspiration in the art that predated the Italian High Renaissance as typified by the painter Raphael Sanzio.

Use the following question for discussion:

How are the two images of the lovers similar and different?
Answer: Both images show the lovers embracing, but the image of them in Hell shows them clutching each other against the wind in a more desperate embrace.

16 Critical Viewing

Possible answer: The artist seems to share Dante's sympathy. He highlights the lovers' devotion by showing them each time in a passionate embrace. He also shows Dante and Virgil looking concerned rather than condemning.

17 Reading Check

Answer: Dante speaks with Francesca.

Differentiated Instruction Solutions for All Learners

Support for Special Needs Students

Discuss Francesca's repetition in lines 97–105. Point out that repetition creates a rhythmic effect that sticks in listeners' minds. Ask students what chants they know. Point out that we remember chants because of repetition. Have students explain why Dante uses this technique here.

Enrichment for Gifted/Talented Students

Tell students that the tale of Paolo and Francesca has inspired artists and musicians such as Lizst, Tchaikovsky, Botticelli, and Dante Gabriel Rossetti. Have students research one work inspired by this story and its relationship to the story and then share their findings.

Enrichment for Advanced Readers

Invite students to think of *Romeo and Juliet* while reading Francesca's tale. Remind students that *Romeo and Juliet* is set in Verona and Mantua, two cities in northern Italy. Have students read the play and then make comparisons and contrasts between it and the tale of Paolo and Francesca.

18 Literary Analysis

Characterization and Allusion

- Remind students that an allusion is a reference within a literary work to something outside the work. Then, read aloud the bracketed passage. **Ask** students to what Francesca is alluding in this passage.
  Answer: Francesca is alluding to an Arthurian romance—specifically the story of Lancelot and Guinevere.
- **Ask** students the Literary Analysis question: How is the *Divine Comedy,* in its message and purpose, quite different from the Arthurian romance Francesca describes?
  Possible response: One of Dante's purposes is to instruct readers in the pitfalls of sin. By contrast, the tale of Lancelot and Guinevere, as it features in Francesca's story, has the effect of capturing the imagination. By making romantic feelings and situations intriguing, the tale inspires readers such as Paolo and Francesca to sin.

ASSESS

Answers

1. **Possible response:** Students may share Dante's sympathy because it seems unfair to punish people for loving.
2. (a) The lustful are trapped in everlasting flight. (b) Everlasting flight mimics being swept away by passion and lust.
3. (a) The sinners relinquished reason. (b) Words and phrases are "debauchery," "depravity," "killed herself for love," "eternal tempest," "sense-drugged," and "such ill." (c) Dante condemns uncontrolled love. Those who put love above reason and control will suffer the consequences.
4. (a) In line 72, Dante experiences pity and confusion. (b) **Possible response:** Dante feels pity and confusion because he understands how human it is to love beyond reason, but he also sees that such love is unhealthy. He is not sure whether to condemn or pity the sinners. In lines 50–51, Dante comments on the terrible torment of the sinners and in lines 113–114, he states his feelings. In line 71, he

18

our caution and our hearts. For when we read
 how her fond smile was kissed by such a lover,
 he who is one with me alive and dead

breathed on my lips the tremor of his kiss.
 That book, and he who wrote it, was a pander.[20]
 That day we read no further." As she said this,

the other spirit, who stood by her, wept
 so piteously, I felt my senses reel
 and faint away with anguish. I was swept

by such a swoon as death is, and I fell,
as a corpse might fall, to the dead floor of Hell.

20. **That book . . . pander** *Galeotto,* the Italian word for "pander," is also the Italian rendering of the name of Gallehault, who, in the French Romance Dante refers to here, urged Lancelot and Guinevere on to love. A pander is a go-between in a love affair.

Literary Analysis
Characterization and Allusion How is the *Divine Comedy,* in its message and purpose, quite different from the Arthurian romance Francesca describes?

Critical Reading

1. **Respond:** Do you share Dante's sympathy for Paolo and Francesca? Why or why not?
2. **(a) Recall:** What punishment do the lustful suffer? **(b) Analyze:** In what ways does this punishment match their sins? Explain.
3. **(a) Recall:** In line 39, what does Dante say the sinners relinquished in favor of "appetite"? **(b) Classify:** In lines 55 through 67, note words and phrases that liken sensual indulgence to madness.
   (c) Evaluate: What kind of love does Dante condemn in this Canto? Explain.
4. **(a) Recall:** In line 72, what two emotions does Dante experience in reaction to the sight of the carnal sinners? **(b) Interpret:** Why does Dante feel each of these emotions? Support your answer with details from the text.
5. **(a) Recall:** According to Francesca, what motivates her descent into sin? **(b) Infer:** What does Dante suggest about the effects of certain kinds of literature? **(c) Take a Stand:** Do you agree with Dante's assessment?

Go Online
Author Link
For: More about Dante Alighieri
Visit: www.PHSchool.com
Web Code: ete-9503

Answers continued

refers to the sinners as "the great knights and ladies of dim time," so clearly he admires them.

5. (a) Reading the story of Lancelot motivates Francesca's sin. (b) Dante suggests that some literature can have damaging moral effects.
   (c) **Possible response:** Perhaps literature can influence people's views, but ultimately people are responsible for their actions.

Go Online Author Link For additional information about Dante Alighieri, have students type in the Web Code, then select A from the alphabet, and then select Dante Alighieri.

⓳ ⓴ Canto XXXIV

NINTH CIRCLE: COCYTUS[1] — *Compound Fraud*

ROUND FOUR: JUDECCA — *The Treacherous to Their Masters*

THE CENTER — *Satan*

"On march the banners of the King,"[2] Virgil begins as the Poets face the last depth. He is quoting a medieval hymn, and to it he adds the distortion and perversion of all that lies about him. "On march the banners of the King—of Hell." And there before them, in an infernal parody of Godhead, they see Satan in the distance, his great wings beating like a windmill. It is their beating that is the source of the icy wind of Cocytus, the exhalation of all evil.

All about him in the ice are strewn the sinners of the last round, *Judecca*, named for Judas Iscariot.[3] These are the *Treacherous to Their Masters*. They lie completely sealed in the ice, twisted and distorted into every conceivable posture. It is impossible to speak to them, and the Poets move on to observe Satan.

He is fixed into the ice at the center to which flow all the rivers of guilt; and as he beats his great wings as if to escape, their icy wind only freezes him more surely into the polluted ice. In a grotesque parody of the Trinity, he has three faces, each a different color, and in each mouth he clamps a sinner whom he rips eternally with his teeth. *Judas Iscariot* is in the central mouth: *Brutus* and *Cassius*[4] in the mouths on either side.

Having seen all, the Poets now climb through the center, grappling hand over hand down the hairy flank of Satan himself—a last supremely symbolic action—and at last, when they have passed the center of all gravity, they emerge from Hell. A long climb from the earth's center to the Mount of Purgatory awaits them, and they push on without rest, ascending along the sides of the river Lethe, till they emerge once more to see the stars of Heaven, just before dawn on Easter Sunday.

"On march the banners of the King of Hell,"
my Master said. "Toward us. Look straight ahead:
can you make him out at the core of the frozen shell?"

Like a whirling windmill seen afar at twilight,
or when a mist has risen from the ground—
just such an engine rose upon my sight

stirring up such a wild and bitter wind
I cowered for shelter at my Master's back,
there being no other windbreak I could find.

I stood now where the souls of the last class
(with fear my verses tell it) were covered wholly;
they shone below the ice like straws in glass.

1. **Cocytus** (kō sit′ əs) Greek: "river of wailing."
2. **On . . . King** This hymn was written in the sixth century by Venantius Fortunatus, Bishop of Poitiers. The original celebrates the Holy Cross and part of the service for Good Friday, to be sung at the moment of uncovering the cross.
3. **Judas Iscariot** (is ker′ ē ət) disciple who betrayed Jesus; see the Bible, Matthew 26:14, 48.
4. **Brutus and Cassius** They took part in a plot to assassinate Julius Caesar.

㉑ 

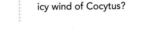

Reading Check

What is the source of the icy wind of Cocytus?

Facilitate Understanding

Before students read Dante's version of Satan, have them speculate on how he will be depicted. Give each student a chance to explain why he or she anticipates some special detail in the portrait of evil.

⓳ About the Selection

In this riveting end to Dante's odyssey into Hell, he and his guide reach its lowest depths. Shaken by what he sees there, Dante escapes from the underworld and emerges to find a brightening, star-studded sky.

⓴ Critical Thinking

Relate

- Tell students that in this canto, the climax of the *Inferno,* they will come face to face with Satan, the symbol of everything evil for Dante.
- Ask students to describe other representations of Satan they have seen or read.
- Then **ask** them to speculate on how he will be depicted in this canto. **Possible response:** Satan may be depicted as grotesque, terrifying, and monstrous.

㉑ Reading Check

Answer: The beating of Satan's wings as he tries to escape creates the icy wind of Cocytus.

Differentiated Instruction

Solutions for All Learners

Background for Special Needs Students

Ask students whether they have ever seen a movie whose ending suggests that a sequel is likely. Offer *Star Wars* as one example, in which evil is overcome but not entirely conquered. Use this familiar example to explain that Canto XXXIV is the end of the *Inferno* section of Dante's work, but it introduces the beginning of the *Purgatorio* section.

Background for Less Proficient Readers

Explain that this canto is the last in the *Inferno* but that it also introduces the second section, *Purgatorio*. Thus, Purgatory is a kind of sequel. Tell students that the work is called a comedy not because it is funny but because at the end, all is well. Ask students to predict what will happen to Dante at the end of this canto.

Background for Advanced Readers

Tell students that this last canto serves as both a beginning and an ending to sections of Dante's epic. Challenge students to find images that present this dual role. Urge them to find any other signs from Dante that convey this message. Invite volunteers to read on in the beginning of *Purgatorio* and report on how, if at all, it echoes Canto XXXIV.

㉒ Humanities

Dante in Hell,
by Gustave Doré

Gustave Doré is remembered today for the volumes of illustrated literary works he published during his career. Here, Virgil and Dante encounter evil-doers punished by immersion in ice up to their necks.

Use the following question for discussion:

What role does the landscape play in creating the mood of this drawing?
Answer: The landscape is icy, harsh, and forbidding. It adds to the despairing mood of the image.

㉓ Critical Viewing

Answer: Dante kneels, while Virgil stands watching. Clues include lines 18–19, in which Dante says "he made me stop, and, stepping aside, he said: 'Now see the face of Dis!'" Also, Dante has shown himself interested in and sympathetic to the tortures of the damned, whereas Virgil has seen them before.

㉒

Some lie stretched out; others are fixed in place
upright, some on their heads, some on their soles;
another, like a bow, bends foot to face.

When we had gone so far across the ice
that it pleased my Guide to show me the foul creature[5]
which once had worn the grace of Paradise,

he made me stop, and, stepping aside, he said:
"Now see the face of Dis![6] This is the place
where you must arm your soul against all dread."

㉓ ▲ **Critical Viewing**
Which figure in this illustration is Dante, and which is Virgil? Explain how you know. **[Distinguish]**

5. **the foul creature** Satan.
6. **Dis** (dis) in Greek mythology, the god of the lower world or the lower world itself. Here, it stands for Satan.

Enrichment

The Role of Satan

Throughout the *Divine Comedy,* Dante uses mythological figures to represent the various sins. Each gets its own perfectly designed appropriate punishment, which focuses readers' attention on the nature of the sin. For example, in Canto V, Francesca and Paolo are swept around the circle of hell just as they were swept away by their passions in life. In Canto XXXIV, readers come face to face with Satan, the symbol of evil for Dante. In the Bible, Satan is represented as a slithering serpent, hissing his treachery to Eve.

Dante depicts Satan as a hideous three-faced monster, the "Emperor of Universal Pain." However, he is frozen at the very bottom of Hell, isolated as far as possible from God and humanity, a suitable punishment for the cold-hearted betrayal of the ultimate good.

Satan also becomes one of the bridges that Dante uses to move his character from one stage of the journey to the next. Virgil carries Dante as he literally climbs up Satan's body into the next world.

(24) Do not ask, Reader, how my blood ran cold
and my voice choked up with fear. I cannot write it:
this is a terror that cannot be told.

I did not die, and yet I lost life's breath:
imagine for yourself what I became,
deprived at once of both my life and death.

(25) The Emperor of the Universe of Pain
jutted his upper chest above the ice;
and I am closer in size to the great mountain

the Titans[7] make around the central pit,
than they to his arms. Now, starting from this part,
imagine the whole that corresponds to it!

If he was once as beautiful as now
he is hideous, and still turned on his Maker,
well may he be the source of every woe!

(26) With what a sense of <u>awe</u> I saw his head
towering above me! for it had three faces:[8]
one was in front, and it was fiery red;

the other two, as weirdly wonderful,
merged with it from the middle of each shoulder
to the point where all converged at the top of the skull;

the right was something between white and bile;
the left was about the color one observes
on those who live along the banks of the Nile.

Under each head two wings rose terribly,
their span proportioned to so gross a bird:
I never saw such sails upon the sea.

They were not feathers—their texture and their form
were like a bat's wings—and he beat them so
that three winds blew from him in one great storm:

it is these winds that freeze all Cocytus.
He wept from his six eyes, and down three chins
the tears ran mixed with bloody froth and pus.[9]

---

7. **Titans** giant deities who were overthrown by Zeus and the Olympian gods of Greece.
8. **three faces** There are many interpretations of these three faces. The common theme in all of them is that the faces are a perversion of the qualities of the Trinity.
9. **bloody froth and pus** the gore of the sinners he chews, which is mixed with his saliva.

Reading Strategy
Distinguishing Between the Speaker and the Poet In what ways does Dante the character's direct address to the reader intensify both the drama and the sense of reality of this scene? Explain.

Literary Analysis
Characterization and Allusion Why is an allusion to the Titans an appropriate detail in Satan's characterization? Explain.

Vocabulary Builder
awe (ô) *n.* feelings of reverence, fear, and wonder

Reading Check (27)
In what substance are the souls of the damned trapped?

(24) Reading Strategy
Distinguishing Between the Speaker and the Poet

- **Ask** students how they think direct address affects readers.
  Possible response: It grabs readers' attention as a break in the narrative and makes readers feel closer to the story by including them in conversation with the author.
- Have a volunteer read the bracketed text aloud. Then, **ask** the Reading Strategy question: In what ways does Dante the character's direct address to the reader intensify both the drama and the sense of reality of this scene? Explain.
  Possible response: The direct address, by drawing attention to the moment, increases drama. By mimicking a conversation with the reader, the direct address makes the scene seem more real.

(25) Literary Analysis
Characterization and Allusion

- Use footnote 7 to clarify that the Titans were giants.
- Direct students to read the bracketed text, paying careful attention to details about size.
- **Ask** students the Literary Analysis question: Why is an allusion to the Titans an appropriate detail in Satan's characterization?
  Possible response: The Titans were giants. Alluding to huge creatures emphasizes Satan's enormity.

(26) Vocabulary Builder
Words Related to *Awe*

- Call students' attention to the word *awe* in line 36 and its definition.
- Point out that *awe* can be positive, as in "feelings of reverence," or negative, as in "feelings of fear."
- Ask student pairs to list things that create feelings of awe. Invite them to explain their choices and connect each to the definition.

(27) Reading Check

Answer: The souls of the damned are trapped in ice.

Differentiated Instruction — Solutions for All Learners

Support for Special Needs Students
Play this section of the selection on **Listening to Literature Audio CDs.** Direct students' attention to line 39, in which Dante uses alliteration, or repeated consonants, to create poetic effects. Here, the effect emphasizes both descriptions—*weirdly* and *wonderful.* To give students practice in recognizing alliteration, have them find another example (line 47).

Support for English Learners
Explain that Dante uses alliteration, the technique of using repeated consonants to achieve poetic effects. Read line 47 aloud to students; then, have them read the line aloud. Urge students to try to "hear" the effect of the sounds. Discuss what the poet might have wanted to accomplish with these lines. Point out that the repetition of the *s* sound mimics the sound of wind blowing through the sails of a ship on the sea.

28 Humanities

Judecca — Lucifer, Inferno XXXIV, by Gustave Doré

This is a fine example of the illustrations Doré produced for his deluxe edition of Dante. The artist's use of strong contrasts between light and dark allows the rendering of fine details without sacrificing the overall darkness of the composition. Doré's Lucifer (Satan) is a nightmarish figure who blends into the dark background and appears to the viewer almost as a surprise. His lurking presence dwarfs the human souls before him.

Use the following questions for discussion:

- How does Doré's Devil compare with others you have seen? **Possible response:** This Devil has wings; others are more serpentlike.
- How does this drawing make you feel? Explain. **Possible response:** The drawing may make students feel like backing up. Satan is so intense and so immediate that viewers instinctively cringe.

29 Critical Viewing

Answer: Both Dante and Doré depict Satan with giant wings, frozen in ice. Dante, however, describes Satan as having three crying faces, and as having a broken sinner in each of his three mouths. Doré's depiction has only one head, no tears, and just one sinner in his mouth. The tears of Dante's Satan suggest regret or at least grief, whereas Doré's Satan seems ominous and threatening.

30 Critical Thinking

Relate

- Read aloud the bracketed text.
- Point out that the guiding principle of Dante's Hell is that a sinner's punishment matches the sin.
- **Ask** students how punishment of sinners in the lowest part of Hell is appropriate for their wrongdoing. **Possible response:** They betrayed their legitimate masters; now they are tortured by their "master," Satan.

28

Judecca - Lucifer, Inferno XXXIV, 1862, Gustave Doré

In every mouth he worked a broken sinner
between his rake-like teeth. Thus he kept three
in eternal pain at his eternal dinner.

For the one in front the biting seemed to play
no part at all compared to the ripping: at times
the whole skin of his back was flayed away.

30

"That soul that suffers most," explained my Guide,
"is Judas Iscariot, he who kicks his legs
on the fiery chin and has his head inside.

Of the other two, who have their heads thrust forward,
the one who dangles down from the black face
is Brutus: note how he writhes without a word.

29 ▲ **Critical Viewing**
How does the artist's depiction of Lucifer in this engraving compare and contrast with Dante's description? Explain. **[Compare and Contrast]**

Vocabulary Builder
writhes (rīthz) *v.* twists and turns the body, as in agony

Enrichment

Dante's Cosmology

The description of how Dante and Virgil leave Hell (lines 69–119) can be confusing. The difficulty is caused partly by Dante's medieval cosmology, or conception of the universe. This view dates back to the second-century astronomer Ptolemy and persisted well into Dante's time. In the thirteenth century, Thomas Aquinas adapted Ptolemy's ideas to Christianity. Ptolemy's concept of the universe rested on a stationary Earth at the center of the universe, with the sun, moon, stars, and planets traveling around the Earth. As a result, the "point to which all gravities are drawn" is the center of the Earth. When Dante and Virgil pass this point, they are on the other side of the Earth, looking at Satan's legs sticking out of the ice on the other side. Ask interested students to research Ptolemy's ideas further to learn how Dante's view of the structure of the universe compares with that understood by modern science. Have students give brief visual presentations to show and explain their findings.

And there, with the huge and sinewy arms, is the soul,
of Cassius,—But the night is coming on[10]
and we must go, for we have seen the whole."

Then, as he bade, I clasped his neck, and he,
watching for a moment when the wings
were opened wide, reached over dexterously[11]

and seized the shaggy coat of the king demon;
then grappling matted hair and frozen crusts
from one tuft to another, clambered down.

When we had reached the joint where the great thigh
merges into the swelling of the haunch,
my Guide and Master, straining terribly,

turned his head to where his feet had been
and began to grip the hair as if he were climbing;[12]
so that I thought we moved toward Hell again.

"Hold fast!" my Guide said, and his breath came shrill
with labor and exhaustion. "There is no way
but by such stairs to rise above such evil."

At last he climbed out through an opening
in the central rock, and he seated me on the rim;
then joined me with a nimble backward spring.

I looked up, thinking to see Lucifer
as I had left him, and I saw instead
his legs projecting high into the air.

Now let all those whose dull minds are still vexed
by failure to understand what point it was
I had passed through, judge if I was perplexed.

"Get up. Up on your feet," my Master said.
"The sun already mounts to middle tierce,[13]
and a long road and hard climbing lie ahead."

10. **the night is coming on** It is now Saturday evening.
11. **dexterously** *adv.* skillfully.
12. **as if he were climbing** They have passed the center of gravity and so must turn around and start climbing.
13. **middle tierce** According to the church's division of the day for prayer, tierce is the period from about six to nine A.M. Middle tierce, therefore, is seven-thirty. In going through the center point, Dante and Virgil have gone from night to day. They have moved ahead twelve hours.

Reading Strategy
Distinguishing Between the Speaker and the Poet
What spiritual and emotional change does the poet express through a physical description? Explain.

Vocabulary Builder
nimble (nim′ bəl) *adj.* able to move quickly and lightly; agile

Reading Check
What torture do Judas Iscariot, Brutus, and Cassius suffer?

31 Background

History

The Cassius who betrayed Caesar was more generally described as having a "lean and hungry look." Another Cassius is described by Cicero (Catiline II) as huge and sinewy.

32 Reading Strategy

Distinguishing Between the Speaker and the Poet

- Review with students where Dante and Virgil are in Hell, noting that they face a mountainous Satan in Hell's innermost region.
- Remind students that Dante's journey will take him through Hell, through Purgatory, and finally to Heaven. Thus, having reached the bottom of Hell, he is ready to travel to Purgatory.
- Then, **ask** the Reading Strategy question: What spiritual and emotional change does the poet express through a physical description? Explain.
  Answer: The poet describes Dante's spiritual and emotional change from despair to hope through the physical description of climbing over Satan and out of Hell.

33 Reading Check

Answer: Judas Iscariot, Brutus, and Cassius are forever being chewed by the mouths of the three-headed Satan.

Differentiated Instruction

Solutions for All Learners

Support for Special Needs Students

Work with students to help them understand the scene in which Dante and Virgil climb out of Hell. Explain that Dante, the poet, uses sensory imagery to help readers envision and experience the scene. Read lines 69–119 aloud as students list details that help them experience the physical sensation of the climb.

Strategy for Gifted/Talented Students

Discuss the physical challenge that Dante and Virgil undertake to literally climb their way out of Hell. Review with students the information about Dante's conception of the universe in Enrichment on the previous page. Then, have students review lines 69–119 to identify words that signal movement or spatial relationship. Finally, have each student write a journal entry expressing Virgil's reactions to the climb. Invite students to share their work with classmates.

34 Themes in World Literature

Literary Views of the Underworld

Not only are there many literary excursions into the underworld, there are many different versions of Dante's excursion. This text uses a translation by John Ciardi, but modern writers such as Dorothy L. Sayers and poet Allen Mandelbaum have created their own versions. One recent translation is by American poet laureate Robert Pinsky. Begun in 1993 for a collaborative reading of the *Inferno,* Pinksy's translation gives the poem a natural feeling in English. In order to do this, the translator adopted a "more flexible definition of rhyme," which allowed him to follow Dante's rhyming pattern without straining. Pinksy drew heavily on previous translations, such as those by Henry Wadsworth Longfellow (1865) and Charles S. Singleton (1970). Then, he added idiomatic English—as Dante had once added idiomatic Italian—to create a work accessible to modern readers.

Connect to the Literature Have students reread the canto. Encourage them to focus on the most vivid details in Dante's description of Hell. After students write their sentences, suggest that they exchange papers with a partner and evaluate each other's work. Then ask volunteers to read their sentences to the class.

Possible response: Hell is a whirling anguish of icy wind, with sinners trapped below the ice and hideous views of Satan chewing his victims.

35 Critical Thinking

Analyze

- Explain that Dante's rhyme scheme is known as terza rima—or *aba, bcb, cdc*—and so on through each canto. The middle line of each tercet determines the rhyme of the next, thus linking the entire canto in this manner.
- Have students look at the bracketed passage while a volunteer reads it aloud.
- **Ask** students what rhyme scheme John Ciardi, the translator, has used. How is it similar to and different from terza rima?

  Answer: Ciardi uses what he calls "dummy terza rima." The pattern is *aba, cdc, efe,* and so on. Unlike terza rima, the middle line of a tercet does not determine the rhyme scheme of the next.

It was no hall of state we had found there,
but a natural animal pit hollowed from rock
with a broken floor and a close and sunless air.

"Before I tear myself from the Abyss,"
I said when I had risen, "O my Master,
explain to me my error in all this:

where is the ice? and Lucifer—how has he
been turned from top to bottom: and how can the sun
have gone from night to day so suddenly?"

And he to me: "You imagine you are still
on the other side of the center where I grasped
the shaggy flank of the Great Worm of Evil

which bores through the world—you *were* while
I climbed down,
but when I turned myself about, you passed
the point to which all gravities are drawn.

You are under the other hemisphere where you stand;
the sky above us is the half opposed
to that which canopies the great dry land.

Under the midpoint of that other sky
the Man[14] who was born sinless and who lived
beyond all blemish, came to suffer and die.

35

You have your feet upon a little sphere
which forms the other face of the Judecca.
There it is evening when it is morning here.

And this gross Fiend and Image of all Evil
who made a stairway for us with his hide
is pinched and prisoned in the ice-pack still.

On this side he plunged down from heaven's height,
and the land that spread here once hid in the sea
and fled North to our hemisphere for fright;[15]

Themes in World Masterpieces

34 Literary Views of the Underworld

Although the *Divine Comedy* is probably the most famous literary excursion into the afterlife, there are many others. The Sumerian-Babylonian epic of *Gilgamesh* contains a vivid description of an underworld in which people sit in darkness and eat dust and clay. In Homer's *Odyssey,* Odysseus visits the Greek underworld, where he converses with the shades of mortals. In Plato's *Apology,* Socrates is optimistic about the afterlife, saying that death may be a state of nothingness, a kind of sleep, or a journey to a place where he will meet all who have gone before him. John Milton's *Paradise Lost* and Goethe's *Faust* present images of Heaven and Hell in which goodness on earth is rewarded and excessive pride and egoism are punished. However, Dante's version of Hell, with its clear structure, sharp physical descriptions, and fully realized characters, remains perhaps the most detailed and vividly imagined of all the literary underworlds.

Connect to the Literature

Write one or two sentences summarizing Dante's version of the ninth circle of Hell in this Canto.

14. the Man Jesus, who suffered and died in Jerusalem, which was thought to be the middle of the Earth.

15. fled North . . . for fright Dante believed that the Northern Hemisphere was mostly land and the Southern Hemisphere, mostly water. Here, he explains the reason for this state of affairs.

Enrichment

Jerusalem

The city of Jerusalem, which Dante references with his mention of Jesus in line 115, is of central importance to three of the world's great religions. It is revered by Christians because it is where Jesus was crucified; by Jews because it is the site of Solomon's temple, of which only a portion at the Western Wall remains; and by Muslims because it is the site from which the prophet Muhammad ascended into heaven. The eastern part of the city is known as the Old City. To the east of the Old City lie the Garden of Gethsemane and the Mount of Olives.

These mutual claims on the city have led to much historical tension and conflict, which continue today. In 1922, the League of Nations gave control of Jerusalem to Great Britain. After World War II, the UN suggested transforming the city into an international city shared by Palestinian Arabs (Christian and Muslim) and Israeli Jews. Palestinians rejected this idea and continue to contest it today as both Israel and the Palestinian Authority claim Jerusalem as their capital.

Poets emerge from Hell, Inferno XXXIV, 139, Gustave Doré

◀ Critical Viewing 37
Which details in this illustration suggest that the poets are no longer in hell? **[Interpret]**

And it may be that moved by that same fear,
the one peak[16] that still rises on this side
fled upward leaving this great cavern[17] here."

Down there, beginning at the further bound
of Beelzebub's[18] dim tomb, there is a space
not known by sight, but only by the sound

16. the one peak the Mount of Purgatory.
17. this great cavern the natural animal pit of line 98. It is also "Beelzebub's dim tomb," line 130.
18. Beelzebub's (bē elʹ zə bubzʹ) Beelzebub, which in Hebrew means "god of flies," was another name for Satan.

Reading Check
What "stairway" did Virgil take to climb out of Hell?

36 Humanities

Poets Emerge From Hell, Inferno XXXIV, 139, by Gustave Doré

Drawing in perfect scale and proportion seems to have come naturally to Gustave Doré (1832–1883). Rock climbing was a favorite pastime of Doré's, and his familiarity with rock formations and aerial views is evident in this scene.

Use the following questions for discussion.

- What does this picture suggest about the relationship between Virgil (on the far left) and Dante? Explain.
  Possible reponse: Virgil stands higher than Dante and, with his arm raised, appears to be instructing or advising him in some way. Also, Dante is looking upward at Virgil with a demeanor of awe or respect.
- In your opinion, would this engraving be more or less effective if it were in color? Explain.
  Possible reponse: The muted black and white tones of the engraving seem effective in communicating the imagery of the poem.

37 Critical Viewing

Answer: The poets' exit from Hell is suggested by the stars, the moonlight shining on the water, and Virgil pointing upward toward Heaven rather than downward toward Hell.

38 Reading Check

Answer: Virgil climbs the "stairway" of Satan's body to get out of Hell.

Differentiated Instruction Solutions for All Learners

Support for Special Needs Students

Review the definition of characterization on page 674. Have students identify and list the four names for Satan that appear on these facing pages: Lucifer, Great Worm of Evil, Fiend and Image of all Evil, Beelzebub. Then have students complete a Satan character web based on Dante's observations of the evil monster.

Support for English Learners

Point out that Lucifer and the Great Worm of Evil refer to the same being. On these pages alone, Satan is given four names: Lucifer, Great Worm of Evil, Fiend and Image of all Evil, and Beelzebub. Ask students what names they know for Satan, and have volunteers list these on the board.

Strategy for Advanced Readers

Point out that Virgil describes Satan as "the Great Worm of Evil," and Dante compares Satan to a bat. Discuss the feelings that students associate with worms and bats. Then, discuss why Dante portrays Satan through these negative animal images and how doing so transfers readers' feelings of disgust to Satan.

39 Critical Thinking

Speculate

- Have students read the bracketed text.
- Point out that the canto and the entire poem end with a couplet, thus betraying the repetition of the tercet throughout.
- **Ask** what reason Dante may have had to end the canto with a different line form.
  Answer: It signals closure.

ASSESS

Answers

1. **Possible response:** The sinners trapped in ice may be the most horrible because the punishment suggests complete paralysis within a horrible nightmare.
2. (a) Dante cannot write or describe the horror of Satan. (b) Dante describes Satan.
3. (a) The three figures in Satan's mouth are Judas Iscariot, Brutus, and Cassius. (b) All share the sin of betraying a legitimate master. (c) Dante situates the three sinners in a frozen lake to symbolize the cold, frozen heart of each traitor.
4. (a) In line 65, Virgil emphasizes that Brutus suffers without the ability to speak. (b) **Possible response:** Language might be denied to inhabitants of Hell's ninth circle because they must suffer complete paralysis in their punishment. Their sins were unspeakable, so now they cannot speak.
5. (a) At the beginning of his journey through Hell, Dante the character has sympathy for the sinners in Hell. By the end of his journey, he has no sympathy and feels nothing but disgust. (b) **Possible response:** Dante the poet may be saying that although sin should not be tolerated because it has awesome and terrible consequences, some sins are worse than others.
6. **Possible response:** Students may name an admired family member or mentor, or they may cite a literary character who inspires confidence.

of a little stream[19] descending through the hollow
it has eroded from the massive stone
in its endlessly entwining lazy flow."

My Guide and I crossed over and began
to mount that little known and lightless road
to ascend into the shining world again.

He first, I second, without thought of rest
we climbed the dark until we reached the point
where a round opening brought in sight the blest

39 and beauteous shining of the Heavenly cars.
And we walked out once more beneath the Stars.[20]

---

19. **a little stream** Lethe (lē´ thē); in classical mythology, the river of forgetfulness, from which souls drank before being born. In Dante's symbolism, it flows down from Purgatory, where it has washed away the memory of sin from the souls who are undergoing purification. That memory it delivers to Hell, which draws all sin to itself.
20. **Stars** As part of his total symbolism, Dante ends each of the three divisions of the *Divine Comedy* with this word. Every conclusion of the upward soul is toward the stars, symbols of hope and virtue. It is just before dawn of Easter Sunday that the Poets emerge—a further symbolism.

Critical Reading

1. **Respond:** Which aspect of the ninth circle of Hell do you find most horrible? Why?
2. **(a) Recall:** In lines 22–23, what does Dante say he cannot write or describe? **(b) Interpret:** How does he succeed nevertheless in communicating his experience?
3. **(a) Recall:** Who are the three figures in Satan's mouth?
   (b) Infer: What sin do all three have in common? **(c) Analyze:** Why do you think Dante chooses to situate the punishment for such sin in a frozen lake?
4. **(a) Recall:** In line 65, which aspect of Brutus' suffering does Virgil emphasize? **(b) Generalize:** Why might language be denied to the inhabitants of the ninth circle of Hell?
5. **(a) Evaluate:** In what ways do you think Dante the character's feelings about the lost inhabitants of Hell have changed since the beginning of the Inferno? **(b) Analyze:** What message about tolerance for sin might Dante the poet be expressing through his character's emotional evolution?
6. **Hypothesize:** If you were to undertake a journey such as Dante's, whom would you choose as your guide? Explain your answer.

For: More about Dante Alighieri
Visit: www.PHSchool.com
Web Code: ete-9503

Go Online Author Link For additional information about Dante Alighieri, have students type in the Web Code, then select *A* from the alphabet, and then select Dante Alighieri.

Apply the Skills

from the *Divine Comedy: Inferno*

Literary Analysis

Characterization

1. Which words and phrases in Francesca's first statements to Dante provide **direct characterization** of Dante the character?
2. Use a chart like the one shown to analyze the **indirect characterization** of Dante in the *Inferno.*

Method of Characterization	Example	Trait Revealed
Dante's Actions	He questions Francesca.	curiosity; sympathy
Dante's Words	"I cowered for shelter."	
Other Characters' Behavior Toward Dante	Virgil carries him.	

3. **(a)** Cite two statements another character makes about Virgil. **(b)** In what ways do each of these statements add to your understanding of Virgil's character?

Connecting Literary Elements

4. In Canto V, Francesca mentions "him who took our lives." **(a)** To whom is she referring with this **allusion**? **(b)** How does this allusion increase the realism of the *Inferno*?
5. At the beginning of Canto XXXIV, Virgil cites a line from a hymn. **(a)** How does Virgil change the line? **(b)** How does this allusion add to the reader's understanding of Hell as a world of distortions?

Reading Strategy

Distinguishing Between the Speaker and the Poet

6. At key transitional points in the story, Dante, **the speaker** of the poem, loses consciousness. In what ways does this solve literary problems for Dante **the poet**?
7. In lines 105–135 of Canto XXXIV, Dante the poet has Virgil explain where the two travelers are standing. **(a)** Why does Dante the character need this explanation? **(b)** Why does the reader need it?

Extend Understanding

8. **Psychology Connection:** At the banks of the river Acheron, Charon tells the souls to "Bury / here and forever all hope of Paradise." Is hope necessary for happiness? Explain your answer.

QuickReview

Characterization is the art of revealing character. Writers use both **direct** and **indirect** characterization to reveal the personalities of their characters.

An **allusion** is a reference within a literary work to a well-known person, place, event, story, work of literature, or work of art.

To **distinguish between the speaker and the poet** as you read, make a distinction between the speaker's feelings and reactions and the overall meaning and purpose of a poem.

Go Online
Assessment
For: Self-test
Visit: www.PHSchool.com
Web Code: eta-6504

Go Online Assessment Students may use the **Self-test** to prepare for **Selection Test A** or **Selection Test B.**

Answers

1. Francesca provides direct characterization of Dante with the words "gracious, kind, and good."
2. **Trait Revealed:** timidity; emotional weakness and dependence. Another sample answer can be found on **Literary Analysis Graphic Organizer B,** p. 124 in ***Graphic Organizer Transparencies.***
3. (a) **Possible responses:** Minos, speaking about Virgil, warns Dante to "watch to whom you turn." Francesca says that Virgil knows that "the double grief of a lost bliss is to recall its happy hour in pain." Dante says that Virgil "reached over dexterously." (b) **Possible response:** The statements show that Virgil may know of sin himself, that he has experienced pain, and that he is skilled.
4. (a) Francesca alludes to Giovanni Malatesta, her husband, who killed her and Paolo for their betrayal. (b) Francesca's allusion increases the *Inferno's* realism by referring to a real, historical figure.
5. (a) Virgil adds the words "of Hell" to the hymn. (b) The allusion to the hymn emphasizes that Hell is a distortion of Heaven and that evil is a distortion of good.
6. When Dante the speaker loses consciousness, Dante the poet can skip over details of how his character gets from one stage of the journey to another. The poet can also change themes as he shows his character's evolution from pity to hardness in reaction to sinners.
7. (a) Dante the character is confused because he believes himself to be still at the bottom of Hell. (b) The reader needs the explanation because readers in Dante's time believed Earth to be stationary and at the center of the universe.
8. **Possible response:** Students may say that hope is necessary for happiness, because without hope people might see no reason to live. Without this reason, happiness is elusive. Others may say that those who are content in their lives do not think about hope.

EXTEND/ASSESS

Answers

❶ Vocabulary Lesson

Related Words: *awe*

1. amazing, inspiring awe; can be both positive and negative
2. filled with awe
3. restrained or subdued by awe
4. inspiring awe, extremely disagreeable; can be both positive and negative

Spelling Strategy

1. lovely
2. graceful
3. truly
4. translation

Vocabulary Builder: Matching

1. h
2. f
3. d
4. b
5. a
6. c
7. e
8. g

❷ Grammar and Style Lesson

1. had finished; past actions
2. had brought; past actions
3. had favored; past condition
4. had translated; past actions
5. had thought; past actions

Writing Application

Sample dialogue: Mark asked, "Had you known about Dante's life before you read the *Inferno?*" Lisa answered, "He had been active in Florentine life before he was exiled. I had read that in my book. Canto V had always been my favorite until I read Canto XXXIV."

WG **Writing and Grammar Platinum Level**

For support in teaching the Grammar and Style Lesson, use Chapter 22, Section 1.

Build Language Skills

❶ Vocabulary Lesson

Related Words: *awe*

Some words formed with the word *awe* have either positive or negative meanings, depending upon their context. *Awful,* for example, can mean either "bad" or "awe-inspiring." Define each of the following words, and determine which of them, if any, possess both positive and negative meanings.

1. awesome
2. awestruck
3. overawed
4. awfully

Spelling Strategy

For most words ending in *e*, make no change when adding a suffix beginning with a consonant (*care* + *-ful* = *careful*). Add the indicated suffix to each word below.

1. love + *-ly*
2. grace + *-ful*
3. true + *-ly*
4. translate + *-tion*

Vocabulary Builder: Synonyms

Review the vocabulary list on page 674. Then, complete the activity below by matching each of the words in the left column with the correct synonym in the right column.

1. grotesque
2. degree
3. anguish
4. tempest
5. perilous
6. awe
7. writhes
8. nimble

a. dangerous
b. storm
c. reverence
d. agony
e. twists
f. level
g. agile
h. distorted

❷ Grammar and Style Lesson

Past Perfect Verb Tense

The **past perfect verb tense** expresses actions that were completed before a specific moment in the past. Use the past perfect tense to show a connection between two past actions or conditions.

Past Actions: And when I had heard those world-offended lovers I bowed my head.

Past Condition: He had been beautiful until he turned on his Maker.

Practice Identify examples of the past perfect tense in each item below, and explain whether they connect past actions or past conditions.

1. We had finished reading the *Inferno* before we went on to the *Purgatorio*.
2. We were able to compare translations because our teacher had brought three different ones to class.
3. Previously, Martina had favored the Sayers translation.
4. Before we read it in English, I had translated some of the Italian text myself.
5. I had never thought I would love medieval literature until I read Dante.

Writing Application Write a dialogue in which two people discuss the *Inferno*. Use at least three examples of the past perfect tense.

WG *Prentice Hall Writing and Grammar Connection: Platinum Level, Chapter 22, Section 1*

Assessment Practice

Evaluate and Make Judgments **(For more practice, see *Test Preparation Workbook*, p. 31.)**

Explain that judgment is a conclusion reached after examining and evaluating facts. Standardized tests often require students to read a sample passage and make judgments about its characters. Use the following sample test item to help students.

The other is Dido; faithless to the ashes of Sichaeus, she killed herself for love.

In describing the lustful with those words from Canto V of the *Inferno* (lines 61–62), what judgment does Virgil make of them?

A They are worthy of sympathy.
B They must be condemned.
C They should be ignored.
D They should be admired.

Lead students to recognize that the correct answer is *B*. The words "faithless" and "killed herself" suggest Virgil's negative judgment. Choices *A*, *C*, and *D* do not fit the language of the excerpt.

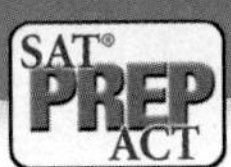

❸ Writing Lesson

Timed Writing: Response to Criticism

Dorothy Sayers, one of Dante's finest translators, wrote that Dante's depiction of Francesca balances good and evil with "a deadly accuracy." Sayers notes, "All the good is there; . . . but also all the evil; the easy yielding, the inability to say No, the intense self-pity." Write an essay responding to Sayers's criticism. ***(40 minutes)***

Prewriting *(10 minutes)* Brainstorm for responses to Sayers's statement by writing freely about these questions: Are good and evil balanced in Francesca? Does she yield easily? Is she self-pitying or merely human? Then, reread Canto V, gathering details to support your opinions.

Drafting *(20 minutes)* Quote Sayers's statement in your introduction. Then, assert your own opinion of Francesca. In your body paragraphs, elaborate on your opinion, using evidence from the poem. When you use quotations from the text, tie each one directly to the point you are making.

Model: Elaborating Using Supporting Quotations

Sayers pinpoints Dante's portrayal of Francesca as a sinner who feels sorry for herself. She has not accepted her guilt and wallows in "intense self-pity." This is shown in line 100 when Francesca blames her downfall on "Love, which permits no loved one not to love." She is saying she is a victim.

Quotations from the text are most effective when directly connected to the writer's point.

Revising *(10 minutes)* Review your essay, making sure that you have supported each point with quotations, examples, or reasons.

WG *Prentice Hall Writing and Grammar Connection: Platinum Level, Chapter 13, Section 3*

❹ Extend Your Learning

Listening and Speaking Develop and present a **movie proposal** for a screen adaptation of the *Inferno*. Use these tips to prepare:

- Reread the poem, taking notes about the setting, characters, and plot.
- Identify opportunities for special effects.
- Summarize the plot, emphasizing the thrills, drama, and adventure of the tale.

Deliver your pitch to classmates as they play the role of the producers you seek to convince.

Research and Technology With a small group, use print and electronic sources to research Dante's politics and the real-life characters who appear in the *Inferno*. Then, create a **biographical analysis chart** that reveals the connections between Dante's political and literary lives. **[Group Activity]**

For: An additional research activity
Visit: www.PHSchool.com
Web Code: etd-7503

Assessment Resources

The following resources can be used to assess students' knowledge and skills.

Unit 5 Resources
Selection Test A, pp. 79–81
Selection Test B, pp. 82–84

General Resources
Rubrics for Response to Literature, pp. 55–56

Go Online Assessment Students may use the **Self-test** to prepare for **Selection Test A** or **Selection Test B.**

❸ Writing Lesson

You may use this Writing Lesson as a timed-writing practice, or you may allow students to develop the response essay as a writing assignment over several days.

- To give students guidance in writing this essay, give them **Support for Writing**, p. 76 in ***Unit 5 Resources.***
- Tell students that a response essay is a written analysis of a specific viewpoint, in this case a literary criticism.
- Review the Writing Lesson model, and clarify how to elaborate through the use of supporting quotations. Then encourage students to use the Outline graphic organizer in ***Graphic Organizer Transparencies***, p. 279, to plan their essays.
- Use the Response to Literature rubrics in ***General Resources***, pp. 55–56, to evaluate students' work.

WG **Writing and Grammar Platinum Level**

For support in teaching the Writing Lesson, use Chapter 13, Section 3.

❹ Research and Technology

- In groups, have students divide sections of the *Inferno* to find and list real-life characters.
- Assign research by source, providing each group member with the character list. Review likely research sources with students. Stress the importance of evaluating research sources, particularly those online.
- The **Support for Extend Your Learning** page (***Unit 5 Resources***, p. 77) provides guided note-taking opportunities to help students complete the Extend Your Learning activities.

Go Online Research Have students type in the Web Code for another research activity.

Standard Course of Study

LT.5.01.3 Analyze literary devices and explain their effect on the work of world literature.

GU.6.01.2 Analyze author's use of language to demonstrate understanding of expression.

GU.6.01.3 Use recognition strategies to understand vocabulary and exact word choice.

Humanities

***Dante Explaining the* Divine Comedy**, 1465, by Domenico di Michelino

This depiction of Dante is part of a larger panel that appears in Santa Maria del Fiore (often called "The Duomo"), the cathedral of Florence, Italy. Michelino's larger painting shows Dante flanked by the architecture of Florence, as well as by the mountain of *Purgatorio* and the great pit of the *Inferno.*

Background

Dante's Language

Dante broke with tradition by writing the *Divine Comedy* in the Italian vernacular, or language of the people. By opting for clear, simple, nearly conversational language instead of Latin (the literary language of the day), Dante made his masterpiece accessible not only to the learned but also to anyone who read Italian.

Critical Viewing

Possible response: Dante appears to be displaying the content of the book to an audience. His serious expression and demonstrative gesture suggest that he is expounding on the content.

A Closer Look

The Art of Translation

When Dante started the *Divine Comedy,* did he write these lines?

Midway in our life's journey, I went astray
from the straight road and woke to find myself
alone in a dark wood.

Or did he write these lines?

Halfway along the road we have to go,
I found myself obscured in a great forest,
bewildered, and I knew I had lost the way.

Then again, perhaps he started out with these words:

Midway this way of life we're bound upon,
I woke to find myself in a dark wood,
Where the right road was wholly lost and gone.

Actually, Dante began his masterpiece with these lines:

Nel mezzo del cammin di nostra vita,
mi ritrovai per una selva oscura,
che la diritta via ere smarrita.

For those of us who do not read medieval Italian, translators are essential to our understanding of Dante. The three English versions shown above—by John Ciardi, C. H. Sisson, and Dorothy L. Sayers—are just a few of the many attempts to make Dante's personal adventure and his medieval worldview clear to modern readers.

▲ Critical Viewing
Which details in this painting of Dante explaining the *Divine Comedy* suggest that the poet is trying to educate or teach people? **[Analyze]**

> "Translation requires the skills of a writer who can make the work sing in the new language."

A translation is an interpretation of a work in literature. When we read Dante, the translator of his work serves as our own personal Virgil—our guide and interpreter. Whatever the text, a great translator conveys both the meaning and the musical sense of the original.

The Levels of Meaning A translator must be conscious of several levels of meaning—the literal, the idiomatic, and the symbolic.

- **Literal:** A literal translation is a word-for-word rendition of the original text. Usually, such translations are stiff and awkward; they do not fully capture the meaning or music of the original.
- **Idiomatic:** Each culture has distinct **idioms**—expressions that are unique to a particular language and cannot be understood literally. A translator must be aware of idiomatic meanings in both languages.

Enrichment

Translators

The Italian proverb *traduttore, traditore* ("A translator is a traitor.") suggests the treacherous task of accurately and artistically translating a literary work. Michael Palma, a translator of the *Inferno,* acknowledges the specific hurdles of Dante.

> The *Inferno* is a poem of stunning originality, complexity, subtlety, and power. It speaks to many different audiences on many different levels. Dante himself, in the dedicatory letter to Can Grande that formforms the preface to the *Paradiso,* identifies several levels of meaning in the *Comedy,* the literal, allegorical, moral, and anagogical, to which we might add the autobiographical, historical, political, mythical, philosophical, psychological, and so on. And all of these levels interact to generate further dimensions and possibilities in our reading of the poem. Given the inexhaustible richness of Dante's achievement, perhaps we should wonder not why there are so many versions available, but why there are not even more.

- **Symbolic:** Symbolic meanings involve the figures of speech, images, and ideas that an author may use to convey an artistic or a philosophical vision. For example, Dante's word *via* may be translated literally as "road." However, a translator may also try to suggest the symbolic meaning of Dante's faith in the road to Heaven.

Capturing the Music Every language has its unique sound, its particular beauties, and its quirks. Translation requires the skills of a writer who can make the work sing in the *new* language. Translation is an art of compromises, as every Dante translation attests. Some translators favor meaning and accuracy over music and style. Others blur meaning for poetic effect. Still others simply want to make a vital, readable modern English poem.

Each age needs its own Dante. Today, we can still admire the formal translation written by Henry Wadsworth Longfellow in the nineteenth century:

Midway upon the journey of our life,
I found myself within a forest dark,
For the straightforward pathway had been lost.

Yet we respond more intensely to the voices of our own time. Here is the compressed but fluid version of Robert Pinsky, former Poet Laureate of the United States:

Midway on our life's journey, I found myself
In dark woods, the right road lost.

As the centuries have passed, one of the continuing lessons of the *Commedia*, whether Dante intended it or not, is that every age needs not only great writers but also great translators.

Activity

Translating Your Own English

Translating Dante into English takes extraordinary artistry to make the language come alive for contemporary American readers. Yet Americans speak English using a variety of dialects, accents, and idioms that reflect ethnic, regional, cultural, and generational differences. Some Americans even speak more than one English—a regional or ethnic dialect with family or friends and a more formal English at school or work.

With a group, discuss your thoughts about the ways you communicate in English. Use these questions to guide your discussion:

- How is your way of speaking English distinctive? Give some examples of idioms or slang that you use, and then provide a translation.
- Do you have more than one way of speaking English? If so, give an example of how you would translate one style of English into another.

Choose a point person to share your thoughts with the class.

Background

Pinsky's Translation

Robert Pinsky began his translation of Dante's *Inferno* for a collaborative reading of the work held in May 1993. The reading included nineteen of America's most highly regarded poets. Once he began, Pinsky said, "It just gripped me, like a child with a new video game. I literally could not stop working on it."

Pinsky drew heavily on previous translations of the *Inferno* by Henry Wadsworth Longfellow (1865) and by Charles S. Singleton (1970). Pinsky sought to create a work that would sound more natural to contemporary English speakers. Pinsky draws on idiomatic English to capture the vitality and earthiness of the original for today's audiences.

Critical Thinking

1. Which of the five translations from the *Divine Comedy* do you prefer? Why? **[Make a Judgment]**
   Possible response: Robert Pinsky's translation may be the most appealing because it is simple, straightforward, and thus the easiest to understand.
2. Do you agree that each age needs its own translation of Dante? Explain. **[Assess]**
   Possible response: Yes; past translations may not correspond to or reflect changes in language and culture.

Activity

Discuss with students the inappropriate use of informal speech in situations that require formal speech, such as public speaking, job interviews, and interactions with elders and other authority figures. Ask volunteers to give examples of the context in which they have inappropriately used informal speech.

Then, suggest that members in each group take responsibility for collecting examples of dialects, accents, slang, or idioms used in conversational American English. Advise students to avoid examples of profanity and crude expressions that may be offensive. Emphasize the importance of attaching the context in which each example is used. Group members should then organize their information for presentation to the class.

Standard Course of Study

WL.1.03.9	Analyze effects of author's craft and style in reflection.
CT.4.02.3	Examine how elements such as irony and symbolism impact theme.
LT.5.01.5	Analyze archetypal characters, themes, and settings in world literature.

Prewriting

- To give students guidance in developing this assignment, give them the **Writing About Literature** support, pp. 85–86 in ***Unit 5 Resources.***
- Have students work in groups of four to identify selections in which a quest is a dominant theme. Then, have them review these selections.
- As students review the selections, have them keep in mind the questions in the Prewriting section. Point out that students need to select works that will provide sufficient material for their essays.
- Review the graphic organizer. Have students use the organizer or one that is similar as they review the selections.
- Remind students that they need to choose two selections as a basis for this essay.

Tips for Test Taking

A writing prompt on the SAT or ACT test may assess students' ability to write an analytical essay that evaluates literary themes, to state a point of view regarding the topic, and to support the point of view with evidence. When writing under timed circumstances, students will need to quickly clarify a point of view (the thesis statement) and the evidence that supports it. Because they will not be able to refer to a text, their evidence must be based on their own experiences, readings, or observations.

Evaluate Literary Themes

One of the most characteristic themes of the literature of the Middle Ages is the quest, or search. In a world filled with mysterious forces, characters embark on quests with goals such as the discovery of the Holy Grail or proof of true love. Heroes test their courage as they go beyond the apparent objects of their quests to discover insights about God, love, and loyalty. Far from being the inert, inactive era that people had long considered it to be, the medieval period was one of political, social, and religious change. Perhaps this is why the theme of the quest for meaning in an unstable world held such allure for writers of this period.

To evaluate the theme of the quest in medieval literature, complete the assignment described in the box at right.

Assignment: The Quest in Medieval Literature

Write an analytical essay that evaluates the theme of the quest in the literature of the Middle Ages, as revealed in the selections in this unit.

Criteria:

- Include a thesis statement that evaluates the theme of the quest in the Middle Ages.
- Evaluate this theme in each of the works you discuss by answering these questions: Does the theme create narrative interest? Does it have relevance for modern readers?
- Support your evaluations with detailed analyses of this theme in at least two of the selections.
- Approximate length: 700 words

Prewriting

Review the selections. Identify the selections in which a quest is a dominant theme. Then, describe the object of the quest. To narrow the focus of your essay, ask yourself questions such as the following:

- How do plot and characterization reveal the quest theme?
- In what ways does the quest theme reveal the values and concerns of writers of the Middle Ages?
- Does the quest make the story interesting, even gripping, or does it lead to a predictable or undramatic story?
- As it appears in the selection, does the quest theme shed light on life or people in general? Or is its relevance limited to the Middle Ages?

Find a focus for your essay by jotting down notes in a format similar to the example below.

Read to Write

As you reread the texts, ask yourself what the main character desires more than anything else. That desire prompts the character's search, or quest.

Model: Identifying Evidence of the Quest Theme

Selection	Object of Quest	Details	Quotes
"The Grail" from *Perceval*	Holy Grail; true faith	Perceval prays to God; help of fisherman	"'There's something I would ask of you, / some things I wanted to inquire, / some information I desire.'"

Choose selections. Reread your notes, and choose two selections that illuminate the theme of the quest or that might make an interesting thematic contrast.

Teaching Resources

The following resources can be used to extend or enrich the instruction for Writing About Literature.

Unit 5 Resources
Writing About Literature, pp. 85–86

General Resources
Response to Literature rubrics, pp. 55–56

Graphic Organizer Transparencies
Five-column Chart, p. 278

Drafting

Use a logical order. Follow an organization that makes sense. For instance, you might discuss one point of evaluation for both selections, and then move to the next point.

Present clear evaluations. For each selection you discuss, show how the quest theme adds to or detracts from the story's excitement. For instance, you might argue that the mysteries surrounding the quest in *Perceval* add interest. Also, discuss whether the quest theme has relevance for modern readers. For instance, you might argue that Dante's thirst for answers about life reflects a desire that everyone feels.

Provide specific support. For each evaluation you give, quote specific passages in support. It is not enough to say that *Perceval* is "slow-moving." To support such an evaluation, you must first quote a relevant passage and then explain why it slows the story down.

Write to Learn
Do not force the examples you have chosen to fit your thesis statement. Be willing to choose other examples or to revise your thesis statement if necessary.

Revising and Editing

Review content: Check the accuracy of details. Your responsibility to readers includes absolute accuracy of content. Check the examples you used in your paper to make sure they are accurate. Make sure that quotations are complete and accurately spelled and punctuated.

Review style: Vary sentence length. One way to make your writing livelier and more interesting is to vary the length of your sentences. Short sentences add emphasis. Longer sentences flow smoothly. Read your paper aloud and split or combine sentences as needed.

Write to Explain
Make sure that the arguments you make and the conclusions you draw are clear. Remember, readers can follow only what is on paper, not what is in your mind.

Model: Revising to Vary Sentence Length

As for most ordinary people of the Middle Ages, ^Faith in God animates ^the character ^Perceval's life and his journey. ~~In this way, Perceval as a character is like most people in the Middle Ages.~~ In ordinary speech, Perceval constantly refers to God. He says such phrases as "Oh God Almighty! It would seem, I'd find my mother, if she's living."

Publishing and Presenting

Oral presentation. Choose one of the works you analyzed in your essay, and read an excerpt to your classmates. Then, explain how the excerpt illuminates an aspect of the theme of the quest.

Writing and Grammar Connection: Platinum Level, Chapter 13

Differentiated Instruction
Solutions for All Learners

Support for Less Proficient Writers
Review with students how to use quotation marks when including examples from the text. Point out that students also need to cite the source in context or use parenthetical documentation to indicate the source of the material.

Support for English Learners
Explain to students the difference between direct quotations and paraphrasing and summarizing. Explain how to use and punctuate direct quotations. Then, show students how these types of specific support can be incorporated in the body of an essay.

Strategy for Advanced Writers
Have students focus on smoothly integrating their quotations and paraphrases into their essays. Point out that the support should not interrupt the flow of the essay. Have them check and revise their essays as necessary to create a smooth integration of the materials.

Drafting

- Remind students that readers can better understand the theme when it is tied to universal ideas or problems. Point out that if the writer of the essay does not clearly understand the examples, the reader will not understand them either.
- Tell students to use proper quotation format and citations when citing material from the text.

Revising and Editing

- Emphasize that quoted material must be quoted exactly. If quotation marks are used, the material should be taken word for word from the text. When quotation marks are not used, the material must be paraphrased (with appropriate parenthetical citation) or summarized.
- Have students return to their groups of four, where they will read their papers aloud. Ask group members to provide feedback about sentences that could be combined or revised for clarity.

Publishing and Presenting

- Have students practice reading their excerpts, adding expression to hold listeners' interest. Suggest that students record themselves reading to help them evaluate their delivery.
- Allow students to use note cards for their explanation of the theme of the quest.

Writing and Grammar Platinum Level
Students will find additional instruction on writing an analytical essay in Chapter 13.

Writing and Grammar Interactive Textbook CD-ROM
Students can use the following tools as they complete the analytical essay:

- Story Map Organizer
- Descriptive Word Bin

Six Traits Focus

✓	Ideas		Word Choice
✓	Organization	✓	Sentence Fluency
	Voice	✓	Conventions

Assessing the Essay

To evaluate students' analytical essays, use the Response to Literature rubrics in *General Resources,* pp. 55–56.

PRETEACH

Standard Course of Study

FA.3.01.2	Research and summarize printed data about a controversial issue.
FA.3.01.4	Compile response and research data to organize argument about controversial issues.
GU.6.01.6	Use correct format for writing.

 **From the Scholar's Desk**

Marilyn Stokstad

- Show students Segment 3 on Marilyn Stokstad on ***From the Author's Desk DVD.*** Discuss her research process, how she decides what she needs to include in her books, and how to describe art in words.

Writing Genres

Using the Form Point out to students that research writing is often incorporated into other types of writing. Point out these examples:

- Persuasive writing may include research to help support a point.
- Research may play an important part in a problem-and-solution speech.
- Newspaper writers often research an article for background on a story.

 **Online Essay Scorer**

A writing prompt for this mode of writing can be found on the ***PH Online Essay Scorer*** at PHSuccessNet.com.

Writing Workshop

Research: Research Paper

The world is full of fascinating questions. How did the ancient Egyptians embalm their dead? Why do different types of birds build different kinds of nests? Which were the most controversial presidential elections? How have the films of Steven Spielberg changed since *Jaws*? In preparing a **research paper,** a writer hunts for answers to questions like these—questions that inspire curiosity and motivate people to investigate a new field of knowledge. Follow the steps outlined in this workshop to write your own research paper.

Assignment Write a research paper investigating a question that interests you, presenting a viewpoint based on your research, and supporting that main idea with factual evidence.

What to Include Your research paper should feature the following elements:

- a clear thesis statement presenting a viewpoint about the topic
- factual information from a variety of sources
- a comparison of information, including a consideration of the reliability of the sources
- a consistent and effective organization
- a correctly formatted list of works consulted

To preview the criteria on which your research paper may be assessed, see the rubric on page 707.

Standard Course of Study

- Demonstrate comprehension of main idea and supporting details in answering research questions. (IR.2.01.4)
- Research and summarize printed data about a controversial issue. (FA.3.01.2)
- Edit for appropriate and correct mechanics. (GU.6.02.2)

Using the Form

You may use elements of research writing in these writing situations:

- statistical reports
- multimedia presentations
- annotated bibliographies
- travel brochures

To see how research information can be presented, read "The Art of Translation" on page 694.

Teaching Resources

The following resources can be used to enrich or extend the instruction for the Writing Workshop.

Unit 5 Resources
- **Writing Workshop: Research,** pp. 87–88

General Resources
- **Rubrics for Research: Research Report,** pp. 51–52

Graphic Organizer Transparencies
- **Rubric for Self-Assessment,** p.125
- **Web,** p. 287

From the Author's Desk DVD
- **Marilyn Stokstad,** Segments 3 and 4

Prewriting

Choosing Your Topic

Use one of these strategies to choose a topic suitable for a research paper:

- **List questions.** Using five or six sheets of paper, write a very broad heading at the top of each, such as *Animals, Computers, Movies, Television, History,* or *Sports.* Then, for five minutes per page, list any questions you have about that broad subject. If you run out of questions, move on to a new subject. After you have generated questions for all the headings, review your lists, and star the questions that interest you. Then, choose the question you would *most* like to investigate.
- **Create a web.** To help you generate ideas for possible topics, create a web like the one shown. Select a topic from the web.

Narrowing Your Topic

Consider whether your topic is narrow enough to develop fully in a short paper. If your topic can be divided into significant subheads, each with its own focus, it is probably too broad. To narrow your topic, use looping. Based on what you already know or have learned in preliminary research, write freely on your topic for two or three minutes. Read what you have written, and circle the most important or compelling idea. Then, write for a few minutes on that idea. Again, read what you have written, and circle the most important or interesting idea. Continue this process until you arrive at a topic that is narrow enough for your paper.

Gathering Information

Do the research. Look in the library for secondary sources such as books and encyclopedias. Use the Internet for secondary sources such as newspapers and magazines, and also for primary sources such as letters and interviews.

Primary sources: historical documents such as speeches, letters, Congressional bills, reports from the Census Bureau, books, or articles
Secondary sources: books, articles, and other materials written about your subject.

Consult a variety of sources—do not rely solely on Web pages or an encyclopedia. Use a minimum of five credible and varied sources.

Use notecards and source cards. On source cards, record the author, title, publisher, city, and publication date of each source you consult. Then, make individual notecards recording each relevant fact or opinion you find. Get the exact wording of any quotations you may want to use, right down to the punctuation. Link source cards to the notes you take by using key words, such as the author's name, to identify the source for each idea.

Tips for Using Rubrics

- Before students begin work on this assignment, have them preview the Rubric for Self-Assessment, p. 707, to know what is expected.
- Review the Assessment criteria in class. Before students use the Rubric for Self-Assessment, work with them to rate the student model by applying one or two criteria to it.
- If you wish to assess students' research papers with a 4-point, 5-point, or 6-point scoring rubric, see ***General Resources***, pp. 51–52.

Prewriting

- Explain to students that they will later refine their initial questions according to the results of their research.
- Remind students that if their topic is too narrow, they will have difficulty finding enough support, but if the topic is too broad, they may be unable to manage a vast array of sources.
- Make sure students understand the difference between and value of primary and secondary sources.
- Point out that some Internet sources are unreliable. Students should use only reliable sites, taking care to avoid personal sites and *.com* sources in favor of *.gov* or *.edu* sources.
- Remind students to write all copyright information as they do their research. Because Internet sources often disappear or change, students should print all documentation as they find it.
- Emphasize the importance of filling out note and source cards. Although some students may find this process tedious, tell them that by completing the cards now, they will save time and avoid frustration during drafting and revising.

Six Traits Focus

✓	Ideas		Word Choice
✓	Organization		Sentence Fluency
	Voice		Conventions

Writing and Grammar Platinum Level

Students will find additional instruction on prewriting for a research paper in Chapter 12, Section 2.

Writing and Grammar Interactive Textbook CD-ROM

Students can use the following tools as they complete their research papers:

- Note cards
- Topic Bank
- Transition Word Bin
- Unity and Coherence Revising Tool

Drafting

- Explain to students that a thesis statement must present an idea that can be debated; a thesis statement cannot be a list of facts about which there is nothing to argue for or against.
- Have students read the "Effective Organizations" chart. Tell students that their information may determine their organizational plan. For example, if a topic is likely to draw serious opposition, the writer may wish to draw conclusions after presenting information from sources. This plan will provide readers with the argument's reasoning before they can reject the conclusions.
- As students provide elaboration, they may have quotations from numerous experts about the same issue. Instruct students to choose only the quotations that are well written, concise, and truly support the thesis statement.
- Remind students to document sources as they write. Students who try to integrate sources after they have written a paper usually do so with great difficulty and provide sloppy documentation.

Six Traits Focus

✓	Ideas		Word Choice
✓	Organization		Sentence Fluency
	Voice		Conventions

WG Writing and Grammar Platinum Level

Students will find additional instruction on drafting a research paper in Chapter 12, Section 3.

Drafting

Shaping Your Writing

Create a thesis statement. After you have read a few sources, jot down a rough thesis statement—an idea or a viewpoint that your paper will develop. As you do more research, refine your rough thesis to reflect your increased knowledge. Present your thesis in your introductory paragraph, and use the statement to direct what you include in your paper.

Decide on an organizational plan. Think about whether you will present conclusions about your information at the start or build toward them throughout the paper. Use one of the plans shown here.

Effective Organizations

Introduction	Introduction
present thesis statement explain/give background for topic DRAW CONCLUSION	present thesis statement explain/give background for topic
Body	**Body**
PROVE CONCLUSION present/analyze/compare sources	present/analyze/compare sources LEAD TO CONCLUSION
Closing	**Closing**
summarize	DRAW CONCLUSION

Providing Elaboration

Choose and use your information well. After reading several sources, you will have a great deal of information. Select the elements that most effectively develop your thesis statement:

- **Details** Specific and unusual details make your research paper more compelling, grounding it in reality.
- **Facts and statistics** Much of what you will present will be objective, factual information or numerical data. Support your thesis well, but do not drown your reader in data. Always interpret your facts and statistics, adding perspective rather than presenting them raw.
- **Expert testimony** Informed opinions by experts on the topic are extremely important in guiding your reader through your information. Indicate the significance of each quotation you provide, as well as the conclusions that you draw from it.

Prepare to document your sources. As you draft your paper, underline information or quotations that you will need to document. At the end of each underlined passage, indicate in parentheses the author's last name. Later, you can go back and set up citations according to a standard format, such as MLA style.

Differentiated Instruction Solutions for All Learners

Strategy for English Learners

Encourage students to select topics that have ample material for research and that are written in language that is accessible to them. When students have compiled a list of topics, help them eliminate those topics that are too technical or too abstract for their language skills.

Strategy for Advanced Writers

Encourage students to gather at least ten sources. Challenge students to find three different perspectives on their research topic and to incorporate an evaluation of the positive and negative attributes of each of the perspectives. As they use sources that disagree with one another, remind students to state clearly the author's perspective, reasons why the author holds his or her opinion, and an evaluation of whether the student believes that the author is correct. Remind students to support their evaluations with appropriate source material.

From the Scholar's Desk
Marilyn Stokstad on Cutting Unnecessary Words

Marilyn Stokstad

In the Introduction to my book *Art History,* I ask the question "Why do we need art?" In one answer, under the heading "Art and the Search for Meaning," I compare a European chalice and an African bowl, two cups used to hold offerings in religious ceremonies. Art historians argue about the date of the cup and the authenticity of parts of its twelfth-century setting, but in this paragraph, I focus on the use and significance of the chalice.

> *"Writing is hard work; revising is fun."*
> — Marilyn Stokstad

Professional Model:

from *Art History*

~~Much of the~~ Works of art that move~~s~~ us most deeply today ~~was~~ often express ~~originally created as an expression of~~ a people's spiritual experience ~~and an object of devotion~~. Consider, for example, the Chalice of Abbot Suger (1137–1140). In twelfth-century France, Abbot Suger, head of the monastery dedicated to Saint Denis near Paris, found an ancient agate vase in the storage chests of the abbey. He ordered his goldsmiths to add a foot, a rim, and handles as well as semiprecious stones and medallions to the vase, turning an entirely secular piece—an object of prestige and delight—into a chalice to be used at the altar of the church ~~that was the birthplace of Gothic architecture.~~ Today, Suger's ~~chalic~~e no longer functions ~~in the liturgy of the Mass~~ in a church as a cup to hold the communion wine. It has ~~taken on~~ a new ~~secular life, enshrined~~ role as a precious work of art in ~~a museum~~ the National Gallery of Art in Washington, D.C. Here, instead of linking the ~~congregation~~ Christian community with God, now it links the modern viewer with ~~the past,~~ the Middle Ages ~~of some 850 years ago~~.

I revised the opening sentence to make it tighter and more direct.

I eliminated a repetitious phrase: "and an object of devotion."

The phrase "that was the birthplace of Gothic architecture" is unnecessary because Gothic architecture is a different subject.

I replaced "in the liturgy of the Mass" because I wanted to use simpler language so the reader would better understand my point.

Here I wanted to be specific. It's not just any museum.

From the Scholar's Desk
Marilyn Stokstad

- Show students Segment 4 on Marilyn Stokstad on ***From the Author's Desk DVD.*** Discuss how writing is important to the preservation of art and how writing can be an important tool for discovering knowledge.
- Point out that Stokstad eliminated unnecessary words and revised her text to make the meaning more specific and easier for her readers to understand. Urge students to keep their audience in mind as they revise and to eliminate any wording that confuses or obscures meaning.
- Review Stokstad's comments about her revision to her model from *Art History.* Ask students to explain how cutting unnecessary or unclear wording strengthened the writing.
- Note that Stokstad made five different revisions that did the following: tightened the writing, eliminated repetition, focused the subject, used simple language, and made a general example more specific. Have students review their drafts and revise them in these five ways.

Tips for Making Writing More Concise

Give students these suggestions for revising for conciseness:

1. Use a verb instead of "there is" or "there are." For example, *There are different ways that artists see their subjects* becomes *Artists see their subjects in different ways.*
2. Taking the example one step further, tell students to use single adverbs or adjectives rather than clauses or phrases. *In different ways* becomes *differently.*
3. Use the active voice whenever possible. *The portrait was painted by Pablo Picasso* becomes *Pablo Picasso painted the portrait.*
4. Avoid useless adverbs and adjectives, especially *very* and *many.*

Revising

- When students review their opening and closing paragraphs, have them write the answers to the questions listed on this page in the student book, citing examples from their paper that support their answers. If they cannot substantiate their answers with examples from the papers, they need to revise.
- Remind students that some sources are better than others are, and even respectable sources can contain bias. Tell students that identifying the presence of bias in an otherwise respectable source can add to the credibility of their papers and can strengthen their argument.
- Explain that writers are usually too familiar with the content and style of their papers to revise them effectively without input from others. Therefore, have each student trade papers with a partner for a peer review. Reviewers should check that ideas, sentences, and paragraphs flow smoothly and contain useful and logical transitions. If they do not, have reviewers circle problem areas and return papers to the writers to incorporate appropriate changes.

Six Traits Focus

✓	Ideas	✓	Word Choice
✓	Organization	✓	Sentence Fluency
	Voice		Conventions

Writing and Grammar Platinum Level

Students will find additional instruction on revising a research paper in Chapter 12, Section 4.

Writing Workshop

Revising

Revising Your Paragraphs

Improve your introduction and conclusion. Review your opening and closing paragraphs. Ask the following questions, and use the answers to revise your draft.

- Does your introduction grab your readers' attention by presenting the topic as interesting or important?
- Does the introduction include your thesis statement?
- Does your thesis statement direct the rest of the paper?
- Does your conclusion grow naturally from the material in the rest of the paper—and does it refer back to your thesis statement?
- Does the information in your conclusion support or contradict your introduction?
- Does your paper end in a memorable way?

Add comments about sources. Add information to note any special qualifications a source may have. If a source has a particular slant, include details to explain this bias or perspective. If a source is especially credible, explain why you consider it authoritative or trustworthy.

Model: Adding the Qualifications of a Source

Draft: Acccording to Ruth Kander, however, Schindler cared only about his own welfare.

Revision: However, Ruth Kander, *who knew Schindler personally,* has maintained that he cared only about his own welfare.

To read the complete student model, see page 704.

Remember your audience. Add information as needed for your audience's benefit. For example, if your audience is new to your subject, define any terms that may be unclear or too technical. Revise any diction, or word choice, that may be inappropriate for your readers.

Revising Sentences

Add transitions. A research paper is an extensive piece of writing. Transitions will help your paper hang together and keep the reader on track by signaling how one item relates to the next and how each sentence or paragraph follows from the previous one. Consider transitional words and phrases like *because, as a result, if, therefore, in addition, despite,* and *recently* to link your sentences.

Peer Review: Have a classmate read your draft to look for places where the connections need to be stronger or clearer. Add transitional words or phrases to clarify the flow of ideas.

Tips for Using Technology in Writing

Remind students that although they can find much information on the Internet, many sites are unreliable. Personal biases and inaccuracies often appear on Web sites. Consequently, students should use only reliable sites, particularly those from universities, libraries, government agencies, and well-known organizations. Individuals' personal Web sites should never be used in a research paper.

Developing Your Style

Quotations and Source Material

Introduce quotations. Every time you include a quotation in your research paper, tell your reader *who* is being quoted, *why* that source is being quoted, and *how* the quotation relates to the thesis of your paper. Here are some ways of making a smooth integration of quotations and other source material into your research paper:

Identify the expert: Professor Megan Byte, who has written extensively about computers, describes their evolution in this way: "Early computers . . . "

Make the quotation part of your own sentence: Reviewer Fred Filmbuff says that Steven Spielberg's films could be interpreted as a "search for . . . "

Avoid plagiarism. Whenever you use someone else's words, you must give credit to the original source. Failure to do so is known as *plagiarism,* a serious offense. Commonly known facts need not be credited within the body of the paper, but for lesser-known facts, quotations, and writers' opinions, always credit your sources. After checking your paper yourself, follow these steps:

1. Have a partner read your draft and star any passages for which the source of the information seems missing.
2. Supply additional citations where needed.
3. Reread your draft. Combine and condense information as necessary to avoid excessive or repetitious references.

Find It in Your Reading Read or review "The Art of Translation" on page 694.

1. Find one quotation in this essay.
2. Determine who is being quoted and what the point of the quotation is.
3. Also notice how the quotation is introduced and how it is followed up.

Apply It to Your Writing Review the draft of your research paper. Challenge yourself to improve the way you integrate quotations from your sources. Find a paragraph that includes a quotation, and follow these steps:

1. Read the paragraph without the quotation and then with it. Ask yourself what information the quotation adds.
2. Note how you identify the author of the quotation.
3. Analyze the paragraphs that lead up to the quotation. If you have not integrated the text properly, revise your writing.
4. Differentiate between short and long quotations.
   - Introduce short quotations with a comma, and run them in with your own sentences, setting them off with quotation marks.
   - Introduce quotations that are five lines or longer with a colon. Start a new line and indent the quotation. Do not use quotation marks.

WG *Prentice Hall Writing and Grammar Connection: Platinum Level, Chapter 28, Section 4*

Developing Your Style

- Tell students that poorly incorporated quotations can ruin a well-researched paper. Point out the second example of incorporating a quotation, and explain that although some quotations will be too long to include as part of a sentence, many other quotations will be short and can easily be blended into a sentence. In the second example, have students note how the writer seamlessly incorporated the quotation as the direct object in the sentence.
- Tell students that if they are in doubt about whether a fact is commonly known, it is better to cite the source than to risk plagiarism.
- After students complete **Find It in Your Reading,** elicit their responses, and write them on the board. **Ask** students for suggestions of other ways that the material could have been cited.
  Possible responses: The author could have used footnotes or parenthetical references to cite the quotations.
- When students have completed **Apply it to Your Writing,** suggest that they review their entire paper and note how they have integrated the quotations. If necessary, have them revise their writing to integrate the quotations more smoothly.

WG **Writing and Grammar Platinum Level**

Students will find additional instruction on quotations and source material in Chapter 28, Section 4.

Student Model

- Explain to students that the Student Model is a sample and that their research papers may be longer.
- **Ask** students to name the topic of Marcus's essay and the particular point for which his thesis statement argues.
  Answer: The topic is the film *Schindler's List.* The thesis statement argues that the film "manages to attain a true historical value" due to the ways in which the film was made.
- Point out that Marcus's inclusion of background information provides context about the film. **Ask** students why this context may be especially helpful for some readers.
  Possible response: The context will enable readers who have not seen the film to understand Marcus's paper.
- Marcus includes Spielberg's motives for making the movie. **Ask** students why this inclusion is important.
  Possible response: Knowing how important the film was to Spielberg helps readers understand why he wanted all details to be accurate.
- **Ask** students to comment on how Marcus's research paper is organized so far and why his thesis statement is effective.
  Possible response: Marcus has provided enough background for the reader to understand his thesis statement and to remain engaged as he develops his first point.

Writing Workshop

Student Model: Marcus Martin, Chilhowie, Virginia

"He Who Saves a Single Life Saves the World Entire"

Sixty years ago, the world experienced one of the darkest periods in human history—the Holocaust. Fifty years later, director Steven Spielberg achieved the goal of creating a biographical drama set during the Holocaust by making *Schindler's List.* Although the film is a Hollywood production about a horrific tragedy, *Schindler's List* manages to attain a true historical value because of Spielberg's realistic filming techniques, accuracy of setting, and honesty of characterization.

> Marcus identifies his thesis in his opening paragraph.

Winner of Best Film at the 1993 Academy Awards, *Schindler's List* tells the story of Oskar Schindler, a German entrepreneur who "saw his chance" during World War II and opened a factory employing Jews "at starvation wages" (Ebert). After defrauding the Nazis for months with a factory that never produced anything of use to the German army, Schindler became a hero. Outfoxing the evil prison commandant Amon Goeth and other Nazis through the creation of a list of "necessary" Jewish workers, Schindler and Jewish accountant Itzhak Stern were able to protect and save more than 1,100 workers ("Behind the Scenes").

> Next, Marcus provides general background on his subject.

Schindler's remarkable story first came to world attention through the publication of Thomas Keneally's book *Schindler's Ark* in 1982. Steven Spielberg immediately saw the movie potential in a book that "faithfully recounts episodes from the lives of its characters. . . . Poldek Pfefferberg really did escape a roundup by convincing Goeth he had been detailed to collect strewn suitcases; and, just as the book records, Oskar Schindler did play for the life of Goeth's maid Helen Hirsch in a single game of blackjack" ("Behind the Scenes"). According to Spielberg, he had been wanting to document the story of Schindler for public record for over ten years: "No one can do anything to fix the past — that's already happened. . . . But a picture like this can impact on us, delivering a mandate about what must never happen again" ("Behind the Scenes"). Spielberg's goal in creating the film was for viewers to "see the Holocaust in a vivid and terrible way," and to give the victims of the Holocaust a voice that they had been robbed of for so long (Ebert).

> Marcus provides a detailed explanation of Spielberg's motives for making the film.

Spielberg was able to accomplish his goal of not merely making a movie but also creating a timeless record of history through specific film-making choices. Spielberg explained that he filmed in black and white because most news film and photographs of the Holocaust are in black and white and that his vision of the Holocaust had "largely been stark black-and-white images" ("Behind the Scenes"). Shooting forty percent of the film with hand-held

> Marcus now addresses his first major point.

cameras also added to the realistic feel of the film. Through both of these filming techniques, Spielberg was able to achieve an effect more like a historical documentary than a Hollywood movie. "The black-and-white and hand-held camera gives the film a sort of *cinéma vérité*, documentary feel. It embodied the truth we were trying to explore and communicate[d] what happened. It made it seem real, somehow" ("Behind the Scenes").

In addition to using special filming techniques, Spielberg was attentive to historical accuracy in choosing the movie's locations and sets. A nationally diverse crew began filming on March 1, 1993, in Krakow, one of the few Polish cities to survive World War II. "One of the great historical cities of the world," Krakow offered streets and buildings that gave the movie an authentic setting ("Behind the Scenes"). Actual locations that were part of Schindler's life, such as his old factory and apartment, were used for filming as much as possible. After meeting resistance to shooting inside Auschwitz/Birkenau, Spielberg was able to film a scene of prisoners entering Auschwitz by shooting outside the camp's actual guardhouse (Royal). Because the forced-labor camp Plaszow was no longer intact, Spielberg had a replica of the camp constructed next to the site of the original camp. Using plans from the old camp, the production company built thirty-four barracks, seven watchtowers, and a replica of the villa that Goeth occupied during his rule of the camp. The company also "recreated the road into the camp that was paved with Jewish tombstones" ("Behind the Scenes"). The feeling of authenticity in the film comes from the fact that it was shot where events actually happened (Royal).

Points here are presented in the same sequence as Marcus presented them in his thesis statement.

Spielberg was also realistic in his presentation of Schindler's character and behavior of Schindler throughout the movie. Instead of depicting Schindler as a noble hero, the film shows him as vice-driven and self-indulgent. He is portrayed as a man who wanted only to maintain his own lavish lifestyle, yet he is shown as having a caring side as well (*Schindler's List*). Most accounts of the real-life Schindler resemble the character in the movie (Ebert). However, some critics argue that Spielberg did not go far enough in exploring Schindler's true motivation for saving the Jews. Those closest to him would say that greed was his chief motivation, but Schindler himself said there was simply no choice but to do what he could: "I felt that the Jews were being destroyed. I had to help them; there was no choice" (Roberts 91). However, Ruth Kander, a German who knew Schindler personally, has maintained that he cared only about his own good (Roberts 89–90). Whatever Schindler's motivation, it is a question that Spielberg does not probe deeply.

Sources are cited throughout the paper. At the end, Marcus properly identifies sources on his Works-Cited list, following MLA style. (See *Developing Your Style*, p. 703)

- **Ask** students why Marcus presents his supporting information in the same order as it appears in his thesis statement.
  Possible response: By maintaining the same order throughout his paper, Marcus keeps the organization clear and makes it easier for the reader to follow the paper's reasoning.
- Point out to students that carefully developing each point in the thesis statement will help to ensure that no extraneous information appears in the essay.
- Explain parenthetical documentation to students and the reasons it is necessary. Then explain that MLA stands for Modern Language Association. Point out that MLA style usually is used for papers dealing with language arts. Tell students that other styles of documentation, such as APA (American Psychological Association), are used in other disciplines.

Differentiated Instruction Solutions for All Learners

Strategy for Less Proficient Writers

To help students understand the organization of Marcus's paper, have them outline the student model using the Outline organizer in ***Graphic Organizer Transparencies,*** p. 279. Instruct students to include the introduction, the thesis statement, the main points of the essay, and the conclusion. Then, have students write one-sentence summaries for each paragraph in the model. Next, have each student trade his or her work with a partner and check each other's work for accuracy. After students have reviewed their partners' work, have them return the papers to their owners. Finally, invite volunteers to explain their papers' organization and how the organization helps to develop the thesis statement.

- Point out that through his organization of this paper and the evidence that he provided, Marcus has supported his thesis and has led the reader to the paper's conclusion.
- Marcus's paper ends with an effective quotation.
Ask: What effect does this quotation have on your impression of Marcus's paper?
Possible response: Since the quotation also functions as the paper's title, the quotation ties the paper together. The quotation also highlights the heroism of Schindler and makes Spielberg's movie—and Marcus's paper—seem like worthwhile endeavors. The quotation also is uplifting, powerful, and nearly impossible to dispute.
- Point out to students the importance of documenting all sources. Remind them of the consequences that your school or classroom guidelines have for plagiarism and that using someone's words without properly citing them is unethical because it is a form of theft.
- Remind students that to follow a style, they must pay attention not only to the material included but also to the indentations in each entry and all of the correct punctuation.

Writing Genres

Research Writing in the Workplace

Explain to students that research writing can be a part of many jobs. Writers conduct research for nonfiction writing and for newspaper articles. Other types of professionals may use it to argue for a policy change, as a basis for purchasing new equipment, or to explain the consequences of an event. Discuss other uses for research writing in the workplace. Then have students consider jobs that they have or with which they are familiar and discuss how research writing may be a part of these jobs.

Is *Schindler's List* an accurate account of a tragic period of a time, or is it just another of Spielberg's box-office hits? Through the use of black-and-white film and hand-held cameras, the accurate re-creation of settings, and the honest portrayal of Schindler, Spielberg was able to create a timeless film of historical value. Just as Schindler touched hundreds of lives with his actions, the cinematic retelling of his efforts continues to touch lives today.

Marcus clearly states his conclusions.

Perhaps the true effect of Schindler and the film is best shown in the scene in which Schindler parts from the people he saved. An inmate at Brinnlitz volunteered his gold dental bridgework to be made into a ring for Schindler when the Jews were liberated. Inside the ring was inscribed a verse from the book of Jewish laws, the Talmud, which read, "He who saves a single life saves the world entire" (*Schindler's List*).

The report ends with a powerful quotation.

Works Cited

Marcus provides a complete, detailed, and properly formatted list of all the works he has cited in his report.

Ebert, Roger. "Schindler's List." *Chicago Sun Times.* 15 Dec 1993. 17 Mar. 2003 <www.suntimes.com/ebert/ebert_reviews/1993/12/894536.html>

Leventhal, Robert S. "Romancing the Holocaust, or Hollywood and Horror: Steven Spielberg's *Schindler's List.*" 1995. The Institute for Advanced Technology in the Humanities, University of Virginia. 17 Mar. 2003 <http://www.iath.virginia.edu/holocaust/schinlist.html>

Marcus follows MLA style in documenting his sources.

Roberts, Jack. *The Importance of Oskar Schindler.* San Diego, CA: Lucent Books, 1996.

Royal, Susan. "*Schindler's List:* An Interview With Steven Spielberg." *Inside Film Magazine Online.* 6 Dec. 1999. 17 Mar. 2003 <http://insidefilm.com/spielberg.htm>

Schindler's List. Dir. Steven Spielberg. Perf. Ralph Fiennes, Ben Kingsley, and Liam Neeson. Universal, 1993.

"*Schindler's List*: Behind the Scenes." PBS Online. 17. Mar. 2003 <http:www.pbs.org/holocaust/schindler/behindthescenes.html>

Thompson, Bruce, ed. *Oskar Schindler.* San Diego, CA: Greenhaven Press, 2002

Editing and Proofreading

Review your research paper to eliminate errors in grammar, usage, punctuation, and spelling.

Focus on Accuracy: As you proofread your work, consult your notecards and source cards to make sure you have quoted material exactly. Confirm the spelling of names, and check all dates and statistics that you include.

Publishing and Presenting

Consider one of the following ways to share your writing.

Create a works-cited list. Your research paper should end with a works-cited list that provides readers with full bibliographic information on each source you cite. Standards for documentation are set by several organizations, such as MLA and APA. Following the format your teacher prefers, check that each entry is complete and properly punctuated. (For more information, see Citing Sources, pages R27–R29.)

Submit your paper to a magazine or newspaper. Select a magazine that publishes student writing or that specializes in the topic you wrote about. Submit your paper for possible publication.

Reflecting on Your Writing

Writer's Journal Jot down your thoughts on the experience of writing a research paper. Begin by answering these questions:

- What have you learned about the process of doing research?
- What new areas of interest did you uncover as you wrote your paper?

 *Prentice Hall Writing and Grammar Connection: Platinum Level, Chapter 12*

Rubric for Self-Assessment

Evaluate your research paper *using the following criteria and rating scale, or, with your classmates, determine your own reasonable evaluation criteria.*

NC Criteria	Rating Scale (not very – very)
Focus: How clear and accurate is your thesis statement?	1 2 3 4 5
Organization: How consistent and effective is the organization?	1 2 3 4 5
Support/Elaboration: How well do you support your thesis with factual information from a variety of sources?	1 2 3 4 5
Style: How well do you consider and explain the reliability of your sources?	1 2 3 4 5
Conventions: According to an accepted format, how complete and accurate are your citations?	1 2 3 4 5

Tips for Test Taking

Tell students that some of the same skills that they use to research and draft a research paper are necessary to respond successfully to writing prompts on standardized tests. The same type of planning required to write a research paper, for instance, is critical for insuring an organized and well-written essay on a standardized test. Therefore, suggest that students spend a quarter of their time prewriting, half their time drafting, and the remaining quarter of their time revising and editing. Encourage students to apply the skills that they learned in this writing workshop, such as using a web to quickly generate ideas in the prewriting stage or an organizational chart to decide how to present information. Also, tell students that writing a brief outline will help keep them focused during the drafting stage, as they formulate an introduction and conclusion and use details to elaborate in the body of their essays.

Editing and Proofreading

- Remind students that they cannot rely on a spelling and grammar checker to find their errors. They must proofread carefully.
- Point out to students that they must be sure that they cited their sources and copied quotations accurately. Failure to do so will destroy the credibility of their papers.

Six Traits Focus

	Ideas		Word Choice
	Organization		Sentence Fluency
	Voice	✓	Conventions

ASSESS

Publishing and Presenting

- Tell students to list their sources alphabetically on note cards. Students can use this information as they type their works-cited list.
- Have students check the library to learn what magazines publish student writing. If students choose to submit their papers for publication, suggest that they write cover letters to accompany the submissions.
- Remind students to review the magazine's guidelines for submission and to follow those guidelines carefully.

Reflecting on Your Writing

- Suggest that students reflect on what they could do differently to make the task easier the next time they write a research paper. Have students share these ideas with the class.
- Review the assessment criteria with students.
- Place the Rubric for Self-Assessment transparency on an overhead projector. Then, have students assess their papers using the rubric. When students have finished, refer to the overhead transparency as students discuss how they applied the rubrics to their papers.

Writing and Grammar Platinum Level

Students will find additional guidance for editing and proofreading and publishing and presenting a research paper in Chapter 12, Sections 5 and 6.

Standard Course of Study

WL.1.03.4	Demonstrate comprehension of main idea and supporting details in personal reflection.
FA.3.04.6	Make inferences and draw conclusions based on argumentative text.
LT.5.03.8	Make connections between works, self and related topics in world literature.

Know Your Terms: Analyzing

Explain that the terms listed under Terms to Learn will be used in standardized-test-taking situations when students are asked to recall information from a reading passage.

Terms to Learn

- Review *categorize.* Tell students that a category is a division of a large group. All members of a category have characteristics in common. When students categorize items, encourage them to ask themselves, "What qualities do these things have in common?" or "How is this idea like that group of ideas?" The reading passage on which students base their categories should provide enough details for them to see the similarities among the members of each category.
- Review *differentiate.* Emphasize that differentiation is a process of dividing or finding differences among two or more items or ideas. When students are asked to differentiate, they are being asked to find the dissimilarities of items or ideas or how each item or idea is unique.

Vocabulary Workshop

High-Frequency Academic Words

High-frequency academic words are words that appear often in textbooks and on standardized tests. Though you may already know the meaning of many of these words, they usually have a more specific meaning when they are used in textbooks and on tests.

Know Your Terms: Analyzing

Each of the words listed is a verb that tells you to break down information and look at the parts of a topic. The words indicate the specific kinds of details and information you should include in your answer.

Standard Course of Study

- Demonstrate comprehension of main idea and supporting details in personal reflection. (WL.1.03.4)
- Make connections between works, self and related topics in world literature. (LT.5.03.8)

Terms to Learn

Categorize Identify groups and explain the shared traits.

Sample test item: ***Categorize*** the symbols in the poem.

Differentiate Identify and explain the qualities that distinguish two items or ideas.

Sample test item: ***Differentiate*** between symbol and archetype.

Practice

Directions: *Read the passage, and then answer questions 1– 4.*

Every language has its unique sound, its particular beauties, and its quirks. Translation requires the skills of a writer who can make the work sing in the *new* language. Translation is an art of compromises, as every Dante translation attests. Some translators favor meaning and accuracy over music and style. Others blur meaning for poetic effect. Still others simply want to make a vital, readable modern English poem.

Each age needs its own Dante. Today, we can still admire the formal translation written by Henry Wadsworth Longfellow in the nineteenth century:

Midway upon the journey of our life
I found myself within a forest dark,
For the straightforward pathway had been lost.

Yet, we respond more intensely to the voices of our own time. Here is the compressed but fluid version of Robert Pinsky, former Poet Laureate of the United States:

Midway on our life's journey, I found myself
In dark woods, the right road lost.

1. *Differentiate* between the translations by Longfellow and Pinsky.
2. *Differentiate* between an original work and a translation.
3. *Categorize* the different types of translations described in this essay.
4. Using information from this passage, *categorize* the skills of a translator.

ASSESS

Answers

1. Pinsky's translation is more direct and shorter than Longfellow's translation. For example, Pinsky shortens "our life's journey" to "our journey," and he eliminates the passive voice in Longfellow's third line to "the right road lost."
2. An original work reflects exactly what the author wants to say. A translation reflects the translator's view of the literature, which may not exactly match the author's meaning.
3. The types of translations in this essay include literal, poetic, prose, and readable.
4. The skills of a translator include language skills, poetic skills, grammar skills, and a sense of sound.

Answers continued

Go Online Vocabulary **For:** An Interactive Crossword Puzzle
Visit: www.PHSchool.com
Web Code: etj-5501

This crossword puzzle contains vocabulary that reflects the concepts in Unit 5. After students have completed Unit 5, give students the Web Code and have them complete the crossword puzzle.

Assessment Workshop

Critical Reading: Comparing and Contrasting

In the reading sections of some tests, you may be required to make comparisons and contrasts within a passage or between passages. The following strategies will help you answer such test questions:

- Identify similarities and differences in the passages.
- Demonstrate and summarize likenesses and differences in a few words.

Standard Course of Study

- IR.2.01.5
- CT.4.03.2
- CT.4.03.3

Practice

Directions: *Read the passages, and then choose the letter of the best answer to the questions that follow.*

Passage 1: The chivalrous ideal of courtly love grew from the poems of Ovid and the songs of the troubadours. Courtly love, which thrived mostly in England and France during the Middle Ages, required that a man fall in love with a highborn but unavailable woman.

Passage 2: In contemporary society, songs, stories, and poems celebrate the concept of ideal love. Two people meet, fall in love, marry, and their love grows ever stronger. The fact that many contemporary people marry later in life may testify to the difficulty of attaining this ideal.

1. What main topic is addressed by both of these passages?

- **A** the strength of marriage
- **B** stories and poems of love
- **C** contemporary society
- **D** ideals of love

Directions: *Read the passages, and then choose the letter of the best answer to the questions that follow.*

Passage 1: Is that small amphibian you see resting on a lily pad a frog or a toad? Take a good look at its skin. Frogs have smooth, wet skin. Look inside the amphibian's mouth. Frogs have tiny teeth in their upper and lower jaws. They also have long hind legs, so they can jump quite a distance. Frogs lay eggs in clumps.

Passage 2: It's easy to distinguish toads from frogs. If you spy a small, disgruntled amphibian with warty, dry skin, it can only be a toad. Toads have stubby back legs—they can't jump; they hop. Can you look in the animal's mouth? Toads have no teeth at all. Toads lay their eggs in long strings.

1. What is the most obvious difference between frogs and toads?

- **A** their eggs
- **B** their teeth
- **C** their skin
- **D** none of the above

2. In what way are frogs and toads identical?

- **A** They are green.
- **B** They are amphibians.
- **C** They like to jump.
- **D** They have stubby legs.

Test-Taking Strategies

- If topics, themes, and other elements are similar, identify contrasting details.

Standard Course of Study

IR.2.01.5	Summarize key events and/or points from research text.
CT.4.03.2	Analyze how writers choose and incorporate significant, supporting details.
CT.4.03.3	Analyze how writers relate the organization to the ideas.

Critical Reading

- Correctly comparing or contrasting two or more things depends greatly on paying attention to the details about those things in a reading passage. Emphasize to students that they must read carefully when asked to compare or contrast.
- Remind students that they can never assume that two or more things are similar or different. Students must find evidence for similarities or differences in the reading passage.
- After students have read the Practice passages and have answered the questions, point out that in question 1 following the first pair of passages, although A, B, and C appear in either Passage 1 or Passage 2, D is the only answer that appears in both passages.
- Point out that question 1 following the second pair of passages asks for the most *obvious* difference. Although answers A, B, and C are all differences, C, the skin, is more obvious than A, teeth, which may be difficult to see, or B, eggs, which may be difficult to find or to observe.
- Point out that in question 2, B is the only way that frogs and toads are identical.

ASSESS

Answers

1. D
2. C
3. B

Tips for Test Taking

- When students are asked to differentiate on a standardized test, tell them that they have to distinguish what makes an idea or item different from another. Remind them that they can look for transitions or key words and phrases that signal differences. *However, but, unlike, on the other hand, different,* and *in contrast* are words that signal differences.
- Remind students that categorizing is the opposite; they need to look for similarities rather than differences. Some key words and phrases that indicate similarities are *like, in the same way, similarly, along the same lines,* and *as.*

Standard Course of Study

WL.1.02.5 Demonstrate an understanding of media's impact on analyses and personal reflection.

IR.2.03.1 Access cultural information from media sources.

CT.4.05.7 Identify and analyze influences, contexts, or biases in critical text.

Analyze Explicit Influence

- Explain to students that editorials are explicit statements of a journalist's views and contain opinions, not facts or unbiased news.
- Explain to students that debate forums are similar to friends talking about an issue. Each member gives his or her own opinion and tries to persuade the others in the group.

Analyze Implicit Influence

- Point out that news editors decide which stories are run and which are not. **Ask** students whether a news editor might be encouraged to drop or bury a story regarding an important advertiser or politician.
 Possible response: An ethical news editor would not be affected by political or economic pressure.
- Point out to students that the questions journalists ask leaders can shape the public image of that leader. If the leader is asked only certain questions, he or she may not have the opportunity to address more important issues in the media.
- Have students complete the Activity, using the chart to analyze media coverage. Then, lead students in a discussion about what they have discovered by analyzing the news story throughout the week.

Assess the Activity

To evaluate students' analyses, use the Listening: Analyzing a Media Presentation rubric, p. 85 in *General Resources.*

Analyzing the Impact of Media

The influence of the media on the democratic process is a topic of current and vigorous debate. As a future voter, you need to develop critical listening and viewing skills in order to **analyze the impact of media** on the public. The strategies described below will help you understand some aspects of media influence.

Standard Course of Study
- Demonstrate an understanding of media's impact. (WL.1.02.5)
- Access cultural information from media sources. (IR.2.03.1)

Analyze Explicit Influence

News commentators and various "experts" seek to affect the political process with direct statements of opinion. Familiarize yourself with the most common opinion forums.

- **Identify editorials.** Be aware that any printed or televised feature billed as an "editorial" or as "commentary" will present a persuasive case for one side of an issue. In addition, news shows may host discussions in which the participants express opinions. Learn to recognize such segments by listening for words such as *views, thoughts,* or *comments.* Consider whether participants express multiple perspectives on an issue.
- **Recognize opinion forums.** Debate forums in which journalists express opposing views offer you an opportunity to hear several opinions. Note, however, that each speaker is using persuasive techniques to influence you to share his or her views.

News Story:__________
Dates Followed:__________
Program 1:__________

Format: Editorial / News Hour / Opinion Forum/ Other__________
Placement: Main Story / Lead Story / Close / Other__________
Issues Addressed __________
Key Phrases Used __________
Images Used__________
Direct Influence? Y/N
Views stated__________
Support offered__________
Indirect Influence? Y/N
Views implied__________
Ways in which views are implied:__________
 Loaded language__________
 Provocative images__________
 Story placement__________
 Choice of questions__________

Analyze Implicit Influence

Media makers also exert indirect influence on public opinion. Learn to identify these forms of indirect influence:

- **Reporting priorities** Media makers exert influence through the stories they choose to report and the sequence in which they present the stories. For example, the lead story on a television news show usually attracts the largest audience—and so may distract public attention from stories run later in the show. Consider whether the choice of lead story reflects a true sense of priorities.
- **Images of leaders** When the media show politicians or CEOs appearing strong, the media transmit a positive message. If these people look tired or distracted, the media telegraph a lack of confidence. Consider the influence such images may have on public perceptions of leaders.
- **Shaping attitudes** As journalists conduct interviews, the questions they ask determine the information readers or viewers receive. Consider whether an interviewer's questions will uncover a complete picture or whether they fail to probe important issues.

Activity *View and Analyze the Media* For at least one week, analyze the coverage of an important news story in different media outlets. Use the chart shown to analyze the coverage of the story each day.

Differentiated Instruction
Solutions for All Learners

Strategy for Less Proficient Readers
Provide students with background about a national issue, and then show them videotaped commentary on the issue. Stop the tape during the speaker's opening remarks and point out any use of opinion. Show the remainder of the tape, and have students point out additional uses of opinion.

Strategy for English Learners
Provide students with short news articles and editorials about a local or national issue. Have each student compare the two texts and underline words in the editorial that express an opinion.

Enrichment for Gifted/Talented Students
Have each student select a local issue and write a commentary about it. Students must clearly indicate that their work presents opinions they have formed while reading about the issue. Then, have them practice the commentary and present it to the class.

Suggestions for Further Reading

Featured Titles:

The Divine Comedy: Paradiso

Dante Alighieri, *translated by Mark Musa, Penguin Classic, 1986*

Epic The *Paradiso* is the last of the three volumes that form *The Divine Comedy,* Dante's allegory of his journey through the afterlife. In the *Inferno,* Dante travels through Hell under the guidance of the Roman poet Virgil. In the *Purgatorio,* Dante and Virgil ascend the Mount of Purgatory. At the mountain's summit, Virgil departs, and Beatrice, a woman Dante had loved before her death, becomes his guide. The *Paradiso* begins as Dante soars into Heaven with Beatrice. Like Hell and Purgatory, Dante's Heaven has its own geography and order. The lowest level is the Moon, followed by Mercury, Venus, the Sun, Mars, Jupiter, Saturn, the Stars, and the *Primum Mobile*—the source of all time and motion. The highest level is the Empyrean, the dwelling place of God.

Egil's Saga

Snorri Sturluson, *translated by Hermann Pálsson and Paul Edwards, Penguin Classic, 1977*

Epic Composed in the thirteenth century by a master storyteller, this tale is set in tenth-century Iceland, Norway, and England. Egil, the hero of the book, is a formidable man, even by the standards of his dangerous Viking world. A brooding outsider, he has the courage to defy kings and to battle with the crazed warriors known as berserkers. Yet behind his impressive appearance is an equally impressive mind. Egil is loyal and intelligent, a poet who can lament the death of his son in eloquent verse. When this fierce and complex man dies shortly before Iceland is converted to Christianity, his death seems to mark the passing of an era.

Works Presented in Unit Five:

If sampling a portion of the following texts has built your interest, treat yourself to the full works.

The Nibelungenlied

Anonymous, *translated by A. T. Hatto, Penguin Classic, 1965*

The Song of Roland

Anonymous, *translated by Glyn S. Burgess, Penguin Classic, 1990*

Related British Literature:

The Canterbury Tales

Geoffrey Chaucer, *translated by Nevill Coghill, Penguin Classic, 2003*

In this array of storytellers and their rhymed stories, a great poet portrays the many-sided life of medieval England.

Related American Literature:

A Connecticut Yankee in King Arthur's Court

Mark Twain, *Signet Classic, 1963*

Making a fictional journey backward in time, America's greatest humorist casts a satirical but affectionate eye on the doings of King Arthur's court.

***Many of these titles are available in the* Prentice Hall/Penguin Literature Library.**
Consult your teacher before choosing one.

Planning Students' Further Reading

Discussions of literature can raise sensitive and often controversial issues. Before you recommend further reading to your students, consider the values and sensitivities of your community as well as the age, ability, and sophistication of your students. It is also good policy to preview literature before you recommend it to students. The notes below offer some guidance on specific titles.

The Divine Comedy by Dante Alighieri

On his visionary pilgrimage, Dante repeats an anti-Semitic belief, common in his day, that the Jews were responsible for the crucifixion of Jesus. In addition, there is a mention of the rape of the Sabine women, as well as references to suicide. To prepare students to read Dante's epic, discuss the medieval Christian traditions in which it is rooted.

Lexile: NP

Egil's Saga by Snorri Sturluson

Because this Norse tale grows out of a male-oriented, warrior culture, there are frequent depictions of violence and drunkenness, allusions to slavery and the mistreatment of women, and, in one instance, frank and direct language regarding one character's diminished sexual powers. To prepare students, discuss the values of warrior cultures.

Lexile: Appropriate for high school students

The Nibelungenlied

This epic includes descriptions of the hero Siegfriend's physical coercion and sexual conquest of Brunhild and references to lovemaking, couched in mild, non-explicit language. Kriemhild's ultimate revenge for Siegfried's death leads to numerous bloody acts.

Lexile: Appropriate for high school students

The Song of Roland

This epic poem includes scenes of bloody violence and death. In addition, the poem depicts non-Christians negatively. To prepare students, discuss with them the worldview of medieval Europe.

Lexile: NP

The Canterbury Tales by Geoffrey Chaucer

The tales contain ribald remarks, adultery, rape, and other sexual content; crude humor; gender bias; anti-Semitism and other ethnic slurs; clergy who break their vows; and other bad behavior, often for purposes of satire.

Lexile: Appropriate for high school students

A Connecticut Yankee in King Arthur's Court by Mark Twain

Twain's novel contains strong criticism of both organized religion in general and, specifically, the Roman Catholic Church. Some of his humorous descriptions of the Church's positions and customs might be considered sacrilegious. Some readers may feel that Twain's depiction of religion lacks dignity and open-mindedness. Others will feel that Twain's perspective as a rationalist is honestly presented and carefully justified.

Lexile: 1080L

RESOURCES

Reading and Vocabulary Handbook

Literary Handbook

Writing Handbook

Communications Handbook

Indexes

INDEX OF AUTHORS AND TITLES

Note: Nonfiction selections and informational text appear in red. Page numbers in *italic text* refer to background or biographical information.

L

M

N

O

P

Q

R

S

T

V

W

Y

Z

INDEX OF SKILLS

Note: Page numbers in **boldface** refer to pages where terms are defined.

Literary Analysis

Reading Strategies

Vocabulary

Grammar and Style

Critical Reading

Critical Viewing

Writing

Timed Writing Applications

Writing Strategies

Listening and Speaking

Research and Technology

INDEX OF FEATURES

Note: Page numbers in **boldface** refer to pages where terms are defined.

ACKNOWLEDGMENTS

American University in Cairo Press."Haiku: "Clouds come from time to time...," and "The sun's way...," two haikus by Matsuo Basho from *An Introduction to Haiku* by Harold G. Henderson, copyright © 1958 by Harold G. Henderson. Used by permission of Doubleday, a division of Random House, Inc.

Dutton Signet, a division of Penguin Group (USA), Inc. "A Doll House," from *The Complete Major Prose Plays of Henrik Ibsen* by Henrik Ibsen, translated by Rolf Fjelde, copyright © 1965, 1970, 1978 by Rolf Fjelde. Used by permission of Dutton Signet, a division of Penguin Group (USA), Inc.

Everyman's Library "The Lay of the Werewolf," (originally titled "VIII: The Lay of the Werewolf"), by Marie de France, translated by Eugene Mason from *Lays of Marie de France and Other French Legends*.

Farrar, Straus & Giroux, Inc. "When in early summer," by Nelly Sachs translated by Ruth and Matthew Mead from The Seeker and Other Poems. Copyright © 1970 by Farrar, Straus & Giroux, Inc. "Freedom to Breathe," by Alexander Solzhenitsyn translated by Michael Glenny from Alexander Solzhenitsyn: Stories and Prose Poems. Translation copyright © 1970, 1971 by Michael Glenny. "The Grownup," by Ranier Maria Rilke, translated by Randall Jarrell from *An Anthology of German Poetry from Hoderine to Rilke in English Translation*. "Comrades" from *Jump and Other Stories* by Nadine Gordimer. Copyright © 1991 by Felix Licensing B.V. All rights reserved. "from Annie John: from A Walk to the Jetty," from *Annie John* by Jamaica Kincaid. © 1985 by Jamaica Kincaid. "Also All" and "Assembly Line" by Shu Ting, translated by Donald Finkel and Jinsheng Yi. "All" by Bei Dao, translated by Donald Finkel and Xueliang Chen from *A Splintered Mirror, Chinese Poetry from the Democracy*. Translation copyright © 1991 by Donald Finkel. Excerpt from Nobel Lecture by Alexander Solzhenitsyn, translated by F.D. Reeve. Copyright © 1972 by the Nobel Foundation. Translation copyright © 1972 by Farrar, Straus & Giroux. "The Bracelet" from *The Collected Stories of Colette* by Colette. Translation copyright © 1957, 1966, 1983 by Farrar, Straus & Giroux, Inc. "from The Expiation: Russia 1812," from Imitations translated by Robert Lowell. Copyright © 1958, 1959, 1960, 1961 by Robert Lowell.

The Estate of Angel Flores c/o The Permissions Company "Ophelia," translated by Daisy Alden, from Angel Flores, ed., *An Anthology of French Poetry from Nerval to Valery in English Translation with French* Originals (New York: Anchor Books, 1958). Copyright © 1958 and renewed 1986 by Angel Flores. Reprinted with permission of the Estate of Angel Flores, c/o The Permissions Company, High Bridge, New Jersey.

David R. Godine, Publisher, Inc. "The Albatross," from *Les Fleurs Du Mal* by Charles Baudelaire, translated from the French by Richard Howard, illustrations by Michael Mazur. Copyright © 1982 by Charles Baudelaire. Reprinted by permission of David R. Godine, Publisher, Inc.

Grove/Atlantic, Inc. "I Built My House Near Where Others Dwell," by T'ao Ch'ien, translated by William Acker from *Anthology of Chinese Literature: From early times to the fourteenth century.* Copyright © 1965 by Grove Press, Inc. All rights reserved. Used by permission of Grove/Atlantic, Inc.

Harcourt, Inc. "Invitation to the Voyage," (originally titled "Charles Baudelaire: L'Invitation au Voyage"), from *Things of this World*, English translation, copyright © 1956 and renewed 1984 by Richard Wilbur. "The End and the Beginning," from *View with a Grain of Sand*, copyright © 1993 by Wislawa Szymborska, English translation by Stanislaw Baranczak and Clare Cavanagh, copyright © 1995 by Harcourt, Inc. This material may not be reproduced in any form or by any means without prior written permission of the publisher. Reprinted by permission of the publisher.

HarperCollins Publishers, Ltd. "The Handsomest Drowned Man in the World," from *Leaf Storm and Other Stories* by Gabriel Garcia Marquez. Copyright © 1971 by Gabriel Garcia Marquez. "A Song on the End of the World," from *The Collected Poems, 1931-1987* by Czeslaw Milosz and translated by Robert Hass. Copyright © 1988 by Czeslaw Milosz Royalties, Inc. Reprinted by permission of HarperCollins Publishers, Inc. "From The Gulistan: From The Matter of Kings," by Sa´di, translated by Edward Rehatsek from *The Gulistan, or Rose Garden, of Sa´di.* Reprinted by permission of HarperCollins Publishers.

Hill and Wang, an imprint of Farrar, Straus & Giroux, Inc. From *Night* by Elie Wiesel translated by Stella Rodway. Copyright © 1960 by MacGibbon & Kee; originally published in French by Les Eiditions de Minuit, copyright © 1958.

Hispanic Society of America "The Guitar," by Federico Garica Lorca from Translations from Hispanic Poets. Copyright © 1938 by The Hispanic Society of America. Reprinted with the permission of The Hispanic Society of America.

Barbara Hogenson Agency, Inc. "The Tiger Who Would Be King," by James Thurber from *Further Fables for Our Time*. Copyright © 1956 by James Thurber. Copyright © renewed 1984 by Rosemary A. Thurber.

Houghton Mifflin Company "Sent to Li Po as a Gift," by Tu Fu, translated and edited by Amy Lowell and Florence Ayscough from *Fir-Flower Tablets, Poems translated from the Chinese.* Copyright © 1921, copyright renewed 1949 by Ada D. Russell. Reprinted by permission of Houghton Mifflin Co. All rights reserved.

Indiana University Press "from Metamorphoses: The Story of Daedalus and Icarus," (originally titled "from Book 8: The Story of Daedalus and Icarus") by Ovid from *Ovid: Metamorphoses*, translated by Rolfe Humphries. Copyright © 1955 by Indiana University Press. Reprinted by permission of Indiana University Press.

International African Institute "African Proverbs: Liberia: The Jabo: "The one who listens . . ."," "Children are the wisdom . . ."," "Daring talk . . ."," "One who cannot pick up an ant . . ."," "The butterfly that flies among . . ."," "A man's ways are good . . ."," from *Jabo Proverbs from Liberia: Maxims in the Life of Native Tribe*. Published for the International Institute of African Languages & Cultures by Oxford University Press, London: Humphrey Milford, 1936.

The Estate of Alta Jablow "African Proverbs: Nigeria: The Yoruba: "One does not set. . ."," from *Yes and No: The Intimate Folklore of Africa: Dilemma Tales, Proverbs and Stories of Love, and Adult Riddles* by Alta Jablow. Copyright © 1961 by Alta Jablow.

The Jewish Publication Society "from The Bible: Genesis: 1-3: The Creation and the Fall," (originally titled "Genesis: 1-3"), "from The Bible: Genesis 6-9: The Story of the Flood," (originally titled "Genesis: 6-9"), "The Book of Ruth," (originally titled "Ruth: 1-4"), "Psalm 8," "Psalm 19," "Psalm 23," and "Psalm 137," reprinted from the *Tanakh: A New Translation of the Holy Scriptures According to the Hebrew Text.* Copyright date © 1985, by the Jewish Publication Society. Reprinted by permission.

John & Alcock Ltd. "I have visited again," by Alexander Pushkin, translation © 1982 by D.M. Thomas, from *The Bronze Horseman: Selected Poems of Alexander Pushkin*, The Viking Press, New York, 1982. Used with permission of Johnson & Alcock Ltd.

Kensington Publishing Corp. "The Lorelei" by Heinrich Heine from The Poetry and Prose of Heinrich Reine, edited by Frederic Ewen. Copyright © 1948, 1976 by The Citadel Press. All rights reserved. Reprinted by arrangement with Kensington Publishing Corp. www.kensingtonbooks.com.

Alfred A. Knopf, Inc, a division of Random House, Inc. "The Guest," from *Exile and the Kingdom* by Albert Camus, translated by Jusin O'Brien, copyright © 1957, 1958 by Alfred A. Knopf, Inc. a division of Random House, Inc. "from *Hiroshima*," by John Hersey, copyright © 1946 and renewed 1974 by John Hersey. "Ancestral Voices" and "Substance" from *The Vixen* by W.S. Merwin, copyright © 1995 by W.S. Merwin. Used by permission of Alfred A. Knopf, a division of Random House, Inc.

L. R. Lind "from Canzoniere: Laura," "from Canzoniere: Spring," by Francesco Petrarch, translated by Morris Bishop, reprinted by permission of L.R. Lind, Editor, from *Lyric Poetry of the Italian Renaissance*, copyright 1954. Used by permission.

Macmillan Education Christopher Marlowe, *The Tragical History of Doctor Faustus*. Text of 1604, with Introduction and Notes by William Modlen (London: Macmillan & Co., repr. 1966).

Maypop Books "The Guest House," "Elephant in the Dark," "Two Kinds of Intelligence," "Which is Worth More" by Coleman Barks translated from *The Essential Rumi*. Copyright © 1995 by Coleman Barks. All rights reserved. Reprinted by permission.

The Modern Library, an imprint of Random House, Inc. "from Candide: Chapter I and Chapter II," (originally titled "from Candide: Chapter I: How Candide was brought up in a noble castle and how he was expelled from the same and Chapter II: What Happened to Candide among the Bulgarians") from *Candide; And Philosophical Letters* by Voltaire, translated by Richard Aldington, copyright © 1928, 1956, 1984 by Random House, Inc.

Jonathan Musere "African Proverbs: Uganda: The Bagada: "A small deed out of friendship . . .," "Two people can keep the words a secret . . .," "One who loves you, warns you . . .," "The one who is hopeful . . .," "The one who has not made the journey . . .," "The one who travels is the one who sees things . . .," "Words are easy, but friendship is difficult . . .," and "Where there are no dogs . . ." from *African Proverbs and Proverbial Names* by Jonathan Musere. Copyright © 1999 by Ariko Publications. Reprinted by permission.

New Directions Publishing Corporation "Jade Flower Palace," by Tu Fu, translated by Kenneth Rexroth, from *One Hundred Poems from the Chinese*, copyright © 1971 by Kenneth Rexroth. "The River-Merchant's Wife: A Letter," by Ezra Pound, from *Personae*, copyright © 1926 by Ezra Pound. "The Prayer," by Gabriella Mistral, translated by Donald Devenish Walsh, from *Anthology of Contemporary Latin-American Poetry*, copyright © 1942, 1947 by New Directions Publishing Corp. Reprinted by permission of New Directions Publishing Corp.

New York Times Co. "Leonardo: The Eye, the Hand, the Mind" by Holland Cotter from *The New York Times*, January 24, 2003. Copyright © 2003 by the New York Times Co. Reprinted by permission.

Harold Ober Associates, Incorporated "Marriage is a Private Affair," from *Girls at War and Other Stories* by Chinua Achebe, copyright © 1972, 1973 by Chinua Achebe. Reprinted by permission of Harold Ober Associates, Incorporated.

Oxford University Press, Inc. and David Higham Associates Ltd. "from Faust: from The First Part of the Tragedy: Night," and "from Faust: Prologue in Heaven," (originally titled "from *Faust, Part I & 2*"), by Johann Wolfgang von Goethe, translated by Louis MacNeice, copyright © 1951, 1954 by Federick Louis MacNeice; renewed 1979 by Hedi MacNeice. Used by permission of Oxford University Press, Inc.

Oxford University Press, UK "How Much Land Does a Man Need?" by Leo Tolstoy from *The Raid and Other Stories*, translated by Louise an Aylmer Maude (1935). Reprinted by permission of Oxford University Press.

Oxford University Press, UK and Columbia University Press "from The Pillow Book of Sei Shonagon: The Cat Who Lived in the Palace," "Things That Arouse a Fond Memory of the Past," "I Remember a Clear Morning," from *The Pillow Book of Sei Shonagon* by Sei Shonagon, translated and edited by Ivan Morris. Copyright (c) Ivan Morris 1967. Reprinted by permission.

Pearson Education, Inc. publishing as Pearson Prentice Hall "What is an Insect?" from *Prentice Hall Biology* by Kenneth R. Miller, Ph.D., and Joseph Levine, Ph.D. © 2002 Pearson Education, Inc. publishing as Pearson Prentice Hall. Used by permission.

Pearson Education Ltd. "from Sundiata: An Epic of Old Mali: from The Lion's Awakening," from *Sundiata: An Epic of Old Mali* by D.T. Niane, translated by G.D. Pickett. Copyright © Presence Africaine, 1960(original French version: *Soundjata, ou L'Epopee Mandingue*). © 1965 Longman Group Ltd. (English). Reprinted by permission of Pearson Education Limited. "from Sundiata: An Epic of Old Mali: Childhood," from *Sundiata: An Epic of Old Mali* by D.T. Niane, translated by G.D. Pickett. Copyright © Presence Africaine, 1960(original French version: *Soundjata, ou L'Epopee Mandingue*). © 1965 Longman Group Ltd. (English).

Penguin Books Ltd., London "from The Annals: from The Burning of Rome," from *The Annals of Imperial Rome* by Tacitus, translated by Michael Grant(Penguin Classics 1956, Sixth revised edition 1989) copyright © Michael Grant Publications Ltd., 1969. "From Tales from the Thousand and One Nights: The Fisherman and the Jinnee," from *Tales from the Thousand and One Nights* translated by N.J. Dawood (Penguin Classics 1954, Revised edition 1973) translation copyright © N.J. Dawood, 1954, 1973. "from The Rig Veda: "Creation Hymn" and "Night,"" from *The Rig Veda, An Anthology* translated by Wendy Doniger O'Flaherty (Penguin Classics, 1981). Copyright © Wendy Doniger O'Flaherty, 1981. "Visit," by Yevgeny Yevtushenko from *Yevtushenko: Selected Poems*, translated by Robin Milner-Gulla and Peter Levi, S.J. (Penguin Books, 1962) copyright © Robin Milner-Gulla and Peter Levi, 1962. "The Qur'an," (originally titled "from The Koran) from *The Koran*, translated by N.J. Dawood (Penguin Classics, 1956, Fifth revised edition 1990). Copyright © N.J. Dawood, 1956, 1959, 1966, 1968, 1974, 1990. "Prayer to Masks," by Leopold Sedar Senghor, translated by Gerald Moore and Ulli Beier from *The Penguin Book of Modern African Poetry* edited by Gerald Moore and Ulli Beier, first published as *Modern Poetry from Africa*, 1963 (Penguin Books, 1984). Copyright © Gerald Moore and Ulli Beier, 1963, 1968, 1984. "from The Decameron: Federigo's Falcon," (originally titled "Ninth Story") by Giovanni Boccaccio from *The Decameron*, translated by G.H. McWilliam (Penguin Classics, 1972 Second Edition, 1995). Copyright © G.H. McWilliam, 1972, 1995. "From History of the Peloponnesian War: Pericles' Funeral Oration," by Thucydides from *History of the Peloponnesian Wars*, translated by Rex Warner (Penguin Classics, 1954). Translation copyright © Rex Warner, 1954. "from The Epic of Gilgamesh: Prologue," (originally titled "from Prologue: Gilgamesh King in Uruk"), "The Battle with Humbaba," (originally titled "from The Forest Journey"), "The Death of Enkidu," (originally titled "from

The Death of Enkidu"), "The Story of The Flood," and "The Return," from *The Epic of Gilgamesh*, translated by N.K. Sanders (Penguin Classics 1960, Third Edition 1972). Copyright © N.K. Sanders, 1960, 1964, 1972. "from the Tao Te Ching: I, III, IX & XLIII," from *Tao Te Ching: The Book of Meaning and Life* by Lao Tzu, translated by Richard Wilhelm, translated by H.G. Ostwald (Arkana, 1989) copyright © Eugen Diederichs Verlad GmBh & Co, Koln, 1985. English translation copyright © Routeledge & Kegan Paul, 1985. "from **The Nibelungentilied:** How Siegfried Was Slain," (originally titled "Chapter 16. How Siegfried Was Slain") from *The Nibelungenlied* translated by A.T. Hatto (Penguin Classics, 1965, revised edition 1969) copyright © A.T. Hatto, 1965, 1969. Reproduced by permission of Penguin Books Ltd.

Peter Pauper Press, Inc. "African Proverbs: Nigeria: The Yoruba: "The day on which one starts out . . .," "He who is being carried does not realize . . .," "Time destroys all things." and "Little is better than nothing."" Reprinted by permission. "African Proverbs: Ghana: The Ashanti: "Rain beats a leopard skin . . .," "If you are in hiding . . .," "One falsehood . . .," and "No one tests the depth of a river . . . "" from *African Proverbs*, compiled by Charlotte and Wolfe Leslau. Copyright © 1962, Peter Pauper Press.

Princeton University Press "Ithaka," by C.P. Cavafy, from *C.P. Cavafy: Selected Poems*, translated by Edmund Keeley and Philip Sherrard. Copyright © 1972 by Edmund Keeley and Philip Sherrard. Reprinted by permission of Princeton University Press.

Random House, Inc. "from The Aeneid: from Book II: How They Took the City," by Virgil from *The Aenid*, translated by Robert Fitzgerald, copyright © 1980, 1982, 1983 by Robert Fitzgerald. Used by permission of Random House, Inc.

Rupert Crew Limited on behalf of Steve and Megumi Biddle From "The Origins of Origami" by Steve and Megumi Biddle from *Origami: Inspired by Japanese Prints*. Copyright © 1998 by The Metropolitan Museum of Art. Introduction, instructions, diagrams and models © 1998 by Steve and Megumi Biddle. All rights reserved. Reprinted by permission.

The Sheep Meadow Press "Pride," by Dahlia Ravikovitch from A Dress of Fire translated by Chana Bloch, The Sheep Meadow Press, Riverdale-on-Hudson. Reprinted by permission.

Simon & Schuster Adult Publishing Group "The Wooden People," (originally titled "from Popol Vuh"), reprinted with permission of Simon & Schuster Adult Publishing Group from *Popol Vuh: The Definative Edition of the Mayan Book of the Dawn of Life and the Glories of Gods and Kings* translated by Dennis Tedlock. Copyright © Dennis Tedlock, 1985, 1996.

William Jay Smith "The Sleeper in the Valley," by Arthur Rimbaud, translated by William Jay Smith, in *Collected Translations: Italian, French, Spanish, Portuguese*, published by New Rivers Press, copyright © 1985 by William Jay Smith. Reprinted by permission.

Elyse Sommer "CurtainUp Review: A Doll's House," copyright April 1997, Elyse Sommer. Reprinted courtesy of www.curtainup.com, online theater magazine.

David Spencer "A Doll's House by Henrik Ibsen, a new version by Frank McGuinness," reviewed by David Spencer from www.aislesay.com. Reprinted by permission of the author, David Spencer.

Story Line Press "Autumn Song," by Paul Verlaine, translated by Louis Simpson from *Modern Poets of France, A Bilingual Anthology*. Copyright © 1997, 1998 by Louis Simpson. Reprinted by permission of the author and Story Line Press.

Tufts University, Perseus Project, Classics Department "from The Perseus Digital Library (http://www.perseus.tufts.edu/Olympics/)," reproduced by kind permission of Tufts University, Perseus Project.

Charles E. Tuttle Co, Inc. of Boston, Massachussetts and Tokyo, Japan "Zen Parables: "A Parable," "The Taste of Banzo's Sword" and "Publishing the Sutras," from *Zen Flesh, Zen Bones: A Collection of Zen & Pre-Zen Writings* compiled by Paul Reps. Reprinted by permission.

The University of California Press "He is More Than a Hero," and "You Know the Place: Then," by Sappho from Sappho: A New Translation, translated by Mary Barnard. Copyright © 1958, by The Regents of the University of California. "Green" by Juan Ramon Jimenez from *Juan Ramon Jimenez: Fifty Spanish Poems*, translated by J. B. Trend. "The Diameter of the Bomb," and "From The Book of Esther I Filtered the Sediment," by Yehuda Amichai from *The Selected Poetry of Yehuda Amichai*, translated by Chana Boch and Stephen Mitchell. English translation copyright © 1986 by Chana Boch and Stephen Mitchell. Reprinted by permission.

The University of Chicago Press "Olympia 11," by Pindar from *The Odes of Pindar, Second Edition*, translated by Richmond Lattimore. Copyright © 1947, 1976 by The University of Chicago Press. "He is More Than a Hero," by Sappho from Greek Lyrics, translated by Richmond Lattimore. Copyright © 1949 and 1955 by Richmond Lattimore. "from The Panchatantra: Numskull and the Rabbit," from *The Panchatantra*, translated by Arthur W. Ryder. Copyright © 1925 by The University of Chicago. Copyright renewed 1953 by Mary E. Ryder and Winifred Ryder. "Oedipus the King," by Sophocles, D. Grene, translator, from *The Complete Greek Tragedies: Oedipus the King, Oedipus at Colonus, Antigone, Volume II*, D. Grene and Richmond Lattimore, editors, pp. 11-76. Copyright © 1942 by The University of Chicago. All rights reserved. Reprinted by permission of The University of Chicago Press.

The University of Georgia Press from "Perceval or The Story of the Grail" translated by Ruth Harwood Cline. Copyright © 1983 by Ruth Harwood Cline. Used by permission of the University of Georgia Press.

Vedanta Society of Southern California "from The Bhagavad-Gita: The Yoga of Knowledge," from *The Song of God: Bhagavad-Gita*, translated by Swami Prabhavananda and Christopher Isherwood. Copyright © 1944, 1951 by The Vedanta Society of Southern California. Reprinted by permission.

Viking Penguin, a division of Penguin Group (USA) Inc. "from Book 1: The Quarrel (originally titled "from Book 1: The Rage of Achilles")," "from Book 6: The Meeting of Hector and Andromache (originally titled "from Book 6: Hector Returns to Troy")," "from Book 24: Achilleus and Priam," "from Book 22: The Death of Hector," from *The Iliad* by Homer, translated by Robert Fagles, copyright © 1990 by Robert Fagles. "The Fox and the Crow," copyright © 1952 by Marianne Moore, renewed © 1980 by Lawrence E. Brinn and Louise Crane, Executors of the Estate, "The Oak and the Reed," from *The Fables of La Fontaine*, translated by Marianne Moore, copyright © 1952, 1953, 1954, © 1964 by Marianne Moore, renewed © 1980, 1981, 1982 by Lawrence Brinn and Louise Crane, Executors of the Estate. "On the Bottom," from *If This is a Man* (Survival in Auschwitz)," by Primo Levi, translated by Stuart Woolf, copyright © 1959 by Orion Press, Inc., © 1958 by Giulio Einaudi editore, s.p.a. "from The Ingenious Gentleman Don Quixote de la Mancha," (originally titled "from The Ingenious Gentleman Don Quixote de la Mancha, Part 1, Chapter 1") from *Don Quixote* by Miguel de Cervantes Saavedra, translated by Samuel Putnam, copyright © 1949 by The Viking Press, Inc. "from The Ramayana: Rama and Ravana in the Battle," from *The Ramayana* by R.K. Narayan, copyright © 1972 by R.K. Narayan. Used by permission of Viking Penguin, a division of Penguin Group (USA), Inc.

Visva-Bharati Publishing Department, Visva Bharati University "The Artist," by Rabindranath Tagore from *The Housewarming and Other Selected Writings*, translated by Amiya Chakravarty, Mary Lago and Tarun Gupta. Copyright © 1965 Amiya Chakravarty. All rights reserved. Used by permission.

W. W. Norton & Company, Inc. From *The Song of Roland*, translated by Frederick Goldin. Copyright © 1978 by W.W. Norton & Company, Inc. "from The Inferno: Cantos I: The Dark Wood of Error," "from The Inferno: Cantos III: Vestibule of Hell / The Opportunists," "from The Inferno: Cantos V: Circle Two / The Carnal," "from The Inferno: Cantos XXXIV: Circle Nine / Cocytus," from *The Divine Comedy* by Dante Alighieri, translated by John Ciardi. Copyright © 1954, 1957, 1959, 1960, 1965, 1967, 1970 by the Ciardi Family Publishing Trust. This selection may not be reproduced, stored in a retrieval system or transmitted in any form or by any means without prior written permission of the publisher. Used by permission of W.W. Norton & Company, Inc.

The Arthur Waley Estate "from The Book of Songs: 34," "from The Book of Songs: 24," from *Translations from the Chinese* and "from *The Analects of Confucius*," translated by Arthur Waley, George Allen & Unwin, Ltd. London. All rights reserved. Reprinted by permission of the Arthur Waley Estate.

Washington Post Writers Group "A Lot of Baggage for Nora to Carry: After a History of Misinterpretation, Ibsen's Leave-Taking Heroine Finally Gets Her Due," by Lloyd Rose from *The Washington Post, April 20, 1997.* Copyright © 1997, The Washington Post. Reprinted with permission.

Gwendoline Mary Watkins "Comme on void sur la branche ("Roses")," by Pierre Ronsard, translated by Vernon Watkins. Reprinted by permission.

Witswatersrand University Press "African Proverbs: South Africa: The Zulu: "You cannot chase two gazelles."," "The one offended never forgets . . ."," "No dew ever competed . . ."," "It never dawns in the same way."," "Look as you fell a tree."," "Do not speak of rhinoceros . . ."," "Eyes do not see all."," "There is no foot . . ."," "What has happened before . . ."," from *Zulu Proverbs* edited by C.L. Sibusiso Nyembezi, M.A. Copyright 1954 Witswaterarand University Press. All rights reserved. Reprinted by permission.

Yale University Press "To Helene," (originally titled "Le Second Livre des Sonnets pour Helene, XLIII"), by Pierre de Ronsard from *Lyrics of the French Renaissance: Marot, Du Bellay, Ronsard*, translated by Norman R. Shapiro. Copyright © 2002 by Yale University. All rights reserved. This book may not be reproduced in whole or in part, in any form (except by reviewers for the public press) without written permission from the publishers. Reprinted by permission.

Note: Every effort has been made to locate the copyright owner of material reprinted in this book. Omissions brought to our attention will be corrected in subsequent editions.

CREDITS

Cover: Werner Forman/Art Resource, NY; **i:** Werner Forman/Art Resource, NY; **iv: t.** Christopher Felver/CORBIS; **iv: m (1).** Prentice Hall; **iv: m (2).** Prentice Hall; **iv: m (3).** Getty Images; **iv: b.** Prentice Hall; **v: t.** Prentice Hall; **v: m (1).** Prentice Hall; **v: m (2).** Miriam Berkley/Authorpix; **v: m (3).** Photo © Sigrid Estrada; **v: b.** Reuters Pictures; **vii:** Royalty-Free/CORBIS; **viii:** Christopher Felver/CORBIS; **ix:** *The Creation of Adam,* (detail), 1510, Fresco, 280x570 cm. Michelangelo de Lodovico Buonarroti Simoni (Italian, 1475–1564). Cappella Sistina, Vatican. Canali Photobank Milan/Superstock; **x:** Prentice Hall; **xi: t.** Prentice Hall; **xi: b.** Arjuna and Krishna in the Chariot, Between the Two Armies, Illustration from Bhagavad-Gita, Photo by Lynn Saville; **xii:** © Matthias Kulka/CORBIS; **xiii:** Getty Images; **xiv:** Sei Shonagon, Heibonsha/Pacific Press Service; **xv:** Prentice Hall; **xvi:** Prentice Hall; **xvii:** © Dorling Kindersley; **xviii:** Prentice Hall; **xix:** Corel Professional Photos CD-ROM™; **xx:** Miriam Berkley/Authorpix; **xxi:** © Dorling Kindersley; **xxii:** Photo © Sigrid Estrada; **xxiii:** © Sylvain Grandadam/Photo Researchers, Inc.; **1:** The Art Archive/Archaeological Museum Istanbul/Dagli Orti; **2: t.** Christopher Felver/CORBIS; **2: b.** The Art Archive/Bodleian Library Oxford/The Bodleian Library; **4: m.l.** Head of an Acadion Ruler, Nineveh, 2300–2200 B.C., Bhagdad Museum, Scala/Art Resource, New York; **4: m.r.** Boltin Picture Library; **4: t.r.** Araldo de Luca/CORBIS; **4: b.l.** Founders Society purchase, General Membership Fund/Bridgeman Art Library, London/New York; **4: b.r.** The Palma Collection/Getty Images; **4: t.l.** Astrolabe, Museum fur Kunst und Gewerbe, Hamburg; **5: m.** Art Resource, New York; **5: t.** The Art Archive/Ethnic Jewellery Exhibition Milan/Dagli Orti; **5: b.** Senegalese glass painting used on Sundiata, from the collection of Professor Donal Cruise-O'Brien, Courtesy of Longman International Education; **6: b.** Babylonian globe, c. 5000 B.C., The British Museum, Bridgeman/Art Resource, New York; **6: t.** Astrolabe, Museum fur Kunst und Gewerbe, Hamburg; **8: b.** Page from the Book of the Dead, c. 1100 B.C., Egyptian, The British Museum, Photo by Michael Holford; **8: t.** Astrolabe, Museum fur Kunst und Gewerbe, Hamburg; **9:** Will and Deni McIntyre/Getty Images; **10: b.** Mary Evans/Edwin Wallace; **10: t.** Astrolabe, Museum fur Kunst und Gewerbe, Hamburg; **11:** Bojan Brecelj/CORBIS; **12:** Astrolabe, Museum fur Kunst und Gewerbe, Hamburg; **13:** The Simurgh Brings Zal to Sam, Leaf from Shah-nameh by Ferdowsi, 14th century, The Metropolitan Museum of Art, Rogers Fund, 1969, © Copyright by The Metropolitan Museum of Art; **15:** Erich Lessing/Art Resource, NY; **16:** Colossus of the King holding a lion (Gilgamesh), relief from the Palace of Sargon II at Khorsabada. Assyrian, ca. 725 BCE. Inv.: AO 19861-16. Photo: Herve Lewandowski. Louvre, Paris, France. Reunion des Musees Nationaux/Art Resource, NY **18:** Colossus of the King holding a lion (Gilgamesh), relief from the Palace of Sargon II at Khorsabada. Assyrian, ca. 725 BCE. Inv.: AO 19861-16. Photo: Herve Lewandowski. Louvre, Paris, France. Reunion des Musees Nationaux/Art Resource, NY; **20-21:** Yann Arthus-Bertrand/CORBIS; **22:** Scala/Art Resource, NY; **23:** Kabul Museum, Afghanistan/Bridgeman Art Library, London/New York; **26:** Front of lyre from tomb of Queen Pu-abi, Early Dynastic period, c. 2685–2290 B.C., British Museum, London; **28-29:** Erich Lessing/Art Resource, NY; **30-31:** Academy of Natual Sciences of Philadelphia/CORBIS; **38:** *The Creation of Adam* (detail), 1510, Fresco, 280x 570 cm. Michelangelo de Lodovico Buonarroti Simoni (Italian, 1475–1564). Cappella Sistina, Vatican. Canali Photobank Milan/Superstock; **40-41:** *The Creation of Adam,* 1510, Fresco, 280x 570 cm. Michelangelo de Lodovico Buonarroti Simoni (Italian, 1475–1564). Cappella Sistina, Vatican. Canali Photobank Milan/Superstock; **42:** Scala/Art Resource, NY; **44:** Bettmann/CORBIS; **47:** Corel Professional Photos CD-ROM™; **48:** *Noah's Ark,* Aaron Douglas, Fisk University Fine Art Galleries, Nashville, Tennessee; **54:** Harvey Lloyd/Getty Images; **55:** Dick S. Ramsay Fund, The Brooklyn Museum; **56:** Werner Forman Archive, Liverpool Museum, Liverpool/Art Resource, NY; **60:** Corel Professional Photos CD-ROM™; **62:** Historical Picture Archive/CORBIS; **65:** Chaim Gross (1904–1991). "Ketubbah, (Marriage Contract)", New York, ca. 1970, silkscreen on paper, 24 1/4 x 20 3/4 in. © Chaim Gross Studio Museum. Photo: John Parnell. Photo Credit: The Jewish Museum of New York/Art Resource, NY. The Chaim Gross Studio Museum, New York, NY, USA; **67:** *Il Buon Pastore* (The Good Shepherd), Early Christian, 4th century, Vatican Museum, Scala/Art Resource, New York; **69:** David Composing the Psalms, Illustrated by Paris Psalter, 10th century, Photo Bibliotheque Nationale, Paris; **75:** The Granger Collection, New York; **78:** CORBIS; **79:** Arabic Manuscript: 30,60. Page from a Koran, 8th–9th century. Kufic script H: 23.8 x W: 35.5 cm. Courtesy of the Freer Gallery of Art, Smithsonian Institution, Washington, D.C.: Purchase, F1930.60r; **84:** Scheherazade and King Shahriyar, (detail), Anton Pieck. Illustration from Stories of the Arabian Nights. Retold by Naomi Lewis. Illus. © 1984 by B.V. Elsevier. Uitgeversmaatschappij, Amsterdam. Photo by Rex Joseph.; **86:** Nick Koudis/Getty Images; **89:** Illustration from Arabian NIghts, for the story "The Fisherman and the Genie", Edmund Dulac, NY, Scribner's & Sons: 1907, Photo courtesy of the New York Public Library, Astor, Lenox and Tilden Foundations/Art Resource, NY; **90:** Monique le Luhandre/© Dorling Kindersley; **93:** George Hood/The Palma Collection/Getty Images; **94-95:** Christie's Images/CORBIS; **100: l.** Bettmann/CORBIS; **100: r.** Courtesy of the Freer Gallery of Art, Smithsonian Institution, Washington, D.C.: Gift of the Art and History Trust in honor of Ezzat-Malek Soudavar, F1998.5.6a; **103:** *Rubáiyát of Omar Khayyám,* Edmund Dulac, Photo by John Lei/Omni-Photo Communications, Inc.; **104:** *Rubáiyát of Omar Khayyám,* Edmund Dulac, Photo by John Lei/Omni-Photo Communications, Inc.; **107:** National Gallery Collection; By kind permission of the Trustees of the National Gallery, London/CORBIS; **109:** The Art Archive/Biblioteca Nazionale Marciana Venice/Dagli Orti; **114: b.** Scala/Art Resource, NY; **114: t.** Christopher Felver/CORBIS; **115:** Courtesy of the Trustees of British Library; www.bl.uk/imagesonline.; **116:** The Art Archive/Dagle Orti (A); **118:** Pococke 400 folio 99r/The Art Archive/Bodleian Library Oxford/The Bodleian Library; **120:** The Art Archive/Museum of Islamic Art Cairo/Dagli Orti; **123:** Bildarchiv Preussischer Kulturbesitz/Art Resource, NY; **124:** The Art Archive/Bodleian Library Oxford/The Bodleian Library; **128:** Private Collection/Heine Schneebeli/Bridgeman Art Library, London/New York; **130:** Werner Forman/Art Resource, NY; **133:** Pearson Education/PH School Division; **134:** Cover of SUNDIATA by David Wisniewski. Copyright © 1992 by David Wisniewski. Reprinted by permission of Clarion Books/Houghton Mifflin Company. All rights reserved.; **137:** © Michael Melford; **139:** Monique le Luhandre/© Dorling Kindersley; **145: t.** Photograph by J.D. Dallet, (c) 2002 Board of Trustees, National; Gallery of Art, Washington; **145: m.** The Art Archive/Egyptian Museum, Cairo/Dagli Orti; **150:** Bananastock/PictureQuest; **153:** Christopher Felver/CORBIS; **162-163:** The Art Archive/Victoria and Albert Museum London/Eileen Tweedy; **164: m.** Prentice Hall; **164: b.** Bildarchiv Preussisher Kulturbesitz/Art Resource, NY; **164: t.** Astrolabe, Museum fur Kunst und Gewerbe, Hamburg; **166 m.m.** Kanch Mandir/B.P.S. Walia/© Dorling Kindersley; **166: m.l.** The Granger Collection, New York; **166: m.r.** Buddha Standing, bronze, 1st half of 7th century, The Metropolitan Museum of Art, Purchase, Bequest of Florance Waterbury, 1969, © Copyright by The Metropolitan Museum of Art; **166: b.l.** Bridgeman Art Library, London/New York; **166: b.r.** Attic Red Figure Nolan Amphora: Hephaestus Making Armor for Achilles, The Dutuit painter, Francis Bartlett Fund, Courtesy, Museum of Fine Arts, Boston; **166: t.** Astrolabe, Museum fur Kunst und Gewerbe, Hamburg; **167: t.r.** © Christie's Images., 2004; **167: t.l.** Scala/Art Resource, New York; **167: b.** Werner Forman/Art Resource, NY; **168: t.** Astrolabe, Museum fur Kunst und Gewerbe, Hamburg; **170: t.** Astrolabe, Museum fur Kunst und Gewerbe, Hamburg; **171: r.** Scala/Art Resource, NY; **171: l.** David Buffington/Getty Images; **172: r.** *Zero,* 1980–1996, Robert Indiana, Morgan Art Foundation Limited/Art Resource, NY, © Copyright ARS, NY; **172: l.** Astrolabe, Museum fur Kunst und Gewerbe, Hamburg; **173:** Rama and Lakshman Confer with the Animal Armies, from the Adventures of Rama, Courtesy of the Freer Gallery of Art, Smithsonian Institution, Washington, D.C., fol. 194v, full view. Gift of Charles Lang Freer, F1907.271.194; **174: b.** Dinodia/Omni-Photo Communications, Inc.; **174: t.** Astrolabe, Museum fur Kunst und Gewerbe, Hamburg; **176: b.** Victoria & Albert Museum, London/Art Resource, NY; **176: t.** Prentice Hall; **177:** Lindsay Hebberd/CORBIS; **178:** Ann and Bury Peerless Picture Library/Bridgeman Art Library, London/New York; **180:** © Matthias Kulka/CORBIS; **180-181:** © Matthias Kulka/CORBIS; **182:** © Otto Rogge/Stock Photos/CORBIS; **187:** Bibliotheque National, Paris, France, Flammarion; Giraudon/The Bridgeman Art Library, London/New York; **188: b.** Victoria and Albert Museum, London/Art Resource, NY; **188: t.** Astrolabe, Museum fur Kunst und Gewerbe, Hamburg; **190:** Krishna on a Swing, Scala/Art Resource, NY; **192:** Indra, engraved by Marlet et Cie, 1841. Private Collection/The Stapleton Collection/Bridgeman Art Library, London/New York; **194:** Vishnu and Lakshmi Riding on Garuda, Ann & Bury Peerless Picture Library/Bridgeman Art Library, London/New York; **197:** A Hawk, Indian Mughal, 18th century miniature, Victoria and Albert Museum, Photo by Michael Holford; **198:** King Sibi's Sacrifice to the God Indra, Gandharan Art, c. 2nd century, Courtesy of the Trustees of the British Museum; **200:** © Art Resource, New York; **202:** Arjuna and Krishna in the Chariot, Between the Two Armies, Illustration from Bhagavad-Gita, Photo by Lynn Saville; **205:** © Werner Forman/Art Resource, NY; **211:** Corel Professional Photos CD-ROM™; **212:** Ingo Jezierski/Getty Images; **213:** Rama and Lakshmana shooting arrows at the demon Ravana. gouache on paper. Dehle of Jaipur school. 19th century, © Victoria & Albert Museum, London/Art Resource, NY; **214:** Lyndsay Hebberd/CORBIS; **220:** Kangra Valley Painting, New York Public Library; **223:** *A Lion at Rest,* The Metropolitan Museum of Art, The Alice and Nasli Heeramaneck Collection, Gift of Alice Heeramaneck, 1985. (1985.221); **225:** Monique le Luhandre/© Dorling Kindersley; **230:** Royalty-Free/CORBIS; **231:** Bettmann/CORBIS; **234:** © Dorling Kindersley; **238:** Gary Conner/PhotoEdit Inc.; **241:** Prentice Hall; **250-251:** Katsusika Hokusai (1760–1849). *The Great Wave of Kanagawa,* from 36 Views of Mount Fuji. Private Collection. Art Resource, NY.; **252: m.** Prentice Hall; **252: b.** Bettmann/CORBIS; **252: t.** Astrolabe, Museum fur Kunst und Gewerbe, Hamburg; **254: m.r.** Mary Evans Picture Library; **254: b.** Pawel Kumelowski/Omni-Photo Communications, Inc.; **254: m.l.** Pearson Education EMG Education Management Group; **254: t.** Astrolabe, Museum fur Kunst und Gewerbe, Hamburg; **255: t.** *First Landing at Kurihama,* July 14, 1853, Gessan Ogata, Courtesy of United States Naval Academy Museum; **255: b.** Reuters NewMedia Inc./CORBIS; **255: m.** © Will and Deni McIntyre/Photo Researchers, Inc.; **256:** Astrolabe, Museum fur Kunst und Gewerbe, Hamburg; **257:** Dallas and John Heaton/CORBIS; **258: b.** Tokyo National Museum; **258: t.** Astrolabe, Museum fur Kunst und Gewerbe, Hamburg; **259:** Pearson Education Corporate Digital Archive; **260: b.** *The Poet Li Po Admiring a Waterfall,* Hokusai, Honolulu Academy of Arts, Gift of James A. Michener (21,892); **260: t.** Astrolabe, Museum fur Kunst und Gewerbe, Hamburg; **262:** Astrolabe, Museum fur Kunst und Gewerbe, Hamburg; **263:** Asian Art & Archaeology, Inc./CORBIS; **264: r.** The Granger Collection, New York; **264: l.** Foto Marburg/Art Resource, NY; **267:** *Poet on a Mountain Top,* Shen Chou, The Nelson-Atkins Museum of Art, Kansas City, Missouri; **268:** *Old Trees by Cold Waterfall,* 1470–1559, Wen Zhengming. Ming dynasty, dated 1531, hanging scroll, ink and colored paper, 86 1/2 x 17 1/8 in. The Los Angeles County Museum of Art, The Ernest Larsen Blancok Memorial Fund. Museum No. 55.67.1. Photograph © 2004 Museum Associates/LACMA; **274:** The Granger Collection, New York; **275:** *Benjamin Franklin* (detail), c.1790, Pierre Michel Alix, National Portrait Gallery, Smithsonian Institution, Washington, D.C./Art Resource, New York; **278: b.l.** T'ao Ch'ien, Collection of the National Palace Museum, Taipei, Taiwan, Republic of China; **278: t.** © New York Public Library/Art Resource, NY; **278: b.r.** New York Public Library Picture Collection; **281:** *Fishing Village in the Wind and Rain,* hanging scroll painting, 1955, Li K'e-jan, Werner Forman/Art Resource, NY; **283:** *A Myriad of Trees on Strange Peaks,* Yen Wen-Kuei (Northern Sung Dynasty), The Granger Collection, New York; **285:** *River and Mountains in Autumn Color,* 1120–1182, Zhao Boju, Imerial Palace Museum, Beijing, China.; **287:** *River Village in a Rainstorm,* Hanging scroll, ink and slight color on silk, 169.2 x 103.5 cm, Lü Wenying, Chinese, active ca. 1490–1507, © The Cleveland Museum of Art, John L. Severance Fund, 70.76; **288-289:** Eyewire/Getty Images; **290:** Corel Professional Photos CD-ROM™; **294: b.** *Landscape with a Solitary Traveler,* c. 1780. Japan, Edo Period (1615–1868) Hanging Scroll, ink and light colors on silk 40 x 14 3/8 in. (101.5x36.4 cm), Copyright © 2005 by Kimbell Art Museum; **294: t.** Prentice Hall; **296: m.r.** Yosa Buson, Heibonsha/Pacific Press Service; **296: b.r.** Kobayashi Issa, Heibonsha/Pacific Press Service; **296: t.r.** Basho, The Granger Collection, New York; **296: m.l.** Onono-komachi, Heibonsha/Pacific Press Service; **296: t.l.** Kino Tsurayuki, Heibonsha/Pacific Press Service; **296: b.l.** Jakuren Houshi, Heibonsha/Pacific Press Service; **298:** *Snow at Senso-ji Temple in Asakusa,* Victoria and Albert Museum, London/Art Resource, NY; **300:** *The Monkey Bridge in Koshu Province,* 1841, Hiroshige Hitsu, © Christie's Images, Inc., 2004; **301:** *Sudden Shower on Ohashi Bridge,* Hiroshige, Art Resource, New York; **302:** Artville/Getty Images; **306:** Sei Shonagon, Heibonsha/Pacific Press Service; **309:** *Triptych of Snow, Moon, and Flower* (Center Panel), c.1780's, Shunsho, Museum of Art, Tami, Japan; **311:** Sei Shonagon, Heibonsha/Pacific Press Service; **316:** Astrolabe, Museum fur Kunst und Gewerbe, Hamburg; **317:** *The Celebrated Beauty of the Teahouse, Kagiya, at Kasamori Shrine,* Suzuki Harunobu, 18th century, The Metropolitan Museum of Art, the Henry L. Phillips Collection, Bequest of Henry L. Phillips, 1940, © Copyright by The Metropolitan Museum of Art; **318:** Large Enso, hanging scroll, Torei Enji, Gitter-Yelen Art Center; **320:** CORBIS; **321:** Monique le Luhandre/© Dorling Kindersley; **327-330:** Instructions, diagram and models © 1998 by Steve and Megumi Biddle. Models photograph by Les Morsillo. Photograph ©1998 The Metropolitan Museum; **334:** John Neubauer/PhotoEdit Inc.; **337:** Prentice Hall; **346-347:** *Aeneas at Delos,* Claude Lorrain, © National Gallery Collection; By kind permission of the Trustees of the National Gallery, London/CORBIS; **348: t.** Getty Images; **348: b.** Photo by Janine Norton; **350: m.l.** Mimmo Jodice/CORBIS; **350: b.l.** Ann & Bury Peerless Picture Library/Bridgeman Art Library, London/New York; **350: b.r.** Seattle Art Museum/CORBIS; **350: t.r.** Antonio M. Rosario/Getty Images; **350: t.l.** Astrolabe, Museum fur Kunst und Gewerbe, Hamburg; **351: t.l.** Roman Mosaic: Gladiator with Leopard, Galleria Borghese, Scala/Art Resource, New York; **351: t.r.** Bettmann/CORBIS; **351: b.** Michael S. Yamashita/CORBIS; **352:** Astrolabe, Museum fur Kunst und Gewerbe, Hamburg; **354: r.** The Apollo Belvedere, Roman marble copy probably of Greek original of late 4th (or 1st) century BC, Vatican Museums, Rome, Scala/Art Resource, New York; **354: l.** Astrolabe, Museum fur Kunst und Gewerbe, Hamburg; **355:** Erich Lessing/Art Resource, NY; **356: b.** Richard Quataert/Folio, Inc.; **356: t.** Astrolabe, Museum fur Kunst und Gewerbe, Hamburg; **357:** *Circe Meanwhile Had Gone Her Ways...,* 1924, From THE ODYSSEY by Homer, William Russell Flint, Collection of the New York Public Library; Astor, Lenox and Tilden Foundations; **358: b.** The Art Archive/Biblioteca Braidense Milan/Dagli Orti; **358: t.** Astrolabe, Museum fur Kunst und Gewerbe, Hamburg; **359:** The Art Archive/Dagli Orti; **360:** Bettmann/CORBIS; **363:** Mimmo Jodice/CORBIS; **364:** Mimmo Jodice/CORBIS; **365:** Historical Picture Archive/CORBIS; **366:** Kimbell Art Museum/CORBIS; **369:** Hirmer Verlag Munchen; **370:** *Minerva restrains Achilles from killing Agamemnon,* Giambattista Tiepolo, Scala/Art Resource, New York; **372:** Liz McAulay/© Dorling Kindersley; **374:** Mimmo Jodice/CORBIS; **377:** *Hector Taking Leave of Andromache,* Angelica Kauffmann, Tate Gallery, London/Art Resource, NY; **379:** Odysseus' Mission to Achilles, Cleophrades Painter, 485–475 B.C., Staatliche Antikensammlungen und Glyptothek, Munich; **383:** Mimmo Jodice/CORBIS; **386:** Araldo de Luca/CORBIS; **389:** Monique le Luhandre/© Dorling Kindersley; **391:** *Achilles defeating Hector,* Peter Paul Rubens, Musee des Beaux-Arts, Giraudon/Art Resource, New York; **392:** *Achilles Deciding to Resume Fighting Upon the Death of Patroclus,* 1620, Dirck van Baburen/Bridgeman Art Library, London/New York; **395:** *Andromache and Astyanax,* 1789, Richard Cosway, Courtesy of the Trustees of Sir John Soane's Museum, London/Bridgeman Art Library, London/New York; **397: t.** Mimmo Jodice/CORBIS; **397: b.** *"Achilles"* detail from the fresco *"Thetis consoling Achilles",* Giovanni Battista Tiepolo, Scala/Art Resource, New York; **401:** The Granger

Collection, New York; **402:** Nationalmuseet, Copenhagen, Denmark/Bridgeman Art Library, London/New York; **407:** *Andromache mourning Hector,* Jacques Louis David, Peter Willi/Bridgeman Art Library, London/New York; **412: l.** Bettmann/CORBIS; **412: r.** The Granger Collection, New York; **414:** Sir Lawerence Alma-Tadema, *Sappho and Alcaeus,* 1881, oil on panel, 66 cm x 122 cm. The Walters Art Museum, Baltimore; **415:** Staatliche Antikensammlungen und Glypthothek, Munich. Photograph by Koppermann; **417:** Sappho and Alcaeus, Staatliche Antikensammlungen und Glyptothek, Munich; **418: t.** Lauros/Giraudon/Bridgeman Art Library, London/New York; **422:** Bust of Thucydides, National Museum, Naples, Scala/Art Resource, New York; **427:** Bildarchiv Preussischer Kulturbesitz; **429:** Boltin Picture Library; **430:** Monique le Luhandre/© Dorling Kindersley; **431:** Antikenmuseum Basel; **436:** CORBIS; **437:** Courtesy of the Library of Congress; **438:** Bust of Plato, fourth century B.C., marble, Capitoline Museum, Rome, Scala/Art Resource, New York; **441:** Joachim Blauel, Artothek/Neue Pinakothek, Munich; **442-443:** Steve Vidler/SuperStock; **445:** Alinari/Art Resource, N.Y.; **448-449:** Alan Schein/CORBIS; **451:** Mosaic, *The School of Plato,* National Museum, Naples, Scala/Art Resource, New York; **453:** *The Death of Socrates,* Jacques Louis David, The Metropolitan Museum of Art, Wolfe Fund, 1931, Catharine Lorillard Wolfe Collection, © Copyright by The Metropolitan Museum of Art; **454:** Monique le Luhandre/© Dorling Kindersley; **462: b.** The Metropolitan Museum of Art, NY, Hewitt Fund, 1911, Rogers Fund, 1921, Munsey Fund, 1936, and Anonymous Gift, 1951, (11.185); **462: t.** Astrolabe, Museum fur Kunst und Gewerbe, Hamburg; **463: b.** Oedipus at the Guthrie Theater, 2005. A new version of the Sophocles play by Ellen McLaughlin. Photo by T. Charles; Erickson; **463: t.** Getty Images; **464:** Oedipus at the Guthrie Theater, 2005. A new version of the Sophocles play by Ellen McLaughlin Photo by T. Charles; Erickson; **466:** Archivo Iconografico/CORBIS; **468:** False door flanked by two sphinxes surmounted by two lions, limestone. 450 B.C., Egyptian, Gable end from a relief from a tomb at Xanthos, The British Museum, London/Bridgeman/Art Resource, New York; **470-471:** Pictor Images/ImageState/International Stock Photography Ltd.; **471: t.** Archivo Iconografico/CORBIS; **472:** Fotopic/Omni-Photo Communications, Inc.; **475:** Roman Mosaic: Theatre masks, Capitoline Museum, Rome, Scala/Art Resource, New York; **479:** © AFP/CORBIS Sygma; **481:** Jeffrey M. Spielman/Getty Images; **483:** Archivo Iconografico, S.A./CORBIS; **484-485:** Robbie Jack/CORBIS; **488:** Relief of a seated Poet (Menander) with masks of new comedy, early Imperial, 1st c. B.C., white marble, probably Italian, but perhaps different from that of some restored parts, which should be Cattara; H. 44.3 cm; w. 59.5 cm; depth at right foot of poet 8.5 cm. Princeton University Art Museum. Museum purchase, Caroline G. Mather Fund. Photo credit: Bruce M. White; **490:** Robbie Jack/CORBIS; **492:** © Pizzoli Alberto/CORBIS Sygma; **495: b.** Michael Nicholson/CORBIS; **495: t.** Bettmann/CORBIS; **503:** False door flanked by two sphinxes surmounted by two lions, limestone. 450 B.C., Egyptian, Gable end from a relief from a tomb at Xanthos, The British Museum, London/Bridgeman/Art Resource, New York; **504:** Pictor Images/ImageState/International Stock Photography Ltd.; **506-507:** © AFP/CORBIS Sygma; **508:** © AFP/CORBIS Sygma; **510:** Robbie Jack/CORBIS; **513:** Monique le Luhandre/© Dorling Kindersley; **514-515:** Robbie Jack/CORBIS; **520-521:** Robbie Jack/CORBIS; **532:** Roger Wood/CORBIS; **534:** *Aeneas and Dido,* Pierre Narcisse Guerin, Photo: Herve Lewandowski. The Louvre, Paris, Reunion des Musees Nationaux/Art Resource, New York; **537:** National Gallery Collection; By kind permission of the Trustees of the National Gallery, London/CORBIS; **539:** © Getty Images Inc, Hulton Archive Photos; **540:** The Wooden Horse of Troy, Limoges Master of the Aeneid, Louvre, Paris, © Reunion des Musees Nationaux/Art Resource, NY; **542-543:** Araldo de Luca/CORBIS; **548:** Bettmann/CORBIS; **550:** Réunion des Musées Nationaux/Art Resource, NY; **556:** Bettmann/CORBIS; **559:** Giraudon/Art Resource, NY; **560:** Museo Capitolino, Rome/Bridgeman Art Library, London/New York; **561:** Paolo Koch/Photo Researchers, Inc.; **562:** Massimo Listri/CORBIS; **570:** Tom Stewart/CORBIS; **573:** Getty Images; **582-583:** Corel Professional Photos CD-ROM™; **584: m.** Prentice Hall; **584: b.** AKG LONDON; **584: t.** Astrolabe, Museum fur Kunst und Gewerbe, Hamburg; **586: m.l.** Courtesy of the Trustees of British Library; **586: m.r.** Werner Forman/Art Resource, NY; **586: b.** Index Stock Photography, Inc.; **586: t.** Astrolabe, Museum fur Kunst und Gewerbe, Hamburg; **587: m.** Philip Gatward/© Dorling Kindersley; **587: b.** The Granger Collection, New York; **587: t.** Mary Evans Picture Library; **588: b.** Franz-Marc Frei/CORBIS; **588: t.** Astrolabe, Museum fur Kunst und Gewerbe, Hamburg; **589:** Geoff Dann/© Dorling Kindersley/By Kind Permission of the Trustees of the Wallace Collection, London; **590: b.** *The Crowning of Charlemagne and Other Scenes from His Life,* V. de Beauvais, 15th century, Réunion des Musées Nationaux/Art Resource, New York, Musée Condé, Chantilly, France; **590: t.** Astrolabe, Museum fur Kunst und Gewerbe, Hamburg; **592: b.** Russell Thompson/Omni-Photo Communications, Inc.; **592: m.** Giraudon/Art Resource, NY; **592: t.** Astrolabe, Museum fur Kunst und Gewerbe, Hamburg; **593:** Geoff Dann/© Dorling Kindersley. Museum of Order of St. John; **594: b.** The Art Achive/University Library Heidelberg/Dagli Orti; **594: t.** Astrolabe, Museum fur Kunst und Gewerbe, Hamburg; **595:** The Granger Collection, New York; **597:** Giraudon/Art Resource, NY; **598:** *Death of Roland,* Vincent de Beauvais, Giraudon/Art Resource, NY; **600:** © Dorling Kindersley; **601:** Giraudon/Art Resource, NY; **603:** The Granger Collection, New York; **604:** © Hulton/Archive Photos; **606:** Geoff Dann/© Dorling Kindersley; **607:** *Death of Roland,* Vincent de Beauvais, Giraudon/Art Resource, NY; **608:** Geoff Dann/© Dorling Kindersley/By Kind Permission of the Trustees of the Wallace Collection, London; **610-611:** The Granger Collection, New York; **612:** Simone End/© Dorling Kindersley; **613:** Kenneth Lilly/© Dorling Kindersley; **614:** *Siegfried's Death,* Staatsbibliothek Preussischer Kulturbesitz, Berlin; Photo Bildarchiv Preussischer Kulturbesitz; **617:** *The Buriel of Siegfried,* Richard Jack, City of New York Art Gallery/SuperStock; **623:** Shane L. Amaya, www.rolandcomic.com; **624:** Shane L. Amaya, www.rolandcomic.com; **626: b.** Derek Croucher/CORBIS; **626: t.** Prentice Hall; **628:** English Greenwich, Field and tournament armor for man, 1527, Made in the royal workshops at Greenwich, steel and gold, G. 73 in. (185.5 cm); Wt. 80 lb, 4 oz. (36.7 kg): The Metropolital Museum of Art, Purchase, William H. Riggs Gift and Rogers Fund, 1919. (19.131.1-2). Photograph © 1987 The Metropolitan Museum of Art.; **630:** Courtesy of Joyce Patti/Morgan Gaynin, Inc.; **632:** *Parsifal Sees the Grail's Castle,* 1934, Martin Wiegand (early 20th c.) Private Collection, Munich, Germany/A.K.G., Berlin/SuperStock; **634:** Monique le Luhandre/© Dorling Kindersley; **635:** Bayerische Staatsbibliothek Munchen; **636:** *The Damsel of Sanct Grael,* 1857, Dante Gabriel Rossetti, Tate Gallery, London/Art Resource, NY; **639:** Perceval at Amfortas, wall painting from the "Parsifal saga", Ferdinand Piloty, The Younger, AKG London; **641:** Art Resource, NY; **642:** © Judith Miller/Dorling Kindersley/Barry Davies; **643:** The Granger Collection, New York; **644:** Diantha York-Ripley/SuperStock; **645:** Jim Stamates/Getty Images; **646:** Giraudon/Art Resource, NY; **647:** The Granger Collection, New York; **653:** *Sir Galahad,* George Frederick Watts, Trustees of the National Museums & Galleries of Merseyside/Bridgeman Art Library, London/New York; **654:** The Granger Collection, New York; **655:** *Alfred Lord Tennyson* (detail), c.1840, S. Laurence, by courtesy of the National Portrait Gallery, London; **656:** *Dante,* Andrea del Castagno, Firenze, Santa Apollonia, Scala/Art Resource, New York; **658:** *The Forest, Inferno I,* 1862, Gustave Dore, New York Public Library Special Collections, L'Enfer de Dante Alighieri avec dessins de Gustave Dore, 1862. The New York Public Library/Art Resource, NY; **660:** University of Texas at Austin; **661: t.** University of Texas at Austin; **661: b.** University of Texas at Austin; **662:** The Granger Collection, New York; **665:** University of Texas at Austin; **669:** Monique le Luhandre/© Dorling Kindersley; **670:** The Granger Collection, New York; **676:** The Granger Collection, New York; **678:** The Granger Collection, New York; **681:** *Paolo and Francesca,* 1855, Dante Gabriel Rossetti, Tate Gallery, London/Art Resource, NY; **684:** Mary Evans Picture Library; **686:** *Judecca - Lucifer, Inferno XXXIV,* 1862, Gustave Dore, New York Public Library Special Collections, L'Enfer de Dante Alighieri avec dessins de Gustave Dore, 1862. The New York Public Library/Art Resource, NY; **689:** *Poets emerge from Hell, Inferno XXXIV*, 139, Gustave Dore, 1862, New York Public Library Special Collections, L'Enfer de Dante Alighieri avec dessins de Gustave Dore, 1862. The New York Public Library/Art Resource, NY; **694:** John Heseltine/© Dorling Kindersley. Duomo and Bapistry, Florence/John Hestletine; **698:** David Young-Wolff/PhotoEdit Inc.; **701:** Prentice Hall; **712-713:** *The School of Athens,* Raphael, Scala/Art Resource, NY; **714: m.** Prentice Hall; **714: b.** Getty Images; **716: m(1).** Scala/Art Resource, NY; **716: m(2).** Bettmann/CORBIS; **716: b.** Philip Blenkinsop/© Dorling Kindersley; **716: m(3).** Boltin Picture Library; **716: t.** Astrolabe, Museum fur Kunst und Gewerbe, Hamburg; **717: t.l.** NASA; **717: t.r.** Night of August 4, 1789, or "Patriotic Delirium", Bibliotheque Nationale, Paris, Giraudon/Art Resource, New York; **717: b.l.** Réunon des Musées Nationaux/Art Resource, NY; **717: b.l.** View of the Imperial Bank and environs, Giraudon/Art Resource, New York; **718:** Astrolabe, Museum fur Kunst und Gewerbe, Hamburg; **719:** Leonardo da Vinci (1452–1519), Mona Lisa. Oil on wood (1503 and 1506) 77 x 53 cm., Leonardo da Vinci (1452–1519), Inv. 779. Photo R.G. Ojeda. Louvre, Paris. Reunion des Musees Nationaux/Art Resource, NY; **720: b.** The Granger Collection, New York; **720: t.** Astrolabe, Museum fur Kunst und Gewerbe, Hamburg; **722: b.** Florence Museo delle Scienze/AKG London; **722: t.** Astrolabe, Museum fur Kunst und Gewerbe, Hamburg; **723:** *Lorenzo il Magnifico,* G. Vasari, Scala/Art Resource, New York; **724: b.** *The Trinity* (detail), 1426–28, fresco, 667 x 317 cm. Masaccio (1401–1428), Duomo, Florence. Nicolo Orsi Battaglini/Art Resource, NY; **724: t.** Astrolabe, Museum fur Kunst und Gewerbe, Hamburg; **725:** The Granger Collection, New York; **728: l.** *Petrarch,* Alinari/Art Resource, New York; **728: r.** *Portrait of Ronsard,* Anonymous artist, early 17th century, Giraudon/Art Resource, New York; **730:** *Three Graces* (detail), Botticelli, Giraudon/Art Resource, New York; **731:** *Three Graces* (detail), Botticelli, Giraudon/Art Resource, New York; **732: r.** Monique le Luhandre/© Dorling Kindersley; **732: l.** D. Robert & Lorri Franz/CORBIS; **733:** Corel Professional Photos CD-ROM™; **735:** Cameraphoto Arte, Venice/Art Resource, NY; **736:** Corel Professional Photos CD-ROM™; **741:** *William Shakespeare,* (detail), attributed to John Taylor, by courtesy of the National Portrait Gallery, London; **742:** Giovanni Boccaccio, Scala/Art Resource, New York; **744:** © Dorling Kindersley; **745:** *Robert Cheseman,* Hans Holbein the Younger. Muritshuis, The Hague. Scala/Art Resource, New York; **746:** Réunion des Musées Nationaux/Art Resource, NY; **748:** The Granger Collection, New York; **749:** Monique le Luhandre/© Dorling Kindersley; **754: b.** CORBIS; **754: t.** Prentice Hall; **755:** The Granger Collection, New York; **756:** Bettmann/CORBIS; **759:** NASA; **760:** The Science Museum/Science & Society Picture Library; **761:** Eckhard Slawik/Photo Researchers, Inc.; **762:** Academy of Natural Sciences of Philadelphia/CORBIS; **763:** Colin Keates/© Dorling Kindersley; **768:** The Granger Collection, New York; **771:** *Don Quixote,* Honore Daumier, Scala/Art Resource, NY; **772:** The Palma Collection/Getty Images; **775:** *Don Quixote Hanging from the Window and Preparing His Armour*; two scenes from the novel by Cervantes, Zacarias Velazquez Gonzalez, Caylus Anticuario, Madrid, Spain/Bridgeman Art Library, London/New York; **776:** *Dulcinea Del Toboso* from Cervantes, Don Quixote, 1839, Charles Robert Leslie, Art Resource, NY; **779:** *Don Quixote and Sancho Panza Riding Clavileno,* Zacarias Velazquez Gonzalez, Caylus Anticuario, Madrid, Spain/Bridgeman Art Library, London/New York; **780:** Monique le Luhandre/© Dorling Kindersley; **783:** *Don Quixote and the Windmill,* Francisco J. Torrome (fl. 1890–1908), Bonhams, London/Bridgeman Art Library, London/New York; **788:** John de la Fontaine, The Bettmann Archive; **791:** *"The Crow and the Fox",* Felix Lorioux, illustration for "Fables' by Jean de La Fontaine, Private Collection/Roger Perrin/The Bridgeman Art Library. Copyright © Artists Rights Society (ARS), New York; **792:** Alan Kearney/Getty Images; **798: b.** The Granger Collection, New York; **798: m.** *Niccolo Macchiavelli,* Florence Uffizi, Art Resource, New York; **798: t.** Astrolabe, Museum fur Kunst und Gewerbe, Hamburg; **799: t.** Bettmann/CORBIS; **799: b.** The Granger Collection, New York; **800:** *Voltaire in 1718,* 18th century French school after N. de Largilliere, Paris, Musee Carnavalet, Giraudon, Erich Lessing/Art Resource, New York; **803:** Bibliotheque Nationale, Paris, France/Bridgeman Art Library, London/New York; **805:** Josef Beck/Getty Images; **811:** *A Rider on a Rearing Horse in a Profile View,* Leonardo da Vinci, Fitzwilliam Museum, University of Cambridge; **813:** *Head of the Virgin in Three-Quarter View Facing to the Right,* Black and colored chalks on paper, Leonardo da Vinci, The Metropolitan Museum of Art, Harris Brisbane Dick Fund, 1951. (51.90) Photograph © 1992 The Metropolitan Museum of Art; **818:** Bonnie Kamin/PhotoEdit Inc.; **821:** Prentice Hall; **830-831:** *Sunday Afternoon on the Island of La Grande Jatte,* 1884–86, oil on canvas, George Pierre Seurat/Art Institute of Chicago, IL/The Bridgeman Art Library, London/New York; **832: m.** Prentice Hall; **832: b.** © Alamy Images; **832: t.** Astrolabe, Museum fur Kunst und Gewerbe, Hamburg; **834: m.r.** *Napoleon Bonaparte as First Consul,* Jean Aguste Dominque Ingres, Musee des Beaux-Arts, Liege, Belgium, Scala/Art Resource, New York; **834: m.m.** Photofest; **834: m.r.** *The Stone Breakers,* Gustave Courbet/SuperStock; **834: b.l.** Joseph Sohm; Visions of American/CORBIS; **834:** *Fuji from Noge in Yokohama,* Musashi, Ando Hiroshige, The Newark Museum, John Cotton Dana Collection/Art Resource, NY; **834: t.** Astrolabe, Museum fur Kunst und Gewerbe, Hamburg; **835: t.** Private Collection/Bridgeman Art Library, London/New York; **835: b.r.** *A Berber of Southern Tunis,* c. 1898, Harry Hamilton Johnston, Private Collection/Bridgeman Art Library, London/New York; **835: b.l.** The Granger Collection, New York; **836:** Astrolabe, Museum fur Kunst und Gewerbe, Hamburg; **838: b.** Erich Lessing/Art Resource, NY; **838: t.** Astrolabe, Museum fur Kunst und Gewerbe, Hamburg; **839:** Burstein Collection/CORBIS; **840: b.** *The Wanderer Above the Sea of Fog,* 1818, (oil on canvas), Friedrich, Caspar-David (1774–1840) / Hamburger Kunsthalle, Hamburg, Germany; / Bridgeman Art Library, London/New York; **840:** Astrolabe, Museum fur Kunst und Gewerbe, Hamburg; **841:** *Ludwig van Beethoven,* portrait by Joseph Karl Stieler, 1820. Beethoven-Haus Bonn.; **842:** Astrolabe, Museum fur Kunst und Gewerbe, Hamburg; **843:** On the Bank of the Seine, Bennecourt, 1868, Claude Monet, Potter Palmer Collection, 1922.427, reproduction, The Art Institute of Chicago. All Rights Reserved.; **844:** *Johann Wolfgang von Goethe,* J. K. Stieler, The Granger Collection, New York; **846-847:** © Joseph Sohm/Photo Researchers, Inc.; **849:** *Mephistopheles,* 1863, Eugène Delacroix, Giraudon/Art Resource, New York; **851:** © Thomas Wiewandt/Photo Researchers, Inc.; **852:** The Granger Collection, New York; **855:** The Granger Collection, New York; **857:** Monique le Luhandre/© Dorling Kindersley; **859:** *Dunstanburgh Castle in a Thunderstorm,* Thomas Girtin, Ashmolean Museum, Oxford, UK/Bridgeman Art Library, London/New York; **860:** *Vanitas,* Edwaert Collier, Johnny van Haeften Gallery, London, UK/Bridgeman Art Library, London/New York; **866:** Corel Professional Photos CD-ROM™; **869:** *Mephistopheles Appears Before Faust,* Eugène Delacroix, Reproduced by the permission of the Trustees of the Wallace Collection; **870-871:** Corel Professional Photos CD-ROM™; **870:** Corel Professional Photos CD-ROM™; **871:** The Granger Collection, New York; **873:** *Green Jade Vine (Stongylodon Macrobotrys),* 1991, Jessica Tcherpnine, Private Collection/The Bridgeman Art Library, London/New York; **874: l.** *Alexander Pushkin,* Orest Kiprensky, The Granger Collection, New York; **874: r.** Mary Evans Picture Library; **876:** Raymond Gehman/CORBIS; **877:** *Lake Scene in France,* oil on canvas, Josephine Bowes, The Bowes Museum, Barnard Castle, County Durham, UK/Bridgeman Art Library, London/New York; **879:** Uwe Schmid/CORBIS; **880:** © Gregory G. Dimijian/Photo Researchers, Inc.; **884: r.** The Granger Collection, New York; **884: b.l.** The Granger Collection, New York; **884: t.l.** © Bettmann/CORBIS; **887:** *Erminia in the Rough Sea,* 1869, National Trust Photographic Library/John Hammond/Bridgeman Art Library, London/New York; **888:** Kenneth Lilly/© Dorling Kindersley; **889:** The Granger Collection, New York; **890:** *Ophelia,* John Everett Millais, Tate Gallery, London/Art Resource, New York; **892:** The Granger Collection, New York; **898: t.** Prentice Hall; **898: b.** Zephyr Picture/Index Stock Imagery, Inc.; **899:** *Haystack at Giverny,* Claud Monet, Scala/Art Resource, NY; **901:** © Alamy Images; **902: inset.** Paul Nicklen/National Geographic Society; **902:** George F.

Mobley/National Geographic Society; **904: m.** Getty Images Inc./Hulton Archive Photos; **904: b.** L. N. Tolstoy, I. E. Repin, Sovfoto/Eastfoto; **904: t.** CORBIS-Bettmann; **907:** *Les Maisons Cabassud à la Ville d'Avray,* Camille Corot, The Louvre, Paris, Scala/Art Resource, New York; **909:** Stephen Oliver/© Dorling Kindersley; **910:** The Granger Collection, New York; **913:** TK; **914:** Vladmir Stozharov, *The Village of Andreikovo* (detail), 1958, Vladmir Stozharov, The Tretyakov Gallery, Moscow, © Estate of Vladimir Stozharov; **917:** Dallas and John Heaton/CORBIS; **918-919:** *Cornfield at Ewell,* William Holman Hunt, Art Resource; **920:** Frank Greenway/© Dorling Kindersley; **923:** Monique le Luhandre/© Dorling Kindersley; **924-925:** David Brookover/Getty Images; **928:** *The Library at Windsor Castle,* Joseph Nash, National Trust Photographic Library/John Hammond/Bridgeman Art Library, London/New York; **931:** *Ball at the Moulin de la Galette,* 1876, Pierre Auguste Renoir, Collection of Mr. and Mrs. John Hay Whitney, New York, USA/Bridgeman Art Library, London/New York; **932:** *E. Duranty,* 1879, Edgar Degas, Glasgow Museums: The Burrell Collection; **935:** Corel Professional Photos CD-ROM™; **940:** *Henrik Ibsen,* George T. Tobin, The Granger Collection, New York; **942:** Private Collection/Bridgeman Art Library, London/New York; **944:** Paramount Pictures. The Kobal Collection, New York; **946:** *A Lark, Archibald Thorburn,* John Spike Fine Watercolours, London, UK/Bridgeman Art Library, London/New York; **949:** Artville/Getty Images; **951:** © Judith Miller/Dorling Kindersley/Bonhams; **953:** Paramount Pictures. The Kobal Collection, New York; **955:** Artville/Getty Images; **956-957:** Paramount Pictures. The Kobal Collection, New York; **958:** Dave King/© Dorling Kindersley; **961:** Paramount Pictures. The Kobal Collection, New York; **964:** Artville/Getty Images; **968:** © Hulton/Archive Photos; **975:** Private Collection/Bridgeman Art Library, London/New York; **977:** *Lady with a Fur Muff,* Theodor Bruckner, Whitford & Hughes, London, UK/Bridgeman Art Library, London/New York; **980:** Paramount Pictures. The Kobal Collection, New York; **983:** Steve Cole/Getty Images; **986:** Owaki-Kulla/CORBIS; **988:** © Judith Miller/Dorling Kindersley/Axtell Antiques; **990-991:** Paramount Pictures. The Kobal Collection, New York; **993:** Artville/Getty Images; **996:** Dave King/© Dorling Kindersley; **1001:** Private Collection/Bridgeman Art Library, London/New York; **1003:** Paramount Pictures. The Kobal Collection, New York; **1005:** Paramount Pictures. The Kobal Collection, New York; **1006:** Owaki-Kulla/CORBIS; **1009:** Paramount Pictures. The Kobal Collection, New York; **1012:** Paramount Pictures. The Kobal Collection, New York; **1014:** *A Lark, Archibald Thorburn,* John Spike Fine Watercolours, London, UK/Bridgeman Art Library, London/New York; **1019:** Private Collection/Bridgeman Art Library, London/New York; **1020:** © National Gallery Collection; By kind permission of the Trustees of the National Gallery, London/CORBIS; **1026:** Astrolabe, Museum fur Kunst und Gewerbe, Hamburg; **1027: b.** John Heseltine/CORBIS; **1027: t.** Wolfgang Kaehler/CORBIS; **1029:** background istockphoto.com; **1030:** Robbie Jack/CORBIS; **1030:** background istockphoto.com; **1031:** background istockphoto.com; **1032:** background istockphoto.com; **1036:** Mary Kate Denny/PhotoEdit Inc.; **1039:** Prentice Hall; **1048-1049:** Ypres after First Bombardment, Christopher Richard Wynne Nevinson/Sheffield Galleries and Museums Trust, UK/The Bridgeman Art Library, London/New York; **1050: b.** Giraudon/Art Resource, NY; **1050: m.** Miriam Berkley/Authorpix; **1050: t.** Astrolabe, Museum fur Kunst und Gewerbe, Hamburg; **1052: m.l.** Bettmann/CORBIS; **1052: m.m.** Ewing Galloway/Index Stock Photography, Inc.; **1052: m.r.** "Shattering a German Charge", From "The Literary Digest", Culver Pictures, Inc.; **1052: b.** The Granger Collection, New York; **1052: t.** Astrolabe, Museum fur Kunst und Gewerbe, Hamburg; **1053: t.l.** The Granger Collection, New York; **1053: t.m.** Bettmann/CORBIS; **1053: t.r.** Getty Images; **1053: b.** Photofest; **1054: b.** © Science VU/National Laboratory of Medicine/Visuals Unlimited; **1054: t.** Astrolabe, Museum fur Kunst und Gewerbe, Hamburg; **1055: b.** Pablo Picasso, Les Demoiselles d'Avignon, 1907 (detail), oil on canvas, 8' x 7'8". Acquired through the Lille P. Bliss Bequest. (333.1939). Digital Image © The Museum of Modern Art/Licensed by Scala/Art Resource, NY. © 2004 Estate of Pablo Picasso; Artists Rights Society (ARS), NY; **1055: t.** Davis Factor/CORBIS; **1056: inset.** Bettmann/CORBIS; **1056:** Heinrich Hoffmann/TIMEPIX; **1056: t.** Astrolabe, Museum fur Kunst und Gewerbe, Hamburg; **1057:** View of Terezin, paper collage, Hanus Weinberg, State Jewish Museum, Prague; **1058:** Astrolabe, Museum fur Kunst und Gewerbe, Hamburg; **1059:** The Art Archive/Conservatoire Prague/Dagli Orti; **1060:** Astrolabe, Museum fur Kunst und Gewerbe, Hamburg; **1061:** La condition humaine (The Human Condition), 1933, Rene Magritte, Copyright 1997 Board of Trustees, National Gallery of Art, Washington, Gift of the Collectors Committee, 1933. © 1998 C. Herscovici, Brussels/Artists Rights Society (ARS), New York; **1063:** Royalty-Free/CORBIS; **1064:** The Granger Collection, New York; **1066: l.** Steve Gorton/© Dorling Kindersley; **1067: r.** Steve Gorton/© Dorling Kindersley; **1068:** Pictor/ImageState; **1070:** Walking Man, bronze statue 150 x 60 x 133 cm, Rick Amor, Niagara Galleries; **1072:** Steven Rothfeld/Getty Images; **1075:** Martha Swope Photography; **1076:** © Dorling Kindersley; **1080:** Steve Gorton/© Dorling Kindersley; **1081:** Verlag Klaus Wagenbach; **1082:** Steve Gorton/© Dorling Kindersley; **1083:** Monique le Luhandre/© Dorling Kindersley; **1084:** Martha Swope Photography; **1087:** Steve Gorton/© Dorling Kindersley; **1088:** © Dorling Kindersley; **1091:** Susan Watkins, Lady in Yellow (Eleanor Reeves), ca. 1905. Oil on canvas, 44 1/2 x 35 1/2 inches. Chrysler Museum of Art, Norfolk, VA, Bequest of Goldsborough Serpell (46.76.137); **1094:** USDA Photo; **1095:** Steve Gorton/© Dorling Kindersley; **1096:** Steve Gorton/© Dorling Kindersley; **1098:** Gjon Mili/TimePix; **1101:** Monique le Luhandre/© Dorling Kindersley; **1102:** Steve Gorton/© Dorling Kindersley; **1105:** Museum of Czech Literature, Prague; **1107:** Verlag Klaus Wagenbach; **1113:** Frank Greenaway/© Dorling Kindersley; **1116:** Henri Manuel/CORBIS; **1119:** Madame Mayden, Amedeo Modigliani/SuperStock; **1120:** © Sotheby's/CORBIS SYGMA; **1121:** Artville/Getty Images; **1126:** Luigi Pirandello, Primo Conti, Giraudon/Art Resource, New York; **1129:** A Star Shell, exh. 1916, Christopher R.W. Nevinson, © Tate Gallery, London 2004/Art Resource, NY; **1130:** Italian Soldiers, Karl Fahringer, Heeresgeschichtliches Museum, Vienna, Austria; **1131:** Burstein Collection/CORBIS; **1136:** Royalty-Free/CORBIS; **1139:** The Hailstorm, Thomas Hart Benton, Joslyn Art Museum, Omaha, Nebraska, Gift of James A. Douglas Foundation; **1140:** H. Armstrong Roberts/CORBIS; **1141:** Bettmann/CORBIS; **1142:** Miriam Berkley/Authorpix; **1143:** Lester Lefkowitz/CORBIS; **1144: t.l.** The Granger Collection, New York; **1144:b.l.** The Granger Collection, New York; **1144: t.r.** CORBIS-Bettmann; **1144: b.r.** AP/Wide World Photos; **1146:** The Old Guitarist, 1903, Pablo Picasso, Spanish, 1881–1973, oil on panel 122.9 x 82.6 cm, Helen Birch Bartlett Memorial Collection, 1926.253. Reproduction, The Art Institute of Chicago, © 2004 Estate of Pablo Picasso/Artists Rights Society (ARS), New York; **1150:** Woman and Child, Pablo Picasso, Estate of Pablo Picasso/Artists RIghts Society (ARS), New York. Museo Picasso, Barcelona, Spain. Scala/Art Resource, NY; **1152:** The Revolution, Manuel Rodriguez Lozano, Museo Nacional de Arte Moderno, Mexico City, Photo Laurie Platt Winfrey; **1158: b.** AFP/CORBIS; **1158: m.** AFP/CORBIS; **1158: t.** Astrolabe, Museum fur Kunst und Gewerbe, Hamburg; **1160:** The Granger Collection, New York; **1162:** © Danny Lehman/CORBIS; **1163:** © Gerry Charm/SuperStock; **1164:** Monique le Luhandre/© Dorling Kindersley; **1165:** © Carmen jRedondo/CORBIS; **1166:** Two Gazelles, miniature from the "Babar Nama", 1530, fol. 269 v. Mohgul manuscript. National Museum, New Delhi, Delhi India. Borromeo/Art Resource, New York; **1167:** © Danny Lehman/CORBIS; **1174:** AP/Wide World Photos; **1177:** Miriam Berkley/Authorpix; **1186-1187:** Dynamism of a Cyclist, 1913, oil on canvas, Umbert Boccioni/Mattioli Collection, Milan, Italy/Bridgeman Art Library; **1188: t.** Photo © Sigrid Estrada; **1190: m.l.** Division of Computer Research and Technology, National Institute of Health/Science Photo Library/Photo Researchers, Inc.; **1190: m.r.** NASA; **1190: t(2).** © Getty Images, Inc. - Hulton Archive Photos; **1190: m.m.** From THINGS FALL APART (JACKET COVER) by Chinua Achebe. Copyright and used by permission of Doubleday, a division of Random House, Inc.; **1190: b.** © Bettmann/CORBIS; **1190: t.** Astrolabe, Museum fur Kunst und Gewerbe, Hamburg; **1191: t.l.** © Dorling Kindersley; **1191: b.** AP/Wide World Photos; **1191: t.r.** AP/Wide World Photos; **1192: b.** NASA; **1192: t.** Astrolabe, Museum fur Kunst und Gewerbe, Hamburg; **1193:** © 2001 The Record (Bergen County, NJ), Thomas E. Franklin, Staff Photographer; **1194: b.** Earthworks; **1194: m.** Shanachie Entertainment Corp.; **1194: t.** Astrolabe, Museum fur Kunst und Gewerbe, Hamburg; **1195:** Los Papagayos ("The Parrots"), 1986, Beatriz Gonzalez, Courtesy of the artist, Bogota, Columbia. Photo by Julio Cesar Florez; **1196: b.** Joseph Van Os/Getty Images; **1196: t.** Astrolabe, Museum fur Kunst und Gewerbe, Hamburg; **1198: b.** Herrmann/Starke/CORBIS; **1198: t.** Astrolabe, Museum fur Kunst und Gewerbe, Hamburg; **1199:** Round of Friendship Dedicated to the Virgin of..., Pablo Picasso. © 2004 Estate of Pablo Picasso/Artists Rights Society (ARS), New York. Museo de la Abadia, Montserrat, Catalonia/Index/Bridgeman Art Library, London/SuperStock; **1200:** Susan Meiselas/Magnum Photos, Inc.; **1202:** CORBIS; **1203:** Waves, 1917, Christopher Nevinson, Phillips, The International Fine Art Auctioneers, UK/Courtesy of the Christopher Richard Wynne Estate/Bridgeman Art Library, London/New York; **1204:** Geoffrey Clements/CORBIS; **1205:** Siede Preis/Getty Images; **1206-1207:** Hiroshi Takano/Omni-Photo Communications, Inc.; **1208:** David David Gallery/SuperStock; **1209:** Monique le Luhandre/© Dorling Kindersley; **1214:** Astrolabe, Museum fur Kunst und Gewerbe, Hamburg; **1215:** Italian Landscape, Ben Shahn, © Estate of Ben Shahn/Licensed by VAGA, New York, NY. Burstein Collection/CORBIS; **1216:** Photo © Sigrid Estrada; **1217:** Getty Images; **1218:** Photo © Sigrid Estrada; **1220:** Vista II, 1987, oil on canvas, 24 x 32. Hughie Lee-Smith. Art © Estate of Hughie Lee-Smith/Licensed by VAGA, New York, NY; **1221:** C Squared Studios/Getty Images; **1222:** San Antonio de Oriente. Collection of the Art Museum of the Americas. Organization of American States; **1223:** © Judith Miller/Dorling Kindersley/Woolley and Wallis; **1225:** Daniel Mackie/Getty Images; **1230:** Bettmann/CORBIS; **1232-1233:** Eugene Delacroix, Album de voyage: Spain, Morocco, Algeria, 1834, Chantilly. Musee Conde, Chantilly, France. Giraudon/Art Resource, NY; **1235:** Arab at the Door of His House, Eugene Delacroix, Rijksmuseum, Amsterdam; **1236:** The Ear of Grain, (L'espiga de blat) 1922–1923, oil on canvas, 14 7/8 x 18 1/8, Joan Miro, Purchase. (11.1939). Digital Image © The Museum of Modern Art/Licensed by Scala/Art Resource, NY. The Museum of Modern Art, New York, NY. USA. © Copyright ARS, NY; **1238:** Auguste Raffet, Album Afrique 1835–1845. Arab of Constantine. Musee Conde, Chantilly, France. Giraudon/Art Resource, NY; **1241:** Arabe assis de face, les mains croisees (Seated Arab), Eugene Delacroix, Louvre, D.A.G. © Photo RMN - J.G. Berizzi. Réunion des Musées Nationaux/Art Resource, NY; **1242:** Monique le Luhandre/© Dorling Kindersley; **1244-1245:** © Sylvain Grandadam/Photo Researchers, Inc; **1252: t.l.** Bernard Gotfryd/Hulton Archive/Getty Images Inc.; **1252: b.l.** AP/Wide World Photos; **1252: r.** © Getty Images, Inc. - Hulton Archive Photos; **1254:** © Getty Images Inc. - Hulton Archive Photos; **1255:** CORBIS; **1256:** Hellmut Bachrach-Barée, Concentration Camp Inmates, February 1945, Pencil and watercolor on paper, Gift of the artist. Courtesy of the Yad Vashem Art Museum, Jerusalem; **1257:** Guard with Stick, a collage of paper cut from an office ledger, Soña Spitzova, Jewish Museum in Prague, Courtesy of the United States Holocaust Memorial Museum; **1258:** Drawing for the Transportation Bas Relief, Dee Clements; **1261:** To the Victims of Fascism, 1947, Hans Grundig, Galerie Neue Meister. Staatliche. Kunstsammlungen Dresden; **1263:** Bettmann/CORBIS; **1264:** 1943 A.D, c, 1943, Ben Shahn, Courtesy of The Syracuse University Art Collection, © Estate of Ben Shahn/Licensed by VAGA, New York, NY; **1267:** © CORBIS; **1268: t.** Portrait of an Unknown Prisoner, ca. 1942–43, Franciszek Jazwiecki, Auschwitz Museum; **1268: b.** Auschwitz Museum; **1275: inset.** The Wolloch Haggadah: Pessach Haggadah in Memory of the Holocaust. Rare book, Manuscript, and Special Collections Library, Duke University; **1275: border.** istockphoto.com; **1276: border.** istockphoto.com; **1278: l.** Corbis-Bettmann; **1278: r.** AP/Wide World Photos; **1280:** Leslye Borden/PhotoEdit; **1283:** Aftermath, 1945, Karl Hofer, Hamburg Kunsthalle, Hamburg, Germany/Bridgeman Art Library, London/New York; **1288: l.** © Pascal Le Segretain/CORBIS Sygma; **1288: r.** AP/Wide World Photos/Ron Frehm; **1292:** Horace Bristol/CORBIS; **1295:** Wolfgang Kaehler/CORBIS; **1300:** Barry Iverson/TIMEPIX; **1302:** Will and Deni McIntyre/Getty Images; **1304:** Salvador Dali, The Persistence of Memory, 1931, oil on canvas, 9 1/2 x 13 in. © The Museum of Modern Art/Licensed by Scala/Art Resource, NY. Given anonymously. © 2002 Kingdom of Spain, Gala-Salvador Dali Foundation/Artists Rights Society (ARS), New York; **1305:** Thomas Hartwell/CORBIS; **1310: l.** Dina Gona; **1310: r.** Inge Morath/Magnum Photos, Inc.; **1312:** G. R. Roberts/Omni-Photo Communications, Inc.; **1318:** FPG International Corp.; **1319:** Courtesy National Archives; **1320:** FPG International Corp.; **1321:** AP/Wide World Photos; **1322: l.** © Thomas Victor/Harriet Spurlin; **1322: r.** AP/Wide World Photos; **1325:** Ulli Michel/CORBIS; **1326:** Heini Schneebeli/Bridgeman Art Library, London/New York; **1331:** The Old African, The Medal, and the Statue, 1988, Fodé Camara, Museum of African American Art, Collection: Abourahim Agne; **1332:** Monique le Luhandre/© Dorling Kindersley; **1338:** Reuters Pictures; **1339:** LWA-Stephen Welstead/CORBIS; **1340: l.** Dorothy Alexander; **1340: r.** Dorothy Alexander; **1342:** Morning Rain, 2001, oil on canvas, Bich Nguyet, Courtesy of Galeria La Vong Ltd.; **1344:** Peacefulness, Tran Nguyen Dan, Indochina Arts Project; **1346:** Royalty-Free/CORBIS; **1347:** Royalty-Free/CORBIS; **1354:** Getty Images; **1357:** Photo © Sigrid Estrada; **1365: t.l.** From THINGS FALL APART (JACKET COVER) by Chinua Achebe. Copyright and used by permission of Doubleday, a division of Random House, Inc.

MAP AND ART CREDITS

All graphic organizers: In-House Pros; all maps by Mapping Specialist, except where noted

STAFF CREDITS

Ernie Albanese, Diane Alimena, **Rosalyn Arcilla,** Jasjit Arneja, **Nancy Barker, Amy Baron,** Rachel Beckman, Betsy Bostwick, **Ellen Bowler,** Jennifer Brady, Evonne Burgess, Pradeep Byram, Rui Camarinha, **Pam Carey,** Lisa Carrillo, Jaime Cohen, Allison Cook, **Irene Ehrmann,** Leanne Esterly, Steve Frankel, Philip Fried, **Maggie Fritz,** Michael Ginsberg, **Elaine Goldman,** Patricia Hade, **Monduane Harris, Martha Heller,** Beth Hyslip, Vicki A. Kane, **Kate Krimsky,** Mary Sue Langan, Monica Lehmann, **Mary Luthi, George Lychock,** Gregory Lynch, Daniela Mastria, John McClure, Jim McDonough, Kathleen Mercandetti, Kerrie Miller, Karyl Murray, Ken Myett, Kim Ortell, Carolyn Pallof, Sal Pisano, Jackie Regan, Erin Rehill-Seker, Bruce Rolff, **Laura Ross,** Carolyn Sapontzis, **Melissa Shustyk, Robert Siek, Rita Sullivan, Cynthia Summers,** Patrice Titterington, Jane S. Traulsen

ADDITIONAL CREDITS

Additional Credits: Susan C. Ball, William Bingham, Andrea Brescia, Donna Chappelle, Jennifer Ciccone, Jason Cuoco, Florrie Gadson, Judith Gaelick, Phillip Gagler, James Garratt, Allen Gold, Kristan Hoskins, Lisa Iozzia, Mohamed Kaptan, Barbara Kehr, Terry Kim, Stuart Kirschenbaum, Linda Latino, Julian Liby, Karen Mancinelli, Ginidir Marshall, Bill McAllister, Patrick J. McCarthy, Caroline McDonnell, Meg Montgomery, Gita Nadas, Lesley Pierson, Rachel Ross, Lloyd Sabin, James Savakis, Donna Schindler, Debi Taffet, Elizabeth Torjussen, Ryan Vaarsi, Gina M. Wangrycht, Lindsay White